Soviet Asia:
Bibliographies

Edward Allworth

 Published in cooperation with the
Program on Soviet Nationality Problems,
Columbia University

The Praeger Special Studies program—utilizing the most modern and efficient book production techniques and a selective worldwide distribution network—makes available to the academic, government, and business communities significant, timely research in U.S. and international economic, social, and political development.

Soviet Asia: Bibliographies

A Compilation of Social Science and Humanities Sources on the Iranian, Mongolian, and Turkic Nationalities

With an Essay on the Soviet-Asian Controversy

PRAEGER SPECIAL STUDIES IN INTERNATIONAL POLITICS AND GOVERNMENT

Praeger Publishers New York Washington London

Library of Congress Cataloging in Publication Data

Allworth, Edward.
  Soviet Asia, bibliographies.

  (Praeger special studies in international politics and government)
  1. Minorities--Soviet Center Asia--Bibliography.
  2. Ethnology--Soviet Central Asia--Bibliography.
  3. Soviet Central Asia--Bibliography. 4. Minorities--Russia--Bibliography. 5. Ethnology--Russia--Bibliography. I. Title.
  Z3414.M54A44 [DK855.4]   016.30145'1'0958   73-9061
  ISBN 0-275-28740-8

PRAEGER PUBLISHERS
111 Fourth Avenue, New York, N.Y. 10003, U.S.A.

Published in the United States of America in 1975
by Praeger Publishers, Inc.

All rights reserved

© 1975 by Praeger Publishers, Inc.

Printed in the United States of America

PREFACE

A startling proliferation in the publishing of Soviet materials about the USSR's non-Russians, especially since World War II, matches the growing need in the West for more systematic analysis of the insufficiently studied Soviet Asian people and region. The present bibliography of bibliographies and essay about the area are meant to aid scholars in gaining access to the multiplicity of sources and to emphasize the importance of advancing research about the eastern USSR. About 5,200 bibliographies relating to the humanities or social sciences and published in Czarist Russia or the USSR up to 1970 are listed.

Indispensable assistance in preparing this work came from many persons in Columbia University. John Hanselman, Anna Procyk, John Kohan and Susan D. Friedman helped intelligently both with the organizing and the myriad of details in the manuscript. Azamat Altay, Robert A. Barrett, Gideon Braude, Richard Green, Frederick Jahn, Robert Scott and Vrej Ter-Gevorkian aided in compiling and verifying certain portions of the entries. Rado L. Lencek and Richard Sorich generously gave attention to some problems arising in the essay. Paul G. Rubel helped locate Kalmyk bibliographies. Hubbard W. Ballou photographed the documents reproduced in the opening chapter. Rita Keckeissen, Eileen McIlvaine, William Young and other members of the Columbia University Libraries' remarkable reference staff repeatedly surmounted difficulties in locating needed sources. Only the steadfast encouragement of Janet Allworth and Richard C. Rowson, Director of the Special Projects Division, Praeger Publishers, Inc., along with the support of the Program on Soviet Nationality Problems have made the completion of this large endeavor possible. To them all the author is most grateful.

CONTENTS

	Page
PREFACE	v
THE CONTROVERSIAL STATUS OF SOVIET ASIA	xvi
Russian Mapmakers' Terminology for Asia	xx
Rising Asian Consciousness	xxiv
Organized Search for an Asian Identity	xxx
Soviet Easterners in Foreign Affairs	xxxvii
USSR's Asianness Challenged	xliii
Growing Soviet Asia	xlvii
Russian Ambivalence	li
SOURCES AND METHODS FOR THE BIBLIOGRAPHY	lx

PART I: SOVIET ASIA

Chapter

1   SOVIET ASIA

General	1
Anthropology, Ethnography	8
Architecture, Art, Music	9
Economics	9
Education	10
Geography	11
History, Archaeology	12
Language, Literature	14
Philosophy, Religion	19
Political Science, Law	21

PART II: BLACK SEA & WEST CASPIAN LITTORAL
(Up to the Kuma River)

2   AZERBAIJAN

General	25
Anthropology, Ethnography	36
Architecture, Art, Music	36
Economics	40
Education	43
Geography	45
History, Archaeology	46
Language, Literature	53
Philosophy, Religion	69
Political Science, Law	70
Social Organization	74

Chapter		Page
3	CAUCASUS	
	General	75
	Anthropology, Ethnography	84
	Architecture, Art, Music	87
	Economics	87
	Education	89
	Geography	89
	History, Archaeology	93
	Language, Literature	98
	Philosophy, Religion	99
	Political Science, Law	100
	Social Organization	101
4	CRIMEA & CRIMEAN TATAR	
	General	102
	Economics	103
	Geography	104
	History, Archaeology	105
	Language, Literature	106
	Political Science, Law	107
5	DAGESTAN	
	General	108
	Anthropology, Ethnography	111
	Architecture, Art, Music	111
	Economics	111
	Education	113
	Geography	114
	History, Archaeology	114
	Language, Literature	115
	Philosophy, Religion	116
	Political Science, Law	117
	Social Organization	117
6	GAGAUZ	
	General	118
	Anthropology, Ethnography	118
	History, Archaeology	118
	Language, Literature	118
7	KARACHAY-BALKAR	
	General	119
	Anthropology, Ethnography	121
	Economics	121
	Geography	123
	History, Archaeology	123
	Language, Literature	124
	Philosophy, Religion	125

Chapter		Page
	Political Science, Law	126
	Social Organization	126
8	KARAIM	
	General	127
	Anthropology, Ethnography	127
	History, Archaeology	127
	Language, Literature	128
	Philosophy, Religion	128
	Political Science, Law	128
9	KUMYK	
	History, Archaeology	129
	Language, Literature	129
10	KURD	
	General	131
	Anthropology, Ethnography	131
	History, Archaeology	132
	Language, Literature	133
	Social Organization	134
11	NOGAI	
	History, Archaeology	135
	Language, Literature	135
12	NORTH CAUCASUS (See also CAUCASUS, TRANSCAUCASUS)	
	General	136
	Anthropology, Ethnography	136
	Architecture, Art, Music	137
	Economics	137
	Geography	138
	History, Archaeology	138
	Political Science, Law	139
13	OSSET	
	General	140
	Anthropology, Ethnography	142
	Architecture, Art, Music	142
	Economics	143
	Education	143
	Geography	144
	History, Archaeology	144
	Language, Literature	145
	Political Science, Law	148
	Social Organization	148

Chapter		Page
14	TALYSH	
	Anthropology, Ethnography	149
	History, Archaeology	149
	Language, Literature	149
15	TAT	
	Language, Literature	150
16	TRANSCAUCASUS (See also CAUCASUS, NORTH CAUCASUS)	
	General	151
	Architecture, Art, Music	151
	Economics	151
	Geography	152
	History, Archaeology	152
	Philosophy, Religion	153

PART III: VOLGA BASIN
(Down to the Kuma River Mouth)

17	VOLGA BASIN	
	General	157
	Anthropology, Ethnography	157
	Economics	158
	Education	158
	Geography	158
	History, Archaeology	159
	Volga Basin: Bulgar, History, Archaeology	160
	Volga Basin: Bulgar, Language, Literature	160
	Volga Basin: Khazar, History, Archaeology	161
18	BASHKIRS (See also URALS)	
	General	162
	Anthropology, Ethnography	167
	Economics	168
	Geography	169
	History, Archaeology	170
	Language, Literature	173
	Political Science, Law	179

Chapter		Page
19	CHUVASH	
	General	181
	Anthropology, Ethnography	185
	Architecture, Art, Music	186
	Economics	186
	Education	187
	History, Archaeology	187
	Language, Literature	189
	Philosophy, Religion	194
	Political Science, Law	195
	Social Organization	195
20	KALMYK	
	General	196
	Architecture, Art, Music	196
	Economics	197
	History, Archaeology	197
	Language, Literature	198
21	URALS (See also SIBERIA & MONGOLIA; BASHKIR)	
	General	200
	Anthropology, Ethnography	204
	Architecture, Art, Music	204
	Economics	205
	Education	208
	Geography	208
	History, Archaeology	211
	Language, Literature	214
	Political Science, Law	214
	Social Organization	216
22	VOLGA TATAR	
	General	217
	Anthropology, Ethnography	224
	Architecture, Art, Music	225
	Economics	226
	Education	227
	Geography	229
	History, Archaeology	230
	Language, Literature	235
	Philosophy, Religion	246
	Political Science, Law	247

Chapter		Page

PART IV: CENTRAL ASIA

23 CENTRAL ASIA

General	251
Anthropology, Ethnography	258
Architecture, Art, Music	261
Economics	262
Education	267
Geography	268
History, Archaeology	278
Language, Literature	294
Philosophy, Religion	296
Political Science, Law	297
Social Organization	302

24 KARAKALPAK

General	303
Anthropology, Ethnography	303
Architecture, Art, Music	304
Economics	304
Education	305
History, Archaeology	305
Language, Literature	306
Political Science, Law	308

25 KAZAKH

General	309
Anthropology, Ethnography	321
Architecture, Art, Music	323
Economics	326
Education	333
Geography	336
History, Archaeology	339
Language, Literature	347
Philosophy, Religion	358
Political Science, Law	359
Social Organization	363

26 KIRGIZ

General	365
Anthropology, Ethnography	373
Architecture, Art, Music	374
Economics	376
Education	382
Geography	384
History, Archaeology	389
Language, Literature	394

Chapter			Page
		Philosophy, Religion	403
		Political Science, Law	404
		Social Organization	407
27	TAJIK		
		General	408
		Anthropology, Ethnography	417
		Architecture, Art, Music	418
		Economics	419
		Education	421
		Geography	424
		History, Archaeology	426
		Language, Literature	435
		Philosophy, Religion	446
		Political Science, Law	447
		Social Organization	449
28	TURKMEN		
		General	450
		Anthropology, Ethnography	456
		Architecture, Art, Music	457
		Economics	458
		Education	460
		Geography	462
		History, Archaeology	464
		Language, Literature	470
		Philosophy, Religion	476
		Political Science, Law	477
		Social Organization	479
29	UYGHUR		
		General	481
		Anthropology, Ethnography	481
		History, Archaeology	481
		Language, Literature	482
30	UZBEK		
		General	483
		Anthropology, Ethnography	495
		Architecture, Art, Music	496
		Economics	499
		Education	506
		Geography	509
		History, Archaeology	510
		Language, Literature	522
		Philosophy, Religion	532
		Political Science, Law	533
		Social Organization	538

Chapter		Page

PART V: SIBERIA & MONGOLIA

31	ALTAY	
	General	541
	Anthropology, Ethnography	542
	Architecture, Art, Music	542
	Economics	543
	Education	544
	Geography	544
	History, Archaeology	546
	Language, Literature	547
32	BURIAT	
	General	549
	Anthropology, Ethnography	552
	Architecture, Art, Music	553
	Economics	554
	Education	555
	Geography	556
	History, Archaeology	557
	Language, Literature	561
	Philosophy, Religion	565
	Political Science, Law	565
33	DOLGAN	
	General	568
34	KHAKASS	
	General	569
	Economics	570
	History, Archaeology	570
	Language, Literature	571
35	MONGOLIA	
	General	573
	Anthropology, Ethnography	576
	Architecture, Art, Music	577
	Economics	577
	Education	578
	Geography	578
	History, Archaeology	581
	Language, Literature	583
	Philosophy, Religion	585
	Political Science, Law	586
	Social Organization	587

Chapter		Page
36	SIBERIA	
	General	588
	Anthropology, Ethnography	601
	Architecture, Art, Music	606
	Economics	607
	Education	613
	Geography	615
	History, Archaeology	623
	Language, Literature	634
	Philosophy, Religion	638
	Political Science, Law	639
	Social Organization	642
37	TUVAN	
	General	644
	Anthropology, Ethnography	645
	Economics	645
	Geography	646
	History, Archaeology	646
	Language, Literature	647
	Philosophy, Religion	649
	Political Science, Law	649
38	YAKUT	
	General	650
	Anthropology, Ethnography	653
	Archaeology, Architecture, Art	654
	Economics	655
	Education	657
	Geography	657
	History, Archaeology	659
	Language, Literature	662
	Philosophy, Religion	666
	Political Science, Law	667
	Social Organization	669

PART VI: SUPPLEMENT

SOVIET ASIA		671
BLACK SEA & WEST CASPIAN LITTORAL (up to the Kuma River)		673
	Azerbaijan	673
	Caucasus	674
	Dagestan	675
	Karachay-Balkar	675
	North Caucasus	676

	Page
VOLGA BASIN (down to Kuma River)	678
Bashkir	676
Chuvash	677
Kalmyk	677
Urals	677
Volga Tatar	678
CENTRAL ASIA	678
Kazakh	679
Kirgiz	681
Tajik	681
Turkmen	682
Uzbek	682
SIBERIA & MONGOLIA	683
Altay	683
Mongolia	685
Siberia	685
Tuva	686

THE CONTROVERSIAL STATUS OF SOVIET ASIA

> "Woe, woe to Europe, if she fails
> to heed the voice of righteousness,
> the voice of Asia." (Sadvoukas
> Saifullin, Kazakh poet, 1922)

Modernity and Marxism are said to have levelled Soviet society thoroughly while they unified politics from the western to the eastern reaches of the USSR. These two forces did away with whatever regional inequality may have existed previous to 1917, assert Soviet authorities. But even before this equalization could have been effected, a senior Russian academician widely-known for scholarship respecting the Orient had expressed the idea that in the USSR "the East and the West are one," a close reflection of his country's official position on the matter. Simultaneously, he attributed to Europe, thereby implicitly distinguishing it from Russia, an insistence that the entire East and West "are two completely different worlds, opposed to each other. . ."[1] Within this formulation contends a set of contradictions as yet unresolved by the Soviet Union. Quite aside from the tangible factors-- location, concentration, distinguishing characteristics of people--which signify very much in the unity or polarities of a country, these contradictory attitudes erect an enduring obstacle to real solution of the problem of the concept or terminology embracing the eastern USSR. The academician's contention that the primary difficulty centers upon Europe's "wrong" way of seeing East-West relations, allows for only two points of view in the controversy regarding them. But three main intangibles complicate the question of Soviet Asia's status: the standpoint of the local Asians themselves, views held by Russians high and low, and the perceptions and orientation of outsiders, especially those in Asia proper. Normally, all three attitudes could be expected to undergo significant alteration as time passed. Their interrelations have become increasingly intricate.

How far, then, by the onset of the 1970's has the combination of time, modern development, and official policies succeeded in detaching the Asians of the USSR and their territory from an ancient continental, cultural identity, reorienting them toward a newer pole of attraction? To answer means to understand the effect those forces exerted upon the Asians, upon international relations, and how the Russians reacted to them. Above all, until recently, what accounts for the paradox of a continued Russian preoccupation, perennially ambivalent, with the idea of preserving a palpable domestic Asia, distinct, vital, once within the domains of St. Petersburg and now of Moscow?--All this despite the impact of the drives for homogeneity and unity, and regardless of repeated claims for East-West sameness. The multitude of measures and policies already undertaken or applied provide evidence, if nothing else, of the great concern on the Russian part with their domestic East-West dilemma. Claiming sameness persistently, the terms in which these Eastern Slavs thought of the lands and people to the east of Moscow nevertheless give clues to the sense of awareness the Russians nurtured of Asia's special character. That cognition of a separate Asia inevitably absorbed a certain coloration from Russia's own self identity.

Earlier Russian mapmakers, military leaders, and geographers graphically recorded a range of these ideas. Some famed Russian literary voices also declared insistently in the nineteenth century that Russia should not be confused with either Europe or Asia. Especially during the Polish rising in 1830-1831, Aleksandr Pushkin wrote sarcastically about what he calls an enfeebled Europe, far removed from Russia. His letters to friends often speak about news of a Europe distinct from his Russia. Only a few years after distinguishing Russia from lands to the West, Pushkin perfected his delimitation of Russia by commenting upon an "Asiatic poverty," or "Asiatic swinishness" which he claimed to have discerned during 1829 in an East which in his view contrasted unfavorably with the poorest Russian village.[2] In the fourth quarter of the century, Fedor M. Dostoevsky at certain times emphasized his country's un-European character: ". . .a Russian can never be converted into a true European as long as he remains even slightly Russian; this being so, Russia is something quite independent and special, not like Europe at all. . ." The difference between Russians and Europeans, thought Dostoevsky, forcefully obtruded whenever the chronic "Eastern question" revived.[3] Russia's identity, at least in times of stress (change), was relative, as these eminent writers grasped it. Compared with Europe, Russia was eastern; beside Asia, Russia was western. Praising the Czarist slaughter of the Turkmens at Gok-Tepe, in Central Asia, Dostoevsky wrote in 1881, near the end of his diary and his days: "In Europe we were Tatars, whereas in Asia even we are Europeans. Our civilizing mission in Asia will bribe our spirit and drive us there. . ."[4] This remark seems to express a Russian longing to secure unequivocal status as Europeans through dominating Asians.

The changing outlook among Asians living under Czarist and Soviet Russian governments is revealed, likewise, in their actions and writings stimulated first by the proselytizing and modernizing pressures felt to some extent from inside the Empire. New ways of thinking were also aroused through contact with Middle Eastern, Japanese, and Indian cultural, social or political figures--mostly intellectuals and reformists. Moreover, large-scale Russian colonization in the Asian parts of the Empire begun under the Czars and expanded by the Soviet regime, has, some observers feel, measurably de-Asianized a large portion of the eastern USSR. Later, the impetus forcing further revision of traditional Asian notions about group identity and its roots came mainly as a response to the Russian imposition of demographic-administrative divisions in Asia ordered according to ethno-linguistic classifications of people.

From the second half of the nineteenth to the early twentieth century informed Asians within the Russian perimeter had awakened gradually to the need for communication among themselves if their groups were to survive the assimilative pressures exerted throughout the Czarist domain. Among educated Asians, this quickening awareness of the peril imminent in remaining isolated from each other prompted efforts--initially in the Volga-Kama and Crimean regions, and later in the Transcaucasus and Central Asia--to combine their people, usually along religious, cultural, linguistic, or regional lines, into larger communities and bodies. A pan-Islamic drive among many of the Empire's Asians developed into one of the largest reactions to the threat of a Russification which included conversion to Christianity.[5] With this came a slow upturn of concern with more general levels of identity among Muslims, for example. The social reform movements of the period gained strength both from these threats of assimilation and the surprised recognition, mainly by Asian cultural leaders, that the East would remain subordinate to Russia and Europe if it allowed itself to stay far behind them in educational and technical progress.

As a result, among the Empire's Eastern subjects more concrete ideas about distinctions between Russia and Asia had begun to circulate. They were now being articulated by an emerging class of modernizers who used, in addition to their own tongues, Slavic languages. These skills enabled them to communicate freely with intellectuals and officials of the ruling Russian group. Outstanding as such an Asian innovator and spokesman was Ismail-Bey Gaspirali (Gasprinskii), Crimean Tatar social and religious reformist. Writing for the Russian-language press in the same years Dostoevsky was expressing such concern over the "Eastern question," Gaspirali in 1881, and at many other times, warned Czarist readers against Russifying the nationalities within the Empire, if that meant assimilation. Domination for the sake of domination, without leading the Czarist Asians toward progress and civilization, perceived and received through their own tongues, he said, would make Russian rule rate even below the despotic Chinese (in other words, "Asian") rule. Rather, Gaspirali suggests, Russia should make

CONTROVERSIAL STATUS OF SOVIET ASIA

partners of her Asians:

> I believe. . .that sooner or later Russian Muslims, brought up by Russia, will stand in the forefront of the intellectual development and civilization of the remaining Muslims. . . .If the Romans and Arabs established Eastern civilization in the West, perhaps Providence meant Russians and Tatars to establish that of the West in the East.[6]

That idea of partnership between Russia and her Orient evidently failed to achieve wide acceptance. These messages about the hazard of refusing to modernize were borne in upon the Asian mind painfully beyond the Crimea and Kazan after 1800 by the successive encroachments of disciplined Russian army troops. They were relatively small in number but carried overwhelming firepower, for that time, into the militarily and technologically backward Transcaucasus and the Central Asian areas.

Penetration of Kazakhstan and more southerly regions deeply affected the outlook of the Russians themselves, especially men of the armed services, respecting the identity and character of the conquered people and land stretching east-southeast beyond the Muscovite heartland. These strong new impressions in turn altered in a practical manner previous conceptions held by Russians regarding their entire eastern territory. The decisive Russian assault of Tashkent in mid-June 1865 truly qualified in their minds as a victory of West over East.[7] Compared with this and other nineteenth-century military gains in the Transcaucasus and Central Asia--in what many Russians regarded as the prolonged contest between East and West--the much commemorated medieval success of Russian arms at Kulikovo field against the Golden Horde in September 1380 won only momentary respite. Nevertheless, the relatively easy conquests achieved against the demoralized northern Kazakhs and Kirgiz in Central Asia by the 1850s stimulated Russian historians in the nineteenth century to think of that distant defeat of Mongol-Tatar troops at Kulikovo, inspiring some, at least, to see in it Europe's ascendance:

> . . .the Kulikovo victory. . .was a sign of the triumph of Europe over Asia; it has in the history of Eastern Europe exactly the same significance as the victories of Catalan and Tours in the history of Western Europe, and bears with them the identical character, the character of terrible, bloody slaughter, of a desperate conflict of Europe with Asia, which has necessitated deciding the great question of humanity in history--which of these parts of the world is to triumph over the other?[8]

SOVIET ASIA: BIBLIOGRAPHIES

After the Mongol-Tatar Golden Horde had destroyed itself through unending internal strife and its wars with Timur, the small successor khanates centered at Kazan and Astrakhan barring routes to the East were readily pushed aside. By the mid-1500's, from Moscow's vantage point it must have seemed that the Asia represented by Russia's long-domineering Tatar masters had virtually disappeared. The more so, since, to the East, Czarist involvement with the elusive khanate of Sibir (Siberia) preoccupied Moscow's attention until the sixteenth century ended with the death of the khanate's chieftain, Kuchum.

RUSSIAN MAPMAKERS' TERMINOLOGY FOR ASIA

Thus, in the mapping of eastern lands, Russia's earliest known cartographers refer rarely if ever, specifically to the "Asia" within which most of the new Czarist lands lay. The terminology they adopted reflected not only their immediate experience, however, but the ideas filtering into them from the West. In two medieval maps of "Russia" connected with the names of contemporary Russians (Dmitri Gerasimov, 1525 and Ivan Liatskii, 1534), neither a cartographer, the lands east of Moscovy are designated "Tartary." This Tartary reaches boldly from west of the Volga eastward to China on the 1525 map, seeming to be shifted somewhat to the south on the map of 1534. Only the second of these shows a Siberia. It appears as a small dot designating the town of Sibir close to the Ob river just east of the Urals. Though both maps were drawn by Europeans on the basis of advice or information from their Russian informants, neither visualizes Siberia as an area or region.[9]

In the early seventeenth century on maps prepared by Europeans who spent some time in Russia, "Tartary" dominated the eastern portions of the barely charted terrain. Both Isaac Massa, from the Netherlands, and Hessel Gerritsz, his publisher, maintained this terminology on their maps of 1633 (Massa) and 1614 (Gerritsz) for the territory east of the Volga and Ob. Siberia yet appears to be only a town of the Tobol district--"Tobol Metropolis Sibiria"--as Massa shows it in his map first printed in the supplement to Mercator's Atlas.[10] The "Tartary" favored by the Europeans--generally the terrain running east from about the Pechora in the north and Yaik river to the south--became "Siberia" for Russian cartographers before the eighteenth century had begun. Both Peter I. Godunov's map of Siberia (1667) and Semen U. Remezov's (ca.1698) appear to refer, north of today's Central Asia, approximately to the same space that the maps linked to Gerasimov, Liatskii and Massa had designated "Tartary" up to a few decades earlier. On these two seventeenth century maps, Tartary goes unmentioned. Each depiction of Siberia begins at the western margin with a line

Semyon Remezov's map of Siberia, ca.1698 (detail), south at top, from ATLAS AZIATSKOI ROSSII, 1914, plate 3

stretching from about the Pechora river down to the lower
Volga. Godunov shows the more westerly Dvina river as
well.
  But "Tartary" meant something yet to Russians, in an
ethnographic sense. A rare ethnic-political map of
"Siberia" drawn and unusually brightly colored to delineate
the various nationality groups in visible contrast was
evidently based upon information compiled around 1673 by
and for Cornelius, Orthodox Metropolitan of Siberia and
Tobolsk. This flamboyant rendering based upon Remezov's
general map of Siberia (ca.1698), called itself, on a
special title page, "Map and Likeness; a Prospect of all
Siberia's Lands, of the Town of Tobolsk and of all the
Different Townships and Localities and Steppes." Notwithstanding such an emphasis, the map portrays Tartary
prominently. Here, the draftsman reconciles the two contenders for one expanse--Tartary vs. Siberia--by depicting
Tartary as a very large, irregular area shaped like a crude
parallelogram located immediately east of the Urals. It
is surrounded by stronger-hued patches representing Ostiaks,
Tepter-Bashkirs, Voguls (Mansis) and many others, placed
exactly midway between the map's northern and southern
limits. Moscovy (Russia is not mentioned) is contained
entirely west of the Volga. Siberia, ostensibly the
primary subject of the map, apparently reaches from somewhere just east of the Volga to the mostly unnamed seas
seen washing the lands of the Chukchis, Kamchadals and
Giliaks shown inhabiting patches of coastline along the
fringe of the far east. This massive stretch completely
encompasses a much-shrunken Tartary occupying approximately
western Siberia. Nonetheless, the name of the Siberian
region plus some of its components both figure small in the
inscription dominating the map's face, beneath the boldest
crimson heading which reads: "Great Tartary" (VELIKAIA
TARTARIIA).[11]
  This may have been a final emphatic use of "Tartary"
on contemporary Russian maps. The "Siberia" which supplanted it has now been traced back to deep antiquity in
its connections to people along the middle course of the
Irtysh river. In adopting "Siberia" for the Czarist East,
the Russians followed the lead, probably unwittingly, of
medieval Chinese sources (YUAN CHAO PI SHI--SECRET HISTORY
OF THE MONGOL DYNASTY) as well as Middle East historians.
Rashid ad-Din (1247-1318) mentions in his collection of
chronicles both people and districts called Siberia
located not far from the river Irtysh and bordering on
Kirgiz lands. Tribal names "Sabir," "Sybyr," and the
like, as well as denominations of a whole region so named
in the same area constituted the local practice. The
Asian people who lived in the path of Russian expansion,
therefore, provided an example accepted in the Russian
chronicles starting from the fifteenth century and in
Russian cartography by the second half of the seventeenth

century for labeling all or a good part of the former Tartary "Siberia." A Russian contribution to the application of this terminology came with their extending of the Siberian concept and name to most of the Asian expanse conquered by Czarist forces east of Russia proper, and popularizing the name in the West. Evidence provided by the maps shows that this generalization of "Siberia" must have occurred (excluding the Ugric lands along the lower Ob) around the middle of the seventeenth century, or a few years later.[12] The Asian Siberians who originated the term and imprinted it on people and land had long since disappeared. Russian adherence to the changed designation continues in some usages to the present. But, as an appellation for the entire Czarist East, "Siberia" lasted not quite 200 years.

Imprecise as the early Russian maps are, these, and later ones repeatedly portray a Siberia stretching eastward from the north-south flowing rivers, the Pechora, the Volga, and others draining the area immediately west and south of the Urals. The widely-circulated Academy of Sciences atlas of 1745 refers specifically to Siberia and details a small western part of it in one of many plates. Here again, however, the map implies a Siberia beginning from a river west of the Urals, the Kama, within the territory of the Tobolsk administrative unit of the time (TOBOLSKAIA PROWINCIIA). "Tartary" and "Asia" are not specified at all, nor is the extent of Siberia explicitly outlined upon the one general map portraying Russia's dominions. Neither Siberia nor Asia is mentioned in the contents or plates of two succeeding important atlases produced in Russia in 1792 and 1827.[13] Through the first quarter of the nineteenth century, primarily by subtraction from the minuend of all the Empire could the limits for the western reaches of that eastern territory be cartographically differentiated. The term "Russian Asia" sporadically appeared in geographical studies of 1848 and later. A new Russian atlas (1851), however, in both plates and table of contents details the subtrahend, "European Russia," explicitly. "Europe's" eastern boundaries appear as clearly as scale and space, together with contemporary techniques of mapmaking, could make them. In a map of "Siberia and North-American Russia," the atlas shows the southwestern Siberia portion plainly meeting "European Russia" above the "Kazakh plains." The border between "Europe" and "Siberia," here, follows the Ural mountains southward from the Kara river, down to the Ural (earlier Yaik) river, and thence into the Caspian sea, all of whose western shore--the Caucasus-Transcaucasus included--remains in "Europe."[14]

The perplexing question of where the Caucasus-Transcaucasus belongs in this grand division of the Empire into East and West was raised more pointedly now that a Russian Asia had entered the thinking and vocabulary of the Russians. But, for the next half-century, at least, the query was usually answered by keeping the area extending all the way to the Persian border within "European Russia." That inclusion mirrored the subtractive process of thought by which Asiatic Russia finally emerged as a positive idea replacing its negative (non-Russia), or Tartary-Siberia. Leaving the Caucasus-Transcaucasus on the European side of the East-West scheme also offered a hint of the related tendency which subsequently grew more noticeable: the European continent's frontiers were apparently drifting to the East at the expense of non-Russia.

Not only did the 1851 military atlas exclude the whole region of the Caspian sea from Asia, but its "Europe" captured a huge salient to the east across the Ural mountains as well. This bulge reached a good way toward Omsk, on the Irtysh river. The fact that the 1851 atlas was prepared for military training schools and approved personally by the Adjutant General, Jacob I. Rostovtsov, for publication, suggested an absence of official change in the Asian concept. Between the date that atlas was published and the appearance of the MAP OF ASIATIC RUSSIA (KARTA AZIATSKOI ROSSII) prepared by the General Staff Headquarters in 1865, however, a fundamental alteration had occurred in the conception entertained and designations used for the Czarist lands east of Russia proper. By 1860 the Siberian Branch of the Imperial Russian Geographical Society had printed a MAP OF ASIATIC RUSSIA dated 1860 (unavailable for examination in the U.S.) In 1865, the yearly Report (OTCHET) of the parent geographical society had started to employ the terminology "Asiatic Russia" (AZIATSKAIA ROSSIIA) regularly in official publications.[15] That heading subsumed the Caucasus, Orenburg Krai, Turkistan Oblast', Siberia, and Russian Manchuria. Also, the General Staff map prepared exactly the year in which Russian troops first captured a major city in an old, organized state in the heart of Asia reflected this toponymic metamorphosis. The approach to and taking of Tashkent may be regarded as a major turning point in Russia's official understanding of her eastern Empire. "Siberia" remained, of course, as a territorial designation, but from the pivotal year 1865 until 1917 was nearly always included as but one part of the Asiatic Russia signaled and demarked by geographers and military cartographers.[16]

RISING ASIAN CONSCIOUSNESS

These Russian advances into adjacent Eastern lands naturally attracted international attention, especially in England and China; however, none of the alterations in the names applied to Czarist Asian regions appears to have been dictated by concern with what the foreign response might have been to one concept or another. Such naming remained essentially a domestic matter related to a

Title page, First "ATLAS OF ASIATIC RUSSIA," 1914

combination of traditions and St. Petersburg's view of its own position relative to West or East. To designate an official East in the form of "Asiatic Russia" was to reinforce the non-Asianness (Europeaness?) of the remainder, something many influential Russians quite earnestly favored at the time for Russia. The choice of "Asiatic Russia" could refer back to the putative Oriental character of Russia itself, said to stem from prolonged, close interaction, lasting at least up through the fifteenth century, even before Russian expansion beyond the Volga, with Khwarazmians, Khazars, Pechenegs, Cumans (Polovetsians), and other Asians. That hardly seems to have been what the Russian leadership had in mind. Either way, the effect of openly recognizing a domestic Asia promised to be serious.

Czarist Russians and Russia's Asians both arrived at the twentieth century schooled explicitly by the official terminology and policies behind it to the division between them as Westerners and Easterners, and--when only the two groups were concerned--as Europeans and Asians. A brief outspoken period had in fact foreshadowed this new outburst when the local press which came into existence for a few years around the 1905 uprising which shook Czarist Russia's government temporarily into a somewhat moderate stance respecting its non-Russians. Newspapers like THE RUSSIAN EAST (SHARQ-I RUSS), 1903-1904 at Tiflis, and ASIA (AZIYA) at Tashkent during part of 1908, with their pan-Islamic, pan-Turkic views, were unceremoniously shut down by regional Czarist authorities disturbed over the stirrings among their Asians.[17] Among members of the Czarist Orientalist Society on the eve of the second Russian revolution, "East" and "Oriental studies" had become "merely geographical-ethnographic terms not relating at all to the degrees of longitude at which the person who uses the terms lives, writes and speaks."[18] That liberation from tyranny of the compass functioned in both directions, however. The official ATLAS OF ASIATIC RUSSIIA (ATLAS AZIATSKOI ROSSII) (1914) drew a firm line along the Caucasus range and the Ural mountains, excluding both the Caucasus-Crimea-Kalmykia area as well as the Volga-Kama region from Russia's Asian domains.[19] After 1917, the new Russian masters of the Soviet government managed to remove from themselves somewhat the stigma or label attached to "Europeans." The Asians received an alternative identity as well. The transformation in both instances may yet have been only tentative, for the brief time elapsed provides an inconclusive test.

This change throughout the Soviet Union by 1925 provoked by the application of Leninist-Stalinist nationality policies had drastically affected the areal designations and organization of societies in the eastern USSR. In place of ethnically-heterogeneous communities of the past, western-style nationalities were emphasized now particularly through a process of territorial gerrymandering. These policies had the intention of countering active or latent urges among the Asians, at least, to unite in supra-nationality bodies like pan-Iranian, pan-Mongolian, or pan-Turkic combinations. A similar indigenous move toward maintaining the inhabitants and area of the Uralic people in the USSR located roughly in the north between the Pechora river, the Kama, and the Urals in the south, as a single group and unit was also thwarted. Measures were soon taken by the authorities to segregate the local population of the region according to ethnic group into at least four "nationalities" and their eponymous administrative units (Komi, Komi-Permyak, Udmurt, Nenets).[20] Nationalizing people and lands, in that sense, together with the government's propagandizing anti-colonialism actively inside and outside the Russian Soviet Federated Socialist Republic (RSFSR), coming on the heels of liberation from Czarist Russian domination, brought to the surface and perhaps focused attitudes among the Asians within Soviet Russia which had seldom been openly expressed in the past, at least in public or print.

An extraordinary opportunity for spreading ideas of Asian uniqueness within the Russian republic presented itself at the huge First Congress of Eastern Peoples, held in Baku as if to demonstrate, among other things, that the Transcaucasus belongs to Asia. Meeting in September 1920, nearly 1900 delegates are reported to have heard many Russians and Asians address the sessions, including Tashbulatbek Narbutabek-oghli, a non-Communist politician from Tashkent. He insisted, in a speech to the Congress on September 4th, that ". . .the East is quite different, its interests different, from those in the West!" He went on to stir stormy applause, even shouts of "bravo," from the predominantly Asian audience, when he warned the Soviet government to get its "counter revolutionaries," "aliens," "colonizers masked as communists" (all three euphemisms for Russians) out of Turkistan. Narbutabek-oghli explained that this measure was imperative if the varied and special traits of the Caucasus and Central Asia were to be protected properly.[21]

That gathering symbolized a veering toward Asia and away from Europe of the Soviet leadership's main ideological focus. This turnabout shook the confidence of some Russians then supporting the new regime. A foreign guest of Maxim Gorky in Petrograd during September 1920, just after the "Eastern Peoples" sessions were held (Sept. 1-8) in Azerbaijan, reports that "This Baku Conference has depressed Gorky profoundly. He is obsessed by a nightmare of Russia going East."[22] Possibly Gorky's beginnings in Nizhni Novgorod (now Gorky) a city very near the Chuvash and Tatars of Asia's western reaches, colored his feelings. Certainly the accents heard from local Asians at this time would not have contradicted the Russian writer.

Soon, among some Asian communists and non-communists

alike within the USSR the strange new tone began to be struck in both press and book publishing. There, symbolic, aesopean language provided a thin camouflage for ideas of protest and dissent. Saken Saifullin's poem "ASIA (TO EUROPE)" ["ASIYA (YEVROPAGHA)"] (1922) appearing in his volume of verse and songs entitled WILD CHARGER (ASAU TULPAR) stressed the invidious differences he saw between East and West:

> Perfidious Europe--land of violence, exploitation
>   and cruelty,
> Many times I directed thee into the way of truth,
> Many a clever man I sent thee. . .
> I sent my Huns, Magyars, Bolgars, Moors and Arabs,
> Thou sawest my Tatars, Turks and Mongols. . .
> Days and years passed; thou renounced not evil. . . .
> Woe, woe to Europe if she fails to heed the voice of
>   righteousness, the voice of Asia.[23]

"Europe," in Saifullin's poem, is probably a code word for "Russia." Russians were the non-Asians whom the Kazakhs had known and were experiencing significant contact with, and against which "Europeans," Kazakhs know, the "Mongols" had struck many heavy blows during the thirteenth to fifteenth centuries. This poem, "ASIA," reached a very wide audience in Kazakhstan when it was reprinted in at least four periodicals and newspapers, including the main communist journal of the republic QIZIL QAZAQSTAN, during 1922.[24] Saifullin's poetry about Asia was not a solitary literary expression of this anti-European/Russian feeling in the Soviet East. That sharp distinction found forceful expression likewise in the Kazakh writings of Magjan Jumabay-uli through poems like "THE EAST," and here in a fragment from "THE PROPHET," where Jumabay-uli idealizes the East and condemns the West:

> The Prophet of the East: I come, I come,
>   Son of the sun--of the fire, descendant of the
>   glorious Hun.
> I am the prophet. I come, the prophet, I bring
>   The light of the fire, of the sun.
> Expect me, oh West, and learn your prayer of
>   contrition by heart.[25]

The detestation of Europe/Russia articulated in these poems evidently became widely shared among the eastern populations of the young Soviet state. An idea that Asia as a whole was different from the West and should belong to its own people revived in that atmosphere and gained some added impetus from the energetic promotion of the notion by Japan in the 1920s. A Japanese journalist traveling around the USSR during 1924-25 personally tried out his country's call, "Asia for Asiatics," the year Japan formally recognized the USSR. He spoke with Trotsky, Stalin and no doubt the many Uzbeks, Turkmens, Caucasus people and other Soviet easterners he reported meeting in Moscow during the Third Congress of Soviets of the USSR (1925).[26] Soviet Easterners comprised over 16 percent of the 834 full and partial members on the Central Executive committee for that Congress. The traveler felt that there was much in common between Japan's policy and Soviet demands for liberating Eastern nationalities. That "Asia for Asiatics" was not what the Soviet leaders had in mind, they quickly explained to the East Asian visitor. Lenin had evidently made clear several years earlier to the same journalist that the West differed significantly from the East when the Soviet leader told him that ". . .true communism can be successful only in the West. . ."[27] Stalin in his interview with the Japanese correspondent acknowledged that Russia had been the "terror" and "gendarme" of the Eastern people, but was now transformed along with her social system.[28] In fact, from the early 1920s Asians of the USSR who argued for a certain uniqueness of the East, in contrast with the West/Russia, were soon accused publicly of adopting "theories smelling strongly of the influence of Japanese imperialism's ideologists." By extension, such an attitude was equated not exactly with nationalism but with supra-nationality tendencies said to exist in the Soviet East. Atajan Hashimov, a prominent younger Uzbek Communist theoretician, writer and editor suffered just such a denunciation from critics who said his idea that "the East developed in isolation from Europe" resembled the claims of the Japanese. "This 'theory' was close to the hearts of the pan-Turkists. . . ," his accusers charged.[29]

The rise of strong sentiment among people of the Soviet East for identifying themselves assertively as Asians was not easily stifled, as the evidence shows, though the three Soviet Asian voices just cited were permanently silenced in the terrible Soviet purges of local Asian intellectuals in the 1920s and 1930s. The Soviet leadership, nevertheless, experienced some ambivalence regarding the Asians' attitudes, hoping to employ those feelings for its purposes in two ways. The obvious convenience of utilizing the domestic Asians and their facilities in foreign relations directed toward the non-Soviet East constituted one of their important functions for the state.

Meetings assembling domestic and foreign Asians together were common in the Soviet East between 1917 and 1926. The authorities soon afterward moved to curtail the calling of congresses which assembled such heterogeneous bodies. A second "Turkological Congress" planned during the first one in 1926 at Baku, where Turkish and other visitors actively participated, was quietly forgotten.

SOVIET ASIA: BIBLIOGRAPHIES

Equally definite had been the measures implementing Soviet nationality policies which required partitioning the eastern conglomerations of the USSR into ethnic nationalities or sub-nationalities (NARODNOSTI). "Turkistan" became a dirty political word not long after the delimitation of the Turkistan Autonomous Soviet Socialist Republic and additional segments of Central Asia very late in 1924 and had not reentered the acceptable vocabulary until long after Stalin's demise in 1953.

Beyond these administrative measures, mainly negative in the sense that they were undertaken to halt the prevailing custom or natural coalescing of people on a scale larger than the Soviet politicians felt they could manage, official actions became less sure. Positive steps toward re-identification among the variegated easterners uncertainly approached the finding and establishing of a broader conception of the East needed to replace the previously attractive pan-Islamic, pan-Mongolian, pan-Turkic and other supra-nationality movements. Most political figures among the eastern Soviet people in public at least remained discreetly mute upon this issue. They and the central authorities left the open discussion to scholars and the bureaucracy. A series of associations sponsoring related publications record the faltering progress and ultimate failure of this contingent to discover a lasting solution. A significant part of the difficulty lay in the inherited territorial, ethnic or racial concepts, not so much amidst the easterners themselves, but the Russians directing affairs. "Siberia" may have waned after the Czarist adoption of "Asiatic Russia" following the mid-1800s, but habit and the sheer magnitude of Siberia's expanse now dominated the deliberations of academic or bureaucratic organizers.

ORGANIZED SEARCH FOR ASIAN IDENTITY

One of the early bodies established for the advancement of conceptual and practical knowledge regarding the East of the USSR was the "Society for the Study of the Ural area, Siberia, and the Far East." Emphasizing mainly economics, its major effort probably went into the issuing of the magazine NORTH ASIA (SEVERNAIA AZIIA) published by the Society beginning in 1925. In the first number, the fact that the term "Northern Asia" received two somewhat conflicting definitions, presaged the dilemmas just ahead. "Northern Asia," it was claimed, "comprises three of the most huge regions: the Ural area, Siberia, and the Far East. . . .[a] great expanse. . .bounded on the west by the Ural mountains, on the east by the Pacific Ocean, limited in the north by the Arctic Ocean and on the south by the borders of Turkistan, Mongolia, and Manchuria." In later pages of NORTHERN ASIA, No. 1/2, however, Siberia is described as". . .Siberia itself, the Kazakh territory, and the Far East," thus immediately extending Siberia southward while overlapping segments of what had been called "Northern Asia."[30]

Organizations devoted to the eastern USSR multiplied, and each faced the problem of defining jurisdiction, terrain, and function. As these bodies grew, the image of the eastern USSR became more varied and less focused. The Central Bureau of Area Studies attached to the Peoples' Commissarit for Education of the Russian SFSR entered the field, prompting work which was not so professional as the tasks undertaken by the scholars, but probably reached a much wider public. When the magazine AREA STUDIES (KRAEVEDENIE), first appeared in 1924 it immediately divided the materials relating to the Russian SFSR into European and Asian parts, including in the second, Siberia, Central Asia with Kazakhstan, and the Caucasus plus Transcaucasus. A Committee for the Study of the Languages and Ethnic Cultures of the Eastern People of the USSR simultaneously started around the mid-twenties to release a series of separate volumes concerning mainly the Caucasus nationalities. An Institute for Ethnic and Nationality Cultures of the Peoples of the East also published a learned journal labeled UCHENYE ZAPISKI during these years. The Department and Center for the Soviet East of the Scientific Research Association for the Study of Nationality and Colonial Problems prepared statistics and other materials concerning the East up to at least 1934.[31]

Meanwhile, the political-social magazine NEW EAST (NOVYI VOSTOK), put out by the Learned Society for Oriental Studies of the USSR since 1922, had started, from 1927 on, to provide space for a section specifically entitled "The Soviet East." The same editorial change occurred two years later in the political magazine REVOLUTIONARY EAST (REVOLIUTSIONNYI VOSTOK), which instituted a "Soviet East" department with No. 7, 1929, destined to appear off and on through the journal's final issue, No. 41, in 1937. The Soviet Eastern area envisioned by NEW EAST, unlike the target pointed out by many of the earlier publications and organizations, included the people of the Volga-Kama region such as the Chuvash, for example. That broadened to the West the scope of the "East" then customarily employed in the USSR.

By the time the magazine NORTHERN ASIA issued its final number in 1930, at the end of a five-year existence, a new concept and different organization had appeared to supplant the idea it embodied. The periodical SOVIET ASIA (SOVETSKAIA AZIIA) replacing it was sponsored by the Society for the Study of Soviet Asia which acted as the publisher of the new magazine during 1930-31. SOVIET ASIA designated an even larger portion of the USSR as its terrain than any recent predecessors had claimed: the Ural region, Siberia, Far East, Central Asia, and, when

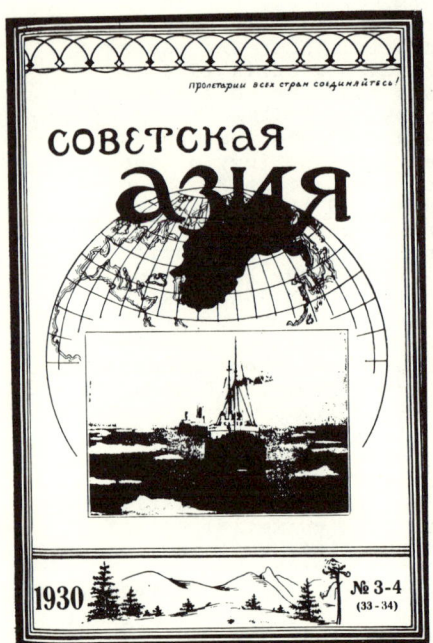 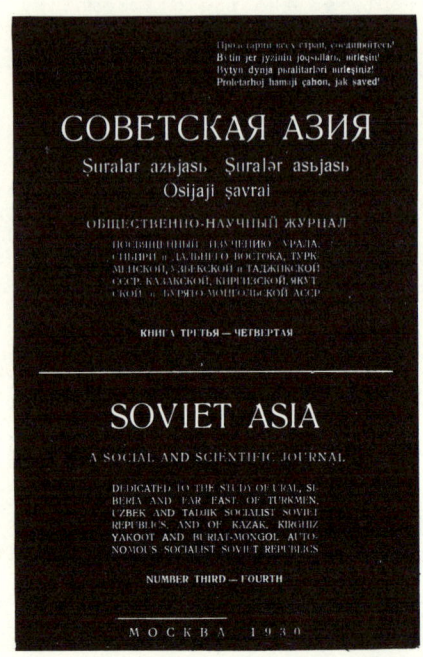

Cover and Title Page, "SOVIET ASIA" magazine, 1930

CONTROVERSIAL STATUS OF SOVIET ASIA

No. 3/4, 1931, added the Bashkir ASSR, a substantial nationality and its territory west of the Ural mountains in the Volga-Kama region had been introduced. The Society for the Study of Soviet Asia, headquartered in Moscow, elaborated a formal structure regulated by published statutes and notable for both frequent seminars and numerous books, such as AIRPLANE OVER YAKUTIA (SAMOLET NAD IAKUTIEI) and AIR ROUTES OF THE NORTH (VOZDUSHNYE PUTI SEVERA), printed up through 1933. Nevertheless, the magazine of the Society suffered a characteristic fate in the general search for an acceptable denomination appropriate to the eastern USSR. Though the Society itself carried on with its chosen name several years after 1930, the magazine suddenly ceased publication under the title SOVIET ASIA in 1931. Evidently, the connotations of "Asia" became especially unsettling for Russian sensibilities at this time because of the intense propaganda for Asianism being directed toward all easterners from Japan. Superseding SOVIET ASIA in 1932 came a more proletarian-sounding heading, FOR INDUSTRIALIZATION OF THE SOVIET EAST (ZA INDUSTRIALIZATSIIU SOVETSKOGO VOSTOKA). Definition of Soviet Asia's territory seemingly had nothing to do with this name change. FOR INDUSTRIALIZATION... was a magazine whose purview extended to the identical geographical areas covered by the previous magazine. It was jointly published by the Central Bureau for Area Studies and the Society for the Study of Soviet Asia. This periodical, too, survived only briefly, disappearing in 1934, when the popularity of focusing upon the nationalities, and especially those of the East, rapidly declined in Russian circles as political repression spread. By the end of 1937 the study groups had largely dispersed and no magazines at all were being published in the USSR's political center bearing names and expressing the all-embracing concepts Soviet East, Soviet Asia, or their analogues.[32]

While that succession of magazines--some, like FOR INDUSTRIALIZATION OF THE SOVIET EAST with Asians of the USSR sitting on their boards--worked piecemeal toward establishing an acceptable version of "Soviet Asia," several leading Soviet specialists in the field of Eastern studies were separately arriving at an understanding of what comprised Soviet Asia, so far as their subjects of concentration were concerned. I. Borozdin, in his analysis of eastern art, was one of the earliest to advocate a detailed system of comprehensive areal-ethnic categories for the treatment of the USSR's "East." His outline of 1927 begins with the Tatars, including the Crimean Tatars, adding Chuvash and Bashkirs as well, at once defining his version of the Soviet East from its westernmost outposts. He started much this side of most dividing lines placed between East and West during the nineteenth century in Czarist Russia. Emphasizing his conviction that the Volga-Kama cluster of nationalities belongs to the East, rather than West, Borozdin includes as easterners, without special comment, the Komi, Mari and Udmurt (Votiak) people of that region. His Soviet East also embraced Kalmyks and Buriat Mongols, all the indigenous nationalities of the Caucasus, North Caucasus and Transcaucasus, thus adding Armenians, Georgians, Ossets and the like, and of course Central Asia's Kazakhs, Tajiks, Uzbeks and other groups.

Discussing the obligatory reforms and change of alphabets affecting all literate eastern nationalities of the USSR except Armenians and Georgians, a linguist, Professor Nikolai F. Iakovlev, between 1925 and 1928 repeated in various verbal and printed forums his set of categories broadly defining the "Eastern People" of the Soviet Union. They are: 1. All the people of Muslim culture; 2. The non-Muslims of relatively developed eastern culture, including Armenians, Georgians, cultured people of the Far East, and the like; 3. All the sub-nationalities (NARODNOSTI) having relatively undeveloped nationality culture best characterized by the absence or weak development of their own written language. His broad system had real importance in distinguishing Soviet Asia from the remainder of the USSR, for Professor Iakovlev determined that "The characteristic trait of all these groups may be considered their relative distance from European [Russian and Soviet Western] culture." From the standpoint of language affiliation, his categories comprehend: 1. All Turkic groups; 2. All non-Turkic Caucasus people, including Armenians, Georgians, and the like; 3. "Eastern Finno-Ugrians divided from the bulk of the Finno-Ugric people by their geographic position and relative backwardness of nationality culture;" 4. All Iranians; All Mongolians; and 6. The small subnationalities of the North and Siberia, including the Tungus-Manchu, Paleoasiatic, Samoyed, and American tribes. This system, based partly upon language families, actually enlarged the list Borozdin proposed, adding, again, the Volga-Kama cluster, the Mordvins and Komi-Permiaks as well as all other small northern and eastern groups, including the Lapps, to the makeup of the Soviet East. Moreover, Iakovlev introduced an economic factor into his definition of "easterners" by concluding that

> The distribution of the eastern people about the map of the [Soviet] Union shows that as a result of the process of Russian colonization they were either shunted to the more backward, poor regions or were kept in localities less suitable for the 'dry' 'dry' (i.e., 'without artificial irrigation') agriculture employed among the Russians. . . . This unpropitious territorial and economic situation inherited by the Soviet East from the past impressed

CONTROVERSIAL STATUS OF SOVIET ASIA

its mark also upon the cultural condition of the eastern people.[34]

Iakovlev's categories as well as his recognition of the disabilities suffered by the easterners--which he believed had helped create aspects of their "easternness"--were also reflected in publications and discussions offered by other individuals about the East in the period immediately ahead. An important bibliographical study of the war issued in 1934 and entitled MATERIALS FOR A BIBLIOGRAPHY OF THE HISTORY OF THE CIVIL WAR IN THE SOVIET EAST, again found it natural to treat an East which encompassed the Volga-Kama nationalities and areas, including Komis, Mordvins, Udmurts, Chuvash, and others, Crimean Tatars, the Kalmyks along the Lower Volga, all the Caucasus-Transcaucasus people, Central Asians, Buriat Mongols, Altays, Khakass, and others of Siberia.[35]
But Iakovlev's procedure, and that of like-minded specialists, in classifying easterners ethnically and linguistically before long drove some Russians to emotional resistance against the whole idea of a "Soviet Asia" or "Soviet East." Comparable notions had caused a reaction in Czarist times when the "aliens" (certain non-Russians) of the Empire were strongly felt to be inferior to Russians and entitled to no separate recognition or protection at all. By the mid-1930's the strain of trying to reach a consensus upon this potentially volatile terminology and principle soon manifested itself in that recriminatory atmosphere through polemics dangerous for all sides of the exchange. The last word was spoken, temporarily, in the name of politics when a new ideological concept of Asia was demanded which virtually destroyed the usefulness of the name as a term for study or identification. Now, "The East" was to be conceived as ". . .a purely conventional term for the convenient designation of the entire colonial world and countries of the East, foreign and Soviet. . . ." In attempting to define the East in this sweeping manner there was an assertion that "Marxist science [was] struggling against unscientific, racial-geographical theories. . . ."[36]
An economically-defined East seemed temporarily not so far from Professor Iakovlev's version of it, but the hostility now displayed toward ethnic or territorial designations for the East disrupted his contention basically. The rising tension required both name and vision unfraught with what politicians regarded as threats of territorial plus ethnic-linguistic ties broader than those advanced in the name of a single nationality. What seemed a neutral and therefore unspecific designation finally resulted from the decade of effort started around the mid-1920s. That solution was achieved by semantically disconnecting ethnicity from geography, or simply through looking at territory alone in search for an umbrella to hold over the entire East. Typically, in the heading on a new map of the Soviet East issued exactly in 1953 appears the formula "Asiatic Part of [the]

USSR." This phrasing seemed to be acceptable because it suggested only a continental designation and the word "part" implied nothing about compass direction or content, no language or ethnic families. If the terminology had changed, the East meant by it evidently had also. This new 1935 cartography shows an "Asiatic Part" in clear distinction from what lies west of it beginning in the north along the Barents and Kara seas reaching east from approximately 43° E Longitude and including the Nenets area. Below, however, the designated Asiatic frontier makes a sharp detour to the East varying between 54° and 58° Longitude E, and, by following that general line south, avoids the Volga-Kama nationality region entirely, tracing on down to the Kazakhstan administrative border and southwest along it to the Caspian Sea. Major exclusions from this "Asia" are all nationalities of the Volga-Kama knot, regardless of ethnic or language affinity, the Kalmyk ASSR, and the entire Caucasus-Transcaucasus, the whole procedure a return almost to the "Russian Asia" of 1848-1851.[37]

The triumph of the wording "the Asian part of the USSR," acknowledged publicly to be a replacement for the last Czarist usage, "Asiatic Russia," reflected a Soviet reaction against the development of too-sympathetic or liberal attitudes respecting the Soviet easterners and offering them recognition as one community.[38] Russian conservatives most of all appeared to deplore what seemed to them a callous indifference to the importance of the enlarged "European Russia" which had expanded to the eastern edge of the Urals and the Caspian Sea before the end of the nineteenth century. This negation of any idea about regional ethnic unification or a larger Soviet Asia received unmistakable confirmation promptly in government action. In 1936 the USSR's sole Asian federated republic, the Transcaucasus SFSR, was abolished. Only a Five-Year Plan's length after Moscow's disastrous "purges" of 1937-1938 had destroyed the mature intellectual, political, and cultural leadership of most Soviet Asian groups, further drastic Russian measures altered the very configurarion and size of the Soviet East substantially. The eight Asian groups forcibly uprooted during 1943-1944 and exiled far to the East from their native soil in the Crimea, Kalmykia west of the lower Volga, and along the northern and western edge of the Caucasus (Balkars, Chechens, Crimean Tatars, Ingush, Kalmyks, Karachays, Karapapakhs, and Meskhetian Turks) amounted to nearly one million people. Until then they occupied about 130,000 square kilometers of territory fronting mainly on Russia. The sole "European" group treated similarly in this period was the Volga German nationality. Preemptively removed from the middle Volga, it was dispersed into Soviet Asia in 1941, serving to dilute further the concentration of eastern people there.[39]

CONTROVERSIAL STATUS OF SOVIET ASIA

SOVIET EASTERNERS IN FOREIGN AFFAIRS

Had this conservative attitude continued to prevail after World War II, the Russian view of its Asia might easily have remained committed to publicizing an indefinitely expanding Europe/Russia at the expense of the Soviet East. Several developments soon acted to slow or reverse this tendency. The triumph of communism in China in 1949 spurred increased Russian communist missionary activity elsewhere in non-Soviet Asia, especially after Stalin's death. Widely advertized visits by Soviet leaders to India and other parts of Asia during 1955 and thereafter initiated this new effort. In connection with this vigorous campaign, the Kremlin then began utilizing a number of its own Asians, like Tajik or Uzbek politicians Mirza Tursun-Zada, chairman of the Soviet committee for Solidarity of the Countries of Asia and Africa, Nuretdin A. Muhitdinov, member of the Central Committee Presidium of the CPSU, and Sharaf R. Rashidov, deputy chairman, Supreme Soviet, USSR, in foreign contacts and events such as the Cairo Asian-African Conference of December-January 1957-1958. A major role in the Soviet-sponsored Tashkent Conference of Writers from Asia and Africa (sequel to a similar event held in Delhi, 1956) was of course played by Soviet Asians in a very active 1958.

The executive secretary to the Soviet Afro-Asian Solidarity Committee reported in a Cairo-based magazine that delegates from his organization had visited nineteen Asian and African countries during 1958 alone. Soviet members included Tursun-Zada, Rashidov, Mukhtar Auezov (the eminent Kazakh writer), Zulfiya Israilov, and Mufti Babakhanov (head of the Muslim ecclesiastical center in Tashkent). They received visitors to the USSR from thirty-six foreign Asian and African lands.[40] Even more momentous was the participation in Tashkent of a large delegation from the People's Republic of China. An omen of things to come then perhaps not perceived came from Mao Tun, renowned Chinese novelist and head of his delegation. Speaking about "Chinese Literature in the Fight for National Independence and the Matter of Mankind's Progress," he developed at some length several historical connections between East and West Asia such as those which had linked China with Tashkent and Uzbekistan via the famous Silk Route beginning centuries B.C. The Chinese writer made no reference at all in his speech to "the Soviet people," the USSR, or to the Russians.[41]

These two developments--communization of China and a resurgence of Soviet interest in the foreign East--which had begun changing the USSR's attitude toward Soviet Asia, soon helped exert pressure for correcting some past excesses attributable to the government and party in dealing with their Asians. Together with the incentive supplied by Moscow's wish to ingratiate itself in foreign Asian capitals, this tentative reappearance of moderation led to "rehabilitation" (often posthumous) or reinstatement, first of some individuals falsely denounced, imprisoned and in too many instances killed, mainly during the 1930s. Equally crucial for the status of Soviet Asia, however, became the return of five out of eight eastern nationalities deported during 1943-1944 to Siberia and Central Asia from their homelands along the Volga and in the Caucasus. Back came what remained, after unspeakable treatment during exile--which evidently cut thier numbers substantially--of the surviving Balkars, Chechens, Ingush, Kalmyks, and Karachays. At least some of their former space in the Caucasus now had to be vacated to allow repatriation. The "homelands" reverting to them had therefore shrunk in most cases. At the same time, the Soviet government and party prevented the Meskhetian Turks and presumably the neighboring Karapapakhs from returning to their native Georgian regions, and prohibited the Tatars from repossessing any of the 26,000 square kilometers of their former autonomous republic in the Crimea. Though Soviet Asia filled out again somewhat during the 1950s, it regained in this fashion only about 100,000 of the approximately 130,000 square kilometers confiscated during World War II.[42] This final de-Asianizing of the Crimea by Soviet authorities pushed the westernmost configuration of the Soviet Asian frontier 325 kilometers farther to the east.

    The temporary Russian desire to make a good impression abroad in external Asia was accompanied by a revival of the public attempt at home to define Soviet Asia precisely. That effort, which had been abruptly suspended in the mid-1930s after stimulating some systematic proposals, once again received active attention from specialists in many fields. In the controversy among the Russians an implied distinction arose between the Soviet East (Russian: SOVETSKII VOSTOK) and Soviet Asia (Russian: SOVETSKAIA AZIIA). Those discussing Asia concerned themselves with the attenuated but still abiding force of the traditional continental identifications. Like many Europeans, the Russians retain a deep feeling that the Ural mountains, inconsiderable as their elevation may be (the highest peak reaches only 1894 meters and most Urals are much lower), form continental limits. This vague conviction could stem from primordial, unreasoned, perhaps mythical identification of the Urals corridor as the edge of the known land. Actually, the mountains probably do mark the collision point, western geologists now theorize, between two mighty tectonic plates, the Russian and the Siberian, which smashed together obliquely in the process of continental change and drift which closed off the dividing sea between them over 300 million years ago.[43] Despite a strong Russian belief in that physical division between the contiguous continents, the usage of "West" and "East," "Europe/Russia and Asia" seems to denote fairly synonymous antipodes.

    The views of Soviet Asians regarding the location of

CONTROVERSIAL STATUS OF SOVIET ASIA

Asia's limits seldom became publicly evident during Stalin's era after 1937. One of the first reported instances following World War II indirectly delineated a portion of that boundary as early as 1947. Possibly this resulted from the wartime momentum for linking USSR's Asia with Asia at large via propaganda built up by Soviet officials in order to strengthen all possible beneficial international ties for defense. In this case, 12 Soviet Asians plus two delegates from the Mongolian People's Republic attended the First Asian Relations Conference held in New Delhi, March-April 1947, as observers. Though the Mongolians, Turkmen and Kirgiz arrived late owing to travel and other difficulties, certain of the Soviet Asian delegates present promptly moved to establish their non-Western credentials for attendance. The representative from Armenia, Prof. L. Kalantar, said: "Being an Asian people and at the same time living at the crossing point of two worlds--the Asian and the European--the Armenian people succeeded in the creation of a culture in which the best traditions of the East merged with cultural achievements of the West." Azerbaijanian delegate Ibrahimov of the Academy of Sciences in Baku described the former Azerbaijan as ". . .one of the most backward corners of Asia [whose]. . .connections. . .with the other peoples of the East were rich and many sided." Mme. M. Tairova, from Stalinabad talked in a similar vein.[44]

Even rarer than that post-War reaffirmation abroad of Soviet Asianness seemed a comparable instance in domestic affairs which happened in 1955-1956. Again, Armenian and Azerbaijanian plus Georgian spokesmen, this time from the geographical sections of the Transcaucasian scholarly community, separately defined Asia's limits in their part of the world, apparently acting at the request of the Soviet Academy of Sciences in Moscow. Armenia's and Azerbaijan's geographical establishments declared their area to be part of Asia, setting its northwestern limits along the Kuma river and Manych lowlands, excluding the Azov Sea and Crimea. Georgian views differed completely. Spokesmen for that republic's geographical circle placed themselves entirely within Europe, designating the Araks river (marking the Soviet-Iranian frontier) as the beginning of Asia.[45] This disagreement among representatives of the Transcaucasian intelligentsia poses a question about how much weight must be given in defining Asia's limits to the beliefs or attitudes of the people involved. In determining nationality, it is now usually felt that the will of the group is crucial. Regarding the East-West and Asia-Russia/ Europe distinction, the popular voice probably has to be heard, though supra-nationality clusters patently differ from fundamental ethnic nationality. It seems unlikely that a nationality such as the Georgian, which insists upon its Westernness in opposition to a more general acceptance today of Transcaucasian Asianness, would unilaterally be

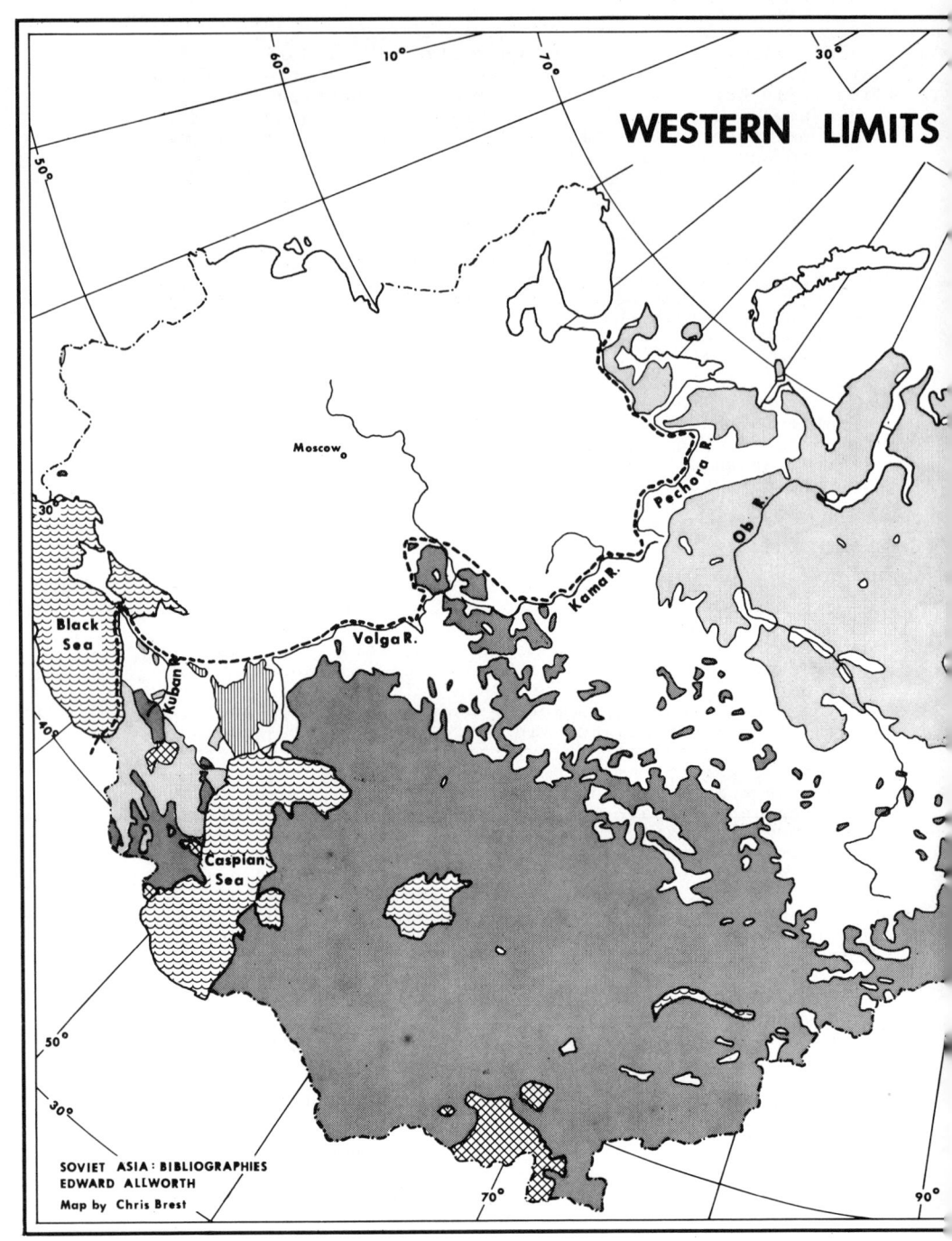

Source: ATLAS SSSR (Moscow: Glavnoe Upravlenie Geodezii

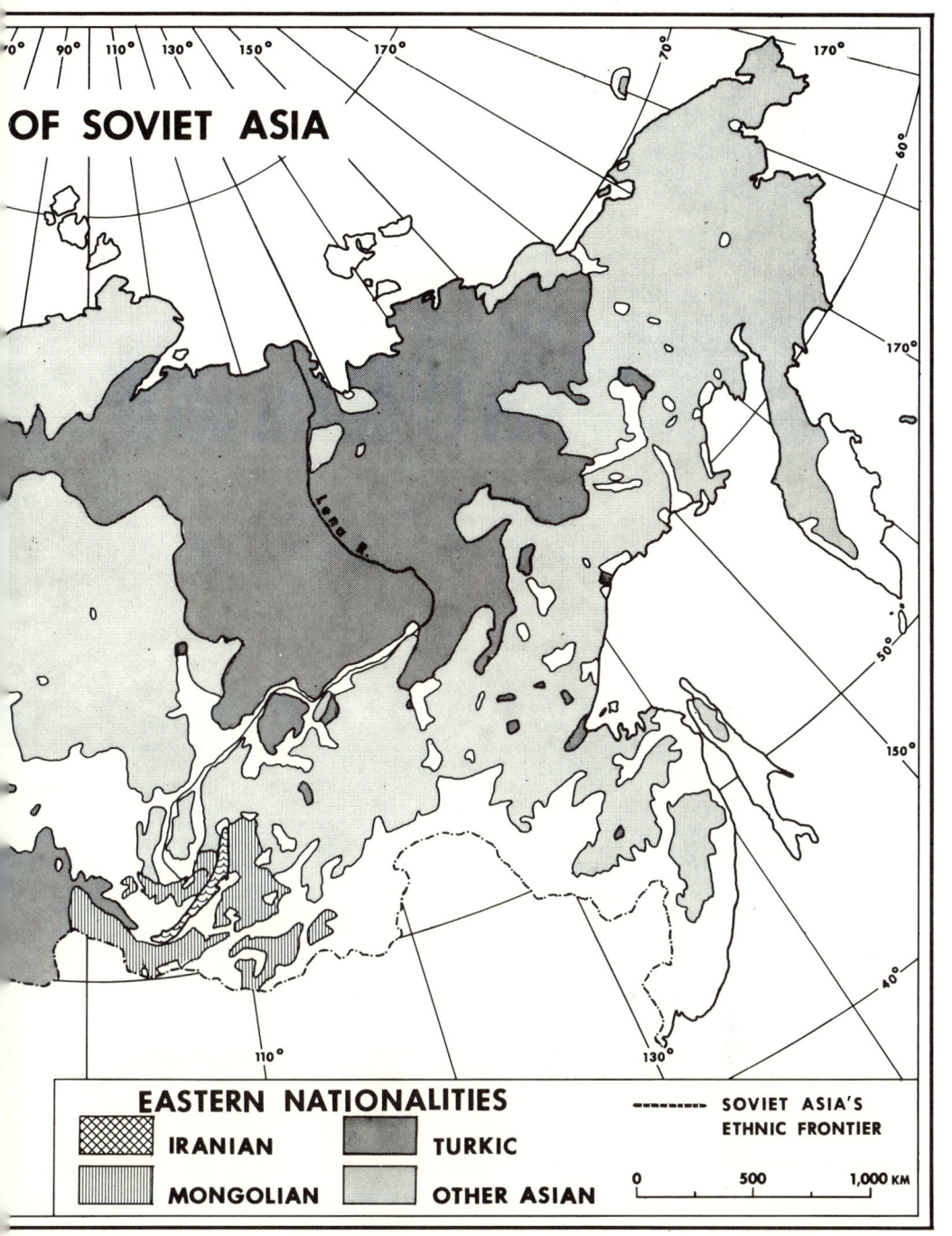

i Kartografii pri Sovete Ministrov SSR, 1969) pp. 6-7, 98-99

able to fix the limits of (Soviet) Asia.

Among those not so directly concerned with the position of the Asian frontier the debate at that time nevertheless assumed an actively polemical character. Eduard Bagramov, long-time Soviet political commentator specializing on the nationality question, categorically denied the usefulness of "West" and "East" as ideas in the history of social development or world civilization, insisting that these were entirely geographical concepts. He seemed to contradict that view, however, by seeing substantial political differences distinguishing the two areas, for in 1958 he promptly paraphrased Mao Tse-Tung's Moscow speech of Nov. 18, 1957, without acknowledgement, in asserting that "A revolutionary wind from the East is borne irrepresibly throughout the whole world, overcoming the wind from the West." In this assertion both men were attempting to equate "East" with communism ("socialism").[46]

Here the political theorist disagreed directly with other Soviet specialists. A conference held by the Moscow branch of the USSR's Geographical Society, also exactly in 1958, adopted a resolution, to which some geographers objected, agreeing "...to consider that the border between Europe and Asia is not a physical-geographical concept...but a cultural-historical one." The Russian geographers also sharply criticized the large Soviet ATLAS OF THE WORLD (ATLAS MIRA) because it placed the entire Caucasus-Transcaucasus on the "European" side of the dividing line instead of running the border along the Kuma-Manych depression. Designating the entire Caucasus, Central Asia, and all Siberia as the Asiatic part of the USSR, the Soviet capital's geographical circle agreed with anthropologists in the Academy of Sciences at the center in specifying the areas included in Asia. Both groups were at odds with some cultural or literary historians of their country who at the same time claimed, besides the three large regions already named, both the Volga basin and Ural vicinity (Priural'e) for the Soviet East.[47]

The Soviet scholars' last word in this round of the controversy seems to have been heard when a distinguished geographer, E. M. Murzaev, himself born at Simferopol and bearing a last name usually associated with Crimean Tatar nobility, spoke to the point. On March 5, 1963, he gave a report and recommendations about an East-West division to the Learned Council of the Institute of Geography, USSR Academy of Sciences. Murzaev argued that no satisfactory separation can be based upon physical geographical lines. He also rejected the possibility of determining the dividing line by recourse to history, anthropology, or linguistics, declaring that "Asian" languages, ethnic types, or economies are non-existent. Nevertheless, he acknowledged, convention demands an Asia and a Europe, and the problem comes down to supplying a more or less arbitrary separation point between them. Utilizing the political-

CONTROVERSIAL STATUS OF SOVIET ASIA

administrative boundaries circumscribing SSRs and ASSRs would serve the purpose, Murzaev states, for these borders "are drawn according to the nationality factor and thus reflect historical-ethnographic variations. . ." Clearly Murzaev's method is feasible only when the various administrative units have already been classified as "European" or "Asian." The Soviet geographer demonstrates this by criticizing previous proposals, often adopted in published works, to follow south from the Ural mountains along either the Emba or Ural rivers, alternatively the Mugojar Hills, because such delimitations, he points out, cut part of Kazakhstan off from Asia. This should be avoided, he thinks, for ". . .in respect to nationality the Kazakhs represent a unified nation, the historical development of which is intimately connected with the Asiatic expanses." By recognizing the importance of making a prior ethnic determination of who is Asian, Murzaev indirectly modifies his previous ruling that cultural history, linguistics, and anthropology cannot provide any basis for locating Soviet Asia. Presumably, the Soviet geographer allocated the Chuvash, Tatar and Bashkir republics to the European side of his line on the theory that their historical development was intimately linked to Russia/Europe's mountains or urban areas. That idea hardly seems defensible in the case of the Tatars and Bashkirs, at least. During discussion arranged at the Institute of Geography, Murzaev's recommendations underwent attacks or were defended by the many commentators, but Academician I. P. Gerasimov, the chairman, apparently trying to establish a definitive position, finally approved the proposed line along administrative unit borders, leaving Kalmyks, Chuvash, Tatars, Bashkirs, Adygeis, Circassians, Nogays and others to the north and west of this Soviet Asian frontier. At the Institute of Ethnography of the USSR Academy of Sciences in 1963, "a majority of the coworkers of the Institute. . .came out for drawing the line along the Caucasus mountain range, the Ural river and Ural mountains, but agreed to accept Murzaev's line skirting the administrative units 'for planning and statistical efforts'."[48]

USSR'S ASIANNESS CHALLENGED

Against this background of domestic uncertainty regarding the issue of Soviet Asianness, China, and the USSR (represented by some Soviet Asians), served together at the Afro-Asian Peoples' Solidarity Conference in Conakry, Africa, April 1-15, 1960. Oddly enough, though the creation of a communist China realized a long-stated Soviet aim, it soon began to generate a rivalry between the USSR and PRC which bore directly upon the Soviet Union's ambition to be an Asian country. This hope was based explicitly on the possession of extensive territory in the Asian continent. By early 1963, if not before, the Chinese government was openly challenging Soviet claims to being Asian. In February, 1963 Chinese delegates to the Third Afro-Asian Peoples' Solidarity Conference in Tanganyika reportedly singled out the visiting Soviet representatives as "whites." Peking protested in July that year against articles in RED STAR (KRASNAIA ZVEZDA), the Soviet military publication, saying that the Chinese Communist Party lay claim to a dominant role in world history for the "yellow peoples." In response, the Soviet journal KOMMUNIST, also in July 1963, editorially accused the Chinese Communist Party of referring to the "putrid" or "feeble" West (or North), and of praising nationalism and race.[49]

A Chinese representative had defended the USSR's participation at the Cairo Asian-African conference in 1958. But Marshal Ch'en Yi, head of the Chinese delegation to the preparatory meeting in Jakarta, Indonesia, which ended April 17, 1964, commended the session for rejecting an Indian delegation proposal for inviting the USSR to participate in the second African-Asian Conference. The Chinese official said: "This proposal is improper, because, as everybody knows, the Soviet Union is not an African or Asian country."[50] This rejection sparked a round of openly acrimonious exchanges which to some degree detailed what each of the two contestants believe determines the Asianness of a country. The official declaration of the Soviet government, May 5, 1964, sent to all independent governments of Asia and Africa and published in the capital of the USSR, replying to Vice Premier Ch'en Yi's statement issued earlier in Jakarta, faulted the Marshal's understanding of geography. It claimed the USSR to be both the largest Asian and European power. The Soviet statement cited possession of about 40 percent of Asia's territory, a piece almost twice the size of all China, as its main proof of Asian identity. A marker near Sverdlovsk was said to designate the border dividing Europe/Russia from ". . . .the huge territory [reaching] beyond the Caspian Sea and the Urals to the Pacific Ocean." Existence of the more than 7,000 kilometers of common Soviet-Chinese border was another proof, asserted the Soviet government newspaper IZVESTIIA, that the Peoples Republic of China was advancing a racist, that is, ethnic, argument to define the community of interests in Asia.[51]

Soviet Asia quickly served again to support Moscow's contention that it spoke for an Asian country. May 9th and May 10th, for example, in the name of the government (PRAVITEL'STVO) of the Turkmen Soviet Socialist Republic and the government of the Uzbek SSR, separate public declarations were made asserting their Asianness. It derived, they said, from a position bordering Afghanistan,

CONTROVERSIAL STATUS OF SOVIET ASIA

from their "sovereignty" as Soviet republics, and the "voluntary" nature of their unity with "other equal Soviet republics." An assertion that two-thirds of the USSR's land is located on the Asian continent, the growth of cultural and economic ties between Turkmenistan, Uzbekistan and especially Asian and African countries, plus Uzbekistan's role hosting important international meetings, and activity of specialists from the Soviet Central Asian area working on the Aswan dam project in Egypt and Jelalabad canal in Afghanistan were cited as additional proofs of the USSR's Asian identity by the official newspapers of these two constituent republics. The Central Asian press avoided available ethnic claims to Asianness except to repeat Moscow's charge that using the argument of ethnicity was racist.[52] While selected Soviet Asian politicians were identifying themselves abroad as Asians at the various international conferences of the period, a noticeable change in outlook was emerging within the USSR. Mme. Halima I. Ussupova, mayor of Tashkent in 1954, expressed the revised attitude when she enjoined a visiting European to think less about Central Asia's early history and more of the present and near future: ". . .now we are a nation learning and growing quickly. . . .The center of gravity is swinging back to Asia, and Uzbekistan will again be as famous as in the days of Tamerlane."[53]

Writers from the Soviet East also articulated a comparable but nevertheless unusual image through their almost uniformly tendentious literature. Perhaps for the first time since the Uzbek Ghafur Ghulam and his peers had spoken cautiously during World War II in verse of "coming from the East," Soviet Asian poets were again publishing verses like these composed in 1956:

> The little stream of my villages
>   The stream is lively, ebullient,
> With the voice of Asia's streams
>   It is in tune, in harmony. . . .
> From the edge of this stream,
>   From my darling village
> My heart's singing began,--
>   My sweet singing bird.
> It joined the voice of Asia,
>   It accompanied it,
> It took its place
>   In the line of happiness' creators.[54]

There could be no doubt that this vaguely familiar tone, identifying Soviet easterness with all Asia, though not like some Soviet Asian poetry of the 1920s simultaneously attacking Europe/Russia, had the sanction of Soviet leaders. Its Tajik author, Mirza Tursun-Zada, won the

SOVIET ASIA: BIBLIOGRAPHIES

Lenin prize in 1960 specifically for writing "Asia's Voice" and related poems. In this vein, Tursun-Zada's was not a lonely voice from Soviet Asia at that moment. Others, like Zulfiya Israilova, an Uzbek poet, remained active in literary circles and personally represented the Soviet East on visits through South Asia and the Middle East during the late 1950s and 1960s. She helped to revive the use of the "Asian" idiom and concept for easterners in the USSR. In "Greetings, Egypt," an Uzbek poem written after the Suez crisis of 1956, for example, she declared:

> From Soviet Asia's fervent heart
> I've brought you greetings,
>   heroic people.[55]

Repeatedly, Soviet Asians in verse and polemics and communist Chinese in politics both stress the significance of their Asianness for the question of defining Asia's provenance. Asia is where Asians are concentrated. Those people are Asians who have the tradition of non-Russian, non-European identification plus ethnic, linguistic, cultural and other links with the East. The Chinese, like many non-Westerners, definitely speak of skin color, as well. Describing the USSR's East-West duality, no Russian official would successfully label the ethnic Russians "Asian" today though millions of Russians reside or work in the Eastern USSR. That claim demands the existence of the Soviet Asians. The ethnic boundary between Russia and Soviet Asia, therefore, follows the main outline of the westernmost concentrations of Asians in the USSR. In the Sino-Soviet argument over hegemony in Asia, for ideological reasons the Russians felt compelled to deny themselves the ethnic basis for defining Asia. Their denunciation of these links, as racism and nationalism not only set in motion the mutual recriminations which helped ruin relations between the USSR and PRC, but seriously weakened their position in the dispute over an Asian identity for the Soviet Union. The Soviet Asians, though their state-controlled press was obliged to repeat Moscow's stand, were naturally caught in no such ambivalence as the Russians at any time in the course of the recent dispute with China. Both in domestic and foreign affairs the Russians evidently feared alliances with Asians of dubious (pro-Asian) reliability, and thus turned again to out-dated calls for proletarian class solidarity rather than appeals to whole people for resolution of the dilemma over their confrontation with external Asia. This has at the very least produced an ambiguity concerning the status of Soviet Asia and noticeably reduced Russian enthusiasm for the active recognition they accorded Soviet Asia during the decade beginning around 1955-1957. Not the simplest problem for the Russians, looming

GROWING SOVIET ASIA

In sheer bulk and numbers there were several compensatory additions to Soviet Asia's size and population at the expense of Asia proper during and shortly after World War II. The USSR annexed Tannu Tuva's 170,000 square kilometers in October 1944, complementing the Soviet population with thousands of Tuvans (97,996 in 1959 census; 135,306 in 1970). Additional Khakass's likewise accompanied this new piece of ground. Soviet annexations from Asia proper around 1946 also included the Kurile islands (1945) and Sakhalin island south of 50° N latitude from Japan, and a rich pistachio-nut growing area around Kushka from Afghanistan. That Soviet action in 1946 rescinded a treaty dated Feb. 28, 1921 in which the Russian SFSR had agreed to relinquish Afghan territory held by Czarist Russia during the nineteenth century, in accordance with "the opinion of the majority of the permanent residents of the population" in the area. Provisions in that same document announced approval of freedom and self-determination for the "nations of the East" and specifically for Bukhara and Khiva. Russian adherence to the agreement regarding the independence of those two young Eastern republics lasted only until 1924.[56] Asian populations acquired with those lands were small. The Russian attempt to seize northwest Iran would have added perhaps another three million Azerbaijanians plus Iranians and others, to the USSR's Asians, but the annexation was thwarted.

As a phase in the Soviet regime's upgrading of its Asians during the vigorous Soviet foreign efforts of the 1950s and 1960s, the recently incorporated Tuvans in their Autonomous Oblast were elevated one step to the status of autonomous Soviet socialist republic in 1961. That promotion constituted the most recent such change in level of eponymous unit recognition effected anywhere in the USSR. (The Kalmyk Autonomous Oblast reestablished in 1957 at the time of the mass "rehabilitation" of Kalmyks had been promoted to an ASSR in 1958).[57]

These rehabilitations of deported Asians produced some affirmative results, but only partially made up for earlier losses. Major new developments positively affecting Soviet Asia's place in the USSR as well as outside it included the rise of numerous, young generations of educated easterners concentrated in most of the Asian capitals of the Soviet Union (40 of the 53 eponymous administrative units in the USSR are Asian). The twenty-eight eponymous Asian nationalities of the autonomous oblasts, ASSRs, and SSRs increased their quantity of students in higher educational institutions (VUZ) over

SOVIET ASIA: BIBLIOGRAPHIES

84 percent on the average between 1962/63 and 1970/71. At the same time, the USSR-wide increase for the same categories of administrative units and period reached only 51.3 percent. The presence of this expanding Asian intelligentsia helps solidify the identity of contemporary Asian nationalities in a modern sense by providing them with new leaders who can enunciate their collective interests, however informally, in Soviet affairs.[58] Another development of great importance to Soviet Asia's future is the substantial growth in population of the Asian nationalities compared with nearly all those of the Soviet West and Russia itself.

Asians comprised 15.07 percent of the USSR's population as recently as 1959. Their proportion rose to 18.77 percent by 1970. That reflects an absolute increase from 32.14 to 45.28 million Asian people. Continuing high birth rates could enlarge that Asian share of the Soviet aggregate further by 1980. Asians are, moreover, located almost totally well to the East and South of the USSR's off-center Russian core. Soviet Asia made up around 82.3 percent of the USSR's land area in both 1959 and 1970. Among the Soviet Asian nationalities, in 1970 the Turkic were most populous though not distinguishable in the largest quantity of groups--32.27 million people and 22 nationalities recognized separately in the census. Iranians totalled 2.76 million divided into six groups; the three Mongolian nationalities (Buriat, Kalmyk, Khalka-Mongol) came to almost half a million altogether; and other Asians all told (mainly Caucasus-Transcaucasus, Ugric and Paleoasiatic) 9.8 millions dispersed in 43 nationalities recorded individually in the latest population census. Altogether, 71 out of the 102 USSR groups specified were Asian. Besides the Asians living in the Soviet East, substantial numbers of Slavs, Balts, Germans, Jews and Moldavians, in 1970, over 12.7 million westerners and 47.9 million Russians, were counted there. These non-Asians are often widely dispersed in the East and have a relatively weak identification with the areas where Asians are strongest. Nonetheless, if the proportions of these migrants greatly increased, the present configuration of Soviet Asia could undergo a change. Instead of a conventional East-West polarization, the eastern Soviet Union would probably become separated into six great Asian nationality areas by such colonization. Coherent Asian regions would then be: 1. the Volga-Kama; 2. the Caucasus-North Caucasus-Transcaucasus; 3. Central Asia including Kazakhstan; 4. the South Siberia of the Altays, Buriats, Khakass, Shors, and Tuvans; 5. East Siberia, with its Evens, Evenks, Yakuts, and others; 6. the Northlands from the Nenets to the Chukchis. The western limits of Soviet Asia, however, should remain quite stable.[59]

Not only population growth but notable stability in

location (relative group immobility) strongly distinguishes the main USSR Asian nationalities in general today from the Russians. Those migrating Soviet Asians giving their names to SSRs (persons who had lived in their small census district less than two consecutive years before January 1970) totalled 638,635. They comprised under 5 percent of all the USSR's "migrants" (defined by such inter-district movement) identified with their respective SSRs. This meant at the same time that though over 14 percent of the entire eponymous population of the SSRs, including all Russians, was Asian, that segment provided only 2.07 percent of the Soviet Union's SSR migrants. A percentage of Russians more than three times as large, 6.74, and of SSR Soviet Westerners, twice the Asian proportion, 4.87 qualified as migrants in January 1970. Average rates of migration combining eponymous Asians and Westerners of the SSRs with all Soviet Russians thus reached 29.13 percent for the two years up to January 1970. This revealed the Soviet Asians' 4.6 percent to be strikingly low, followed by the 20.21 percent of the much more mobile Westerners, both in feeble competition with the virtually nomadic Russians moving on the average high above the mean with 62.5 percent of all migrants reported according to ethnic affiliation.[60] Stability or instability among Asians not identified with SSRs (Avars, Kalmyks, and Karakalpaks, for example), cannot be specified for lack of published data. Because most are identified with their own administrative units, and all are surrounded by or living adjacent to some other Asians, it is likely that their pattern of migration resembles the modest degree of mobility shown by the SSR Asians.

Soviet Asian stability may to some degree correlate with the unurbanized status of a large percentage among their population as late as 1970. Only five Soviet Asian groups exceeded the USSR average of 56.3 percent urban, as officials defined it. Above 60 percent of most Asian nationalities in fact remained rural dwellers in 1970. The Tajiks, for example, were 74 percent, Yakuts 78.9 percent, and Kirgiz 85.4 percent. Russia and the Soviet West contrast sharply with the East in this respect as well, being much more highly urbanized. In fields of publishing, education, broadcasting, and other attributes of modern cultural life, Soviet Asians likewise participate to a noticeably smaller degree than do the Russians and the western USSR nationalities, especially at the advanced levels of activity or schooling.[62]

Nevertheless, the collective Asian self-consciousness stimulated in the USSR by improving communications and reengagement with the foreign East, after Stalin, persisted through the decade of the 1960s. Continuing Chinese-Russian controversy helped sustain this supra-nationality awareness of Soviet Asians as they actively participated in external relations with foreign Asia. Some, like

SOVIET ASIA: BIBLIOGRAPHIES

Sarvar Azimov, sent from Tashkent as ambassador to Beirut, served as diplomats to the Middle East and Africa. Others, including the senior Uzbek author, Kamil Yashin, in September 1968 welcomed visiting Eastern intellectuals to Tashkent and similar cities in the area where, he said, "the. . .guests could see. . .how old Asia (ESKI ASIYA) has been completely changed. . . .[into] young and vigorous Soviet Asia (SOVET ASIYASI)." Yashin made clear, too, that he saw Uzbekistan as only a portion of the USSR's Asia.[62] Local Asian scholars and journalists in the USSR focusing upon today's Soviet Central Asia similarly describe that huge region more and more as only a fraction of the Soviet East. Perhaps this usage will dispose for good of a confusing habit formed in the USSR after the mid-1930s, and often copied abroad since then (except during World War II), of considering the Soviet East to be coextensive only with Soviet Central Asia. Judging from the specialized periodical press, the attitude at the center at first agreed. The series, SOVIET ORIENTAL STUDIES (SOVETSKOE VOSTOKOVEDENIE), six volumes of which came out between 1940 and 1949, never used "Soviet East" or "Soviet Asia" in a heading, though the editors mentioned the Soviet East in the introduction to the first issue. The sequel to this irregular serial, which the Academy of Sciences put out from 1955 to 1958 under the same titles, SOVIET ORIENTAL STUDIES, printed "Soviet East" on only two article titles during the time its 36 issues were appearing. In both cases, however, the term referred to Mongolian, Turkic and other Soviet Asian groups outside and inside Central Asia. Subsequently, the main Soviet learned journals concentrating upon contemporary affairs in the East, PROBLEMS OF ORIENTAL STUDIES (PROBLEMY VOSTOKOVEDENIIA), 1959-1960, and PEOPLES OF ASIA AND AFRICA (NARODY AZII I AFRIKI), 1961-1974, at first called Central Asia, alone, "the Soviet East." More recently that terminology was extended to cover the Caucasus-Transcaucasus as well. In no article title published during that time in those bi-monthly journals, did "Soviet East," encompass Siberia, the Volga-Kama or the North Caucasus, including Kalmykia, however. Twice in the period merely "the East" in a title designated the Soviet East, and in no heading was "Soviet Asia" employed. If there is a pattern of change discernible over these 34 years, it tends toward specifying only the Transcaucasus and Central Asia as the Soviet East. In a parallel series of publications, called LANDS AND PEOPLES OF THE EAST (STRANY I NARODY VOSTOKA), neither "Soviet Asia" nor "the Soviet East" appeared in any article titles between the publication of No. 1 (1959) and No. 15 (1973), though Asian nationalities of the USSR were treated frequently in all these periodicals.

Although Soviet Asians today ordinarily employ "Soviet Asia" and "Soviet East" interchangeably to designate the

CONTROVERSIAL STATUS OF SOVIET ASIA

same people and area, in practice they emphasize "Soviet Asia" when community or comparison with foreign Asia is meant. Purely domestic concerns more regularly elicit a preference for the term "Soviet East." This tendency goes back to the drastic official suppression, starting about mid-1930s, of the concept "Asia" for any Soviet territory. That terminological distinction between "East" and "Asia" has been strengthened since the late 1950s by the Russian competition with the Chinese, already discussed, for influence throughout Asia. Regardless of the word choice, in the early 1970s local Asians were complaining openly that European (Russian?) colonialists habitually considered Asia/the East to be eternally weak and backward, but Asia and her people represent "the cradle of mankind [in which] a great civilization originally came into existence and exerted a very strong influence upon all subsequent development." These Soviet commentators, unconsciously echoing Nariman Narimanov's remarks made at the first session of the Baku Congress of Eastern Peoples over fifty years earlier, also expressed resentment toward western attitudes which suggested that strong contradictions divide the East (SHARQ) and West (GHARB) and imply an Eastern inferiority.[63] These historical arguments citing the East's human equality and cultural precedence on the East-West spectrum are presently linked in turn to Soviet Asia's relatively advanced socio-economic status, routinely said to have resulted from the 1917 Russian revolution and activity of the Soviet communist party.

Here is an unmistakeable claim that Asianness is ineradicable. This affirmation of sustained Asianness/Easterness persisting throughout history, extending into contemporary times, has extraordinary importance. In the eyes of the Asians, the jolts of past humiliating discrimination following military or economic conquest, and, most crucial of all now, great scientific and political change, have not caused the Soviet East to lose its essential character. This continuity of strong Asian self-awareness within the Czarist Empire, the Russian SFSR and USSR through the past centuries despite increasingly heavy pressure for Russification and, recently, rapid technological modernization, conveys a profound message about the Soviet East's striking adaptability and the consequent durableness of its identity. The message sounds overtones for the future of all Asia as it increasingly adopts modern ways.

RUSSIAN AMBIVALENCE

Also intimately involved in the existence of Soviet Asia are the Russians themselves, who control it politically. Contradictory attempts to deemphasize their Asia for domestic purposes and accentuate it in external affairs

SOVIET ASIA: BIBLIOGRAPHIES

have intensified the ambiguities they seemingly feel respecting "their" East. Russian circles again cautiously acknowledge a geographical Soviet Asia. Its limits, they say without explanation, are continually shifting eastward. Quite ignoring the crucial awareness of the Asians themselves, these circles offer but one basic reason for distinguishing "Asia" from "Europe" (including Russia) today: this conventional division they call "too deeply imbedded in the [people's] consciousness" to be dislodged.64 Possibly this refers to a mystical belief grounded in the continental separation between "Russian" and "Siberian" earth plates of pre-human eras discovered by geologists in recent times. In practice, the Soviet Asia recognized in the Soviet geographer's mind around 1970 includes the Caucasus-Transcaucasus, Central Asia with Kazakhstan, the Northlands, Artic region, and Siberia plus the Soviet Far East. The Bashkirs, Chuvash, Kalmyks, Nenets and Tatars are thereby unaccountably detached from Asia.

Russia's preoccupation with the proximity of its domestic Asia, along with the penetration of this Asia into the Russian subconscious, has been sharply mirrored in the early 1970s by a recognized Russian novelist. Unlike the foreboding expressed by Maxim Gorky in 1920 about Russia's "going Asian," Grigorii Konovalov, in his recent book THE BOUNDARY (PREDEL) confidently employs a short stretch of Asian/Russian threshold as a rich complex of symbols denoting the Easterness and Westernness natural in these fictional Soviet personages. Konovalov, born himself in Orenburg oblast's southwest corner near Kazakhstan, an area with large patches of Bashkirs and Tatars, convincingly describes the two worlds interacting. The narrative focuses on a hybrid village, Predel-Tashla, half-Russian, half-Turkic, through which the frontier passes, each side remaining largely true to what can be called its "historical memory." Chuvash, Kalmyks and Tatars populating THE BOUNDARY, the very people regularly excluded from the domestic East created by Soviet ideology and official geography, are specifically identified with the Asian side of Konovalov's microcosm. They exist across the river from his Slavs, whose leading contemporary Russian, meant unobtrusively to be a blend of East and West, is suggestively surnamed Tolmachev (The Russian lexicon borrowed the word TOLMACH centuries ago from the Turkic languages) signifying "interpreter (go between?)." A Tatar, on the other hand, is presented as a purely ethnic type: "But Tugan somehow, in a terribly sly-Asiatic way (KHITRO-AZIATSKI), grinned ironically with his whole lemon-fresh face. . ." There, in a single sentence, among a number of such passages, the author weakens any misapprehension that today's Russians may be oblivious to the physical traits, including skin color, differentiating Soviet Asians from Slavs, or that those visible characteristics are noticed without prejudice.65 The long, close

CONTROVERSIAL STATUS OF SOVIET ASIA

interrelation between Asians and Russians of the Volga-Kama region acknowledged so evocatively by Konovalov conveys an acute sense of living on the periphery that refutes the arguments for East-West homogeneity and confounds the standard Russian definition of the identity and limits of the Soviet East. This difficulty further complicates Moscow's conception of internal and therefore external Asia.

Russia's vacillating opinions concerning its identification with or inferiority to Europe have hardly been matched as yet by a comparable Soviet Asian indecision over community with Asia at large. But confronting the East with consistently assertive Russian self-consciousness contributes notably to maintaining Soviet Asians' well-developed sense of ethnic contrast within the USSR. Should the Russians submerge their group feeling completely beneath an acceptable identity, such as the "Soviet people" presently offered--today a most unlikely step--the longevity and health of Soviet Asia would still merit an excellent prognosis, modernizing forces and ideology notwithstanding. The shape Soviet Asia may assume, the precise name it will ultimately acquire, depend equally upon shifts or stability of population and retention or changes of identity. Over fifty years of practice have established the easterners' habit of recognizing their collective Asianness. Hardly any doubt remains that Soviet Asia will survive as a unifying idea, though by 1970, in comparison with 1920, Russia's enthusiasm for its Asia had obviously subsided. The considerable fluctuation evident in Russian opinion regarding the non-whites of Asia over the decades suggests a great uncertainty about their own status. Perhaps this doubt is rooted in a partly submerged racism often expressed as a highly conscious feeling of superiority over the East based on power alone and asserted repeatedly at least from the day in 1489 when Ivan III first officially claimed part of Siberia for Moscow Czardom.[66] The persistent Russian fear and suspicion of potential supra-nationality conglomerations' forming among the Easterners may be traced back to the Middle Ages, when "the great question of humanity" concerned which part of the world would conquer the other. This memory works against official sponsorship of an appropriate Soviet Asia now. That ambivalence reflects itself in policies which in turn may affect the factors of stability or identity among the Asians. In this sense, above and beyond the vigorous Russian ethnocentrism, Kremlin attitudes will continue to exert influence upon the definition of a Soviet Asia, even while its people grow stronger, more populous, more self-aware and self-reliant every year.

> "'When the Chinese come, they'll straighten you out' is a cry often heard by me and others in our Central Asian cities." (Igor Shafaravich, Russian mathematician, ca.1974)

NOTES

1. Akademik S. F. Ol'denburg, VOSTOK I ZAPAD V SOVETSKIKH USLOVIIAKH (Moscow-Leningrad: Gosudarstvennoe Sotsial'no-Ekonomicheskoe Izdatel'stvo, 1931), p. 14.
2. A. S. Pushkin, "KLEVETNIKAM ROSSII [1831]," POLNOE SOBRANIE SOCHINENII (Moscow: Izdatel'stvo Akademii Nauk, 1957), Vol. 3, p. 223; IBID., Vol. 10 (1958), pp. 301, 335, 352 (letters to Mme. E. M. Khitrova and P. A. Viazemskii); A. Pushkin, "PUTESHESTVIE V ARZRUM," SOVREMENNIK No. 1 (1836), p. 75.
3. F. M. Dostoevskii, "DNEVNIK PISATELIA ZA 1876 G.," POLNOE SOBRANIE SOCHINENII (St. Petersburg: Tipografiia P. F. Pantelieeva, 1905, 6th ed.), Vol. 11, pp. 203, 206-207, 276-277.
4. IBID., Vol. 12 (1906), p. 505.
5. Alexandre Bennigsen; Chantal Lemercier-Quelquejay, ISLAM IN THE SOVIET UNION, trans. Geoffrey E. Wheeler, Hubert Evans (London: Pall Mall Press, 1967), pp. 11-20; Edward Allworth, ed., CENTRAL ASIA: A CENTURY OF RUSSIAN RULE (New York: Columbia University Press, 1967), pp. 349-370.
6. G. Gasprinskii, RUSSKOE MUSUL'MANSTVO (a collection of articles originally issued separately in the newspaper TAVRIDA in 1881), quoted by M. A. Miropiev, O POLOZHENII RUSSKIKH INORODTSEV (St. Petersburg: Sinodal'naia Tipografiia, 1901), pp. 6-7 (Gasprinskii, pp. 8-9, 13, 30, 35-36).
7. Edward Allworth, "ENCOUNTER," CENTRAL ASIA: A CENTURY OF RUSSIAN RULE, pp. 1-59.
8. S. M. Solov'ev, ISTORIIA ROSSII S DREVNEISHIKH VREMEN (Moscow: Izdatel'stvo Sotsial'no-Ekonomicheskoi Literatury, 1963), Book 2 (originally pub. as Vols. 3 and 4, 1854), p. 287.
9. Leo Bagrow, "AT THE SOURCES OF THE CARTOGRAPHY OF RUSSIA," IMAGO MUNDI Vol. 16 (1962), pp. 38-40, 43-45, especially plates opposite pp. 40, 44, 45.
10. V. Kordt, MATERIALY PO ISTORII RUSSKOI KARTOGRAFII (Kiev: Izdanie Kievskoi Kommissii dlia Razbora Drevnikh Aktov, 1899), No. 1, pp. 13-14 and plate XXIX.
11. ATLAS AZIATSKOI ROSSII (St. Petersburg: Izdanie Pereselencheskago Upravleniia Glavnago Upravleniia Zemleustroistva i Zemledieliia, 1914), pp. 1-2, 4 and plate 3; Semen U. Remezov, THE ATLAS OF SIBERIA ('sGravenhage: Mouton & Co., 1958), plate 4 (Godunov's map); Leo Bagrow, "SEMYON REMEZOV--A SIBERIAN CARTOGRAPHER," IMAGO MUNDI Vol. XI (1954), p. 118 and plate opposite p. 111; John F. Baddeley, RUSSIA, MONGOLIA, CHINA. . . (London: Macmillan & Co., Ltd., 1919), Vol. I, plate 7 following p. cxxxviii.
12. K. V. Viatkina, "K VOPROSU O TERMINE 'SIBIR'," SOVETSKAIA ETNOGRAFIIA No. 1 (1935), pp. 91-92; Z. Ia. Boiarshinova, "O PROISKHOZHDENII SLOVA 'SIBIR',"

ISTORICHESKIE NAUKI No. 3 (1959), p. 110; S. M. Seredonin, "ISTORICHESKII OCHERK ZAVOEVANIIA AZIATSKOI ROSSII," AZIATSKAIA ROSSIIA (St. Petersburg: Izdanie Pereselencheskago Upravleniia Glavnago Upravleniia Zemleustroistva i Zemledieliia, 1914), Vol. I, p. 4; Rashid ad-Din, SBORNIK LETOPISEI trans. L. A. Khetagurov (Moscow-Leningrad: Izdatel'stvo Akademii Nauk SSSR, 1952), Vol. 1, Book 1, pp. 73, 150; E. Bretschneider, MEDIAEVAL RESEARCHES FROM EASTERN ASIATIC SOURCES. . . (London: Kegan Paul, Trubner & Co., Ltd., 1910), Vol. 2, pp. 88, 37 n. 811.
 13. ATLAS RUSSICUS (Petropoli: Academiae Imperialis Scientiarum Petropolitanae, 1745), plates XII, XX; ROSSIISKOI ATLAS (n.p.: Sochin. Gravir. i Pechat. pri Gornom Uchilishche, 1792), 44 maps; Piadyshev, GEOGRAFICHESKII ATLAS ROSSIISKOI IMPERII, TSARSTVA POL'SKAGO I VELIKAGO KNIAZHESTVA FINLIANDSKAGO (n. p.: n. pub., 1820-1827).
 14. Aleksandr Voshchinin, GEOGRAFICHESKII ATLAS ROSSIISKOI IMPERII. . .(St. Petersburg: Shtaba Ego Imperatorskago Vysochestva Glavnago Nachal'nago Voennago Uchebnago Zavedeniia, approved Mar. 9, 1851), 16 plates-- see plates 3 and 15 especially.
 15. OTCHET RUSSKAGO GEOGRAFICHESKAGO OBSHCHESTVA ZA 1864 GOD (St. Petersburg) (1865), cited in UKAZATEL' K IZDANIIAM IRGO I EGO OTDIELOV S 1846 PO 1875 GOD (St. Petersburg: V Tipografii V. Bezobrazova i Komp., 1886), p. 58.
 16. KARTA AZIATSKOI ROSSII. SOSTAVLENA PO NOVIEISHIM SVIEDIENIIAM. . . (n.p.: Voenno-Topograficheskaia Chast' Glavnago Upravleniia General'nago Shtaba, 1865, corrected 1869), 1 sheet.
 17. Alexandre Bennigsen; Chantal Lemercier-Quelquejay, LA PRESSE ET LE MOUVEMENT NATIONAL CHEZ LES MUSULMANS DE RUSSIE AVANT 1920 (Paris: Mouton & Co., 1964), pp. 44-45, 164.
 18. "IMPERATORSKOE OBSHCHESTVO VOSTOKOVIEDIENIIA," VIESTNIK IMPERATORSKAGO OBSHCHESTVA VOSTOKOVIEDIENIIA No. 1 (Aug. 1916), p. 14.
 19. M. A. Tsvietkov, "PROSTRANSTVO I GRANITSY AZIATSKOI ROSSII," AZIATSKAIA ROSSIIA, Vol. I, p. 39.
 20. Walter Kolarz, RUSSIA AND HER COLONIES (n.p.: Archon Books, 1967 repr. of 1953 ed.), pp. 56-58.
 21. 1-YI S"EZD NARODOV VOSTOKA, BAKU, 1-8 SENT. 1920 G. STENOGRAFICHESKIE OTCHETY (Petrograd: Izdatel'stvo Kommunisticheskogo Internatsionala, 1920, 2d ed.), pp. 87, 90-91.
 22. H. G. Wells, RUSSIA IN THE SHADOWS (New York: George H. Dovan Co., 1921), p. 101.
 23. S. Saifullin (Saken), ASAU TULPAR (Orenburg: Izdatel'stvo Kirgizskogo Gosizdata, 1922), p. 98, cited by N. Tiurakulov in Russian translation, reviewing the book for ZHIZN' NATSIONAL'NOSTEI No. 2. (1923), pp. 167-169.
 24. E. Baybolov, B. Qoyshibaeva, A. Narimbetov,

E. El'konina, comp., SAKEN SEYFULLIN. (TUGHANINA 70 JIL TOLUINA ARNALGHAN ADEBIETTERDING KORSETKISHI) (Alma Ata: "Qazaqstan Baspasi, 1965), p. 2.
25. A. B., "ZHUMABAEV, MAGZHAN (1896)," LITERATURNAIA ENTSIKLOPEDIIA Vol. 4 (Moscow: Izdatel'stvo Kommunisticheskoi Akademii, 1930), p. 203.
26. TRETII S"EZD SOVETOV SOIUZA SOVETSKIKH SOTSIALISTICHESKIKH RESPUBLIK. POSTANOVLENIIA (Moscow: Izdanie TsIK SSSR, 1925), pp. 45-56.
27. "IZ BESEDA V. I. LENINA S IAPONSKIM KORRESPONDENTOM KATSUCHZHI FUSE. . . . ," SOVETSKOE VOSTOKOVEDENIE No. 1 (1958), p. 14.
28. I. V. Stalin, "O REVOLIUTSIONNOM DVIZHENII NA VOSTOKE," SOCHINENIIA (Moscow: OGIZ Gosudarstvennoe Izdatel'stvo Politicheskoi Literatury, 1947) Vol. 7, p. 228.
29. Katsuji Fuse, SOVIET POLICY IN THE ORIENT (East Peking: Enjinsha, 1924), pp. 74-77, 395-397; Dzh. Baibulatov, CHAGATAIZM-PANTIURKIZM (Moscow-Tashkent: OGIZ, 1932), p. 20.
30. Vl. Vilenskii-Sibiriakov, ZADACHI IZUCHENIIA SEVERNOI AZII," SEVERNAIA AZIIA No. 1/2 (1925), p. 7; N. Zdobnov, "SOVREMENNOE SOSTOIANIIE I ZADACHI URALO-SIBIRSKOI BIBLIOGRAFII," IBID., p. 114.
31. REVOLIUTSIONNYI VOSTOK No. 4 (1934), p. 201 f.
32. PERIODICHESKAIA PECHAT' SSSR. 1917-1949. BIBLIOGRAFICHESKII UKAZATEL'. ZHURNALY, TRUDY I BIULLETENI, SVODNYE UKAZATELI (Moscow: Izdatel'stvo Vsesoiuznoi Knizhnoi Palaty, 1963), Vols. I, I Book 1, II, and VIII.
33. I. Borozdin, "IZUCHENIE KUL'TUR SOVETSKOGO VOSTOKA (NEKOTORYE ITOGI K 10-LETIIU OKTIABRIA)," NOVYI VOSTOK No. 19 (1927), pp. XLVII-LIX.
34. Prof. N. Iakovlev, "RAZVITIIA NATSIONAL'NOI PIS'MENNOSTI U VOSTOCHNYKH NARODOV SOVETSKOGO SOIUZA I ZAROZHDENIE IKH NATSIONAL'NYKH ALFAVITOV," REVOLIUTSIONNYI VOSTOK No. 3 (1928), pp. 206-212.
35. N. Ia. Vitkind, MATERIALY K BIBLIOGRAFII ISTORII GRAZHDANSKOI VOINY NA SOVETSKOM VOSTOKE (Moscow: Izdanie Nauchno-Issledovatel'skoi Assotsiatsii po Izucheniiu Natsional'nykh i Kolonial'nykh Problem, 1934).
36. I. V. Vladislavlev, "IAPONIIA I DRUGIE STRANY VOSTOKA V BURZHUAZNOI I SOVETSKOI BIBLIOGRAFII (K VOPROSU O BLIZHAISHIKH ZADACHAKH NASHEI VOSTOKOVEDNOI BIBLIOGRAFII)," SOVETSKAIA BIBLIOGRAFIIA No. 3/4 (7/8) (1934), p. 105.
37. MAP OF THE ASIATIC PART OF [sic] USSR (Moscow: Mezhdunarodnaia Kniga, 1935), 1 sheet in color, 1 side.
38. "AZIATSKAIA ROSSIIA," SIBIRSKAIA SOVETSKAIA ENTSIKLOPEDIIA (Novosibirsk: Sibirskoe Kraevoe Izdatel'stvo, 1929), Vol. 1, p. 30.
39. ITOGI VSESOIUZNOI PEREPISI NASELENIIA 1959 GOD. SSSR (SVODNYI TOM) (Moscow: Gosstatizdat, 1962), p. 186;

Frank Lorimer, THE POPULATION OF THE SOVIET UNION: HISTORY AND PROSPECTS (Geneva: League of Nations, 1946), pp. 63, 138-139, 242-243; Walter Kolarz, pp. 74-75, 185; VSESOIUZNAIA PEREPIS' NASELENIIA 17 DEKABRIA 1926 G., KRATKIE SVODKI. Vol. IV, NARODNOST' I RODNOI IAZYK NASELENIIA SSSR (Moscow: Izdanie TsSU SSSR, 1928), p. 71.

40. A. Sofronov, "SOVIET UNION IN THE AFRO-ASIAN SOLIDARITY MOVEMENT," AFRO-ASIAN QUARTERLY Vol. I, Nos. 2/3 (Jan.-June 1959), pp. 135-137.

41. Mao Tun', "KITAISKAIA LITERATURA V BOR'BE ZA NATSIONAL'NUIU NEZAVISIMOST' I DELO PROGRESSA CHELOVECHESTVA," TASHKENTSKAIA KONFERENTSIIA PISATELEI STRAN AZII I AFRIKI (Tashkent: Gosudarstvennoe Izdatel'stvo Khudozhestvennoi Literatury UzSSR, 1960), p. 104 f.

42. Robert Conquest, THE NATION KILLERS. THE SOVIET DEPORTATION OF NATIONALITIES (London: Macmillan, 1970), pp. 48, 64-66, 145-152, 160-163, 186-189; ATLAS SSSR (Moscow: Glavnoe Upravlenie Geodezii i Kartografii pri Sovete Ministrov SSSR, 1969), p. 150; Frank Lorimer, pp. 138-139.

43. Warren Hamilton, "THE URALIDES AND THE MOTION OF THE RUSSIAN AND SIBERIAN PLATFORMS," BULLETIN OF THE GEOLOGICAL SOCIETY OF AMERICA Vol. 81 (1970), pp. 2553-2576.

44. ASIAN RELATIONS. BEING REPORT OF THE PROCEEDINGS AND DOCUMENTATION OF THE FIRST ASIAN RELATIONS CONFERENCE, NEW DELHI, MARCH-APRIL, 1947 (New Delhi: Asian Relations Organization, 1948), pp. 5, 8, 33-35, 60.

45. E. M. Murzaev, "GDE ZHE PROVODIT' GEOGRAFICHESKUIU GRANITSU EVROPY I AZII?" IZVESTIIA AN SSSR, seriia geograficheskaia No. 4 (1963), p. 115.

46. Eduard A. Bagramov, MIF O PROTIVOPOLOZHNOSTI ZAPADA I VOSTOKA (Moscow: Izdatel'stvo "Znanie," 1958), pp.3, 40; John Gittings, SURVEY OF THE SINO-SOVIET DISPUTE. A COMMENTARY AND EXTRACTS FROM THE RECENT POLEMICS, 1963-1967 (London: Oxford University Press, 1968), pp. 82-83;"TALK AT A MEETING WITH CHINESE STUDENTS AND TRAINEES IN MOSCOW (EXCERPTS)," in "LONG LIVE MAO TSETUNG THOUGHT (A COLLECTION OF STATEMENTS BY MAO TSE-TUNG)," trans. and pub. in CURRENT BACKGROUND (Hong Kong: American Consulate General, Oct. 8, 1969), No. 891, p. 26.

47. Iu. K. Efremov, "OBSUZHDENIE VOPROSA O GRANITSY EVROPY I AZII V MOSKOVSKOM FILIALE GEOGRAFICHESKOGO OBSHCHESTVA SSSR," IZVESTIIA AKADEMII NAUK SSSR. seriia geograficheskaia No. 4 (July-Aug. 1958), pp. 145-146; ATLAS MIRA (Moscow: Glavnoe Upravlenie Geodezii i Kartografii MVD SSSR, 1954), maps 18-19; V. I. Prokaev, "ESHCHE RAZ O GRANITSE MEZHDU EVROPOI I AZIEI V SVIAZI S VOPROSOM O KRUPNYKH EDINITSAKH FIZIKO-GEOGRAFICHESKOI KHARAKTERISTIKI," IZVESTIIA VSESOIUZNOGO GEOGRAFICHESKOGO OBSHCHESTVA Vol. XCII, No. 4 (1960), pp. 361-365; S. P. Tolstov et al, eds., OCHERKI OBSHCHEI ETNOGRAFII.

AZIATSKAIA CHAST' SSSR (Moscow: Izdatel'stvo Akademii Nauk SSSR, 1960), pp. 3, 366; L. Klimovich, IZ ISTORII LITERATUR SOVETSKOGO VOSTOKA (Moscow: Gosudarstvennoe Izdatel'stvo Khudozhestvennoi Literatury, 1959), p. 5.

48. E. M. Murzaev, "GDE ZHE PROVODIT' GEOGRAFICHESKUIU GRANITSU EVROPY I AZII?" pp. 112-114 , 116; A. G. Chikishev, "OBSUZHDENIE VOPROSA O GRANITSE EVROPY I AZII," IBID., pp. 154-155.

49. "ZA TORZHESTVO TVORCHESKOGO MARKSIZMA-LENINIZMA, PROTIV REVIZII KURSA MIROVOGO KOMMUNISTICHESKOGO DVIZHENIIA," KOMMUNIST (Moscow) No. 11 (July 1963), pp. 6, 23; Peter Berton, comp., THE CHINESE-RUSSIAN DIALOGUE: A COLLECTION OF LETTERS EXCHANGED BETWEEN THE COMMUNIST PARTIES OF CHINA AND THE SOVIET UNION AND RELATED DOCUMENTS (Los Angeles: Research Institute on Communist Strategy and Propaganda, School of International Relations, University of Southern California, 1964), chronology.

50. "VICE PREMIER CH'EN YI'S WRITTEN STATEMENT BEFORE LEAVING DJAKARTA," Jakarta: New China News Agency release, April 17, 1964; Hong Kong, American Consulate General's report No. 3204, April 23, 1964, pp. 41-42.

51. "SPLACHIVAT', A NE RAZ"EDINIAT' BORTSOV PROTIV IMPERIALIZMA. ZAIAVLENIE SOVETSKOGO PRAVITEL'STVA," IZVESTIIA (May 5, 1964), pp. 1-2.

52. "ZAIAVLENIE PRAVITEL'STVA TURKMENSKOI SSR PROTIV POPYTOK RUKOVODITELEI KNR NE DOPUSTIT' SSSR K UCHASTIIU VO VTOROI KONFERENTSII AFRO-AZIATSKIKH STRAN," TURKMENSKAIA ISKRA (May 9, 1964), p. 1; "SPLACHIVAT', A NE RAZ"EDINIAT' BORTSOV PROTIV IMPERIALIZMA. ZAIAVLENIE PRAVITEL'STVA UZBEKSKOI SOVETSKOI SOTSIALISTICHESKOI RESPUBLIKI," PRAVDA VOSTOKA (May 10, 1964), p. 1.

53. Patrick Sergeant, ANOTHER ROAD TO SAMARKAND (London: Hodder and Stoughton, 1955), p. 115.

54. Mirzo Tursunzoda, "SADOI OSIYO," ASARHON MUNTAKHAB Vol. 2 (Dushanbe: Nashriyoti Davlatii Tojikiston, 1962), p. 271, Manouchehr Kasheff kindly helped with this translation from Tajik; Mirzo Tursun-Zade, GOLOS AZII. KHASAN-ARBAKESH, STIKHOTVORENIIA I POEMY, trans. from Russ. (Moscow: Gosudarstvennoe Izdatel'stvo Khudozhestvennoi Literatury, 1960), pp. 20-21; H. Yaqubov, GHAFUR GHULAM. HAYATI VA IJADI (Tashkent: OzSSR Dawlat Badiiy Adabiyati Nashriyati, 1959), p. 73.

55. Zulfiya, "SALAM, MISR!," TANLANGAN ASARLAR (Tashkent: OzSSR Davlat Badiiyat Adabiyat Nashriyati, 1959), p. 194.

56. SOVETSKO-AFGHANSKIE OTNOSHENIIA 1919-1969 GG. DOKUMENTY I MATERIALY (Moscow: Izdatel'stvo Politicheskoi Literatury, 1971), pp. 30, 100; KEESINGS CONTEMPORARY ARCHIVES (June 22-29, 1946), p. 7982.

57. "O PREOBRAZOVANII TUVINSKOI AVTONOMNOI OBLASTI V TUVINSKUIU AVTONOMNUIU SOVETSKUIU RESPUBLIKU," VEDOMOSTI VERKHOVNOGO SOVETA RSFSR No. 41 (162) (Oct. 19, 1961),

articles 572-573, pp. 610-611; "O PREOBRAZOVANII KALMYTSKOI AVTONOMNOI OBLASTI V KALMYTSKUIU AVTONOMNUIU SOVETSKUIU SOTSIALISTICHESKUIU RESPUBLIKU," VEDOMOSTI VERKHOVNOGO SOVETA RSFSR No. 8 (11) (Aug. 14, 1958), article 401, p. 339.

58. Edward Allworth, "REGENERATION IN CENTRAL ASIA," THE NATIONALITY QUESTION IN SOVIET CENTRAL ASIA (New York: Praeger Publishers,1973), pp. 3-18; NARODNOE KHOZIAISTVO SSSR V 1970 G. STATISTICHESKII EZHEGODNIK (Moscow: Izdatel'stvo "Statistika," 1971), p. 651.

59. ITOGI. . .1970 GODA, Vol. IV, pp. 9-15, 61-151. Nicholas Dima, graduate student in population geography, kindly prepared some of the data cited here.

60. ITOGI. . .1970 GODA. MIGRATSIIA NASELENIIA. . . (Moscow: "Statistika," 1974), Vol. VII, pp. 184-85; ITOGI. . .1970 GODA Vol. IV, p. 9.

61. Edward Allworth, "MAINSTAY OR MIRROR OF IDENTITY--THE PRINTED WORD IN CENTRAL ASIA AND OTHER SOVIET REGIONS TODAY," CANADIAN SLAVONIC PAPERS Vol. XVII, Nos. 2/3 (spring, 1975); Robert A. Lewis, Richard Rowland, Ralph S. Clem, NATIONALITY AND POPULATION CHANGE IN RUSSIA AND THE USSR: 1897-1970 (New York, unpublished manuscript, 1975) Table 5-4; ITOGI. . .1970 GODA, Vol. IV, pp. 20-42.

62. Kamil Yashin, "DOSTLIK ANJUMANI," OZBEKISTAN MADANIYATI (Sept. 20, 1968), p. 1.

63. H. Tursunov (Professor of History), "SOVET SHARQI," SOVET OZBEKLSTANI (June 27, 1971), p. 2; I-YI S"EZD NARODOV VOSTOKA, p. 27.

64. E. M. Murzaev, "IZUCHENIE SOVETSKOI AZII," ISTORIIA OTKRYTIIA I ISSLEDOVANIIA SOVETSKOI AZII (Moscow: Izdatel'stvo Mysl', 1969), pp. 7-8.

65. Grigorii Konovalov, "PREDEL. ROMAN," MOSKVA No. 3 (1974), pp. 4-5, 37-40; IBID., No. 4 (1974), pp. 33-34; Maks Fasmer, ETIMOLOGICHESKII SLOVAR' RUSSKOGO IAZYKA (Moscow: Izdatel'stvo "Progress," 1973), Vol. IV, p. 72; V. Luk'ianin, "VLAST' PAMIATI," LITERATURNOE OBOZRENIE No. 11 (Nov. 1974), pp. 36-37.

66. Donald W. Treadgold, THE GREAT SIBERIAN MIGRATION. . . (Princeton: Princeton University Press, 1957), p. 17.

**SOURCES AND METHODS
FOR THE BIBLIOGRAPHY**

The search for the bibliographies making up this list begins with 1850 and ends in 1970. The earlier date seems approximately to mark an appropriate starting point for modern bibliographical treatment in the Czarist Empire of the nationalities and regions concerned. The closing date is the most recent for which substantial sources are available and for which sufficient time has elapsed to permit rewarding verification efforts. Two main kinds of sources provide the majority of entries for the following bibliography of bibliographies. From 1850 until 1938, the main lists of bibliographies concerning Czarist and Soviet Asia have appeared in separate bibliographies, and toward the last decades of the period, especially in periodical bibliographies. World War II curtailed bibliographical publishing greatly in the USSR. After the 1940s, Soviet bibliographies began coming out again more rapidly in a variety of forms. In the post-War era the annual BIBLIOGRAPHY OF SOVIET BIBLIOGRAPHIES (BIBLIOGRAFIIA SOVETSKOI BIBLIOGRAFII), which had started publication, covering 1939, in 1941 but was immediately interrupted, became increasingly effective. The BSB has evolved into the major source for Soviet bibliographies issued since 1950, at least. A valuable cross-check upon that central compilation and earlier efforts has been furnished by 14 specialized bibliographies of bibliographies which have appeared in the USSR since 1920, all of them entered below, devoted to particular Asian regions or nationalities. The number of entries enumerated and listed in 12 of them (quantities in the other two are unknown) totals 3,583.

In addition, certain encyclopedias were searched for the purpose of adding system and filling in the gaps between coverage offered by separate bibliographies. Excellent for the earlier time have been the ENCYCLOPEDIC DICTIONARY (ENTSIKLOPEDICHESKII SLOVAR') published in St. Petersburg, 1890-1907, in 82 volumes or books, the JEWISH ENCYCLOPEDIA (EVREISKAIA ENTSIKLOPEDIIA) 1906-1913, in 16 volumes, and the MILITARY ENCYCLOPEDIA (VOENNAIA ENTSIKLOPEDIIA), Petrograd, 1911-1915, 18 volumes. Subsequently, the SIBERIAN SOVIET ENCYCLOPEDIA (SIBIRSKAIA SOVETSKAIA ENTSIKLOPEDIIA), 1929-1932, in three volumes (four were announced) and the URALS SOVIET ENCYCLOPEDIA (URAL'SKAIA SOVETSKAIA ENTSIKLOPEDIIA) 1933, only one volume published, have been extremely rich in bibliographies. Finally, the LITERARY ENCYCLOPEDIIA (LITERATURNAIA ENTSIKLOPEDIIA), first edition, 1929-1939, 11 volumes (No. 10 not published), and the first two editions of the LARGE SOVIET ENCYCLOPEDIA (BOL'SHAIA SOVETSKAIA ENTSIKLOPEDIIA), 1926-1947, 65 volumes, and 1950-1957, 51 volumes, also supplement and double-check the annual BIBLIOGRAPHY OF SOVIET BIBLIOGRAPHIES.

Another serial source exploited for augmenting those already cited has been the BIBLIOGRAPHIC ANNUAL (BIBLIOGRAFICHESKII EZHEGODNIK), Moscow 1911-1914, 1922-1924, the ANNUAL OF THE CENTRAL STATE BOOK CHAMBER OF THE RSFSR (EZHEGODNIK GOSUDARSTVENNOI TSENTRAL'NOI KNIZHNOI PALATY RSFSR), 1925-1929, and BOOK ANNUAL OF THE USSR (EZHEGODNIK KNIGI SSSR), 1935, 1941-. These publications have been very useful in providing coverage of book publishing for periods of upheaval like the Second World War. Periodicals treating the fields of press, area, nationality, and Oriental studies complement the above-listed sources considerably. Some of those journals surveyed for this compilation include PRESS AND REVOLUTION (PECHAT' I REVOLIUTSIIA), 1921-1930, AREA STUDIES (KRAEVEDENIE), 1924-1929, and its successor, SOVIET AREA STUDIES (SOVETSKOE KRAEVEDENIE), 1930-1936, NORTHERN ASIA (SEVERNAIA AZIIA), 1925-1930, SOVIET ASIA (SOVETSKAIA AZIIA), 1930-1931, the SOVIET NORTH (SOVETSKII SEVER'), 1930-1935, and sequels. Several bibliographical magazines were also important in the research. Two are BIBLIOGRAPHY FOR THE EAST (BIBLIOGRAFIIA VOSTOKA), 1932-1936, and SOVIET BIBLIOGRAPHY (SOVETSKAIA BIBLIOGRAFIIA), 1933-. Although Czarist and Soviet bibliographic sources have been of primary value for this endeavor, a number of western guides were helpful. Among them, Karol Maichel's GUIDE TO RUSSIAN REFERENCE BOOKS, several volumes, 1962-, Paul L. Horecky's BASIC RUSSIAN PUBLICATIONS: AN ANNOTATED BIBLIOGRAPHY ON RUSSIA AND THE SOVIET UNION, 1962, and Chauncy D. Harris' new GUIDE TO GEOGRAPHICAL BIBLIOGRAPHIES AND REFERENCE WORKS IN RUSSIAN OR ON THE SOVIET UNION, 1975, which reaches far beyond geography into history, travels, and general topics, are especially notable. They and others like them perform the essential function of correcting the slant, tilt or inefficiencies of Soviet bibliography with its pervasive ideological censorship and massive bureaucracy. Many bibliographies issued since 1900 have been ignored or forgotten in Soviet bibliographical research because their authors or subject matter have fallen from favor. Soviet bibliographies frequently deliberately avoid listing entries which have become politically sensitive. That is why going beyond retrospective Soviet works to use bibliographies produced in earlier days or contemporaneously, plus consulting the guides of American and European authors, continues to be crucial in scholarly, objective research concerning Czarist Russia and the USSR.

This bibliography of bibliographies aims to present bibliographies in the humanities and social sciences, published in the Czarist Empire and its Soviet successor, and pertaining directly to the Iranian, Mongolian, and Turkic nationalities and the regions of Czarist Russia and the USSR associated with them. They make up a substantial part of Asiatic Russia or Soviet Asia, and relate closely to areas and people just across those borders. It is hoped that someone will prepare a list of bibliographies for the other Soviet Asian nationalities as well.

The five main regional divisions used here cover all areas of the Czarist or Soviet East. One Turkic group not in the East, the Gagauz of Moldavia and the Ukraine, has also been included. Bibliographies about Mongolia and the Mongolian People's Republic are likewise added, because they supply many entries regarding the Soviet Buriats and Kalmyks. Thus, under regional headings such as Dagestan or Volga Basin appears coverage of territories and often groups in addition to the Iranian, Mongolian and Turkic ones of primary interest in this work. But general bibliographies covering the entire Czarist Empire or USSR have been omitted. Entries classified within the principal divisions are further sub-divided into five smaller regions, 28 living nationalities, and two long-defunct groups (Bulgar and Khazar).

Within various regional or nationality sections, ten subject categories may be found: general; architecture, art, music; anthropology, ethnography; economics; education; geography; history, archaeology; language, literature; political science (government), law; social organization. In practice, bibliographies are often lacking in some of these subject areas, usually for very small nationalities. Subject fields necessarily overlap because bibliographies duplicate topical or areal coverage; therefore, bibliographies about economics should also be sought under geography headings and vice versa. History, if recent, may appear as well in the political science category. "General" ordinarily includes bibliographies offering undifferentiated subject treatment of a nationality and region or differentiated subject fields when the fields number over three, plus materials relating specifically to publishing, bibliography itself, and the press. "Social organization" regularly combines bibliographies regarding particular classes or social groups such as farmers, women, and children, plus organized entertainment and sports, as well as public health problems. Few bibliographies specifically about Soviet Asian nationalities relate strictly to social structure itself.

A complete entry in the ensuing list of bibliographies offers seven items of information about the book or article in which the bibliography appears: 1. name of author, editor or compiler, sometimes both of the latter; 2. title of the work, along with the name and number of the journal or volume if it comprises only part of a larger work; 3. place published; 4. publisher's name; 5. date published; 6. total number of pages in book or separate volume; and 7. number of copies of the book published. About the bibliography itself, complete annotations shown in square brackets provide information about 1. the language employed by the "text" (the book or article itself); 2. the number of entries making up the bibliography; 3. the main languages

SOURCES AND METHODS FOR THE BIBLIOGRAPHY

of the entries within the bibliography; 4. the period covered by the entries and the inclusive dates during which those entry titles were published; and 5. exact page numbers of each bibliography. Every entry is not complete, but a serious attempt has been made to verify each entry and its attributes in holdings of the Columbia University Libraries. An asterisk placed before an entry signals that its location was verified in those libraries. Verified entries should be virtually complete, though the number of titles in a bibliography is shown here only when the bibliography's entries are numbered or when the total is provided in the Soviet source. The size of the press run is rarely known for pre-1917 publications. The many unverified entries are listed in the expectation that they will help guide research in other libraries and can be completed whenever the bibliographies are discovered. Abbreviations used in the sources have customarily been adopted in these entries, as well. Transliteration follows a modification of the system and tables published in Edward Allworth, NATIONALITIES OF THE SOVIET EAST (1971).

Section Heading "The Soviet East" Introduced in the magazine NEW EAST, 1927

PART

I

SOVIET ASIA

1 SOVIET ASIA

GENERAL

*Bartol'd, V. ISTORIIA IZUCHENIIA VOSTOKA V EVROPE I ROSSII. Leningrad: (TsIK SSSR. Leningradskii Institut Zhivykh Vostochnykh Iazykov. 7), 1925 2nd ed. (1911, 1st ed.), 318 pp., 3000 copies. [Russ. text; scattered titles]

*_____. SOCHINENIIA. Vols. 1-6. Moscow: Izdatel'stvo Vostochnoi Literatury. Izdatel'stvo "Nauka," (Vol. 1) 1963, 760 pp.; (Vol. 2, Part 1) 1963, 1020 pp.; (Vol. 2, Part 2)1964, 657 pp.; (Vol. 3) 1965, 711 pp.; (Vol. 4) 1966, 495 pp.; (Vol. 6) 1966, 784 pp., 4600 copies. [Russ. text; Russ., Europ., Arabic, Turkic, Iranian titles (Vol. 1) 613-688 pp.; (Vol. 2, Part 1) 881-947 pp.; (Vol. 2, Part 2) 562-604 pp.; (Vol. 3) 577-646 pp.; (Vol. 4) 411-461 pp.; (Vol. 6) 679-729 pp.]

*"BARTOL'D, VASILII VLADIMIROVICH," BOL'SHAIA SOVETSKAIA ENTSIKLOPEDIIA. Vol. 4. Moscow: Aktsionernoe Obshchestvo "Sovetskaia Entsiklopediia," 1926 (1st ed.), p. 791. [Russ. text and titles, p. 791]

*BIBLIOGRAFIIA VOSTOKA. Nos. 1-10, 1932-1937. [Russ. text; scattered Russ., Europ. titles, especially No. 8/9 (1936), pp. 152-194]

*Drikker, Kh. N. "NOVYE KNIGI PO GUMANITARNYM NAUKAM V RESPUBLIKAKH SOVETSKOGO VOSTOKA (BIBLIOGRAFICHESKIE ZAMETKI)," PROBLEMY VOSTOKOVEDENIIA. No. 6. 1960. [Russ. text; Sov. Asian, Russ. titles, pub.: 1957-1960, pp. 140-150]

*Grande, B. "UNIFIKATSIIA ALFAVITOV," BOL'SHAIA SOVETSKAIA ENTSIKLOPEDIIA. Vol. 56. Moscow: Gosudarstvennyi Institut "Sovetskaia Entsiklopediia," (Ogiz RSFSR), 1936, 1st ed., 106-107 pp. [Russ. text and titles, p. 107]

Iadrintsev, N. ed. BIBLIOGRAFIIA "VOSTOCHNAGO OBOZRENIIA" ZA 1882, 1883, 1884, 1885 I 1886 GG. [PRILOZHENIE K "VOSTOCHNOE OBOZRENIE." No. 9; 7] 1887, 12 pp. [Russ. text; titles pub.: 1882-1886]

Soviet Asia: General

*Iakovleva, E.; N. Vitkind. "SISTEMATICHESKII UKAZATEL' STATEI I ZAMETOK, POMESHCHENNYKH V 'REVOLIUTSIONNOM VOSTOKE' 1927-1930 GG., No. 1-10," REVOLIUTSIONNYI VOSTOK. No. 11/12. 1931. [Russ. text; 30 Russ. titles, pub.: 1927-1930, pp. 352-353]

*INORODCHESKOE OBOZRENIE. PRILOZHENIE K ZHURNALU PRAVOSLAVNYI SOBESIEDNIK. 1912-1917. [Russ. text; titles pub.: 1912-1917] [NNC has 1912-1915]

Kagarov, E. "OBZOR INOSTRANNOI LITERATURY," SOVETSKII SEVER. No. 1/2. 1932, 241-247 pp. [Russ. text; 1932 (1/2) 58 titles]

_____. "OBZOR NOVEISHEI INOSTRANNOI LITERATURY PO VOPROSAM GEOGRAFII, EKONOMIKI I ETNOGRAFII SEVERA," SOVETSKII SEVER. No. 9. 1931, 159-168 pp. [Russ. text; 38 titles, pub.: 1929-1930]

_____. "OBZOR (No. 6) NOVEISHEI INOSTRANNOI LITERATURY PO SOVETSKOMU I ZARUBEZHNOMU SEVERU," SOVETSKII SEVER. No. 3. 1932, 138-142 pp. [Russ. text; 56 titles]

Katanov, Nikolai Fedorovich. VOSTOCHNAIA BIBLIOGRAFIIA. OBZORY KAZANSKIKH IZDANII NA IAZYKAKH TURETSKOM, TATARSKOM I KIRGIZSKOM. Kazan, 1896-1903. [Russ. text; Tatar, Kazakh, Turkish titles]

Konogorov, P. "KNIZHNYE NOVOSTI PO SOVETSKOI AZII," SOVETSKAIA AZIIA. No. 9/10, 1931, 228-237 pp.; No. 11/12, 1931, 259-267 pp. [Russ. text and titles, pub.: 1931, (9/10) 184 titles: (11/12) 157 titles]

*_____. "KNIZHNYE NOVOSTI PO SOVETSKOI AZII," ZA INDUSTRIALIZATSIIU SOVETSKOGO VOSTOKA. No. 1, 1932, 181-188 pp.; No. 2, 1932, 274-282 pp.; No. 3, 1932, 306-315 pp.; No. 4, 1932, 176-184 pp.; No. 1, 1933, 202-214 pp.; No. 2, 1933, 225-244 pp.; No. 3, 1933, 299-304 pp.; [No. 1] 1934, 283-288 pp. [Russ. text;1932, (1) 158; (2) 131; (3) 163; (4) 160; 1933 (1) 215; (2) 351; (3) 80; 1934 (1) 106 Russ. titles, pub.: 1931-1932] [NNC has 1-4, 1932]

_____. "NOVAIA LITERATURA PO SOVETSKOMU SEVERU. KNIGI IZDANNYE V [1929-1932] G.," SOVETSKII SEVER. No. 1, 1930, 179-182 pp.; No. 2, 1930, 163-166 pp.; No. 3, 1930, 173-175; No. 4, 1930, 113-115 pp.; No. 5, 1930, 140-141 pp.; No. 7/8, 1930, 134-137 pp.; No. 3/4, 1931, 288-291 pp.; No. 11/12, 1931, 162-169 pp.; No. 1/2, 1932, 237-241 pp.; No. 2, 1933, 126-128 pp. [Russ. text and titles, pub.: 1929-1932]

Soviet Asia: General

Konogorov, P. F. "NOVOSTI LITERATURY PO SOVETSKOI AZII," SOVETSKAIA AZIIA/SHURALAR AZIYASI. No. 3/4, 1930, 355-366 pp.; No. 5/6, 1930, 373-383 pp.; No. 1/2, 1931, 322-328 pp.; No. 3/4, 1931, 278-286 pp.; No. 5/6, 1931, 290-298 pp.; No. 7/8, 1931, 262-270 pp. [Russ. text; 1930 (3/4) 149; (5/6) 137; 1931 (1/2) 117; (3/4) 133; (5/6) 155; (7/8) 152 Russ. titles]

*Kozlova, M. A. comp. "PREDMETNYI UKAZATEL' STATEI, POMESHCHENNYKH V ZHURNALE 'NOVYI VOSTOK' (S NO. 1 PO NO. 15)," NOVYI VOSTOK. No. 16/17. 1927. [Russ. text and titles, pub.: 1922-1926, pp. 421-429]

*_____. comp. "SISTEMATICHESKII PERECHEN' STATEI, POMESHCHENNYKH V ZHURNALE 'NOVYI VOSTOK' V No. No. 16/17, 18, 19, 20/21, 22, 23/24, 25, 26/27, 28," NOVYI VOSTOK. No. 29, 1930. [Russ. text and titles, pub.: 1927-1930, 280-286 pp.]

KRATKII OTCHET O DEIATEL'NOSTI O-VA IZUCHENIIA URALA, SIBIRI I DAL'NEGO VOSTOKA ZA PERIOD 1924-1927 GG. PRILOZHENIE: KRATKII UKAZATEL' STATEI OSNOVNOGO OTDELA "SEVERNOI AZII" ZA 1925-1926 GG. I PERVUIU POLOVINU 1927 G. Moscow: [Severnaia Aziia] 1927, 48 pp. [Russ. text; 98 Russ. titles, pub.: 1925-1927, pp. 44-48]

*Krymskii, A. "IBN-FODLAN (FEDLAN AKHMED I. ABBAS I.-RASHID I.-KHEMMAD)," ENTSIKLOPEDICHESKII SLOVAR'. Vol. 12A. St. Petersburg: F. A. Brokgauz, I. A. Efron, 1894, 742-743 pp. [Russ. text; Russ., Europ. titles, pp. 742-743]

*L. SH-G. "TIURKO-TATARY. III.TURETSKO-TATARSKIE NARODY," ENTSIKLOPEDICHESKII SLOVAR'. Vol. 34. St. Petersburg: F. A. Brokgauz, I. A. Efron, 1902, 347-350 pp. [Russ. text; Russ., Europ. titles, p. 350]

*Likhachev, N. P. KNIGOPECHATANIE V KAZANI ZA PERVOE PIATIDESIATILIETIE SUSHCHESTVOVANIIA V ETOM GORODIE TIPOGRAFII. St. Petersburg: Tipografiia V. S. Balasheva i Ko., 1895, 100 pp. [Russ. text and titles, p. 63-69]

*Livotova, O. E.; V. B. Portugal'. VOSTOKOVEDENIE V IZDANIIAKH AKADEMII NAUK. 1726-1917. BIBLIOGRAFIIA. Moscow: "Nauka," 1966, 144 pp., 1000 copies. [Russ. text; 1813 Russ., Europ. titles, per.: 1726-1917]

Soviet Asia: General

Mal'tsev, A. M. SPISOK PECHATNYKH RABOT SOTRUDNIKOV
TSENTRAL'NOI SELEKTSIONNOI STANTSII SOIUZNIKHI
(ZA 1930-1935 GG.) 1936. [Russ. text; titles pp. 78-
92]

MATERIALY DLIA BIOGRAFICHESKOGO SLOVARIA DEISTVITEL'NYKH
CHLENOV IMP. AKADEMII NAUK [V. V. RADLOV] Vol. 2.
Petrograd, 1917. [Russ. text; titles pp. 121-136]

Matveev, Z. CHTO CHITAT' O DAL'NE-VOSTOCHN. OBLASTI.
OPYT SISTEMATICHESKOGO UKAZATELIA LITERATURY.
Vladivostok, 1926, 248 pp. [Russ. text]

*"MELIORANSKII, PLATON MIKHAILOVICH," BOL'SHAIA
SOVETSKAIA ENTSIKLOPEDIIA. Vol. 38. Moscow:
Gosudarstvennyi Institut "Sovetskaia Entsiklopediia"
(Ogiz RSFSR), 1938, 1st ed., p. 736. [Russ. text
and titles, p. 736]

Mezhov, V. I. BIBLIOGRAFIA ASIATICA (BIBLIOGRAFIIA
AZII). UKAZATEL' KNIG I STATEI OB AZII NA RUSSKOM
IAZYKIE I ODNEKH TOL'KO KNIG NA INOSTRANNYKH IAZYKAKH,
KASAIUSHCHIKHSIA OTNOSHENII ROSSII K AZIATSKIM
GOSUDARSTVAM. Vol. 1. VOSTOK VOOBSHCHE...
SREDNEAZIATSKIE KHANSTVA I RUSSKIE VLADENIIA V
SREDNEI AZII. Vol. 2. INORODTSY FINSKOGO,
TATARSKOGO I MONGOLSKOGO PROISKHOZHDENIIA,
OBITAIUSHCHIE V ROSSII. KAVKAZSKIE INORODTSY.
St. Petersburg, 1891-1892 (vol. 1), 389 pp.; 1892-1894
(Vol. 2), 257 pp. [Russ. text; (Vol. 2) 6314 Russ.,
Europ. titles, pub.: up to 1890]

*"MUSUL'MANSKAIA KNIZHNAIA LIETOPIS'," MIR ISLAMA.
Vol. 2, No. 11, 1913; Vol. 2, No. 12, 1914.
[Russ. text; Tatar, Kazakh, Uzbek, Russ. titles,
pub.: ca.1912-1913, (Vol. 2, No. 11, 1913) 825-830 pp.;
(Vol. 2, No. 12, 1914) 906-914 pp.]

*"MUSUL'MANSKAIA PERIODICHESKAIA PECHAT' V ROSSII,"
MIR ISLAMA. Vol. 2, No. 3. 1913. [Russ.
text; titles pub.: ca.1912-1913, pp. 193-194]

NOVAIA INOSTRANNAIA LITERATURA PO VOSTOKOVEDENIIU.
Moscow: (Akad. Nauk SSSR. Fundament. B-ka Obshchestv.
Nauk), 1949-1952. [Russ. text; Europ. titles]

"NOVAIA LITERATURA PO KRAEVEDENIIU, POSTUPIVSHAIA V
BIBLIOTEKU TSENTRAL'NOGO BIURO KRAEVEDENIIA V
LENINGRADE S I MAIA 1924 G. DO I IANVARIA 1925 G.,"
KRAEVEDENIE. No. 4. 1924, 494-513 pp. [Russ. text;
152 titles]

Soviet Asia: General

NOVAIA SOVETSKAIA I INOSTRANNAIA LITERATURA PO
RESPUBLIKAM SOVETSKOGO VOSTOKA. Moscow: (Akad.
Nauk SSSR. Fundam. B-ka Obshchestv. Nauk) 1953[-1958]
(monthly), 1953, 150 pp.; 1955, 153 pp.; 1956, 142 pp.;
1957, 149 pp.; 1958, 154 pp. [Russ. text; Sov. Asian,
Russ., Foreign titles]

NOVAIA SOVETSKAIA LITERATURA PO VOSTOKOVEDENIIU...
Moscow: (Akad. Nauk SSSR. Fundament. B-ka Obshchestv.
Nauk), 1949-1952. [Russ. text]

"NOVYE·IZDANIIA PO VOSTOKU," VESTN. NAUCHN. OB-VA
TATAROVEDENIIA. No. 7. 1927. [Russ. text; titles
pp. 203-205]

"NOVYE KNIGI," SOVETSKII SEVER. No. 3, 1934, 129-
131 pp.; No. 5, 1934, 107-109 pp.; No. 6, 1934,
136-138 pp.; No. 1, 1935, 128-129 pp.; No. 2, 1935,
118-119 pp. [Russ. text]

"NOVYIA MUSUL'MANSKIE KNIGI," MIR ISLAMA. Vol.2, No. 5,
1913; Vol. 2, No. 6, 1913; Vol. 2, No. 7, 1913;
Vol. 2, No. 8, 1913, Vol. 2, No. 9, 1913, Vol. 2,
No. 10, 1913. [Russ. text; Tatar, Kazakh, Uzbek,
Russ. titles, pub.: 1911-1913, (5) pp. 348-350;
(6) pp. 422-429; (7) pp. 505-512; (8)pp. 574-580;
(9) pp. 642-654; (10) pp. 725-728

*Obruchev, V. "PRZHEVAL'SKII, NIKOLAI MIKHAILOVICH,"
BOL'SHAIA SOVETSKAIA ENTSIKLOPEDIIA. Vol. 46.
Moscow: Gosudarstvennyi Institut "Sovetskaia
Entsiklopediia" (Ogiz RSFSR), 1940, 2nd ed., 774-775 pp.
[Russ. text and titles, p. 775]

*"PERVAIA SERIIA KNIG, IZDANNYKH NA NOVOM LATINIZIROVANNOM
TIURKSKOM ALFAVITE RESPUBLIKANSKIMI KOMITETAMI ZA
SCHET SREDSTV, OTPUSHCHENNYKH VTSK NTA V 1924-1928
BUDZHETNYI GOD," KUL'TURA I PISMENNOST' VOSTOKA.
Book 4. 1929. [Russ. text; 208 Azeri, Uzbek,
Turkmen titles, pp. 198-203]

"PERECHEN' KNIG I KART PO AZII," SBORNIK GEOGRAFICHESKIKH,
TOPOGRAFICHESKIKH I STATISTICHESKIKH MATERIALOV PO
AZII. No. 10, 11, 12. St. Petersburg, 1884.
[Russ. text; 1545 Russ., Europ. titles, supplement,
pp. 1-45, etc.]

Soviet Asia: General

Petri. PERECHEN' ZAPADNO-EVROPEISKIKH SOCHINENII OB AZIATSKIKH VLADIENIIAKH ROSSII ZA 1884 I 1885 GODA," SIBIRSKII SBORNIK. Book 2. 1886. [Russ. text; ca.70 Europ. titles, pub.: 1884-1885, pp. 178-182]

*Samoilovich, A. "MUSUL'MANSKAIA PERIODICHESKAIA PECHAT'," MIR ISLAMA. Vol. 1, No. 2. 1912. [Russ. text; titles pub.: ca.1911-1912, pp. 257-287]

* _____. "MUSUL'MANSKAIA PERIODICHESKAIA PECHAT'. PECHAT' RUSSKIKH MUSUL'MAN," MIR ISLAMA. Vol. 1, No. 3, 1912. [Russ. text; titles, pub.: ca.1911-1912, pp. 463-492]

* _____. "MUSUL'MANSKAIA PERIODICHESKAIA PECHAT'," MIR ISLAMA. Vol. 1, No. 4. 1912. [Russ. text; titles, pub.: ca.1911-1912, pp. 611-644]

*Smirnov, V. "MUSUL'MANSKIIA PECHATNYIA IZDANIIA V ROSSII," ZAPISKI VOSTOCHNAGO OTDIELENIIA IMPERATORSKAGO RUSSKAGO ARKHEOLOGICHESKAGO OBSHCHESTVA. Vol. 3, 5-8. 1888-1893/4. [Russ. text; Chaghatay, Arabic, Persian titles, pub.: 1885-1893, (3) pp. 97-114; 395-398; (5) pp. 139-145; (6) pp. 389-396; (7) pp. 389-393; (8) pp. 195-201; 391-398]

*SPISOK KNIG I PERIODICHESKIKH IZDANII, POSTUPIVSHIKH V REDAKTSIIU," ZHIZN' NATSIONAL'NOSTEI. Nos. 2, 3/4, 5. 1923-1924. [Russ. text; Sov. Asian, Russ. titles, (2) pp. 170-175; (3/4) pp. 233-235; (5) pp. 216-218]

*"UKAZATEL' GLAVNIEISHIKH ISTOCHNIKOV I POSOBII PO AZIATSKOI ROSSII," AZIATSKAIA ROSSIIA. Vol. 3. St. Petersburg: Izdanie Pereselencheskago Upravleniia Glavnago Upravleniia Zemleustroistva i Zemledieliia, 1914, CLV pp. [Russ. text; Russ., Europ. titles, pp. LXXI-CXLI]

*"UKAZATEL' STATEI, POMESHCHENNYKH V ZHURNALE 'REVOLIUTSIONNYI VOSTOK' ZA 1936 GOD," REVOLIUTSIONNYI VOSTOK. No. 1(41). 1937, 126-129 pp. [Russ. text and titles, pub.: 1936, pp. 127-128]

Veselovskii, N. I. V.V. GRIGOR'EV PO EGO PIS'MAM I TRUDAM, 1816-1881. St. Petersburg: Izd. Imperatorskago Russkago Arkhivnago Obshchestva, 1887. [Russ. text; titles, per.: 1816-1881]

Soviet Asia: General

VTORAIA SERIIA KNIG, IZDANNYKH NA NOVOM
LATINIZIROVANNOM TIURKSKOM ALFAVITE RESPUBLIKANSKIMI
KOMITETAMI ZA SCHET SREDSTV, OTPUSHCHENNYKH VTSK NTA
V 1927-28 BIUDZHETNOM GODU," KUL'TURA I PIS'MENNOST'
VOSTOKA. Book 5. 1929. [Russ. text; Sov. Asian,
(Turkic) titles, pp. 203-208]

Zaleman, K. G. KO DNIU SEMIDESIATILETIIA V. V. RADLOVA.
St. Petersburg, 1907. [Russ. text; titles, per.: 70th
birthday, pp. 3-25]

_____. 75-LETNII IUBILEI DNIA ROZHDENIIA
AKADEMIKA V. V. RADLOVA. St. Petersburg, 1912.
[Russ. text; titles, 75th birthday, pp. 5-8]

*Zdobnov, N. V. "OBZOR ZHURNAL'NOI LITERATURY O SOVETSKOI
AZII ZA 1931 [-1933] G. (Prodolzhenie)III [IV, V,
VI, VII, VIII, IX] ZA INDUSTRIALIZATSIIU SOVETSKOGO
VOSTOKA. No. 1, 1932, 162-180 pp.; No. 2, 1932,
252-273 pp.; No. 3, 1932, 283-305 pp.; No. 4, 157-
175 pp.; No. 1, 1933, 176-201 pp.; No. 3, 1933,
248-298 pp.; [No. 1], 1934, 255-282 pp. [Russ. text;
1932, (1)   393; (2)   485; (3)   521; (4)   402;
1933 (1)   571; (3)   1123; 1934 [1]   559 Russ.
titles, pub.: 1931-1932]

Zdobnov, N. "OBZOR ZHURNAL'NOI LITERATURY PO SOVETSKOI
AZII," SOVETSKAIA AZIIA. [begins here:] No. 9-10,
1931; 207-227 pp.; No. 11-12, 1931, 236-258 pp.
[Russ. titles, (9/10   539; (11/12)   528, pub.:
1931]

_____. UKAZATEL' STATEI, ZAMETOK I ILLIUSTRATSII,
POMESHCHENNYKH V ZHURNALE "SEVERNAIA AZIIA" ZA
PERVOE PIATILETIE EGO SUSHCHESTVOVANIIA (1925-1929 GG.)
Moscow: Izdatel'stvo "Sovetskaia Aziia," 1931, 32 pp.,
1000 copies. [Russ. text; 437 titles, pub.: 1925-1929]

ANTHROPOLOGY, ETHNOGRAPHY

*Ivanovskii,A. "LITERATURA PO ANTROPOLOGII INORODTSEV ROSSII," RUSSKII ANTROPOLOGICHESKII ZHURNAL. No. 1. 1902. [Russ. text; 45 titles]

*Kagarov, E. G. "INOSTRANNAIA LITERATURA O NARODAKH SSSR ZA 15 LET," SOVETSKAIA ETNOGRAFIIA. No. 1/2. 1934. [Russ. text; Europ. titles, pp. 245-257]

_____. "OBZOR NOVEISHEI LITERATURY PO VOPROSAM ETNOGRAFII SEVERA. I.," SOVETSKII SEVER. No. 2. 1931, (2) 205-214 pp. [Russ. text]

*Ostrovskikh, P. E. NARODY SSSR. OCHERKI TRUDA, BYTA, I PRIRODY...NARODY SEVERA, ALTAIA I SREDNEI AZII. Moscow-Leningrad: Gosudarstvennoe Izdatel'stvo, 1929, 124 pp., 15,000 copies. [Russ. text; 6 Russ. lists, scattered]

*Permiakov, G. L. IZBRANNYE POSLOVITSY I POGOVORKI NARODOV VOSTOKA. Moscow: "Nauka," 1968, 376 pp., 10,000 copies. [Russ. text; 99 Russ. titles, pp. 368-372]

*Petrov, G. I. "I. A. IARKHO," SOVETSKAIA ETNOGRAFIIA. No. 1. 1936, 136-138 pp. [Russ. text; 36 Russ. titles, pub.: ca.1925-1934, p. 138]

*Tolstov, S. P.; M. G. Levin; N. N. Cheboksarov. eds. OCHERKI OBSHCHEI ETNOGRAFII. AZIATSKAIA CHAST' SSSR. Moscow: Izdatel'stvo Akademii Nauk SSSR, 1960, 366 pp., 4000 copies. [Russ. text and titles, pp. 359-365]

*Zelenin, D. K. BIBLIOGRAFICHESKII UKAZATEL' RUSSKOI ETNOGRAFICHESKOI LITERATURY O VNIESHNEM BYTIE NARODOV ROSSII. 1700-1910 GG. ZAPISKI IMPERATORSKAGO RUSSKAGO GEOGRAFICHESKAGO OBSHCHESTVA PO OTDIELENIIU ETNOGRAFII. Vol. 40. No. 1. 1913, 733 pp. [Russ. text; many Russ., scattered titles, per.: 1700-1910]

Soviet Asia

ARCHITECTURE, ART, MUSIC

*A. S-V. "MUSUL'MANSKOE ILI MAGOMETANSKOE ISKUSSTVO," ENTSIKLOPEDICHESKII SLOVAR'. Vol. 20. St. Petersburg: F. A. Brokgauz, I. A. Efron, 1897, 231-240 pp. [Russ. text; Russ., Europ. titles, p. 240]

*Borshchevskii, Iu. E. [supplement to] "'ISLAMIC ART AND ARCHEOLOGY.' A REGISTER OF WORKS PUBLISHED IN THE YEAR 1954. COMPILED BY J. D. PEARSON AND D. S. RICE. CAMBRIDGE, 1956, 38 PP.," SOVETSKOE VOSTOKOVEDENIE. No. 6. 1957, 173-177 pp. [Russ. text; 8 Russ. lists, pub.: 1954, pp. 174-177]

Denike, B. ISKUSSTVO VOSTOKA. OCHERK ISTORII MUSUL'MANSKOGO ISKUSSTVA. Kazan, 1923. [Russ. text; Russ., Europ. titles, pp. 178-181; 246-247]

ECONOMICS

*Fekhner, M. V. TORGOVLIA RUSSKOGO GOSUDARSTVA SO STRANAMI VOSTOKA V XVI VEKE. TRUDY GOS. IST. MUZEIA. No. 31. Moscow, 1956, 119 pp. [Russ. text; 254 titles, per.: 16th c., pp. 114-120]

*Iamzin, I. L.; V. P. Voshchinin. UCHENIE O KOLONIZATSII I PERESELENIIAKH. Moscow: Gosudarstvennoe Izdatel'stvo, 1926, 328 pp. [Russ. text; 76 Russ. titles, pp. 325-328]

Soviet Asia

EDUCATION

*Livotova, O. E. comp. "BIBLIOGRAFIIA IZDANII AZIATSKOGO MUZEIA I INSTITUTA VOSTOKOVEDENIIA AKADEMII NAUK SSSR (1917-1958)," OCHERKI PO ISTORII RUSSKOGO VOSTOKOVEDENIIA. SBORNIK III. Moscow: Izdatel'stvo Vostochnoi Literatury, 1960, 196-311 pp., 1300 copies [Russ. text; 15 Russ., Europ. lists, pub.: 1917-1958, pp. 198-297]

Ostroumov, N. P. ISLAMOVEDENIE. 4. "SHARIAT PO SHKOLE: (MAZKHAB) ABU-KHANIFY." Tashkent, 1912. [Russ. text; 37 titles]

SISTEMATICHESKII UKAZATEL' KNIG I-X KUL'TURY I PIS'MENNOST' VOSTOKA. No. 1/2. 1932, pp. 188-192 [Russ. text]

"SPISOK UCHENNYKH TRUDOV AKADEMIKA A. N. SAMOILOVICHA," TURKMENOVEDENIE. No. 5. 1929. [Russ. text; 84 titles, pp. 29-31]

*Znamenskii, P. NA PAMIAT' O NIKOLAIE IVANOVICHIE IL'MINSKOM K 25 LETIIU BRATSTVA SVIATITELIA GURIIA. Kazan: Izdanie Bratstva Sviatitelia Guria, 1892, 403 pp. [Russ. text and titles, 25-year anniv., pp. 310-315]

Soviet Asia

GEOGRAPHY

*Azat'ian, A. A.; M. I. Belov; N. A. Gvozdetskii; L. G.
 Kamanin; E. M. Murzaev; R. L. Iugai. ISTORIIA
 OTKRYTIIA I ISSLEDOVANIIA SOVETSKOI AZII. Moscow:
 Izdatel'stvo "Mysl'," 1969, 536 pp., 13,000 copies.
 [Russ. text; 5 Russ., Europ. lists, per.: Ancient to
 contemporary pp. 495-507]

 Bagrov, L. S. MATERIALY K ISTORICHESKOMU OBZORU KART
 KASPIISKAGO MORIA. St. Petersburg: Tipografiia
 Morskago Ministerstva, 1912, 112 pp. [Russ. text;
 51 titles, per.: 1854-1874, pp. 65-66]

*Dorn, B. KASPII: O POKHODAKH DREVNIKH RUSSKIKH V
 TABARISTAN, S DOPOLNITEL'NYMI SVIEDIENIIAMI O
 DRUGIKH NABIEGAKH IKH NA PRIBEREZH'IA KASPIISKAGO
 MORIA. St. Petersburg: Prilozhenie k XXVI-mu Tomu
 Zapisok Imp. Akademii Nauk, 1875, 718 pp. [Russ.
 text; Arabic, Turkic, Persian, Russ., Europ. titles,
 pp. 225-294]

*Iakhnenko, V. "BIBLIOGRAFIIA V TRUDAKH AKADEMIKA V. A.
 OBRUCHEVA," BIBLIOTEKAR'. No. 7. July 1954. [Russ.
 text; Russ. survey, pp. 30-33]

*Karataev, N. M. NIKOLAI MIKHAILOVICH PREZHEVAL'SKII.
 PERVYI ISSLEDOVATEL' PRIRODY TSENTRAL'NOI AZII.
 Moscow-Leningrad: Izdatel'stvo Akademii Nauk SSSR,
 1948, 284 pp., 8000 copies. [Russ. text; 29 Russ.
 titles, pp. 274-281]

*Murzaev, E. M. "GDE ZHE PROVODIT' GEOGRAFICHESKUIU
 GRANITSU EVROPY I AZII?," IZVESTIIA AKADEMII NAUK SSSR.
 SERIIA GEOGRAFICHESKAIA. No. 4. 1963, 111-119 pp.
 [Russ. text; Russ., Europ. titles, p. 119]

*Obruchev, V. V. "SPISOK GEOGRAFICHESKIKH TRUDOV V. A.
 OBRUCHEVA," VOPROSY GEOGRAFII. SBORNIK 35--FIZICHESKAIA
 GEOGRAFIIA AZII. Moscow: Gosudarstvennoe Izdatel'stvo
 Geograficheskoi Literatury, 1954, 352 pp., 3000
 copies. [Russ. text; ca.350 Russ., Europ. titles,
 pub.: 1886-1954, pp. 328-350]

Soviet Asia: Geography

*Semenov, P. P.; I. D. Cherskii; G. G. Petts. comps.
ZEMLEVIEDIENIE AZII KARLA RITTERA. GEOGRAFIIA
STRAN VKHODIAKHSHCHIKH V SOSTAV AZIATSKOI ROSSII ILI
POGRANICHNYKH S NEIU. VOSTOCHNAIA SIBIR'; OZERO
BAIKAL I PRIBAIKAL'SKAIIA STRANY, ZABAIKAL'E I STEP'
GOBI. NOVIEISHIIA SVIEDIENIIA OB ETIKH STRANAKH
(1832-1893 G.) SLUZHASHCHIIA POSLIEDUIUSHCHIMI
VYPUSKAMI K RUSSKOMU TEKSTU RITTERA, IZDANNOMU POD
PRIVEDENNYM ZAGLAVIEM V 1879 GODU. St. Petersburg:
[Imperatorskoe Russkoe Geograficheskoe Obshchestvo]
Part 1, 1894, 605 pp; Part 2, 1895, 629 pp. [Russ.
text; Russ., German titles, (Part 2) pp. 51-59 +
47-51]

*SISTEMATICHESKII UKAZATEL' STATEI KASAIUSHCHIKHSIA
MATERIKA AZII, POMIESHCHENNYKH V IZDANIIAKH
IMPERATORSKOGO RUSSKOGO GEOGRAFICHESKOGO OBSHCHESTVA
S 1846 PO 1897 GODA. Irkutsk: Tipo-litografiia P. I.
Makushina, 1898, 245 pp. [Russ. text; 1450 titles,
pub.: 1846-1897, pp. 5-124]

"SPISOK PECHATNYKH RABOT P. P. SEMENOVA TIAN-SHANSKOGO,"
P. P. SEMENOV TIAN-SHANSKII, MEMUARY. Vol. 2.
PUTESHESTVIIE V TIAN'SHAN' V 1856-1857 G. G. Moscow,
1948. [Russ. text; 86 Russ., Europ. titles, pub.:
1850-1947, pp. 373-378]

Tillo, A. A.; Iu. M. Shokal'skii. ISCHISLENIE
POVERKHNOSTI AZIATSKOI ROSSII S POKAZANIEM
PLOSHCHADEI BASSEINOV: OKEANOV, MOREI, RIEK I OZER, A
RAVNO I ADMINISTRATIVNYKH PODRAZDIELENII V
TSARSTVOVANIE IMPERATORA NIKOLAIA II. St. Petersburg,
1905. [Russ. text]

"TRUDY PO CHASTI DREVNEI GEOGRAFII RUSSKOI AZII,"
GEOGRAFICHESKIE IZVIESTIIA. 1848. [Russ. text and
titles]

HISTORY, ARCHAEOLOGY

*Drabkina, E. A. NATSIONAL'NYI I KOLONIAL'NYI VOPROS V
TSARSKOI ROSSII. Moscow: Kommunisticheskaia Akademiia.
Komissiia po Izucheniiu Natsional'nogo Voprosa,
1930, 67-144 pp., 5000 copies. [Russ. text; 167
titles]

Soviet Asia: History, Archaeology

*Egorov, D. N. ed. BIBLIOGRAFIIA VOSTOKA. No. 1.
ISTORIIA (1917-1925). Moscow: (Nauchnaia Assotsiatsiia
Vostokovedeniia pri TsIK SSSR), 1928, 300 pp., 2500
copies. [Russ. text and titles, pub.: 1917-1925,
pp. 66-67, 78-96, 109-119, 120-125, 126-135, 183-212]

*L. Sh-G. "TIURKI," ENTSIKLOPEDICHESKII SLOVAR'.
Vol. 35. St. Petersburg: F. A. Brokgauz, I. A. Efron,
1902, 344-347 pp. [Russ. text; Russ., Europ. titles,
pp. 346-347]

Mamet, L. P.; I. I. Polessa. eds. [SOVETSKII VOSTOK]
SBORNIK PROGRAMM PO ISTORII, EKONOMIKE I
PRAVITEL'STVU V NATSIONAL'NYKH RESPUBLIKAKH I
OBLASTIAKH. Moscow: Izd. KUTB. im. Stalina, 1930,
2nd ed.. [Russ. text]

*"MATERIALY DLIA BIBLIOGRAFII MUSUL'MANSKOI ARKHEOLOGII.
IZ BUMAG BAR. V. G. TIZENGAUZENA...II. SREDNIAIA
AZIIA...BASHKIRIIA. KIRGIZSKIIA STEPI. SIBIR'...
BOLGARSKOE, KAZANSKOE I KASIMOVSKOE TSARSTVO...
ZOLOTAIA ORDA I ASTRAKHANSKOE TSARSTVO...KAVKAZSKII
PERESHEEK...KRYM, NOVOROSII I PR.," ZAPISKI
VOSTOCHNAGO OTDIELENIIA IMPERATORSKAGO RUSSKAGO
ARKHEOLOGICHESKAGO OBSHCHESTVA. Vol. 16 (1904-1905).
1906. [Russ. text; Russ., Europ. titles, pp. 0213-
0268; 0285-0299]

Mikhalkin, I. I.; P. P. Khoroshikh. OPYT UKAZATELIA
LITERATURY PO ARKHEOLOGII ZABAIKAL'IA. Irkutsk-Chita:
Chitinskii Kraev. Muzei im. A. K. Kuznetsova, 1929,
22 pp. [Russ. text]

*"NOVYE KNIGI PO VOSTOKOVEDENIIU. NEPOLNYI SPISOK KNIG I
PUBLIKATSII PO VOSTOKOVEDENIIU, VYSHEDSHIKH V 1954 G.,"
SOV. VOSTOKOVEDENIE. No. 1. 1955. [Russ. text;
52 Russ., other USSR titles, pub.: 1954, pp. 179-182]

PIS'MENNYE PAMIATNIKI I PROBLEMY ISTORII KUL'TURY
NARODOV VOSTOKA. Leningrad: (AN SSSR. In-t Narodov
Azii. Leningr. Otd-nie), 1968, 132 pp., 250 copies.
[Russ. text; titles pp. 39-40]

Sidorov, A. L. ed. VYSSHII POD"EM REVOLIUTSII 1905-
1907 GG. VOORUZHENNYE VOSTANIIA. NOIABR' - DEKABR'
1905 G. Part 3, Book 2. (ZAKAVKAZ'E--SREDNIAIA AZIIA
I KAZAKHSTAN). Moscow, 1956. [Russ. text; 707 titles,
per.: Nov.-Dec. 1905, pp. 1141-1179]

Soviet Asia: History, Archaeology

*Smirnov, A. P. SKIFY. Moscow: "Nauka," 1966, 200 pp.,
   47,000 copies. [Russ. text; Russ., Western titles,
   pp. 186-188]

"SPISOK STATEI PO VOSTOKOVEDENIIU," (IZV. ROSS. AKAD.
   NAUK.) AZIATSKII SBORNIK. 1918. [Russ. text;
   titles pub.: 1895-1917 pp. III-XV]

*Umniakov, I. I. "BIBLIOGRAFIIA RABOT O V. V. BARTOL'DE,"
   NARODY AZII I AFRIKI. No. 1. 1970. [Russ. text;
   ca.100 titles, pp. 211-215]

*Umniakov, I. I. "V. V. BARTOL'D. (PO POVODU 30-LETIIA
   PROFESSORSKOI DEIATEL'NOSTI)," BIULL. SR. AZIATSK.
   GOSUD. UNIV. Vol. 14. Tashkent: Tipografii Uzgiza
   No. 2, 1926, 281 pp., 1500 copies. [Russ. text;
   titles per.: 30th Anniversary of Professorship,
   pp. 175-202]

*"VEL'IAMINOV-ZERNOV, VLADIMIR VLADIMIROVICH,"
   IMPERATORSKAIA AKADEMIIA NAUK. 1889-1914. III.
   MATERIALY DLIA BIOGRAFICHESKAGO SLOVARIA DIESTVITEL'NYKH
   CHLENOV IMPERATORSKOI AKADEMII NAUK. Part 1.
   Petrograd: Tipografiia Imperatorskoi Akademii Nauk,
   1915, 143-146 pp. [Russ. text; 35 Russ., Europ.
   titles, pub.: 1850-1893, pp. 144-146]

*Vitkind, N. Ia. MATERIALY K BIBLIOGRAFII ISTORII
   GRAZHDANSKOI VOINY NA SOVETSKOM VOSTOKE. (TRUDY.
   No. 8 [13]). Moscow: Izdanie Nauchno-Issledovatel'skoi
   Assotsiatsii po Izucheniiu Natsional'nykh i
   Kolonial'nykh Problem, 1934, 91 pp., 1500 copies.
   [Russ. text and titles, per.: 1917-1921, pub.:
   1919-1933]

LANGUAGE, LITERATURE

Aidarov, G. IAZYK ORKHONSKOGO PAMIATNIKA BIL'GE-KAGANA.
   Alma Ata: "Nauka," 1966, 93 pp., 3500 copies. [Russ.
   text; 54 titles, pp. 90-92]

Soviet Asia: Language, Literature

*Aliev, G. Iu. "BIBLIOGRAFIIA NAUCHNYKH TRUDOV CHLENA-
KORRESPONDENTA AN SSSR E. E. BERTEL'SA," SOVETSKOE
VOSTOKOVEDENIE. No. 1. 1958. [Russ. text; 295
Tajik, Russ., Europ., Persian titles, pub.: 1918-1957,
pp. 115-124]

*Baskakov, N. A. TIURKSKIE IAZYKI. Moscow: Izd. Vost.
Lit., 1960, 242 pp. [Russ. text; 80 Russ., Europ.
titles, per.: 1780-1959, pp. 6-20]

*Batmanov, I. A. ed. ISTOCHNIKI FORMIROVANIIA TIURSKIKH
IAZYKOV SREDNEI AZII I IUZHNOI SIBIRI. Frunze:
Izdatel'stvo "Ilim," 1966, 360 pp., 500 copies.
[Russ. text; Cent. Asian Turkic, Siberian Turkic,
p. 359, and at end of articles]

Charyiarov, B. VREMENA GLAGOLA V TIURKSKIKH IAZYKAKH
IUGO-ZAPADNOI GRUPPY. Ashkhabad, 1969. [Turkmen
text; ca.220 titles, pp. 339-346]

*Dmitriev, N. K. STROI TIURSKIKH IAZYKOV. Moscow:
Izdatel'stvo Vostochnoi Literatury, 1962, 607 pp.,
1400 copies. [Russ. text; 160 Sov. Asian, Russ.,
Europ. titles, pp. 599-603]

Ianchuk, N. A. ed. IUBILEINYI SBORNIK V CHEST' V. F.
MILLERA, IZDANNYI EGO UCHENIKAMI I POCHITATELIAMI.
Moscow: Tip.-Lit. A. V. Vasil'eva, 1900. [Russ.
text; pp. XIII-XVII]

*Isengalieva, V. A. TIURKSKIE GLAGOLY S OSNOVAMI,
ZAIMSTVOVANNYMI IZ RUSSKOGO IAZYKA. (PROIZVODNYE
GLAGOLY SINTETICHESKOGO I ANALITICHESKOGO
OBRAZOVANIIA). Alma Ata: Izdatel'stvo "Nauka"
Kazakhskoi SSR, 1966, 247 pp., 2000 copies. [Russ.
text; ca.280 Uzbek, Kazakh, Russ., Europ. titles,
pp. 237-245]

Ismailov, I. A. TERMINY RODSTVA V TIURKSKIE IAZYKAKH.
Tashkent: "Fan," 1966, 150 pp., 1500 copies. [Uzbek
text; 81 titles, pp. 146-149]

ISTORICHESKOE RAZVITIE LEKSIKI TIURSKIKH IAZYKOV.
Moscow: AN SSSR, 1961, 467 pp. [Russ. text; 141
titles, per.: 1844-1954, pp. 463-467]

*Ivanov, S. N. NIKOLAI FEDOROVITCH KATANOV 1862-1962.
OCHERK ZHIZNI I DEIATEL'NOSTI. Moscow-Leningrad:
Izdatel'stvo Akademii Nauk SSSR, 1962, 106 pp.,
2500 copies. [Russ. text; 217 Russ., Europ. titles,
pub.: 1885-1958, pp. 94-106]

Soviet Asia: Language, Literature

K KONFERENTSII PISATELEI STRAN AZII I AFRIKI. No. 2.
SOVETSKIE RESPUBLIKI I AVTONOMNYE OBLASTI--
UCHASTNITSY KONFERENTSII. Moscow: (Vsesoiuznye
Ob"edinenie Knizhnoi Torgovli "Soiuzkniga"), 1958,
69 pp. [Russ. text]

Katanov, N. F. ETNOGRAFICHESKII OBZOR TURETSKO-
TATARSKIKH PLEMEN. Kazan, 1894, 22 pp. [Russ.
text; 60 titles, pub.: 1827-1893, pp. 17-22]

*Kononov, A. N. TIURKSKAIA FILOLOGIIA. Moscow: "Nauka,"
1967, 53 pp. [Russ. text; Russ., English titles,
pp. 25-52]

*Krymskii, A. "TURETSKIIA NARIECHIIA I LITERATURY,"
ENTSIKLOPEDICHESKII SLOVAR'. Vol. 34. St. Petersburg:
F. A. Brokgauz, I. A. Efron, 1902, 159-168 pp.
[Russ. text; Russ., Europ. titles, pp. 167-168]

LENIN I STALIN V TVORCHESTVE NARODOV SSSR. Leningrad:
B-ka Vyborg. Doma Kul'tury, 1939, 20 pp., 1000 copies.
[Russ. text; 132 titles]

*Letiagina, N. I. "TRUDY ALEKSANDRA KONSTANTINOVICHA
BOROVKOVA," TIURKOLOGICHESKIE ISSLEDOVANIIA. Moscow-
Leningrad: Izdatel'stvo Akademii Nauk SSSR, 1963,
298 pp. [Russ. text; Uzbek, Russ. titles, pub.:
1928-1961, pp. 294-298]

*Malov, S. E. PAMIATNIKI DREVNETIURKSKOI PIS'MENNOSTI.
TEKSTY I ISSLEDOVANIIA. Moscow-Leningrad:
Izdatel'stvo Akademii Nauk SSSR, 1951, 451 pp.,
3000 copies. [Russ. text; Russ., Oriental, Europ.
titles, profuse, scattered, per.: Ancient]

Meliev, K. IMENA DEISTVIIA V SOVREMENNYKH TIURKSIKH
IAZYKAKH. Tashkent, 1969. [Uzbek text; ca.90
titles, pp. 159-162]

*Nasilov, V. M. DREVNE-UIGURSKII IAZYK. Moscow:
Izdatel'stvo Vostochnoi Literatury, 1963, 122 pp.,
1700 copies. [Russ. text; titles, per.: Ancient,
pp. 119-121]

*"NEVAI," LITERATURNAIA ENTSIKLOPEDIIA. Vol. 7.
Moscow: Gosudarstvennoe Slovarno-Entsiklopedicheskoe
Izdatel'stvo "Sovetskaia Entsiklopediia," 1934,
642-643 pp. [Russ. text; Chaghatay, Russ., Europ.
titles, per.: Medieval, p. 643]

Soviet Asia: Language, Literature

*"NOVYI ALFAVIT," LITERATURNAIA ENTSIKLOPEDIIA. Vol. 8.
Moscow: Gosudarstvennoe Slovarno-Entsiklopedicheskoe
Izdatel'stvo "Sovetskaia Entsiklopediia" (Ogiz RSFSR),
1934, 139-142 pp. [Russ. text; Turko-Tatar, Russ.
titles, p. 142]

*Oranskii, I. M. IRANSKIE IAZYKI. Moscow: Izd-vo
Vostochnoi Literatury, 1963, 203 pp., 3200 copies.
[Russ. text; Russ., Europ., Persian titles, pp. 191-
198]

Polumordvinov, I. T. SPISOK P'ES NA RUSSKOM, TATARSKOM,
AISORSKOM, GRECHESKOM, OSETINSKOM, ESTONSKOM,
POL'SKOM I SARTSKOM IAZYKAKH, RAZRESHENNYKH K
PREDSTAVLENIIU NA STENAKH KAVKAZSKAGO KRAIA PO 1
IANVARIA 1914 G. Tiflis, 1914, 17 pp. [Russ. text;
titles pub.: up to 1914]

*Potseluevskii, E. A. TIURKSKII TREKHCHLEN. Moscow:
"Nauka," 1967, 136 pp., 1400 copies. [Russ. text and
titles, pp. 131-135]

*"RADLOV, VASILII VASIL'EVICH," IMPERATORSKAIA AKADEMIIA
NAUK. 1889-1914. Vol. 3. MATERIALY DLIA
BIOGRAFICHESKAGO SLOVARIA DIEISTVITEL'NYKH CHLENOV
IMPERATORSKOI AKADEMII NAUK. Part 2. Petrograd:
Tipografiia Rossiiskoi Akademii Nauk, 1917, 121-136 pp.
[Russ. text; 141 Russ., Europ. titles, pub.: 1860-1912,
pp. 129-136]

*Riasianen, M. MATERIALY PO ISTORICHESKOI FONETIKE
TIURKSKIKH IAZYKOV. Moscow: I * L Izdatel'stvo
Inostrannoi Literatury, 1955, 221 pp. [Russ. text;
Sov. Asian, Russ., Europ., Turkish, Hung. titles,
pp. 207-211]

Samoilovich, A. N. "MATERIALY DLIA UKAZATELIA
LITERATURY PO ENISEISKO-ORKHONSKOI PISMENNOSTI,"
TRUDY TROITSKO-SAVSKO-KIAKHTINSKOGO OTDIELA PRIAMUR.
OTDIELA RUSSKAGO GEOGRAFICHESKAGO OBSHCHESTVA.
Vol. 15. No. 1 (1912). 1914. [Russ. text; 292 Russ.
Europ. titles, pp. 55-80]

*"SISTEMATICHESKII UKAZATEL' STATEI, RETSENZII I DOKLADOV
K TOMAM I-XX ZAPISOK VOSTOCHNAGO OTDIELENIIA
IMPERATORSKAGO RUSSKAGO ARKHEOLOGICHESKAGO OBSHCHESTVA
1886-1896," ZAPISKI VOSTOCHNAGO OTDIELENIIA
IMPERATORSKAGO RUSSKAGO ARKHEOLOGICHESKAGO OBSHCHESTVA.
Vol. 10, 1896. 1897. [Russ. text and titles, pub.:
1886-1896, pp. 235-237; 241-247; 251-253; 258-260]

Soviet Asia: Language, Literature

*SISTEMATICHESKII UKAZATEL' STATEI, RETSENZII I DOKLADOV
K TOMAM XI-XX ZAPISOK VOSTOCHNAGO OTDIELENIIA
IMPERATORSKAGO RUSSKAGO ARKHEOLOGICHESKAGO OBSHCHESTVA.
1897-1910," ZAPISKI VOSTOCHNAGO OTDIELENIIA
IMPERATORSKAGO RUSSKAGO ARKHEOLOGICHESKAGO OBSHCHESTVA.
Vol. 20,1910. 1912. [Russ. text and titles, pub.:
1897-1910, pp. 0119-0129; 0132-0133; 0136-0139]

*"SPISOK TRUDOV V. A. ZHUKOVSKAGO," ZAPISKI VOSTOCHNAGO
OTDIELENIIA RUSSKAGO ARKHEOLOGICHESKAGO OBSHCHESTVA.
Vol. 25. 1921. [Russ. text; 68 Russ. titles,
pp. 420-422]

*"TIURKSKIE IAZYKI," LITERATURNAIA ENTSIKLOPEDIIA. Vol. 11.
Moscow: Gosudarstvennoe Izdatel'stvo "Khudozhestvennaia
Literatura," 1939, 467-468 pp. [Russ. text; Turk.,
Russ., Europ. titles, p. 468]

*Ubriatova, E. I. "IZUCHENIE DIALEKTOV TIURKSKIKH IAZYKOV,
[OBZOR]," VOPROSY DIALEKTOLOGII TIURKSKIKH IAZYKOV.
Vol. 2. Baku: Akad. Nauk Azerb. SSR, 1960. [Russ.
text; survey, pp. 7-22]

*_____. "TRUDY SERGEIA EFIMOVICHA MALOVA.--
MATERIALY K BIOGRAFII S. E. MALOVA," TIURKOL.
SBORNIK, No. 1. Moscow, 1951. [Russ. text; 163 Russ.,
Europ. titles, pub.: 1904-1949, pp. 22-30]

*Veselovskii, N. "KAZEMBEK, ALEKSANDR KASIMOVICH,"
ENTSIKLOPEDICHESKII SLOVAR'. Vol. 13A.
St. Petersburg: F. A. Brokgauz, I. A. Efron, 1894,
925 pp. [Russ. text; Russ., Europ. titles, p. 925]

*"ZALEMAN, KARL GERMANOVICH [SALEMANN]," IMPERATORSKAIA
AKADEMIIA NAUK. 1889-1914. Vol. 3, MATERIALY DLIA
BIOGRAFICHESKAGO SLOVARIA DIESTVITEL'NYKH CHLENOV
IMPERATORSKOI AKADEMII NAUK. Part 1. Petrograd:
Tipografiia Imperatorskoi Akademii Nauk, 1915,
293-298 pp. [Russ. text; 38 Russ., Europ. titles,
pub.: 1874-1914, pp. 295-298]

*Vinogradov, V. V. ed. IAZYKI NARODOV SSSR. Vol. 1,
INDOEVROPEISKIE IAZYKI, 1966, 658 pp.; Vol. 2,
TIURKSKIE IAZYKI, 1966, 530 pp.; Vol. 5, MONGOL'SKIE
TUNGUSO-MAN'CHZHURSKIE I PALEOAZIATSKIE IAZYKI, 1968,
524 pp., 6200 copies. [Russ. text; Sov. Asian, Russ.
Europ. scattered titles]

Soviet Asia

PHILOSOPHY, RELIGION

Andrei [Episkop]; N. V. Nikol'skii. eds. NAIBOLIEE VAZHNYIA STATISTICHESKIIA SVIEDIENIIA OB INORODTSAKH VOSTOCHNOI ROSSII I ZAPADNOI SIBIRI PODVERZHENNYKH VLIIANIIU ISLAMA. Kazan: Tipografiia Gubernskago Pravleniia, 1912, 80 + 320 pp. [Russ. text; titles per.: 19th - 20th cc., pp. 242-320: pp. 242-243 Bashkirs (pp. 244-245 in Bashkir); pp. 259-269 Kreshchen Tat.(pp. 263-269 in Tatar); pp. 280-312 Chuvash (pp. 306-312 in Chuvash); pp. 319-320 Volga & Siberia Regions]

Arsharuni, A. M. "BIBLIOGRAFIIA PO ISLAMU," ISLAM. Moscow: Tsentral'nyi Sovet Soiuza Voinstvuiushchikh Bezbozhnikov SSSR, 1931. [Russ. text; 94 Russ. titles, per.: 1917-1931, pp. 156-167]

*_____.; Gabidullin, Kh. OCHERKI PANISLAMIZMA I PANTIURKIZMA V ROSSII. n. p. Izdatel'stvo "Bezbozhni," 1931, 140 pp., 5000 copies. [Russ. text; Russ., Turkish titles, (incl. archives), pp. 139-140]

*Bernfel'd, S. "Islam," EVREISKAIA ENTSIKLOPEDIIA. Vol. 8. St. Petersburg: Izdanie Obshchestva Dlia Nauchnykh Evreiskikh Izdanii i Izdatel'stva Brokgauz-Efron, n. d., 340-354 pp. [Russ. text; Europ. titles, p. 354]

*Gidulianov, P. "TALAK," ENTSIKLOPEDICHESKII SLOVAR'. Vol. 32A. St. Petersburg: F. A. Brokgauz, I. A. Efron, 1901, 531-532 pp. [Russ. text; Russ., Europ. titles, p. 532]

*Gil'fanov, Ibragim Gil'fanovich. O MUSUL'MANSKOI RELIGII. Kazan: Tatarstan Kitap Nashriyati, 1965, 86 pp., 8000 copies. [Tatar text; Tatar, Russ. titles, pp. 84-85]

"IZDANIIA PEREVODCHESKOI KOMMISSII PRAVOSLAVNAGO MISSIONERSKAGO OBSHCHESTVA ZA 1881-1912 G.," INORODCHESKOE OBOZRENIE (PRILOZH. K 'PRAVOSLAVNYI SOBESIEDNIK'). Book 2. 1913. [Russ. text; titles pub.: 1881-1912, pp. 155-159]

Soviet Asia: Philosophy, Religion

*KORAN. (TRANS. I. IU. KRACHKOVSKII). Moscow: Izd. Vostoch. Liter., 1963, 713 pp. [Russ. text; ca.300 Russ., Europ. Mid-East titles, pp. 677-682, 686-709]

*"KORAN," EVREISKAIA ENTSIKLOPEDIIA. Vol. 9. St. Petersburg: Izdanie Obshchestva Dlia Nauchnykh Evreiskikh Izdanii i Izdatel'stva Brokgauz-Efron, n.d., 736-740 pp. [Russ. text; Europ., Yiddish, Russ. titles, p. 740]

*Krymskii, A. "SHIITSTVO ILI SHIIZM," ENTSIKLOPEDICHESKII SLOVAR'. Vol. 39A. St. Petersburg: F. A. Brokgauz, I. A. Efron, 1903, 617-619 pp. [Russ. text; Russ., Europ. titles, p. 619]

* _____. "SUNNA (SONNA, SIUNNA)," ENTSIKLOPEDICHESKII SLOVAR'. Vol. 32. St. Petersburg: F. A. Brokgauz, I. A. Efron, 1901, 77-78 pp. [Russ. text; Russ., Europ. titles, p. 78]

* _____. "SUNNITY," ENTSIKLOPEDICHESKII SLOVAR'. Vol. 32. St. Petersburg: F. A. Brokgauz, I. A. Efron, 1901, 78-79 pp. [Russ. text; Russ., Europ. titles, p. 79]

*M. T. "PRAVO MUSUL'MAN," ENTSIKLOPEDICHESKII SLOVAR'. Vol. 24 A. St. Petersburg: F. A. Brokgauz, I. A. Efron, 1898, 896-899 pp. [Russ. text; Russ., Europ. titles, pp. 898-899]

Popov, A. A. MATERIALY DLIA BIBLIOGRAFII RUSSKOI LITERATURY PO IZUCHENIIU SHAMANSTVA SEVERO-AZIATSKIKH NARODOV. Leningrad: Izd. Instituta Narodov Severa TsIK SSSR, 1932, 117 + 14 pp., 1500 copies. [Russ. text and titles]

Purygina, G. D. comp. ISLAM I EGO REAKTSIONNAIA SUSHCHNOST'. (KRATKII SPISOK LITERATURY, REK. PROPAGANDISTAM AGITATORAM, KUL'TPROSVETRABOTNIKAM). Kuibyshev: (Kuibyshevskaia Oblastnaia Biblioteka), 1966, 6 pp., 300 copies. [Russ. text]

Soviet Asia

POLITICAL SCIENCE, LAW

*Iakushkin, E. I. OBYCHNOE PRAVO RUSSKIKH INORODTSEV--
MATERIALY DLIA BIBLIOGRAFII OBYCHNOGO PRAVA. Nos. 1-4.
No. 1, Iaroslavl: Tip. Gubernskogo Upravleniia,
1875 (2nd ed. 1910), 46 + 249 pp.; 191 pp. (2nd ed.);
No. 2, Iaroslavl: Tip.-Lit. Gub. Zemsk. Upravl.,
1896, 37 + 544 pp.; No. 3, Moscow: T-vo Tip. A. I.
Mamontova, 1908, 546 pp.; No. 4, Moscow: T-vo Tip.
A. I. Mamontova, 1909; Moscow: Universitetskaia
Tipografiia, 1899, 366 pp. [Russ. text; (1899)
1197 Russ., Europ. titles, pub.: 19 c.; (1899) pub.:
1875-1890] [NNC has 1899 vol.]

Iamzin, I. L. SPISOK IZDANII PERESELENCHESKAGO
UPRAVLENIIA S RISUNKAMI. St. Petersburg:
(Pereselencheskoe Upravlenie), 1914, 141 pp. [Russ.
text; pub.: 1908-1914]

SPISOK IZDANII PERESELENCHESKOGO UPRAVLENIIA,
VYSHEDSHIKH V SVET V 1912 I 1913 GG. VOPROSY
KOLONIZATSII. No. 14, 1914; No. 16, 1914. [Russ.
text and titles, pub.: 1912-1913, (No. 14) pp. 220-
222; (No. 16) pp. 170-172]

*"TEKUSHCHAIA BIBLIOGRAFIIA," REVOLIUTSIIA I
NATSIONAL'NOSTI. No. 2, 1937, 90-95 pp.; No. 3, 1937,
77-83 pp.; No. 4, 1937, 107-108 pp.; No. 6/7, 1937,
129-131 pp.; No. 9/10, 1937, 129-131 pp. [Russ.
text and titles] [NNC has 9/10 1957]

Veniukov, M. OPYT VOENNAGO OBOZRENIIA RUSSKIKH
GRANITS V AZII. Nos. 1, 2. St. Petersburg: Tip.
V. Bezobrazova i Komp., (No. 1) 1873; (No. 2) 1876.
[Russ. text; titles (1873) pp. 274-275, 319-320,
383-320, 383-384, 438-440, 487; (1876) pp. 50, 148]

*Zharov, F. I. PODVIGI KRASNYKH LETCHIKOV. Moscow:
Voennoe Izdatel'stvo Ministerstva Oborony SSSR,1963,
119 pp., 26,000 copies. [Russ. text; 25 Russ.
titles, + archives, per.: 1918-1924, pp. 118-119]

PART II

BLACK SEA & WEST CASPIAN LITTORAL

2 AZERBAIJAN

GENERAL

*Agadzhanova, L. E., H. G. Amirkhasova, S. S. Gomel'skaia, M. K. Muradova, M. M. Fitukhi, comp. UCHENYE AZERBAIDZHANA V MIROVOI PECHATI. BIBLIOGRAFIIA. Baku: "Elm," 1970, 110 pp., 1800 copies. [Russ. text: 515 Europ. and other titles, pub. 1923-69]

Agaev, N., A. Alekperov, comp. LETOPIS' ZHURNAL'NYKH STATEI (1931-1938). Baku: (Respublikanskaia Knizhnaia Palata), 1965, 174 pp., 1500 copies. [Azerb. and Russ. text; 2256 Azerb. and Russ. titles, pub. 1931-8]

*Agaeva, N., A. Alekperov, comp. LETOPIS' ZHURNAL'NYKH STATEI. 1942-1946. Baku: (Resp. Knizhnaia Palata) (Respublika Kitab Palatasi), 1965, 91 pp., 1500 copies. [Azerb. and Russ. text; 800 Azerb. and Russ. titles, magazine articles pub. 1942-6, pp. 7-72]

*Akhundov, Nazim. PERIODICHESKAIA PECHAT' V AZERBAIDZHANE. (1832-1920). BIBLIOGRAFIIA. Baku: AN AzSSR. (Inst. Lit. i Iazyka im. Nizami), 1965, 178 pp., 2250 copies. [Azerb. text; 405 Azerb., Russ., Armenian, Georg., Polish, and German titles, per. 1832-1920]

*"ALFAVITNYI PERECHEN' STATEI, OCHERKOV I RASSKAZOV, POMESHCHENNYKH V ZHURNALAKH I SBORNIKAKH, IZDANNYKH NA TERRITORII AZERB. SSR V 1931-M GODU," LETOPIS' PECHATI AZERBAIDZHANA. No. 12, Dec. 1931. [Azerb., Russ. text and titles, pub. 1931, pp. 255-90]

*Aliev, A. Ia., comp. AZERBAIDZHANSKAIA KNIGA (BIBLIOGRAFIIA). Vol. 1: 1780-1920. Baku: (Knizhnaia Palata AzSSR), 1963, 220 pp., 3000 copies. [Azerb. text; 1329 Azerb., Pers., Russ., and Arabic titles, pub. 1780-1920]

Aliyev, Z. H. "AZARBAYJAN MATBUAT LETOPISI" VA CHAP KARTOCHKALARINDAN ISTIFADA OLUNMASI. Baku: (Azarb. SSR Madaniyyat Nazirl. Azarb. SSR Dovlat Kitab Palatasi. M. F. Akhundov Ad. Azarb. Resp. Kitabkhanasi), 1962, 36 pp., 1500 copies. [Azerb. text]

Azerbaijan: General

*"AZERBAIDZHANSKAIA SOV. SOTSIALIST.RESPUBLIKA,"
BOL'SHAIA SOVETSKAIA ENTSIKLOPEDIIA. Vol. 1. Moscow:
Aktsionernoe Obshchestvo "Sovetskaia Entsiklopediia,"
1926. 1st ed. [Russ. text; Azerb., Russ., Europ.
titles, pp. 659-665]

*"AZERBAIDZHANSKAIA SOV. SOTSIALIST. RESPUBLIKA,"
BOL'SHAIA SOVETSKAIA ENTSIKLOPEDIIA. Vol. 1. Moscow:
Aktsionernoe Obshchestvo "Sovetskaia Entsiklopediia,"
1926. 1st ed. [Russ. text; Azerb., Russ. titles, pp.
658-9]

*"AZERBAIDZHANSKAIA SOVETSKAIA SOTSIALISTICHESKAIA
RESPUBLIKA," BOL'SHAIA SOVETSKAIA ENTSIKLOPEDIIA. Vol.
1. Moscow: Gosudarstvennoe Nauchnoe Izdatel'stvo
"Bol'skaia Sovetskaia Entsiklopediia," 1949, 2nd ed.
[Russ. text and titles, pp. 452, 455, 456, 462, 467,
472, 476, 478-9, 480]

AZARBAYJAN MATBU'ATININ ELLI ILLIGI. "EKINCHI," (1875-
1925). Baku, 1926, 48 pp. [Azerb. text; pub. 1875-
1925]

AZERBAIDZHANSKAIA KNIGA. (BIBLIOGRAFIIA). Baku:
(Azerbaidzh. Gos. Kn. Palata), 1951, 196 pp.
[Azerb. text; ca.2000 Azerb. titles, per. 1940-50]

AZERBAIDZHANSKII GOSUDARSTVENNYI UNIVERSITET IMENI
V. I. LENINA. NAUCHNYE IZDANIIA 1919-1929. Baku:
Tip. "III Internatsional," 1929. [Russ. text;
pub. 1919-29, pp. 17-22]

AZERBAIDZHANSKII UNIVERSITET IM. S. M. KIROVA.
MATERIALY NAUCHNOI KONFERENTSII ASPIRANTOV. Baku:
(Az. Univ. im. S. M. Kirova), 1967, 225 pp., 500
copies. [Russ. text; Azerb., Russ. titles at end of
articles]

Bagrii, A. V.   MATERIALY DLIA BIBLIOGRAFII
AZERBAIDZHANA. Vyp. 1, 1924; Vyp. 2, 1924; Vyp. 3,
1925, 1926 "PREDMETNYI UKAZATEL' K PERVYM TREM
VYPUSKAM" Baku: Izdanie "Doma Rabotnikov
Prosveshcheniia," 1924-6; Vyp. 1: 86 + 1 pp.; Vyp. 2:
66 pp.; Vyp. 3: 92 pp. [Russ. text; 1205 titles in
Vyp. 1, 1659 titles in Vyp. 2, 2029 titles in Vyp. 3]

"BIBLIOGRAFIIA AZERBAIDZHANSKOI SSR," BIBLIOGRAFIIA.
No. 1, 1929. [Russian text; titles pp. 95-6]

BIBLIOGRAFII RETSENZII (1946-1959). Baku: Azerbaidzh.
Resp. B-ka im. Akhundova, 1961, 107 pp., 3000 copies.
[Azerb. text; 977 Azerb. titles pub. 1946-59 in AzSSR]

Azerbaijan: General

Bogoslovskii, Evg. Al. "BAKINSKAIA PECHAT' POSLE
17 OKTIABRIA 1905 G. (PO IIULIA 1907 G.),
BIBLIOGRAFICHESKII ETIUD." Baku, 1907, 28 pp.
[Russ. text; titles pub. Oct. 17, 1905-July 1907]

_____. BAKINSKAIA PECHAT' V 1907 G. (S 1-GO IIULIA PO
31 DEKABRIA), BIBLIOGRAFICHESKII ETIUD. Baku:
Tip. A. N. Tarasova i A. D. Mirzaiantsa, 1908, 38 pp.
[Russ. text; titles pub. 1907]

Bogoslovskii, E. BAKINSKAIA PECHAT' V 1908 GODU (S
1 IANVARIA PO 31 DEKABRIA), BIBLIOGRAFICHESKII ETIUD.
Baku, 1909, 86 pp. [Russ. text; titles, pub 1908]

*BOL'SHEVISTSKAIA PERIODICHESKAIA PECHAT' AZERBAIDZHANA
(1904-APREL' 1920 GG.). SPRAVOCHNIK. Baku:
Azerbaidzhanskoe Gosudarstvennoe Izdatel'stvo, 1964,
78 pp., 1000 copies. [Russ. text; 61+ Azerb., Russ.,
Armen. titles pub. 1904-20, pp. 9-63, 71-7]

*EZHEGODNIK KNIGI AZERBAIDZHANA. 1960. Baku: Ob"edin.
Izd., 1961, 162 pp., 1000 copies. [Azerb, Russ.
pub. 1960]; 1962, 174 pp., 1000 copies [1522 Azerb.,
Russ. titles pub. 1961]; 1963, 207 pp., 1500 copies
[1726 Azerb., Russ. titles pub. 1962]; 1964, 186 pp.,
1500 copies [Azerb., Russ., pub. 1963]; 1965, 202 pp.,
1500 copies [1864 Azerb, Russ., Armen. titles pub.
1964]; 1966, 147 pp., 1500 copies [Azerb., Russ.];
1968, 205 pp., 1500 copies [Azerb., Russ.];
189 pp, 2000 copies [Azerb, Russ., pub. 1967]; 1969,
211 pp., 2000 copies [Azerb., Russ. pub. 1968]; 1970,
206 pp., 2500 copies [Azerb., Russ., pub. 1969]. [NNC
has 1962, 1964]

EZHEGODNIK KNIZHNOI PRODUKTSII AZERBAIDZHANSKOI SSR.
1939. Baku: (Azerb. Gos. Knizh. Palata), 1941, 92 pp.,
500 copies. [Azerb., pub. 1939]

*Gadzhieva, T. D., et al., comp. BIBLIOGRAFIIA IZDANII
AKADEMII NAUK AZERBAIDZHANSKOI SSR. 1945-1959 GG.
Baku: (AN AzSSR Tsentr. Nauch. B-ka), 1962, 676 pp.,
2000 copies. [Russ. text; ca.10,000 Azerb., Russ.
titles pub. 1945-59]

Gamidova, A. M., S. M. Alieva, comp. M. F. NAGIEV.
BIOBIBLIOGRAFIIA. Baku: Izd. AN AzSSR, 1968, 144 pp.,
2000 copies. [Russ. text]

*Gurko-Kriazhin, V. "AZERBAIDZHANSKAIA SOVETSKAIA
SOTSIALISTICHESKAIA RESPUBLIKA," BOL'SHAIA SOVETSKAIA
ENTSIKLOPEDIIA, Vol. 1. Moscow: Aktsionernoe
Obshchestvo "Sovetskaia Entsiklopediia," 1926, 1st ed.,
pp. 638-665. [Russ. text and titles, pp. 659, 665]

Azerbaijan: General

*Guseinov, A. A., N. A. Mangasarova. BOL'SHEVISTSKAIA
  PERIODICHESKAIA PECHAT' AZERBAIDZHANA (1904-APREL'
  1920 GG.) SPRAVOCHNIK. Baku: Azerbaidzhanskoe
  Gosudarstvennoe Izdatel'stvo, 1964, 78 pp., 1000 copies
  [Russ. text; ca.171 Azerb., Russ., Armen. titles,
  pp. 71-7]

Guseinov, S. ANNOTIROVANNAIA BIBLIOGRAFIIA GAZETY
  "EKINCHI." Baku: (Azerbaidzhanskaia Respublika.
  Biblioteka im. Akhundova), 1963, 94 pp., 1400 copies.
  [Azerb. text; 837 Azerb. titles pub. 1875-77]

Imanova, D. K. S. M. KULIEV DEIATELI NAUKI I KUL'TURY
  AZERBAIDZHANA. Baku: Izd. AN AzSSR, 1968, 100 pp.,
  2000 copies. [Russ. text]

*IU. G. MAMEDALIEV. 1905-1961. BIBLIOGRAFIIA. Baku:
  Izdatel'stvo Akademii Nauk Azerbaidzhanskoi SSR,
  1965, 91 pp., 2800 copies. [Russ. text; Azerb., Russ.
  titles per. 1905-61]

KATALOG IZDANII NA RUSSKOM IAZYKE IZDATEL'STVA
  AKADEMII NAUK AZERBAIDZHANSKOI SSR (1961-1964 GG.)
  Baku: Izdatel'stvo Akademii Nauk Azerbaidzhanskoi
  SSR, 1964, 24 pp., 3000 copies. [Russ. text;
  Russ. titles pub. 1961-64]

Khalafov, A. T. PROIZVEDENIIA N. K. KRUPSKOI NA
  AZERBAIDZHANSKOM IAZYKE. Baku: (M-vo Kul'tury
  AzSSR Azerbaidzh. Resp. B-ka im. M. F. Akhundova),
  1968, 49 pp., 3000 copies. [Russ. text; Azerb. titles]

KNIZHNAIA LETOPIS'. 1920-1925. Baku: (Knizhnaia
  Palata AzSSR), 1962, 67 pp., 1000 copies. [Azerb.
  text; 641 titles pub. 1920-25]

KNIZHNAIA LETOPIS' AZERBAIDZHANA, 1940 (monthly).
  [Azerb., Russ., pub. 1940]

KNIZHNAIA LETOPIS' AZERBAIDZHANA, 1941 (monthly).
  [Azerb., Russ., pub. 1941]

KNIZHNAIA LETOPIS' AZERBAIDZHANA. No. 1/2, 1942.
  [Azerb., Russ., pub. 1942]

KNIZHNAIA LETOPIS' AZERBAIDZHANA, 1946 (2 issues).
  [Azerb., Russ., pub. 1946]

KNIZHNAIA LETOPIS' AZERBAIDZHANA. No. 1/2; 2/4, 1947.
  [Azerb., Russ., pub. 1947]

KNIZHNAIA LETOPIS' AZERBAIDZHANA, 1948 (3 nos.).
  [Azerb., Russ., pub. 1948]

Azerbaijan: General

KNIZHNAIA LETOPIS' AZERBAIDZHANA, 1949 (quarterly).
[Azerb., Russ. text and titles, pub. 1949]

KNIZHNAIA LETOPIS' AZERBAIDZHANA, 1950 (quarterly).
[Azerb., Russ. text and titles, pub. 1950]

KNIZHNAIA LETOPIS' AZERBAIDZHANA, 1951 (quarterly).
[Azerb., Russ. text and titles, pub. 1951]

KNIZHNAIA LETOPIS' AZERBAIDZHANA, 1952 (quarterly),
[Azerb., Russ. text and titles, pub. 1952]

KNIZHNAIA LETOPIS' AZERBAIDZHANA, 1953 (quarterly),
[Azerb., Russ. text and titles, pub. 1953]

KNIZHNAIA LETOPIS' AZERBAIDZHANA, 1954 (quarterly),
[Azerb., Russ. text and titles, pub. 1954]

KNIZHNAIA LETOPIS' AZERBAIDZHANA, 1955 (quarterly),
[Azerb., Russ. text and titles, pub. 1955]

KNIZHNAIA LETOPIS' AZERBAIDZHANA, 1956 (quarterly),
[Azerb., Russ. text and titles, pub. 1956]

KNIZHNAIA LETOPIS' AZERBAIDZHANA, 1957 (quarterly),
[Azerb., Russ. text and titles, pub. 1957]

KNIZHNAIA LETOPIS' AZERBAIDZHANA, 1958 (quarterly),
[Azerb., Russ. text and titles, pub. 1958]

KNIZHNAIA LETOPIS' AZERBAIDZHANA, 1959 (bimonthly),
[Azerb., Russ. text and titles, pub. 1959]

KNIZHNAIA LETOPIS' AZERBAIDZHANA ZA 1942-1946 GG.
  Baku: (Azerbaidzh. Gos. Kn. Palata), 1951, 140 pp.,
  500 copies. [Azerb. text; ca.1500 Azerb., Russ.
  titles, pub. 1942-6]

Kuliev, G. I. FRONTOVYE GAZETY (1941-1945 GG.). Baku:
  Azernashr, 1965, 142 pp., 1500 copies. [Azerb. text;
  serials contents pub. 1941-5]

*Kuliev, N. M., T. D. Gadzhieva, Kh. A. Zulalova, Kh. Z.
  Makhmudov, comp. VELIKII OKTIABR' I AZERBAIDZHAN
  (1917-1967). BIBLIOGRAFIIA. Baku: Izd. AN AzSSR,
  1967, 172 pp., 2750 copies. [Russ. text; ca.1600
  Azerb., Russ. titles, per. 1917-67, pp. 38-162]

*LETOPIS' AZERBAIDZHANSKOI GOSUDARSTVENNOI KNIZHNOI
  PALATY. No. 1-5, 1926 (Jan.-Dec.). [Azerb., Russ.
  text; Azerb. titles, pub. 1926]

Azerbaijan: General

*LETOPIS' AZERBAIDZHANSKOI GOSUDARSTVENNOI KNIZHNOI
PALATY. No. 1-6, 1927 (bimonthly). [Azerb., Russ.
text; Azerb. titles, pub. 1927]

*LETOPIS' PECHATI AZERBAIDZHANA, 1928 (monthly). [Azerb.,
Russ. text; Azerb. titles, pub. 1928; NNC has 1-7,9-12]

*LETOPIS' PECHATI AZERBAIDZHANA, 1929 (monthly). [Azerb.,
Russ. text; Azerb. titles, pub. 1929; NNC has 1-12]

*LETOPIS' PECHATI AZERBAIDZHANA, 1930 (monthly). [Azerb.,
Russ. text; Azerb. titles, pub. 1930; NNC has 1-3,5-12]

*LETOPIS' PECHATI AZERBAIDZHANA, 1931 (monthly). [Azerb.,
Russ. text; Azerb. titles, pub. 1931; NNC has 1-12]

*LETOPIS' PECHATI AZERBAIDZHANA, 1932 (monthly). [Azerb.,
Russ. text; Azerb. titles, pub. 1932; NNC:3-5,7,10-12]

*LETOPIS' PECHATI AZERBAIDZHANA, 1933 (monthly). [Azerb.,
Russ. text; Azerb. titles, pub. 1933; NNC: 1-6, 9-12]

*LETOPIS' PECHATI AZERBAIDZHANA, 1934 (monthly). [Azerb.,
Russ. text; Azerb. titles, pub. 1934; NNC has 1-4]

LETOPIS' PECHATI AZERBAIDZHANA, 1935 (monthly). [Azerb.,
Russ. text; Azerb. titles, pub. 1935]

LETOPIS' PECHATI AZERBAIDZHANA, 1936 (monthly). [Azerb.,
Russ. text; Azerb. titles, pub. 1936]

LETOPIS' PECHATI AZERBAIDZHANA, 1937 (monthly). [Azerb.,
Russ. text; Azerb. titles, pub. 1937]

LETOPIS' PECHATI AZERBAIDZHANA, 1938 (monthly). [Azerb.,
Russ. text; Azerb. titles, pub. 1938]

LETOPIS' PECHATI AZERBAIDZHANA, 1939 (monthly). [Azerb.,
Russ. text; Azerb. titles, pub. 1939]

LETOPIS' PECHATI AZERBAIDZHANA. 1960 (monthly). [Azerb.,
Russ. text and titles, pub. 1960]

LETOPIS' PECHATI AZERBAIDZHANA. [1961] (monthly).
[Azerb., Russ. text and titles, pub. 1961]

LETOPIS' PECHATI AZERBAIDZHANA. [1962] (monthly).
[Azerb., Russ. text and titles, pub. 1962]

LETOPIS' PECHATI AZERBAIDZHANA. [1963] (monthly).
[Azerb., Russ. text and titles, pub. 1963]

Azerbaijan: General

LETOPIS' PECHATI AZERBAIDZHANA. 1964 (monthly).
[Azerb., Russ. text and titles, pub. 1964]

LETOPIS' PECHATI AZERBAIDZHANA. [1965] [monthly]
[Azerb., Russ. text and titles, pub. 1965]

LETOPIS' PECHATI AZERBAIDZHANA. [1966] [monthly]
[Azerb., Russ. text and titles, pub. 1966]

LETOPIS' PECHATI AZERBAIDZHANA. [1967] [monthly]
[Azerb., Russ. text and titles, pub. 1967]

LETOPIS' PECHATI AZERBAIDZHANA. [1968] [monthly]
[Azerb., Russ. text and titles, pub. 1968]

LETOPIS' PECHATI AZERBAIDZHANA. [1969] [monthly]
[Azerb., Russ. text and titles, pub. 1969]

LETOPIS' PECHATI AZERBAIDZHANA. [1970] [monthly]
[Azerb., Russ. text and titles, pub. 1970]

LETOPIS' GAZETNYKH STATEI AZERBAIDZHANA (NA
AZERBAIDZHANSKOM IAZYKE). 1938 (quarterly).
[Azerb. text and serials contents pub. 1938]

LETOPIS' GAZETNYKH STATEI AZERBAIDZHANA (NA
AZERBAIDZHANSKOM IAZYKE). 1939 (quarterly).
[Azerb. text and serials contents pub. 1939]

LETOPIS' GAZETNYKH STATEI AZERBAIDZHANA (NA
AZERBAIDZHANSKOM IAZYKE). 2 nos., 1940. [Azerb.
text and serials contents pub. 1940]

LETOPIS' GAZETNYKH STATEI AZERBAIDZHANA (NA
AZERBAIDZHANSKOM IAZYKE). 1941 (monthly). [Azerb.
text and serials contents pub. 1941]

LETOPIS' GAZETNYKH STATEI AZERBAIDZHANA (NA
AZERBAIDZHANSKOM IAZYKE). 3 nos., 1942. [Azerb. text
and serials contents pub. 1942]

LETOPIS' GAZETNYKH STATEI AZERBAIDZHANA (NA
AZERBAIDZHANSKOM IAZYKE). 2 nos., 1946. [Azerb. text
and serials contents pub. 1946]

LETOPIS' GAZETNYKH STATEI AZERBAIDZHANA (NA
AZERBAIDZHANSKOM IAZYKE). 1947 (bimonthly). [Azerb.
text and serials contents pub. 1947]

LETOPIS' GAZETNYKH STATEI AZERBAIDZHANA (NA RUSSKOM
IAZYKE). 1938 (quarterly). [Russ. text and serials
contents pub. 1938]

Azerbaijan: General

LETOPIS' GAZETNYKH STATEI AZERBAIDZHANA (NA RUSSKOM
    IAZYKE). 1939 (quarterly). [Russ. text and titles,
    serials contents pub. 1939]

LETOPIS' GAZETNYKH STATEI AZERBAIDZHANA (NA RUSSKOM
    IAZYKE). 1940 (quarterly). [Russ. text and titles,
    serials contents pub. 1940]

LETOPIS' GAZETNYKH STATEI AZERBAIDZHANA (NA RUSSKOM
    IAZYKE). Baku, 1941. [Russ. text and titles, serials
    contents pub. 1941]

LETOPIS' GAZETNYKH STATEI AZERBAIDZHANA (NA RUSSKOM
    IAZYKE). 1 no., 1942. [Russ. text and titles;
    serials contents pub. 1942]

LETOPIS' GAZETNYKH STATEI AZERBAIDZHANA (NA RUSSKOM
    IAZYKE). 1946 (triannually). [Russ. text and titles,
    serials contents pub. 1946]

LETOPIS' GAZETNYKH STATEI AZERBAIDZHANA (NA RUSSKOM
    IAZYKE). 1947 (triannually). [Russ. text and titles,
    serials contents pub. 1947]

LETOPIS' GAZETNYKH STATEI AZERBAIDZHANA. 1948 (monthly).
    [Azerb., Russ. text and titles; serials contents pub.
    1948]

LETOPIS' GAZETNYKH STATEI AZERBAIDZHANA. 1949 (monthly).
    [Azerb., Russ. text and titles; serials contents pub.
    1949]

LETOPIS' GAZETNYKH STATEI AZERBAIDZHANA. 1950 (monthly).
    [Azerb., Russ. text and titles; serials contents pub.
    1950]

LETOPIS' GAZETNYKH STATEI AZERBAIDZHANA. 1951 (monthly).
    [Azerb., Russ. text and titles; serials contents pub.
    1951]

LETOPIS' GAZETNYKH STATEI AZERBAIDZHANA. 1952 (monthly).
    [Azerb., Russ. text and titles; serials contents pub.
    1952]

LETOPIS' GAZETNYKH STATEI. 1953 (monthly). [Azerb.,
    Russ. text and titles, serials contents pub. 1953]

LETOPIS' GAZETNYKH STATEI. 1954. [Azerb., Russ. text
    and titles, serials contents pub. 1954]

LETOPIS' GAZETNYKH STATEI. 1955. [Azerb., Russ. text
    and titles, serials contents pub. 1955]

Azerbaijan: General

LETOPIS' GAZETNYKH STATEI. 1956. [Azerb., Russ. text and titles, serials contents pub. 1956]

LETOPIS' GAZETNYKH STATEI. [1957] (monthly). [Azerb., Russ. text and titles, serials contents pub. 1957]

LETOPIS' GAZETNYKH STATEI. [1958] (monthly). [Azerb., Russ. text and titles, serials contents pub. 1958]

LETOPIS' GAZETNYKH STATEI. 1959 (monthly). [Azerb., Russ. text and titles, serials contents pub. 1959]

LETOPIS' ZHURNAL'NYKH STATEI. 1938 (biannual). [Azerb. text; serials contents pub. 1938]

LETOPIS' ZHURNAL'NYKH STATEI. 1939 (biannual). [Azerb. text; serials contents pub. 1939]

LETOPIS' ZHURNAL'NYKH STATEI AZERBAIDZHANA. 1940 (biannual). [Azerb. text; serials contents pub. 1940]

LETOPIS' ZHURNAL'NYKH STATEI. 1941 (quarterly). [Azerb. text; serials contents pub. 1941]

LETOPIS' ZHURNAL'NYKH STATEI AZERBAIDZHANA. 1947 (quarterly). [Azerb. text; serials contents pub. 1947]

LETOPIS' ZHURNAL'NYKH STATEI AZERBAIDZHANA. 1948 (quarterly). [Azerb. text; serials contents pub. 1948]

LETOPIS' ZHURNAL'NYKH STATEI AZERBAIDZHANA. 1949 (quarterly). [Azerb. text; serials contents pub. 1949]

LETOPIS' ZHURNAL'NYKH STATEI AZERBAIDZHANA. 1950 (quarterly). [Azerb. text; serials contents pub. 1950]

LETOPIS' ZHURNAL'NYKH STATEI AZERBAIDZHANA. 1951 (quarterly). [Azerb. text; serials contents pub. 1951]

LETOPIS' ZHURNAL'NYKH STATEI AZERBAIDZHANA. 1952 (quarterly). [Azerb. text; serials contents pub. 1952]

LETOPIS' ZHURNAL'NYKH STATEI AZERBAIDZHANA. 1953 (quarterly). [Azerb. text; serials contents pub. 1953]

Azerbaijan: General

LETOPIS' ZHURNAL'NYKH STATEI AZERBAIDZHANA. 1954 (quarterly). [Azerb. text; serials contents pub. 1954]

LETOPIS' ZHURNAL'NYKH STATEI AZERBAIDZHANA. 1955 (quarterly). [Azerb. text; serials contents pub. 1955]

LETOPIS' ZHURNAL'NYKH STATEI AZERBAIDZHANA. 1956 (quarterly). [Azerb. text; serials contents pub. 1956]

LETOPIS' ZHURNAL'NYKH STATEI AZERBAIDZHANA. 1957 (quarterly). [Azerb. text; serials contents pub. 1957]

LETOPIS' ZHURNAL'NYKH STATEI AZERBAIDZHANA. 1958 (quarterly). [Azerb. text; serials contents pub. 1958]

LETOPIS' ZHURNAL'NYKH STATEI AZERBAIDZHANA. 1959 (quarterly). [Azerb. text; serials contents pub. 1959]

Mamedov, V. UKAZATEL' GAZETY "EKINCHI." Baku: (Azerbaidzh. Gos. Un-t im. Kirova), 1963, 40 pp., 1500 copies. [Azerb. text and titles, 456 serials contents pub. 1875-7]

*Mirzoian, G. G., V. M. Rustambeili, comp. PERIODICHESKIE I PRODOLZHAIUSHCHIESIA IZDANIIA AZERBAIDZHANSKOGO GOSUDARSTVENNOGO UNIVERSITETA IM. S. M. KIROVA (1921-1962 GG.). Baku: (Azerbaidzh. Gos. Un-t im. Kirova), 1964, 303 pp., 3000 copies. [Russ. text; 2587 Azerb., Russ. serials pub. 1921-62]

*"PERECHEN' PERIODICHESKIKH IZDANII VYKHODIVSHIKH NA TERRITORII ASSR V 1931-MU GODU I POSTUPIVSHIKH V KNIZHNUIU PALATU PO 31 DEKABRIA 1931 G.," LETOPIS' PECHATI AZERBAIDZHANA. No. 12, Dec. 1931. [Azerb., Russ. text; Azerb., Talysh, Tatar, Armen., Russ. titles, pub. 1931, pp. 247-55]

*"PERECHEN' PERIODICHESKIKH IZDANII, VYKHODIVSHIKH NA TERRITORII ASSR V 1932 GODU I POSTUPIVSHIKH V KNIZHNUIU PALATU PO 31-E DEKABRIA 1932 GODA," LETOPIS' PECHATI AZERBAIDZHANA. No. 11/12, Nov.-Dec. 1932. [Azerb., Russ. text; Azerb., Tatar, Talysh, Armen., Russ. titles pub. 1932, pp. 30-36]

"PERIODICHESKIE IZDANIIA, VYKHODIVSHIE V 1928 G. NA TERRITORII AZSSR, ZAREGISTRIROVANNYE AZ. GOS. KNIZHNOI PALATY PO 1 SENTIABRIA TEKUSHCHEGO GODA," LETOPIS' PECHATI AZERBAIDZHANA. No. 8, 1928. [Azerb., Russ. text and titles, 79 serials pub. 1928, pp. 73-81]

*"PERIODICHESKIE IZDANIIA, VYKHODIVSHIE NA TERRITORII AZSSR V 1929 GODU, ZAREGISTRIROVANNYE AZ. GOS. KNIZHNOI PALATY PO 31 DEKABRIA 1929 G.," LETOPIS'

Azerbaijan: General

PECHATI AZERBAIDZHANA, No. 12, Dec. 1929. [Azerb., Russ. text; 88 Azerb., Armen, Russ. serials pub. Dec. 1929, pp. 207-17]

*"PERIODICHESKIE IZDANIIA, VYKHODIVSHIE V AZERBAIDZHANSKOI SSR V 1930-M GODU. (ZHURNALY I VEDOMSTVENNYE IZDANIIA)," LETOPIS' PECHATI AZERBAIDZHANA. No. 11/12, Nov.-Dec. 1930. [Azerb., Russ. text and titles; 37 serials pub. 1930, pp. 249-52]

REKOMENDATEL'NAIA BIBLIOGRAFIIA. Baku: Azerb. Gos. Kn. Palata, 1938, 28 pp., 500 copies. [Azerb., Tatar text and titles; 61 titles pub. 1937]

Riumin, V. A. AZERBAIDZHANOVEDENIE. KRATKII ISTORICHESKII I ETNOGRAFICHESKII OCHERK AZERBAIDZHANA. Baku: Izd. Osoboi Komiissii Pri AZTsIKE, 1924, pp. 384-6. [Russ. text; 60 titles at end of article]

Safarov, I. MIR-ALI KASHKAI. BIBLIOGRAFIIA. Baku: Izd. AN AzSSR, 1967, 162 pp., 3000 copies. [Russ. text]

Sokol'skii, N. A. MATERIALY PO IZUCHENIIU NAKHICHEVANSKOI SSR. Tiflis: Zakgiz, 1933, 2nd ed. [Russ. text; pp. 182-4]

40 LET SO DNIA USTANOVLENIIA SOVETSKOI VLASTI V AZERBAIDZHANE. (METOD. I BIBLIOGR. MATERIALY). Baku: (Azer. Resp. B-ka im. Akhundova), 1960, 86 pp., 3000 copies. [Azerb. text; Sov. period]

*"UKAZATEL' STATEI, POMESHCHENNYKH V PERIODICHESKIKH IZDANIIAKH NAUCHNYKH UCHREZHDENII ASSR, VYKHODIASHCHIKH V NEOPREDELENNYE SROKI, KOTORYE OPISANY V NASTOIASHCHEM (NO. 5) NOMERE 'LETOPIS'," LETOPIS' PECHATI AZERBAIDZHANA. No. 5, May 1929. [Russ. text and titles; serials contents pub. May 1929, pp. 75-9]

*"UKAZATEL' STATEI, POMESHCHENNYKH V PERIODICHESKIKH IZDANIIAKH NAUCHNYKH UCHREZHDENII ASSR, VYKHODIASHCHIKH V NEOPREDELENNYE SROKI, KOTORYE OPISANY V NASTOIASHCHEM (NO. 7/8) NOMERE 'LETOPISI'," LETOPIS' PECHATI AZERBAIDZHANA. No. 7/8, 1929. [Azerb., Russ. text; Russ. titles, serials contents pub. July-Aug. 1929, pp. 128-30]

ZHURNAL'NAIA LETOPIS' AZERBAIDZHANSKOI SSR (ZA 1920-1930 GG.). Baku: Azerbaidzhanskaia Gosudarstvennaia Knizhnaia Palata, 1932, 278 pp. [Azerb. text and titles, pub. 1920-30]

Azerbaijan: General

ZHURNAL'NAIA LETOPIS' AZERBAIDZHANSKOI SSR. 1934.
[Azerb. text; serials contents pub. 1931]

ZHURNAL'NAIA LETOPIS' AZERBAIDZHANSKOI SSR. 1934.
[Azerb. text; serials contents pub. 1932]

ANTHROPOLOGY, ETHNOGRAPHY

*Anserov, N. I.   TIURKI SOVETSKOGO AZERBAIDZHANA (K KHARAKTERISTIKE IKH FIZICHESKOGO TIPA). Baku: Izdanie.Azerbaidzhanskii Gosudarstvennyi Nauchno-Issledovatel'skii Institut, 1930, 73 pp. [Russ. text; 32 Russ. titles, pp. 67-8]

*Guliev, G. A.   BIBLIOGRAFIIA ETNOGRAFII AZERBAIDZHANA. CH. 1. [LIT.], IZD. NA RUS. IAZ. DO 1917 G. Baku: Izdatel'stvo Akademii Nauk Azerbaidzhanskoi SSR, 1962, 127 pp., 750 copies. [Russ. text; 1742 Russ. titles pub. pre-1917]

ARCHITECTURE, ART, MUSIC
(For ARCHAEOLOGY, see HISTORY)

*Abasova, E. G., K. A. Kasimov.   OCHERKI MUZYKAL'NOGO ISKUSSTVA SOVETSKOGO AZERBAIDZHANA. 1920-1956. Baku: "Elm," 1970, 178 pp., 1600 copies. [Russ. text; ca.200 Azerb., Russ. titles, per. 1920-56, pp. 171-7]

Abasova, E.   OPERA "KEROGLY" UZEIRA GADZHIBEKOVA. Baku: Azerneshr, 1966 [on cover 1965], 57 pp., 700 copies. [Russ. text; titles at end of book]

_____.   OPERY I MUZYKAL'NYE KOMEDII UZEIRA GADZHIBEKOVA. Baku: (Akad. Nauk AzSSR. In-t Arkhitektury i Iskusstva), 1961. [Russ. text; 83 Azerb. and Russ. titles, pp. 190-3]

Abasova, E. G., D. Kh. Danilov, L. V. Karagicheva, eds., comp.   SOIUZ KOMPOZITOROV AZERBAIDZHANA. Baku:

Azerbaijan: Architecture, Art, Music

Azerneshr, 1965, 124 pp., 2000 copies. [Russ. text; 60 lists]

Agaeva, Kh. UZEIR GADZHIBEKOV (ZHIZN', DEIATEL'NOST' I TVORCHESTVO VELIKOGO AZERBAIDZH. KOMPOZITORA). Baku: (Azerbaidzh. Teatr. O-vo), 1955. [Russ. text; 178 Azerb., Russ. titles, per. 1904-45, pp. 145-51]

AZERBAIDZHANSKII POLITEKHNICHESKII INSTITUT. UCHENYE ZAPISKI. SERIIA 10. ARKHITEKTURA, STROITEL'STVO, TRANSPORT I LEGKAIA PROM-ST'. No. 1(9). Baku: (M-vo Vyssh. i Sred. Spets. Obrazovaniia AzSSR.), 1967, 192 pp., 500 copies. [Russ. text; titles at end of articles]

AZERBAIDZHANSKII POLITEKHNICHESKII INSTITUT. UCHENYE ZAPISKI SERIIA 10. ARKHITEKTURA, STROITEL'STVO, TRANSPORT I LEGKAIA PROM-ST'. No. 3 (11). Baku: (M-vo Vyssh. i Sred. Spets. Obrazovaniia AzSSR), 1967, 189 pp., 500 copies. [Russ. text; titles at end of articles]

AZERBAIDZHANSKII POLITEKHNICHESKII INSTITUT. UCHENYE ZAPISKI SERIIA 10. ARKHITEKTURA. Baku: (M-vo Vyssh. i Sred. Spets. Obrazovaniia AzSSR), 1967, 170 pp., 500 copies. [Russ. text; titles at end of articles]

Bretanitskii, L. S. "K PROBLEME IZUCHENIIA ARKHITEKTURNYKH NAPRAVLENII SREDNEVEKOGO AZERBAIDZHANA." DOKL. AKAD. NAUK. AZERBAIDZH. SSR., Vol. 2, No. 1. Baku: Akad. Nauk. Azerbaidzh. SSR, 1946. [Russ. text; 21 titles, pub. 1851-1946; per. medieval, pp. 30-3]

Efendi, Rasim. KHUDOZHESTVENNOE REMESLO AZERBAIDZHANA. (METALL I IUVELIRNOE ISKUSSTVO). Baku: Azerneshr, 1966, 38 pp., 2000 copies. [Azerb. text; 39 Azerb. titles, pp. 37-8]

Efendiev, V. A., comp. ISKUSSTVO. (PAMIATKA CHITATELIU). Baku: (Azerbaidzh. Resp. B-ka im. Akhundova. Chto Chitat' ob Azerbaidzhane. Vyp. 3), 1964, 18 pp., 500 copies. [Russ. text]

*Gabibov, N., M. Nadzhafov. ISKUSSTVO SOVETSKOGO AZERBAIDZHANA. ZHIVOPIS', SKUL'PTURA, GRAFIKA. Moscow: "Iskusstvo," 1960, 198 pp. [Russ. text; 78 Russ. titles, Sov. per., pp. 190-2]

_____, et. al. OCHERKI IZOBRAZITEL'NOGO ISKUSSTVA SOVETSKOGO AZERBAIDZHANA. ZHIVOPIS', SKUL'PTURA, GRAFIKA. Baku: (Akad. Nauk AzSSR. In-t Arkhitektury i Iskusstva), 1960. [Russ. text; ca.120 Azerb. and Russ. titles, Sov. per., pp. 137-9]

Azerbaijan: Architecture, Art, Music

*Gadzhiev, Dzh., D. Danilov, D. Zhitomirskii, K. Karaev,
S. Rustamov, N. Usubova, eds. AZERBAIDZHANSKAIA
MUZYKA. SBORNIK STATEI. Moscow: Gosudarstvennoe
Muzykal'noe Izdatel'stvo, 1961, 376 pp., 2300 copies.
[Russ. text; 24 Azerb., Russ. titles, pp. 374-5]

*Gadzhiev, P. A. AZERBAIDZHANSKAIA SOVETSKAIA GRAFIKA
(1920-1940 GG.). Baku: Izdatel'stvo Akademii Nauk
Azerbaidzhanskoi SSR, 1962, 139+ pp., 750 copies.
[Russ. text; Azerb., Russ. titles, per. 1920-40, pp.
126-30]

Gubad. UZEIR GADZHIBEKOV. BIBL. UKAZATEL'. Baku:
Azerbaidzh. Gos. Knizh. Palata), 1941, 68 pp.,
5100 copies. [Azerb. text]

*Ibragimova, M., A. Isazade, Kh. Mamedova, comp.
KARA KARAEV. BIBLIOGRAFIIA. Baku: Izdatel'stvo
Akademii Nauk Azerbaidzhanskoi SSR (AN AzSSR. Fundam.
B-ka. Deiateli Nauki i Kul'tury Azerbaidzhana), 1969,
143 pp., 2000 copies. [Russ. text; 719 Azerb., Russ.
titles, pub. 1937-68]

*Isazade, A. INSTRUMENTAL'NOE TVORCHESTVO KOMPOZITOROV
SOVETSKOGO AZERBAIDZHANA (DLIA STRUNNOSMYCHKOVYKH
INSTRUMENTOV). Baku: Izdatel'stvo Akademii Nauk
Azerbaidzhanskoi SSR, 1961, 147 pp., 1200 copies.
[Azerb. text; 68 Azerb., Russ. titles, pp. 145-7]

_____. ZHIZN' I TVORCHESTVO NARODNOGO ARTISTA
SSSR BIUL'-BIULIA. Baku, 1967. [Azerb. text; ca.200
titles, pp. 112-21]

*ISKUSSTVO SOVETSKOGO AZERBAIDZHANA. ZHIVOPIS'. GRAFIKA.
SKUL'PTURA. Moscow: Sovetskii Khudozhnik, [1970],
200 pp., 6700 copies. [Russ. text; ca.200 Azerb.,
Russ. titles, pp. 194-9]

Karagicheva, L. V. AZERBAIDZHANSKAIA SSR. Moscow:
Muzgiz, 1956. [Russ. text; 25 Russ. titles, pp. 100-1]

Karagicheva, L. AZERBAIDZHANSKAIA SSR. Moscow:
Muzgiz, 1957. [Russ. text: 51 Russ. titles, Sov. per.,
pp. 159-62]

_____. BALETY KARA KARAEVA "SEM' KRASAVITS,"
"TROPOIU GROMA." Moscow: Muzgiz, 1959. [Russ. text;
42 Azerb., Russ. titles, Sov. per., pp. 86-7]

Kasimov, K. UZEIR GADZHIBEKOV. Baku: (Akad. Nauk
Azerbaidzh. SSR. In-t Azerbaidzh. Iskusstva im.
Gadzhibekova), 1945. [Russ. text; 478 Azerb., Russ.
titles, pub. 1907-45, pp. 73-93]

Azerbaijan: Architecture, Art, Music

Kasimova, S.   DZHANGIR DZHANGIROV.   Baku, 1964, 65 pp.
[Russ. text; 19 titles]

Kasim-zade, E. A., Iu. S. Iaralov.   DADASHEV. USEINOV.
Moscow: Gos. Izd. Lit. po Stroit-vu i Arkhitekture,
1951. [Russ. text; 25 titles, pp. 126, 128]

*Kasim-zade, E.   PROBLEMY RAZVITIIA AZERBAIDZHANSKOI
SOVETSKOI ARKHITEKTURY NA SOVREMENNOM ETAPE. Baku:
Azerbaidzhanskoe Gosudarstvennoe Izdatel'stvo, 1967,
234 pp., 1580 copies. [Russ. text; ca.140 Russ.
titles, pub. 1925-61, pp. 230-3]

Kaziev, A. Iu.   NARODNYI KHUDOZHNIK AZIM AZIMZADE.
Baku: (Akad. Nauk Azerbaidzh. SSR In-t Arkhitektury i
Iskusstva), 1953. [Russ. text; 24 Azerb., Russ.
titles, per. 1880-1943, pp. 51-2]

*Kerimova, Rafiga Kerim Kyzy.   AZERBAIDZHANSKAIA
SOVETSKAIA PORTRETNAIA ZHIVOPIS'. Baku: Azarbayjan
SSR Elmlar Akademiyasi Nashriyyati, 1964, 130+ pp.,
1400 copies. [Azerb. text; Azerb., Russ. titles,
Soviet per., pp. 117-20]

Khan-Mogomedov, S. O.   DERBENT. Moscow: Gosstroiizdat,
1958. [Russ. text; 33 titles, pp. 121-2]

Mekhtieva, N.   KINOMUZYKA KARA KARAEVA. Baku: Azerneshr,
1966, 98 pp., 1000 copies. [Russ. text; 48 titles,
pp. 96-7]

*Nadzhafov, Mursal.   AZIMZADE. Baku: Azerbaidzhanskoe
Gosudarstvennoe Izdatel'stvo, 1965, 148 pp., 1000
copies. [Russ. text; 63 Azerb., Russ. titles, pp.
117-19]

Nadzhafova, N. N.   KHUDOZHESTVENNAIA KERAMIKA
AZERBAIDZHANA XII-XV VV. Baku, 1964. [Russ. text;
87 titles, per. 12th-15th cc., pp. 95-8]

Nadzhafova, S., comp.   ISKUSSTVO (ANNOT. BIBLIOGR.
UKAZATEL'). Baku: (Azerbaidzh. Resp. B-ka im.
Akhundova), 1963, 42 pp., 500 copies. [Azerb. text;
102 titles]

NOTY. PROIZVEDENIIA AZERBAIDZHANSKIKH KOMPOZITOROV.
Baku: Azmuzgiz, 1951, 14 pp., 500 copies. [Russ. text;
99 titles]

"Opublikovannye Trudy [M. Mamedova]."   Dzhafarov, D.
ISKUSSTVO REZHISSERA. O TVORCHESKOM PUTI M. MAMEDOVA.
Baku, 1969. [Russ. text; 51 titles pub. 1948-68, pp.
iv-vi]

Azerbaijan: Architecture, Art, Music

Salamzade, A. V. ARKHITEKTURA AZERBAIDZHANA XVI-XIX
VV. Baku, 1964. [Russ. text; ca.340 titles, per.
16-19cc, pp. 248-54]

Sarabskii, A. G.   VOZNIKNOVENIE I RAZVITIE
AZERBAIDZHANSKOGO MUZYKAL'NOGO TEATRA (DO 1917 G.).
Baku, 1968. [Russ. text; ca.300 titles, per. up to
1917, pp. 259-71]

Sarkisov, N. A. "OSOBENNOSTI TEKHNIKI POLIKHROMNYKH
MAIOLIKOVYKH MOZAIK AZERBAIDZHANA. (K ORGANIZATSII
STROITEL'STVA I OTDELOCHNYKH RABOT IZ KERAMIKI)."
UCHENYE ZAPISKI. (Azerb. Politekh. In-t), No. 3,
1964. [Russ. text; 46 titles, pp. 42-3]

*Useinov, M., L. Bretanitskii, A. Salamzade.   ISTORIIA
ARKHITEKTURY AZERBAIDZHANA. Moscow: Gos. Izd-vo
Lit-ry po Stroit., Arkhitekt. i Stroit. Materialam.,
1963, 395 pp. [Russ. text; ca.450 Azerb., Russ.,
Europ. titles, pp. 381-8]

*Useinov, M. A.   PAMIATNIKI AZERBAIDZHANSKOGO ZODCHESTVA.
Moscow: Gosizdat Arkhitektury i Gradostroit-va, 1951,
162 pp. [Russ. text; 30 titles, p. 158]

ECONOMICS

Abdurakhmanov, B. E.   TRANSPORT I EGO VLIIANIE NA
RAZVITIE I RAZMESHCHENIE PROIZVODSTVA AZERBAIDZHANSKOI
SSR. Baku: Izd. AN AzSSR, 1966, 174 pp., 850 copies.
[Russ. text; 62 titles, pp. 171-3]

Airapetova, S. A.   BIBLIOGRAFIIA OPUBLIKOVANNYKH
RABOT PO OVOSHCHE-BAKHCHEVYM KUL'TURAM I KARTOFELIU V
AZERBAIDZHANSKOI SSR. Baku: (Azerbaidzh. NII
Ovoshchevodstva Gos. Proizvod. Kom. Soveta Ministrov
AzSSR.), 1967, 42 pp., 1000 copies. [Russ. text]

ALFAVITNYI UKAZATEL' K TRUDAM S"EZDA BAKINSKIKH
NEFTEPROMYSHLENNIKOV. Baku, 1-24, 1908. [Russ. text]

*Aliev, Gadi Bedal Ogly.   EKONOMICHESKAIA GEOGRAFIIA
AZERBAIDZHANSKOI SSR. Baku: Azarbayjan Dovlat
Tadrispedagozhi Adabiyyati Nashriyyati, 1963, 216 pp.,
3000 copies. [Azerb. text; 17 Azerb. titles, p.214]

Azerbaijan: Economics

Aminova, N. A., comp. PROMYSHLENNOST' AZERBAIDZHANA. Baku: (Azerbaidzh. Resp. B-ka im. Akhundova. Chto Chitat' ob Azerbaidzhane. Vyp. 4), 1965, 19 pp., 1000 copies. [Russ. text; 172 titles]

Atamali, F. V. SPRAVOCHNYE MATERIALY PO ERGONOMIKE. Baku: Azerneshr, 1968, 183 pp., 1000 copies. [Russ. text; 154 titles, pp. 178-82]

Avdeev, Mikh. "BIBLIOGRAFIIA MUGANI." MUGAN' I SAL'IANSKAIA STEP'. NASELENIE, ZEMLEPOL'ZOVANIE, VODNOE KHOZIASTVO. Baku: (Obshchestvo Obsledovaniia i Izucheniia Azerbaidzhana), 1927, 136 pp., 1500 copies. [Russ. text; 48+ titles, pp. 134-6]

Bagrii, A. "BIBLIOGRAFIIA PO EKONOMIKE AZERBAIDZHANA." IQTISADI KHABARLAR, Nos. 8/9, 10/11, 12, 13, 14, 1924; Nos. 1/2, 3, 4/5, 6, 7/8, 9/10, 11, 1925. [Russ. text; 1163 Russ. titles pub. 1924-1925: No. 8/9, pp. 43-4, No. 10/11, pp. 33-4, No. 12, pp. 27-30, No. 13, pp. 22-3, No. 14, p. 24. In 1925, No. 1/2, pp. 31-2, No. 3, p. 26, No. 4/5, pp. 29-30, No. 7/8, pp. 30-1, No. 11, p. 41]

*Buniatov, Teimur Amiraslan Ogly. K ISTORII RAZVITIIA ZEMLEDELIIA V AZERBAIDZHANE. Baku: Azarbayjan SSR Elmlar Akademiyasi Nashriyyati, 1964, 152 pp., 2850 copies. [Azerb. text; Azerb., Russ. titles, pp. 144-52]

EKONOMICHESKII VESTNIK. ORGAN VYSSHEGO EKONOMICHESKOGO SOVETA ASSR. Baku, 1922-1925 (twice monthly). [Russ. text; section "Bibliogr." for titles]

Faradzhev, A. S. "SPISOK TRUDOV PROFESSORA FARADZHEVA ALI KULI SATTAR OGLY," VOSPOMINANIIA IZ ISTORII PODGOTOVKI EKON. KADROV V AZERBAIDZH. SSR. Baku, 1968. [Russ. text; 43 titles, pub. 1926-67, pp. 18-20]

Gadzhiev, S., A. Kuliev, A. Sultanov, et al. OBSHCHAIA TEORIIA STATISTIKI. Baku: (M-vo Vyssh. i Sred. Spets. Obrazovaniia AzSSR), 1968, 83 pp., 1000 copies. [Russ. text; Azerb. titles, p. 82]

Imanova, D. K., comp. S. M. KULIEV. BIBLIOGRAFIIA. Baku: Izd. AN AzSSR, 1968, 100 pp., 2000 copies. [Russ. text; 350 + 87 Azerb., Russ. titles, pub. 1932-68]

Ismailov, M. A. KAPITALIZM V SEL'SKOM KHOZIASTVE AZERBAIDZHANA NA ISKHODE XIX-NACHALE XX V. Baku, 1964. [Russ. text; ca.470 titles per. ca.1900, pp. 3-16, 288-304]

Azerbaijan: Economics

IZVESTIIA VYSSHEGO EKONOMICHESKOGO SOVETA. ORGAN VYSSHEGO EKONOMICHESKOGO SOVETA ASSR. Baku, 1922-5 (twice monthly). [Azerb. text; titles in section "Bibliogr."]

*Kashkai, M. A., P. M. Alampiev, eds.   AZERBAIDZHANSKAIA SSR. EKON.-GEOGR. KHARAKTERISTIKA. Moscow: (In-t Geografii Akad. Nauk Azerbaidzh. SSR. In-t Geografii Akad. Nauk SSSR), 1957, 444 pp. [Russ. text; ca.210 titles, pp. 434-43]

*Makhmudov, G.Z., comp.; T. D. Gadzhieva, ed.   G. A. ALIEV. BIBLIOGRAFIIA. Baku: Izdatel'stvo Akademii Nauk Azerbaidzhanskoi SSR, 1968, 1500 copies. [Azerb., Russ. text; 349 Azerb, Russ. titles pub. 1925-67, pp. 37-78]

Mekhtiev, D.M., T. A. Susoeva, comp.   NEFTIANYE KAMNI. BIBLIOGRAFICHESKII UKAZATEL' LITERATURY O MORSKOM NEFTIANOM MESTOROZHDENII V AZERBAIDZHANE. Baku: Azerbaidzh. Institut Nauch.-Tekhn. Informatsii, 1962, 52 pp., 900 copies. [Russ. text; 150 Azerb., Russ. titles]

Mirzoev, Sultan.   RAZMESHCHENIE I SPETSIALIZATSIIA SEL'SKOGO KHOZIAISTVA AZERBAIDZHANSKOI SSR. Baku: Azerneshr, 1967, 320 pp., 1700 copies. [Russ. text; titles pp. 313-18]

Pavlova, T. V., Z. I. Agalarova, comp.   ORGANIZATSIIA I METODIKA TRUDA INZHENERNOTEKHNICHESKIKH RABOTNIKOV. Baku: (Gosplan AzSSR. Azerbaidzh. Inti. Resp. Nauch.-Tekhn. B-ka), 1967, 27 pp., 500 copies. [Russ. text]

PERECHEN' STATEI, POMESHCHENNYKH V ZHURNALE "EKONOMICHESKII VESTNIK AZERBAIDZHANA" ZA 1926-7 GOD. Baku: Tip. "Azgiz"'a (Prilozhenie k Zhurnalu "Ekonomicheskii Vestnik Azerbaidzhana"), 1928, 30 pp. [Russ. text; titles pub. 1926-7]

Pishcherskii, Ia.   UKAZATEL' STATEI I ZAMIETOK, POMESHCHENNYKH V TBORTO S 1886 G. PO 1904 G. TRUDY BAKINSKAGO OTDIELENIIA RUSSKAGO TEKHNICHESKAGO OBSHCHESTVA, No. 5, 1904. [Russ. text; Russ. titles pub. 1886-1904]

SISTEMATICHESKII UKAZATEL' STATEI I ZAMIETOK, POMESHCHENNYKH V ZHURNALE NEFTIANOE DIELO ZA 1899-1907 gg. chast' I-IX)...ZA 1908-1909 GG. Baku, 1908-10. [Russ. text; titles pub. 1899-1909]

Slepov, I. A.   V. I. LENIN I NAUCHNAIA ORGANIZATSIIA TRUDA. Baku: Azerneshr, 1967, 59 pp., 7000 copies.

Azerbaijan: Economics

[Russ. text; 25 titles, pp. 57-8]

[Strel'tsov, E. N., Iu. Danilova, comps.]. V. I. LENIN I NEFTIANAIA PROMYSHLENNOST' AZERBAIDZHANA. BIBLIOGR. SPRAVKA. Baku: (Azerb. NII Nauch.-Tekhn. Informatsii i Nauch. Organizatsii Truda Gosplana AzSSR. Resp. NTB Bibliogr. Informatsiia. 1970, 7 pp., 400 copies. [Russ. text; 63 titles pub. 1920-69]

*Sumbatzade, A. S. PROMYSHLENNOST' AZERBAIDZHANA V XIX V. Baku: Izdatel'stvo Akademii Nauk Azerbaidzhanskoi SSR, 1964, 498 pp. 1200 copies. [Russ. text; ca.160 Russ. titles, 19th century, pp. 491-6]

EDUCATION

Abdullaev, A. IZ ISTORII PREPODAVANIIA AZERBAIDZHANSKOGO IAZYKA (V SHKOLE). Baku, 1966. [AZERB. TEXT: 183 titles, pp. 326-31]

Abramov, K. I. ISTORIIA BIBLIOTECHNOGO DELA V SSSR. Baku: (M-vo Vyssh. i Sred. Spets. Obrazovaniia AzSSR. Azerbaidzh. Gos. Un-t im. S. M. Kirova.), 1967, 29 pp., 1000 copies. [Russ. text; Azerb. titles at end of chapters]

Agaian, Ts. P. P. A. BAKIKHANOV. Baku: (In-t Istorii im Bakikhanova), 1948. [Russ. text; 173 titles, including archives, pub. 1829-1947, pp. 131-54]

Aliev, A. CHTO CHITAT'. (UKAZATEL' KNIG). Baku, 48 pp. [Azerb. text; ca.900 Azerb. titles, pub. 1940-8]

AZERBAIDZHANSKII PEDAGOGICHESKII INSTITUT IAZYKOV IM. M. F. AKHUNDOVA. UCHENYE ZAPISKI. SERIIA 12. IAZYK I LITERATURA. No. 1. Baku: (M-vo Vyssh. i Sred. Spets. Obrazovaniia AzSSR...), 1966, 117 pp., 500 copies. [Russ. text; Azerb., Russ. titles, pp. 78-9]

Baisheva, Kh. A. "RASHID EFENDIEV--AZERBAIDZHANSKII PEDAGOG I PROSVETITEL' (1863-1942)," SOVETSKAIA PEDAGOGIKA, No. 8, 1957. [Russ. text; 15 Azerb., Russ. titles, per. 1863-1942, p. 84]

Efendieva, Sh. M. CHTO CHITAT' MOLODEZHI O KOMMUNISTICHESKOM VOSPITANII. Baku: (Azerbaidzh.

Azerbaijan: Education

  Resp. Publ. B-ka im. Akhundova), 1956, 16 pp., 1500
  copies. [Azerb. text; 166 titles]

Gasanov, A. M.   BIBLIOGRAFICHESKII UKAZATEL' PO KURSU
  PEDAGOGIKI. (METOD. POSOBIE DLIA ZAOCHNIKOV).
  Baku: (Azerbaidzh. Gos. Zaoch. Ped. In-t), 1954 (3rd.
  ed.), 19 pp., 1500 copies. [Azerb. text; ca.200 Azerb.
  titles, Sov. per.]

*Hasanov, Muzaffar.   ROL' BIBLIOTEKI V KOMMUNISTICHESKOM
  VOSPITANII CHITATELEI. Baku: (Azarbayjan Respublika
  Kitabkhanasi Elmi-Metodik Kitabkhanashunaslig Sho'-
  basi), 1962, 46 pp., 3000 copies. [Azerb. text;
  Azerb. titles, pp. 44-5]

Kazymova, M.   VOSPITANIE V SEM'E I SHKOLE. KRATKAIA
  BIBLIOGR. PAMIATKA. Baku: Azerbaidzh. Resp. Publ.
  B-ka im. Akhundova, 1954, 8 pp., 1000 copies. [Azerb.
  text; 39 titles]

Khalafov, A. T.   PROIZVEDENIIA N. K. KRUPSKOI NA
  AZERBAIDZHANSKOM IAZYKE. BIBLIOGRAFIIA. (K 100-
  LETNIIU SO DNIA ROZHDENIIA.). Baku: (Azerbaidzh.
  Resp. B-ka im. Akhundova), 1968, 49 pp., 3000 copies.
  [Azerb. text; ca.525 Azerb. titles, pub. 1923-67]

KNIGA V ESTAFETE KUL'TURY. Baku: (Tsentr. Bibliotech.
  Peredvizhnoi Fond im. Gor'kogo. K 40-Letiiu
  VLKSM.), 1958, 31 pp., 1200 copies. [Azerb. text;
  Azerb. titles, pub. 1952-7]

[LERMAN, A. N.]   KNIGA V ESTAFETE KUL'TURY. Baku:
  (Tsentr. Bibliotech. Peredvizhnoi Fond im. Gorkogo
  k 46-Letiiu VLKSM), 1958, 36 pp.,4000 copies. [Russ.
  text]

Magerramov, M.   O VOSPITANII VOLI SHKOL'NIKOV. Baku:
  Azerneshr, B-ka Uchitelia, 1953. [Azerb. text; 30
  Azerb., Russ. titles, p. 112]

METODICHESKIE MATERIALY K PROVEDENIIU SEKTSIONNYKH
  RABOT NA... RAIONNYKH SOVESHCHANIIAKH UCHITELEI
  NACHAL'NYKH, SEMILETNIKH I SREDNIKH SHKOL V 1954 GODU.
  Baku: Azerbaidzh. In-t Usovershenstvovaniia Uchitelei,
  Jan., Aug., 1954. Jan.: 58 pp.; Aug.: 84 pp. [Azerb.
  text; Jan.: 11 lists; Aug.: 16 lists, Azerb., Russ.]

Rzaev, A.   IZ ISTORII VYSSHEGO PEDAGOGICHESKOGO
  OBRAZOVANIIA V AZERBAIDZHANE. Baku: Azernesher, 1957.
  [Russ. text; 46 titles, pp. 99-101.

*Safarov, Ismet, comp.   MIR-ALI KASHKAI. BIBLIOGRAFIIA.
  Baku: Izdatel'stvo Akademii Nauk Azerbaidzhanskoi SSR,

Azerbaijan: Education

1967, 162 pp., 3000 copies. [Russ. text; 543 + 128 Azerb., Russ. titles, pub. 1933-66]

"SPISOK MATERIALOV, POMESHCH.,'V 1939 G. V ZH. V POMOSHCH' UCHITELIU',"MIUELIME KEMEK, No. 11-12, 1939. [Azerb. text; 114 titles, pub. 1939, pp. 126-8]

Sumbat-zade, A. S., ed. VOSTOKOVEDENIE V SOVETSKOM AZERBAIDZHANE. Baku: (AN AzSSR. Institut Vostokovedeniia), 1964, 47 pp., 2000 copies.

Tsitovich, V. A. VOSPITANIE V SEM'E I SHKOLE. KRATKAIA BIBLIOGR. PAMIATKA. Baku: Azerbaidzh. Resp. Publ. B-ka im. Akhundova, 1954, 10 pp., 1000 copies. [Russ. text; 59 titles]

*"ZADACHI UCHITELEI RUSSKOGO IAZYKA V 1960-1961 UCHEBNOM GODU," RUSSKII IAZYK V NERUSSKOI SHKOLE (PRILOZHENIE K ZHURNALU "AZERBAIDZHAN MEKTEBI"), No. 7 (135), July, 1960, 98 pp., 5100 copies. [Russ. text; 6 lists, Russ., pp. 3-13]

GEOGRAPHY

*AZERBAIDZHANSKOE GEOGRAFICHESKOE OBSHCHESTVO. TRUDY. Vol. 3. Baku: Izdatel'stvo Akademii Nauk Azerbaidzhanskoi SSR, 1966, 224 pp., 600 copies. [Russ. text; Azerb., Russ. titles at end of articles]

AZERBAIDZHANSKOE GEOGRAFICHESKOE OBSHCHESTVO. TRUDY. Vol. 4. Baku: Izd. AN AzSSR, 1968, 252 pp., 500 copies. [Russ. text; Azerb., Russ. titles at end of articles]

Gadzhieva, G. A. LANDSHAFTHO-ZONAL'NOE RAIONIROVANIE SEVERO-VOSTOCHNOGO SKLONA MALOGO KAVKAZA V SEL'SKOKHOZIAISTVENNYKH TSELIAKH. Baku, 1965. [Azerb. text; 155 titles, pp. 100-6]

*Gadzhizade, Abduragim Mamediia Ogly. NASELENIE AZERBAIDZHANSKOI SSR I EGO RASSELENIE. Baku: Azarbayjan Dovlat Nashriyyati, 1965, 116 pp., 3000 copies. [Azerb. text; Azerb., Russ. titles, per. 1897-1964, p. 116]

*Golubiatnikov, D. "BAKINSKAIA NEFTIANAIA PROMYSHLENNOST'," BOL'SHAIA SOVETSKAIA ENTSIKLOPEDIIA, Vol. 4, Moscow: Aktsionernoe Obshchestvo "Sovetskaia

Azerbaijan: Geography

Entsiklopediia," 1926 (1st ed.), pp. 382-96. [Russ. text; Russ. titles, p. 396]

*Iuzbashev, Ramzi. AZERBAIDZHANSKIE GEOGRAFICHESKIE TERMINY. (ISSLEDOVANIIA.). Baku: Izd. AN AzSSR., 1966, 158 pp., 2200 copies. [Azerb. text; ca.130 Azerb., Russ. titles, pub. 1863-1960, pp. 152-6]

Kashkai, Mir-ali, G. Aliev, eds. FIZICHESKAIA GEOGRAFIIA AZERBAIDZHANSKOI SSR. Baku: Izdatel'stvo Azfan, 1945, 279 pp., 3000 copies. [Russ. text; 9 Russ. lists, pp. 263-9]

Mekhtiev, N. N. DINAMIKA I MORFOLOGIIA ZAPADNOGO POBEREZH'IA IUZHNOGO KASPIIA. Baku: Izd. AN AzSSR, 1966, 112 pp., 550 copies. [Russ. text; titles pp. 108-12]

Sumbat-zade, A. S. "PROGRESSIVNOE VLIANIE PRISOEDINENIIA AZERBAIDZHANA K ROSSII NA ROST NARODONASELENIIA STRANY V XIX V," IZVESTIIA AKAD. NAUK AZERBAIDZH. SSR., No. 3, 1952. [Russ. text; 44 titles, pp. 89-90]

HISTORY, ARCHAEOLOGY

*Abdullaev, Gasi. AZERBAIDZHAN V XVIII VEKE I VZAIMOOTNOSHENIIA EGO S ROSSIEI. Baku: Izdatel'stvo Akademii Nauk Azerbaidzhanskoi SSR, 1965, 621 pp., 1950 copies. [Russ. text; Azerb., Russ., Turkish, Persian, Europ. titles, per. 18th c., bibl. essay, pp. 31-52]

*Abibullaeva, O. A. "NEKOTORYE ITOGI IZUCHENIIA KHOLMA KIUL'-TEPE V AZERBAIDZHANE," SOVETSKAIA ARKHEOLOGIIA, No. 3, 1963, 319 pp., 1965 copies. [Russ. text; 41 Russ., Europ. titles, pp. 167-8]

"ADERBEIDZHAN (AZERBEIDZHAN)," VOENNAIA ENTSIKLOPEDIIA, Vol. 1. St. Petersburg: T-vo I. D. Sytina, 1911, pp. 138-143. [Russ. text; Russ., Europ. titles, pp. 142-3]

Agaian, Ts. P. KREST'IANSKAIA REFORMA V AZERBAIDZHANE V 1870 GODU. Baku: (Akad. Nauk Azer. SSR. In-t Istorii), 1956. [Russ. text; ca. 300 Azerb., Armen., Russ. titles, per. 1870, pp. 385-97]

Azerbaijan: History, Archaeology

*Aliev, F. M. GORODA SEVERNOGO AZERBAIDZHANA VO VTOROI
POLOVINE XVIII VEKA. Baku: Izdatel'stvo Akademii
Nauk Azerbaidzhanskoi SSR (Akademiia Nauk AzSSR
Institut Istorii), 1960, 136 pp., 500 copies. [Azerb.
text; 202 Azerb, Russ., Mid-East, Europ. titles, per.
second half of 18th cent., pp. 127-35]

Aliev, Kh. "K VOPROSU ISTORIOGRAFII DVIZHUSHCHIKH SIL
REVOLIUTSII V AZERBAIDZHANE. OBZOR," UCHEN. ZAP.
(AZERBAIDZH. UN-T) SERIIA IST. I FILOSOF. NAUK.,No. 1,
1967. [Russ. text; titles pp. 3-13]

Alieva, L. M. RABOCHIE-TEKSTIL'SHCHIKI BAKU V NACHALE
XX V. Baku, 1969. [Russ. text; ca. 330 titles, per.
beginning 1900's, pp. 177-92]

*Alizade, Abdul K. SOTSIAL'NO-EKONOMICHESKAIA I
POLITICHESKAIA ISTORIIA AZERBAIDZHANA XIII-XIV VV.
Baku: Izdatel'stvo AN AzSSR, 1956, 420 pp., 1000 copies.
[Russ. text; Azerb., Russ. titles, per. 13-14 cent.,
pp. 400-6]

Arsharuni, A. "AZERBAIDZHANSKAIA KHUDOZH. LIT-RA I
FOL'KLOR,"--CHTO CHITAT',No. 10/11, 1939. [Russ. text;
10 titles, pub. 1935-9, pp. 49-51]

*Arutiunov, G. A. RABOCHEE DVIZHENIE V ZAKAVKAZ'E V
PERIOD NOVOGO REVOLIUTSIONNOGO POD'EMA (1910-1914 GG).
Baku: Izd-vo Akadem. Nauk Azerb. SSR, 1963, 461 pp.,
1500 copies. [Russ. text; ca.470 Russ. titles, per.
1910-1914, pp. 15-21, 431-53]

Ashurbeili, S. B. OCHERK ISTORII SREDNEVEKOVOGO BAKU
(VIII-NACHALO XIX VV). Baku, 1964. [Russ. text; ca.
430 titles, per. 8th-19th cent., pp. 317-35]

"AZERBAIDZHANSKAIA SSR," SOVETSKAIA VOENNAIA
ENTSIKLOPEDIIA, Vol. 1. Moscow: Gosudarstvennoe
Slovarno-Entsiklopedicheskoe Izdatel'stvo
"Sovetskaia Entsiklopediia" OGIZ RSFSR, 1932, pp. 329-
32. [Russ. text; Russ. titles, p. 332]

AZERBAIDZHANSKAIA SSR.--SOTSIALISTICHESKII BAKU.
(PAMIATKA CHITATELIU). Baku: (Upr. Kul'tury Bakin.
Gor. Ispolkoma. Fond Tsentr. Peredvizhnoi B-ki im.
Gor'kogo), 1957, 18 pp., 3000 copies. [Azerb. text;
ca. 100 titles]

*Azizbekova, Pista A. V. I. LENINA I SOTSIALISTICHESKIE
PREOBRAZOVANIIA V AZERBAIDZHANE (1920-1923 GG).
Moscow: Izdatel'stvo Akademii Nauk SSSR, 1962, 364 pp.,
2500 copies. [Russ. text; Azerb, Russ titles, per.
1920-3, pp. 339-54]

Azerbaijan: History, Archaeology

*"BAKU," BOL'SHAIA SOVETSKAIA ENTSIKLOPEDIIA, Vol. 4. Moscow: Aktsionernoe Obshchestvo "Sovetskaia Entsiklopediia." 1926 (1st ed.), pp. 433-40. [Russ. text; Russ., Azerb. titles, p. 440]

*"BAKU," ENTSIKLOPEDICHESKII SLOVAR', Vol. 2A. St. Petersburg: F. A. Brokgauz, I. A. Efron, 1891, pp. 770-2. [Russ. text; Russ., Europ. titles, p. 772]

*Bekzadi, Ismail Pasha Ogly. PROIZVEDENIE RAVANDI "RAKHET-US-SUDUR VE AIET-US-SURUR" KAK ISTORICHESKII ISTOCHNIK. Baku: Azarbayjan SSR Elmlar Akademiyasi Nashriyyati, 1963, 147 pp., 1250 copies. [Azerb. text; Azerb., Russ., Mid-East., Europ. titles, pp. 139-46]

Buniatov, T. OCHERKI AZERBAIDZHANSKOI ARKHEOLOGII. Baku: Azerneshr, 1960. [Azerb. text; ca.250 Azerb., Russ. titles, pp. 225-35]

*Buniatov, T. A. ZEMLEDELIE I SKOTOVODSTVO V AZERBAIDZHANE V EPOKHU BRONZY. Baku: (Akad. Nauk Azerbaidzh. SSR. In-t Istorii), 1957, 136 pp., 500 copies. [Russ. text; ca.330 Russ., Europ. titles, Bronze Age, pp. 127-37]

*Buniiatov, Z. M. OBZOR ISTOCHNIKOV PO ISTORII AZERBAIDZHANA. ISTOCHNIKI ARABSKIE. Baku: Izdatel'stvo Akademii Nauk Azerbaidzhanskoi SSR, 1964, 36 pp., 1000 copies. [Russ. text; 76 Azerb., Russ., Arab., Europ. titles, incl. mss.]

*Buniiatov, Ziia. AZERBAIDZHAN V VII-IX VV. Baku: Izdatel'stvo Akademii Nauk Azerbaidzhanskoi SSR, 1965, 380 pp., 1000 copies. [Russ. text; ca.620 Russ., Turk., Europ. titles, per. 7th-9th cent., pp. 340-61]

*Chaikin, K. I., ed. UKAZY KUBINSKIKH KHANOV, Kn. 3. Tbilisi: Izdatel'stvo Gruzinskogo Filiala AN SSSR, 1937, 109 pp., 1000 copies. [Russ. text; 36 Azerb., Russ., Pers. titles, per. 1705-1819, pp. 105-7]

Dzhafarzade, I. M. ISTORIKO-ARKHEOLOGICHESKII OCHERK STAROI GANDZHI. Baku: (Akad. Nauk Azerbaidzh. SSR; In-t Istorii im. Bakikhanova), 1949, 103 pp. [Russ. text; 33 Russ., foreign titles, incl. archives, pub. 1844-1940]

Dzhiddi, G. A. KREPOST' GIULISTAN. (SHEMAKHIN. DEVICH'IA KREPOST'). Baku: Izd. AN AzSSR, 1967, 116 pp. 1200 copies. [Russ. text; Azerb. titles, pp. 92-9]

*Efendiev, O. A. OBRAZOVANIE AZERBAIDZHANSKOGO GOSUDARSTVA SEFEVIDOV V NACHALE XVI VEKA. Baku:

Azerbaijan: History, Archaeology

(Akad. Nauk AzSSR Institut Istorii) Izdatel'stvo Akademii Nauk Azerbaidzhanskoi SSR, 1961, 208 pp., 1350 copies. [Russ. text; ca.170 Azerb., Russ., Persian, Turkish, Europ. titles, per. early 16th cent., pp. 200-7]

Gamidova, G. M., comp.   26 BAKINSKIKH KOMISSAROV. (BIBLIOGRAFIIA). Baku: (Azerbaidzh. Gos. Resp. B-ka im. Akhundova), 1968, 34 pp., 3000 copies. [Azerb. text; ca.420 titles]

_____. ISTORIIA AZERBAIDZHANA. (ANNOT. BIBLIOGR. UKAZATEL'), No. 1. Baku: (Azerbaidzh. Resp. B-ka im. Akhundova), 1963, 20 pp., 500 copies. [Azerb. text; 71 titles]

Gasanov, K. G., A. Aliev, comp.   MAMED EMIN ADIL' OGLY KAZIEV. Baku: (Azerbaidzh. Gos. Un-t im. Kirova. Fundam B-ka. Vidnye Uchenye Un-ta. Deiateli Nauki i Kul'tury Azerbaidzhana), 1969, 62 pp., 1000 copies. [Azerb., Russ. text; 424 titles, pub., 1938-69]

*Geidarov, M. Kh.   REMESLENNOE PROIZVODSTVO V GORODAKH AZERBAIDZHANA V XVII V. Baku: Izdatel'stvo Akademii Nauk Azerbaidzhanskoi SSR, 1967, 200 pp., 750 copies. [Russ. text; ca.200 Azerb., Russ., Armen., Persian, Europ, titles, per. 17th cent., pp. 191-9]

Guliyev, N. M., T. D. Hajieva, et al., comps.   VELIKII OKTIABR' I AZERBAIDZHAN (1919-1967). BIBLIOGRAFIIA. Baku: Izdatel'stvo Akademii Nauk Azerbaidzhanskoi SSR, 1967, 170 pp., 2750 copies. [Azerb., Russ. text; Azerb., Russ. titles, pub. 1917-67]

*Guseinov, I. A. [& others], eds.   ISTORIIA AZERBAIDZHANA. Vol. 1. "S DREVNEISHIKH VREMEN DO PRISOEDINENIIA AZERBAIDZHANA K ROSSII." Baku: Izdatel'stvo Akademii Nauk Azerbaidzhanskoi SSR, 1958, 423 pp., 20,000 copies. [Russ. text; ca.500 Azerb., Russ., other titles, per. up to annexation by Russia, pp. 402-19]

* _____, ed.   ISTORIIA AZERBAIDZHANA. Vol. 2. "OT PRISOEDINENIIA AZERBAIDZHANA K ROSSII DO FEVRAL'SKOI BURZHUAZNO-DEMOKRATICH. REVOLIUTSII 1917 GODA." Baku: Izdatel'stvo Akademii Nauk Azerbaidzhanskoi SSR, 1960, 953 pp., 20,000 copies. [Russ. text; ca.1000 Azerb., Russ. titles, per. from annexation of Azerb. by Russia to 1917, pp. 912-50]

* _____, eds.   ISTORIIA AZERBAIDZHANA, Vol. 3, part 2. Baku: Izdatel'stvo Akademii Nauk Azerbaidzhanskoi SSR, 1963, 529 pp., 10,000 copies.

Azerbaijan: History, Archaeology

   [Russ. text; ca.1500 Azerb., Russ. titles, Sov. per.,
   pp. 469-525]

*Guseinov, Akhmed.   AZERBAIDZHANO-RUSSKIE OTNOSHENIIA.
XV-XVII VEKOV. Baku: Izdatel'stvo Akademii Nauk
Azerbaidzhanskoi SSR, 1963, 237 pp., 1100 copies.
[Russ. text; ca.290 Russ., Mid-East., English titles,
archives, per. 15th-17th cent., pp. 14-42, 219-36]

*Guseinzade, Ali.   AZERBAIDZHANSKAIA ISTORIOGRAFIIA
VTOROI POLOVINY XIX VEKA. Baku: Izd. AN AzSSR, 1967,
219 pp., 1500 copies. [Azerb. text; ca.300 Azerb.
titles, pp. 187-205]

*Iampol'skii, Z.   "DREVNIAIA ISTORIIA V NAUCHNYKH
IZDANIIAKH AZERBAIDZHANSKOI SSR. (1952-1957). OBZOR,"
VESTNIK DREVNEI ISTORII, No. 3, 1958. [Russ. text;
Russ. titles, pub. 1952-7, pp. 214-19]

*Ibragimbeili, Kh. M.   ROSSIIA I AZERBAIDZHAN V PERVOI
TRETI XIX VEKA. (IZ VOENNO-POLIT. ISTORII). Moscow:
"Nauka," 1969, 288 pp., 2200 copies. [Russ. text;
ca.500 Russ., Pers., Turk., Europ. titles, per.
1st 1/3 of 19th cent., pp. 258-75]

 Ibragimov, D.   OCHERKI PO ISTORII AZERBAIDZHANA XV
VEKA. Baku: (Azerbaidzh. Gos. Ped. In-t im. Lenina),
1958. [Azerb. text; 185 Azerb., Russ., Europ. titles,
per. 15th cent., pp. 202-8]

*Ibragimov, Dzhafar.   FEODAL'NYE GOSUDARSTVA NA
TERRITORII AZERBAIDZHANA XV VEKA. Baku:
(Azerbaidzhanskii Gosudarstvennyi Pedagogicheskii
Institut im. V. I. Lenina), 1962, 111 pp., 800 copies.
[Russ. text; 131 Russ. titles, per. 15th cent., pp.
106-10]

 Ismizade, O. Sh.   IALOILUTEPINSKAIA KULTURA. Baku:
(AN AzSSR In-t Istorii i Filosofii), 1956. [Russ.
text; 99 titles, pp. 128-31]

 ISTOCHNIKI I OSNOVNAIA LITERATURA DLIA IZUCHENIIA
ISTORII AZERBAIDZHANA. Baku: Azerneshr, 1945, 9 pp.,
1000 copies. [Azerb. text; Azerb. titles]

 Karaulov, N. A.   "SVEDENIIA ARABSKIKH PISATELEI O
KAVKAZIE, ARMENII I AZERBAIDZHANE," SBORNIK MATERIALOV
DLIA OPISANIIA MESTNOSTEI I PLEMEN KAVKAZA, Vol.
29, 1901; Vol. 31, 1902; Vol. 32, 1903; Vol. 38, 1908.
[Russ. text; per. medieval]

*Kerimova, D. Iu., comp.   26 BAKINSKIKH KOMISSAROV.
(BIBLIOGRAFIIA). Baku: (Azerbaidzhanskaia

Azerbaijan: History, Archaeology

Gosudarstvennaia Respublikanskaia Biblioteka im.
M. F. Akhundova), 1968, 69 pp., 3000 copies. [Russ.
text; ca.840 Russ. titles]

_____.   ISTORIIA AZERBAIDZHANA (PAMIATKA
CHITATELIU). Baku: (Azerbaidzh. Resp. B-ka im.
Akhundova.), 1963, 12 pp., 500 copies. [Russ. text]

Khadzhi-Murat, Ibragimbeili. "ZARUBEZHNAIA
ISTORIOGRAFIIA O VOENNOPOLITICHESKIKH VOPROSAKH
PRISOEDINENIIA AZERBAIDZHANA K ROSSII (OBZOR),"
VESTN. STD-NIIA OBSHCHESTV. NAUK., No. 3 (AN Gruz.
SSR), 1966. [Russ. text; titles pp. 85-102]

Khalafov, A.   PERVAIA RUSSKAIA REVOLIUTSIIA (1905-1907
GG). KRATKII BIBLIOGR. UKAZATEL' LIT. Baku:
(Azerbaidzh. Resp. Publ. B-ka im. Akhundova), 1955, 28
pp., 1500 copies. [Azerb. text; 82 titles, pub. 1941-
54, per. 1905-7]

Khalilov, D. A.   ARKHEOLOGICHESKIE PAMIATNIKI
ZAPADNOGO AZERBAIDZHANA V EPOKHU BRONZY I NACHALA
ZHELEZNOGO VEKA. Baku: (Akad. Nauk. AzSSR In-t
Istorii), 1959. [Azerb. text; ca.150 Azerb., Russ.,
Europ. titles, per. Bronze & Iron Ages, pp. 164-8]

Kaziev, M.   "KRATKII PERECHEN' OPUBLIKOVANNYKH RABOT N.
NARIMANOVA-KRATKAIA BIBLIOGRAFIIA RABOT O N.
NARIMANOVE," NARIMAN NARIMANOV. Baku, 1970. [Russ.
text; 278 titles, pp. 168-77]

*Kuliev, Agamir Agasi Ogly.   VYDAIUSHCHIISIA
AZERBAIDZHANSKII UCHENYI-PUTESHESTVENNIK G. Z.
SHIRVANI. Baku: Azarbayjan SSR Elmlar Akademiyasi
Nashriyyati, 1964, 211 pp., 3700 copies. [Azerb. text;
Azerb., Russ., Mid-East. 250...titles, pp. 195-210]

Kuliev, N. M.   ISTORIIA AZERBAIDZHANA. (1920-1961)
BIBLIOGRAFIIA. Baku: "Elm" (AN AzSSR. Fundam. B-ka),
1970, 287 pp., 1400 copies. [Russ. text; ca.3000 Azerb.,
Russ. titles, pub. 1920-61]

Lerman, A.   AZERBAIDZHANSKAIA SSR--BAKU
SOTSIALISTICHESKII (PAMIATKA CHITATELIU). Baku:
(Tsentr. Peredvizhnoi Bibliotech. Fond im. Gor'kogo),
1957, 15 pp., 4000 copies. [Russ. text; ca.100 titles,
Sov. per.]

Lerman, A. N., comp.   NAVEKI YMESTE. K 150-LETIIU
VKHOZHDENIIA AZERBAIDZHANA V SOSTAV ROSSII. PAMIATKA
CHITATELIU. Baku: (Azerbaidzhanskaia Resp. B-ka im.
Akhundova), 1964, 22 pp., 1000 copies. [Russ. text;
ca.180 titles]

Azerbaijan: History, Archaeology

Leviatov, V. N.   OCHERKI IZ ISTORII AZERBAIDZHANA V XVIII VEKE. Baku, 1948.   [513 Azerb., Russ., other titles and archives, per. 1718-1948, pp. 200-25]

Makhmudov, G. Z., comp.   A. S. SUMBATZADE. BIBLIOGRAFIIA. Baku: Izd. AN AzSSR, 1967, 47 pp., 1300 copies. [Russ. text; 126 + 32 Azerb., Russ. titles, pub. 1924-67]

Minorskii, V. F.   ISTORIIA SHIRVANA I DERBENDA X--XI VEKOV. Moscow, 1963.   [Russ. text; ca.320 titles, per. 10th-11th cent., pp. 15-26, 231-44]

[Moscheili] Mosgeim.   "SOCHINENIE O TATARAKH NA LATINSKOM IAZYKE (BIBLIOGRAFICHESKIE ZAMETKI)," MAIAK, Vol. 17, 1844.   [Russ. text; Latin titles, p. 20]

Nasirli, M. N.   SEL'SKIE POSELENIIA I KREST'IANSKIE ZHILISHCHA NAKHICHEVANSKOI ASSR. Baku: (Akad. Nauk AzSSR. Muzei Istorii Azerbaidzhana), 1959.   [Russ. text; ca.160 titles, pp. 134-9]

Melikset-Bekov, L. M.   "ISTOCHNIKI GRUZINSKIE," OBZOR ISTOCHNIKOV PO ISTORII AZERBAIDZHANA. Baku: Izd-vo AzFAN, 1939, 28 pp., 1000 copies.   [Russ. text; 49 Georgian titles]

Pakhomov, E. A., L. M. Melikset-Bekov.   OBZOR ISTOCHNIKOV PO ISTORII AZERBAIDZHANA. 2 Vols. Baku: (Azerbaidzhanskii Filial AN SSSR. Institut Istorii, Arkheologii i Etnografii), 1939-40.   [Russ. text; Georgian, Greek, Latin titles]

Petrushevskii, I. P.   OCHERKI PO ISTORII FEODAL'NYKH OTNOSHENII V AZERBAIDZHANE I ARMENII V XVI-NACHALE XIX VV. Leningrad: (Leningr. Gos. Un-t im. Zhdanova; Vost. Fak Vost. Nauch-Issled In-t), 1949, 384 pp. [Russ. text; ca.350 Azerb., Russ., foreign titles and archives, per. 16th-19th cent., pp. 365-78]

*Raevskii, A.   ANGLIISKAIA INTERVENTSIIA I MUSAVATSKOE PRAVITEL'STVO. IZ ISTORII INTERVENTSII I KONTR-REVOLIUTSII V ZAKAVKAZ'E. Baku: (Istpart. Otdel TSK i BK AKP(B)), 1927, 195 pp., 1500 copies.   [Russ. text; 36 Russ. titles, archives, pp. 193-4]

*Rakhmani, A.   "TARIKH-I ALAM ARAI-I ABBASI KAK ISTOCHNIK PO ISTORII AZERBAIDZHANA. Baku: Izdatel'stvo Akademii Nauk Azerbaidzhanskoi SSR, 1960, 191 pp., 500 copies. [Russ. text; ca.100 Azerb., Russ., Persian, other titles, per. 1560-1633, pp. 175-9]

Azerbaijan: History, Archaeology

*Samedov, V. Iu. RASPROSTRANENIE MARKSIZMA-LENINIZMA V
 AZERBAIDZHANE. Part 2: GODY PERVOI RUSSKOI REVOLIUTSII.
 Baku: Azer. Gos. Izd., 1966, 634 pp., 2500 copies.
 [Russ. text; ca.400 Azerb., Russ. titles, per. 1905,
 pp. 603-20]

SHARK FAKULTANIN KHABARLARI, No. 1, 1926, 330 pp., 400
 copies. [Azerb., Russ. text; 1439 titles]

*Sumbat-zade, A. S. "RAZVITIE ISTORICHESKOI NAUKI V
 AZERBAIDZHANSKOI SSR ZA GODY SOVETSKOI VLASTI. [OBZOR],"
 VOPROSY ISTORII, No. 11, 1957, 222 pp., 50,000 copies.
 [Russ. text; Azerb., Russ. titles, Sov. per., pp. 206-18]

_____. SEL'SKOE KHOZIAISTVO AZERBAIDZHANA V XIX V.
 Baku: (Akad. Nauk Azerbaidzh. SSR. In-t Istorii), 1958.
 [Russ. text; ca.100 titles, archives, per. 19th cent.,
 pp. 357-61]

*TRUDY AZERBAIDZHANSKOI (OREN-KALINSKOI) ARKHEOLOGICHESKOI
 EKSPEDITSII. Vol. 3: SREDNEVEKOVYE PAMIATNIKI
 AZERBAIDZHANA. Moscow-Leningrad: (Materialy i
 Issledovaniia po Arkheologii SSSR. No. 133) Izdatel'stvo
 "Nauka," 1965, 111 pp., 1300 copies. [Russ. text; 65
 Russ. titles, per. medieval, pp. 108-9]

LANGUAGE, LITERATURE

*A. Dzh. "RADZHI, GADZHI ABDUL GASAN," LITERATURNAIA
 ENTSIKLOPEDIIA, Vol. 9. Moscow: Gosudarstvennyi
 Institut "Sovetskaia Entsiklopediia"/OGIZ RSFSR, 1935,
 p. 486. [Russ. text; Azerb., Russ. titles, p. 486]

* _____. "RAFILI, MIKAEL'," LITERATURNAIA
 ENTSIKLOPEDIIA, Vol. 9. Moscow: Gosudarstvennyi
 Institut "Sovetskaia Entsiklopediia"/OGIZ RSFSR, 1935,
 p. 544. [Russ. text; Azerb., Russ. titles, p. 544]

Abdullaev, A. K ISTORII PREPODAVANIIA AZERBAIDZHANSKOGO
 IAZYKA. Baku: Azerneshr, 1958. [Azerb.text; 109 Azerb.,
 Russ. titles, pp. 201-4]

ABDURRAGIM AKHVERDOV. Baku: (Azarbayjan SSR Nazirlar
 Soveti Madani-Maarif Ishlari Metodkabinasi), 1947, 16
 pp. [Azerb. text]

Azerbaijan: Language, Literature

ABDURRAGIMBEK AKHVERDOV (BIBLIOGRAFIIA). Baku: (Gos. Kom. Soveta Ministrov AzSSR po Pechati), 1964, 75 pp., 2000 copies. [Azerb., Russ. text]

Abid, Emin. "FIRDOUSI I AZERBAIDZHANSKAIA LITERATURA," FIRDOVSI, A.-K. SHAHNAMA. SECHILMISH DASTANLAR. Baku, 1934. [Azerb. text; titles pp. xciv-cvii]

Agaev, S., G. B. Gasanov. OBRAZ NEFTIANIKA V KHUDOZHESTVENNOI LITERATURE. Baku: (Azerbaidzh. Resp. B-ka im. Akhundova), 1958, 36 pp., 3000 copies. [Azerb. text; ca.140 titles]

*AGAMALY-OGLY, SAMED AGA," LITERATURNAIA ENTSIKLOPEDIIA, Vol. 1. n.p.: Izdatel'stvo Kommunisticheskoi Akademii, 1929. [Russ. text; Azerb., Russ. titles, p. 648]

*Agazade, N. G. K VOPROSU O KATEGORII NAKLONENIIA I MODAL'NOSTI V SOVREMENNOM AZERBAIDZHANSKOM IAZYKE. Baku: Izdatel'stvo Akademii Nauk Azerbaidzhanskoi SSR, 1965, 111 pp., 500 copies. [Russ. text; ca.110 Russ., Turk., Europ. titles, pp. 107-11]

Akhundov, A. VREMENA GLAGOLA. Baku, 1961. [Azerb. text; ca.100 titles, pp. 135-8]

Akhundov, I. DZHAFAR-DZHABARLY. BIBLIOGRAFIIA. Baku: (Azerb. Resp. Publ. B-ka im. Akhundova), 1950, 64 pp., 1000 copies. [Azerb., Russ. text; ca.400 Azerb., Russ. titles]

Akhundov, M. F. (Sabukhi). K 125-LETIU SO DNIA ROZHDENIIA M. F. AKHUNDOVA (1812-1889). Baku: (Kn. Palata AzSSR Bibliogr. Pamiatka #1), 1938, 20 pp., 4000 copies. [Azerb. text; 51 titles, pub. 1857-1938]

Akhundov, N. JAFAR JABBARLI (BIBLIOGRAFIYA). Baku: (M. F. Akhundov Adina Azarbayjan Respublika Kitabkhanasi), 1956, 64 pp. [Azerb. text]

_____, comp. JAFAR JABBARLI (QISA ADABIYYAT GOSTARIJISI). Baku: (M. F. Akhundov Adina Azarbayjan Respublika Kitabkhanasi), 1947, 12 pp. [Azerb. text]

_____, comp. MIRZA FATALI AKHUNDOV (MUKHTASAR ADABIYYAT GOSTERIJISI). Baku: (M. F. Akhundov Adina Azerbayjan Respublika Kitabkhanasi), 1948, 13 pp. [Azerb. text]

_____. SAMED VURGUN. (BIBLIOGRAFIIA). Baku: (Pub. B-ka AzSSR im. Akhundova), 1949, 52 pp. [Azerb. text; 453 titles, pub. 1927-49, 1932-48]

Azerbaijan: Language, Literature

* _____, comp. SAMED VURGUN. 1906-1956. BIBLIOGRAFIIA. Baku: Izdatel'stvo Akademii Nauk Azerbaidzhanskoi SSR, 1965, 190 pp., 3300 copies. [Azerb. text; 1434 Azerb., Russ. titles, pub. 1926-63, pp. 20-162]

*Akhundov, Nazim, comp. DZHAFAR DZHABARLY. (BIBLIOGRAFIIA). Baku: (Resp. Knizhnaia Palata), 1965, 110 pp., 2000 copies. [Azerb. text; 838 Azerb., Russ. titles, pub. 1915-60, pp. 5-100]

* _____. M. A. SABIR. BIBLIOGRAFIIA. Baku: (Azerbaidzh. Resp. B-ka im. Akhundova), 1958, 110 pp., 3000 copies. [Azerb. text; 720 Azerb., Russ. titles, pub. 1903-55]

*Akrem, Dzh. "NESIMI, SEID IMAD-ED-DIN," LITERATURNAIA ENTSIKLOPEDIIA, Vol. 8. Moscow: Gosudarstvennoe Slovarno-Entsiklopedicheskoe Izdatel'stvo "Sovetskaia Entsiklopediia" (OGIZ RSFSR), 1934, pp. 27-8. [Russ. text; Azerb., Russ., Turk. titles, p. 28]

Aliev, F. ZARUBEZHNAIA LITERATURA. (REK. UKAZATEL'). Baku: (Azerbaidzh. Resp. B-ka im. Akhundova), 1959, 65 pp., 3000 copies. [Azerb. text; ca.550 Azerb. titles]

Aliev, N., comp. MIRZA ALEKPER SABIR (K 100-LETIIU SO DNIA ROZHDENIIA). Baku, 1962. [Azerb. text; 35 titles, per. ca.1861-1961, pp. 52-6]

Alieva, D. IZ ISTORII AZERBAIDZHANSKO GRUZINSKIKH LITERATURNYKH SVIAZEI. Baku: (In-t Lit. i Iazyka im. Nizami), 1958. [Russ. text; ca.160 Azerb., Russ., Georg. titles, pp. 171-5]

Alisultan, A. "BIBLIOGRAFIIA," OBRAZ STALINA V AZ. LITERATURE. Baku: (AN AzSSR In-t Literatury im. Nizami), 1949. [Russ. text; 383 titles, pp. 187-223]

*Arasly, G. "FIZULI, MOGAMED SULEIMAN OGLY [1500 (1502?)-1563]," LITERATURNAIA ENTSIKLOPEDIIA, Vol. 11. Moscow: Gosudarstvennoe Izdatel'stvo "Khudozhestvennaia Literatura," 1939, pp. 716-17. [Russ. text; Azerb., Russ., Turk., Arab., Europ. titles, per. 1500-63, p. 717]

Arasly, G. ISTORIIA AZERBAIDZHANSKOI LITERATURY XVII-XVIII VEKOV. Baku: (Az. Gos. Universiteta im. Kirova), 1956. [Azerb. text; 246 Azerb., Russ. titles, per. 17th, 18th cent., pp. 317-25]

Azerbaijan: Language, Literature

*Arasly, Gamid M. VELIKII AZERBAIDZHANSKII POET FUZULI.
Baku: Detiunizdat, 1958, 312 pp., 16,000 copies.
[Azerb. text; 178 Azerb., Mid-East. titles, per.
400th anniv., pp. 301-11]

*Arif, M., ed. ISTORIIA AZERBAIDZHANSKOI SOVETSKOI
LITERATURY V 2-KH T., Vol. 2. Baku: Izd. AN AzSSR,
1967, 501 pp., 5500 copies. [Azerb. text; Azerb.,
Russ. titles, pub. 1920-66, pp. 452-90]

_____. TVORCHESKII PUT' DZHAFARA DZHABARLY. Baku:
(Az. Gos. Un-t im. Kirova), 1956. [Azerb. text; 82
Azerb., Russ. titles, pub. 1923-54, pp. 345-7]

*Arif, Mamed. TVORCHESTVO DZHAFARA DZHABARLY. Baku:
Izdatel'stvo Akademii Nauk Azerbaidzhanskoi SSR, 1961,
237 pp., 2000 copies. [Russ. text; 32 Azerb. Russ.
titles, per. 1899-1934, pp. 235-6]

*"ASI, ABDULLA-BEK," LITERATURNAIA ENTSIKLOPEDIIA, Vol. 1.
n.p.: Izdatel'stvo Kommunisticheskoi Akademii, 1929,
pp. 270-1. [Russ. text; Azerb., Russ. titles, per.
19th cent., p. 271]

*Aslanov, A. A., ed. ISSLEDOVANIE PO SINTAKSISU
AZERBAIDZHANSKOGO IAZYKA (PORIADOK SLOV V ODNOSLOZHNOM,
NEZAKONCH. I PROSTOM PREDLOZHENIIAKH). Baku:
Azarbayjan SSR Elmlar Akademiyasi Nashriyyati, 1963,
189 pp., 2700 copies. [Azerb. text; 70 Azerb., Russ.
titles, pp. 185-7]

*Aslanov, Aslan. KATEGORII OTRITSANIIA I CHISLA V
SOVREMENNOM AZERBAIDZHANSKOM IAZYKE. Baku: Azarbayjan
SSR Elmlar Akademiyasi Nashriyyati, 1963, 92 pp., 3200
copies. [Azerb. text; Azerb., Russ. titles, pp. 90-1]

Babaev, G. AZERBAIDZHANSKIE LITERATURNYE SVIAZI.
(1920-1959 GG.) BIBLIOGRAFIIA. Baku: Izd-vo Akad.
Nauk AzSSR, 1959, 112 pp., 500 copies. [Russ. text;
974 Azerb., Russ. titles, per. 1920-59]

_____. V. MAIAKOVSKII I AZERBAIDZHAN. (K 65-
LETIIU SO DNIA ROZHDENIIA). BIBLIOGR. UKAZATEL'.
Baku: (Resp. B-ka im. Akhundova), 1958, 44 pp., 2000
copies. [Azerb. text; ca.455 titles, pub. 1926-58]

Babaeva, R. A., comp. M. SH. SHIRALIEV. BIBLIOGRAFIIA.
Baku: "Elm," 1968, 66 pp., 1800 copies. [Azerb. text;
233 Azerb., Russ. titles, pub. 1938-69]

Bagirov, A. "KRATKAIA BIBLIOGRAFIIA AZERBAIDZHANSKOI
LITERATURY XIX-XX STOLETIIA," ISTORIIA AZERBAIDZHANSKOI
LITERATURY. Vol. 2. Baku: (Institut Lit. i Iazyka im.

Azerbaijan: Language, Literature

Nizami), 1960. [Azerb. text; ca.570 Azerb., Russ., other titles, per. 19th, 20th cent. to 1959, pp. 888-904]

Bairamov, F. A.   DZHALIL MAMEDKULIZADE. BIBLIOGRAFIIA. 1866-1966. Baku: Azerneshr, 1966, 267 pp., 3500 copies. [Azerb. text; Azerb. titles, per. 1866-1966]

*Bairamov, Gusein. SLOZHNOSOCHINENNYE PREDLOZHENIIA V SOVREMENNOM AZERBAIDZHANSKOM IAZYKE. Baku: Izdatel'stvo Akademii Nauk Azerbaidzhanskoi SSR, 1960, 122 pp., 1000 copies. [Azerb. text; Azerb., Russ. titles, pp. 117-20]

*Begdeli, Gulamgusein.   ZHIZN' I TVORCHESTVO AVKHADI. Baku: Azarbayjan SSR Elmlar Akademiyasi Nashriyyati-1962, 192 pp., 2200 copies. [Azerb. text; Azerb., Russ., Mid-East. titles, per. 13-14th cent., pp. 187-91]

*Bertel's,   E.   "NIZAMI, NIZAMUDDIN ABU-MUKHAMED IL'IAS IBN-IUSUF IBN-ZEKI-MUAIIAD," BOL'SHAIA SOVETSKAIA ENTSIKLOPEDIIA, Vol. 41. Moscow: Gosudarstvennyi Institut "Sovetskaia Entsiklopediia" (OGIZ RSFSR), 1939 (1st ed.), pp. 93-4. [Russ. text; Azerb., Russ., Europ. titles, p. 94]

*Bertel's, E. E.   NIZAMI. TVORCHESKII PUT' POETA. Moscow: (AN SSSR Nauch. Popul. Seriia.), 1956, 260 pp., 15000 copies. [Russ. text; 80 Russ., Persian, other titles, per. 1141-1202, pp. 257-61]

*Bertel's, Evgenii Eduardovich.   IZBRANNYE TRUDY. NIZAMI I FUZULI. Vol. 2. Moscow: Izdatel'stvo Vostochnoi Literatury, 1962, 555 pp., 2400 copies. [Russ. text; 55+ Chaghatay, Russ., Pers. titles, pub. 1923-60, pp. 15-26, 534-6]

"BIBLIOGRAFIIA PO AZERBAIDZHANSKOMU SOVETSKOMU LITERATUROVEDENIIU. (1920-1966)," ISTORIIA AZERBAIDZH. SOVETSKOI LIT., Vol. 2. Baku, 1967. [Azerb. text; ca.1100 Azerb., Russ. titles, per. 1920-66, pp. 452-90]

*Budagova, Z. I., G. A. Bairamov, eds.   SLOVOSOCHETANIIA V SOVREMENNOM AZERBAIDZHANSKOM IAZYKE. Baku: Izdatel'stvo Akademii Nauk Azerbaidzhanskoi SSR, 1961, 148 pp., 1800 copies. [Azerb. text; 46 Azerb., Russ. titles, pp. 145-6]

*Budagova, Zarifa.   PROSTOE PREDLOZHENIE V SOVREMENNOM AZERBAIDZHANSKOM LITERATURNOM IAZYKE. Baku: Azarbayjan SSR Elmlar Akademiyasi Nashriyyati, 1963, 222 pp., 3700 copies. [Azerb. text; 276 Azerb., Sov. As., Russ., Europ. titles, contemporary, pp. 207-19]

Azerbaijan: Language, Literature

*Chobanzade, B.   TIURKO-TATARSKAIA DIALEKTOLOGIIA
(VVEDENIE). Baku: Izdanie Obshchestva Obsledovaniia
i Izucheniia Azerbaidzhana, 1927, 135 pp., 1000 copies.
[Azerb., Russ. text; 96 Sov. Asian, Russ., Europ.
titles, pp. 92-9]

Dadash-zade, Aras.   MOLLA PANAKH VAGIF. (ZHIZN' I
TVORCHESTVO). Baku: Izd. AN AzSSR, 1966, 190 pp.,
1700 copies. [Azerb. text; ca.140 Azerb. titles, pp.
183-9]

*Dadashzade, Araz Mamed Arif Ogly.   ZHIZN' I TVORCHESTVO
VAGIFA. Baku: Azarbayjan SSR Elmlar Akademiyasi
Nashriyyati, 1966, 190 pp., 1700 copies. [Azerb. text;
Azerb., Sov. Asian, Russ., Turk., Europ. titles, pp.
183-9]

*Daronian, Sergei K.   MIRZA IBRAGIMOV; KRITIKO-
BIOGRAFICHESKII OCHERK. Moscow: Sovetskii Pisatel',
1960, 156 pp. [Russ. text; Russ. titles, pp. 154-6]

DEKADA AZERBAIDZHANSKOI LITERATURY. KATALOG KNIG. Baku:
Azerneshr, 1950, 31 pp., 10,000 copies. [Russ. text;
28 Russ. titles]

*Demirchizade, A. M., Z. Kh. Tagizade. "AZERBAIDZHANSKOE
SOVETSKOE IAZYKOZNANIE ZA 40 LET. [OBZOR]." VOPROSY
IAZYKOZNANIIA, No. 5. 1961, 160 pp., 5465 copies.
[Russ. text; 32 Azerb., Russ. titles, Sov. per., pp.
141-4]

Devitt, V. V., comp.   26 BAKINSKIKH KOMISSAROV V
KHUDOZHESTVENNOI LITERATURE. (BIBLIOGRAFIIA). Baku:
(Azerbaidzhanskaia Resp. B-ka im. Akhundova), 1964, 41
pp., 2000 copies. [Azerb., Russ. text; 284 Azerb.,
Russ. titles, pub. 1919-63]

*Dubrovinskaia, A.   "BAKINSKAIA TIPOGRAFIIA," BOL'SHAIA
SOVETSKAIA ENTSIKLOPEDIIA, Vol. 4. Moscow: Aktsionernoe
Obshchestvo "Sovetskaia Entsiklopediia," 1926, pp. 397-
398. [Russ. text; Russ. titles, p. 398]

Dzhafarov, S.   SOVREMENNYI AZERBAIDZHANSKII IAZYK.
(IMENA I OBRAZUIUSHCHIE IKH AFFIKSY). Baku, [ca. 1949].
[Russ. text; 42 Azerb., Russ. titles, contemporary,
pp. 95-6]

*Dzhafarov, Selim Abdulliatif Ogly.   SLOVOOBRAZOVANIE
V AZERBAIDZHANSKOM IAZYKE. Baku: (Azerbaidzh. Gos.
Universitet im. Kirova), 1960, 204 pp., 5000 copies.
[Azerb. text; 200 Azerb., Russ., Turk. titles, pp.
196-202]

Azerbaijan: Language, Literature

*Dzhangidze, V. T.   DMANISSKII GOVOR KAZAKHSKOGO
  DIALEKTA AZERBAIDZHANSKOGO IAZYKA.   Baku: Izd-vo
  Akademii Nauk Azerbaidzhanskoi SSR, 1965, 153 pp.,
  1200 copies. [Russ. text; 96 titles, pp. 148-51]

Efendiev, E.   AZERBAIDZHANSKAIA LITERATURA NA IAZYKAKH
  NARODOV SSSR. BIBLIOGRAFIIA. Baku: (Azerbaidzh.
  Resp. B-ka im. Akhundova), 1960, 88 pp., 5000 copies.
  [Azerb. text; ca.1000 titles]

Efendieva, Sh. M., M. N. Meil'man.   ABDULLA SHAIG
  TALYB-ZADE (K 75-LETIIU SO DNIA ROZHDENIIA). PAMIATKA.
  Baku: (Az. Resp. Publ. B-ka im. Akhundova), 1956, 10 pp.,
  500 copies. [Azerb., Russ. text; 31 titles, pub. 1940-
  55]

_____, V. A. Tsitovich.   SAMED VURGUN. (K 50-
  LETIIU SO DNIA ROZHDENIIA). PAMIATKA. Baku:
  (Azerbaidzhan Res. Publ. B-ka im. Akhundova), 1956,
  11 pp., 500 copies. [Azerb., Russ. text; 56 titles,
  pub. 1942-56]

*Erevanly, Akper Iunus Ogly.   SVIAZI ARMIANO-
  AZERBAIDZHANSKOI NARODNOI USTNOI LITERATURY. Erevan:
  Armianskoe Gosudarstvennoe Izdatel'stvo, 1958, 270 pp.,
  6000 copies. [Azerb. text; ca.150 Azerb., Armen.,
  Russ. titles, pp. 261-9]

*"FIZULI, MOGAMED SULEIMAN OGLU," LITERATURNAIA
  ENTSIKLOPEDIIA, Vol. 11. Moscow: Gosudarstvennoe
  Izdatel'stvo 'Khudozhestvennaia Literatura,' 1939, pp.
  716-17. [Russ. text; Azerb., Russ., Europ. titles,
  p. 717]

Gadzhiev, A. A.   PREDMET, SODERZHANIE, FORMA
  KHUDOZHESTVENNOI LITERATURY. Baku: (M-vo Vyssh. i
  Sred. Spets. Obrazovaniia AzSSR), 1967, 76 pp., 500
  copies. [Russ. text; titles pp. 72-6]

Gasanov, K.   OBRAZ LENINA V AZERBAIDZHANSKOI SOVETSKOI
  POEZII (KRATKAIA BIBLIOGRAFIIA) POSVIASHCHAETSIA 95-
  LETIIU SO DNIA ROZHDENIIA V. I. LENINA. Baku:
  (Azerbaidzh. Resp. B-ka im. Akhundova), 1965, 26 pp.,
  1000 copies. [Azerb. text; 225 titles]

Gasanov, K. M.   SINTAKSIS. "DEKHNAME" (OPREDELITEL'NYE
  SLOVOSOCHETANIIA). Baku: Izd. AN AzSSR, 1967, 116 pp.,
  800 copies. [Russ. text; Azerb. titles, pp. 113-16]

*Gasanov, T. B., D. Iu. Kerimov, comp.   KASUM BEK ZAKIR
  (1784-1857) (REKOMENDATEL'NYI SPISOK LITERATURY).
  Baku: (Azerbaidzhanskaia Respublikanskaia Biblioteka
  im. M. F. Akhundova), 1970, 23 pp., 1000 copies. [Azerb.,

Azerbaijan: Language, Literature

Russ. text; 64 Azerb., Russ. titles, per. 1784-1857, pp. 10-13, 21-23]

*Gasanova, M. M., comp. MAMED ARIF DADASHZADE. BIBLIOGRAFIIA. Baku: Izdatel'stvo Akademii Nauk Azerbaidzhanskoi SSR, 1965, 83 pp., 2500 copies. [Azerb. text; 630 Azerb., Russ. titles, pub. 1923-64]

[Guliev, A.] Quliyev, A., H. Rzaquliyev, ed. MAMMAD RAHIM (BIBLIOGRAFIYA). Baku: (Azarbayjan SSR Madaniyyat Nazirliyi, Respublika Metodkabinasi), 1958, 96 pp. [Azerb. text]

Guliev, A. K., G. A. Rzakuliev. NARODNYI POET SAMED VURGUN (KRATKAIA BIBLIOGR.). Baku: (Resp. Metod. Kabinet Kul't.-Prosvet Raboty), 1956, 73 pp., 3000 copies. [Azerb. text; 514 titles, pub. 1927-56]

Guliev, A. K. SULEIMAN RUSTAM. BIBLIOGRAFIIA. Baku: (Resp. Metod. Kabinet Kul't-Prosvet. Raboty), 1950, 96 pp., 1000 copies. [Azerb. text; 729 Azerb. titles]

_____. SULEIMAN RUSTAM (KRATKII UKAZATEL' LIT.). Baku: (M-vo Kul'tury Azerbaidzh. SSR), 1954, 75 pp., 3000 copies. [Azerb. text; 474 titles, pub. 1925-54]

*Gurbanov, A. M. MUASIR AZARBAYJAN DILININ GRAFIKA VA ORFOGRAFIYASI (OKHUNMUSH MUHAZIRANIN GISA IJMALI). Baku: V. I. Lenin Adina Azarbayjan Dovlat Pedagozhi Institutu, 1963, 67 pp., 600 copies. [Azerb. text; 41 Azerb., Russ. titles, pp. 64-5]

Guseinov, A., comp. MIRMEKHTI SEIDZADE (PAMIATKA CHITATELIU). Baku: (Azerbaidzh. Resp. Det. B-ka im. Kocharli. K 50-Letiiu Komsomola), 1968, 11 pp., 3000 copies. [Azerb. text]

Guseinov, A. U. ZADACHI DETSKIKH I SHKOL'NYKH BIBLIOTEK V SVIAZI S 50-LETIEM VELIKOGO OKTIABRIA. Baku: (M-vo Kul'tury AzSSR. Azerbaidzh. Res. Det. B-ka), 1967, 18 pp., 3000 copies. [Russ. text; Azerb. titles, pp. 16-18]

Ibragimov, A. A. OPISANIE ARKHIVA M. F. AKHUNDOVA. Baku: Izd-vo Akad. Nauk Azerbaidzh. SSR, 1955, 295 pp., 1000 copies. [Azerb. text; Azerb., Russ. titles, per. 1812-78]

* _____. OPISANIE ARKHIVA M. F. AKHUNDOVA. Baku: Izdatel'stvo Akademii Nauk Azerbaidzhanskoi SSR, 1962, 274 pp., 900 copies. [Azerb. text; 3 lists, Azerb., Russ., Pers., Arab, per. 1812-78, pp. 258-67]

Azerbaijan: Language, Literature

Ibragimov, B. I.   NEKOTORYE LEKSICHESKIE OSOBENNOSTI
GRUPPY GOVOROV NAKHICHEVANA. Baku: (Azerbaidzh. Gos.
Ped. In-t im. Lenina), 1960. [Azerb. text; 37 Azerb.,
Russ. titles, pp. 32-3]

Ibragimova, M., comp. MIRZA IBRAGIMOV. BIBLIOGRAFIIA.
Baku: Izd. AN AzSSR, 1966, 130 pp., 3100 copies.
[Azerb. text; 1050 Azerb., Sov. nat. lang., Russ.,
foreign titles, pub. 1930-65]

Isazade, Akhmed.   ZHIZN' I TVORCHESTVO NARODNOGO ARTISTA
SSSR BIUL'-BIULIA. Baku: Izd. AN AzSSR, 1967, 122 pp.,
3000 copies. [Russ. text; Azerb. titles, pp. 112-21]

Islamov, Musa.   NUKHINSKII DIALEKT AZERBAIDZHANSKOGO
IAZYKA. Baku: Izd. AN AzSSR, 1968, 274 pp., 1000 copies.
[Russ. text; ca.140 Azerb. titles, pp. 267-71]

*Ismailova, A. M.   ANTICHNYI TEATR. Baku: (M-vo Vyssh.
i Sred. Spets. Obrazovaniia AzSSR), 1967, 64 pp. 500
copies. [Azerb. text; Azerb., Russ. titles, pub.
1892-1962, per. ancient, pp. 60-4]

JALIL MAMMADQULUZADA (MOLLA NASRADDIN) METODIKI
GOSTARISHLAR VA BIBLIOGRAFIYA. Baku: (Azarb. SSR
Nazirlar Soveti Madani-Maarif Ishlari Metodkabinesi),
1947, 18 pp. [Azerb. text]

Kagramanov, A. G.   AZERBAIDZHANSKAIA LITERATURA V DNI
VELIKOI OTECHESTVENNOI VOINY. (1941-1945 GG.).
BIBLIOGR. UKAZATEL'. Baku: (Azerb. Gos. Knizh. Palata),
1946, 161 pp., 1000 copies. [Pub. during W. W. II]

_____. BIBLIOGRAFIIA AZERBAIDZHANSKOI LITERATURY.
(1920-1953). Baku: Azer. Gos. Knizhnaia Palata, 1954,
98 pp., 3000 copies. [Azerb., Russ. text; ca.990
Azerb., Russ. titles, pub. 1920-53]

_____. BIBLIOGRAFIIA RUSSKOI LITERATURY.
(PROIZVEDENIIA RUSSKOI KLASSICHESKOI LITERATURY I
RUSSKOI SOVETSKOI LITERATURY, PEREVEDENNYE NA
AZERBAIDZHANSKII IAZYK). 1953.

_____. LITERATURA BRATSKIKH NARODOV.
(BIBLIOGRAFICHESKII UKAZATEL'). Baku: (Az. Gos. Kn.
Palata), 1948, 95 pp. [Azerb. text; ca.640 Azerb.
titles, pub. 1928-48]

_____. VELIKII AZERBAIDZHANSKII POET NIZAMI
GIANDZHEVI. Baku: Izd. Azerbaidzhanskoi
Gosudarstvennoi Knizhnoi Palaty, 1947, 88 pp. [Azerb.
text]

Azerbaijan: Language, Literature

Kasimzade, F.   M. F. AKHUNDOV. ZHIZN' I TVORCHESTVO
Baku: (Az. Filial. AN SSSR, In-t, Lit-ry i Iaz. im.
Nizami), 1939. [Azerb. text; 220 Azerb., Russ.,
Europ. titles, pub. 1837-1938, pp. 133-40]

Kasim-zade, F.   ZHIZN' I TVORCHESTVO MIRZA FATALI
AKHUNDOVA. Baku, 1962. [Azerb. text; ca.320 Azerb.,
Russ., other titles, pp. 356-71]

*Kazimov, R. A.   SOSTOIANIE I RAZVITIE BIBLIOGRAFII
KHUDOZHESTVENNOI LITERATURY I LITERATUROVEDENIIA V
AZERBAIDZHANE (1946-1964 GG.). Baku: (Azarbayjan SSR
Nazirlar Sovetinin Dovlat Matbuat Komitasi...), 1965,
74 pp., 2000 copies. [Azerb. text; Azerb. titles,
per. 1946-64, pp. 71-4]

Kedrina, Z. S., G. B. Babaev, eds.   OCHERK ISTORII
AZERBAIDZHANSKOI SOVETSKOI LITERATURY. Moscow, 1963.
[Russ. text; ca.360 titles, Sov. per., pp. 551-63]

Khalafov, A.   AZERBAIDZHANSKAIA SOVETSKAIA LITERATURA.
Baku: (Azerbaidzh. Resp. Publ. B-ka im. Akhundova),
1954, 68 pp., 1500 copies. [Azerb. text; 58 lists,
19 titles, per. 1941-54]

_____.   MUKHAMMED FUZULI (K 400-LETIIU SO DNIA
SMERTI), KRATKII BIBLIOGR. UKAZATEL'. Baku:
(Azerbaidzh. Resp. B-ka im. Akhundova), 1958, 30 pp.,
2000 copies. [Azerb. text; Azerb., Russ. titles]

_____, M. N. Meil'man.   DZHAFAR DZHABARLY. Baku:
(Azerbaidzh. Resp. Publ. B-ka im. Akhundova), 1954,
12 pp., 1000 copies. [Azerb., Russ. text; 13 Azerb.,
Russ. titles]

Khalafov, A. T.   GUSEIN MEKHTI, K 50-LETIIU SO DNIA
ROZHDENIIA. (BIBLIOGRAFIIA). Baku: (Azerbaidzh. Resp.
B-ka im. Akhundova), 1959, 63 pp., 3000 copies.
[Azerb. text; 298 titles, per. 1927-58]

_____.   KOLKHOZNOE SELO V AZERBAIDZHANSKOI
SOVETSKOI LITERATURE. (KRATKII ANNOT. REK. BIBLIOGR.
UKAZATEL' LIT.). Baku: (Azer. Resp. B-ka im.
Akhundova), 1958, 43 pp., 3000 copies. [Azerb. text;
ca.200 titles, Sov. per.]

Kuliev, A. K., A. T. Khalafov.   NARODNYI PISATEL'
SULEIMAN RAGIMOV. (KRATKII UKAZATEL' LIT.). Baku:
(Azerbaidzhanskii Resp. B-ka im. Akhundova), 1963, 56
pp., 3000 copies. [Azerb. text; 318 titles]

*Kuliev, M.   "NARIMANOV, NARIMAN," LITERATURNAIA
ENTSIKLOPEDIIA, Vol. 7. Moscow: Gosudarstvennoe

Azerbaijan: Language, Literature

　　Slovarno-Entsiklopedicheskoe Izdatel'stvo "Sovetskaia
　　Entsiklopediia," 1934 (1st ed.), pp. 591-2. [Russ.
　　text; Russ. titles, p. 592]

*Kurbanov, A. M.　SOVREMENNYI AZERBAIDZHANSKII
　　LITERATURNYI IAZYK. Baku: "Maarif," 1967, 375 pp.,
　　7000 copies. [Azerb. text; 85 Azerb., Russ. titles,
　　pub. 1911-65, pp. 267-70]

*Kurbanov, Afat Mamed Ogly.　SEMASIOLOGY SOVREMENNOGO
　　AZERBAIDZHANSKOGO IAZYKA. Baku: (Azarbayjan Dovlat
　　Pedagozhi Institutu), 1964, 51 pp., 1000 copies.
　　[Azerb. text; Azerb., Sov. Asian, Russ. titles, pp.
　　47-50]

*Kurbanov, Sh.　ETAPY RAZVITIIA AZERBAIDZHANSKO-RUSSKIKH
　　LITERATURNYKH SVIAZEI V XIX VEKE. Baku:
　　Azerbaidzhanskoe Gos. Izdatel'stvo, 1969, 312 pp.,
　　3000 copies. [Azerb. text; ca.320 Azerb., Russ.
　　titles, per. 19th cent., pp. 299-309]

*Lerman, A. N.　MIRZA FATALI AKHUNDOV V RUSSKOI PECHATI.
　　1837-1962 GG. BIOBIBLIOGRAFIIA. Baku: (Azer. Resp.
　　B-ka im. Akhundova), 1962, 233 pp., 5000 copies.
　　Russ. text; 1724 Russ. titles, pub. 1837-1962, pp.
　　204-12]

　Mamedov, A.　SHAKH ISMAIL KHATAI. Baku: Detiunizdat,
　　1961. [Azerb. text; 71 Azerb., Russ. titles, per. 16th
　　cent., pp. 152-9]

　Mamedov, K.　KASUMBEK ZAKIR. Baku: (In-t Lit. i
　　Iazyka im. Nizami), 1957. [Azerb. text; 66 Azerb.,
　　Russ. titles, pp. 253-7]

　Mamedov, Kamran.　ABDURRAGIM AKHVERDOV. Baku:
　　Detiunizdat, 1955 (2nd ed.) [Azerb. text; 40 Azerb.,
　　Russ. titles, per. 1870-1933, pp. 190-3]

*Mamedov, Mamed Makhmud Ogly.　KHUDOZHESTVENNAIA PROZA
　　DZHALILA MAMEDKULIZADE. Baku: Azarbayjan SSR Elmlar
　　Akademiyasi Nashriyyati, 1963, 156 pp., 2750 copies.
　　[Azerb. text; ca.150 Azerb. titles, pub. 1904-61,
　　pp. 151-6]

*Mamedov, N.　KHUDOZHESTVENNOE TVORCHESTVO M. F.
　　AKHUNDOVA. Baku: Izd-vo AN Azer. SSR, 1962, 150 pp.,
　　2400 copies. [Russ. text; 160 Azerb., Russ., Europ.
　　titles, pub. 1837-62, pp. 143-50]

*Marr, N. Ed.　"AZERBAIDZHANSKII IAZYK," BOL'SHAIA
　　SOVETSKAIA ENTSIKLOPEDIIA, Vol. 1. Moscow:
　　Aktsionernoe Obshchestvo "Sovetskaia Entsiklopediia,"

Azerbaijan: Language, Literature

1926 (1st ed.), pp. 665-6. [Russ. text; Azerb., Russ. titles, p. 666]

*Meil'man, M. N.   AZERBAIDZHANSKAIA LITERATURA. REKOMENDATEL'NYI UKAZATEL'. Moscow: (Gosudarstvennaia Ordena Lenina Biblioteka SSR imeni Lenina...), 1958, 118 pp., 3000 copies. [Russ. text; Russ. titles, per. 12th-20th cent., pp. 9-112]

_____. SAMED VURGUN. Baku: Azerbaidzh. Resp. Publ. B-ka im. Akhundova, 1951, 81 pp., 1000 copies. [Russ. text; ca.300 Azerb., Russ. titles, pub. 1928-50]

Melikov, Kh.   OSOBENNOSTI STILIA I DRAMATURGIIA MUZYKAL'NYKH KOMEDII UZEIRA GADZHIBEKOVA. Baku, 1963. [Russ. text; 70 titles, pp. 158-60]

*Mir Akhmedov, A.   SABIR. Baku: Izdatel'stvo Akademii Nauk Azerbaidzhanskoi SSR, 1958, 443 pp., 6000 copies. [Azerb. text; ca.100 Azerb., Sov. Asian, Russ., Pers. titles, pp. 439-42]

Mirzaeva, V., comp.   ABDURRAGIMBEK AKHVERDOV (BIBLIOGRAFIIA). Baku: (Azerbaidzhanskaia Respublikanskaia Knizhnaia Palata), 1964, 75 pp., 2000 copies. [Azerb. text; 406 Azerb., Russ. titles, pub. 1899-1962]

_____, N. Agaeva, comps.   RASUL RZA 50-LETIE SO DNIA ROZHDENIIA. (BIBLIOGRAFIIA). Baku: (Azer. Gos. Knizhnaia Palata), 1960, 68 pp., 5000 copies. [Azerb. text; 879 Azerb., Russ., other titles]

*Nabiev, Bekir Akhmed Ogly.   VYDAIUSHCHIISIA KRITIK I LITERATUROVED (ZHIZN' I TVORCHESTVO F. KOCHARLINSKOGO). Baku: Azarbayjan SSR Elmlar Akademiyasi Nashriyyati, 1963, 163 pp., 2800 copies. [Azerb. text; ca.180 Azerb., Russ. titles, archives, pp. 154-62]

Nadzhafova, M. Iu., M. N. Meil'man.   SULEIMAN RUSTAM. Baku: (Az. Resp. Publ. B-ka im. Akhundova), 1956, 13 pp., 500 copies. [Azerb., Russ. text; 57 titles, pub. 1942-56]

Nadzhafova, M. Iu., I. V. Peregonets.   NAVSTRECHU RESPUBLIKANSKOMU, VSESOIUZNOMU I VI VSEMIRNOMU FESTIVALIU MOLODEZHI (KRATKII REK. UKAZATEL' LIT. V POMESHCH' KHUDOZH. SAMODEIATEL'NOSTI). Baku, 1957, 32 pp., 1000 copies. [Azerb., Russ. text; ca.450 Azerb., Russ. titles]

Azerbaijan: Language, Literature

*Nazim, A. "DZHAVID, GUSEIN," LITERATURNAIA ENTSIKLOPEDIA, Vol. 3. N.P.: Izdatel'stvo Kommunisticheskoi Akademii, 1930, pp. 233-4. [Russ. text; Azerb., Turkish titles, p. 234]

NIZAMI GANJAVININ 800 ILLIYI (METODIK VASAIT VA ADABIYYAT SIYAHISI). Baku: (Azarbayjan SSR Nazirlar Soveti Madani-Maarif Muassisalari Metodkabinese), 1947, 13 pp. [Azerb. text; per. 800th anniv. of Nizami]

*Orudzhev, A. A. NAUCHNYE OSNOVY FILOLOGICHESKOGO TOLKOVOGO SLOVARIA AZERBAIDZHANSKOGO IAZYKA. Baku: Azarbayjan SSR Elmlar Akademiyasi Nashriyyati, 1965, 123 pp., 1200 copies. [Azerb. text; ca.160 Azerb., Sov. Asia., Russ., Turkish titles, pp. 115-22]

Pepinova, Sevda Akhmed Kyzy. STRUKTURNO-SISTEMATICHESKIE (VIDO-VREMENNYE) OSOBENNOSTI FORM PROSHEDSHEGO VREMENI V NEMETSKOM I AZERBAIDZHANSKOM IAZYKAKH. Baku: "Maarif," 1966, 176 pp., 1000 copies. [Russ. text; titles, pp. 166-75]

Rafili, M. AKHUNDOV (ZHIZN' ZAMECHATEL'NYKH LIUDEI. SERIIA BIOGRAFII. Vyp. 2 (268). Moscow: "Molodaia Gvardiia," 1959, 191 pp. [Russ. text; 17 Russ. titles]

_____. MIRZA SHAFI V MIROVOI LITERATURE. (K VOPROSU O LIT. NASLEDII MIRZA SHAFI I PLAGIATE FRIDRIKHA BODENSHTEDTA). Baku: Azerneshr, 1958. [Russ. text; 37 Azerb., Russ., Europ. titles, pp. 118-19]

_____. NIZAMI. ZHIZNI I TVORCHESTVO. Baku, 1939. [Separate editions in Azerb. and Russ.; 178 Azerb., Russ., Europ. titles, pub. 1809-1939, pp. 121-30 in Russ. ed., pp. 100-6 in Azerb. ed.]

Rustamov, R., Z. Budagova. "AZERBAIDZHANSKOE IAZYKOZNANIE ZA 20 LET," IZVESTIIA AN AZSSR. SERIIA OBSHCHESTV. NAUK, No. 3. 1965. [Russ. text; titles pp. 33-51]

*Rustamov, R. A. KUBINSKII DIALEKT. Baku: Izdatel'stvo Akademii Nauk Azerbaidzhanskoi SSR, 1961, 281 pp., 500 copies. [Azerb. text; ca.60 Azerb., Sov. Asian, Russ. titles, pp. 275-7]

* _____, Z. I. Budagova, eds. GRAMMATIKA AZERBAIDZHANSKOGO IAZYKA. Ch. 1. (MORFOLOGIIA). Baku: Izdatel'stvo Akademii Nauk Azer. SSR, 1960, 334 pp., 7000 copies. [Azerb. text; 67 Azerb., Russ. titles, pp. 323-5]

*Rustamov, Rasul Ali-Abas Ogly. GLAGOL V DIALEKTAKH I

Azerbaijan: Language, Literature

GOVORAKH AZERBAIDZHANSKOGO IAZYKA. Baku: Azarbayjan SSR Elmlar Akademiyasi Nashriyyati, 1965, 320 pp., 1500 copies. [Azerb. text; 101 Azerb., Sov. Asian, Russ., Turk. titles, pp. 312-16]

*_____. STRUKTURNYE TIPY GLAGOLA V DIALEKTAKH I GOVORAKH AZERBAIDZHANSKOGO IAZYKA. Baku: Azarbayjan SSR Elmlar Akademiyasi Nashriyyati, 1963, 106 pp., 3200 copies. [Azerb. text; 55 Azerb., Russ., Europ. titles, pp. 99-101]

*_____. ZHELATEL'NOE I SOSLAGATEL'NOE NAKLONENIIA V DIALEKTAKH I GOVORAKH AZERBAIDZHANSKOGO IAZYKA. Baku: Azarbayjan SSR Elmlar Akademiyasi Nashriyyati, 1962, 60 pp., 2200 copies. [Azerb. text; Azerb., Sov. Asian, Russ. titles, pp. 56-57]

*S.-Z. "AKHUNDOV (AKHUN-ZADE). MIRZA-FETKH-ALI," LITERATURNAIA ENTSIKLOPEDIIA. Vol. 1, N.P.: Izdatel'stvo Kommunisticheskoi Akademii, 1929 (1st ed.), pp. 285-7. [Russ. text; Azerb., Russ., Europ. titles, p. 287]

*S.-Z. "VEZIR-ZADE, NEDZHEF-BEK," LITERATURNAIA ENTSIKLOPEDIIA. Vol. 2, N.P.: Izdatel'stvo Kommunisticheskoi Akademii, 1929, pp. 122-3. [Russ. text; Azerb., Russ. titles, p. 123]

*S.-Z., A.-A. "VIDADI," LITERATURNAIA ENTSIKLOPEDIIA. Vol. 2, N.P.: Izdatel'stvo Kommunisticheskoi Akademii, 1929. [Russ. text; Azerb., Russ. titles, pp. 210-11]

Saadiev, Sh. BIBLIOGRAFIIA LITERATURY PO AZERBAIDZHANSKOMU IAZYKOZNANIIU. (SOVETSKII PERIOD). Baku: (Azerb. Gos. Un-t im. Kirova), 1960, 144 pp., 3000 copies. [Azerb. text; 1442 Azerb., Russ. titles, Sov. period]

Salmanov, Sh. M. MIKAIL RAFILI. (K 60-LETIIU SO DNIA ROZHDENIIA). Baku: (Azerbaidzh. Resp. B-ka im. Akhundova), 1965, 80 pp., 500 copies. [Azerb. text]

Seidov, Iakh'ia. TVORCHESKII PUT' MEKHTI GUSEINA. Baku: Izd. AN AzSSR, 1966, 252 pp., 2200 copies. [Azerb. text; 94 Azerb. titles, pub. 1930-65, pp. 248-51]

*Sevortian, E. V. AFFIKSY IMENNOGO SLOVOOBRAZOVANIIA V AZERBAIDZHANSKOM IAZYKE. Moscow: "Nauka," 1966, 437 pp., 1000 copies. [Russ. text; 167 Azerb., Russ., Europ. titles, pp. 370-7]

*Shamkhalov, A. "DAGESTANSKIE IAZYKI," BOL'SHAIA SOVETSKAIA ENTSIKLOPEDIIA. Vol. 20, Moscow: Aktsionernoe

Azerbaijan: Language, Literature

Obshchestvo "Sovetskaia Entsiklopediia," 1930 (1st ed.), pp. 165-6. [Russ. text; Azerb., Russ., Dargyn, Avar., Europ. titles, p. 166]

Shiraliev, M. A. BAKINSKII DIALEKT. Baku: (AN AzSSR In-t Iazyka), 1947/1949. [Azerb. text; 43 Azerb., Russ., titles, per. 1836-1944, pp. 248-9]

*Shiraliev, M. Sh., ed. NAKHICHEVANSKAIA GRUPPA DIALEKTOV I GOVOROV AZERBAIDZHANSKOGO IAZYKA. Baku: Izdatel'stvo Akademii Nauk Azerbaidzhanskoi SSR, 1962, 326 pp., 1000 copies. [Azerb. text; 98 Azerb., Sov. Asian, Russ., Turk. titles, pp. 318-321]

*Shiraliev, Mamedaga Shirali Ogly. OSNOVY AZERBAIDZHANSKOI DIALEKTOLOGII UCHEBNOE POSOBIE DLIA VUZOV. Baku: Azeruchpedgiz, 1962, 423 pp., 2500 copies. [Azerb. text; Azerb., Sov. Asian, Russ., Turk. titles, pp. 415-18]

*Sokolov, Iu. M., ed. AZERBAIDZHANSKIE TIURKSKIE SKAZKI. [Moscow]: Academia, 1935, 667 pp., 10,300 copies. [Russ. text; 51+ Azerb., Russ. titles, pp. 629-50, 651-5]

SPISOK LITERATURY PO ISTORII AZERBAIDZHANSKOI LITERATURY I AZERBAIDZHANSKOGO IAZYKOZNANIIA. Baku: Az. Gos. Zaoch. Ped. In-ta, 16 pp. [Azerb. text; ca.200 titles, pub. 1924-49]

SULEYMAN RUSTAM (QISA TOVSIYA ADAB. GOSTARIJISI). Baku: (Azerbayjan SSR Madaniyyat Nazirliyi, Respublika Metodkabinesi), 1959, 75 pp. [Azerb. text]

Tagiev, G. BIBLIOGRAFIIA M. F. AKHUNDOVA. Baku: (Azerb. Resp. Publ. Bib-ka im. Akhundova), 1948, 112 pp., 1000 copies. [Azerb. text]

_____. BIBLIOGRAFIIA PROIZVEDENII M. S. ORDUBADY. Baku: Az. Gos. Kn. Palata, 1951, 96 pp., 500 copies. [Azerb. text; 1253 Azerb., Russ. titles, pub. 1903-49]

_____. M. F. AKHUNDOV. BIBLIOGRAFIIA. (1837-1957 GG). Baku: (Azer. Resp. B-ka im. Akhundova), 1960, 103 pp., 3000 copies. [Azerb. text; 710 titles, pub. 1837-1957]

Taghiyev, H., ed. M.-F. AKHUNDOV HAQQINDA BIBLIOGRAFIYA (1837-1947-JI ILLAR). Baku: (M. F. Akhundov Adina Azarbayjan Respublika Kitabkhanasi), 1948, 110 pp. [Azerb. text; Azerb. titles, per. 1837-1947]

Talybov, F. T. OSMAN SARYVELLI (KRATKII UKAZATEL' LITERATURY). Baku: (M-vo Kul'tury AzSSR. Azerbaidzh.

Azerbaijan: Language, Literature

Resp. B-ka im. M. F. Akhundova. Nauch.-Metod. Otd. Bibliotekovedeniia), 1966, 19 pp., 1000 copies. [Azerb. text; 143 + 44 Azerb. titles, pub. 1934-66]

Teimurova, N. M., comp. MIR DZHALAL. BIBLIOGRAFIIA. Baku: (AN AzSSR. Fundam. B-ka. Deiateli Nauki i Kul'tury Azerbaidzhana), 1968, 139 pp., 3000 copies. [Azerb. text; 944 Azerb., Russ., Europ. other titles, pub. 1926-68]

*"VAKYF, MOLLA PENAKH," LITERATURNAIA ENTSIKLOPEDIIA. Vol. 2, N.P.: Izdatel'stvo Kommunisticheskoi Akademii, 1929, pp. 80-1. [Russ. text; Azerb., Russ. titles, per. 18th cent., p. 81]

Veliev, V. AZERBAIDZHANSKOE USTNOE NARODNOE TVORCHESTVO. Baku, 1970. [Azerb. text; ca.170 titles, pp. 433-8]

Veliev, V. A. NARODNYE DASTANY. Baku: (M-vo Vyssh. i Sred. Spets. Obrazovaniia AzSSR), 1966, 52 pp., 1000 copies. [Russ. text; 20 Azerb. titles, pp. 51-2]

*Vurgun, S., ed. ISTORIIA AZERBAIDZHANSKOI LITERATURY. Vol. I: S DREVNEISHIKH VREMEN DO KONTSA XVIII VEKA. Baku: (In-t Lit. i Iazyka im. Nizami), 1960. [Azerb. text; ca.400 Azerb., Russ., other titles, per. antiquity to end of 18th cent., pp. 577-89]

* _____, and others, eds. ISTORIIA AZERBAIDZHANSKOI LITERATURY. Vol. 3: SOVETSKII PERIOD. Baku: (In-t Lit. i Iazyka im. Nizami), 1957. [Azerb. text; ca.100 titles, Sov. per., pp. 558-60]

*Vurghun, Samad, Mirza Ibrahimov, M. Arif Dadashzada, eds. ISTORIIA AZERBAIDZHANSKOI LITERATURY. V TREKH TOMAKH. Vol. 1: S DREVNEISHIKH VREMEN DO KONTSA XVIII VEKA. Vol. 2: S NACHALA XIX VEKA DO 1917 GODA. Vol. 3: SOVETSKII PERIOD. Baku: Izdatel'stvo Akademii Nauk Azerbaidzhanskoi SSR. Vol. 1, 1960, 590 pp., 20,000 copies. Vol. 2, 1960, 906 pp., 20,000 copies. Vol. 3, 1957, 562 pp., 10,000 copies. [Azerb. text; 411+ Azerb., Russ., Europ., Mid-East. titles, pp. 577-89 (Vol. 1), 888-904 (Vol. 2), 558-60 (Vol. 3)]

*Zarinezade, G. G. AZERBAIDZHANSKIE SLOVA V PERSIDSKOM IAZYKE (PERIOD SEFEVIDOV). Baku: Izdatel'stvo Akademii Nauk Azerbaidzhanskoi SSR, 1962, 436 pp, 1750 copies. [Azerb. text; 218 Azerb., Russ., Sov. Asian, Mid-East., Europ. titles, Safavid per., pp. 421-34]

Zeinalov, F. P. PRINTSIPY KLASSIFIKATSII IMENNYKH CHASTEI RECHI. Baku: (Azerbaidzh. Gos. Un-t im. Kirova), 1959. [Russ. text; 130 Azerb., Russ. titles, pre-rev.

Azerbaijan: Language, Literature

§ Sov. per., pp. 7-72, 210-14]

*Zeinalova, Kh. A., N. S. Grigor'ian, comp. N. B. VEZIROV (1854-1926). (REKOMENDATEL'NYI SPISOK LITERATURY). Baku: (Azerbaidzhanskaia Respublikanskaia Biblioteka im. M. F. Akhundova), 1970, 23 pp., 1000 copies. [Azerb., Russ. text; 51 Azerb., Russ. titles, pp. 11-14, 22-3]

*Zhirmunskii, V. M., A. N. Kononov, eds. KNIGA MOEGO DEDA KORKUTA. OGUZSKII GEROICHESKII EPOS. Moscow: Izdatel'stvo Akademii Nauk SSSR, 1962, 299 pp., 3100 copies. [Russ. text; 72 Azerb., Russ., Turkish, Europ. titles, pp. 281-3]

*Zulalova, G., comp. F. S. KASUM-ZADE. BIBLIOGRAFIIA. Baku: Izdatel'stvo Akademii Nauk Azerbaidzhanskoi SSR, 1968, 68 pp., 3600 copies. [Azerb. text; 388 Azerb., Russ. titles, pub. 1930-67]

PHILOSOPHY, RELIGION

*Geiushev, Z. B., comp. "TRUDY GASAN-BEKA MELIKOVA-ZARDABI-O ZARDABI," MIROVOZZRENIE G. B. ZARDABI. Baku: Izdatel'stvo AN Azerb. SSR, 1962, 402 pp., 1400 copies. [Russ. text; ca.260 Azerb., Russ. titles, pub. 1877-1903, pp. 392-402]

*_____, Sh. F. Mamedov, A. M. Agakhi, A. A. Amin-zade, F. K. Kocharli, Z. A. Kuli-zade, D. V. Mustafaev, S. D. Rza-kuli-zade, eds. OCHERKI PO ISTORII AZERBAIDZHANSKOI FILOSOFII. Vol. 1. Baku: Izdatel'stvo Akademii Nauk Azerbaidzhanskoi SSR, 1966, 348 pp., 1400 copies. [Russ. text; ca.330 Azerb., Russ., Mid-East., Europ. titles, 11-18th cent., pp. 337-47]

Kerimov, G. M. AL'-GAZALI I SUFIZM. Baku, 1969. [Russ. text; ca.70 titles, pp. 5-21, 105-8]

Khalafov, A. NAUKA I RELIGIIA. Baku: (Azerb. Resp. Publ. B-ka im. Akhundova), 1954, 40 pp., 1500 copies. [Russ. text; 95 titles, Sov. per.]

Kuli-zade, Z. KHURUFIZM I EGO PREDSTAVITELI V AZERBAIDZHANE. Baku, 1970. [Russ. text; titles pp. 6-41]

Azerbaijan: Philosophy, Religion

*Makhmudov, Panakh Gusein Ogly. ATEIZM I RELIGIIA.
Baku: Azarbayjan Dovlat Nashriyyati, 1963, 151 pp.,
5000 copies. [Azerb. text; Azerb., Russ. titles,
pp. 149-50]

Mamedbeili, G. D., comp. "SPISOK NAUCHNYKH TRUDOV
NASIREDDINA," OSNOVATEL' MARAGINSKOI OBSERVATORII
MUKHAMMED NASIREDDIN TUSI. Baku, 1961. [Russ. text;
76 titles, pp. 179-92]

Mamedov, Gulam. FORMY PROPAGANDY NAUCHNOGO ATEIZMA
KHUDOZHESTVENNOI LITERATUROI V MASSOVYKH BIBLIOTEKAKH.
Baku: (M-vo Kul'tury AzSSR Azerbaidzh. Resp. B-ka im.
M. F. Akhundova), 1967, 41 pp., 2000 copies. [Russ.
text; Azerb. titles, pp. 38-40]

*Mamedov, Sh. F. MIROVOZZRENIE M. F. AKHUNDOVA. Moscow:
Izd-vo Moskovskogo Universiteta, 1962, 260 pp., 1350
copies. [Russ. text; ca.360 Azerb., Russ. titles, per.
1812-1877, pp. 246-59]

Rzaev, A. K. OCHERKI OB UCHENYKH I MYSLITELIAKH
AZERBAIDZHANA XIX V. Baku, 1969. [Russ. text; 391
Russ, Mid-East., Europ. titles, per. 19th cent., pp.
77-107]

UKAZATEL' NAUCHNO-ATEISTICHESKOI LITERATURY. Baku:
Obedin. Izd. (Otd. Propagandy i Agitatsii TsK KP
Azerbaidzhana), 1958, 8 pp., 5000 copies. [Azerb. text;
ca.60 titles, Sov. per.]

POLITICAL SCIENCE, LAW

Akhmedov, F. N. ISTORIIA SOVETSKOGO GOSUDARSTVA I
PRAVA. Baku: Azeruchpedgiz, 1961. [Azerb. text; ca.
200 Azerb., Russ. titles, pp. 271-81]

*Ali-zade, Abdul-kerim. SOTSIAL'NO-EKONOMICHESKAIA I
POLITICHESKAIA ISTORIIA AZERBAIDZHANA XIII-XIV VV.
Baku: Izdatel'stvo Akademii Nauk Azerbaidzhanskoe SSR,
1956, 420 pp., 1000 copies. [Russ. text; ca.225 Russ.,
Mid-East., Europ. titles, per. 13-14th cent., pp. 10-
24, 400-6]

Asadov, A. I. SOVETSKOE GRAZHDANSKOE PRAVO. Baku:
(Azerbaidzh. Gos. Un-t im. Kirova), 1957. [Azerb. text;

Azerbaijan: Political Science, Law

32 Russ., Azerb. titles, pp. 250-1]

*Azizbekova, P. A.   RUKOVODSTVO V. I. LENINA
SOTSIALISTICHESKOM STROITEL'STVOM V AZERBAIDZHANE V
1920-1923 GG. Baku: Izdatel'stvo Akademii Nauk
Azerbaidzhanskoi SSR, 1960, 267 pp., 2000 copies.
[Russ. text; ca.350 Azerb., Russ. titles, archives, per.
1920-23, pp. 229-52]

_____. V. I. LENIN I SOTSIALISTICHESKIE
PREOBRAZOVANIIA V AZERBAIDZHANE. (1920-1923 GG).
Moscow, 1962. [Russ. text; 470 titles, per. 1920-23,
pp.· 3-30, 349-54]

Badalov, E. V.   V. I. LENIN AD. UMUMITTIFAQ PIONER
TASHKILATI. (40 ILLIYI MUNASIBATI ILA METODIK VASAIT).
Baku: (Azarb. SSR Madaniyyat Nazirl. M. F. Akhundov
Ad. Azarb. Resp. Kitabkhanasi. Elmi-metodik Kitabkhana
Shunasliq Shob'asi), 1962, 19 pp., 1000 copies. [Azerb.
text; per. 40th anniv.]

*D. K.   "BAKINSKIE KOMISSARY," BOL'SHAIA SOVETSKAIA
ENTSIKLOPEDIIA, Vol. 4. Moscow: Aktsionernoe
Obshchestvo "Sovetskaia Entsiklopediia," 1926 (1st ed.),
pp. 400-403. [Russ. text; Russ., Europ. titles, p.403]

*Efendiev, Kh. S.   "PROIZVEDENIIA V. I. LENINA I I. V.
STALINA NA AZERBAIDZHANSKOM IAZYKE," SOVETSKAIA KNIGA,
No. 1, 1951. [Russ. text; Azerb. titles, per. 20th
cent., pp. 18-23]

Efendieva, Sh. F.   SLAVNYI PUT' KOMSOMOLA. (BIBLIOGR. I
METOD. MATERIALY V CHEST' 40-LETIIA VLKSM). Baku:
(Metod. Kabinet Bibliotech. Raboty pri Tsentr. Gor.
B-ke im. Lenina. V Pomoshch' Massovym B-kam), 1958, 39
pp., 1200 copies. [Azerb. text; Sov. per.]

Efendieva, Sh. M.   K VYBORAM V VERKHOVNYI SOVET
AZERBAIDZHANSKOI SSR I MESTNYE SOVETY DEPUTATOV
TRUDIASHCHIKHSIA. PAMIATKA CHITATELIU. Baku:
(Azerbaidzh. Resp. Publ. B-ka im. Akhundova), 1955, 8
pp., 1000 copies. [Azerb. text; 58 titles, Sov. per.]

_____.   MOLODEZH' V BOR'BE ZA MIR. Baku:
(Azerbaidzh. Resp. Publ. B-ka im. Akhundova), 1953, 71
pp., 1000 copies. [Azerb. text; 119 Azerb. titles]

Gamidova, G. M., comp.   26 BAKINSKIKH KOMISSAROV
(BIBLIOGRAFIIA). Baku: (M-vo Kul'tury AzSSR. Azerbaidzh.
Gos. Resp. B-ka im. M. F. Akhundova), 1968, 34 pp.,
3000 copies. [Azerb. text]

_____.   SLAVNYI PUT' AZERBAIDZHANSKOGO KOMSOMOLA

Azerbaijan: Political Science, Law

(REK. UKAZATEL' LITERATURY). Baku: (M-vo Kul'tury AzSSR. Azerbaidzhanskaia Gosudarstvennaia Resp. Biblioteka im. M. F. Akhundova), 1968, 56 pp., 2000 copies. [Azerb. text; ca.570 Azerb. titles]

Gavrilova, S. A., comp. "GRUZINSKAIA SSR, AZERBAIDZHANSKAIA SSR, ARMIANSKAIA SSR," EKONOMICHESKIE ADMINISTRATIVNYE RAIONY SSSR. UKAZATEL' NOVOI LIT. PO PRIRODE, RESURSAM I KHOZIAISTVU. No. 13. Moscow: (Akad. Nauk SSSR. In-t Nauch. Informatsii), 1958, 122 pp., 500 copies. [Russ. text; ca.1500 titles, Sov. per.]

Guseinov, A., comp. KHALIDA GASILOVA. (PAMIATKA CHITATELIU). Baku: Azerbaidzh. Resp. Det. B-ka im. Kocharli. K 50-Letiiu Komsomola), 1968, 10 pp., 3000 copies. [Azerb. text.]

_____, comp. SULEIMAN SANI AKHUNDOV. (PAMIATKA CHITATELIU). Baku: (Azerbaidzh. Resp. Det. B-ka im. Kocharli. K 50-Letiiu Komsomola), 1968, 11 pp., 3000 copies. [Azerb. text]

*Ibragimov, Dzhafar. FEODAL'NYE GOSUDARSTVA NA TERRITORII AZERBAIDZHANA XV VEKA. Baku: (Komitet Vysshego i Srednego Spetsial'nogo Obrazovaniia, Sovet Ministrov Azerbaidzhanskoi SSR), 1962, 112 pp., 800 copies. [Russ. text; 131 Russ., Mid-East. titles, archives, per. 15th cent., pp. 106-10]

Kagramanov, V. SOVETSKOE UGOLOVNOE PRAVO. Baku: "Maarif," 1967, 216 pp., 5000 copies. [Russ. text; Azerb. titles at end of chapters]

Kagramanov, V. P. SOVETSKOE UGOLOVNOE PRAVO. OBSHCHAIA CHAST'. Baku: Azerbaidzh. Gos. Un-t im. Kirova, 1953. [Azerb. text; 112 Azerb., Russ. titles, pp. 156-9]

Kerimov, I. A. METODICHESKOE UKAZANIE PO IZUCHENIIU SOVETSKOGO STROITEL'STVA. Baku: (M-vo Vyssh. i Sred. Spets. Obrazovaniia AzSSR), 1968, 70 pp., 500 copies. [Russ. text; Azerb. titles, pp. 68-9]

*Kerimova, D. Iu., comp. 26 BAKINSKIKH KOMISSAROV. (BIBLIOGRAFIIA). Baku: (M-vo Kul'tury AzSSR. Azerbaidzh. Gos. Resp. B-ka im. M. F. Akhundova), 1968, 69 pp., 3000 copies. [Russ. text; Russ. titles]

Khalafop, A. K VYBORAM V VERKHOVNYI SOVET SSSR [14 MARTA 1954 GODA]. PAMIATKA CHITATELIU. Baku: Azerbaidzh. Resp. Publ. B-ka, 1954, 8 pp., 1000 copies. [Azerb. text; 41 Azerb. titles, per. 1954]

Azerbaijan: Political Science, Law

Khalafov, A. T.   BIBLIOGRAFICHESKII UKAZATEL'
PROIZVEDENII K. MARKSA I F. ENGEL'SA.   Baku:
(Azerbaidzhanskaia Respublikanskaia B-ka im. Akhundova),
1965, 55 pp., 3000 copies.   [Azerb. text; 582 Azerb.
titles]

*Khalafov, M. S., et al., ed.   ISTORIIA GOSUDARSTVA I
PRAVA AZERBAIDZHANSKOI SSR.   Vol. 1.   VELIKAIA
OKTIABR'SKAIA SOTSIALISTICHESKAIA REVOLIUTSIIA I
SOZDANIE SOVETSKOI GOSUDARSTVENNOSTI V AZERBAIDZHANE.
Baku: Izdatel'stvo Akademii Nauk Azerbaidzhanskoi SSR,
1964, 313 pp., 1100 copies.   [Russ. text; ca.340 titles,
archives, pp. 300-11]

*Kocharli, Firudin Kasum Ogly.   NARIMAN NARIMANOV.   Baku:
Azarbayjan SSR Elmlar Akademiyasi Nashriyyati, 1965,
340 pp., 5000 copies.   [Azerb. text; 178 + 62 Azerb.
titles, pub. 1894-1925, pp. 331-9]

LENINSKIE UROKI V SISTEME POLITICHESKOGO PROSVESHCHENIIA
MOLODEZHI.   Baku: Azerneshr, 1966, 30 pp., 2000 copies.
[Russ. text, Azerb. titles, pp. 22-8]

*Makhmudov, Kh. Z., comp.   GEIDAR GUSEINOV.   1908-1950.
BIBLIOGRAFIIA.   Baku: Izdatel'stvo Akademii Nauk
Azerbaidzhanskoi SSR, 1965, 48 pp., 2800 copies.
[Azerb. text; 198, 50, 14 Azerb., Russ. titles, pub.
1934-62, pp. 18-40]

Mamedli, G.   KHIABANI.   (IZ ISTORII BORBY AZERB. NARODA
ZA NATS. OSVOBOZHDENIE).   Baku: Azerneshr, 1949.
[Azerb. text; ca.30 Azerb., Russ. titles, pp. 159-60]

Melikset-Bekov, L. M.   UKAZATEL' LITERATURY PO ISTORII
GOSUDARSTVA I PRAVA, OBYCHNOMU PRAVU I IURIDICHESKIM
DREVNOSTIAM GRUZII, ARMENII I AZERBAIDZHANA.   Tiflis,
1939.   [Russ. text]

MORAL'NYI KODEKS STROITELIA KOMMUNIZMA.   POSOBIE DLIA
PROPAGANDISTOV I SLUSHATELEI SISTEMY POLIT.
PROSVESHCHENIIA.   Baku: Azerneshr, 1966, 181 pp., 8000
copies.   [Russ. text, Azerb. titles, pp. 177-9]

Peregonets, I. V.   K VYBORAM V VERKHOVNYI SOVET
AZERBAIDZHANSKOI SSR. I MESTNYE SOVETY DEPUTATOV
TRUDIASHCHIKHSIA.   PAMIATKA CHITATELIU.   Baku:
(Azerbaidzh. Resp. Publ. B-ka im. Akhundova), 1955, 8
pp., 1000 copies.   [Russ. text; 61 titles, Sov. per.]

Petrushevskii, I. P.   "GOSUDARSTVA AZERBAIDZHANA V XV
VEKE," SBORNIK STATEI PO ISTORII AZERBAIDZHANA.   No. 1.
Baku, [1949].   [Russ. text; 106 Russ., foreign titles,
per. 15th cent., pub. 17th cent., 1821-1942, pp.210-13]

Azerbaijan: Political Science, Law

PRIMERNYE SPISKI LITERATURY, REKOMENDUEMOI SAMOSTOIATEL'NO IZUCHAIUSHCHIM MARKSISTKO-LENINSKUIU TEORIIU. Baku, [1949], 15 pp. [Azerb., Russ. text; Russ. titles]

S. M. KIROV. (1886-1934) KRATKII UKAZATEL' LIT. Baku: Azerbaidzhan. Resp. Publ. B-ka im. Akhundova, 1952, 39 pp., 5000 copies. [Azerb. text; 63 Azerb., Russ. titles]

*Samedov, V. Iu. RASPROSTRANENIE MARKSIZMA-LENINIZMA V AZERBAIDZHANE. Baku: Azerbaidzhanskoe Gos. Izd-vo, 1962, 762 pp. [Russ. text; ca.400 Azerb., Russ. titles, 19-20th cents., pp. 728-45]

Shcherbina, R. V., comp. K 40-LETIIU KOMMUNISTICHESKOI PARTII AZERBAIDZHANA I POBEDY SOVETSKOI VLASTI V AZERBAIDZHANE. (REK. SPISOK LIT.). Baku: (Tsentr. Gor. B-ka im. Lenina), 1960, 39 pp., 1500 copies. [Russ. text; ca.400 titles, Sov. per.]

_____. K 40-LETIIU VLKSM. Baku: (Tsentr. Gor. B-ka im. Lenina), 1958, 50 pp., 1500 copies. [Sov. per.]

Sliusarenko, E. A., comp. A. O. MAKOVEL'SKII. BIBLIOGRAFIIA. Baku: Izdatel'stvo Akademii Nauk Azerbaidzhanskoi SSR, 1964, 68 pp., 2500 copies. [Russ. text; 175 titles, mss., pub. 1904-62]

Teimurov, Kh., M. Mirzoev. CHTO CHITAT' O DRUZHBE NARODOV SSSR. Baku: (Res. Pub. B-ka im. Akhundova), 88 pp. [Azerb. text; 39 books, articles, pub. 1935-47]

UKAZATEL' PERVOISTOCHNIKOV DLIA IZUCHAIUSHCHIKH KRATKII KURS ISTORII VKP (B). 1941.

SOCIAL ORGANIZATION

Airapetova, R. A., comp. M. A. MIR-KASIMOV. 1883-1958. BIBLIOGRAFIIA. Baku: Izdatel'stvo AN Azerbaidzhanskoi SSR, 1964, 51 pp., 2600 copies. [Russ. text; 148 Azerb., Russ. titles, pub. 1914-62]

Gornik, L. N., T. S. Davtian, comp. KURORTY I MINERAL'NYE ISTOCHNIKI AZERBAIDZHANA. FIZIOTERAPIIA. BIBLIOGRAFICHESKII UKAZATEL' LITERATURY ZA 1920-1964 GG. Baku: (Ministerstvo Zdravookhraneniia AzSSR. Azerbaidzh. NII Kurortologii i Fiz. Metodov Lechenii im. S. M. Kirova...), 1965, 126 pp., 1000 copies. [Russ. text; titles pub. 1920-64]

Mammadov, F. QADINLAR KOMMUNIZMIN FAAL QURUJULARIDIR. METODIK VASAIT VA ADABIYYAT SIYAHISI. Baku: (Azarb. SSR Madaniyyat Nazirl. M. F. Akhundov Ad. Azarb. Resp. Kitabkhanasi. Elmi-Metodik Kitabkhanashunasliq Shobasi, 1961, 27 pp.,2000 copies. [Azerb. text]

3 CAUCASUS

GENERAL

A. A. P. "NOVYE ZHURNALY NA KAVKAZE," KAVKAZSKII KNIZHNYI VIESTNIK, No. 2, 1900. [Russ. text; titles pp. 13-16]

*A.Th.S. "TERSKAIA OBLAST'," ENTSIKLOPEDICHESKII SLOVAR', Vol. 33, St. Petersburg: F. A. Brokgauz, I. A. Efron, 1901, pp. 82-90. [Russ. text; Russ, Europ. titles, p.90]

Aliev, U. A. "KNIGOIZDATEL'SKOE DELO NA NATSIONAL'NYKH IAZYKAKH SEVERNOGO KAVKAZA," ZAPISKI GORSKOGO KRAEVOGO NAUCHNO-ISSLEDOVATEL'SKOGO INSTITUTA, Vol. 1, 1928. [Russ. text; Sov. Asian titles, pub. 1925-28, pp. 236-243]

Arkhangelov, N. A. "BIBLIOGRAFICHESKII UKAZATEL' LITERATURY O KUBANSKOI OBLASTI, KUBANSKOM KAZACH'EM VOISKE I CHERNOMORSKOM OKRUGE IZ STAVROPOL'SKOI GAZETY 'SEVERNYI KAVKAZ' ZA PERVOE DESIATILETIE (1884-1893) EE IZDANIIA," TRUDY STAVROPOL'SKOI UCHENOI ARKHIVNOI KOMISSII (PRILOZHENIE), No. 2, 1910, 78 pp. [Russ. text; 1494 titles, pub. 1884-93]

BIBLIOGRAFICHESKIE EZHEGODNIKI. Rostov N/D: (Severokavkazs'kaia Kraev. B-ka im. Karla Marksa), No. 1, 1932. [Russ. text]

Bibliofil [Gorodetskii, B. M.] "KAVKAZ V RUSSKIKH ZHURNALAKH," NA KAVKAZIE, No. 6, 1909. [Russ. text; 37 titles, pub. 1880-1909, pp. 212-14]

"BIBLIOGRAFICHESKIE ZAMIETKI O STAT'IAKH, OTNOSIASHCHIKHSIA DO KAVKAZA," KAVKAZ, Nos. 42, 43, 51/52, 56, 58, 1867. [Russ. text]

BIBLIOGRAFICHESKII UKAZATEL' STAT'IAM, POMESHCHENNYM V GAZETE "KAVKAZ" ZA 1872 GOD. Tiflis: Tipografiia Chantseva i Ko., 1874, 41 +2 +3 pp. [Russ. text; titles pub. 1872]

BIBLIOGRAFIIA SEVERNOGO KAVKAZA. UKAZATEL' KNIG I ZHURNAL'NYKH STATEI O SEVEROKAVKAZSKOM KRAIE ZA 1931 G. Rostov N/D: Knigoizdatel'stvo "Severnyi Kavkaz" (Sev.-Kavk. Kraev. B-ka im. K. Marksa. Bibliograficheskii Ezhegodnik; Vypusk 1), 1932, 79 +5 pp., 500 copies. [Russ. text; titles pub. 1931]

Biegichev, K. N. OB IASNITEL'NYI KATALOG BIBLIOTEKI E. I. V. VELIKAGO KNIAZIA GEORGIIA ALEKSANDROVICHA V ABASTUMANIE KAVKAZ I SOSIEDNIIA S NIM STRANY. Tiflis, 1894. [Russ. text; 500 titles]

Caucasus: General

Dmitrenko, I. I. KHRONOLOGICHESKII UKAZATEL' 'KUBANSKIKH OBLASTNYKH VIEDOMOSTEI' (1863-1898 GG.)," IZVIESTIIA OBSHCHESTVA LIUBITELEI IZUCHENIIA KUBANSKOI OBLASTI, No. 2, 1900. [Russ. text; titles pub. 1863-8 (survey not completed), pp. 235-49]

Dzagurov, G. A. "UKAZATEL' STATEI PO KAVKAZOVEDENIIU, POMESHCHENNYKH V GAZETE TERSKIE VIEDOMOSTI (S 1883 PO 1916 GOD)," IZVESTIIA GORSKOGO INSTITUTA NARODNOGO OBRAZOVANIIA, No. 1, 1923. [Russ. text; titles pub. 1883-1916, pp. 78-95]

Eritsov, A. D. "KRATKII OBZOR RABOT RUSSKIKH UCHENYKH PO KAVKAZOVEDENIIU ZA 1885 GOD," KAVKAZ, No. 176, 1886. [Russ. text; Russ. titles, pub. 1885, pp. 1-2]

_____. "NACHALO PERIODICHESKOI LITERATURY NA KAVKAZIE," KAVKAZ, No. 133, 1879. [Russ. text, titles]

*"GAZETY I ZHURNALY, IZDAVAVSHIES'IA NA KAVKAZIE," KAVKAZSKII KALENDAR' NA 1885 G.: NA 1886 G.; NA 1887 G.: NA 1888 G.; NA 1892 G.; NA 1893 G.; NA 1895 G.; NA 1896 G.; NA 1897 G.; NA 1899 G.; NA 1900 G.; NA 1901 G.; NA 1902 G.; NA 1903 G.; NA 1904 G.; NA 1905 G. 1885-1905. [Russ. text; Azerb., Russ., Persian, Tatar, Arab, Armenian, Georgian titles, pub. 1885-1905. (1885) pp. 283-5; (1886) pp. 184-6; (1887) pp. 238-9; (1888) pp. 143-4; (1892) p. 39; (1893) p. 155; (1895) p. 112; (1896) p. 308; (1897) p. 106; (1899) p. 88; (1900) pp. 75-6; (1901) pp. 99-100; (1902) pp. 70-1; (1903) pp. 103-4; (1904) pp. 96-7; (1905) pp. 98-9] [NNC has 1896]

*Genko, A. "KAVKAZOVEDENIE," BOL'SHAIA SOVETSKAIA ENTSIKLOPEDIIA. Moscow: Gosudarstvennyi Institut "Sovetskaia Entsiklopediia," Vol. 30, 1937 (1st ed.), pp. 481-3. [Russ. text; Russ. titles p. 483]

*Gizetti, A., comp. "SODERZHANIE PERVYKH VOSEMNADTSATI [DEVIATNADTSATYI] TOMOV 'KAVKAZSKAGO SBORNIKA,'" KAVKAZSKII SBORNIK, Vol. 19, 20, 1898-1899. [Russ. text; titles pub. 1876-95. 19 (supplement) pp. 1-5; 20, pp.1-5]

* _____. "UKAZATEL' STATEI PERVYKH TOMOV KAVKAZSK. SBORNIKA," KAVKAZSKII SBORNIK, Vol. 19, 1898, p. 463 + (53). [Russ. text; ca.80 Russ. titles, per. 17-18th cent. pp. (1-5)]

Gorodetskii, B. ISTORIK I IZSLEDOVATEL' KUBANSKAGO KRAIA (PO POVODU SOROKALETIIA NAUCHNOLITERATURNOI DEIATEL'NOSTI F. A. SHCHERBINY), I. V. [IZVIESTIIA

Caucasus: General

VOSTOCHNAGO FAKUL'TETA AZERBAIDZHANSKAGO GOSUDARSTVENNAGO UNIVERSITETA...], No. 3, 1913. [Russ. text; titles pp. 1025-33]

_____. "LITERATURA NA KAVKAZIE V 1910 GODU," KUBANSKII KUR'ER, Nos. 677, 678, 680. 1911. [Russ. text; Russ. titles pub. 1910, (No. 677), p. 5; (No. 678), pp. 2-3; (No. 680), p. 3]

Gorodetskii, B. M. "BIBLIOGRAFICHESKAIA LITERATURA O KAVKAZE," SEVERO-KAVKAZSKII KRAI. (BIBLIOGRAFIIA-BIBLIOGRAFII), No. 2, 1927. [Russ. text; 167 bibl., pp. 128-37]

_____. "BIBLIOGRAFICHESKII OBZOR LITERATURY O SEVERNOM KAVKAZIE ZA 1906-1907 GG.," IZVIESTIIA OBSHCHESTVA LIUBITELEI IZUCHENIIA KUBANSKOI OBLASTI, No. 4 [Also publ. separately at Ekaterinodar, 43 pp.]. [Russ. text; pub. 1906-7, pp. 93-135]

_____. "GDE PISALOS' O KAVKAZSKOM ZEMSTVE," NA KAVKAZIE, No. 4, 1909. [Russ. text; titles pp. 527-8]

_____. MATERIALY DLIA BIBLIOGRAFII SEVERNAGO KAVKAZA. IZVIESTIIA OBSHCHESTVA LIUBITELEI IZUCHENIIA KUBANSKOI OBLASTI, No. 4--BIBLIOGRAFICHESKII OBZOR LITERATURY O SEVERNOM KAVKAZIE ZA 1906-1907 GG. 1909 [Also separate offprint, 1909]. [Russ. text; 538 Russ. titles, pub. 1906-7, pp. 93-135 (43)]

_____. NASH KRAI. ISTOCHNIKI DLIA IZUCHENIIA KUBANI I CHERNOMOR'IA, No. 1, Krasnodar: Tip. im. Limanskogo Iuvkraiizdata "Burevestnik," 1924, 132 pp. [Russ. text; 219 titles]

_____. "OBZOR LITERATURY O SEVERNOM KAVKAZIE ZA 1906-1908 G.," KUBANSKII KUR'ER, nos. 24, 25, 26. 1908. [Russ. text; titles pub. 1906-8, (No. 24) pp. 3-4; (No. 25), p. 3; (No. 26) p. 3]

_____. PERIODIKA KUBANO-CHERNOMORSKOGO KRAIA. 1863-1925. Krasnodar: Obshchestvo Liubitelei Izucheniia Kubanskogo Kraia, 1927, 72 pp. [Russ. text; 347 Sov. Asian, Russ. titles pub. 1863-1925]

"IZDANIIA PRAVITEL'STVENNYKH UCHREZHDENII I UCHENYKH OBSHCHESTV NA KAVKAZIE, VYSHEDSHIIA V 1891 I 1892 G.G. S PEREIMENOVANIEM VSIEKH SOCHINENII, VOSHEDSHIKH V ETI IZDANIIA," KAVKAZSKII KALENDAR' NA 1893. 1892. [Russ. text; titles pub. 1891-2, pp. 57-63]

K. F. "UKAZATEL' NEKOTORYKH BIBLIOGRAFICHESKIKH ISTOCHNIKOV O SEVERO-KAVKAZSKOM KRAE," SOVETSKOE KRAEVEDENIE NA SEVERNOM KAVKAZE--SBORNIK KRAEVEDCHESKIKH

Caucasus: General

MATERIALOV. Rost.-na-Donu Knigoizdatel'stvo "Severnyi Kavkaz," 1932, 91 pp., 600 copies. [Russ. text; 26 Russ. titles, pp. 83-4]

KAVKAZ. SPRAVOCHNAIA KNIGA STAROZHILA. No. 5. "RUSSKAIA LITERATURA O KAVKAZIE: TUZEMNAIA LITERATURA: TEATR." (Tiflis), 1888. [Russ. text]

KAVKAZSKII KNIZHNYI VIESTNIK. Tiflis: K. N. Begichev, 1900. [Russ. text]

Kazbek, G. N. "INOSTRANNYE ZHURNALY O KAVKAZIE," KAVKAZ, Nos. 59-63, 1868. [Russ. text; Europ. titles]

*Khoruev, Iu. 109 GOLOSOV. SPRAVOCHNIK PERIODICHESKIKH IZDANII NA TEREKE (1863-1917 GG.). Ordzhonikidze: Severo-Osetinskoe Knizhnoe Izdatel'stvo, 1966, 127 pp., 3500 copies. [Russ. text; 109 Osset, Russ. titles, pub. 1863-1917, pp. 13-111]

"KNIGI I BROSHIURY IZDANNYE V TIFLISIE S 1862 G. PO 1868 G." SBORNIK STATISTICHESKIKH SVEDENII O KAVKAZIE, Vol. 1, Part 2. (Tiflis): (Kavkazskii Otdiel Russkago Geograficheskago Obshchestva), 1869. [Russ. text, titles pp. 165-73]

"KNIGI O KAVKAZ.," BIBLIOGR. VIESTN. T-VA 'V. A. BERZOVSKII,' No. 244, 1918. [Russ. text; titles pp.22-3]

Kobianov, D. A. UKAZATEL' GEOGRAF., ISTOR., STATIST., I ETNOGRAF. MATER'IALA, ZAKLIUCHAIUSHCHEGOSIA V STAVROPOL'SKIKH GUBERNSKIKH VIEDOMOSTIAKH ZA 1850-55 GG. Izviestiia Kavkazskago Otdiela Imperatorskago Russkago Geograficheskago Obshchestva 4-5 (v Prilozhenii) [Russ. text; titles pub. 1850-55]

*Kompanskii, K. A. "BIBLIOGRAFICHESKII UKAZATEL' KNIG I STATEI, OTNOSIASHCHIKHSIA DO KAVKAZA I ZAKAVKAZSKAGO KRAIA," [KAVKAZSKII KALENDAR' NA 18...]. (Tiflis), 1866 (Vol. 22); 1867, No. 2; 1868. (1867) 407 pp. [Russ. text; (1867) 369 Russ. titles, (1868) 47 Russ. titles; pub. 1863-66 in Tiflis. (1867) pp. 231-55, (1868) pp. 476-479, NNC has 1867]

Kompanskii, K. A. BIBLIOGRAFICHESKII UKAZATEL' KNIG I STATEI OTNOSIASHCH. DO KAVK. I ZAKAVK. KRAIA, K XXI-XXX VYP. SBORNIK MATERIALOV DLIA OPISANIIA MESTN. I PLEMEN KAVKAZA. Tiflis, 1883-1909. [Russ. text]

Kozubskii, E. I. K ISTOCHNIKOVEDENIIU KAVKAZA. KAVKAZ, Nos. 225, 227, 1893. [Russ. text, titles pub. 1893, (No. 225) p. 3, (No. 227) p. 3]

_____. "MATERIALY DLIA BIBLIOGRAFICHESKAGO KAVKAZOVEDENIIA," IZVIESTIIA KAVKAZSKAGO OTDIELA

Caucasus: General

RUSSKAGO GEOGRAFICHESKAGO OBSHCHESTVA, Vol. XVI, No. 4. [Russ. text; titles pp. 68-72]

*"KRATKII PERECHEN' GAZET I ZHURNALOV, VYKHODIVSHIKH NA KAVKAZIE S 1870 PO 1889 G., S PEREIMENOVANIEM REDAKTOROV IKH I S POKAZANIEM VREMENI VOZNIKNOVENIIA GAZET I KOLICHESTVA PECHATAVSHIKHSIA NOMEROV I EKZEMPLIAROV ETIKH IZDANII," KAVKAZSKII KALENDAR' NA 1891 GOD, Part I, 1890. [Russ. text; Azerb., Russ., Armen., Georgian, French titles, pub. 1870-89, pp. 239-54]

*KRATKII· SPISOK GAZET I ZHURNALOV, VYKHODIVSHIKH NA KAVKAZE S 1870 PO 1889 GG.... KAVKAZSKII KALENDAR', Vol. 46, 1891, 261 pp. [Russ. text; 56 Cauc., Russ. titles, pp. 239-54]

L. M.-B. "PERIODICHESKIE IZDANIIA SPETSIAL'NO OBSLUZHIVAIUSHCHIE KAVKAZOVEDENIE," IZVIESTIIA ODESSKAGO BIOBIBLIOGRAFICHESKAGO OBSHCHESTVA, Vol. 4, No. 1, 1915. [Russ. text; Russ., Europ. titles, pp. 16-17]

"LITERATURNYE NOVOSTI," NA KAVKAZIE, No. 6, 1909; No. 7/8, 1910. [Russ. text, titles, (1909) pp. 216-17; (1910) pp. 363-4]

*Miansarov, M. M., comp. BIBLIOGRAPHIA CAUCASICA ET TRANSCAUCASICA. OPYT SPRAVOCHNAGO SISTEMATICHESKAGO KATALOGA PECHATNYM SOCHINENIIAM O KAVKAZIE, ZAKAVKAZ'IE I PLEMENAKH, ETI KRAIA NASELIAIUSHCHIKH, Vol. 1, Part 2. St. Petersburg: Tipografii O. I. Baksta i Gogenfel'den i Komp., 1874-76; 1967 (2nd ed), 804 pp. [Russ. text; 4840 Russ., Armen., Europ. titles]

"NAZVANIIA GLAVNEISHIKH KNIG I BROSHIUR, RAZRESHENNYKH KAVKAZSKIM TSENZURNYM KOMITETOM V 1896 I 1897 (PO IIUN') G.," KAVKAZSKII KALENDAR' NA 1898 G., Part 2, [1898]. [Russ. text; Cauc., Russ., Europ. titles, pp. 125-30]

"O SODERZHANII KAVKAZSK. KALENDARIA NA 1846-69 GG.," KAVKAZSKII KALENDAR', 1893. [Russ. text; titles pub. 1846-69]

"OBZOR IZDANII O KAVKAZIE V 1899 G.," KAVKAZSKII KNIZHNYI VIESTNIK 1-3. 1900. [Russ. text; titles pub. 1899, (No. 2) pp. 16-21; (No. 3) pp. 12-23]

"OBZOR IZDANII PO KAVKAZOVEDENIIU, NAPECHATANNYKH NE NA KAVKAZIE, ZA 1-OE POLUGODIE 1899 G.," KAVKAZSKII KNIZHNYI VIESTNIK, Nos. 1-3. 1900. [Russ. text; titles pub. 1899-1900, (No. 1) pp. 23-8; (No. 2) pp. 25-7; (No. 3) pp. 12-24]

Caucasus: General

*"OBZOR STATEI, POMESHCHENNYKH V GAZETE 'KAVKAZ,'" KAVKAZ, No. 48, Nov. 26; No. 49, Dec. 3; No. 50, Dec. 10; No. 51, Dec. 17; No. 52, Dec. 24, 1849. [Russ. text; survey Russ. titles pub. 1846-49. (No. 48) pp.190-1; (No. 49) pp.195-6; (No. 50) pp.199-200; (No. 51) pp.202-3; (No. 52) pp.206-8]

"PERECHEN' NOVEISHIKH KNIG, BROSHIUR, NAUCHNYKH STATEI I RAZLICHNYKH ZAMIETOK O KAVKAZIE," KAVKAZSKII KALENDAR' NA 1898 G. [1898] [Russ. text; titles pub. 1898, pp. 65-95]

"PERECHEN' PECHATNYKH TRUDOV E. D. FELITSINA," IZVIESTIIA OBSHCHESTVA LIUBITELEI IZUCHENIIA KUBANSKOI OBLASTI, No. 1, 1899. [Russ. text; 38 Russ. titles pub. 1879-98, pp. 139-42]

PERIODICHESKAIA PECHAT' NA KAVKAZIE. Tiflis: Elektropechatnia Gruz. Izd. T-va, 1901, 52 pp. [Russ. text; titles p. 51]

"PERIODICHESKIE IZDANIIA I GAZETY, VYSHEDSHIE NA KAVKAZIE V 1891 G.," KAVKAZSKII KALENDAR' NA 1893 G. [1893] [Russ. text; Georg., Armen., Russ., French titles, pub. 1891, pp. 56-7]

"PERIODICHESKIE IZDANIIA V TIFLISIE S 1856 G. PO 1869 G. NA RUSSKOM, ARMIANSKOM I GRUZINSKOM IAZYKAKH," SBORNIK STATISTICHESKIKH SVEDENII O KAVKAZIE, IZD. KAVKAZSKIM OTDIELOM RUSSKAGO GEOGRAFICHESKAGO OBSHCHESTVA, Vol. 1. Tiflis, 1869. [Russ. text; Armen., Georg., Russ. titles pub. 1856-69, pp. 161-4]

*Politovskii, V. N. "SISTEMATICHESKII UKAZATEL' NAIBOLIEE VYDAIUSHCHIKHSIA STATEI I ZAMIETOK, POMIESHCHENNYKH V GAZETIE 'KAVKAZ' ZA VSIE 50 LIET IZDANIIA (S 1844 PO 1895 G.)," KAVKAZSKII KALENDAR' NA 1896 GOD [Others, more detailed, in 1893, 1894, 1895], 1895. [Russ. text; Russ. titles pub. 1844-95, pp. 49-100]

Potskhverdov, D. UKAZATEL' K XXXI-XL VYPUSKAM "SBORNIKA MATERIALOV DLIA OPISANIIA MESTNOSTEI I PLEMEN KAVKAZA." Tiflis: Tip. Kantseliarii Namiestnika Ego I. V. Na Kavkazie, 1910, 66 pp. [Russ. text; titles pub. 1902-9]

*Pul'ner, I. M. "MATERIALY DLIA BIBLIOGRAFII BIBLIOGRAFII KAVKAZA," SOVETSKAIA ETNOGRAFIIA, No. 4/5, 1936, 303 pp. 2500 copies. [Russ. text; 297 Russ. titles pub. 19-20th cent., pp. 230-70]

Semenov, L. P. GOSUDARSTVENNYI NAUCHNYI MUZEI GORODA VLADIKAVKAZA PRI SEVERO-KAVKAZSKOM INSTITUTE KRAEVEDENIIA. Vladikavkaz: Sev.-Kavkazskii Institut Kraevedeniia, 1925. [Russ. text; titles pp.16-18, 20]

Caucasus: General

Shamrai, V. S. "PERECHEN' PECHATNYKH TRUDOV E. D. FELITSINA," IZVIESTIIA KAVKAZSKAGO OTDIELA IMPERATORSKAGO RUSSKAGO GEOGRAFICHESKAGO OBSHCHESTVA, Vol. 19, 1909. [Russ. text; 102 Russ. titles, pp.82-8]

──────────. SPISOK STATEI I VYDAIUSHCHIKHSIA ZAMIETOK POMIESHCHENNYKH V IZDANIIAKH KAVKAZSKIKH UCHENYKH [ZAVEDENII] OBSHCHESTV, RAZNYKH PRAVITEL'STV. UCHREZHDENII NA KAVKAZIE I V GAZETAKH, IZDAVAVSHIKHSIA V ZAKAVKAZ'E, ZA VSE VREMIA IKH DIEIATEL'NOSTI PO 1891 G. KAVKAZSKII KALENDAR' 1892, 1893. [Russ. text; titles pub. 1846-91]

"SISTEMATICHESKII SPISOK GLAVNEISHIKH STATEI NAPECHATANYKH V 'TERSKIKH VIEDOMOSTIAKH' V PERIOD 1869-1892 G.G.," TERSKII SBORNIK, No. 3, Book 2, 1893. [Russ. text; 235 Russ. titles pub. 1869-92, pp. 174-83]

Sokolov, L. T. "PERECHEN' TRUDOV KUBANSKAGO OBLASTNAGO STATISTICHESKAGO KOMITETA, IZDANNYKH OSOBYMI SBORNIKAMI," KUBANSKII SBORNIK, Vol. 14, 1909. [Russ. text; titles pub. 1875-81, pp. 491-9]

Sollogub, V. A. "OB ISTOCHNIKAKH DLIA POZNANIIA KAVKAZA," KAVKAZ, Nos. 48-49, 1852. [Russ. text, titles. (No.48) pp. 203-5, (No. 49) pp. 206-9]

"SPISOK BOLEE VYDAIUSHCHIKHSIA STATEI I ZAMIETOK, POMESHCHENNYKH V 'KAVKAZSKOM KALENDARE' ZA VSIE 50 LET EGO IZDANIIA, S 1846 G. PO 1895 G.," KAVKAZSKII KALENDAR NA 1895 G. [Russ. text, titles pub. 1846-95, pp. 102-11]

SPISOK GLAVNYKH STATEI I ZAMIETOK, POMESHCHENNYKH V 'KAVKAZSKOM KALENDARE' ZA VSIE 64 GODA EGO IZDANIIA (S 1846 PO 1910 GG), KAVKAZSKII KALENDAR' NA 1910 G. [Russ. text; titles pub. 1846-1910, pp. 923-8]

"SPISOK GLAVNYKH STATEI I ZAMIETOK, POMESHCHENNYKH V 'KAVKAZSKOM KALENDARE' ZA VSE 63 GODA EGO IZDANIIA S 1846 PO 1909 GG.," KAVKAZSKII KALENDAR' NA 1910 G. [Russ. text; titles pub. 1846-1909]

"SPISOK KNIG I BROSHIUR, VYSHEDSHIKH V 1891 [I 1892 GG.] NA KAVKAZIE," KAVKAZSKII KALENDAR' NA 1893 G. [Russ. text; Azerb., Arm., Georg., Russ., Pers., French titles pub. 1891-2, pp. 42-50]

"SPISOK KNIG I STATEI, VYSHEDSHIKH OTDEL'NYMI IZDANIIAMI V 1892 G. NA KAVKAZIE (PO 6-E NOIABRIA VKLIUCHITEL'NO)," KAVKAZSKII KALENDAR' NA 1893 G. [Russ. text; Azerb., Russ., Pers., Europ. titles pub. 1892, pp. 50-6]

Caucasus: General

"SPISOK NAI BOLEE VYDAIUSHCHIKHSIA STATEI I ZAMIETOK, POMIESHCHENNYKH V "KAVKAZSKOM KALENDARE" ZA VSIE 50 LET EGO IZDANIIA, (S 1846 PO 1895 GG)," KAVKAZSKII KALENDAR' NA 1895 G. 1894. [Russ. text, titles, pub. 1846-95]

SPISOK STATEI I VYDAIUSHCHIKHSIA ZAMIETOK POMESHCHENNYKH V GAZETIE 'KAVKAZ' ZA 1852-1860 GG. KAVKAZSKII KALENDAR' 1894, 1895. [Russ. text; titles pub. 1852-60]

SPISOK STATEI I ZAMIETOK, POMESHCHENNYKH V GAZETIE 'KAVKAZIE' ZA 1852-57 G. KAVKAZSKII KALENDAR', 1894. [Russ. text; titles pub. 1857-7]

"SPISOK STATEI I ZAMIETOK, VOSHEDSHIKH V 'KAVKAZSKII KALENDAR' NA 1846-1869 G.," KAVKAZSKII KALENDAR' NA 1893. 1892. [Russ. text; titles pub. 1846-1869]

"SPISOK STATEI I ZAMIETOK, VOSHEDSHIKH V GAZETU 'KAVKAZ' ZA 1846-1857 G.," KAVKAZSKII KALENDAR' NA 1893 I 1894 G.G. 1892, 1893. [Russ. text; titles pub. 1846-57]

"SPISOK VYDAIUSHCHIKHSIA STATEI I ZAMIETOK, POMESHCH. V GAZ. 'KAVKAZ' ZA VREMIA S 1846 PO 1851 G.," KAVKAZSKII KALENDAR'. 1893. [Russ. text; titles pub. 1846-51]

Starozhil. RUSSKAIA LITERATURA O KAVKAZIE. SPRAVOCHNAIA KNIGA STAROZHILA (No. 5. PRILOZHENIE). Kavkaz: (Tiflis Tip. L. G. Kramarenko), 1888. [Russ. text, titles, pp. 241-72]

"STAT'I I ZAMIETKI, POMESHCHENNYE V IZDANIIAKH KAVKAZSKAGO OTDIELA IMPERATORSKAGO RUSSKAGO GEOGRAFICHESKAGO OBSHCHESTVA S 1892 PO 1897 G.," KAVKAZSKII KALENDAR' NA 1898 G. [Russ. text; titles pub. 1892-7, pp. 122-5]

"STAT'I, POMESHCHENNYE V SBORNIKE MATERIALOV DLIA OPISANIIA MESTNOSTEI I PLEMEN KAVKAZA (VYPUSKI XX-XXIII)," KAVKAZSKII KALENDAR' NA 1898 G. [Russ. text; titles pp. 96-9]

Sutugin, A. P. BIBLIOGRAFIIA BASSEINA OZERA GOKCHI (SEVANA). Leningrad: Akademiia Nauk (Materialy Komissii Ekspeditsionnykh Issledovanii, Vyp. 3), 1928, 81 pp. [Russ. text; 119 titles]

*"SVEDENIIA O PERIODICHESKIKH IZDANIIAKH, VYKHODIVSHIKH V TIFLISIE I DRUGIKH GORODAKH KAVKAZKAGO I ZAKAVKAZSKAGO KRAIA," KAVKAZSKII KALENDAR' NA 1867-1868, 1871, 1872, 1873, 1875, 1876, 1877, 1878, 1879-1882, 1886-1889, 1891, 1893, 1895, 1898, 1902, 1905, 1910, 1912-1916.(1873) 279 pp. [Russ. text; (1873) 22 Azerb., Armen., Georg.,

Caucasus: General

Russ. titles pub. 1863-1916 (1873: pub. 1872). (1867)
pp.255-7; (1871) pp.375-7; (1872) p.83; (1873) pp.
224-5; (1875) pp.284-6; (1876) pp.65-6; (1877) pp.271-
2; (1878) pp.306-7; (1879) pp.168-9; (1880) pp.176-7;
(1881) pp.216-17; (1882) pp.308-10; NNC has 1873]

Tokarev, G. "OB ISTOCHNIKAKH SVIEDIENII O KAVKAZIE,"
KAVKAZ. Nos. 27, 28, 1847; Nos. 5, 6, 24-26, 35, 36,
1848. [Russ. text; titles: No.27, pp.107-8; No.28,
pp.111-12; No.5, pp.19-20; No.6, pp.23-24; No.24, pp.94-
6; No.25, pp.98-100; No.26, pp.102-4; No.35, pp.138-40;
No.36, pp.143-4]

"UKAZATEL' STATEI O KAVKAZIE," ZAPISKI KAVK. OTD.
GEOGR. OBSHCH., Vol. 9, 1875. [Russ. text]

"UKAZATEL' VSIEKH STATEI I ZAMIETOK, POMIESHCHENNYKH V
ZAPISKAKH I IZVIESTIIAKH KAVKAZSKAGO OTDIELA RUSSKAGO
GEOGRAFICHESKAGO OBSHCHESTVA S NACHALA IKH IZDANIIA PO
1892-01 GOD," KAVKAZSKII KALENDAR' NA 1893 G. 1892.
[Russ. text; titles pub. up to 1892, pp. 1-89]

Veidenbaum, E. G. "MATERIALY DLIA BIBLIOGRAFII KAVKAZA,"
KAVKAZSKII KNIZHNYI VIESTNIK (PRILOZHENIE), No. 2, No.3,
1900; No.4, 1901. [Russ. text; 77 titles; No. 2, pp.
1-16; No.3, pp.17-32; No.4, pp.33-40]

Vezirov. "MUSUL'MANSKAIA LITERATURA V TIFLISIE,"
NOVOE OBOZRENIE (GAZETA), No. 4003. 1895. [Russ. text]

Vorob'ev, N. I. UKAZATEL' SOCHINENII O CHERNOMORSKOM
POBEREZH' I KAVKAZA (ANAPA-TURETSKAIA GRANITSA), No. 1.
Petrograd: Tip. Sirius, 1915, xiv +244 pp. [Russ. text]

Voronov, N. I. "'KAVKAZSKII KALENDAR' ZA 1863-1866
GODY," ZAPISKI KAVKAZSKAGO OTDIELA RUSSKAGO
GEOGRAFICHESKAGO OBSHCHESTVA, Vol. 7, Part 2. 1866.
[Russ. text, titles, pub. 1863-66, pp. 78-97]

"VYDAIUSHCHIESIA STAT'I, ZAMIETKI, POMESHCHENNYE V
GAZETIE 'KAVKAZ' V 1895, 1896 I 1897 (PO IIUL')
GODAKH," KAVKAZSKII KALENDAR' NA 1898 G. Part 2.
[Russ. text, titles pub. 1895-97]

"VYDAIUSHCHIESIA STAT'I I ZAMIETKI, POMESHCHENNYE V
GAZETIE 'NOVOE OBOZRENIE' S 1886 PO 1896 G." KAVKAZSKII
KALENDAR' NA 1898 G. Part 2. [Russ. text, titles
pub. 1886-96, pp. 99-118]

Zagurskii, L. P. "KRATKII SPISOK KNIGAM, STAT'IAM I
IZDANIIAM, OTNOSIASHCHIMSIA K KAVKAZOVIEDIENIIU,"
KAVKAZSKII KALENDAR' NA 1890, 1889; KAVKAZSKII

Caucasus: General

KALENDAR' NA 1891, 1890, (NA 1890 G.) 48 pp. [Russ. text; 211 Russ. titles pub. 1890-91]

Z-skii [Zagurskii, L.] "KRATKII SPISOK KNIGAM, STAT'IAM I IZDANIIAM, OTNOSIASHCHIMSIA K KAVKAZOVIEDIENIIU," VES' KAVKAZ (SBORNIK), No. 1. Tiflis, 1903. [Russ. text, titles, pp. 1-20]

ANTHROPOLOGY, ETHNOGRAPHY

*Aristova, T. "ANNOTIROVANNYI SPISOK LITERATURY PO ETNOGRAFII ZAKAVKAZ'IA, OPUBLIKOVANNOI V 1964 GODU," SOVETSKAIA ETNOGRAFIIA, No. 2. 1966. [Russ. text; 87 Azerb., Georg., Armen., Russ. titles pub. 1964, pp. 168-77]

* _____. "ANNOTIROVANNYI SPISOK LITERATURY PO ETNOGRAFII ZAKAVKAZ'IA, OPUBLIKOVANNOI V 1962 G.," SOVETSKAIA ETNOGRAFIIA, No. 6. 1963, 182 pp., 1910 copies. [Russ. text; 47 Armen., Georg., Russ. titles, pub. 1962, pp. 168-72]

* _____. "ANNOTIROVANNYI SPISOK LITERATURY PO ETNOGRAFII ZAKAVKAZIIA, OPUBLIKOVANNOI V 1963 GODU," SOVETSKAIA ETNOGRAFIIA, No. 6. 1964. [Russ. text; 64 Azerb., Armen., Georg., Russ. titles pub. 1963, pp. 182-8]

Beliaev. "BIBLIOGRAFIIA PO ETNOGRAFII I LINGVISTIKE KAVKAZA," KUL'TURA I PIS'MENNOST' GORSKIKH NARODOV SEVERNOGO KAVKAZA. Rostov, 1931. [Russ. text; titles pp. 71-145]

*Berzhe, A. P., comp. "ETNOGRAFICHESKOE OBOZRENIE KAVKAZA," TRUDY TRET'AGO MEZHDUNARODNAGO S'IEZDA ORIENTALISTOV V S. PETERBURG. 1876, Vol. 1. 1879-1880, pp. 291-326. [Russ. text; 41 +54 + Russ., Europ. titles pub. 1876, pp. 312-26]

*Gardanov, B. A., et al, ed. NARODY KAVKAZA, Vol. 2. Moscow: Izdatel'stvo Akademii Nauk SSSR, 1962, 682 pp., 5000 copies. [Russ. text; ca.400 Cauc., Russ. titles pub. 19-20th cent., pp. 621-36]

Gorodetskii, B. M., ed. "BIBLIOGRAFIIA KUBANSKOGO KRAIA. SISTEMATICHESKII UKAZATEL' LITERATURY O

KUBANSKOI OBLASTI S RETSENZIIAMI I REFERATAMI," TRUDY SOVETA OBSLEDOVANIIA I IZUCHENIIA KUBANSKOGO KRAIA, Vol. 1, Nos. 1-4. 1918-1919, viii + 192 pp., 2000 copies. [Russ. text]

*"IZDANIIA UPRAVLENIIA KAVKAZSKAGO UCHEBNAGO OKRUGA," SBORNIK MATERIALOV DLIA OPISANIIA MIESTNOSTEI I PLEMEN KAVKAZA, Nos. 22, 28. Tiflis, 1897, 1900. [Russ. text, titles pub. 1890-96, 1895-1900. No.22 Supplement I-VI; No.28 pp. 49-52]

*Kagarov, E. G. "INOSTRANNAIA LITERATURA PO ETNOGRAFII KAVKAZA ZA POSLEDNIE 10 LET," SOVETSKAIA ETNOGRAFIIA, No. 4/5. 1936, pp. 274-7. [Russ. text; 36 Europ. titles per. 1924-34, pp. 274-5]

*Kamenetskaia, R. V., comp. "NOVAIA LITERATURA PO NARODAM KAVKAZA," SOVETSKAIA ETNOGRAFIIA, No. 3. 1967. [Russ. text; Azerb., Armen., Georg., Russ. titles pub. 1965-6, pp. 183-8]

* _____ "NOVAIA LITERATURA PO NARODAM KAVKAZA," SOVETSKAIA ETNOGRAFIIA, no. 4. 1968. [Russ. text; ca.200 Azerb., Armen., Kalmyk, Balkar, Georg., Ingush, Kabardian, Abkhaz, Russ., Greek titles, pub. 1965-67, pp. 176-83]

*Khakhanov, A. S. "KAVKAZSKAIA BIBLIOGRAFIIA. UKAZATEL' ETNOGRAFICHESKIKH STATEI I ZAMIETOK V KAVKAZSKIKH IZDANIIAKH OT NACHALA IKH SUSHCHESTVOVANIIA," ETNOGRAFICHESKOE OBOZRENIE. 1892, Nos. 2-3; 1893, Nos. 1,4; 1894, Nos. 1-2; 1895, Nos. 1, 4; 1896, No. 4; 1899, Nos. 1-2; 1900, Nos. 2,4. [Russ. text, titles pub. 19th cent. (1892:2,3) pp.84-95; (1893:1) pp.210-14; (1893:4) pp.240-5; (1894:1) pp.21-6; (1894:2) pp.27-8; (1895:4) pp.193-4; (1896:4) pp.197-8; (1899:1/2) pp. 375-9; (1900:2) pp.184-5; (1900:4) pp.157-8: NNC lacks 1894 (I)]

_____ "NESKOL'KO SLOV O KNIGAKH, KASAIUSHCHIKHSIA NARODNOSTEI KAVKAZA," NOVOE OBOZRENIE. 1890. [Russ. text; titles pp. 31-41]

* _____, comp. "UKAZATEL' ETNOGRAFICHESKIKH STATEI I ZAMIETOK V KAVKAZSKIKH IZDANIIAKH OT NACHALA IKH SUSHCHESTVOVANIIA. KAVKAZ," ETNOGRAFICHESKOE OBOZRENIE No. 2/3, 1892; No. 1, 1893. [Russ. text, titles. No. 2/3 pub. 1846-1853; No. 1 pub. up to 1892. No. 2/3, pp. 84-95; No. 1, pp. 210-15]

*Kosven, M. "MATERIALY PO ISTORII ETNOGRAFICHESKOGO IZUCHENIIA KAVKAZA V RUSSKOI NAUKE," KAVKAZSKII ETNOGRAFICHESKII SBORNIK, No. 1. Moscow: Izd-vo AN SSSR, 1955, 374 pp., 2000 copies. [Russ. text, titles,

Caucasus: Anthropology, Ethnography

per. up to 1850's, pp. 265-374]

*Kosven, M. O.   "MATERIALY PO ISTORII ETNOGRAFICHESKOGO IZUCHENIIA KAVKAZA V RUSSKOI NAUKE," KAVKAZSKII ETNOGRAFICHESKII SBORNIK, No. 3. Moscow-Leningrad: (Trudy In-ta Etnografii im. Miklukho-Maklaia, Vol. 79), 1962, 288 pp., 1500 copies. [Russ. text, titles per. 1880-1917, pp. 158-288]

* _____, L. I. Lavrova, G. A. Nersesova, Kh. O. Khashaeva, eds.   NARODY KAVKAZA. Vol. 1. Moscow: Izdatel'stvo Akademii Nauk SSSR, 1960, 611 pp., 5000 copies. [Russ. text; ca.340 Russ., Europ. titles, pp. 565-74]

Kozubskii, E., comp.   UKAZATEL' K I-XX VYPUSKAM "SBORNIKOV [SBORNIKA] MATERIALOV DLIA OPISANIIA MIESTNOSTEI I PLEMEN KAVKAZA" (1881-1894 G.). Tiflis: Tip. K. Kozlovskago, 1895, 2 + ii + 177 pp. [Russ. text, titles pub. 1881-94]

Kozubskii, E. I., [D. Potskhverdov].   UKAZATEL' K 1-20 [21-40] VYPUSKAM "SBORNIK MATERIALOV DLIA OPISANIIA MIESTNOSTEI I PLEMEN KAVKAZA" 1881-1894 G. [1895-1902 G.; 1903-1909 G.]. Tiflis, 1895, 1902, 1910, 177 pp. (1895), 60 pp. (1902).[Russ. text, titles pub. 1881-1909]

Liaister, A. F.   "PROF. G. F. CHURSIN. NEKROLOG I SPISOK TRUDOV," SOVETSKAIA ETNOGRAFIIA, No. 3/4. 1931, pp. 193-5. [Russ. text; 99 titles]

*Nadezhdin, P. P.   KAVKAZSKII KRAI: PRIRODA I LIUDI. Tula: Tipografiia Vlad. Mk. Sokolova. 1901 (3rd ed.), 521 pp. [Russ. text; Russ., Europ. titles pub. 1839-1898, pp. 487-96]

*"NOVAIA LITERATURA PO NARODAM KAVKAZA," SOVETSKAIA ETNOGRAFIIA, No. 6, 1969. [Russ. text; ca.200 Azerb., Abkhaz, Georg., Adygei, Armen., Uzbek, Russ., Greek titles pub. 1966-69, pp. 173-80]

Semenov, Leonid P.   "OBZOR RUSSKOI ETNOGRAFICHESKOI LITERATURY O KAVKAZE ZA 1917-1927 GG.," ETNOGRAFIIA. 1928, No. 2 (6); 1929, No. 1 (7). [Russ. text, titles pub. 1917-27, (1928) pp. 125-32; (1929) pp. 141-64]

"TRUDY PO ETNOGRAFII I GEOGRAFII KAVKAZA (POIAVIVSHIESIA V 1879 G.)," IZVIESTIIA KAVKAZSKAGO OTDIELA RUSSKAGO GEOGRAFICHESKAGO OBSHCHESTVA, Vol. 6. [Russ. text, titles pub. 1879, pp. 104-14]

Caucasus: Anthropology, Ethnography

Veidenbaum, E. G. "KAVKAZSKIE AMAZONKI. MATERIALY DLIA DREVNEI ETNOGRAFII KAVKAZA," ZNANIE, Vol. 8, Nos. 9, 10. 1847. [Russ. text; per. ancient, pp. 245-98]

ARCHITECTURE, ART, MUSIC

KAVKAZSKAIA MUZYKA. BIBLIOGRAFICHESKIE ZAMIETKI. Tiflis, 1900. [Russ. text]

ECONOMICS

*"BAKINSKIE NEFTIANNYE PROMYSLY," ENTSIKLOPEDICHESKII SLOVAR', Vol. 2A, St. Petersburg: F. A. Brokgauz, I. A. Efron, 1891, pp. 773-4. [Russ. text, titles, p. 774]

Ivanov, A. "OBZOR IZSLEDOVANII NEFTENOSNYKH RAIONOV KAVKAZA, PROIZVEDENNYKH GEOLOGICHESKIM KOMITETOM V 1901-1905 G.," NEFTIANOE DIELO, No. 13, 14 (Baku), 1907. [Russ. text; per. 1901-1909, pp. 955, 1015]

*Konstantinov, O. A., comp. EKONOMICHESKAIA GEOGRAFIIA SSSR PO RAIONAM. SEVERNYI KAVKAZ (SEVERO-KAVKAZSKII KRAI I DAGESTAN), Moscow-Leningrad: Gosudarstvennoe Izdatel'stvo, 1928; 1930 (2nd ed.), (1928) 148 pp. (1928) 4000 copies. [Russ. text; (1928) 145, (1930) 158 Russ. titles, (1928) pp. 142-7, (1930) pp.152-8]

"KRATKII OBZOR LITERATURNYKH ISTOCHNIKOV, KASAIUSHCHIKHSIA POLOZHENIIA KUSTARNOI PROMYSHLENNOSTI NA KAVKAZIE," TRUDY PERVAGO S"EZDA DEIATELEI PO KUSTARNOI PROMYSHLENNOSTI KAVKAZA V G. TIFLISIE V 1902 G. Tiflis: Tip. Kants. Glavnonach. Gr. Ch. Na Kavkazie, 1902. [Russ. text; 32 titles, per. 1902, pp. 165-84]

Caucasus: Economics

"KRATKII UKAZATEL'. PEREDOVYIA STAT'I O ZHELIEZNYKH
DOROGAKH S KAVKAZA V PERSIIU," IZVIESTIIA KAVKAZSKAGO
RUSSKAGO GEOGRAFICHESKAGO OBSHCHESTVA, Vol. 1 (Tiflis)
1872-3. [Russ. text; pub. 1872]

Kumykov, T. Kh. VOVLECHENIE SEVERNOGO KAVKAZA VO
VSEROSSIISKII RYNOK V XIX V. Nal'chik, 1962. [Russ.
text; titles per. 19th cent., pp. 8-15]

Mezhov, V. "TRUDY TSENTRAL'N. I GUBERNSKIKH STATISTICH.
KOMIT. BIBLIOGRAF. UKAZATEL' KNIG I ZALIUCHAIUSHCHIKHSIA
V NIKH STATEI, OBNIMAIUSHCHII DEIATEL'NOST' STATIST.
KOMITETOV SAMOGO NACHALA IKH UCHREZHDENII VPLOT'
DO 1873 G. IZVESTIIA IMPERATORSKAGO RUSSKAGO
GEOGRAFICHESKAGO OBSHCHESTVA, 1873, No. 3. [Russ.
text; titles per. up to 1873]

PERECHEN' STATEI, OCHERKOV I OBZOROV POMESHCHENNYKH V
'EKONOMICHESKOM VESTNIKE ZAKAVKAZ'IA' ZA 1927 GOD.
Tiflis: Tip.-Lit. KKA, 1928. [Russ. text; 10 serials
cont. pub. 1927, pp. 1-6, 12]

*"PERECHEN' STATEI, POMESHCHENNYKH V PIATI TOMAKH 'SVOD
MATERIALOV BYTA GOSUDARSTVENNYKH KREST'IAN ZAKAVKAZSKAGO
KRAIA'," SVOD MATERIALOV PO IZUCHENIIU EKONOMICHESKAGO
BYTA GOSUDARSTVENNYKH KREST'IAN ZAKAVKAZSKAGO KRAIA,
Vol. 5. Tiflis: Tipografii: A. A. Mikhel'sona;
Rotin'iantsa; Libermana, 1888, 347 pp. [Russ. text,
titles pp. 339-47]

Popov, Sergei. OPYT SISTEMATICHESKAGO UKAZATELIA
LITERATURNYKH DANNYKH PO KAVKAZSKIM MIN. VODAM. St.
Petersburg, 1889. [Russ. text]

"UKAZATEL' STATEI POMESHCHENNYKH V TOMAKH I-XII TRUDOV I
I-VI IZVESTII KAVKAZSK. SHELKOVODSTVEN. STANTSII,"
IZVESTIIA KAVK. SHELKOV. STANTS., Vol. 7, No. 2.
[Russ. text]

Voronov, N. I. "OBZOR STATISTICHESKIKH TRUDOV NA
KAVKAZIE ZA POSLEDNIE 25-LETIE," SBORNIK SVEDENII O
KAVKAZIE, Vol. 1. Tiflis, 1869. [Russ. text; titles
pub. 1844-68]

Caucasus

EDUCATION

"SODERZHANIE ZHURNALA 'VOPROSY PROSVESHCHENIIA NA SEVERNOM KAVKAZE' ZA 1926, 1927, 1928 I 1929 GODY," VOPROSY PROSVESHCHENIIA NA SEVERNOM KAVKAZE, No. 12, No. 12/13, No. 20, No. 19/20. 1926, 1927, 1928, 1929. [Russ. text; Russ. titles pub. 1926-29, (1926) pp. 92-5; (1927) pp. 81-7; (1928) pp. 56-64; (1929) pp. 87-96]

UKAZATEL' IZDANII KAVKAZSKAGO UCHEBNAGO OKRUGA. Tiflis: Izd. Kavk. Uch. Okr. 1912 (2nd ed., supplemented), 1913,(3rd ed.), 1914,(4th ed.) 3rd. ed. 16 pp., 4th ed., 16 pp. [Russ. text]

UKAZATEL' SODERZHANIIA K SBORNIKAM RASPORIAZHENII PO KAVKAZSKOMU UCHEBNOMU OKRUGU. Vols. 1-5. 1867-81. [Russ. text]

"'VOPROSY PROVESHCHENIIA NA SEVERNOM KAVKAZE'. SODERZHANIE ZHURNALA 'VOPROSY PROSV. NA SEV. KAVKAZE' ZA 1926 GOD.'," VOPROSY PROSVESHCHENIIA NA SEVERNOM KAVKAZE, No. 12, 1926. [Russ. text; titles pub. 1926, pp. 92-5]

GEOGRAPHY

*Ardzhevanidze, I. A. VOENNO-GRUZINSKAIA DOROGA (KRAEVEDCHESKII OCHERK S PRILOZHENIEM SKHEMAT. KARTY MARSHRUTA I BIBLIOGRAFII), Tbilisi: Kombinat Pechati Glavpoligrafizdata Ministerstva Kul'tury Gruzinskoi SSR, 1954, 250 pp., 10,000 copies. [Russ. text; Georgian, Russ. titles, pp. 234-49]

Arsenin, V., N. Bondarev, E. Sergievskii. GORNYE PUTESHESTVIIA PO ZAPADNOMU KAVKAZU. Moscow: "Fizkul'tura i Sport," 1968, 152 pp., 25,000 copies. [Russ. text; titles at end of book]

"BIBLIOGRAFICHESKII UKAZATEL' VYSHEDSHIKH V 1861 I 1862 GODAKH KNIG I STATEI, KASAIUSHCHIKHSIA GEOGRAFII I ISTORII KAVKAZA," ZAPISKI KAVKAZSKAGO OTDIELA IMPERATORSKAGO RUSSKAGO GEOGRAFICHESKAGO OBSHCHESTVA, Book 6, Part 3, 1864. [Russ. text; titles pub. 1861-62, pp. 79-132]

"BIBLIOGRAFICHESKII UKAZATEL' PO GEOGRAFII I ISTORII KAVKAZA ZA 1852 GODA," ZAPISKI KAVKAZSK. OTDIEL. GEOGR. OBSHCH. Vol. 2, 1853. [Russ. text; titles pub. 1852]

Caucasus: Geography

Biegichev, K. N. "KRATKII OBZOR GEOGRAFICHESKIKH TRUDOV RUSSKIKH IZSLEDOVATELEI KAVKAZA KONTSA 18-GO STOLIETIIA," KAVKAZSKII KNIZHNYI VIESTNIK, No. 2, 3. 1900. [Russ. text; titles pub. late 18th cent., (No. 2) pp. 9-13; (No. 3) pp. 8-11]

_____. "KRATKII OBZOR GEOGRAFICHESKIKH TRUDOV RUSSKIKH IZSLEDOVATELEI KAVKAZA 1-OI POLOVINY XIX STOLIETIIA," KAVKAZ, No. 262, No. 264, 1901. [Russ. text; titles pub. 1800-1850, serials cont., (No. 262) p. 3, (No. 264) p. 2]

Demchenko, M. A. "K ISTORII FIZIKO-GEOGRAFICHESKIKH I OSOBENNO GLIATSIOLOGICHESKIKH ISSLEDOVANII BOL'SHOGO KAVKAZA," UCHENYE ZAPISKI (KHAR'K. UN-T.), Vol. 81; TRUDY GEOGR. FAK., Vol. 3. 1957. [Russ. text; ca.462 titles pp. 270-84]

*Dobrynin, B. "KAVKAZ," BOL'SHAIA SOVETSKAIA ENTSIKLOPEDIIA, Vol. 30. Moscow: Gosudarstvennyi Institut "Sovetskaia Entsiklopediia" (OGIZ RSFSR),1937, 1st ed. pp.451-81. [Russ. text; Russ., Europ. titles, pp. 480-1]

"GEOGRAFICHESKAIA LITERATURA KAVKAZA, AZIATSKOI TURTSII I IRANA PO DANNYM BIBLIOTEKI KAVKAZSKAGO OTDIELA IMPERATORSKAGO RUSSKAGO GEOGRAFICHESKAGO OBSHCHESTVA. Vol. 13, Supplement to Nos. 1-3, 5. Vol. 14, Supplement to No. 3. 1900-1901. [Russ. text; titles pub. 1900, (XIII, No. 2) pp. 9-17; (No. 3) pp. 19-31; (No. 5) pp. 33-40; (XIV, No. 3) pp. 41-53]

*GEOGRAFIIA KHOZIAISTVA RESPUBLIK ZAKAVKAZ'IA. Moscow: Izdatel'stvo "Nauka," 1966, 283 pp., 1700 copies. [Russ. text, titles, pp. 278-81]

*Gerasimov, I. P., ed. KAVKAZ. PRIRODNYE USLOVIIA I ESTESTVENNYE RESURSY SSSR. Moscow: Izdatel'stvo "Nauka," 1966, 482 pp., 2200 copies. [Russ. text, titles, pp. 446-70]

"GIMRY (GUMRY)," VOENNAIA ENTSIKLOPEDIIA, Vol. 8. Petersburg: T-vo I. D. Sytina, 1912, 321 pp. [Russ. text, titles, p. 321]

Gren, A. "BIBLIOGRAFICHESKII SPISOK KART, KARTIN, SOCHINENII I STATEI, OTNOSIASHCHIKHSIA K TERSKOI OBLASTI," TERSKII SBORNIK, No. 2, Book 2, Part 8. (Vladikavaz), 1892. [Russ. text; 451 titles pub. up to 1891, pp. 1-28]

*Gvozdetskii, N. A. FIZICHESKAIA GEOGRAFIIA KAVKAZA. KURS LEKTSII. No. 1, OBSHCHAIA CHAST'. No. 2, BOL'SHOI KAVKAZ PREDKAVKAZ'E; ZAKAVKAZ'E. Moscow:

Caucasus: Geography

Izdatel'stvo Moskovskogo Universiteta. No. 1, 1954.
No. 2, 1958. I: 208 pp., 8000 copies. II: 264 pp.,
4000 copies. [Russ. text, titles. I: pp. 202-5;
II: pp. 257-62]

*Kalesnik, S. V. SEVERNYI KAVKAZ I NIZHNII DON. FIZIKO-
GEOGRAFICHESKAIA KHARAKTERISTIKA. Moscow-Leningrad:
Izdatel'stvo Akademii Nauk SSSR, 1946, 131 pp., 5000
copies. [Russ. text, titles, p. 123]

*KAVKAZ. Moscow: Izdatel'stvo "Nauka," 1966, 481 pp.,
2200 copies. [Russ. text, titles, pp. 446-70]

KAVKAZ. PERVOE POLUGODIE 1874 G. (NOS. 1-74). IZVESTIIA
KAVKAZSKAGO OTDIELA IMPERATORSKAGO RUSSKAGO
GEOGRAFICHESKAGO OBSHCHESTVA, No. 3. [Russ. text;
titles pub. 1874, pp. 101-10]

Kazbek, G. "BIBLIOGRAFIIA SOCHINENII O KAVKAZIE.
ITAL'IANTSY O KAVKAZIE. RELIATSII PUTESHESTVENNIKOV,
S XI PO XVII V.," KAVKAZ, Nos. 4, 6, 35, 36, 40, 41, 42,
54, 1867; No. 72, 1868. [Russ. text; Europ. titles,
per. 11-17th cent. 1867: (No. 4) pp. 25-6; (No. 6) pp.
35-6; (No. 35) pp. 201-2; (No. 36) pp. 207-8; (No. 40)
p. 230; (No. 41) pp. 235-6; (No. 42) pp. 241-2; (No. 54)
pp. 311-12. 1868 (No. 72) p. 3]

_____. "ZHURNALY 'NOUVELLES ANNALES DES VOYAGES,
DE LA GEOGRAPHIE, DE L'HISTOIRE ET DE L'ARCHEOLOGIE'
I 'JOURNAL ASIATIQUE' O KAVKAZIE," KAVKAZ, Nos. 59, 61,
63, 1868. [Russ. text; Fre. titles, (No. 59) p. 3;
(No. 61) pp. 3-4; (No. 63) p. 3]

Kharitonov, A. "BIBLIOGRAFIIA. UKAZATEL' KNIG I
ZHURNAL'NYKH STATEI O KAVKAZIE, GEOGRAFICHESKAGO
STATISTICHESKAGO I ETNOGRAFICHESKAGO SODERZHANIIA ZA
1852 G.," ZAPISKI KAVKAZSKAGO OTDIELA IMPERATORSKAGO
RUSSKAGO GEOGRAFICHESKAGO OBSHCHESTVA, Vol. 2, 1853.
[Russ. text, titles pub. 1852, pp. 170-87]

Liaister, A. F. "UKAZATEL' LITERATURY O PRIRODE KAVKAZA
ZA 1912 G.," LIUBIT.TIFLISSKOGO O-VA LIUBIT. PRIRODY,
No. 1, 1913. [Russ. text; titles pub. 1912, pp. 84-90]

*Merkulov, V. A., comp. PUTEVODITEL' PO GORAM KAVKAZA.
St. Petersburg: Izdanie Krymsko-Kavkazskago Gornago
Kluba, 1904, 32 pp. [Russ. text; 77 Russ. titles +
maps, pp. 26-31]

Pagirev, D. D. "PERECHEN' NIEKOTORYKH KNIG, STATEI I
ZAMIETOK O KAVKAZIE," ZAPISKI KAVKASKAGO OTDIELA IMP.
RUSSKAGO GEOGR. O-VA. [Also separate publication in
D. D. Pagirev, ALFAVITNYI UKAZATEL' PIATIVERSTNOI KARTE

Caucasus: Geography

KAVKAZSKAGO KRAIA, published in Tiflis, 1913 by
Kavkazskii Voenno-Tipograficheskii Otdiel.] Vol. 30
(PRILOZHENIE). Tiflis, 1913. [Russ. text; 8000 titles,
pp. 309-530]

_____. "UKAZATEL' STATEI I ZAMIETOK POMESHCHENNYKH
V IZDANIIAKH KAVKAZSKAGO OTDIELA IMPERATORSKAGO RUSSKAGO
GEOGRAFICHESKAGO OBSHCHESTVA ZA VREMIA S 1852 PO 1906-OI
GOD, VKLIUCHITEL'NO," IZVIESTIIA KAVKAZSKAGO OTDIELA
IMPERATORSKAGO RUSSKAGO GEOGRAFICHESKAGO OBSHCHESTVA
Vol. 19, No. 3 (PRILOZHENIE), Tbilisi, 1908, 51 pp.
[Russ. text; 1273 titles pub. 1852-1906, pp. 1-37]

"UKAZATEL' GEOGRAFICHESKAGO MATERIALA,
ZAKLIUCHAIUSHCHAGOSIA V KAVKAZSKIKH PERIODICHESKIKH
IZDANIIAKH ZA 1871 GOD," IZVIESTIIA KAVKAZSKAGO OTDIELA
IMPERATORSKAGO RUSSKAGO GEOGRAFICHESKAGO OBSHCHESTVA.
Vol. I (PRIBAVLENIE). Tiflis, 1872-73. [Russ. text;
titles pub. 1871]

*Vilenkin, V. L. PO TSENTRAL'NOMU KAVKAZU I ZAPADNOMU
ZAKAVKAZ'IU. PUTEVYE ZAMETKI I NABLIUDENIIA. Moscow:
Geografgiz, 1966, 263 pp. [Russ. text; 58 Russ. titles
pub. 20th cent., pp. 260-2]

Viskovatov, A. A. "OBZOR GEOGRAFICHESKIKH RABOT NA
KAVKAZIE V 1863 G.," ZAPISKI KAVKAZSKAGO OTDIELA
IMPERATORSKAGO RUSSKAGO OBSHCHESTVA. Vol. 6, Part 5.
1864. [Russ. text; titles pub.: 1863, pp. 97-122]

Voronov, N. I. "KRITIKO-BIBLIOGRAFICHESKII OBZOR
GEOGRAFICHESKO-STATISTICHESKAGO MATERIALA
NAKOPIVSHEGOSIA V GAZETIE KAVKAZ V 1863-1865 GODAKH,"
ZAPISKI KAVKAZSKAGO OTDIELA IMP. RUSSKAGO
GEOGRAFICHESKAGO OBSHCHESTVA, Vol. 7, Part 2. 1866.
[Russ. text; titles pub. 1863-65, pp. 1-78]

*Zanina, A. A. KAVKAZ. KLIMAT SSSR, No. 2. Leningrad:
Gidrometeorologicheskoe Izdatel'stvo, 1961, 290 pp.,
1000 copies. [Russ. text, titles, pp. 220-2]

Zeidlits, N. K. UKAZATEL' GEOGRAFICHESKAGO, ISTOR.,
STATIS., I ETNOGRAF., MATERIALA, ZAKLIUCHAIUSHCHAGOSIA
V KUBANSKIKH VIEDOMOSTIAKH (ZA GG. 1863-1874). IZVESTIIA
KAVKAZSKAGO OTDIELA IMPERATORSKAGO RUSSKAGO
GEOGRAFICHESKAGO OBSHCHESTVA. Vol. 3 (PRILOZHENIE).
Tiflis, 1874-1875. 113 +9, 68 +6 pp. [Russ. text,
titles pub. 1863.]

HISTORY, ARCHAEOLOGY

Alekseeva, E. P. "POZDNE-KOBANSKAIA KUL'TURA TSENTRAL'NOGO KAVKAZA," UCHENYE ZAPISKI LENINGR. GOS. UN-T IM. ZHDANOVA. No. 85--SERIIA IST. NAUK, No. 13, 1949. [Russ. text; 70 Russ., Europ. titles pub. 1879-1941, pp. 254-257]

[Bentkovskii, I. V.] "BIBLIOGRAFICHESKII UKAZATEL' ISTORIKO-STATISTICHESKIKH MATERIALOV I STATEI I. V. BENTKOVSKOGO," KUBANSKII SBORNIK, Vol. 1. Ekaterinodar, 1910. [Russ. text; 80 titles pp. 79-86]

Beriketov, Kh. G. ISTORICHESKAIA NAUKA NA SEVERNOM KAVKAZE (1959-1963 GG.). Nal'chik: Kabard.-Balkar. Kn. Izd., 1964, 58 pp., 1000 copies. [Russ. text; titles pub. 1959-63]

Berzhe, Adol'f P., D. A. Kobiakov, Evgenii G. Veidenbaum. "KAVKAZSKIE DEIATELI NA GRAZHDANSKOM I VOENNOM POPRISHCHAKH: BIOGRAFICHESKIE SVIEDENIIA," AKTY, SOBRANNYE KAVKAZSKOIU ARKHEOGRAFICHESKOIU KOMMISSIEIU (TIFLIS), Vols. 6, 8, 9, 10, 11, 12. 1874-1904. [Russ. text]

BIBLIOGRAFICHESKII UKAZATEL' KNIG I STATEI, OTNOSIASHCHIKHSIA K STATISTIKE, ISTORII I ETNOGRAFII SEVERNOGO KAVKAZA. SBORNIK STATISTICHESKIKH SVEDENII O STAVROPOL'SKOI GUBERNII, No. 3. Stavropol', 1870. [Russ. text; titles pub. 1728-1816]

"BIBLIOGRAFICHESKII UKAZATEL' KNIG, SOCHINENII I STATEI OTNOSIASHCHIKHSIA K STATISTIKIE, ISTORII I [ETNOGRAFII] GEOGRAFII SIEVERNAGO KAVKAZA," SBORNIK STATISTICHESKIKH SVIEDENII O STAVROPOL'SKOI GUBERNII, Vol. 3. Stavropol', 1870. [Russ. text; 399 titles publ. 1850-1869, pp. 119-150]

"BIBLIOGRAFIIA VOENNYKH DIESTVII NA KAVKAZIE, POIAVLIAVSHIKHSIA V 'VOENNOM SBORNIKIE' 1859-1862 GG. S PRILOZHENIEM SODERZHANIIA I NIEKOTORYMI ZAMIETKAMI," VOENNYI SBORNIK, No. 2, 1863. [Russ. text; titles pub. 1859-62, serials cont., pp. 497-519]

*Butkov, P. G. MATERIALY DLIA NOVOI ISTORII KAVKAZA S 1722 PO 1803 GOD. Part 3. St. Petersburg: Tipografiia Imperatorskoi Akademii Nauk, 1869, 620 pp. [Russ. text; Russ., Europ. titles per. 1722-1803, pp. ix-xxx]

*Degen-Kovalevskii, B. E. "OBZOR LITERATURY PO ETNOGRAFII I ARKHEOLOGII KAVKAZA ZA TRI GODA, 1933-1936," SOVETSKAIA ETNOGRAFIIA, No. 4/5. 1936, 303 pp., 2500 copies. [Russ. text; 153 Russ., Europ. titles pub. 1933-36, pp. 277-303]

Caucasus: History, Archaeology

Egoriev, V., M. Svechnikov, M. Lifshits. "BAKU,"
SOVETSKAIA VOENNAIA ENTSIKLOPEDIIA, Vol. 2. Moscow:
Gosudarstvennoe Slovarno-Entsiklopedicheskoe
Izdatel'stvo "Sovetskaia Entsiklopediia" OGIZ RSFSR,
1933, pp. 102-5. [Russ. text, titles, p. 105]

*"ERMOLOV, ALEKSEI PETROVICH," VOENNAIA ENTSIKLOPEDIIA,
Vol. 10. Peterburg: T-vo I. D. Sytina, 1912, pp. 341-7.
[Russ. text, titles, p. 347]

*Fadeev, A. V. ROSSIIA I KAVKAZ PERVOI TRETI XIX V.
N.P.: Izdatel'stvo Akademii Nauk SSSR, 1960, 398 pp.,
2500 copies. [Russ. text; Russ., Europ. titles, per.
early 19th cent., pp. 375-8]

*Felitsin, E. D., V. S. Shamrai [Shamrai alone, from Vol.
XIV]. "BIBLIOGRAFICHESKII UKAZATEL' LITERATURY O
KUBANSKOI OBLASTI, KUBANSKOM KAZACH'EM VOISKIE I
CHERNOMORSKOI GUBERNII," KUBANSKII SBORNIK, Vols. 5,
6, 10, 14, 15, 19. Ekaterinodar: Tipografiia Kubanskago
Oblastago Pravleniia, 1899-1914. (Vol. 6) 217 pp.,
(Vol. 15) 663 pp. [Russ. text; (Vol. 6) 1168 Russ.
titles; (Vol. 15) 544 Russ. titles. (Vol. 6) pp. 121-217;
(Prilozhenie K...15) pp. 554-585); NNC has 6, 15]

*Genko, A. "KAVKAZOVEDENIE," BOL'SHAIA SOVETSKAIA
ENTSIKLOPEDIIA, Vol. 30. Moscow: Gosudarstvennyi
Institut "Sovetskaia Entsiklopediia" (OGIZ RSFSR), 1937,
pp. 481-3. [Russ. text; Russ., Europ. titles p. 483]

Gizetti, A. BIBLIOGRAFICHESKII UKAZATEL' PECHATNYM NA
RUSSKOM IAZYKIE SOCHINENIIAM I STAT'IAM O VOENNYKH
DEISTVIAKH RUSSKIKH VOISK NA KAVKAZIE. St. Petersburg:
Ekonomicheskaia Tip.-Litografiia, 1901, vi + 250 pp.
[Russ. text; 1319 Russ. titles]

_____. UKAZATEL' LITERATURY O VOENNYKH DEISTVIIAKH
RUSSKIKH VOISK NA KAVKAZIE. St. Petersburg, 1900.
[Russ. text]

Golovenchenko, F., ed. 1917 GOD V STAVROPOL'SKOI GUBERNII.
Stavropol': Istpartotdel Okrkoma VKP(B) i Iubileinoi
Komissii, 1927, 102 pp. [Russ. text; titles per. 1917,
at end of book]

* _____, F. Emel'ianov. GRAZHDANSKAIA VOINA V
STAVROPOL'SKOI GUBERNII (1918-1920 G.G.) ISTORICHESKII
OCHERK. Stavropol': Stavropol'skaia Okruzhnaia
Oktiabr'skaia Komissiia i Istpart Okrkoma VKP(B), 1928,
226 pp., 3000 copies. [Russ. text; 28, incl. archives,
Russ. titles, per. 1918-20, p. 225]

Caucasus: History, Archaeology

*I. O. KAVKAZSKIIA VOINY," ENTSIKLOPEDICHESKII SLOVAR',
Vol. 13A. St. Petersburg: F. A. Brokgauz, I. A. Efron,
1894, pp. 854-62. [Russ. text; titles p. 862]

*Ibragimbeili, Kh. M. STRANITSY ISTORII BOEVOGO
SODRUZHESTVA RUSSKOGO I KAVKAZSKIKH NARODOV (1853-1856
GG.). Baku: Azerb. Gos. Iz-vo, 1970, 233 pp., 4100
copies. [Russ. text; ca.180 Georg., Arm., Russ.,
Turk., Europ. titles, per.: 1853-56; pub. 1854-1969,
pp. 218-24]

Ismailov, I. Z. LENINSKAIA TEORIIA NEKAPITALISTICHESKOGO
RAZVITIIA I NARODNOSTI KAVKAZA. Baku: Azerneshr, 1968,
166 pp., 2500 copies. [Russ. text; titles pp. 27-45]

*"KAVKAZ," EVREISKAIA ENTSIKLOPEDIIA, Vol. 9.
St. Petersburg: Izdanie Obshchestva dlia Nauchnykh
Evreiskikh Izdanii i Izdatel'stva Brokgauz-Efron, n.d.
pp. 61-7. [Russ. text; Tat., Russ., Europ. titles
pp. 66-67]

*KAVKAZ: (VNUTRENNIAIA ZHIZN' K-KH EVREEV," EVREISKAIA
ENTSIKLOPEDIIA, Vol. 9. St. Petersburg: Izdanie
Obshchestva dlia Nauchnykh Evreiskikh Izdanii i
Izdatel'stva Brokgauz-Efron, n.d., pp. 67-72. [Russ.
text: Tat.. Russ.. Hebrew titles. pp. 71-72]

KAVKAZSKAIA STARINA. EZHEMESIACH. ZHURNAL, No. 1-2, 1872;
No. 3-8, 1873. (Tiflis). [Russ. text]

"KAVKAZSKAIA VOINA," VOENNAIA ENTSIKLOPEDIIA, Vol. 11.
Peterburg: T-vo I. D. Sytina, 1913, pp. 220-42. [Russ.
text, titles, pp. 241-2]

"KAVKAZSKII VOENNYI OKRUG," VOENNAIA ENTSIKLOPEDIIA, Vol.
11, Peterburg: T-vo I. D. Sytina, 1913, pp. 249-50.
[Russ. text, titles, p. 250]

*"KAZI-MULLA (MULLA-MAGOMET)," VOENNAIA ENTSIKLOPEDIIA, Vol.
11. Peterburg: T-vo I. D. Sytina, 1913, p. 298. [Russ.
text, titles, p. 298]

Khakhanov, A. S. "TRUDY," IMPERATORSKOE MOSKOVSKOE
ARKHEOLOGICHESKOE OBSHCHESTVO V PERVOE PIATIDESIATILETIE
EGO SUSHCHESTVOVANIIA (1864-1914), Vol. 2. Moscow,
1915. [Russ. text; titles per. 1864-1914, pp. 233-4]

[Korolenko, P. P.]. "[BIBLIOGRAFICHESKII OTDEL]. TRUDY
DEISTVITEL'NOGO CHLENA OBSHCHESTVA LIUBITELEI IZUCHENIIA
KUBANSKOI OBLASTI P. P. KOROLENKO," IZVIESTIIA
OBSHCHESTVA LIUBITELEI IZUCHENIIA KUBANSKOI OBLASTI, No.
1. 1879. [Russ. text; 21 Russ. titles, pp. 121-8]

Caucasus: History, Archeology

Korol'kov, I. V. BOR'BA ZA VLAST' SOVETOV NA SEVERNOM KAVKAZE. Chita, 1962. [Russ. text; ca.80 titles, per. Civil War, pp. 180-3]

*Kushnareva, K. Kh., T. N. Chubinishvili. "ISTORICHESKOE ZNACHENIE IUZHNOGO KAVKAZA V III TVSIACHIELETII DO N. E.," SOVETSKAIA ARKHEOLOGIIA, No. 3. 1963. [Russ. text; 59 Russ. titles, per. 3rd mil., B. C., pp. 23-4]

*Latyshev, V. V. "SCYTHICA ET CAUCASICA...IZVIESTIIA DREVNIKH PISATELEI GRECHESKIKH I LATINSKIKH O SKITHII I KAVKAZIE...," ZAPISKI IMPERATORSKAGO RUSSKAGO ARKHEOLOGICHESKAGO OBSHCHESTVA, Vol. 2. St. Petersburg: Akademiia Nauk, 1893-1906 and 1890 (Repr. 1947-1949 in VESTNIK DREVNEI ISTORII). [Russ. text; Russ., Greek, Latin titles per. ancient, scattered, 296 pp.]

Lifshits, M. "BAKINSKIE KOMISSARY," SOVETSKAIA VOENNAIA ENTSIKLOPEDIIA, Vol. 2. Moscow: Gosudarstvennoe Slovarno-Entsiklopedicheskoe Izdatel'stvo "Sovetskaia Entsiklopediia" OGIZ RSFSR, 1933, pp. 98-100. [Russ. text, titles, p. 100]

Lunin, B. V. "BIBLIOGRAFICHESKII UKAZATEL' LITERATURY PO ISTORII KUL'TURY SEVERNOGO KAVKAZA (S 1917 PO 1927 G. VKL.)," BIULLETEN' SEVERNO-KAVKAZSKOGO KRAEVEDCHESKOGO GORSKOGO NAUCHNO-ISSLEDOVATEL'SKOGO INSTITUTA KRAEVEDENIIA, No. 2/4. (Rostov N-D),1927, pp. 63-9. [Russ. text; 104 titles pub. 1917-27]

_____. "BIBLIOGRAFICHESKII UKAZATEL' STATEI, ZAMETOK I KORRESPONDENTSII PO VOPROSAM ARKHEOLOGII SEVERNOGO KAVKAZA, OPUBLIKOVANNYKH V GAZETAKH 'SOVETSKII IUG' I 'MOLOT' V 1926 I 1927 GG.," ZAPISKI SEVERO-KAVKAZSKOGO KRAEVOGO OBSHCHESTVA ISTORII ARKHEOLOGII I ETNOGRAFII. Vol. 3, Book 1, No. 3/4. 1927-28. [Russ. text; titles pub. 1926-27, pp. 78-89]

_____. "LITERATURNYE NOVINKI 1930 I 1931 GG. PO ARKHEOLOGII I ISTORII MATERIAL'NOI KUL'TURY SEVERNOGO KAVKAZA (BIBLIOGRAFICHESKII OBZOR)," SOVETSKOE KRAEVEDENIE NA SEVERNOM KAVKAZE. Rostov-na-Donu: Knigoizdatel'stvo "Severnyi Kavkaz," 1932. [Russ. text; survey Russ., Ukr. titles pub. 1930-31, pp. 84-7, 90]

*Manukian, R. A. REVOLIUTSIONNAIA RABOTA BOL'SHEVIKOV V KAVKAZSKOI ARMII (FEVR. 1917 G.-FEVR. 1918 G.). Erevan: "MITK," 1969, 272 pp., 2000 copies. [Armen. text; ca.100 Armen., Russ. titles, per. 1917-18, pp. 257-61]

Markovin, V. I. V USHCHEL'IAKH ARGUNA I FORTANGI. Moscow, 1965. [Russ. text; 40 titles, pp. 124-6]

Caucasus: History, Archaeology

*Melikian, G. S. OKTIABR'SKAIA REVOLIUTSIIA I
KAVKAZSKAIA ARMIIA. Erevan: "AIASTAN," 1970, 615 pp.,
3000 copies. [Armenian text; ca.200 Armenian, Russ.
titles, per. October Rev., pub. 1917-69, pp. 604-13]

*Mishchenko, F. "SARMATY, SAVROMATY," ENTSIKLOPEDICHESKII
SLOVAR', Vol. 28A. St. Petersburg: F. A. Brokgauz,
I. A. Efron, 1900, pp. 439-42. [Russ. text; Russ.,
Europ. titles, p. 442]

Mourier (J.). L'ARCHEOLOGIE AU CAUCASE. Tiflis:
Tip. Martirosiantsa, 1885, 44 pp. [French text]

*Polievktov, M. A. EVROPEISKIE PUTESHESTVENNIKI
XIII-XVIII VV. PO KAVKAZU. 2 vols. Tiflis:
(Akademiia Nauk SSSR. Nauchno-Issledovatel'skii
Institut Kavkazovedeniia Imeni Akademika N. Ia. Marra),
1935-1936, Vol. 1: 224 pp. Vol. 2: 153 pp. 1000
copies. [Russ. text; Russ., Europ. titles, per.
13-18th cent., Vol. 1, pp. 14-18] [NNC has Vol. 1]

*Shilling, E. "ZAKAVKAZSKAIA SOTSIALISTICHESKAIA
FEDERATIVNAIA SOVETSKAIA RESPUBLIKA"/ZSFSR/
BOL'SHAIA SOVETSKAIA ENTSIKLOPEDIIA, Vol. 26. Moscow:
Gosudarstvennoe Slovarno-Entsiklopedicheskoe
Izdatel'stvo "Sovetskaia Entsiklopediia"/OGIZ RSFSR/,
1933, pp. 31-34. [Russ. text, titles, p. 34]

Shimkevich, F. ISTORIOGRAFICHESKIE ZAPISKI O STRANAKH,
LEZHASHCHIKH MEZHDU MORIAMI CHERNYM I KASPIISKIM.
St. Petersburg, 1810. [Russ. text]

*"SPISOK NAUCHNYKH TRUDOV ANATOLIIA VSEVOLODOVICHA
FADEEVA," ISTORIIA SSSR, No. 6. 1965. [Russ. text;
100 Russ. titles, pub. 1930-65, pp. 230-32]

*Tokarev, G. "OB ISTOCHNIKAKH SVIEDIENII O KAVKAZIE
(STAT'IA BIBLIOGRAFICHESKAIA)," SBORNIK GAZETY KAVKAZ,
Vol. 2. Tiflis: O. I. Konstantinov, v Tipografii
Kantseliarii Namiestnika Kavkazskago, 1848, 244 pp.
[Russ. text; Greek, Latin titles, per. ancient, pp.
1-19]

*V. M. "KAVKAZSKII KRAI," ENTSIKLOPEDICHESKII SLOVAR',
Vol. 13A, St. Petersburg: F. A. Brokgauz, I. A. Efron,
1894, pp.818-49. [Russ. text; Russ., Europ. titles,
pp. 848-9]

"VLADIKAVKAZ," VOENNAIA ENTSIKLOPEDIIA, Vol. 6, St.
Petersburg: T-vo I. D. Sytina, 1912, pp. 427-8.
[Russ. text, titles, p. 428]

Caucasus

LANGUAGE, LITERATURE

Avaliani, S. V. "V. F. MILLER--KAVKAZOVED," IZVESTIIA ODESSKAGO BIBLIOGRAFICHESKAGO OBSHCHESTVA. Vol. 3, No. 2, 1914. [Russ. text; titles pub. 1881-1906, pp. 89-92]

*Bagrii, A. V. "NARODNAIA SLOVESNOST' KAVKAZA (MATERIALY DLIA BIBLIOGRAFICHESKOGO UKAZATELIA)," IZVESTIIA VOSTOCHNOGO FAKUL'TETA AZERBAIDZHANSKOGO GOSUDARSTVENNOGO UNIVERSITETA IMENI V. I. LENINA, Vol. 1 (PRILOZHENIE). (Baku), 1926, 500 copies. [Russ. text; 1439 local langs., Russ. titles, pp. 204-330]

Beliaev, M. V. "KAVKAZSKOE IAZYKOVEDENIE (BIBLIOGRAFICHESKII OBZOR)," SBORNIK. KUL'TURA I PIS'MENNOST' GORSKIKH NARODOV SEVERNOGO KAVKAZA. Vladikavkaz, 1930. [Russ. text; titles pp. 145-66]

*Bogdanov, Vl. "SPISOK UCHENYKH TRUDOV VSEVOLODA FEDOROVICHA MILLERA," ETNOGRAFICHESKOE OBOZRIENIE. No. 3/4, 1913, 1914. [Russ. text; 209 Russ. titles pub. 1871-1913, pp. xxix-xlii]

Dzagurov, G. A. "VS. MILLER, KAK SOBIRATEL' I ISSLEDOVATEL' PAMIATNIKOV NARODNOI SLOVESNOSTI KAVKAZSKIKH GORTSEV," IZVESTIIA SEVERO-KAVKAZSKOGO PEDAGOGICHESKOGO INSTITUTA. Vol. 2, 1924. [Russ. text; 14 titles pub. 1881-1902, p. 79]

Dzhaukian, G. B. VZAIMOOTNOSHENIE INDOEVROPEISKIKH KHYRRITSKO-URARTSKIKH I KAVKAZSKIKH IAZYKOV. Erevan, 1967. [Russ. text; 384 titles, pp. 195-214]

Gorodetskii, B. M. "BIOBIBLIOGRAFICHESKIE MATERIALY O SIEVERNOM KAVKAZE. LITERATURNYE DEIATELI SIEVERNAGO KAVKAZA," SIEVERO-KAVKAZSKII ALMANAKH NA 1908-1909 G.G. Ekaterinodar: Tip. "Osnova," 1908. [Russ. text; titles pp. 248-273]

_____. "MATERIALY DLIA BIBLIOGRAFII KAVKAZA. LITERATURNYE I OBSHCHESTVENNYE DEIATELI SEVERNAGO KAVKAZA," KUBAN. SBORNIK. Vol. 18 [separate offprint:] Ekaterinodar, 1913. [Russ. text]

*Kaloev, B. A. V. F. MILLER--KAVKAZOVED (ISSLEDOVANIE I MATERIALY). Ordzhonikidze: Severo-Osetinskoe Knizhnoe Izdatel'stvo, 1963, 198 pp., 2000 copies. [Russ. text; 66+ Russ., Europ. titles, pp. 192-6]

*Klimov, Georgii Andreevich. KAVKAZSKIE IAZYKI. Moscow: Izdatel'stvo "Nauka," 1965, 112 pp., 2700 copies.

Caucasus: Language, Literature

[Russ. text; Georg., Russ., Europ. titles pub. 1914-1964, pp. 109-12]

Kozubskii, E. I. "R. F. FON ERKERT I EGO SOCHINENIE: 'DIE SPRACHEN DES CAUCASISCHEN STAMMES,' MATERIALY DLIA BIBLIOGRAFII KAVKAZOVEDENIIA," IZVESTIIA KAVKAZSKAGO OTDIELA IMPERATORSKAGO RUSSKAGO GEOGRAFICHESKAGO OBSHCHESTVA, Vol. 16, No. 4. [Russ. text; titles pp.68-72]

Markov, A. V. "SPISOK UCHENYKH TRUDOV V. F. MILLERA, KASAIUSHCHIKHSIA KAVKAZA," IZVIESTIIA KAVKAZSKAGO OTDIELA IMPERATORSKAGO RUSSKAGO GEOGRAFICHESKAGO OBSHCHESTVA, Vol. 22, No. 2, 1913-1914. [Russ. text; 42 Russ. titles, pp. 179-81]

*"MILLER, VSEVOLOD FEODOROVICH," MATERIALY DLIA BIOGRAFICHESKAGO SLOVARIA DIESTVITEL'NYKH CHLENOV IMPERATORSKOI AKADEMII NAUK, Part 2. Petrograd: Tipografiia Rossiiskoi Akademii Nauk, 1917, pp. 34-43. [Russ. text; 194 Russ., Europ. titles pub. 1871-1913, pp. 37-43]

*Treskov, Ilia V. FOL'KLORNYE SVIAZI SEVERNOGO KAVKAZA. Nal'chik: Kabardino-Balkarskoe Knizhnoe Izdatel'stvo, 1963, 341 pp., 1000 copies. [Russ. text; Balkar, Osset., other nat. langs., Russ., Europ. titles, pp. 284-315]

*Vinogradov, V. V., ed.   IAZYKI NARODOV SSSR. Vol. 4. IBERIISKO-KAVKAZSKIE IAZYKI. Moscow: "Nauka," 1967, 712 pp., 6400 copies. [Russ. text; titles at end of chapters]

PHILOSOPHY, RELIGION

*"KAVKAZ," EVREISKAIA ENTSIKLOPEDIIA, Vol. 9. St. Petersburg: Izdanie Obshchestva Dlia Nauchnykh Evreiskikh Izdanii i Izdatel'stva Brokgauz-Efron, 1911, pp. 61-77. [Russ. text; Hebrew, Russ., Europ. titles, pp. 66-7]

Popov, I. "SISTEMATICHESKII UKAZATEL' SODERZHANIIA 'VLADIKAVKAZSKIKH EPARKHIAL'NYKH VIEDOMOSTEI' ZA SHEST' LET IKH IZDANIIA (1895-1900)," VLADIKAVKAZSKIE EPARKHIAL'NYE VIEDOMOSTI, No. 4 (PRILOZHENIE). 1901, 29 pp. [Russ. text, titles pub. 1895-1900]

Caucasus

POLITICAL SCIENCE, LAW

*Chaikin, K. I., ed.   UKAZY KUBINSKIKH KHANOV, KNIGA III,
SERIIA PAMIATI. Tbilisi: Izdatel'stvo Gruzinskogo
Filiala AnSSSR, 1937, 109 pp., 1000 copies. [Russ.
text; 36 Russ. titles per. 1705-1819, pp. 105-7]

Dubrovin, N.   ISTORIIA VOINY I VLADYCHESTVA RUSSKIKH
NA KAVKAZIE. Vol. 1.   OCHERK KAVKAZA I NARODOV,
EGO NASELIAIUSHCHIKH. Kn. 3.   BIBLIOGRAFICHESKII
UKAZATEL' ISTOCHNIKOV K PERVYM DVUM KNIGAM. St.
Petersburg: Tip. Departamenta Udelov, 1871/1886.
(1871) 2+ 1v + 451; (1886) 550 pp. [Russ. text;
2355 Russ. titles pub. 19th cent.]

[Ermolov, A.]   BIBLIOGRAFICHESKII UKAZATEL' SOCHINENII,
ZHURNAL'NYKH STATEI I ZAMIETOK OB A. P. ERMOLOVE S
PRILOZHENIEM PERECHNIA EGO PORTRETOV K 50-LETIIU SO
DNIA EGO KONCHINY. PRILOZHENIE. 1911, 35 + 1 pp.
[Russ. text; 415 Russ. titles]

KAVKAZ. GAZETA POLITICHESKAIA I LITERATURNAIA.   Nos.
130, 145, 150, 1872; Nos. 1-23, 1873. [Russ. text,
titles pub. 1872-3, pp. 92-95]

*"KUTAISSKOE DIELO," EVREISKAIA ENTSIKLOPEDIIA," Vol. 9.
St. Petersburg: Izdanie Obshchestva dlia Nauchnykh
Evreiskikh Izdanii i Izdatel'stva Brokgauz-Efron, n.d.
pp. 938-40. [Russ. text, titles pp. 939-40]

*P. G.   "KHANSTVO DAGESTANA I KH. ZAKAVKAZ'IA,"
ENTSIKLOPEDICHESKII SLOVAR'. Vol. 37.   St. Petersburg:
F. A. Brokgauz, I. A. Efron, 1903, pp. 52-4. [Russ.
text, titles, p. 54]

Poznanskii, M. A.   "UKAZATEL' LITERATURY O VOENNO-
SUKHUMSKOI DOROGE I PRILEZHASHCHEI MESTNOSTI,"
ZAPISKI KRYMSKO-KAVKAZSKAGO GORNAGO KLUBA. No. 3.
1913. [Russ. text; 115 Russ., Europ. titles, pp.29-33]

Shigabudinov, M. Sh.   BOR'BA RABOCHIKH SEVERNOGO KAVKAZA
NAKANUNE I V PERIOD REVOLIUTSII 1905-1907 GG.
Makhachkala, 1964. [Russ. text; ca.250 titles per.
1905-1907, pp. 5-20, 249-56]

"UKAZATEL' STATEI I KORRESPONDENTSII, NAPECHATANNYKH V
ZHURNALE 'PUT' SOVETOV' ZA 1931 GOD," PUT' SOVETOV.
No. 24.   1931. [Russ. text, titles pub. 1931, pp.45-9]

UKAZATEL' STATEI I OBZOROV, POSTANOVLENII, PISEM I
TSIRKULIAROV KRAIKOMA VKP(B) I DRUGIKH MATERIALOV,
POMESHCHENNYKH V 'IZVESTIIAKH SEVERO-KAVKAZSKOGO

Caucasus: Political Science, Law

KRAEVOGO KOMITETA VKP(B)' ZA 1928 GOD. [Rostov-na-Donu]: Gos. Tip. im. Kominterna (Prilozhenie k No. 24 Izvestiia SKKRK), 1928, 16 pp. [Russ. text; titles pub. 1928]

UKAZATEL' STATEI, OBZOROV I POSTANOVLENII TSK I KRAIKOMA VKP(B) I DRUGIKH MATERIALOV, POMESHCHENNYKH V 'IZVESTIIAKH' ZA PERVUIU POLOVINU 1930 GODA. [Rostov-na-Donu]: Gos. Tip. im. Kominterna. Sevkraipoligraf Ob"-edineniia (Prilozhenie k No. 13 Izvestiia Severo-Kavkazskogo Kraevogo Komiteta VKP(B)), [1930], 8 pp. [Russ. text; titles pub. 1930]

"UKAZATEL' STATEI, POMESHCHENNYKH V ZHURNALE 'PUT' SOVETOV' ZA 1930 GOD," PUT' SOVETOV, No. 24. 1930. [Russ. text; titles pub. 1930, pp. 45-8]

SOCIAL ORGANIZATION

*Bagrii, A. V. "MATERIALY PO BIBLIOGRAFII KAVKAZA (K VOPROSU O BYTE ZHENSHCHINY KAVKAZA)," IZVESTIIA VOSTOCHNOGO FAKUL'TETA AZERBAIDZHANSKOGO GOSUDARSTVENNOGO UNIVERSITETA IMENI V. I. LENINA. Vol. 2 (PRILOZHENIE). 1928. [Russ. text; 57 Russ. titles pub. 1881-1914, pp. 1-3]

Gorodetskii, B. M. "MATERIALY DLIA BIBLIOGRAFII SEVERNAGO KAVKAZA. LITERATURNYE I OBSHCHESTVENNYE DEIATELI SEVERNAGO KAVKAZA. BIO-BIOBLIOGRAFICHESKIE OCHERKI," KUBANSKII KUR'ER. Vol. 18. 1913. (separate) 62 pp. [Russ. text; titles pp. 333-96]

*SOVETSKOE CHERNOMOR'E. Moscow: Izdatel'stvo "Morskoi Transport," 1955, 367 pp., 50,000 copies. [Russ. text, titles, pp. 362-3]

4 CRIMEA & CRIMEAN TATAR

GENERAL

*A. A. "GASPRINSKII, ISMAIL-BEI," LITERATURNAIA
ENTSIKLOPEDIIA, Vol. 2, n. p.: Izdatel'stvo
Kommunisticheskoi Akademii, 1929. [Russ. text;
Crimean Tatar. Russ. titles, p. 403]

*Gopshtein, E. E. BIBLIOGRAFIIA BIBLIOGRAFICHESKIKH
UKAZATELEI LITERATURY O KRYME. Simferopl': Izdanie
OPIK Obshchestvo po Izucheniiu Kryma, 1930, 15 pp.,
400 copies. [Russ. text; 28 Russ. titles]

Gorodetskii, B. "KUBAN' I CHERNOMOR'E V LITERATURE
1925 GODA," BIULLETEN' OBSHCHESTVA IZUCHENIIA
KUBANSKOGO KRAIA, No. 1, 1926. [Russ. text; 268
titles pub. 1925, pp. 29-39]

*"KRYM," EVREISKAIA ENTSIKLOPEDIIA, Vol. 9, St. Petersburg:
Izdanie Obshchestva dlia Nauchnykh Evreiskikh Izdanii
i Izdatel'stva Brokgauz-Efron, n.d., pp. 888-92.
[Russ. text;Hebrew, Europ, Russ. titles, p. 892]

*"KRYMSKAIA AVTONOMNAIA SOVETSKAIA SOTSIALISTICHESKAIA
RESPUBLIKA (KRYM)," BOL'SHAIA SOVETSKAIA ENTSIKLOPEDIIA.
Vol. 35, Moscow: Ogiz RSFSR Gosudarstvennyi Institut
"Sovetskaia Entsiklopediia," 1937, 1st ed., pp. 279-324.
[Russ. text, titles pp. 301, 319, 320]

*"KRYMSKAIA AVTONOMNAIA SOVETSKAIA SOTSIALISTICHESKAIA
RESPUBLIKA" (KRYM). BOL'SHAIA SOVETSKAIA
ENTSIKLOPEDIIA, Vol. 35, Moscow: Gosudarstvennyi
Institut "Sovetskaia Entsiklopediia" (Ogiz RSFSR), 1937,
pp. 279-94. [Russ. text, titles, pp. 293-4]

LITERATURA O KRYMSKOI OBLASTI. (IIUL' 1961-MART 1962 GG.).
Simferopol': Krymizdat, 1963, 107 pp. [Russ. text;
titles pub. 1961-62]

Crimea & Crimean Tatar: General

Markevich, A. I. "TAURICA. OPYT UKAZATELIA SOCHINENII, KASAIUSHCHIKHSIA KRYMA I TAVRICHESKOI GUBERNII VOOBSHCHE," IZVESTIIA TAVRICHESKOI UCHENO-ARKHIVNOI KOMISSII, Nos. 20, 28, 32-33. [Also, separate publication at Simferopol' by Tavricheskaia Uchennaia Arkhivnaia Kommissiia No. 1, 1894; No. 2, 1898; No. 3, 1902] [Russ. text; 10,000+ Russ., Europ. titles]

NOVAIA LITERATURA O KRYME. BIBLIOGRAFICHESKII UKAZATEL', No. 1 (Sept. 1960-June 1961). Simferopol': (Krymskaia Obl. B-ka im. I. Ia. Franko), 1961, 77 pp. [Russ. text; titles pub. 1960-61]

*ROSSIIA. POLNOE GEOGRAFICHESKOE OPISANIE NASHEGO OTECHESTVA. Vol. 14. NOVOROSSIIA I KRYM. St. Petersburg: Izdanie A. F. Devriena, 1910, 983 pp. [Russ. text, titles, pp. 911-41]

Simakovskii, V. "KNIGI, POSVIASHCHENNYE DESIATILETIIU SOVETIZATSII KRYMA," EKONOMIKA I KUL'TURA KRYMA, No. 2, 1931, pp. 102-6. [Russ. text; titles pub. 1930-31]

Simonovskii, Viktor V. "BIBLIOGRAFIIA PO KRYMOVEDENIIU," VES' KRYM, 1920-1925. IUBILEINYI SBORNIK. Simferopol', 1926. [Russ. text; 720 titles per. 1917-1926, pp.517-34]

Simonovskii, V. [Simakovskii, V.] "MATERIALY PO BIBLIOGRAFII LITERATURY, VYKHODIASHCHEI V KRYMSKOI ASSR ILI KASAIUSHCHEISIA KRYMA," EKONOM. I KUL'TURA KRYMA, No. 3 (2) [4(3)], 1931 [1931]. [No. 3: 106-143. No. 4: 110-113]. [Russ. text; titles pub. 1930-1931]

V. S. "UKAZATEL' STATEI I KRITICHESKIKH OTZYVOV, POMESHCHENNYKH V ZAPISKAKH KRYMSKO-KAVKAZSKAGO GORNAGO KLUBA V TECHENIE 25 LET (1891-1915 GG.)," ZAPISKI KRYMSKO-KAVKAZSKAGO GORNAGO KLUBA. No. 3/4, 1915, pp. 93-106 [Russ. text]

ECONOMICS

*"KRYMSKAIA AVTONOMNAIA SOVETSKAIA SOTSIALISTICHESKAIA RESPUBLIKA (KRYM)," BOL'SHAIA SOVETSKAIA ENTSIKLOPEDIIA, Vol. 35. Moscow: Gosudarstvennyi Institut "Sovetskaia Entsiklopediia" (Ogiz RSFSR), 1937, pp. 294-301. [Russ. text, titles, p. 301]

Crimea & Crimean Tatar: Economics

SEL'SKOKHOZIAISTVENNAIA NAUKA-PROIZVODSTVU. Simferopol:
"Krym," 1966, 176 pp., 1000 copies. [Russ. text;
titles at end of articles]

"SPISOK NAUCHNYKH TRUDOV S.A. USOVA," KRYM, No. 1 (5)
vyp. 1, 1928, pp. 7-8. [Russ. text; 19 Russ. titles]

GEOGRAPHY

*"BAKHCHISARAI," ENTSIKLOPEDICHESKII SLOVAR'. Vol. 3,
St. Petersburg: F. A. Brokgauz, I. A. Efron, 1891,
pp. 214-15. [Russ. text; Russ., Europ. titles, p. 215]

*Baranov, Bor. KRYM. PUTEVODITEL'. Moscow: Fizkul'tura
i Turizm, 1935, 303 pp., 21,000 copies. [Russ. text;
15 Russ. titles, pp. 300-301]

*Gol'dfail', L., B. Shustov. "IALTA," BOL'SHAIA
SOVETSKAIA ENTSIKLOPEDIIA. Vol. 65. Moscow:
Gosudarstvennoe Slovarno-Entsiklopedicheskoe
Izdatel'stvo "Sovetskaia Entsiklopediia" (Ogiz RSFSR),
1931, pp. 512-15. [Russ. text, titles, p. 515]

*"IALTA," ENTSIKLOPEDICHESKII SLOVAR'. Vol. 41A. St.
Petersburg: F. A. Brokgauz, I. A. Efron, 1904, pp. 644-
47. [Russ. text, titles, p. 647]

Kostritskii, M. E., V. I. Terekhova. "ISTORIIA
ISSLEDOVANNII PRIRODY KRYMA," IZVESTIIA KRYMSKOGO
PED. IN-TA. Vol. 22, 1956. [Russ. text; 144 titles,
pp. 72-80]

*Maslov, E. P. KRYM. EKONOMIKO-GEOGRAFICHESKAIA
KHARAKTERISTIKA. Moscow: Gosudarstvennoe Izdatel'stvo
Geograficheskoi Literatury. 1954, 173 pp., 30,000
copies. [Russ. text, titles, pp. 170-72]

Shul'ts, N. PLANERSKOE. (KOKTEBEL') OCHERK-PUTEVODITEL'.
Simferopol: "Krym," 1966, 72 pp., 25,000 copies.
[Russ. text; titles pp. 69-71]

*"THEODOSIIA," ENTSIKLOPEDICHESKII SLOVAR'. Vol. 41A.
St. Petersburg: F. A. Brokgauz, I. A. Efron, 1904,
pp. 918-20. [Russ. text, titles, p. 920]

Crimea & Crimean Tatar

HISTORY, ARCHAEOLOGY

*Bashkirova, A. S.   PROSHLOE KRYMA. ISTORICHESKII ESKIZ.
Moscow: Izdatel'stvo Sodruzhestva Krymskikh
Kul'turnykh Rabotnikov. "Chatyrdag" (Biblioteka Kryma,
No. 2). 1923, 40 pp., 3000 copies. [Russ. text; Russ.,
Europ. titles, p. 38]

*Berlin, I. "KRYMCHAKI INACHE KRYMSKIE EVREI,"
EVREISKAIA ENTSIKLOPEDIIA. Vol. 9. St. Petersburg:
Izdanie Obshchestva dlia Nauchnykh Evreiskikh Izdanii i
Izdatel'stva Brokgauz-Efron, n.d., pp. 887-88. [Russ.
text; Tatar, Hebrew, Russ. titles, p. 888]

*Ermolenko, L. A., ed. Margolina, R. V., E. M. Norman,
T. L. Shostak, comp.   KRYM V VELIKOI OTECHESTVENNOI
VOINY. BIBLIOGRAFICHESKII UKAZATEL' LITERATURY.
Simferopol': Izdatel'stvo "Krym," 1966, 87 pp., 1500
copies. [Russ. text; 690 Russ. titles, per. W. W. II
(1941-1944), pp. 5-58]

Gennadi, G. "SPISOK SOCHINENII O KRYME," VIESTNIK SPB.
RUSSKAGO GEOGRAFICHESKAGO OBSHCHESTVA. Vol. 15, No. 6,
1855; Vol. 16, No. 1, 1856. [Russ. text; titles Vol.
15, No. 6: 55-62]

_____. "SPISOK SOCHINENII O KRYME," ZAP. ODESS.
O-VA IST. I DREVN. Vol. 6, 1867. Reprint of 1855-56
ed. [Russ. text; titles pp. 623-44]

GOROD NEMERKNUSHCHEI SLAVY (K 20-LETIIU OSVOBOZHDENIIA
SEVASTOPOLIA OT NEMETSKO-FASHISTSKIKH ZAKHVATCHIKOV.
REKOMEND. SPISOK LITERATURY). Sevastopol': (Krymskaia
Obl. B-ka im. I. Ia. Franko. Sevastopol'skaia Tsentr.
Gor. B-ka im. L. N. Tolstogo), 1964, 22 pp. [Russ. text]

IKH IMENAMI NAZVANY...REKOMENDATEL'NYI SPISOK LITERATURY
O GEROIAKH 2-I OBORONY SEVASTOPOLIA, CH'IMI IMENAMI
NAZVANY ULITSY, GORODA. Sevastopol':(Tsentr. Gor.
B-ka im. L. N. Tolstogo), 1960, 12 pp. [Russ. text]

ISTORIIA GORODOV I SEL KRYMSKOI OBLASTI. BIBLIOGRAFICHESKII
UKAZATEL' LITERATURY. V 2-KH CH. Part 1. Simferopol',
1964. [Russ. text]

Korobkov, N. I.   GEROICHESKII SEVASTOPOL'. 1854-1855 GG.
1941-1942 GG. UKAZATEL' LITERATURY. Moscow: (Vsesoiuz.
Kn. Palata), 1942, 47 pp. [Russ. text; titles per.
1854-1855, 1941-1942]

Crimea & Crimean Tatar: History, Archaeology

*"KRYMSKIE POKHODY: (1662-69 GG., 1687 I 1689 GG., I 1735-38 GG.)," VOENNAIA ENTSIKLOPEDIIA. Vol. 14, Petrograd: T-vo I. D. Sytina, 1914, pp. 326-33. [Russ. text; Russ. titles per. 1662-89, 1735-38, p. 333]

*"KRYMSKIIA VOINY," VOENNAIA ENTSIKLOPEDIIA. Vol. 14, Petrograd: T-vo I. D. Sytina, 1914, pp. 334-37. [Russ. text, titles, p. 337]

*N. V. "KRYMSKOE KHANSTVO," NOVYI ENTSIKLOPEDICHESKII SLOVAR'. Vol. 23. Petrograd: Izdanie Aktsionernago Obshchestva "Izdatel'skoe Dielo Byvshee Brokgauz-Efron," n.d., pp. 512-521. [Russ. text; Cr. Tatar, Russ. titles, p. 521]

LEGENDARNYI SEVASTOPOL'-SIMVOL DOBLESTI, MUZHESTVA I GEROISTVA. KRATKII UKAZATEL' LITERATURY. (K 20-LETIIU OSVOBOZHDENIIA GORODA-GEROIA OT FASHISTSKIKH ZAKHVATCHIKOV). Sevastopol': (Morskaia B-ka), 1964, 11 pp. [Russ. text]

"LITERATURA I PERIODICHESKAIA PECHAT' O BOIAKH ZA KRYM, IZDANNAIA ZA GODY VELIKOI OTECHESTVENNOI VOINY (BIBLIOGRAFIIA SOSTAVLENA KRYMSKOI OBL. B-KOI I KRYMSKOI KOMISSIEI PO ISTORII VELIKOI OTECHESTVENNOI VOINY)," SOVETSKII KRYM. No. 1. 1945. [Russ. text; titles per. 1941-45, pp. 205-16]

LANGUAGE, LITERATURE

*Al-y, Al. "IPCHI, U.," LITERATURNAIA ENTSIKLOPEDIIA. Vol. 4. n.p.: Izdatel'stvo Kommunisticheskoi Akademii, 1930, pp. 560-61. [Russ. text; Cr. Tatar titles, p.561]

*"GAFAROV,D.," LITERATURNAIA ENTSIKLOPEDIIA. Vol. 2, n.p.: Izdatel'stvo Kommunisticheskoi Akademii, 1929. [Russ. text; Cr. Tatar titles, p. 413]

*"KRYMSKO-TATARSKAIA LITERATURA," BOL'SHAIA SOVETSKAIA ENTSIKLOPEDIIA. Vol. 35, Moscow: Gosudarstvennyi Institut "Sovetskaia Entsiklopediia" (Ogiz RSFSR), 1937, pp. 319-20. [Russ. text; Crimean, Russ. titles, p. 320]

*"KRYMSKO-TATARSKII IAZYK," BOL'SHAIA SOVETSKAIA ENTSIKLOPEDIIA. Vol. 35. Moscow: Gosudarstvennyi Institut "Sovetskaia Entsiklopediia" (OGIZ RSFSR), 1937, pp. 318-319. [Russ. text;Cr. Tat., Russ. titles, p. 319]

Crimea & Crimean Tatar: Language, Literature

Samoilovich, A. "O MATERIALAKH RADLOVA PO NARODNOI SLOVESNOSTI KRYMSKIKH TATAR I KARAIMOV," ZAPISKI KRYMSKAGO OBSHCHESTVA ESTESTVOISPYTATELEI I LIUBITELEI PRIRODY. Vol. 6, 1916. [Russ. text; titles pp. 1-7]

*"TATARSKII IAZYK KRYMA," LITERATURNAIA ENTSIKLOPEDIIA. Vol. 11. Gosudarstvennoe Izdatel'stvo "Khudozhestvennaia Literatura," 1939, p. 203. [Russ. text; Cr. Tatar, Russ., Europ. titles, p. 203]

POLITICAL SCIENCE, LAW

Atlas, M. L. BOR'BA ZA SOVETY. OCHERKI PO ISTORII SOVETOV V KRYMU 1917-18 G.G. [Simferopol']: Krymgosizdat, [1933], 144 pp. [Russ. text; titles, per. 1917-18, p. 144]

*Bunegin, M. F. REVOLIUTSIIA I GRAZHDANSKAIA VOINA V KRYMU, 1917-1922 GG. Simferopol': Krymgosizdat, 1927, 336 pp. [Russ. text, titles per. 1917-22, pp. 333-4]

Kal'vari, M. INTERVENTSIIA V KRYMU. n.p.: Krymskoe Gosudarstvennoe Izdatel'stvo, 1930, 180 pp. [Russ. text; titles per. 1917-20, end of book]

*Machanov, A. F. BOR'BA TSARSKOI ROSSII I TURTSII ZA OBLADANIE KRYMSKIM KHANSTVOM. Simferopol': Krymskoe Gosudarstvennoe Izdatel'stvo, 1929, 67 pp., 2000 copies. [Russ. text, titles, pub. mainly 18th cent., p. 66]

*N. V. "KHANSTVO KRYMSKOE," ENTSIKLOPEDICHESKII SLOVAR'. Vol. 37. St. Petersburg: F. A. Brokgauz, I. A. Efron, 1903, pp. 45-52. [Russ. text, titles, p. 52]

"OBZOR LITERATURY PO ISTORII OKTIABRIA V KRYMU," REVOLIUTSIIA V KRYMU, Sb. 10, 1932. [Russ. text; titles per. 1917, pp. 96-121]

Rempel', L. I. KRASNAIA GVARDIIA V KRYMU. 1917-1918. [Simferopol']: Krymgosizdat, 1931, 158 pp. [Russ. text; titles per. 1917-18, p. 152]

REVOLIUTSIIA V KRYMU, Sb. 7-01. Simferopol': (Istpart Otdel Krymsk. Komiteta VKP(B) po Izucheniiu Istorii Oktiabr'skoi Revoliutsii i VKP(B)), 1927, 288 pp. [Russ. text; titles per. 1917-18, pp. 287-8]

"UKAZATEL' TSITIRUEMYKH LIT. ISTOCHNIKOV," I. STALIN, MARKSIZM I NATSIONAL'NO-KOLONIALNYI VOPROS. Simferopol', 1939. [Cr. Tatar text; titles pp. 316-19]

5 DAGESTAN

GENERAL

Anzarova, Iu. I. MATERIALY DLIA BIBLIOGRAFII DASSR. VTOROI GOD RABOTY. Piatigorsk: Severo-Kavkazskoe Kraevoe Gosudarstvennoe Izdatel'stvo Dagestanskogo Nauchno-Issledovatel'skogo Instituta Natsional'nostei pri TSIK DASSR. No. 1. 1934. [Russ. text; 339 Russ. titles pub. 1934, pp. 31-48]

"BIBLIOGRAFIIA," BIULLETEN' DAGESTANSKOGO MUZEIA. No. 1. 1924. [Russ. text, titles, pub. 1924, pp. 20-1]

"BIBLIOGRAFIIA NEPERIODICHESKIKH IZDANII PO DAGESTANOVEDENIIU," BIULLETEN' DAGESTANSKOGO MUZEIA. No. 2. 1926. [Russ. text; titles pp. 53-6]

Bodrov, A. I. "SISTEMATICHESKII UKAZATEL' STATEI, POMESHCHENNYKH V ZHURNALE 'REVOLIUTSIIA I GORETS' ZA 1928-1932 GG." REVOLIUTSIIA I GORETS. No. 3/4, 1933. [Russ. text; titles pub. 1928-1932, pp. 113-32]

*"DAGESTANSKAIA ASSR," BOL'SHAIA SOVETSKAIA ENTSIKLOPEDIIA. Vol. 20, Moscow: Aktsionernoe Obshchestvo "Sovetskaia Entsiklopediia," 1930, pp. 118-28, 128-63. [Russ. text, titles pp. 128, 162-3]

Gorodetskii, B. M. DAGESTAN V SOVETSKOI LITERATURE. ISTOCHNIKI DLIA IZUCHENIIA DAGESTANSKOI ASSR. Makhachkala: Daggosizdat, 1933, viii+ 232 pp. [Russ. text; 1,895 titles]

Izmailov, B. NOVAIA LITERATURA O DAGESTANE (IANVAR'-IUN' 1960 G.) Makhachkala, 1961, 48 pp. [Titles pub. 1960]

*Kanarsh, V. I., L. N. Sedova, comp. DAGESTAN V RUSSKOI LITERATURE. REKOMENDATEL'NYI UKAZATEL' LITERATURY. Makhachkala: Dagestanskoe Knizhnoe Izdatel'stvo, 1960, 68 pp., 1000 copies. [Russ. text; ca.100 Russ. titles, pp. 8-47]

Kargina, K. I., Dmitrii M. Pavlov. "BIBLIOGRAFIIA DAGESTANA ZA POSLEREVOLIUTSIONNYI PERIOD, 1917-1928 GG. PERECHEN' LITERATURY, SPISOK RUKOPISEI," (SBORNIK) 10 LET NAUCHNYKH RABOT V DAGESTANE. Makhachkala: Izdatel'stvo Dagestanskogo Nauchno-Issledovatel'skogo Instituta. Podotdel Bibliografii. 1928. [Russ. text; 372; 140 (incl. mss.) Russ. titles pub. 1917-1928, pp. 8-18]

Kozubskii, E. I. DAGESTANSKII SBORNIK. Nos. 1,2. Temir-Khan-Shura, 1902-1904. [Russ. text]

Dagestan: General

*Kozubskii, E. I. MATERIALY DLIA BIBLIOGRAFII
DAGESTANSKOI OBLASTI," DAGESTANSKII SBORNIK. No. 2.
[1904]. [Russ. text; titles pp. 249-257] ["A
SUPPLEMENT AND CONTINUATION OF 'MATERIALY' PRINTED IN
'PAMIATNAIA KNIGA DAGESTANSKOI OBLASTI' 1895, AND IN
'DAGESTANSKII SBORNIK,' VYP. 1."]

Kozubskii, Evgenii I. OPYT BIBLIOGRAFII DAGESTANSKOI
OBLASTI. Temir-Khan-Shura: "Russkaia Tipografiia"
V. M. Sorokina, 1895, 268 pp. [Russ. text; 1508 Russ.,
Europ. titles]

_____, comp. "OPYT BIBLIOGRAFII DAGESTANSKOI
OBLASTI ZA 1895-1902 G.G.," DAGESTANSKII SBORNIK.
No. 1-2, 1902-1904. [Russ. text; titles pub. 1895-1902,
(no. 1) pp. 373-415]

_____. PAMIATNAIA KNIZHKA DAGESTANSKOI OBLASTI
IZDANA PO RASPORIAZHENIIU G. VOENNAGO GUBERNATORA
DAGESTANSKOI OBLASTI. Temir Khan Shura, 1895. [Russ.
text]

Krotova, V. MOI GOROD RODNOI (BESEDA O KNIGAKH.)
Makhachkala: Dagknigoizdat, 1966, 10 pp., 2000 copies.
[Russ. text]

*Kuznetsov, N. "DAGESTAN," ENTSIKLOPEDICHESKII SLOVAR'.
Vol. 10. St. Petersburg: F. A. Brokgauz, I. A. Efron,
1893, pp. 26-32. [Russ. text; Russ., Europ. titles, p.
32]

LETOPIS' PECHATI DAGESTANA. MAI-DEK. 1960 G. 1961, 94 pp.,
1000 copies. [Russ. text; titles pub. May-Dec. 1960]

LETOPIS' PECHATI DAGESTANA. 1962. Makhachkala: (Dagest.
Resp. B-ka im. Pushkina), 1965, 87 pp., 1000 copies.
[Russ. text; 87 titles pub. 1962]

LETOPIS' PECHATI DAGESTANA. 1963. Makhachkala: (Dagest.
Resp. B-ka im. Pushkina), 1965, 108 pp., 1000 copies.
[Russ. text; titles pub. 1963]

LETOPIS' PECHATI DAGESTANA. 1964. Makhachkala: (Dagest.
Resp. B-ka im. Pushkina); 1965, 107 pp., 1000 copies.
[Russ. text; titles pub. 1964]

LETOPIS' PECHATI DAGESTANA. 1965. Makhachkala: (Dagest.
Resp. B-ka im. Pushkina), 1966, 102 pp., 1000 copies.
[Russ. text; titles pub. 1965]

LETOPIS' PECHATI DAGESTANA. 1966. Makhachkala: (Dagest.
Resp. B-ka im. Pushkina), [1967], 1000 copies. [Russ.
text; titles pub. 1966]

Dagestan: General

LETOPIS' PECHATI DAGESTANA. 1968 (quarterly), 1000 copies. [Russ. text; titles pub.: 1967]

NOVAIA LITERATURA O DAGESTANE 1960, Vyp. 1. 1960 (semiannual). [Russ. text; titles pub. 1960]

NOVAIA LITERATURA O DAGESTANE. 1961. Vyp. [3]-5. 1962. [Russ. text; titles pub. 1961]

NOVAIA LITERATURA O DAGESTANE. 1962. Vyp. 1 (6). 1963. [Russ. text; titles pub. 1962]

NOVAIA LITERATURA O DAGESTANE. Makhachkala: (Dagest. Resp. B-ka im. Pushkina), 1964. [Russ. text; titles pub. 1964]

NOVAIA LITERATURA O DAGESTANE. Makhachkala: (Dagest. Resp. B-ka im. Pushkina), 1966. [Russ. text; titles pub. 1965]

Paulova, D. M., A. A. Takho-Godi, ed. "SPISOK VAZHNEISHIKH RUKOPISEI PO DAGESTANU S 1917-1928," DESIAT' LET NAUCHNYKH RABOT V DAGESTANE. Piatigorsk-Makhachkala: "Terek," 1928. [Russ. text; titles pub. 1917-28]

*Skazin, E. V.   DAGESTAN V SOVETSKOI ISTORICHESKOI LITERATURE. Makhachkala: (Dagestanskii Filial AN SSSR. Institut Istorii, Iazyka i Literatury), 1963, 196 pp., 1000 copies. [Russ. text; 1400 Russ. titles, per: pre-1962]

*_____. LITERATURA O DAGESTANE NA ZAPADNOEVROPEISKIKH IAZYKAKH. Makhachkala: (Dagestanskii Filial AN SSSR. Institut Istorii, Iazyka i Literatury), 1964, 135 pp., 500 copies. [Russ. text; 709 Europ. titles per: pre-1959]

"SOKRASHCHENNYI SPISOK LITERATURY PO DAGESTANU, VYSHEDSHEI S 1917-1928 G.," DESIAT' LET NAUCHNYKH RABOT V DAGESTANE. Piatigorsk-Makhachkala: "Terek," 1928. [Russ. text; titles pub. 1917-28, pp. 8-18]

"SPISOK IZDANII DAGESTANSKOGO MUZEIA, ASSOTSIATSII SEVERO KAVKAZSKIKH GORSKIKH KRAEVEDCHESKIKH ORGANIZATSII, DAGESTANSKOGO NAUCHNO-ISSLEDOVATEL'SKOGO INSTITUTA I SOVETA OBSLEDOVANIIA I IZUCHENIIA DAGESTANA," PLANOVOE KHOZIAISTVO DAGESTANA. No. 5/6, 1928. [Russ. text; 32 titles pp. 115-16]

*Trunov, D.   DOROGA K SVETU. Makhachkale: Dagestanskoe Knizhnoe Izdatel'stvo, 1962, 505 pp., 6500 copies. [Russ. text; 211 Russ. titles, pp. 491-501]

Dagestan

ANTHROPOLOGY, ETHNOGRAPHY

*Aliev, A. K. NARODNYE TRADITSII, OBYCHAI I IKH ROL' V
  FORMIROVANII NOVOGO CHELOVEKA. Makhachkala:
  (Dagestanskii Filial Akademii Nauk SSSR), 1968, 290 pp.,
  1000 copies. [Russ. text, titles pp. 266-88]

*NARODY DAGESTANA. SBORNIK STATEI. Moscow: (Akad. Nauk
  SSSR. In-t Etnografii im. Miklukho-Maklaia.), 1955,
  245 pp., 6000 copies. [Russ. text; 137 Russ. titles
  pub. 19-20th cents., pp. 241-6]

ARCHITECTURE, ART, MUSIC

(for ARCHAEOLOGY see HISTORY)

*Debirov, P. M.   ARKHITEKTURNAIA REZ'BA DAGESTANA.
  Moscow: Izdatel'stvo "Nauka," 1966, 95 pp., 2500 copies.
  [Russ. text; 93 Russ. titles pub. 1810-1962, pp. 92-4]

* _____ .   REZ'BA PO KAMNIU V DAGESTANE. Moscow:
  Izdatel'stvo "Nauka," 1966, 208 pp., 2000 copies.
  [Russ. text; ca.150 Russ., Europ. titles pp. 81-4]

ECONOMICS

Aliev, M. A.   SPETSIALIZATSIIA VINOGRADARSKIKH SOVKHOZOV.
  Makhachkala: Dagknigoizdat, 1967, 64 pp., 1000 copies.
  [Russ. text; titles p. 63]

Bedelov, G. B.   ORGANIZATSIIA, NORMIROVANIE I
  ISPOL'ZOVANIE OBOROTNYKH SREDSTV PROMYSHLENNYKH
  PREDPRIIATII. Makhachkala: Dagknigoizdat, 1967, 29 pp.,
  200 copies. [Russ. text; 11 titles at end of book]

DAGESTANSKII NAUCHNO-ISSLEDOVATEL'SKII INSTITUT SEL'SKOGO
  KHOZIAISTVA. TRUDY MOLODYKH UCHENYKH. Kn. 2.
  Makhachkala: Dagknigoizdat, 1966, 208 pp., 500 copies.
  [Russ. text; titles at end of articles]

Dagestan: Economics

DAGESTANSKII S.-KH INSTITUT. TRUDY. Vol. 17, No. 1.
  Makhachkala: Dagknigoizdat, 1966, 92 pp., 600 copies.
  [Russ. text; titles at end of articles]

DAGESTANSKII S.-KH. INSTITUT. TRUDY. Vol. 18. Makhachkala:
  Dagknigoizdat, 1968, 284 pp., 500 copies. [Russ. text;
  titles at end of articles]

DAGESTANSKII S.-KH. INSTITUT TRUDY. Vol. 19. Makhachkala:
  Dagknigoizdat, 1968, 311 pp., 600 copies. [Russ. text;
  titles at end of articles]

Daniialova, N. V. SOTSIALISTICHESKAIA REKONSTRUKTSIIA
  NARODNOGO KHOZIAISTVA DAGESTANA (1926-1932 GG.).
  Makhachkala, 1962. [Russ. text; ca.100 titles per.
  1926-32, pp. 146-51]

Kerimov, I. K. ISTORIIA PROFSOIUZNOGO DVIZHENIIA V
  DAGESTANE. (1905 G.--IIUNE' 1941 G.). Makhachkala,
  1963. [Russ. text; ca.120 titles per. 1905-1941, pp.
  285-90]

Osmanov, G. G. SOTSIAL'NO-EKONOMICHESKOE RAZVITIE
  DAGESTANSKOGO DOKOLKHOZNOGO AULA. Moscow, 1965.
  [Russ. text; titles pp. 6-13]

Rakhmatulaev, M. D. EKONOMICHESKIE PROBLEMY POVYSHENIIA
  KACHESTVA, NADEZHNOSTI I DOLGOVECHNOSTI PROMYSHLENNOI
  PRODUKTSII. Makhachkala: Dagknigoizdat, 1966, 20 pp.,
  200 copies. [Russ. text; 12 titles pp. 19-20]

Shamov, A. A. MATERIAL'NYE INTERESY OBSHCHESTVA I
  POOSHCHRITEL'NYE FONDY PREDPRIIATIIA. Makhachkala:
  Dagknigoizdat, 1966, 32 pp., 2000 copies. [Russ. text;
  40 titles pp. 31-2]

Shein, M. Ia. "SPISOK PECHATNYKH RABOT, OPUBLIKOVANNYKH
  V TRUDAKH DAGESTANSKOGO SEL'SKOKHOZIAISTVENNOGO
  INSTITUTA TT. XIII-XVIII (1963-1967)," TRUDY DAGEST. S.-
  KH. IN-TA. Vol. 19. 1968. [Russ. text; titles pub.
  1963-1967, pp. 293-308]

"SISTEMATICHESKII PERECHEN' STATEI I PROCHIKH MATERIALOV,
  OPUBLIKOVANNYKH V ZHURNALE 'PLANOVOE KHOZIAISTVO
  DAGESTANA' ZA 1927-28 GG.," PLANOVOE KHOZIAISTVO
  DAGESTANA. No. 1, 1929. [Russ. text; 234 titles pub.
  1927-1928, pp. 87-97]

Tananakin, P. T. SEBESTOIMOST' I RENTABEL'NOST' V
  PROMYSHLENNOSTI. Makhachkala: Dagknigoizdat, 1966, 37
  pp., 2000 copies. [Russ. text; titles pp. 36-7]

Dagestan: Economics

Viktorov, A. F. et al. DAGESTANSKAIA ASSR FIZ.-GEOG. I
EKON.-GEOG. OBZOR. Makhachkala: (M-vo Prosveshcheniia
Dagest.ASSR. Nauch.-Issled In-t Shkol....), 1958.
[Russ. text; 53 titles pp. 242-4]

EDUCATION

Aliev, A. NOVAIA ZHIZN'--NOVYE TRADITSII. Makhachkala:
Dagknigoizdat, 1966, 96 pp., 2000 copies. [Russ. text;
titles pp. 95-6]

El'darov, M. M. KRAEVEDENIE I DETSKII TURIZM V SHKOLAKH
DAGESTANA. [Makhachkala], 1968. [Russ. text; 56
titles pp. 58-63]

*Ismailov, A. R. LIKVIDATSIIA NEGRAMOTNOSTI V DAGESTANE.
Makhachkala: (Dagest. Filial AN SSSR In-t Ist., Iaz.,
i Lit. im. G. Tsadasy), 1970, 134 pp., 1000 copies.
[Russ. text; 114 titles, per: Soviet, pub.: 1897-1969,
pp. 129-33]

Khasbulatov, Sh. D. BIBLIOGRAFICHESKII SPRAVOCHNIK PO
VOPROSAM METODIKI PREPODAVANIIA UCHEBNYKH DISTSIPLIN V
DAGESTANSKOI SHKOLE I RAZVITIIA NARODNOGO OBRAZOVANIIA
V RESPUBLIKE. Makhachkala: Daguchpedgiz, 1960, 111 pp.,
1000 copies. [Russ. text; Dagestan, Russ. titles]

METODICHESKIE POSOBIIA V POMOSHCH' UCHITELIU DAGESTANSKOI
NERUSSKOI SHKOLY. KATALOG. [ANNOT.]. No. 1. ["ZA
1958-1959 GG."]. 1959; No. 2. ["ZA 1960-1961 GG."].
Makhachkala. No. 1, 1959, 19 pp., 2500 copies. No. 2,
1962, 17 pp., 1700 copies. [Russ. text; (No. 1) 29
titles, (No. 2) 26 titles, per. 1958-1961]

"SPISOK IZDANII NARKOMPROSA (DASSR), LITERATURY
(NEPOSREDSTVENNO I CHEREZ TSK NOVOGO DAGESTANSKOGO
ALFAVITA)," PLANOVOE KHOZIAISTVO DAGESTANA. No. 10/11/12.
1928. [Russ. text; 98 Azerb., Kumyk, Sov. Asian, Russ.
titles pp. 112-14]

Dagestan

GEOGRAPHY

Krymina, E. G. "BIBLIOGRAFICHESKII SPISOK RABOT SOTRUDNIKOV DAGESTANSKOGO NIISKH ZA 1962-1963 GG.," TRUDY DAGEST. NII SEL. KHOZ-VA, Vol. 3, Book 2, 1965. [Russ. text; 145 Dagest. langs. titles, pub. 1962-63, pp. 152-8]

Skachko, A. N. DAGESTAN. Moscow: Izdatel'stvo "Vlast' Sovetov" pri Prezidiume v TsIK, 1931, 157 pp. [Russ. text; titles pp. 155-7]

TRUDY ESTESTVENNO-GEOGRAFICHESKOGO FAKUL'TETA. No. 3. Makhachkala: Dagestanskii Pedagogicheskii Institut im. Gamzata Tsadasy, 1968, 155 pp., 500 copies. [Russ. text, titles at end of articles]

HISTORY, ARCHAEOLOGY

*Aliev, B., Sh. Akhmedov, M. S. Ymakhanov. IZ ISTORII SREDNEVEKOVOGO DAGESTANA. Makhachkala: [Dag. Fil. An SSSR, In-t Ist., Iaz., i Lit.], 1970, 235 pp., 600 copies. [Russ. text; ca.300 Dargin, Russ. titles, per. Middle Ages, pub. 1760-1969, pp. 218-32]

"DAGESTANSKAIA MILITSIIA," VOENNAIA ENTSIKLOPEDIIA. Vol.8, Petrograd: T-vo I. D. Sytina, 1912, pp. 572-3. [Russ. text, titles, p. 573]

*ISTORIIA DAGESTANA. Vol. 1, Moscow: Izdatel'stvo "Nauka," 1967, 431 pp., 7000 copies. [Russ. text; ca.370 Russ., Europ. titles, per. ancient times to 18th cent., pp. 417-28]

*ISTORIIA DAGESTANA. Vol. 2, Moscow: Izdatel'stvo "Nauka," 1968, 368 pp., 7000 copies. [Russ. text; ca.250 Russ. titles, per. 19th cent. to beg. 20th cent., pp. 359-66]

*ISTORIIA DAGESTANA. Vol. 3, Moscow: Izdatel'stvo "Nauka," 1968, 426 pp., 7000 copies. [Russ. text; ca.280 Russ. titles, per. 1917-45, pp. 416-24]

*ISTORIIA DAGESTANA. Vol. 4, Moscow: Izdatel'stvo "Nauka," 1969, 302 pp., 7000 copies. [Russ. text; ca.160 Russ. titles, per. 1946-69, pp. 295-300]

Dagestan: History, Archaeology

Izmailova, B., V. I. Kanarsh, L. N. Sedova. SOVETSKII
 DAGESTAN. REKOMENDATEL'NYI UKAZATEL' LITERATURY PO
 ISTORII DAGESTANA. Makhachkala: Dagknigoizdat, 1960,
 74 pp. [Russ. text; ca.200 titles; pub. 1957-1960]

Kazbekova, F. "BIBLIOGRAFIIA TRUDOV INSTITUTA ISTORII,
 IAZYKA I LITERATURY DAGESTANSKOGO FILIALA AN SSSR ZA
 1963 GOD," UCHEN. ZAP. (IN-T ISTORII, IAZ., I LIT. IM.
 TSADASY,), Vol. 14. 1965. [Russ. text; 51 Dagest.
 langs., Russ. titles, pub. 1963, pp. 375-83]

Kichev, M. IZ ISTORII BOR'BY ZA UPROCHENIE SOVETSKOI
 VLASTI V DAGESTANE. Makhachkala, 1963. [Russ. text;
 44 titles pp. 100-101]

Lunin, B. V. "POREVOLIUTSIONNAIA LITERATURA PO
 ARCHEOLOGII I ISTORII MATERIAL'NOI KUL'TURY DAGESTANA
 (BIBLIOGRAFICHESKII OBZOR)," SOVETSKOE KRAEVEDENIE NA
 SEVERNOM KAVKAZE. SBORNIK KRAEVEDCHESKIKH MATERIALOV.
 Rostov-na-Donu: Knigoizdatel'stvo "Severnyi Kavkaz,"
 1932. [Russ. text; Russ., Europ. titles, pp. 87-90,
 90-8]

Magomedov, R. M. ISTORIIA DAGESTANA. S DREVNEISHIKH
 VREMEN DO NACHALA XIX V. Makhachkala, 1961. [Russ.
 text; ca.300 titles, ancient times up to 19th cent.,
 pp. 279-89]

*"SHAMIL'," ENTSIKLOPEDICHESKII SLOVAR'. Vol. 39, St.
 Petersburg: F. A. Brokgauz, I. A. Efron, 1903, pp. 125-
 32. [Russ. text, titles, p. 132]

Sotavov, N.-K. A. K ISTORIOGRAFII VOPROSA
 "VNESHNEPOLITICHESKIE OTNOSHENIIA DAGESTANA SO STRANAMI
 BLIZHNEGO VOSTOKA (TURTSIIA, IRAN) V PERVOI POLOVINE
 XVIII VEKA." (KRATKII OBZOR ISTOCHNIKOV I LIT.),"
 SBORNIK ASPIRANTSKIKH RABOT (DAGEST. UN-T). GUMANITARNYE
 NAUKI, no. 2. 1966. [Russ. text; titles per. 1700-1750,
 pp. 74-98]

LANGUAGE, LITERATURE

*"DAGESTANSKIE IAZYKI," BOL'SHAIA SOVETSKAIA ENTSIKLOPEDIIA.
 Vol. 13, Moscow: Gosudarstvennoe Nauchnoe Izdatel'stvo
 "Bol'shaia Sovetskaia Entsiklopediia," 1952 (2nd ed.).
 pp. 294-5. [Russ. text, titles p. 295]

Dagestan: Language, Literature

[Gazurova, B.] NARODNYI POET DAGESTANA ZAGID GADZHIEV. REK. UKAZATEL' LIT. Makhachkala: (Resp. B-ka im. Pushkina), 1968, 16 pp., 1000 copies. [Russ. text; 111 Russ., other Soviet titles]

Nazarevich, A. EPOS, TVORIMYI V NASHI DNI. PUTI SOZDANIIA KHUDOZH. OBRAZA I. V. STALINA V USTNOI POEZII I LITERATURE NARODOV DAGESTANA. Makhachkala: Daggiz, 1950. [Russ. text; ca.50 titles pp. 66-8]

*Shamkhalov, A. "DAGESTANSKIE IAZYKI," BOL'SHAIA SOVETSKAIA ENTSIKLOPEDIIA. Vol. 20, Moscow: Aktsionernoe Obshchestvo "Sovetskaia Entsiklopediia," 1930 (1st ed.), pp. 165-6. [Russ. text; Russ., Europ. titles, p. 166]

* _____. "DAGESTANSKIE LITERATURY," BOL'SHAIA SOVETSKAIA ENTSIKLOPEDIIA. Vol. 20, Moscow: Aktsionernoe Obshchestvo "Sovetskaia Entsiklopediia," 1930 (1st ed.), pp. 164-5. [Russ. text; Dagest. langs., Russ., Europ. titles, p. 165]

*Shamkhalov, A. P. "DAGESTANSKIE IAZYKI," LITERATURNAIA ENTSIKLOPEDIIA. Vol. 3, n.p.: Izdatel'stvo Kommunisticheskoi Akademii, 1930, pp. 132-5. [Russ. text; Russ., Europ. titles, p. 135]

*Syprun, V., comp. LUCHSHIE KNIGI PISATELEI DAGESTANA (METODICHESKIE I BIBLIOGRAFICHESKIE MATERIALY V POMOSHCH' BIBLIOTECHNYM RABOTNIKAM). Makhachkala: Dagknigoizdat, 1968, 52 pp., 1000 copies. [Russ. text, titles, at end of articles]

PHILOSOPHY, RELIGION

*Abdullaev, M. A. IZ ISTORII FILOSOFSKOI OBSHCHESTVENNO-POLITICHESKOI MYSLI NARODOV DAGESTANA V XIX V. Moscow: Izdatel'stvo "Nauka," 1968, 336 pp., 7000 copies. [Russ. text; ca.200 Dargin, Lezgin, Russ., Arabic, Lak., French titles, per. 19th cent., pp. 324-31]

K VOPROSU O KHARAKTERE DVIZHENIIA MIURIDIZMA I SHAMILIA. KRATKII SPISOK LITERATURY. Moscow: Gos. Publ. Ist. B-ka, 1950, 4 pp., 2000 copies. [Russ. text; 18 titles, per. 19th cent.]

Dagestan

POLITICAL SCIENCE, LAW

[Amintaeva, S. T., comp. GEROI GRAZHDANSKOI VOINY
DAGESTANA (KRATKII ANNOT. REK. SPISOK LITERATURY).
Makhachkala: Dagknigoizdat, 1966, 11 pp., 2000 copies.
[Russ. text; 14 titles]

Bigaev, Iu. K. IZDANIE PROIZVEDENII K. MARKSA, F.
ENGEL'SA I V. I. LENINA NA IAZYKAKH NARODOV DAGESTANA.
(UKAZATEL' LIT.). Makhachkala: Dagknigoizdat, 1969,
31 pp., 1000 copies. [Russ. text; 102 Dagestan langs.
titles pub. 1925-60]

*Bushuev, S. K. BOR'BA GORTSEV ZA NEZAVISIMOST' POD
RUKOVODSTVOM SHAMILIA. Moscow-Leningrad: Izdatel'stvo
Akademii Nauk SSSR, 1939, 184 pp., 5000 copies. [Russ.
text; Russ., Europ. titles, pp. 167-84]

Kulish-Amirkhanova, A. S. ROL' KRASNOI ARMII V
KHOZIASTVENNOM I KUL'TURNOM STROITEL'STVE V DAGESTANE
(1920-1923 GG.). Makhachkala, 1964. [Russ. text;
ca.200 (incl. archives) titles, per. 1920-23, pp. 145-52]

*Osmanov, A. KOMSOMOL DAGESTANA V GODY KOLLEKTIVIZATSII.
Makhachkala: Dagknigoizdat, 1968, 48 pp., 1000 copies.
[Russ. text; 11 Russ. titles, per. 1928-38, p. 47]

SOCIAL ORGANIZATION

Gasanova, A. I. RASKREPOSHCHENIE ZHENSHCHINY-GORIANKI
V DAGESTANE (1920-1940 GG.). Makhachkala, 1963.
[Russ. text; ca.120 titles, per. 1920-40, pp. 152-6]

6 GAGAUZ

GENERAL

*S. R-o. "GAGAUZY," NOVYI ENTSIKLOPEDICHESKII SLOVAR'.
Vol. 12. St. Petersburg: F. A. Brokgauz, I. A.
Efron, n.d., 320-21 pp. [Russ. text; Russ., Bulgarian,
Europ. titles, p. 321]

ANTHROPOLOGY, ETHNOGRAPHY

*Derzhavin, N. S. "O NAIMENOVANII I ETNICHESKOI
PRINADLEZHNOSTI GAGAUZOV," SOVETSKAIA ETNOGRAFIIA.
No. 1. 1937, 80-87 pp. [Russ. text; 18 Russ.,
Europ. titles, p. 86]

HISTORY, ARCHAEOLOGY

*"GAGAUZY," BOL'SHAIA SOVETSKAIA ENTSIKLOPEDIIA. Vol. 14,
Moscow: Aktsionernoe Obshchestvo "Sovetskaia
Entsiklopediia," 1929, 1st ed., pp. 196-7. [Russ. text,
titles, p. 197]

*Meshcheriuk, I. I. ANTIKREPOSTNICHESKAIA BOR'BA
GAGAUZOV I BOLGAR BESSARABII V 1812-1820 GG. Kishinev:
Gos. Izd-vo Moldavii, 1957, 118 pp., 3000 copies.
[Fuss. text; Ukr., Russ., Bulgarian titles per. 1812-20,
pp. 115-17]

LANGUAGE, LITERATURE

*Dmitriev, N. "GAGAUZSKII IAZYK," BOL'SHAIA SOVETSKAIA
ENTSIKLOPEDIIA. Vol. 14, Moscow: Aktsionernoe Obshchestvo
"Sovetskaia Entsiklopediia," 1929, p. 196. [Russ. text;
Gagauz, Russ. titles, p. 196]

*"GAGAUZSKII IAZYK," BOL'SHAIA SOVETSKAIA ENTSIKLOPEDIIA.
Vol. 9, n.p.: Gosudarstvennoe Nauchnoe Izdatel'stvo
"Bol'shaia Sovetskaia Entsiklopediia," 1951, 2nd ed.,
p. 608. [Russ. text, titles, p. 608]

7 KARACHAY-BALKAR

GENERAL

Balkarov, K., comp. "KNIGI, IZDANNYE KABARDINO-BALKARSKIM KNIZHNYM IZDATEL'STVOM," KABARDA, Book 10, 1957. [Russ. text; titles pub. 1954-57, pp. 229-37]

Galkina, I. A., M. N. ELINOVA, T. A. KUMAKHOVA, T. B. NAGAEVA, A. G. SOZAEVA, L. G. FAL'KO, comp. CHTO CHITAT' O KABARDINO-BALKARSKOI ASSR. REK. UKAZATEL' LIT. Nal'chik: Kabard-Balkar. Kn. Izd., 1967, 110 pp., 3000 copies. [Russ. text; 671 titles]

*"KABARDINO-BALKARSKAIA AVTONOMNAIA SOVETSKAIA SOTSIALISTICHESKAIA RESPUBLIKA," BOL'SHAIA SOVETSKAIA ENTSIKLOPEDIIA. Vol. 30, Moscow: Gosudarstvennyi Institut "Sovetskaia Entsiklopediia," 1937, 1st ed., pp. 401-18. [Russ. text, titles, pp. 407, 418]

KABARDINO-BALKARSKII UNIVERSITET. SBORNIK NAUCHNYKH RABOT ASPIRANTOV. No. 2, Nal'chik: (M-vo Vyssh. i Sred. Spets. Obrazovaniia RSFSR), 1968, 468 pp., 500 copies. [Russ. text; titles at end of articles]

KABARDINO-BALKARSKII UNIVERSITET. OTCHET O NAUCHNOI RABOTE ZA 1964 I 1965 GODY. Nal'chik: (M-vo Vyssh. i Sred. Spets. Obrazovaniia RSFSR), 1966, 250 pp., 500 copies. [Russ. text; titles per. 1964-65, at end of chapters]

KABARDINO-BALKARSKII UNIVERSITET. SBORNIK STUDENCHESKIKH NAUCHNYKH RABOT. No. 4, Nal'chik: (M-vo Vyssh. i Sred. Spets. Obrazovaniia RSFSR), 1966, 174 pp., 500 copies. [Russ. text; titles at end of articles]

*"KARACHAEVSKAIA AVTONOMNAIA OBLAST'," BOL'SHAIA SOVETSKAIA ENTSIKLOPEDIIA. Vol. 31, Moscow: Gosudarstvennyi Institut "Sovetskaia Entsiklopediia" (Ogiz RSFSR), 1937, 1st ed., pp. 470-9. [Russ. text, titles, p. 479]

*KARACHAILY, ISLAM," LITERATURNAIA ENTSIKLOPEDIIA. Vol. 5, n.p.: Izdatel'stvo Kommunisticheskoi Akademii, 1931, pp. 119-20. [Russ. text, titles, p. 120]

Kerefov, K. N., ed. KABARDINO-BALKARSKAIA ASSR. Nal'chik: (Kabard.-Balkar. Nauch.-Issled. In-t), 1957, 620 pp. [Russ. text; 13 lists of titles, per.: Soviet]

LETOPIS' PECHATI KBASSR. 1959. Nal'chik: (Resp. B-ka im. Krupskoi), 1961, 54 pp., 500 copies. [Balkar, Kabardin, Russ. text; Balkar, Kabard., Russ. titles pub. 1959]

LETOPIS' PECHATI KBASSR. 1960. Nal'chik: (Resp. B-ka im. Krupskoi), 1961, 47 pp., 300 copies. [Balkar, Kabardin, Russ. text; Balkar, Kabard., Russ. titles pub. 1960]

Karachay-Balkar: General

LETOPIS' PECHATI KBASSR [1961]. Nal'chik: (Resp. B-ka im. Krupskoi), 1962, 40 pp., 300 copies. [Balkar., Kabardin, Russ. text; Balkar, Kabard., Russ. titles pub. 1961]

LETOPIS' PECHATI KBASSR. No. 5, 1963. Nal'chik: (Resp. B-ka im. Krupskoi), 1964, 32 pp., 300 copies. [Balkar., Kabard., Russ. text; Balkar, Kabard., Russ. titles pub. 1963]

LETOPIS' PECHATI KBASSR. No. 6, 1964. Nal'chik: (Resp. B-ka im. Krupskoi), 1966, 400 copies. [Balkar, Kabard., Russ. text; Balkar, Kabard., Russ. titles pub. 1964]

LETOPIS' PECHATI KBASSR. No. 7, 1965. Nal'chik: (Resp. B-ka im. Krupskoi), 1966. [Balkar, Kabard, Russ. text; Balkar, Kabard., Russ. titles pub. 1965]

LETOPIS' PECHATI KBASSR. No. 8, 1966. Nal'chik: (Resp. B-ka im. Krupskoi), 1969, 400 copies. [Balkar, Kabard., Russ. text; Balkar, Kabard., Russ. titles pub. 1966]

LETOPIS' PECHATI KBASSR. No. 9, 1967. Nal'chik: (Resp. B-ka im. Krupskoi), 1969, 400 copies. [Balkar, Kabard., Russ. text; Balkar, Kabard., Russ. titles pub. 1967]

LETOPIS' PECHATI KBASSR. No. 10, 1968. Nal'chik: (Resp. B-ka im. Krupskoi), 1970, 400 copies. [Balkar, Kabard., Russ. text; Balkar, Kabard., Russ. titles pub. 1968]

*Merzhanov, G. "KABARDINO-BALKARSKAIA AVTONOMNAIA SOVETSKAIA SOTSIALISTICHESKAIA RESPUBLIKA," BOL'SHAIA SOVETSKAIA ENTSIKLOPEDIIA. Vol. 30, Moscow: Gosudarstvennyi Institut "Sovetskaia Entsiklopediia" (Ogiz RSFSR), 1937, 1st ed., pp. 401-7. [Russ. text, titles p. 407]

Sarakhan, D. A. BIBLIOGRAFIIA KABARDY I BALKARII. Nal'chik: (Leningr. [Leninskii] Uchebnyi Gorodok, Kabinet Kraevedeniia, No. 1 [No. III]), [1930], 1931, iii+ 114 pp., 500 copies. [Russ. text]

Sergievskaia, I. S., G. Kh. Tantasheva, B. Saatova, comp. UKAZATEL' LITERATURY NA DUNGANSKOM, KARACHAEVO-BALKARSKOM I CHECHENO-INGUSHSKOM IAZYKAKH, IZDANNOI V KIRGIZII (1930-1960 GG). Frunze: (Kirgiz. Gos. Knizhnaia Palata), 1962, 16 pp., 500 copies. [Russ. text; 177 Karachay, Dungan, Chechen, Russ. titles pub. 1930-60]

Shpileva, N. S., comp. "KNIGI, IZDANNYE KABARDINO-BALKARSKIM NII. BIBLIOGR. UKAZATEL'," UCHENYE ZAPISKI

Karachay-Balkar: General

(KABARD.-BALKAR. NII). Vol. 24, 1967 (1966). [130 Balkar, Kabard., Russ. titles pp. 279-89]

Tuganov, R. U., comp. BIBLIOGRAFIIA KABARDINO-BALKARII, KARACHAEVO-CHERKESII I ADYGEI. (S DREVNEISHIKH VREMEN PO 1917 G.). Nal'chik: Kabard.-Balkar. Kn. Izd., 1967, 679 pp., 500 copies. [Russ. text; 5,664 Russ., Europ. titles per.: ancient times to 1917]

ANTHROPOLOGY, ETHNOGRAPHY

Chechenov, I. M. DREVNOSTI KABARDINO-BALKARII. Nal'chik, 1969. [Russ. text; 186 titles, pp. 142-49]

Shchukin, I. S. "MATERIALY DLIA IZUCHENIIA KARACHAEVTSEV," RUSSKII ANTROPOLOGICHESKII ZHURNAL. Nos. 1/2, 1913. [Russ. text; 14 titles p. 98]

ECONOMICS

Anan'eva, E., comp. KABARDINO-BALKARIIA V SEMILETKE. REK. UKAZATEL' LIT. Nal'chik: (Kabard.-Balkar. Resp. B-ka im. Krupskoi.), 1960, 22 pp., 500 copies. [Russ. text; ca.90 titles, per.: late 1950's]

KABARDINO-BALKARSKII UNIVERSITET. UCHENYE ZAPISKI. No. 24. SERIIA SEL'SKOKHOZIAISTVENNAIA I KHIMIKO-BIOLOGICHESKAIA. Nal'chik: (M-vo Vyssh. i Sred. Spets. Obrazovaniia RSFSR.), 1966, (No. 24) 510 pp., (No. 29) 452 pp., 500 copies. [Russ. text; titles at end of articles]

KABARDINO-BALKARSKII UNIVERSITET. UCHENYE ZAPISKI. No. 35 (SERIIA SEL'SKOKHOZIAISTVENNAIA). Nal'chik: (M-vo Vyssh. i Sred. Spets. Obrazovaniia RSFSR), 1967, 372 pp., 500 copies. [Russ. text; titles at end of articles]

Kardanov, Z., M. Shevkhuzhev. SPETSIALIZATSIIA I KONTSENTRATSIIA SEL'SKOKHOZIAISTVENNOGO PROIZVODSTVA.

Karachay-Balkar: General

PO MATERIALAM KHOZ.- KARACHAEVO-CHERKES. AVT. OBL. Stavropol: Kn. Izd., 1968, 144 pp., 1000 copies. [Russ. text; titles pp. 140-3]

*Khakuashev, E. T.   KABARDINO-BALKARIIA V GODY VOSSTANOVLENIIA NARODNOGO KHOZIASTVA SSSR. (1921-1925 GG.). Nal'chik: Kabardino-Balkarskoe Knizhnoe Izdatel'stvo, 1962, 135 pp., 1000 copies. [Russ. text; ca.150 Russ. titles, per. 1921-25, pp. 128-35]

Kumykov, T. Kh.   EKONOMICHESKOE I KUL'TURNOE RAZVITIE KABARDY I BALKARII V XIX VEKE. Nal'chik, 1965. [Russ. text; titles per. 19th cent., pp. 7-29]

Mambetov, G. Kh.   KREST'IANSKIE PROMYSLY V KABARDE I BALKARII VO VTOROI POLOVINE XIX--NACHALE XX VEKA. Nal'chik, 1962. [Russ. text; ca.120 titles per.: 19th to early 20th cent., pp. 107-10]

Mutalipova, A. Kh., G. I. Naurzokov.   RENTABEL'NOST' PROIZVODSTVA V KOLKHOZAKH I SOVKHOZAKH KABARDINO-BALKARSKOI ASSR. Nal'chik: (Kabard.-Balkar. NII), 1966 (vyp. dan 1967), 176 pp., 500 copies. [Russ. text; 18 titles, p. 174]

*Nastaev, V. S., P. P. Iakovlev, comp. PROIZVODSTVENNIKAM O NAUCHNOI ORGANIZATSII TRUDA. Nal'chik: Kabard.-Balkar. Kn. Izd., 1966, 146 pp., 3000 copies. [Russ. text, titles, pub. 1961-66, pp. 144-5]

Taov, P. K.   UGLUBLENIE SPETSIALIZATSII I PROIZVODSTVENNYE TIPY KOLKHOZOV BAKSANSKOGO I CHEGEMSKOGO RAIONOV KABARDINO-BALKARSKOI ASSR. Nal'chik: "El'brus," 1968, 160 pp., 700 copies. [Russ. text; titles pp. 157-60]

Temirzhanov, V. Kh.   PUTI ISPOL'ZOVANIIA ZAKONA STOIMOSTI V KOLKHOZNOM PROIZVODSTVE. Nal'chik: Kabard.-Balkar. Kn. Izd., 1967, 196 pp., 500 copies. [Russ. text; titles pp. 190-5]

Zhakomikhov, T. A.   ISTORIIA NARODNOGO KHOZIAISTVA KABARDINO-BALKARII. Part 1. Nal'chik, 1965. [Russ. text; titles pp. 3-10]

_____.   ISTORIIA NARODNOGO KHOZIAISTVA KABARDINO-BALKARII. Part 2. Nal'chik: Kabard.-Balkar. Kn. Izd., 1967, 390 pp., 500 copies. [Russ. text; titles pp. 379-87]

Karachay-Balkar

GEOGRAPHY

PRIRODA KABARDINO-BALKARII I EE OKHRANA. Nal'chik, 1966, 270 pp. [Russ. text; titles at end of articles]

HISTORY, ARCHAEOLOGY

Alekseeva, E. P. KARACHAEVTSY I BALKARTSY-DREVNII NAROD KAVKAZA. Cherkessk, 1963. [Russ. text; ca.80 titles, pp. 88-92]

Berbekov, Kh. M. PEREKHOD K SOTSIALIZMU NARODOV KABARDINO-BALKARII. Nal'chik, 1963. [Russ. text; ca.400 titles, pp. 25-33, 522-35]

*Dobruskin, L. NARODNOE OBRAZOVANIE,...ISTORICHESKII OCHERK...," BOL'SHAIA SOVETSKAIA ENTSIKLOPEDIIA. Vol. 30. Moscow: Gosudarstvennyi Institut "Sovetskaia Entsiklopediia," (OGIZ RSFSR), 1937, 1st ed., pp. 407-418. [Russ. text and titles, p. 418]

Kardanov, Ch. E. AGRARNOE DVIZHENIE V KABARDE I BALKARII. (KONETS XIX--NACHALO XX V.). Nal'chik, 1963. [Russ. text; ca.170 titles, late 19th & early 20th cents., pp. 8-16, 169-75]

Kasumov, A. Kh. RAZNYE SUD'BY. Nal'chik: Kabard.-Balkar. Kn. Izd., 1967, 88 pp., 1000 copies. [Russ. text; titles pp. 85-8]

Nevskaia, V. P. SOTSIAL'NO-EKONOMICHESKOE RAZVITIE KARACHAIA V XIX VEKE. (DOREFORMENNYI PERIOD). Cherkessk: (Karachaevo-Cherkes. Nauch.-Issled. In-t Istorii, Iazyka i Lit.), 1960. [Russ. text; 65 titles, per. 18th cent. to 1960's, pp. 3-12, 153-6]

Tekuev, A. K. PUT' K NOVOI ZHIZNI. Nal'chik: "El'brus," 1968, 112 pp., 1000 copies. [Russ. text; titles pp. 108-12]

Karachay-Balkar

LANGUAGE, LITERATURE

*A. B. "KARACHAEVSKII IAZYK," BOL'SHAIA SOVETSKAIA
ENTSIKLOPEDIIA. Vol. 31, Moscow: Gosudarstvennyi
Institut "Sovetskaia Entsiklopediia" (Ogiz RSFSR),
1937, pp. 480-1. [Russ. text; Karachay, Russ., Europ.
titles p. 481]

*Akhmatov, I. Kh. GLAVNYE CHLENY PREDLOZHENIIA I SREDSTVA
IKH VYRAZHENIIA V SOVREMENNOM KARACHAEVO-BALKARSKOM
IAZYKE. Nal'chik: Knizhnoe Izdatel'stvo "El'brus,"
1968, 164 pp., 500 copies. [Russ. text; 145 Karachay,
Russ. titles pub. 1930-67, pp. 156-62]

*Baskakov, N. A., ed. GRAMMATIKA KARACHAEVO-BALKARSKOGO
IAZYKA. FONETIKA. MORFOLOGIIA. SINTAKSIS. Nal'chik:
Kabard.-Balkar. Kn. Izd., 1966, 400 pp., 1000 copies.
[Kabard. text; 129 Karachay, Russ., Europ. titles,
pp. 386-92]

Budaev, A. Zh. SISTEMA FONEM SOVREMENNOGO KARACHAEVO-
BALKARSKOGO IAZYKA. Nal'chik, 1968. [Russ. text; 173
titles pp. 145-51]

KARACHAEVO-CHERKESSKII NAUCHNO-ISSLEDOVATEL'SKII INSTITUT
EKONOMIKI, ISTORII, IAZYKA I LITERATURY. TRUDY. No. 5
(SERIIA FILOLOGICHESKAIA). Cherkessk: Stavrop. Kn. Izd.
Karachaevo-Cherkes. Otd-nie., 1968, 368 pp., 500 copies.
[Russ. text; titles at end of articles]

*Karachaily, Islam. "KARACHAEVSKAIA LITERATURA,"
LITERATURNAIA ENTSIKLOPEDIIA. Vol. 5. n.p.: Izdatel'stvo
Kommunisticheskoi Akademii, 1931, 1st ed., pp. 117-19.
[Russ. text, titles, p. 119]

*Karaeva, A. I. OCHERK ISTORII KARACHAEVSKOI LITERATURY.
Moscow: Izdatel'stvo "Nauka," 1966, 320 pp., 2500
copies. [Russ. text; Karachay titles, pp. 313-19]

Khabichev, M. A. MESTOIMENIE V KARACHAEVO-BALKARSKOM
IAZYKE. Cherkessk: Karachaevo-Cherkes. Kn. Izd., 1961.
[Russ. text; ca.200 Karachay-Balkar, Russ. titles, pp.
203-9]

Khadzhilaev, Kh.-M. I. POSLELOGI I POSLELOZHNO-IMENNYE
SLOVA V KARACHAEVO-BALKARSKOM IAZYKE. Cherkessk, 1962.
[Russ. text; ca.175 titles, pp. 150-7]

*Khubiev, M. KARACHAEVO-BALKARSKIE NARODNYE PESNI
SOVETSKOGO PERIODA. Cherkessk: Karachaevo-Cherkesskoe
Otdelenie Stavropol'skogo Knizh. Izd-a, 1968, 188 pp.,
1500 copies. [Balkar text; 160 Balkar, Russ., Ukr.
titles, per.: Soviet; pub.: 1842-1966, pp. 180-5]

Karachay-Balkar: Language, Literature

Shumakhova, A., comp. KERIM SARAMURZAEVICH OTAROV. (50 LET SO DNIA ROZHDENIIA) BIOBIBLIO. PAMIATKA. Nal'chik: (Resp. B-ka im. Krupskoi), 1962, 14 pp., 340 copies. [Russ. text]

*Shumakhova, A. S., ed.; Sozaeva, A. G., T. B. Nagoeva, comp. PISATELI. KABARDINO-BALKARII. (BIOBIBLIOGRAFICHESKII UKAZATEL'). Nal'chik: Kabardino-Balkarskoe Knizhnoe Izdatel'stvo, 1965, 135 pp., 700 copies. [Russ. text; 48 lists Balkar, Russ., other titles]

Sottaev, A. Kh. IMIA SUSHCHESTVITEL'NOE V KARACHAEVO-BALKARSKOM IAZYKE. Nal'chik: "El'brus," 1968, 84 pp., 500 copies. [Russ. text; titles at end of book]

*Suiunchev, Kh. I., I. Kh. Urusbiev, eds. RUSSKO-KARACHAEVO-BALKARSKII SLOVAR'. Moscow: Izdatel'stvo "Sovetskaia Entsiklopediia," 1965, 744 pp., 10,000 copies. [Russ. text; Karachay, Balkar, Russ., Europ. titles, pp. 10-11]

*Urusbiev, I. Kh. SPRIAZHENIE GLAGOLA V KARACHAEVO-BALKARSKOM IAZYKE. Cherkessk: Karachaevo-Cherkesskoe Knizhnoe Izdatel'stvo, 1963, 232 pp., 1000 copies. [Russ. text; ca.175 Karachay-Balkar, Russ., Europ. titles, pp. 224-30]

*V. M. "KARACHAEVSKII IAZYK," LITERATURNAIA ENTSIKLOPEDIIA. Vol. 5. n.p.: Izdatel'stvo Kommunisticheskoi Akademii, 1931, 1st ed. [Russ. text; Russ., Europ. titles, p.119]

PHILOSOPHY, RELIGION

Tsavkilov, B. Kh. MORAL' ISLAMA. Nal'chik: Kabard.-Balkar. Kn. Izd., 1967, 327 pp., 4000 copies. [Russ. text; titles pp. 316-25]

Karachay-Balkar

POLITICAL SCIENCE, LAW

*Berbekov, Kh. M. PEREKHOD K SOTSIALIZMU NARODOV KABARDINO-BALKARII. Nal'chik: Kabardino-Balkarskoe Knizhnoe Izdatel'stvo, 1963, 536 pp., 1500 copies. [Russ. text, titles, incl. archives, pp. 25-33, 522-34]

_____. SOVETSKAIA AVTONOMIIA KABARDY I BALKARII. Nal'chik: Kabard.-Balkar. Kn. Izd., 1961. [Russ. text; ca.45 titles, pp. 124-6]

Sorokin, comp. ISTORIIA KOMSOMOLA KARACHAEVO-CHERKESII (REK. SPISOK LITERATURY). Cherkessk: (Karachaevo-Cherkes. Obkom. VLKSM...)

Tekuev, A. BOR'BA KABARDINO-BALKARSKOI PARTORGANIZATSII ZA SOTSIALISTICHESKOE PREOBRAZOVANIE SEL'SKOGO KHOZIAISTVA. Nal'chik: Kabard-Balkar. Kn. Izd., 1960. [Russ. text; ca.50 titles Sov. per., pp. 149-51]

SOCIAL ORGANIZATION

*Pushkin, V. N., M. M. Shueva-Filatova. PSIKHOLOGIIA I VOPROSY NAUCHNOI ORGANIZATSII TRUDA. Nal'chik: Kabard.-Balkar. Kn Izd., 1968, 159 pp., 800 copies. [Russ. text; 15 Russ. titles pub. 1960-67, p. 158]

8 KARAIM

GENERAL

*A. G. "KARAIMY," ENTSIKLOPEDICHESKII SLOVAR'. Vol. 14, St. Petersburg: F. A. Brokgauz, I. A. Efron, 1895, pp. 426-31. [Russ. text; Russ., Europ. titles, p. 431]

*A. G. "KARAIMY," EVREISKAIA ENTSIKLOPEDIIA. Vol. 9, St. Petersburg: Izdanie Obshchestva dlia Nauchnykh Evreiskikh Izdanii i Izdatel'stva Brokgauz-Efron, n.d., pp. 268-90. [Russ. text; Russ., Europ. titles, p. 290]

*Balaban, M. "KARAIMY: (...V GALITSII)," EVREISKAIA ENTSIKLOPEDIIA. Vol. 9, St. Petersburg: Izdanie Obshchestva dlia Nauchnykh Evreiskikh Izdanii i Izdatel'stva Brokgauz-Efron, n.d., pp. 290-1. [Russ. text; Europ. titles, p. 291]

ANTHROPOLOGY, ETHNOGRAPHY

*S. P. "VENIAMIN BEN-ILIIA," EVREISKAIA ENTSIKLOPEDIIA. Vol. 5, St. Petersburg: Izdanie Obshchestva dlia Nauchnykh Evreiskikh Izdanii i Izdatel'stva Brokgauz-Efron, n.d., pp. 481-2. [Russ. text; Hebrew, Russ., Europ. titles, pp. 481-2]

HISTORY, ARCHAEOLOGY

*"FIRKOVICH, AVRAAM BEN-SHAMUIL," EVREISKAIA ENTSIKLOPEDIIA. Vol. 15, St. Petersburg: Izdanie Obshchestva dlia Nauchnykh Evreiskikh Izdanii i Izdatel'stva Brokgauz-Efron, n.d., pp. 289-93. [Russ. text; Hebrew, Russ., Europ. titles, p. 293]

"KIRIMI, AVRAAM," EVREISKAIA ENTSIKLOPEDIIA. Vol. 9, St. Petersburg: Izdanie Obshchestva dlia Nauchnykh Evreiskikh Izdanii i Izdatel'stva Brokgauz-Efron, n.d., pp. 483-4. [Russ. text; Europ. titles, p. 484]

*"SULTANSKII, MORDEKHAI BEN IOSIF," EVREISKAIA ENTSIKLOPEDIIA. Vol. 14, St. Petersburg: Izdanie Obshchestva dlia Nauchnykh Evreiskikh Izdanii i Izdatel'stva Brokgauz-Efron, n.d., p. 637. [Russ. text; Russ., Europ. titles, p. 637]

Karaim

LANGUAGE, LITERATURE

G. S. "KRATKII OCHERK TIURKSKO-KARAIMSKOI LITERATURY,"
IZVESTIIA KARAIMSKAGO DUKHOVNAGO PRAVLENIIA. Vol. 1,
No. 1, No. 2, 1918. [Russ. text; titles (1) pp.6-10;
(2) pp. 13-17]

*Musaev, K. M. GRAMMATIKA KARAIMSKOGO IAZYKA, FONETIKA
I MORFOLOGIIA. Moscow: Izdatel'stvo "Nauka," 1964,
344 pp., 2100 copies. [Russ. text; Karaim, Turkic,
Russ., Polish titles, p. 340]

*S. P. "ILIIA BEN-BARUKH," EVREISKAIA ENTSIKLOPEDIIA.
Vol. 8, St. Petersburg: Izdanie Obshchestva dlia
Nauchnykh Evreiskikh Izdanii i Izdatel'stva Brokgauz-
Efron, n.d., pp. 100-1. [Russ. text; Karaim, Europ.
titles, p. 101]

PHILOSOPHY, RELIGION

S. P. "BEIM, SOLOMON ABRAMOVICH," EVREISKAIA
ENTSIKLOPEDIIA. Vol. 4, St. Petersburg: Izdanie
Obshchestva dlia Nauchnykh Evreiskikh Izdanii i
Izdatel'stva Brokgauz-Efron, n.d., pp. 41-2. [Russ.
text; Hebrew, Russ., Europ. titles, p. 42]

POLITICAL SCIENCE, LAW

*Gessen, Iu. "KARAIMY: PRAVOVOE POLOZHENIE K. V
ROSSII," EVREISKAIA ENTSIKLOPEDIIA. Vol. 9, St.
Petersburg: Izdanie Obshchestva dlia Nauchnykh
Evreiskikh Izdanii i Izdatel'stva Brokgauz-Efron, n.d.,
pp. 291-8. [Russ. text, titles, p. 298]

*S. P. "AGA, VENIAMIN BEN-SAMUIL," EVREISKAIA
ENTSIKLOPEDIIA. Vol. 1, St. Petersburg: Izdanie
Obshchestva dlia Nauchnykh Evreiskikh Izdanii i
Izdatel'stva Brokgauz-Efron, n.d., pp. 382-3. [Russ.
text; Hebrew, Russ. titles, pp. 382-3]

9 KUMYK

HISTORY, ARCHAEOLOGY

*Gadzhieva, S. Sh. KUMYKI. ISTORIKO-ETNOGRAFICHESKOE
ISSLEDOVANIE. Moscow: Izdatel'stvo Akademii Nauk
SSSR, 1961, 387 pp., 3300 copies. [Russ. text;
Russ., Europ. titles, pp. 4-16, 378-385]

*"KUMYKI," ENTSIKLOPEDICHESKII SLOVAR' Vol. 17.
St. Petersburg, F. A. Brokgauz, I. A. Efron, 1896,
p. 14. [Russ. text; Russ. titles, p. 14]

LANGUAGE, LITERATURE

*A. S. "MAGOMED EFENDI OSMANOV," LITERATURNAIA
ENTSIKLOPEDIIA, Vol. 6. Moscow: Gosudarstvennoe
Slovarno-Entsiklopedicheskoe Izdatel'stvo "Sovetskaia
Entsiklopediia," 1932, 1st ed. [Russ. text; Kumyk,
Russ. titles, pp. 683-684 pp.]

*Anisimov, N.; A. Shamkhalov. "KUMYKSKAIA LITERATURA,"
LITERATURNAIA ENTSIKLOPEDIIA, Vol. 5. n. p.
Izdatel'stvo Kommunisticheskoi Akademii, 1931, 1st ed.,
725-729 pp. [Russ. text and titles, p. 729]

*Choban-Zade, B. ZAMETKI O IAZYKE I SLOVESNOSTI KUMYKOV.
Baku: Izdanie O-va "Obsledovaniia i Izucheniia
Azerbaidzhana," 1926, 105 pp., 1000 copies. [Azeri
text; 49 Kumyk titles, per. ca.1883-1925, pp. 24-26]

*Dzhanmavov, Iu. D. DEEPRICHASTIIA V KUMYKSKOM
LITERATURNOM IAZYKE. (SRAVNITEL'NO S DRUGIMI TIURK.
IAZ.), Moscow: Izdatel'stvo "Nauka," 1967, 330 pp.,
1700 copies. [Russ. text; Sov. Asian, Russ. titles,
pp. 321-328]

Kumyk: Language, Literature

*"KUMYKSKII IAZYK," BOL'SHAIA SOVETSKAIA ENTSIKLOPEDIIA.
Vol. 35. Moscow: Gosudarstvennyi Institut "Sovetskaia
Entsiklopediia" (OGIZ RSFSR), 1937 1st ed., 482 p.
[Russ. text; Kumyk, Russ., Europ. titles, p. 482]

*"SULEIMANOV, ABDUL-VAGAB," LITERATURNAIA ENTSIKLOPEDIIA.
Vol. 11. Moscow: Gosudarstvennoe Izdatel'stvo
"Khudozhestvennaia Literatura," 1939, 1st ed., p. 107.
[Russ. text; Kumyk, Russ. titles, p. 107]

10 **KURD**

GENERAL

Aleksanian, N. A. comp. BIBLIOGRAFIIA SOVETSKOI KURDSKOI KNIGI (1921-1960). Erevan: (AN Arm. SSR. Sektor Vostokovedeniia), 1962, 124 pp., 1000 copies. [Kurd, Russ. text; 238 Kurd titles]

Kartsev, "ZAMIETKI O KURDAKH," ZAPISKI KAVKAZKAGO OTDIELA IMPERATORSKAGO RUSSKAGO GEOGRAFICHESKAGO OBSHCHESTVA. Vol 19., 1897. [Russ. text; 29 Russ. Europ. titles, pp. 337-338]

*"KURDISTAN," ENTSIKLOPEDICHESKII SLOVAR'. Vol. 17. St. Petersburg: F. A. Brokgauz, I. A. Efron, 1896, p. 69. [Russ. text; Europ. titles, p. 69]

*[Rostopchin, F. B.] comp. "BIBLIOGRAFIIA PO KURDSKOI PROBLEME [SISTEMATICHESKII UKAZATEL' LITERATURY S PREDISL. K VASILEVSKOGO]," REVOLIUTSIONNYI VOSTOK. Nos. 3/4 (19/20), 5. 1933. [Russ. text; 732 Russ. Europ., Mid-East. titles, (No. 3/4) pp. 292-326; (No. 5) pp. 159-173]

ANTHROPOLOGY, ETHNOGRAPHY

*Krymskii, A. "KURDY," ENTSIKLOPEDICHESKII SLOVAR'. Vol. 17. St. Petersburg: F. A. Brokgauz, I. A. Efron, 1896, 69-71 pp. [Russ. text; Russ., Europ. titles, p. 71]

*"KURDY," BOL'SHAIA SOVETSKAIA ENTSIKLOPEDIIA. Vol 35. Moscow: Gosudarstvennyi Institut "Sovetskaia Entsiklopediia" (OGIZ RSFSR), 1937, 532-535 pp. [Russ. text; Kurd, Russ., Europ. titles, p. 535]

HISTORY, ARCHAEOLOGY

*Dzhalil, Dzhalile. VOSSTANIE KURDOV 1880 GODA. Moscow: Izdatel'stvo "Nauka," 1966, 132 pp., 1700 copies. [Russ. text; Kurd, Armenian, Russ., Europ., Arab. titles, per.: 1880, pp. 129-132]

*Khalfin, N. A. BOR'BA ZA KURDISTAN (KURDSKII VOPROS V MEZHDUNARODNYKH OTNOSHENIAKH XIX VEKA). Moscow: Izdatel'stvo Vostochnoi Literatury, 1963, 170 pp., 4000 copies. [Russ. text; Russ., Europ. titles, pp. 154-162]

*"KURDISTAN," EVREISKAIA ENTSIKLOPEDIIA. Vol. 9. St. Petersburg: Izdanie Obshchestva Dlia Nauchnykh Evreiskikh Izdanii i Izdatel'stva Brokgauz-Efron, n. d. 924-925 pp. [Russ. text; Europ. titles, p. 925]

*Lazarev, M. S. KURDISTAN I KURDSKAIA PROBLEMA (90-E GODY XIX VEKA--1917 G.) Moscow: Izdatel'stvo "Nauka," 1964, 400 pp., 400 copies. [Russ. text; Kurd, Russ., Europ., Turkish titles, per.: 1890's-1917, pp. 376-384]

Lerkh, P. IZSLEDOVANIIA OB IRANSKIKH KURDAKH I IKH PREDKAKH, SEVERNYKH KHALDEIAKH. St. Petersburg: Tip. Akademii Nauk, Kn. 1, 1856; Kn. 2, 1858. [Russ. text; Russ., Europ. titles, (1) pp. 5-19; (2) pp. I-XXXV]

*Musaelian, Zh. S. BIBLIOGRAFIIA PO KURDOVEDENIIU. Moscow: Izd. Vost. Lit., 1963, 184 pp., 900 copies. [Russ. text; 2690+79 Azeri, Armen., Georgian, Russ., Europ. titles, pub.: 18th cent. to 1963]

Kurd

LANGUAGE, LITERATURE

*B. M. "KURDSKII IAZYK," BOL'SHAIA SOVETSKAIA
ENTSIKLOPEDIIA. Vol. 35, 1937, 1st ed., 531-532 pp.
[Russ. text; Russ., Europ. titles, p. 532]

Dzhndi, A. "KURDSKAIA LITERATURA SOVETSKOI ARMENII,"
NAUCH-MAS. B-KA OBSHCHESTVENNYKH NAUK. No. 8.
Erevan: (AN ArmSSR), 1954. [Kurd. text; 42 Kurd
titles, pp. 91-94]

*Khaznadar, Maruf. OCHERKI ISTORII SOVREMENNOI KURDSKOI
LITERATURY. Moscow: Izdatel'stvo "Nauka," 1967,
232 pp., 1300 copies. [Russ. text; Russ., Europ.,
Turk. titles, per.: 1890-1960's, pp. 217-220]

*Kurdoev, K. K. GRAMMATIKA KURDSKOGO IAZYKA (KURMANDZHI).
Moscow-Leningrad: (Akad. Nauk SSSR. Institut
Vostokovedeniia), 1957, 343 pp., 1700 copies. [Russ.
text; 67 Russ., Kurd, Europ. titles, pp. 336-338]

*Kurdoev, K. K. KURDSKII IAZYK. Moscow: Izdatel'stvo
Vostochnoi Literatury, 1961, 81 pp., 1500 copies.
[Russ. text; Kurd, Russ., Europ. titles, p. 80]

*Miller, B. "KURDSKAIA LITERATURA," LITERATURNAIA
ENTSIKLOPEDIIA. Vol. 5. n. p. Izdatel'stvo
Kommunisticheskoi Entsiklopedii, 1931, 1st ed.,
751-753 pp. [Russ. text; Russ., Europ. titles,
p. 753]

*_____. "KURDSKII IAZYK," LITERATURNAIA ENTSIKLOPEDIIA.
Vol. 5. n. p. Izdatel'stvo Kommunisticheskoi
Akademii, 1931, 1st ed., 753-754 pp. [Russ. text;
Europ. titles, p. 754]

*Vil'chevskii, O. "BIBLIOGRAFICHESKII OBZOR ZARUBEZHNYKH
KURDSKIKH PECHATNYKH IZDANII V XX STOLETII," IRANSKIE
IAZYKI. Vol. 1. Moscow-Leningrad: Izdatel'stvo
Akademii Nauk SSSR, 1954, 181 pp., 2000 copies. [Russ.
text; Kurd, Europ., Middle East titles, pub.: 20th
century, pp. 147-181]

Kurd

SOCIAL ORGANIZATION

*Nikitin, B. Kurdy. Moscow: Izdatel'stvo "Progress,"
  1964, 432 pp. [Russ. text; Russ., Mid-East, European
  titles, pp. 412-427]

11 NOGAI

HISTORY, ARCHAEOLOGY

*"NOGAITSY," BOL'SHAIA SOVETSKAIA ENTSIKLOPEDIIA.
  Vol. 42. Moscow: Gosudarstvennyi Institut "Sovetskaia
  Entsiklopediia" (OGIZ RSFSR), 1939, 1st ed.,
  281-282 pp. [Russ. text; Nogai, Russ., Europ. titles,
  p. 282]

LANGUAGE, LITERATURE

*N. B. "NOGAISKII IAZYK," BOL'SHAIA SOVETSKAIA
  ENTSIKLOPEDIIA. Vol. 42. Moscow: Gosudarstvennyi
  Institut "Sovetskaia Entsiklopediia" (OGIZ RSFSR),
  1939, 1st ed., 280-281 pp. [Russ. text; Nogay.,
  Russ. titles, p. 281]

12 NORTH CAUCASUS

GENERAL

[Funtikova, T. I. comp.] STAVROPOL'E V VELIKOI OTECHESTVENNOI VOINE. 1941-1945. UKAZATEL' LIT. Stavropol': Kn. Izd., 1968, 51 pp., 1000 copies. [Russ. text; ca.560 titles]

Iampol'skii, M. L. "OBZOR LITERATURY PO SEVERO-KAVKAZSKOMU KRAIU," VOPR. PROSV. NA SEV. KAVK. No. 5, 1927. [Russ. text; titles, pp. 92-94]

Sarakhan, D. A. "LITERATURA O SEV.-KAVK. KRAE. (S I/XII-25 G. PO I/1 26 6.)," SEV.-KAVK. KRAI No. 5, 1926. [Russ. text; titles pp. 179-190, pub. 1925-1926]

ZA VLAST' SOVETOV NA STAVROPOL'E [BIBLIOGRAFICHESKIE] PAMIATKI-ZAKLADKI. Stavropol': Knizhnoe Izdatel'stvo, 1966, [30] pp., 1000 copies. [Russ. text]

ANTHROPOLOGY, ETHNOGRAPHY

*Sergeeva, G. "ANNOTIROVANNYI SPISOK LITERATURY PO ETNOGRAFII SEVERNOGO KAVKAZA, OPUBLIKOVANNOI V 1964-1965 GG." SOVETSKAIA ETNOGRAFIIA. No. 3, 1966. [Russ. text; 103 Azerb., Georg., Arm., Russ. titles, pp. 175-184, pub. 1964-1965]

North Caucasus

ARCHITECTURE. ART. MUSIC

*EPIGRAFICHESKIE PAMIATNIKI SEVERNOGO KAVKAZA NA ARABSKOM, PERSIDSKOM I TURETSKOM IAZYKAKH. PART 1. NADPISI X-XVII VV. Moscow: Izdatel'stvo "Nauka," 1966, 300 pp., 1600 copies. [Russ. text; 223-240 pp., per. X-XVII cent.]

ECONOMICS

Potapova, P. A. comp. EKONOMICHESKAIA RABOTA NA PREDPRIIATIIAKH. KRATKII UKAZATEL' LITERATURY. (SEV. KAVKAZSKII SOVNARKHOZ.) Rostov N/D: (Sev.-Kavkazskii Sovnarkhoz. Tsbti. Tsentr. Nauch.-Tekhn. B-ka.), 1966, 40 pp., 1000 copies. [Russ. text]

Runchev, M. S. REZERVY IUZHNOI STEPNOI ZONY. NA OPYTE KHOZ-V ZERNOVO-ZHIVOTNOVODCHESKOGO NAPRAVLENIIA SEV. KAVKAZA. Rostov-N/D: Kn. Izd., 1967, 191 pp., 4000 copies. [Russ. text; titles pp. 188-189]

SEVERNYI KAVKAZ. Moscow: (Akad. Nauk SSSR. In-t Geografii), 1957. [Russ. text; ca.160 titles, pp. 500-504]

GEOGRAPHY

*Maslov, E. P. PROIZVODITEL'NYE SILY SEVERNOGO KAVKAZA. (PROBLEMY GEOGRAFII KHOZ-VA I OSVOENIIA RESURSOV.) Moscow: "Nauka," 1966, 264 pp., 1200 copies. [Russ. text; ca.170 Russ. titles, pub.: 1927-1965, pp. 257-262]

Safronov, I. N. GEOMORFOLOGIIA SEVERNOGO KAVKAZA. Rostov N/D, 1969. [Russ. text; ca.250 titles, pp. 206-217]

HISTORY, ARCHAEOLOGY

"BIBLIOGRAFICHESKII UKAZATEL' KNIG, SOCHINENII I STATEI OTNOSIASHCHIKHSIA K STATISTIKIE, ISTORII I ETNOGRAFII SIEVERNAGO KAVKAZA," SBORNIK STAT. SVIED O STAVROP. GUB. TRUDY STAVROPOL'SKOI UCHENOI ARKHIVNOI KOMISSII. No. 1, 1911. [Russ. text; titles pp. 1-7]

Kusheva, E. N. NARODY SEVERNOGO KAVKAZA I IKH SVIAZI S ROSSIEI. VTORAIA POLOVINA XVI--30-E GODY XVII V. Moscow, 1963. [Russ. text; titles, pp. 22-36, per.: 16th-17th cent]

Vinogradov, V. B. TAINY MINUVSHIKH VREMEN. [ARKHEOL. PAMIATNIKI SEV. KAVKAZA]. Moscow, 1966. [Russ. text; 33 titles, pp. 166-167]

North Caucasus

POLITICAL SCIENCE, LAW

UKAZATEL' LITERATURY K TEMATIKE LEKTSII, DOKLADOV,
BESED POLITUPRAVLENIIA... Piatigorsk: "Krasnyi
Kavalerist," 1941, 36 pp., 1500 copies. [Russ. text]

13 OSSET

GENERAL

Abaev, V. I. KLASSIFITSIROVANNYI PERECHEN' RABOT VSEV. F. MILLERA PO OSETINOVEDENIIU (K STO LETIIU SO DNIA ROZHDENIIA). IZVESTIIA IUGO-OSETINSK. NAUCHNO-ISSLED. IN-TA AN GRUZINSKOI SSR. No. 6, 1948. [Russ. text; 39 titles, per.: 1881-1934, pp. 28-30]

Alborov, B. "PERVAIA PECHATNAIA OSETINSKAIA KNIGA," IZVESTIIA GORSKOGO PEDAGOGICHESKOGO INSTITUTA. Vol. 5, 1929. [Russ. text; 21 titles, p. 182]

*Gireev, D. A.; M. T. Lukashenko, comp. OSETIIA V RUSSKOI LITERATURE. Ordzhonikidze: Severo-Osetinskoe Knizhnoe Izdatel'stvo, 1963, 480 pp., 5000 copies. [Russ. text and titles, pp. 443-477]

*"IUGO-OSETINSKAIA AVTONOMNAIA OBLAST'," BOL'SHAIA SOVETSKAIA ENTSIKLOPEDIIA. Vol. 49. Moscow: Gosudarstvennoe Nauchnoe Izdatel'stvo "Bol'shaia Sovetskaia Entsiklopediia," 1957, 2nd ed., pp. 301-306. [Russ. text and titles, pp. 303, 304]

KATALOG IZDANII SEVERO-OSETINSKOGO KNIZHNOGO IZDATEL'STVA ZA 1956 GOD. Ordzhonikidze: Sev.-Oset. Kn. Izd., 1957, 24 pp., 1000 copies. [Russ. text; pub.: 1956]

KATALOG IZDANII SEVERO-OSETINSKOGO KNIZHNOGO IZDATEL'STVA ZA 1957 GOD. Ordzhonikidze, 1958, 27 pp., 1000 copies. [Russ. text; pub.: 1957]

LETOPIS' PECHATI. 1959. Ordzhonikidze: (Resp. B-ka im. Kirova.), 1960, 500 copies. [Osset. text; pub.:1959]

LETOPIS' PECHATI. 1960. Ordzhonikidze: (Resp. B-ka im. Kirova.), 1961, 40 pp., 300 copies. [Osset., Russ. text; pub.: 1960]

LETOPIS' PECHATI. Ordzhonikidze: (Resp. B-ka im. Kirova), 1962, 34 pp., 300 copies. [Osset, Russ. text; pub.: 1961]

Osset: General

LETOPIS' PECHATI. 1962. Ordzhonikidze: (Resp. B-ka im. Kirova), 1963, 37 pp., 300 copies. [Osset., Russ.text; pub. 1962]

LETOPIS' PECHATI. 1963. Ordzhonikidze: (Resp. B-ka im. Kirova), 1964, 35 pp., 300 copies. [Osset, Russ. text; pub.: 1963]

LETOPIS' PECHATI. 1964. Ordzhonikidze: (Resp. B-ka im. Kirova), 1965, 32 pp., 300 copies. [Osset, Russ. text; pub.: 1964]

LETOPIS' PECHATI. 1965. Ordzhonikidze: (Resp. B-ka im. Kirova), 1966. [Osset, Russ. text and titles, pub.: 1965]

LETOPIS' PECHATI. 1966. Ordzhonikidze: (Resp. Gos. Nauch. B-ka im. Kirova), 1967, 500 copies. [Osset, Russ. text and titles, pub.: 1966]

LETOPIS' PECHATI. 1967. Ordzhonikidze: (Resp. Gos. Nauch. B-ka im. Kirova), 1969, 500 copies. [Osset, Russ. text and titles, pub: 1967]

LETOPIS' PECHATI. 1968. Ordzhonikidze: (Resp. Gos. Nauch. B-ka im. Kirova), 1970, 500 copies. [Osset, Russ. text and titles, pub.: 1968]

*Miller, Vs. "OSETINY," ENTSIKLOPEDICHESKII SLOVAR'. Vol. 22. St. Petersburg: F. A. Brokgauz, I. A. Efron, 1897, 263-266 pp. [Russ. text and titles, p. 266]

*_____. OSETINSKIE ETIUDY. CHAST' VTORAIA: IZSLIEDOVANIIA. UCHENYE ZAPISKI IMPERATORSKAGO MOSKOVSKAGO UNIVERSITETA OTDIEL ISTORIKO-FILOLOGICHESKII, No. 2, 1882, 301 pp. [Russ. text; 88 Osset, Russ., Europ. titles, pp. III-VII]

*"OSETINY," BOL'SHAIA SOVETSKAIA ENTSIKLOPEDIIA. Vol. 31. Moscow: Gosudarstvennoe Nauchnoe Izdatel'stvo "Bol'shaia Sovetskaia Entsiklopediia," 1955, 2nd ed. 279-280 pp. [Russ. text and titles, p. 280]

Pchelina, E. "'OSSETICA' (OPYT BIBLIOGRAFII)," UCHENYE ZAPISKI INSTITUTA ETNICHESKIKH I NATSIONAL'NYKH KUL'TUR [NARODOV] VOSTOKA. Vol. 2, 1930 [Russ. text; 1050 Russ., Europ. titles, pp. 169-232]

Osset: General

*"SEVERO-OSETINSKAIA AVTONOMNAIA SOVETSKAIA
SOTSIALISTICHESKAIA RESPUBLIKA," BOL'SHAIA SOVETSKAIA
ENTSIKLOPEDIIA. Vol. 38. Moscow: Gosudarstvennoe
Nauchnoe Izdatel'stvo "Bol'shaia Sovetskaia
Entsiklopediia," 1955 2nd ed., 345-355 pp. [Russ.
text; Osset, Russ. titles, pp. 350, 351, 354]

Tlatova, L. K.; E. M. Ramonova. BIBLIOGRAFIIA RABOT I
STATEI PO ISTORII, EKONOMIKE, O PRIRODE, PO
IAZYKOZNANIIU, LITERATURE, KULTURE I ISKUSSTVU
SEVERNOI OSETII, OPUBLIKOVANNYKH VO VTOROM POLUGODII
1953 G. I V 1954 G.," IZVESTIIA SEV.-OSET. NAUCH.-
ISSLED. IN-TA, Vol. 17, 1956. [Russ. text; 890
titles, pub. 1953-4, pp. 329-377]

ANTHROPOLOGY, ETHNOGRAPHY

Chursin, G. F. "OSETINY. ETNOGRAFICHESKII OCHERK,"
TRUDY ZAKAVKAZSKOI NAUCHNOI ASSOTSIATSII, SERIIA 1.
No. 1. MATERIALY PO IZUCHENIIU GRUZII. IUGO-OSETIIA.
n.p., 1925. [Russ. text; 65 titles, pp. 228-232]

Gagloeva, Z. D. "BIBLIOGRAFIIA PO ETNOGRAFII OSETII,"
IZVESTIIA (IUGO-OSET. NII). No. 11, 1962. [(Russ.)
text; 894 titles, pub. 19th and 20th cent., pp. 326-401]

Vaneev, Z. N. IZ ISTORII RODOVOGO BYTA V IUGO-OSETII.
Tiflis: (Akademiia Nauk Gruz. SSR Iugo-Oset. Nauch.-
Issled. In-t) [1955]. [Russ. text; 39 titles, pp.
100-101]

ARCHITECTURE, ART, MUSIC

Isaeva, D. A. comp. PREKRASNOE--VSEM! Ordzhonikidze:
(Resp. B-ka im. Kirova), 1963. [Russ. text; ca.220
Osset, Russ. titles]

Osset: Architecture, Art, Music

*Muldarov, Gaimuraz. KHUDOZHNIKI IUGO-OSETII
(BIOBIBLIOGR. DANNYE). Tskhinvali: Iugo-Osetinskoe
Izdatel'stvo, 1967, 114 pp., 1000 copies [Osset text]

ECONOMICS

GORSKII S.-KH INSTITUT. TRUDY. Vol. 26. Ordzhonikidze:
Sev.-Oset. Kn. Izd., 1966, 202 pp., 550 copies. [Russ.
text; titles at end of articles]

GORSKII S.-KH INSTITUT. TRUDY. Vol. 27. Ordzhonikidze:
Sev.-Ost. Kn. Izd., 1967, 404 pp., 550 copies. [Russ.
text; titles at end of articles]

Karbelashvili, L. A. IUGO-OSETIIA. EKONOMICHESKO-
GEOGRAFICHESKII OBZOR I BIBLIOGRAFIIA. Tiblisi:
Izdatel'stvo Akademii Nauk Gruzinskoi SSR, 1962, 426 pp.
[Russ. text]

*Pchelina, Evg. [Reviewer] "KRAEVEDENIE...," PECHAT' I
REVOLIUTSIIA. No. 4, May-June, 1928, [Russ. text;
7 Russ. titles, pub.: 1925-1927]

Smol'skii, Ia. V.; L. P. Altunina; I. L. Larshina,
F. N. Evstropova, comp. SEVERO-OSETINSKAIA S.-KH
OPYTNAIA STANTSIIA. UKAZATEL' OPUBLIKOVANNYKH RABOT.
(1928-1968 GG.). Ordzhonikidze: (MSKH RSFSR.), 1968,
43 pp., 500 copies. [Russ. text; pub.: 1928-1968]

EDUCATION

Sarishvili, T. SHKOLA I NARODNOE OBRAZOVANIE V
DOREVOLIUTSIONNOI OSETII. Tiblisi-Staliniri:
Gosizdat Iugo-Osetii, 1956. [Georgian text; 185
Georgian, Russ. titles, per.: pre.-1917, pp. 210-216]

Osset: Education

SEVERO-OSETINSKII PEDAGOGICHESKII INSTITUT IM. K. L. KHETAGUROVA. UCHENYE ZAPISKI. Vol. 27, No. 5, 1967, 80 pp., 500 copies. [Russ. text; titles at end of articles]

*Sheinberg, A. "SEVERO-OSETINSKAIA ASSR--NARODNOE OBRAZOVANIE," BOL'SHAIA SOVETSKAIA ENTSIKLOPEDIIA. Vol. 50. Moscow: Gosudarstvennyi Nauchnyi Institut "Sovetskaia Entsiklopediia," (OGIZ RSFSR), 1944, 1st ed., 604-613 pp. [Russ. text; Osset., Russ., titles, p. 613]

GEOGRAPHY

Shan'ko, T. B. NASH GORNYI KRAI. KRATKII REK. UKAZATEL' LITERATURY PO GEOGRAFII SEVERNOI OSETII. Ordzhonikidze: (Ministerstvo Kul'tury Sev.-Oset. ASSR. Sev.-Oset. Resp. B-ka Bibliogr. Otd....), 1967, 19 pp., 500 copies. [Russ. text]

HISTORY, ARCHAEOLOGY

Fardzinova, Z. B. "BIBLIOGRAFIIA RABOT I STATEI PO ISTORII OSETII OPUBLIKOVANNYKH V 1956-1960 GG.," IZVESTIIA SEV.-OSET. NAUCH.-ISSLED. IN-TA. Vol. 22, No. 4. 1960. [Russ. text; ca.310 titles, pub. 1956-1960, pp. 220-231]

Kazbekov, G. V. FORMIROVANIE I RAZVITIE RABOCHEGO KLASSA V SEVERNOI OSETII. (1860-1940 GG.). Ordzhonikidze, 1963. [Russ. text; 80 titles per.: 1860-1940, pp. 134-137]

Osset: History, Archaeology

LITERATURA O SEVERNOI OSETII. Ordzhonikidze: (Resp. B-ka im. Kirova), [1961] (semiannual), 400 copies [Russ. text; titles pub.: 1961]

Tekhov, B. V. POZDNEBRONZOVAIA KUL'TURA LIAKHVSKOGO BASSEINA. Staliniri: Gosizdat Iugo-Osetii, 1957. [Russ. text; 169 Georgian, Russ., Europ. titles, per.: Bronze Age, pp. 160-172]

LANGUAGE, LITERATURE

*Abaev, V. "OSETINSKII IAZYK," LITERATURNAIA ENTSIKLOPEDIIA. Vol. 8. Moscow: Gosudarstvennoe Slovarno-Entsiklopedicheskoe Izdatel'stvo "Sovetskaia Entsiklopediia" (OGIZ RSFSR), 1934, 1st ed., 337-338 pp. [Russ. text; Osset., Russ., Europ. titles, p. 338]

Abaev, V. D. KOSTA. K 90-LETIIU SO DNIA ROZHDENIIA KOSTA (KHETAGUROVA). Stalinin: Gosizdat Iugo-Osetii, 1950. [55 titles, pp. 126-129]

*Abaev, V. I. ISTORIKO-ETIMOLOGICHESKII SLOVAR' OSETINSKOGO IAZYKA. Vol. 1, A-K. Moscow-Leningrad: Akademiia Nauk SSSR, 1958, 655 pp., 3500 copies. [Russ. text; Sov. Asian, Russ., Persian titles, pp. 10-18]

Ardasenov, Kh. N. "GEORGII MALIEV," IZVESTIIA SEV-OSET. NAUCHNO-ISSLEDOVATEL'NOGO INSTITUTA. Vol. 22, No. 2. 1960, 48 pp. [Russ. text; 18 Osset, Russ. titles, pub.: 1907-1958]

Bigulaev, B. B. KRATKAIA ISTORIIA OSETINSKOGO PIS'MA. Dzaudzhikau: Gosizdat Sev.-Oset. ASSR, 1952. [Russ. text; 31 titles, pp. 75-76]

*Bolaev, A. "KULAEV, SOZYRYKO," LITERATURNAIA ENTSIKLOPEDIIA. Vol. 5. n. p. Izdatel'stvo Kommunisticheskoi Akademii, 1931, 1st ed., 710-711 pp. [Russ. text; Osset, Russ. titles, p.711]

Osset: Language, Literature

*Eremeeva, N. M. comp. LAUREATY LENINSKOI PREMII V
OBLASTI LITERATURY (1957-1965). Ordzhonikidze:
Sev.-Oset. Kn. Izd., 1966, 26 pp., 500 copies.
[Russ. text and titles, per.: 1957-1965]

Gabaraev, Nikolai. comp. BIBLIOGRAFICHESKII SBORNIK
TVORCHESTVA PISATELEI IUGO-OSETII. 1940-1967 GG.
Tskhinvali: "Iryston," 1968, 121 pp., 1000 copies.
[Osset text; per.: 1940-1967]

Gagkaev, K. E. SINTAKSIS OSETINSKOGO IAZYKA.
Ordzhonikidze: Sev.-Oset. Kn. Izd., 1956. [Russ.
text; 139 Osset, Russ. titles, pp. 268-274]

Gudieva, K. M.; V. S. Kreidenko; N. M. Pastukhova.
comp. ISKUSSTVO SEVERNOI OSETII. KRATKII UKAZATEL'
LIT. Ordzhonikidze: (Resp. B-ka im. Kirova), 1959,
120 pp., 500 copies. [Osset, Russian text; ca.600
titles]

Isaev, M. I. OCHERK FONETIKI OSETINSKOGO
LITERATURNOGO IAZYKA. Ordzhonikidze: Sev.-Oset. Kn.
Izd., 1959. [Russ. text; 45 Osset, Russ., Europ.
titles, pp. 81-84]

Khadartseva, A. A. PEVETS SOVREMENNOSTI (O TVORCHESTVE
TATARI EPKHIEVA). Ordzhonikidze: Sev.-Oset. Kn. Izd.,
1966, 96 pp., 600 copies. [Russ. text; titles,
pp. 90-95]

Khadartseva, A. A. "TVORCHESKII PUT' DAVIDA TUAEVA,"
IZVESTIIA SEV.-OSET. NAUCH. ISSLED. IN-TA, Vol. 22,
No. 2, 1960. [Russ. text; 35 Osset, Georgian, Russ.
titles, p. 99, pub.: 1944-1959]

Khetagurov, K. L. SOBRANIE SOCHINEII V 3-KH T. Vol. 1.
OSETINSKAIA LIRA--KHETAG. Dzaudzhikau: Gosizdat
Sev.-Oset ASSR, 1951. [Osset, Russ., text; Osset,
Russ. titles, per.: 1859-1900, pp. 145-146]

Kochisov, K. L.; V. S. Kreidenko. IAKOV KHOZIEV (1916-
1938). Ordzhonikidze: (Sev.-Oset. Resp. B-ka im.
Kirova.), 1956, 8 pp. [Russ. text; 8 Osset. Russ.
titles, pub. 1939-1954, per.: 1916-1938]

*Korzun, V. KOSTA KHETAGUROV. OCHERK ZHIZNI I
TVORCHESTVA. Moscow: "Sov. Pisateli," 1957, 204 pp.,
10,000 copies. [Russ. text; ca.60 Osset, Russ.
titles, per.: 1859-1906, pp. 200-203]

Osset: Language, Literature

*"KOSTA KHETAGUROV" (KONSTANTIN LEVANOVICH KHETAGUROV),
BOL'SHAIA SOVETSKAIA ENTSIKLOPEDIIA. Vol. 34.
Moscow: Gosudarstvennyi Institut "Sovetskaia
Entsiklopediia," (OGIZ RSFSR), 1937, 1st ed., p. 411.
[Russ. text; Russ. titles, p. 441]

[Kreidenko, V. S.; K. L. Kochisov] KOSTA KHETAGUROV.
K 100-LETIIU SO DNIA ROZHDENIIA. 1859-1959. REK.
UKAZATEL' LIT. Ordzhonikidze: Sev.-Oset Kn. Izd.,
1959, 92 pp., 700 copies. [Osset, Russ. text; 558
Osset, Russ., other Sov. langs., per.: 1859-1959]

Kreidenko, V. S.; K. L. Kochisov. KOSTA LEVANOVICH
KHETAGUROV (1859-1906). Ordzhonikidze: (Resp. B-ka
im. Kirova.), 1956, 29 pp., 800 copies. [Russ.
text; 149 Osset, Russ. titles, per.: 1859-1906]

_____. OSETINSKAIA
SOVETSKAIA DRAMATURGIIA. KRATKII UKAZATEL' LIT.
Ordzhonikidze: (Resp. B-ka im. Kirova), 1960, 94 pp.,
700 copies. [Russ. text; Osset, Russ. titles, Sov.
per.]

Kulaev, N. Kh. SOIUZY V SOVREMENNOM OSETINSKOM IAZYKE.
Ordzhonikidze: Sev.-Oset. Kn. Izd., 1959. [Russ.
text; 53 Osset, Russ., Europ. titles, pp. 98-100]

*Lutsenko, Ivan. K. KHETAGUROV I UKRAINA. Stalinir:
Gosizdat, 1959, 103 pp., 3000 copies. [Russ. text;
Ukr., Russ., titles, pp. 101-103]

*Malinkin, A. MATERIALY DLIA BIBLIOGRAFII KOSTA
KHETAGUROVA," KOSTA KHETAGUROV. SBORNIK PAMIATI
VELIKOGO OSETINSKOGO POETA. Moscow: OGIZ Gosizdat
Khudozhestvennoi Literatury, 1941, 255 pp., 10,000
copies. [Russ. text; Osset., Russ. titles, pub.:
1887-1940, pp. 227-251]

*Miller, Vsev. DIGORSKIIA SKAZANIIA. TRUDY PO
VOSTOKOVIEDIENIIU IZDAVAEMYE LAZAREVSKIM INSTITUTOM
VOSTOCHNYKH IAZYKOV. No. 11, 1902, 147 pp. [Russ.
text; Osset, Russ. titles, pp. III-IV]

*Shifner, A. OSETINSKIE TEKSTY. St. Petersburg:
(Prilozhenie k XIV-mu Tomu Zapisok Imp. Akademii Nauk.
No. 4), 1868, 104 pp. [Russ. text; 9 Osset titles,
pp. 2-3]

*Tskhovrebova, L. E. comp. KOSTA KHETAGUROV (1859-1906)
BIBLIOGRAFIIA. Stalinir: Gosizdat Iugo-Osetii, 1959,
98 pp., 2000 copies. [Russ. text; 912 Osset, Russ.
titles, per.: 1859-1906, pub.: 1887-1958]

Osset: Language, Literature

*V. A. "OSETINSKII IAZYK," BOL'SHAIA SOVETSKAIA
ENTSIKLOPEDIIA. Vol 43. Moscow: Gosudarstvennyi
Institut "Sovetskaia Entsiklopediia" (OGIZ RSFSR),
1939, 1st ed., p. 438. [Russ. text; Osset., Russ.
Europ. titles p. 438]

*"OSETINSKII IAZYK," BOL'SHAIA SOVETSKAIA ENTSIKLOPEDIIA.
Vol. 31. n. p. Gosudarstvennoe Nauchnoe Izdatel'stvo
"Bol'shaia Sovetskaia Entsiklopediia," 1955, 2nd ed.,
p. 279. [Russ. text and titles, p. 279]

POLITICAL SCIENCE, LAW

Eremeeva, N. M.; T. A. Tsomaeva. KOMSOMOL SEVERNOI
OSETII. REKOMENDATEL'NYI UKAZATEL' LITERATURY (1918-
1965 GG.). Ordzhonikidze: (Sev.-Oset. Obkom VLKSM.
Sev.-Oset. Resp. B-ka im. S. M. Kirova...), 1967, 51
pp., 1000 copies. [Russ. text; ca.570 Osset, Russ.
titles, per.: 1918-1965]

SOCIAL ORGANIZATION

*Kazbekov, Gadzo V. FORMIROVANIE I RAZVITIE RABOCHEGO
KLASSA V SEVERNOI OSETII (1860-1940 GG.).
Ordzhonikidze: Severo-Osetinskoe Knizhnoe Izdatel'stvo,
1963, 137 pp., 1500 copies. [Russ. text; 53 Russ.
titles, per.: 1860-1940, pp. 134-137]

14 TALYSH

ANTHROPOLOGY, ETHNOGRAPHY

Anserov, N. I. TALYSHI. MEDIKO-ANTROPOLOGICHESKOE ISSLEDOVANIE. Baku: Azerbaidzhanskii Gosudarstvennyi Nauchno-Issledovatel'skii Institut, 1932, [Russ. text; 46 titles, pp. 72-3]

HISTORY, ARCHAEOLOGY

*"TALYSHSKOE KHANSTVO," BOL'SHAIA SOVETSKAIA ENTSIKLOPEDIIA. Vol. 41. n.p., 1956, 2nd ed., 562-563 pp. [Russ. text and titles, p. 563]

LANGUAGE, LITERATURE

*Miller, B. "TALYSHSKII IAZYK" (TOLYSHA ZYVON), BOL'SHAIA SOVETSKAIA ENTSIKLOPEDIIA. Vol. 53. Moscow: Gosudarstvennyi Nauchnyi Institut "Sovetskaia Entsiklopediia" (OGIZ RSFSR), 1946, 1st ed., 515-516 pp. [Russ. text; Russ., Europ. titles, p. 516]

"TALYSHSKII IAZYK," BOL'SHAIA SOVETSKAIA ENTSIKLOPEDIIA. Vol. 41. n.p., GOSUDARSTVENNOE NAUCHNOE IZDATEL'STVO "BOL'SHAIA SOVETSKAIA ENTSIKLOPEDIIA," 1956, 2nd ed., p. 562. [Russ. text and titles, p. 562]

15 ᵀᴬᵀ

LANGUAGE, LITERATURE

*B. M. "TATSKII IAZYK," LITERATURNAIA ENTSIKLOPEDIIA.
Vol. 11. n. p. Gosudarstvennoe Izdatel'stvo
"Khudozhestvennaia Literatura," 1939, 1st ed., 202 pp.
[Russ. text; Tat, Russ. titles, pp. 207-208]

Miller, Vsev. MATERIALY DLIA IZUCHENIIA EVREISKO-
TATSKAGO IAZYKA. St. Petersburg, 1892. [Russ. text;
30 titles, pp. III-IV, Chapter: "Bibliografiia"]

*TATSKII IAZYK," BOL'SHAIA SOVETSKAIA ENTSIKLOPEDIIA.
Vol. 53. Moscow: Gosudarstvennyi Nauchnyi Institut
"Sovetskaia Entsiklopediia" (OGIZ RSFSR), 1946, 669-
670 pp. [Russ. text; Tat, Russ., Europ. titles,
pp. 669-670]

16 TRANSCAUCASUS

GENERAL

Avaliani, S. "BIBLIOGRAPHIA TRANSCAUCASICA. MATERIALY ZA 1912 G.," IZVESTIIA ODESSKAGO BIBLIOGRAFICHESKAGO OBSHCHESTVA. Vol. 2, No. 8, 1913. [Russ. text; titles pp. 373-376, per.: 1912]

ARCHITECTURE, ART, MUSIC

*BABENCHIKOV, M. V. NARODNOE DEKORATIVNOE ISKUSSTVO ZAKAVKAZ'IA I EGO MASTERA. Moscow: Gosudarstvennoe Arkhitekturnoe Izdatel'stvo, 1948, 174 pp., 5000 copies. [Russ. text; 115 Georgian, Ukr., Russ. titles, pp. 169-174, pub: 1866-1948]

ECONOMICS

"EKONOMICHESKAIA LITERATURA," TRUDY ZAKAVKAZSK. EKON. SOVESHCHANIIA. Tiflis, 1923. [Russ. text; titles per.: 1921-1923]

Klupt, V. S. EKONOMICHESKAIA GEOGRAFIIA SSSR PO RAIONAM. ZAKAVKAZ'E. Moscow-Leningrad: Gosudarstvennoe Izdatel'stvo RSFSR, 1929, 160 pp. [Russ. text; titles, pp. 156-157]

Transcaucasus

GEOGRAPHY

*Liaister, A. F.; G. F. Chursin. GEOGRAFIIA
ZAKAVKAZ'IA. OCHERKI PO FIZICHESKOI GEOGRAFII I
ETNOGRAFII ZSFSR. n. p. Zakkniga, 1929, 339 pp.,
4000 copies. [Russ. text; 130+ scattered lists,
Georgian, Armenian, Russ., Europ. titles, scattered
and pp. 328-331]

HISTORY, ARCHAEOLOGY

*[Alagardian, S. G.; N. N. Stepanishvili. comp.] V. I.
LENIN O ZAKAVKAZ'E. ANNOT. BIBLIOGR. Tbilisi:
"Sabchota Sakartvelo," 1969, 197 pp., 5000 copies.
[Russ. text; 723 Russ. titles, pp. 7-161]

Azizbekova, P.; A. Manatsakanian; M. Traskunov.
SOVETSKAIA ROSSIIA I BOR'BA ZA USTANOVLENIE I
UPROCHENIE VLASTI SOVETOV V ZAKAVKAZ'E. Baku, 1969.
[Russ. text; ca.300 titles, pp. 314-321]

*Bagdasarian, O. BOR'BA PARTIINYKH ORGANIZATSII
ZAKAVKAZ'IA ZA EDINSTVO KPSS. 1920-1936. Erevan:
"Aiastan," 1969, 556 pp., 3000 copies. [Armenian
text; ca.330 Armenian, Russ. titles, pp. 534-549,
per.: 1920-1936, pub.: 1920-1968]

*Basilaia, Sh. I. ZAKAVKAZ'E V GODY PERVOI MIROVOI
VOINY. Sukhumi: Izdatel'stvo "Alashaka," 1968, 363 pp.,
1000 copies. [Russ. text; ca.350 Russ. titles, per.:
1914-1918]

Kharmandarian, S. V. LENIN I STANOVLENIE ZAKAVKAZSKOI
FEDERATSII. 1921-1923. Erevan, 1969. [Russ. text;
titles pp. 444-452, per.: 1921-1923]

Transcaucasus: History, Archaeology

Melikishbili, G. A. "DREVNIAIA ISTORIIA ZAKAVKAZ'IA
  V SOVETSKOI ISTORICHESKOI NAUKE (OBZOR)," VESTNIK
  DREVNEI ISTORII. No. 3., 1957. [Russ. text; titles
  pp. 66-75, per.: ancient[

PHILOSOPHY, RELIGION

*Apresian, G. Z. ESTETICHESKAIA MYSL' NARODOV
  ZAKAVKAZ'IA. DOMARKSISKII PERIOD. Moscow:
  "Iskusstvo," 1968, 336 pp., 2500 copies. [Russ.
  text; 230 Russ. titles, pp. 324-330, per.:
  pre-Marxist]

PART III
VOLGA BASIN

17 VOLGA BASIN

GENERAL

*Ganeizer, E. "ASTRAKHANSKAIA GUBERNIIA," BOL'SHAIA SOVETSKAIA ENTSIKLOPEDIIA, Vol. 3 Moscow: Aktsionernoe Obshchestvo "Sovetskaia Entsiklopediia," 1926, 1st ed., pp. 651-655. [Russ. text, titles, p. 655]

LITERATURA OB ASTRAKHANSKOI OBLASTI ZA 1963 GOD. (KRAEVEDCHESKII KATALOG). Astrakhan: (Obl. B-ka im. Krupskoi), 1965, 117 pp. 800 copies. [Russ. text; 1196 titles, pub. 1963]

LITERATURA OB ASTRAKHANSKOI OBLASTI ZA 1964 GOD. (KRAEVED. KATALOG). Astrakhan: (Obl. Nauch. B-ka im. Krupskoi), 1966, 57 pp., 1000 copies. [Russ. text; 454 titles, pub. 1964]

LITERATURA OB ASTRAKHANSKOI OBLASTI ZA 1965 GOD. (KRAEVEDCHESKII KATALOG). Astrakhan: (Obl. Nauch. B-ka im. Krupskoi), 1966, 79pp. 1000 copies. [Russ. text; 627 titles, pub. 1965]

ANTHROPOLOGY, ETHNOGRAPHY

*Belitser, V. N.; N. I. Vorob'eva; L. N. Terent'eva; N. N. Cheboksarova; N. V. Shlygina, ed. NARODY EVROPEISKOI CHASTI SSSR, Vol. 2. Moscow: Izdatel'stvo "Nauka" 1964, 918 pp. 4000 copies. [Russ. text, titles; pp. 848-853]

Bogdanovich, A. E. IAZYK ZEMLI. NASELENIE VERKH. POVOLZH'IA, OKI I KAMY. ETNOL. OCHERK PO DANNYM VODO-RECHNOI NOMENKLATURY I DR. MATERIALAM, Iaroslavl: Verkh-Volzh. Kn. Izd., 1966, 143 pp., 1000 copies. [Russ. text; pp. 122-142]

Volga Basin

ECONOMICS

Kliukin, N. V. "RAZVITIE PROIZVODITEL'NYKH SIL ASTRAKHANSKOI OBLASTI ZA GODY SOVETSKOI VLASTI," UCHEN. ZAP. ASTRAKH. PED. IN-TA, Vol. 16, 1969. [Russ. text; per. 1917-; ca.100 titles; pp. 42-49]

Mel'kov, V. D. ISPOL'ZOVANIE TRUDOVYKH RESURSOV V KOLKHOZAKH. Astrakhan: N.-Volzh. Kn. Izd., 1966, 56 pp., 1000 copies. [Russ. text; 29 titles; pp. 54-55]

EDUCATION

REKOMENDATEL'NYI SPISOK LITERATURY V POMOSHCH' RABOTNIKAM SHKOL I VNESHKOL'NYKH UCHREZHEDNII PO VOSPITANIIU UCHASHCHIKHSIA NA PRIMERE ZHIZNI I DEIATEL'NOSTI V. I. LENINA V REVOLIUTSIONNYKH, BOEVYKH I TRUDOVYKH TRADITSIIAKH SOVETSKOGO NARODA. Astrakhan; (Obl. Otd. Nar. Obrazovaniia), 1967, 14 pp. 1000 copies. [Russ. text]

GEOGRAPHY

*"BASKUNCHAKSKOE (SOLENOE) OZERO," BOL'SHAIA SOVETSKAIA ENTSIKLOPEDIIA, Vol. 5. Moscow: Aktsionernoe Obshchestvo "Sovetskaia Entsiklopediia," 1927 1st ed., pp. 33-35. [Russ. text, titles; p. 35]

*Beliavskii, P. "KAMA (AK-IDEL')," ENTSIKLOPEDICHESKII SLOVAR", Vol. 14. St. Petersburg: F. A. Brokgauz, I. A. Efron, 1895, pp. 123-131. [Russ. text, titles; p. 131]

Kliukin, N. V., ed. "NEKOTORYE VOPROSY GEOGRAFII ASTRAKHANSKOI OBLASTI," ASTRAKH. GOS. PED. IN-T IM. S. M. KIROVA, UCHEN. ZAPISKI, Vol.11, No. 2. Astrakhan: (M-vo Prosveshcheniia RSFSR), 1967, 172 pp., 500 copies. [Russ. text; bibliography at end of articles]

*Kriukov, A. S., ed. VOPROSY GEOGRAFIII GORODOV (NIZHNEGO POVOLZH'IA). Volgograd: (Volgogr. Pedagogicheskii Institut im. A. S. Serafimovicha), 1967, 180 pp., 700 copies. [Russ. text, titles; bibliography at end of articles]

Volga Basin: Geography

PUTEVODITEL' PO ASTRAKHANI I OBLASTI. Volgograd:
N.-Volzh. Kn. Izd., 1967, 127 pp. 25000 copies.
[Russ. text; pp. 123-125]

HISTORY, ARCHAEOLOGY

Alikina, N. A.; I. G. Gorovaia, comp. REVOLIUTSIONERY
PRIKAM'IA. 150 BIOGRAFII DEIATELEI REVOLIUTS.
DVIZHENIIA RABOTAVSHIKH V PRIKAM'E. Perm: Perm'
Kn. Izd., 1966, 823 pp., 5000 copies. [Russ. text;
pp. 747-758; 779-782]

"ASTRAKHAN'," SOVETSKAIA VOENNAIA ENTSIKLOPEDIIA,
Vol. 1. Moscow: Gosudarstvennoe Slovarno-
Entsiklopedicheskoe Izdatel'stvo "Sovetskaia
Entsiklopediia," 1932, 881-884 pp. [Russ. text,
titles; p. 884]

"ASTRAKHANSKII VOENNYI PORT," VOENNAIA ENTSIKLOPEDIIA,
Vol. 3. St. Petersburg: T-vo. I. D. Sytina, 1911,
194-195 pp. [Russ. text, titles; p. 195]

Irmuratov, Kh. OKTIABR' V AULE. Volgograd: N.-Volzh.
Kn. Izd., 1967 (Vyp. Dan. 1968), 190 pp., 3000
copies. [Russ. text; pp. 187-189]

Nikitina, N. I.; V. S. Kryshina; L. Iu. Sycheva, comp.
LENIN V POVOLZH'E. 1870-1893 GG. BIBLIOGR. UKAZ.
Ul'ianovsk: Privolzh. Kn. Izd.-vo., 1970, 126 pp.
4000 copies. [Russ. text; ca. 800 titles; per.
1870-1893]

Stasevich, P. "ASTRAKHANO-KASPIISKAIA FLOTILIIA
RKKF," SOVETSKAIA VOENNAIA ENTSIKLOPEDIIA, Vol. 1.
Moscow: Gosudarstvennoe Slovarno-Entsiklopedicheskoe
Izdatel'stvo "Sovetskaia Entsiklopediia" Ogiz RSFSR,
1932, 880-881 pp. [Russ. text; p. 881]

*Suponitskaia, P. A.; A. Ia. Il'ina. LITERATUROVEDENIE
V POVOLZH'E. BIBLIOGRAFICHESKII UKAZATEL' TRUDOV
LITERATUROVEDOV. (1953-1964 GG) Saratov:
Izdatel'stvo Saratovskogo Universiteta, 1967, 118 pp.,
1000 copies. [Russ. text; 1321 Bashkir, Tatar,
Uzbek, Russ. titles pub. 1953-1964]

Volga Basin: Bulgar

HISTORY, ARCHAEOLOGY

*"BOLGAR VELIKII," BOL'SHAIA SOVETSKAIA ENTSIKLOPEDIA.
Vol. 5. n. p. Gosudarstvennoe Nauchnoe Izdatel'stvo
"Bol'shaia Sovetskaia Entsiklopediia," 1950, 2nd ed.,
396-97 pp. [Russ. text and titles, pp. 396-97]

*"BOLGARY," BOL'SHAIA SOVETSKAIA ENTSIKLOPEDIIA. Vol. 6.
Moscow: Aktsionernoe Obshchestvo "Sovetskaia
Entsiklopediia," 1927, 1st ed., p. 774. [Russ. text;
Tatar, Russ. titles, p. 774]

*Iakovlev, A. "BOLGARY VOLZHSKIE," BOL'SHAIA SOVETSKAIA
ENTSIKLOPEDIA. Vol. 6. Moscow: Aktsionernoe
Obshchestvo "Sovetskaia Entsiklopediia," 1927, 1st ed.,
774-76 pp. [Russ. text; Russ., Europ. titles,
pp. 776]

Smirnov, A. P. VOLZHSKIE BULGARY. Moscow: (Trudy Gos.
Ist. Muzeia. No. 19), 1951, 277 pp. [Russ. text;
9 lists]

*Smirnov, Kirill A. VELIKIE BOLGARY: PUTEVODITEL' PO
GORODISHCHU. Moscow: Izdatel'stvo Akademii Nauk
SSSR, 1960, 36 pp., 4000 copies. [Russ. text and
titles, p. 36]

*V. P. "BULGARY," ENTSIKLOPEDICHESKII SLOVAR'. Vol. 4A.
St. Petersburg: F. A. Brokgauz, I. A. Efron, 1891,
895-898 pp. [Russ. text; Russ., Europ. titles, p. 898]

LANGUAGE, LITERATURE

*"BULGARSKII IAZYK," BOL'SHAIA SOVETSKAIA ENTSIKLOPEDIIA.
Vol. 6. n. p. Gosudarstvennoe Nauchnoe Izdatel'stvo
"Bol'shaia Sovetskaia Entsiklopediia," 1951, 2nd ed.,
260-61 pp. [Russ. text; Russ., Europ. titles,
p. 261]

Volga Basin: Khazar

HISTORY, ARCHAEOLOGY

*L. V. "KHOZARY," EVREISKAIA ENTSIKLOPEDIIA, Vol. 15. St. Petersburg: Izdanie Obshchestva Dlia Nauchnykh Evreiskikh Izdanii i Izdatel'stva Brokgauz-Efron, n. d., 648-652 pp. [Russ. text; Hebrew, Russ. Europ. titles, p. 652]

*Luchinskii, G. "KHOZARY," ENTSIKLOPEDICHESKII SLOVAR', Vol. 37A. St. Petersburg: F. A. Brokgauz, I. A. Efron, 1903, 484-485 pp. [Russ. text; Russ., Europ. titles, p. 485]

*Zakharov, A. "KHAZARY," BOL'SHAIA SOVETSKAIA ENTSIKLOPEDIIA, Vol. 59. Moscow: Gosudarstvennyi Institut "Sovetskaia Entsiklopediia" (Ogiz RSFSR), 1935, 1st ed., 380-381 pp. [Russ. text; Hebrew, Russ. titles, p. 381]

18 BASHKIRS

GENERAL

Artem'eva, R. comp. LITERATURA O BASHKIRSKOI ASSR
Vyp. 11 (ZA 1962 G.). Ufa: (Resp. B-ka im. Krupskoi),
1964, 111 pp., 1200 copies. [Russ. text; 1108
titles; pub. 1962]

_____. comp. LITERATURA O BASHKIRSKOI ASSR.
Vyp. 15 (ZA 1964 G.). Ufa: (Resp. B-ka im. Krupskoi),
1967, 144 pp., 600 copies. [Russ. text; 1418 titles,
pub. 1964]

BASHKIRIIA V RUSSKOI LITERATURE, Vol. 2. Ufa: 1964
[Russ. text; ca.200 titles; per. 19th c.; pp. 456-465]

*"BASHKIRSKAIA AVTONOMNAIA SOTSIALISTICHESKAIA
SOVETSKAIA RESPUBLIKA," BOL'SHAIA SOVETSKAIA
ENTSIKLOPEDIIA, Vol 5. Moscow: Aktsionernoe
Obshchestvo "Sovetskaia Entsiklopedii," 1927,
1st ed., 106-136 pp. [Russ. text; titles, p. 136]

*"BASHKIRSKAIA AVTONOMNAIA SOVETSKAIA
SOTSIALISTICHESKAIA RESPUBLIKA," BOL'SHAIA
SOVETSKAIA ENTSIKLOPEDIIA, Vol. 4. Moscow:
Gosudarstvennoe Nauchnoe Izdatel'stvo "Bol'shaia
Sovetskaia Entsiklopediia," 1950, 2nd ed., pp. 336-359.
[Russ. text; titles; pp. 341, 348, 353, 356.]

Cherdantsev, A. A. "BASHKIRSKAIA KRAEVAIA
BIBLIOGRAFIIA. VYP. VI ZA APREL'-IIUN' 1931 G.,"
KHOZIAISTVO BASHKIRII, No. 3/4, No. 11/12, 1931,
(No. 3/4) pp. 102-116; (No. 11/12) pp. 76-97. [Russ.
text; 3/4 208 titles, 11/12 346 titles; pub. 1931]

_____. "TEKUSHCHAIA BIBLIOGRAFIIA PO
KRAIU," KHOZIAISTVO BASHKIRII, Vypuski 1-3, 5-6,
Nos. 8/9, 10/12, 1929, (8/9) pp. 113-142; (10/12)
pp. 195-222. [Russ. text]

Filonenko, V. BASHKIRY. BIBLIOGRAFICHESKII UKAZATEL'
LITERATURY O BASHKIRAKH," VIESTNIK ORENB. UCHEBN.
OKR. ZA 1913-1914 GG., [1914]

Bashkir: General

Iagudina, G., comp. LITERATURA O BASHKIRSKOI ASSR.
No. 10 (ZA 1961 G.). Ufa: (Resp. B-ka im. Krupskoi),
1965, 115 pp., 1200 copies. [Russ. text; 1307 titles,
pub. 1961]

KATALOG GAZET I ZHURNALOV BASHKIRSKOI ASSR....NA 1967
GOD. Ufa: (M-vo Sviazi SSSR Bashk. Upr. Resp. Otd.
Rasprostraneniia Pechati "Soiuzpechat'"), 1966,
18 pp., 15000 copies. [Russ. text; pub. 1967]

KNIZHNAIA LETOPIS' BASHKIRSKOI TSENTRAL'NOI KNIZHNOI
PALATY. Ufa: (Knizhnaia Palata Bashkirskoi ASSR),
1935, (annual or semi-annual). [Bashk., Russ. text;
pub. 1934]

KNIZHNAIA LETOPIS' BASHKIRSKOI TSENTRAL'NOI KNIZHNOI
PALATY. Ufa: (Knizhnaia Palata Bashkirskoi ASSR),
1936, (annual or semi-annual). [Bashk., Russ. text;
pub. 1936]

KNIZHNAIA LETOPIS' BASHKIRSKOI TSENTRAL'NOI KNIZHNOI
PALATY. Ufa: (Knizhnaia Palata Bashkirskoi ASSR),
1937, (annual or semi-annual). [Bashk., Russ. text;
pub. 1937]

KNIZHNAIA LETOPIS' BASHKIRSKOI TSENTRAL'NOI KN. PALATY.
Ufa: (Kn. Palata Bash. ASSR), 1938, (semi-annual),
1938, (No. 1-2) 31 pp., 250 copies; (No. 3-4) 31 pp.,
300 copies. [Bashk., Russ. text; (No. 1-2) 250
Bashk., Russ. titles; (No. 3-4) 300 Bashk., Russ.
titles, pub. 1938]

KNIZHNAIA LETOPIS' BASH. TSENT. KN. PALATY. Ufa:
(Kn. Palata Bash. ASSR), 1939, (semi-annual),
(No. 1-2) 36 pp.; (No. 3) 21 pp., 250 copies.
[Bashk., Russ. text; 477 Bashk., Russ. titles,
pub. 1939]

KNIZHNAIA LETOPIS'. No. 1-4. Ufa: (Kn. Palata Bash.
ASSR), 1950 (quarterly), 23 pp., 300 copies. [Bashk.
text; 96 Bashk., Russ. titles, pub. 1944]

KNIZHNAIA LETOPIS'. No. 1-4. Ufa: (Kn. Palata Bash.
ASSR), 1951, (quarterly), 22 pp., 250 copies.
[Bashk. text; pub. 1945]

KNIZHNAIA LETOPIS'. No. 1-4. Ufa: (Kn. Palata Bash.
ASSR), 1952, (quarterly), 28 pp., 250 copies.
[Bashk. text; pub. 1946]

Bashkir: General

KNIZHNAIA LETOPIS'. No. 1-4. Ufa: (Kn. Palata Bash. ASSR), 1951, (quarterly), 30 pp., 300 copies. [Bashk. text; pub. 1950]

KNIZHNAIA LETOPIS'. No. 1-4. Ufa: (Kn. Palata Bash. ASSR), 1952, (quarterly), 31 pp., 300 copies. [Bashk. text; pub. 1951]

KNIZHNAIA LETOPIS'. No. 1-4. Ufa: 1949-1950, (quarterly). [Bashk. text; 223 Bashk., Tatar, Russ. titles, pub. 1949]

KNIZHNAIA LETOPIS'. No. 1-4. Ufa: (Knizhnaia Palata Bashk. ASSR), 1953, (quarterly), 42 pp., 300 copies. [Bashk., Russ. text; Bashk., Russ. titles, pub. 1952]

KNIZHNAIA LETOPIS'. No. 1-4. Ufa: (Knizhnaia Palata Bashk. ASSR), 1954, (quarterly), 44 pp., 500 copies. [Bashk., Russ. text, Bashk., Russ. titles, pub. 1953]

KNIZHNAIA LETOPIS'. No. 1-4. Ufa: (Knizhnaia Palata BASSR), 1954, (quarterly), 300 copies. [Bashk., Russ. text, Bashk., Russ. titles, pub. 1954]

KNIZHNAIA LETOPIS'. No. 1-4. Ufa: (Bashknigoizdat), 1956, (quarterly), 52 pp., 500 copies. [Bashk., Russ. text;, Bashk., Russ. titles, pub. 1955]

KNIZHNAIA LETOPIS'. No. 1-4. Ufa: Bashknigoizdat, 1957, (quarterly), 60 pp., 500 copies. [Bashk., Russ. text; Bashk., Russ titles, pub. 1956]

KNIZHNAIA LETOPIS'. No. 1-4. Ufa: Bashknigoizdat (Gos. Knizhnaia Palata BASSR), 1958, (quarterly), 62 pp., 500 copies. [Bashk., Russ. text; Bashk. Russ. titles, pub. 1957]

KNIZHNAIA LETOPIS'. No. 1-4. Ufa:.Bashknigoizdat (Gos. Knizhnaia Palata BASSR), 1959, (quarterly), 72 pp., 1000 copies. [Bashk., Russ. text; Bashk. Russ. titles, pub. 1958]

KNIZHNAIA LETOPIS'. No. 1-4. Ufa: Bashknigoizdat, 1960, 91 pp., 1000 copies. [Bashk., Russ. text, Bashk., Russ. titles, pub. 1959]

KNIZHNAIA LETOPIS'. No. 1-4. Ufa: Bashknigoizdat, 1961 (quarterly), 91 pp., 1000 copies. [Bashk., Russ. text; Bashk., Russ. titles, pub. 1960]

Bashkir: General

KNIZHNAIA LETOPIS'. Ufa: Bashknigoizdat, 1962, 72 pp., 1000 copies. [Bashkir, Russ. text; Bashkir, Russ. titles, pub. 1961]

KNIZHNAIA LETOPIS'. Ufa: Bashknigoizdat, 1963, 76 pp., 1000 copies. [Bashkir, Russ., text, Bashkir, Russ. titles, pub. 1962]

KNIZHNAIA LETOPIS'. Ufa: Bashknigoizdat, 1964, 95 pp., 1000 copies. [Bashkir, Russ. text; Bashkir, Russ. titles, pub. 1963]

KNIZHNAIA LETOPIS'. Ufa: Bashknigoizdat, 1965, 95 pp. 1000 copies. [Bashkir, Russ. text; Bashkir, Russ. titles, pub. 1964]

KNIZHNAIA LETOPIS'. Ufa: Bashknigoizdat, 1966, 95 pp. 1000 copies. [Bashkir, Russ. text; Bashkir, Russ. titles, pub. 1965]

KNIZHNAIA LETOPIS'. Ufa: Bashknigoizdat, 1969, 88 pp., 1000 copies. [Bashkir, Russ. text; Bashkir, Russ. titles, pub. 1967]

KRAEVAIA BIBLIOGRAFIIA. Ufa: (Tsentr. Knizhnaia Palata Bashkir. ASSR), No. 1-6 [No. 4 did not appear] 1929-1931. [Russ. text]

LETOPIS' PERIODICHESKIKH IZDANII BASHKIRSKOI ASSR. Ufa: (Bash. Tsentr. Kn. Palata), 1938, 24 pp., 250 copies. [Russ. text; ca.175 Bashkir, Tatar, Russ., and other titles, pub. 1937]

LETOPIS' PERIODICHESKIKH IZDANII BASHKIRSKOI ASSR. Ufa: (Bash. Tsentr. Kn. Palata), 1939, 21 pp., 300 copies. [Russ. text; ca.175 Bashkir, Tatar, Russ., and other titles, pub. 1938]

LITERATURA O BASHKIRSKOI ASSR ZA 1958 GOD. (REK. UKAZATEL'). Ufa: (Resp. B-ka), 1959, 64 pp., 1500 copies. [Russ. text; ca.700 titles, pub. 1958]

LITERATURA O BASHKIRSKOI ASSR. No. 2(6). Ufa: (Resp. B-ka im.Krupskoi), 1962, 68 pp. 300 copies. [Bashkir text, 890 Bashkir titles, pub. 1959]

LITERATURA O BASHKIRSKOI ASSR. No. 4. Ufa: (Resp. B-ka im. Krupskoi), 1960, 64 pp., 1500 copies. [Russ. text; 677 Russ. titles, pub. 1958]

Bashkir: General

LITERATURA O BASHKIRSKOI ASSR. No. 5. Ufa: (Resp.
B-ka im. Krupskoi), 1961, 74 pp., 2000 copies.
[Russ. text; 966 Russ titles, pub. 1959]

LITERATURA O BASHKIRSKOI ASSR. No. 7. Ufa: (Resp.
B-ka im. Krupskoi), 1963, 110 pp., 1200 copies.
[Russ. text; 1228 Russ. titles, pub. 1960]

LITERATURA O BASHKIRSKOI ASSR. No. 10. Ufa: (Resp.
B-ka im. Krupskoi), 1965, 115 pp., 1200 copies.
[Russ. text, 1307 titles, pub. 1961]

LITERATURA O BASHKIRSKOI ASSR. No. 5(12). Ufa:
(Resp. B-ka im. Krupskoi), 1964, 104 pp., 600 copies.
Bashk. text, 1425 Bashk. titles, pub. 1962]

LITERATURA O BASHKIRSKOI ASSR. No. 14. Ufa: (Resp.
B-ka im. Krupskoi), 1966, 104 pp., 1200 copies.
[Russ. text; 1160 Russ. titles, pub. 1963]

LITERATURA O BASHKIRSKOI ASSR. No. 15. Ufa: (resp.
B-ka im. Krupskoi), 1967, 144 pp., 600 copies.
[Russ. text; 1418 titles, pub. 1965]

*Nikol'skii, D. P., comp. "BIBLIOGRAFICHESKII UKAZATEL'
LITERATURY O BASHKIRAKH (S 1730 PO 1899 G.),"
BASHKIRY. St. Petersburg [Reprinted in
Etnograficheskoe Obozrenie (Moscow) No. 4 Za (1900),
Pribavlenie pp. 1-26] 1899. [Russ. text; Russ.,
Europ. titles, pub. 1730-1899, pp. 348-365]

*Rudenko, S. "BASHKIRY," NOVYI ENTSIKLOPEDICHESKII
SLOVAR'. Vol. 5. St. Petersburg: F. A. Brokhauz,
I. A. Efron, 1910, 483-504 pp. [Russ. text; 23
Russ., Europ. titles, pp. 503-504]

*"SPISOK TRUDOV, OPUBLIKOVANNYKH NAUCHNYMI SOTRUDNIKAMI
BFANSSSR." ANNOT. BIULLETEN' NAUCH. RABOT, No. 1.
[Russ. text, 313 Bashk., Russ. titles, pp. 93-104,
pub. 1952-1957]

Bashkir

ANTHROPOLOGY, ETHNOGRAPHY

*"BASHKIRY," URAL'SKAIA SOVETSKAIA ENTSIKLOPEDIIA, Vol. 1. Sverdlovsk-Moscow: Izdatel'stvo Uraloblispolkoma, 1933, 277-287 pp. [Russ. text; Russ. titles, pp. 286-287]

Kuzeev, R. OCHERKI ISTORICHESKOI ETNOGRAFII BASHKIR. Part I, "RODO-PLEMENNYE ORGANIZATSII BASHKIR V XVII-XVIII VV." Ufa: (Akad. Nauk SSSR. Bashkir. Filial. In-t Istorii Iazyka i Lit.), 1957. [Russ. text; ca.140 titles, per. 17th and 18th centuries, pp. 178-83]

Kuzeev, R. G.; S. N. Shitova. BASHKIRY. IST.-ETNOG. OCHERK. Ufa: 1963. [Russ. text; 58 titles, pp. 147-150]

*Mazhitov, N. A. BAKHMUTINSKAIA KUL'TURA. ETNICHESKAIA ISTORIIA NASELENIIA SEVERNOI BASHKIRII SEREDINY 1 TYSIACHELETIIA NASHEI ERY. Moscow: Izdatel'stvo "Nauka," 1968, 162 pp., 2300 copies. [Russ. text; 119 Russ. titles, pub. 1869-1966, pp. 114-118]

Nikol'skii, D. P. BASHKIRY. ETNOGRAFICHESKOE I SANITARNO-ANTROPOLOGICHESKOE IZSLIEDOVANIE. St. Petersburg, 1899, 377 pp. [Russ. text, ca.100 titles, pp. 348-365]

*Rudenko, S. I. BASHKIRY. ISTORIKO-ETNOGRAFICHESKIE OCHERKI. Moscow-Leningrad: Izdatel'stvo Akademii Nauk SSSR, 1955, 393 pp., 3500 copies. [Russ. text; ca.130 Russ., Europ. titles, pp. 382-6, pub.: 1952-54]

_____. BASHKIRY. OPYT ETNOLOGICHESKOI MONOGRAFII. ZAPISKI IMPERATORSKAGO (GOSUDARSTVENNOGO) RUSSKAGO GEOGRAFICHESKAGO OBSHCHESTVA PO OTDELENIIU ETNOGRAFII. Vol. 43, No. 1. Petrograd: 1916, X+312 pp. [Russ. text; 71 titles, pp. 309-312]

_____. BASHKIRY. OPYT ETNOLOGICHESKOI MONOGRAFII. ZAPISKI IMPERATORSKAGO (GOSUDARSTVENNOGO) RUSSKAGO GEOGRAFICHESKAGO OBSHCHESTVA PO OTDELENIIU ETNOGRAFII. Vol. 43, No. 2. Leningrad: 1926, VI+330 pp. [Russ. text, 54 titles, pp. 328-330]

Bashkir

ECONOMICS

*Khismatov, M. F. BASHKIRIIA. EKON.-GEOGR.
KHARAKTERISTIKA. Ufa: Bashknigoizdat, 1968, 387 pp.,
7000 copies. [Russ. text; ca.250 Russ. titles,
pub. 1950-1956, pp. 273-285]

*Khismatov, Mukhammed'ian Fazyl'ianovich. BASHKIRIIA.
Ufa: Bashqortostan Kitap Nashriate, 1962, 191 pp.,
3000 copies. [Bashkir text; 55 Bashkir titles,
pp. 188-190]

KHOZIAISTVO URALA. POLITIKO-EKONOMICHESKII ZHURNAL
[PREDMETNYI UKAZATEL' MATERIALOV, POMESHCHENNYKH V
ZHURNAL'E KHOZIAISTVO URALA ZA 1925, 1926, 1927 I
1928 G. G.]. Sverdlovsk: "Khoziaistvo Urala," 1929,
40 pp. [Russ. text, pub. 1925-1928]

Parkhomenko, I. I. comp. RAIONY URALA. Moscow:
Akademiia Nauk SSSR. Institut Nauchnoi Informatsii.
Ekonomicheskie Administrativnye Raiony SSSR.
Ukazatel' Novoi Literatury po Prirode, Resursam, i
Khoziaistvu, No. 5, 1958, 48 pp. [Russ. text]

"SPISOK VYSHEDSHIKH V 1931 G. KNIG PO URAL'SKOI CHASTI
UKK," KHOZIAISTVO URALA. No. 1/2, 3. 1933,
(No. 1/2) 107-110 pp.; (No. 3) 73-76 pp. [Russ. text;
(No. 1/2) 109 Russ. titles; (No. 3) 78 Russ. titles]

Takhaev, Kh. Ia. BASHKIRIIA. EKON.-GEOGR.
KHARAKTERISTIKA. Moscow: Geografgiz, 1950. [Russ.
text; 139 titles, pp. 318-325]

Timergalina, R. BASHKIRSKOI ASSR - 40 LET (UKAZATEL'
LIT.). Ufa: (Resp. B-ka), 1959, 20 pp. [Bashkir
text;, ca.200 titles, Sov. per.]

Timergalina, R. Kh., comp. BASHKIRIIA V 1958 GODU.
(UKAZATEL' LIT.). Ufa: (M-vo Kul'tury BASSR.),
1960, 74 pp., 400 copies. [Bashkir text; 660 titles,
pub. 1958]

Timergalina, R. Kh.; M. Kh. Zakirov. BASHKIRIIA V
SEMILETKE. REK. UKAZATEL' LIT. Ufa: Bashknigoizdat,
1960, 23 pp., 2000 copies. [Bashkir, Russ. text;
168 Bashkir, Russ. titles]

*Usmanov, Kh. F. STOLYPINSKAIA AGRARNAIA REFORMA V
BASHKIRII. Ufa: (Akad. Nauk SSSR. Bashkir. Filial.
In-t Istorii, Iazyka i Lit.), 1958, 173 pp., 2000
copies. [Russ. text; ca.140 Russ. titles, per. early
20th cent., pp. 169-174]

Bashkir: Economics

Zakirov, M. Kh. BASHKIRIIA V SHESTOI PIATILETKE. REK. UKAZATEL' LIT. Ufa: (Resp. B-ka), 1958, 19 pp., 1,500 copies. [Russ. text; ca.100 titles, per. Post-WW II]

_____. BASHKIRSKOI ASSR - 40 LET. (REK. UKAZATEL' LIT). Ufa: (M-vo Kul'tury BASSR. Resp. B-ka), 1959, 12 pp., 1500 copies. [Russ. text; 76 titles, Sov. per.]

GEOGRAPHY

*A. Th. S. "UFA," ENTSIKLOPEDICHESKII SLOVAR'. Vol. 35. St. Petersburg: F. A. Brokgauz, I. A. Efron, 1902, 87-89 pp. [Russ. text; Russ. titles, p. 89.]

* _____. "UFIMSKAIA GUBERNIIA," ENTSIKLOPEDICHESKII SLOVAR', Vol. 35. St. Petersburg: F. A. Brokgauz, I. A. Efron, 1902, 90-96 pp. [Russ. text; Russ. titles, p. 96]

Drozdov, G. N. "BIBLIOGRAFIIA URAL'SKOGO OKRUGA (UKAZATEL' PECHATNYKH RABOT ZA PERIOD 1762-1929 GG.)," URAL'SKII OKRUG I EGO RAIONY. No. 2. 1929. [Russ. text; titles, pp. 49-216]

Kadil'nikov, I. P. LANDSHAFTY RAIONA G. UFY," ZAPISKI BASHKIR. FILIALA GEOGR. O-VA SSSR. No. 3. 1960. [Russ. text; 59 titles, pp. 44-66]

"KRATKII UKAZATEL' LITERATURY PO URALU," SOVETSKOE KRAEVEDENIE. No. 11. 1935, 117-120 pp. [Russ. text; pub. 1932-1935]

Kucherov, E. V. OKHRANA PRIRODY V BASHKIRII. Ufa: Bashknigoizdat, 1958. [Russ. text; 58 titles, pp. 47-50]

_____. OKHRANA PRIRODY V BASHKIRII. Ufa: Bashknigoizdat, 1959. [Bashkir text; 66 Bashkir, Russ. titles, pp. 52-55.

Bashkir: Geography

Novogorodtsev, D. PO REKE UFE. PUTEVODITEL' DLIA TURISTOV. Cheliabinsk: Iuzh.-Ural'skoe Kn. Izd., 1968, 88 (10) pp., 2000 copies. [Russ. text; titles, pp. 97]

*Takhaev, Kh. Ia. PRIRODNYE USLOVIIA I RESURSY BASHKIRSKOI ASSR. Ufa:(Akad. Nauk SSSR. Bashkir. Filial.), 1959, 296 pp., 10,000 copies. [Russ. text; ca.400 Russ. titles, Sov. per., pp. 279-295]

Zaplatin, G. N., et al ed. GEOGRAFIIA BASHKIRII ZA 50 LET. UCHEN. ZAPISKI No. 30. SERIIA GEOGR. Ufa: (Bashk. Gos. Un-t im. 40-Letiia Oktiabria), 1967, (vyp. dan. 1968), 223 pp., 1000 copies. [Russ. text; titles at end of articles]

HISTORY, ARCHAEOLOGY

Amirov, M. V; A. A. Cherdantsev. BIBLIOGRAFICHESKII UKAZATEL' MATERIALOV O SALAVATE IULAEVA. (K 200-LETIIU SO DNIA ROZHDENIIA). Ufa: Bashgosizdat, 1952, 23 pp., 8000 copies. [Russ. text; 176 Bashkir, Tatar, Russ., and other titles]

"BASHKIRSKOE VOISKO," VOENNAIA ENTSIKLOPEDIIA. Vol. 4. Petersburg: T-vo I. D. Sytina, 1911, 428-429 pp. [Russ. text and titles, p. 429]

*"BASHKIRY," ENTSIKLOPEDICHESKII SLOVAR'. Vol. 3. St. Petersburg: F. A. Brokgauz, I. A. Efron, 1891, 225-240 pp. [Russ. text; Russ. and Europ. titles, pp. 238-240]

*Iuldashbaev, B. OBRAZOVANIE BASHKIRSKOI ASSR. Ufa: Bashknigoizdat, 1958, 156 pp., 4000 copies. [Russ. text; ca.20 Russ. titles, early Sov. per., pp. 3-10]

Konogorova-Shirinkina, A. M. "ANNOTIROVANNAIA BIBLIOGRAFIIA PO ARKHEOLOGII URALA," No. 2. UCHENYE ZAPISKI (PERMSKII GOS. UNIVERSITET). Vol. 12, No. 1. 1960. [Russ. text; 177 titles, pub. 1918-1940, pp. 278-297]

Bashkir: History, Archaeology

Kuzeev, R. G.; K. V. Sal'nikova, eds. ARKHEOLOGIIA I ETNOGRAFIIA BASHKIRII. Vol. 2. Ufa, 1964. [Russ. text; ca.370 titles, pp. 271-279]

*Kuzeev, Rust. G.; Kh. S. Sairanov; D. A. Chugaev, eds. OCHERKI PO ISTORII BASHKIRSKOI ASSR. Vol. II, (SOVETSKII PERIOD). Ufa: Bashkirskoe Knizhnoe Izdatel'stvo, 1966, 643 pp., 10000 copies. [Russ. text; ca.400 Russ. titles, Sov. per., pp. 598-620]

*MATERIALY PO ISTORII BASHKIRSKOI ASSR. Part I- BASHKIRSKIE VOSSTANIE V XVII I PERVOI POLOVINE XVII VV. Moscow-Leningrad: Izdatel'stvo Akademii Nauk SSSR, 1936, 631 pp., 3000 copies. [Russ. text and titles, incl. archives, maps, per. up to 1798, pp. 497-536]

NAUCHNAIA SESSIIA PO ISTORII SOVETSKOGO RABOCHEGO KLASSA BASHKIRSKOI ASSR. Ufa: (AN. SSSR. Ufim. In-t Istorii, Iazyka i Literatury), 1967, 68 pp., 500 copies. [Russ. text]

Nimvitskii, B. "BASHKIRSKAIA ASSR," SOVETSKAIA VOENNAIA ENTSIKLOPEDIIA. Vol. 2. Moscow: Gosudarstvennoe Slovarno-Entsiklopedicheskoe Izdatel'stvo "Sovetskaia Entsiklopediia" Ogiz RSFSR, 1933, 258-263 pp. [Russ. text and titles]

OCHERKI PO ISTORII BASHKIRSKOI ASSR. Vol. 2. SOVETSKII PERIOD. Ufa: Bashknigoizdat, 1966, 643 pp., 10,000 copies. [Russ text; titles pp598-620]

*Raimov, R. M. OBRAZOVANIE BASHKIRSKOI AVTONOMNOI SOVETSKOI SOTSIALISTICHESKOI RESPUBLIKI. Moscow: Izdatel'stvo Akademii Nauk SSSR, 1952, 524 pp., 4000 copies. [Russ. text and titles, pub. 1914-1949, pp. 519-520]

*Rudenko, S. "BASHKIRY," BOL'SHAIA SOVETSKAIA ENTSIKLOPEDIIA. Vol. 5. Moscow: Aktsionernoe Obshchestvo "Sovetskaia Entsiklopediia," 1927, 1st ed. pp. 140-141. [Russ. text and titles, p. 141]

Shirinkina, A. M. "ANNOTIROVANNAIA BIBLIOGRAFIIA LITERATURY PO ARKHEOLOGII URALA," No.1 (1941-1953 GG.) UCHENYE ZAPISKI MOLOTOVSKOGO GOS. UN-TA. Vol. 2, No. 3. 1956. [Russ. text; 251 titles, pub. 1941-1953, pp. 139-161]

Bashkir: History, Archaeology

*Smirnov, A. P.; N. V. Ustiugov; A. I. Kharisov;
  G. F. Shafikov; R. G. Kuzeev, eds. OCHERKI PO
  ISTORII BASHKIRSKOI ASSR, Vol. 1, Part 1. Ufa:
  Bashkirskoe Knizhnoe Izdatel'stvo, 1956, 303 pp.,
  10,000 copies. [Russ. text; 268 Tatar, Russ. titles,
  inc. archives, up to begin. of 20th century,
  pp. 289-300]

UFIMSKII INSTITUT ISTORII, IAZYKA I LITERATURY.
  ITOGOVAIA NAUCHNAIA SESSIIA UFIMSKOGO INSTITUTA
  ISTORII, IAZYKA I LITERATURY AN SSSR ZA 1965 G.
  MART 1966 G. TEZISY DOKLADOV. Ufa: (AN SSSR.)
  1966, 104 pp., 500 copies. [Russ. text; titles at
  end of reports, per. 1965-1966]

Usmanov, A. PRISOEDINENIE BASHKIRII K MOSKOVSKOMU
  GOSUDARSTVU. Ufa: (Bash. Nauch. Isled. In-t Iazyka,
  Literatury i Istorii im. Gafuri), 136 pp. [Russ.
  text; 140 Bashkir, Russ. titles, including archives,
  pub. 1737-1947, pp. 128-135]

*Usmanov, A. N. PRISOEDINENIE BASHKIRII K RUSSKOMU
  GOSUDARSTVU. Ufa: Bashknigoizdat, 1960, 193 pp.,
  3000 copies. [Russ. text; ca.140 Russ. titles,
  per. 16th century, pp. 3-24, 176-81]

*Ustiugov, N. V. BASHKIRSKOE VOSSTANIE 1737-1739 GG.
  Moscow-Leningrad: Izdatel'stvo Akademii Nauk SSSR,
  1950, 155 pp., 3000 copies. [Bashkir text; Russ.
  titles, incl. archives, per. 1737-39, pp. 11-16]

*Vasil'ev, S. M.; G. M. Derenkovskii; R. G. Kuzeev;
  N. V. Ustiugov; A. I. Kharisov, eds. OCHERKI PO
  ISTORII BASHKIRSKOI ASSR. Vol. 1, Part 1. Ufa:
  Bashkirskoe Knizhnoe Izdatel'stvo, 1959, 539 pp.,
  10,000 copies. [Russ. text; ca.500 Bashkir, Tatar,
  Russ. titles, including archives, per. 1798-1917,
  pp. 472-88]

Zhuchkova, L. Ia., comp. URAL V PERIOD VELIKOI
  OKTIABR'SKOI SOTSIALISTICHESKOI·REVOLIUTSII,
  INOSTRANNOI VOENNOI INTERVENTSII I GRAZHDANSKOI
  VOINY. (MART 1917-AVG. 1919 GG.) UKAZATEL' LIT.
  No. 1. ZA 1957-1962 GG. Sverdlovsk: Sred.-Ural'skoe
  Kn. Izd., 1965, 127 pp., 2000 copies. [Russ. text;
  950 +8 titles, per. 1917-1919, pub. 1957-1962]

Bashkir

LANGUAGE, LITERATURE

*Absaliamova, Gainiia, G. "BIBLIOGRAFIIA PROIZVEDENII SAGITA AGISHA," TVORCHESTVO SAGITA AGISHA. Ufa: Bashqortostan Kitap Nashriate, 1964, 104 pp., 1000 copies. [Bashkir text; 149 Bashkir, Russ. titles, pub. 1927-1963, pp. 98-104]

Akhmerov, K. SINTAKSIS PROSTOGO PREDLOZHENIIA V BASHKIRSKOM IAZYKE. Ufa: (Akad. Nauk SSSR. Bashkir. Filial, In-t Istorii, Iazyka i Lit), 1957. [Bashkir text; 53 Bashkir, Russ. titles, pp. 259-261]

_____. SINTAKSIS SLOZHNOSOCHINENNOGO PREDLOZHENIIA V BASHKIRSKOM IAZYKE. Ufa: (Akad. Nauk SSSR. Bashkir. Filial In-t Istorii, Iazyka i Lit.), 1960. [Bashkir text; ca.100 Bashkir, Russ. titles, pp. 76-79]

Amantai, G. IZBRANNYE PROIZVEDENIIA. Ufa: Bashknigoizdat, 1960. [Bashkir text; titles pp. 176-77]

*Aznabaev, Akhmer Mukhamedinovich. OSOBLENNYE VTOROSTEPENNYE CHLENY PREDLOZHENIIA V BASHKIRSKOM IAZYKE. Ufa: Bashqortostan Kitap Nashriate, 1965, 83 pp., 2000 copies. [Bashkir text; 80 Bashkir, Russ. titles, pp. 79-82]

Baraga, L. G., et al ed. ISTORIIA BASHKIRSKOI SOVETSKOI LITERATURY. OCHERKI. Part 2, 1941-1964. Ufa: Bashknigoizdat, 1966, 422 pp., 2000 copies. [Russ. text; ca.850 Bashkir, Tatar, Russ. titles, per. 1941-1964, pp. 369-420]

*"BIBLIOGRAFIIA PEREVODOV (1917-1940). PEREVODY PROIZVEDENII BASHKIRSKOI LITERATURY NA RUSSKII IAZYK....PEREVODY PROIZVEDENII RUSSKOI, ZARUBEZHNOI LITERATURY I LITERATURY NARODOV SSSR NA BASHKIRSKII I NA TATARSKII IAZYK," ISTORIIA BASHKIRSKOI SOVETSKOI LITERATURY. UCHENYE ZAPISKI Vyp. 11. SERIIA FILOLOGICHESKIKH NAUK No. 4(8) (Bashkirskii Gosudarstvennyi Universitet im. 40-letiia Oktiabria), 1963, 503 pp., 1000 copies. [Russ. text and titles; pub. 1920-1940, pp. 465-472; 473-501.

*Bilialov, M.; V. Moskalev. "BASHKIRSKII IAZYK," LITERATURNAIA ENTSIKLOPEDIIA. Vol. 1. n. p. Izdatel'stvo kommunisticheskoi Akademii, 1929, 376-377 pp. [Russ. text; Bashkir, Russ., Europ. titles, p. 377]

Bashkir: Language, Literature

*Dmitriev, N. "BASHKIRSKII IAZYK," BOL'SHAIA SOVETSKAIA ENTSIKLOPEDIIA. Vol. 5. Moscow: Aktsionernoe Obshchestvo "Sovetskaia Entsiklopediia," 1927, 137-139 pp. [Russ. text; Russ., Europ. titles, p. 139]

Dmitriev, N. K. BIBLIOGRAFIIA PO BASHKIRSKOMU IAZYKU I FOL'KLORU. Ufa: Bashkirskii Nauchno-Issledovatel'skii Institut Iazyka i Literatury, 1936, 12 pp. [Russ. text]

Gainullin, M.; G. Khusainov. PISATELI SOVETSKOI BASHKIRII. BIOBIBLIOGR. SPRAVOCHNIK. Ufa: Bashknigoizdat, 1969, 408 pp., 10,000 copies. [Russ. text; per. Soviet]

*Gainullin, M. F.; G. B. Khusainov. BASHKIRSKIE SOVETSKIE PISATELI [BIOBIBLIOGR. SPRAVOCHNIK]. Ufa: Bashknigoizdat, 1967, 464 pp., 5000 copies. [Bashkir text; Bashkir, Russ. titles, bibliography at end of articles]

Galin, S. A.; F. A. Nadrshina. ANNOTIROVANNYI BIBLIOGRAFICHESKII UKAZATEL' PO BASHKIRSKOMU USTNO-POETICHESKOMU TVORCHESTVU. Ufa: (AN SSSR. Ufim. In-t Istorii, Iaz. i Literatury), 1967, 100 pp., 500 copies. [Russ. text; 632 Bashkir, Russ. titles]

Garipov, T. M., comp. BASHKIRSKAIA LEKSIKA. TEMAT. SBORNIK. Ufa: Bashknigoizdat, 1966, 223 pp., 500 copies. [Russ. text; titles at end of articles]

* _____. BASHKIRSKOE IMENNOE SLOVOOBRAZOVANIE. Ufa: (Akademiia Nauk SSSR. Bashkirskii Filial. Institut Istorii, Iazyka i Literatury), 1959, 224 pp., 500 copies. [Russ. text; Bashkir, Uzbek, Tatar, Russ., Turkish, Europ. titles, pp. 215-219]

* _____., comp. "BIBLIOGRAFIIA PO BASHKIRSKOMU IAZYKOZNANIIU, VYPUSK 1," VOPROSY BASHKIRSKOI FILOLOGII. Moscow: Izdatel'stvo Akademii Nauk SSSR, 1959, 159 pp., 1200 copies. [Russ. text; Russ., Europ. titles, incl. mss., per. pre-1917, pp. 153-157]

_____. "TRUDY N. K. DMITRIEVA PO BASHKIROVEDENIIU," VOPROSY BASHKIRSKOI FILOLOGII. Moscow: (Akad. Nauk SSSR. Bashkir. Filial. In-t Istorii, Iazyka i Lit.), 1959. [Russ. text; 73 Bashkir, Russ., other titles, pp. 12-16]

Bashkir: Language, Literature

*Garipov, T. M.; M. L. Rafikov; Z. G. Uraksin.
BIBLIOGRAFIIA PO BASHKIRSKOMU IAZYKOZNANIIU
(1917-1967). Ufa: (AN SSSR. Bashk. Filial. In-t
Istorii, Iaz. i Lit.), 1969, 141 pp., 500 copies.
[Russ. text; ca.800 Bashkir, Tatar, Russ. titles,
pub. 1917-1967, pp. 13-126]

Ishbulatov, N. Kh. SOVREMENNYI BASHKIRSKII IAZYK.
Ufa, 1962. [Bashkir text; ca.100 titles,
pp. 123-127]

*ISTORIIA BASHKIRSKOI SOVETSKOI LITERATURY. Ufa:
Bashknigoizdat, 1967, 711 pp., 3000 copies.
[Bashkir text; 37 Bashkir, Russ. titles, pub.
1923-1967, pp. 708-709]

*Iuldashev, A. A. SISTEMA SLOVOOBRAZOVANIIA I
SPRIAZHENIIA GLAGOLA. Moscow: AN SSSR. Inst.
Iazykoznaniia. Bashk. Filial, 1958, 194 pp.
[Bashkir text; ca.100 Russ., other titles,
pp. 192-93]

"IZDANIIA PROIZVEDENII DAUTA IULTYIA--LITERATURNO-
KRITICHESKIE I PUBLITSISTICHESKIE STAT'I DAUTA
IULTYIA O KUL'TURE I LITERATURE," I. KHUSAINOV,
DAUT IULTYI. Ufa, 1963. [Bashkir text; 178
Bashkir, Tatar, Russ., titles, pub. 1921-1961,
pp. 212-219]

Kaiumova, N. BASHKIRSKII NARODNYI POET MAZHIT
GAFURI. Ufa: (Bashkir. Otd-nie Resp. B-ki
Bashkir. ASSR), 1955, 35 pp., 1000 copies.
[Bashkir text; 70 Bashkir, Tatar titles, pub.
1941-55]

Kaiumova, N.; M. Zakirov. BASHKIRSKII POET SAIFI
KUDASH. (UKAZATEL' LIT.). Ufa: (Resp. B-ka
BASSR. Poety Bashkirii), 1957, 48 pp., 1000 copies.
[Bashkir, Russ. text; 202 Bashkir, Russ. titles]

Karipov, N. IZBRANNYE PROIZVEDENIIA. Ufa:
Bashknigoizdat, 1956. [Bashkir text; 11 titles,
pp. 169-70]

Karnai, A. IZBRANNYE PROIZVEDENIIA. Ufa:
Bashknigoizdat, 1956. [Bashkir text; 40 titles,
pp. 448-51]

Khusainov, G. NARODNYI POET NIGMATI. Ufa:
Bashknigoizdat, 1960. [Bashkir text; 121 titles,
pub. 1929-59, pp. 248-54]

Bashkir: Language, Literature

Khusainov, G. TVORCHESTVO SAIFI KUDASHA. Ufa:
(Akad. Nauk SSSR. Bashkir Filial, In-t Istorii,
Iazyka i Lit.), 1959. [Bashkir text; ca.180
Bashkir, other titles, pp. 221-228]

Kiekbaev, Dzh. G. FONETIKI BASHKIRSKOGO IAZYKA.
Ufa: Bashknigoizdat, 1958. [Bashkir text; 90
Bashkir, Russ., foreign titles, pp. 206-208]

"KRATKAIA BIBLIOGRAFIIA PROIZVEDENII MAZHITA GAFURI. -
KRITICHESKAIA LITERATURA O MAZHITE GAFURI,"
TVORCHESTVO MAZHITA GAFURI. Ufa, 1965. [Bashkir
text; ca.250 Bashkir, Tatar, Ukr., Russ. titles,
per. 1904-1963, pp. 437-446]

*"KRITICHESKAIA LITERATURA O PROIZVEDENIIAKH SAGITA
AGISHA," ISTORIIA BASHKIRSKOI SOVETSKOI LITERATURY.
UCHENYE ZAPISKI, Vyp. 11, SERIIA FILOLOGICH. NAUK
No. 4(8). Ufa: Bashkirskii Gosudarstvennyi
Universitet im. 40-letiia Oktiabria, 1963, 503 pp.,
1000 copies. [Russ. text; 43 Bashkir, Tatar, Russ.
titles, pub. 1917-60, pp. 419-420]

*"KRITICHESKAIA LITERATURA O PROIZVEDENIAKH M. GAFURI,"
ISTORIIA BASHKIRSKOI SOVETSKOI LITERATURY,
UCHENYE ZAPISKI, Vyp. 11, SERIIA FILOLOGICH. NAUK
No. 4(8). Ufa: Bashkirskii Gosudarstvennyi
Universitet im. 40-letiia Oktiabria, 1963,
503 pp., 1000 copies. [Russ. text; 154 Bashkir,
Tatar, Russ. titles, pub. 1917-60, pp. 152-157]

*"KRITICHESKAIA LITERATURA O PROIZVEDENIIAKH D.
IULTYIA," ISTORIIA BASHKIRSKOI SOVETSKOI LITERATURY.
UCHENYE ZAPISKI, Vyp. 11, SERIIA FILOLOGICH. NAUK
No. 4(8). Ufa: Bashkirskii Gosudarstvennyi
Universitet im. 40-letiia Oktiabria, 1963, 503 pp.,
1000 copies. [Russ. text; 22 Bashkir, Russ., titles,
pub. 1917-60, p. 198]

*"KRITICHESKAIA LITERATURA O PROIZVEDENIIAKH ALI
KARNAIA," ISTORIIA BASHKIRSKOI SOVETSKOI LITERATURY.
UCHENYE ZAPISKI, Vyp. 11, SERIIA FILOLOGICH. NAUK
No. 4(8). Ufa: Bashkirskii Gosudarstvennyi
Universitet im. 40-letiia Oktiabria ,1963, 503 pp.,
1000 copies. [Russ. text; 11 Bashkir, Tatar, Russ.
titles, pub. 1917-60, p. 380]

Bashkir: Language, Literature

*"KRITICHESKAIA LITERATURA O PROIZVEDENIIAKH SAIFI KUDASHA," ISTORIIA BASHKIRSKOI SOVETSKOI LITERATURY. UCHENYE ZAPISKI, Vyp. 11, SERIIA FILOLOGICH. NAUK No. 4(8). Ufa: Bashkirskii Gosudarstvennyi Universitet im. 40-letiia Oktiabria, 1963, 503 pp., 1000 copies. [Russ. text; 65 Bashkir, Tatar, Russ. titles, pub. 1917-60, pp. 263-265]

*"KRITICHESKAIA LITERATURA O PROIZVEDENIIAKH SAGITA MIFTAKHOVA," ISTORIIA BASHKIRSKOI SOVETSKOI LITERATURY. UCHENYE ZAPISKI, Vyp. 11, SERIIA FILOLOGICH. NAUK No. 4(8). Ufa: Bashkirskii Gosudarstvennyi Universitet im. 40-letiia Oktiabria, 1963, 503 pp., 1000 copies. [Russ. text; 18 Bashkir, Tatar, Russ. titles, pub. 1917-1960, p. 462]

*"KRITICHESKAIA LITERATURA O PROIZVEDENNIAKH IMAIA NASYRI," ISTORIIA BASHKIRSKOI SOVETSKOI LITERATURY. UCHENYE ZAPISKI, Vyp. 11, SERIIA FILOLOGICH. NAUK No. 4(8). Ufa: Bashkirskii Gosudarstvennyi Universitet im. 40-letiia Oktiabria, 1963, 503 pp., 1000 copies. [Russ. text; 11 Bashkir titles, pub. 1917-60, p. 356]

*"KRITICHESKAIA LITERATURA O PROIZVEDENNIAKH GALIMOVA SALIAMA," ISTORIIA BASHKIRSKOI SOVETSKOI LITERATURY. UCHENYE ZAPISKI, Vyp. 11, SERIIA FILOLOGICH. NAUK No. 4(8). Ufa: Bashkirskii Gosudarstvennyi Universitet im. 40-letiia Oktiabria, 1963, 503 pp., 1000 copies. [Russ. text; 23 Bashkir, Tatar, Russ. titles, pub. 1917-60, pp. 440-441]

*"KRITICHESKAIA LITERATURA O PROIZVEDENNIAKH AFZALA TAGIROVA," ISTORIIA BASHKIRSKOI SOVETSKOI LITERATURY. UCHENYE ZAPISKI, Vyp. 11, SERIIA FILOLOGICH. NAUK No. 4(8). Ufa: Bashkirskii Gosudarstvennyi Universitet im. 40-letiia Oktiabria, 1963, 503 pp., 1000 copies. [Russ. text; 60 Bashkir, Tatar, Russ., titles, pub. 1917-60, pp. 232-234]

*Mergen, K.; F. Nadrshina, comp. BASHKIRSKIE NARODNYE ZAGADKI. Ufa: Bashknigoizdat, 1968, 255 pp., 4000 copies. [Russ. text, 16 Bashkir titles, pub. 1930-1967, p. 254]

Novikova, L. M. RUSSKII IAZYK V BASHKIRII. UCHEN. ZAPISKI No. 23, SERIIA FILOL. NAUK No. 10(14). Ufa: Bash. Gos. Un-t im. 40-letiia Oktiabria, 1968, 237 pp., 1000 copies. [Russ. text, titles pp. 229-236]

Bashkir: Language, Literature

PISATELI SOVETSKOI BASHKIRII. Ufa: Bashknigoizdat, 1955, 124 pp, 10,000 copies. [Russ. text; 48 lists, Sov. per.]

*Rakhimkulov, M. G. comp. BASHKIRIIA V RUSSKOI LITERATURE. Vol. 1. Ufa: Bashkirskoe Knizhnoe Izdatel'stvo, 1961, 455 pp., 15,000 copies. [Russ. text; Bashkir, Russ. titles, pp. 447-453]

_____. comp. BASHKIRIIA V RUSSKOI LITERATURE V 5-TI T. Vol. 4. Ufa: 1966. [Russ. text; ca.140 titles, pp. 512-517]

Rakhimkulova, M. G. BASHKIRIIA V RUSSKOI LITERATURE V 5-TI TOMAKH. Vol. 5. Ufa: Bashknigoizdat, 1968, 550 pp., 5000 copies. [Russ. text; titles pp. 538-546]

*Ramazanov, Gilemdar Z. TVORCHESTVO MAZHITA GAFURI. Ufa: Bashqortostan Kitap Nashriate, 1965, 448 pp., 2000 copies. [Bashkir text; Bashkir, Tatar, Ukrainian, Russ. titles, per. 1880-1934, pp. 437-446]

*Saadi, A. "BASHKIRSKAIA LITERATURA," LITERATURNAIA ENTSIKLOPEDIIA. Vol. 1. n. p. Izdatel'stvo Kommunisticheskoi Akademii, 1929, 373-376 pp. [Russ. text; Bashkir titles, p. 376]

Safuanov, S. ALI KARNAI. Ufa: (Bashkir. Filial Akad. Nauk SSSR. In-t Istorii, Iazyka i Lit.), 1960. [Bashkir text; ca.160 Bashkir, Tatar, Russ. titles, pp. 148-59]

_____. comp. TUKAI V BASHKIRII. VOSPOMINANIIA, STIKHI, RASSKAZY I STAT'I. Ufa: Bashknigoizdat, 1966, 208 pp., 3000 copies. [Russ. text; 149 Bashkir titles, pp. 199-205]

Saiargaliev, B. S. SLUZHEBNYE SLOVA V BASHKIRSKOM IAZYKE. Ufa: (Akad. Nauk SSSR. Bashkir. Filial.), 1960. [Bashkir text; 53 Bashkir, Tatar, Russ. titles, pp. 105-06]

Saitbattalov, G.G. SINTAKSIS SLOZHNOGO PREDLOZHENIIA BASHKIRSKOGO IAZYKA. Ufa: (Akad. Nauk SSSR. Bashkir. Filial. In-t Istorii, Iazyka i Lit.), 1961. [Bashkir text, 137 Bashkir, Russ., other titles, pp. 292-96]

Bashkir: Language, Literature

Shastina, N. P. "SPISOK NAUCIINYKH TRUDOV AKADEMIKA B. IA. VLADIMIRTSOVA.--LITERATURA OB AKADEMIKE B. IA. VLADIMIRTSOVE," FILOLOGIIA I ISTORIIA MONGOL'SKIKH NARODOV. Moscow: (Akad. Nauk SSSR. In-t Vostokovedeniia.), 1958. [Russ. text; 94 Bashkir, Russ., foreign titles, pub. 1909-1934, pp. 8-11]

Siunchelei, S. A. ANNOTIROVANNAIA BIBLIOGRAFIIA PO BASHKIRSKOMU IAZYKU. n. p. [194?], 92 pp. [Russ. text]

Timergalina, R. Kh. PISATELI BASHKIRII. Ufa: Bashknigoizdat, 1968, 498 pp., 1500 copies. [Bashkir text and titles]

*VOPROSY BASHKIRSKOI FILOLOGII. Moscow: Izdatel'stvo Akademii Nauk SSSR, 1959, 159 pp., 1200 copies. [Russ. text; Bashkir, Russ., Hung., Europ. titles, pp. 153-155; 156-157]

"VOPROSY LEKSIGOLOGII I SINTAKSISA," UCHENYE ZAPISKI (BASHKIR. GOS. UN-T). SERIIA FILOL. NAUK. No. 8. Ufa: 1964. [Russ. text; 94 titles, pp. 62-63; 107-109]

*VOPROSY METODOLOGII I METODIKI LINGVISTICHESKIKH ISSLEDOVANII. Ufa: (M-vo Vyssh. i Sred. Spets. Obrazovaniia RSFSR.), 1966, 267 pp., 800 copies. [Russ. text; titles at end of articles]

Zaripov, Nur. ODIN IZ PERVYKH GVARDEITSEV (OB IMAE NASYRI). Ufa: Bashknigoizdat, 1968, 160 pp., 2000 copies. [Russ. text; Bashkir titles, pp. 155-159]

POLITICAL SCIENCE, LAW

Aleksandrov, F. A. BOR'BA ZA VLAST' SOVETOV V BASHKIRII V 1917 GODU. Ufa: (Bashkir. Nauch.-Issled. In-t Iazyka, Lit. i Istorii im. Gafuri), 1951. [Russ. text; ca.65 titles, per. 1917, pp. 186-187]

Bashkir: Political Science, Law

Amirov, M. V. BIBLIOGRAFIIA PROIZVEDENII KLASSIKOV MARKSIZMA-LENINIZMA, IZDANNYKH NA BASHKIRSKOM IAZYKE. Ufa: Knizhnoe Izdatel'stvo, 1954, 27 pp., 1000 copies. [Bashkir text; 131 Bashkir titles, pub. 1919-53]

*"BASHKIRSKAIA ASSR," URAL'SKAIA SOVETSKAIA ENTSIKLOPEDIIA. Vol. 1. Sverdlovsk-Moscow: Izdatel'stvo Uraloblispolkoma, 1933, 267-277 pp. [Russ. text and titles, pub. 1930s, p. 277]

*Karimova. "OBZOR LITERATURY POSVIASHCHENNOI OKTIABRIU I GRAZHDANSKOI VOINY V BASHKIRII," REVOLIUTSIONNYI VOSTOK No. 6(28). 1934, 226-231 pp. [Russ. text; Russ. survey, per. 1917-1920, pp. 226-227]

Kuzyev, R. U. SHAGIT KHUDAIBERDIN. Ufa: 1964. [Russ. text; ca.40 titles, pp. 91-94]

*Murtazin, M. L. BASHKIRIIA I BASHKIRSKIE VOISKA V GRAZHDANSKUIU VOINU. Leningrad:Shtab RKKA, Nauchno-Ustavnoi Otdel. Izdanie Voennoi Tipografii Upravleniia Delami Narkomvoenmor i RVS SSSR, 1927, 214 pp., 2500 copies. [Russ. text; Russ. titles, including archives, per. 1734-1921; pub. 1734-1926, pp. 9-11]

Podshivalov, I. GRAZHDANSKAIA BOR'BA NA URALE 1917-1918 (OPYT VOENNO-ISTORICHESKOGO ISSLEDOVANIIA), Moscow: Gosudarstvennoe Voennoe Izdatel'stvo, 1925, 221 pp. [Russ. text; per. 1917-1918, pp. 218-221]

*Raimov, R. M. OBRAZOVANIE BASHKIRSKOI AVTONOMNOI SOVETSKOI SOTSIALISTICHESKOI RESPUBLIKI. Moscow: (Akad. Nauk SSSR), 523 pp., 4000 copies. [Russ. text; ca.260 Bashkir, Tatar, Russ. titles, pp. 512-520]

19 CHUVASH

GENERAL

Chernova, G. M. CHUVASHSKAIA ASSR. UKAZATEL' LITERATURY. Cheboksary: Chuvashgosizdat, 1953, 127 pp., 2000 copies. [Russ. text; ca.1750 Chuvash, Russ. titles, pub.: Sov. per.]

*"CHUVASHSKAIA AVTONOMNAIA SOVETSKAIA SOTSIALISTICHESKAIA RESPUBLIKA," BOL'SHAIA SOVETSKAIA ENTSIKLOPEDIIA. Vol. 61. Moscow: OGIZ RSFSR. Gosudarstvennoe Slovarno-Entsiklopedicheskoe Izdatel'stvo "Sovetskaia Entsiklopediia," 1934, 1st ed., 700-718 pp. [Russ. text and titles, pp. 708, 718]

*"CHUVASHSKAIA AVTONOMNAIA SOVETSKAIA SOTSIALISTICHESKAIA RESPUBLIKA," BOL'SHAIA SOVETSKAIA ENTSIKLOPEDIIA. Vol. 47. Moscow: Gosudarstvennoe Nauchnoe Izdatel'stvo "Bol'shaia Sovetskaia Entsiklopediia," 1957, 2nd ed., pp. 447-454. [Russ. text and titles, pp. 450, 453, 454]

Danilov, S. D. comp. CHUVASHSKAIA KNIGA DO 1917 GODA. n.p. (Knizhnaia Palata Bashkirii), 1950. [titles pub.: pre-1917]

Gorbachevskaia, N. F. comp. BIBLIOGRAFIIA KRAEVEDCHESKOI BIBLIOGRAFII RSFSR. (ANNOT. UKAZATEL'). No. 2. BIBLIOGRAFIIA GEOGR. I EKON. RAIONOV, KRAEV, OBLASTEI AVTONOMNYKH RESPUBLIK RSFSR. No. 3. VOLGO-VIATSKII RAION. Leningrad: (Gos. Publ. B-ka im. Saltykov-Shchedrina), 1964, (No. 3) 118 pp., 200 copies. [Russ. text; (No. 3) 348 Russ. titles, pub.: 1858-1960]

INFORMATSIIA O NOVYKH KNIGAKH, IZDAVAEMYKH V CHUVASHSKOI ASSR. Cheboksary: (Knizhnaia Palata Chuvash. ASSR. Chuvash. Resp. B-ka im. Gor'kogo), [1963] (bimonthly), 500 copies. [Chuvash text; titles, pub.: 1962]

INFORMATSIIA O NOVYKH KNIGAKH, IZDAVAEMYKH V CHUVASHSKOI ASSR. [1963] (bi-weekly), 500 copies. [Chuvash text and titles, pub.: 1963]

Chuvash: General

INFORMATSIIA O NOVYKH KNIGAKH, IZDAVAEMYKH V CHUVASHSKOI ASSR. Cheboksary: (Knizhnaia Palata Chuvashskoi ASSR), 1964 (monthly), 500 copies. [Chuvash text; titles, pub.: 1964]

INFORMATSIIA O NOVYKH KNIGAKH IZDAVAEMYKH V CHUVASHKOI ASSR. [1965] (monthly), 500 copies. [Chuvash text and titles, pub.: 1965]

INFORMATSIIA O NOVYKH KNIGAKH IZDAVAEMYKH V CHUVASHSKOI ASSR. Cheboksary: (Knizhnaia Palata Chuvash. ASSR. Chuvash. Resp. B-ka im. Gor'kogo), [1966] (monthly), 500 copies. [Chuvash text and titles, pub.: (1966)]

INFORMATSIIA O NOVYKH KNIGAKH, IZDAVAEMYKH V CHUVASHSKOI ASSR. Cheboksary: (Knizhnaia Palata Chuvash. ASSR. Chuvash. Resp. B-ka im. Gor'kogo) [1967] (monthly), 500 copies. [Chuvash text; titles pub.: (1967)]

INFORMATSIIA O NOVYKH KNIGAKH, IZDAVAEMYKH V CHUVASHSKOI ASSR. Cheboksary: (Knizhnaia Palata Chuvash. ASSSR. Chuvash. Resp. B-ka im. Gor'kogo), [1968] (monthly), 500 copies. [Chuvash text; titles pub.: (1968)]

INFORMATSIIA O NOVYKH KNIGAKH, IZDAVAEMYKH V CHUVASHSKOI ASSR. Cheboksary: (Knizhnaia Palata Chuvash. ASSR. Chuvash. Resp. B-ka im. Gor'kogo), [1969] (monthly), 500 copies. [Chuvash text; titles pub.: (1969)]

INFORMATSIIA O NOVYKH KNIGAKH, IZDAVAEMYKH V CHUVASHSKOI ASSR. Cheboksary: (Knizhnaia Palata Chuvash. ASSR. Chuvash. Resp. B-ka im. Gor'kogo), [1970] (monthly), 500 copies. [Chuvash text; titles pub.: (1970)]

*Ivanov, Antonii. "UKAZATEL' KNIG, BROSHIUR, ZHURNAL'NYKH I GAZETNYKH STATEI I ZAMIETOK NA RUSSKOM IAZYKIE O CHUVASHAKH, V SVIAZI S DRUGIMI INORODTSAMI SREDNAGO POVOLZH'IA, S 1756 GG. PO 1906 GG.," IZVESTIIA OBSHCHESTVA ARKHEOLOGII, ISTORII I ETNOGRAFII PRI KAZANSKOM UNIVERSITETIE. Vol. 23, Nos. 2, 4. 1907., (separately) 63 pp. [Russ. text; 562 Russ. titles, (2) pp. 1-32; (4) pp. 33-63, pub.: 1756-1906]

Kagan, A. S.; L. D. Kalinina; G. M. Chernova. CHUVASHSKAIA ASSR. UKAZATEL' LIT. Cheboksary: Chuvashknigoizdat, 1969, 143 pp., 1000 copies. [Russ. text; ca.1900 Chuvash, Russ. titles, pub.: 1954-1968]

Chuvash: General

KATALOG KNIG, IMEIUSHCHIKHSIA V PRODAZHE V TSENTRAL'NOM KNIZHNOM MAGAZINE TORGOVOGO P/OTD. CHUVASHKOGO OBLASTNOGO OTDELA PO NAR. OBRAZ. Cheboksary: Tip. Gostipografiia, 1922, 4 pp. [titles]

KNIZHNAIA LETOPIS' CHUVASHSKOI ASSR (1919-1928). Cheboksary: (Knizhnaia Palata Chuvashskoi ASSR), 1960, 95 pp. [Chuvash text; titles pub.: 1919-1928]

KNIZHNAIA LETOPIS' CHUVASHSKOI ASSR (1929-1938). Cheboksary: (Knizhnaia Palata Chuvashskoi ASSR), 1964, 274 pp. [Chuvash text; titles pub.: 1929-1938]

KNIZHNAIA LETOPIS' CHUVASHSKOI ASSR (1939-1940). Cheboksary: (Knizhnaia Palata Chuvashskoi ASSR), 1949, 50 pp. [Chuvash text; 325 Chuvash, Russ. titles, pub.: 1939-1940]

KNIZHNAIA LETOPIS' CHUVASHSKOI ASSR (1941-1945). Cheboksary: (Knizhnaia Palata Chuvashskoi ASSR), 1949, 96 pp. [Chuvash text; 834 Chuvash, Russ. titles, pub.: 1941-1945]

KNIZHNAIA LETOPIS' CHUVASHSKOI ASSR (1946-1949). Cheboksary: (Knizhnaia Palata Chuvashskoi ASSR), 1950, 100 pp., 450 copies. [Chuvash text; 627 + 29 + 52 Chuvash, Russ. titles, pub.: 1946-1949; pub.: 1939-1950]

KNIZHNAIA LETOPIS' CHUVASHSKOI ASSR. 1952. [Chuvash text; Chuvash, Russ. titles pub.: 1950]

KNIZHNAIA LETOPIS' CHUVASHSKOI ASSR. 1952. [Chuvash text; Chuvash, Russ. titles pub.: 1951]

KNIZHNAIA LETOPIS'. 1953. [Chuvash, Russ. text and titles, pub.: 1952]

KNIZHNAIA LETOPIS'. 1954. [Chuvash, Russ. text and titles, pub.: 1953]

KNIZHNAIA LETOPIS'. 1955. [Chuvash, Russ. text and titles, pub.: 1954]

KNIZHNAIA LETOPIS'. 1956. [Chuvash, Russ. text and titles, pub.: 1955]

KNIZHNAIA LETOPIS'. 1957. [Chuvash, Russ. text and titles, pub.: 1956]

Chuvash: General

LETOPIS' GAZETNYKH STATEI. 1954. [Chuvash, Russ. text; titles pub.: 1954]

LETOPIS' GAZETNYKH STATEI. 1955-1956, 600 copies. [Chuvash, Russ. text; titles pub.: 1955]

LETOPIS' GAZETNYKH STATEI. [1957] (quarterly). [Chuvash, Russ. text; pub.: 1956]

LETOPIS' PECHATI. 1959 (quarterly). [Chuvash, Russ. text and titles, pub.: 1957]

LETOPIS' PECHATI. 1958. (quarterly). [Chuvash, Russ. text and titles, pub.: 1958]

LETOPIS' PECHATI. 1959 (quarterly). [Chuvash, Russ. text and titles, pub.: 1959]

LETOPIS' PECHATI. [1960] (quarterly). [Chuvash, Russ. text and titles, pub.: 1960]

LETOPIS' PECHATI. [1961] (quarterly). [Chuvash, Russ. text and titles, pub.: 1961]

LETOPIS' PECHATI. 1962-1963 (quarterly). [Chuvash, Russ. text and titles pub.: 1962-1963]

LETOPIS' PECHATI. 1964 (quarterly). [Chuvash, Russ. text and titles pub.: 1964]

LETOPIS' PECHATI. [1965; (quarterly)] [Chuvash, Russ. text and titles pub.: 1965]

LETOPIS' PECHATI. 1966 (quarterly) [Chuvash, Russ. text and titles pub.: 1966]

LETOPIS' PECHATI. 1967 (quarterly). [Chuvash, Russ. text and titles pub.: 1967]

LETOPIS' PECHATI. [1968] (quarterly). [Chuvash, Russ. text and titles pub.: (1968)]

LETOPIS' PECHATI. [1969] (quarterly). [Chuvash, Russ. text and titles pub.: (1969)]

LETOPIS' ZHURNAL'NYKH STATEI. 1952. [Chuvash text; 432 Chuvash, Russ. titles, pub.: 1951]

LETOPIS' ZHURNAL'NYKH STATEI. 1953. [Chuvash, Russ. text and titles, pub.: 1952]

Chuvash: General

LETOPIS' ZHURNAL'NYKH STATEI. 1954. [Chuvash, Russ. text and titles, pub.: 1953]

LETOPIS' ZHURNAL'NYKH STATEI. 1954. [Chuvash, Russ. text and titles, pub.: 1954]

LETOPIS' ZHURNAL'NYKH STATEI. 1956. [Chuvash, Russ. text and titles, pub.: 1955]

LETOPIS' ZHURNAL'NYKH STATEI. 1957. [Chuvash, Russ. text and titles, pub.: 1956]

*Petrova, M. I.; F. D. Dmitrieva. comps. KNIZHNAIA LETOPIS'. ORGAN GOSUDARSTVENNOI BIBLIOGRAFII CHUVASHSKOI ASSR 1929-1938. Cheboksary: (Upravlenie po Pechati pri Sovete Ministrov Chuvashskoi ASSR. Knizhnaia Palata Chuvashskoi ASSR), 1964, 274 pp., 500 copies. [Chuvash text, 2323 + 23 + 97 Chuvash, Russ. titles, pub.: 1929-1938]

Petrova, M. I.; F. E. Efimova. REKOMENDATEL'NYI KATALOG SEL'SKOI I KOLKHOZNOI BIBLIOTEKI-KNIGI, IZD. CHUVASHGOSIZDATOM. Cheboksary: Chuvashgosizdat, 1954, 216 pp., 1500 copies. [Chuvash text; 518 Chuvash, Russ. titles]

ANTHROPOLOGY, ETHNOGRAPHY

*Smirnov, I. "CHUVASHI," ENTSIKLOPEDICHESKII SLOVAR'. Vol. 38A (76). St. Petersburg: Tipografiia Akts. Obshch. Brokgauz-Efron, 1903, 933-938 pp. [Russ. text; 8 Russ. titles, p. 938]

Vorob'ev, N. I. CHUVASHI. ETNOGR. ISSLEDOVANIE. Part 1. "[MATERIAL'NAIA KUL'TURA]." Cheboksary: (Nauch.-Issled. In-t Iazyka. Lit., Istorii i Ekonomiki pri Sovete Ministrov Chuvash. ASSR), 1956. [Russ. text; ca.600 titles, pp. 389-407]

Chuvash

ARCHITECTURE, ART, MUSIC

LETOPIS' MUSIKAL'NOI LITERATURY. Cheboksary: Chuvashgosizdat, 1960, 56 pp., 300 copies. [Chuvash, Russ. text; 306 titles, pub.: mainly 1917-1952]

ECONOMICS

Akhmeev, G. N. PRIMENENIE MATEMATICHESKIKH METODOV V EKONOMICHESKOM ANALIZE. Cheboksary: (M-vo Vyssh. i Sred. Spets. Obrazovaniia RSFSR), 1968, 37 pp., 500 copies. [Russ. text; 13 titles, p. 36]

Andreev, M. A. SOTSIALISTICHESKOE PREOBRAZOVANIE SEL'SKOGO KHOZIAISTVA CHUVASHSKOI ASSR. Cheboksary: Chuvashgosizdat, 1956. [Russ. text; ca.130 titles, pp. 247-253]

CHUVASHSKII S.-KH. INSTITUT. TRUDY. Vol. 6, No. 2. 1966. [Russ. text; titles at end of articles]

CHUVASHSKII S.-KH. INSTITUT. TRUDY. Vol. 7. 1968. [Russ. text; titles at end of articles]

*Matveev, G. P. EKONOMIKO-GEOGRAFICHESKII OCHERK CHUVASHII. Cheboksary: Chuvashskoe Gosudarstvennoe Izdatel'stvo, 1959, 210 pp., 1500 copies. [Russ. text; ca.90 Russ. titles, pub.: Sov. period, pp. 206-209]

OPYT PEREDOVIKOV V SEL'SKOM KHOZIAISTVE CHUVASHSKOI ASSR. (BIBLIOGRAFICHESKIE I METODICHESKIE MATERIALY). Cheboksary: Chuvashgosizdat, 1954, 56 pp., 1000 copies. [Russ. text; 153 Chuvash, Russ. titles]

40-LETIIU CHUVASHII--DOSTOINUIU VSTRECHU. Cheboksary: Chuvashgosizdat, 1960, 88 pp., 1500 copies. [Russ. text; titles pub.: Sov. period]

Chuvash

EDUCATION

Makarov, M. P. IL'IA NIKOLAEVICH UL'IANOV I
  PROSVESHCHENIE CHUVASH. Cheboksary: Chuvashgosizdat,
  1958. [Russ. text; 23 titles, per.: 2nd half 19th c.,
  pp. 156-157]

Volkov, G. N. CHUVASHSKAIA NARODNAIA PEDAGOGIKA.
  Cheboksary: Chuvashgosizdat, 1958. [Russ. text; 70
  titles, pp. 260-262]

*_____. ETNOPEDAGOGIKA CHUVASHSKOGO NARODA. (V
  SVIAZI S PROBLEMOI OBSHCHNOSTI NARODNYKH
  PEDAGOGICHESKIKH KUL'TUR). Cheboksary: Chuvashskoe
  Knizhnoe Izdatel'stvo, 1966, 341 pp., 500 copies.
  [Russ. text; 146 Chuvash, Russ., other titles,
  pp. 335-339]

HISTORY, ARCHAEOLOGY

*Alekseev, A. A. "BIBLIOGRAFIIA PROIZVEDENII V. I.
  LENINA, OPUBLIKOVANNYKH I IZDANNYKH NA CHUVASHSKOM
  IAZYKE V 1918-1920 GG.," V. I. LENIN I CHUVASH.
  NAROD. (UCHEN. ZAP. NII PRI SOVETE MINISTROV CHUVASH.
  ASSR. No. 44). Cheboksary, 1969, 256 pp., 1000
  copies. [Russ. text; 52 Chuvash titles, pub.: 1918-
  1920, pp. 151-155]

*Dmitriev, V. D. ISTORIIA CHUVASHII XVII VEKA (DO
  KREST'IANSKOI VOINY 1773-1775 GG.) Cheboksary:
  Chuvashgosizdat, 1959, 531 pp., 1000 copies. [Russ.
  text and titles (incl. archives), per.: 17th c.- 1775,
  pp. 3-22, 528-529]

*Dolgov, V. A. VERNAIA DRUZHBA. (SEM'I UL'IANOVYKH S
I. IA. IAKOVLEVYM). IST. OCHERK. Cheboksary:
Chuvashknigoizdat, 1966, 115 pp., 3500 copies.
[Chuvash text; Chuvash, Russ. titles, pub.: 1935-1965,
pp. 112-114]

Kakhovskii, V. F. PAMIATNIKI MATERIAL'NOI KUL'TURY
CHUVASHSKOI ASSR. Cheboksary: Chuvashgosizdat, 1957,
[Russ. text; 60 titles, pp. 157-159]

_____. PROISKHOZHDENIE CHUVASHSKOGO NARODA.
[Cheboksary] 1965. [Russ. text; ca.460 titles,
pp. 466-482]

*Kuznetsov, I. "NARODNOE OBRAZOVANIE...ISTORICHESKII
OCHERK," BOL'SHAIA SOVETSKAIA ENTSIKLOPEDIIA. Vol. 61.
Moscow: (OGIZ RSFSR) Gosudarstvennoe Slovarno-
Entsiklopedicheskoe Izdatel'stvo "Sovetskaia
Entsiklopediia," 1934, 708-718 pp. [Russ. text;
Chuvash, Russ. titles, p. 718]

_____. KREST'IANSTVO CHUVASHII V PERIOD
KAPITALIZMA. Cheboksary, 1963. [Russ. text; ca.200
titles, per.: pre-1917, pp. 12-17, 559-570]

* _____. OCHERKI PO ISTORII CHUVASHSKOGO
KREST'IANSTVA. Cheboksary: Chuvashskoe
Gosudarstvennoe Izdatel'stvo, 1957, 343 pp., 3000
copies. [Chuvash text; 120 Chuvash, Russ., Europ.
titles, per.: pre-20th c., pp. 324-328]

_____. OCHERK PO ISTORII I ISTORIOGRAFII
CHUVASHII. Cheboksary: Chuvashgosizdat, 1960.
[Russ. text; 100 Chuvash, Russ. titles, pub.: 1925-
1959, pp. 374-378]

* _____., et al, eds. ISTORIIA CHUVASHSKOI
ASSR. Vol. 1. S DREVNEISHIKH VREMEN DO VELIKOI
OKTIABR'SKOI SOTSIALISTICHESKOI REVOLIUTSII.
Cheboksary: Chuvashskoe Knizhnoe Izdatel'stvo, 1966,
259 pp., 13,000 copies. [Russ. text; 73 Russ.
titles, per.: up to 1917, pp. 238-239]

* _____., et al, eds. ISTORIIA CHUVASHSKOI
ASSR. Vol. 2. OT VELIKOI OKTIABR'SKOI
SOTSIALISTICHESKOI REVOLIUTSII DO NASHIKH DNEI.
Cheboksary: Chuvashskoe Knizhnoe Izdatel'stvo,
1967, 279 pp., 8000 copies. [Russ. text; 83 Russ.
titles, per.: 1917-1967, pp. 250-251]

Chuvash: History, Archaeology

Petrov, I. E. CHUVASHIIA V PERVYE GODY DIKTATURY
PROLETARIATA. Cheboksary: Chuvashgosizdat, 1961.
[Russ. text; ca.220 titles, per.: early Sov.,
pp. 3-10, 345-354]

Romanov, N. R. "OCHERKI PO ISTORII BURLACHESTVO V XVIII
VEKOV I PERVOI POLOVINE XIX VEKA," ZAPISKI NAUCHNOGO
ISSLEDOVATEL'SKOGO INSTITUTA IAZYKA, LITERATURY I
ISTORII PRI SOVETE MINISTROV CHUVASHSKOI ASSR. No. 2.
[ca.1949] [Russ. text; 135 titles, per.: 1771-1947,
pp. 106-109]

Rumiantsev, M. V. PERVYE SHAGI KOMMUNISTOV CHUVASHII
(U ISTOKOV PART. I NATS. STROITEL'STVA). Cheboksary:
Chuvashknigoizdat, 1967, 132 pp., 1000 copies. [Russ.
text; 35 Chuvash titles, pp. 130-131]

Smirnov, A. P. ZHELEZNYI VEK CHUVASHSKOGO POVOLZH'IA.
(AKAD. NAUK SSSR. IN-T ARKHEOLOGII SSSR. No. 95).
Moscow: (Akad. Nauk SSSR. Inst. Arkheologii SSSR),
1961. [Russ. text; 67 titles, pp. 168-169]

*Studenetskii, A. ZNAKOM'TES': CHEBOKSARY. Cheboksary:
Chuvashknigoizdat, 1967, 223 pp., 15,000 copies.
[Russ. text and titles, pp. 220-222]

LANGUAGE, LITERATURE

Bassargin, B. "IZDANIIA OSNOVNYKH PROIZVEDENII IAKOVA
UKHSAIA--LITERATURNO-KRITICHESKIE STAT'I OB UKHSAE,"
IAKOV UKHSAI. Cheboksary, 1965. [Russ. text; 115
Chuvash, Russ. titles, pub.: 1934-1965, pp. 110-114]

"BIBLIOGRAFICHESKI UKAZATEL' LITERATURY PO
CHUVASHSKOMU IAZYKU," NAUCHNO-PEDAGOGICHESKII SBORNIK.
1930. [Russ. text; titles pp. 90-121]

Chernov, M. F. OBOSOBLENNYE OPREDELENIIA V SOVRM.
CHUVASHSKOM IAZYKE. Cheboksary, 1962. [Russ. text;
38 titles, per.: contemporary, pp. 44-45]

Chuvash: Language, Literature

CHUVASHSKAIA LITERATURA MEZHDU DVUMIA S"EZDAMI
PISATELEI. (APR. 1963--MART 1967).
BIBLIOGRAFICHESKII UKAZATEL'. Cheboksary:
Chuvashknigoizdat, 1967, 99 pp., 500 copies. [Russ.
text; titles pub.: 1963-1967]

CHUVASHSKAIA SOVETSKAIA LITERATURA POSLE XX S"EZDA KPSS.
PERECHEN' PROIZVEDENII CHUVASH. PISATELEI ZA 1956-
1957 GG.) Cheboksary: (Pravl. Soiuza Pisatelei
Chuvash. ASSR), 1958, 36 pp., 1000 copies. [Russ.
text; ca.500 Chuvash, Russ., Europ. titles, pub.:
1956-1957]

*"CHUVASHSKII IAZYK," BOL'SHAIA SOVETSKAIA ENTSIKLOPEDIIA,
Vol. 47. Moscow: Gosudarstvennoe Nauchnoe
Izdatel'stvo "Bol'shaia Sovetskaia Entsiklopediia,"
1957, 2nd ed., p. 455. [Russ. text and titles, p. 455]

*Danilov, D. "CHUVASHSKAIA LITERATURA," BOL'SHAIA
SOVETSKAIA ENTSIKLOPEDIIA. Vol. 61. Moscow:
Gosudarstvennoe Slovarno-Entsiklopedicheskoe
Izdatel'stvo "Sovetskaia Entsiklopediia," (OGIZ RSFSR),
1934, 1st ed., 718-720 pp. [Russ. text and titles,
pp. 720]

*_____. "MAKSIMOV-KOSHKINSKII, I. S.,"
LITERATURNAIA ENTSIKLOPEDIIA. Vol. 6. Moscow:
Gosudarstvennoe Slovarno-Entsiklopedicheskoe
Izdatel'stvo "Sovetskaia Entsiklopediia," 1932.
[Russ. text; Chuvash titles, p. 724]

*_____. "OSIPOV, PETR NIKOLAEVICH," LITERATURNAIA
ENTSIKLOPEDIIA. Vol. 8. Moscow: Gosudarstvennoe
Slovarno-Entsiklopedicheskoe Izdatel'stvo
"Sovetskaia Entsiklopediia" (OGIZ RSFSR), 1934, 1st ed.,
339-340 pp. [Russ. text; Chuvash, Russ. titles,
p. 340]

*_____. "PAVLOV, FEDOR PAVLOVICH," LITERATURNAIA
ENTSIKLOPEDIIA. Vol. 8. Moscow: Gosudarstvennoe
Slovarno-Entsiklopedicheskoe Izdatel'stvo
"Sovetskaia Entsiklopediia," (OGIZ RSFSR), 1934,
p. 395. [Russ. text; Chuvash, Russ. titles, p. 395]

*Dedushkin, N. S. CHUVASHSKAIA LITERATURA PERIODA
VELIKOI OTECHESTV. VOINY. Cheboksary: Chuvashskoe
Knizhnoe Izdatel'stvo, 1962, 154 pp., 1500 copies.
[Russ. text; 71 Russ. titles, per.: WW II, pp. 152-155]

P. V. Denisov. ed.-comp. VESTNIKI. Cheboksary, 1961.
[Chuvash text; 46 titles, pp. 267-269]

Chuvash: Language, Literature

Efimova, F. E. P. P. KHUZANGAI.[BIBLIOGR. PAMIATKA]. Cheboksary: Chuvashgosizdat, 1957, 16 pp., 1500 copies. [Chuvash text]

*_____.: L. D. Kalinina; M. I. Petrova. V. I. LENIN V CHUVASHSKOI KHUDOZHESTVENNOI LITERATURE. BIBLIOGR. UKAZ. Cheboksary: Chuvashknigoizdat, 1970, 56 pp., 1000 copies. [Chuvash text; 624 Chuvash, Russ. titles, pp. 6-51]

*Egorov, V. "CHUVASHSKII IAZYK," BOL'SHAIA SOVETSKAIA ENTSIKLOPEDIIA. Vol. 61. Moscow: Gosudarstvennoe Slovarno-Entsiklopedicheskoe Izdatel'stvo "Sovetskaia Entsiklopediia," (OGIZ RSFSR), 1934, 1st ed., 720-722 pp. [Russ. text; Chuvash, Russ. titles, p. 722]

_____. BIBLIOGRAFICHESKII UKAZATEL' LITERATURY PO CHUVASHSKOMU IAZYKU. Cheboksary: (Chuvashskii Nauchno-Issledovatel'skii Institut), 1931, 76 pp., 700 copies. [Russ. text]

_____. N. I. ASHMARIN KAK ISSLEDOVATEL' CHUVASHSKOGO IAZYKA. K 75-LETIIU SO DNIA ROZHDENIIA. Cheboksary, 1948.

Fetisov, M. I. NARODNYI POET CHUVASHII P. P. KHUZANGAI. Cheboksary: Chuvashgosizdat, 1957. [Russ. text; 337 Chuvash, Russ., other titles, pp. 256-275]

*Gorskii, S. P. OCHERKI PO ISTORII CHUVASHSKOGO LITERATURNOGO IAZYKA DOOKTIABR'SKOGO PERIODA. Cheboksary: Chuvashgosizdat, 1959, 271 pp., 2000 copies. [Russ. text; 58 Russ. titles, pp. 268-269]

Iur'ev, M. CHUVASHSKIE PISATELI. BIOBIBLIOGR. SPRAVOCHNIK. Cheboksary: Chuvashknigoizdat, 1968, 371 pp., 6000 copies. [Chuvash text; 134 Chuvash titles]

Ivanov, K. SOBRANIE SOCHINENII. Cheboksary, 1957. [Chuvash, Russ. text; 33 Chuvash, Russ., other Sov. Lang. titles, pp. 446-448]

Kalinina, L. comp. OBRAZ V. I. LENINA V CHUVASHSKOI LITERATURE. (SPISOK PROIZVEDENII). Cheboksary: (Chuvash. Obkom VLKSM. Chuvash. Resp. B-ka im. Gor'kogo. Molodezhi o V. I. Lenine), 1969, 5 pp., 1000 copies. [Chuvash text; 33 Chuvash, Russ. titles]

Chuvash: Language, Literature

Kaniukov, V. Ia. MARFA TRUBINA. Cheboksary: (Nauch.-Issled. In-t Iazyka, Lit. Istorii i Ekonomiki), 1959. [Chuvash text; ca.140 Chuvash, Russ. titles, pp. 84-91]

"KHUDOZHESTVENNYE PROIZVEDENIIA, VYPUSHCHENNYE CHUVASHSKIM GOSUDARSTVENNYM IZDATEL'STVOM V 1953 GODU," DRUZHBA. Book 5. 1954. [Russ. text; 70 Chuvash, Russ. titles, pub.: 1953, pp. 230-232]

*Khuzangai, Peder. KNIGA DRUZHBY. (LIT. SVIAZI NARODOV SSSR. SBORNIK.) Cheboksary: Chuvashknigoizdat, 1966, 199 pp., 2000 copies. [Russ. text; titles pp. 198-199]

Kuz'min, A. I. "BIBLIOGRAFIIA LITERATURNYKH PROIZVEDENII F. P. PAVLOVA," F. PAVLOV, SOBRANIE SOCH. Vol. 1. Cheboksary, 1962, 220 pp. [Chuvash, Russ. text; 33 titles, pub.: 1918-1946]

Mikhailov, M. M. KUL'TURA RECHI LEKTORA. Cheboksary: Chuvashknigoizdat, 1968, 35 pp., 1500 copies. [Russ. text; titles pp. 32-34]

Muchi, I. IZBRANNOE. Cheboksary: Chuvashgosizdat, 1960. [Chuvash text; 175 titles pp. 152-158]

Pavlova, L.; I. S. TUKTASH. K 50-LETIIU SO DNIA ROZHDENIIA. V POMOSHCH' CHITATELIAM. Cheboksary: (Chuvash. Resp. B-ka im. Gor'kogo. Pisateli Chuvashii), 1957, 26 pp., 1500 copies. [Chuvash text]

_____. KOMSOMOL V CHUVASHSKOI KHUDOZHESTVENNOI LITERATURE. (K 40-LETIIU VLKSM). [METOD. I BIBLIOGR. MATERIALY.] Cheboksary: (Gos. Resp. B-ka im. Gor'kogo), 1958, 27 pp., 1500 copies. [Chuvash. text; titles,Sov. per.]

_____.: A. F. Sergeeva. TRUBINA MARKHVI. 1888-1956 [PAMIATKA]. Cheboksary: Chuvashgosizdat, 1958, 16 pp., 1000 copies. [Chuvash text; titles, per.: 1888-1956]

"PERECHEN' PROIZVEDENII CHUVASHSKIKH PISATELEI, SOZDANNYKH V PERIOD MEZHDU IV I V S"EZDAMI PISATELEI (IIUN' 1954 - SENTIABR' 1958 G.)," CHUVASHSKAIA SOVETSKAIA LITERATURA MEZHDU DVUMIA S"EZDAMI. Cheboksary, 1958. [Russ. text; ca.800 Chuvash, Russ., other titles, pub.: 1954-1958, pp. 3-28]

Chuvash: Language, Literature

Petrov, N. P. BIBLIOGRAFICHESKII UKAZATEL' LITERATURY PO DIALEKTOLOGII CHUVASHSKOGO IAZYKA, IZDANNOI NA RUSSKOM I CHUVASHSKOM IAZYKAKH (1827-1967). MATERIALY PO CHUVASH. DIALEKTOLOGII. No. 3. 1969. [Russ. text; 102 Chuvash, Russ. titles, pub.: 1827-1967, pp. 189-206]

*_____. "BIBLIOGRAFICHESKII UKAZATEL' LITERATURY PO FONETIKE CHUVASHSKOGO IAZYKA, IZDANNOI NA RUSSKOM I CHUVASHSKOM IAZYKAKH," VOPROSY CHUVASHSKOI LITERATURY I IAZYKA. (NII PRI SOVETE MINISTROV CHUVASH ASSR. UCHEN. ZAPISKI. No. 32.) Cheboksary: Chuvashskoe Knizhnoe Izdatel'stvo, 1966, 235 pp., 700 copies. [Russ. text; 191 Chuvash, Russ. titles, per.: 1756-1966, pp. 209-235]

Petrova, M. I. comp. CHUVASHSKAIA LITERATURA MEZHDU DVUMIA S"EZDAMI PISATELEI (APR. 1963-MART 1967). BIBLIOGR. UKAZATEL'. Cheboksary: Chuvashknigoizdat, 1967, 199 pp., 500 copies. [Russ. text; 2759 titles, pub.: 1963-1967]

_____.; F. E. Efimova. BIBLIOGRAFIIA TRUDOV M. IA. SIROTKINA. UCHEN. ZAPISKI (NII IAZYKA, LIT., ISTORII I EKONOMIKI PRI SOVETE MINISTROV CHUVASH. ASSR), No. 21. n. p. 1962. [Russ. text; ca.135 titles, pub.: 1928-1958, pp. 385-389]

Plaskin, G. PROPAGANDA PROIZVEDENII CHUVASHSKIKH PISATELEI. SBORNIK METOD. UKAZANII. Cheboksary: Chuvash. Resp. B-ka im. Gor'kogo, 1952, 56 pp., 3000 copies. [Chuvash text; 9 lists]

"PROIZVEDENIIA A. M. GOR'KOGO NA CHUVASHSKOM IAZYKE," M. GOR'KII. SOCHINENIIA. Cheboksary: Chuvashgosizdat, 1953. [Chuvash text; 70 Chuvash titles, pub.: 1925-1951, pp. 693-695]

N. P. Prokop'ev, comp. SESPEL' MISHSHI. Cheboksary: (Chuvash. Resp. B-ka im. Gor'kogo), 1962, 23 pp., 1000 copies. [Chuvash text]

REKOMENDATEL'NYI SPISOK DOREVOLIUTSIONNOI, SOVETSKOI I INOSTRANNOI KHUDOZHESTVENNOI LITERATURY DLIA PARTIINO-KOMSOMOL'SKOGO AKTIVA NA RUSSKOM IAZYKE. Cheboksary: Dom Partprosa, 1936, 23 pp. [Russ. text and titles]

Chuvash: Language, Literature

Rimanov, I. F. IAROSLAV GASHEK SREDI CHUVASHSKIKH
KRASNOARMEITSEV. Cheboksary: Chuvashknigoizdat,
1968, 159 pp., 2000 copies. [Russ. text; 25 Chuvash
titles, p. 158]

Romanov, N. R. comp. CHUVASHSKIE POSLOVITSY, POGOVORKI
I ZAGADKI. Cheboksary: (Nauch.-Issled. In-t Iazyka,
Lit., Istorii i Ekonomiki), 1960. [Chuvash, Russ.
text; ca.140, 46 Chuvash, Russ. titles, pub.: 1923-
1959, pp. 334-340, 341-344]

Sespel', M. SOBR. SOCH. Cheboksary: Chuvashgosizdat,
1959. [Chuvash, Russ. text; 56 Chuvash, Ukrainian,
Russ. titles, pub.: 1918-1958, pp. 342-346]

Taer, Timkki (Semenov, T. S.) STIKHOTVORENIIA I
RASSKAZY. Cheboksary: Chuvashgosizdat, 1959.
[Chuvash text; 16 Chuvash, Russ. titles, pp. 91-94]

*Vasil'ev, N. V. [Shubossinni] comp. CHUVASHSKIE
SKAZKI. Moscow: Gosudarstvennoe Izdatel'stvo
"Khudozhestvennaia Literatura," 1937, 298 pp., 8000
copies. [Russ. text; Russ. survey, pp. 6-16]

PHILOSOPHY, RELIGION

Denisov, P. PROISKHOZHDENIE RELIGII. Cheboksary,
1962. [Chuvash text; 67 Russ. titles, pp. 146-148]

Feizov, E. Z.; E. N. Sokolov. MATERIALIZM I IDEALIZM O
DUSHE I TELE. Cheboksary: (O-vo "Znanie" RSFSR.
Chuvash. Resp. Organizatsiia. V Pomosch' Lektoru), 1967,
39 pp., 500 copies. [Russ. text; 10 titles, p. 38]

*Kudriashov, G. ATEIZM I MOLODEZH'. Cheboksary:
Chuvashknigoizdat, 1968, 128 pp., 3000 copies.
[Russ. text and titles, pub.: 1955-1967, pp. 110-127]

*Nikol'skii, N. V. KHRISTIANSTVO SREDI CHUVASH SREDNIAGO
POVOLZH'IA V XVI-XVII VIEKAKH. ISTORICHESKII OCHERK.
Kazan: Tipo-Litografiia Imperatorskago Universiteta
(Izviestiia Obshch. Arkheologii, Ist., Etnografii
pri Imp. Kazanskom Universitetie za 1912), 1912,
416 + 4 pp. [Russ. text; Tatar, Russ., Europ. titles
(incl. archives), pp. 4-6, 24-27]

POLITICAL SCIENCE, LAW

Grigor'ev, S.; A. Tokarev. PO STUPENIAM POLITICHESKIKH ZNANII. Cheboksary: Chuvashknigoizdat, 1968, 99 pp., 2000 copies. [Russ. text; titles p. 98]

SOCIAL ORGANIZATION

Kalinin, A. I. RAZDELENIE TRUDA I VSESTORONNEE RAZVITIE LICHNOSTI V USLOVIIAKH STROITEL'STVA KOMMUNIZMA. Cheboksary: (Chuvash. Resp. Organizatsiia O-va "Znanie" RSFSR), 1968, 64 pp., 1000 copies. [Russ. text; titles p. 63]

_____.; K. V. Kalinina. PEREMENA TRUDA I VSESTORONNEE RAZVITIE LICHNOSTI V USLOVIIAKH STROITEL'STVA KOMMUNIZMA. Cheboksary: (Chuvashknigoizdat), 1967, 42 pp., 1000 copies. [Russ. text; titles at end of book]

Sergeev, T.; V. Sergeeva. ROST KUL'TURY CHUVASHSKOI DEREVNI ZA GODY SOVETSKOI VLASTI. Cheboksary: Chuvashknigoizdat, 1968, 26 pp., 1500 copies. [Russ. text; titles p. 26]

20 KALMYK

GENERAL

Ivanov, I. S. DOPOLNENIE K KHRONOLOGICHESKOMU UKAZATELIU LITERATURY OB ASTRAKHANSKOM KRAIE FR. SHPERKA. Astrakhan, 1898. [Russ. text]

——————. DOPOLNENIE K OPYTU KHRONOLOGICHESKOGO UKAZATELIA LITERATURY OB ASTRAKHANSKOM KRAIE FR. SHPERKA. Astrakhan: Pamiat. Knizhka Astr. Gub. na 1889 g. [Russ. text]

——————. TRET'E DOPOLNENIE K OPYTU SISTEMATICHESKOGO UKAZATELIA LITERATURY OB ASTRAKHANSKOM KRAIE FR. SHPERKA. Astrakhan, 1905. [Russ. text]

Khristenko, Konst., comp. UKAZATEL' LITERATURY O KALMYTSKOM NARODE. Elista: Kalmgosizdat, 1941, 1350 copies, 67 pp. [Russ. text and 966 Russ. titles, per. 1728-1916]

LETOPIS' PECHATI KALMYTSKOI ASSR. Elista: (Kalm. Resp. B-ka im. Amur-Sanana), 1969, 500 copies. [Russ. text; pub. 1968]

ARCHITECTURE, ART, MUSIC

Orekhov, I. I., et al ed. O KALMYTSKOM PRIKLADNOM ISKUSSTVE. Volgograd: N.-Volzh. Kn. Izd., 1967, 52 pp., 1000 copies. [Russ. text; 19 titles, pp. 51-52]

Kalmyk

ECONOMICS

Bakaev, P. D. PUTI INTENSIFIKATSII SEL'SKOGO
KHOZIAISTVA KALMYKII. Elista: Kalmizdat, 1968,
100 pp., 1000 copies. [Russ. text; titles pp. 99-100]

*Kudriavtsev, I.; E. Davydov. "KALMYTSKAIA AVTONOMNAIA
SOVETSKAIA SOTSIALISTICHESKAIA RESPUBLIKA
(KALMYTSKAIA ASSR, KALMYKIIA)," BOL'SHAIA SOVETSKAIA
ENTSIKLOPEDIIA, Vol 30. Moscow: Gosudarstvennyi
Institut "Sovetskaia Entsiklopediia" (Ogiz RSFSR),
1937, 1st ed., 748-755 pp. [Russ. text; Kalmyk,
Russ. titles, pp. 754-755]

Nominkhanov, D. V EDINOI SEM'E. Elista: Kalmizdat,
1967, 108 pp., 2000 copies. [Russ. text; titles
pp. 102-107]

HISTORY, ARCHAEOLOGY

*"ASTRAKHAN', UIEZD I GUBERNIIA," ENTSIKLOPEDICHESKII
SLOVAR', Vol. 2. St. Petersburg: F. A. Brokgauz,
I. A. Efron, 1890, 351-364 pp. [Russ. text; Russ.,
Europ. titles, p. 364]

Badmaev, G. D. ZAIA-PANDITA. Elista: Kalmizdat,
1968, 77 pp., 1000 copies. [Russ. text; titles,
pp. 75-76]

*IZ ISTORII KUL'TURY DOREVOLIUTSIONNOI KALMYKII.
Volgograd: Nizhne-Volzhskoe Izdatel'stvo, 1967,
73 pp., 1000 copies. [Russ. text; 77 Russ. titles,
pp. 70-72]

*Kichikov, Mergen L. ISTORICHESKIE KORNI DRUZHBY
RUSSKOGO I KALMYTSKOGO NARODOV. OBRAZOVANIE
KALMYTSKOGO GOSUDARSTVA V SOSTAVE ROSSII. Elista:
Kalmytskoe Knizhnoe Izdatel'stvo, 1966, 152 pp.,
800 copies. [Russ. text; Mongol, Russ., Europ.
titles, per.: 1607-1637, pp. 143-149]

Kalmyk: History, Archaeology

* _____.: B. S. Sandzhiev; Iu. O. Oglaev, comp.
KALMYKIIA V VELIKOI OTECHESTVENNOI VOINE. 1941-1945.
DOKUMENTY I MATERIALY. Elista: Kalmizdat, 1966,
551 pp., 4000 copies. [Russ. text; per.: 1941-1945,
titles, p. 547]

Magidovich, I. "DZHUNGARIIA," BOL'SHAIA SOVETSKAIA
ENTSIKLOPEDIIA, Vol. 21. Moscow: Gosudarstvennoe
Slovarno-Entsiklopedicheskoe Izdatel'stvo
"Sovetskaia Entsiklopediia" (OGIZ RSFSR), 1931,
1st ed., pp. 832-838. [Russ. text; Russ., Europ.
titles, p. 838]

LANGUAGE, LITERATURE

Alekseeva, E. I. comp., ANTON MUDRENOVICH AMUR-SANAN.
(PAMIATKA CHITATELIU. K 80-LETIIU SO DNIA
ROZHDENIIA.) Elista: (Kalm. Resp. B-ka im. A. M.
Amur-Sanana), 1968, 8 pp., 500 copies. [Russ. text]

Badmaev, Bata Badmaevich. GRAMMATIKA KALMYTSKOGO
IAZYKA. MORFOLOGIIA. Elista: Kalmytskoe Knizhnoe
Izdatel'stvo, 1966, 115 pp., 1000 copies. [Russ.
text and titles, p. 113]

Dzhimgirov, M. IZ ISTORII IZUCHENIIA KALMYTSKOGO
FOL'KLORA. ZAPISKI KALMYTSKOGO NII IAZYKA,
LITERATURY I ISTORII. No. 2. 1962. [Russ. text;
survey, pp. 77-93]

Dzhimgirov, M. E. PISATELI SOVETSKOI KALMYKII.
(BIOBIBLIOGR. SPRAVOCHNIK.) Elista: Kalmizdat, 1966,
223 pp., 3000 copies. [Russ. text; ca.240 Kalmyk,
Russ. titles]

*G. S. "OIRATSKII IAZYK," BOL'SHAIA SOVETSKAIA
ENTSIKLOPEDIIA, Vol. 42. Moscow: Gosudarstvennyi
Institut "Sovetskaia Entsiklopediia" (OGIZ RSFSR),
1939, 1st ed., pp. 786-787. [Russ. text; Oirat,
Kalmyk, Russ., Europ. titles, p. 787]

Kalmyk: Language, Literature

Kabachenko, E. ANTON AMUR-SANAN. ZHIZN' I TVORCHESTVO. Elista, 1967. [Russ. text; 29 titles, pp. 126-129]

KALMYTSKII NAUCHNO-ISSLEDOVATEL'SKII INSTITUT IAZYKA, LITERATURY I ISTORII. VESTNIK INSTITUTA, No. 3. Elista: (Kalm. NII Iaz., Literatury i Istorii pri Sovete Ministrov Kalm. ASSR), 1968, 212 pp., 500 copies. [Russ. text; titles at end of articles]

*Poppe, N. "KALMYTSKAIA LITERATURA," LITERATURNAIA ENTSIKLOPEDIIA, Vol. 5. n. p. Izdatel'stvo Kommunisticheskoi Akademii, 1931 66-68 pp. [Russ. text; Kalmyk, Russ., Europ. titles, p. 68]

*_____. "KALMYTSKII IAZYK," LITERATURNAIA ENTSIKLOPEDIIA, Vol. 5. n. p. Izdatel'stvo Kommunisticheskoi Akademii, 1931, 68-70 pp. [Russ. text; Russ., Europ. titles, p. 70]

*Pozdneev, A. "KALMYTSKIE IAZYK I LITERATURA" ENTSIKLOPEDICHESKII SLOVAR', Vol. 14. St. Petersburg: F. A. Brokgauz; I. A. Efron, 1895, 71-72 pp. [Russ. text; Russ., Europ. titles, pub. 1804-1885]

Sangadzhieva, N. B. DZHANGARCHI. Elista: Kalmizdat, 1967, 36 pp., 1000 copies. [Russ. text; 26 titles, p. 35]

*Veselovskii, N. I. "K BIBLIOGRAFII KALMYTSKYKH SKAZOK," ZAPISKI VOSTOCHNAGO OTDIELENIIA IMPERATORSKAGO RUSSKAGO ARKHEOLOGICHESKAGO OBSHCHESTVA. Vol. 5. 1890(1891). [Russ. text; survey notes, pp. 112-113]

21 URALS

GENERAL

A. I. M. SISTEMATICHESKOE OGLAVLENIE SBORNIKA PERMSKAGO ZEMSTVA ZA 1872-1883 G. G. Perm': 1884, 35 pp. [Russ. text; pub. 1872-1883]

"ALFAVITNYI SPISOK LITERATURY," NARODNOE KHOZIAISTVO ZHELEZNOI DOROGI. Sverdlovsk: 1926. [Russ. text]

ALFAVITNYI UKAZATEL' STATEI I NIEKOTORYKH ZAMIETOK POMIESHCHENNYKH V 'PERMSKOI ZEMSKOI NEDIELIE' ZA 1914 G. (S I PO 26 NO. VKLIUCHITEL'NO), PERMSKAIA ZEMSKAIA NEDIELIA No. 28, 1914 (prilozhenie) stolb. 1-16 [Russ. text]

ALFAVITNYI UKAZATEL' STATEI I NIEKOTORYKH ZAMIETOK POMIESHCHENNYKH V PERMSKOI ZEMSKOI NEDIELIE ZA 1915 G. (S I PO 26 NO. VKLIUCHITEL'NO), PERMSKAIA ZEMSKAIA NEDIELIA, No. 27, 1916 (prilozhenie) stolb. 1-12 [Russ. text]

ALFAVITNYI UKAZATEL' STATEI I NIEKOTORYKH ZAMIETOK POMIESHCHENNYKH V PERMSKOI ZEMSKOI NEDIELIE ZA 1916 G. (S I PO 26 NO. VKLIUCHITEL'NO), PERMSKAIA ZEMSKAIA NEDIELIA, 1917. [Russ. text]

*Azanova, G. A.; L. A. Briushinkina; V. D. Inzel'berg; K. G. Shatunova comp., BIBLIOGRAFICHESKII UKAZATEL' NAUCHNYKH RABOT SOTRUDNIKOV PGU. 1916-1965 G. G. Perm': (Permskii Orden Trudovogo Krasnogo Znameni, Gosudarstvennyi Universitet im. A. M. Gor'kogo. Fundamental'naia Biblioteka), 1966, 451 pp., 1500 copies. [Russ. text; 6270 Russ. titles, pub. 1916-1965, pp. 3-414]

BIBLIOTEKA PERMSKAGO PROMYSHLENNAGO MUZEIA, No. 1, KATALOG KNIG O PERMSKOM KRAIE. Perm': (Permskii Nauchno-Promyshlennyi Muzei), 1907, 2+104 pp. [Russ. text]

Blium, A. V. ALEKSANDR ANDREEVICH SHMAKOV. BIBLIOGRAFICHESKII UKAZATEL'. Cheliabinsk: Cheliabinskoi Oblastnaia Publichnaia Biblioteka. Bibliograficheskii Otdel. Pisateli Cheliabnskoi Oblasti), 1958. [Russ. text]

Urals: General

*Borodin, N. "URAL'SKAIA OBLAST'," ENTSIKLOPEDICHESKII
SLOVAR', Vol. 34 A. St. Petersburg: F. A. Brokgauz,
I. A. Efron, 1902, 864-870 pp. [Russ. text; Russ.,
Europ. titles, p. 870]

*Cheremnykh, V. G.; F. A. Aleksandrov; I. S. Kaptsugovich;
V. P. Krasavin; A. N. Fadeev. eds. ISTORIIA URALA,
Vol. 2--PERIOD SOTSIALIZMA. Perm': Permskoe Knizhnoe
Izdatel'stvo, 1965, 611 pp., 5000. [Russ. text;
Russ. titles incl. arch., Sov. period, pp. 599-609]

D. S. [Smyshliaev, D. D.] "EZHEGODNIKI PERMSKOI
GUBERNII," PAMIATNAIA KNIZHKA I ADRES-KALENDAR'
PERMSKOI GUBERNII NA 1892 G. Otd. V, No. III. Perm',
n. p. 1891. [Russ. text, pub. 1863-1891, pp. 97-101]

_____. "UKAZATEL' STATEI PO
ARKHEOLOGII, ISTORII I ETNOGRAFII PERMSKOI GUBERNII,
POMIESHCHENNYKH V PERMSKIKH EPARKHIAL'NYKH
VIEDOMOSTIAKH 1867-1889 G. G.," PAMATNAIA KNIZHKA I
ADRES-KALENDAR' PERMSKOI GUBERNII NA 1892 G. Perm:
(Otd. I, SBORNIK MATERIALOV DLIA OZNAKOMLENIIA S
PERMSKOI GUBERNIEI, No. III), 1891. [Russ. text;
112 titles, pub. 1867-1889, pp. 102-107]

Dunin-Gorkavich, A. A. "PREDMETNYI BIBLIOGRAFICHESKII
UKAZATEL' PECHATNYKH TRUDOV PO TOBOL'SKOMU SEVERU,"
NASH KRAI (ZHURN.), No. 3, 1924. [Russ. text]

*Kirilin, G. N. et al. ROSSIIA. POLNOE GEOGRAFICHESKOE
OPISANIE NASHEGO OTECHESTVA, Vol. V. URAL I PRIURAL'E.
St. Petersburg: Izdatel'stvo A. F. Davriena, 1914,
669 pp. [Russ. text; ca.700 Russian titles,
pp. 599-619]

LITERATURA O SVERDLOVSKOI OBLASTI. 1951-1956.
Sverdlovsk: (Gosudarstvennaia Publichnaia Biblioteka
Imeni V. G. Belinskogo), 1952-1957 (annually). [Russ.
text]

*Makhanek, K. S.; S. F. Nikolaev; I. S. Sandler; V. F.
Tiunov; B. A. Chazov eds. PERMSKAIA OBLAST'.
PRIRODA. ISTORIIA. EKONOMIKA. KUL'TURA. Perm':
Permskoe Knizhnoe Izdatel'stvo, 1959, 407 pp., 5000
copies. [Russ. text; Russ. titles, including
archives, pp. 399-406]

Malakhov, M. "UKAZATEL' KNIG I STATEI O PERMSKOM
KRAIE, 1866-1884," EKATERINBURGSKAIA NEDIELIA, 1884,
Nos. 26, 28, 32, 35-41, 46-49; 1885, Nos. 8-10, 15,
22-29, 32,33. [Russ. text; 975 Russ. titles, pub.
1866-1884]

Urals: General

Nekliudov, I. "UKAZATEL' KNIG I STATEI, NAPECHATANNYKH V RAZLICHNYKH ZHURNALAKH I GAZETAKH O CHERDYNSKOM KRAE," CHERDYNSKII KRAI, No. 2, 1927. [Russ. text; 218 titles]

NOVAIA LITERATURA O KUIBYSHEVSKOI OBLASTI, Nos. 1-4, 1958-1959 (quarterly bulletin). [Russ. text]

"NOVOSTI URALO-SIBIRSKOI LITERATURY," SEVERNAIA AZIIA. Nos. 1/2, 1925, 153-158 pp.; No. 3, 1925, 149-153 pp.; No. 4, 1925, 133-143 pp.; No. 1, 1926, 137-144 pp.; No. 2, 1926, 133-142 pp.; No. 3, 1926, 124-128 pp.; No. 4, 1926, 135-142 pp.; Nos. 5/6, 1926, 191-202 pp.; No. 1, 1927, 154-162 pp.; No. 2, 1927, 135-142 pp.; No. 3, 1927, 120-128 pp.; No. 4, 1927, 124-128 pp.; Nos. 5/6, 1927, 208-217 pp.; No. 1, 1928, 124-131 pp.; No. 2, 1928, 136-140 pp.; No. 3, 1928, 131-138 pp.; No. 4, 1928, 149-158 pp.; Nos. 5/6, 1928, 213-227 pp.; No. 1, 1929, 150-158 pp.; No. 2, 1929, 146-152 pp.; No. 3, 1929, 148-152 pp.; No. 4, 1929, 125-132 pp.; Nos. 5/6, 1929, 169-178 pp.; Nos. 1/2, 1930, 180-188 pp.; [Russ. text; 1926 (1) 104 titles; (2) 128 titles; (3) 67 titles, (4) 81 titles, (5/6) 156 titles; 1927 (1) 97 titles, (2) 90 titles, (3) 90 titles; (4) 51 titles, (5/6) 108 titles; 1928 (1) 85 titles, (2) 56 titles, (3) 76 titles, (4) 102 titles, (5/6) 174 titles; 1929 (1) 101 titles, (2) 73 titles, (3) 47 titles, (4) 86 titles, (5/6) 110 titles; 1930 (1/2) 103 titles]

"OGLAVLENIE ZHURNALA 'SERP I MOLOT' ZA 1920 GOD," SERP I MOLOT, No. 30, 1920. [Russ. text; pub. 1920, (prilozhenie) I-X pp.]

Pavlov, V. A. "PERIODICHESKIE IZDANIIA URALA XIX VEKA. (KRATKII KRAEVED. IST-BIBLIOGR. OBZOR)," V POMOSHCH' KRAEVEDU. Sverdlovsk, 1966. [Russ. text; per. 19th cent., titles, pp. 119-126]

Sharts, A. K. "IUNYI PROLETARII URALA" (BIBLIOGRAFICHESKII UKAZATEL' [ZHURNALA]). Perm': (Zapadno-Ural'skaia Naucho-Tekhnicheskaia Biblioteka), 1966, 68 pp., 200 copies. [Russ. text; pub. 1918-1924]

──────────. LEONID NAUMOVICH BOL'SHAKOV (BIBLIOGR. MATERIALY). Perm: (Zap.-Ural'skaia Nauch. Tekh. B-ka), 1966, 32 pp. [Russ. text]

Shestakov, I. UKAZATEL' STATEI PO ISTORII ARKHEOLOGII I ETNOGRAFII, POMIESHCHENNYKH V PERMSKIKH EPARKHIAL'NYKH VIEDOMOSTIIAKH SO VREMENI IKH VYKHODA PO AVGUST 1915 G. (ISTOCHNIKI I POSOBII PRI IZUCHENII PRIKAMSKAGO KRAIA) Sarapul: Izd. Obshchestva Izucheniia Prikamskago Kraia) 1915, 35 pp. [Russ. text]

Urals: General

*Shmidt, A. "AKADEMIIA NAUK I EE RABOTA NA URALE,"
URAL'SKAIA SOVETSKAIA ENTSIKLOPEDIIA. Vol. I.
Sverdlovsk-Moscow: Izdatel'stvo Uraloblispolkoma, 1933,
82-87 pp. [Russ text; p. 87]

Skalozubova, A. V. "SISTEMATICHESKII UKAZATEL' STATEI,
POMIESHCHENNYKH V 'SBORNIKIE PERMSKAGO ZEMSTVA' V
PERIOD S 1883 PO 1893 G.," SBORNIK PERMSKAGO ZEMSTVA,
No. 5, 1893; Nos. 2/3, 5/6, 1894; Nos. 1/2, 3, 4, 5/6,
1895; Nos. 1, 4, 5/6 1896; Nos. 1, 2, 3, 4/5, 1897.
[Russ. text; pub. 1883-1893; (1893) pp. 106-120;
(1894) 2/3 pp. 60-64, 5/6 pp. 85-88; (1895) 1/2
p. 196, 3, p. 116, 4 pp. 102-104, 5/6 pp. 167-168;
(1896) 1 pp. 132-144, 4 pp. 40-48, 5/6 pp. 73-80;
(1897) 1 pp. 42-48, 2 pp. 56-64, 3 pp. 43-56, 4/5
pp. 35-48]

Smyshliaev, D. D. "UKAZATEL' STATEI, KASAIUSHCHIKHSIA
PERMSKOI GUBERNII I NAPECHATANNYKH V NEOFITSIAL'NOM
OTDIELIE 'PERMSKIKH GUBERNSKIKH VIEDOMOSTEI' V
TECHENII 1841-1880 GODOV," SBORNIK STATEI,
KASAIUSHCHIKHSIA PERMSKOI GUBERNII, No. 1. Perm': n.
p. 1882, 83 pp. (separately). [Russ. text; pub.
1841-1880, 1420 titles, pp. 1-83]

S. [Smyshliaev, D. D.] "UKAZATEL' STATEI O PERMSKOI
GUBERNII NAPECHATANNYKH V PERMSKIKH IZVESTIIAKH
(1811-1820), PERMSKII SBORNIK, Vol. II. Moscow: n. p.
1860. [Russ. text; 97 titles, (prilozhenie) pp. XVII-
XXI]

S. [Smyshliaev, D. D.] "UKAZATEL' STATEI O PERMSKOI
GUBERNII, NAPECHATANNYKH V PERMSKIKH GUBERNSKIKH
VIEDOMOSTIAKH. 1839-1858," PERMSKII SBORNIK, Vol. II.
Moscow: n. p. 1860. [Russ. text; 93 titles,
(prilozhenie) pp. XXI-XXVII]

Smyshliaev, D. D. "UKAZATEL' STATEI, POMESHCHENNYKH V
NEOFITSIAL'NOI CHASTI 'PERMSKIKH GUBERNSKIKH VIEDOMOSTEI'
ZA 1881-1884 GG.," PERMSKIE GUBERNSKIE VIEDOMOSTI.
No. 13. PRILOZHENIE, 1885, 27 pp. [Russ. text;
pub. 1881-1884]

UKAZATEL' STATEI O EKATERINBURGSKOI EPARKHII,
POMIESHCHENNYKH V NEOFITSIAL'NOM OTDIELIE PERMSKIKH
EPARKHIAL'NYKH VIEDOMOSTIAKH S 1867 PO 1885 G.
EKATERINBURGSKIIA EPARKHIAL'NYIA VIEDOMOSTI, Nos. 17-49,
1895, 80 pp. (separately). [Russ. text, pub. 1867-1885]

Urals: General

UKAZATEL' STATEI POMIESHCHENNYKH V ZAPISKAKH URAL'SKAGO OBSHCHESTVA LIUBITELEI ESTESTVOZNANIIA V G. EKATERINBURGIE. S 1871 PO 1895 G. ZAPISKI URAL'SKAGO OBSHCHESTVA LIUBITELEI ESTESTVOZNANIIA. Vol. XVII, No. 1. 1896. [Russ. text; pub. 1871-1895, pp. 119-154]

*Zdobnov, N. V. URAL'SKAIA SOVETSKAIA ENTSIKLOPEDIIA Vol. I. Sverdlovsk-Moscow: Izdatel'stvo Uraloblispolkoma, 1933, 368-383 pp. [Russ. text and titles, pp. 373-383]

_____. UKAZATEL' BIBLIOGRAFICHESKIKH POSOBII PO URALU (SO VKLIUCHENIEM BASHKIRII I SIBIRSKIKH OKRUGOV URAL'SKOI OBLASTI). No. 1. Moscow: Izdanie Russkogo Bibliograficheskogo Obshchestva Pri Moskovskom Gosudarstvennom Universitete. No. 116, 1927, 72 pp., 700 copies. [Russ. text; 243 Russ. titles]

ANTHROPOLOGY, ETHNOGRAPHY

Fisl'strup, F. A. ETNICHESKII SOSTAV NASELENIIA PRIURAL'IA. Leningrad: Izd. Akademii Nauk SSSR (Trudy Komissii po Izucheniiu Plemennogo Sostava Naseleniia SSSR i Sopredel'nykh Stran. No. 11), 1926, 37 pp. [Russ. text; 19 titles, pp. 22-23]

ARCHITECTURE, ART, MUSIC

Budrina, A. G. URAL'SKII PLAKAT VREMEN GRAZHDANSKOI VOINY. Perm: n. p. 1968. [Russ. text; 98 titles, pp. 81-93]

Urals

ECONOMICS

Bobylev, D. M. EKSPORTNOE KHOZIAISTVO URALA, KAK EKONOMICHESKAIA PROBLEMA. Ekaterinburg: Izd. Uralkniga (Ural'skaia Ekonomika, Vyp. VIII), 1924, 112 pp. [Russ. text; 38 titles, pp. 110-111]

*Chernysh, Mikhail I. RAZVITIE KAPITALIZMA NA URALE I PERMSKOE ZEMSTVO. Perm': Permskoe Knizhnoe Izdatel'stvo, 1959, 239 pp., 2000 copies. [Russ. text and titles, including archives, pp. 232-237]

*Dubenskii, M. M. comp. EKONOMICHESKAIA GEOGRAFIIA SSSR PO RAIONAM. SREDNEE POVOLZH'E. Moscow-Leningrad: Gosudarstvennoe Izdatel'stvo, 1928 (2nd ed., supplemented), 83 pp., 3000 copies. [Russ. text and titles; pub. 1901-1927, pp. 81-82]

Fedorovich, I. URALO-KUZNETSKAIA PROBLEMA. Moscow-Leningrad: Tsentral'noe Upravlenie Pechati VSNKH SSSR, 1926, 94 pp. [Russ. text; 16 titles, p. 94]

*Fersman, A. E. BOGATSTVA URALA. Sverdlovsk: OGIZ. Sverdlovskoe Oblastnoe Gosudarstvennoe Izdatel'stvo, 1944, 67 pp., 10,000 copies. [Russ. text and titles; p. 66]

*Gapeev, A. "KRAEVEDENIE...," PECHAT' I REVOLIUTSIIA, Kn. 6, Sept., 1927, 200-202 pp. [Russ. text; Russ. survey, pp. 201-202]

Ievlev, P. P. NA URAL'SKOM SEVERE. (KOMMUNISTICH. STROITEL'STVO V SVERDL. OBL.) Sverdlovsk: Sred.-Ural'skoe Kn. Izd., 1966, 123 pp., 4000 copies. Russ. text; titles pp. 121-122]

*Komar, I. V. URAL: EKONOMIKO-GEOGRAFICHESKAIA KHARAKTERISTIKA. Moscow: Izdatel'stvo Akademii Nauk SSSR, 1959, 367 pp., 2500 copies. [Russ. text; Russ. Europ. titles, pp. 352-366]

Konstantinov, O. A. EKONOMICHESKAIA GEOGRAFIIA SSSR PO RAIONAM. URAL'SKAIA OBLAST' (S PRILOZHENIEM KRATKOGO OCHERKA BASHKIRSKOI RESPUBLIKI). Moscow-Leningrad: Gosudarstvennoe Izdatel'stvo RSFSR, [1926 (1st ed.)]; 1929 (3rd ed.), 155 pp. [Russ. text; 149 titles (1st ed. 35), pp. 152-153]

Laskina, A. KUIBYSHEVSKAIA OBLAST' NAVSTRECHU XXI S"EZDU KPSS (KRATKII REKOMENDATEL'NYI UKAZATEL' LITERATURY OB USPEKHAKH KOMMUNISTICHESKOGO STROITEL'STVA V OBLASTI). Kinel': (Kuibyshevskaia Oblastnaia Biblioteka), 1958, 14 pp. [Russ. text]

Urals: Economics

Makurin, P. I. OKHRANA TRUDA. Sverdlovsk: (M-vo Vyssh. i Sred. Spets. Obrazovaniia RSFSR.), 1967, 88 pp., 1000 copies. [Russ. text; 12 titles, p. 86]

Murzaev, A.; E. Kharitonov. SETEVOE PLANIROVANIE NA PREDPRIIATIIAKH SREDNEGO URALA. Sverdlovsk: Sred.-Ural'skoe Kn. Izd., 1966, 83 pp., 4000 copies. [Russ. text; titles pp. 77-79]

NARODNOE KHOZIAISTVO RAIONA PERMSKOI ZHELEZNOI DOROGI. STATISTIKO-EKONOMICHESKOE OPISANIE. Sverdlovsk: Izd. Pravleniia Permskoi Zheleznoi Dorogi, 1926. [Russ. text; titles pp. 1-18]

*NATSIONALIZATSIIA PROMYSHLENNOSTI NA URALE (OKTIABR' 1917-IIUL' 1918 GG.) SBORNIK DOKUMENTOV. Sverdlovsk: Sverdlovskoe Knizhnoe Izdatel'stvo, 1958, 328 pp., 3000 copies. [Russ. text; 30+ Russ. titles, per. 1917-1918, pp. 308-311]

*Polishchuk, P. N.; B. I. Shaitan. VNUTRIKHOZIAISTVENNYI RASCHET V KOLKHOZAKH I SOVKHOZAKH. Sverdlovsk: Sred.-Ural'skoe Kn. Izd., 1967, 98 pp., 2500 copies. [Russ. text and titles; pub. 1960-1966, pp. 96-97]

"PREDMETNYI UKAZATEL' MATERIALOV, POMESHCHENNYKH V ZHURNALE 'KHOZIAISTVO URALA' S NO. 1 (IIUN' 1925 G.) PO NO. 19 (DEKABR' 1926 G.)," KHOZIAISTVO URALA, No. 19. 1926. [Russ. text; titles pub. 1925-1926, pp. 153-166]

Rott, M. E.; A. S. Koriukova, comp. NAUCHNAIA ORGANIZATSIIA TRUDA. BIBLIOGR. UKAZATEL'. Sverdlovsk: (Sred.-Ural'skoe Tsbti. Tsentr. Nauch-Tekhn. B-ka.), 1968, 31 pp., 2000 copies. [Russ. text]

Semchenkov, G. G. ROL' PROFSOIUZOV V EKONOMICHESKOI RABOTE ZAPADNOGO URALA. Perm: Kn. Izd., 1966, 64 pp., 1000 copies. [Russ. text; titles pp. 62-63]

Semenov, K. S. LESNOE KHOZIAISTVO URALA. Sverdlovsk: Izd. Uralkniga (Ural'skaia Ekonomika, Vyp. II), 1925, 118 pp. [Russ. text; titles pp. 115-117]

Shikhalov, A. ESTESTVENNO-ISTORICHESKIE USLOVIIA I SEL'SKOE KHOZIAISTVO RAIONA PERMSKOI ZHELEZNOI DOROGI. Sverdlovsk: Permskaia Zheleznaia Doroga, 1926, VII+124 pp. [Russ. text; titles pp. V-VII]

*Shuvalov, L. URAL: EKONOMIKO-GEOGRAFICHESKII OCHERK. Moscow: Izdatel'stvo "Prosveshchenie," 1966, 199 pp. 30,000 copies. [Russ. text; titles p. 198, pub. 1951-1964]

Urals: Economics

Smyshliaev, D. D. UKAZATEL' DOKUMENTOV, ZAPISOK I STATEI
O NAPRAVLENII URAL'SKOI ZHELIEZNOI DOROGI. PERMSKIIA
GUBERNSKIIA VIEDOMOSTI. Nos. 4-6, 8. 1877. [Russ.
text; 56 titles]

*Stepanov, P. N. URAL'SKAIA OBLAST' S PRILOZHENIEM
OCHERKA: BASHKIRSKAIA ASSR. Moscow: Izdatel'stvo
"Planovoe Khoziaistvo," 1928, 116 pp., 8100 copies.
[Russ. text and titles, pp. 115-116, pub. 1922-1927]

"STROITEL'STVO URALO-KUZNETSKOGO KOMBINATA,"
BOL'SHEVITSKAIA PECHAT', Nos. 1-5, 1931; Nos. 1-4,
1932. [Russ. text]

Tikhonovych, N.; A. Zamiatin. NEFTENOSNYI RAION
URAL'SKOI OBLASTI. IZVIESTIIA GEOLOGICHESKAGO
KOMITETA. No. 9, 1912. [Russ. text; 31 titles,
including notes, pp. 548-550]

Tikhonovich, N. N. "URAL'SKII NEFTENOSNYI RAION,"
ESTESTVENNYE SILY ROSSII. Vol. 4. Petrograd: Izd.
KEPS pri Akademii Nauk, Vypusk 22, 1919. [Russ. text;
20 titles, pp. 102-103]

*Tiunov, V. PROMYSHLENNOE RAZVITIE ZAPADNOGO URALA.
KNIGA TRET'IA. Perm: Permskoe Knizhnoe Izdatel'stvo,
1958, 335 pp., 3000 copies. [Russ. text and titles,
pp. 330-334]

URALO-KUZNETSKII KOMBINAT. MATERIALY PO BIBLIOGRAFII.
Leningrad: Gos. Nauch.-Tekhn. Izd. (Nauchno-Issled.
Sektor VSNKH SSSR), 1931, 126 pp. [Russ. text;
1583 titles]

URAL'SKII NAUCHNO-ISSLEDOVATEL'SKII PROEKTNYI INSTITUT
STROITEL'NYKH MATERIALOV. ANNOTATSII I BIBLIOGRAFIIA
1956-1966 GG. Cheliabinsk: Iuzhn.-Ural'skoe Kn. Izd.,
1966, 75 pp., 1000 copies. [Russ. text; per. 1956-1966]

Vasiutin, V.; T. Raikov eds. URALO KUZNETSKII KOMBINAT.
REFERATIVNAIA BIBLIOGRAFIIA LITERATURY. 1927-1931 GG.
No. 1. ENERGETIKA METALL, KHIMIIA, TRANSPORT. Moscow:
"Sovetskaia Aziia," 1933, 384 pp. [Russ. text]

"VODNYI RECHNOI TRANSPORT," URAL'SKAIA SOVETSKAIA
ENTSIKLOPEDIIA, Vol I. Sverdlovsk-Moscow:
Izdatel'stvo Uraloblispolkoma, 1933, 694-711 pp.
[Russ. text and titles, p. 711]

Urals: Economics

Vorob'ev, A. SEL'SKOE KHOZIAISTVO URALA. Sverdlovsk: Izd. Uralkniga (Ural'skaia Ekonomika, Vyp. III), 1926, 120 pp. [Russ. text; 26 titles, p. 120]

EDUCATION

*Abramov, I. I. "BIBLIOTECHNAIA RABOTA," URAL'SKAIA SOVETSKAIA ENTSIKLOPEDIIA, Vol. I. Sverdlovsk-Moscow: Izdatel'stvo Uraloblispolkoma, 1933, 383-390 pp. [Russ. text and titles, pp. 389-390]

Abramov, I. "TEMATICHESKII UKAZATEL' STATEI, POMESHCHENNYKH V ZHURNALE 'URAL'SKII UCHITEL'' S 1-GO IANVARIA 1925 G. PO 1-E IANVARIA 1926 G.," URAL'SKII UCHITEL' Nos. 1 (11), 2(12), 1926. [Russ. text; pub. 1925, (1) pp. 71-74; (2) pp. 81-82]

*Perel', I. A. "VSEOBSHCHEE NACHAL'NOE OBUCHENIE," URAL'SKAIA SOVETSKAIA ENTSIKLOPEDIIA. Vol I. Sverdlovsk-Moscow: Izdatel'stvo Uraloblispolkoma, 1933, pp. 783-797. [Russ. text and titles, p. 797]

GEOGRAPHY

Afinogenov, A. A., et al. PO SOVETSKOMU URALU. PUTEVODITEL'. Sverdlovsk: n. p., 1930 (2nd ed.) [Russ. text; 113 titles]

Biriukov, V. P. "LITERATURA O SHADRINSKOM KRAE," PRIRODA I NASELENIE SHADRINSKOGO KRAIA. Shadrinsk: n. p., 1926. [Russ. text]

Chepkasov, P. N. SOPUTNIKI GORODA PERMI. EKON.-GEOGR. OCHERK PERM. AGLOMERATSII V SVIAZI S PROBLEMAMI RASSELENIIA. UCHEN. ZAP. (PERM. UN-T). 1966. [Russ. text; 35 titles, pp. 63-64.

Urals: Geography

Chupin, Narkiz. UKAZATEL' SOCHINENII, V KOTORYKH ZAKLIUCHAIUTSIA GEOGRAFICHESKIIA I STATISTICHESKIIA SVIEDIENIIA O PERMSKOI GUBERNII. PERMSKII SBORNIK, Vol. 2. Moscow: n. p., 1860. [Russ. text; 57 titles, pub. up to 1841, (prilozhenie) pp. I-XVII]

EKONOMICHESKAIA GEOGRAFIIA ZAPADNOGO URALA. No. 3. Perm: (Uchen. Zap. (Perm. Un-t im. Gor'kogo). Vyp. 144), 1966, 217 copies. [Russ. text]

*GEOGRAFICHESKII SBORNIK. SVERDLOVSKII GOSUDARSTVENNYI PEDAGOGICHESKII INSTITUT. UCHENYE ZAPISKI. SBORNIK 34. Sverdlovsk: Ministerstvo Prosveshcheniia RSFSR, 1966, 118 pp. 550 copies. Russ. text and titles, end of articles]

*Komar, I. V. GEOGRAFIIA KHOZIAISTVA URALA. Moscow: Izdatel'stvo "Nauka," 1964, 395 pp., 1300 copies. Russ. text and titles; pub. 1852-1962, pp. 386-394]

*_____.; A. G. Chikishev, comp. URAL I PRIURAL'E. Moscow: Izdatel'stvo "Nauka," 1968, 461 pp., 2600 copies. [Russ. text; Russ. Europ. titles, pp. 432-447]

Konogorov, P.F. KARTOGRAFIIA SEVERNOI AZII. (1917-1927 GG.) BIBLIOGRAFICHESKII UKAZATEL'. Moscow: Tip. "Transpechat'." (O-vo Izucheniia Urala, Sibiri i Dal'nego Vostoka...), 1928, 78 pp., 1000 copies. [Russ.text; 293 Russ. titles, pub. 1917-1927]

Lovyreva, D. L. ed. SEL'SKOKHOZIAISTVENNYE RAIONY I ZEMEL'NYE NORMY ORENBURGSKOI GUBERNII, Part I. Orenburg: n. p., 1927. [Russ. text]

Malakhov, M. V. GEOGRAFICHESKIE KARTY I PLANY PERMSKOI GUBERNII, NAKHODIASHCHIESIA V 'MOSKOVSKOM GLAVNOM ARKHIVE MINISTERSTVA INNOSTRANNYKH DIEL. ZAPISKI UOLE. Vol. 9, No. 1, 1887. [Russ. text; 17 titles]

Moskaleva, Z. N. "ISSLEDOVANIIA BASSEINA URALA," NAUCH. ZAPISKI. No. 9. Ural'sk: (Geogr. O-vo SSSR. Zap.-Kazakst. Otd.), 1957. [Russ. text; ca.80 titles, pp. 70-73]

Mozel', Kh. PERMSKAIA GUBERNIIA. Part I. St. Petersburg: n. p. 1864, XVI + 367 + 60 pp. [Russ. text; titles, incl. MSS., pp. II-XV]

Urals: Geography

Neustroeva, S. S. "VAZHNEISHIE SOCHINENIIA KASAIUSHCHIESIA GEOGRAFII ORENBURGSKOI GUBERNII," ESTESTVENNYE RAIONY ORENBURGSKOI GUBERNII. Orenburg: Izd. Soiuza Koop. Soiuzov "Narodnoe Dielo," 1918, 169 + X + 3 pp. [Russ. text; titles pp. III-X]

PROBLEMY FIZICHESKOI GEOGRAFII URALA. TRUDY MOSK. O-VA. ISPYTATELEI PRIRODY. Vol. 18. Moscow: Izd.-vo Mosk. Un-ta, 1966, 295 pp., 2000 copies. [Russ. text; titles end of articles]

Semetkovskii, V. EKSKURSIIA NA URAL. Moscow-Leningrad: Gosudarstvennoe Izdatel'stvo, 1926, 72 pp. [Russ. text; 12 titles, pp. 70-71]

Sergieev, S. "VIEDOMOST' O KOLICHESTVIE IZDANII URAL'SKAGO OBSHCHESTVA LIUBITELEI ESTESTVOZNANIIA, NAKHODIASHCHIKHSIA V MUZEIE OBSHCHESTVA K 11 FEVRALIA 1889 G.," ZAPISKI URAL'SKAGO OBSHCHESTVA LIUBITELEI ESTESTVOZNANIIA. Vol. 12, No. 11, 1889. [Russ. text; pub. up to 1888, pp. 104-111]

Sergieev, S. I. "SISTEMATICHESKII UKAZATEL' STATEI, POMIESHCHENNYKH V ZAPISKAKH URAL'SKAGO OBSHCHESTVA LIUBITELEI ESTESTVOZNANIIA. T. I-XI. 25 VYPUSKOV S 1876 PO 1888 G.," ZAPISKI URAL'SKAGO OBSHCHESTVA LIUBITELEI ESTESTVOZNANIIA. Vol. XII, No. 2, 1891. [Russ. text; pub. 1871-1888, pp. 112-115]

*Shuvalov, E. L. URAL. EKONOMIKO-GEOGRAFICHESKII OCHERK. Moscow: "Prosveshchenie," 1966, 199 pp., 30,000 copies. [Russ. text; 21 Russ. titles, p. 198, pub. 1961-1964]

*"URAL'SKII KHREBET," ENTSIKLOPEDICHESKII SLOVAR', Vol. 34 A. St. Petersburg: F. A. Brokgauz, I. A. Efron, 1902, 871-883 pp. [Russ. text: Russ., Europ. titles, p. 883]

VOPROSY FIZICHESKOI GEOGRAFII IUZHNOGO URALA. No. 1. Cheliabinsk: n. p., 1966, 204 pp. [Russ. text; titles end of articles]

VOPROSY GEOGRAFII IUZHNOGO URALA. (SBORNIK STATEI.) Cheliabinsk: (M-vo Prosveshcheniia RSFSR.), 1968, 199 pp., 500 copies. [Russ. text; titles end of articles]

HISTORY, ARCHAEOLOGY

Bobylev, D. M. "UKAZATEL' NIEKOTORYKH ISTORIKO-STATISTICHESKIKH I DRUGIKH MATERIALOV PO IZUCHENIIU PERMSKAGO KRAIA, POMIESHCHENNYKH V 'SBORNIKIE PERMSKAGO ZEMSTVA' ZA VREMIA SO 1873 G. PO 1903 G.," TRUDY PERMSKOI UCHENOI ARKHIVNOI KOMISSII. No. 6, 1903. [Russ. text; 177 Russ. titles, pp. 130-135, pub. 1873-1903]

Briukhanova, L. I.; V. I. Kuznetsov. RAZVEDCHIK NIKOLAI KUZNETSOV. Sverdlovsk: Sred.-Ural'skoe Kn. Izd., 1967, 231 pp.,100,000 copies. [Russ. text; titles p. 230]

*Chernetsov, V. N. NASKAL'NYE IZOBRAZHENIIA URALA. Moscow: Izdatel'stvo "Nauka," 1964, 52 pp., 1000 copies. [Russ. text; Russ., Europ. titles, pp. 50-51, pub. 1785-1959]

Chufarov, V. G. DEIATEL'NOST' PARTIINYKH ORGANIZATSII URALA PO OSUSHCHESTVLENIIU KUL'TURNOI REVOLIUTSII (1920-1937 GG.). Sverdlovsk: n. p., 1970. [Russ. text; ca.300 titles, pp. 8-16; 366-378; per. 1920-1937]

Dmitriev, A. "BIBLIOGRAFICHESKII UKAZATEL'," PERMSKAIA STARINA, Perm': No. 5, 1894; No. 7, 1897. [Russ. text; 17 titles, (5) pp. VII-XII; (7) pp. VII-XIV]

Futorianskii, L. I. ed. PLAMENNYE GODY. DATY, TSIFRY I FAKTY IZ ISTORII ORENB. OBL. KOMSOMOL'SKOI ORGANIZATSII. Cheliabinsk: Iuzhn.-Ural. Kn. Izd., 1968, 95 pp., 5000 copies. [Russ. text; titles pp. 78-93]

*Gorovoi, F. S.; F. A. Aleksandrov; L. M. Gantman; I. S. Kaptsugovich. URAL V OGNE REVOLIUTSII. PROLETARSKAIA REVOLIUTSIIA V PERM. GUBERNII. Perm: Permskoe Knizhnoe Izdatel'stvo, 1967, 234 pp., 3000 copies. [Russ. text; 52 Russ. titles, pp. 231-233]

KAMYSHLOV. Sverdlovsk: n. p., 1968. [Russ. text; 33 titles, pp. 85-86]

Urals: History, Archaeology

*Khudiakov, M. "ARKHEOLOGICHESKIE ISSLEDOVANIIA V U. O. [URAL'SKOI OBLASTI] I PRIURAL'E," URAL'SKAIA SOVETSKAIA ENTSIKLOPEDIIA. Vol. 1. Sverdlovsk-Moscow: Izdatel'stvo Uraloblispolkoma, 1933, 179-184 pp. [Russ. text; Russ., Europ. titles, pp. 183-184]

Koverda, A.; A. Brylin. NASH GOROD ARTEMOSSKII. Sverdlovsk: Sred.-Ural'skoe Kn. Izd., 1966, 106 pp., 10,000 copies. [Russ. text; 21 titles, pp. 104-105]

*Makhanek, K. S.; V. V. Mukhin; P. I. Khitrov eds. ISTORIIA URALA V DVUKH TOMAKH. Vol. 1. PERVOBYTNOOBSHCHINNYI STROI. PERIOD FEODALIZMA. PERIOD KAPITALIZMA. Perm': Permskoe Knizhnoe Izdatel'stvo, 1963, 499 pp., 5000 copies. [Russ. text and titles, pp. 488-495, per. ancient to 1917]

*Markusenko, I. S. comp. ISTORIIA DONA OT VELIKOI OKTIABR'SKOI SOTSIALISTICHESKOI REVOLIUTSII DO NASHIKH DNEI. Rostov-N/D: Izdatel'stvo Rostovskogo Universiteta, 1967, 356 pp., 10,000 copies. [Russ. text; 88 Russ. titles, pp. 350-354, per. 1917-1967]

*Popov, P.; Iu. Buranov; I. Shakinko. PO PRIKAZU REVOLIUTSII. Sverdlovsk: Sredne-Ural'skoe Knizhnoe Izdatel'stvo, 1966, 182 pp., 15,000 copies. [Russ. text and titles, pp. 180-181, pub. 1943-1962]

*Repin, M. E. KASLI; ISTORICHESKII OCHERK. Cheliabinsk: Cheliabinskoe Oblastnoe Izdatel'stvo, 1940, 200 pp., 8000 copies. [Russ. text and titles, incl. archives, pp. 196-200]

Ryzhikov, A. URAL'SKII RABOCHII SOIUZ. 1896-1899 GG. Cheliabinsk: n. p., 1967. [Russ. text; ca.60 titles, pp. 75-77, per. 1896-1899]

*Sal'nikov, K. V. OCHERKI DREVNEI ISTORII IUZHNOGO URALA. Moscow: Izdatel'stvo "Nauka," 1967, 408 pp., 2300 copies. [Russ. text; ca.400 Russ., Europ. titles, pp. 392-405]

S[myshliaev, D. D.] "STAT'I O PERMSKOI GUBERNII ISTORICHESKAGO I ETNOGRAFICHESKAGO SODERZHANIIA, NAPECHATANNYIA V PERMSKIKH EPARKHIAL'NYKH VIEDOMOSTIAKH," PERMSKIIA GUBERNSKIIA VIEDOMOSTI. Nos. 21, 23, 1882; No. 9, 1883. [Russ. text; pub. 1880-1882]

Urals: History, Archaeology

Temerova, A. Ia.; T. E. Korshunova; T. A. Tsvetkova, comp. CHELIABINSKAIA OBLAST'. (KATALOG NOVYKH KNIG I STATEI ZA IANV.-MART 1965 G. PO ISTORII, REVOLIUTSIONNOMU PROSHLOMU, KOMMUNISTICHESKOMU STROITEL'STVU I GEOGRAFII IUZHNOGO URALA). Cheliabinsk: (Cheliabinskaia Oblastnaia Publichnaia Biblioteka. Bibliograficheskii Otdel...), 1966, 145 pp., 250 copies. [Russ. text; pub. 1965]

Tokmakov, I. UKAZATEL' MATERIALOV DLIA IZUCHENIIA ISTORII I STATISTIKI PERMSKOI GUBERNII. SBORNIK PERMSKAGO ZEMSTVA. No. 5/6, Section II, 1882, 19 pp. (separately). [Russ. text; including archives, pp. 137-153]

"UKAZATEL' STATEI PO ARKHEOLOGII, ISTORII, I ETNOGRAFII PERMSKOI GUBERNII, POMIESHCHENNYKH V PERMSKIKH EPARKHIAL'NYKH VIEDOMOSTIIAKH 1867-1899 G. G.," ADRES-KALENDAR' I PAMIATNAIA KNIZHKA PERMSKOI GUBERNII NA 1900 G. Perm: n. p., 1900. [Russ. text; pub. 1867-1899, pp. 38-46]

*[Uvarov, A. S.] PERM' I PERMSKAIA GUBERNIIA. BIBLIOGRAFIIA. DREVNOSTI. TRUDY MOSKOVSKAGO ARKHEOLOGICHESKAGO OBSHCHESTVA. Vol. 3, No. 3. Moscow: V Sinodal'noi Tipografii, 1873, 31-34 pp. [Russ. text; 53 Russ. Europ. titles, pub. 1752-1861]

Urals

LANGUAGE, LITERATURE

*Biriukov, Vladimir P. URAL SOVETSKII: NARODNYE
   RASSKAZY I USTNOE POETICHESKOE TVORCHESTVO. [Kurgan]:
   Izdatel'stvo Gazeta "Krasnyi Kurgan," [1958], 195 pp.
   10,000. [Russ.text and titles, pp. 187-190]

[Elistratova, M. (comp.)] LENINSKAIA TEMA V LITERATURE
   I ISSKUSTVE IUZHNOGO URALA. (REK. SPISOK LIT.).
   Cheliabinsk: (Cheliab. Obl. Publ. B-ka), 1970, 8 pp.,
   1000 copies. [Russ. text; 48 titles]

Matveev, A. K. "OSNOVNYE ZADACHI IZUCHENIIA URAL'SKOI
   TOPONIMIKI," VOPROSY TOPONOMASTIKI. Sverdlovsk:(Uchenye
   Zapiski. Ural'skii Gos. Un-t im. Gor'kogo. No. 48,
   Seriia Filol. Vyp. 3), 1967. [Russ. text; 44 titles,
   pp. 10-12]

*Podol'skaia, A. P.; I. I. Mikhlina; E. M. Doroshenko;
   M. A. Elistratova, comp. PISATELI IUZHNOGO URALA.
   BIBLIOGRAFICHESKII SPRAVOCHNIK. Cheliabinsk:
   Iuzhno-Ural'skoe Knizhnoe Izdatel'stvo, 1966, 311 pp.,
   7000 copies. [Russ. text, titles scattered]

POLITICAL SCIENCE, LAW

*Bykov, P. M.; N. G. Niporkin. RABOCHAIA REVOLIUTSIIA
   NA URALE. EPIZODY I FAKTY. Ekaterinburg:
   Gosudarstvennoe Izdatel'stvo. Ural'skoe Oblastnoe
   Upravlenie, 1921, 185 pp., 10,000 copies. [Russ.
   text; Russ. archives, pp. IV-V]

*Bystrykh, Fedor P. BOL'SHEVITSKIE ORGANIZATSII URALA I
   REVOLIUTSIIA 1905-1907 GODOV. [Sverdlovsk]:
   Sverdlovskoe Knizhnoe Izdatel'stvo, 1959, 363 pp.,
   1500 copies. [Russ. text; 9 lists, incl. archives,
   pp. 339-347, per. 1905-1907]

Urals: Political Science, Law

Dubrovin, N. "BIBLIOGRAFICHESKII UKAZATEL' STATEI I KNIG, OTNOSIASHCHIKHSIA DO PUGACHEVSKAGO BUNTA," PUGACHEV I EGO SOOBSHCHNIKI. Vol. III. St. Petersburg: n. p. 1884. [Russ. text; titles pp. 379-403, per. 18th cent.]

Fedorova, L. I. comp. ISTORIIA PARTIINYKH ORGANIZATSII URALA. UKAZATEL' LITERATURY, IZDANNOI V 1956-1964 GG. No. 1. Sverdlovsk: Sred.-Ural'skoe Knizhnoe Izdatel'stvo, 1967, 268 pp., 2300 copies. [Russ. text; 2244 titles, pub. 1956-1964]

Ionova, Z. A. comp. KOMSOMOL--NASHEI DOBLESTNOI PARTII SYN (KATALOG LITERATURY O KOMSOMOLE CHELIABINSKOI OBLASTI). Cheliabinsk: (Cheliabinskaia Oblastnaia Publichnaia Biblioteka. Cheliabinskii Obkom VLKSM), 1967, 35 pp., 2000 copies. [Russ. text]

*Liubimov, V.; B. Iuldashbaev. LENIN I SAMOOPREDELENIE NATSII. (NA PRIMERE NARODOV SREDNEGO POVOLZH'IA I PRIURAL'IA.) Cheboksary: Chuvashskoe Knizhnoe Izdatel'stvo, 1967, 239 pp., 4000 copies. [Russ. text; 341 Russian titles, pp. 214-238]

[Mal'gina, N. A. comp.] ISTORIIA PERMSKOGO KOMSOMOLA (REK UKAZATEL' LIT.) Perm: (Perm. Obkom VLKSM. Perm. Gos. Publ. B-ka im. Gor'kogo. Navstrechu 50-letiiu VLKSM), 1968, 79 pp., 3000 copies. [Russ. text; 540 titles]

*Petrov, S. M. "BOEVIKI," URAL'SKAIA SOVETSKAIA ENTSIKLOPEDIIA. Vol 1. Sverdlovsk-Moscow: Izdatel'stvo Uraloblispolkoma, 1933, 427-436 pp. [Russ. text and titles, per. 1905-1918, pp. 435-436]

Podshivalov, I. GRAZHDANSKAIA VOINA NA URALE. 1917-1918 (OPYT VOENNO-ISTORICHESKOGO ISSLEDOVANIIA). Moscow: Gosudarstvennoe Voennoe Izdatel'stvo (Nauchno-Voennoe Obshchestvo), 1925, 221 pp. [Russ. text; 50 titles, per. 1917-1918, pp. 218-220]

*Popov, V. T.; A. A. Orlov. "VYBORY V SOVETY," URAL'SKAIA SOVETSKAIA ENTSIKLOPEDIIA. Vol. 1. Sverdlovsk-Moscow: Izdatel'stvo Uraloblispolkoma, 1933, 808-821 pp. [Russ. text and titles, p. 821]

*Preobrazhenskii, Aleksandr A. OCHERKI KOLONIZATSII ZAPADNOGO URALA V XVII--NACHALE XVIII V. Moscow: Izdatel'stvo Akademii Nauk SSSR, 1956, 302 pp., 1800 copies. [Russ. text and titles, including archives, pp. 276-283]

Urals: Political Science, Law

*Smykov, Iu. "MATERIALY O POVOLZH'E I URALE V 'KOLOKOLE'. (ANNOTIROVANNYI UKAZATEL')," A. I. GERTSEN, N. P. OGAREV I OBSHCHESTVENNOE DVIZHENIE V POVOLZH'E I NA URALE. Kazan': Izdatel'stvo Kazanskogo Universiteta, 1964, 211 pp., 600 copies. [Russ. text and titles, pp. 176-207, pub. 1855-64]

*Zhilin, A.; A. Kolupaev. "ADMINISTRATIVNOE DELENIE URALA," URAL'SKAIA SOVETSKAIA ENTSIKLOPEDIIA Vol. 1. Sverdlovsk-Moscow: Izdatel'stvo Uraloblispolkoma, 1933, 62-73 pp. [Russ. text and titles, pp. 72-73]

*Zhurina, V. I. comp. IAKOV MIKHAILOVICH SVERDLOV NA URALE (REKOMENDATEL'NYI UKAZATEL' LITERATURY). Sverdlovsk: (Sverdlovskaia Gosudarstvennaia Publichnaia Biblioteka im. V. G. Belinskogo), 1966, 39 pp., 2000 copies. [Russ. text; ca.140 Russ. titles, pp. 6-28]

SOCIAL ORGANIZATION

"SODERZHANIE ZHURNALA 'URAL'SKII OKHOTNIK' ZA 1924 GOD," URAL'SKII OKHOTNIK. No. 12, 1924. [Russ. text; titles, pp. I-VI.

"SODERZHANIE ZHURNALA 'URAL'SKII OKHOTNIK' ZA 1925 GOD," URAL'SKII OKHOTNIK. No. 12, 1925. [Russ. text; titles, pp. I-XI]

22 VOLGA TATAR

GENERAL

Abramov, P. V. TATARSKAIA ASSR. Kazan: Tatknigoizdat, 1960. [Russ. text; 40 titles, pp. 229-30, Sov. per.]

Abramov, P. V.; N. Kh. Kaldiev; F. G. Shagi-Mukhametov. NASH KRAI TATARSTAN. Kazan: n. p., 1970. [Russ. text; 36 titles, pp. 187-188]

"BIBLIOGRAFIIA TATARSTANA," TRUDY OBSHCHESTVA IZUCHENIIA TATARSTANA. Vol. 1, 1930. [Russ. text; pub. 1928, pp. 181-203]

BIBLIOGRAFIIA TATARSTANA. 1917-1927, No. 1 Kazan: Tatizdat, 1930, 76 pp., 500 copies. [Russ. text; 710 Russ. titles, pub. 1917-27]

[Gabidullin, R. M.; Z. N. Akchurina, comp. IZDANIIA KAZANSKOGO FILIALA AN SSSR. 1946-1957. (BIBLIOGR. UKAZATEL'). Moscow: (B-ka Akad. Nauk SSSR. B-ka Kazan. AN SSSR), 1958, 131 pp., 200 copies. [Russ. text; 601 Tatar, Russ. titles, pub. 1946-57]

Kaliagina, N. A. UKAZATEL' STATEI K UCHENYM ZAPISKAM KAZANSKOGO ORDENA TRUDOVOGO KRASNOGO ZNAMENI GOSUDARSTVENNOGO UNIVERSITETA IMENI V. I. UL'IANOVA-LENINA ZA 1900-1950 GG. Kazan: (Kazansk. Un-t Nauchn. Biblioteka), 1955, 132 pp., 2000 copies. [Russ. text; 1538 titles, pub. 1900-1950]

KATALOG IZDANII [KAZANSKOGO FILIALA AKADEMII NAUK SSSR] NO. 2. "(1948-1955)." Kazan: (AN SSSR. Kazan. Filial), 1956, 13 pp., 4000 copies. [Russ. text; pub. 1948-1955]

KATALOG KNIG, IMEIUSHCHIKHSIA V PRODAZHE V TORGOVOM OTDELE TATGOSIZDATA. Kazan: Tip. im. Tukaeva, 1922, 80 pp.

*KAZANSKII UNIVERSITET IM. V. I. LENINA. VESTNIK STUDENCHESKOGO NAUCHNOGO OBSHCHESTVA. VYP. 4. OBSHCHESTVENNYE I GUMANITARNYE NAUKI. Kazan: (Izd. Kazan. Un-ta), 1967, 117 pp., 500 copies. [Russ. text; titles at end of articles]

Volga Tatar: General

KNIZHNAIA LETOPIS'. 1938, No. 1/2. Kazan: (Gosudarstvennaia Knizhnaia Palata Tatarskoi SSR), 1939. [Tatar, Russ. text; 198 Tatar, Russ. titles, pub.: 1st half 1938, p. 23]

KNIZHNAIA LETOPIS'. 1938 1 NENUM. VYP. 2-E POLUGODIE. Kazan: (Gosudarstvennaia Knizhnaia Palata Tatarskoi SSR), 1939. [Tatar, Russ. text; titles, pub.: 2nd half 1938]

KNIZHNAIA LETOPIS'. 1939 1 NENUM. VYP. ZA 1-I KVARTAL. Kazan: Tatgosizdat (Gosudarstvennaia Knizhnaia Palata Tatarskoi SSR), 1939, 20 pp., 650 copies. [Tatar, Russ. text; ca.130 Tatar, Russ. titles, pub.: 1st quarter 1939]

KNIZHNAIA LETOPIS'. 1939 NO. 2/3 ZA 2-3 KVARTALY. Kazan: (Gosudarstvennaia Knizhnaia Palata Tatarskoi SSR), 1940. [Tatar text; titles, pub.: 2nd, 3rd quarters 1939]

KNIZHNAIA LETOPIS'. 1939 1 NENUM. VYP. ZA 4-I KVARTAL. Kazan: (Gosudarstvennaia Knizhnaia Palata Tatarskoi SSR), 1941. [Tatar, Russ. text; titles, pub.: 4th quarter 1939]

KNIZHNAIA LETOPIS'. 1940 2 NENUM. VYP. (IANV./SENT.-OKT./DEK.) Kazan: (Gosudarstvennaia Knizhnaia Palata Tatarskoi SSR), 1941. [Tatar, Russ. text; titles, pub.: 1940]

KNIZHNAIA LETOPIS'. 1941 NENUM. VYP. (ZA IANV./MART). Kazan: (Gosudarstvennaia Knizhnaia Palata Tatarskoi SSR), 1941. [Tatar, Russ. text; titles, pub.: 1st quarter 1941]

KNIZHNAIA LETOPIS'. 1941 NENUM. VYP. (ZA APR./IIUN'). Kazan: Tatgosizdat (Gosudarstvennaia Knizhnaia Palata Tatarskoi SSR), 1946, 23 pp., 695 copies. [Tatar, Russ. text; 198 Tatar, Russ. titles, pub.: 2nd quarter 1941]

KNIZHNAIA LETOPIS'. 1941 NENUM. VYP. (ZA IIUL'/DEK). Kazan: (Gosudarstvennaia Knizhnaia Palata Tatarskoi SSR), 1945. [Tatar, Russ. text; titles, pub.: 2nd half 1941]

KNIZHNAIA LETOPIS'. (ZA 1945). Kazan: (Gosudarstvennaia Knizhnaia Palata Tatarskoi SSR), 1948. [Tatar, Russ. text; titles, pub.: 1945]

Volga Tatar: General

KNIZHNAIA LETOPIS'. (ZA 1946 G.) Kazan:
(Gosudarstvennaia Knizhnaia Palata Tatarskoi SSR),
1948. [Tatar, Russ. text; titles, pub.: 1946]

KNIZHNAIA LETOPIS'. 1947. Kazan: (Gos. Kn. Palata Tat.
ASSR), 1950, 1105 copies. [Tatar text; 457 Tatar,
Chuvash, Russ. titles, pub.: 1947]

KNIZHNAIA LETOPIS' TATARII. (ZA 1948). Kazan:
Tatgosizdat (Gosudarstvennaia Knizhnaia Palata
Tatarskoi SSR), 1952, 68 pp., 829 copies. [Tatar,
Russ. text; titles, pub.: 1948]

KNIZHNAIA LETOPIS' TATARII. (ZA 1949). Kazan:
Tatgosizdat (Gosudarstvennaia Knizhnaia Palata
Tatarskoi SSR), 1952, 75 pp., 855 copies. [Tatar,
Russ. text; titles, pub.: 1949]

KNIZHNAIA LETOPIS' TATARII. (ZA 1950). Kazan:
Tatgosizdat (Gosudarstvennaia Knizhnaia Palata
Tatarskoi SSR), 1952, 104 pp., 750 copies. [Tatar,
Russ. text; titles, pub.: 1950]

KNIZHNAIA LETOPIS' TATARII. ZA 1951 G. Kazan: Tatgosizdat,
1953, 104 pp., 750 copies. [Tatar, Russ. text;
titles, pub.: 1951]

KNIZHNAIA LETOPIS' TATARII. ZA 1952 G. Kazan:
Tatknigoizdat, 1954, 116 pp., 750 copies. [Tatar,
Russ. text; titles, pub.: 1952]

KNIZHNAIA LETOPIS' TATARII. ZA 1953 GOD. Kazan:
Tatknigoizdat, 1955, 143 pp., 1000 copies. [Tatar,
Russ. text; titles, pub.: 1953]

KNIZHNAIA LETOPIS' TATARII. ZA 1954 GOD. Kazan:
Tatknigoizdat, 1955, 135 pp., 1000 copies. [Tatar,
Russ. text; titles, pub.: 1954]

KNIZHNAIA LETOPIS' TATARII. ZA 1955 G. Kazan: (Gos.
Knizhnaia Palata Tatar. ASSR), 1957, 130 pp., 1000
copies. [Tatar, Russ. text; titles, pub.: 1955]

KNIZHNAIA LETOPIS' TATARII. 1956. Kazan: Tatknigoizdat,
1960, 115 pp., 500 copies. [Tatar, Russ. text;
titles, pub.: 1956]

KNIZHNAIA LETOPIS' TATARII. 1958. Kazan: Tatknigoizdat,
1960, 121 pp., 1000 copies. [Tatar, Russ., text;
titles, pub.: 1958]

Volga Tatar: General

KNIZHNAIA LETOPIS' TATARII. 1959. Kazan: Tatknigoizdat, 1960, 139 pp., 1000 copies. [Tatar, Russ. text; titles, pub.: 1959]

Kryshina, V. S. comp. SOVETSKAIA TATARIIA. PAMIATKA CHITATELIU, AGITATORU, LEKTORU. Kazan: (Tatar. Obkom VLKSM.), 1960, 11 pp., 2000 copies. [Russ. text; Sov. per.]

[Leont'ev, N.] SPISOK KNIG, BROSHIUR I PERIODICHESKIKH IZDANII, PECHATAVSHIKHSIA V ASTRAKHANSKIKH TIPOGRAFIIAKH S 1797 PO 1868 G. Astrakhan: n. p. 1869. [Russ. text; pub. 1797-1868]

LETOPIS' PECHATI. ORGAN GOS. BIBLIOGRAFII TATAR. ASSR. Kazan: (Knizhnaia Palata Tatar. ASSR) [1961] (quarterly), 500 copies. [Tatar, Russ. text; titles, pub.: 1961]

LETOPIS' PECHATI TATARII. ORGAN GOS. BIBLIOGRAFII TATAR ASSR. Kazan: (Knizhnaia Palata Tatar. ASSR) [1962] (quarterly), 500 copies. [Tatar, Russ. text; titles, pub.: 1962]

LETOPIS' PECHATI TATARII. ORGAN GOS. BIBLIOGRAFII TATAR. ASSR. Kazan: (Knizhnaia Palata Tatar. ASSR) [1963] (quarterly), 500 copies. [Tatar, Russ. text; titles, pub.: 1963]

LETOPIS' PECHATI TATARII. Kazan: (Knizhnaia Palata Tatarskoi ASSR), 1964 (quarterly), 500 copies. [Tatar, Russ. text; titles, pub.: 1964]

LETOPIS' PECHATI TATARII. Kazan: (Knizhnaia Palata Tatar ASSR) [1965; quarterly] 500 copies. [Tatar, Russ. text; titles, pub.: 1965]

LETOPIS' PECHATI TATARII. Kazan: (Knizhnaia Palata Tatar. ASSR), 1966 (quarterly), 500 copies. [Tatar, Russ. text; Tatar, Russ. titles, pub.: 1966]

LETOPIS' PECHATI TATARII. Kazan: (Knizhnaia Palata Tatar. ASSR), 1967 (quarterly), 500 copies. [Tatar, Russ. text; Tatar, Russ. titles, pub.: 1967]

LETOPIS' PECHATI TATARII. Kazan: (Knizhnaia Palata Tatar. ASSR), 1968 (quarterly), 500 copies. [Tatar, Russ. text; Tatar, Russ. titles, pub.: 1968]

LETOPIS' PECHATI TATARII. Kazan: (Knizhnaia Palata Tatar. ASSR), 1969 (quarterly), 1000 copies. [Tatar, Russ. text; Tatar, Russ. titles, pub.: 1969]

Volga Tatar: General

LETOPIS' PECHATI TATARII. Kazan: (Knizhnaia Palata
Tatar. ASSR), 1970 (quarterly), 1000 copies. [Tatar,
Russ. text; Tatar, Russ. titles, pub.: 1970]

LETOPIS' PERIODICHESKIKH IZDANII TATARSKOI ASSR ZA
1938 G. Kazan: Tatgosizdat, 1939, 20 pp., 650 copies.
[Tatar, Russ. text; ca.160 Tatar, Chuvash, Udmurt,
Russ. titles]

LETOPIS' PERIODICHESKIKH IZDANII TATARSKOI ASSR ZA
1939 G. Kazan: (Gosudarstvennaia Knizhnaia Palata
Tatarskoi ASSR), 1940. [Tatar, Russ. text; titles,
pub.: 1939]

LETOPIS' PERIODICHESKIKH IZDANII TATARSKOI ASSR ZA
1941 G. Kazan: Tatgosizdat, 1946, 28 pp., 695 copies.
[Tatar, Russ. text; 152 Tatar, Russ. titles, pub.:
1941]

LETOPIS' PERIODICHESKIKH IZDANII TATARSKOI ASSR ZA
1945 G. Kazan: (Gosudarstvennaia Knizhnaia Palata
Tatarskoi ASSR), 1947. [Tatar, Russ. text; titles,
pub.: 1945]

LETOPIS' PERIODICHESKIKH IZDANII TATARSKOI ASSR ZA
1946 G. Kazan: (Gosudarstvennaia Knizhnaia Palata
Tatarskoi ASSR), 1947. [Tatar, Russ. text; titles,
pub.: 1946]

LETOPIS' PERIODICHESKIKH IZDANII TATARSKOI ASSR ZA
1942-1944, 1947 I 1948 GG. Kazan: Tatgiz.
(Gosudarstvennaia Knizhnaia Palata Tatarskoi ASSR),
1950, 32 pp., 1065 copies. [Tatar, Russ. text; 162
Tatar, Chuvash, Udmurt, Russ. titles, pub.: 1942-1944,
1947, 1948]

LETOPIS' RETSENZII ZA 1953 GOD. Kazan: Tatknigoizdat,
1955, 36 pp., 1000 copies. [Tatar, Russ. text; 234
titles, pub.: 1953]

LETOPIS' RETSENZII ZA 1954 G. Kazan: Tatknigoizdat,
1956, 32 pp., 1500 copies. [Tatar, Russ. text; 185
titles, pub.: 1954]

LETOPIS' RETSENZII ZA 1955 G. Kazan: Tatknigoizdat,
1957, 33 pp., 1500 copies. [Tatar, Russ. text;
titles, pub.: 1955]

LETOPIS' RETSENZII ZA 1957 GOD. Kazan: (Gos. Knizhnaia
Palata Tatar. ASSR) Tatknigoizdat, 1959, 38 pp.,
1500 copies. [Tatar, Russ. text; titles, pub.: 1957]

Volga Tatar: General

LETOPIS' RETSENZII ZA 1958 GOD. Kazan: Tatknigoizdat, 1960, 39 pp., 1000 copies. [Tatar, Russ. text; titles, pub.: 1958]

LETOPIS' RETSENZII ZA 1959 GOD. Kazan: Tatknigoizdat, 1960, 45 pp., 1000 copies. [Tatar, Russ. text; titles, pub.: 1959]

LETOPIS' ZHURNAL'NYKH, GAZETNYKH STATEI I RETSENZII. ORGAN GOS. BIBLIOGRAFII TATAR. ASSR. 1955. Kazan: (Knizh. Palata Tatar. ASSR), 1956, 1500 copies. [Tatar, Russ. text; titles, pub.: 1955]

LETOPIS' ZHURNAL'NYKH I GAZETNYKH STATEI. ORGAN GOS. BIBLIOGRAFII TATAR. ASSR. Kazan: Tatknigoizdat (Knizhnaia Palata Tatar. ASSR), 1959, Tatar - 160 pp., Russ. - 148 pp., 500 copies. [Tatar, Russ. text; titles, pub.: 1956]

LETOPIS' ZHURNAL'NYKH I GAZETNYKH STATEI. ORGAN GOS. BIBLIOGRAFII TATAR. ASSR. Kazan: (Knizhnaia Palata Tatar ASSR), 1957 (quarterly), 500 copies. [Tatar, Russ. text; titles, pub.: 1957]

LETOPIS' ZHURNAL'NYKH I GAZETNYKH STATEI. ORGAN GOS. BIBLIOGRAFII TATAR. ASSR. 1958. Kazan: (Gos. Knizhnaia Palata Tatar. ASSR), 1960, 251 pp., 500 copies. [Tatar text; titles, pub.: 1958]

LETOPIS' ZHURNAL'NYKH STATEI. ORGAN GOS. BIBLIOGRAFII TATAR. ASSR. 1958. Kazan: (Gos. Knizhnaia Palata Tatar. ASSR), 1961, 135 pp., 300 copies. [Russ. text; titles, pub.: 1958]

LETOPIS' ZHURNAL'NYKH I GAZETNYKH STATEI. ORGAN GOS. BIBLIOGRAFII TATAR. ASSR. Kazan: (Gos. Knizhnaia Palata Tatar. ASSR), 1960, 256 pp., 500 copies. [Tatar text; titles, pub.: 1959]

LETOPIS' ZHURNAL'NYKH I GAZETNYKH STATEI. ORGAN GOS. BIBLIOGRAFII TATAR. ASSR. 1959. Kazan: (Gos. Knizhnaia Palata Tatar. ASSR), 1961, 129 pp., 500 copies. [Russ. text; titles, pub.: 1959]

LETOPIS' ZHURNAL'NYKH I GAZETNYKH STATEI. ORGAN GOS. BIBLIOGRAFII TATAR. ASSR. Kazan: (Gos. Knizhnaia Palata Tatar. ASSR), 1962, 199 pp., 500 copies. [Tatar text; titles, pub.: 1960]

Volga Tatar: General

Mishina, E. M., comp. SISTEMATICHESKII UKAZATEL' STATEI K PERIODICHESKIM IZDANIIAM KAZANSKOGO ORDENA TRUDOVOGO KRASNOGO ZNAMENI GOSUDARSTVENNOGO UNIVERSITETA IM. V. I. UL'IANOVA-LENINA 1815-1947 GG. Kazan:, n. p. 1960, 280 pp., 1000 copies. [Russ. text; 4659 Russ., other titles, pub. 1815-1947]

*Mukhariamov, M. K.; Iu. I. Smykov; V. V. Kuz'min, ed. TATARIIA NA PUTI K KOMMUNIZMU. Kazan: Tatarskoe Knizhnoe Izdatel'stvo, 1965, 324 pp., 1000 copies. [Russ. text; Tatar, Russ. titles, pp. 259-281]

Rakhim, A. "MATERIALY DLIA BIBLIOGRAFII PO TATAROVEDENIIU. (1918-1929).". "TRUDY DOMA TATARSK. KUL'TURY. T. 1 OCHERKI PO IZUCHENIIU MESTNOGO KRAIA." Kazan: n. p. 1930. [Russ. text; titles, pp. 342-395, pub. 1918-1929]

Rameev, I. VAQITLI TATAR MATBUGATIY. 1905-1925. AL'BOM TATARSKOI PERIODICHESKOI PECHATI. 1905-1925. Kāzan: Izd. "Gazhur," 1926, 231 pp. [Tatar text; pub. 1905-1925]

*Semenov, V. P. ed. ROSSIIA. POLNOE GEOGRAFICHESKOE OPISANIE NASHEGO OTCHESTVA. Vol.6 SREDNEE I NIZHNEE POVOLZH'E I ZAVOLZH'E. St. Petersburg: Izdanie A. F. Devriena, 1901, 599 pp. [Russ text; Russ. titles, pp. 550-558]

Shperk, F. Th. OPYT KHRONOLOGICHESKAGO UKAZATELIA LITERATURY OB ASTRAKHANSKOM KRAIE S 1473 PO 1887 GOD VKLIUCHITEL'NO. St. Petersburg: Izd. Astrakhanskago Gubernskago Statisticheskago Komiteta, 1892, VII+249. [Russ. text; 5848 Russ., Europ. titles, pub. 1473-1887]

[Sinegulov, A. ed., comp.] SPUTNIK. 1968. [Kazan] [Tatknigoizdat] [1969] 30 pp., 4000 copies. [Tatar text]

Volga Tatar: General

Skopin, G. A. SPISOK PECHATNYKH RABOT NIKOLAIA
FILIPPOVICHA KALININA. Kazan: (Gos. Muzei TASSR),
1958, 16 pp. [Russ. text and titles, Sov. per.]

Tagirova, S. Sh. NAUCHNAIA BIBLIOGRAFIIA KNIG NA
TATARSKOM IAZYKE, IZDANNYKH V 1925 G. Kazan: Izd. Doma
Tatarskoi Kul'tury, 1928/1929 102 pp., 2000 copies.
[Tatar text and titles, pub. 1925]

*TATARIIA na puti k kommunizmu. Kazan: Tatarskoe
Kniżhnoe Izdatel'stvo, 1965, 324 pp., 1000 copies.
[Russ. text; Tatar, Russ. titles, pp. 259-281]

"TATARSKAIA AVTONOMNAIA SOVETSKAIA SOTSIALISTICHESKAIA
RESPUBLIKA," BOL'SHAIA SOVETSKAIA ENTSIKLOPEDIIA. Vol.
41. Moscow: Gosudarstvennoe Nauchnoe Izdatel'stvo
"Bol'shaia Sovetskaia Entsiklopediia," 1956, 2nd ed.
642-656 pp. [Russ. text; Tatar, Russ. titles, pp.
647, 653, 654]

TATARSTAN BIBLIOGRAFIYASE. (1918-1929). Kazan:
Tatizdat, 1930, 40 pp. [Tatar text and titles,
pub. 1929]

Vlasova, I, V. et al. comp. DISSERTATSII
ZASHCHISHCHENNYE V KAZANSKOM GOSUDARSTVENNOM
UNIVERSITETE. BIBLIOGR. UKAZATEL'. Kazan: (Kazan Gos.
Un-t im. Ulianova-Lenina.), 1960, 202 pp., 700 copies.
[Russ. text; 642 titles, per. 1934-58]

ANTHROPOLOGY, ETHNOGRAPHY

Kriukova, T. A. UKAZATEL' ETNOGRAFICHESKIKH KOLLEKTSII
NARODOV POVOLZH'IA. Kazan: n. p., 1958, 48 pp.
[Russ. text]

Trofimova, T. A. "ETNOGENEZ TATAR SREDNEGO POVOLZH'IA
V SVETE DANNYKH ANTROPOLOGII," SOV. ETNOGRAFIIA.
No. 3, 1946, 51-74 pp. [Russ. text; ca.40 titles,
pub. 1829-1941]

Volga Tatar: Anthropology, Ethnography

*Trofimova, T. A. ETNOGENEZ TATAR POVOLZH'IA V SVETE DANNYKH ANTROPOLOGII. (TRUDY AN SSSR. INSTITUT ETNOGRAFII N. N. MIKHLUKHO-MAKLAIA. NOVAIA SERIIA. Vol. VII). Moscow-Leningrad: Izdatel'stvo Akademii Nauk SSSR, 1949, 264 pp., 2000 copies. [Russ. text; Turkish, Russ., Europ. titles, pp. 250-253]

*Trofimova, T. A. ETNOGENEZ TATAR POVOLZH'IA V SVETE DANNYKH ANTROPOLOGII. Moscow-Leningrad: Izdatel'stvo Akademii Nauk SSSR. (Trudy Institut Etnografii im. N. N. Mikhlukho-Maklaia. Novaia Seriia, Tom VII), 1949, 264 pp., 2000 copies. [Russ. text; Turkish, Russ., Europ. titles, pp. 250-253]

Vishnevskii, B. "SPISOK RABOT, DAIUSHCHIKH PREDSTAVLENIE O FIZICHESKOM TIPE NARODNOSTEI KAZANSKOI GUBERNII," KAZANSK. MUZEINYI VESTN. No. 3/4, 1920. [Russ. text; titles, pp. 25-27]

*Vorob'ev, N. I. KAZANSKIE TATARY (ETNOGR. ISSLEDOVANIE MATERIAL'NOI KUL'TURY DOOKTIABR'SKOGO PERIODA.) Kazan: (Akad. Nauk SSSR. Kazan. Filial. Int. Iazyka, Lit. i Istorii), 1953, 380 pp. [Russ. text; 432 Tatar, Russ. titles, pp. 366-381, per. pre-1917]

ARCHITECTURE, ART, MUSIC

*Dul'skii, P. "TATARSKOE ISKUSSTVO," BOL'SHAIA SOVETSKAIA ENTSIKLOPEDIIA. Vol. 53. Moscow: Gosudarstvennyi Nauchnyi Institut "Sovetskaia Entsiklopediia" (OGIZ RSFSR), 1946. 659-663 pp. [Russ. text and titles, p. 663]

Dunaeva, T. G.; L. M. Aver'ianova; V. S. Kryshina; G. A. Mustafina, comp. KALENDAR' ZNAMENATEL'NYKH I PAMIATNYKH DAT PO TATARII....NA 1966 GOD. Kazan: (M-vo Kul'tury Tatar. ASSR.), 1966, 75 pp. [Russ. text; titles at end of chapters]

Faizi, Dzhaudat. MUZYKAL'NYE VECHERA. Kazan: Tatknigoizdat, 1966, 176 pp., 5000 copies. [Russ. text; 13 Tatar titles p. 175]

Volga Tatar: Architecture, Art, Music

[Litinskii, G. I., ed.] MUZYKAL'NAIA KUL'TURA SOVETSKOI TATARII. Moscow: Muzgiz, 1959. [Russ. text; 39 Tatar, Russ. titles, pp. 244-245]

Lotsmanova, A. P.; Z. Sh. Khabibullina. N. G. ZHIGANOV. LAUREAT STALINSKOI PREMII, KOMPOZITOR. Kazan: Tatknigoizdat, 1954, 35 pp., 2000 copies. [Russ. text; 141 titles, pub. 1937-54]

[Melikhovskii, V. M.; G. A. Skopin, comp.] PLAKATY PERVYKH LET SOVETSKOI VLASTI. (1918-1922 GG.) KATALOG. Kazan: (Gos. Muzei Tatar. ASSR), 1959, 78 pp., 300 copies. [Russ. text; per. 1918-1922]

[Privalova, V. S.; R. I. Faibusovich.] ODENEM GORODA I SELA TATARII V ZELENYI UBOR. Kazan: (Tatar. Obl. Kom-t VLKSM. Resp. B-ka Tatar. ASSR im. Lenina), 1958, 18 pp., 1500 copies. [Russ. text]

Safina, G. B. OSNOVOPOLOZHNIK TATARSKOI SOVETSKOI MUZYKI KOMPOZITOR SALIKH SAIDASHEV. (UKAZATEL' LIT.) Kazan: (Tatar. Resp. B-ka im. Lenina), 1958, 34 pp., 1000 copies. [Tatar, Russ. text; 37 Tatar, Russ. titles]

Skopin, G. A. IZDANIIA MUZEIA. 1894-1956. Kazan: (Gos. Muzei TASSR), 1957, 35 pp. [Russ. text; pub. 1894-1956]

_____. SPISOK KNIG I STATEI NAPECHATANNYKH V 1949 GODU PO VOPROSAM ARKHITEKTURY. [Kazan]: (Soiuz Sov. Arkhitektorov SSSR. Tatarskoe Otd-nie), [1950], 26 pp., 300 copies. [Tatar text; 238 titles, pub. 1949]

Valeev, F. Kh. ORNAMENT KAZANSKIKH TATAR. Kazan: 1969. [Russ. text; ca.150 titles, pp. 198-202]

ECONOMICS

Abramov, P. V. SOVETSKAIA TATARIIA. EKON.-GEOGR. OCHERK. Kazan: Tatknigoizdat, 1956. [Russ. text, 47 titles, pp. 161-2]

Volga Tatar: Economics

Andreev, I. A. BIUDZHETNYI UCHET. Kazan: Izd. Kazan. Un-ta, 1966, 284 pp., 500 copies. [Russ. text; 28 titles, pp. 281-282]

*Belialov, U. B. RUKOVODSTVO KHOZIASTVENNYM STROITEL'STVOM V TATARII V GODY GRAZHDANSKOI VOINY (1918-1920). Kazan: Izdatel'stvo Kazanskogo Universiteta, 1963, 210 pp., 1000 copies. [Russ. text; ca.220 Russ. titles, per. 1918-1920, pp. 201-209]

Berman, S. I. comp. VO IMIA CHELOVEKA, DLIA BLAGA CHELOVEKA. Kazan: (Lektorskaia Gruppa Tatar. Obkoma KPSS.), 1966, 24 pp., 1000 copies. [Russ. text; titles pp. 23-24]

[Khabibullina, Z. Sh.] TRIDTSAT' LET TATARSKOI RESPUBLIKI. (REK. SPISOK LIT.) Kazan: (Resp. B-ka TatASSR im. Lenina), 1950, 10 pp. [Tatar text; 37 Tatar titles]

Kondakov, V. V. PRIBYL' PROMYSHLENNOGO PREDPRIATIIA. Kazan: Tatknigoizdat, 1967, 75 pp., 1000 copies. [Russ. text; titles p. 74]

Tagirov, Z. "OBZOR FONDA KAZANSKOGO EKONOMICHESKOGO OBSHCHESTVA," TSENTR. ARKHIV TATARSTANA. No. 1 (22), 1933. [Russ. text; titles pp. 76-80]

Tazetdinov, A. KUL'TURA SELA. Kazan: Tatknigoizdat, 1968, 120 pp., 1500 copies. [Russ. text; titles pp. 117-119]

EDUCATION

Bolgarskii, B. V. KAZANSKAIA SHKOLA MATEMATICHESKOGO OBRAZOVANIIA (V KHARAKTERISTIKAKH EE GLAVNEISHIKH DEIATELEI). CH. I. RAZVITIIA ELEMENTARNOI MATEMATIKI DO VELIKOI OKTIABR'SKOI SOTS. REVOLIUTSII. Kazan: n. p. 1966. [Russ. text; 183 titles, pp. 254-260]

Gizatullin, Kh. G. BIBLIOGRAFIIA PO ISTORII KAZANSKOGO VETERINARODNOGO INSTITUTA (V KHRONOL. PORIADKE). UCHENYE ZAPISKI. KAZAN. VET. IN-TA, T. 101. [Russ. text; 14 titles, p. 283]

Volga Tatar: Education

Islamov, F. F. INTERNATSIONAL'NOE VOSPITANIE UCHASHCHIKHSIA PRI IZUCHENII TATARSKOI LITERATURY. (5-8 KLASSY). Kazan: n. p., 1968. [Tatar text; 89 titles, pp. 167-174]

*"KAZANSKII UNIVERSITET," ENTSIKLOPEDICHESKII SLOVAR' Vol. 13A. St. Petersburg, F. A. Brokgauz, I. A. Efron, 1894, 903-905 pp. [Russ. text and titles, p. 905]

Mikheeva, A. A.; L. Z. Shakirova. SOCHINENIIA NA RUSSKOM IAZYKE V TATARSKIKH SHKOLAKH. Kazan: n. p. 1969. [Russ. text; 50 titles, pp. 91-94]

Mukhtarov, Kh. M. VOSPITANIE DETEI V SEM'E. Kazan: Tatknigoizdat, 1955. [Tatar text; 29 Tatar, Russ. titles, pp. 102-103]

Privalova, V. S. KUL'TURA I ISKUSSTVO TATARSKOI ASSR. PAMIATKA CHITATELIU, AGITATORU, LEKTORU. Kazan: (Tatar. Obkom VLKSM. Resp. B-ka TASSR im. Lenina), 1960, 16 pp., 2000 copies. [Russ. text]

Sattarov, G. F. KUL'TURA RECHI V SHKOLE. Kazan: n. p., 1965. [Tatar text; ca.130 titles, pp. 144-149]

Shofman, A. S. IZ ISTORII KAZANSKOGO UNIVERSITETA IMENI V. I. UL'IANOVA-LENINA. [150-LETIIU SO DNIA OSNOVANIIA.] Kazan: n. p., 1954. [Russ. text; 130 titles, pp. 19-25]

Tahirova S. "TATAR MADANIIYATE IORTY TURYNDA BASYLGAN MATERIYALLAR BIBLIOGRAFIIYASE," TRUDY DOMA TATARSK. KUL'TURY. T. I. "OCHERKI PO IZUCHENIIU MESTN. KRAIA." Kazan: n. p., 1930. [Tatar text; titles, pp. 42-49]

_____. "BIBLIOGRAFIIA PECHATNYKH MATERIALOV O DOME TATARSK. KUL'TURY," TRUDY DOMA TATARSKOI KUL'TURY. T. I. "OCHERKI PO IZUCHENIIU MESTNOGO KRAIA." 1930. [Russ. text; titles, pp. 42-49]

Taibinskii, S. T. OKTIABR' I POVYSHENIE UROVNIA ZHIZNI TRUDIASHCHIKHSIA. Kazan: (Otd. Propagandy i Agitatsii Obkoma KPSS), 1967, 31 pp., 1042 copies. [Russ. text; titles p. 31]

Tazetdinov, A. VELIKII OKTIABR' I KUL'TURNAIA REVOLIUTSIIA V TATARII. Kazan: (Otd. Propagandy i Agitatsii Tatar OK KPSS.), 1967, 33 pp.; 1042 copies. [Russ. text; 17 titles, pp. 32-33]

Volga Tatar: Education

Tuishev, Iu. A. OBSHCHESTVENNO-PEDAGOGICHESKAIA
DEIATEL'NOST' GABDULLY TUKAIA. Kazan: n. p., 1963.
[Russ. text; 28 titles]

*Zalkind, G. M.; M. K. Korbut; M. A. Vasil'ev, comp.
"BIBLIOGRAFICHESKII UKAZATEL'," KORBUT, M. K.
KAZANSKII GOSUDARSTVENNYI UNIVERSITET IMENI V. I.
UL'IANOVA-LENINA ZA 125 LET. 1804/05-1929/30.
Vol. 2. Kazan: Izdanie Kazanskogo Universiteta, 1930,
(II) 385 pp. [Russ. text; Russ., Europ. titles (II)
pp. 337-364]

*Znamenskii, P. NA PAMIAT' O NIKOLAE IVANOVICHE
IL'MINSKOM: K 25 LETIIU BRATSTVA SV. GURIIA.
Kazan: Bratstvo Sv. Guriia, Gurii Bratstvo, 1892.
[Russ. text; titles pp. 310-315]

GEOGRAPHY

Chupin, N. "OBOZRENIA KNIG I ZHURNAL'NYKH STATEI
ZAKLIUCHAIUSHCHIKH V SEBE GEOGRAFICHESKIE I
STATISTICHESKIE SVEDENIIA O KAZANSKOI GUBERNII,"
KAZ. GUB. VIED., Nos. 10-27, 36, 51-52, 1851. [Russ.
text; pub. 1851]

Melikhovskii, V. M., comp. KARTY I PLANY KAZANSKOI
GUBERNII I TATARSKOI ASSR. KATALOG. Kazan:
(Gos. Muzei Tatar ASSR), 1957, 44 pp., 300 copies.
[Russ. text; 125 titles]

Stupishin, A. V. ed. GEOGRAFICHESKII SBORNIK. No. 1.
ZA 1965 G. Kazan: Izd. Kazan. Un-ta im. V. I.
Ul'ianova-Lenina, 1966, 146 pp., 500 copies. [Russ.
text; titles at end of articles]

Stupishina, A. V. ed. GEOGRAFICHESKII SBORNIK. No. 2.
Kazan: Izd. Kazan. Un-ta, 1967, 170 pp., 500 copies.
[Russ. text; titles at end of articles]

*Tikhvinskaia, E. I. GEOLOGIIA. Kazan: UCHENYE ZAPISKI
Kazanskogo Gosudarstvennogo Universiteta, T. 99.
KNIGA 3. No. 13, 1939, 238 pp. [Russ. text; 107
Russ. titles, pp. 234-238]

Volga Tatar: Geography

"UKAZATEL' GLAVNEISHIKH LITERATURNYKH ISTOCHNIKOV PO PO TATARSKOI RESPUBLIKE," GEOGRAFICHESKOE OPISANIE TATARSKOI ASSR. PART I, PRIRODA KRAIA. Kazan: n. p., 1921. [Russ. text; titles pp. 251-270]

HISTORY, ARCHAEOLOGY

"ALALYKIN, TEMIR," VOENNAIA ENTSIKLOPEDIIA. Vol. 1. Petersburg: T-vo I. D. Sytina, 1911, p. 229. [Russ. text and titles, p. 229]

Al'fonsov, I. A. UKAZATEL' K "IZVESTIIAM OBSHCHESTVA ARKHEOLOGII, ISTORII I ETNOGRAFII PRI KAZANSKOM UNIVERSITETE" ZA 1878-1905 GG. (T.I-XXI). Kazan: n. p., 1906, 143 pp. [Russ. text; pub. 1878-1905]

*Bakhrushin, S. "KAZANSKOE KHANSTVO" BOL'SHAIA SOVETSKAIA ENTSIKLOPEDIIA. Vol. 30. Moscow: Gosudarstvennyi Institut "Sovetskaia Entsiklopediia (OGIZ RSFSR), 1937, 545-550 pp. [Russ. text; Tatar, Russ. titles, p. 550]

BIBLIOGRAFIIA ZOLOTOI ORDY. ZAPISKI VOSTOCHNAGO OTDIELA RUSSKAGO GEOGRAFICHESKAGO OBSHCHESTVA. Vol. XX, No. 4., 1912. [Russ. text]

Bushkanets, E. G. KAZAN' V VOSPOMINANIIAKH SOVREMENNIKOV. ANNOT. UKAZATEL'. No. 1, "1800-1850 GG." Kazan: (Gos. Muzei Tatar. ASSR.), 1955, 18 pp., 300 copies. [Russ. text; 56 titles, per. 1800-1850]

Chernyshev, E. "SPISOK TRUDOV N. N. FIRSOVA," VESTN. NAUCH. O-VA TATAROVEDENIIA. No. 9/10, 1930. [Russ. text; per. 1864-1934, pp. 17-24]

*Daishev, S. I., ed. ISTORIIA TATARSKOI ASSR (S DREVNEISHIKH VREMEN DO NASHIKH DNEI). UKAZATEL' SOVETSKOI LIT. 1917-1959. Kazan: (Kazan. Gos. Univ. im. Ul'ianova-Lenina.), 1960, 320 pp., 1000 copies. [Tatar and Russ. text; 5,777 Tatar, Russ. titles, per. antiquity to 1959, pub. 1917-1959]

Volga Tatar: History, Archaeology

Elert, A. A. OCHERK STUDENCHESKOGO DVIZHENIIA V KAZANI NAKANUNE REVOLIUTSII 1905-1907 GG. Kazan: (Kazan. Fin.-Ekon. In-t. im Kuibysheva), 1961. [Russ. text; ca.80 titles, per. early 20th cent., pp. 110-13]

*Firsov, M.; A. Tarasov. "KAZAN!" BOL'SHAIA SOVETSKAIA ENTSIKLOPEDIIA. Vol. 30. Moscow: Gosudarstvennyi Institut "Sovetskaia Entsiklopediia' (OGIZ RSFSR), 1937, 551-557 pp. [Russ. text; Tatar, Russ. titles, p. 557]

*G. G. "ZOLOTAIA ORDA," BOL'SHAIA SOVETSKAIA ENTSIKLOPEDIIA. Vol. 27, Moscow: Gosudarstvennoe Slovarno-Entsiklopedicheskoe Izdatel'stvo "Sovetskaia Entsiklopediia," (OGIZ RSFSR), 1933, 100-104 pp. [Russ. text; Russ., Europ. titles, p. 104]

[Gabidullin, R. M.] TRIDTSAT' LET TATARSKOI ASSR. (REK. SPISOK LIT). Kazan: Resp. B-ka TatASSR im. Lenina, 1950, 11 pp., 500 copies. [Russ. text; 45 titles.]

*Gening, V. F.; V. E. Stoianov; T. A. Khlebnikova; I. S. Vainer; E. P. Kazakov; R. K. Valeev. ARKHEOLOGICHESKIE PAMIATNIKI U SELA ROZHDESTVENO. Kazan: Izdatel'stvo Kazanskogo Universiteta, 1962, 127 pp., 600 copies. [Russ. text; 31 Russ. titles, pub. 1871-1959, per. Bronze Age to 14th c., pp. 125-126]

[Gimadi, Kh. G., ed.] ISTORIIA TATARSKOI ASSR. Vol. 1. "S DREVNEISHIKH VREMEN DO VELIKOI OKTIABR'SKOI SOTS. REVOLIUTSII." Kazan: (Akad. Nauk SSSR. Kazan Filial In-t Iazyka, Lit. i Istorii), 1959. [Tatar text; ca.260 Tatar, Russ. titles, per. antiquity to 1917, pp. 577-584]

Gimadi, K. G., ed. ISTORIIA TATARSKOI ASSR. Vol. 1. "S DREVNEISHIKH VREMEN DO VELIKOI OKTIABR'SKOI SOTS. REVOLIUTSII," 1955. [Russ. text; ca.260 Tatar, Russ. titles, per. antiquity to Revolution, pp. 532-40]

Gimadi, Kh. G. ISTORIIA TATARSKOI ASSR. V. 2 (OT VELIKOI OKTIABR'SKOI SOTS. REVOLIUTSII DO NASHIKH DNEI). Kazan: (Akad. Nauk SSSR. Kazan. Filial. In-t Iazyka, Lit. i Istorii.), 1960. [Russ. text; ca.250 titles, per. 1917-1959, pp. 574-81]

_____; M. K. Mukhariamov. SOVETSKAIA TATARIIA-- DETISHCHE OKTIABRIA. Kazan: Tatknigoizdat, 1957. Russ. text; 70 titles, pp. 170-73]

Volga Tatar: History, Archaeology

*Grekov, B. D.; A. Iu. Iakubovskii. ZOLOTAIA ORDA I EE
PADENIE. Moscow-Leningrad: Izdatel'stvo Akademii
Nauk SSSR, 1950, 478 pp., 10000 cop. [Russ. text; Russ.
Europ. titles, pp. 431-443]

Ianguzov, Z.; L. Iudkevich. SKOVZ' OGNENNOE KOL'TSO
(REID IUZHN. -URAL. PARTIZANSKOI ARMII, 1918 G).
Kazan: Tatknigoizdat, 1968, 183 pp., 16,000 copies.
[Russ. text; titles, p. 181]

Ionenko, I. M. KRES'TIANSTVO SREDNEGO POVOLZH'IA
NAKANUNE VELIKOGO OKTIABRIA. Kazan: Tatknigoizdat,
1957. [Russ. text; ca.300 titles, pp. 241-251]

Ionenko, I.; I. Tagirov. OKTIABR' V KAZANI. Kazan: n. p.
1967. [Russ. text; 86 titles, pp. 267-271]

ISTORIIA TATARSKOI ASSR. (S DREVNEISHIKH VREMEN DO
NASHIKH DNEI). UKAZ. SOV. LIT. (1960-1967). Kazan:
(Kazan. Gos. Un-t im. Ul'ianova-Lenina. Nauch. B-ka
im. Lobachevskogo), 1970, 160 pp., 700 copies.
[Tatar, Russ. text; pub. 1960-1967, 2172 titles]

Kalinin, N. F. KAZAN'. ISTORICHESKII OCHERK. Kazan:
Tatknigoizdat, 1955, 2nd ed. [Russ. text; ca.340
Tatar, Russ. titles, pp. 394-408]

KATALOG IZDANII TATGOSIZDAT. Kazan: Tip. "Vostok,"
1923, 56+12 pp., 1000 copies. [Tatar, Russ. text;
ca.110 Tatar, Russ. titles, pub. 1919-1922]

*"KAZAN'," ENTSIKLOPEDICHESKII SLOVAR'. Vol. 13A.
S.-Petersburg: F. A. Brokgauz, I. A. Efron, 1894,
910-912 pp. [Russ. text and titles, p. 912]

"KAZAN' I KAZANSKIE POKHODY," VOENNAIA ENTSIKLOPEDIIA.
Vol. 2. Petersburg: T-vo I. D. Sytina, 1913, 282-286
pp. [Russ. text and titles, p. 286]

*Khalikov, A. Kh.; Sh. F. Mukhamed'iarov; E. I. Chernyshov.
ISTORIIA TATARSKOI ASSR. Kazan: Tatknigoizdat, 1968,
719 pp., 9000 copies. [Russ. text; ca.470 Tatar, Russ.
titles, pp. 681-700, pub. 1884-1967]

*Khasanov, Kh. Kh. REVOLIUTSIIA 1905-1907 GG. V TATARII.
Moscow: Izdatel'stvo "Nauka,"1965, 341 pp., 1800
copies. [Russ text; ca.300 Tatar, Russ. titles, incl.
archives, per. 1905-1907, pp. 3-10, 329-338]

Khudiakov, M. OCHERKI PO ISTORII KAZANSKOGO KHANSTVA.
Kazan: Gosudarstvennoe Izdatel'stvo, 1923. [Russ. text,
titles, pp. 294-300]

Volga Tatar: History, Archaeology

*Klimov, I. M. OBRAZOVANIE I RAZVITIE TATARSKOI ASSR.
(1920-1926). Kazan: Izd-vo Kazan. Un-ta, 1960,
367 pp., 3000 cop. [Russ. text: ca.250 Tatar, Russ.
titles, pp. 347-58. per. 1920-1926]

"KRATKII UKAZATEL' LITERATURY PO ISTORII TATARII. (V
POMOSHCH' PROPAGANDISTU)," KOMMUNIST TATARII, No. 9,
1958. [Russ. text]

Kryshina, V. S.; G. B. Safina; L. Sh. Sakmarova, comp.
BIBLIOGRAFICHESKIE MATERIALY K PAMIATNYM DATAM PO
TATARII NA 1960 GOD. Kazan: n. p., 1960, 39 pp.,
2000 copies. [Tatar, Russ. text and titles, per. 1960]

"KULIKOVSKAIA BITVA," VOENNAIA ENTSIKLOPEDIIA. Vol. 14.
Petersburg: T-vo I. D. Sytina, 1914, 377-382 pp.
[Russ. text and titles, p. 382]

*Kuz'min, V. V.; V. I. Shishkin. "BIBLIOGRAFIIA
[OKTIABR'SKOI REVOLIUTSII V KAZANSKOI GUBERNII]"
TATARIIA V PERIOD VELIKOGO OKTIABRIA. Kazan: (AN SSSR,
Ins-t Iaz., Lit., i Ist. im. Galimdzhana, 1970,
216 pp., 500 copies. [Russ. text; 310 Russ. titles,
pub. 1917-67; per. 1917-20, pp. 199-214]

Mukhariamov, M. GRAZHDANSKAIA VOINA V TATARII (1918-1919).
Kazan: n. p. 1969. [Russ. text; ca.400 titles,
per. 1918-1919, pp. 5-15; 274-293]

*Mukhariamov, M. K. OKTIABR' I NATSIONAL'NYI VOPROS V
TATARII (OKT. 1917-1918). Kazan: (Akad. Nauk SSSR,
Kazan. Filial In-t Iazyka, Lit. i Istorii), 1958,
275 pp. [Russ. text; ca.270 Tatar, Russ. titles,
per. Oct. 1917 - July 1918, pp. 3-11; 264-276]

*_____. OKTIABR' I NATSIONAL'NO-
GOSUDARSTVENNOE STROITEL'STVO V TATARII (OKT. 1917 G.
1920 G). Moscow: "Nauka", 1969, 288 pp., 2000 copies.
[Russ. text; ca.370 Tatar, Bashkir, Russ. titles,
lit. pub. to 1968, pp. 265-279]

*Mun'kov, N. P. "SPISOK NAUCHNYKH RABOT E. I.
USTIUZHANINA -- IZDANIIA, VYSHEDSHIE POD REDAKTSIEI
E. U. USTIUZHANINA. UCHEN. ZAP. KAZAN. PED. IN-TA.
VYP. 71 SB. 4. Kazan, 1969, 343-348 pp., 1000
copies. [Russ. text; 39 Russ. titles, pub. 1941-1965,
pp. 346-348]

*N. D. "KASYMOVSKO-TATARSKOE NARECHIE," BOL'SHAIA
SOVETSKAIA ENTSIKLOPEDIIA, Vol. 31. Moscow:
Gosudarstvennyi Institut "Sovetskaia Entsiklopediia,"
(OGIZ RSFSR), 1937, p. 693. [Russ. text; Tatar.,
Russ. titles, p. 693]

Volga Tatar: History, Archaeology

*Neguliaev, A. P. ZAVOD-VETERAN. IZ ISTORII KAZAN. Z-DA "SERP I MOLOT" 1851-1967, Kazan: Tatknigoizdat, 1968, 143 pp., 2000 copies. [Russ. text and titles, per. 1851-1967, pp. 133-139]

*Saidashcva, M. A. LENIN I SOTSIALISTICHESKOE STROITEL'STVO V TATARII. 1918-1923. Moscow: "Nauka," 1969, 328 pp., 4500 copies. [Russ. text; ca.380 Tatar, Russ. titles, per. 1918-1923, pub. 1918-1969, pp. 307-321]

*Shakirzianov, M. Kh.; R. I. Idiatullin. VOLZHSKIE KOMMUNARY. IST. OCHERK. Kazan: Tatknigoizdat, 1966, 64 pp., 6000 copies. [Tatar text and titles, pp. 62-63, per. 1919-1920]

Sharapov, Ia. Sh. NATSIONAL'NYE SEKTSII RKP (B). Kazan: n. p., 1967. [Russ. text; ca.430 titles, pp. 254-271]

Shishkin, V. I. comp. VOPROSY ISTORIOGRAFII VSEOBSHCHEI ISTORII. VYP. 2, "ISTORIOGRAFIIA ISTORII VTOROI MIROVOI VOINY." Kazan: Izd. Kazan. Un-ta, 1967, 189 pp., 600 copies.[Russ. text; titles, pp. 175-185]

*Shpilevskii, S. M. DREVNIE GORODA I DRUGIE BULGARSKO-TATARSKIE PAMIATNIKI V KAZANSKOI GUBERNII. Kazan: V Universitetskoi Tipografii, 1877, 585+16 pp. [Russ. text; Tatar, Russ., Mid-East titles, pp. 3-191]

*Silaeva, N. M. "OBZOR MATERIALOV TSGA TASSR PO ISTORII OBRAZOVANIIA TASSR (1917-1921 GG)," IZ ISTORII KLASSOVOI BOR'BY I OBSHCHESTV. MYSLI V POVOLZH'E I PRIURAL'E. (UCHEN. ZAPISKI KAZAN. UN-TA, T. 122 Kn. 2). Kazan: (Kazan. Un-t), 1962, 198 pp. [Russ. text and titles, per. 1917-21, pp. 179-199]

Tagirov, R. Sh. "BIBLIOGRAFICHESKII UKAZATEL' DOKTORSKIKH I KANDIDATSKIKH DISSERTATSII," KOMMUNIST TATARII, No. 9, 1958. [Russ. text; 57 titles, pub. 1939-1957, pp. 90-93]

*"TATARSKAIA AVTONOMNAIA SOVETSKAIA SOTSIALISTICHESKAIA RESPUBLIKA," BOL'SHAIA SOVETSKAIA ENTSIKLOPEDIIA, Vol. 53. Moscow: Gosudarstvennyi Nauchnyi Institut "Sovetskaia Entsiklopediia" (OGIZ RSFSR), 1946, pp. 618-640. [Russ. text; Tatar, Russ., titles, p. 640]

"TATARSTAN TARIKHY BUENCHA KISKACHA ADABIYAT KURSATKECHE," TATARSTAN KOMMUNISTY. No. 9, 1958. [Tatar text]

Volga Tatar: History, Archaeology

*TATARY SREDNEGO POVOLZH'IA I PRIUARL'IA. Moscow: "Nauka," 1967, 538 pp., 6300 copies. [Russ. text; ca.550, Tatar, Turk, Russ. titles, pp. 514-531]

Vorob'ev, N. I. "UKAZATEL' K IZVESTIIAM OBSHCHESTVA ARKHEOLOGII, ISTORII I ETNOGRAFII PRI KAZANSKOM GOSUDARSTVENNOM UNIVERSITETE ZA 1906-1927 GODY. (TOMY 22-23)," TRUDY O-VA ARKHEOL., ISTORII I ETNOGRAF. T. 34, No. 1/2, 1928, [Russ. text; pub. 1906-1927, pp. 1-21]

*Zakirov, Salikh. DIPLOMATICHESKIE OTNOSHENIIA ZOLOTOI ORDY S EGIPTOM (XII-XIV VV.). Moscow: "Nauka," 1966, 160 pp., 2200 copies. [Russ. text; Cent. As., Russ., Europ. titles, per. XIII-XIV pp. 147-159]

LANGUAGE, LITERATURE

*Abdrazakov, K. S.; G. S. Amirov; A. Sh. Asadullin; et al. comp. TATARSKO-RUSSKII SLOVAR'. OKOLO 38,000 SLOV. Moscow: "Sov. Entsiklopediia," 1966, 863 pp., 21,000 copies. [Russ. text; 33 Tatar, Russ. titles, pub. 1833-1960, p. 78]

*Abdullin, I. A. IAZYK DRAM G. KAMALA. Kazan: "Tatarstan," 1968, 198 pp., 2000 copies. [Tatar text; 53 Tatar, Russ. titles, pub. 1948-1967, pp. 192-197]

*Akhatov, G. Kh. DIALEKT ZAPADNO SIBIRSKIKH TATAR. Ufa: (Ministerstvo Vysshego i Srednego Spetsial'nogo Obrazovaniia RSFSR...), 1963, 195 pp., 800 copies. [Russ. text; 244 Sov. Asian, Russ. Europ. titles, profuse, scattered]

_____. IAZYK SIBIRSKIKH TATAR. CH. I. "FONETICH. OSOBENNOSTI." Kazan: (Bashkir. Gos. Un-t im. 40-let. Oktiab. Rev.), 1960. [Tatar text; 60 Tatar, Russ. titles, pp. 68-69]

*Akhmadullin, A.; F. Musin. "KRATKAIA BIBLIOGRAFIIA TRUDOV PO TATARSKOI SOVETSKOI LITERATURY. Moscow: Izdatel'stvo "Nauka," 1965, 569 pp., 3500 copies. [Russ. text; ca.710 Tatar, Russ. titles, pp. 548-569]

Volga Tatar: Language, Literature

*Akhmetov, Abdulla. IZBRANNOE. Kazan: Tatarstan
Kitap Nashriyati, 1964, 354 pp., 13,000 copies.
[Tatar text; 30+ Tatar titles, pp. 352-353]

Akhunzianov, E. M. RUSSKIE ZAIMSTVOVANIIA V TATARSKOM
IAZYKE. Kazan: Izd. Kazan. Un-ta, 1968, 367 pp.,
[Russ. text; pp. 347-363]

*Arsharuni, A. "IBRAGIMOV, GALIMDZHAN," LITERATURNAIA
ENTSIKLOPEDIIA. Vol. 4. n. p. Izdatel'stvo
Kommunisticheskoi Akademii, 1930, 384-387 pp. [Russ.
text; Tatar, Russ. titles, p. 387]

*Barskaia, K. A. MUSA DZHALIL'. Leningrad:
"Prosveshchenie," 1968, 96 pp., 75,000 copies.
[Russ. text; titles, p. 95]

*B-G, G. "NIGMATI, GALIMDZHAN AMIRDZHANOVICH,"
LITERATURNAIA ENTSIKLOPEDIIA, Vol. 8. Moscow:
Gosudarstvennoe Slovarno-Entsiklopedicheskoe
Izdatel'stvo "Sovetskaia Entsiklopediia," (OGIZ
RSFSR), 1934, p.46. [Russ. text; Tatar, Russ.
titles, p. 46]

Bashirov, G. NASHE VREMIA (KRATKAIA BIBLIOGRAFIIA
PROIZVEDENII G. BASHIROVA.) Kazan: Tatgosizdat,
1953. [Tatar text; 39 Tatar, Russ., other titles,
pp. 335-337]

"BIBLIOGRAFIIA PROIZVEDENII KAVI NADZHIMI," SVETLAIA
TROPA. Kazan: Tatgosizdat, 1953. [Tatar text;
115 Tatar, Russ. titles, pub. 1924-1951, pp. 550-555]

Burganova, N. B; L. T. Makhmutova. "K VOPROSU OB ISTORII
OBRAZOVANIIA I IZUCHENIIA TATARSKIKH DIALEKTOV I
GOVOROV," MATERIALY PO TATARSKOI DIALEKTOLOGII.
No. 2. Kazan: n. p., 1962. [Russ. text; 56 titles,
pp. 13-15]

*Dzhalilov, M. "MAKSUD, MAKHMUT" LITERATURNAIA
ENTSIKLOPEDIIA. Vol. 6. Moscow: Gosudarstvennoe
Slovarno-Entsiklopedicheskoe Izdatel'stvo "Sovetskaia
Entsiklopediia," 1932, 724-726 pp. [Russ. text;
Tatar titles, p. 726]

*Faizullin, S. "KAMAL, GALIASKAR GALIASKAROVICH,"
LITERATURNAIA ENTSIKLOPEDIIA. Vol. 5. n. p.
Izdatel'stvo Kommunisticheskoi Akademii, 1931, 77-79 pp.
[Russ. text; Tatar titles, p. 79]

*Faseev, F. S. OSNOVY TERMINOLOGII V TATARSKOM IAZYKE.
Kazan: "Tatarstan Kitap Neshriiaty," 1969, 200 pp.,
2000 copies. [Tatar text; ca.130 Tatar, Russ.
titles, pub. 1917-1966, pp. 195-199]

Volga Tatar: Language, Literature

*Faseev, F. S. OSNOVY TERMINOLOGII V TATARSKOM IAZYKE.
Kazan: "Tatarstan Kitap Neshriiaty," 1969, 200 pp.,
2000 copies. [Tatar text; ca.130 Tatar, Russ. titles,
pub. 1917-1966, pp. 195-199]

Fattakhova, D. SOVETSKAIA LITERATURA -- BORETS ZA MIR.
Kazan: Tatar Resp. B-ka im. Lenina, 1952, 8 pp.,
750 copies. [Tatar text; 79 titles]

Gabidullin, R. M.; A. P. Lotsmanova. MUSA DZHALIL'.
1906-1944. Moscow: (Gos. B-ka SSSR im. Lenina;
Resp. B-ka Tatar ASSR im. Lenina), 1956, 30 pp.,
5000 copies. [Russ. text; 18 titles, per. 1906-1944]

Gainullin, M. KAIUM NASYRI. Kazan: Tatgosizdat, 1945,
112 pp. [Tatar text; per. 19th c., titles section
of book]

_____. NASYRI, KAIUM. IZBR. PROIZVEDENIIA.
(BIBLIOGRAFICHESKAIA SPRAVKA). Kazan: (Akad. Nauk
SSSR. Kazan. Filial In-t Iazyka, Lit. i Istorii),
1953. [Tatar text; ca.131 Tatar, Russ. titles,
pub. 1895-1950, pp. 409-415]

_____. KAIUM NASYRI (EGO NAUCHNAIA, LITERATURNAIA
I PROSVETITEL'SKAIA DEIATEL'NOST') K 120-LETIIU SO
DNIA ROZHDENIIA. Kazan: Tatgosizdat, 1945, 84 pp.
[Russ. text, per. 19th c., titles separate section of
book]

*Gali, Gumer. "NADZHMI, KAVI," LITERATURNAIA
ENTSIKLOPEDIIA. Vol. 7. Moscow: Gosudarstvennoe
Slovarno-Entsiklopedicheskoe Izdatel'stvo "Sovetskaia
Entsiklopediia," 1934, pp. 569-571. [Russ. text and
titles, p. 571]

*Ganiev, F. A. VIDOVAIA KHARAKTERISTIKA GLAGOLOV
TATARSKOGO IAZYKA. Kazan: n. p., 1963, 179 pp.
[Russ. text; 81 Tatar, Russ. titles, pp. 175-178]

Gaziz, G. "KRATKAIA BIBLIOGRAFIIA PROIZVEDENII G.
GAZIZA," RASSKAZY. Kazan: Tatknigoizdat, 1958.
[Tatar text; 94 Tatar, other USSR lang., Russ. titles,
p. 94]

*Giniiatullina, A. PISATELI SOVETSKOGO TATARSTANA.
BIBLIOGR. SPRAVOCHNIK. Kazan: Tatknigoizdat, 1957,
486 pp., 5000 copies. [Russ. text; 126 Russ. titles,
pub. 1940-56]

Volga Tatar: Language, Literature

Giniiatulina, A. PISATELI SOVETSKOGO TATARSTANA.
BIOBIBLIOGR. SPRAVOCHNIK. Kazan: Tatknigoizdat,
1970, 511 pp., 9000 copies. [Russ. text]

_____. TATARSKIE SOVETSKIE PISATELI.
BIOBIBLIOGR. MATERIALY. Kazan: Tatknigoizdat, 1958,
740 pp., 5000 copies. [Tatar text; 113 titles]

Gizatullin, N. KAVI NADZHMI. Kazan: Tatknigoizdat,
1956. [Tatar text; 244 Tatar, Russ., other titles,
pub. 1919-56, pp. 77-88]

*_____. KAVI NADZHMI. Kazan: Tatknigoizdat,
1957, 131 pp. [Russ. text; 61 Russ., other titles,
per. 1901-1957, pp. 129-32]

*Iarmi, Khemid. TATARSKOE NARODNOE POETICHESKOE
TVORCHESTVO. Kazan: Tatknigoizdat, 1967, 308 pp.,
5000 copies. [Tatar text; ca.430 Tatar titles,
pub. 1859-1963, pp. 290-307]

*Ibragimov, G. "GALIMJAN 'IBRAHIMOFNING BASILIB
CHIQQAN ADABIY ASARLARI,'" TIREN TAMYRLAR. Kazan:
Tatarstan Davlat Nashriyyati, 1928, 200 pp., 5000
copies. [Tatar text; 21 Tatar titles, p. 200]

*Ibragimov, Sagadat Mugallimovich. ANALITICHESKIE
KONSTRUKTSII. Kazan: Izdatel'stvo Kazanskogo
Universiteta, 1964, 134 pp., 600 copies. [Tatar
text; 60 Tatar, Russ. titles, pp. 130-132]

*"IL'MINSKII, NIKOLAI IVANOVICH," BOL'SHAIA SOVETSKAIA
ENTSIKLOPEDIIA, Vol. 27. Moscow: Gosudarstvennoe
Slovarno-Entsiklopedicheskoe Izdatel'stvo
"Sovetskaia Entsiklopediia" (OGIZ RSFSR), 1933, p. 785.
[Russ. text; Tatar. Kazakh (Kirghiz) titles, p. 785]

*Isanbet, G. "BIBLIOGRAFICHESKII UKAZATEL' PROIZVEDENII
N. ISANBETA -- KARIMULLIN A. DOPOLNENIIA K
BIBLIOGRAFII PROIZVEDENII N. ISANBETA," PISATEL'
I UCHENYI. Kazan: n. p., 1969. [Tatar text; 197
Tatar, Bashkir, Kazakh, Uzbek, Russ. titles, pub.
1914-1968, pp. 95-123]

Karimullin, A. G. BIBLIOGRAFIIA LITERATURY PO
TATARSKOMU IAZYKOZNANIIU. Kazan: (Kazan. Gos. Un-t
im. Ul'ianova-Lenina. Nauch. B-ka im. Lobachevskogo),
1957, 39 pp., 500 copies. [Russ. text; 276 Russ.
titles, pub. end of 18th cent. to 1956]

Volga Tatar: Language, Literature

Karimullin, A. G. BIBLIOGRAFIIA LITERATURY PO TATARSKOMU IAZYKOZNANIIU. Kazan: Tatknigoizdat, 1958, 115 pp., 600 copies. [Tatar text; 973 Tatar titles, pub. end 18th cent.--1958]

*_____. BIBLIOGRAFIIA TATARSKOI KHUDOZHESTVENNOI LITERATURY(1917-1960). Kazan: Izd-vo Kazan Un-ta, 1964, 155 pp., 5000 copies. [Tatar text and titles, pub. 1917-1960]

*_____. comp. "KRATKAIA BIBLIOGRAFIIA PROIZVEDENII M. DZHALILIA I LITERATURY O NEM NA IAZYKAKH NARODOV SSSR I ZARUBEZHNYKH STRAN," DZHALIL, M. SOCHINENIIA. Kazan: Tatarskoe Knizhnoe Izdatel'stvo, 1962, 606 pp., 50,000 copies. [Russ. text; Tatar, Sov. Asian, Russ., Europ. titles, pp. 581-600]

*_____. comp. LITERATURA, FOL'KLOR I ISKUSSTVO NARODOV SSSR I ZARUBEZHNYKH STRAN V PEREVODAKH NA TATAR. IAZYK. BIBLIOGRAFIIA. 1917-1962. Kazan: Izdatel'stvo Kazanskogo Universiteta, 1963, 337 pp., 6000 copies. [Tatar text; 4906 Tatar titles, pub. 1917-1962]

_____. comp. MUSA DZHALIL'. (BIBLIOGRAFIIA. 1919-1961). Kazan: (Kazan. Gos. Univ. im. Ul'ianova-Lenina.), 1961, 77 pp., 700 copies. [Russ. text; ca.987 Tatar, Russ., other titles, pub. 1919-1961]

_____. TATARSKAIA LITERATURA. (FOL'KLOR, LITERATUROVEDENIE I ISTORIIA LIT.) BIBLIOGRAFIIA. 1917-1959. Kazan: Tatknigoizdat, 1961, 216 pp., 600 copies. [Tatar text; 2445 titles, pub. 1917-59]

_____. TATARSKAIA LITERATURA V PEREVODAKH NA RUSSKII IAZ. (BIBLIO. UKAZATEL'. 1917-1960). Kazan: Izd-vo Kazan. Un-ta, 1962, 91 pp., 5000 copies. [Russ. text; 818 titles, pub. 1917-1960]

KATALOG KHUDOZHESTVENNOI LITERATURY. Kazan: Tatgiz, 1950, 12 pp., 2065 copies. [Tatar text; ca.150 Tatar, Russ. titles, pub. 1947-1950]

Kaverin, F. N. SOVETY RUKOVODITELIU DRAMATICHESKOGO KRUZHKA. Kazan: (Tatar. Dom. Nar. Tvorchestva), [ca. 1949]. [Tatar text; 23 Tatar, Russ. titles, pub. 1936-1949, pp. 66-67]

Khabibullina, Z. Sh. GABDULLA TUKAI. BIBLIOGR. SPRAVKA. Kazan: (Resp. B-ka Tatar. ASSR im. Lenina.), 1951, 4 pp., 500 copies. [Tatar text; 37 Tatar titles]

Volga Tatar: Language, Literature

[Khabibullina, Z. Sh.] GUMER BASHIROV, LAUREAT STALINSKOI PREMII. (BIBLIOGR.UKAZATEL'), Kazan: (Tatar. Resp. B-ka im. Lenina), 1952, 12 pp., 750 copies. [Tatar text; 17 Tatar titles]

_____. KAVI NADZHMI, LAUREAT STALINSKOI PREMII (BIBLIOGR. UKAZATEL'), Kazan: (Tatar Resp. B-ka im. Lenina), 1952, 12 pp., 750 copies. [Tatar text; 40 Tatar, Russ., titles]

_____. KLASSIK TATARSKOI LITERATURY SHARIF KAMAL (1884-1942). UKAZATEL' LIT. Kazan: (Tatar. Resp. B-ka im. Lenina), 1952, 12 pp., 1000 copies. [Tatar text; 30 Tatar titles, per. 1884-1942]

_____. LAUREATY STALINSKOI PREMII (SPISOK PROIZVEDENII KHUDOZH. LIT. NA TATAR. IAZ.). Kazan: (Tatar Resp. B-ka im. Lenina), 1952, 18 pp., 500 copies. [Tatar text; 34 Tatar titles]

_____. NARODNYI POET MADZHIT GAFURI (1880-1934). UKAZATEL' LIT. Kazan: (Tatar. Resp. B-ka im. Lenina), 1952, 8 pp., 1037 copies. [Tatar text; 23 titles, per. 1880-1934]

_____. TATARSKII NARODNYI DRAMATURG GALIASKAR KAMAL (1879-1933) UKAZATEL' LIT. Kazan: (Tatar. Resp. B-ka im. Lenina), 1953, 14 pp., 1000 copies. [Tatar text; 26 titles, per. 1879-1933]

_____. TATARSKII NARODNYI POET GABDULLA TUKAI. (1886-1913). UKAZATEL' LIT. Kazan: (Tatar. Resp. B-ka im. Lenina), 1953, 20 pp., 1000 copies. [Tatar text; 70 Tatar, Russ. titles]

_____. TATARSKII SOVETSKII PISATEL' ADEL' KUTUI. UKAZATEL' LIT. Kazan: (Tatar. Resp. B-ka im. Lenina), 1953, 10 pp., 1000 copies. [Tatar text; 17 Tatar titles, per. 1903-1945]

_____. VYDAIUSHCHIISIA TATARSKII SOVETSKII POET FATIKH KARIM (1909-1945). Kazan: Tatknigoizdat, 1955, 15 pp., 1000 copies. [Tatar text; 41 titles, per. 1909-1945]

*Khakov, V. Kh. VVEDENIE V STILISTIKU TATARSKOGO IAZYKA. Kazan: Izdatel'stvo Kazanskogo Universiteta, 1963, 168 pp., 600 copies. [Tatar text; Tatar, Russ., Europ. titles, pp. 166-167]

Volga Tatar: Language, Literature

Khanbikova, Sh. SINONIMY TATARSKOGO IAZYKA. Kazan:
(Kazan. Filial Akad. Nauk SSSR. Institut Iazyka, Lit.
j Istorii.), 1961. [Tatar text; 66 Tatar, Russ.
titles, pp. 66-68]

Khangil'din, V. N. GRAMMATIKA TATARSKOGO IAZYKA. Kazan:
(Akad. Nauk SSSR. Kazan Filial In-t Iazyka, Lit. i
Istorii), 1959. [Tatar text; ca.100 Tatar, Russ.
titles, pp. 636-638]

Khasanov, M. "BIBLIOGRAFIIA PROIZVEDENII G.
IBRAGIMOVA," GALIMDZHAN IBRAGIMOV. Kazan: n. p.,
1964. [Tatar text; 772 Tatar, Russ. titles; pub.
1907-1963, pp. 302-331]

Khatipov, F. "BIBLIOGRAFIIA LITERATURNO-KRITICHESKIKH
PROIZVEDENII O TVORCHESTVE M. AMIRA," MIRSAI AMIR.
Kazan: n. p., 1964. [Tatar text; 43 titles, pp. 177-
179]

*Khismatullin, A. GALIASKAR KAMAL. Kazan: Tatarstan
Kitap Neshriaty, 1969, 116 pp., 2500 copies. [Tatar
text; ca.50 Tatar titles, pub. up to 1961, pp. 109-114]

*Klimentovskii, V. A. RUSSKIE PISATELI V TATARSKOI ASSR.
Kazan: Tatknigoizdat, 1960, 190 pp. [Russ. text;
90 Russ. titles, Sov. per., pp. 187-191]

KRATKAIA BIBLIOGRAFIIA PROIZVEDENII SH. KAMALA," Sh.
Kamal, Izbr. PROIZVEDENIIA. Kazan: Tatknigoizdat,
1954. [Tatar text; 45 titles, per. 1906-1951,
pp. 595-597]

Kulakhmetov, G. BIBLIOGRAFIIA PROIZVEDENII GAFURA
KULAKHMETOVA," IZBR. PROIZVEDENIIA. Kazan: Tatgosizdat,
1952, 2nd ed. [Tatar text; 26 titles, pub. 1904-1947,
pp. 118-119]

Lopushanskaia, S. A. OCHERKI PO ISTORII GLAGOL'NOGO
FORMOOBRAZOVANIIA V RUSSKOM IAZYKE. Kazan:
Tatknigoizdat, 1967, 175 pp., 1000 copies. [Russ.
text; 127 titles, pp. 167-174]

[Lotsmanova, A. P.] KHUDOZHESTVENNAIA LITERATURA K
30-LETIIU TATARSKOI SSR (REK. SPISOK LIT.). Kazan:
(Resp. B-ka TatASSR im. Lenina), 1950, 8 pp., 500
copies. [Russ. text; 43 Tatar, Russ. titles]

Volga Tatar: Language, Literature

Lotsmanova, A. P.; Z. Sh. Khabibullina. POET - PATRIOT MUSA DZHALIL. UKAZATEL' LIT. Kazan: Tatknigoizdat, 1956, 54 pp., 2000 copies. [Tatar text; 161 Tatar, Russ. titles, pub. 1935 - Sept. 1, 1955]

MUSA DZHALIL'. K 60-LETIIU SO DNIA ROZHDENIIA POETA-GEROIA. Kazan: Gaz.-Zhurn. Izd., 1966, 42 pp., 5000 copies. [Russ. text; titles pp. 39-42]

Nadzhmi, K. SOCHINENIIA. Vol. 4. Kazan: Tatknigoizdat, 1960. [Tatar text; 460 Tatar, Russ., other titles, pp. 348-362]

*Nasretdinov, Gamir. IZBRANNYE PROIZVEDENIIA. Kazan: Tatarstan Kitap Nashriyati, 1966, 284 pp., 9000 copies. [Tatar text and titles, pp. 280-282]

Nasyri, Kaium. IZBR. PROIZVEDENIIA. Kazan: (Akad. Nauk SSSR. Kazan: Filial In-t Iazyka, Lit., i Istorii), 1956, 2nd ed. [Tatar text; 130 Tatar, Russ. titles, pub. 1895-1950, pp. 409-15]

Nigmati, G. IZBRANNYE PROIZVEDENIIA. Kazan: Tatknigoizdat, 1958. [Tatar text; 75 titles, pub. 1922-36, pp. 272-277]

*Nigmati, G. "RAMIEV, SAGIT LUTFULLOVICH," LITERATURNAIA ENTSIKLOPEDIIA. Vol. 9. Moscow: Gosudarstvennyi Institut "Sovetskaia Entsiklopediia," (OGIZ RSFSR), 1935, 516-517 pp. [Russ. text; Tatar, Russ. titles, p. 517]

*Nigmatullin, A. "BIBLIOGRAFIIA IZBRANNYKH PROIZVEDENII SH. KAMALA," SHARIF KAMAL. Kazan: n. p., 1964. [Tatar text; 109 Tatar, Russ. titles, pub. 1905-1957, pp. 167-172]

*Nigmatullin, Akhat. SHARIF KAMAL. Kazan: Tatarstan Kitap Nashriyati, 1964, 172 pp., 3000 copies. [Tatar text and titles, pp. 167-172]

Popov, V. I.; N. S. Travushkin. ASTRAKHAN'--KRAI LITERATURNYI. BIBLIOGRAFICHESKII UKAZATEL' S PRIL. "LIT. KARTY ASTRAKH. OBL." Astrakhan: ["Volga"], 1968, 66 pp., 5000 copies. [Russ. text]

"PROIZVEDENIIA AKHMETA FAIZI. (KRATKAIA BIBLIOGR.)" A. S. Faizi, VOSKHODIT SOLNTSE. Kazan: Tatknigoizdat, 1954. [Tatar text; 38 Tatar, Russ. titles, pub. 1929-1953, pp. 522-523]

Volga Tatar: Language, Literature

Rakhmankulov, Sh. O ROMANE "CHEST'" GUMERA BASHIROVA.
Kazan: (M-vo Kul'tury Tatar ASSR), 1954, 31 pp.
[Tatar text; 12 Tatar, Russ. titles, pub. 1941-1952]

*Sabirov, K. S. ZNAKI PREPINANIIA V TATARSKOM IAZYKE.
Kazan: Tatknigoizdat (Akad. Nauk SSSR. Kazan. Filial.
In-t Istorii, Iazyka i Lit.), 1956, 184 pp., 3000
copies. [Tatar text; 49 Tatar, Russ. titles, pp. 182-
183]

Safina, G. B. KHADI TAKTASH. 1901-1931. (UKAZATEL'
LIT.). Kazan: (Tatar. Resp. B-ka im. Lenina), 1957,
22 pp., 1000 copies. [Tatar text; 87 Tatar, Russ.
titles, per. 1901-1931]

Safuanov, Sufiian. IBRAGIM GAZI. KNIGA O PISATELE.
Kazan: Tatknigoizdat, 1968, 168 pp., 2500 copies.
[Russ. text; 41 Tatar titles, pp. 165-168]

Safuanov, S. IBRAGIM GAZI. KNIGA O PISATELE. Kazan,
1968. [Tatar text; 41 titles, pp. 165-168]

Saiganov, A. D. ROMAN SHARIFA KAMALA "KOGDA
ROZHDAETSIA PREKRASNOE." Kazan: Tatknigoizdat, 1966,
56 pp., 4000 copies. [Russ. text; 20 Tatar titles,
p. 56]

Shamukov, G. NAKI ISANBET. Kazan: Tatknigoizdat, 1959.
[Tatar text; ca.360 Tatar, Russ., other titles,
pp. 53-76]

Shirokova, N. A. IZ ISTORII SOIUZNYKH KONSTRUKTSII,
VYRAZHAIUSHCHIKH OTNOSHENIIA SRAVNENIIA. Kazan:
Izd. Kazan Un-ta, 1966, 185 pp., 1000 copies. [Russ.
text; titles pp. 177-184]

*SOVREMENNYI TATARSKII LITERATURNYI IAZYK. LEKSIKOLOGIIA,
FONETIKA, MORFOLOGIIA. Moscow: "Nauka," 1969, 383 pp.,
3200 copies. [Russ. text; ca.160 Tatar, Bashkir,
Russ.,German titles, pub. to 1966, pp. 371-377]

*Tagirov, R.; G. Mukhamedova. comp. "BIBLIOGRAFIIA
PROIZVEDENII GALIMDZHANA IBRAGIMOVA," VESTNIK
NAUCHNOGO OBSHCHESTVA TATAROVEDENIIA. No. 8
[published annually or slightly oftener] (Kazan):
Izdanie Doma Tatarskoi Kul'tury, 1928, 278 pp.,
600 copies. [Russ. text; 5 lists Tatar, Russ. titles,
pp. 49-54]

Volga Tatar: Language, Literature

Tahirov, R. Sh. "DOKTORLYK HAM KANDIKATLYK
DISSERTATSIIALARENENG BIBLIOGRAFIK KURSATKECHE,"
TATARSTAN KOMMUNISTY, No. 9, 1958. [Tatar text;
per. 1939-1957, pp. 90-93]

Tahirov, R. "TATAR TELENDA BASILGAN MATUR ADABIYAT,
ANING TARIKHII HAM TANKIYT' BIBLIOGRAFIYASE," UN EL
ECHENDE TATAR MATUR ADABIYATI. Kazan: Tatgosizdat,
1930, 472 pp. [Tatar text; 476 Tatar titles, pub.
1920-1930, pp. 443-470]

Tahirov, Rifagat'. TATARSTAN TURINDAGI ADABIYAT
BIBLIOGRAFIYASE. 1-2 KISAKLAR. Kazan: "Magarif,"
1928, 23 pp. [Tatar text and titles]

*"TAKHTASH, KHADI," LITERATURNAIA ENTSIKLOPEDIIA. Vol. 11.
Moscow: Gosudarstvennoe Izdatel'stvo "Khudozhestvennaia
Literatura," 1939, 176-177 pp. [Russ. text; Tatar,
Russ. titles, p. 177]

*"TATARSKIE IAZYKI," BOL'SHAIA SOVETSKAIA ENTSIKLOPEDIIA.
Vol. 53. Moscow: Gosudarstvennyi Nauchnyi Institut
"Sovetskaia Entsiklopediia," (OGIZ RSFSR), 1946,
656-657 pp. [Russ. text; Tatar, Russ., Europ. titles,
p. 657]

*"TATARSKIE IAZYKI," LITERATURNAIA ENTSIKLOPEDIIA. Vol.
11. Moscow: Gosudarstvennoe Izdatel'stvo
"Khudozhestvennaia Literatura," 1939, p. 201. [Russ.
text; Russ., Europ. titles, p. 201]

*"TATARSKII IAZ. POVOLZH'IA," LITERATURNAIA ENTSIKLOPEDIIA.
Vol. 11. Moscow: Gosudarstvennoe Izdatel'stvo
"Khudozhestvennaia Literatura," 1939, 201-203 pp.
[Russ. text; Tatar, Russ. Europ. titles, pp. 202-203]

*"TATARSKII IAZYK ZAPADNOI SIBIRI," LITERATURNAIA
ENTSIKLOPEDIIA. Vol. 11. Moscow: Gosudarstvennoe
Izdatel'stvo "Khudozhestvennaia Literatura," 1939, 203-
204 pp. [Russ. text; Tatar, Russ., Europ. titles,
p. 204]

*TATARSKO-RUSSKII SLOVAR'. Moscow: Izdatel'stvo
"Sovetskaia Entsiklopediia," 1966, 863 pp., 21000
copies. [Tatar, Russ. text; 33 Tatar, Russ. titles,
pp. 7-8]

*"TUKAI, ABDULLA," LITERATURNAIA ENTSIKLOPEDIIA. Vol. 11.
Moscow: Gosudarstvennoe Izdatel'stvo "Khudozhestvennaia
Literatura," 1939, 410-412 pp. [Russ. text; Tatar,
Russ. titles, p. 412]

Volga Tatar: Language, Literature

Tukai, G. PROIZVEDENIIA. Vol. 4. Kazan: (AN SSSR Filial. In-t Iazyka, Lit. i Istorii), 1956. [Tatar text; 476 Tatar, Russ., other titles, pp. 257-276, pub. 1907-1956]

Usmanov, Kh. TATARSKAIA POEZIIA 20-KH GODOV. Kazan, 1964. [Tatar text; ca.670 titles, per. 1920's, pp. 376-396]

Usmanova, Z. ADEL' KUTUI. ZHIZN' I TVORCHESTVO. Kazan: Tatknigoizdat, 1966, 96 pp., 3000 copies. [Russ. text; titles at end of book]

*Valiullina, Z. M. SOPOSTAVITEL'NAIA GRAMMATIKA RUSSKOGO I TATARSKOGO IAZYKOV. KAZANSKII GOSUDARSTVENNYI PEDAGOGICHESKII INSTITUT. UCHENYE ZAPISKI, No. 52. Kazan: (Ministerstvo Prosveshcheniia RSFSR) "Tatpoligraf," 1968, 126 pp., 1000 copies. [Russ. text; 32 Tatar, Russ. titles, pub. 1927-1965, pp. 123-124]

*VOPROSY TATARSKOGO IAZYKOZNANIIA, KN. 2. Kazan: Izdatel'stvo Kazanskogo Universiteta, 1965, 456 pp., 2000 copies. [Russ. text; titles at end of articles]

VOPROSY TATARSKOGO IAZYKOZNANIIA. KNIGA 3-IA. [Kazan] 1969, 210 pp. [Tatar text; titles at end of articles]

*Zakiev, M. Z. SINTAKSICHESKII STROI TATARSKOGO IAZYKA. Kazan: Izdatel'stvo Kazanskogo Universiteta, 1963, 464 pp., 1500 copies. [Russ. text; 284 Tatar, Bashkir, Russ., Europ. titles, pp. 445-456]

Zaliai, L.; N. Burganova, L. Makhmutova, comp. TATARSKAIA FRAZEOLOGIIA, POSLOVITSY I POGOVORKI. Kazan: Tatknigoizdat, 1957. [Tatar text; ca.50 Tatar, Russ. titles, pp. 241-242]

Zalialieva, M. OBRAZ CHELOVEKA V DREVNETATARSKOI LITERATURE. Kazan: Tatknigoizdat, 1968, 91 pp., 3000 copies. [Russ. text; Tatar titles, pp. 90-91]

*Zinnatullina, K. Z. ZALOGI GLAGOLA V SOVREMENNOM TATARSKOM LITERATURNOM IAZYKE. Kazan, 1969. [Russ. text; 177 titles, pp. 221-229]

Volga Tatar

PHILOSOPHY, RELIGION

Berman, S. I. OBSHCHESTVENNYI PROGRESS. Kazan: Gaz.-Zhurn. Izd., 1966, 60 pp., 600 copies. [Russ. text; titles at end of book]

Faseev, K. F. NATSIONAL'NYE OTNOSHENIIA I ISLAM. Kazan: Tatknigoizdat, 1968, 88 pp., 4000 copies. [Russ. text; Tatar titles, pp. 86-87]

*Gil'fanov, I.; R. Baltanov. REAKTSIONNAIA SUSHCHNOST' KORANA. Kazan: Tatarstan Kitap Nashriyati, 1962, 36 pp., 6000 copies. [Tatar text; 15 Tatar, Russ. titles, p. 36]

*"IZDANIIA PEREVODCHESKOI KOMISSII PRAVOSLAVNAGO MISSIONERSKAGO OBSHCHESTVA ZA 1881-1912 GODY," INORODCHESKOE OBOZRENIE. PRILOZHENIE K ZHURNALU PRAVOSLAVNYI SOBESIEDNIK ZA DEKABR' 1912 GODA. KNIGA 1-AIA. Kazan, 1912. [Russ. text; 63 Kreshchen-Tatar titles, pub. 1881-1912, pp. 155-159]

Kalaganov, A.; I. Svetlov; Sh. Saifutdinov. NA PUTI K ATEIZMU. Kazan: Tatknigoizdat, 1967, 162 pp., 2500 copies. [Russ. text; titles pp. 159-161]

Khabibullina, Z. Sh. V POMOSHCH' PROPAGANDE NAUCHNO-ATEISTICHESKOI LITERATURY. (UKAZATEL' LIT.) Kazan: Tatknigoizdat, 1955, 11 pp., 1000 copies. [Tatar text; 75 titles, Sov. per.]

Sokolov, P. LITERATURA DLIA LEKTOROV--ATEISTOV. Kazan: TASSR, 1952. [Russ. text; 15 titles, pub. 1951, pp. 7-8]

TELYAKLYAR. CHASOSLOV NA TATARSKOM IAZYKIE. n. p. Pravoslavnoe Missionerskoe Obshchestvo, Tipografiia M. A. Chirkovoi, 1893. [Tatar text; Tatar titles, pp. I-II]

Volga Tatar

POLITICAL SCIENCE, LAW

Bulatov, A. comp. VLADIMIR IL'ICH LENIN. PROIZVEDENIIA V. I. LENINA V PEREVODE NA TATARSKOM IAZYKE I LITERATURE O NEM. 1917-1966. Kazan: Tatknigoizdat, 1966, 52 pp., 2000 copies. [Tatar text; Tatar, Russ. titles, pub. 1917-1966]

*Enaleev, Sh. M. OSUSHCHESTVLENIE LENINSKOI NATSIONAL'NOI POLITIKI V TATARII. (1929-1937 GG.) Kazan: Izd-vo Kazan. Un-ta, 1960, 106 pp. [Russ. text; ca.140 Tatar, Russ. titles, per. 1929-1937, pp. 101-106]

[Khabibullina, Z. Sh.] ZHIZN' ZAMECHATEL'NYKH LIUDEI V KAZANI. Kazan: (Resp. B-ka TatASSR im. Lenina), 1950, 16 pp., [Tatar text; 100 Tatar titles]

Khasanov, Kh. KHUSAIN IAMASHEV [BOL'SHEVIK. 1882-1912] Kazan: Tatknigoizdat, 1954. [Russ. text; ca.140 Tatar, Russ., titles, pp. 166-171]

_____. REVOLIUTSIONER--BOL'SHEVIK KHUSAIN IAMASHEV. Kazan: Tatknigoizdat, 1959. [Tatar text; ca.110 Tatar, Russ. titles, pp. 208-213]

Kibardin, M. S. BOL'SHEVIKI KAZANSKOI GUBERNII VO GLAVE AGRARNYKH PREOBRAZOVANII 1917-1919 GODOV. Kazan, 1963. [Russ. text; ca.340 titles, per. 1917-1919, pp. 215-226]

*Korbut, M. "OB IZUCHENII ISTORII OKTIABR'SKOI REVOLIUTSII V TATARSTANE (OBZOR LITERATURY, VYSHEDSHII NA RUSSKOM IAZYKE)." KATORGA I SSYLKA. No. 4-5, 1933. [Russ. text and titles, pp. 126-144]

[Kryshina, V. S.; G. B. Safina] VLADIMIR IL'ICH LENIN V KAZANI. REK. UKAZATEL' LIT. Kazan: (Resp. B-ka Tatar. ASSR im. Lenina), 1958, 26 pp., 1500 copies. [Russ. text; 40 Tatar, Russ. titles]

Nafigov, R. MULLANUR VAKHITOV. Kazan: Tatknigoizdat, 1960. [Russ. text; ca.250 Tatar, Russ. titles, per. early 20th cent., pp. 3-23, 142-154]

Volga Tatar: Political Science, Law

Nafigov, R. I. KAZANSKAIA SOTSIAL-DEMOKRATICHESKAIA
 ORGANIZATSIIA V 1907-1914 GODAKH. Kazan, 1961.
 [Russ. text; ca.100 titles, per. 1907-1914, pp. 95-97]

Seleznev, N. A. POLVEKA BEZUPRECHNOI SLUZHBY RODINE.
 Kazan: (Tatar. Resp. Organizatsiia O-va "Znanie"
 RSFSR), 1967, 48 pp., 342 copies. [Russ. text;
 titles, p. 48]

Tahirov, R. MULLANUR VAKHITOV (MAKALALAR HAM KITAPLAR
 BIBLIOGRAFIYASE)," BEZNENG YUL. No. 7/8, 1926.
 [Tatar text; Tatar titles, pp. 42-44]

PART IV
CENTRAL ASIA

23 CENTRAL ASIA

GENERAL

*I. Ia. "KIRGIZY I KIRGIZ-KAISAKI," ENTSIKLOPEDICHESKII SLOVAR' Vol. 15. St. Petersburg: F. A. Brokgauz, I. A. Efron, 1895, 103-108 pp. [Russ. text; Russ. Europ. titles, pp. 107-108]

Aleksandrova, V. S. "MATERIALY DLIA UKAZATELIA SREDNEAZIATSKIKH PERIODICHESKIKH IZDANII NA RUSSKOM IAZYKE ZA 1917-1934 GG.," TRUDY GOSUDARSTVENNOI PUBLICHNOI BIBLIOTEKI UzSSR, Vol. 1--IUBILEINYI, 1870-1935. [Tashkent], 1935. [Russ. text; 423 Russ. titles, pub.: 1917-1934, pp. 157-241]

*Amitin-Shapiro, Z. L.; O. D. Morozov. "'TURKESTANSKIE VEDOMOSTI' KAK ISTOCHNIK PO ISTORII KIRGIZII," TRUDY INSTITUTA ISTORII. No. 1. Frunze: Izdatel'stvo Akademii Nauk Kirgizskoi SSR (Akademia Nauk Kirgizskoi SSR, Institut Istorii), 1955, 153 pp. 500 copies. [Russ. text and Survey; pp. 113-123]

Avsharova, M. P.; M. S. Viridarskii. EVGENII KARLOVICH BETGER (1887-1956). OCHERK ZHIZNI I DEIATEL'NOSTI. Tashkent: Uzgosizdat, 1960. [Russ. text; titles, pp. 27-43]

* _____. RUSSKAIA PERIODICHESKAIA PECHAT' V TURKESTANE (1870-1917). BIBLIOGRAFICHESKII UKAZATEL' LITERATURY. Tashkent: Gosizdat UzSSR, 1960, 200 pp., 750 copies. [Russ. text; ca.200 Russ. titles, pub.: 1870-1917]

Bartol'd, V. V. ed. SREDNIAIA AZIA V UCHREZHDENIIAKH AK. NAUK. 1917-1927. Leningrad: Izd.-vo Ak. Nauk, 1927, 34 pp., 1000 copies. [Russ. text and titles, per.: 1917-1927]

* _____. "TURKESTAN," ENTSIKLOPEDICHESKII SLOVAR' Vol. 67(34). St. Petersburg: Izd.-vo F. A. Brokgauza i I. A. Efrona, 1902, 174-204 pp. [Russ. text; 70 Russ., Europ. titles, pp. 201-263, pub.: 1880-1901]

Central Asia: General

Berg, L. RUSSKAIA BIBLIOGR. PO TURKESTANU "Priroda,"
1925 No. 7-9. Kazan: Izd-vo AN SSSR, 1925. [Russ.
text and titles; publ.: pp. 253-254]

"BIBLIOGRAFICHESKII PERECHEN' LITERATURY PO SREDNEI
AZII. (V EE GEOGRAFICHESKIKH GRANITSAKH),"
NARODNOE KHOZIAISTVO SREDNEI AZII, No. 12. Tashkent,
1929. [Russ. text; 622 Russ., Europ. titles, pub.:
mainly 1900-1928, pp. 125-174]

BIBLIOGRAFIIA...BIBLIOGRAFICHESKII UKAZATEL' ZHURNAL'NYKH
I GAZETNYKH STATEI O SREDNEI AZII... TURKESTANSKIE
VIEDOMOSTI. No. 38. Tashkent, 1871, 5 pp. (separately).
[Russ. text; 36 titles]

*Bisnek, A. G.; K. I. Shafranovskii. "BIBLIOGRAFIIA
BIBLIOGRAFII SREDNEI AZII," BIBLIOGRAFIIA VOSTOKA,
No. 8-9. Moscow-Leningrad: (Izd. AN SSSR), 1935,
(sep. ed. 1936). [Russ. text; 284 Russ., Europ.
titles, pp. 152-194, pub. 1852-1935]

*"BUKHARA," EVREISKAIA ENTSIKLOPEDIIA. Vol. 5. St.
Petersburg: Izdanie Obshchestva Dlia Nauchnykh
Evreiskikh Izdanii i Izdatel'stva Brokgauz-Efron n. d.,
119-123 pp. [Russ. text; Russ., Europ. titles,
p. 123]

*Burov, N. A. "DOREVOLIUTSIONNAIA PECHAT' TURKESTANA."
No. 1, 1868-1879 GG. NAUCHNYE TRUDY (TASHKENTSKII
GOSUDARSTVENNYI UN-T), No. 261. BIBLIOGRAFIIA,
No. 10. 1964, 62-87 pp. [Russ. text; 231 Uzbek,
Russ. titles, pub.: 1868-1879 in Turkistan, pp. 65-87]

Burov, N. A.; A. A. Garritskii. KRATKII
BIBLIOGRAFICHESKII UKAZATEL' PO TURKESTANU.
Tashkent: Izdanie Turkestanskogo Ekonomicheskogo
Soveta. Tsentral'noe Statisticheskoe Upravlenie
Turkestanskoi Respubliki. Prilozhenie k
Statisticheskomu Ezhegodniku, 1924, 112 pp. [Russ.
text; 3,626 Russ., Europ. titles, per.: 1917-1923]

[Burov, N. A. comp.] UKAZATEL' IZDANII SREDNE-AZIATSKOGO
GOSUDARSTVENNOGO UNIVERSITETA. No. 1, 1922-1929;
No. 2, 1930-1933. Tashkent: Izdatel'stvo
Sredneaziatskogo Gosudarstvennogo Universiteta, 1930,
1934, No. 1, 34 pp.; No. 2, 8 pp.. No. 1, 2500 copies.
[Russ., Eng. text; (No. 1) 112 titles,(No.2) 36
titles, pub.: 1922-1933]

Central Asia: General

*Dmitrovskii, N. V. "BIBLIOGRAFICHESKII UKAZATEL' SOCHINENII O SREDNEI AZII, NAPECHATANNYKH V ROSSII, NA RUSSKOM IAZYKIE, S 1692 PO 1870 GOD." MATERIALY DLIA STATISTIKI TURKESTANSKOGO KRAIA. No. 3. [REPR. FROM TURKESTANSKIE VIEDOMOSTI Nos. 7, 16: 1874] St. Petersburg: Izdanie Turkestanskago Statisticheskago Komiteta, 1874, 452 pp. [Russ. text; 796 Russ. titles, pp. 181-250, pub.: 1692-1870]

*G. Gr. Gr. "DUNGANSKOE VOZSTANIE," ENTSIKLOPEDICHESKII SLOVAR', Vol. 11. St. Petersburg: F. A. Brokgauz, I. A. Efron, 1893, 238-239 pp. [Russ. text and titles, p. 239]

KATALOG RESPUBLIKANSKIKH I RAIONNYKH GAZET I ZHURNALOV, VYKHODIASHCHIKH V TURKMENSKOI SSR I OSNOVNYKH IZDANII SR.-AZ. RESPUBLIK. [Ashkhabad], 1931, 14 pp. [Russ. text]

*Kozlova, M. A. comp. "ALFAVITNYI PERECHEN' AVTOROV, POMESHCHENNYKH V 'NOVOM VOSTOKE' (S No. 1 PO No. 15)" NOVYI VOSTOK, 16/17, 1927. [Russ. text and titles, pub.: 1922-1926, pp. 406-420]

* _____. "ALFAVITNYI PERECHEN' STATEI, POMESHCHENNYKH V ZHURNALE 'NOVYI VOSTOK' V NO. NO. 16/17, 18, 19, 20/21, 22, 23/24, 25, 26/27, 28," NOVYI VOSTOK, No. 29, 1930. [Russ. text and titles, pub.: 1927-1930, pp. 268-279]

"KUL'TURNOE STROITEL'STVO V SREDNEI AZII. ANNOT. BIBLIOGRAFIIA," PROSVESHCHENIE NATSIONAL'NOSTEI. No. 6., 1934. [Russ. text; ca.200 Russ. titles, pub.: 1929-1934, pp. 132-149]

*"KUL'TURNOE STROITEL'STVO V SREDNEI AZII. ANNOTIROVANNAIA BIBLIOGRAFIIA." PROSVESHCHENIE NATSIONAL'NOSTEI. No. 6. Nov.-Dec. 1934, 132-149 pp. [Russ. text; 381 Russ., Cent. Asian Lang. titles, pub.: 1929-1934]

*L. Sh. "TURKMENY," ENTSIKLOPEDICHESKII SLOVAR'. Vol. 34. St. Petersburg: F. A. Brokgauz, I. A. Efron, 1902, 206-208 pp. [Russ. text; Russ., Europ. titles, p. 208]

Lidskii, S. "MATERIALY DLIA BIBLIOGRAFII SREDNEI AZII I SOSEDNIKH STRAN," RUSSKII TURKESTAN. SBORNIK. Vol. 1. Tashkent, 1899. [Russ. text; 125 titles, pp. 1-6]

Central Asia: General

LITERATURA O SOVETSKIKH SOTSIALISTICHESKIKH RESPUBLIKAKH: UZBEKISTAN, TURKMENISTAN, TADZHIKISTAN. No. 4. Moscow, 1935. [Russ. text; Sov. per.]

*Livotova, O. E. "BIBLIOGRAFIIA IZDANII AZIATSKOGO MUZEIA I INSTITUTA VOSTOKOVEDENIIA AKADEMII NAUK SSSR (1917-1958)," OCHERKI PO ISTORII RUSSKOGO VOSTOKOVEDENIIA. SB. 3. Moscow: (Akad. Nauk SSSR. In-t Narodov Azii), 1960, 196-311 pp., 1300 copies. [Russ. text; ca.380 Russ., Sanskrit, Tibetan, Europ. titles, pub.: 1917-1958, pp. 198-297]

Lunin, B. V. NAUCHNYE OBSHCHESTVA TURKESTANA I IKH PROGRESSIVNAIA DEIATEL'NOST'. KONETS XIX--NACHALO XX V. Tashkent: Izd.-vo Akad. Nauk Uz. SSR, 1962, 344 pp. [Russ. text; 1092 Russ. titles, per.: end 19th - beg. 20th cent., pp. 279-342]

*Masal'skii. V. "BUKHARA" ILI "BOKHARA" ENTSIKLOPEDICHESKII SLOVAR'. Vol. 5. St. Petersburg: F. A. Brokgauz, I. A. Efron, 1891, 97-108 pp. [Russ. text; Russ., Europ. titles, pp. 107-108]

*Masal'skii, V. I. "UKAZATEL' GLAVNEISHIKH ISTOCHNIKOV I POSOBII PO TURKESTANSKOMU KRAIU," V. P. SEMENOVA-TIAN-SHANSKOGO. ED. ROSSIIA. POLNOE GEOGRAFICHESKOE OPISANIE NASHEGO OTECHESTVA. "TURKESTANSKII KRAI," Vol. 19. St. Petersburg, 1913. [Russ. text; 840 titles, pub.: 19th and early 20th cent., pp. 781-803, 856]

* ———————. comp. ROSSIIA. POLNOE GEOGRAFICHESKOE OPISANIE NASHEGO OTECHESTVA. TURKESTANSKII KRAI. Vol. 19. St. Petersburg: Izdanie A. F. Devriena, 1913, 861 pp. [Russ. text and titles, pp. 781-803]

[Maslova, O. V.] SISTEMATICHESKII UKAZATEL' K IZDANIIAM SREDNEAZIATSKOGO GOSUDARSTVENNOGO UNIVERSITETA S 1922-1950 GG. Tashkent: (Sredneaziat. Gos. Un-t. Materialy k Bibliografii, No. 2), 1952, 119 pp., 1200 copies. [Russ. text; 1500 titles, pub: 1922-1950]

Maslova, O. V.; V. A. Viatkina; A. I. Kormilitsyn. SISTEMATICHESKII UKAZATEL' K IZDANIIAM SREDNEAZIATSKOGO GOSUDARSTVENNOGO UNIVERSITETA IM. V. I. LENINA (1922-1956). Tashkent: (M-vo Vyssh. Obrazovaniia SSSR. Sredneaz. Gos. Un-t im. V. I. Lenina. Materialy k Bibliografii. No. 8), 1958. [Russ. text; 2026 Uzbek, Russ. titles, pub.: 1922-1950]

Central Asia: General

*Mezhov, V. I. RUSSKAIA ISTORICHESKAIA BIBLIOGRAFIIA
ZA 1865-1876 VKLIUCHITEL'NO. Vols. 1-8.
Vol. 1, No. 1-10036 "ISTORIIA OBLASTEI I GUBERNII.
ISTORIIA INORODTSEV." Vol. 3, No. 26250-36810
"PRAVOSLAVII, TSIVILIZATSII, PROSVESHCHENII. PO
ISTORII TURKESTANSKOI EPARKHII." Vol. 5, No. 44706-
51692. "ISTORIIA POLITIKI. PO ISTORII SNOSHENII
ROSSII S SREDENEI AZIEI. Vol. 6, No. 54693-66021
"VSEOBSHCHAIA ISTORIIA. PO ISTORII SREDNEI AZII."
St. Petersburg, 1882-1890. [Russ. text; 314 titles,
pub. 1865-1876, (Vol. 1) p. 436; (Vol. 3), pp. 143,295;
(Vol. 5), pp. 33-40; 136-146, 299; (Vol. 6) pp. 271-
273]

Mezhov, Vladimir Izmailovich. TURKESTANSKII SBORNIK
SOCHINENII I STATEI, OTNOSIASHCHIKHSIA DO SREDNEI
AZII VOOBSHCHE I TURKESTANSKOGO KRAIA V OSOBENNOSTI,
SOSTAVLIAEMYI PO PORUCHENIIU G. TURKESTANSKAGO
VOENNAGO GENERAL GUBERNATORA K. P. FON KAUFMANA
V. I. MEZHOVYM. SISTEMATICHESKII I AZBUCHNYI
UKAZATEL' SOCHINENII I STATEI NA RUSSKOM I
INOSTRANNYKH IAZYKAKH K "TURKESTANSKOMU SBORNIKU."
Vols. 1-3. [T. 1. k tomam 1-150, 192 pp. (1878); Vol.
2. K Tomam 151-300, 175 pp. (1884); Vol. 3,
k tomam 300-416, 140 pp., (1888)] St. Petersburg:
Tip. V. Bezobrazova i Komp., 1878-1888. [Russ. text;
4714 titles, pub.: 19th cent.]

*Mysovskii, I. V. PO SREDNEI AZII. OT TASHKENTA DO
KRASNOVODSKA. PUTEVODITEL'. Moscow-Leningrad:
Fizkul'tura i Turizm, 1933, 128 pp., 10,000 copies.
[Russ. text and titles, pp. 124-126]

"NOVEISHIE SOCHINENIIA O TURKESTANE," PUTEVODITEL' PO
TURKESTANU I SREDNE-AZIATSKOI ZHELEZNOI DOROGE. St.
Petersburg, 1901. [Russ. text; 77 Russ. titles,
pp. 136-138]

Pankov, A. V. "BIBLIOGRAFICHESKII UKAZATEL' KNIG I
STATEI PO TURKESTANOVEDENIIU. S I-GO OKTIABRIA 1912
G. PO I IANVERIA 1914 G.," IZV. TURK. OTD. RUSSK.
GEOGR. O-VA. Vol. 10, No. 1 Tashkent, 1914. [Russ.
text; 262 Russ., Europ. titles, pub.: 1912-1914,
pp. 257-279]

Pankov, A. V.; E. K. Betger. "BIBLIOGRAFICHESKII
UKAZATEL' SOCHINENII PO TURKESTANOVEDENIIU ZA
1914-1915 GODY," IZVESTIIA TURKESTANSKAGO OTDIELA
RUSSKAGO GEOGRAFICHESKAGO OBSHCHESTVA. Vol 12, No. 2,
Vol. 13, No. 1, 1916-1917. [Russ. text; 360 titles,
pub.: 1914-1915. (1916) pp. 311-339; (1917) pp. 28-34]

Central Asia: General

_____. "BIBLIOGRAFICHESKII PERECHEN' STATEI I KNIG PO TURKESTANOVEDENIIU S 1-GO IANVARIA 1914 GODA DO 1-GO IANVARIA 1915 G." IZV. TURK. OTD. RUS. GEOGR. O-VA. Vol. 11, No. 1., 1915. [Russ. text; 212 titles, pub.: 1914-1915, pp. 92-111]

Penkina, Z. M. ZAKASPIISKII KRAI. 1865-1885. SISTEMATICHESKII SBORNIK BIBLIOGRAFICHESKIKH UKAZANII KNIG I STATEI O ZAKASPIISKOM KRAIE I SOPREDEL'NYKH STRANAKH. St. Petersburg: Tip.-Lit. S. Muller i I. Bogel'man, 1888, 127 pp. [Russ. text; 2,416+ 238 Russ., Europ. titles, per.: 1865-1885]

"PERIODICHESKAIA PECHAT' I KNIZHNOE DIELO V TRUK STANSKOM KRAIE V 1896 GODU," TURKESTANSKIE VIEDOMOSTI, No. 4, 1897. [Russ. text; 14 titles, per. 1896]

*Pul'ner, I. M.; Ia. B. Dobrin. "MATERIALY DLIA BIBLIOGRAFII SREDNEI AZII (BIBLIOGRAFICHESKIE UKAZATELI ISTORIKO-ETNOGRAFICHESKOI LITERATURY I SMEZHNYKH DISTSIPLIN)," SOVETSKAIA ETNOGRAFIIA, No. 6, 1935, 146-165 pp. [Russ. text; 144 Russ. titles, pp. 146-160]

* "SARTY," ENTSIKLOPEDICHESKII SLOVAR', Vol. 28 A. St. Petersburg: F. A. Brokgauz, I. A. Efron, 1900, 449-451 pp. [Russ. text and titles, p. 451]

Semenov, G. M.; P. V. Vil'koshevkii. UKAZATEL' LITERATURY PO SAMARKANDU I SAMARKANDSOMU KRAIU. Samarkand: Uzbekistanskii Gosudarstvennyi Universitet imeni T. Ikramova, 1935, IV+225 pp. [Russ. text; 970 titles]

Shvets, I. G. BIBLIOGRAFICHESKII UKAZATEL' IZDANII GOSIZDATA UZSSR. No. 1. Tashkent: GIZ UZSSR, 1935, 203+3 pp. [Russ. text; Uzbek, Uyghur, Kazakh, Tajik, C. A. Hebrew, Russ., pub.: 1925-1934]

Sivers, V. AZIIA. St. Petersburg, 1908. [Russ. text]

*SPISOK OPUBLIKOVANNYKH NAUCHNYKH RABOT M. S. ANDREEVA," PAMIATI MIKHAILA STEPANOVICHA ANDREEVA. SBORNIK STATEI PO ISTORII I FILOLOGII NARODOV SREDNEI AZII. Stalinabad: Izdatel'stvo Akademii Nauk Tadzhikskoi SSR (Trudy AN Tadzhikskoi SSR. Institut Istorii, Arkheologii i Etnografii, Vol. 120, 1960, 245 pp., 500 copies. [Russ. text; 54 Russ. titles, pub.: 1893-1958, pp. 20-23]

Central Asia: General

SREDNIAIA AZIIA V IZDANIIAKH AKADEMII NAUK SSSR.
TEMATICHESKII SPISOK 1940 GODA. Moscow: Izdatel'stvo
Akad. Nauk SSSR, 1940, 23 pp. [Russ. text and titles,
pub.: 1940]

TRUDY BIBLIOGRAFICHESKOI KOMISSII BYVSH. PRI SNK TSSR.
Tashkent, 1925. [Russ. text]

TURKESTANSKII SBORNIK SOCHINENII I STATEI,
OTNOSIASHCHIKHSIA DO SREDNEI AZII VOOBSHCHE I
TURKESTANSAGO KRAIA V OSOBENNOSTI. Vols. 300-416.
SISTEMATICHESKIE I AZBUCHNYE UKAZATELI SOCHINENII I
STATEI NA RUSSKOM I INOSTRANNOM IAZYKAKH. St.
Petersburg: Tip. V. Bezobrazova, 1888, 134 pp.
[Russ. text]

UKAZATEL' PUBLIKATSII N. S. LYKOSHINA S 1890 G. PO
1922 G. TRUDY SREDNEAZ. GOS. UN-TA IM. LENINA.
NOVAIA SERIIA. No. 3. IST. NAUKI. BOOK 25. 1956.
[Russ. text; 750 titles, pub.: 1890-1922, pp. 197-230]

*Ul'ianov, G. K. OBZOR LITERATURY PO VOPROSAM KUL'TURY I
PROSVESHCHENIIA NARODOV SSSR. Moscow-Leningrad:
Gos. Izdat., 1930 248 pp. [Russ. text; 132 Russ.
titles, pp. 93-94, 221-225]

UZBEKISTAN, KAZAKHSTAN, TURKMENIIA, TADZHIKISTAN I
KIRGIZIIA V VELIKOI OTECHESTVENNOI VOINE.
BIBLIOGRAFIIA MATERIALOV, OPUBLIKOVANNYKH V SREDNEI
AZII. Moscow: (Fundamental'naia Biblioteka
Obshchestvennykh Nauk Akademii Nauk SSSR), 1942-1945.
Nos. 1-10 (1942), 1-12 (1943), 1-12 (1944), 1/5 (1945).
[Russ. text]
*V. M. "TURKESTAN," ENTSIKLOPEDICHESKII SLOVAR', Vol.
34. St. Petersburg: F. A. Brokgauz, I. A. Efron,
1902, 174-203 pp. [Russ. text; Russ., Europ. titles,
pp. 201-203]

*N. Ia. Vitkind. BIBLIOGRAFIIA PO SREDNEI AZII
(UKAZATEL' LITERATURY PO KOLONIAL'NOI POLITIKE
TSARISMA V SREDNEI AZII) (TRUDY NAUCHNO-
ISSLEDOVATEL'SKOI ASSOTSIATSII PRI KOMMUNISTICHESKOM
UNIVERSITETE TRUDIASHCHIKHSIA VOSTOKA IMENI I. V.
STALINA, No. 4). Moscow: Izdanie Komm. Un-ta
Trudiashchikhsia Vostoka imeni I. V. Stalina, 1929,
166 pp., 1,050 copies. [Russ. text; ca.1275 Russ.,
other titles, per.: 2nd half 19th cent. to 1917, pp.
9-152; 162-165]

Central Asia: General

*Vorontsovskii, P. A. comp. "SPISOK IZDANII ORENBURGSKAGO OTDIELA IMPERATORSKAGO RUSSKAGO OBSHCHESTVA I UKAZATEL' POMIESHCHENNYKH V NIKH TRUDOV," IZVIESTIIA ORENBURGSKAGO OTDIELA IMPERATORSKAGO RUSSKAGO GEOGRAFICHESKAGO OBSHCHESTVA. No. 23 (supplement), 1912. [Russ. text and titles, pub.: 1870-1912, (supplement) pp. 1-11]

Zav'ialov, V. V. OB ISTOCHNIKAKH I POSOBIIAKH DLIA IZUCHENIIA ORENBURGSKAGO KRAIA I SOSIEDSTVENNYKH ZEMEL' SREDNEI AZII. ORENBURGSKIE GUBERNSKIE VIEDOMOSTI. 1852: Nos. 1, 2, 22, 27, 32, 34, 35, 38, 42, 51; 1853: Nos. 1, 2, 33, 34; 1854: Nos. 26, 27, 43, 51 [Nos. 1-51] 1852-1854. [Russ. text; 294+ titles]

Zimin, L. "BIBLIOGRAFIIA," SREDNIAIA AZIIA. KN. 2, 3, 4, 6, 8., 1911. [Russ. text; 183 Sov. Eastern, Russ. titles, (2) pp. 130-133; (3) pp. 130-132; (4) pp. 115-116; (6) pp. 169-170; (8) pp. 155-157]

ANTHROPOLOGY, ETHNOGRAPHY

Ginzburg, V. V. "RASOVYE TIPY SREDNEI AZII I IKH FORMIROVANIE V PROTSESSE ETNOGENEZA EE NARODOV," NAUCHNYE TRUDY TASHKENTSKOGO GOSUDARSTVENNOGO UNIVERSITETA IMENI V. I. LENINA. NOVAIA SERIIA, No. 235, ISTORICHESKIE NAUKI, BOOK 49. 1964. [Russ. text; ca.100 Russ. titles, per. 2nd half 19th cent. to 1963, pp. 142-146]

Ivanovskii, A. A. "UKAZATEL' ETNOGRAFICHESKIKH STATEI I ZAMIETOK, POMIESHCHENNYKH V TURKESTANSKIKH VIEDOMOSTIAKH S No. 1 ZA 1870 G. PO No. 47 ZA 1888 G.," ETNOGRAFICHESKOE OBOZRENIE, Book 9, No. 4. 1891· [Russ. text; 234 titles, pub: 1870-1888, pp. 267-279]

*Kamenetskaia, R. V. comp. NOVAIA LITERATURA PO NARODAM SREDNEI AZII I KAZAKHSTANA," SOVETSKAIA ETNOGRAFIIA. No. 2, 1967. [Russ. text; ca.180 local, Russ., Europ. titles, pub.: 1965-1966, pp. 195-202]

Central Asia: Anthropology, Ethnography

* _____. "NOVAIA LITERATURA PO NARODAM SREDNEI AZII I KAZAKHSTANA," SOVETSKAIA ETNOGRAFIIA. Moscow: "Nauka," No. 3, 1968, 198S pp.; No. 5, 1969, 213S pp. [Russ. text; ca.490 Uzbek, Kazakh, Dungan, Kirgiz, Turkmen, Tajik, Karakalpak, Uigur, Russ., Eng., Esperanto, Arabic, Sp., Fr. titles, pub.: 1966-1968, (No. 3) pp. 165-177; (No. 5) pp. 178-184]

*Kharuzin, A. N. BIBLIOGRAFICHESKII UKAZATEL' KNIG I STATEI KASAIUSHCHIKHSIA ETNOGRAFII KIRGIZOV I KARAKIRGIZOV 1737 PO 1891 GOD. ETNOGRAFICHESKOE OBOZRENIE. 1891. [Russ. text; Russ., Foreign titles, pp. 1-68]

*Kormilitsyn, A. I. "EKSPEDITSII KAFEDRY ANTROPOLOGII BIOLOGO-POCHVENNOGO FAKUL'TETA TASHGU ZA 1923-1959 GG." NAUCHNYE TRUDY (TASHK. UN-T), No. 261. BIBLIOGRAFIIA, No. 10. Tashkent, 1964. [Russ. text; 29 Russ. lists, per.: 1923-1959, pp. 26-61]

*Lunin, B. V. comp. "SPISOK PECHATNYKH RABOT L. V. OSHANINA, OPUBLIKOVANNYKH V 1922-1960 GG." IZVESTIIA AKADEMII NAUK UZSSR. SERIIA OBSHCHESTVENNYKH NAUK, No. 3, 1960. [Russ. text; 32 Russ. titles, pub.: 1922-1960, pp. 62-64]

Masanov, E. A. "NAUCHNYE TRUDY SH. M. IBRAGIMOVA," VESTNIK AKAD. NAUK KIRGIZ. SSR. No. 9, 1964. [Russ. text; 19 Russ. titles, pub.: 1870-1904, pp. 59-60]

Oshanin, L. V. ANTROPOLOGICHESKII SOSTAV NASELENIIA SREDNEI AZII I ETNOGENEZ EE NARODOV. Ch. 1-3. Erevan: (Sredneaziatskii Gosudarstvennyi Universitet. Trudy. Novaia Seriia, No. 96. Istoricheskie Nauki, Book 16; No. 97. Istoricheskie Nauki Book. 17; No. 98, Istoricheskie Nauki Book 18), 1957-1959. [Russ. text; 326 Russ., Europ. titles, (No. 96) pp. 135-138; (No. 97) pp. 140-145; (No. 98) pp. 188-194]

_____.; V. Ia. Zezenkova. "ANTROPOLOGICHESKII SOSTAV NASELENIIA SREDNEI AZII I ETNOGENEZ EE NARODOV V SVETE DANNYKH ANTROPOLOGII," VOPROSY ETNOGENEZA NARODOV SREDNEI AZII V SVETE DANNYKH ANTROPOLOGII. Tashkent: (Akad. Nauk UzSSR. In-t Istorii i Arkheologii), 1953. [Russ. text; 65 titles, pp. 54-56]

_____. VOPROSY ETNOGENEZA NARODOV SREDNEI AZII V SVETE DANNYKH ANTROPOLOGII, 1953. [Russ. text]

Central Asia: Anthropology, Ethnography

*"OSNOVNYE PECHATNYE RABOTY M. M. D'IAKONOVA,"
SOVETSKAIA ETNOGRAFIIA. No. 3, 1954. [Russ. text and
titles, pub.: 1934-1953, pp. 123-124]

*Rusiaikina, S. P. "MUZEINYE ETNOGRAFICHESKIE FONDY KAK
ISTOCHNIK DLIA SOSTAVLENIIA ISTORIKO-ETNOGRAFICHESKOGO
ATLASA SREDNEI AZII I KAZAKHSTANA," MATERIALY K ISTORIKO-
ETNOGRAFICHESKOMU ATLASU SREDNEI AZII I KAZAKHSTANA.
(TRUDY INST. ETNOG. IM. MIKLUKHOMAKLAIA. N. S.
Vol. 48). Moscow-Leningrad: Izdatel'stvo Akademii
Nauk SSSR. [Russ. text; titles pp. 36-85]

Semenov, A. A. "BIBLIOGRAFICHESKII UKAZATEL' PO KOVROVYM
TKANIAM AZII," TRUDY BIBLIOGRAFICHESKOI KOMISSII PRI SNK
TSSR. No. 1. Tashkent, 1925, 21 pp. [Russ. text; 199
titles]

_____. "UKAZATEL' LITERATURY O KOVRAKH AZII.
KOVRY RUSSKOGO TURKESTANA," ETNOGRAFICHESKOE OBOZRENIE.
Book LXXXVIII-LXXXIX. No. 1/2, 1911. [Russ. text;
121 titles, pp. 168-179]

*Tolstov, S. "SPISOK PECHATNYKH TRUDOV A. N. BERNSHTAMA,"
SOVETSKAIA ETNOGRAFIIA. No. 1, 1957. [Russ. text;
148 Russ. titles, pub.: 1929-1957, pp. 180-183]

*Tolstov, S. P.; T. A. Zhdanko; S. M. Abramzona; N. A.
Kisliakova, eds. NARODY SREDNEI AZII I KAZAKHSTANA.
[V DVUKH TOMAKH] Moscow: Izdatel'stvo Akademii Nauk
SSSR, (Vol. 1) 1962, 768 pp.; (Vol. 2) 1963, 778 pp.,
3750 copies. [Russ. text; (Vol. 1) ca.600 titles,
pp. 685-704; (Vol. 2) ca.250 titles, pp. 699-707]

Vasileva, G. P.; E. I. Makhova. "PROGRAMMA SBORA
MATERIALA PO ZHILISHCHU SEL'SKOGO NASELENIIA SREDNEI
AZII I KAZAKHSTANA DLIA ISTORIKO-ETNOGRAFICHESKOGO
ATLASA," TRUDY IN-TA ETNOGRAFII IM. MIKLUKHO-MAKLAIA.
Vol. 48, 1961. [Russ. text; 50 titles, pp. 130-132]

*Vorob'eva, M. G. "OPYT KARTOGRAFIROVANIIA GONCHARNYKH
PECHEI DLIA ISTORIKO-ETNOGRAFICHESKOGO ATLASA SREDNEI
AZII I KAZAKHSTANA," (TRUDY INST. ETNOG. IM. MIKLUKHO-
MAKLAIA. NOVAIA SERIIA: TOM XLVII). MATERIALY K
ISTORIKO-ETNOGRAFICHESKOMU ATLASU SREDNEI AZII I
KAZAKHSTANA. Moscow-Leningrad: Izdatel'stvo Akademii
Nauk SSSR, 1961, pp. 147-179, 1700 copies. [Russ. text
and titles, pp. 175-178]

Voznesenskaia, E. A.; A. B. Piotrovskii. MATERIALY DLIA
BIBLIOGRAFII PO ANTROPOLOGII I ETNOGRAFII KAZAKSTANA I
SREDNEAZIATSKIKH RESPUBLIK. Leningrad: Izdatel'stvo
Akad. Nauk SSSR. (Trudy [No. 14] Komissii Po
Izucheniiu Plemennogo Sostava Naseleniia SSSR i
Sopredel'nykh Stran), 1927, pp. 21; 247. [Russ. text
and 2,917 Russ., Europ. titles, pub.: up to Jan. 1926]

Central Asia: Anthropology, Ethnography

*[Zaleman, K. G.] Salemann, C. "TRUDY V. V. RADLOVA V KHRONOLOGICHESKOM PORIADKE. RADLOFF'S DRUCKSCHRIFTEN IN CHRONOLOGISCHER ORDNUNG," KO DNIU SEMIDESIATILIETIIA VASILIIA VASIL'EVICHA RADLOVA. 5 IANVARIA 1907 GODA. St. Petersburg: Tipografiia Imperatorskoi Akademii Nauk, 1907, 111 pp. [Russ. text; 99 Russ., Europ. titles, pub.: 1860-1906, pp. 3-25]

ARCHITECTURE, ART, MUSIC

*Al'baum, L. I. BALALYK-TEPE. K ISTORII MATERIAL'NOI KUL'TURY I ISKUSSTVA TOKHARISTANA. Tashkent, 1960. [Russ. text; Russ., Europ. titles, pub.: pre-rev. and Soviet, pp. 220-228]

*Denike, B. "KOVER," BOL'SHAIA SOVETSKAIA ENTSIKLOPEDIIA. Vol. 33. Moscow: Gosudarstvennyi Institut "Sovetskaia Entsiklopediia," (OGIZ RSFSR), 1938, 208-211 pp. [Russ. text; Russ., Europ. titles, p. 211]

*Dolinskaia, V. G. "KHUDOZHNIK MINIATIURIST MUKHAMMED MURAD SAMARKHANDI," IZVESTIIA AKADEMII NAUK UzSSR. No. 9, 1955, 65 pp. [Russ. text; 13 Russ., Europ. titles, pp. 63-64]

ENEOLIT IUZHNYKH OBLASTEI SREDNEI AZII. CH. Z. I. N. KHOLPIN. PAMIATNIKI RAZVITOGO IUGO-VOST. TURKMENII. Leningrad, 1969. [Russ. text; 98 titles, pp. 52-53]

Semenov, A. A. BIBLIOGRAFICHESKII UKAZATEL' PO KOVROVYM TKANIAM SREDNEI AZII. Tashkent: (Bibliogr. Komis. pri SNK TSSR. Trudy. No. 1), 1925. [Russ. text; 199 Russ., foreign titles, pub.: 1906-1924, p. 21]

[Morozov, I. S.] SPISOK NAUCHNYKH RABOT I PUBLIKATSII ZASLUZHENNOGO DEIATELIA NAUKI UZBEKSOI SSR, DOKTORA ISKUSSTVOVEDENIIA, PROFESSORA L. I. REMPELIA. K 60-LETIIU SO DNIA ROZHDENIIA I 40-LETIIU NAUCH.-ISSLED. DEIATEL'NOSTI. BIBLIOGR. UKAZATEL'. Tashkent: (In-t Iskusstvoznaniia im. Khamzy. Tashk. Teatr-Khudozh. In-t im. Ostrovskogo. Soiuz Khudozhnikov Uzbekistana), 1968, 13 pp., 150 copies. [Russ. text; 150 titles, pub.: 1927-1967]

Central Asia: Architecture, Art, Music

*Nil'sen, V. A. MONUMENTAL'NAIA ARKHITEKTURA BUKHARSKOGO OAZISA XI-XII VV. K VOPROSU O VOZNIKNOVENII SREDNEVEKOVOI ARKHITEKTURY V SREDNEI AZII. Tashkent: (Akad. Nauk Uzbek. SSR. In-t Istorii i Arkheologii) Izdatel'stvo Akademii Nauk Uzbekskoi SSR, 1956, 154 pp., 650 copies. [Russ. text; 169 Russ., Europ. titles, pub.: 19th c.-1953; per.: 11th-12th c., pp. 149-155]

*Saiko, E. V. GLAZURI KERAMIKI SREDNEI AZII VIII-XII VV. (PO MATERIALAM KERAMICHESKIKH KOMPLEKSOV KHUTTALIA, SOGDA, FERGANY). Dushanbe: Izdatel'stvo Akademii Nauk Tadzhikskoi SSR (Akademiia Nauk Tadzhikskoi SSR. Institut Istorii im. Akhmed Donisha. Trudy, Vol. 36), 1963, 114+ pp., 500 copies. [Russ. text; survey Russ. Europ., per. 8th-12th cc, pp. 3-9]

Voronina, V. L. "SOVETSKIE UCHENYE OB ARKHITEKTURE SREDNEI AZII. OBZOR RABOT PO IZUCHENIIU ARKHITEKTURY SREDNEI AZII ZA 25 LET (1917-1942 GG.)," SOOBSHCHENIIA KABINETA TEORII I ISTORII ARKHITEKTURY. Moscow: (Akad. Arkhitektury SSSR), No. 3, 1943, 12-25 pp. [Russ. text; pub.: 1917-1942, pp. 16-21]

Zalesskaia, L. S. OZELENENIE GORODOV SREDNEI AZII. Moscow: (Akad. Arkhitektury SSSR) [1949]. [Russ. text; 93 titles, pub.: 1822-1949, pp. 92-94]

*Zasypkin, B. N. ARKHITEKTURA SREDNEI AZII. Moscow, 1948, 159 pp., 10,000 copies. [Russ. text; 20 Russ. titles, pub.: 1920-1940, p. 154]

ECONOMICS

*AKADEMIIA NAUK SSSR RESPUBLIKAM SREDNEI AZII 1924-1934; K DESIATILETIIU NATIONAL'NAGO RAZMEZHEVANIIA SREDNEI AZII. Moscow-Leningrad: Izdatel'stvo Akademii Nauk SSSR. Sovet po Izucheniiu Prirodnykh Resursov, 1934, 217 pp. [Russ. text; scattered titles, per.: 1924-1934]

Central Asia: Economics

*Aminov, A. M. EKONOMICHESKOE RAZVITIE SREDNEI AZII (SO VTOROI POLOVINY XIX STOLETIIA DO PERVOI MIROVOI VOINY). Tashkent: Gos. Izd.-vo Uzbekskoi SSR, 1959, 298 pp., 5000 copies. [Russ. text; ca.300 Russ. titles, per.: 2nd half 19th cent. - WWI, pp. 282-286]

*ANNOTIROVANNYI KATALOG IZDANII VYPUSHCHENNYKH IZDATEL'STVOM "SOVETSKAIA AZIIA" ZA 1925-1933 GG. Moscow: Izdatel'stvo "Sovetskaia Aziia," (Tsentral'noe Biuro Kraevedeniia RSFSR. Obshchestvo Izucheniia Sovetskoi Azii), 1933, 81 pp., 2000 copies. [Russ. text and titles, pub. 1925-1933]

*Arkhipov, N. B. EKONOMICHESKAIA GEOGRAFIJA SSSR PO RAIONAM. SREDNE-AZIATSKIE RESPUBLIKI. Moscow-Leningrad: Gosudarstvennoe Izdatel'stvo, 1930 3rd ed. with supplement [ca.1927/28 1st ed.] 160 pp. (1st ed.: 139 pp.), 10,000 copies. [Russ. text and titles, pp. 157-159]

_____. "UKAZATEL' VAZHNEISHIKH POSOBII." SREDNE-AZIATSKIE RESPUBLIKI. Moscow-Leningrad, 1927 (2nd ed. 1928; 3rd ed. 1930). [Russ. text; 68 titles]

*Balashev, N. I. UZBEKISTAN I SOPREDEL'NYE RESPUBLIKI I OBLASTI. GEOGRAFICHESKII I EKONOMICHESKII OCHERK. Tashkent: Uzbekskoe Gosudarstvennoe Izdatel'stvo, 1925, 99 pp. [Russ. text and titles, p. 97]

Balkov, V. "BIBLIOGRAFIIA MELKOI PROMYSHLENNOSTI SREDNEI AZII (RUSSKAIA LITERATURA)," KUSTARNO-REMESLENNAIA PROMYSHLENNOST' SREDNEI AZII. Tashkent, 1927. [Russ. text; 87 Russ. titles, pub.: 1866-1926 (no newsp. since 1917), pp. 189-194]

*Baratov, P. REKI SREDNEI AZII I IKH KHOZIAISTVENNOE ZNACHENIE. Tashkent, 1967. [Uzbek text; 78 titles, pp. 100-102]

Betger, E. K. UKAZATEL' K SBORNIKAM, IZDANNYM STATISTICHESKIMI KOMITETAMI TURKESTANSKOGO KRAIA. Tashkent, 1930. [Russ. text; 454 titles, per.: 1872-) 1915]

_____. O. V. Maslova. UKAZATEL' K ZHURNALU "NARODNOE KHOZIAISTVO SREDNEI AZII" ZA VREMIA EGO SUSHCHESTVOVANIIA. 1924-1930. Tashkent, 1932. [Russ. text; pub. 1924-1930]

Central Asia: Economics

Cherdantsev, G. N. "UKAZATEL' LITERATURY,"
SREDNE-AZIATSKIE RESPUBLIKI, EKONOMIKO-GEOG. OCHERKI
SSSR. Moscow: "Planovoe Khoz-vo," 1928. [Russ. text;
74 Russ. titles, pp. 166-168]

Gavrilova, S. A.; I. I. Parkhomenko, compilers.
EKONOMICHESKIE ADMINISTRATIVENYE RAIONY SSSR--UKAZATEL'
NOVOI LITERATURY PO PRIRODE, RESURSAM I KHOZIAISTVU.
No. 11: UZBEKSKAIA SSR, KIRGIZSKAIA SSR, TADZHIKSKAIA
SSR, TURKMENSKAIA SSR. Moscow, 1958, 161 pp.,
1,500 copies. [Russ. text; ca.2,300 Sov. Asian, Russ.
titles, pub. (journals), 1953-1956; other pub.]

Igamberdyev, R. OSUSHCHESTVENIE LENINSKIKH IDEI OB
OROSHENII I OSVOENII GOLODNOI STEPI. Tashkent, 1969.
[Russ. text; ca.220 titles, pp. 10-14; 168-178]

ISTORIIA OROSHENIIA GOLODNOI STEPI, ANNOTIROVANNYI
UKAZATEL' LITERATURY 1937-1945 GG. Tashkent: GPB UzSSR,
1947. [Russ. text; pub.: 1937-1945]

*"KASPIISKOE MORE," BOL'SHAIA SOVETSKAIA ENTSIKLOPEDIIA.
Vol. 31. Moscow: Gosudarstvennyi Institut
"Sovetskaia Entsiklopediia" (OGIZ RSFSR), 1937
pp. 699-701. [Russ. text and titles, p. 701]

"KATALOG IZDANII SYR-DAR'INSKOGO OBLASTNOGO
STATISTICHESKOGO KOMITETA," Stupakov, I. E. ADRES-
SPRAVOCHNIK TURKESTANSKGO KRAIA. Tashkent, 1910.
[Russ. text; 39 titles, supplement pp. 1-8, pub.: 1887-
1910]

*Kostenko, L. comp. SREDNIAIA AZIIA I VODVORENIE V NEI
RUSSKOI GRAZHDANSTVENNOSTI. St. Petersburg:
Tipografiia V. Bezobrazova i Komp., 1870, 358+ pp.
[Russ. text; 122 Russ., Europ. titles, pp. VII-XIII]

Mamontov, I. I. UKAZATEL' IZDANII MINISTERSTVA
ZEMLEDELIIA I GOSUDARSTVENNYKH IMUSHCHESTV PO SEL'SKO-
KHOZIAISTVENNOI I LESNOI CHASTI. 1894-1903. [For
1894-1900. 2nd ed.--1900, XII+830+1. For 1901--1903
282 pp.; For 1902-1904 228 pp.; For 1903-1906 249 pp.]
St. Petersburg: M. Z. i G. I Departament Zemledeliia,
1900-1906. [Russ. text; pub. 1894-1903]

ROSSIIA. MINISTERSTVO ZEMLEDELIIA. OTDEL ZEMEL'NYKH
ULUCHSHENII. SPISOK IZDANII OTDIELA ZEMEL'NYKH
ULUCHSHENII. Petrograd, 1914-1917. [Russ. text;
pub.: 1914-1917]

Central Asia: Economics

ROSSIIA. MINISTERSTVO ZEMLEDELIIA. IZDANIIA VEDOMSTVA ZEMLEDELIIA (SVEDENIIA PO 1-OE IIUNIA 1914 G.) St. Petersburg, n. d., 41 pp. [Russ. text; pub.: up to June 1914]

ROSSIIA. DEPARTAMENT ZEMLEDELIIA. SISTEMATICHESKII KATALOG IZDANII IMEIUSHCHIKHSIA V SKLADE DEPARTAMENTA ZEMLEDELIIA. St. Petersburg. [Russ. text; pub.: 1912-1916]

Savitskaia, M. A. "UKAZATEL' LITERATURY PO IRRIGATSII I MELIORATSII SREDNE-AZIATSKIKH RESPUBLIK I KAZAKHSTANA," MATERIALY KOMISSII EKSPEDITSIONNYKH ISSLEDOVANII. Vol.1. Leningrad: Akad. Nauk SSSR. Materialy Komissii Ekspeditsionnykh Issledovanii, 1928, 230 pp. [Russ. text; 1,853 Russ. titles, pub.: up to 1926]

"SISTEMATICHESKII UKAZATEL' STATEI POMESHCHENNYKH V ZHURNALE 'NARODNOE KHOZIAISTVO SREDNEI AZII' V 1924, 1925, 1926 GG." NAR. KHOZ.-VO SREDNEI AZII. No. 11, 1926. [Russ. text; 294 titles, pub.: 1924-1926, pp. 143-145]

"SISTEMATICHESKII UKAZATEL' STATEI POMESHCHENNYKH V ZHURNALE 'NARODNOE KHOZIAISTVO SREDENEI AZII' ZA 1927 GOD," NAR. KHOZ.-VO SREDNEI AZII. No. 10/12, 1927. [Russ. text; 112 titles, pub.: 1927, pp. 213-219]

"SISTEMATICHESKII UKAZATEL' STATEI POMESHCHENNYKH V ZHURNALE 'NARODNOE KHOZIAISTVO SREDNEI AZII' ZA 1928 G." NAR. KHOZ.-VO SREDNEI AZII. No. 1, 1929. [Russ. text; 66 titles, pub.: 1928, pp. 197-200]

"SISTEMATICHESKII UKAZATEL' STATEI POMESHCHENNYKH V ZHURNALE 'NARODNOE KHOZIAISTVO SREDNEI AZII' ZA 1929 GOD," NAR. KHOZ.-VO SREDNEI AZII. No. 12, 1929. [Russ. text; 96 Russ. titles, pub.: 1929, pp. 119-124]

*"SISTEMATICHESKII UKAZATEL' STATEI POMESHCHENNYKH V ZHURNALE 'NARODNOE KHOZIAISTVO SREDNEI AZII' V 1924, 1925 I 1926 GG.," NARODNOE KHOZIAISTVO SREDNEI AZII. No. 11/12. 1926. [Russ. text; 312 Russ. titles, per.: 1924-1926, pp. 143-145]

"SPISKI KNIG PO EKONOMIKE SREDNEI AZII," BIBLIOGRAFICHESKAIA ZHIZN' SREDNEI AZII V 1928 GODU. BIBLIOGRAFIIA, No. 1. 1929, 98 pp. [Russ. text]

Central Asia: Economics

SPISOK NAUCHNYKH RABOT I PUBLIKATSII ZASLUZHENNOGO
DEIATELIA NAUKI UZSSR DOKTORA ISKUSSTVOVEDENIIA
PROFESSORA G. A. PUGACHENKOVOI. K 50-LETIIU SO DNIA
ROZHDENIIA I 25-LETIIU NAUCH.-ISSLED. DEIATEL'NOSTI.
Tashkent: (In-t Iskusstvoznaniia im. Khamzy. Soiuz
Arkhitektorov Uzbekistana, 1965, 10 pp., 300 copies.
[Russ. text; 160 titles, pub. 1941-1964]

*SREDNIAIA AZIIA. EKON.-GEOGR. KHARAKTERISTIKA I PROBLEMY
RAZVITIIA KHOZ-VA. Moscow: "Mysl'," 1969, 504 pp.,
4000 copies. [Russ. text; ca.180 Russ. titles, works
pub.: 1915-1968, pp. 493-502]

*Stokasimov, Kniaz'. comp. VOENNO-STATISTICHESKOE
OPISANIE TURKESTANSKAGO OKRUGA. FERGANSKII RAION.
Tashkent: Izdanie Shtaba Turkestanskago Voennago
Okruga, 1912. [Russ. text; titles, pp. 159-165]

*Suvorov, V. A. ISTORIKO-EKONOMICHESKII OCHERK RAZVITIIA
TURKESTANA. (PO MATERIALAM ZH.-D STROITEL'STVA V 1880-
1917 GG.) Tashkent, 1962, 171 pp., 2000 copies. [Russ.
text; 66 Russ. titles, per.: 1880-1917, pp. 150-159]

*Tulepbaev, B. A. OSUSHCHESTVLENIE LENINSKOI AGRARNOI
POLITIKI PARTII V RESPUBLIKAKH SREDNEI AZII. Moscow:
"Mysl'," 1967, 325 pp. [Russ. text; ca.300 Russ.
titles, pp. 310-323]

"UKAZATEL' KNIG PO EKONOMIKE SREDNEI AZII IZDANNYKH V
1928 GODU," TURKMENOVEDENIE. No. 12, 1928; No. 1, 1929;
No. 2/3, 1929; No. 4, 1929; 1928-1929. [Russ. text;
134 titles, pub.: 1928, (1928 No. 12) 80-82 pp.;
(1929 No. 1) 49-50 pp., (No. 2/3, 1929) 58 p.; (No. 4,
1929) 39-40 pp.]

*Valentini, G. G.; L. G. Popova; T. M. Tsyganova, comp.
BIBLIOGRAFICHESKII UKAZATEL'. 1923-1967. Tashkent:
(Sredneaziatskii Nauchno-Issledovatel'skii Institut
Irrigatsii im. V. D. Zhurina. Ministerstvo
Melioratsii i Vodnogo Khoziaistva SSSR...), 1968, 319 pp.,
500 copies. [Russ. text; per. 1923-1967]

VOPROSY EKONOMICHESKOI GEOGRAFII I ISTORII GEOGRAFICHESKOGO
IZUCHENIIA SREDNEI AZII. Tashkent: (Nauchnye Zapiski.
Tashkentskii Institut Narodnogo Khoziaistva, No. 26),
1964, 283 pp. [Russ. text; titles scattered]

Voznesenskaia, E. A. "BIBLIOGRAFICHESKII UKAZATEL' PO
KHLOPKOVODSTVU TURKESTANA," TRUDY PO PRIKLADNOI
BOTANIKE I SELEKTSII. Vol. 15, No. 5. Leningrad, 1925.
[Russ. text; 1,942 Russ. titles, pub.: to Fall, 1925,
pp. 395-497]

Central Asia: Economics

Voznesenskaia E. A.; A. I. Rabinerson. UKAZATEL'
LITERATURY PO GIDROLOGII SREDNEAZIATSKIKH RESPUBLIK I
KAZAKHSTANA. Leningrad: (AN SSSR. Komissiia po
Izucheniiu Proizvoditel'nykh Sil Soiuza), 1928, 115 pp.
[Russ. text; 1,113 titles].

EDUCATION

*Bendrikov, K. E. OCHERKI PO ISTORII NARODNOGO
OBRAZOVANIIA V TURKESTANE. (1865-1924 GG.) Moscow:
(Akad. Ped. Nauk RSFSR. In-t Teorii i Istorii
Pedagogiki.), 1960, 512 pp. [Russ. text; ca.220 Russ.
titles, per.: 1865-1924, pp. 499-510]

Betger, E. K. "UKAZATEL' GLAVNEISHEI LITERATURY O
TURKESTANSKOI GOSUDARSTVENNOI BIBLIOTEKE (OPYT
BIBLIOGRAFII)," Betger, E. K. OTCHET TURKESTANSKOI
GOSUDARSTVENNOI BIBLIOTEKI ZA 1923 GOD. Tashkent:
Tip. No. 2 Sredne Aziatskogo Gosudarstvennogo
Izdatel'stva, 1924-1926. [Russ. text; 333 titles,
pub.: 1870-1923, (1924) 22-24 pp.; (1925) 33-42 pp.;
(1926) 31-37 pp.]

*Libova, F. M.; P. S. Shats, comp. "BIBLIOGRAFIIA.
VOPROSY KUL'TURNOGO STROITEL'STVA V NATSIONAL'NYKH
RESPUBLIKAKH, KRAIAKH I OBLASTIAKH," REVOLIUTSIIA I
NATSIONAL'NOSTI. No. 3. 1935, 90-94 pp. [Russ. text;
pub.: 1934-1935]

Matvievskaia, G. P. K ISTORII MATEMATIKI SREDNEI AZII
IX-XV VEKOV. Tashkent, 1962. [Russ. text; 310 Russ.,
Europ. titles, pub.: up to 1961; per.: 9th-15th cc.,
pp. 82-100]

*L. A. Mukhin, Z. F. Trudoliubova, N. Z. Khotimskaia,
M. E. Shumskaia. "ANNOTATSII NA KNIGI VYSHEDSHIE V
RESPUBLIKAKH SOVETSKOGO VOSTOKA (1956-1957 GG.),"
SOVETSKOE VOSTOKOVEDENIE. No. 1, 1958. [Russ. text;
Russ. titles, pp. 168-175]

Ostroumov, N. P. OTCHET TURKESTANSKOI UCHITEL'SKOI
SEMINARII ZA XXV LET EE SUSHCHESTVOVANIIA (30 AVGUSTA
1879 GODA--30 AVGUSTA 1904 GODA). Tashkent: Tip.-Lit.
V. M. Il'ina, 1904. [Russ. text; titles, appendix,
pp. 39-47]

Central Asia: Education

*Perepelitsyna, L. A. "O VLIIANII KUL'TURY RUSSKOGO NARODA NA KUL'TURU NARODOV TURKESTANSKOGO KRAIA," TRUDY SREDNE-AZIAT. UN-TA, No. 51. (FILOL. NAUKI), KN. 5. 1954. [Russ. text; ca.70 titles (in notes), pp. 106-108]

*_____. "VLIIANIE RUSSKOI KUL'TURY NA KUL'TURU NARODOV SREDNEI AZII." (TASHK. GOS. UN-T IM. LENINA. TRUDY. [NOVAIA SERIIA]. No. 165 [FILOL NAUKI]. KN. 22). Tashkent, 1960, 170 pp., 2,800 copies. [Russ. text; ca.190 Russ. titles (archive mat.), pp. 102-107]

*Rosliakov, A. A. "K ISTORII NARODNOGO KHOZIAISTVA TURKMENISTANA." IZVESTIIA AKAD. NAUK TURKM. SSR. No. 1. n. p. (Akad. Nauk Turkm. SSR.), 1953, 195 pp. [Russ. text; 37 Turk., Russ., titles, Sov. per., p. 53]

*Shukrullah-Oghli, Hajji Mu'in. "FIWRAL INQILABIGHACHA SAMARQAND WILAYATIDA CHIQGHAN YANGI ASRLAR," INQILAB (TASHKENT), No. 1. February, 1922. [Uzbek text; 49 Uzbek, Tajik, Persian titles, pub.: 1904-1916, pp. 42-43]

"SPISOK LITERATURY PO ISTORII NAUKI I KUL'TURY SREDNEI AZII I KAZAKHSTANA," VELIKIE UCHENYE SREDNEI AZII I KAZAKHSTANA. (VIII-XIX VV). Alma Ata, 1965. [Russ. text; 68 Russ. titles, per.: 8th to 19th cc., pp. 235-237]

GEOGRAPHY

*A. N. "KOPAL," ENTSIKLOPEDICHESKII SLOVAR'. Vol. 16. St. Petersburg: F. A. Brokgauz, I. A. Efron, 1895, 161-162 pp. [Russ. text and titles, p. 162]

*"AMU ILI AMU-DAR'IA," ENTSIKLOPEDICHESKII SLOVAR'. Vol. IA. St. Petersburg: F. A. Brokgauz, I. A. Efron, 1890, 676-677 pp. [Russ. text; Russ., Europ. titles, p. 677]

Andrianov, B. V. DREVNIE OROSITEL'NYE SISTEMY PRIARAL'IA: V SVIAZI S ISTORIEI VOZNIKOVENIIA I RAZVITIIA OROSHAEMOGO ZEMLEDELIIA. Moscow: Izdatel'stvo "Nauka," 1969, 254 pp. [Russ. text; ca.900 titles, pp. 234-250]

Central Asia: Geography

*"ARALO-KASPIISKAIA NIZMENNOST'," ENTSIKLOPEDICHESKII SLOVAR', Vol. 2. St. Petersburg: F. A. Brokgauz, I. A. Efron, 1890, 10-12 pp. [Russ., Europ. titles, p. 12]

"ARAL'SKOE MORE," SOVETSKAIA VOENNAIA ENTSIKLOPEDIIA. Vol 1. Moscow: Gosudarstvennoe Slovarno-Entsiklopedicheskoe Izdatel'stvo "Sovetskaia Entsiklopediia," OGIZ RSFSR, 1932, 589-590 pp. [Russ. text and titles, p. 590]

Azat'ian, A. A. "VVEDENIE V ISTORIIU GEOGRAFICHESKOGO IZUCHENIIA SREDNEI AZII V DOREVOLIUTSIONNYI PERIOD," NAUCHNYE ZAPISKI (TASHK. FIN-EKON. IN-T) No. 15, 1961, 7-59 pp. [Russ. text; 27 Russ. titles, per.: pre-rev., pub.: 1856-1961, p. 59]

*_____. VYDAIUSHCHIESIA ISSLEDOVATELI PRIRODY SREDNEI AZII (VTORAIA POLOVINA XIX V.), CHAST' I-IA. Tashkent: Izdatel'stvo "Sredniaia i Vysshaia Shkola," UzSSR, 1960, 172 pp., 3,000 copies. [Russ. text and titles, per.: 19th c. 63-67pp.; 137-140 pp.; 168-169 pp.]

*_____. VYDAIUSHCHIESIA ISSLEDOVATELI PRIRODY SREDNEI AZII. (VTORAIA POLOVINA XIX V.) CH. 2. Tashkent: Izdatel'stvo "Uchitel'," 1966, 224 pp., 3,000 copies. [Russ. text; ca.500 Russ. titles, per.: 1850-1900, pp. 202-222]

Babushkin, L. G., N. A. Kogai. "NEKOTORYE VOPROSY FIZIKO-GEOGRAFICHESKOGO RAIONIROVANIIA RESPUBLIK SREDNEI AZII DLIA TSELEI SEL'SKOGO KHOZIAISTVA," NAUCHNYE ZAPISKI (TASHK. FIN-EKON. IN-T). No. 15, 1961, 87-118 pp. [Russ. text; 47 Russ. titles, pub.: 1929-1959, pp. 117-118]

*"BALKHASH ILI BALKASH," ENTSIKLOPEDICHESKII SLOVAR', Vol. 2A. St. Petersburg: F. A. Brokgauz, I. A. Efron, 1891; 834-835. [Russ. text and titles, p. 835]

*Baranskii, N. "AMU-DAR'INSKII RAION," BOL'SHAIA SOVETSKAIA ENTSIKLOPEDIIA. Vol. 2. Moscow: Aktsionernoe Obshchestvo "Sovetskaia Entsiklopediia," 1926, 555-557 pp. [Russ. text and titles, p. 557]

*Baratov, P. ESTESTVENNAIA VODNAIA LABORATORIIA SREDNEI AZII. Tashkent: "Fan," 1968, 50 pp., 2,000 copies. [Russ. text; Uzbek titles, p. 49]

Central Asia: Geography

Baratov, P. "ISTORIIA GEOGRAFICHESKOI IZUCHENNOSTI DOLINY ZARAFSHANA," VOPR. IZUCHENIIA I ISPOL'ZOVANIIA PRIRODY I PRIRODNYKH RESURSOV SREDNEI AZII I SOPREDEL'NYKH STRAN. Tashkent, 1970. [Russ. text; 61 titles, pp. 98-99]

_____. ed. OCHERKI GEOGRAFII SREDNEI AZII. TASH. PED. IN-T IM. NIZAMI. UCHEN. ZAPISKI. Vol. 59. Tashkent: "Fan," 1966, 97 pp., 1000 copies. [Russ. text; Uzbek titles, pp. 22-23]

Beber, V. POLEZNYE ISKOPAEMYE TURKESTANA. BIBLIOGRAFICHESKII UKAZATEL'. St. Petersburg, 1913. [Russ. text]

*Berg, L. "AMU-DAR'IA," BOL'SHAIA SOVETSKAIA ENTSIKLOPEDIIA. Vol. 2. Moscow: Aktsionernoe Obshchestvo "Sovetskaia Entsiklopeiia," 1926, 554-557 pp. [Russ. text and titles, p. 557]

* _____. "ARAL'SKOE MORE," BOL'SHAIA SOVETSKAIA ENTSIKLOPEDIIA. Vol. 3. Moscow: Aktsionernoe Obshchestvo "Sovetskaia Entsiklopediia," 1926, 234-240 pp. [Russ. text and titles, p. 240]

* _____. "ARAL'SKOE MORE," ENTSIKLOPEDICHESKII SLOVAR' Vol. 1, (supplement). St. Petersburg: F. A. Brokgauz, I. A. Efron, 1905, 138-141 pp. [Russ. text and titles, p. 141]

* _____. "RUSSKAIA BIBLIOGRAFIIA PO TURKESTANU," PRIRODA. Nos.: 7/9. 1925. [Russ. text; titles, columns 253-254]

Betger, E. K. UKAZATEL' STATEI I ZAMETOK PO GEOGRAFII, METEOROLOGII, SEISMOGRAFII I GIDROLOGII TURKESTANA POMESHCHENNYKH V GAZETE "TURKESTANSKIE VIEDOMOSTI," ZA VREMIA EE SUSHCHESTVOVANIIA (1870-1917) 2 Parts. n. p., 220 pp. [Russ. text; 4,800 titles, pub.: 1870-1917]

"BIBLIOGRAFIIA. [NOVAIA] LITERATURA PO KRAEVEDENIIU, POSTUPIVSHAIA V [BIBLIOTEKU] TSENTRAL'NOGO BIURO KRAEVEDENIIA ZA [APREL'-DEKABR' 1925 G.]" IZVESTIIA TSENTRAL'NOGO BIURO KRAEVEDENIIA. 1926, No. 3, pp. 88-95; No. 6, 201-214 pp; No. 7 246-262 pp; No. 9, 319-326 pp.; No. 10, 355-360 pp. [Russ. text and titles]

Central Asia: Geography

*"BIBLIOGRAFIIA. NOVYE KNIGI," REVOLIUTSIIA I NATSIONAL'NOSTI. 1936. No. 4, 94-96 pp.; No. 5, 95-97 pp; No. 6, 90-93 pp.; No. 7, 97-101 pp.; No. 8, 85-87 pp.; No. 10, 104-106 pp.; No. 11, 139-142 pp. [Russ. text]

*Chelpanova, O. M. SREDNIAIA AZIIA. KLIMAT SSSR. No. 3. Leningrad: Gidrometeorologicheskoe Izdatel'stvo, 1963, 447 pp., 1,700 copies. [Russ. text; 197 Russ. titles]

*Cherniavskii, V. I. PETR PETROVICH SEMENOV--TIAN-SHANSKII I EGO TRUDY PO GEOGRAFIZ. Moscow: Geografigz, 1955, 296 pp. [Russ. text; 224 Russ., Europ. titles, pub. 1850-1947, pp. 285-296]

*Chetyrkin, V. M. SREDNIAIA AZIIA. OPYT KOMPLEKSNOI GEOGR. KHARAKTERISTIKI I RAIONIROVANIIA. (TASHK. GOS UN-T IM. LENINA. TRUDY. [NOVAIA SERIIA]. No. 182. [GEOGR. NAUKI]. KN. 19). Tashkent, 1960. [Russ. text; 48 titles, pp. 237-238]

*Dobrovol'skii, A. D. KASPIISKOE MORE. Moscow: Izd. Mosk. Un-ta, 1969, 264 pp., 1,550 copies. [Russ. text; titles, pp. 265-263]

*Dubrovina, E. I.; R. I. Niiazova; N. S. Khabirova. ZEMLETRIASENIIA V SREDNEI AZII. UKAZATEL' LITERATURY PO SEISMOLOGII I SEISMOLOGICHESKIM METODAM ISSLEDOVANIIA STROENIIA ZEMNOI KORY V SREDNEI AZII. Tashkent: (Fundam. Biblioteka AN UzSSR. Fundam B-ka Tashk. Gos. Un-ta), 1967, 164 pp., 500 copies. [Russ. text]

*Dumitrashko, N. "KARAKORUM," BOL'SHAIA SOVETSKAIA ENTSIKLOPEDIIA. Vol. 31. Moscow: Gosudarstvennyi Institut "Sovetskaia Entsiklopediia," (OGIZ RSFSR), 1937, 452-453 pp. [Russ. text; Europ. titles, p. 453]

*Dzens-Litovskii, A. I. KARA-BOGAZ-GOL. Leningrad: "Nedra," 1967, 95 pp., 4000 copies. [Russ. text; titles pp. 91-94]

*Dzhordzhio, Z. V. "OPYT DOLGOSROCHNYKH PROGNOZOV STOKA REK SREDNEI AZII." SREDNE AZIAT. GOS. UN-T IM. LENINA. TRUDY. (NOVAIA SERIIA) No. 107 (GEOGR. NAUKI) KN. 11. Tashkent: (Sredneaziat. Gos. Un-t im. Lenina), 1957. [Russ. text; 192 Russ., other titles, pp. 192-200]

Fedchenko, A. P. PUTESHESTVIE V TURKESTAN. Moscow: Geografgiz, 1950. [Russ. text; 85 Russ. titles, pub.: 1868-1939, pp. 462-466]

Central Asia: Geography

*G. N. "KARAKORUM," ENTSIKLOPEDICHESKII SLOVAR'. Vol. 14. St. Petersburg: F. A. Brokgauz, I. A. Efron, 1895, 436-437 pp. [Russ. text; Russ., Europ. titles, p. 437]

"GEOGRAFICHESKAIA LITERATURA ROSSII EVROPEISKOI I AZIATSKOI I PRILEZHASHCHIKH STRAN, IZVESTIIA RUS. GEOGR. O-VA." Vol. 29, No. 4, 1893, 24-25 pp.; Vol. 30, No. 1, 1894, 142 pp.; No. 2, 1894, 327-328 pp.; No. 6, 1894, 803-804 pp.; Vol. 31, No. 2, 1895, 249-250 pp. [Russ. text and titles]

*Gerasimov, I. P. ed. SREDNIAIA AZIIA. Moscow: "Nauka," 1968, 484 pp., 2,800 copies. [Russ. text; titles 455-469 pp.]

Gorodetskii, V. D.; M. N. Gorodetskaia, compilers. BIBLIOGRAFIIA TURKESTANA. Vol. 1. [See also: BIBLIOGRAFICHESKII UKAZATEL' KNIG I STATEI PO TURKESTANOVEDENIIU]. Tashkent: Tipo-Lit. V. M. Il'ina, 1913, 166 pp. [Russ. text; 3,642 titles, pub: to Oct., 1912]

*Grum -Grzhimailo, G. E. "ILIISKII KRAI," ENTSIKLOPEDICHESKII SLOVAR'. Vol. 12A. St. Petersburg, F. A. Brokgauz, I. A. Efron, 1894, 920-922 pp. [Russ. text and titles, p. 922]

*_____. "TIAN'-SHAN'" ENTSIKLOPEDICHESKII SLOVAR'. Vol. 34. St. Petersburg: F. A. Brokgauz, I. A. Efron, 1902, 390-394 pp. [Russ. text; Russ., Europ. titles, p. 394]

Gvozdetskii, N. A. LEV SEMENOVICH BERG KAK ISSLEDOVATEL' SREDNEI AZII. VOPROSY GEOGRAFII. Sb. 24. 1951. [Russ. text; 59 Russ. titles, pp. 50-51]

_____. "PRIRODNO-GEOGRAFICHESKOE RAIONIROVANIE SREDNEI AZII," FIZIKO-GEOGRAFICHESKOE RAIONIROVANIE SSSR. Moscow, 1960, 169-207 pp. [Russ. text; 107 Russ. titles, pub.: 1926-1957, pp. 202-207]

I. V. MUSHKETOV (RUSSKIE UCHENYE-ISSLEDOVATELI SREDNEI AZII. T. 3). Tashkent: Gosizdat, UzSSR, 1960. [Russ. text; 79 Russ. titles, per.: 1876-1915, pp.294-302]

Central Asia: Geography

Iakovkin, Inn. I. "LITERATURA PO MINERAL'NOMU SYR'IU
SREDNEI AZII. (MATERIALY DLIA BIBLIOGRAFII),"
MINERAL'NYE BOGATSTVO SREDNEI AZII. Leningrad:
(Tadzhiksko-Pamirskaja ekspeditsiia pri SNK SSSR.
Narkomtiazhprom NIS Tekhprom), 1935. [Russ. text;
969 titles, per.: 1867-1933, pp. 517-568]

*Islamov, O. I. "IZ ISTORII GORNOGO DELA I
GEOLOGICHESKIKH PREDSTAVLENII V NARODOV SREDNEI AZII
S DREVNEISHIKH VREMEN DO XVII V." OCHERKI PO ISTORII
GEOLOGICHESKIKH ZNANII. No. 4. Moscow: Izdatel'stvo
Akademii Nauk SSSR, 1955. [Russ. text and titles,
pp. 68-69]

*"ISSYK-'KUL'" ENTSIKLOPEDICHESKII SLOVAR'. Vol. 13.
St. Petersburg: F. A. Brokgauz, I. A. Efron, 1894,
460-462. [Russ. text and titles, p. 462]

*"IZDANIIA TURKESTANSKOGO OTDELA RUSSKOGO GEOGRAFICHESKOGO
OBSHCHESTVA, 1898-1926. BIULLETEN; SAGU. No. 18.
Tashkent: (Sredne-Aziatskii Otdel Gos. Russkogo
Geograficheskogo Obshchestva, 1929, 228 pp. [Russ.
text; 50 Russ. titles, pub.: 1898-1926; pp. 180-182
(separate: 23 pp.)]

Kariev, M. FIZICHESKAIA GEOGRAFIIA SREDNEI AZII.
Tashkent: Uchpedgiz UzSSR, 1959. [Uzbek text; 115
Russ. titles, pp. 251-254]

*Kaufman, A. "AKMOLINSKAIA OBLAST,'" ENTSIKLOPEDICHESKII
SLOVAR'. Supplementary Vol. 1. St. Petersburg:
F. A. Brokgauz, I. A. Efron, 1905, 57-61 pp.
[Russ. text and titles, p. 61]

*_____. "TURGAISKAIA OBLAST'" ENTSIKLOPEDICHESKII
SLOVAR'. Vol 34. St. Petersburg: F. A. Brokgauz,
I. A. Efron, 1902, 88-95 pp. [Russ. text and titles,
p. 95]

*Kogai, N. A. FIZIKO-GEOGRAFICHESKOE RAIONIROVANIE
TURANSKOI CHASTI SREDNEI AZII. Tashkent: "Fan,"
1969, 132 pp., 500 copies. [Russ. text; 282 Russ.,
Eng. titles, pub.: 1865-1967, pp. 117-130]

Korzhenevskii, N. L. "LITERATURNYE UKAZANIIA.
FIZIKO-GEOGRAFICHESKII OCHERK SREDNEI AZII,"
Korzhenevskii, N. L. TURKESTAN. Tashkent, 1922, 1925
(1st and 2nd eds.), 1941 (3rd ed.). [Russ. text;
336 titles, (1st ed.) pp. 67-74; (2nd ed.) pp. 89-98]

Central Asia: Geography

*Kuznetsov, N. T. VODY TSENTRAL'NOI AZII. Moscow: Izdatel'stvo "Nauka," 1968, 272 pp., 1150 copies. [Russ. text; Russ., Mongolian, Chinese, Europ. titles, pp. 260-271]

*Lagovskaia, E. I. SOIUZNYE RESPUBLIKI SREDNEI AZII. POSOBIE DLIA UCHITELEI. Moscow: Gosudarstvennoe Uchebno-Pedagogicheskoe Izdatel'stvo Ministerstva Prosveshcheniia RSFSR, 1959, 191 pp., 12,000 copies. [Russ. text and titles, pp. 185-186]

*Massal'skii, V. "PAMIR, PAMIRY," ENTSIKLOPEDICHESKII SLOVAR'. Vol. 22A. St. Petersburg: F. A. Brokgauz, I. A. Efron, 1897, 664-671 pp. [Russ. text; Russ., Europ. titles, p. 671]

"MERV," EVREISKAIA ENTSIKLOPEDIIA. Vol. 10. St. Petersburg: Izdanie Obshchestva Dlia Nauchnykh Evreiskikh Izdanii i Izdatel'stva Brokgauz-Efron, n. d., 887 pp. [Russ. text; Europ. titles, p. 887]

Minaev, I. "BIBLIOGRAFICHESKII UKAZATEL'", Minaev, I. SVEDENIIA O STRANAKH PO VERKHOV'IAM AMU-DAR'I. (OTCHET RUSSKOGO GEOGRAFICHESKOGO OBSHCHESTVA ZA 1880 G.). St. Petersburg: Izd. Russk. Geogr. Obshch., 1879. [Russ. text; 168 titles, pub.: 1878, pp. 43-45]

_____. SVEDENIIA O STRANAKH PO VERKOV'IAM AMU-DAR'I. St. Petersburg: Tip. V. S. Balasheva, 1879. [Russ. text; Russ., Europ. titles, pp. 243-254]

*Molchanov, L. A. "SPISOK GLAVNEISHEI LITERATURY PO OZERAM SREDNEI AZII," TRUDY SREDNEAZIATSKOGO GOS. UNIVERSITETA. SERIIA XII-A "GEOGRAFIIA." No. 3. Tashkent, 1929. [Russ. text; 199 titles, pp. 62-72, 81]

*Murzaev, E. M. SKHEMA FIZIKO-GEOGRAFICHESKOGO RAIONIROVANIIA SREDNEI AZII. IZVESTIIA AKADEMII NAUK SSSR. SERIA. GEOGRAFICHESKAIA. No. 6, 1953. [Russ. text; 42 Russ. titles, pp. 29-30; 17-30]

_____. SREDNIAIA AZIIA. Moscow: Geografgiz, 1961. [Russ. text; ca.100 Russ. titles, pub.: 1913-1960, pp. 235-239]

* _____. SREDNIAIA AZIIA. FIZ-GEOGR. OCHERK. Moscow: Geografgiz, 1957, 269 pp., 10,000 copies. [Russ. text; 100 Russ. titles, Sov. per., pp. 258-262]

Central Asia: Geography

[Murzaev, E. M. ed.] SREDNIAIA AZIIA. FIZ.-GEOGR. KHARAKTERISTIKA. Moscow: (Akad. Nauk SSR In-t Geografii), 1958. [Russ. text; ca.500 titles, pp. 611-624]

Mushketov, I. V. SBORNIK DOKUMENTOV. Tashkent: Gosizdat UzSSR, 1960, 335 pp. [Russ. text; titles per.: pre-1917, pp.294-302]

*Nikol'skii, A. M. "SEMIRIECHENSKAIA OBLAST'," ENTSIKLOPEDICHESKII SLOVAR'. Vol. 29. St. Petersburg: F. A. Brokgauz, I. A. Efron, 1900, 457-461 pp. [Russ. text; Russ., Europ. titles, p. 461]

N. M. PRZHEVAL'SKII. (1839-1888-1939). PERVYI ISSLEDOVATEL' TSENTR. AZII... Tomsk: Nauch. B-ka pri Tomskom Gos. Un-te im. V. V. Kuibysheva, 1939, 8 pp., 500 copies. [Russ. text; 103 titles, pub.: 1869-1939]

*Nikol'skii, A. M. "ILI," ENTSIKLOPEDICHESKII SLOVAR'. Vol. 12A. St. Petersburg: F. A. Brokgauz, I. A. Efron, 1894, 916-917 pp. [Russ. text and titles, p. 917]

*Obruchev, V. "TSENTRAL'NAIA AZIIA," BOL'SHAIA SOVETSKAIA ENTSIKLOPEDIIA. Vol. 60. Moscow: Gosudarstvennoe Slovarno-Entsiklopedicheskoe Izdatel'stvo "Sovetskaia Entsiklopediia" (OGIZ RSFSR), 1934, 482-487 pp. [Russ. text; Russ., Europ. titles, pp. 486-487]

*_____. PO GORAM' I PUSTYNIAM SREDNEI AZII. Moscow-Leningrad: Izdatel'stvo Akademii Nauk SSSR, 1948, 244 pp., 7000 copies. [Russ. text; Turkmen, Russ. titles, pub.: 1887-1940, pp. 241-242]

Omarov, O. Iu. OTVAZHNYI ISSLEDOVATEL' KASPIISKOGO MORIA. Makhachkala, 1965. [Russ. text; 49 titles, pp. 77-80]

Pankov, A. V. "SPISOK IZDANII TURKESTANSKOGO OTDELA RUSSKOGO GEOGRAFICHESKOGO OBSHCHESTVA," IZVESTIIA TURKESTANSKOGO OTDELA RUSSKOGO GEOGRAFICHESKOGO OBSHCHESTVA. Vol. XV, 1922. [Russ. text; 42 titles, pp. 11-12]

*Perevalov, V. A. "SREDNIAIA I TSENTRAL'NAIA AZIIA V TRUDAKH RUSSKOGO GEOGRAFICHESKOGO OBSHCHESTVA," PRIRODA. No. 8, 1946. [Russ. text; 40 Russ. titles, per.: 1831-1940 pp. 77-80]

*PERVYE RUSSKIE NAUCHNYE ISSLEDOVANIIA USTIURTA. Moscow: Izdatel'stvo Akademii Nauk SSSR, 1963, 326 pp., 800 copies. [Russ. text; Russ., Europ. titles, per.: 1825-1853, pp. 301-305]

Central Asia: Geography

*Petrov, M. P. PUSTYNI TSENTRAL'NOI AZII. V 2-KH T.
Vol. 1. ORDOS, ALASHAN', BEISHAN'. Moscow-Leningrad:
"Nauka" (Leningr. Otd-nie), 1966, 274 pp., 1300 copies.
[Russ. text; ca.220 titles, pp. 256-263]

*_____. PUSTYNI TSENTRAL'NOI AZII. V 2-KH T.
Vol. 2. KORIDOR KHESI, TSAIDAM, TARIMSKAIA VPADINA.
Moscow-Leningrad: "Nauka," 1967, 288 pp., 1200 copies.
[Russ. text; ca.220 titles, pp. 273-279]

Pogrebetskii, M. "BIBLIOGRAFIIA," Pogrebetskii, M.
PRAKTIKA TURIZMA I PUTESHESTVII. Moscow-Leningrad,
1930. [Russ. text; 64 titles, pp. 231-234]

Popov, V. L. "SPISOK NEKOTORYKH ISTOCHNIKOV PO SREDNEI
AZII," Popov, V. L. VOENNAIA GEOGRAFIIA. OBZOR
RUSSKOI PRIGRANICHNOI POLOSY AZII. Book 2.
SREDNEAZIATSKII FRONT. Moscow: Voennaia Akademiia
RKKA im. M. V. Frunze, 1926. [Russ. text; 46 titles,
pp. 163-164]

Rabinerson, A. I. BIBLIOGRAFICHESKII UKAZATEL' PO
GEOGRAFII TURKESTANA. n. d. [Russ. text; 1045 titles,
pub.: to 1928]

Rakhimbekov, R. U. "PUSTYNI SREDNEI AZII V TRUDAKH
UCHENYKH SREDNEAZIATSKOGO UNIVERSITETA," NAUCH.
TRUDY TASHK. UN-TA. No. 344., 1969. [Russ. text;
56 titles, pp. 83-84]

*Rudakov, V. "KARABUGAZSKII ZALIV," ENTSIKLOPEDICHESKII
SLOVAR'. Vol. 14A. St. Petersburg: F. A.
Brokgauz, I. A. Efron, 1895, 670-672 pp. [Russ. text;
Russ., Europ. titles, p. 672]

Rusanova, T. A. "A I. VOEIKOV O PREOBRAZOVANII PRIRODY
SREDNEI AZII," NAUCHNYE ZAPISKI (LENINGR. FIN-EKON.
IN-T), No. 12, 1956. [Russ. text; 56 Russ., foreign
titles, pp. 32-34]

SBORNIK AFTOREFERATOV NEOPUBLIKOVANNYKH RABOT SAGU. ZA
1939-1944 GG. (BIUL. SREDNEAZ. GOS. UN-TA). No. 23.
Tashkent, 1946, 199 pp., 2000 copies. [Russ. text;
231 titles, per.: completed 1939-1944]

SBORNIK GEOGRAFICHESKIKH, TOPOGRAFICHESKIKH I
STATISTICHESKIKH MATERIALOV PO AZII. No. 10.
(No. 18 covers 1883-1914 publications). St.
Petersburg, 1885. [Russ. text; pub. 19th c.]

Central Asia: Geography

Semenov-Tian-Shanskii, P. P. PUTESHESTVIE V TIAN'-SHAN'. 1856-1857. Moscow: Geografgiz, 1958, 277 pp. [Russ. text; 81 Russ. titles, per: 1856-1857, pp. 271-275]

_____. MEMUARY. [Vol. 2] PUTESHESTVIE V TIAN'-SHAN'. Moscow, 1946. [Russ. text; 81 Russ., other titles, pub.: 1850-1946, pp. 251-254]

*Severtsov, N. A. PUTESHESTVIIA PO TURKESTANSKOMU KRAIU. Moscow: Gosudarstvennoe Izdatel'stvo Geograficheskoi Literatury, 1947 (2nd ed., first pub. 1873), 304 pp., 10,000 copies. [Russ. text; 74+24 Russ., Europ. titles]

Shchukin, I. S. OCHERKI FIZICHESKOI GEOGRAFII SREDNEI AZII. CH 1. Moscow: (Mosk. Gos. Un-t im. Lomonosova. Geogr. Fak.), 1956. [Russ. text; 206 titles, Sov. per., pp. 390-404]

*Shchukina, N. M. KAK SOZDAVALAS' KARTA TSENTRAL'NOI AZII. Moscow: Geografgiz, 1955, 237 pp., 10,000 copies. [Russ. text; ca.230 Russ. titles, pub.: 19th and 20th c., pp. 226-235]

_____. "OSNOVNYE RABOTY V. A. OBRUCHEVA PO SREDNEI AZII I KAZAKHSTANU," UCHEN. ZAPISKI (ALMA-AT. PED. IN-T) Vol. 6. 1955. [Russ. text; 17 titles, pub.: 1887-1952, p. 105]

*Shpindler, I. "KASPIISKOE MORE," ENTSIKLOPEDICHESKII SLOVAR'. Vol. 14A. St. Petersburg: F. A. Brokgauz, I. A. Efron, 1895, 667-670 pp. [Russ. text; Russ. Europ. titles, p. 670]

*Shokal'skii, Iu., M. Pervukhin. "KASPIISKOE MORE," BOL'SHAIA SOVETSKAIA ENTSIKLOPEDIIA. Vol. 31. Moscow: Gosudarstvennyi Institut "Sovetskaia Entsiklopediia," (OGIZ RSFSR), 1937, 694-699 pp. [Russ. text and titles, p. 699]

*Sinitsyn, V. M. TSENTRAL'NAIA AZIIA. Moscow: Gosudarstvennoe Izdatel'stvo Geograficheskoi Literatury, 1959, 456 pp., 4000 copies. [Russ. text; ca.140 Russ., Europ. titles, pp. 450-455]

*SREDNIAIA AZIIA. FIZIKO-GEOGRAFICHESKAIA KHARAKTERISTIKA. Moscow: Izdatel'stvo Akademii Nauk SSSR, 1958, 648 pp., 5000 copies. [Russ. text; ca.450 Russ., Europ. titles, pub. 1867-1955, pp. 611-624]

Central Asia: Geography

*Tikhmenev, General-Maior ed. OPYT VOENNO-STATISTICHESKAGO OPISANIIA ILIISKAGO KRAIA. Part 1. Tashkent: Izdanie Shtaba Turkestanskago Voennago Okruga, 1903, 299 pp. [Russ. text and titles, pp. V-VII]

*V. M. "ZERAVSHAN," ENTSIKLOPEDICHESKII SLOVAR'. Vol. 12A. St. Petersburg: F. A. Brokgauz, I. A. Efron, 1894, 554-556 pp. [Russ. text and titles, pp. 555-556]

VOPROSY GEOGRAFICHESKOGO RAIONIROVANIIA SREDNEI AZII. Tashkent: (Nauch. Trudy Tashk. Un-t im. Lenina. No. 307), 1967. [Russ. text; titles at end of articles]

Voznesenskaia, E. A.; A. B. Piotrovskii. MATERIALY PO ANTROPOLOGII I ETNOGRAFII KAZAKHSTANA I SREDNEAZIATSKIKH RESPUBLIK. Leningrad, 1927. [Russ. text]

Zabelin, I. M., et al. KAZAKHSKAIA SSR. UZBEKSKAIA SSR. KIRGIZSKAIA SSSR. TADZHIKSKAIA SSR. TURKMENSKAIA SSR. Moscow: Geografgiz, 1956, 112 pp., 5000 copies. [Russ. text; 48 Russ. titles, Sov. per., pp. 109-111]

Zatulovskii, D. M. SREDI SNEGOV I SKAL. Moscow: Geografgiz, 1957. [Russ. text; 85 titles, Sov. per. pp. 554-556]

Zolotnitskaia, R. L. "BIBLIOGRAFIIA TRUDOV N. A. Severtsov I LITERTURA O EGO ZHIZNI I DEIATEL'NOSTI," Zolotnitskaia, R. L.; N. A. Severtsov. Moscow, 1953. [Russ. text; 174 Russ., Europ. titles, pub.: 1850-1952, pp. 196-209]

HISTORY. ARCHAEOLOGY

*Ageeva, E. I.; T. N. Zadneprovskaia. "BIBLIOGRAFIIA PO ARCHEOLOGII I DREVNEI ISTORII SYR-DAR'I I SEMIRECH'IA." TRUDY IN-TA ISTORII ARKHEOLOGII I ETNOGRAFII AKADEMII NAUK, KAZAKHSKOI SSR). Vol. 7. ARKHEOLOGIIA. n. p. 1959, 307 pp., 320 copies. [Russ. text; 597 Russ. titles, pub.: 1821-1956; per.: ancient, pp. 270-307]

Central Asia: History, Archaeology

*"AKHAL-TEKINSKIIA EKSPEDITSII," VOENNAIA ENTSIKLOPEDIIA.
Vol. 3. St. Petersburg: T-vo I. D. Sytina, 1911, 283-
291 pp. [Russ. text and titles, p. 291]

"AKHALTEKINSKIE EKSPEDITSII," SOVETSKAIA VOENNAIA
ENTSIKLOPEDIIA. Vol. 1. Moscow: Gosudarstvennoe
Slovarno-Entsiklopedicheskoe Izdatel'stvo "Sovetskaia
Entsiklopediia," Ogiz RSFSR, 1932, 954-955 pp. [Russ.
text and titles, p. 955]

*AKHUN, M.; V. A. Petrov. MATERIALY PO ISTORII
UZBEKSKOI, TADZHIKSKOI I TURKMENSKOI SSR. Part 1.
Leningrad: Izd-vo Akad. Nauk SSSR, 1932, 506 pp.,
1500 copies. [Russ. text; ca.250 Russ., Europ.
titles, per.: XVI-XVII c., pub.: up to 1930]

[Ashin, V. D.] "ALEKSANDR NIKOLAEVICH SAMOILOVICH (1880-
1938)," NARODY AZII I AFRIKI. Vol. 2, 1963, 243-264 pp.,
[Russ. text; titles pp. 253-264]

*"AMU-DAR'IA," VOENNAIA ENTSIKLOPEDIIA. Vol. 2.
St. Petersburg: T-vo I. D. Sytina, 1911, 400 pp. [Russ.
text and titles, p. 400]

*"ARAL'SKAIA FLOTILIIA," VOENNAIA ENTSIKLOPEDIIA. Vol. 3.
St. Petersburg: T-vo I. D. Sytina, 1911, 1 p. [Russ.
text and titles, p. 1]

*Babakhodzhaev, A. Kh. PROVAL AGRESSIVNOI POLITIKI
ANGLIISKOGO IMPERIALIZMA V SREDNEI AZII V 1917-1920 GG.
Tashkent: (Akad. Nauk Uzbek SSR. In-t Vostokovedeniia.),
1955, 157 pp., 2000 copies. [Russ. text; 93 Russ.
titles, pp. 155-157]

*"BADAKHSHAN," VOENNAIA ENTSIKLOPEDIIA, Vol. 4.
St. Petersburg: T-vo I. D. Sytina, 1911, 334-335 pp.
[Russ. text; Russ., Europ. titles, p. 335]

*Barthold, W. "BUKHARA," THE ENCYCLOPAEDIA OF ISLAM.
Vol. 1, 1913, 776-783 pp. [Russ. text; Russ.,
European titles, p. 783]

*"BARTOL'D, VASILII VLADIMIROVICH," IMPERATORSKAIA
AKADEMIIA NAUK. 1889-1914. Vol. 3. MATERIALY DLIA
BIOGRAFICHESKAGO SLOVARIA DIESTVITEL'NYKH CHLENOV
IMPERATORSKOI AKADEMII NAUK. Petrograd: Tipografiia
Imperatorskoi Akademii Nauk, 1915, 19-24 pp. [Russ.
text; 168 Russ., Europ. titles, pub.: 1892-1913, pp.20-24]

*Bartol'd, V. "TIMUR (TAMERLAN)," ENTSIKLOPEDICHESKII
SLOVAR'. Vol. 33. St. Petersburg: F. A. Brokgauz,
I. A. Efron, 1901, 195-197 pp. [Russ. text; Russ.
Europ. titles, pp. 196-197]

"BASMACHESTVO," SOVETSKAIA VOENNAIA ENTSIKLOPEDIIA.
Vol. 2. Moscow: Gosudarstvennoe Slovarno-
Entsiklopedicheskoe Izdatel'stvo "Sovetskaia
Entsiklopediia," Ogiz RSFSR, 1933, pp. 22-226. [Russ.
text and titles, pp. 225-226]

*Batrakov, V. S. "O RAZDELENII TRUDA MEZHDU KOCHEVYMI I
OSEDLYMI RAIONAMI," TRUDY SREDNEAZIAT. UN-TA. No. 75.
(EKON. NAUKI), Book 1, 1955. [Russ. text; 53 titles,
pp. 137-138]

Betger, E. K.; A. V. Pankov. BIBLIOGRAFICHESKII
UKAZATEL' LITERATURY PO TURKESTANOVEDENIIU ZA 1914-
1915 GG. IZVIESTIIA TURKESTANSKAGO OTDIELA RUSSKAGO
GEOGRAFICHESKAGO OBSHCHESTVA. Vol. XII, No. 2, 1916;
Vol. 13, No. 1, 1917. [Russ. text; titles (1916) p. 9.
(1917) pp. 28-32, pub.: 1914-1915]

_____. "ROSPIS' STAT'IAM I ZAMETKAM PO ARKHEOLOGII
I ISTORII SREDNEI AZII, POMESHCHENNYM V GAZETE
'TURKESTANSKIE VEDOMOSTI' ZA VREMIA EE SUSHCHESTVOVANIIA.
APR. 1870--DEC. 1917," V. V. BARTOL'DU. TURKESTANSKIE
DRUZ'IA, UCHENIKI I POCHITATELI. Tashkent, 1927, 55 pp.
[Russ. text; 772 titles, pub.: 1870-1917, pp. 481-531]

_____. "SPISOK TRUDOV VASILIIA LAVRENT'EVICHA
VIATKINA," TRUDY TASHKENTSKOGO GOSUDARSTVENNOGO
UNIVERSITETA IM. I. V. LENINA. ARKHEOLOGIIA SREDNEI
AZII. 5. NOVAIA SERIIA, No. 172. ISTORICHESKIE
NAUKI, Book 37, 1960. 212 pp. [Russ. text; titles
per. 1859-1932]

_____. UKAZATEL' K GAZETE "TURKESTANSKIE VIEDOMOSTI"
ZA 1870-1892 GG. 193 pp. [Russ. text; 2,759 titles,
pub. 1870-1892]

Bisnek, A. G. SREDNIAIA AZIIA (TURKESTAN) NA
STRANITSAKH ZHURNALA "VOENNYI SBORNIK" 1858-1917,
n. p., n. d. [Russ. text; 306 titles, pub.: 1858-1917]

*Borodovskii, L. "CHZHUNGARIIA, DZHUNGARIIA, DZIUNGARIIA,"
ENTSIKLOPEDICHESKII SLOVAR'. Vol. 38A. St. Petersburg:
F. A. Brokgauz, I. A. Efron, 1903, 805-809 pp. [Russ.
text; Russ., Europ. titles, p. 809]

Braginskii, I. S.; L. M. Landa; N. A. Khalfin.
SOVETSKOE ISSLEDOVANIE PO ISTORII SREDNEI AZII I
KAZAKHSTANA. Moscow: "Nauka," 1967, 39 pp. [Russ.
text; 16 English titles, pp. 37-39]

Central Asia: History, Archaeology

*"BUKHARA," NOVYI ENTSIKLOPEDICHESKII SLOVAR'. Vol. 8.
n. d. 739-754 pp. [Russ. text; Russ., Europ. titles,
pp. 751-752]

"BUKHARA," SOVETSKAIA VOENNAIA ENTSIKLOPEDIIA. Vol. 2.
Moscow: Gosudarstvennoe Slovarno-Entsiklopedicheskoe
Izdatel'stvo "Sovetskaia Entsiklopediia" Ogiz, RSFSR,
1933, 867-872 pp. [Russ. text and titles, p. 872]

*"BUKHARA," VOENNAIA ENTSIKLOPEDIIA. Vol. 5. St.
Petersburg: T-vo I. D. Sytina, 1911, 171-174 pp.
[Russ. text and titles, p. 174]

Burov, N. A. TOCHNYE NAUKI V TURKESTANE V 1917-1922 GG.
UKAZATEL' LITERATURY PO ESTESTVOZNANIIU I
MATEMATIKE, VYSHEDSHEI V TURKESTANE ZA UKAZANNYI PERIOD
VREMENI. IZVESTIIA TURKESTANSKOGO OTDELA RUSSKOGO
GEOGRAFICHESKOGO OBSHCHESTVA. Vol. 17. (Tashkent)
1924. [Russ. text; titles, pp. 227-244]

_____. UKAZATEL' LITERATURY PO ESTESTVOZNANIIU
I MATEMATIKE, VYSHEDSHEI V TURKESTANE ZA 1917-1922 GG.
IZVESTIIA TURKESTANSKOGO OTDELA RUSSKOGO
GEOGRAFICHESKOGO OBSHCHESTVA. Vol. 17. 1924. [Russ.
text; pub. : 1917-1922, titles pp. 229-244]

Chekaninskii, I. A. "LITERATURA PO VOPROSY VOSSTANIIA
TUZEMTSEV SREDNEI AZII V 1916 GODU. (BIBLIOGR.
ZAMETKA)," ZAPISKI SEMIPALAT. OTD. O-VA IZUCHENIIA
KAZAKHSTANA," Vol. 1, No. 18. 1929. [Russ. text; 79
Kazakh, Russ. titles, per.: 1917, pp. 105-109]

Chernovskii, A. "BIBLIOGRAFIIA NELEGAL'NOI LITERATURY.
S PRED. S. MURAVEISKOGO." KOMMUNIST. ("BIBLIOGRAFIIA
TURKESTANSKOI NELEGAL'NOI PECHATI" 1905-1909.) No. 7/8.
Tashkent, 1922. [Russ. text; titles pp. 7-8, 95-112,
per.: 1905-1909]

Dobrosmyslov, A. I. TASHKENT V PROSHLOM I NASTOIASHCHEM.
ISTORICHESKII OCHERK. Tashkent, 1911. [Russ. text;
titles, pp. 286-296, per.: 1870--Apr. 1911]

*"DOPOLNENIIA K BIBLIOGRAFII NAUCHNYKH TRUDOV AKADEMIKA
AN TADZHIKSKOI SSR A. A. SEMENOVA," PROBLEMY
VOSTOKOVEDENIIA. No. 1. Moscow, 1959. Russ. text;
22 Russ. titles, pub.: 1953-1958, pp. 242-243]

*"DZHIZAK," VOENNAIA ENTSIKLOPEDIIA. Vol. 9.
St. Petersburg, T-vo I. D. Sytina, 1912, 84-85.
[Russ. text and titles, p. 85]

Central Asia: History, Archaeology

*Egorov, D. N. "BIBLIOGRAFIIA SREDNEI AZII," NAUCHNAIA ASSOTSIATSIIA VOSTOKOVEDENIIA. BIBLIOGRAFIIA VOSTOKA. Vol. 1. "ISTORIIA (1917-1925)." Moscow: (Nauch. Assotsiatsiia Vostokovedeniia pri TsIK SSSR), 1928, 302 pp. [Russ. text; 82 Russ. titles, per.: 1917-1925, pp. 109-119]

Fedorov, E. "BIBLIOGRAFIIA NELEGAL'NOI LITERATURY REVOLIUTSII 1905 GODA V SREDNEI AZII," IZVESTIIA SRED.-AZ. KOM. PO DELAM MUZEEV I OKHRANY PAMIATNIKOV STARINY ISSKUSTVA I PRIRODY "SREDAZKOMSTARIS." No. 1. 1926. [Russ. text; 245 Russ. titles, per.: 1905, pp. 280-297]

Gurevich, A. "O POLOZHENII NA ISTORICHESKOM FRONTE SREDNEI AZII," REVOLIUTSIIA I KUL'TURA V SREDNEI AZII. SBORNIK PERVYI. Tashkent, 1934. [Russ. text; 4-13 pp.]

*I. Kh. "KHIVA," BOL'SHAIA SOVETSKAIA ENTSIKLOPEDIIA. Vol. 59, 1935 (1st ed.), 528-535 pp. [Russ. text and titles, p. 535]

*Iakubovskii, A. Iu. "PAVEL PETROVICH IVANOV KAK ISTORIK SREDNEI AZII," SOVETSKOE VOSTOKOVEDENIE. Vol. 5. Moscow-Leningrad, 1948, 313-320 pp. [Russ. text; Russian survey, pub.: 1893-1942, p. 316]

*"ILIISKII KRAI," VOENNAIA ENTSIKLOPEDIIA. Vol. 10. St. Petersburg: T-vo I. D. Sytina, 1912, 586-587 pp. [Russ. text and titles, p. 587]

*INNOSTRANNAIA VOENNAIA INTERVENTSIIA I GRAZHDANSKAIA VOINA V SREDNEI AZII I KAZAKHSTANE. Vols. 1-2. Alma Ata: Izd-vo Akad. Nauk Kaz. SSR, 1963-1964, Vol. 1 701 pp., 4,500 copies; Vol. 2 724 pp., 4,240 copies. [Russ. text; ca.100 Russ. titles, Sov. per. (Vol. 1) pp. 698-700; (Vol. 2) pp. 722-723]

*Inoiatov, Kh. Sh. OTVET FAL'SIFIKATORAM ISTORII SOVETSKOI SREDNEI AZII I KAZAKHSTANA. Tashkent: Gosudarstvennoe Izdatel'stvo Uzbekskoi SSR, 1962, 198 pp., 5000 copies. [Russ. text; ca.130 Russ. titles, pub.: 1955-1961, pp. 192-197]

"IRDZHAR," VOENNAIA ENTSIKLOPEDIIA. Vol. 11. St. Petersburg: T-vo I. D. Sytina, 1913, 22-23 pp. [Russ. text and titles, p. 23]

Ishanov, A. I. BUKHARSKAIA NARODNAIA SOVETSKAIA RESPUBLIKA. Tashkent, 1969. [Russ. text; ca.160 titles, pp. 9-16, 381-390]

Central Asia: History, Archaeology

*Iuldashbaeva, F. Kh. IZ ISTORII ANGLIISKOI KOLONIAL'NOI POLITIKI V AFGANISTANE I SREDNEI AZII (70-80-E GODY XIX V). Tashkent, 1963, 190 pp., 2000 copies. [Russ. text; ca.200Russ., Europ. titles, per.: 1870's-1880's, pp. 181-190]

Iunuskhodzhaeva, M. Iu. IZ ISTORII ZEMLEVLADENIIA V DOREVOLIUTSIONNOM TURKESTANE. Tashkent, 1970. [Russ. text; ca.160 titles, pp. 104-111]

*Ivanov, P. P. OCHERKI PO ISTORII SREDNEI AZII. (XVI-SEREDINA XIX V.) Moscow: Izdatel'stvo Vostochnoi Literatury (Akad. Nauk SSSR, In-t Vostokovedeniia), 1958, 247 pp., 3,800 copies. [Russ. text; ca.250 Russ., Europ. titles, per.: XV-mid XIX c., pp. 227-246]

*Kn. V. M. "TURKESTAN," ENTSIKLOPEDICHESKII SLOVAR'. Vol. 34, 1902, 174-203 pp. [Russ., Europ. titles, pp. 201-203]

"K VOPROSU O NAUCHOI RAZRABOTKE ISTORII OKTIABR'SKOI SOTSIALISTICHESKOI REVOLIUTSII V TURKESTANE (OBZOR OPUBLIKOVANNOI LITERATURY)," IZVESTIIA AKADEMII NAUK UZSSR, SERIIA OBSHCHESTVENNYKH NAUK. No. 4. 1957. [Russ. text; survey, per.: 1917-1918, pp. 63-79]

Kadyrova, T. IZ ISTORII KREST'IANSKIKH VOSSTANII V MAVERANNAKHRE I KHORASANE V VIII-NACHALE IX V. Tashkent, 1965. [Russ. text; ca.350 titles, per.: 8th - 9th c., pp. 13-32, 195-213]

KARAKUMSKIE DREVNOSTI. SBORNIK STATEI. No. 1. PREDVARITEL'NYE SOOBSHCHENIIA OB ARKHEOLOGICHESKIKH RABOTAKH V 1967 G. V ZONE OROSHAEMYKH ZEMEL' III OCHEREDI KARAKUMSKOGO KANALA IM. V. I. LENINA. Ashkhabad: (An TSSR. In-t Istorii im. Sh. Batyrova), 1968, 66 pp., 500 copies. [Russ. text; titles at end of articles]

*"KASHGARIIA (VOSTOCHNYI ILI KITAISKII TURKESTAN)," VOENNAIA ENTSIKLOPEDIIA. Vol. 12. St. Petersburg: T.-vo I. D. Sytina, 1913, 468-473 pp. [Russ. text and titles, p. 473]

*"KASPIISKOE MORE (KHVALYNSKOE)," VOENNAIA ENTSIKLOPEDIIA Vol. 12. St. Petersburg: T-vo I. D. Sytina, 1913, 440-442 pp. [Russ. text and titles, p. 442]

Central Asia: History, Archaeology

*"KAUFMAN, KONSTANTIN PETROVICH," VOENNAIA
ENTSIKLOPEDIIA. Vol. 12. St. Petersburg: T-vo I. D.
Sytina, 1913, 461-462 pp. [Russ. text and titles,
p. 462]

Khakimov, M. Kh., Ia. M. Seryi. "BOR'BA BOL'SHEVIKOV
TURKESTANA ZA UPROCHENIE MESTNYKH SOVETOV (NOIABR'
1917 G.--OKTIABR' 1918 G.)" TRUDY (TASHK. GOS. UN-T)
ISTORIIA KPSS. NOVAIA SERIIA. No. 199. IST. NAUKI.
Book 40, 1962, 70-89 pp. [Russ. text; 87 Russ.
titles, per.: 1917-1918; pub.: 1917-1960, pp. 86-89]

*Khalfin, N. A. PRISOEDINENIE SREDNEI AZII K ROSSII.
(60-90-E GODY XIX V.) Moscow: Izdatel'stvo "Nauka."
Glavnaia Redaktsiia Vostochnoi Literatury, 1965,
448 pp., 1,750 copies. [Russ. text; ca.560 Russ.
Europ. titles, incl. archives, per.: 1860's-1890's,
pp. 9-45, 445-467]

Khasanov, K. TSK VKP(B) V BOR'BE ZA POSTROENIE
SOTSIALIZMA V SREDNEI AZII. (1924-1937 GG.)
Tashkent, 1968. [Russ. text; ca.350 titles, pp. 7-11;
201-214]

Kliashtornyi, S. G. DREVNETIURKSKIE RUNICHESKIE
PAMIATNIKI KAK ISTOCHNIK PO ISTORII SREDNEI AZII.
Moscow, 1964. [Russ. text; titles, pp. 181-211]

*"KORANDSKAIA EKSPEDITSIIA 1875-76 GG," VOENNAIA
ENTSIKLOPEDIIA. Vol. 13. St. Petersburg, T-vo I. D.
Sytina, 1913, 23-25 pp. [Russ. text and titles,
p. 25]

*"KOKANSKOE KHANSTVO," ENTSIKLOPEDICHESKII SLOVAR'."
Vol. 15A, 1895, 621-624 pp. [Russ. text; Russ.
Europ. titles, pp. 623-624]

*Kostenko, L. SREDNIAIA AZIIA I VODVORENIE V NEI
RUSSKOI GRAZHDANSTVENNOSTI. St. Petersburg: Izdanie
A. Th. Bazunova, 1870, 358+ pp. [Russ. text; 122
Russ., Europ. titles, pp. VII-XIII]

Kovalev, P. A. TYLOVYE RABOCHIE TURKESTANA V GODY
PERVOI MIROVOI VOINY. (1916-MAI 1917 G.) Tashkent:
Gosizdat UzSSR, 1957. [Russ. text; ca.400 titles,
per.: 1916-1917, pp. 172-186]

Krylova, V. G. "K VOPROSU O PERVYKH SOTSIALISTICHESKIKH
PREOBRAZOVANIIAKH V SOVETSKOM TURKESTANE," TRUDY
SREDNEAZIAT. UN-TA. No. 101. IST. NAUKI. Book 19.
1957. [Russ. text; ca.40 titles, Sov. per., pp. 113-
114]

Central Asia: History, Archaeology

*L. Sh-G. "UZBEKI," ENTSIKLOPEDICHESKII SLOVAR'.
Vol. 34A. St. Petersburg: F. A. Brokgauz, I. A.
Efron, 1902, pp. 608-610. [Russ. text; Russ., Europ.
titles, pp. 608-610]

*Landa, L. M. "SOVETSKAIA ISTORIOGRAFIIA NATSIONAL'NO-
GOSUDARSTVENNOGO RAZMEZHEVANIIA SREDNEI AZII,"
ISTORIIA SSSR. No. 6. 1964. [Russ. text; (survey)
pp. 66-80]

*Logofet, D. N. BUKHARSKOE KHANSTVO POD RUSSKIM
PROTEKTORATOM. Vol. 2. St. Petersburg: Izdatel'stvo
V. Berezovskii, 1911, 357 pp. [Russ. text; titles
pp. 351-355]

Lunin, B. V. "BIBLIOGRAFICHESKII, IMENNOI I
GEOGRAFICHESKII UKAZATEL' K PROTOKOLAM I SOOBSHCHENIIAM
TURKESTANSKOGO KRUZHKA LIUBITELEI ARKHEOLOGII (1895-
1917 GG.) CH. 1. BIBLIOGR. UKAZATEL'" ISTORIIA
MATERIAL'NOI KUL'TURY UZBEKISTANA. Tashkent: (Akad.
Nauk UzSSR. In-t Istorii i Arkheologii), 1959.
[Russ. text; pub.: 1895-1917, titles, pp. 231-256]

_____. "ISTORIIA I PAMIATNIKI MATERIAL'NOI
KUL'TURY KUSHANSKOGO PERIODA V SOVETSKOI LITERATURE.
BIBLIOGR. UKAZATEL'." OBSHCHESTVENNYE NAUKI V
UZBEKISTANE. No. 8. 1968. [Russ. text; ca.280
Russ. titles, pp. 65-82]

* _____. "ISTORIIA, KUL'TURA I ISKUSSTVO VREMENI
TIMURIDOV V SOVETSKOI LITERATURE. (BIBLIOGR.
UKAZATEL')" OBSHCHESTV. NAUKI V UZBEKISTANE. No. 8-9.
Tashkent: "Fan," 1969, 101-145 pp., 1,569 pp.,
[Russ. text; ca.830 Uzbek, Russ. titles, pub.: 1917-
1968, pp. 101-145]

* _____. IZ ISTORII RUSSKOGO VOSTOKOVEDENIIA I
ARKHEOLOGII V TURKESTANE. Tashkent: (Akad. Nauk
Uzbek SSR. In-t Istorii i Arkheologii), 1958,
319 pp., 650 copies. [Russ. text; ca.1250 Russ.
titles, pp. 247-319]

_____. "IZ NOVYKH PUBLIKATSII PO ISTORII
SREDNEI AZII DREVNIKH I SREDNIKH VEKOV," IZVESTIIA
AN UZSSR. No. 3. 1949. [Russ. text; survey
pp. 80-88]

_____. SREDNIAIA AZIIA V DOREVOLIUTSIONNOM I
SOVETSKOM VOSTOKOVEDENII. Tashkent, 1965. [Russ.
text; 1412 Russ. titles, pub.: 1867-1964, pp. 311-398]

Central Asia: History, Archaeology

* _____. "UKAZATEL' PECHATNYKH RABOT I. I. UMNIAKOVA S 1923 PO 1960 GODY," ISTORIIA MATERIAL'NOI KUL'TURY UZBEKISTANA. No. 3. Tashkent: Izd-vo Akad. Nauk Uzbek SSR, 1962, 158-168 pp., 1000 copies. [Russ. text; 53 Russ., Europ. titles, pub.: 1923-1960 pp. 165-168]

* _____. "UKAZATEL' PECHATNYKH RABOT I. I. UMNIAKOVA S 1923 PO 1960 GG." ISTORIIA MATERIAL'NOI KUL'TURY UZBEKISTANA. No. 3. Tashkent: Izdatel'stvo Akademii Nauk SSSR, 1962, 169 pp., 1000 copies. [Russ. text; 53 Russ. titles, pub.: 1923-1960, pp. 165-168]

Makarova, T. I. comp. PERVOBYTNOOBSHCHINNYI STROI. DREVNEISHIE GOSUDARSTVA ZAKAVKAZ'IA I SRED. AZII. DREVNIAIA RUS'. (DO NACHALA XIII V.) ISTORIIA SSSR. S DREVNEISHIKH VREMEN DO NASHIKH DNEI. Vol. 1. Moscow, 1966. [Russ. text; ca.450 titles, per. before XIII c., pp. 695-708]

*Mal'kevich, B. A. "MATERIALY K BIBLIOGRAFII TRUDOV N. IA. BICHURINA," BICHURIN (IAKINF), N. IA. SOBRANIE SVEDENII O NARODAKH OBITAVSHIKH V SREDNEI AZII V DREVNIE VREMENA. III PRILOZHENIIA. Moscow-Leningrad: Izdatel'stvo Akademii Nauk SSSR, 1953. 326 pp., 5000 copies. [Russ. text; 116+ Russ. titles incl. archives, pub.: 1827-1906; up to 1905, pp. 87-101]

*Masal'skii, V. "VIERNENSKOE ZEMLETRIASENIE," ENTSIKLOPEDICHESKII SLOVAR," Vol. 7A, St. Petersburg: F. A. Brokgauz, I. A. Efron, 1892, 641-642 pp. [Russ. text; Russ., Europ. titles, p. 642]

Maslova, O. V.; V. A. Viatkina; A. I. Kormilitsin, comps. "SISTEMATICHESKII UKAZATEL' K IZDANIIAM SREDNEAZIATSKOGO GOSUDARSTVENNOGO UNIVERSITETA IM. V. I. LENINA (1922-1956 GG.)" (SREDNEAZIAT. GOS. UN-T IM LENINA. MATERIAL K BIBLIOGRAFII, No. 8). Tashkent: (Sredneaziatskii Gosudarstvennyi Universitet Im. V. I. Lenina.), 1958 (2nd., revised and supplemented), 192 pp., 500 copies. [Russ. text; 2,026 Uzbek, Russ. titles, pub.: 1922-1956)

Masson, V. M. ARKHEOLOGIIA SREDNEI AZII. Moscow, "Nauka," 1967, 30 pp. [Russ. text; 100 English titles, pp. 21-30]

Central Asia: History, Archaeology

*Matveev, A. M.; G. B. Nikol'skaia. "VYKHODTSY IZ ZARUBEZHNYKH STRAN V KOMMUNISTICHESKOI PARTII TURKESTANA (1918-1920 GG.)," NAUCHNYE TRUDY (TASHK. GOS. UN-T) No. 238. MATERIALY PO ISTORII SREDNEI AZII I UZBEKISTANA. 1964, 32-49 pp. [Russ. text; 87 Russ., foreign titles, per.: 1918-1920, pub.: 1918-1963, pp. 45-49]

METALLICHESKIE IZDELIIA ENEOLITA I BRONZOVOGO VEKA V SREDNEI AZII. Moscow: Izdatel'stvo "Nauka," 1966, 151 pp., 900 copies. [Russ. text; ca.490 titles, per.: bronze and eneolit c., pub.: before 1964, pp. 110-116]

Mezhov, V. I. BIBLIOGRAFIIA ASIATICA. BIBLIOGRAFIIA AZII. UKAZATEL' KNIG I STATEI OB AZII NA RUSSKOM IAZYKE I ODNYKH TOL'KO KNIG NA INOSTRANNYKH IAZYKAKH, KASAIUSHCHIKHSIA OTNOSHENII ROSSII K AZIATSKIM GOSUDARSTVAM. Vol. 1-3. Vol. 1, "VOSTOK VOOBSHCHE," Vol. 2, "INORODTSY." St. Petersburg: Glavn. Stab, 1891-1894, (Vol. 1) 234 pp; (Vol. 2) 623 pp; (Vol. 3) 274 pp. [Russ. text; 2,228 Russ., other titles]

Milovanov, V. "UKAZATELI KHRONOLOGICHESKII I PREDMETNYI K PROTOKOLAM ZASEDANII I SOOBSHCHENII CHLENOV TURKESTANSKOGO KRUZHKA LIUBITELI ARKHEOLOGII S II/XII 1895 PO II/XII 1915 G.," PROTOKOLY ZASED. I SOOBSHCH. CHLEN. TURK. KRUZHKA LIUBIT. ARKHEOL. GOD 20-1 Vol. 1. n. d. [Russ. text; pub.: 1895-1915]

_____. "ZA DVADSTAT' LET," PROTOKOLY ZASEDANII I SOOBSHCHENII CHLENOV TURKESTANSKOGO KRUZHKA LIUBITELEI ARKHEOLOGII. Tashkent, 1915. [Russ. text; 227 titles, per.: 1914-1915, pp. i-XXIII]

*Mints, I. I. ed. POBEDA SOVETSKOI VLASTI V SREDNEI AZII I KAZAKHSTANE. Tashkent: "Fan," 1967, 771 pp., 5,000 copies. [Russ. text and titles, pub.: 1907-1920, pp. 739-741]

*Mukhamedzhanov, A. R.; T. Nigmatov. NEKOTORYE ISTOCHNIKI K ISTORII VZAIMOOTNOSHENII BUKHARY I KHIVY S ROSSIEI. Tashkent: (Akad. Nauk Uzbek. SSR. In-t Vostokovedeniia), 1957, 223 pp. [Uzbek text; ca.280 Uzbek, Oriental, Russ., Europ. titles, pp. 211-221, per.: 1820's-1850's (entire book surveys sources)]

*Mishchenko, F. "SKITHY," ENTSIKLOPEDICHESKII SLOVAR', Vol. 30. St. Petersburg: F. A. Brokgauz, I. A. Efron, 1900, 202-206 pp. [Russ. text; Russ., Europ. titles, pp. 205-206]

Central Asia: History, Archaeology

*Myrkhanov, T. "ZHIZN' I DEIATEL'NOST' VYDAIUSHCHEGOSIA
RUSSKOGO KITAEVEDA N. IA. BICHURINA (O. IAKINF)
(1777-1853)," SBORNIK STUDENCHESKIKH RABOT
SREDNE AZIATSKOGO UNIVERSITETA. No. 7, 1954. [Russ.
text; 32 Russ. titles, per.:1777-1853, p. 27]

"N. I. VESELOVSKII...(TRUDY)," BIOGRAFICHESKII SLOVAR'
PROFESSOROV I PREPODAVATELEI S PETERSBURGSKAGO
UNIVERSITETA ZA ISTEKSHUIU TRET'IU CHETVERT VEKA
EGO SUSHCHESTVOVANIIA. 1869-1894. Vol. I.
St. Petersburg, 1896. [Russ. text; titles, p. 152]

Novoselov, K. PROTIV BURZHUAZNYKH FAL'SIFIKATOROV
ISTORII SREDNEI AZII. Ashkhabad, 1962. [Russ.
text; ca.150 foreign titles, pp. 311-316]

*Osetrov, V. "ENVER-PASHA," BOL'SHAIA SOVETSKAIA
ENTSIKLOPEDIIA. Vol. 64. Moscow: Gosudarstvennoe
Slovarno-Entsiklopedicheskoe Izdatel'stvo "Sovetskaia
Entsiklopediia," (Ogiz RSFSR), 1933, 231-232 pp.
[Russ. text; Russ., Europ. titles, p. 232]

*"PAMIR," VOENNAIA ENTSIKLOPEDIIA. Vol. 17. Petrograd:
T-vo I. D. Sytina, 1914, 273-275 pp. [Russ. text;
Russ., Europ. titles, p. 275]

"PAMIRSKIE POKHODY," VOENNAIA ENTSIKLOPEDIIA, Vol. 17.
Petrograd: T-vo I. D. Sytina, 1914, 271-273 pp.
[Russ. text; Russ., Europ. titles, p. 273]

"PERECHEN' NAUCHNYKH RABOT CHLENOV KAFEDRY ARKHEOLOGII
SREDNEI AZII, POSVIASHCHENYKH VOPROSAM ISTORII
MATERIAL'NOI KUL'TURY SREDNEI AZII XV VEKA S 1940
PO 1950 GG." TRUDY SREDNEAZIAT. UN-TA. No. 49.
(GUMANITARNYE NAUKI). Book 6. 1953. [Russ. text;
ca.70 titles, per.: 15th c., pub.: 1940-1950,
pp. 12-15]

PERECHEN' NAUCHNYKH RABOT I PUBLIKATSII MIKHAILA
EVGEN'EVICHA MASSONA. K 50-LETIIU NAUCH.-ISSLED.
DEIATEL'NOSTI. Tashkent. (Sredneaz. Gos. Un-t. Ist.
Fak.), 1954. [Russ. text; ca.226 Russ. titles,
pub.: 1924-1954, p. 33]

PERECHEN' NAUCHNYKH RABOT I PUBLIKATSII DOKTORA
ISTORICHESKIKH NAUK MIKHAILA EVGEN'EVICHA MASSONA.
K PIATDESIAT-LETIIU NAUCHNO-ISSLEDOVATEL'SKOI
DEIATEL'NOSTI. Tashkent: Izd-vo Akad. Nauk Uzbek SSSR,
1954, 33 pp., 300 copies. [Russ. text; ca.290,titles,
pub.: 1924-1954]

Central Asia: History, Archaeology

*Pozdneev, A. "KIRGIZ-KAISAKI," ENTSIKLOPEDICHESKII SLOVAR'. Vol. 15. St. Petersburg: F. A. Brokgauz, I. A. Efron, 1895, 95-101 pp. [Russ. text; Russ. Europ. titles, p. 101]

* _____. "KIRGIZY," ENTSIKLOPEDICHESKII SLOVAR'. Vol. 15. St. Petersburg: F. A. Brokgauz, I. A. Efron, 1895, 101-103 pp. [Russ. text; Russ., Europ. titles, p. 103]

*"PUBLIKATSIIA RABOT KAFEDRY ARKHEOLOGII SREDNEI AZII PO LINII SAGU." TRUDY TASHK. UN-TA, No. 172, 1960. [Russ. text; 50 Russ. titles, pub. 1945-1957, pp. 207-209]

*Pulatov, I. IZ ISTORII UCHASTIIA NARODOV SREDNEI AZII V VELIKOI OTECHESTVENNOI VOINE. Tashkent: Izdatel'stvo "Fan," 1966, 228 pp., 2,000 copies. [Russ. text; ca.140 Russ. titles, pp. 222-227]

*Rasul'-Zade, P. N. IZ ISTORII SREDNEAZIATSKO-INDIISKIKH SVIAZEI VTOROI POLOVINY XIX-NACHALA XX VEKA. Tashkent: "Fan," 1968, 170 pp., 1000 copies. [Russ. text; ca.300 Uzbek, Russ., Western titles, per.: 1850-1900, pp. 155-169]

Rosliakov, A. A. K VOPROSU O POLITIKE TSK RKP(B) I SOVETSKOGO PRAVITEL'STVA V OTNOSHENII KHIVY. (OB ISTINNOI DATE NACHALA KHOREZMSKOI REVOLIUTSII). DOKLAD NA I NAUCHNOI KONFERENTSII PO ISTORII KPSS. "TRUDY," (In-t Istorii Partii pri TsK KP Turkmenistana. Filial In-ta Marksizma-Leninizma pri TsK KPSS), 1959. [Russ. text; 17 titles, pp. 5-13]

Sadykov, Kh. U. BIRUNI I EGO RABOTY PO ASTRONOMII I MATEMATICHESKOI GEOGRAFII. Moscow, 1953. [Russ. text; 64 Russ., Europ. titles, pp. 148-151]

Saliamov, M. Iu. POBEDA LENINSKOI PLATFORMY V KOMMUNISTICHESKOI PARTII TURKESTANA V PERIOD PROFSOIUZNOI DISCUSSII. Tashkent, 1969. [Russ. text; 46 titles, pp. 134-135]

Seryi, Ia. M. "IZ ISTORII PARIINOGO STROITEL'STVA V TURKESTANE (INOSTRANNYE KOM. GRUPPY I SEKTSII KPT V 1920-1921 GODY)," NAUCHNYE TRUDY (TASHK. GOS. UN-T) No. 244. IST. NAUKI. Book. 51. ISTORIIA KPSS, 1964, 39-52 pp. [Russ. text; 74 Russ. titles, per.: 1920-1921; pub.: 1950's-1960's, pp. 50-52]

Central Asia: History, Archaeology

_____. "IZ ISTORII SOZDANIIA INOSTRANNYKH GRUPP PRI TSK RKP(B) I PARTIINOI ORGANIZATSII KOMMUNISTOV V SREDNEI AZII. (SEREDINA 1918--NACHALO 1920 GG.)" TRUDY. (TASHK. GOS. UN-T) ISTORIIA KPSS. NOVAIA SERIIA. No. 199. IST. NAUKI. Book. 40. 1962, 50-69 pp. [Russ. text; 86 Russ. titles, per.: 1918-1920, pub. 1918-1960, pp. 67-69]

*Sher, Ia. A. KAMENNYE IZVAIANIIA SEMIRECH'IA. Moscow-Leningrad: Izdatel'stvo "Nauka," 1966, 139 pp., 1700 copies. [Russ. text; 188 Russ., Europ. titles, pp. 130-136]

*Shmurlo, E. "KENISARA (KASIMOV)," ENTSIKLOPEDICHESKII SLOVAR'. Vol. 14A. St. Petersburg: F. A. Brokgauz, I. A. Efron, 1895, p. 938. [Russ. text and titles, p. 938]

SPISOK NAUCHNYKH PUBLIKATSII BORISA VLADIMIROVICHA LUNINA. K 60 LETIIU SO DNIA ROZHDENIIA. Tashkent: (AN UzSSR. In-t Istorii i Arkheologii), 1967, 32 pp., 290 copies. [Russ. text; 316 titles, pub.: 1924-1967]

*"SPISOK OSNOVNYKH NAUCHNYKH TRUDOV PROFESSORA, DOKTORA ISTORICHESKIKH NAUK B. N. ZAKHODERA. (K 60-LETIIU SO DNIA ROZHDENIIA), PROBLEMY VOSTOKOVEDENIIA. No. 1. Moscow, 1959. [Russ. text; 41 Turkmen, Russ., Europ. titles, pp. 227-228]

*"SPISOK OSNOVNYKH PECHATNYKH RABOT A. N. BERNSHTAMA," KRATKIE SOOBSHCHENIIA O DOKLADAKH I POLEVYKH ISSLEDOVANIIAKH INSTITUTA ISTORII MATERIAL'NOI KUL'TURY. (AKADEMIIA NAUK SSSR), No. 80. 1960. [Russ. text; Russ. titles, pub.: 1929-1959, pp. 9-16]

"SPISOK PECHATNYKH TRUDOV A. IU. IAKUBOVSKOGO," KRATKIE SOOBSHCHENIIA O DOKLADAKH I POLEVYKH ISSLEDOVANIIAKH INSTITUTA ISTORII MATERIAL'NOI KUL'TURY. AKADEMIIA NAUK SSSR. No. 51. Moscow, 1953. [Russ. text; 91 Russ. titles, pub.: 1923-1953 pp. 169-172]

"SPISOK PECHATNYKH TRUDOV M. M. D'IAKONOVA," KRATKIE SOOBSHCHENIIA O DOKLADAKH I POLEVYKH ISSLEDOVANIIAKH INSTITUTA ISTORII MATERIAL'NOI KUL'TURY. AKADEMIIA NAUK SSSR. No. 55, Moscow, 1954. [Russ. text; 63 titles, pub.: 1932-1954, pp. 159-162]

Central Asia: History, Archaeology

*Staviskii, B. Ia. MEZHDU PAMIROM I KASPIEM. (SREDNIAIA AZIIA V DREVNOSTI.) [ARKHEOL. PAMIATNIKI.] Moscow: Izdatel'stvo "Nauka," 1966, 327 pp., 7000 copies. [Russ. text; Russ. titles, pp. 319-322]

*_____.; B. I. Vaiberg; N. G. Gorbunova; E. A. Novgorodova. SOVETSKAIA ARKHEOLOGIIA SREDNEI AZII I KUSHANSKAIA PROBLEMA. ANNOTIROVANNAIA BIBLIOGRAFIIA. Vol. 1 and 2. Moscow: Izdatel'stvo "Nauka," (Mezhdunarodnaia Konferentsiia po Istorii, Arkheologii i Kul'ture Tsentr. Azii v Kushan. Epokhu. Dushanbe 1968), 1968, (Vol. 1) 163 pp., (Vol. 2) 195 pp., 1000 copies. [Russ. text; 720 Russ. titles, pub.: before 1968]

*Struve, V. V. ETIUDY PO ISTORII SEVERNOGO PRICHERNOMOR'IA KAVKAZA I SREDNEI AZII. Leningrad: "Nauka," 1968, 355 pp., 2000 copies. [Russ. text; titles, pp. 216-268]

Sukhina, M. D. SOVETSKAIA BIBLIOGRAFIIA ISTORII SREDNEI AZII I KAZAKHSTANA. AVTOREFERAT DISS.... Leningrad: (Leningradskii Gos. Bibliotechn. Institut im. N. K. Krupskoi), 1956. [Russ. text; titles, p. 20]

*Suvorov, V. A. TURKESTANSKII EKONOMICHESKII RAION V PERVYE GODY NEPA (1921-1925 GG.) Tashkent: "Fan," 1968, 207 pp., 650 copies. [Russ. text and titles, pp. 202-206, per.: 1921-1925]

*Temirkhodzhaev, P. S. UKREPLENIE LENINSKOGO SOIUZA RABOCHEGO KLASSA I TRUDOVOGO DEKHKANSTVA TURKESTANA V 1921-1924 GG. Tashkent: "Fan," 1969, 184 pp., 1500 copies. [Russ. text; ca.150 Russ. titles, per.: 1921-1924, pub.: 1921-1968, pp. 175-181]

*Terent'ev, Gen.-Leit. M. A. ISTORIIA ZAVOEVANIIA SREDNEI AZII S KARTAMI I PLANAMI. Vol. 1. St. Petersburg: Tipo-Litografiia V. V. Komarova, 1906. [Russ. text; 150 titles, per.: 19th c., pub.: 1832-1903, pp. XI-XIV]

*Tolstov, S. "IZMAILITY," BOL'SHAIA SOVETSKAIA ENTSIKLOPEDIIA. Vol. 27. Moscow: Gosudarstvennoe Slovarno-Entsiklopedicheskoe Izdatel'stvo "Sovetskaia Entsiklopediia," (Ogiz RSFSR), 1933, 599-600 pp. [Russ. text and titles, p. 600]

Central Asia: History, Archaeology

Ubaidullaev, S. NA ZARE REVOLIUTSII (OCHERK REVOLIUT. DVIZHENIIA V SRED. AZII V KANUN OKTIABRIA.). Tashkent: "Uzbekistan," 1967, 181, 5000 copies. [Russ. text; ca.140 titles, pp. 174-180]

"UKAZATEL' STATEI I ZAMETOK, POMESHCHENNYKH V NAUCHNO-LITERATURNOM SBORNIKE SREDNIAIA AZIIA I ZHURN. SREDNE-AZIATSII VIESTNIK ZA 1896 G.," SREDNE-AZIATSKII VIESTNIK. No. 12, 1896. Tashkent, Dec. 1896. [Russ. text; titles, pp. 156-160, pub.: 1896]

*V. B. "UIGURY," ENTSIKLOPEDICHESKII SLOVAR'. Vol. 34A. St. Petersburg: F. A. Brokgauz, I. A. Efron, 1902, 623-624 pp. [Russ. text; Russ., Europ. titles, p. 624]

*V. M. "GERAT," ENTSIKLOPEDICHESKII SLOVAR', Vol. 8. St. Petersburg: F. A. Brokgauz, I. A. Efron, 1892, 448-449 pp. [Russ. text; Russ., Europ. titles, p. 449]

*V. M. "VAMBERI (GERMAN VAMBERY)," ENTSIKLOPEDICHESKII SLOVAR'. Vol. 5A. St. Petersburg: F. A. Brokgauz, I. A. Efron, 1891, 478-479 pp. [Russ. text; Russ., Europ. titles, p. 478-479]

*V. M. "ZAKASPIISKAIA OBLAST'," ENTSIKLOPEDICHESKII SLOVAR'. Vol. 12. St. Petersburg: F. A. Brokgauz, I. A. Efron, 1894, 157-165 pp. [Russ. text; Russ. Europ. titles, pp. 164-165]

*V. R-V "SREDNE-AZIATSKAIIA VLADIENIIA ROSSII," ENTSIKLOPEDICHESKII SLOVAR'. Vol. 31. St. Petersburg: F. A. Brokgauz, I. A. Efron, 1900, 341-342 pp. [Russ. text and titles, p. 342]

*Valiev, A. FORMIROVANIE I RAZVITIE SOVETSKOI NATSIONAL'NOI INTELLIGENTSII V SREDNEI AZII. Tashkent: "Fan," 1966, 159 pp., 1000 copies. [Russ. text; ca.350 Russ. titles, pp. 146-158]

*"VOENNYIA DIESTVIIA V SREDNEI AZII. SISTEMATICHESKII UKAZATEL' VOENNAGO SBORNIKA ZA 1858-1890 G. G.," VOENNYI SBORNIK (SUPPLEMENT) No. 12. St. Petersburg, 1891. [Russ. text; 66 titles, pub.: 1858-1890, pp. 78-82]

Voronovskii, D. G. BIBLIOGRAFIIA NAUCHNYKH RABOT A. A. SEMENOVA. SBORNIK STATEI PO ISTORII I FILOLOGII NARODOV SREDNEI AZII. TRUDY AKAD. NAUK TADZHIK SSR. 1953. [Russ. text; 176, 52 Tajik, Russ., foreign titles, pub. and MSS.: 1892-1953, pp. 7-24]

Central Asia: History, Archaeology

_____. "BIBLIOGRAFIIA RABOT A. A. SEMENOVA," SBORNIK STATEI PO ISTORII I FILOLOGII NARODOV SREDNEI AZII, POSVIASHCHENNYI 80-LETIIU SO DNIA ROZHDENIIA A. A. SEMENOVA. Stalinabad, 1953. [Russ. text; titles, pp. 7-24]

_____. "BIBLIOGRAFIIA NAUCHNYKH RABOT A. A. SEMENOV," SBORNIK STATEI PO ISTORII I FILOLOGII NARODOV SREDNEI AZII POSVIASHCHENNYI 80-LETIIU A. A. SEMENOVA. Stalinabad, 1953. [Russ. text]

Voznesenskaia, E. A. BIBLIOGRAFIIA PO ISTORII SREDNEI AZII. n. d. [ca.1934?] n. p. [Russ. text; 1,985 titles, per.: 1925]

Zadneprovskaia, T. I. "LITERATURA PO PERVOBYTNOI ARKHEOLOGII SREDNEI AZII NA IAZYKAKH NARODOV SSSR.- LITERATURA NA INOSTRANNYKH IAZYKAKH." SREDNAIA AZIIA V EPOKHU KAMNIA I BRONZY. Moscow-Leningrad: Izdatel'stvo "Nauka," 1966, 1300 copies. [Russ. text; ca.550 Sov. and foreign titles, per.: stone and bronze ages, pp. 266-285]

*Zadneprovskii, Iu. A.; V. M. Masson. "LITERATURA PO NUMIZMATIKE SREDNEI AZII V SSSR ZA II LET 1945-1955 GG.)" EPIGRAFIKA VOSTOKA. No. 12, 1958. [Russ. text; 73 Russ. titles, pub.: 1945-1955, pp. 111-118]

Zaslavskaia, F. A. "TERRAKOTOVYE STATUETKI VSADNIKOV S BULAVAMI IZ ATRASIABA V SOBRANII MUZEIA ISTORII UZSSR," TURDY MUZEIA ISTORII UZBEK SSR. No. 3. 1956. [Russ. text; 58 Russ., Europ. titles, pub.: 19th c.- 1954, pp. 115-117]

Zeimal', E. V. KUSHANSKAIA KHRONOLOGIIA. Moscow, "Nauka," 1968, 186 pp., 1000 copies. [Russ. text; titles, pp. 164-184]

*Zevelev A. I. "GRAZHDANSKAIA VOINA V TURKESTANE V SOVETSKOI ISTORICHESKOI LITERATURE," ISTORIIA SSSR. No. 3. 1963. [Russ. text; f. notes, pp. 61-79, per.: 1917-1921]

*Ziiaev, Kh. SREDNIAIA AZIIA I POVOLZH'E (VTORAIA POLOVINA XVI-XIX VV.). Tashkent: Izdatel'stvo "Nauka," UzSSR, 1965, 237 pp., 650 copies. Uzbek text; ca.210 Uzbek, Russ. titles, per.: XVI-XIX c., pp. 226-236]

Central Asia: History, Archaeology

Ziiaev, Kh. SREDNIAIA AZIIA I SIBIR'. (XVI-XIX VV.)
Tashkent, 1962. [Uzbek text; ca.170 titles, per.:
16-19th c., pp. 3-29, 333-341]

Zimin, L. "BIBLIOGRAFIIA. IZDANIIA NEMESTNYE
IZDANIIA MESTNYE. (S 10 OKTIABRIA 1910 G. PO 24
APR. 1911 G.)," SREDNIAIA AZIIA. Nos. 2, 3, 4, 6, 8.
Tashkent, 1910-1911. [Russ. text; 183 Central Asian,
European titles, pub.: 1910-1911. (No. 2) pp. 130-
133, (No. 3), pp. 130-132, (NO. 4) pp. 115-116,
(No. 6) pp. 119-170, (No. 8) pp. 155-157]

LANGUAGE, LITERATURE

*Bertel's, E. "CHAGATAISKAIA LITERATURA," BOL'SHAIA
SOVETSKAIA ENTSIKLOPEDIIA. Vol. 61. Moscow:
Gosudarstvennoe Slovarno-Entsiklopedicheskoe
Izdatel'stvo "Sovetskaia Entsiklopediia," (Ogiz RSFSR),
1934, 18-19 pp. [Russ. text; Russ., Europ. titles,
p. 19]

*Bertel's, Evgenii Eduardovich. IZBRANNYE TRUDY.
NAVOI I DZHAMI. Moscow: Izdatel'stvo "Nauka,"
Glavnaia Redaktsiia Vostochnoi Literatury, 1965,
498 pp., 2,100 copies. [Russ. text; Sov. Asian,
Russ., Europ. titles, per.: 15th-16th cc., pp. 205,
469-481]

*"CHAGATAISKII IAZYK," BOL'SHAIA SOVETSKAIA ENTSIKLOPEDIIA.
Vol. 61. Moscow: Gosudarstvennoe Slovarno-
Entsiklopedicheskoe Izdatel'stvo "Sovetskaia
Entsiklopediia," (Ogiz RSFSR), 1934, 19-20 pp.
[Russ. text; Chagatai, Russ., Europ. titles, p. 20]

*Ivanov, Viach. Vs. "IZ ISTORII IAZYKOZNANIIA.
LINGVISTICHESKIE VZGLIADY E. D. POLIVANOVA,"
Sovetskoe Vostokovedenie. No. 3. May-June, 1957,
pp. 55-76. [Russ. text; 92 Russ., Europ. titles,
pp. 73-76]

Central Asia: Language, Literature

*"KHAKIM SULEIMAN," BOL'SHAIA SOVETSKAIA ENTSIKLOPEDIIA, Vol. 59. Moscow: Gosudarstvennyi Institut "Sovetskaia Entsiklopediia," (Ogiz, RSFSR), 1935, pp. 397-398. [Russ. text and titles, pp. 397-398]

*Kliashtornyi, S. G. DREVNETIURKSKIE RUNICHESKIE PAMIATNIKI KAK ISTOCHNIK PO ISTORII SREDNEI AZII. Moscow: Izdatel'stvo "Nauka," 1964, 215 pp., 1300 copies. [Russ. text; Sov. Asian, Russ., Europ., Turkish titles, per.: ancient, pp. 181-211]

Krukovskii, Iu. "OBORONNAIA TEMATIKA U PISATELEI SREDNEI AZII," SOVETSKAIA LITERATURA NARODOV SREDNEI AZII. No. 1, 1934. [Russ. text and titles, pp. 119-121]

Leont'ev, A. A. comp. "SPISOK RABOT E. D. POLIVANOVA," Polivanov, E. D. STAT'I PO OBSHCHEMU IAZYKOZNANIIU. Moscow: Izdatel'stvo "Nauka," 1968, 376 pp., 4100 copies. [Russ. text; 146+30 titles, pub.: 1914-1937, 1957-1963, pp. 31-43, 46-47]

Nurmakhanova, A. N. TIPY PROSTOGO PREDLOZHENIIA V TIURKSKIKH IAZYKAKH. Tashkent, 1965. [Russ. text; ca.200 titles, pp. 147-154]

Samoilovich, A. N. MATERIALY DLIA UKAZATELIA LITERATURY PO ENISEISKO-ORKHONSKOI PIS'MENNOSTI. Troitskosavsk: Trudy Troitskosavsko-Kiakhtinskago Podotdiela Amurskago Otdiela Imperatorskago Russkago Geograficheskago Obshchestva, Vol. 15, Part 1. 1912, repr. St. Petersburg, 1914. [Russ. text; titles, pp. 55-81]

*Sartbaev, K. K. SRAVNITEL'NAIA GRAMMATIKA TIURKSKIKH IAZYKOV (PO MATERIALAM KIRGIZSKOGO, KAZAKHSKOGO I UZBEKSKOGO IAZYKOV). Part 1. Frunze: Izd-vo Akad. Nauk Kirgiz SSR, 1962, 111 pp., 500 copies. [Kirgiz text; 132 Turkic, Russ. titles, pub.: 1898-1958, pp. 104-109]

"ZAPISKA OB UCHENYKH TRUDAKH A. N. SAMOILOVICHA," IZVESTIIA AKADEMII NAUK. No. 12-8, 1924. [Russ. text and titles, pp. 533-555]

Central Asia

PHILOSOPHY, RELIGION

Khairullaev, M. M. "SPISOK PROIZVEDENII FARABI,"
FARABI I EGO FILOSOFSKIE TRAKTATY. Tashkent, 1963.
[Uzbek text; 269 Soviet, foreign titles, per.: medieval,
pp. 117-135]

Klimovich, Liutsian. ISLAM V TSARSKOI ROSSII. Moscow:
Gosudarstvennoe Antireligioznoe Izdatel'stvo, 1936,
408 pp., 5200 copies. [Russ. text; 127 Russ.
titles, pp. 399-407]

Mirzaev, S. BIBLIOGRAFIIA PROIZVEDENII IBN SINY V
INSTITUTE VOSTOKOVEDENIIA AN UZSSR. n. p.
(Akademiia Nauk Uz SSR. Institut Vostokovedeniia),
1955, 72 pp., 2000 copies. [Uzbek text]

Modestov, N. N. "UKAZATEL' LITERATURY O SELE TABYNSKOM
I TABYNSKOI IKONE BOZHE'EI MATERI," TRUDY ORENBURGSKOI
UCHENOI ARKHIVNOI KOMISSII. No. 31, 1914. [Russ.
text; 19 titles, (prilozhenie)]

Semenov, A. A. ABU-ALI-IBN SINA (AVITSENNA). Stalinabad:
(Tadzh. Fil. A. N. SSSR, Int. Ist. Iaz. i Lit.), 1945.
[Russ. text; 42 titles, pub. or copied 1296-1927,
per.: Middle Ages, pp. 61-69]

"SINA, ABU-ALI IBN KHUSEIN IBN-ABDALLA IBN (VULGO
AVITSENNA, ISKAZHENNOE OT IBN-SINY)," EVREISKAIA
ENTSIKLOPEDIIA. Vol. 14. IZDANIE OBSHCHESTVA DLIA
NAUCHNYKH EVREISKIKH IZDANII I IZDATEL'STVA BROKGAUZ-
EFRON. n. d. p. 254. [Russ. text; Europ. titles,
p. 254]

*Takho-Godi, A. "IMAMAT," BOL'SHAIA SOVETSKAIA
ENTSIKLOPEDIIA. Vol. 27. Moscow: Gosudarstvennoe
Slovarno-Entsiklopedicheskoe Izdatel'stvo "Sovetskaia
Entsiklopediia," (Ogiz RSFSR), 1933, 1st ed. 788-
789 pp. [Russ. text; Russ. titles, p. 789]

Central Asia

POLITICAL SCIENCE, LAW

Ageev, A. I. OKTIABR'SKAIA REVOLIUTSIIA I GRAZHDANSKAIA VOINA V SREDNEI AZII. BIBLIOGRAFICHESKII UKAZATEL'. Tashkent: GPB UzSSR, 1941. [Russ. text; per. 1917-1921]

*Aleskerov, Iu. INTERVENTSIIA I GRAZHDANSKAIA VOINA V SREDNEI AZII. Tashkent: Gosudarstvennoe Izdatel'stvo Uzbekskoi SSR, 1959, 234 pp., 5000 copies. [Russ. text; Russ. titles, pp. 230-231]

*Altmyshbaev, A. A. O NEKOTORYKH OSOBENNOSTIAKH FORM PEREKHODA NARODOV SREDNEI AZII K SOTSIALIZMU. Frunze: Akad. Nauk Kirgiz SSR, 1959. [Russ. text; Russ. titles, pub.: 1918-1959, pp. 95-97]

Antropov, P. G. CHTO I KAK CHITAT' PO ISTORII REVOLIUTSIONNEGO DVIZHENIIA I PARTII V SREDNEI AZII. BIBLIOGRAFICHESKII UKAZATEL' LITERATURY S KRITICHESKIMI OTZYVAMI O NEI I PROGRAMMOI CHTENIIA. Samarkand: Uzbekistanskoe Gosudarstvennoe Izd-vo (Istpart Sr.-Az. Biuro TsKVKP[b]), 1929, 98 pp., 3000 copies. [Russ. text; 121 Russ. titles, per.: early Sov.]

_____. "VTOROI (2-OI) KRAEVOI S"EZD RKP(B) V TURKESTANSKOI RESPUBLIKE," REVOLIUTSIIA V SREDNEI AZII. SB. 1. 1929, 10-42 pp. [Russ. text; titles, p. 42]

Babakhodzhaev, A. Kh. PROVAL ANGLIISKOI ANTISOVETSKOI POLITIKI V SREDNEI AZII I NA SREDNEM VOSTOKE V PERIOD PRIZNANIIA SOVETSKOGO GOSUDARSTVA DE-FAKTO I DE-IURE (1919-1924 GG.). Tashkent: (In-t Vostokovedeniia im. Biruni), 1959. [Uzbek text; 850 Uzbek, Russ. titles (incl. archives), per.: 1919-1924, pp. 304-336]

*_____. PROVAL ANGLIISKOI ANTISOVETSKOI POLITIKI V SREDNEI AZII I NA SREDNEM VOSTOKE V PERIOD PRIZNANIIA SOVETSKOGO GOSUDARSTVA DE-FAKTO I DE-IURE (1921-1924 GG.). Tashkent: Izdatel'stvo Akademii Nauk Uzbekskoi SSR, 1957, 216 pp., 2000 copies. [Russ. text; Russ., Europ., Middle East. titles, (incl. archives)   per.: 1921-1924, pp. 205-214]

Central Asia, Political Science, Law

Bezgin, I. G. KNIAZIA BEKOVICHA-CHERKASSKAGO EKSPEDITSIIA V KHIVU I POSOL'STVA FLOTA PORUCHIKA KHOZHINA I MURZY TEVKELEVA V INDIIU K VELIKOMU MOGOLU (1714-1717 GG). BIBLIOGRAFICHESKAIA MONOGRAFIIA. (MATERIALY DLIA BIBLIOGRAFICHESKAGO SLOVARIA), No. 3-i. St. Petersburg: Tip. R. Golike, 1891, 239 pp. [Russ. text; 110 titles, per.: 1714-1717]

*"BIBLIOGRAFIIA. PEREVODY KLASSIKOV MARKSIZMA-LENINIZMA." REVOLIUTSIIA I NATSIONAL'NOSTI. No. 6, 1937, 103-107 pp.; No. 6/7, 1937, 124-128 pp.; No. 8, 1937, 86-90 pp.; No. 9/10 124-128 pp. [Russ. text and titles, pub.: 1936-1937]

*"BIBLIOGRAFIIA. VOPROSY KORENIZATSII (KNIGI, BROSHIURY I ZHURNAL'NYE STAT'I 1930-1935 GG.)" REVOLIUTSIIA I NATSIONAL'NOSTI. No. 9, 1935, 77-81 pp. [Russ. text and titles, pub. 1930-1935]

Chekaninskii, I. A. "LITERATURA PO VOPROSU VOSSTANIIA TUZEMTSEV SREDNEI AZII V 1916 GODU. (BIBLIOGRAFICHESKAIA ZAMETKA)," ZAPISKI SEMIPALATINSKOGO OTDELA OBSHCHESTVA IZUCHENIIA KAZAKSTANA. Vol. 1, No. 18. Semipalatinsk, 1929. [Russ. text; 81 Kazakh, Russ. titles, per.: 1916, 105-109 pp.]

"CHTO CHITAT' K OKTIABRIU. IV. OKTIABR' I SREDNIAIA AZIIA." PRAVDA VOSTOKA. No. 244 (1440), 1927. Russ. text; 27 titles]

Egorov, D. N. "NEMETSKAIA KOLONIAL'NAIA LITERATURA ZA 1918-1923 G.," TRUDY GOS. KOLONIZ. NAUCHNO-ISSLED. INSTITUTA. Vol. 1. Moscow, 1924. [Russ. text; pub.: 1918-1923]

Fedorov, D. comp. OPYT VOENNO-STATISTICHESKAGO OPISANIIA ILIISKAGO KRAIA. Pt. 1. Tashkent: Izdanie Shtaba Turkestanskago Voennago Okruga, 1903, 299 pp. [Russ. text and titles, pp. V-VII]

Fedorov, E. "BIBLIOGRAFII NELEGAL'NOI LITERATURY REVOLIUTSII 1905 G. V SREDNEI AZII," IZVESTIIA SR. AZIATSKOGO K-TA PO DELAM MUZEEV, OKHRANY PAMIATNIKOV STARINY, ISKUSSTVA I PRIRODY. No. 1. Tashkent, 1926. [Russ. text; 245 [144] titles, pub.: 1905-1907, pp. 280-297]

*Garritskii, A. A. "UKAZATEL' STATEI I ZAMETOK V RUSSKOI SREDNEAZIATSKOI PERIODICHESKOI PECHATI S 1870-1917 G. PO REVOLIUTSIONNOMU I NATSIONAL'NOMU DVIZHENIIAM V SREDNEI AZII," BIBLIOGRAFIIA VOSTOKA, No. 7. 1935. [Russ. text; 812 Russ. titles, pub: 1870-1917]

Central Asia: Political Science, Law

"GENERAL OT INFANTERII NIKOLAI IVANOVICH GRODEKOV," TURKESTANSKIE VIEDOMOSTI. No. 1. 1907. [Russ. text]

*Inoiatov, Kh. Sh.; T. E. Eleuov. INOSTRANNAIA VOENNAIA INTERVENTSIIA I GRAZHDANSKAIA VOINA V SREDNEI AZII I KAZAKHSTANE. Vol. 1 MAI 1918 G.--SENTIABR' 1919 G. Vol. 2 SENTIABR' 1919 G.--DEKABR' 1920 G. Alma Ata: Vol. 1: Izdatel'stvo Akademii Nauk Kazakhskoi SSR, 1963, 701 pp., 4500 copies; Vol. 2: Izdatel'stvo "Nauka," 1964, 724 pp., 4240 copies. [Russ. text; (Vol. 1) 63 + archives,pp. 694-700; (Vol. 2) titles incl. archives, pp. 717-723, per.: 1918-1920]

*"K DESIATILETIIU NATSIONAL'NOGO RAZMEZHEVANIIA SREDNEI AZII (KNIGI,BROSHIURY I ZHURNAL'NYE STAT'I)," VESTNIK KOMMUNISTICHESKOI AKADEMII. No. 5/6, 1934. [Russ. text and titles, per. 1924-1934, pp. 138-149]

K DESIATELETIIU NATIONAL'NOGO RAZMEZHEVANIIA SREDNEI AZII. Moscow-Leningrad: Izdaniia AN SSSR, 1934. [Russ. text; 91 titles, per.: 1924-1934]

KATALOG IZDANII VOENNO-REDAKTSION. SOVETA TURKFRONTA. 5/II 1922 G.--15/II-1923 G. Tashkent: Tip. Shtaba Turkfronta, 1923, 36 pp., 500 copies. [Russ. text; 23 titles, pub.: Feb. 5, 1922--Feb. 15, 1923]

* Khalfin, N. A. POLITIKA ROSSII V SREDNEI AZII. (1857-1868) Moscow: Izdatel'stvo Vostochnoi Literatury (Akad. Nauk SSSR. In-t Vostokovedeniia), 1960, 272 pp., 1900 copies. [Russ. text; ca.410 Russ. titles and archives, pp. 247-261, per.: 1857-1868]

* _____. TRI RUSSKIE MISSII. IZ ISTORII VNESHNEI POLITIKI ROSSII NA SRED. VOSTOKE VO VTOROI POLOVINE 60-KH GODOV XIX V. (SREDNEAZIAT. GOS. UN-T IM. LENINA. TRUDY. NOVAIA SERIIA. No. 87. IST. NAUKI. Book 13). Tashkent, 1956. [Russ. text; 94 Russ., other titles, per.: second half of 1860's, pp. 73-85]

*"KOKANSKOE KHANSTVO," ENTSIKLOPEDICHESKII SLOVAR'. Vol. 15A. St. Petersburg: F. A. Brokgauz, I. A. Efron, 1895, 621-624 pp. [Russ. text; Russ., Europ. titles, pp. 623-624]

Krukovskaia, S. M. "UKAZATEL' LITERATURY PO NATSIONAL'NOMU RAZMEZHEVANIIU SREDNEAZIATSKIKH RESPUBLIK," SOTSIALISTICHESKAIA NAUKA I TEKHNIKA. No. 1/2. Tashkent, 1935. [Russ. text; 194 Russ. titles, pp. 134-143]

Central Asia: Political Science, Law

*Lunin, B. V. V. I. LENIN I NARODY SREDNEI AZII.
Tashkent: Izdatel'stvo "Uzbekistan," 1967, 271 pp.,
5000 copies. [Russ. text; ca.300 Uzbek, Kazak,
Kirgiz, Tajik, Turkmen, Russ., pub.: 1925-1965,
pp. 251-270]

Maslova, O. V. OBZOR RUSSKIKH PUTESHESTVII I
EKSPEDITSII V SREDNIUIU AZIIU. MATERIALY K ISTORII
IZUCHENIIA SRED. AZII. Part 1 (1715-1856.)
Tashkent, 1955, 83 pp. [Russ. text; 38 Russ., other
annotated lists, per.: 1715-1856]

* _____. OBZOR RUSSKIKH PUTESHESTVII I
EKSPEDITSII V SREDNIUIU AZIIU. MATERIALY K ISTORII
IZUCHENIIA SREDNEI AZII.Part 2 (1856-1869).
Tashkent: Izdatel'stvo SAGU, 1956 102 pp. [Russ.
text; 30 Russ., Europ. annotated lists, per.:
1856-1869]

_____. OBZOR RUSSKIKH PUTESHESTVII I EKSPEDITSII
V SREDNIUIU AZIIU. MATERIALY K ISTORII IZUCHENIIA
SREDNEI AZII. Part 3 (1869-1880). Tashkent:
(Tashkentskii Gosudarstvennyi Universitet Imeni V. I.
Lenina. Materialy k Bibliografii. No. 9), 1962,
181 pp. [Russ. text]

Mitiaev, K. L.; E. K. Mitiaeva. ADMINISTRATIVNAIA
DOKUMENTATSIIA (DELOPROIZVODSTVO) V SOVETSKIKH
UCHREZHDENIIAKH. Tashkent: "Uzbekistan," 1968, 230 pp.,
20,000 copies. [Russ. text, titles, pp. 227-228]

*Nikishov, P. P. IZ ISTORII KRAKHA LEVYKH ESEROV V
TURKESTANE. Frunze: Izdatel'stvo "Kyrgyzstan," 1965,
178 pp., 1000 copies. [Russ. text; ca.100 Russ. titles
incl. archives, per.: 1917-1919, pp. 172-177]

"PLAN NAUCHNOI RABOTY SANIIMLA NA 1934 GOD," REVOLIUTSIIA
I KUL'TURA V SREDNEI AZII. SBORNIK 1. Tashkent,
1934. [Russ. text; 26 titles, pub.: 1940s-1950s, pp.124-
125]

Ponomareva A.; R. O. Tal'man; T. Kal'nitskaia. K
50-LETIIU PERVOI RUSSKOI REVOLIUTSII 1905-1907 GODOV.
(UKAZATEL' LIT.). Stalinabad: (Gos. Publ. B-ka
Tadzhik SSR im. Firdousi), 1955, 63 pp., 2000 copies.
[Russ. text; 394 Tajik, Uzbek, Russ. titles]

Seryi, Ia. M. "SREDNEAZIATSKOE BIURO TSK RKP(B) (IZ
ISTORII OBRAZOVANIIA I DEIATEL'NOSTI. MAI 1922-
NACHALO 1923 G.) NAUCHNYE TRUDY (TASHK. GOS. UN-T)
No. 244. IST. NAUKI, 1964, pp. 86-99. [Russ. text
and 58 titles, pub.: 1922-1962, per.: 1922-1923,
pp. 98-99]

Central Asia: Political Science, Law

Sevriugov, S. KRASNAIA KONNITSA V GORNOI VOINE.
Moscow: Gosudarstvennoe Izdatel'stvo, 1931, 166 pp.
[Russ. text; titles, per.: 1921-1926, end of book]

*Sologubov, I. S. INOSTRANNYE KOMMUNISTY V TURKESTANE
(1918-1921 GG.), Tashkent, 1961, 178 pp., 5000
copies. [Russ. text; ca.70 Russ. titles, pp. 175-178,
per. 1918-1921]

*Tursunov, Kh. VOSSTANIE 1916 GODA V SREDNEI AZII I
KAZAKHSTANE. Tashkent: Gosudarstvennoe Izdatel'stvo
Uzbekskoi SSR, 1962, 428 pp., 3000 copies. [Russ.
text; ca.260 Russ. titles (incl. archives), per.:
1916, pp. 412-427]

*Tashmukhamedov, A. "IZ ISTORII PARTIINOGO STROITEL'STVA
V KISHLAKAKH TURKESTANA (1918 G.)" NAUCHNYE TRUDY
(TASHK. GOS. UN-T) No. 238. MATERIALY PO ISTORII
SREDNEI AZII I UZBEKISTANA, 1964, 50-71 pp. [Russ.
text; 81 Russ. titles, per.: 1918, pub.: 1918-1963,
pp. 69-71]

Tutundzhan, T. VOSSTANIE TURKESTANSKIKH SAPEROV V 1912
GODU. Tashkent: Gosizdat UzSSR, 1960. [Russ. text;
39 titles, per.: 1912, pp. 29-30]

*Urazaev, Sh. Z. TURKESTANSKAIA ASSR I EE GOSUDARSTVENNO-
PRAVOVYE OSOBENNOSTI. Tashkent: Gosudarstvennoe
Izdatel'stvo Uzbekskoi SSR, 1958, 219 pp., 5000
copies. [Russ. text; ca.180 Russ. titles (incl.
archives), per.: 1917-1924, pp. 209-217]

*_____. V. I. LENIN I STROITEL'STVO SOVETSKOI
GOSUDARSTVENNOSTI V TURKESTANE. Tashkent: "Fan,"
1967, 518 pp., 2000 copies. [Russ. text and titles,
pp. 501-516]

*Vitkind, N. Ia. "LITERATURA (KNIZHNAIA, ZHURNAL'NAIA I
GAZETNAIA) ZA 1933-1934 G. G. PO ISTORII KOMPARTII
SREDNEAZIATSKIKH RESPUBLIK," REVOLIUTSIONNYI VOSTOK.
No. 2, 1935. [Russ. text and titles, pub.: 1933-1934,
pp. 211-224]

*_____. "LITERATURA (KNIZHNAIA, ZHURNAL'NAIA I
GAZETNAIA) PO ISTORII KOMPARTII SREDNEAZIATSKIKH
RESPUBLIK," REVOLIUTSIONNYI VOSTOK. No. 2(30),
1935. [Russ. text; 244 Russ. titles, pp. 211-224]

*_____. S. A. Siunchelei. "LITERATURA PO
NATSRAZMEZHEVANIIU SREDNEAZIATSKIKH RESPUBLIK,"
REVOLIUTSIONNYI VOSTOK, No. 6(28) 1934. [Russ. text;
230 Russ. titles, pp. 231-243, pub.: 1924-1934]

Central Asia: Political Science, Law

*Zhukovskii, S. V. SNOSHENIIA ROSSII S BUKHAROI I KHIVOI ZA POSLIEDNEE TREKHSOTLIETIE. Petrograd: (Trudy Obshchestva Russkikh Orientalistov, No. 2) 1915, 215 pp. [Russ. text and titles, per.: 16th to 20th c., pp. IX-XII]

SOCIAL ORGANIZATION

*"BIBLIOGRAFIIA. ZHENSHCHINA-NATSIONALKA V SOTSIALISTICHESKOM STROITEL'STVE (1933-1935 GG.)" REVOLIUTSIIA I NATSIONAL'NOSTI. No. 3. 1936, 94-97 pp. [Russ. text and titles, pub.: 1933-1935, pp. 94-97]

Dobrokhotov, V. A. "KRAEVEDCHESKIA DEIATEL'NOST' MEDFAKA SAGU," TURKESTANSKII MEDITSINSKII ZHURNAL. Vol. 4, No. 11. 1925. [Russ. text; 50 titles, pp. 676-678]

24 KARAKALPAK

GENERAL

BIBLIOGRAFICHESKII UKAZATEL' LITERATURY PO KARAKALPAKII. Moscow-Leningrad: (Akademiia Nauk SSSR. SOVET PO IZUCHENIIU PROIZVODITEL'NYKH SIL. SERIIA KARAKALPAKSKAIA, No. 8), 1935, 307 pp. [Russ. text; 2182 titles, pub.: up to 1932]

Morozova, A. S. "BIBLIOGRAFICHESKII UKAZATEL' O KARA-KALPAKSTKOI ASSR," TRUDY KOMPLEKSNOGO NAUCHNO-ISSLEDOVATEL'SKOGO INSTITUTA KKASSR. (SEKTSIIA ISTORICHESKAIA. RAZRIAD BIBLIOGRAFII. No. 1.- Tortkul/Turtkul': Izd. Kompleksnogo Naucho-Issledovatel'skogo Instituta (Trudy...Sektsiia Istoricheskaia. Razriad Bibliografii, No. 1), 1932, XII + 122 pp. [Russ. text; 1113 titles]

Suinov, U. S. "PERIODICHESKAIA PECHAT' KARAKALPAKSKOI AVTONOMNOI OBLASTI," VESTNIK. KARAKALP. FILIALA AN UZSSR. No. 3. 1962. [Russ. text; titles, pp. 62-70]

ANTHROPOLOGY, ETHNOGRAPHY

Zhdanko, T. A. OCHERKI ISTORICHESKOI ETNOGRAFII KARAKALPAKOV. RODO-PLEMEN. STRUKTURA I RASSELENIE V XIX-NACHALE XX VEKA. TRUDY. INT. ETNOGRAFII IM. MIKLUKHO-MAKLAIA. (NOVAYA SER.) No. 9. 1950. [Russ. text; ca.80 titles, per.: 19th-20th c., pp. 11-36]

Karakalpak

ARCHITECTURE, ART, MUSIC

Allamuratov, A. IZ ISTORII ISKUSSTV KARAKALPAKII.
Nukus, 1968. [Karakalpak text; 34 titles, pp. 56-57]

Allamuratov, Agynbai. IZ ISTORII ISKUSSTV KARAKALPAKII.
Nukus: "Karakalpakiia," 1968, 80 pp., 1000 copies.
[Russ. text; Karakalpak titles, pp. 56-57]

ECONOMICS

*EKONOMICHESKIE OSNOVY SPETSIALIZATSII I RAZMESHCHENIIA
VEDUSHCHIKH OTRASLEI NARODNOGO KHOZIAISTVA
KARAKALAPAKSKOI ASSR. Tashkent: "Fan," 1969, 244 pp.,
650 copies. [Russ. text; 114 Russ. titles, pp. 237-241]

Tatarinova, M. M.; N. K. Eremiants. NIZOV'IA AMU DAR'I.
PRIRODNYE USLOVIIA I SEL'SKOE KHOZIAISTVO. UKAZATEL'
LITERATURY. Tashkent: (Ministerstvo Sel'skogo
Khoziastva UzSSR. Tsentral'naia Nauchnaia Sel'sko-
Khoziaistvennaia Biblioteka), 1961, 235 pp. [Russ.
text]

UST'-URT KARAKALPAKSKII. EGO PRIRODA I KHOZIAISTVO.
ITOGI UST'-URTSKOI KOMPLEKSNOI EKSPEDITSII (1941-1945 GG.)
Moscow: (Akad. Nauk UzSSR), 1949, 231 pp. [Russ. text;
5 lists, per.: 1941-1945]

Karakalpak

EDUCATION

*SHAPIRO, I. "NARODNOE OBRAZOVANIE." "ZDRAOOKHRANENIE,"
BOL'SHAIA SOVETSKAIA ENTSIKLOPEDIIA. Vol. 31.
Moscow: Gosudarstvennyi Institut "Sovetskaia
Entsiklopediia," (Ogiz RSFSR), 1937, 446-448 pp.
[Russ. text; Russ. titles, p. 448]

Urmubaev, N. A. OSNOVY METODIKI RUSSKOGO IAZYKA V
KARAKALPAKSKOI SHKOLE. Book. 1. OBSHCH. VOPROSY
METODIKI. Nukus, 1969. [Russ. text; 186 titles, pp.
314-321]

HISTORY, ARCHAEOLOGY

*Dosumov, Ia. M. OCHERKI ISTORII KARA-KALPAKSKOI ASSR.
1917-1927. Tashkent: (Akad. Nauk UzSSR. Kara-Kalp.
Filial), 1960, 314 pp., 1000 copies. [Russ. text;
ca. 350 Russ. titles, incl. archives, per.: 1917-1927,
pp. 302-314]

*Kamalov, S. K. KARAKALPAKI V XVII-XIX VEKAKH. (K
ISTORII VZAIMOOTNOSHENII S ROSSIEI I SREDNEAZ.
KHANSTVAMI). Tashkent: "Fan," 1968, 328 pp.,
5000 copies. [Russ. text; ca.850 Karakalpak, Russ.
titles, per.: 18th-19th c., pp. 283-326]

*KARAKALPAKIIA V PERIOD POBEDY SOTSIALIZMA I
KOMMUNISTICHESKOGO STROITEL'STVA. Tashkent: "Fan,"
1969, 268 pp., 650 copies. [Russ. text; ca.140
Karakalpak, Russ. titles, pp. 259-264, per.: 1938-1966]

*KARAKALPAKSKAIA AVTONOMNAIA SOVETSKAIA
SOTSIALISTICHESKAIA RESPUBLIKA," BOL'SHAIA
SOVETSKAIA ENTSIKLOPEDIIA. Vol. 31, 1937, 1st ed.,
pp. 437-448. [Russ. text and titles, pp. 446, 448]

Karakalpak: History, Archaeology

*"KARAKALPAKSKAIA AVTONOMNAIA SOVETSKAIA SOTSIALISTICHESKAIA
RESPUBLIKA," BOL'SHAIA SOVETSKAIA ENTSIKLOPEDIIA.
Vol. 20, 1953, 2nd ed., 113-123 pp. [Russ. text and
titles, pp. 118, 120]

"OBZOR STATEI PO ISTORII KARAKALPAKII OPUBLIKOVANNYKH V
'VESTNIKE KARAKALPAKSKOGO FILIALA AN UZSSR' ZA 1962
GOD," VESTNIK KARAKALP. FILIALA AN UZSSR. No. 2,
1963. [Russ. text; titles pp. 101-102]

OCHERKI ISTORII KARAKALPAKSKOI ASSR. Vol. 1, S
DREVNEISHIKH VREMEN DO 1917 G.; Vol. 2, (1917-1963 GG.).
Tashkent, 1964. [Russ. text; ca.480, 270 titles,
pp. 414-427, 330-337, per.: (1) to 1917; (2) 1917-1963]

Pal'mov, I. N.; A. I. Ponomarev. "PECHATNYE I
RUKOPISNYE ISTORICHESKIE IZVESTIIA O KARAKALPAKAKH
RUSSKOM IAZYKE," MATERIALY PO ISTORII KARAKALPAKOV.
(TRUDY IV AN SSSR, Vol. 7). Moscow-Leningrad, 1935.
[Russ. text and titles, pp. 145-225]

*Ponomarev, A. I. "BIBLIOGRAFICHESKII MATERIAL NA
RUSSKOM IAZYKE O KARAKALPAKAKH," MATERIALY PO ISTORII
KARAKALPAKOV. SBORNIK. (TRUDY INSTITUTA
VOSTOKOVEDENIIA AN SSSR. Vol. 7.) Moscow-Leningrad:
Izdatel'stvo Akademii Nauk SSSR, 1935. [Russ. text;
202 Russ. titles, pp. 257-277]

LANGUAGE, LITERATURE

Akhmetov, S. OCHERKI ISTORII KARAKALPAKSKOI POEZII.
Nukus: Karakalpakgiz, 1960. [Karakalpak text; 133
Karakalpak, Russ. titles, Sov. per., pp. 286-290]

Allamuratov, Zh. K VOPROSAM FORM PROSHEDSHEGO VREMENI
GLAGOLA IZ"IAVITEL'NOGO NAKLONENIIA V KARAKALPAKSKOM
IAZYKE. Nukus, 1964. [Russ. text; 81 titles,
pp. 137-144]

*Allanazarov, T. KARAKALPAKSII SOVETSKII TEATR. ISTOKI I
FORMIROVANIE. Tashkent, Izdatel'stvo "Fan," 1966,
180 pp., 650 copies. [Russ. text; Karakalpak, Russ.
titles, pp. 178-179]

Karakalpak: Language, Literature

Baskakov, N. "KARA-KALPAKSKII IAZYK," BOL'SHAIA SOVETSKAIA ENTSIKLOPEDIIA. Vol. 31. 1st ed., 449-450 pp. [Russ. text; Russ., Europ. titles, p. 450]

*Baskakov, N. A. KARAKALPAKSKII IAZYK. Vol. 2. FONETIKA I MORFOLOGIIA. Part 1. CHASTI RECHI I SLOVOOBRAZOVANIE. Moscow: Akad. Nauk SSSR. In-t Iazykoznaniia, 1952. [Russ. text; ca.220 Russ., foreign titles, pp. 527-532]

*Baskakov, N. "KARA-KALPAKSKAIA LITERATURA," BOL'SHAIA SOVETSKAIA LITERATURA. Vol. 31. Moscow: Gosudarstvennyi Institut "Sovetskaia Entsiklopediia," (Ogiz RSFSR), 1937, 1st ed., 448-449 pp. [Russ. text; Karakalpak, Russ. titles, p. 449]

Berdimuratov, Esemurat. LEKSIKA SOVREMENNOGO KARAKALPAKSKOGO IAZYKA. UCHEBNOE POSOBIE DLIA VUZOV. Nukus: Qaraqalpaq Mamleket Baspasi, 1964, 168 pp., 3000 copies. [Karakalpak text; 126 Karakalpak, Sov. Asian, Russ. titles, pp. 163-166]

*Berdimuratov, E. LEKSIKOLOGIIA SOVREMENNOGO KARAKALPAKSKOGO IAZYKA. Nukus: "Karakalpak text; ca.170 Karakalpak, Uzbek, Kazakh, Turkmen, Russ. titles, pub.: 1869-1967, pp. 320-326]

Dzhaksybaev, Anvar. VOPROSY KHUDOZHESTVENNOGO PEREVODA. Nukus: "Karakalpakiia," 1967, 130 pp., 1000 copies. [Russ. text; Karakalpak titles, pp. 125-129]

Kutlymuratov, B. IMENA DEISTVIIA V SOVREMENNOM KARAKALPAKSKOM IAZYKE. Nukus: "Karakalpakiia," 1967, 125 pp., 2000 copies. [Russ. text; 101 Karakalpak titles, pp. 119-124]

Nasyrov, D. S. PRICHASTIE V KARAKALPAKSKOM IAZYKE. Nukus, 1964. [Karakalpak text; 117 titles, pp. 163-169]

*Sagitov, I. T. KARAKALPAKSKII GEROICHESKII EPOS. Tashkent: Izdatel'stvo Akademii Nauk Uzbekskoi SSR, 1962, 107 pp., 650 copies. [Russ. text; 87 titles, pp. 103-106]

Karakalpak: Language, Literature

Sagitov, I. TVORCHESTVO BERDAKHA. Nukus: (Akad. Nauk
Uzbek.SSR. Karakalpak. Kompleksnyi Nauch.-Issled.
In-t), 1958. [Karakalpak text; 43 Karakalpak, Russ.
titles, pp. 208-210]

Ubaidullaev, K. SOVREMENNYI KARAKALPAKSKII IAZYK.
FONETIKA. Nukus, 1965. [Karakalpak text; 31 titles,
pp. 104-105]

POLITICAL SCIENCE, LAW

*Dosumov, Ia. M. POBEDA VELIKOI OKTIABR'SKOI
SOTSIALISTICHESKOI REVOLIUTSII V KARA-KALPAKII.
Tashkent: Izdatel'stvo Akademii Nauk Uzbekskoi SSR
(Kara-Kalpak. Nauch.-Issled. Kompleksnyi In-t), 1958,
144 pp., 1000 copies. [Russ. text; ca.90 Russ.
titles, incl. archives, per.: 1917-early 20th c.,
pp. 137-143]

25 KAZAKH

GENERAL

A. F. [Flerov, A. K.] "BIBLIOGRAFICHESKII UKAZATEL' KNIG I STATEI O SEMIRECHENSKOI OBLASTI," PAMIATNAIA KNIZHKA I ADRES-KALENDAR' SEMIRECHENSKOI OBLASTI NA 1898 G. Vol. 1. Vernyi, 1898. [Russ. text; 180 Russ., Europ. titles, pp. 32-48]

*Aitbaev, E. S.; G. P. Tsarev, eds. [SOROK] 40 LET KAZAKHSKOI SOVETSKOI SOTSIALISTICHESKOI RESPUBLIKI. REKOMENDATEL'NYI UKAZATEL'. Alma Ata: (Gosudarstvennaia Respublikanskaia Biblioteka Kazakhskoi SSR im. A. S. Pushkina), 1960, 221 pp., 5000 copies. [Kazakh text; ca.900 Kazakh, Russ. titles, per.: 1920-1960, pub.: ca.1957-1960]

*Akashev, S. A., comp. KAZAKHSTAN. BIBLIOGRAFIIA ZA 1955 GOD. Alma Ata: (Gos. Resp. B-ka Kaz.SSR im. Pushkina), 1960, 341 pp., 2000 copies. [Russ. text; ca.5000 Russ., Kazakh titles, pub.: 1955]

*Akhinzhanova, S. M.; Kh. K. Kanganova, comp. KAZAKHSTAN V RUKOPISNYKH MATERIALAKH FONDA REDKIKH KNIG I RUKOPISEI GOSUDARSTVENNOI RESPUBLIKANSKOI BIBLIOTEKI IM. A. S. PUSHKINA. (ANNOTIROVANNYI UKAZATEL'). Alma Ata: Izdatel'stvo "Kazakhstan," 1966, 71 pp., 1000 copies. [Kazakh text; 46 + 132 Kazakh, Russ. titles, (incl. archives), per.: 1926-1946; 1824-1942, pp. 4-68]

Aleksandriiskii, V. "NOVYE KNIGI," VESTNIK AKADEMII NAUK KAZAKHSKOI SSR. No. 1. 1949. [Russ. text; titles, pp. 106-109]

Alektorov, A. E. UKAZATEL' KNIG, ZHURNAL'NYKH I GAZETNYKH STATEI I ZAMIETOK O KIRGIZAKH. Kazan, 1900. [Russ. text; ca.1000 titles, pub.: 1734-1899]

ANNOTIROVANNYI KATALOG GAZET I ZHURNALOV KAZAKHSKOI SSR. 1966. Alma-Ata: (M-vo Sviazi Kaz. SSR), 1966, 65 pp., 25000 copies. [Russ. text; titles pub.: 1966]

ANNOTIROVANNYI KATALOG IZDANII. Alma Ata: Izdatel'stvo Akademii Nauk Kazakhskoi SSR, 1950, 72 pp., 15000 copies. [Russ. text]

Kazakh: General

Arianina, I. P.; Iu. N. Gerts. KAZAKHSKAIA RESP. NAUCHNO-TEKHNICHESKAIA BIBLIOTEKA...ZA 1964-1967 GG. Alma-Ata: (Gos. Plan Kom. Soveta Ministrov Kaz. SSR. Tsinti. Resp. Nauch-Tekhn. B-ka), 1967, 76 pp. [Russ. text; per.: 1964-1967]

Babintsev, S. M. "ZAMETKI O PERIODIKE SEMIPALATINSKOGO KRAIA," ZAPISKI SEMIPALATINSKOGO OTDELA OBSHCHESTVA IZUCHENIIA KAZAKHSTANA. Vol. 3. 1931. [Russ. text; titles per.: 1869-1931, pp. 77-134]

Bekmukhamedov, K. Sh.; B. Karina. Sh. Bitkenbaeva. KAZAKHSTAN. MATERIALY OBL. GAZET ZA 1956 G. Alma Ata: (Gos. Resp. B-ka im. Pushkina Kaz. SSR), 1960, 129 pp., 1500 copies. [Kazakh text; ca.2000 titles, pub.: 1956]

"BIBLIOGRAFICHESKII OBZOR GAZETY 'ORENBURGSKII LISTOK' ZA 1876-1893 GG." ADRES-KALENDAR' I PAMIATNAIA KNIZHKA ORENBURGSKOI GUBERNII NA 1895 G. Orenburg, 1894. [Russ. text; pub.: 1876-1893, pp. 85-168]

BIBLIOGRAFICHESKII UKAZATEL' PECHATI KAZAKHSKOI SSR. Part 2 (1917-1939 PERIODICHESKAIA PECHAT'). Alma-Ata: Kaz. Ogiz (Knizhnaia Palata Kazakhskoi SSR), 1941, 100 pp., 1000 copies. [Kazakh text; Kazakh, Russ. titles, pub.: 1917-1939]

"BIBLIOGRAFICHESKII UKAZATEL' SOCHINENII I STATEI, KASAIUSHCHIKHSIA NYNESHNEI ORENBURGSKOI GUBERNII," MATERIALY PO STATISTIKI, GEOGRAFII, ISTORII I ETNOGRAFII ORENBURGSKOI GUBERNII. No. 1. Orenburg: Izd. Orenburgskago Gubernskago Statisticheskago Komiteta, 1877. [Russ. text; titles, pp. 51-89]

"BIBLIOGRAFICHESKII UKAZATEL' SOCHINENII I STATEI, POMIESHCHENNYKH V RAZNYKH PERIODICHESKIKH IZDANIIAKH I KASAIUSHCHIKHSIA NYNIESHNEI ORENBURGSKOI GUBERNII," SPRAVOCHNAIA KNIZHKA ORENBURGSKAGO KRAIA NA 1872. Orenburg, 1871. [Russ. text; pub.: 1843-1868, pp. 1-18]

*Demesheva, G. "BIBLIOGRAFIIA IZDANII AKADEMII NAUK KAZAKHSKOI SSR (1956-1957 GG.)," BIBLIOTECHNO-BIBLIOGRAFICHESKII BIULLETEN' AN KAZAKH. SSR. No. 1. n. p. (Akad. Nauk Kazakh SSR. Tsentr. Nauch. B-ka.), 1958, 185 pp. [Russ. text; ca.1,500 Kazakh. Russ. titles, pub.: 1956-1957, pp. 19-186]

Kazakh: General

Drozdov, G. N. "BIBLIOGRAFIIA URAL'SKOGO OKRUGA (UKAZATEL' PECHATNYKH RABOT ZA PERIOD 1770-1929 G. G.)," URAL'SKII OKRUG I EGO RAIONY. No. 2. Ural'sk, 1930. [Russ. text; 1774 titles, pp. 49-214]

*ETAPY BOL'SHOGO PUTI. Alma Ata: "Kazakhstan," 1968, 272 pp., 6000 copies. [Kazakh, Russ. text; ca.2500 Kazakh; Russ. titles]

Etingof, F. I.; M. E. Kornblium. LITERATURA O SOVETSKIKH SOTSIALISTICHESKIKH RESPUBLIKAKH. No. 5. KAZAKHSTAN. KIRGIZSTAN. Moscow: (Narkompros RSFSR. Nauchno-Issledovatel'skii Institut Bibliotekovedeniia i Rekomendatel'noi Bibliografii), 1936, 8 pp., 6000 copies. [Russ. text and titles]

Feokistova, V.; E. Ivanchikova. comp. IZDANIIA AKADEMII NAUK KAZAKHSKOI SSR ZA 1952-1953 GG. BIBLIOGRAFIIA. VESTNIK AKADEMII NAUK KAZAKHSKOI SSR. No. 12. 1953. [Russ. text; pub.: 1952-1953, pp. 107-141]

Gra, A. P. "NAUCHNYE OBSHCHESTVA," TRUDY ORENBURGSKOI UCHENOI ARKHIVNOI KOMISSII. No. 12. 1903. [Russ. text; titles, pp. 95-97]

GUR'EVSKAIA OBLAST' (REK. UKAZATEL' LITERATURY K 50-LETTIU SOVETSKOI VLASTI.) Gur'ev: (Gur'evskaia Obl. B-ka im. N. Ostrovskogo), 1967, 40 pp., 100 copies. [Russ. text]

Iakhnovich, B. M.; S. N. Bekkulava. comp. BIBLIOGRAFIIA IZDANII AKADEMII NAUK KAZAKHSKOI SSR. KNIGI I STAT'I 1946-50. Alma Ata: (Akademiia Nauk Kazakhskoi SSR, Tsentr. Nauch. B-ka), 1952, 148 pp., 2000 copies. [Russ. text; 1733 Kazakh titles, pub.: 1946-1950]

*Ianitskii, N.; T. Zhurgenev; S. Asfendiarov. "KAZAKHSKAIA SOVETSKAIA SOTSIALISTICHESKAIA RESPUBLIKA," BOL'SHAIA RUSSKAIA ENTSIKLOPEDIIA. Vol. 30. Moscow: Gosudarstvennyi Institut "Sovetskaia Entsiklopediia," 1937, 1st ed., pp. 561-599. [Russ. text and titles, pp. 585-586, 599]

*Ivanchikova, E. I. comp. BIBLIOGRAFIIA IZDANII AKADEMII NAUK KAZAKHSKOI SSR. 1932-1959. Alma Ata, 1960, 1,107 pp., 1,450 copies. [Russ. text; ca.13,500 Kazakh, Russ., other titles, pub.: 1932-1959]

* _____.: M. Z. Tsinman. comp. BIBLIOGRAFIIA IZDANII AKADEMII NAUK KAZAKHSKOI SSR. 1951-1955 GG. Alma Ata: Izdatel'stvo Akademii Nauk Kazakhskoi SSR (Akademiia Nauk Kazakhskoi SSR. Tsentral'naia Nauchnaia Biblioteka), 1956, 212 pp., 1,100 copies. [Russ. text; 2,100 Kazakh, Russ. titles, pub.: 1951-1955] 1955]

Kazakh: General

_____.; V. Feokistova. comp. "IZDANIIA AKADEMII NAUK KAZAKHSKOI SSR ZA 1954 GOD. BIBLIOGRAFIIA," VESTNIK AKADEMII NAUK KAZAKHSKOI SSR. No. 5. 1955. [Russ. text; pub. 1954, titles, pp. 72-103]

*K 50-LETIIU VELIKOGO OKTIABRIA (METODICHESKIE MATERIALY V POMOSHCH BIBLIOTEKARIU). n. p. "Qazaqstan," Baspasi, 1966, 80 pp., 4000 copies. [Kazakh text and titles, per.: 1917 Rev. anniv.]

Karina, B.; B. Nusipbekova. comp. GEROICHESKIE TRADITSKII I KUL'TURNOE NASLEDIE NARODA-NASHE BOGATSTVO. Alma-Ata: "Kazakhstan," 1966, 18 pp., 10,000 copies. [Russ. text; Kazakh titles]

KATALOG GAZET I ZHURNALOV KAZAKHSKOI SSR. (1967). Alma-Ata: (M-vo Sviazi Kaz.SSR), 1966. 22 pp., 60,000 copies. [Russ. text]

KATALOG IZDANII KRAEVOGO IZDATEL'STVA OGIZA V KAZAKHSTANE. DEKABR' 1934 G.--MART 1935 G. Alma Ata: Kazkraiizdat, 1935, 10 pp., 1000 copies. [Russ. text; pub. 1934-1935]

KATALOG KNIG, REKOMENDUEMYKH DLIA KOMPLEKTOVANIIA VNOV' ORGANIZUEMYKH SEL'SKIKH, KOLKHOZNYKH I PROFSOIUZNYKH BIBLIOTEK, BIBLIOTEK MTS I SOVKHOZOV KAZAKHSKOI SSR. Alma Ata: Kazgosizdat, 1955, 88 pp., 5,000 copies. [Russ. text; ca.1,100 titles, pub.: prior to March 1954]

KATALOG KNIG, REKOMENDUEMYKH DLIA KOMPLEKTOVANIIA VNOV' ORGANIZUEMYKH SEL'SKIKH, KOLKHOZNYKH I PROFSOIUZNYKH BIBLIOTEK, BIBLIOTEK MTS I SOVKHOZOV KAZAKHSKOI SSR. Alma Ata: Kazgosizdat, 1955, 60 pp., 5000 copies. [Kazakh text; ca.800 titles, pub. prior to March 1954]

KAZAKHSKAIA SSR K 40-LETIIU VELIKOI OKTIABR'SKOI SOTSIALISTICHESKOI REVOLIUTSII: KRATKIE SPRAVOCHNYE SVEDENIIA I UKAZATEL' LITERATURY. Alma Ata: Kazakhskaia SSR. Gosudarstvennaia Respublikanskaia Publichnaia Biblioteka, 1957, 233 pp. 7000 copies. [Russ. text; ca.450 titles pub.: 1920-1956]

*"KAZAKHSKAIA SOVETSKAIA SOTSIALISTICHESKAIA RESPUBLIKA," BOL'SHAIA SOVETSKAIA ENTSIKLOPEDIIA. Moscow: Gosudarstvennoe Nauchnoe Izdatel'stvo "Bol'shaia

Kazakh: General

Sovetskaia Entsiklopediia," Vol. 19, 1953, 2nd ed., 321-359 pp. [Russ. text and titles, pp. 338, 340, 346, 353, 355]

*KAZAKHSTAN. BIBLIOGRAFIIA ZA 1953 GOD. Alma Ata: Izd-vo Akad. Nauk Kazakh. SSR, 1955, 155 pp., 2,000 copies. [Russ. text; 1,668 Russ., other Sov. titles, pub.: 1953]

*KAZAKHSTAN. BIBLIOGRAFIIA ZA 1954 G. Alma Ata: Izd-vo Akad. Nauk Kazakh. SSR, 1956, 232 pp., 2,000 copies. [Russ. text; 2,490 Kazakh, Russ. titles, pub. 1954]

KAZAKHSTAN. BIBLIOGRAFIIA ZA 1955 GOD. Chimkent: Gos. Tip. No. 13. (Qaz. SSR Madeniet Ministrligi), 1960 150 pp. [Kazakh text; pub. 1955]

KAZAKHSTAN. BIBLIOGRAFIIA ZA 1956 GOD. Taldiqorghan: Taldiqorghan Mem. Baspakhanasi, 1960, 130 pp. [Kazakh text; pub.: 1956]

*KAZAKHSKAIA RESP. BIBLIOTEKA IM. A. S. PUSHKINA. KAZAKHSTAN V RUKOPISNYKH MATERIALAKH FONDA REDKIKH KNIG I RUKOPISEI GOSUDARSTVENNOI RESPUBLIKANSKOI BIBLIOTEKI...(ANNOT. UKAZATEL'). Alma-Ata: "Kazakhstan," 1966, 71 pp., 1000 copies. Kazakh text; Kazakh, Russ. titles, pub.: 1824-1942]

*Kazbekova, D., et al. comp. KNIGA SOVETSKOGO KAZAKHSTANA. SVODNYI BIBLIOGRAFICHESKII UKAZATEL' 1917-1945. Alma Ata: Kazgosizdat, 1962, 446 pp., 1000 copies. [Kazakh, Russ. text; 3018 (Kazakh) 2,253 (Russ.) Uygur titles, pub.: 1917-1945]

Khamankulova, A.; D. Kazbekov; Z. Kasymova. comp. KNIGA SOVETSKOGO KAZAKHSTANA. SVODNYI BIBLIOGR. UKAZ. 1956-1965 GG. Alma Ata: "Kazakhstan," 1970, 258 pp., 2,500 copies. [Kazakh text; 5,442 titles, pub.: 1956-1965]

*KNIGA SOVETSKOGO KAZAKHSTANA (SVODNYI BIBLIOGRAFICHESKII UKAZATEL'), Vol. 2. Alma Ata: Kazgosizdat, 1961, 357 pp., 1000 copies. [Kazakh text; 2256 Kazakh, 2475 Russ. titles, pub.: 1917-1945]

Kazakh: General

*KNIGA SOVETSKOGO KAZAKHSTANA. SVODNYI
BIBLIOGRAFICHESKII UKAZATEL'. Alma Ata: (Knizhnaia
Palata Kazakhskoi SSR) Izdatel'stvo "Kazakhstan,"
1966, 558 pp., 3000 copies. [Kazakh, Russ. text;3940
(Kaz.)+ 2015 (Russ.) Uygur titles.
pub.: 1946-1955]

KNIGI KAZAKHSTANA. KNIGI VYSHEDSHIE V [1963 G.]
Alma Ata: (Ministerstvo Kul'tury Kaz SSR. Resp.
Ob"edinenie Knizhnoi Palaty [1963] (monthly)
2000 copies. [Kazakh, Russ. text; pub. 1963]

KNIGI KAZAKHSTANA. KNIGI VYSHEDSHIE V [1964 G.]
Alma Ata: (Gos. Kom. Soveta Ministrov Kaz. SSR po
Pechati), 1964 (monthly) 2000 copies. [Kazakh,
Russ. text; pub.: 1964]

KNIZHNAIA LETOPIS'. 1937, No. 1/2. 1939. [Russ.
text; Kazakh, Russ. titles, pub.: 1937]

KNIZHNAIA LETOPIS'. 1938, No. 1/2 (ZA 1-E POLUGODIE).
1939. [Russ. text; Kazakh, Russ. titles, pub.:
1938]

KNIZHNAIA LETOPIS'. 1938 1 NENUM. VYP. (ZA 2-E
POLUGODIE). 1940. [Russ. text; Kazakh, Russ.
titles, pub.: 1938]

KNIZHNAIA LETOPIS'. 1939, No. 1. [Kazakh, Russ. text;
pub. 1939]

KNIZHNAIA LETOPIS'. 1939, No. 2. 1941. [Russ. text;
pub.: 1939]

KNIZHNAIA LETOPIS'. KNIGI VYSHEDSHIE V 1946, 1947 I
1948. Alma Ata: Kazgosizdat, 1950, 40 pp., 500
copies. [Kazakh text; 540 Kazakh, Uyghur titles,
pub.: 1946-1948]

KNIZHNAIA LETOPIS'. KNIGI VYSHEDSHIE V 1946, 1947 I
1948. Alma Ata: Kazgosizdat, 1950 36 pp., 500
copies. [Russ. text; 490 Russ. titles, pub. 1946-
1948]

KNIZHNAIA LETOPIS' ZA 1949 G. 1951, 24 pp., 500 copies.
Kazakh text; 293 Kazakh titles, pub.: 1949]

KNIZHNAIA LETOPIS' ZA 1949 G. 1951, 19 pp., 500 copies.
[Russ. text; 223 Russ. titles, pub.: 1949]

KNIZHNAIA LETOPIS' ZA 1-E POLUGODIE 1950 G. 1951,
20 pp., 500 copies. [Kazakh text; 260 Kazakh
titles, pub.: 1950 (first half)]

Kazakh: General

KNIZHNAIA LETOPIS' ZA 1-E POLUGODIE 1950 G. 1951,
14 pp., 500 copies. [Russ. text; 153 Russ. titles,
pub.: 1950 (first half)]

KNIZHNAIA LETOPIS' ZA 1950 (IIUL'--DEKABR'). 1951,
32 pp., 500 copies. [Kazakh text; Kazakh titles,
pub.: 1950 (second half)]

KNIZHNAIA LETOPIS'. Alma Ata: (Knizhnaia Palata
Kazakh. SSR), 1952, 68 pp., 500 copies. [Kazakh
text; pub.: 1950-51]

KNIZHNAIA LETOPIS'. Alma Ata: (Knizhnaia Palata Kazakh.
SSR), 1953, 32 pp., 500 copies. [Russ. text;
pub.: 1950-1951]

KNIZHNAIA LETOPIS' ZA 1952 G. 1954, 95 pp., 800 copies
[Russ. text; pub.: 1952]

KNIZHNAIA LETOPIS'. ZA 1953 G. 1955. [Kazakh, Russ.
text; pub.: 1953]

KNIZHNAIA LETOPIS'. ZA 1954 G. 1955. [Kazakh, Russ.
text; pub.: 1954]

KNIZHNAIA LETOPIS'. 1955. [Kazakh, Russ. text; pub.:
1957]

KNIZHNAIA LETOPIS'. 1956. Kazakh, Russ. text; pub.:
1956]

Kopylov, A. comp. SEMIPALATINSK ZA 50 LET (BIBLIOGR.)
PAMIATKA. No. 1. Semipalatinsk: (Obl. B-ka im.
Gogolia), 1967, 24 pp., 600 copies. [Russ. text]

Kovaleva, P. A.; N. Ia. Nasyrova. comp. KNIGA
SOVETSKOGO KAZAKHSTANA. SVODNYI BIBLIOGR. UKAZ. 1956-
1965 GG. Alma Ata: "Kazakhstan," 1970, 556 pp.,
2,500 copies. [Russ. text; 6,833 Russ., other
titles, pub.: 1956-1965]

"LETOPIS' IZOBRAZITEL'NOGO ISKUSSTVA," LETOPIS'
PECHATI KAZAKHSKOI SSR. No. 4, 1961; No. 4, 1962;
No. 4, 1963, No. 1, 1964, No. 1, 1966. [Kazakh,
Russ. text and titles, pub.: 1961, 1962, 1963, 1964,
1965]

LETOPIS' PECHATI KAZAKHSKOI SSR. ORGAN GOS. BIBLIOGRAFII
KAZAKH. SSR. Alma Ata: (Knizhnaia Palata Kaz. SSR),
1957 (quarterly), 1,500 copies. [Kazakh, Russ.
text; pub.: 1957]

Kazakh: General

LETOPIS' PECHATI KAZAKHSKOI SSR. ORGAN GOS. BIBLIOGRAFII
KAZAKH. SSR. Alma Ata: (Knizhnaia Palata Kazakh.
SSR), 1958 (quarterly), 1,500 copies. [Kazakh, Russ.
text]

LETOPIS' PECHATI KAZAKHSKOI SSR. ORGAN GOS. BIBLIOGRAFII
KAZAKH SSR. Alma Ata: (Knizhnaia Palata Kazakh. SSR),
1959 (quarterly) 1,400 copies. [Russ. text]

LETOPIS' PECHATI KAZAKHSKOI SSR. ORGAN GOS. BIBLIOGRAFII
KAZAKH. SSR. Alma Ata: (Knizhnaia Palata Kaz. SSR)
[1960] quarterly, 2,000 copies. [Kazakh, Russ. text;
pub.: 1960]

LETOPIS' PECHATI KAZAKHSKOI SSR. ORGAN GOS. BIBLIOGRAFII
KAZAKH. SSR. Alma Ata: (Knizhnaia Palata Kaz SSR)
[1961] (quarterly) 500 copies. [Kazakh, Russ.
text; pub.: 1957]

LETOPIS' PECHATI KAZAKHSKOI SSR. ORGAN GOS. BIBLIOGRAFII
KAZ. SSR. Alma Ata: (Knizhnaia Palata Kaz. SSR),
1962, 500 copies. [Kazakh, Russ. text; pub.: 1962]

LETOPIS' PECHATI KAZAKHSKOI SSR. [1963] (quarterly).
[Kazakh, Russ. text; pub.: 1963]

LETOPIS' PECHATI KAZAKHSKOI SSR. Alma Ata: (Knizhnaia
Palata Kaz SSR) 1964 (quarterly), 500 copies.
[Kazakh, Russ. text; pub.: 1964]

LETOPIS' PECHATI KAZAKHSKOI SSR. Alma Ata: (Knizhnaia
Palata Kaz.SSR) 1965, (quarterly). [Kazakh, Russ. text;
pub.: 1965]

LETOPIS' PECHATI KAZAKHSKOI SSR. Alma Ata: (Knizhnaia
Palata Kaz. SSR), [1966] (quarterly), 500 copies.
Kazakh, Russ. text; Kazakh, Russ. titles, pub.: [1966]

LETOPIS' PECHATI KAZAKHSKOI SSR. Alma Ata: (Knizhnaia
Palata Kaz.SSR), [1967] (quarterly), 500 copies.
[Kazakh, Russ. text; Kazakh, Russ. titles, pub.: [1967]

LETOPIS' PECHATI KAZAKHSKOI SSR. Alma Ata: (Knizhnaia
Palata Kaz. SSR), [1968] (quarterly), 500 copies.
[Kazakh, Russ. text; Kazakh Russ. titles, pub.: [1968]

LETOPIS' PECHATI KAZAKHSKOI SSR. Alma Ata: (Knizhnaia
Palata Kaz. SSR) [1969] (quarterly), 500 copies.
[Kazakh, Russ. text; Kazakh, Russ. titles, pub.: [1969]

LETOPIS' PECHATI KAZAKHSKOI SSR. Alma Ata: (Knizhnaia
Palata Kaz. SSR), [1970] (quarterly), 500 copies.
[Kazakh, Russ. text; Kazakh, Russ. titles, pub.: [1970]

Kazakh: General

[Kasymova, Z.; E. A. Skurishina. comp.] LETOPIS'
PERIODICHESKIKH IZDANII KAZAKHSKOI SSR. 1940-1955.
BIBLIOGRAFICHESKII UKAZATEL'. Alma Ata: Kazgosizdat,
1957, 61 pp., 1,500 copies. [Kazakh, Russ. text;
702 Kazakh, Russ. titles, pub.: 1940-1955]

LETOPIS' ZHURNAL'NYKH STATEI. 1938, No. 1. Alma Ata:
(Knizhnaia Palata Kazakhskoi SSR), 1939. [Kazakh,
Russ. text; Kazakh, Russ. titles, publ: 1938]

LETOPIS' ZHURNAL'NYKH STATEI. 1939, No. 2. Alma Ata:
(Knizhnaia Palata Kazakhskoi SSR), 1941. [Kazakh,
Russ. text; pub.: 1939]

LETOPIS' ZHURNAL'NYKH STATEI ZA 1947-1948 GG. Alma-Ata:
(Knizh. Palata Kaz. SSR), 1950, 28 +30 pp., 500 + 500
copies. [Kazakh, Russ. text; 706 + 506 Kazakh, Russ.
titles, pub.: 1947-1948]

LETOPIS' ZHURNALNYKH STATEI. 1949. ORGAN GOS.
BIBLIOGRAFII KAZ.SSR. Alma Ata: Kazgosizdat (Kn.
Palata Kaz.SSR), 1951, 500 copies. [Kazakh, Russ.
text; 1,188 Kazakh, Russ. titles, pub.: 1949]

LETOPIS' ZHURNAL'NYKH STATEI. ORGAN GOS. BIBLIOGR.
KAZAKH. SSR. Alma Ata: (Knizhnaia Palata Kazakh. SSR)
1953 (annual), 83 pp., 500 copies. [Kazakh, Russ.
text; pub.: 1950]

LETOPIS' ZHURNAL'NYKH STATEI. ORGAN GOS. BIBLIOGRAFII
KAZAKH SSR. Alma Ata: Kazgosizdat, 1953; (1951) 79 pp.,
500 copies; (1952) 84 pp., 800 copies. [Kazakh, Russ.
text; pub.: 1951-1952]

LETOPIS' ZHURNAL'NYKH STATEI. ORGAN GOS. BIBLIOGRAFII
KAZAKH. SSR. 1953 GOD. Alma Ata: Kazgosizdat, 1955,
107 pp., 500 copies. [Kazakh, Russ. text; pub.: 1953]

LETOPIS' ZHURNAL'NYKH STATEI. ORGAN GOS. BIBLIOGRAFII
KAZAKH. SSR. 1954 GOD. Alma Ata: Kazgosizdat, 1955,
145 pp., 800 copies. [Kazakh, Russ. text; pub.: 1954]

LETOPIS' ZHURNAL'NYKH STATEI. ORGAN GOS. BIBLIOGRAFII
KAZAKH SSR. 1955. Alma Ata: Kazgosizdat, 1956,
168 pp., 800 copies. [Kazakh, Russ. text; pub.: 1955]

LETOPIS' ZHURNAL'NYKH STATEI. ORGAN GOS. BIBLIOGRAFII
KAZAKH. SSR. 1956. Alma Ata: (Knizhnaia Palata
Kazakh. SSR), 1957, 167 pp., 1,500 copies. [Kazakh,
Russ. text; pub.: 1956]

Kazakh: General

LETOPIS' ZHURNAL'NYKH STATEI. ZHURNAL MAKALARYNY
LETOPISI. 1941-1942. [Kazakh, Russ. text; pub.:
1938-1939]

MATERIALY OB"EDINENNOI NAUCHNOI KONFERENTSII KAFEDR
OBSHCHESTVENNYKH NAUK VUZOV G. UST'-KAMENOGORSKA.
Ust' Kamenogorsk: "Znanie," 1968, 154 pp., 550
copies. [Russ. text; titles at end of reports]

*N. M.; N. Iu. "KAZAKSKAIA AVTONOMNAIA SOVETSKAIA
SOTSIALISTICHESKAIA RESPUBLIKA," SIBIRSKAIA SOVETSKAKA
ENTSIKLOPEDIIA. Vol. 2. Novosibirsk: Sibirskoe
Kraevoe Izdatel'stvo, 1932, 431-448 pp. [Russ. text
and titles, p. 448]

Nigmetov, E.; E. Skurishina, comp. LETOPIS'
PERIODICHESKIKH IZDANII KAZAKHSKOI SSR. 1917-1959 GG.
SVODNYI BIBLIOGR. UKAZATEL'. Alma Ata: Knizhnaia
Palata Kazakh. SSR, 1963, 191 pp., 1000 copies.
[Kazakh, Russ. text; 1555 titles. pub.: 1917-1959]

NOVYE KNIGI. EZHEMES. BIBLIOGR. BIULLETEN'. Alma Ata:
(Knizhnaia Palata Kaz. SSR), 1959 (monthly), 8,000
copies. [Kazakh, Russ. text; Kazakh, Russ. titles,
pub.: 1959]

Pak, A. N. comp. KZYL-ORDINSKAIA OBLAST'. (REK.
UKAZATEL' LIT.) Kzyl-Orda: (Kzyl-Ordin. Obl. B-ka im.
Gorkogo), 1960, 59 pp., 1000 copies. [Russ. text;
460 titles]

QAZAQ TILINDA BASILGHAN KITABTARDI KORSATKISH.
Qizil Orda: Qaz. Mamlakat Basbasi, 1926, 112 pp.,
2000 copies. [Kazakh text and titles]

QAZAQ TILINDA BASILGHAN KITABTARDI KORSATKISH. Qizil
Orda: Qaz. Mamlakat Basbasi, 1927, 53 pp., 3000
copies. [Kazakh text and titles]

Radenko, E. L. comp. NAUCHNAIA ORGANIZATSIIA TRUDA.
BIBLIOGR. 1964 (VYBORCHNO) 1965, 1966 GG. Alma Ata:
(Tsinti pri Gosplane Kaz. SSR. Resp. Nauch-Tekhn.
B-ka Kaz. SSR), 1966, 37 pp., 400 copies. [Russ.
text; per.: 1964-1966]

Sh. A. "BIBLIOGRAFICHESKII UKAZATEL' [STATEI, ZAMETOK
I NEKOTORYKH OFITSIAL'NYKH MATERIALOV, POMESHCHENNYKH
V ZHURNALAKH 'SOVETSKAIA KIRGIZIIA', 'SOVETSKII
KAZAKSTAN' I 'NARODNOE KHOZIAISTVO KAZAKSTANA' ZA
VREMIA S 1923 G. PO 1928 G. VKLIUCHITEL'NO]"
NARODNOE KHOZIAISTVO KAZAKSTANA. No. 11/12. 1928.
[Russ. text; Russ. titles, pub.: 1923-1928, pp. 346-370]

Kazakh: General

*Samoilovich, A. N. ed. KAZAKHSTAN V IZDANIIAKH AKADEMII NAUK SSSR 1734-1935. Moscow-Leningrad: Izdatel'stvo AN SSSR(AN SSSR, Kazfilial. Trudy. No. 9), 1936, 72 pp., 1,200 copies. [Russ. text; 654 Russ. titles, pub.: 1734-1935]

Sauraebaev, N. T. "O TIURKOLOGICHESKIKH RABOTAKH SOVETSKIKH UCHENYKH [BIBLIOGRAFIIA]" VESTNIK AN KAZSSR. No. 6. 1948. [Russ. text; titles, pp. 71-76]

Shevich, V. "UKAZATEL' K 'ORENBURGSKIM VIEDOMOSTIAM' ORENBURGSKIE GUBERNSKIE VIEDOMOSTI. Nos. 19, 21, 23, 24, 1865. [Russ. text]

_____. "UKAZATEL' NEOFFITSIAL'NOI CHASTI ORENBURGSKIKH GUBERNSKIKH VIEDOMOSTEI S 1843 PO 1863 GOD," ORENBURGSKIE GUBERNSKIIA VIEDOMOSTI. Nos. 15, 17, 19, 21, 23, 24. 1865. [Russ. text and titles; pub.: 1843-1863]

[Skuchalina, A. Ia.; M. N. Shut'kova. comp.] LITERATURA O TSELINOGRADSKOI OBLASTI I SEVERNYKH OBLASTIAKH KAZAKHSTANA ZA 1965 GOD. No. 3. Tselinograd: (Tselinogr. Obl. B-ka im. Seifullina) 1967, 161 pp., 2000 copies. [Russ. text; ca.2200 titles, pub.: 1965]

*Subkhanberdina, U. MATERIALY OPUBLIKOVANNYE NA STRANITSAKH KAZAKHSKOI DOREVOLIUTSIONNOI PERIODICHESKOI PECHATI. ANNOT. BIBLIOGR. UKAZATEL'. Pt. 2. Alma Ata: Qazaq SSR Ghilim Akademiyasining Baspasi (AN Kaz. SSR. Tsentr. Nauch. B-ka), 1963, 292 pp., 3400 copies. [Kazakh text; 2,040 Kazakh titles, pub.: 1870-1913]

*_____. MATERIALY, OPUBLIKOVANNYE V KAZAKHSKOI DOREVOLIUTSIONNOI PERIODICHESKOI PECHATI. Alma Ata: Kazmembas, 1961, 153 pp., 4000 copies. [Kazakh text; 87 Kazakh (Barlygy 87-88 nomer) lists, pub.: 1911-1915]

_____. STAT'I, PIS'MA I SOOBSHCHENIIA NA STRANITSAKH "AIKAP". ANNOT. BIBLIOGR. UKAZATEL'. Alma Ata: Kazgosizdat, 1961, 155 pp., 4000 copies. [Kazakh titles, pub.: 1911-1915]

"TRUDY ORENBURGSKOI UCHENOI ARKHIVNOI KOMISSII," TRUDY ORENBURGSKOI UCHENOI ARKHIVNOI KOMISSII. No. 12. K 200-LETNEMU IUBILEIU RUSSKOI PRESSY. Orenburg, 1903. [Russ. text; contents of Orenburg press]

Kazakh: General

"TRUDY SOTRUDNIKOV KAZAKHSKOGO FILIALA AN SSSR NAKHODIASHCHIESIA V PECHATI," TRUDY IUBILEINOI SESSII, POSVIASHCHENNOI 25-I GODOVSHCHINE VELIKOI OKTIABR'SKOI SOTSIALISTICHESKOI REVOLIUTSII. Alma Ata, 1943. [Russ. text; titles, pp. 271-274]

UKAZATEL' STATEI, POMIESHCHENNYKH V NEOFFITSIAL'NOI CHASTI 'ORENBURGSKIKH GUBERNSKIKH VIEDOMOSTEI' S 1845 PO 1852 G.G. ORENBURGSKIE GUBERNSKIE VIEDOMOSTI. (PRILOZHENIE). 1852. [Russ. text]

[Vakhmistrova, M. P.; G. P. Tsarev; F. I. El'konina] KAZAKHSTAN. BIBLIOGRAFIIA ZA 1952 G. Alma Ata: Izd.-vo Akad. Nauk Kazakh. SSR. (Gos. Publ. B-ka im. Pushkina), 1953, 108 pp., 1200 copies. [Russ. text; 1,328 Russ., other titles, pub.: 1952]

*Vakhmistrova, M. P.; N. V. Chechulina; F. I. El'konina. KAZAKHSTAN. BIBLIOGRAFIIA ZA 1956 G. Alma Ata: (Gos. Resp. B-ka Kaz. SSR im. Pushkina), 1960, 275 pp., 1500 copies. [Russ. text; ca.4000 Kazakh, Russ. titles, pub.: 1956]

_____. et. al. comp. KAZAKHSTAN. BIBLIOGRAFIIA ZA 1957 G. Alma Ata: (Gos. Resp. B-ka Kaz. SSR im. Pushkina), 1962, 340 pp., 600 copies. [Russ. text; ca.4500 Russ. titles, pub.: 1957]

Vasilenko, R. F.; V. N. Pazdnikov. comp. BIBLIOGRAFICHESKII SBORNIK KAZAKHSKOGO GOSUDARSTVENNOGO UNIVERSITETA IM. S. M. KIROVA. Alma Ata: (Kazakh. Gos. Un-t, im. Kirova, Fundam. B-ka), 1957, 177 pp., 1000 copies. [Russ. text; 2273 Kazakh, Russ. titles, pub.: 1935-1957]

"VELIKAIA OTECHESTVENNAIA VOINA SOVETSKOGO NARODA," BIBLIOGRAFICHESKII UKAZATEL' PECHATI KAZAKHSKOI SSR. 1941-1942 (quarterly). (1941), 128 pp. 1950 2d ed.(1950). 562 pp. [Russ. text; pub. & per.: 1941-1942]

Vorontsovskii, P. A. "SPISOK IZDANII ORENBURGSKAGO OTDIELA I.R.G.O. I UKAZATEL' POMIESHCHENNYKH V NIKH TRUDOV," IZVIESTIIA ORENBURGSKAGO OTDIELA IMPERATORSKAGO RUSSKAGO GEOGRAFICHESKAGO OBSHCHESTVA. No. 22. 1912. [Russ. text; titles (supplement) pp. 1-11]

Zhamankulova, A.; D. Kazbekova; Z. Kazymova. KNIGA SOVETSKOGO KAZAKHSTANA. SVODNYI BIBLIOGR. UKAZATEL'. 1956-1965 GG. Alma Ata, "Kazakhstan," 1970 528 pp., 2500 copies. [Kazakh, Russ. text; pub.: 1956-1965]

Kazakh: General

Zvierinskii, V. "BIBLIOGRAFICHESKII UKAZATEL' SOCHINENII I STATEI, POMIESHCHENNYKH V RAZNYKH PERIODICHESKIKH IZDANIIAKH I KASAIUSHCHIKHSIA NYNIESHNEI ORENBURGSKOI GUBERNII," SPISKI NASELENNYKH MIEST. Vol. 28. ORENBURGSKAIA GUBERNIIA. St. Petersburg, 1871. [Russ. text; 18 lists, pp. CV-CX]

ANTHROPOLOGY, ETHNOGRAPHY

*A. Sh. "KAZAKI, KIRGIZ-KAZAKI," SIBIRSKAIA SOVETSKAIA ENTSIKLOPEDIIA. Vol. 2. Novosibirsk: Sibirskoe Kraevoe Izdatel'stvo, 1932, 429-431 pp. [Russ. text and titles, pp. 430-431]

Akhinzhanov, M. OB ETNOGENEZE KAZAKHSKOGO NARODA. Alma Ata: Kazgosizdat, 1957. [Kazakh text; ca.100 titles, pp. 156-162]

*Alektorov, A. E. UKAZATEL' KNIG, ZHURNAL'NYKH I GAZETNYKH STATEI I ZAMIETOK O KIRGIZAKH. Kazan: Tipo-Litografiia Imperatorskago Universiteta (Prilozhenie k "Izviestiiam Ob-va Arkheologii, Istorii, Etnogr., pri Kazanskom Universitete." Vols. XVI-XX, 1900-1904), 1900-1904, 970 + 12 pp. [12 in Kazakh] + 2. [Russ. text; Kazakh, Russ., Europ. titles, pp. 53-172, 129-432, + 1-12]

Kastan'e, I. A. "UKAZATEL' ISTOCHNIKOV I TRUDOV PO VOPROSU O POKHORONAKH, OBRIADAKH I POMINKAKH KIRGIZ," NADGROBNYE SOORUZHENIIA KIRGIZSKIKH STEPEI. TRUDY ORENBURGSKOI UCHENOI ARKHIVNOI KOMISSII. No. XXVI. 1911. [Russ. text; titles, pp. 98-102]

Kharuzin, Aleksei N. "BIBLIOGRAFICHESKII UKAZATEL'," KIRGIZY BUKEEVSKOI ORDY. No. 1, 2; Part 1. (also in:) IZVIESTIIA OBSHCHESTVA LIUBITELEI ESTESTVOZNANIIA, ANTROPOLOGII I ETNOGRAFII...PRI MOSKOVSKOM UNIVERSITETE. Vols. 63, 72. (also:) TRUDY ANTROPOLOGICHESKOGO OTDIELA. Vols. 10, 14, No. 1 Moscow, 1889-1891. [Russ. text; 875 Russ. titles, pp. (No. 1) I-LIX; (No. 2) I-LI, pub.: 1734-1891]

Kharuzin, A. N. "BIBLIOGRAFICHESKII UKAZATEL' SOCHINENII I STATEI, KASAIUSHCHIKHSIA KIRGIZOV I STRAN, ZANIMAEMYKH IMI," IZV. IMP. O VA LIUB. ESTESTV., ANTROP. I ETNOGR. Vol. 63 1889. [Russ. text; titles, pp. I-LIX]

Kazakh: Anthropology, Ethnography

Kharuzin, Aleksei N. BIBLIOGRAFICHESKII UKAZATEL'
STATEI, KASAIUSHCHIKHSIA ETNOGRAFII KIRGIZOV I
KARAKIRGIZOV S 1734 PO 1891 G. (also in:)
ETNOGRAFICHESKOE OBOZRENIE. Book 9, No. 2, Bk. 11, No.4.
Supplement pp. 1-68. Moscow, 1891, 68 pp. [Russian
text; 764 titles, pub.: 1734 - May, 1891]

Khodzhaeva, R. D. "OB ISTOCHNIKAKH IZUCHENIIA
KAZAKHSKOI NATIONAL'NOI ODEZHDY," VOPROSY ETNOGRAFII
I ANTROPOLOGII KAZAKHSTANA. Alma Ata: (Trudy In-ta
Istorii, Arkheol. i Etnogr. im. Valikhanova. Vol. 16)
1962, 117-137 pp. [Russ. text; 153 titles]

*Krakhalev, A. I. "DOPOLNENIE K UKAZATELIU LITERATURY O
KIRGIZAKH," ETNOGRAFICHESKOE OBOZRENIE. No. 2/3.
1892. [Russ. text; 34 Russ. titles, pp. 71-75]

Masanov, E. A. IBRAI ALTYNSARIN KAK ETNOGRAF
KAZAKHSKOGO NARODA [OBZOR RABOT]. VOPROSY ETNOGRAFII
I ANTROPOLOGII KAZAKHSTANA. Alma Ata: (Trudy In-ta.
Istorii, Arkheologii i Etnografii im. Valikhanova.
Vol. 16), 1962, 95-116 pp. [Russ. text; per.:
19th c.]

——————————. "NAUCHNYE TRUDY SH. M. IBRAGIMOVA,"
VESTNIK AN KAZSSR. No. 9. 1964. [Russ. text; 19
titles, pub.: 1870-1904 pp. 59-60]

Miller, V. F. SISTEMATICHESKOE OPISANIE KOLLEKTSII
DASKOVTSKOGO ETNOGRAFICHESKOGO MUZEIA. No. 1.
Moscow, 1887. [Russ. text; 50 titles, p. 96,
pub.: 1755-1887]

"SPISOK NAUCHNYKH TRUDOV E. A. MASANOVA," IZVESTIIA AN
KAZSSR. SERIIA OBSHCHESTVENNYKH NAUK. No. 4. 1965.
[Russ. text; 40 titles, pp. 86-87, pub.: 1958-1965]

Valikhanov, Ch. Ch. IZ CHERNOVYKH BUMAG. ZAPISKI
RUSSKAGO GEOGRAFICHESKAGO OBSHCHESTVA PO OTDIELENIIU
ETNOGRAFII. Vol. XXIX. No. 1. 1904. [Russ. text;
survey, pp. 179-194]

Veselovskii, N. "DOPOLNENIIA K BIBLIOGRAFICHESKOMU
UKAZATELIU STATEI KASAIUSHCHIKHSIA KIRGIZOV I
KARAKIRGIZOV,SOSTAVLENNOMU A. N. KHARUZINYM,"
ETNOGRAFICHESKOE OBOZRENIE. Book 9, No. 4. 1891.
[Russ. text; 98 titles, pub.: 1773-1891, pp. 285-289]

Kazakh: Anthropology, Ethnography

Voznesenskaia E, A.; A. B. Piotrevskii. "MATERIALY DLIA BIBLIOGRAFII I ANTROPOLOGII KAZAKSTANA ZA 1921-1926 G.G.," GOD RABOTY....Leningrad: Akademiia Nauk SSSR. (Trudy Komissii po Izuch. Plemenn. Sostava Naseleniia SSSR i Sopredel'nykh Stran, No. 14), 1927, pp. XII, 247, 3. [Russ. text; per.: 1921-1926]

ARCHITECTURE, ART, MUSIC

Besenov, T. K. ORNAMENT KAZAKHSTANA V ARKHITEKTURE. Alma Ata: (Akad. Nauk Kazakh. SSR), 1957. [Russ. text; 75 titles, pp. 87-89]

──────────. PRIKLADNOE ISKUSSTVO KAZAKHSTANA. Alma Ata: Kazgoslitizdat, 1958. [Russ. text; 37 titles, p. 22]

Bogatenkova, L. KHADISHA BUKEEVA. Alma Ata, 1965. [Russ. text; 39 titles, pp. 139-140]

*Bugoslavskii, S. "KAZAKHSKAIA MUZIKA," BOL'SHAIA SOVETSKAIA ENTSIKLOPEDIIA. Vol. 30. Moscow: Gosudarstvennyi Institut "Sovetskaia Entsiklopediia," (OGIZ RSFSR), 1937, pp. 601-602. [Russ. text; Kazakh, Russ. titles, p. 602]

Dernova, V. P. comp. NARODNAIA MUZYKA V KAZAKHSTANE. Alma Ata: "Kazakhstan," 1967, 269 pp., 4600 copies. [Russ. text; titles pp. 261-268]

Erzakovich, B. G. ed. IZOBRAZITEL'NOE ISKUSSTVO KAZAKHSTANA. Alma Ata, 1963. [Russ. text; 53 titles, pp. 368-370]

* ──────────. "RUSSKIE UCHENYE O KAZAKHSKOI MUZYKE. OBZOR DOREV. LIT. PO USTNOMU MUZYK. TVORCHESTVU KAZAKH. NARODA," VESTNIK AKAD. NAUK KAZAKH. SSR. No. 9, 1954, 96 pp. [Russ. text; 17 Russ. titles, per.: 1795-1914, pp. 45-60]

Gerasimov, G. G. PAMIATNIKI ARKHITEKTURY DOLINY REKI KARA-KENGIR V TSENTRAL'NOM KAZAKHSTANE. Alma Ata: (Akad. Nauk Kazakhskoi SSR. Institut Arkhitektury, Stroitel'stva i Stroitel'nykh Materialov), 1957. [Russ. text; 31 titles, pp. 59-60]

Kazakh: Architecture, Art, Music

Gizatov, B. KAZAKHSKII GOSUDARSTVENNYI ORKESTR NARODNYKH INSTRUMENTOV IMENI KURMANGAZY. Alma Ata: Kazgoslitizdat, 1957. [Russ. text; ca.100 titles, per.: Sov., pp. 171-175]

ISKUSSTVO I INOSTRANNYE IAZYKI. SBORNIK STATEI ASPIRANTOV I SOISKATELEI. (PO VOPROSAM MUZYKI I INOSTR. IAZ.) Alma Ata: (M-vo Vyssh. i Sred. Spets. Obrazovaniia Kaz. SSR.), 1966 (No. DAN 1967) 205 pp., 500 copies. [Russ. text; titles at end of articles]

Koriakin, I. S. OZELENENIE NASELENNYKH MEST KAZAKHSTANA. Alma Ata: (Kazakh. Gos. Med. In-t), 1959. [Russ. text; 214 titles, pp. 79-85]

Margulan, A.; T. Basenov, M. Mendikulov. ARKHITEKTURA KAZAKHSTANA. Alma Ata: Kazgosizdat, 1959. [Kazakh, Russ. text; ca.130 text; pp. 167-171]

Mendikulov, M. M. PAMIATNIKI ARKHITEKTURY POLUOSTROVA MANGYSHLAKA I ZAPADNOGO USTIURTA. Alma Ata: (AN Kaz. SSR), 1956. [Russ. text; 33 titles, pp. 41-42]

Novozhilov, G. N. ARKHITEKTURNYI PAMIATNIKI KAZAKHSTANA. Alma Ata: "Kazakhstan," 1968, p. 95, 9500 copies. [Russ. text;

*Nurmukhammedov, N. B. ISKUSSTVO KAZAKHSTANA. Moscow: "Isskustvo," 1970, 148 pp., 7000 copies. [Russ. text; 73 Kazakh, Russ., English titles, pub.: 1819-1966, pp. 143-144]

[Plakhotnaia, L. comp.] KATALOG PROIZVEDENII KHUDOZHNIKA URMANCHE BAKI IDRISOVICHA. Alma Ata :(Soiuz Khudozhnikov Kazakhstana. Kazakh Gos. Khudozh. Galereia im. Shevchenko), 1959. [Russ. text; 40 titles, pp. 44, 49-51]

*Sarykulova, G. GRAFIKA KAZAKHSTANA. Alma Ata: Izdatel'stvo "Nauka" Kazakhskoi SSR, 1967, 168 pp., 1700 copies. [Russ. text and titles, pub.: 1934-1964, pp. 83-86]

Turogeldieva, R. comp. IZOBRAZITEL'NOE ISKUSSTVO KAZAKHSTANA. BIBLIOGR. UKAZATEL'. 1938-1959 GG. Alma Ata: Kazgosizdat, 1963, 75 pp., 500 copies. [Kazakh, Russ. text; 1387 Kazakh, Russ. titles, per.: 1938-1959]

Kazakh: Architecture, Art, Music

*Veimarn, B. "KAZAKHSKOE ISKUSSTVO," BOL'SHAIA SOVETSKAIA ENTSIKLOPEDIIA. Vol. 30. Moscow: Gosudarstvennyi Institut "Sovetskaia Entsiklopediia" (Ogiz RSFSR), 1937, 604-605 pp. [Russ. text; Kazakh, Russ., Europ. titles, p. 605]

Zataevich, A. "BIBLIOGRAFICHESKII UKAZATEL' LITERATURY PO VOPROSU O KIRGIZSKOI NARODNOI MUZYKE, KAK RAVNO OPUBLIKOVANNYKH V ETOI OBLASTI NOTNYKH ZAPISEI I KHUDOZHESTVENNYKH OBRABOTOK. 1000 PESEN KIRGIZSKOGO NARODA. Orenburg, 1925. [Russ. text; 9 titles, pub.: 1899-1924]

_____. 500 KAZAKHSKIKH PESEN I KIUIEV (NAPEVY I INSTRUMENTAL'NYE P'ESY) ADAEVSKIKH, BUKEEVSKIKH, SEMIPALATINSKIKH I URAL'SKIKH. Alma Ata, 1931. [Russ. text; 18 Russ. titles, pub.: 1899-1926, pp. 309-312]

_____. [TYSIACHA] 1000 PESEN KIRGIZSKOGO NARODA (NAPEVY I MELODII). TRUDY OBSHCHESTVA IZUCHENIIA KIRGIZSKOGO KRAIA PRI NARKOMPROSE KIRSSR. Orenburg: Kirgizskoe Gosudarstvennoe Izdatel'stvo, 1925, LVIII + 403 pp. [Russ. text; titles end of work]

[Zhamankulova, A.; N. Nasyrova; D. Kazbekova; Z. Kasymova. comp.] MUZYKAL'NAIA LITERATURA SOVETSKOGO KAZAKHSTANA. 1938-1965 GG. SVODNAIA BIBLIOGRAFIIA. Alma Ata: "Kazakhstan," 1969, 162 pp., 1500 copies. [Kazakh, Russ. text; 1297 titles, pub.: 1938-1965]

*Zhanuzakova, Z. comp. KAZAKHSKAIA NARODNAIA INSTRUMENTAL'NAIA MUZYKA. KIUII DLIA DOMBRY, KOBYZA I SYBYZGY. Alma Ata: (Akademiia Nauk Kazakhskoi SSR. Institut Literatury i Iskusstva im. M. O. Auezova. Otdel Muzyki), 1964, 248 pp., 3650 copies. [Kazakh, text; Kazakh, Russ. titles, pp. 239-242]

Zhubanov, A. STRUNY STOLETII. OCHERKI O ZHIZNI I TVORCHESKOI DEIATEL'NOSTI KAZAKH. NAR. KOMPOZITOROV. Alma Ata: Kazgoslitizdat, 1958. [Russ. text; 166 titles, pp. 388-394]

Kazakh

ECONOMICS

Abdullina, M. et al. compilers. KUSTANAISKII EKONOMICHESKII ADMINISTRATIVNYI RAION. BIBLIOGRAFICHESKII UKAZATEL'. BIBLIOTECHNO-BIBLIOGRAFICHESKII BIULLETEN'. No. 2. Alma Ata: Izdatel'stvo Akademii Nauk KazSSR. (Akad. Nauk Kazakh. SSR. Tsentr. Nauch. B-ka), 1959. [Russ. text; 2678 Kazakh, Russ. titles, pub.: 1786-Aug. 1958, pp. 15-260]

*Adamchuk, V. A. BOL'SHOI TURGAI. EKONOMIKO-GEOGRAFICHESKAIA KHARAKTERISTIKA. Moscow: Gosudarstvennoe Izdatel'stvo Geograficheskoi Literatury, 1959, 167 pp., 7500 copies. [Russ. text; 52 Russ. titles, pp. 164-166]

[Akashev, S.] PRIMENENIE METODA T. S. MAL'TSEVA V KOLKHOZAKH SOVKHOZAKH KAZAKHSTANA. (KRATKII SPISOK LIT.) Alma Ata: (Gos. Publ. B-ka Kazakh. SSR im. Pushkina), 1956, 21 pp., 1000 copies. [Kazakh text; 54 titles]

Antropova, Z. L.; L. S. Banshchikova; A. A. Kobycheva. comp. OSVOENIE TSELINY. (UKAZATEL' LIT. PO EKONOMIKE I KULTURE OBLASTEI SEV. KAZAKHSTANA.) Alma Ata: "Kazakhstan," (Gos. Resp. B-ka Kaz. SSR im. Pushkina. Tselinorg. Obl. B-ka.), 1966, 98 pp., 1500 copies. [Russ. text; 1000 titles, pub.: Jan. 1954 - Oct. 1965]

Asanov, K. NAUKA V KOLKHOZE. Alma Ata: "Kainar," 1967, 147 pp., 9000 copies. [Russ. text; titles pp. 145-146]

*Ashimbaev, T. A. VOSPROIZVODSTVO I ISPOL'ZOVANIE OSNOVNYKH PROIZVODSTVENNYKH FONDOV PROMYSHLENNOSTI (NA PRIMERE KAZAKHSTANA). Alma Ata: Izdatel'stvo Akademii Nauk Kazakhskoi SSR, 1963, 258 pp., 1300 copies. [Russ. text and titles, pp. 249-257]

*Aubakirov, Zh. A. ALMA-ATINSKAIA OBLAST' (EKON.-GEOGR. KHARAKTERISTIKA). Alma Ata: (Akad. Nauk KazSSR. Sektor Geografii), 1959, 137 pp. [Russ. text; ca.100 Russ. Kaz. titles, per.: Sov. pp. 133-138]

Kazakh: Economics

Baitasov, A. A.; A. M. Miliutina; E. N. Karaseva; et al. comp. SEL'SKOE KHOZIAISTVO KAZAKHSTANA. BIBLIOGRAFICHESKII UKAZATEL' LITERATURY. 1961-1965 GG. Vol. 1. 1967, 236 pp., 3000 copies. [Russ. text; per.: 1961-1965]

[_____.; Z. P. Stepanova; M. A. Abdulova; G. N. Korotkova. comp.] SEL'SKOE KHOZIAISTVO KAZAKHSTANA. BIBLIOGR. UKAZATEL' LIT. 1961-1965. Vol. 2. Alma Ata: (Resp. Nauch. C.-kh. B-ka), 1968, 315 pp., 3000 copies. [Russ. text; 6517 Kazakh, Russ. titles, pub.: 1961-1965]

Baitasov, A. A.; I. K. Nechipurenko. SEL'SKOKHOZIAISTVENNAIA LITERATURA KAZAKHSTANA. BIBLIOGR. UKAZ. LIT. IZD. "KAINAR." 1969, 238 pp., 2700 copies. [Kazakh, Russ. text; 1007 Kazakh, Russ. titles]

Balandina, A. A. comp. PROSHLOE I NASTOIASHCHEE KARAGANDINSKOI OBLASTI [REK. UKAZATEL' LIT.] Karaganda: (Obl. B-ka im. Gogolia), 1961, 46 pp., 400 copies. [Russ. text; 470 titles]

*[Baranskii N. N. ed.] KAZAKHSKAIA SSR. EKON.-GEOGR. KHARAKTERISTIKA. Moscow: Gosudarstvennoe Izdatel'stvo Geograficheskoi Literatury (Akad. Nauk SSSR. In-t Geografii. Akad. Nauk Kazakh SSR), 1957, 734 pp., 10,000 copies. [Russ. text; ca.650 Russ. titles, per.: Sov., pp. 701-732]

Bazarbaev, K. KUSTANAISKAIA OBLAST' (EKON.-GEOGR. KHARAKTERISTIKA). Alma Ata: (Akad. Nauk KazSSR. Otd. Geografii), 1959. [Russ. text; ca.100 titles, pp. 185-190]

Bessonov, V. A.; K. I. Shafranovskii. "OSNOVNAIA LITERATURA PO DZHEZKAZGANO-ULUTAVSKOMU I SOPREDEL'NYM RAIONAM TSENTRAL'NOGO KAZAKHSTANA," TRUDY KAZAKHSTANSKOI BAZY AN SSSR. No. 7. (BOL'SHOI DZHEZKAZGAN. SBORNIK MATERIALOV PO PROBLEME KOMPLEKSNOGO IZUCHENIIA I OSVOENIIA PRIRODNYKH RESURSOV DZHEZKAZGANO-ULUTAVSKOGO RAIONA TSENTRAL'NOGO KAZAKHSTANA.) 1935. [Russ. text; titles pp. 673-679]

*Chulanov, G. ROL' KAZAKHSTANA V SOZDANII MATERIAL'NO-TEKHNICHESKOI BAZOI KOMMUNIZMA. Alma Ata, 1963, 114 pp. [Russ. text; 70 Russ., Kaz. titles, Sov. per., pp. 113-115]

Kazakh: Economics

Dairova, A. M.; K. Sh. Bekmukhammedov. OPYT OSVOENIIA TSELINNYKH I ZALEZHNYKH ZEMEL' V KAZAKHSTANE. (KRATKII UKAZATEL' REK. LIT.). Alma Ata: (Gos. Resp. B-ka Kazakh. SSR im. Pushkina), 1956, 50 pp., 2000 copies. [Kazakh text; 112 titles]

Deeva, Z. N. GUR'EVSKAIA OBLAST' KAZAKHSKOI SSR. (ESTESTV.-IST. I EKON. KHARAKTERISTIKA I SEL. KHOZIAISTVO). UKAZATEL' LITERATURY. Alma Ata: (Kazakh. Akad. S.-Kh. Nauk Tsentr. Nauch. S.-kh. B-ka), 1960, 54 pp., 500 copies. [Russ. text; 472 titles]

_____. comp. "OSVOENIE TSELINNYKH A ZALEZHNYKH ZEMEL' KAZAKHSTANA. UKAZATEL' LITERATURY," VESTNIK AKADEMII NAUK KAZAKHSKOI SSR. No. 5. 1954. [Russ. text; titles, 92-101 pp.]

Deinekin, S. E. ed. UST' KAMENOGORSKII PEDAGOGICHESKII INSTITUT. MATERIALY VIII NAUCHNOI KONFERENTSII PROFESSORSKO-PREPODAVATEL'SKOGO SOSTAVA. SOTS. EKON. NAUKI. Ust Kamenogorsk: (M-vo Vyssh. i Sred. Spets. Obrazovaniia Kaz.SSR), 1966, 53 pp., 550 copies. [Russ. text; 20 titles at end of book]

Dosymbekov, S. N. GOSUDARSTVENNOE UPRAVLENIE PROMYSHLENNOST'IU V KAZAKHSKOI SSR. Alma Ata, 1964. [Russ. text; ca.350 titles, pp. 239-254]

EKONOMIKA I PRAVO. No. 1. Alma Ata: (M-vo Vyssh. i Sred. Spets. Obrazovaniia Kaz.SSR), 1966, 227 pp., 500 copies. [Russ. text; titles at end of articles]

EKONOMIKA I PRAVO. No. 2. Alma Ata: (M-vo Vyssh. i Sred. Spets. Obrazovaniia Kaz.SSR), 1967, 281 pp., 550 copies. [Russ. text; titles at end of articles]

Erenov, A.; S. Baisalov. PRAVO SEL'SKOKHOZIAISTVENNOGO VODOPOL'ZOVANIIA V KAZAKHSKOI SSR. Alma Ata, 1956. [Russ. text; 94 titles, per.: Sov., pp. 168-171]

Gribanov, L. N.; S. N. Uspenskii. comp. LESA I LESNOE KHOZIAISTVO. BIBLIOGRAFICHESKII UKAZATEL'. 1735-1960. Alma Ata: "Kainar," 1965, 108 pp., 1000 copies. [Russ. text; titles per.: 1735-1960]

*Iarmukhamedov, M. Sh. EKONOMICHESKAIA GEOGRAFIIA KAZAKHSKOI SSR. Alma Ata: Izdatel'stvo "Mektep," 1964, 251 pp., 4400 copies. [Russ. text; ca.90 Russ. titles, pub.: 1954-1962, pp. 247-250]

Kazakh: Economics

INDUSTRIAL'NOE SERDTSE KAZAKHSTANA. Alma Ata: "Nauka," 1968, 110 pp., 1800 copies. [Russ. text; titles pp. 107-109]

ISTORIIA ZHELEZNODOROZHNOGO TRANSPORTA KAZAKHSTANA (UKAZATEL' LITERATURY). Alma Ata: (MPS SSSR. Kaz. Zh. D. Dor. Nauch.-Tekhn. B-ka), 1967, 19 pp., 300 copies. [Russ. text]

IUBILEINOE IZDANIE K 50-LETIIU VELIKOI OKTIABR'SKOI SOTSIALISTICHESKOI REVOLIUTSII. KAZAKHSKII S.-KH. INSTITUT. TRUDY. Vol. 11. Alma Ata: "Kainar," 1968, 392 pp., 1200 copies. [Russ. text; titles at end of articles]

[Ivanchikova, E. I. et al. compilers] KARAGANDINSKII EKONOMICHESKII ADMINISTRATIVNYI RAION. BIBLIOGRAFICHESKII UKAZATEL' LITERATURY. Alma Ata: Izdatel'stvo Akademii Nauk KazSSR (Akad. Nauk KazSSR. Tsentr. Nauch. B-ka), 1959, 458 pp., 1200 copies. [Kazakh, Russ. text; 4488 Kazakh, Russ. titles, pub.: 1860-1958]

Ivanov, P. V. VERBLIUD I EGO IZUCHENIE. TRUDY OBSHCHESTVA IZUCHENIIA KAZAKSTANA (KZYL ORDA). Vol. 7, No. 1. 1926. [Russ. text; 83 titles, pp. 21-25]

Kalashnikova, T. M.; V. G. Kriuchkov. ed. METODIKA ANALIZA RAIONNYKH KOMPLEKSOV NA PRIMERE VOSTOCHNOGO KAZAKHSTANA. Moscow: (Mosk. Gos. Un-t im. M. V. Lomonosova), 1967, 133 pp., 500 copies. [Russ. text; 48 Russ. titles, pub.: 1956-1964, pp. 129-132]

*KNIGA SOVETSKOGO KAZAKHSTANA. SVODNYI BIBLIOGRAFICHESKII UKAZATEL'. 1946-1955 GG. [Vol. II-1] Alma Ata: Izdatel'stvo "Kazakhstan," (Gos. Kom. Soveta Ministrov Kaz.SSR po Pechati...), 1966, 558 pp., 3000 copies. [Kazakh text; 3940 + 2015 Kazakh, Uyghur, Russ., Dungan, Chechen, Korean titles, pub.: 1946-1955]

*Koloskov, P. I. AGROKLIMATICHESKOE RAIONIROVANIE V KAZAKHSTANE. I. TEKST. Moscow-Leningrad: Izdatel'stvo Akademii Nauk SSR, 1947, 268 pp., 2000 copies. [Russ. text; 212 Russ., Europ. titles, pp. 261-266]

Kazakh: Economics

Korobitsyna, T. D.; L. M. Orlianskaia. NAUCHNAIA
ORGANIZATSIIA TRUDA, PROIZVODSTVA I UPRAVLENIIA.
Alma Ata: (Gosplan Kaz.SSR. Tsinti), 1968, 205 pp.,
2600 copies. [Russ. text; titles at end of chapters]

*Kuzembaev, N. POD"EM MATERIAL'NOGO BLAGOSTOIANIIA I
KUL'TURNOGO UROVNIA SEL'SKOGO NASELENIIA KAZAKHSTANA.
Alma Ata, 1964, 180 pp. [Russ. text; 75 Russ.,
Kazakh titles, per.: Sov., pp. 177-179]

*Kuznetsova, Z. V. PAVLODARSKAIA OBLAST' (EKONOMIKO-
GEOGRAFICHESKAIA KHARAKTERISTIKA). Alma Ata:
Izdatel'stvo Akademii Nauk Kazakhskoi SSR, 1958,
181 pp., 1500 copies. [Russ. text and titles,
per.: 1954-1956, pp. 176-180]

Kuznetsova, Z. V.; I. I. Kuritsyn. SEMIPALATINSKAIA
OBLAST'. (EKON-GEOGR. KHARAKTER.) Alma Ata, 1961.
[Russ. text; ca.160 titles, pp. 209-214]

Lapshin, V. A. comp. NAVSTRECHU 40-LETIIU KAZAKHSTANA.
SBORNIK METOD. I BIBLIOGR. MATERIALOV. Kustanai:
(Obl. B-ka im. Tolstogo), 1960 22 pp., 1000 copies.
[Russ. text; per.: Sov.]

"LITERATURA O GOLODNOI STEPI," SEL'SKOE KHOZIAISTVO
KAZAKHSTANA. No. 10, 1956. [Russ. text; 20
titles, pub.: 1921-1956. pp. 34-35]

*Magidovich, I. "DZHETI-SU," BOL'SHAIA SOVETSKAIA
ENTSIKLOPEDIIA. Vol. 21. Moscow: Gosudarstvennoe
Slovarno-Entsiklopedicheskoe Izdatel'stvo
"Sovetskaia Entsiklopediia," (Ogiz RSFSR), 1931,1st ed.,
775-786 pp. [Russ. text and titles, pp. 785-786]

*Malybaev, O. BOR'BA KPSS ZA SOZDANIE I RAZVITIE
TRET'EI UGOL'NOI BAZY SSSR. Alma Ata: Kazgosizdat,
1961, 405 pp. [Russ. text; 326 Russ., other
titles, pp. 339-405]

*Margulan, A. Kh. DREVNIE KARAVANNYE PUTI CHEREZ
PUSTYNIU BETPAK-DALA. VESTNIK AKADEMII NAUK
KAZAKHSKOI SSR. No. 1. [1949] 78 pp. [Russ. text;
28 Russ. titles, pp. 77-78]

Morachevskaia, E. N. comp. BIBLIOGRAFIIA PO RAZVITIIU
PROIZVODITEL'NYKH SIL KUSTANAISKOGO EKONOMICHESKOGO
ADMINISTRATIVNOGO RAIONA I BOL'SHOGO TURGAIA V
TSELOM. (1801-1959 GG.) Moscow: (Akad. Nauk SSSR),
1959, 35 pp., 500 copies. [Russ. text; 1033 titles,
per.: 1801-1959]

Kazakh: Economics

NASELENIE I TRUDOVYE RESURSY GORODOV SEVERNOGO
KAZAKHSTANA. Alma Ata, 1970. [Russ. text; ca.120
titles, pp. 265-273]

Ogneva, N. G. RISOSEIANIE V KZYL-ORDINSKOI OBLASTI.
Kzyl Orda: (Kzyl-Ordin. Obl. B-ka im. M. Gor'kogo),
1965 (Vyp. Dan. 1966) 32 pp., 400 copies. [Kazakh,
Russ. text]

OPYT PEREDOVIKOV SEL'SKOGO KHOZIAISTVA KAZAKHSKOI SSR.
ANNOTIROVANNYI UKAZATEL' LITERATURY. Alma Ata:
Izdatel'stvo Akademii Nauk Kazakhskoi SSR, 1955,
291 pp., 10,000 copies. [Russ. text; ca.500 Kazakh,
Russ. titles, pub.: 1945-1954]

[Parkhomenko, I. I.] comp. EKONOMICHESKIE
ADMINISTRATIVNYE RAIONY SSSR. UKAZATEL' NOVOI LIT.
PO PRIRODE RESURSAM I KHOZIAISTVU. No. 12.
"KAZAKHSKAIA SSR." Moscow: (Akad. Nauk SSSR. In-t
Nauch. Informatsii), 1958, 143 pp., 500 copies.
[Russ. text; ca.2500 titles, pub.: 1950-1957]

*Petrov, G. N. "NEKOTORYE NEOTLOZHNYE ZADACHI VODNOGO
KHOZIAISTVA KAZAKHSTANA," VESTNIK AKAD. NAUK KAZ. SSR.
No. 4. Alma Ata, 1962. [Russ. text; 43 Russ.,
other titles, per.: Sov., pp. 21-22]

*Petrushin, N. I. LENINSKIM KURSOM K SPLOSHNOI
ELEKTRIFIKATSII. Alma Ata: "Znanie," 1968 (Vyp. Dan.
1969) 59 pp., 4500 copies. [Russ. text; pp. 57-58]

POLEZNYE ISKOPAEMYE KAZAKSTANA. MATERIALY PO BIBLIOGRAFII
ZA 1752-1929. Moscow-Leningrad: Geologicheskoe
Izdatel'stvo, 1931, 240 pp. [Russ. text; 1804 titles,
pub.: 1752-1929]

Polovich, A. comp. ALMA-ATINSKAIA OBLAST'. K 40-LETIIU
KAZ. SOTS. RESPUBLIKI. REK. UKAZATEL' LIT. Alma Ata:
(Obl. B-ka), 1960, 74 pp., 1000 copies. [Russ.
text; 611 titles, Sov. per.]

PRIMENENIE METODA T. S MAL'TSEVA V KAZAKHSTANE
(UKAZATEL' LITERATURY). Alma Ata: (M-vo Sel.
Khoziaistva KazSSR), 1957, 27 pp., 7000 copies.
[Russ. text]

PROIZVODITEL'NYE SILY IUZHNOGO KAZAKHSTANA. Vol. 2.
SEL'SKOE KHOZIAISTVO, PISHCHEVAIA I LEGKAIA
PROMYSHLENNOST'. Alma Ata: "Nauka," 1967, 363 pp.,
1150 copies. [Russ. text; titles at end of reports]

Kazakh: Economics

*RAZVITIE I RAZMESHCHENIE PROIZVODITEL'NYKH SIL
KAZAKHSKOI SSR. Moscow: Izdatel'stvo "Nauka,"
1967, 259 pp., 2600 copies. [Russ. text; 72 Russ.
titles, pp. 251-253]

RUDNYI ALTAI. BIBLIOGRAFICHESKII UKAZATEL' LITERATURY.
Alma Ata: Kazgosizdat, 1940, 56 pp., 285 copies.
[Russ. text]

Semenova, M. I. DZHAMBULSKAIA OBLAST'. (PRIRODA,
NASELENIE I KHOZIAISTVO). Alma Ata: (Akademiia Nauk
Kazakhskoi SSR. Otd. Geografii), 1961. [Russ. text;
200 titles, pp. 211-217]

*_____. PRIRODA I KHOZIAISTVO IUZHNO-
KHAZAKHSTANSKOI OBLASTI (EKON.-GEOG. KHARAKTERISTIKA).
Alma Ata: (Akad. Nauk KazSSR. Sektor Geografii),
1959, 143 pp., 3400 copies. [Russ. text; 57 Kazakh,
Russ. titles, per.: Sov., pp. 141-142]

Shaukenbaev, T. URALO-EMBENSKII NEFTENOSNYI RAION.
Alma Ata: Kazgosizdat, 1960. [Russ. text; 185 titles,
pp. 206-214]

Sokolova, N. V.; A. A. Kobycheva; S. M. Akhinzhanova.
compilers. K SOROKALETIIU KAZAKHSKOI SOVETSKOI
SOTSIALISTICHESKOI RESPUBLIKI. (METOD I BIBLIOGR.
MATERIALY V POMOSHCH' B-KAM RESPUBLIKI). SB. 1.
Alma Ata: (Gos. Resp. B-ka KazSSR im. Pushkina), 1960,
35 pp., 5000 copies. [Russ. text; titles, per.: Sov.]

*Suleimenov, B. AGRARNYI VOPROS V KAZAKHSTANE POSLEDNEI
TRETI XIX-NACHALA XX V. (1867-1907 GG.), Alma Ata,
1963, 410 pp. [Russ. text; ca.700 Russ., other titles
(incl. archives), pp. 3-21, 376-409, per.: 1867-1907]

Tolmacheva, A. K.; I. P. Arianina. comp. PROMYSHLENNAIA
ESTETIKA I KUL'TURA PROIZVODSTVA. BIBLIOGR. 1964, 1965.
Alma Ata: (Tsinti pri Gosplane Kaz.SSR), 1966, 18 pp.,
400 copies. [Russ. text; per.: 1964-1965]

Urazova, M. I. comp. MASHINOSTROITEL'NAIA
PROMYSHLENNOST' KAZAKHSTANA. BIBLIOGR. UKAZATEL'
LITERATURY ZA 1961-1967 GG. Alma Ata: (Gosplan Kaz.SSR
Tsinti), 1968, 56 pp., 300 copies. [Russ. text;
per.: 1961-1967]

Vasil'eva, M. S.; A. V. Chigarkii. PRIRODA I KHOZIAISTVO
DZHEZKAZGANSKOGO PROMYSHLENNOGO RAIONA. Alma Ata:
(Akad. Nauk KazSSR. Sektor Geografii), 1959.
[Russ. text; 42 titles, pp. 95-97]

Kazakh: Economics

Voshchinin, V. L. EKONOMICHESKAIA GEOGRAFIIA SSSR PO RAIONAM. KAZAKSTAN. Moscow-Leningrad: Gosudarstvennoe Izdatel'stvo, [ca.1929?]. [Russ. text]

VOSTOCHNO-KAZAKHSTANSKAIA S.-KH. OPYTNAIA STANTSIIA. TRUDY. Vol. 1. Ust-Kamenogorsk: (M-vo Sel. Khoz-va Kaz.SSR), 1967, 224 pp., 2000 copies. [Russ. text; titles at end of articles]

VOZNIKNOVENIE I RAZVITIE ZHIZNI NA ZEMLE (BESEDA O KNIGAKH). Alma Ata: (Izd-vo AN Kaz. SSR), 1952, 23 pp., 3000 copies. [Russ. text]

Zhumagaliev, B. DARY STEPNYKH PROSTOROV. Alma Ata: "Kazakhstan," 1968, 144 pp., 6000 copies. [Russ. text; titles, pp. 140-143]

ZONA STALINGRADSKOGO KANALA (SEVERNAIA CHAST' PRIKASPIISKOI NIZMENNOSTI). PRIRODNYE USLOVIIA, NARODNOE KHOZIAISTVO, PREOBRAZOVANIE PRIRODY, EKONOMICHESKOE OSVOENIE I GIDROTEKHNICHESKOE STROITEL'STVO. BIBLIOGRAFICHESKII UKAZATEL'. n. p. (Akademiia Nauk Kazakhskoi SSR. Tsentral'naia Nauchnaia Biblioteka), 1953, 182 pp. [Russ. text]

EDUCATION

*Abdulkadyrova, M. A.; S. B. Beisembaev; S. S. Golubiatnikov; Kh. Kh. Khabiev. eds. KUL'TURNOE STROITEL'STVO V KAZAKHSTANE (1918-1932 GG.). SBORNIK DOKUMENTOV I MATERIALOV. Vol. 1. Alma Ata: Izdatel'stvo "Kazakhstan," 1965, 566 pp., 2300 copies. [Russ. text; Kazakh, Russ. titles, incl. archives, per.: 1918-1932, pp. 554-560]

*Asfendiarov, S. "NARODNOE OBRAZOVANIE....ISTORICHESKII OCHERK," BOL'SHAIA SOVETSKAIA ENTSIKLOPEDIIA. Vol. 30. Moscow: Gosudarstvennyi Institut "Sovetskaia Entsiklopediia," (Ogiz RSFSR), 1937, 586-599 pp. [Russ. text; Kazakh, Russ. titles, p. 599]

Kazakh: Education

*Borukaev, R. A.; E. D. Shlygin. "TRUDY K. I. SATPAEVA." VESTNIK. AKAD. NAUK KAZAKHSKOI SSR. No. 4. [1949] [Russ. text; 187 Kazakh, Russ. titles, pub.: 1923-1949, pp. 29-33]

Dadabaeva, P. S. OBSHCHESTVENNO-POLEZNYI TRUD UCHASHCHIKHSIA V ISTORII KIRGIZSKOI SOVETSKOI SHKOLY. (1918-1964 GG.) Frunze, 1966. [Russ. text; 133 titles, pp. 138-143]

Erokhina, E. A. PIS'MENNYE RABOTY V X-VII KLASSAKH KAZAKHSKOI SHKOLY V SVIAZI S UROKAMI OB"IASNITEL'NOGO I LITERATURNOGO CHTENIIA. Alma Ata, 1962. [Russ. text; 41 titles, pp. 57-59]

Fridman, Ts. L. BIBLIOGRAFICHESKII SBORNIK. Alma Ata: (Kazakh. Gos. Ped. In-t im. Abaia), 1961, 257 pp., 1000 copies. [Russ. text; 2873 Kazakh, Russ. titles, pub.: 1928-Oct. 1960]

Kantarbaeva, G. M. LITERATURA PO VOPROSAM PREPODAVANIIA RUSSKOGO IAZYKA V KAZAKHSKIKH I DRUGIKH NATSIONAL'NYKH SHKOLAKH (BIBLIOGR. UKAZATEL'). Alma Ata: (Nauch.-Issled. In-t Ped. Nauk M-va Prosveshcheniia Kaz. SSR), 1958, 56 pp., 5000 copies. [Russ. text; ca.450 titles, pub.: 1937-1958]

[Karpunskaia, L. A.] LITERATURA PO VOPROSAM OBUCHENIIA I VOSPITANIIA V SHKOLE I DETSKIKH UCHREZHDENIIAKH. No. 2. Alma Ata: (NII Ped. Nauk M-va Prosveshcheniia Kaz. SSR), 1967, 112 pp., 10,000 copies. [Russ. text; ca.900 Kazakh, Russ. titles, pub.: 1960-1965]

Kovaleva, K. IKH IMENAMI SLAVEN NASH KRAI (KRATKII REK. UKAZATEL' LITERATURY DLIA UCHASHCHIKHSIA 7-8-KH KLASSOV.) Ust Kamenogorsk: (Vost. Kazakhst. Obl. Det. B-ka im. A. P. Gaidara), 1966, 15 pp., 600 copies. [Russ. text]

Krotevich, E. V. RABOTA NAD SLOVOM. Alma Ata: (In-t Shkol. NKProsa KazSSR), 1939, 39 pp. [Russ. text; 28 titles, pub.: 1893-1939]

Lepilov, V. P. METODIKA PREPODAVANIIA RUSSKOGO IAZYKA V 5-8 KLASSAKH KAZAKHSKOI SHKOLY. Alma Ata, 1966. [Russ. text; 52 titles, pp. 119-121]

LITERATURA DLIA UCHITELIA PO VOPROSAM ESTETICHESKOGO VOSPITANIIA UCHASHCHIKHSIA. Alma Ata: (Upr. Shkol M-va Prosveshcheniia KazSSR. Nauch-Issled. In-t Ped. Nauk), 1959, 15 pp., 9000 copies. [Russ. text; 184 Kazakh, Russ. titles]

Kazakh: Education

"LITERATURA O NAUKE I KUL'TURE SREDNEI AZII I KAZAKHSTANA," VELIKIE UCHENYE SREDNEI AZII I KAZAKHSTANA (IX-XIX VEKOV). Alma Ata, 1964. [Kazakh text; 111 titles, per.: 9th -19th c., pp. 298-301]

Meiramov, G. A. SISTEMA OBUCHENIIA RUSSKOMU GRAMMATICHESKOMU UPRAVLENIIU UCHASHCHIKHSIA-KAZAKOV. Alma Ata, 1968. [Russ. text; ca.120 titles, pp. 209-214]

Rakhimbekov, K. K VOPROSU OB IZUCHENII VOSSOZDAIUSHCHEGO VOOBRAZHENIIA. Alma Ata: (Ministerstvo Vysshego i Srednego Spetsial'nogo Obrazovaniia Kazakhskoi SSR. Nauchno-Metodichnyi Kabinet Vysshego i Srednego Spetsial'nogo Obrazovaniia), 1967, 62 pp., 1500 copies. [Russ. text; survey]

_____. K VOPROSU OB IZUCHENII VOSSOZDAIUSHCHEGO VOOBRAZHENIIA. No. 2. Alma Ata: (M-vo Vyssh. i Sred. Spets. Obrazovaniia KazSSR. Nauch.-Metod Kabinet Vyssh. i Sred. Spets. Obrazovaniia, 1967. 48 pp., 1500 copies. [Russ. text]

*Sabitov, N. "BIBLIOGRAFICHESKII UKAZATEL' MATERIALOV O ZHIZNI I DEIATEL'NOSTI KAZAKHSKOGO PEDAGOGA I PROSVETITELIA IBRAGIMA ALTYNSARINA (1841-1889)," VESTNIK AKADEMII NAUK KAZAKHSKOI SSR. No. 5. 1950, 98 pp. [Russ. text; ca.100 Kazakh, Russ. titles, pp. 54-57]

Salikhova, T. comp. TVOI LIUBIMYE KNIGI. Alma Ata, "Kazakhstan," 1967, 13 pp. 10000 copies. [Russ. text; Kazakh titles]

Sitdykov, A. S. PEDAGOGICHESKIE IDEI I PROSVETITEL'NAIA DEIATEL'NOST' I. ALTYNSARINA. Alma Ata: (Nauch.-Issled. In-t Shkol M-va Prosveshcheniia KazSSR) [Russ. text; 48 titles, pub.: 1853-1949, pp. 193-195]

_____. PEDAGOGICHESKIE IDEI I PROSVETITEL'NAIA DEIATELNOST' I. ALTYNSARINA. Alma Ata: (Nauch.-Issled. In-t Shkol M-va Prosveshcheniia KazSSR), 1950. [Kazakh text; 39 Kazakh, Russ. titles, pp. 184-185]

Sufiev, E. NEKOTORYE VOPROSY PSIKHOLOGII OBUCHENIIA RUSSKOMU IAZYKU V KAZAKHSKOI SHKOLE. Alma Ata, 1967. [Russ. text; 114 titles, pp. 73-78]

Kazakh: Education

Sytdykov, A. N. K. KRUPSKAIA. ZHIZN' I DEIATEL'NOST'
I PED. NASLEDIE. Alma Ata: Kazuchpedgiz, 1959.
[Kazakh text; 108 Kazakh titles, pp. 83-88]

Tursunov, D. METODIKA PREPODAVANIIA RUSSKOGO IAZYKA V
STARSHIKH KLASSAKH KAZAKHSKOI SHKOLY. Alma Ata,
1966. [Russ. text; 133 titles, pp. 109-114]

"UKAZATEL' SODERZHANIIA OFFITSIAL'NAGO OTDIELA
'VIESTNIKA ORENBURGSKAGO UCHEBNAGO OKRUGA' ZA 1912
GOD. (Nos. I-VIII)," VIESTNIK ORENBURGSKAGO
UCHEBNAGO OKRUGA. Ufa, No. 7/8, 1912. [Russ. text;
pub.: 1912, pp. 1-17]

"UKAZATEL' STATEI NAUCHNAGO OTDIELA V VIESTNIKIE
ORENBURGSKAGO UCHEBNAGO OKRUGA ZA 1913 GOD (Nos. I-VIII),"
Ufa, No. 7/8. 1913. [Russ. text; pub.: 1913,
p..253]

GEOGRAPHY

Abdrakhmanov, A. GEOGRAFICHESKIE NAZVANIIA KAZAKHSTANA.
Alma Ata: (Akad. Nauk KazSSR In-t Iazyka i Lit.),
1959. [Kazakh text; ca.230 Kazakh, Russ titles,
pp. 206-219]

"AKHTUBA," ENTSIKLOPEDICHESKII SLOVAR' Vol. 2A.
St. Petersburg: F. A. Brokgauz, I. A. Efron, 1891,
539-540 pp. [Russ. text; Russ., Europ. titles,
p. 540]

Chupakhin, V. M. PRIRODNOE RAIONIROVANIE KAZAKHSTANA.
Alma Ata, 1970. [Russ. text; 145 titles, pp. 255-261]

Deeva, Z. N.; M. V. Danilova. GOLODNAIA STEP'.
UKAZATEL' LIT.) Alma Ata: (M-vo Sovkhozov Kazakh.
SSR. Otd. Propagandy), 1956, 40 pp., 1000 copies.
[Russ. text; ca.370 titles, pub.: 1875-1956]

Donich, A. N. "NARODONASELENIE KAZAKSTANA," NARODNOE
KHOZIAISTVO KAZAKSTANA. No. 11/12. 1928. [Russ.
text; 30 titles, p. 56]

Kazakh: Geography

GEOGRAFICHESKIE ISSLEDOVANIIA V KAZAKHSTANE. TRUDY.
No. 33(48). Alma Ata: (Geogr. O-vo SSSR. Kaz.
Filial), 1968, 323 pp., 500 copies. [Russ. text;
titles at end of reports]

*GEOGRAFIIA RAIONOV OSVOENIIA KAZAKHSTANA. Alma Ata:
(Voprosy Geografii Kazakhstana, No. 14), "Nauka,"
1968, 132 pp., 800 copies. [Russ. text; 74 Russ.
titles, pub.: 1913-1967, pp. 23, 50, 72-73, 82, 99,
112, 119, 126-127, 132]

Gladysheva, E. N. SEVERO-KAZAKHSTANSKAIA OBLAST' (EKON.-
GEOG. KHARAKTERISTIKA), Alma Ata: (Akad. Nauk. Kaz. SSR.
Otdel. Geografii), 1959. [Russ. text; ca.170 titles,
pp. 180-185]

*Ianitskii, N. "KAZAKHSKAIA SOVETSKAIA SOTSIALISTICHESKAIA
RESPUBLIKA" (KAZAKHSTAN), BOL'SHAIA SOVETSKAIA
ENTSIKLOPEDIIA. Vol. 30. Moscow: Gosudarstvennyi
Institut "Sovetskaia Entsiklopediia," (Ogiz RSFSR),
1937, 1st ed., 561-586 pp. [Russ. text; Kazakh,
Russ. titles, pp. 585-586]

KAZAKHSTAN. OBSHCHAIA FIZ.-GEOGR. KHARAKTERISTIKA.
Moscow-Leningrad: (Akad. Nauk SSSR. In-t
Geografii. Akad. Nauk KazSSR), 1950. [Russ. text;
ca.260 titles, pp. 462-473]

*KAZAKHSTAN [PRIRODNYE USLOVIIA I ESTESTV. RESURSY].
Moscow: "Nauka," (Akad. Nauk SSSR: In-t Geog.), 1969,
482 pp., 2800 copies. [Russ. text; ca.400 Russ.
titles, pub.: 1878-1968, pp. 457-469]

Konkashpaev, G. K. KAZAKHSKIE NARODNYE GEOGRAFICHESKIE
TERMINY. IZVESTIIA AKAD. NAUK KAZSSR, No. 99.
SERIIA GEOGR. No. 3. 1951. [Russ. text; 85 Russ.,
Sov. Asian titles, pp. 45-47]

*Magidovich, I. "GUR'EVSKII OKRUG," BOL'SHAIA
SOVETSKAIA ENTSIKLOPEDIIA. Vol. 20. Moscow:
Aktsionernoe Obshchestvo "Sovetskaia Entsiklopediia,"
1930, 18-23 pp. [Russ. text and titles, p. 23]

Mil'kov, F. N. ORENBURGSKIE STEPI V TRUDAKH P. I.
RYCHKOVA, E. A. EVERSMANNA, I S. S. NEUSTRUEVA.
Moscow: Geografgiz, 1949. [Russ. text; 55 titles,
per.: 19th c., pp. 411-413]

Mynbaev, K. M. PUSTYNIA BETPAK-DALA. Alma Ata:
(Akad. Nauk. Kazakhskoi SSR), 1948. [Russ. text;
21 titles, pub.: 1894-1947, pp. 96-97]

Kazakh: Geography

*N. Ia. "KARSAKPAISKII RAION," BOL'SHAIA SOVETSKAIA
ENTSIKLOPEDIIA. Vol. 31. Moscow: Gosudarstvennyi
Institut "Sovetskaia Entsiklopediia," (Ogiz RSFSR),
1937, 621-622 pp. [Russ. text and titles, p. 622]

*Pal'gov, N. N. KAZAKHSTAN. POPULIARNYI FIZIKO-
GEOGRAFICHESKII OCHERK. Moscow: Gosudarstvennoe
Izdatel'stvo Geograficheskoi Literatury, 1953,
168 pp., 25,000 copies. [Russ. text and titles,
pub.: 1923 -1950, pp. 166-167]

*_____. KAZAKHSTAN OT URAL'SKA DO ALMA-ATY.
Alma Ata: Izdatel'stvo "Nauka," Kazakhskoi SSR,
1965, 256 pp., 6760 copies. [Russ. text and titles,
pub.: 1934-1963, pp. 251-255]

PROBLEMY FIZICHESKOI, EKONOMICHESKOI I MEDITSINSKOI
GEOGRAFII KAZAKHSTANA. Alma Ata, 1967, 159 pp.
[Russ. text; titles at end of articles]

RAZVITIE GEOGRAFICHESKIKH NAUK V KAZAKHSTANE. Alma Ata:
"Kazakhstan," 1967, 151 pp., 1400 copies. [Russ.
text; titles at end of works]

*Semenov-Tian'-Shanskii, V. P. ed. ROSSIIA.
POLNOE GEOGRAFICHESKOE OPISANIE NASHEGO OTECHESTVA.
Vol. 18. "KIRGIZSKII KRAI." St. Petersburg:
Izdanie A. F. Devriena, 1903, 478 pp. [Russ. text;
676 Russ., Europ. titles, per.: 19 c., pp. 436-453]

Shnitnikov, V. N. "LITERATURA PO SEMIRECHIIU.
OBSHCHAIA GEOGRAFIIA. KLIMAT. GEOLOGIIA.
MINERALOGIIA. POCHVOVEDENIE. BOTANIKA. ZOOLOGIIA.
ETNOGRAFIIA I ANTROPOLOGIIA. ARKHEOLOGIIA. ISTORIIA,"
DZHETYSU (SEMIRECH'E). Tashkent, 1925. [Russ.
text; 510 titles, pp. 215-234]

Titova, A. S. SLOVAR' RUSSKOI TRANSKRIPTSII TERMINOV I
SLOV, CHASTO VSTRECHAIUSHCHIKHSIA V GEOGRAFICHESKIKH
NAZVANIIAKH KAZAKHSKOI SSR. Moscow, (Tsentr.
Nauch.-Issled. In-t Geodezii), 1960. [Russ. text;
46 titles, pp. 59-61]

*VOPROSY GEOGRAFII KAZAKHSTANA. No. 13. ZASUSHLIVYE
ZONY KAZAKHSTANA. Alma Ata: Izdatel'stvo "Nauka"
Kazakhskoi SSR, 1966, 236 pp., 1000 copies.
[Russ. text and titles, at end of articles]

Kazakh: Geography

*VOPROSY GEOGRAFII KAZAKHSTANA. No. 14. GEOGRAFIIA RAIONOV OSVOENIIA KAZAKHSTANA. Alma Ata: Izdatel'stvo "Nauka" Kazakhskoi SSR, 1968, 128 pp., 800 copies. [Russ. text and titles at end of articles]

ZASUSHLINYE ZONY KAZAKHSTANA. Alma Ata: (Voprosy Geografii Kazakhstana. No. 13). 1966, 236 pp. [Russ. text; titles at end of articles]

HISTORY, ARCHEOLOGY

*Abisheva, B. N.; A. A. Baishin; E. L. Vilenskii; et al. comp. ISTORIIA INDUSTRIALIZATSII KAZAKHSKOI SSR. Vol. 2. 1933-IIUN' 1941 GG. Alma Ata: Izdatel'stvo "Nauka," 1967, 434 pp., 2800 copies. [Russ. text; titles per.: 1933-1941, p. 419]

*Abishev, G. KAZAKHSTAN V VELIKOI OTECHESTVENNOI VOINE. Alma Ata: Kazakhskoe Gosudarstvennoe Izdatel'stvo, 1958, 361 pp., 10,000 copies. [Russ. text and titles, per.: 1941-1945 (WW.II) pp. 346-360]

Ageeva, E. I. ed. "ARKHEOLOGICHESKIE ISSLEDOVANIIA NA SEVERNYKH SKLONAKH KARATAU," TRUDY IN-TA ISTORII, ARKHEOLOGII I ETNOGRAFII IM. VALIKHANOVA. Vol. 14. Alma Ata, 1962, 220 pp. [Russ. text]

_____; V. V. Andronnikov; G. I. Semeniuk; G. P. Tsarev; N. V. Chechulina, comp. BIBLIOGRAFIIA PO ISTORII KAZAKHSTANA (ANNOT. UKAZATEL'). No. 1. DOREVOLIUTSIONNYI PERIOD. Alma Ata: Kazgosizdat, 1964, 410 pp., 5000 copies. [Russ. text; 2483 Russ. titles, per.: pre-Sov., pub.: 19th c. - 1960, p. 410]

* _____ et al. BIBLIOGRAFIIA PO ISTORII KAZAKHSTANA. No. 1. DOREVOLIUTSIONNYI PERIOD. Alma Ata: Kazgosizdat, 1964, 410 pp., 5000 copies. [Russ. text; 2483 Kazakh, Russ., foreign titles, per.: pre-1917]

Aitbaev, E., ed. KAZAKHSKAIA SSR K 40-LETIIU VELIKOI OKTIABR'SKOI SOTSIALISTICHESKOI REVOLIUTSII. Alma Ata: (Gos. Resp. B-ka Kazakh. SSR im. Pushkina), 1957, 235 pp., 5000 copies. [Kazakh text; ca.250 titles, per.: Sov.]

Kazakh: History, Archaeology

*Akashev, S.; A. Zhamankulova; P. A. Kovaleva; V. P. Kolesnikova; (comp.). IZDANIE PROIZVEDENII V. I. LENINA V KAZAKHSTANE 1918-1969 GG. (BIBLIOGR. UKAZ.) Alma Ata: "Kazakhstan," 1970, 129 pp., 3000 copies. [Kazakh, Russ. text; 493 Kazakh, Uyghur, Chechen, Russ. titles, pub.: 1918-1969, pp. 29-119]

*Akhmetova, M.; S. S. Safonova; G. I. Semeniuk. CHOKAN VALIKHANOV. (ANNOTIROVANNYI UKAZATEL' LITERATURY). Alma Ata: Izdatel'stvo "Kazakhstan," 1967, 217 pp., 3000 copies. [Kazakh, Russ. text; 826 Kazakh, Russ.titles pub.: 1857-1965]

Andronnikov, V. V.; G. P. Tsarev. "ISTORIIA KAZAKHSTANA. (BIBLIOGRAFIIA ZA 1961 G.)," VOPROSY ISTORII KAZAKHSTANA. (UCHEN. ZAPISKI KAZ. GOS. UN-T IM. KIROVA. Vol. 54.) Alma Ata, 1963. [Russ. text; ca.250 titles, pub.: 1961, pp. 217-227]

Arslanova, F. Kh. SREDNEVEKOVYI MOGIL'NIK IZ PRIIRTYSH'IA. SBORNIK STATEI ASPIRANTOV I SOISKATELEI. [n. p.] (M-vo Vyssh. i Sred. Spets. Obrazovaniia KazSSR), ISTORIIA, FILOSOFIIA, EKONOMIKA. No. 3. 1963. [Russ. text; 31 titles, p. 294]

*Asfendiarov, S. D. ISTORIIA KAZAKSTANA (S DREVNEISHIKH VREMEN). Vol. 1. Alma Ata-Moscow: Qazaqistan olkeliq Baspasi, 1935, 263 pp., 10,000 copies. [Russ. text; Russ., Europ. titles, pp. 253-256]

* _____.; P. A. Kunte. PROSHLOE KAZAKHSTANA V ISTOCHNIKAKH I MATERIALAKH. SBORNIK I. V. DO N. E.-XVIII V.N.E. Alma Ata-Moscow: Kazakhskoe Kraevoe Izdatel'stvo, 1935, 299 pp., 3000 copies. [Russ. text; Russ., Europ. titles, up to 18th c., pp. 292-298]

*Auezov, L. M. "UKAZATEL' PECHATNYKH TRUDOV CH. CH. VALIKHANOVA," VALIKHANOV, CH. CH. IZBRANNYE PROIZVEDENIIA. Alma Ata: Kaz. Gos. Izd-vo Khudozhestvennoi Literatury, 1958, 643 pp., 20,000 copies. [Russ. text; 34 Russ. titles, pub.: 1861-1950; pp. 619-620]

[Bagriantsev et al. compilers] SOVETSKOE STROITEL'STVO V AULAKH I SELAKH SEMIRECH'IA. 1921-1925 GG. Pt. 1. Alma Ata: Alma-Atin. i Taldy-Kurganskii Obl. Gosarkhivy. In-t Istorii, 1957. [Russ. text; ca.40 titles, per.: 1921-1925, pp. 260-264]

Kazakh: History, Archaeology

*Baishev, S. B. ed. ISTORIIA INDUSTRIALIZATSII
KAZAKHSKOI SSR. Vol. 1. (1926-1932 G). Alma Ata:
"Nauka," 1967, 479 pp., 2720 copies. [Russ. text
and titles, per.: 1926-1932, pp. 462-464]

*_____·POBEDA SOTSIALIZMA V KAZAKHSTANE.
(OCHERKI PO TEORII I ISTORII VOPROSA). Alma Ata:
(Akademiia Nauk Kazakhskoi SSR), 1961, 325 pp.,
2500 copies. [Russ. text; ca.470 Russ. titles,
Sov. per., pp. 311-324]

[Begalina, E. comp.] GEROI GRAZHDANSKOI VOINY I
PERIODA USTANOVLENIIA SOVETSKOI VLASTI V KAZAKHSTANE.
PAMIATKA CHITATELIAM--UCHASHCHIMSIA 7-8-KH KLASSOV.
No. 2. Alma Ata: "Kazakhstan," 1968, 12 pp.,
500 copies. [Russ. text]

_____. GEROI V SOLDATSKIKH SHINELIAKH.
Alma Ata: "Kazakhstan," 1967, 16 pp., 10,000 copies.
[Russ. text]

Bekmakhanov, E. OCHERKI ISTORII KAZAKHSTANA XIX V.
Alma Ata: "Mektep," 1966, 191 pp., 7600 copies.
[Russ. text; 65 titles, pp. 187-190]

*_____. PRISOEDINENIE KAZAKHSTANA K ROSSII.
Moscow: (Akad. Nauk SSSR. In-t Istorii. Kazakh. Gos.
Un-t im. S. M. Korova), 1957, 339 pp. [Russ. text;
ca.500 Russ. titles, per.: 18-19th c., pp. 327-341]

Bernshtam, A. N. "PROBLEMY DREVNEI ISTORII I ETNOGENEZA
IUZHNOGO KAZAKHSTANA." IZV. AN KAZSSR. Vol. 67,
(SERIIA ARKHEOLOGICHESKAIA) No. 2. 1949, 99 pp.
[Russ. text; 53 titles, per.: ancient]

"BIBLIOGRAFICHESKII UKAZATEL' STATEI, KASAIUSHCHIKHSIA
RAZVALIN KZYL-KENSHA," ZAPISKI SEMIPALATINSKOGO
OTDELA OBSHCHESTVA IZUCHENIIA KAZAKHSTANA. No. 28,
Part 1. 1929. [Russ. text; 18 titles, pp. 96-98]

[Bikineeva, D. comp.] PEROVSKII OTRIAD KRASNOI
GVARDII. (REK. SPISOK LIT.) Kzyl Orda: (Kzyl-
Ordin. Obl. B-ka ij. Gorkogo. Velikii Oktiabr'. 50)
1967, 350 pp. [Kazakh, Russ. text; 60 Kazakh, Russ.,
titles, p. 32]

Chernikov, S. S. VOSTOCHNYI KAZAKHSTAN V EPOKHU
BRONZY. Moscow-Leningrad: (Akad. Nauk SSSR. In-t
Arkheol. Materialy i Issled. po. Arkheol. SSSR),
1960. [Russ. text; ca.350 Russ., other titles,
pp. 179-194]

Kazakh: History, Archaeology

Chulanov, G. PROMYSHLENNOST' DOREVOLIUTSIONNOGO
KAZAKHSTANA. (IST.-EKON. OCHERK). Alma Ata:
(Akad. Nauk KazASSR. In-t Ekonomiki), 1960. [Russ.
text; ca.100 titles, per.: pre-1917, pp. 98-101]

Chuloshnikov, A. P. OCHERKI PO ISTORII KAZAK-
KIRGIZSKOGO NARODA V SVIAZI S OBSHCHIMI ISTORICHESKIMI
SUD'BAMI DRUGIKH TIURKSKIKH PLEMEN. Part 1.
DREVNEE VREMIA I SREDNIE VEKA. (TRUDY OBSHCHESTVA
IZUCHENIIA KIRGIZSKOGO KRAIA. No. 5, pp. 285-291)
Orenburg: Kirgizskoe Gos. Izdat., 1924, XII; 291; 3 pp.
[Russ. text; 200+ Russ. titles, per.: antiquity to 18th
c., pub.: 1750-1917, pp. 13, 37-38, 58, 78-79, 100-101,
133, 161, 192, 247-248, 285-291]

*Dmitriev, N. "KAZAKSKII IAZYK," LITERATURNAIA
ENTSIKLOPEDIIA. Vol. 5. n. p. Izdatel'stvo
Kommunisticheskoi Akademii, 1931. [Russ. text and
titles, pp. 22-24]

El'chibekov, E. A. "SPISOK TEM DISSERTATSII,
ZASHCHISHCHENNYKH V 1946-1963 GG. NA SOISKANIE
UCHENOI STEPENI KANDIDATA ISTORICHESKIKH NAUK PO
RAZDELU "ISTORIIA KOMMUNISTICHESKOI PARTII
KAZAKHSTANA," PO SOSTAIANIIU NA I IANVARIA 1964 G."
VOPROSY ISTORII KOMPARTII KAZAKHSTANA. No. 2.
Alma Ata, 1964. [Russ. text; 100 titles, pp. 301-308]

*Eleuov, T. USTANOVLENIE I UPROCHENIE SOVETSKOI VLASTI
V KAZAKHSTANE. Alma Ata: Izdatel'stvo Akademii
Nauk Kazakhskoi SSR, 1961, 528 pp., 2600 copies.
[Russ. text and titles, per.: 1917-1918, pp. 511-526]

*_____.; Kım Syn Khva; K. Nurpeisov; et al. comp.
VELIKAIA OKTIABR'SKAIA SOTSIALISTICHESKAIA REVOLIUTSIIA
V KAZAKHSTANE. (LETOPIS' SOBYTII 27 FEVR. 1917 G. -
30 IIUNIA 1918 G.) Alma Ata: "Nauka," 1967, 458 pp.,
4650 copies. [Russ. text; ca.140 Russ. titles, per.:
1917-1918, pp. 444-448]

Erenov, A. E. OCHERKI PO ISTORII FEODAL'NYKH
ZEMEL'NYKH OTNOSHENII U KAZAKHOV. Alma Ata: (Akad.
Nauk KazSSR. In-t Filosofii i Prava), 1960. [Russ.
text; ca.140 titles, pp. 3-9, 152-157]

*F. Sh. "BUKEEVSKAIA ILI VNUTRENNAIA ORDA,"
ENTSIKLOPEDICHESKII SLOVAR'. Vol. 4A. St. Petersburg:
F. A. Brokgauz, I. A. Efron, 1891, 866-871 pp. [Russ.
text and titles, pp. 870-871]

Kazakh: History, Archaeology

*Gabdullin, M.; M. O. Dzhangalin,T. Zhangel'din; A. N.
Nusupbekov; S. N. Pokrovskii. eds. KAZAKHSTAN V
PERIOD VELIKOI OTECHESTVENNOI VOINY SOVETSKOGO
SOIUZA 1941-1945. SBORNIK DOKUMENTOV I MATERIALOV.
V DVUKH TOMAKH. Vol. 1--IIUN' 1941-1943 GG.
Alma Ata: (Institut Istorii, Arkheologii i Etnografii
im. Ch Ch. Valikhanova, Akademiia Nauk Kazakhskoi
SSR...), 1964, 596 pp. 2465 copies. [Russ. text;
Russ. titles, (incl. archives), per.: 1941-1945,
pp. 590-592]

ISTORIIA. SBORNIK STATEI ASPIRANTOV I SOISKATELEI.
No. 1. Alma Ata:(M-vo Vyssh. i Sred. Spets.
Obrazovaniia Kaz.SSR), 1966 (Vyp. DAN 1967), 227 pp.,
500 copies. [Russ. text; titles at end of articles]

ISTORIIA. SBORNIK STATEI ASPIRANTOV I SOISKATELEI.
No. 2. Alma Ata: (M-vo Vyssh. i Sred. Spets.
Obrazovaniia Kaz. SSR. Obshchestv. Nauki), 1967,
200 pp., 550 copies. [Russ. text; titles at end of
articles]

ISTORIIA, FILOSOFIIA, EKONOMIKA, PRAVO. (SBORNIK
STATEI ASPIRANTOV I SOISKATELEI.) OBSHCHESTVENNYE
NAUKI. No. 8. (Pt. 1). Alma Ata: (M-vo Vyssh. i
Sred. Spets. Obrazovaniia Kaz.SSR), 1965 (1966), 194 pp.,
1000 copies. [Russ. text; titles at end of articles]

ISTORIIA KPSS, FILOSOFIIA POLITEKONOMIIA. (OBSHCHESTV.
NAUKI. VYP. 9). Alma Ata: (M-vo Vyssh. i Sred.
Spets. Obrazovaniia Kaz.SSR), 1966 (Vyp. DAN 1967)
213 pp., 500 copies. [Russ. text; titles at end of
articles]

ISTORIIA KPSS. OBSHCHESTV. NAUKI. No. 10. Alma Ata:
(M-vo Vyssh. i Sred. Spets. Obrazovaniia Kaz.SSR),
1966 (Vyp. DAN 1967), 222 pp., 500 copies. [Russ.
text; titles, at end of articles]

ISTORIIA KOMMUNISTICHESKOI PARTII SOVETSKOGO SOIUZA V
6-TI T. Vol. 1. SOZDANIE BOL'SHEVITSKOI PARTII
(1883-1903 GG.). Alma Ata: "Kazakhstan," 1967,
680+LVII pp., 12000 copies. [Russ. text; Kazakh
titles, per.: 1883-1903, pp. 665-676]

[Kalieva, T.; B. Karina. comp.] POLVEKA POBED I
SVERSHENII. (BESEDA O KNIGAKH). Alma Ata:
"Kazakhstan," (Resp. Publ. B-ka Kaz.SSR im. Pushkina.
50 Let Sovetskoi Vlasti), 1966, 28 pp., 5000 copies.
[Kazakh text]

Kazakh: History, Archaeology

*"KARAGANDA," BOL'SHAIA SOVETSKAIA ENTSIKLOPEDIIA.
Vol. 31 Moscow: Gosudarstvennyi Institut
"Sovetskaia Entsiklopediia" (Ogiz RSFSR), 1937,
1st ed., 427-430 pp. [Russ. text and titles,
p. 430]

Keppen, P. "KHRONOLOGICHESKII UKAZATEL' MATERIALOV
DLIA ISTORII INORODTSEV EVROPEISKOI ROSSII,"
POLNOE SOBRANIE ZAKONOV. St. Petersburg, 1861.
[Russ. text; 175 titles, per.: 1568-1859, pp. 312-344]

*Kiuner, N. V. "BIBLIOGRAFIIA KITAISKOI I MAN'CHZHURSKOI
LITERATURY PO ISTORII KAZAKHSTANA. "TRUDY IN-TA
ISTORII, ARKHEOLOGII I ETNOGRAFII (AKAD. NAUK KAZSSR).
Vol. 8. Izdatel'stvo (Akademiia Nauk Kazakhskoi SSR.,
1960. [Russ. text; 115 + 281 Chinese, Manchurian
titles, per.: Antiquity and Middle Ages, pp. 183-218]

*Madzhlisov, A. AGRARNYE OTNOSHENIIA V VOSTOCHNOI
BUKHARE V XIX-NACHALE XX VEKA. Alma Ata - Dushanbe:
"Irfon," 1967, 331 pp., 1000 copies. [Russ. text;
ca.190 Tajik, Uzbek, Russ. titles, per.: 1800-1900,
pp. 319-329]

Margulan, A. Kh. GLAVNEISHIE PAMIATNIKI EPOKHI BRONZY
TSENTRAL'NOGO KAZAKHSTANA. VESTNIK AKADEMII NAUK
KAZAKH.SSR. No. 3. 1956. [Russ. text; 37 titles,
per.: Bronze Age, pp. 31-32]

Mishelevich, I. D. ALMA-ATINSKAIA OBLAST' K 40-LETIIU
VELIKOI OKTIABRSKOI SOTSIALISTICHESKOI REVOLIUTSII.
Alma Ata: (Obl. B-ka), 1957, 14 pp., 700 copies.
[Russ. text; ca.110 titles, per.: Sov.]

Nikitin, V. P. "ISTORICHESKII OCHERK SEMIPALATINSKOI
OBLASTI," PAMIATNAIA KNIZHKA SEMIPALATINSKOI
OBLASTI NA 1897 G. [Russ. text; 47 titles, pp. 131-
183]

*Nurbekova, G. ZHENSHCHINY KAZAKHSTANA - FRONTU.
Alma Ata: "Kazakhstan," 1968, 158 pp., 9000 copies.
[Russ. text and titles, per.: 1941-1945, pp. 151-157]

Pankov, A. V. "MATERIALY DLIA BIBLIOGRAFII PO ISTORII,
ARKHEOLOGII, ETNOGRAFII I ANTROPOLOGII KAZAKSTANA ZA
1921-26 G.G." GOD RABOTY KAZAKSKOGO VYSSHEGO
PEDAGOGICHESKOGO INSTITUTA. Tashkent: Izd.
Kazpedvuza, 1928. [Russ. text; 161 Russ., Europ.
titles, per.: 1921-1926, pp. 101-106]

Kazakh: History, Archaeology

Pokrovskii, S. N. POBEDA SOVETSKOI VLASTI V SEMIRECH'E. Alma Ata: (Akad. Nauk Kaz. SSR. In-t Istorii, Arkheologii i Etnografii), 1961. [Russ. text; ca.250 Russ. titles, per.: Sov., pp. 350-357]

Portnoi, I. L.; A. Ia. Skuchalina. compilers. USPEKHI SOTSIALISTICHESKOGO STROITEL'STVA V AKMOLINSKOI OBLASTI. UKAZATEL' LIT. Akmolinsk: (Akmolinsk. Obl. B-ka), 1960, 43 pp., 1000 copies. [Russ. text; ca.500 titles, per.: Sov.]

Sabitov, N. AMANGEL'DY. BIBLIOGRAFICHESKII UKAZATEL' MATERIALOV O ZHIZNI I DEIATEL'NOSTI, OPUBLIKOVANNYKH ZA 1926-1945 GG. Alma Ata: Izd-vo AN KazSSR, 1946, 40 pp., 300 copies. [Kazakh, Russ. text; pub.: 1926-1945]

_____. BIBLIOGRAFICHESKII UKAZATEL' KAZAKHSKOI LITERATURY (1862-1917). Alma Ata: Izd-vo AN Kaz SSR, 1948, 35 pp., 750 copies. [Kazakh text; pub.: 1862-1917]

_____. "BIBLIOGRAFICHESKII UKAZATEL' MATERIALOV O ZHIZNI I DEIATEL'NOSTI KAZAKHSKOGO UCHENOGO CHOKANA CHINGISOVICHA VALIKHANOVA," VESTNIK AKAD. NAUK KAZ. SSR. No. 2(59). 1950. [Russ. text; 89 Kazakh, Russ. titles, pp. 118-121]

_____. BIBLIOGRAFICHESKII UKAZATEL' MATERIALOV PO ISTORII KAZAKHSTANA (VOSTOCHNYE ISTOCHNIKI OPUBLIKOVANNYE DO 1917 G). Alma Ata: Izd-vo AN KazSSR, 1947, 40 pp., 750 copies. [Russ. text; pub.: before 1917]

*Shalekenov, U. Kh. KAZAKHI NIZOV'EV AMU-DAR'I. K ISTORII VZAIMOOTNOSHENII NARODOV KARAKALPAKII V XVIII-XX VV. Tashkent: "Fan," 1966, 336 pp., 1750 copies. [Russ. text; ca.260 Uzbek, Russ. titles, per.: XVIII-XX VV., 325-335 pp.]

Shaumian, M. OT KOCHEB'IA K SOTSIALIZMU. Alma Ata, 1965. [Russ. text; ca.150 titles, pp. 193-199]

Shnitnikov, V. N. ed. DZHETYSU (SEMIRECH'E). ESTESTVENNO-ISTORICHESKOE OPISANIE KRAIA. Tashkent, 1925, 234 pp. [Russ. text; titles, pp. 216-234]

*"SPISOK KNIG, BROSHIUR, STATEI, RETSENZII I PREDISLOVII CHLENA-KORRESPONDENTA AN KAZSSR E. B. BEKMAKHANOVA." VESTNIK AKADEMII NAUK KAZAKHSKOI SSR. No. 7. 1966. [Russ. text: 107 Russ. titles, pub.: 1938-1965, pp. 74-77]

Kazakh: History, Archaeology

Takenov, A. S. PREDSEDATEL' SOVDEPA (O ZHIZNI I
DEIATEL'NOSTI I. KURMANOVA). Alma Ata: "Kazakhstan,"
1967, 52 pp., 1000 copies. [Russ. text; 16 titles,
p. 50]

Tokareva, N. A.; V. N. Medvedeva. comp.   CHTO
CHITAT' O KUSTANAE I KUSTANAISKOI OBLASTI.
BIBLIOGR. I METOD. MATERIALY. Kustanai: (Kustan. Obl.
Bka im. Tol'stogo), 1960, 39 pp., 1000 copies.
[Russ. text]

*Tolybekov, S. E. OBSHCHESTVENNO-EKONOMICHESKII STROI
KAZAKHOV V XVII-XIX VEKAKH. Alma Ata: Kazgosizdat,
1959, 447 pp. [Russ. text; ca.330 Russ. titles (incl.
archives) per.: 17-19th c., pp. 434-448]

U ISTOKOV KOMMUNISTICHESKOI PARTII KAZAKHSTANA. (LETOPIS'
VAZHNEISHIKH SOBYTII) Pt. 1. KONETS XIX VEKA-
FEVRAL' 1917 GODA. Alma Ata: "Kazakhstan," 1966,
379 pp., 2000 copies. [Russ. text; titles pp. 3-11]

*Valikhanov, Chokan. IZBRANNYE PROIZVEDENIIA. Alma
Ata: Kazakhskoe Gosudarstvennoe Izdatel'stvo
Khudozhestvennoi Literatury, 1958, 643 pp., 20,000
copies. [Russ. text; 34 Kazakh, Russ. titles,
per.: 19th c., pp. 619-620]

_____. STAT'I I PEREPISKA. Alma Ata, n. d.,
170 pp. [Kazakh text; 81 Kazakh, Russ. titles, pub.:
1828-1945, pp. 164-168]

*Viatkin, M. P. BATYR SRYM. Moscow-Leningrad:
Izdatel'stvo Akademii Nauk SSSR, 1947, 391 pp.,
2500 copies. [Russ. text; Russ., Europ. titles, per.:
18th c., pp. 383-388]

_____. OCHERKI PO ISTORII KAZAKHSKOI SSR.
Vol. 1. S DREVNEISHIKH VREMEN PO 1870. Moscow, 1941,
368 pp. [Russ. text; per.: up to 1870, pp. 1-18,
358-67]

Kazakh

LANGUAGE, LITERATURE

*A. B. "ZHUMABAEV, MAGZHAN (1896-). LITERATURNAIA
ENTSIKLOPEDIIA. Vol. 4. Moscow: Izdatel'stvo
Kommunisticheskoi Akademii, 1930, 202-203 pp.
[Russ. text; Kazakh, Russ. titles, p. 203]

*A-NI, A. "ABAI," LITERATURNAIA ENTSIKLOPEDIIA. Vol. 1.
n. p. Izdatel'stvo Kommunisticheskoi Akademii, 1929.
[Russ. text; Kazakh, Russ. titles, p. 5]

Abdrakhmanov, A.; A. Abil'kaev; G. Kaliev. ZHIZN'
I NAUCHNOE NASLEDIE PROFESSORA SARSENA AMANZHOLOVA.
Alma Ata: (O-vo po Rasprostraneniiu Polit. i Nauch.
Znanii KazSSR), 1959. [Kazakh text; 111 Kazakh,
Russ. titles, pub.: 1930-1958, pp. 40-47]

Abetov, G. BIBLIOGRAFICHESKII UKAZATEL' KAZAKHSKOI
SOVETSKOI LITERATURY (1917-1946). Alma Ata: Izd-vo
AN KazSSR, 1950, 191 pp., 1000 copies. [Kazakh,
Russ. text; ca.4000 Kazakh, Russ. titles, pub.:
1917-1946]

Abetov, G. "KRATKAIA BIBLIOGRAFIIA MATERIALOV PO
ISTORII KAZAKHSKOI LITERATURY XVIII-XIX VEKOV,"
ISTORIIA KAZAKHSKOI LITERATURY. Vol. 2. Book 1.
Alma Ata: (Institut Iazyka i Lit. im. Auezova), 1961.
[Kazakh text; ca.560 Kazakh, Russ. titles, per.: 18th-
19th c., pp. 557-580]

Abetov, Gh. QAZAQ SOVET ADEBIETINING BIBLIOGRAFIYALIQ
KORSETKISHI (1917-1946). Alma Ata, 1950. [Kazakh
text; titles pub.: 1917-1946]

*Aitbaev, E. S.; S. A. Akashev, et al. comp.
KHUDOZHESTVENNAIA LITERATURA KAZAKHSTANA. 1946-1957.
(BIBLIOGRAFICHESKII UKAZATEL'). Alma Ata: (Gos.
Resp. B-ka KazSSR im. A. S. Pushkina), 1958, 687 pp.,
5000 copies. [Kazakh, Russ. text; Kazakh, Uyghur,
Russ., other titles, pub.: 1946 to early 1958]

Akhanov, K. OMONIMY V KAZAKHSKOM IAZYKE. Alma Ata:
Kazuchpedgiz, 1958. [Kazakh text; 46 Kazakh, Russ.
titles, pp. 127-129]

Kazakh: Language, Literature

Aralbaev, Zh. A. VOKALIZM KAZAKHSKOGO IAZYKA (OCHERKI PO EKSPERIM. FONETIKE I FONOLOGII). Alma Ata, 1970. [Russ. text; 73 titles, pp. 157-160]

Atimov, M. O KOMPOZITSII KHUDOZHESTVENNYKH PROIZVEDENII. Alma Ata, 1969. [Kazakh text; ca.170 titles, pp. 88-94]

*Auezov, M. O. ABAI KUNANBAEV. STAT'I I ISSLEDOVANIIA. Alma Ata: Izdatel'stvo "Nauka," 1967, 391 pp. 4000 copies. [Kazakh, Russ. text; 57 Kazakh, Russ. titles, pub.: 1922-1961, pp. 386-390]

* _____ ; S. M. Mukanov, et al. eds. OCHERK ISTORII KAZAKHSKOI SOVETSKOI LITERATURY. Alma Ata, Izdatel'stvo Akademii Nauk Kazakhskoi SSR, 1958, 512 pp., 15,500 copies. [Kazakh text; Kazakh, Russ. titles, pp. 502-511]

*Baibulov, E.; B. Koichubaeva; A. Narymbetov; F. El'konina; comp. SAKEN SEIFULLIN. (UKAZATEL' LITERATURY K 70-LETIIU SO DNIA ROZHDENIIA). Alma Ata: Izdatel'stvo "Kazakhstan," 1965, 139 pp., 5000 copies. [Kazakh, Russ. text; 1399 Kazakh, Russ. titles]

Baitugaeva, G. SLOZHNYE OPREDELITEL'NYE KONSTRUKTSII V SOVREMENNOM KAZAKHSKOM IAZYKE. Alma Ata, 1962. [Russ. text; 46 titles. pp. 57-59]

Balakaev, M.; T. Kordabaev. GRAMMATIKA SOVREMENNOGO KAZAKHSKOGO IAZYKA. SINTAKSIS. Alma Ata: "Mektep," 1966, 340 pp., 6200 copies. [Russ. text; 45 titles, pp. 335-336]

*Balakaev, M. B. SOVREMENNYI KAZAKHSKII IAZYK. SINTAKSIS SLOVOSOCHETANIIA I PROSTOGO PREDLOZHENIIA. Alma Ata: Izdatel'stvo Akademii Nauk Kazakhskoi SSR, 1959, 235 pp., 2700 copies. [Russ. text; Kazakh, Russ., Europ. titles, pp. 227-230]

Balanina, Iu. O. DZHAMBUL DZHABAEV. REK. UKAZATEL' LIT. Moscow: (Gos. B-ka SSSR im. Lenina. Gos. B-ka KazSSR im. Pushkina), 1950, 54 pp., 5000 copies. [Russ. text; 43 titles]

Begalina, E. A.; I. K. Nechipurenko; K. T. Tusupov. comp. KAZAKHSKAIA SOVETSKAIA DETSKAIA LITERATURA. (BIOBIBLIOGR. SPRAVOCHNIK. 1945-1964). Alma Ata: "Kazakhstan," 1965, 285 pp., 3000 copies. [Kazakh, Russ. text; 35 lists + 140 Kazakh, Russ. titles, pub.: 1945-1964]

Kazakh: Language, Literature

*Bozheev, M. BIBLIOGRAFICHESKII UKAZATEL' PO
TVORCHESTVU M. O. AUEZOVA. Alma Ata: "Mektep," 1966,
74 pp., 4200 copies. [Kazakh text; 11 Kazakh lists,
pub.: 1917-1965]

Chekaninskii, I. A. BIBLIOGRAFICHESKII UKAZATEL'
STATEI I ZAMETOK, KASAIUSHCHIKHSIA POEMY I PAMIATNIKA
BAIAN-SLU I KOZY-KURPESH. ZAPISKI SEMIPALATINSKOGO
OTDELA OBSHCHESTVA IZUCHENIIA KAZAKHSTANA. Vol. 1
(No. 18), 1929. [Russ. text; 85 titles, pp. 55-63]

"BIBLIOGRAFIIA PO ISTORII I DIALEKTOLOGII KAZAKHSKOGO
IAZYKA," KAZAKHSKAIA DIALEKTOLOGIIA. Vol. 1.
AKADEMIIA NAUK KAZAKHSKOI SSR. INSTITUT IAZYKOZNANIIA.
1965. [Russ. text]

*Demesinova, N. Kh. SOPOSTAVITEL'NAIA GRAMMATIKA
RUSSKOGO I KAZAKHSKOGO IAZYKOV. "SINTAKSIS".
Alma Ata: "Nauka," 1966, 219 pp., 2550 copies.
[Russ. text; Kazakh, Russ. titles, pub.: 1926-1963,
pp. 212-216]

[Doskaraev, Zh.; et al. comp.] DIALEKTOLOGICHESKII
SLOVAR' KAZAKHSKOGO IAZYKA. Alma Ata, 1969. [Kazakh
text; 35 titles, pp. 424-426]

*Duysenbaev, I. T. ed. ISTORIIA KAZAKHSKOI LITERATURY.
Vol. 2, Bk. 2. NACHALO XX VEKA. Alma Ata: "Ghilim"
Baspasi, 1965, 523 pp., 2770 copies. [Kazakh text;
ca.600 Kazakh, Russ. titles, per.: early 20th c.,
pp. 494-522]

*Fetisov, M. I. ZAROZHDENIE KAZAK. PUBLITSISTIKI.
Alma Ata: Kazgoslitizdat, 1961, 438 pp. [Russ. text;
73 Kazakh, Russ. titles, pub.: 1939-1959, pp. 435-438]

Gizatov, B. "PERECHEN' PROIZVEDENII L. KHAMIDI,"
LATYF KHAMIDI. Alma Ata, 1966. [Russ. text; ca.170
titles, pp. 90-100, per.: 1922-1964]

*Isakov, A.; R. Syzdykova; Sh. Sarybaev. ed. KRATKII
ETIMOLOGICHESKII SLOVAR' KAZAKHSKOGO IAZYKA. Alma
Ata: Qazaq SSR-ning "Ghilim"Baspasi, 1966, 240 pp.,
5000 copies. [Kazakh text; Kazakh, Sov. Asian,
Russ., Mid-East, Europ. titles, pp. 235-240]

*Isengalieva, V. A. UPOTREBLENIE PADEZHEI V KAZAKHSKOM
I RUSSKOM IAZYKAKH. Alma Ata: (Akad. Nauk KazSSR.
Institut Iazyka i Literatury), 1961, 165 pp.
[Russ. text; ca.150 Russ., Kazakh titles, pp. 145-150]

Kazakh: Language, Literature

*Isakov, A. NARECHIE V SOVREMENNOM KAZAKHSKOM IAZYKE.
Alma Ata: Izdatel'stvo Akademii Nauk Kazakhskoi SSR,
1950, 142 pp., 1000 copies. [Russ. text; ca.70 Kazakh,
Russ. titles, pp. 139-141]

Ismailov, E. SAKEN SEIFULLIN. Alma Ata: (M-vo
Kul'tury KazSSR. Glav. Upr. Izdatel'stv i Poligr.
Prom-sti), 1958. [Russ. text; 28 Kazakh, Russ.
titles, pp. 29-30]

_____. ed. VOPROSY KAZAKHSKOI SOVETSKOI
LITERATURY. Vol. 2. Alma Ata: (Akad. Nauk KazSSR.
In-t Iazyka i Lit.), 1960. [Kazakh, Russ. text;
ca.60 Kazakh, Russ. titles, per.: Sov., pp. 220-222]

ISTORIIA KAZAKHSKOI LITERATURY. T. I. FOL'KLOR
Alma Ata: (AN KazSSR, In-t Iazyka i Literatury)
[ca.1949] 400 pp. [Russ. text; ca.200 Kazakh, Russ.
titles, pub.: 1812-1847]

Josib-Bek Oli, Qamza. "QASAQ BAY," Kzil Orda:
Gosudarstvennoe Izdatel'stvo K.S.S.R., 1928, 56 pp.,
3000 copies. [Kazakh text and titles]

*Jumaliev, Q. ed. ISTORIIA KAZAKHSKOI LITERATURY.
Vol. 2, KN. 2-IA. KAZAKHSKAIA LITERATURA KONTSA
XVIII I XIX VV. Alma Ata: Izdatel'stvo Akademii
Nauk KazSSR, 1961, 581 pp., 3300 copies. [Kazakh text;
Kazakh, Russ. titles, per.: late 18th and 19th cc.,
pp. 557-580]

*Kaliev, G.; Sh. Sarybaev. KAZAKHSKAIA DIALEKTOLOGIIA.
Alma Ata: "Mektep," 1967, 175 pp., 4900 copies.
[Kazakh text; 223 Kazakh, Russ. titles, pub.: 1861-
1965, pp. 166-172]

*Kamysov, R. RODNOI DLIA VSEKH. Alma Ata: Izdatel'stvo
"Kazakhstan," 1967, 80 pp., 9000 copies. [Russ. text;
27 Russ. titles, pp. 77-79]

KAZAKHSTAN. LAUREATY STALINSKIKH PREMII. BIOBIBLIOGR.
UKAZATEL'. Ch. 1. Alma Ata: Izd-vo Akad. Nauk
Kazakh.SSR), 1954, 202 pp., 2000 copies. [Russ.
text; 82 lists, pub.: 1939 - July 1, 1953]

Kedrina, Z. MUKHTAR AUEZOV. Moscow: Sov. Pisatel',
1951. [Russ. text; 20 Russ. titles, pp. 121-123]

Kazakh: Language, Literature

Kenenova, T.; B. Nusupbekova; F. I. El'konina; A. A. Kobycheva. comp. MUKHTAR AUEZOV. REKOMENDATEL'NYI UKAZATEL' LITERATURY. Alma Ata: "Kazakhstan," 1968, 104 pp., 6000 copies. [Kazakh text; 443 Kazakh, Sov. Russ, Western titles]

*Kenesbaev, S.; T. Zhanuzakov. RUSSKO-KAZAKHSKII SLOVAR' LINGVISTICHESKIKH TERMINOV. Alma Ata: "Nauka," 1966, 208 pp., 7000 copies. [Kazakh, Russ. text; 18 Kazakh, Russ. titles, pub.: 1946-1965, p. 208]

_____.; G. Musabaev. SOVREMENNYI KAZAKHSKII IAZYK. Ch. 1. "LEKSIKA, FONETIKA." Alma Ata, 1962. [Kazakh text; 218 titles, pp. 304-312]

_____., ed. VOPROSY ISTORII I DIALEKTOLOGII KAZAKHSKOGO IAZYKA. No. 4. Alma Ata, 1962. [Kazakh, Russ. text; 84 titles, pp. 236-240]

*Kenzhebaev, B.; U. Esnazarov. KAZAKHSKAIA LITERATURA XX VEKA. Alma Ata: "Mektep," 1966, 300 pp., 5800 copies. [Kazakh text; ca.620 Kazakh titles, pp. 277-299]

*_____. KAZAKHSKIE PISATELI DEMOKRATY NACHALA XX VEKA. Alma Ata: Qazaq Memleket Baspasi, 1958, 308 pp., 10,000 copies. [Kazakh text; ca.180 Kazakh, Russ. titles, per.: early 20th c., pp. 302-307]

_____.; Kh. Suiunshaliev. SULTANMAKHMUT TORAIGYROV. Alma Ata: (Glav. Upr. Izdatel'stv i Poligr. Prom-sti M-va Kul'tury KazSSR), 1958. [Russ. text; 25 titles, pp. 27-28]

*Kereeva-Kanafieva, K. DOREVOLIUTSIONNAIA RUSSKAIA PECHAT' O KAZAKHSTANE. IZ ISTORII RUSSKO-KAZAKH. LIT. SVIAZEI. Alma Ata: Kazgosizdat, 1963, 299 pp., 2700 copies. [Russ. text; Russ. titles, per.: pre-1917, pp. 285-300]

Khasenova, A. PROIZVODNYE GLAGOL'NYE OSNOVY KAZAKHSKOGO IAZYKA S AFFIKSOM "LA/LE". Alma Ata: (Akad. Nauk Kazakh. SSR. In-t Iazyka i Lit.), 1957. [Kazakh text; 100 Kazakh, Russ. titles, pp. 80-83]

*Khasenova, Akkal K. PROIZVODNYE GLAGOL'NYE OSNOVY KAZAKHSKOGO IAZYKA. Alma Ata: Qazaq SSR Ghilim Akademiyasining Baspasi, 1959, 179 pp., 1400 copies. [Kazakh text; ca.110 Kazakh, Russ. titles, pp. 174-177]

Kazakh: Language, Literature

*Kirabaev, Serik. GABIDEN MUSTAFIN. KRITIKO-
BIOGRAFICHESKII OCHERK. Alma Ata: Kazgoslitizdat,
1956, 83 pp., 5000 copies. [Kazakh text; 58
Kazakh, Russ. titles, pub.: 1929-1954, pp. 81-83]

Konratbaev, A. O KAZAKHSKOI POEME "KOZY-KORPESH."
Alma Ata: Kazgoslitizdat, 1959. [Kazakh text;
168 Kazakh, Russ. titles, pp. 144-150]

Kuznetsova, L. comp. PISATELI KAZAKHSTANA-DETIAM.
Alma Ata: "Kazakhstan," 1967, 26 pp., 10,000 copies.
[Russ. text]

*Magauin, Mukhtar. NAPEVY KOBYZA. KAZ. AKYNY I ZHYRAU
XV-XVIII VV. MONOGRAFIIA. Alma Ata: "Zhazushy,"
1968, 156 pp., 7000 copies. [Kazakh text; 126
Kazakh, Russ. titles, per.: 15th - 18th cc., pp. 150-
155]

*"MAILIN, BEIMBEK ZHARMUKHAMETOVICH," LITERATURNAIA
ENTSIKLOPEDIA. Vol. 6. Moscow: Gosudarstvennoe
Slovarno-Entsiklopedicheskoe Izdatel'stvo
"Sovetskaia Entsiklopediia," 1932, 702-703 pp.
[Russ. text; Kazakh, Russ. titles, p. 703]

Mamanov, I. E. VSPOMOGATEL'NYE GLAGOLY V KAZAKHSKOM
IAZYKE. Alma Ata: AN KazSSR [ca.1949]. [Russ.
text; 39 titles, pub.: 1807-1945, pp. 94-95]

*Musabaev, G. G. SOVREMENNYI KAZAKHSKII IAZYK. Part 1.
LEKSIKA. Alma Ata: Izd-vo Akad. Nauk KazSSR.
(In-t Iazyka i Lit), 141 pp., 3900 copies. [Russ.
text; 80 Kazakh, Russ. titles, pp. 135-139]

*Musinov, A.; A. Sarsenbaev; E. Serikkalieva.
KAZAKHSKIE LITERATURNYE SVIAZI. (BIBLIOGRAFICHESKII
UKAZATEL'). Alma Ata: "Nauka," 1968, 412 pp.,
1800 copies. [Russ. text; Kazakh, Sov. Asian, Russ.
Western titles, pub.: 1917-1967]

*Musrepov, G. "MUKANOV, SABIT," LITERATURNAIA
ENTSIKLOPEDIIA. Vol. 7. Moscow: Gosudarstvennoe
Slovarno-Entsiklopedicheskoe Izdatel'stvo
"Sovetskaia Entsiklopediia, 1934, 527-528. [Russ.
text; Kazakh, Russ. titles, p. 528]

*Myrzakhmetov, M.; B. K. Koichubaeva; F. I. El'konina.
comp. ABAI KUNANBAEV. BIBLIOGRAFICHESKII
UKAZATEL'. Alma Ata: Izdatel'stvo "Kazakhstan,"
1956, 291 pp., 5000 copies. [Kazakh text; 2164 and
1123 Kazakh, Russ., other titles, pub.: 1889-1964]

Kazakh: Language, Literature

N. D. "KAZAKHSKII IAZYK," BOL'SHAIA SOVETSKAIA
ENTSIKLOPEDIIA. Vol. 30. Moscow: Gosudarstvennyi
Institut "Sovetskaia Entsiklopediia," (Ogiz RSFSR),
1937, 1st ed., 603-604 pp. [Russ. text; Kazakh,
Russ. titles, p. 604]

*Narymbetov, A. KAZAKHSKAIA SOVETSKAIA LITERATURA.
BIBLIOGR. UKAZ. PO LITERATUROVEDENIIU I KRITIKE.
1917-1940. Vol. 1. Alma Ata: "Gylym," (In-t
Lit. i Iskusstva im. Auezova), 1970, 355 pp.,
2210 copies. [Kazakh, Russ. text; ca.4600 Kazakh,
Russ. titles, per.: 1917-1940, pp. 32-348]

_____. "KRATKAIA BIBLIOGRAFIIA PO KAZAKHSKOI
SOVETSKOI LITERATURE," OCHERK ISTORII KAZAKH.
SOVETSKOI LITERATURY. Alma Ata: (Akad. Nauk KazSSR.
In-t Iazyka i Lit.), 1958. [Russ. text; 650
Kazakh, Russ. titles, per.: Sov., pp. 469-485]

[_____. T. Kenenova, F. I. El'konina]
OBRAZ V. I. LENINA V LITERATURE I ISKUSSTVE
KAZAKHSTANA. (REK. UKAZ. LIT.) Alma Ata: "Kazakhstan,"
1969, 118 pp., 5000 copies. [Kazakh, Russ. text;
ca.700 Kazakh, Russ. titles]

_____. "STAT'I I OTDEL'NYE TRUDY O KAZAKHSKOI
SOVETSKOI LITERATURE." OCHERK ISTORII KAZAKHSKOI
SOVETSKOI LITERATURY. Alma Ata: (Akad. Nauk SSSR.
In-t Iazyka i Lit.), 1958. [Kazakh text; ca.400
Kazakh, Russ. titles, per.: Sov., pp. 502-511]

Nurkatov, A. MUKHTAR AUEZOV. Alma Ata: Kazgosizdat,
1957. [Kazakh text; 75 Kazakh, Russ. titles,
pp. 180-182]

_____. MUKHTAR AUEZOV. Alma Ata: Kazgoslitizdat,
1958. [Russ. text; 51 titles, pp. 129-131]

[Nurtazin, T.; S. Akashev; B. Karina; R. Koichubaeva,
F. I. El'konina. Comp.] BEIMBET MAILIN.
(UKAZATEL' LIT.) Alma Ata: "Kazakhstan," (Gos.
Resp. B-ka Kaz. SSR im. Pushkina), 1968, 181 pp.,
6000 copies. [Kazakh, Russ. text; 2479 Kazakh,
Russ. titles]

_____.; Kh. Suiunshaliev. SABIT MUKANOV.
Alma Ata: (M-vo Kul'tury KazSSR. Glav. Upr.
Izdatel'stv i Poligr. Prom-sti.) 1958, 26 pp.
[Russ. text; ca.20 Kazakh titles]

Kazakh: Language, Literature

*OCHERK ISTORII KAZAKHSKOI SOVETSKOI LITERATURY.
 Alma Ata: Izdatel'stvo Akademii Nauk Kazakhskoi SSR,
 1958, 512 pp., 15,500 copies. [Kazakh text; Kazakh,
 Russ. titles, pub. 1925-1956, pp. 502-511]

OCHERK ISTORII KAZAKH. SOVETSKOI LIT. Moscow: (In-t
 Mirovoi Lit. im. Kor'kogo. Akad. Nauk KazSSR. In-t
 Iazyka i Lit.), 1960. [Russ. text; ca.680 Kazakh,
 Russ. titles, Sov. per., pp. 660-686]

*Qarataev, M. Q. ed. ISTORIIA KAZAKHSKOI LITERATURY.
 Vol. 1, Book 2. KAZAKHSKOE USTNOE POETICHESKOE
 TVORCHESTVO (SOVETSKII PERIOD). Alma Ata:
 Izdatel'stvo Akademii Nauk Kazakhskoi SSR, 1964,
 695 pp., 4000 copies. [Kazakh text; ca.350 Kazakh,
 Russ. titles, Sov. per., pp. 8-58, 679-694]

*Omarbekov, Sapargali. MESTNYE OSOBENNOSTI RAZGOVORNOI
 RECHI KAZAKOV. Alma Ata: Qazaq SSR-ning "Ghilim,"
 Baspasi, 1965, 203 pp., 1940 copies. [Kazakh text;
 ca.160 Kazakh, Sov. Asian, Russ. titles, pp. 195-201]

*S., A. "AKMULLA [AKMYLA]," LITERATURNAIA ENTSIKLOPEDIIA.
 Vol. 1. n. p., Izdatel'stvo Kommunisticheskoi
 Akademii, 1929, 73-74 pp. [Russ. text; Kazakh,
 Tatar, Russ., titles, per.: 19th c., p. 74]

*S., A. "BAITURSUNOV, AKHMED BAITURSUNOVICH,"
 LITERATURNAIA ENTSIKLOPEDIIA. Vol. 1. n. p.
 Izdatel'stvo Kommunisticheskoi Akademii, 1929,
 305-306 pp. [Russ. text and titles, p. 306]

*S. M. "NAUSHABAEV, PURZHAN," LITERATURNAIA
 ENTSIKLOPEDIIA. Vol. 7. Moscow: Gosudarstvennoe
 Slovarno-Entsiklopedicheskoe Izdatel'stvo "Sovetskaia
 Entsiklopediia," 1934. [Russ. text; Kazakh titles,
 per.: up to 1921, p. 626]

Sabitov, N. ABAI. BIBLIOGRAFICHESKII UKAZATEL'
 PROIZVEDENII ABAIA I LITERATURNYKH MATERIALOV O NEM,
 OPUBLIKOVANNYKH ZA 1889-1945 GG. Alma Ata: Izd-vo
 AN KazSSR, 1946, 78 pp., 500 copies. [Kazakh
 text; pub.: 1889-1945]

_____. QAZAQ ADEBIETINING BIBLIOGRAFIYALIQ
 KORSETKISHI. (1862-1917). Alma Ata, 1948. [Kazakh
 text; pub.: 1862-1917]

*SAKEN SEIFULLIN. (UKAZATEL' LITERATURY K 70-LETIIU SO
 DNIA ROZHDENIIA). Alma Ata: Izdatel'stvo
 "Kazakhstan," 1965, 137 pp., 5000 copies. [Kazakh,
 Russ. text; 988 + 411 Kazakh, Russ. titles, per.:
 1894-1964]

Kazakh: Language, Literature

Salikhova, T. comp. TVOI LIUBIMYE KNIGI. (BIBLIOGR. PAMIATKA). Alma Ata: "Kazakhstan," 1967, 14 pp., 10,000 copies. [Russ. text; Kazakh titles]

Sarybaev, Sh. Sh. BIBLIOGRAFICHESKII UKAZATEL' LITERATURY PO KAZAKHSKOMU IAZYKOZNANIIU. Part 1. Alma Ata: (Akad. Nauk Kazakh. SSR. In-t Iazyka i Lit.), 1960 232 pp., 1600 copies. [Kazakh, Russ. text; 3,622 Kazakh, Russ. titles, pub.: last half of 19th c. to 1958]

*_____. BIBLIOGRAFICHESKII UKAZATEL' PO KAZAKHSKOMU IAZYKOZNANIIU. Alma Ata: Izdatel'stvo Akademii Nauk Kazakhskoi SSR (AN KazSSR. In-t Iazyka i Lit.), 1956, 97 pp., 1,600 copies. [Kazakh, Russ. text; ca.1,500 titles, pub.: second half of 19th c. to 1955]

*_____. BIBLIOGRAFICHESKII UKAZATEL' LITERATURY PO KAZAKHSKOMU IAZYKOZNANIIU. Part 1. Alma Ata: "Nauka," 1965 (2nd ed. revised and supplemented), 270 pp., 1400 copies. [Kazakh, Russ. text; ca.4000 Kaz., Russ. titles, pub. late 19th c. to 1963]

_____. "BIBLIOGRAFIIA PO TEME 'PROGRESSIVNOE VLIIANIE RUSSKOGO IAZYKA NA TIURKSKIE IAZYKI'" PROGRESSIVNOE VLIIANIE RUSSKOGO IAZYKA NA KAZAKHSKII. Alma Ata, 1965. [Russ. text; 115 titles, pp. 210-216]

*[Sarybaev, Sh. comp.] FONETIKA KAZAKHSKOGO IAZYKA. Sb.1. Alma Ata: (AN Kazakh.SSR: In-t Iazykoznaniia, 1969, 168 pp., 1860 copies. [Kazakh, Russ. text; 114 Kazakh, Russ. titles, pub.: 1894-1969, pp. 160-166]

Sarybaev, Sh. Sh. "IAZYKOZNANIE V KAZAKHSTANE [OBZOR RABOT]," VOPROSY IAZYKOZNANIIA. No. 5, 1958. [Russ. text; Sov. per., pp. 140-144]

Sauranbaev, N. T., ed. VOPROSY ISTORII I DIALEKTOLOGII KAZAKHSKOGO IAZYKA. No. 1. Alma Ata: (Akad Nauk Kazakh, SSR. In-t Iazyka i Lit), 1958. [Russ. text; 42 Kazakh, Russ. titles, pp. 210-212]

Seitov, S. PUT' POETA. KRITIKO-BIOGR. OCHERK. Alma Ata: Kazgoslitizdat, 1958. [Kazakh text; 39 Kazakh, Russ. titles, pub.: 1932-1957, pp. 73-74]

Shalabaev, B. ISTORIIA KAZAKHSKOI PROZY. SIUZHET I KHARAKTER. Alma Ata: "Zhazushy," 1968, 310 pp., 100,000 copies. [Russ. text; 21 titles, pp. 308-309]

Kazakh: Language, Literature

Shalabaev, K. compiler. IL'IAS DZHANSUGUROV. Alma Ata: (Kazakh. Resp. B-ka im. Pushkina), 1960, 9 pp., 4000 copies. [Kazakh text]

_____.: N. V. Sokolova; U. Maulenberdina. comps. SABIT MUKANOV (K 60-LETIIU SO DNIA ROZHDENIIA). Alma Ata: (Gos Resp. B-ka KazSSR im. Pushkina), 1960, 29 pp., 4000 copies. [Kazakh, Russ. text; Kazakh, Russ. titles, Sov. per.]

Sidel'nikov, V. M. BIBLIOGRAFICHESKII UKAZATEL' PO KAZAKHSKOMU USTNOMU TVORCHESTVU. No. 1. 1771-1916 GG. Alma Ata: (Akad. Nauk Kaz.SSR), 1951, 103 pp., 500 copies. [Kazakh, Russ. text; 885 Kazakh, Russ., foreign titles, per.: 1771-1916]

_____. comp. and ed. KAZAKHSKIE SKAZKI. Vol. 1. Alma Ata: (Akad. Nauk KazSSR. In-t Iazyka i Lit.), 1958. [Russ. text; ca.320 titles, pp. 440-461]

Suiunshaliev, Kh. ABAI KUNANBAEV. Alma Ata: (M-vo Kul'tury KazSSR. Glav. upr. Izdatel'stv i Poligr. Prom-sti), 1958. [Russ. text; 15 Kazakh, Russ. titles, pp. 23-24]

_____. DZHAMBUL DZHABAEV. Alma Ata: (M-vo Kul'tury KazSSR. Glav. Upr. Izdatel'stva i Poligr. Prom-sti), 1958. [Russ. text; 30 Kazakh titles, pub.: 1936-1958, pp. 19-20]

_____.; I. Gabdirov. GABIDEN MUSTAFIN. Alma Ata: (M-vo Kul'tury KazSSR. Glav. Upr. Izdatel'stv i Poligr. Prom-sti), 1958, 26 pp. [Russ. text; 10 titles]

Sydykov, T. S. "BIBLIOGRAFIIA MATERIALOV A. A. DIVAEVA PO USTNOMU TVORCHESTVU KAZAKHOV, IZDANNYKH NA KAZAKHSKOM I RUSSKOM IAZYKAKH," Divaev, A. A. KAZAKHSKAIA NARODNAIA POEZIIA. Alma Ata, 1964. [Russ. text; 154 titles, pp. 234-243]

*T. I.Zh. "KAZAKHSKAIA LITERATURA," BOL'SHAIA SOVETSKAIA ENTSIKLOPEDIIA. Vol. 30. Moscow: Gosudarstvennyi Institut "Sovetskaia Entsiklopediia," (Ogiz RSFSR), 1937, 599-601 pp. [Russ. text; Kazakh, Russ. titles, p. 601]

*Talipov. T. GLASNYE ZVUKI UIGURSKOGO I KAZAKHSKOGO IAZYKOV. Alma Ata: Izdatel'stvo "Nauka," Kazakskoi SSR, 1968, 108 pp., 1100 copies. [Russ. text; 154 Kazakh, Russ., Europ. titles, pp. 101-107]

Kazakh: Language, Literature

*"TAZHIBAEV, ABDIL'DA," BOL'SHAIA SOVETSKAIA
ENTSIKLOPEDIIA. Vol. 53. Moscow: Gosudarstvennyi
Nauchnyi Institut "Sovetskaia Entsiklopediia," 1st ed.
(Ogiz RSFSR), 1946, p. 455. [Russ. text; Kazakh,
Russ. titles, p. 455]

*"TAZHIBAEV, ABDIL'DA," LITERATURNAIA ENTSIKLOPEDIIA.
Vol. 11. Moscow: Gosudarstvennoe Izdatel'stvo
"Khudozhestvennaia Literatura," 1939, p. 174.
[Russ. text; Kazakh, Russ. titles, p. 174]

*Togzhanov, G. KAZAKSKAIA LITERATURA," LITERATURNAIA
ENTSIKLOPEDIIA. Vol. 5 n. p. Izdatel'stvo
Kommunisticheskoi Akademii, 1931, 18-22 pp. [Russ.
text and titles, p. 22]

Tokpanov, Kh.; M. Tsukanov. UNIVERSITETY KUL'TURY.
Alma Ata: Kazgosizdat, 1960. [Russ. text; ca.200
titles, pp. 42-49]

*"TRUDY FILOLOGOV KAZAKHSTANA," KAZAKHSTANSKAIA PRAVDA.
No. 238. Oct. 8, 1954. [Russ. text and titles,
pub.: 1954 (in Izvestiia AN KazSSR, No. 1-2, Ser.
Fil. i Iskusstv.), p. 3]

[Turlina, G. comp.] O TEBE I TVOIKH TOVARISHCHAKH.
PAMIATKA CHITATELIAM--UCHASHCHIMSIA 5-7 KLASSOV.
Alma Ata: "Kazakhstan" (Gos. Resp. Det. B-ka Kaz.SSR.
K 50-letiiu Velikogo Oktiabria), 1967, 14 pp.,
10,000 copies.

[Turlina, G. comp.] PIONERY--GEROI. PAMIATKA
CHITATELIAM--UCHASHCHIMSIA 5-6-KH KLASSOV. Alma Ata:
"Kazakhstan," 1967, 13 pp., 10,000 copies.

Uiukbaev, I. K. comp. BIBLIOGRAFICHESKII UKAZATEL'
PO METODIKE KAZAKHSKOGO IAZYKA. Alma Ata: (M-vo
Prosveshcheniia KazSSR. Upr. Shkol),1961, 43 pp.,
2,000 copies. [Kazakh text]

VOPROSY KAZAKHSKOGO IAZYKA I LITERATURY. (SBORNIK
STATEI SPIRANTOV I SOISKATELEI). No. 5. Alma Ata:
(M-vo Vyssh. i Sred. Spets. Obrazovaniia Kaz.SSR),
1968 (Vyp. Dan.1969), 267 pp., 550 copies. [Russ.
text; Kazakh, Russ. titles, at end of articles]

Zhirenchin, A. G. M. MUSREPOV. Alma Ata: (M-vo
Kul'tury KazSSR. Glav. Upr. Izdatel'stv i Poligr.
Prom-sti), 1958. [Russ. text; 48 Kazakh, Russ.,
foreign titles, pp. 20-23]

Kazakh

PHILOSOPHY, RELIGION

Chekaninskii, I. A. "SLEDY DREVNIKH VEROVANII KAZAKOV," [KRATKII UKAZATEL' LITERATURY, POSVIASHCHENNOI PEREZHITKAM VEROVANII KAZAKOV, KIRGIZOV, UZBEKOV], ZAPISKI SEMIPALATINSKOGO OBSHCHESTVA IZUCHENIE KAZAKSTANA, Vol. 1, No. 18. 1929. Russ. text; 62 titles, per.: Ancient, pp. 85-87]

Chernavskii, N. M. "ORENBURGSKIIA EPARKHIAL'NYIA VIEDOMOSTI," TRUDY ORENBURGSKOI UCHENOI ARKH. KOMISSII. No. 12, 1903, 153-189 pp. [Russ. text; titles, pp. 153, 174-188]

Kalieva, T. O. comp. NAUKA I RELIGIIA (SERIIA KNIZHNYKH ZAKLADOK NA ATEISTICHESKUIU TEMU). [Alma Ata] "Kazakhstan," 1967, 16 pp., 10,000 copies. [Kazakh text]

Kshibekov, D. O ZAKONOMERNOSTIAKH ZAMENY DOKAPITALISTICHESKIKH PROIZVODSTVENNYKH OTNOSHENII SOTSIALISTICHESKIMI (NA PRIMERE KAZAKHSTANA). Alma Ata, 1963. [Russ. text; ca.450 titles, pp. 5-8, 230-248]

*Musabaeva, N. A. PROBLEMA PRICHINNOSTI V FILOSOFII I BIOLOGII. Alma Ata, 1962, 292 pp., 2,400 copies. [(Russ. text), ca.350 Russ., Kazakh, Europ. titles, pp. 278-291]

OGLAVLENIE OFFITSIAL'NOI I NEOFFITSIAL'NOI CHASTI 'ORENBURGSKIKH EPARKHIAL'NYKH VIEDOMOSTEI' ZA 1898 G. VIEDOMOSTEI' ZA 1898 G. ORENBURGSKIIA EPARKHIAL'NYIA VIEDOMOSTI. 1899. ...ZA 1899[-1911] ORENBURGSKIIA EPARKHIAL'NYIA VIEDOMOSTI. 1899-ca.1912 (annually). [Russ. text; (1899) pub.: 1898; (1899-ca.1912) pub.: 1899-1911]

Saprykin, V. et al. KAK MY BOREMSIA S SEKTANTSTVOM. Alma Ata, 1965. [Russ. text; 195 titles (pub. in Kazakhstan), pp. 213-222]

Sulatskov, A. NA ISKHODE NOCHI. (O DEIATEL'NOSTI IL'INTSEV I BAPTISTOV-"RASKOL'NIKOV"). Alma Ata: "Kazakhstan," 1966, 291 pp., 8500 copies. [Russ. text; titles at end of book]

Kazakh

POLITICAL SCIENCE, LAW

[Abubakirova, G. G.; A. A. Kobycheva] MY K
KOMMUNIZMU DERZHIM PUT'! METOD. I BIBLIOGR.
MATERIALY. Alma Ata: (Gos. Resp. B-ka KazSSR im.
Pushkina), 1959, 27 pp., 3000 copies. [Russ. text;
Sov. per.]

Abubakirova, G. G.; et al. comps. SLAVNYI PUT'
LENINSKOGO KOMSOMOLA. (K 40-LETIIU VLKSM).
METODICHESKIE I BIBLIOGRAFICHESKIE MATERIALY V
POMOSHCH' BIBLIOTEKAM. Alma Ata: (Gos. Resp. B-ka
KazSSR im. Pushkina), 1958, 38 pp., 3,000 copies.
[Russ. text]

Akashev, S.; Kh. Kozhakhmetov. V. I. LENIN V SERDTSAKH
MILLIONOV. (REK. UKAZATEL' LIT.) Alma Ata: (Gos.
Resp. B-ka KazSSR im. Pushkina), 1960, 67 pp.,
5,000 copies. [Kazakh text; ca.225 Kazakh titles]

_____; S. Karina; E. Aitabaev; comp. ISTORIIA
KOMMUNISTICHESKOI PARTII KAZAKHSTANA. NAUCH.-INFORM.
BIBLIOGRAFIIA 1903-1963 GG. Alma Ata: (Resp. Gos.
B-ka KazSSR im. Pushkina), 1963, 140 pp., 4,000
copies. [Kazakh text; ca.800 Kazakh, Russ. titles,
per.: 1903-1963]

*Akashev, S. A. comp.; E. S. Aitbaev. ed.
PROIZVEDENIIA VLADIMIRA IL'ICHA LENINA, PEREVEDENNYE
NA KAZAKHSKII IAZYK. (BIBLIOGRAFICHESKII UKAZATEL').
Alma Ata: (Gos. Resp. B-ka KazSSR im. A. S. Pushkina),
1963, 55 pp., 3,000 copies. [Kazakh text; 301
Kazakh titles, pp. 13-47]

Akhinzhanova, S. M.; K. Sh. Bekmukhamedov; Kh. K.
Kozhakhmetova. comps. DEIATELI OKTIABR'SKOI
REVOLIUTSII I GRAZHDANSKOI VOINY V KAZAKHSTANE.
(PAMIATKI). Alma Ata: (Gos. Resp. Biblioteka
KazSSR. im. Pushkina), 1960, 69 pp., 4,000 copies.
[Russ. text; per.: 1917-1921]

Kazakh: Political Science, Law

Andronnikov, V. V.; I. N. Bukhonova; Kh. A. Dzhabasov; N. P. Kalita; E. A. Mikhalishcheva; Sh. Ia. Shafiro. comps. DOKUMENTAL'NYE ISTOCHNIKI PO ISTORII KOMMUNISTICHESKOI PARTII KAZAKHSTANA. NAUCH.-INFORM. BIBLIOGRAFIIA. OKT. 1917 G. - OKT. 1962 G. Alma Ata: Kazgosizdat, 1963, 135 pp., 2,200 copies. [Russ. text; 1,550 Russ titles, pub.: 1917-1962]

[Annenikova, A. A. et al. comps.] RESHENIIA [DVADTSAT' PERVOGO] XXI S"EZDA KPSS - V MASSY! METOD. I BIBLIOGR. MATERIALY. Alma Ata: (Gos. Resp. B-ka KazSSR im. Pushkina), 1959, 51 pp., 3,000 copies. [Russ. text; per.: 21st Congress CPSU]

*Asfendiarov, S. D. NATSIONAL'NO - OSVOBODITEL'NOE VOSSTANIE 1916 GODA V KAZAKHSTANE. Alma Ata - Moscow: Kazakhstanskoe Kraevoe Izdatel'stvo, 1936, 150 pp., 10,000 copies. [Russ. text; Kazakh, Russ. titles, per.: 1916, pp. 141-149]

Baimurzin, G. OTVETSTVENNOST' ZA PRIKOSNOVENNOST' K PRESTUPLENIIU. Alma Ata: "Nauka," 1968, 188 pp., 1900 copies. [Russ. text; pp. 181-187]

Barsukov, N. A. METODICHESKIE SOVETY K IZUCHENIIU BIOGRAFII V. I. LENINA V NACHAL'NYKH POLITICHESKIKH SHKOLAKH. Alma Ata: "Kazakhstan," 1968, 141 pp., 9200 copies. [Russ. text; Kazakh titles at end of theme]

Belokopytova, M. A.; M. S. Vasil'eva; I. A. Tiutiunnikov. KZYL-ORDINSKAIA OBLAST' I EE ADMINISTRATIVNYE RAIONY. Alma Ata: (Akademiia Nauk Kazakhskoi SSR. Otd. Geografii.), 1961. [Russ. text; 125 titles, pp. 172-176]

Bezgin, I. G. AKMOLINSK, GOROD AKMOLINSKOI OBLASTI. PERVYI SBORNIK UKAZANII NA KNIGI, STAT'I I ZAMIETKI, OTNOSIASHCHIESIA K G. AKMOLINSKU. St. Petersburg: Tip. Porokhovshchikovoi, 1905, 8 pp. [Russ. text; 18 titles]

[Bikineeva, D. comp.] GANI MURATBAEV. (PAMIATKA). Kzyl Orda: (Kzyl-Ordin Obl. B-ka im. Gor'kogo), 1968, 13 pp. 300 copies. [Kazakh, Russ. text]

Bulatov, S. Ia. OTVETSTVENNOST' ZA KHOZIAISTVENNYE PRESTUPLENIIA PO UGOLOVNOMU KODEKSU KAZAKHSKOI SSR. Alma Ata, 1965. [Russ. text; 44 titles, pp. 107-109]

Kazakh: Political Science, Law

_____. PONIATIE I SISTEMA OSOBENNOI CHASTI UGOLOVNOGO PRAVA SOIUZA SSR I KAZAKHSKOI SSR. Alma Ata, 1962. [Russ. text; ca.70 titles, pp. 37-44]

*Erenov, A. VOZNIKNOVENIE I RAZVITIE SOTSIALISTICHESKIKH ZEMEL'NYKH PRAVOOTNOSHENII V KAZAKHSKOI SSR. Alma Ata, 1963, 363 pp., 2400 copies. [Russ. text; ca.300 Russ., Kazakh titles, Sov. per., pp. 349-362]

*Elevov, T. USTANOVLENIE I UPROCHENIE SOVETSKOI VLASTI V KAZAKHSTANE. (MART 1917 - IIUN' 1918 GODA). Alma Ata: Izdatel'stvo Akademii Nauk Kazakhskoi SSR (Institut Istorii, Arkheologii i Etnografii im. Valikhanova), 1961, 528 pp., 2600 copies. [Russ. text; ca.380 Russ. titles, (incl. archives), per.: March 1917-June 1918, pp. 511-526]

Ermagambetov, M. OB ISTOCHNIKAKH PO ISTORII DIPLOMATICHESKIKH I MEZHDUNARODNYKH OTNOSHENII KAZAKHSTANA. IZVESTIIA AKADEMII NAUK KAZAKHSKOI SSR. SERIIA IURIDICHESKAIA. No. 1. 1948. [Russ. text; 64 titles, pp. 95-107]

Iakimenko, T. comp. PERVYE ISKRY KOMMUNISTICHESKOGO TRUDA NA VOSTOKE KAZAKHSTANA. (REK. UKAZATEL' LIT.) Ust Kamenogorsk: (Vost.-Kazakhst. Obl. B-ka im. Pushkina), 1961, 19 pp., 500 copies. [Russ. text; ca.100 titles]

Iur'eva, Z. P. comp. SLAVNYE DELA KOMSOMOLA VOSTOCHNOGO KAZAKHSTANA. (REK. UKAZATEL' LIT. K 40-LETIIU KOMSOMOLA KAZAKHSTANA). Ust Kamenogorsk: (Obl. B-ka im. Pushkina), 1961, 32 pp., 1000 copies. [Russ. text; ca.100 titles]

Kalieva, T.; B. Nusipbekova. comp. S LENINYM V SERDTSE. LENINSKAIA NATSIONAL'NAIA POLITIKA I EE TORZHESTVO V KAZAKHSTANE. (RASSKAZY O KNIGAKH). Alma Ata: "Kazakhstan," (Gos. Resp. B-ka Kaz.SSR im. Pushkina), 1966, 14 pp., 5,000 copies. [Kazakh text]

Kozybaev, M. KOMPARTIIA KAZAKHSTANA V PERIOD VELIKOI OTECHESTVENNOI VOINY. Alma Ata, 1964. [Russ. text; 73 titles, per.: 1941-1945, pp. 356-360]

"KRATKII BIBLIOGRAFICHESKII UKAZATEL' LITERATURY PO KAZAKHSKOMU OBYCHNOMU PRAVU," MATERIALY PO KAZAKHSKOMU OBYCHNOMU PRAVU. SB. 1. Alma Ata, 1948. [Russ. text; 105 titles, pub.: 1811-1948, pp. 345-347]

Kazakh: Political Science, Law

"KRATKII UKAZATEL' LITERATURY O REVOLIUTSII 1905-1907 GG. V ROSSII," KOMMUNIST KAZAKHSTANA. No. 3. 1955. [Russ. text; 128 titles, per.: 1905-1907, pp. 62-64]

LITERATURA O PARTIINYKH S"EZDAKH I KONFERENTSIIAKH. Alma Ata: Qazmembas, 1953, 7 pp., 5,000 copies. [Kazakh, Russ. text]

Mamutov, A. M. PRESTUPLENIIA, SOSTAVLIAIUSHCHIE PEREZHITKI PATRIARKHAL'NO-RODOVOGO BYTA. Alma Ata, 1963. [Russ. text; ca.400 titles, pp. 319-335]

Mukhitdinov, N. PRAVOVYE OSNOVY KHOZIAISTVENNOI DEIATEL'NOSTI MEZHKOLKHOZNYKH STROITEL'NYKH ORGANIZATSII. Alma Ata: "Kazakhstan,"1968, 180 pp., 4,000 copies. [Russ. text; 165-179 pp.]

*Petrushin, N.; N. Ul'ianov; O.Cherniavskaia. TRADITSII RABKRINA ZHIVUT. Alma Ata: Izdatel'stvo "Kazakhstan," 1966, 136 pp., 3,000 copies. [Russ. text and titles, pub.: 1964-1965, pp. 133-136]

PROIZVEDENIIA KLASSIKOV MARKSIZMA-LENINIZMA, IZDANNYE KAZGOSIZDATOM NA KAZAKHSKOM IAZYKE. Alma Ata: Kazgosizdat, 1953, 12 pp., 5,000 copies. [Kazakh, Russ. text; 49 Kazakh titles]

Romanov, Iu. I. DRUZHBA, ROZHDENNIA V BOR'BE. Alma Ata, 1964. [Russ. text; ca.120 titles, per.: 1918-1921, pp. 115-119]

Shaibekov, K. A. TEORETICHESKIE PROBLEMY PRAVOVOGO REGULIROVANIIA OPLATY TRUDA V KOLKHOZAKH. Alma Ata: (Kaz. Gos. Un-t im. S. M. Kirova. Iurid. Fak.), 1968, 470 pp., 2,000 copies. [Russ. text; pp. 446-467]

Shevchenko, Z. M. comp. ALAUTDIN MAKHMUDOVICH BOGOUTDINOV. (MATERIALY K BIBLIOGRAFII UCHENNYKH TADZHIKISTANA. No. 1). Dushanbe: Izd-vo AN Tadzhik. SSR., 1961, 47 pp., 500 copies. [Russ. text; 122 Tajik, Russ., Europ. titles, pub.: 1940-1961]

"SODERZHANIE ZHURNALA" 'BOL'SHEVIK KAZAKHSTANA' ZA 1939 G. BOL'SHEVIK KAZAKHSTANA. No. 12. 1939. [Russ. text; 125 titles, pub.: 1939, pp. 93-96]

"TAIMANOV, ISATAI," BOL'SHAIA SOVETSKAIA ENTSIKLOPEDIIA. Vol. 53. Moscow: Gosudarstvennyi Nauchnyi Institut "Sovetskaia Entsiklopediia," (Ogiz RSFSR), 1946, 1st ed., 484-485 pp. [Russ. text and titles, p. 485]

Kazakh: Political Science, Law

"TRUDY ORENBURGSKOI UCHENOI ARKHIVNOI KOMISSII,"
TRUDY ORENBURGSKOI UCHENOI ARKHIVNOI KOMISSII. No. 31
(PRILOZHENIE) [No. 32]. 1914. [Russ. text;
titles (appendix) pp. I-IX]

Ustinov, A. TVOI ESTETICHESKII IDEAL. Alma Ata:
"Kazakhstan," 1967, 64 pp., 10,200 copies. [Russ.
text; titles p. 63]

*VAZHNEISHIE RABOTY I. V. STALINA. BOL'SHEVIK
KAZAKHSTANA. No. 10. 1949. [Russ. text; 78 Russ.
titles, pp. 45-47]

Zhenabilov, E.; R. Tazutdinov. 300 VOPROSOV I OTVETOV
PO TRUDOVOMU ZAKONODATEL'STVU. Alma Ata: "Kazakhstan,"
1967, 347 pp. 40,200 copies. [Russ. text; titles,
pp. 345-346]

*Zimanov, S. Z. POLITICHESKOI STROI KAZAKHSTANA KONTSA
XVIII I PERVOI POLOVINY XIX VEKOV. Alma Ata:
(Akad. Nauk KazSSr. In-t Filosofii i Prava), 1960,
293 pp. [Russ. text; ca.500 Russ titles, per.:
18th and first half of 19th c., pp. 6-28, 280-294]

SOCIAL ORGANIZATION

Donich, A. N. "PROBLEMA 'NOVOGO KAZAKSKOGO AULA,'"
NARODNOE KHOZIAISTVO KAZAKSTANA. No. 4/5. 1928.
[Russ. text; titles pp. 166-168]

Ermachenkov, Vladimir. CHELOVEK S ROMBOM (O RABOTE
KOMSOMOL'SKIKH ORGANIZATSII VUZOV). Alma Ata:
"Kazakhstan," 1968, 211 pp., 9,000 copies. [Russ.
text; titles pp. 206-209]

KATALOG KAZAKHSKOI LITERATURY PO PROFESSIONAL'NOMU
DVIZHENIIU. Kizil Orda: Kazgosizdat, 1926, 16 pp.
[Russ. text]

Grebenshchikov, V. O. ZDRAVOOKHRANENIE I MEDITSINA V
DOREVOLIUTSIONNOM KAZAKHSTANE. BIBLIOGR. UKAZATEL'
LIT. (1731-1917 GG.) Alma Ata: (Gos. Nauch. Med.
B-ka Kazakhstana), 1960, 290 pp., 1,200 copies. [Russ.
text; 2,415 titles, per.: 1731-1917]

Kazakh: Social Organization

Melkova. N. "IGRY KIRGIZOV," TRUDY ORENBURGSKAGO
OBSHCHESTVA IZUCHENIIA KIRGIZSKAGO KRAIA. No. 1.
1921. 46-49 pp. [Russ. text; 37 titles, appendix]

*Pal'gov, N. N. KAZAKHSTAN OT URAL'SKA DO ALMA ATY.
PUTEVODITEL' PO ZHELEZNOI DOROGE. Alma Ata:
Izdatel'stvo "Nauka," Kazakhskoi SSR, 1965, 256 pp.,
6,760 copies. [Russ. text; Russ. titles, pp. 251-255]

ROZHDENIE KOMSOMOLA SEMIRECH'IA (1918-1920). Alma Ata:
Kazgosizdat, 1958. [Russ. text; 21 Russ. titles,
per.: 1918-1920, pub.: 1918-1957, pp. 275-276]

*Togzhanov, G. KAZAKSKII KOLONIAL'NYI AUL. Part 1.
Moscow: Izdanie Nauchno-Issledovatel'skoi Assotsiatsii
po Izucheniiu Natsional'nykh i Kolonial'nykh Problem,
1934, 111 pp., 1,500 copies. [Russ. text; 115 Russ.
titles, pp. 106-109]

*Zharikbaev, K. B. KRATKII BIBLIOGRAFICHESKII UKAZATEL'
PO PSIKHOLOGII. (1917-1967). Alma Ata: (M-vo
Prosveshcheniia Kaz.SSR), 1967 (Vyp DAN 1968), 79 pp.,
4000 copies. [Russ. text; Kazakh, Russ. titles,
per.: 1917-1967]

26 KIRGIZ

GENERAL

*Abubakirova, S. Sh.; Sh. Sadykova; R. S. Shamshiev. comps.
DVAZHDY ORDENONOSNYI KIRGIZSTAN. Frunze: (Ministerstvo
Kul'tury Kirgizskoi SSR. Gosudarstvennaia
Respublikanskaia Biblioteka Kirgizskoi SSR imeni N. G.
Chernyshevskogo), 1966, 126 pp., 600 copies. [Kirgiz
text; ca.734 titles]

Abubakirova S.; Sh. Sadykova; R. Toktobaeva; M. Tynalieva;
R. Shamshiev. comps. SOVETSKII KIRGIZSTAN. KRATKII
ANNOTIROVANNYI UKAZATEL' LITERATURY. Frunze: (Gos.
Resp. B-ka Kirgiz. SSR im. N. G. Chernyshevskogo.
Bibliogr. Otdel), 1961, 263 pp. [Kirgiz text; 1393
Kirgiz titles pub.: up to 1960]

Ainikenov, R. R. PRZHEVAL'SKII GOSUDARSTVENNYI
PEDAGOGICHESKII INSTITUT. Przheval'sk: (M-vo Nar.
Obrazovaniia Kirgiz. SSR), 1963. [Russ. text; ca.80
Russ. titles, pub.: 1954-1962, pp. 58-62]

Akaibaeva, K.; A. K. Tserilova. comps. KNIGA SOVETSKOI
KIRGIZII. SVODNAIA BIBLIOGR. 1924-1938. Frunze:
(Kom. po Pechati pri Sovete Ministrov Kirg.SSR), 1967,
219 pp., 500 copies. [Russ. text; Kirgiz, Russ.
titles, per.: 1924-1938]

_____.; I. S. Sergievskaia. comp. KNIGA
SOVETSKOI KIRGIZII. SVODNAIA BIBLIOGR. 1960-1965.
Frunze: (Kirg. Gos. Knizhnaia Palata), 1970, 518 pp.,
500 copies. [Kirgiz, Russ. text; 5124 Kirgiz, Russ.
titles, pub.: 1960-1965]

_____. KNIGA
SOVETSKOI KIRGIZII. SVODNAIA BIBLIOGR. 1960-1965.
Frunze: (M-vo Kul'tury Kirg. SSR. Kirg. Gos.
Knizhnaia Palata), 1970, 518 pp. [Kirgiz, Russ.
text; pub.: 1960-1965]

Andasheva, A. A.; I. S. Sergievskaia. comps. KNIGA
SOVETSKOI KIRGIZII. 1955-1959 GG. SVODNAIA
BIBLIOGRAFIIA. Frunze: (Kom. po Pechati pri Sovete
Ministrov Kirgizskoi SSR. Kirgizskaia Gosudarstvennaia
Knizhnaia Palata), 1966, 332 pp., 550 copies. [Kirgiz,
Russ. text; 1897 + 1335 Kirgiz, Russ. titles, pub.:
1955-1959]

Kirgiz: General

*Amitin-Shapiro, Z. L. BIBLIOGRAFIIA KIRGIZII. V 4-KH T. Vol. 1. LITERATURA O KIRGIZII (1918-1924). ANNOTIROVANNYI UKAZATEL'. Frunze: (Gos. Resp. B-ka Kirgizskoi SSR im. Chernyshevskogo), 1963, 319 pp., 1500 copies. [Russ. text; 1602 + 151 Russ. titles, pub.: 1918-1924]

*_____. BIBLIOGRAFIIA KIRGIZII. V 4-KH T. Vol. 2, No. 1. LITERATURA O KIRGIZII (1925-1936). ANNOTIROVANNYI UKAZATEL'. Frunze: (Gos. Resp. B-ka Kirgizskoi SSR im. N. G. Chernyshevskogo), 1965, 806 pp., 1,000 copies. [Russ. text; 4137 Russ. titles, pub.: 1925-1936]

*Belitskii, S. "FRUNZE, MIKHAIL VASIL'EVICH," BOL'SHAIA SOVETSKAIA ENTSIKLOPEDIIA. Vol. 59. Moscow: Gosudarstvennyi Institut "Sovetskaia Entsiklopediia" (Ogiz RSFSR), 1935, 1st ed., 261-266 pp. [Russ. text and titles, pp. 266]

*Belkova, G.; E. Diadiuchenko; V. Zvoleva; M. Shvidka. comps. KIRGIZSKAIA SSR V 1963 GODU. BIBLIOGRAFICHESKII UKAZATEL' LITERATURY. Frunze: "Kyrgyzstan," 1968, 383 pp., 1000 copies. [Russ. text; 5320 Russ. titles, pub.: 1963]

DNI, LIUDI, SOBYTIIA, 1969. KALENDAR'--UKAZATEL' LIT. [PO KIRG. SSR] [Frunze] (Gos. Resp. B-ka Kirg. SSR im. Chernyshevskogo. Tsentr. Gos. Arkhiv Kirg. SSR) [1968] 80 pp., 1,000 copies. [Russ. text]

DNI, LIUDI, SOBYTIIA, 1969. KALENDAR'--UKAZATEL' LIT. [PO KIRG. SSR] [Frunze] (Gos. Resp. B-ka Kirg. SSR im. Chernyshevskogo. Tsentr. Gos. Arkhiv Kirg. SSR) [1968] 141 pp., 1000 copies. (annual). [Kirgiz text]

*Erman, L. M.; M. M. Bazhenova; E. G. Eshimbekova. comps. BIBLIOGRAFIIA IZDANII AKADEMII NAUK KIRGIZSKOI SSR. 1960-1961. Frunze: (A. N. Kirgizskoi SSR), 1964, 213 pp., 500 copies. [Russ. text; 1214 Kirgiz, Dungan, Russ. titles, pub.: 1960-1961]

*_____; E. G. Abail'dinova. comps. BIBLIOGRAFIIA IZDANII AKADEMII NAUK KIRGIZSKOI SSR. 1962-1964 GG. Frunze: Izdatel'stvo "Ilim," 1966, 155 pp., 500 copies. [Russ. text; 385 Kirgiz, Russ. titles, pub.: 1962-1964]

Kirgiz: General

*Erman, L. M.; M. M. Gerasimova. comps. BIBLIOGRAFIIA
IZDANII AKADEMII NAUK KIRGIZSKOI SSR. 1943-1956 GG.
(1943-1954 GG.--KIRGIZ. FILIAL AKAD. NAUK SSSR).
Frunze: (Akad. Nauk Kirgiz SSR. Tsentr. Nauch.
B-ka), 1957, 152 pp., 500 copies. [Russ. text; 1,181
Kirgiz, Russ. titles, pub.: 1943-1956]

_____. "BIBLIOGRAFIIA
IZDANII AKADEMII NAUK KIRGIZSKOI SSR ZA 1955 GOD,"
IZVESTIIA AKAD. NAUK KIRGIZ. SSR. No. 3. 1956.
[Russ. text; 230 titles, pub.: 1955, pp. 141-153]

_____. "BIBLIOGRAFIIA
IZDANII AKADEMII NAUK KIRGIZSKOI SSR ZA 1957 GOD,"
IZVESTIIA AKAD. NAUK KIRGIZ. SSR. (SERIIA ESTESTV. I
TEKHN. NAUK). Vol. 1, No. 1. 1959. [Russ. text;
ca.200 Kirgiz, Russ. titles, pub.: 1957, pp. 145-165]

* _____. BIBLIOGRAFIIA
IZDANII AKADEMII NAUK KIRGIZSKOI SSR. 1957-1959 GG.
Frunze: Izdatel'stvo AN Kirgizskoi SSR. Tsentr.
Nauch. B-ka, 1961, 146 pp., 500 copies. [Russ.
text; 934 Kirg., Russ., Dungan titles, pub.: 1957-1959]

Guzhin, G. S.; M. I. Kuznetsova; D. S. Losev; O. D.
Morozov; E. I. Novichenko; O. I. Sal'nikova. comps.
SOVETSKII KIRGIZSTAN. KRATKII ANNOTIROVANNYI
UKAZATEL' LITERATURY. Frunze: Gos. Resp. B-ka
Kirgiz. SSR im. N. G. Chernyshevskogo), 1961, 400 pp.
[Russ. text; 2231 Russ. titles]

KIRGIZIIA V DNI VELIKOI OTECHESTVENNOI VOINY:
BIBLIOGRAFICHESKII UKAZATEL' PECHATI KIRGIZSKOI SSR.
(KNIGI, GAZETNYE I ZHURNAL'NYE STAT'I IIUL' 1941 -
MAI - 1945 G. G.). Frunze: Kirgizgosizdat, 1950,
268 pp., 940 copies. [Russ. text; 5997 Russ.
titles, pub.: June 1941-May 1945]

KNIZHNAIA LETOPIS'. ORGAN GOS. REGISTRATS. BIBLIOGRAFII
KIRGIZSKOI SSR. 1950. Frunze: (Kn. Palata Kirgiz.
SSR), 1951, 48 pp., 5,100 copies. [Kirgiz text;
Kirgiz titles, pub.: 1950]

KNIZHNAIA LETOPIS'. ORGAN GOS. BIBLIOGRAFII KIRGIZ
SSR. Frunze: (Knizhnaia Palata Kirgiz. SSR), 1953,
40 + 40 pp., 790 copies. [Kirgiz, Russ. text and
titles, pub.: 1951-1952]

KNIZHNAIA LETOPIS'. ORGAN GOS. BIBLIOGRAFII KIRGIZ SSR.
1953. Frunze: (Kirgiz Gos. Knizhnaia Palata), 1954,
52 pp. 590 copies. [Kirgiz, Russ. text and titles,
pub.: 1953]

Kirgiz: General

KNIZHNAIA LETOPIS'. ORGAN GOS. BIBLIOGRAFII KIRGIZ. SSR. 1954. Frunze: (Kirgiz. Gos. Knizhnaia Palata), 1955, 63 pp., 590 copies. [Kirgiz, Russ. text and titles, pub.: 1954]

KNIZHNAIA LETOPIS'. ORGAN GOS. BIBLIOGRAFII KIRGIZ. SSR. 1955. Frunze: (Kirgiz Gos. Knizh. Palata), 1956, 86 pp., 700 copies. [Kirgiz, Russ. text and titles, pub.: 1955]

KNIZHNAIA LETOPIS'. ORGAN GOS. BIBLIOGRAFII KIRGIZ. SSR. Frunze: (Kirgiz. Gos. Knizhnaia Palata) [1957] quarterly, 790 copies. [Kirgiz, Russ. text and titles]

KNIZHNAIA LETOPIS'. ORGAN GOS. BIBLIOGRAFII KIRGIZ. SSR. Frunze: (Kirgiz Gos. Knizhnaia Palata) [1958] quarterly, 700 copies. [Kirgiz, Russ. text and titles, pub.: 1958]

KNIZHNAIA LETOPIS'. ORGAN GOS. BIBLIOGRAFII KIRGIZ SSR. Frunze: (Kirgiz Gos. Knizhnaia Palata), 1959, quarterly, 500 copies. [Kirgiz, Russ. text and titles, pub.: 1959]

KNIZHNAIA LETOPIS'. ORGAN GOS. BIBLIOGRAFII KIRGIZ. SSR. Frunze: (Kirgiz. Gos. Knizhnaia Palata), [1960] quarterly, 500 copies. [Kirgiz, Russ. text and titles, pub.: 1960]

KNIZHNAIA LETOPIS'. ORGAN GOS. BIBLIOGRAFII KIRGIZ. SSR. Frunze: (Kirgiz. Gos. Knizhnaia Palata) [1961] quarterly, 500 copies. [Kirgiz, Russ. text and titles, pub.: 1961]

KNIZHNAIA LETOPIS'. ORGAN GOS. BIBLIOGRAFII KIRGIZ. SSR. Frunze: (Kirgiz. Gos. Knizhnaia Palata), [1962] quarterly, 500 copies. [Kirgiz, Russ. text and titles, pub.: 1962]

KNIZHNAIA LETOPIS'. ORGAN GOS. BIBLIOGRAFII KIRGIZ SSR. Frunze: Kirgiz Gos. Knizhnaia Palata. [1963] quarterly, 500 copies. [Kirgiz, Russ. text and titles, pub.: 1963]

KNIZHNAIA LETOPIS'. Frunze: (Kirgizskaia Gosudarstvennaia Knizhnaia Palata), 1964 (quarterly), 500 copies. [Kirgiz, Russ. text and titles, pub.: 1964]

KNIZHNAIA LETOPIS'. Frunze: (Kirgiz. Gos. Knizhnaia Palata) [1965; (quarterly)] 500 copies. [Kirgiz, Russ. text and titles, pub.: 1965]

Kirgiz: General

KNIZHNAIA LETOPIS'. Frunze: (Kir. Gos. Knizhnaia
Palata) [1966] (quarterly) 500 copies. [Kirgiz,
Russ. text and titles, pub.: (1966)]

KNIZHNAIA LETOPIS'. Frunze: (Kir. Gos. Knizhnaia
Palata) [1967] (quarterly) 500 copies. [Kirgiz,
Russ. text and titles, pub.: (1967)]

KNIZHNAIA LETOPIS'. Frunze: (Kir. Gos. Knizhnaia
Palata) [1968] (quarterly) 500 copies. [Kirgiz,
Russ. text and titles, pub.: (1968)]

KNIZHNAIA LETOPIS'. Frunze: (Kir. Gos. Knizhnaia
Palata) [1969] (quarterly) 500 copies. [Kirgiz,
Russ. text and titles, pub.: (1969)]

KNIZHNAIA LETOPIS'. Frunze: (Kir. Gos. Knizhnaia
Palata) [1970] (quarterly) 500 copies. [Kirgiz,
Russ. text and titles, pub.: (1970)]

Kulakov, A. I. "NAUKA, LITERATURA, ISKUSSTVO KIRGIZII V
PERIOD VELIKOI OTECHESTVENNOI VOINY," IZVESTIIA
KIRGIZ. FILIALA AKAD. NAUK SSSR. No. 1, No. 2-3.
1945. [Russ. text; ca.500 titles, pub.: 1941-1945,
(No. 1) pp. 151-168; (No. 2-3) pp. 139-147]

Kuznetsova, M. I. BIBLIOGRAFIIA IZDANII GOSUDARSTVENNOI
RESPUBLIKANSKOI BIBLIOTEKI KIRGIZSKOI SSR IM. N. G.
CHERNYSHEVSKOGO (1948-1958 GODY). Frunze: (Gos.
Resp. B-ka Kirgiz. SSR im. N. G. Chernyshevskogo.
Bibliogr. Otdel) 1959, 14 pp. [Russ. text; 67 Russ.
titles, pub.: 1948-1958]

*Losev, D. S. ed. DVAZHDY ORDENONOSNYI KIRGIZSTAN.
REKOMENDATEL'NYI UKAZATEL' LITERATURY. Frunze:
(M-vo Kul'tury Kirg. SSR. Gosudarstvennaia
Respublikanskaia Biblioteka Kirgizskoi SSR imeni N. G.
Chernyshevskogo. Otdel Natsional'noi Bibliografii),
1966, 136 pp., 600 copies. [Russ. text; 734 Russ.
titles, per.: 1955-1965]

LETOPIS' PECHATI KIRGIZII. BIBLIOGR. UKAZATEL' KNIG,
GAZETNYKH I ZHURNAL'NYKH STATEI. No. 1. Frunze:
(Kn. Palata Kirgizskoi SSR) 1948. [Russ. text;
1,083 titles, pub. 1948]

LETOPIS' PECHATI KIRGIZII. BIBLIOGRAFICHESKII UKAZATEL'
KNIG, GAZETNYKH I ZHURNAL'NYKH STATEI. No. 1.
Frunze: Kn. Palata Kirgizskoi SSR, 1949. [Kirgiz
text; 991 Kirgiz titles (articles)]

Kirgiz: General

KIRGIZSTANDIN BASMA SOZUNUN LETOPISI. (LETOPIS' PECHATI KIRGIZII). Frunze, 1948, 1950. [Kirgiz, Russ. text; pub.: 1948]

*LETOPIS' ZHURNAL'NYKH I GAZETNYKH STATEI. ORGAN GOS. BIBLIOGRAFII KIRGIZ. SSR. Frunze: (Kirgiz. Gos. Knizh. Palata) 1956 [No. 1, Jan - March, first issue] 52 pp., 700 copies. [Kirgiz, Russ. text; 491 Kirgiz, Russ. titles, pub.: 1955-1956]

LETOPIS' ZHURNAL'NYKH I GAZETNYKH STATEI. ORGAN GOS. BIBLIOGRAFII KIRGIZ. SSR. Frunze: (Kirgiz. Gos. Knizhnaia Palata) [1957] (quarterly) 690 copies. Kirgiz, Russ. text and titles, pub.: 1957]

LETOPIS' ZHURNAL'NYKH I GAZETNYKH STATEI. ORGAN. GOS. BIBLIOGRAFII KIRGIZ. SSR. Frunze: (Kirgiz Gos. Knizhnaia Palata) [1958] (quarterly) 700 copies. [Kirgiz, Russ. text and titles, pub.: 1958]

LETOPIS' ZHURNAL'NYKH I GAZETNYKH STATEI. ORGAN GOS. BIBLIOGRAFII KIRGIZ. SSR. Frunze: (Kirgiz. Gos. Knizhnaia Palata) 1959 (quarterly) 500 copies. [Kirgiz, Russ. text and titles, pub.: 1959]

LETOPIS' ZHURNAL'NYKH I GAZETNYKH STATEI. ORGAN GOS. BIBLIOGRAFII KIRGIZ. SSR. Frunze: (Kirgiz Gos. Knizhnaia Palata) [1960] (quarterly) 500 copies. [Kirgiz, Russ. text and titles, pub.: 1960]

LETOPIS' ZHURNAL'NYKH I GAZETNYKH STATEI. ORGAN GOS. BIBLIOGRAFII KIRGIZ. SSR. Frunze: (Kirgiz. Gos. Knizhnaia Palata) [1961] (quarterly) 500 copies. [Kirgiz, Russ. text and titles, pub.: 1961]

LETOPIS' ZHURNAL'NYKH I GAZETNYKH STATEI. ORGAN GOS. BIBLIOGRAFII KIRGIZ. SSR. Frunze: (Kirgiz. Gos. Knizhnaia Palata) [1962] (quarterly) 500 copies. [Kirgiz, Russ. text and titles, pub.: 1962]

LETOPIS' ZHURNAL'NYKH I GAZETNYKH STATEI. ORGAN GOS. BIBLIOGRAFII KIRGIZ. SSR. Frunze: Kirgiz Gos. Knizhnaia Palata [1963] (quarterly) 500 copies. [Kirgiz, Russ. text and titles, pub.: 1963]

LETOPIS' ZHURNAL'NYKH I GAZETNYKH STATEI. Frunze: (Kirgiz. Gos. Knizhnaia Palata) 1964 (quarterly) 500 copies. [Kirgiz, Russ. text and titles, pub.: 1964]

Kirgiz: General

LETOPIS' ZHURNAL'NYKH I GAZETNYKH STATEI. Frunze:
(Kirgiz. Gos. Knizhnaia Palata) [1965; (quarterly)]
500 copies. [Kirgiz, Russ. text and titles, pub.:
1965]

LETOPIS' ZHURNAL'NYKH I GAZETNYKH STATEI. Frunze:
(Kirg. Gos. Knizhnaia Palata) [1966] (quarterly)
500 copies. [Kirgiz, Russ. text and titles, pub.:
(1966)]

LETOPIS' ZHURNAL'NYKH I GAZETNYKH STATEI. Frunze:
(Kirg. Gos. Knizhnaia Palata) [1967] (quarterly)
500 copies. [Kirgiz, Russ. text and titles, pub.:
(1967)]

LETOPIS' ZHURNAL'NYKH I GAZETNYKH STATEI. Frunze:
(Kirg. Gos. Knizhnaia Palata) [1968] (quarterly)
500 copies. [Kirgiz, Russ. text and titles, pub.:
(1968)]

LETOPIS' ZHURNAL'NYKH I GAZETNYKH STATEI. Frunze:
(Kirg. Gos. Knizhnaia Palata) [1969] (quarterly)
500 copies. [Kirgiz, Russ. text and titles, pub.:
(1969)]

LETOPIS' ZHURNAL'NYKH I GAZETNYKH STATEI. Funze:
(Kirg. Gos. Knizhnaia Palata) [1970] (quarterly)
500 copies. [Kirgiz, Russ. text and titles, pub.
(1970)]

*Mukanova, K. comp. KIRGIZSTAN V 1963 GODU (UKAZATEL'
LITERATURY). Frunze: "Kirgizstan" Basmasi, 1966,
273 pp., 600 copies. [Kirgiz text; 3047 Kirgiz
titles, pub.: 1963]

*Novichenko, E. I. BIBLIOGRAFIIA BIBLIOGRAFII O
KIRGIZII. 1852-1967. ANNOTIROVANNYI UKAZATEL'
LITERATURY. Frunze: Izdatel'stvo "Kyrgyzstan,"
1969, 190 pp., 1000 copies. [Russ. text; 1242
Kirg., Russ. titles, pub.: 1852-1967]

Novichenko, E. comp. KIRGIZSKAIA SSR V 1961 GODU.
UKAZATEL' LIT. Frunze: (Gos. Resp. B-ka Kirg. SSR
im. Chernyshevskogo), 1966, 583 pp., 1000 copies.
[Russ. text; 4690 Russ. titles, pub.: 1961]

NOVOE V SEL'SKOKHOZIAISTVENNOI PRAKTIKE. Frunze:
"Kyrgyzstan," 1967, 9 pp., 600 copies. [Russ. text]

Kirgiz: General

NOVYE KNIGI, IZDANNYE V KIRGIZSKOI SSR. 1963 G.
Frunze: (Kirgiz. Gos. Knizhnaia Palata) 1963 (every
two weeks) 150 copies. [Kirgiz, Russ. text and
titles, pub.: 1963]

NOVYE KNIGI, IZDANNYE V KIRGIZSKOI SSR. Frunze:
(Kirgizskaia Gosudarstvennaia Knizhnaia Palata)
1964 (every two weeks) 150 copies. [Kirgiz, Russ.
text and titles, pub.: 1964]

NOVYE KNIGI, IZDANNYE V KIRGIZSKOI SSR. Frunze:
(Kirg. Gos. Knizhnaia Palata) [1966] (every two weeks]
1150 copies. [Kirgiz, Russ. text and titles, pub.:
(1966)]

NOVYE KNIGI, IZDANNYE V KIRGIZSKOI SSR. Frunze: (Kirg.
Gos. Knizhnaia Palata) [1967] (every two weeks)
1150 copies. [Kirgiz, Russ. text and titles, pub.:
(1967)]

NOVYE KNIGI, IZDANNYE V KIRGIZSKOI SSR. Frunze:
(Kirg. Gos. Knizhnaia Palata) [1968] (every two
weeks) 1150 copies. [Kirgiz, Russ. text and
titles, pub.: (1968)]

NOVYE KNIGI, IZDANNYE V KIRGIZSKOI SSR. Frunze:
(Kirg.Gos. Knizhnaia Palata) [1969] (every two weeks)
1150 copies. [Kirgiz, Russ. text and titles,
pub.: (1969)]

NOVYE KNIGI, IZDANNYE V KIRGIZSKOI SSR. Frunze:
(KIRG. GOS. KNIZHNAIA PALATA) [1970] (every two weeks)
1150 copies. [Kirgiz, Russ. text and titles,
pub.:(1970)]

Ozmitelia, E. K. ed. RUSSKIE SOVETSKIE PISATELI O
KIRGIZII. Frunze: (Gos. Resp. B-ka Kirgiz. SSR
im. N. G. Chernyshevskogo) 1963, 83 pp., 1200 copies.
[Russ. text and titles]

Rakitnikov, A. N. TSENTRAL'NYI TIAN'-SHAN' I ISSYK-
KUL'SKAIA KOTLOVINA. VOPROSY POSTROENIIA GORNOGO
ZHIVOTNOVODCHESKOGO KHOZIAISTVA. Moscow-Leningrad:
Izd-vo Akad. Nauk SSSR, 1936, 200 pp. [Russ. text;
22 Russ. titles]

Shamshiev, R. S.; S. Sh. Abubakirova. BIBLIOGRAFIIA
KIRGIZII. V 4-KH TOMAKH. Vol. 3. No. 2. ISTORIIA.
ARKHEOLOGIIA. ETNOGRAFIIA. KOMMUNISTICHESKOE
STROITEL'STVO. ORGANY GOSUDARSTVENNOI VLASTI I
UPRAVLENIIA. Frunze, 1963. [Kirgiz text; 2514 Kirgiz
titles, pub.: 1922-1960]

Kirgiz: General

Shnitnikov, V. N. "LITERATURA," DZHETYSU (SEMIRECH'E). ESTESTVENNO-ISTORICHESKOE OPISANIE KRAIA. Tashkent, 1925. [Russ. text; 510 Russ., Europ. titles, pp. 215-234]

SODERZHANIE VYSHEDSHIKH NO. NO. ZHURNALA "SOVETSKAIA KIRGIZIIA," No. 1, 1923. No. 5/6, 7, 1924. 1923-1924. [Russ. text; 105 titles, pp. 154-159]

SPISOK SPRAVOCHNYKH I BIBLIOGRAFICHESKIKH IZDANII DLIA MASSOVYKH BIBLIOTEK. Frunze: (Gos. Resp. B-ka Kirg. SSR im. Chernyshevskogo) 1968, 77 pp., 800 copies. [Russ. text; ca.520 Kirgiz, Russ. titles]

Tantasheva, Kh., E. I. Savilova; I. S. Sergievskaia. KNIGA SOVETSKOI KIRGIZII. 1939-1949. SVODNAIA BIBLIOGRAFIIA. Frunze: (Kirgiz. Gos. Knizhnaia Palata), 1962, 158 pp., 700 copies. [Kirgiz, Russ. text; 2,010 Kirgiz, Russ. titles, pub.: 1939-1949]

*_____; I. S. Sergievskaia; A. A. Andasheva. comp. KNIGA SOVETSKOI KIRGIZII. SVODNAIA BIBLIOGRAFIIA. 1950-1954. Frunze: (Gosudarstvennyi Komitet Soveta Ministrov Kirgizskoi SSR po Pechati. Kirgizskaia Gosudarstvennaia Knizhnaia Palata), 1964, 184 pp., 550 copies. [Kirgiz, Russ. texts; 1193 + 568 Kirgiz, Russ. titles, pub.: 1950-1954]

Toktobaeva, R. BIBLIOGRAFICHESKIE IZDANIIA GOSUDARSTVENNOI RESPUBLIKANSKOI BIBLIOTEKI KIRGIZSKOI SSR IM. N. G. CHERNYSHEVSKOGO (1951-1957 GG.) Frunze, 1958. [Kirgiz text; 47 Kirgiz titles, pub.: 1951-1957]

ANTHROPOLOGY, ETHNOGRAPHY

Divaev, A. A. "UKAZATEL' ETNOGRAFICHESKOGO MATERIALA NA KIRGIZSKOM IAZYKE," NAUKA I PROSV. No. 2. Tashkent, 1922. [Kirgiz text and titles, pp. 45-46]

Kirgiz: Anthropology, Ethnography

*Mambetalieva, K. BYT I KUL'TURA SHAKHTEROV-KIRGIZOV KAMENNOUGOL'NOI PROMYSHLENNOSTI KIRGIZII. Frunze: Izdatel'stvo Akademii Nauk Kirgizskoi SSR, 1963, 123 pp., 500 copies. [Russ. text; ca.120 Russ. titles, pp. 118-122]

*Sher, Ia. A. "PAMIATNIKI ALTAISKO-ORKHONSKIKH TIUROK NA TIAN' SHANE," SOV. ARKHEOLOGIIA. No. 4. 1963, 165 pp. [Russ. text; 46 Russ. titles, per.: Antiquity, pp. 165-166]

ARCHITECTURE, ART, MUSIC

Amanbaev, A.; N. Davlesov. ABDYLAS MALDYBAEV. Frunze: (Akad. Nauk Kirgiz SSR. Soiuz Sovetskikh Kompozitorov Kirgizii), 1957, 32 pp. [Russ. text; 14 Russ. titles, pub.: 1940's - 1950's]

Amitin-Shapiro, Z. L. "BIBLIOGRAFICHESKII UKAZATEL' SOVETSKOI LITERATURY PO ARKHEOLOGII KIRGIZII (1918-1956)" TRUDY IN-TA ISTORII (AKAD. NAUK KIRGIZ. SSR) No. 2. 1956. [Russ. text; ca.500 Russ. titles, pub.: 1918-1956, pp. 109-152]

Bernshtam, A. N. ARKHITEKTURNYE PAMIATNIKI KIRGIZII. Moscow-Leningrad: (In-t Istorii. Material. Kul'tury Akad. Nauk SSR) 1950. [Russ. text; 44 Russ., foreign titles, pp. 142-144]

_____. "KIRGIZSKII NARODNYI POVESTVOVATEL'NYI UZOR," Ryndin, M. V. KIRGIZSKII NATSIONAL'NYI UZOR. Leningrad-Frunze: (Kirgiz. Filial Akad. Nauk SSSR Gos. Ermitazh), 1948, 3-27 pp. [Russ. text; 71 Russ. foreign titles, pub.: 1902-1943, pp. 23-27]

Diadiuchenko, E. N. comp. SEMEN AFANAS'EVICH CHUIKOV. BIOBIBLIOGR. (ANNOT.) UKAZATEL'. Frunze: (Gos. Resp. B-ka im. Chernyshevskogo), 1965, 34 pp., 600 copies. [Russ. text; 214 Russ., foreign titles, pub.: 1927-1964]

Kirgiz: Architecture, Music, Art

Iankovskii, V. V. MALDYBAEV, ABDRAEV, TULEEV. (KOMPOZITORY KIRGIZII.) Frunze: "Kyrgyzstan," 1967, 26 pp., 5000 copies. [Russ. text; titles at end of chapters]

Imankulov, Dzh. MURATBEK RYSKULOV, NARODNYI ARTIST SSSR. Frunze: "Kyrgyzstan," 1968, 107 pp., 2000 copies. [Russ. text; titles pp. 104-106]

Norkallaev, I. S.; S. D. Mushaeva; Kh. Isamutdinova; R. Kh. Rakhmatullaeva. comps. KALENDAR' ZNAMENATEL'NYKH I PAMIATNYKH DAT TADZHIKSKOI SSR. ...NA 1968G., Dushanbe: "Ifron," 1968, 80 pp., 1000 copies. [Russ. text; Tajik titles at end of chapters]

Novichenko, E. I.; O. I. Sal'nikova. ISKUSSTVO KIRGIZSKOI SSR. ANNOTIROVANNYI UKAZATEL' LITERATURY. Frunze: (Gos. Resp. B-ka Kirgiz. SSR im. N. G. Chernyshevskogo), 1958, 143 pp., 1,100 copies. [Russ. text; 717 Russ. titles, pub.: 1939 - May 1958]

_____. comp. VTORAIA DEKADA KIRGIZSKOGO ISKUSSTVA I LITERATURY V MOSKVE. (14 - 23 OKT. 1958 G.) BIBLIOGR. UKAZATEL'. Frunze: (Gos. Resp. B-ka Kirgiz SSR im. Chernyshevskogo), 1959, 116 pp., 1000 copies. [Russ. text; 732 Russ., other titles, per.: 1958]

Popova, A. E. comp. MUZYKA-DUSHA NARODA. (OBZOR LITERATURY). Frunze: (M-vo Kul'tury Kirg. SSR), 1966, 9 pp., 300 copies. [Russ. text]

Shamaniev, R. comp. SEMEN AFANAS'EVICH CHUIKOV. (BIOBIBLIOGR. UKAZATEL'). Frunze: (Gos. Resp. B-ka Kirg. SSR im. Chernyshevskogo), 1965, 22 pp., 600 copies. [Kirgiz text; 101 Kirgiz titles, pub.: 1936-1964]

*"SPISOK RABOT V. S. VINOGRADOV," ALAGUSHEV, B. DRUG KIRG. MUZYKI. [Frunze] "Kyrgyzstan," 1969, 128 pp., 1500 copies. [Kirgiz text; 112 Russ. titles, pub.: 1938-1969, pp. 117-127]

Tynalieva, M. ISKUSSTVO KIRGIZSTANA. (REK. UKAZATEL' LIT.). Frunze: (Gos. Resp. B-ka Kirgiz. SSR im. Chernyshevskogo), 1958, 126 pp., 1000 copies. [Kirgiz text; 542 titles, pub.: 1939-1958]

_____. comp. VTORAIA DEKADA KIRGIZSKOGO ISKUSSTVA I LITERATURY V MOSKVE. (14 - 23 OKT. 1958 G.) BIBLIOGR. UKAZATEL'. Frunze: (Gos. Resp. B-ka Kirgiz. SSR. im. Chernyshevskogo), 1960, 130 pp., 800 copies. [Kirgiz text; 713 Kirgiz titles, per.: 1958]

ECONOMICS

Abubakirova, S. comp. ENERGETICHESKIE GIGANTY KIRGIZII (UCH-KURGANSKAIA I TOKTOGUL'SKAIA GES) KRATKII REKOMEND. UKAZATEL' LIT. Frunze, 1963. [Kirgiz text; 46 Kirgiz titles, pub.: 1960-1962]

Alyshbaev, D. A.; I. M. Naidich. O PRESPEKTIVAKH RAZVITIIA TIAZHELOI PROMYSHLENNOSTI KIRGIZSKOI SSR NA BAZE OSVOENIIA ENERGETICHESKIKH RESURSOV BASSEINA REKI NARYNA I MESTNOGO MINERAL'NOGO SYR'IA. (PROBLEMA BOL'SHOGO NARYNA). Frunze: (O-vo Rasprostraneniiu Polit. i Nauch. Znanii Kirgiz SSR), 1959. [Russ. text; 64 Russ. titles pub.: 1931-1959, pp. 46-48]

*Amitin-Shapiro, Z. L. "KIRGIZIIA NA STRANITSAKH ZHURNALA 'SEMIRECH'E'" IZV. KIRG. GEOGR. O-VA. No. 8. Frunze: "Ilim," 1970, 72-76 pp., 500 copies. [Russ. text; 49 Russ. titles, pub.: 1915-1917, pp. 72-76]

Arabaev, E. I., A. U. Oruzbaev. SOVKHOZY I IKH ROL' V RAZVITII SEL'SKOGO KHOZIAISTVA KIRGIZII. Frunze: (Akad. Nauk Kirgiz. SSR. In-t Ekonomiki), 1960. [Russ. text; 50 Russ. titles, pub.: 1915-1960, pp. 69-70]

Artamonov, K. F. REGULIROVOCHNYE SOORUZHENIIA I RABOTY NA REKAKH V PREDOGORNYKH RAIONAKH. Frunze: (Akad. Nauk Kirgiz. SSR), 1957. [Russ. text; 61 Russ. titles, pub.: 1922-1956, pp. 169-170]

Bekturganova, K. VOZNIKNOVENIE I RAZVITIE KOLKHOZNO-KOOPERATIVNOI SOBSTVENNOSTI V KIRGIZII. (1917-1932 GG.) Frunze, 1964. [Russ. text; ca.170 Russ. titles, per.: 1917-1932, pub.: 1916-1962, pp. 156-162]

BIBLIOGRAFIIA KIRGIZII. V 4-KH T. Vol. 3. 1946-1955. No. 5. M. I. Kuznetsova. SEL'SKOE KHOZIAISTVO UKAZATEL' LIT. Frunze: "Kyrgyzstan," 1969, 528 pp., 1000 copies. [Russ. text; 9119 Russ. titles, pub. 1946-1955, pp. 1-528]

Kirgiz: Economics

BIBLIOGRAFIIA KIRGIZII. V 4-KH T. Vol. 3. (1946-1955) No. 5. S. Sh. Abubakirva. SEL. KHOZ-VO. UKAZATEL' LIT. Frunze: "Kyrgyzstan," 1969, 563 pp., 800 copies. [Kirgiz text; 5653 Kirgiz titles, pub.: 1946-1955]

Bol'shakov, M. N.; V. G. Shpak. VODOENERGETICHESKIE RESURSY KIRGIZSKOI SSR. Frunze, 1960. [Russ. text; 35 Russ. titles, pub.: 1931-1959, pp. 143-144]

*Bushman, V. V. SPETSIALIZATSIIA KOLKHOZOV I SOVKHOZOV. Frunze: Izdatel'stvo "Kyrgyzstan," 1967, 145 pp., 1500 copies. [Russ. text and titles, pp. 143-144]

*Duishemaliev, T. OCHERK ISTORII KOLLEKTIVIZATSII SEL'SKOGO KHOZIAISTVA KIRGIZII. Frunze: Izdatel'stvo "Ilim," 1965, 205 pp., 500 copies. [Russ. text; ca.260 Russ. titles (incl. archives), pub.: 1929-1963, pp. 192-203]

*Dzhamankaraev, A. B. RAZVITIE TORGOVLI V KIRGIZII V KONTSE XIX--NACHALE XX VV. Frunze: Izdatel'stvo "Ilim," 1965, 132 pp., 500 copies. [Russ. text; ca.170 Russ. titles (incl. archives), per.: 19th - 20th cc., pub.: 1871-1963, pp. 125-131]

Dzhangaziev, I. EKONOMIKA I NOVYI BYT NA SELE (PO MATERIALAM KIRGSSR). Frunze, 1969. [Russ. text; 79 titles, pp. 114-117]

*Dzhunushev, K. RAZVITIE TOVARNO-DENEZHNYKH OTNOSHENII V DOREVOLIUTSIONNOI KIRGIZII. Frunze, Izdatel'stvo "Ilim," 1965, 143 pp., 500 copies. [Russ. text; ca.140 Russ. titles (incl. archives), per.: pre -1917, pp. 136-141]

Efimenko, G. I. comp. SETEVYE METODY PLANIROVANIIA I UPRAVLENIIA STROITEL'STVOM. UKAZATEL' OTECHESTV. LITERATURY ZA 1963-1966 GG. Frunze: (Kirg. Resp. In-t Nauch.-Tekhn. Informatsii i Propagandy pri Gosplane Kirg. SSR), 1966, 24 pp., 500 copies. [Russ. text; per.: 1963-1966]

*EKONOMIKA SEL'SKOGO KHOZIAISTVA KIRGIZII. BIBLIOGR. UKAZATEL'. 1956-1964 GG. Frunze: (Akad. Nauk. Kirgiz. SSR. In-t Ekonomiki.Tsentr. Nauch. B-ka), 1956, 286 pp., 500 copies. [Russ. text; 1811 Kirgiz, Russ. titles, pub.: 1956-1964, p. 237]

Kirgiz: Economics

*Erman, L. M.; E. G. Abail'dinova; M. M. Bazhenova; M. M. Normantovich. comp. EKONOMIKA SEL'SKOGO KHOZIAISTVA KIRGIZII. BIBLIOGRAFICHESKII UKAZATEL'. (1956-1964). Frunze: Izdatel'stvo "Ilim," 1968, 276 pp., 500 copies. [Russ. text; 1811 Kirgiz, Russ. titles, per.: 1956-1964]

Garkavi, L. M.; N. M. Karataev; T. G. Maziukevich; V. V. Uspenskii; N. I. Shafranovskii; N. N. Ianzhul. "SPISOK OSNOVNOI LITERATURY PO IZUCHENIIU PROIZVODITEL'NYKH SIL KIRGIZSKOI ASSR," KIRGIZIIA. TRUDY PERVOI KONFERENTSII PO IZUCHENIIU PROIZVODITEL'NYKH SIL KIRGIZSKOI ASSR. Leningrad: (AN SSSR Sovet po Izucheniiu Proizvoditel'nykh Sil. Sovet Narodnykh Komissarov Kirgizskoi ASSR), 1934. 522 pp. [Russ. text; 392 titles, pp. 495-522]

Grechko, V. V. SEL'SKOE KHOZIAISTVO OSHSKOI OBLASTI. Frunze, 1962. [Russ. text; 48 Russ. titles, pub.: 1882-1962, pp. 72-74]

Guzhin, G. S. "K ISTORII RAZVITIIA TRANSPORTA KIRGIZSKOI SSR," UCHEN. ZAPISKI GEOGR. FAK. (KIRGIZ. GOS. UN-T). No. 2. 1956, 25-36 pp. [Russ. text; 32 Russ. titles, pub.: 1868-1956, p. 37]

Iakovkin, I. I. "BIBLIOGRAFICHESKIE RABOTY PO PROIZVEDITEL'NYM SILAM KIRGIZII," KIRGIZIIA. TRUDY I KONFERENTSII PO IZUCH. PROIZVODITEL'NYKH SIL KIRGIZ.ASSR. Leningrad, 1934. [Russ. text; titles pp. 440-447, 486-487]

*Ianitskii, N. "CHUISKII KAMBINAT," BOL'SHAIA SOVETSKAIA ENTSIKLOPEDIIA. Vol. 61. Moscow: Gosudarstvennoe Slovarno - Entsiklopedicheskoe Izdatel'stvo "Sovetskaia Entsiklopediia," (Ogiz RSFSR), 1934, 1st ed., 745-746. [Russ. text and titles, p. 746]

Il'iasov, S. I. ZEMEL'NYE OTNOSHENIIA V KIRGIZII V KONTSE XIX - NACHALE XX VV. Frunze, 1963. [Russ. text; ca.360 Russ. titles, pub.: 1867-1962, per.: late 19th - early 20th c., pp. 430-444]

Karatov, M. K. Otorbaev. "OB EKONOMIKO-GEOGRAFICHESKIKH ISSLEDOVANIIAKH V KIRGIZSKOI SSR," IZVESTIIA AKAD. NAUK KIRGIZ. SSR. SERIIA ESTESTV. I TEKHN. NAUK. Vol. 4, No. 4. 1962, 40-42 pp. [Russ. text; 51 Russ. titles, pub.: 1913-1960, pp. 40-42]

Kirgiz: Economics

Kartavov, M. M. "OB EKONOMIKO GEOGRAFICHESKOM
RAIONIROVANII KIRGIZSKOI SSR," TRUDY (TASHK. GOS.
UN-T) No. 186, Book 22. 1961, 207-218 pp. [Russ.
text; 31 Russ. titles, pub.: 1954-1959, p. 218]

KIRGIZIIA - V EDINOI BRATSKOI SEM'E NARODOV SSSR.
Frunze: (Resp. B-ka Kirgiz. SSR im. Chernyshevskogo),
1963, 19 pp., 600 copies. [Kirgiz text; 61 titles]

*"KIRGIZSKAIA SOVETSKAIA SOTSIALISTICHESKAIA RESPUBLIKA,"
BOL'SHAIA SOVETSKAIA ENTSIKLOPEDIIA. Vol. 32, 1936,
1st ed., 362-382 pp. [Russ. text and titles, p. 374]

*"KIRGIZSKAIA SOVETSKAIA SOTSIALISTICHESKAIA RESPUBLIKA
(KIRGIZIIA)," BOL'SHAIA SOVETSKAIA ENTSIKLOPEDIIA.
Vol. 21, 1953, 2nd ed., 70-101 pp. [Russ. text and
titles, pp. 75, 83, 91, 96]

Kuznetsova, M. I. comp. NOVAIA SISTEMA OROSHENIIA--
ZALOG DAL'NEISHEGO POD"EMA SOTSIALISTICHESKOGO
ZEMLEDELIIA (KRATKII OBZOR LITERATURY). Frunze:
(Gos. Publ. B-ka Kirgizskoi SSR im. N. G.
Chernyshevskogo. Spravochno-Bibliograficheskii Otdel),
1953, 18 pp., 1075 copies. [Russ. text]

_____. OBZOR LITERATURY PO KHLOPKOVODSTVU.
Frunze: (Gos. Publ. B-ka Kirgizskoi SSR im.
Chernyshevskogo. Spravochno-Bibliogr. Otdel), 1953,
16 pp., 1000 copies. [Russ. text]

"LITERATURA PO VOPROSAM PROIZVODITEL'NOSTI TRUDA,
OPUBLIKOVANNAIA V 1963-1964 GODAKH," PERVAIA
MEZHVUZOVSKAIA NAUCHNO-TEORETICHESKAIA KONFERENTSIIA
KIRGIZ. SSR PO KOMPLEKSNOI PROBLEME "PROIZVODITEL'NOST'
TRUDA V USLOVIIAKH RAZVERNUTOGO STROITEL'STVA
KOMMUNIZMA." Frunze: (M-vo Nar. Obrazovaniia
Kirgiz. SSR), 1964. [Russ. text; 106 Russ. titles,
pub.: 1963-1964, pp. 57-62]

"LITERATURA PO VOPROSAM PROIZVODITEL'NOSTI TRUDA,
OPUBLIKOVANNAIA V 1963-1964 GODAKH," PERVAIA
MEZHVUZOVSKAIA NAUCHNAIA-TEORETICHESKAIA KONFERENTSIIA
KIRGIZSKOI SSR PO KOMPLEKSNOI PROBLEME "PROIZVODITE'NOST'
TRUDA V USLOVIIAKH RAZVERNUTOGO STROITEL'STVA
KOMMUNIZMA." Frunze: (M-vo Narodnogo Obrazovaniia
Kir.SSR), 1964. [Russ. text; 106 titles, pp. 57-62]

*Losev, D. S. BIBLIOGRAFIIA KIRGIZII. V 4-KH T.
Vol. 3, No. 3 [sic] PRIRODNYE USLOVIIA I PRIRODNYE
RESURSY KIRGIZII (1946-1955). Frunze: (Gos. Resp.
B-ka Kirgizskoi SSR im. N. G. Chernyshevskogo), 1963,
275 pp., 1500 copies. [Russ. text; 2142 Kirgiz, Russ.
titles, pub.: 1946-1955]

Kirgiz: Economics

*_____. BIBLIOGRAFIIA KIRGIZII. V 4-KH T. Vol. 3, No. 3, Part 2. PROMYSHLENNOST'. TRANSPORT. SVIAZ'. UKAZATEL' LITERATURY 1946-1955. Frunze: (Gos. Resp. B-ka Kirgizskoi SSR im. Chernyshevskogo), 1965, 242 pp., 1000 copies. [Russ. text; 2349 Russ. titles, pub.: 1946-1955]

_____. CHTO CHITAT' O KIRGIZII. Frunze: (Gos. Publ. B-ka Kirgiz.SSR im. N. G. Chernyshevskogo), 1951, 8 pp., 890 copies. [Kirgiz, Russ. text; 48 Kirgiz, Russ. titles]

_____; O. D. Morozov. GORODA KIRGIZII. KRATKII UKAZATEL' LIT. Frunze: (Gos. Resp. B-ka Kirgiz. SSR im. N. G. Chernyshevskogo. Bibliogr. Otdel), 1958, 135 pp. [Russ. text; 728 Russ. titles, pub.: 1861-1957]

_____. PROMYSHLENNOST' KIRGIZII. ANNOT. UKAZATEL' LIT. Frunze: (Gos. Resp. B-ka Kirgiz. SSR im. N. G. Chernyshevskogo. Bibliogr. Otd.), 1961, 37 pp. [Russ. text; 124 Russ. titles, pub.: 1954-1961]

_____. PROMYSHLENNOST' KIRGIZII. ANNOTIROVANNYI REKOMENDATEL'NYI UKAZATEL' LITERATURY. Frunze: (Gos. Respubl. B-ka Kirgiz. SSR im. Chernyshevskogo. Bibliogr. Otdel), 1961, 38 pp. [Russ. text]

_____. comp. STROIT' BYSTRO, KHOROSHO I DESHEVO. (KRATKII REKOMEND. SPISOK LIT.). Frunze: (M-vo Kul'tury Kirgiz. SSR. Gos. Resp. B-ka im. N. G. Chernyshevskogo. Otd. Nats. Bibliografii), 1964, 14 pp. [Russ. text; 72 Russ. titles, pub.: 1961-1964]

MIKROELEMENTY V ZHIVOTNOVODSTVE I RASTENIEVODSTVE. Frunze: "Ilim," 1966, 158 pp., 500 copies. [Russ. text; titles at end of articles]

Nazarov, M. I. MOSHCHENNYE KANALY. Frunze: (Akad. Nauk Kirgiz. SSR. In-t Energetiki i Vodnogo Khoz-va), 1958. [Russ. text; 31 Russ. titles, pub.: 1929-1956, pp. 104-105]

*Oruzbaev, A.; K. Dzhunushev; S. Mansurkhodzhaev. NARODNOE KHOZIAISTVO KIRGIZII V PERIOD OKTIABR'SKOI REVOLIUTSII, GRAZHDANSKOI VOINY I INOSTRANNOI INTERVENTSII. (1917-1920 GG.). Frunze, 1962, 116 pp. [Russ. text; ca.90 Russ. Kirg. titles, pub.: 1920-1961, per.: 1917-1920, pp. 114-117]

Kirgiz:Economics

Otorbaev, K. DZHALAL-ABADSKAIA OBLAST' KIRGIZSKOI
SSR. (EKON.-GEOGR. KHARAKTERISTIKA). Frunze:
(Akad. Nauk Kirgiz. SSR), 1957. [Russ. text; 139 Russ.
titles, pub.: 1924-1955, pp. 151-156]

Ploskikh, V. M. OCHERKI ZEMEL'NYKH OTNOSHENII V
IUZHNOI KIRGIZII NAKANUNE VKHOZHDENIIA V SOSTAV
ROSSII. Frunze, 1965. [Russ. text; ca.60 titles,
(incl. archives), per.: 19th c., pp. 57-60]

*Riazantsev, S. N.; V. F. Pavlenko. KIRGIZSKAIA SSR.
EKONOMIKO-GEOGRAFICHESKAIA KHARAKTERISTIKA. Moscow:
Gos. Izdat. Geograficheskoi Literatury (Akad. Nauk
SSSR. In-t Geografii), 1960, 485 pp., 6000 copies.
[Russ. text; ca.150 Russ. titles, per.: 1929-1955,
pp. 479-484]

*Sergeev, S. S. RASSHIRENNOE VOSPROIZVODSTVO I NAKOPLENIE
V KOLKHOZAKH CHUISKOI DOLINY. Moscow: Gosizdat
Sel'skokhoziaistvennoi Literatury, 1950, 344 pp.,
5000 copies. [Russ. text; 77 Russ. titles, Sov. per.,
pp. 339-342]

Shamshiev, R. KOMMUNIZMDIN MATERIALDIK-TEKHNIKALIK
BAZASIN TUZOBUZ (SUNUSH KILINGAN ADABIYATTARDIN
ANNOTATSI YALANGAN KISKACHA TIZMESI). Frunze:
(Kirgiz SSRinin N. G. Chernyshevskii Atindagi
Mamlekettik Kitepkanasi. Uluttuk-Bibliografiya
Bolumu), 1963, 18 pp. [Kirgiz text]

_____ ; M. T. Tynalieva. BIBLIOGRAFIIA KIRGIZII.
V 4-KH T. Vol. 3, No. 3. PRIRODNYE USLOVIIA I
PRIRODNYE RESURSY. PROMYSHLENNOST'. ENERGETIKA.
TRANSPORT. SVIAZ' (1946-1955). Frunze: (Gos. Resp.
B-ka Kirgizskoi SSR im. Chernyshevskogo), 1963, 213 pp.,
1000 copies. [Kirgiz text; 1190 titles, pub.: 1946-1955]

*Sherstobitov, V. P. NARODNOE DVIZHENIE ZA OSVOENIE
GOLODNOI STEPI (1939-1941 GG.). Frunze: "Ilim," 1967,
129 pp., 500 copies. [Russ. text and titles, per.:
1939-1941, pp. 117-127]

Shiriiazdanov, Sh. RABOCHII KLASS KIRGIZII V BOR'BE
ZA RAZVITIE PROMYSHLENNOSTI V POSLEVOENNYE GODY (1946-
1953). Frunze, 1962. [Russ. text; ca.160 titles,
per.: 1946-1953, pp. 203-208]

Shopin, A. S. "OSHSKII EKONOMIKO-GEOGRAFICHESKII RAION,"
IZVESTIIA AKAD. NAUK KIRGIZ. SSR. SERIIA ESTESTV. I
TEKHN. NAUK. Vol. 3, No. 5. 1961, 5-30 pp. [Russ.
text; 30 Russ. titles, pub.: 1935-1960, pp. 29-30]

Kirgiz: Economics

"SPISOK OSNOVNOI LITERATURY PO IZUCHENIIU PROIZVODITEL'NYKH SIL KIRGIZSKOI SSR," KIRGIZIIA. TRUDY 1-1 KONFERENTSII PO IZUCHENIIU PROIZVODITEL'NYKH SIL KIRGIZSKOI ASSR. Leningrad, 1934. [Russ. text; 392 Russ. titles, pub.: 1885-1933]

Tokombaev, K. A. "K VOPROSU VYBORA USTANOVLENNYKH MOSHCHOSTEI PROEKTIRUEMYKH ELEKTROSTANTSII S UCHETOM RABOTY IKH V MESTNOI ENERGOSISTEME," IZVESTIIA AKAD. NAUK KIRGIZ. SSR. SERIIA ESTESTV. I TEKHN. NAUK. Vol. 1, No. 4. ENERGETIKA I AVTOMATIKA. 1959, pp. 53-81 [Russ. text; 24 Russ. titles, pub.: 1948-1958, pp. 80-81]

Toktobaeva, R. CHTO CITAT' O PREOBRAZOVANII PRIRODY KIRGIZII. (KRATKII SPISOK LITERATURY). Frunze: (Gos. Publ. B-ka. Kirgiz. SSR im. Chernyshevskogo), 1953, 8 pp., 920 copies. [Kirgiz, Russ. text; 29 Kirgiz, Russ. titles]

Tynalieva, M. PROMYSHLENNOST' KIRGIZII. ANNOT. REK. UKAZATEL' LIT. Frunze, 1961. [Kirgiz text; 98 Kirgiz titles, pub.: 1955-1961]

Zvoleva, V. P. ENERGETICHESKIE GIGANTY KIRGIZII (UCHKURGANSKAIA I TOKTOGUL'SKAIA GES) KRATKII REKOMEND. UKAZATEL' LITERATURY). Frunze: (Gos. Respubl. B-ka Kirgiz. SSR im. N. G. Chernyshevskogo. Otdel Nats. Bibliografii), 1963, 12 pp. [Russ. text]

EDUCATION

*Aitmambetov, D. KUL'TURA KIRGIZSKOGO NARODA VO VTOROI POLOVINE XIX I NACHALE XIX V. Frunze: Izdatel'stvo "Ilim," 1967, 309 pp., 1000 copies. [Russ. text; ca.600 Kirgiz, Russ. titles (incl. archives), per.: late 19th - 20th c., pp. 288-308]

Amitin-Shapiro, Z. L.; A. S. Stakeeva. BIBLIOGRAFIIA IZDANII KIRGIZSKOGO NAUCHNO-ISSLEDOVATEL'SKOGO INSTITUTA PEDAGOGIKI (1952-1958). Frunze: (Kirgiz. Nauch.-Issled. In-t Pedagogiki), 1959, 64 pp., 2000 copies. [Russ. text; 284 Kirgiz titles, pub.: 1952-1958]

Kirgiz: Education

CHTO CHITAT' O NOT. BIBLIOGRAFICHESKII PERECHEN'. Frunze: (Kirgizskii Respublikanskii Institut Nauchno-Tekhnicheskoi Informatsii i Propagandy pri Gosplane Kirgizskoi SSR), 1967, 8 pp., 250 copies. [Russ. text]

*Daniiarov, S. S. KUL'TURNOE STROITEL'STVO V SOVETSKOM KIRGIZISTANE (1918-1930). Frunze: (Akad. Nauk Kirgiz. SSR In-t Istorii), 1963, 181 pp. [Russ. text; ca.300 Kirgiz, Russ. titles, per.: 1918-1930, pp. 170-182]

Evdokimov, M. E. comp. OBZOR IZDANII GRB IM. N. G. CHERNYSHEVSKOGO O PEREDOVOM OPYTE V BIBLIOTECHNOM DELE KIRGIZII ZA 1962-1964 GG. Frunze: (Gos. Resp. B-ka im. Chernyshevskogo. V Pomoshch' Shkolam Peredogo Opyta), 1965, 10 pp., 600 copies. [Russ. text; pub.: 1962-1964]

Iusupov, S. OCHERK ISTORII KUL'TURNO-PROSVETITEL'NOI RABOTY V SOVETSKOM KIRGIZSTANE (1918-1965 GG.) Frunze, 1965. [Russ. text; ca.200 Russ. titles, per.: 1919-1965, pp. 231-239]

Izmailov, A. E. O VYBORE PROFESII. Frunze: Kirgizuchpedgiz, 1960. [Russ. text; ca.340 Kirgiz, Russ. titles, pub.: 1935-1958, pp. 221-236]

Karakeev, K. K. IZ ISTORII KULTURNOGO STROITEL'STVA V KIRGIZSTANE. Frunze: "Kyrgyzstan," 1968, 176 pp., 2000 copies. [Russ. text; titles pp. 171-175]

Koichumanov, D. I. IDEI VOSPITANIIA V TVORCHESTVE TOGOLOKA MOLDO. Frunze, 1964. [Russ. text; ca.190 titles, pp. 178-186]

Musabaev, D. IZUCHENIE SLUZHEBNYKH SLOV [V SHKOLE]. Frunze, 1968. [Kirgiz text; 85 titles, pp. 116-119]

Osmonkulov, A. METODIKA PREPODAVANIIA FONETIKI V SHKOLE. Frunze, 1967. [Russ. text; ca.280 titles, pp. 249-257]

Petrov, V. P.; L. A. Sheiman; N. S. Kucherenko. VOPROSY PREPODAVANIIA RUSSKOGO IAZYKA I LITERATURY V KIRGIZSKOI SHKOLE. (KRATKII ANNOT. SPISOK KNIG I STATEI V POMOSHCH UCHITELIU). Frunze: (Kirgiz. Nauch.-Issled. In-t Pedagogiki), 1959, 147 pp., 1500 copies. [Russ. text; 359 Russ. titles, pub.: 1938-1958]

Kirgiz: Education

PISATELI KIRGIZII--DETIAM. ANNOTIROVANNYI REKOMENDATEL'NYI UKAZATEL' LITERATURY DLIA UCHASHCHIKHSIA 5-8-GO KLASSOV. Frunze: "Kyrgyzstan," 1967, 42 pp., 2000 copies. [Kirgiz text]

Shatmanov, S. NEKOTORYE VOPROSY PREPODAVANIIA IMENI SUSHCHESTVITEL'NOGO. Frunze, 1965. [Kirgiz text; 49 titles, pp. 126-127]

Timina, A. A. comp. PISATELI KIRGIZII--DETIAM. ANNOT. REK. UKAZATEL' LITERATURY DLIA UCHASHCHIKHSIA 5-8-KH KLASSOV. Frunze: "Kyrgyzstan," 1966, 36 pp., 2000 copies. [Russ. text]

Toktosunov, A. TRUDOVOE I POLITEKHNICHESKOE OBUCHENIE V SHKOLAKH KIRGIZII NA NOVOM ETAPE. Frunze, 1964. [Russ. text; ca.140 Kirg., Russ. titles, pub. 1953-1963, pp. 227-234]

*Ulasovets, G. N.; L. I. Smirnov; A. V. Kalachev. BIBLIOGRAFIIA KIRGIZII V 4-KH T. Vol. 3. No. 4. NAUKA, KUL'TURA, PROSVESHCHENIE, PECHAT', BIBLIOTECHNOE DELO, KUL'TPROSVETRABOT, ZDRAVOOKHRANENIE I MEDITSINA KIRGIZII (1946-1955). Frunze: Ukazatel' Literatury (Ministerstvo Kul'tury Kirg. SSR...) 1966, 262 pp., 1000 copies. [Russ. text; 2239 Russ. titles, per.: 1946-1955, pp. 7-238]

Zabirova, R. D.; V. A. Blagoobrazova. BASSEIN REKI NARYN. Frunze: (Akad. Nauk Kirgiz. SSR. Otd. Geografii), 1960. [Russ. text; 155 titles, pp. 223-229]

GEOGRAPHY

Azykova, E. K. "LANDSHAFTY TSENTRAL'NOGO TIAN'-SHANIA NA PRIMERE BASSEINA P. SARY-CHAT," IZVESTIIA AKAD. NAUK KIRGIZ. SSR. SERIIA ESTESTV. I TEKHN. NAUK. Vol. 2, No. 10, 1960, 15-35 pp. [Russ. text; 26 Russ. titles, pub.: 1875-1956, pp. 34-35]

Kirgiz: Geography

Baiguttiev, S. "KRATKII OCHERK ISTORII ISSLEDOVANII VERKHNE-NARYNSKIKH I SARY-CHATSKIKH SYRTOV VNUTRENNEGO TIAN'-SHANIA," IZVESTIIA KIRGIZ. FILIALA GEOGR. O-VA SSSR, No. 1. 1959, pp. 13-27. [Russ. text; 62 Russ. titles, pub.: 1858-1958, pp. 25-27]

Blagoobrazov, V. A. TIAN'-SHAN'SKAIA FIZIKO-GEOGRAFICHESKAIA STANTSIIA. BIBLIOGR. UKAZATEL' LIT. Frunze, 1965, 224 pp. [Russ. text; 426 Russ. titles, pub.: 1947-1964]

*Bol'shakov, M. N. et al (authors); S. U. Umurzakov, comp. PRIRODA KIRGIZII. Frunze: Kirgiz. Gos. Izd-vo, 1962, 299 pp., 1500 copies. [Russ. text; 470 Russ. titles, pub.: 1858-1960, pp. 279-297]

*Chupakhin, V. M. FIZICHESKAIA GEOGRAFIIA TIAN'-SHANIA (PRIRODNO-GEOGR. OSOBENNOSTI OSNOVNYE VOPROSY LANDSHAFTNOGO KARTIROVANIIA I KOMPLEKSNOGO FIZIKOGEOGRAFICHESKOGO RAIONIROVANIIA). Alma Ata: Izd-vo Akad. Nauk Kaz. SSR, 1964, 373 pp., 1300 copies. [Russ. text; ca.270 Russ. titles, pub.: 1950-1960, pp. 361-372]

_____. "FIZIKO-GEOGRAFICHESKOE RAIONIROVANIE IUGO-ZAPADNOI CHASTI VNUTRENNEGO TIAN'-SHANIA," UCHEN. ZAPISKI GEOGR. FAK. (KIRGIZ. GOS. UN-T). No. 2, 1956, 39-45 pp. [Russ. text; 31 Russ. titles, pub.: 1909-1954, p. 45]

_____. VNUTRENNII TIAN'SHAN'. Frunze: (Kirgiz. Gos. Un-t Kafedra Fiz. Geografii), 1959. [Russ. text; 118 Russ. titles, pub.: 1860-1958, pp. 124-128]

FIZICHESKAIA GEOGRAFIIA TIAN'-SHANIA. (AN KIRG. SSR. RABOTY TIAN'-SHAN. FIZ.-GEOGR. STANTSII. No. 12). Frunze: "Ilim," 1966, 116 pp., 500 copies. [Russ. text; titles at end of articles]

Galitskii, V. Ia., S. U. Umurzakov. "NAUCHNO-ISSLEDOVATEL'SKAIA DEIATEL'NOST' A. M. FETISOVA V KIRGIZII," TRUDY GEOGR. FAK. (KIRGIZ. GOS. UN-T). No. 4. 1964, 21-34 pp. [Russ. text; 44 Russ. titles, pp. 33-34]

GEOGRAFICHESKIE ISSLEDOVANNIA VYSOKOGORNYKH VPADIN KIRGIZII V SVIAZI S IKH OSVOENIEM. Frunze: "Ilim," 1965. [Russ. text; 226 Russ. titles, pub.: Sov. per., titles at end of articles]

Kirgiz: Geography

Gerasimov, I. P. "SPISOK PECHATNYKH NAUCHNYKH RABOT, VYPOLNENNYKH NA TIAN'-SHAN'SKOI FIZIKO-GEOGRAFICHESKOI STANTSII," IZVESTIIA KIRGIZ. FILIALA AKAD. NAUK SSSR, No. 3(13), 154. [Russ. text; 40 Russ. titles, pub.: 1946-1953, pp. 131-133]

*"ISSYK-KUL'," BOL'SHAIA SOVETSKAIA ENTSIKLOPEDIIA. Vol. 29. Moscow: Gosudarstvennyi Institut "Sovetskaia Entsiklopediia," (Ogiz RSFSR), 1935, 630-632 pp. [Russ. text and titles, pp. 631-632]

Kartavov, M. M. "PRIRODNYE USLOVIIA FRUNZENSKOI OBLASTI," UCHEN. ZAPISKI GEOGR. FAK. (KIRGIZ. UN-T), No. 1. 1955, 3-38 pp. [Russ. text; 44 Russ. titles, pub.: 1886-1951, pp. 37-38]

Kashkarov, D. N. REZUL'TATY EKSPEDITSII GLAVNOGO SREDNE-AZIATSKOGO MUZEIA V RAION OZERA SARY-CHELEK. Part 1. Tashkent: (Izvestiia Sred.-Az. Kom. po Delam Muzeev i Okhrany Pamiatnikov Stariny, Iskusstva i Prirody. No. 11), 1927. [Russ. text; 59 Russ. titles, p. 126]

*KIRGIZSKOE GEOGRAFICHESKOE OBSHCHESTVO. IZVESTIIA. No. 7. Frunze: "Ilim," 1968, 100 pp., 500 copies. [Russ. text; titles at end of articles]

(Losev, D. S.) ISSLEDOVATELI KIRGIZII. (P. P. SEMENOV-TIAN-SHANSKII, N. A. SEVERTSOV, A. P. FEDOCHENKO, I. V. MUSHKETOV). UKAZATEL' LITERATURY. No. 1. Frunze: (Gos. Publ. B-ka Kirgiz. SSR im. N. G. Chernyshevskogo), 1955, 15 pp. [Russ. text; ca.90 Russ. titles]

Lunin, B. A. "GEOGRAFICHESKIE ISSLEDOVANIIA N. M. PRZHEVAL'SKOGO V TIAN'-SHANE," UCHENYE ZAPISKI (KIRGIZ. ZHENSKII PED. IN-T). No. 1. 1955, 85-92 pp. [Russ. text; 12 Russ. titles, pp. 91-92]

_____. "K STOLETIIU PERVOGO PUTESHESTVIIA P. P. SEMENOVA-TIAN-SHANSKOGO V TIAN'SHAN'," UCHEN. ZAPISKI GEOGR. FAK. (KIRGIZ UN-T). No. 2. 1956. [Russ. text; ca.152 Russ. titles, pub.: 1856-1955, pp. 16-20]

_____. "NEKOTORYE VOPROSY FIZIKO-GEOGRAFICHESKOGO RAIONIROVANIIA KIRGIZII, IZVESTIIA KIRGIZ. FILIALA GEOGR. O-VA SSSR," No. 1. 1959, 55-62 pp. [Russ. text; 47 Russ. titles, pub.: 1906-1957, pp. 61-62]

_____. "OSNOVNYE PUTI ISTORII GEOGRAFICHESKIKH ISSLEDOVANII V KIRGIZII V SOVETSKII PERIOD," TRUDY (KIRGIZ. GOS. PED. IN-T IM. M. V. FRUNZE). Vol. 11, No. 1. 1947, 77-111 pp. [Russ. text; 330 Russ., foreign titles, Sov. per., pp. 95-111]

Kirgiz: Geography

———————. "ROL' L. S. BERGA V IZUCHENII GEOGRAFII KIRGIZII," TRUDY (KIRGIZ. GOS. PED. IN-T IM. M. V. FRUNZE) Vol. 1, No. 1. 1946 (1947), pp. 9-16. [Russ. text; 36 titles, pub.: 1904-1937, pp. 15-16]

———————. "SEVERNAIA TIAN'-SHAN'SKAIA FIZIKO-GEOGRAFICHESKAIA PROVINTSIIA V PREDELAKH KIRGIZII," TRUDY (TASHK. GOS. UN-T) No. 186. GEOGR. NAUKI. Book 22. 1961, 128-142 pp. [Russ. text; 32 Russ. titles, pub.: 1934-1960, p. 142]

Mysovskii, I. "BIBLIOGRAFIIA PO TIAN'SHANIU." TIAN'-SHAN'. PUTEVODITEL'. KAZAKHSTAN. KIRGIZIIA. Moscow-Leningrad, 1931. [Russ. text; 65 Russ. titles, pub.: up to 1930, pp. 140-142]

NA PROSTORAKH RODINY CHUDESNOI. Khark'kov: Izd-vo Khar'k. Un-ta, 1959. [Russ. text; 68 titles, per.: 19th cent., pp. 329-332]

Naudich, I. M.; R. D. Zabirov. "IZUCHENIE TSENTRAL'NOGO TIAN'-SHANIA, OTKRYTIE I POKORENIE PIKA POBEDY," TRUDY OTDELA GEOGRAFII. AKAD. NAUK KIRGIZ. SSR. No. 1. 1958, 5-21 pp. [Russ. text; 21 Russ. titles, pub.: 1887-1957, pp. 20-21]

Orozaliev, S. "IZ ISTORII ISSLEDOVANIIA BASSEINA R. KOKOMERENA," UCHEN. ZAPISKI GEOGR. FAK. (KIRGIZ. UN-T), No. 1. 1955, 39-92 pp. [Russ. text; 77 Russ. titles, pub.: 1885-1951, pp. 90-92]

———————. "PRIRODNYE USLOVIIA BASSEINA REKI KOKOMEREN," UCHENYE ZAPISKI GEOGR. FAK. (KIRGIZ. GOS. UN-T) No. 2. 1956, 47-65 pp. [Russ. text; 29 Russ. titles, pub.: 1909-1955, pp. 64-65]

Orozgozhoev, B. O. PRIRODA VYSOKOGORNYKH PASTBISHCH VNUTRENNEGO TAN'-SHANIA (AK-SAI I ARPA). Frunze, 1968. [Russ. text; ca.180 titles, pp. 139-146]

Otorbaev, E. "ITOGI I ZADACHI GEOGRAFICHESKIKH I POCHVENNYKH ISSLEDOVANII V KIRGIZII," IZVESTIIA KIRGIZ. FILIALA GEOGR. O-VA SSSR," No. 2, 1960, pp. 5-22. [Russ. text; 24 Russ. titles, pub.: 1906-1958, pp. 21-22]

Otorbaev, K. O. "GEOGRAFICHESKIE ISSLEDOVANIIA V KIRGIZII," PERVAIA NAUCHNAIA SESSIIA AKADEMII NAUK KIRGIZSKOI SSR. Frunze, 1955, pp. 171-179. [Russ. text; 26 Russ. titles, pub.: 1945-1954, pp. 178-179]

Kirgiz: Geography

Otorbaev, K. O. "OSOBENNOSTI GEOGRAFII NASELENIIA DZHALAL-ABADSKOI OBLASTI KIRGISKOI SSR," IZVESTIIA AKAD. NAUK KIRGIZSKOI SSR. No. 2. 1956. [Russ. text; 34 titles, p. 72]

_____. "PETR PETROVICH SEMENOV-TIAN-SHANSKII," IZVESTIIA KIRGIZ. FILIALA O-VA SSSR," No. 1. 1959, pp. 3-27. [Russ. text; 62 Russ. titles, pub.: 1868-1957]

[Postinikova, M. M. comp.] PETR PETROVICH SEMENOV-TIAN-SHANSKII. (1827-1914) BIBLIOGR. PAMIATKA. Frunze: "Kyrgyzstan," 1968, 8 pp., 800 copies. [Kirgiz, Russ. text; titles per.: 1827-1914]

*Rakitnikov, A.; V. Belousov. "KIRGIZSKAIA SOVETSKAIA SOTSIALISTICHESKAIA RESPUBLIKA," (KIRGIZSTAN), BOL'SHAIA SOVETSKAIA ENTSIKLOPEDIIA. Vol. 32. Moscow: Gosudarstvennyi Institut "Sovetskaia Entsiklopediia," (Ogiz RSFSR), 1936, 1st ed., 362-374 pp. [Russ. text; Kirgiz, Russ., titles, p. 374]

REL'EF KIRGIZII. Frunze, 1964. [Russ. text; ca.100 Russ. titles, pub.: 1929-1960, pp. 140-144]

*Riazantsev, S. N. KIRGIZIIA. Moscow: (Akad. Nauk SSSR. In-t Geografii), 1951 (2nd ed.), 249 pp. [Russ. text; ca.140 Kirgiz, Russ. titles, Sov. per., pp. 245-250]

*"TIAN'-SHAN'" BOL'SHAIA SOVETSKAIA ENTSIKLOPEDIIA. Vol. 55. Moscow: Gosudarstvennyi Nauchnyi Institut "Sovetskaia Entsiklopediia," (Ogiz SSSR), 1947, 475-484 pp. [Russ. text; Russ., Europ. titles, pp. 483-484]

Ulasovets, G., R. Shamshiev. AKADEMIK K. I. SKRIABIN V KIRGIZII. PAMIATKA. Frunze: (Gos. Resp. B-ka Kirgiz. SSR im. N. G. Chernyshevskogo), 1962. [Kirgiz, Russ. text and titles, pub.: 1943-1951]

Umurzakov, S. "IZ ISTORII RUSSKIKH GEOGRAFICHESKIKH I KARTOGRAFICHESKIKH PREDSTAVLENII O PRIRODE KIRGIZII," UCHENYE ZAPISKI (KIRGIZ, ZAOCH. PED. IN-T) No. 3. 1957, 132-152 pp. [Russ. text; titles per.: XVII - first half XIX c.]

_____. "ROL' RUSSKIKH UCHENYKH V GEOGRAFICHESKOM IZUCHENII KIRGIZII," TRUDY GEOGR. FAK. (KIRGIZ. GOS. UN-T) NO. 4. VOPROSY FIZICHESKOI GEOGRAFII TIAN'-SHANIA, 1964, 3-11 pp. [Russ. text; 21 Russ. titles, pub.: 1896-1963, pp. 10-11]

Kirgiz: Geography

VOPROSY FIZICHESKOI GEOGRAFII TIAN'-SHANIA. Frunze: (Trudy Geogr. Fak. (Kirg. Gos. Un-t), No. 4. 1964, 74 pp. [Russ. text; titles at end of articles]

Voznesenskaia, E. A. "UKAZATEL' LITERATURY PO GEOGRAFII, GEOLOGII, I POLEZNYM ISKOPAEMYM SEVERNOI I TSENTRAL'NOI KIRGIZII," MATERIALY PO GEOLOGII I GEOKHIMII TIAN'-SHANIA. Part 2. (ANSSSR. TRUDY SOVETA PO IZUCHENIIU PROIZVODITEL'NYKH SIL. [SERIIA KIRGIZSKAIA]). No. 1. Leningrad, 1931. [Russ. text; 930 Russ. titles, pub.: up to 1930, pp. 111-125]

HISTORY, ARCHAEOLOGY

Abramzon, S. M. OCHERK KUL'TURY KIRGIZSKOGO NARODA. Frunze: (Kirgiz. Filial Akad. Nauk SSR. Int. Iaz. Lit. i Ist.), 1946. [Russ. text; 137 Russ. titles, pub.: 1856-1946, pp. 116- 122]

Aitbaev, M. T. ISTORIKO-KUL'TURNYE SVIAZI KIRGIZSKOGO I RUSSKOGO NARODOV. Frunze: Izdatel'stvo Akad. Nauk Kirgiz. SSR (Akad. Nauk Kirgiz. SSR. In-t Istorii), 1957. [Russ. text; 276 Kirgiz, Russ. titles, pub.: 1829-1955, pp. 162-170]

Aitmambetov, D. DOREVOLIUTSIONNYE SHKOLY V KIRGIZII. Frunze: (Akademiia Nauk Kirgizskoi SSR. Institut Istorii), 1961. [Russ. text; ca.160 Russ. titles, pub.: 1874-1958, per.: pre-1917, pp. 123-128]

_____. KUL'TURA KIRGIZSKOGO NARODA VO VTOROI POLOVINE XIX I NACHALE XX V. Frunze: "Ilim," 1967, 309 pp., 1000 copies. [Russ. text; Kirgiz, Russ. titles, per.: 1850-1900, pp. 288-308]

Kirgiz: History, Archaeology

Akaibaeva, G. comp. VLADIMIR IL'ICH LENIN. BIBLIOGR. 1924-1968. Frunze: "Kyrgyzstan," 1970, 97 pp., 1500 copies. [Kirgiz text; 1593 Kirgiz titles, pub.: 1924-1968]

*Amitin-Shapiro, Z. L. ANNOTIROVANNYI UKAZATEL' LITERATURY PO ISTORII, ARKHEOLOGII I ETNOGRAFII KIRGIZII (1750-1917). Frunze: (Akad. Nauk Kirgiz. SSR. In-t Istorii) Izdatel'stvo Akademii Nauk Kirgizskoi SSR, 1958, 349 pp., 500 copies. [Russ. text; 2,002 Russ. titles, pub.: 1750-1917]

_____. "BIBLIOGRAFICHESKII UKAZATEL' SOVETSKOI LITERATURY PO ARKHEOLOGII KIRGIZII (1918-1954 GG.)," TRUDY IN-TA ISTORII (AKAD. NAUK KIRGIZ. SSR), No. 2. Frunze, 1956. [Russ. text; 427 titles, pub.: 1918-1954, pp. 109-152]

_____. "BIBLIOGRAFIIA DOREVOLIUTSIONNOI RUSSKOI LITERATURY PO ISTORII I EKONOMIKE ISSYK'KUL'SKOI OBLASTI. (1768-1917 GG.)," TRUDY PRZHEVAL'SKOGO UCHITEL'SKOGO IN-TA. No. 2. 1953. [Russ. text; 503 Russ. titles, pub.: 1768-1917, pp. 111-189]

_____. "K ISTORII BIBLIOGRAFICHESKOGO IZUCHENIIA KIRGIZSKOGO NARODA I KIRGIZII," TRUDY PRZHEVAL'SKOGO UCHITEL'SKOGO IN-TA. No. 1. 1952. [Russ. text; pub.: 1891-1952, pp. 57-76]

_____. BIBLIOGRAFIIA DOREVOLIUTSIONNOI RUSSKOI LITERATURY O ENISEISKIKH KIRGIZAKH (1750-1917 GG.) TRUDY INSTITUTA IAZYKA I LITERATURY I INSTITUTA ISTORII AKADEMII NAUK KIRGIZSKOI SSR. No. 5. 1956. [Russ. text; titles, per.: 1750-1917, pp. 133-166]

_____. KRATKII BIBLIOGRAFICHESKII UKAZATEL' [SOVETSKOI LITERATURY] PO ISTORII ARKHEOLOGII I ETNOGRAFII KIRGIZII. TRUDY. KIRGIZSKII GOS. PED. INSTITUT. Vol. 2, No. 2. 1948. [Russ. text; 280 Russ. titles, pub.: 1924-1947, Sov. per.]

Attokurov, S. ISTORIIA INDUSTRIAL'NOGO RAZVITIIA KIRGIZII. (1917-1937 GG.). Frunze, 1965. [Russ. text; 580 titles (incl. archives) per.: 1917-1937, pp. 5-40, 430-461]

Baibulatov, B. BOR'BA PARTORGANIZATSII KIRGIZII ZA PROVEDENIE OSEDANIIA KOCHEVOGO NASELENIIA. Frunze: "Kyrgyzstan," 1965. [Russ. text; ca.170 Russ. titles (Incl. archives), pub.: 1930-1963, pp. 213-222]

Kirgiz: History, Archaeology

Dzhamgerchinov, B. DOBROVOL'NOE VKHOZHDENIE KIRGIZII
 V SOSTAV ROSSII. Frunze, 1963. [Russ. text; ca.220
 Russ. titles, pub.: 1824-1962, pp. 427-435]

* _____. PRISOEDINENIE KIRGIZII K ROSSII.
 Moscow: Sotsekgiz., 1959, 432 pp. [Russ. text;
 ca.220 Kirgiz, Russ. titles, per.: late 19th c.,
 pp. 411-418]

Dzhunushev, K. EKONOMICHESKIE PREDPOSYLKI VOZNIKNOVENIIA
 TOVARNOGO KHOZIAISTVA V DOREVOLIUTSIONNOI KIRGIZII.
 Frunze, 1962, 124-128 pp. [Russ. text; ca.120 titles,
 per.: pre-1917]

GEROI SOVETSKOGO SOIUZA GENERAL-MAIOR IVAN VASIL'EVICH
 PANFILOV. Frunze, 1948. [Russ. text; 25 Russ.
 titles, per.: WW II, pub.: 1941-1946, p. 105]

Il'iasov, S. ISTORIIA, ARKHEOLOGIIA I ETNOGRAFIIA
 KIRGIZII V TRUDAKH RUSSKIKH UCHENYKH. IZVESTIIA
 KIRGIZSKOGO FILIALA AKADEMII NAUK SSSR. No. 2/3.
 1945. [Russ. text and titles, pp. 89-93]

*Kadyrov, Sh. ZAPISKI I OTCHETY RUSSKIKH PUTESHESTVENNIKOV
 KAK ISTOCHNIK PO ISTORII KIRGIZII VTOROI POLOVINY XIX
 VEKA. Frunze: Kirgizgosizdat, 1961, 3000 copies,
 107 pp. [Russ. text; 46 Russ. titles, per.: 1850-1900,
 pub.: 1856-1946, pp. 103-105]

* _____. ZAPISKI I OTCHETY RUSSKIKH PUTESHESTVENNIKOV
 KAK ISTOCHNIK PO ISTORII KIRGIZII VTOROI POLOVINY XIX
 VEKA. Frunze: Kirgizgosizdat, 1961, 104 pp. [Russ.
 text; 47 Russ. titles, per.: 19th c., pp. 103-105]

*Khasanov, A. EKONOMICHESKIE I POLITICHESKIE SVIAZI
 KIRGIZII S ROSSIEI. Frunze: Kirgizgosizdat, 1960,
 92 pp., 3500 copies. [Russ. text; 64 Russ. titles,
 pub.: 1851-1957, pp. 90-92]

* _____. EKONOMICHESKIE I POLITICHESKIE SVIAZI
 KIRGIZII S ROSSIEI. Frunze: Kirgizgosizdat, 1960,
 91 pp. [Russ. text; ca.80 Russ., Kirgiz titles,
 pub.: 1851-1957, pp. 89-92]

*Kozhemiako, P. N. RANNESREDNEVEKOVYE GORODA I
 POSELENIIA CHUISKOI DOLINY. Frunze: (Akad. Nauk
 Kirgiz. SSR), 1959, 183 pp. [Russ. text; Kirgiz, Russ.
 titles, per.: early medieval, pp. 6-19]

Lachko, A. F. "KNIGI, IZDANNYE V KIRGIZII V 1956-1957 GG.
 PO ISTORII I OBSHCHESTVENNO-POLITICHESKIM NAUKAM,"
 UCHEN. ZAPISKI IST. FAK. (KIRGIZ. UN-T) No. 6. 1958.
 [Russ. text; 38 Russ. titles, pub.: 1956-1957, pp. 336-339]

Kirgiz: History, Archaeology

[Losev, D. S.] TRIDTSAT' LET KIRGIZSKOI SSR. (1926-1956)
UKAZATEL' LIT. Frunze: (Gos. Resp. B-ka Kirgiz SSR im.
Chernyshevskogo), 1956, 27 pp., 1500 copies. [Kirgiz,
Russ. text; 198 Kirgiz, Russ. titles, per.: 1926-1956]

MATERIALY K BIBLIOGRAFII RUSSKOI LITERATURY PO
ARKHEOLOGII ISSYK-KUL'SKOI KOTLOVINY," TRUDY IN-TA
ISTORII (AKAD. NAUK KIRGIZ. SSR). No. 3. n. p.
(Akad. Nauk Kirgiz SSR), 1957. [Russ. text; 103
Russ. titles, pub.: 1851-1955, pp. 117-125]

Morozov, O. D. MIKHAIL VASIL'EVICH FRUNZE (1885-1925 GG.)
UKAZATEL' LIT. Frunze: (Gos. Resp. B-ka Kirgiz.
SSR im. Chernyshevskogo. Bibliogr. Otdel), 1961, 188 pp.
[Russ. text; 1265 Russ. titles, per.: 1885-1925, pub.:
1936-1960]

ONI BOROLIS' ZA SOVETSKUIU VLAST' V KIRGIZII
ANNOTIROVANNYI UKAZATEL' KNIG I STATEI NA RUSSKOM
IAZYKE ZA 40-60-E GODY. Frunze, 1966. [Kirgiz text;
per.: Sov., pub.: 1940's - 1960's]

ONI BOROLIS' ZA SOVETSKUIU VLAST' V KIRGIZII. REKOMEND.
UKAZATEL' LIT. Frunze: (Gos. Resp. B-ka Kirgiz SSR
im. N. G. Chernyshevskogo. Otd. Nats. Bibliografii),
1966, 21 pp. [Russ. text and titles, per.: Sov.,
pub.: 1940's - 1960's]

*Ploskikh, V. M. OCHERKI PATRIARKHAL'NO-FEODAL'NYKH
OTNOSHENII V IUZHNOI KIRGIZII (50-70-E GODY XIX V.)
Frunze: Izdatel'stvo "Ilim," 1968, 150 pp., 500
copies. [Russ. text and titles, per.: 1950-1970 gg.,
pp. 146-149]

* _____ . PERVYE KIRGIZSKO-RUSSKIE POSOL'SKIE
SVIAZI. (1784-1827 GG.) Frunze: "Ilim," 1970, 132 pp.,
500 copies. [Russ. text; 71 Russ. titles, per.: 1784-
1827, pub.: 1762-1968, pp. 88-92]

*Ryskulov, T. R. KIRGIZSTAN. Moscow-Leningrad:
Gosudarstvennoe Izdatel'stvo, 1929, 116 pp., 3000
copies. [Russ. text; 11 Russ. titles (incl. archives),
p. 114]

Sadykova, Sh. MIKHAIL VASIL'EVICH FRUNZE (1885-1925 GODY).
BIBLIOGR. UKAZATEL'. Frunze, 1960. [Kirgiz text; 230
Kirgiz titles, per.: 1885-1925; pub.: 1935-1960]

*Sannikov, T. V.; V. N. Semenkov. GEROI SOVETSKOGO
SOIUZA--KIRGIZSTANTSY. Frunze: Kirgizskoe Gos. Izd-vo,
1963, 234 pp., 4000 copies. [Russ. text; 230 Russ.
titles, per.: WW II, pp. 222-231]

Kirgiz: History, Archaeology

*Sapelkin, A. A. K ISTORII FEODALIZMA V KIRGIZII V KONTSE XIX--NACHALE XX VV. (ADM. USTROISTVO I NALOGOVAIA SISTEMA). Frunze: "Ilim," 1968, 126 pp., 500 copies. [Russ. text and ca.190 Russ. titles, pub.: 1859-1967, per.: end 19th - early 20th c., pp. 114-124]

*Semichaevskii, M. A. "KNIGI O VELIKOM BRATSTVE NARODOV," ISTORIIA SSSR. No. 1. 1964, 207 pp. [Russ. text; titles footnotes pp. 167-169]

Shamshiev, R. comp. KIRGIZSTAN V BRATSKOI SEM'E NARODOV SSSR. Frunze: 1963. [Kirgiz text; ca.40 Kirgiz titles, pub.: 1950's-1960's]

Sherstiuk, I. N. IZUCHENIE ISTORII KIRGIZII V OBSHCHEOBRAZOVATEL'NOI SHKOLE. Frunze, 1964. [Russ. text; 52 Russ. titles, pub.: 1940-1963, pp. 99-101]

Shiriiazdanov, Sh. Kh. RABOCHII KLASS KIRGIZII V BOR'BE ZA RAZVITIE PROMYSHLENNOSTI V POSLEVOENNYE GODY (1946-1953). Frunze, 1962. [Russ. text; 157 Russ. titles, per.: 1946-1953, pub.: 1940's - 1960's, pp. 203-208]

*Shofler, Z. G.; G. P. Li. ISTORIIA KOMMUNISTICHESKOI PARTII KIRGIZII. ANNOT. UKAZATEL' LIT. Part 2. 1946-1967 GG. Frunze: "Kyrgyzstan," 1969, 403 pp., 1500 copies. [Russ. text; 4021 + 24 Russ. titles, pub.: 1946-1967, pp. 1-403]

_____. comp. IULIUS FUCHIK V KIRGIZII. REKOMEND. UKAZATEL'. Frunze: (M-vo Kul'tury Kirgiz. SSR. Gos. Resp. B-ka Kirgiz. SSR im. N. G. Chernyshevskogo), 1963, 31 pp. [Russ. text; 50 Russ. titles, per.: 1921-1941, pub.: 1940's - 1960's]

_____. comp. KIRGIZSTAN V BRATSKOI SEM'E NARODOV SSSR (K 100-LETIIU DOBROVOL'NOGO VKHOZHDENIIA KIRGIZII V SOSTAV ROSII). KRATKII REKOMENDATEL'NYI SPISOK LITERATURY. Frunze: (Gos. Respubl. B-ka Kirgiz. SSR im. N. G. Chernyshevskogo. Otdel Nats. Bibliografii), 1963, 23 pp. [Russ. text; 53 Russ. titles, per.: 1863-1963, pub.: 1950-1960]

*Tatybekova, Zh. S. ISTORIIA KAMENNOUGOL'NOGO RUDNIKA "KY-ZYL-KIIA" (1917-1963 GG.) Frunze: "Ilim," 1964, 143 pp., 500 copies. [Russ. text; ca.100 Russ. titles, per.: 1917-1963, pub.: 1902-1962, pp. 138-142]

Kirgiz: History, Archaeology

*Tatybekova, Zh. S. RASKREPOSHCHENIE ZHENSHCHINY-KIRGIZKI VELIKOI OKTIABR'SKOI SOTSIALISTICHESKOI REVOLIUTSIEI (1917-1936 GG.). Frunze: Izd-vo Akad. Nauk Kirgiz. SSR, 1963, 137 pp., 500 copies. [Russ. text; ca.100 Russ. titles, per.: 1917-1936, pub.: 1874-1962, pp. 132-136]

Umurzakov, S. NEPROTORENNYMI PUTIAMI. IZ ISTORII ISSLEDOVANIIA KIRGIZII. Frunze, 1963. [Kirgiz text; Kirgiz, Russ. titles at end of articles]

*Usenbaev, K. OBSHCHESTVENNO-EKONOMICHESKIE OTNOSHENIIA KIRGIZOV V PERIOD GOSPODSTVA KOKANDSKOGO KHANSTVA. (XIX VEK DO PRISOEDINENIIA KIRGIZII K ROSSII). Frunze: (Akad. Nauk Kirgiz SSR. Institut Istorii), 1961, 164 pp. [Russ. text; ca.260 Kirgiz, Russ. titles, per.: 19th c., pp. 155-164]

*_____. PRISOEDINENIE IUZHNOI KIRGIZII K ROSSII. Frunze: (Akad. Nauk Kirgiz. SSR. In-t Istorii), 1960, 188 pp. [Russ. text; ca.200 Kirg.,Russ. titles, per. 19th c., pp. 177-189]

*_____. REVOLIUTSIONNOE DVIZHENIE V KIRGIZII NAKANUNE OKTIABR'SKOI REVOLIUTSII. Frunze: Izdatel'stvo "Kyrgyzstan," 1965, 75 pp., 1500 copies. [Russ. text; 77 Russ. titles (incl. archives), pp. 71-74]

*_____. VOSSTANIE 1916 GODA V KIRGIZII. Frunze: "Ilim," 1967, 339 pp., 1500 copies. [Russ. text; ca. 360 Kirgiz, Russ. titles; per.: 1916; pp. 308-326]

LANGUAGE, LITERATURE

ABDRASUL TOKTOMUSHEV. PAMIATKA. Frunze: (Gos. Resp. B-ka im. N. G. Chernyshevskogo), 1962. [Kirgiz, Russ. text; 45 Kirgiz, Russ. titles; pub.: 1936-1958]

Abdullaev, E. CHATKAL'SKII GOVOR KIRGIZSKOGO IAZYKA. Frunze, 1956. [Kirgiz text; 116 Kirgiz, Russ. titles; pub.: 1894-1954, pp. 131-133]

Kirgiz: Language, Literature

Abduldaev, E. CHATKAL'SKII GOVOR KIRGIZSKOGO IAZYKA. Frunze: (Akad. Nauk Kirgiz. SSR. In-t Iazyka i Lit.), 1956. [Kirgiz text; 116 Kirgiz Russ. titles, pp. 131-133]

Abubakirova, S; A. I. Koshmanova. comp. OSMONKUL BOLOBALAEV (ESKERTKICH). Frunze: (Kirgiz SSRinin N. G. Chernyshevskii Atindagi Mamlekettik Respublikalik Kitepkanasi Uluttuk-Bibliografiyalik Bolum), 1963, 8 pp. [Kirgiz text and titles]

Akhmatov, T. K. TALASSKII GOVOR KIRGIZSKOGO IAZYKA. Frunze: (Kirgiz Gos. Un-t), 1959. [Kirgiz text; 130 Kirgiz, Russ. titles, pp. 145-148]

Aly Kul Osmonov. BIBLIOGRAFIIA PROIZVEDENII I LITERATURY O NEM. Frunze: "Kyrgyzstan," 1967. [Kirgiz text; ca.400 Kirgiz, Russ. titles, pub.: 1932-1965]

Amitin-Shapiro, Z. L.; O. D. Morozov. "MATERIALY DLIA BIBLIOGRAFII PO KIRGIZSKOMU LITERATUROVEDENIIU," TRUDY PRZHEVAL'SKOGO UCHITEL'SKOGO INSTITUTA. No. 2, 1956. [Russ. text; 302 Russ. titles, pub.: 1934-1952, pp. 115-147]

Askarov, T. ESTETICHESKAIA PRIRODA KHUDOZHESTVENNOI USLOVNOSTI. (V LITERATURE I ISKUSSTVE.) Frunze: "Ilim," 1966, 157 pp., 700 copies. [Russ. text; bib. survey pp. 3-16]

*"BAIALIN, KASYM," LITERATURNAIA ENTSIKLOPEDIIA. Vol. 1. n. p., Izdatel'stvo Kommunisticheskoi Akademii, 1929. [Russ. text; Kirgiz, Russ. titles, pp. 377-378]

Beishekeev, N. ADABIIATTARDYN BIBLIOGRAFIIALYK KORSOTKUCHU 1929-1959 ZHZH. Frunze: Kyrgyz SSR Ilimder Akademiiasy. Til Zhana Adabiiat Institutu., 1961, 152 pp., 500 copies. [Kirgiz text; titles pub.: 1929-1959]

──────────. KIRGIZSKII IAZYK 1929-1959 GG. BIBLIOGR. UKAZATEL' LIT. Frunze, 1961. [Kirgiz text; 900 Kirgiz, Russ. titles, pub.: 1929-1959]

*[Belkova, G. N.] LENIN I TEPER' ZHIVEE VSEKH ZHIVYKH. OBRAZ V. I. LENINA V PROIZVEDENIIAKH KIRG. ISKUSSTVA. (REK. UKAZ. LIT.) Frunze: "Kyrgyzstan," 1970, 36 pp., 1000 copies. [Russ. text; ca.130 Russ. titles, pub.: 1943-1969, pp. 8-9, 12-13, 16-21, 23-24, 27-28]

Kirgiz: Language, Literature

*Berkov, P. N.; E. K. Sagidova. "BIBLIOGRAFICHESKII
UKAZATEL' LITERATURY O 'MANASE'," KIRGIZSKII
GEROICHESKII EPOS MANAS. Moscow: Izdatel'stvo
Akademii Nauk SSSR, 1961. [Russ. text; 695 Kirgiz,
Russ. titles, pub.: 1849-1960, pp. 298-368]

Bogdanova, M. KIRGIZSKAIA LITERATURA. OCHERK.
Moscow, 1947. [Russ. text; ca.350 Russ. titles,
pub.: 1925-1946, pp. 261-288]

Borovkov, A. "O NARODNOSTI KIRGIZSKOGO EPOSA 'MANAS',"
DRUZHBA NARODOV, No. 5, 1952. [Russ. text; ca.50
titles, pp. 243-244]

CHINGIZ AITMATOV. PAMIATKA. Frunze: (Gos. Resp. B-ka
Kirgiz. SSR im. N. G. Chernyshevskogo), 1962.
[Kirgiz, Russ. text; 18 Kirgiz, Russ. titles, pub.:
1956-1962]

*Chonbashev, K. S. O NEKOTORYKH TIPAKH
SLOZHNOPODCHINENNYKH PREDLOZHENII RUSSKOGO IAZYKA I
SOOTVETSVUIUSHCHIKH IM KONSTRUKTSIIAKH V KIRGIZSKOM
IAZYKE. Frunze: Uchebno-Pedagogicheskoe Izdatel'stvo,
1964, 83 pp., 2500 copies. [Russ. text; Kirgiz,
Russ. titles, pp. 80-82]

_____. SLOZHNYE PREDLOZHENIIA V RUSSKOM I
KIRGIZSKOM IAZYKAKH. Frunze: "Mektep," 1968, 215 pp.,
1700 copies. [Russ. text; titles pp. 201-213]

_____. SLOZHNYE PREDLOZHENIIA V RUSSKOM I
KIRGIZSKOM IAZYKAKH (S PRIDATOCHNYMI IZ"IASNITEL'NYMI,
PRICHINY I VREMENI) Part 1. Frunze, 1968. [Russ.
text; ca.280 titles, pp. 201-211]

*Daronian, S. TUGEL'BEI SYDYKBEKOV: KRITIKO-
BIBLIOGRAFICHESKII OCHERK. Moscow: "Sovetskii
Pisatel'," 1966, 143 pp., 4600 copies. [Russ. text;
74 Russ. titles, pub.: 1953-1966, pp. 138-142]

*Dzhaparov, Abdykul. SOVREMENNYI KIRGIZSKII IAZYK.
Part 2. SINTAKSIS PROSTOGO PREDLOZHENIIA. Frunze:
"Mektep," 1966, 344 pp., 1200 copies. [Russ.
text; 205 Kirgiz, Uzbek, Russ. titles, pp. 337-342]

DZHUSUP TYRYSBEKOV. PAMIATKA. Frunze, 1954. [Kirgiz
text; 11 Kirgiz titles, pub.: 1932-1953]

[Isakova, Zh.] AALY TOKOMBAEV. Frunze, 1954. [Russ.
text; 15 Kirgiz titles, pub.: 1941-1952]

Kirgiz: Language, Literature

[Isakova.] AVTORSKIE TABLITSY. Frunze: (Gos. Publ. B-ka Kirgiz.SSR im. Chernyshevskogo), 1952, 34 pp., 1120 copies. [Kirgiz text]

[Isakova, Zh.] DZHOOMART BOKONBAEV. PAMIATKA. Frunze, 1954. [Kirgiz text; 14 Kirgiz titles, pub.: 1942-1950]

[Ishenov, S.; I. P. Smolianskii; A. A. Timina] KIRGIZSKAIA DETSKAIA LITERATURA. (1926-1966 GG.) BIOBIBLIOGR. SPRAVOCHNIK. Frunze: "Mektep," 1969, 484 pp., 4000 copies. [Kirgiz, Russ. text; 711 Kirgiz, Russ. titles, pub.: 1926-1966]

Iunusaliev, B. M. KIRGIZSKAIA LEKSIKOLOGIIA. Part 1. "RAZVITIE KORNEVYKH SLOV." Frunze: (Kirgiz. Gos. Un-t), 1959. [Russ. text; 170 Russ., foreign titles, pp. 241-246]

K. MALIKOV. PAMIATKA. Frunze, 1961. [Kirgiz text; 14 Kirgiz titles, pub.: 1950-1958]

KASYMALY BAIALINOV. PAMIATKA. Frunze: (Gos. Resp. B-ka Kirgiz. SSR im. N. G. Chernyshevskogo), 1962. [Russ. text; 19 Kirgiz, Russ. titles, pub.: 1946-1960]

Khumadylov, S. OTRAZHENIE IDEI DRUZHBY NARODOV V KIRGIZSKOI SOVETSKOI LITERATURE. Frunze, 1967. [Kirgiz text; ca.110 Kirgiz titles, pp. 209-215]

*Klimovich, L. "OB IZUCHENII EPOSA 'MANAS'," DRUZHBA NARODOV. No. 5, 1952. [Russ. text; 80 titles (in notes), pp. 264-266]

*"KNIGI O KIRGIZSKOI LITERATURE, VYSHEDSHIE ZA POSLEDNIE GODY V IZDATEL'STVE AN KIRGIZSKOI SSR," IZVESTIIA AKAD. NAUK KIRGIZ. SSR. SERIIA OBSHCHESTV. NAUK. Vol. 6. LITERATUROVEDENIE. No. 2. 1964. [Russ. text; 21 Kirgiz, Russ. titles, pub.: 1963, p. 90]

Koichumanov, D. I. IDEI VOSPITANIIA V TVORCHESTVE TOGOLOKA MOLDO. Frunze, 1964. [Russ. text; ca.200 Kirgiz, Russ. titles, pub.: 1938-1963, pp. 178-186]

Koshmanova, A. I.; K. Mukanova. comp. RAIKAN SHUKURBEKOV (1913-1962). PAMIATKA. Frunze: (Gos. Resp. B-ka im. N. G. Chernyshevskogo), 1963, 9 pp. [Kirgiz text]

Kirgiz: Language, Literature

Kydyrbaeva, R. Z. LIRIKA ALYKULA OSMONOVA. Frunze: (Akad. Nauk Kirgiz. SSR. In-t Iazyka i Lit.), 1957. [Russ. text; 122 Kirgiz, Russ. titles, pub.: 1870-1957, pp. 109-113]

Losev, D. S.; R. Toktobaeva. KHUDOZHESTVENNAIA LITERATURA V PEREVODE NA KIRGIZSKII IAZYK. BIBLIOGR. UKAZATEL' IZD. Frunze, 1958, 2nd ed. [Kirgiz text; ca.960 Kirgiz titles, pub.: 1934-1957]

* _____.: O. D. Morozov. KIRGIZSKAIA LITERATURA. REKOMENDATEL'NYI UKAZATEL'. Moscow: (Gosudarstvennaia Ordena Lenina Biblioteka SSSR imeni V. I. Lenina), 1958, 78 pp., 3500 copies. [Russ. text and titles, Sov. per.]

_____. LITERATURA KIRGIZII. BIOBIBLIOGRAFICHESKII UKAZATEL'. (K DEKADE KIRGIZ. ISKUSSTVA I LITERATURY V MOSKVE). Frunze: (Gos. Resp. B-ka Kirgiz SSR im. N. G. Chernyshevskogo), 1958, 186 pp., 1100 copies. [Russ. text and titles, pub.: 1904-1957]

_____. PROIZVEDENIIA RUSSKIKH PISATELEI NA KIRGIZSKOM IAZYKE (UKAZATEL' LIT.). Frunze: (Gos. Publ. B-ka Kirgiz. SSR im. Chernyshevskogo), 1953, 17 pp., 920 copies. [Kirgiz text; 161 Kirgiz titles]

Morozov, O. D. CHEKMENOV NIKOLAI SIMONOVICH (BIBLIOGR. PAMIATKA). Frunze: (Gos. Resp. B-ka Kirgiz. SSR im. N. G. Chernyshevskogo. Russkie Pisateli o Kirgizii, No. 5), 1957, 14 pp. [Russ. text; 51 Russ. titles, pub.: 1925-1926]

_____. SYTIN ALEKSANDR PAVLOVICH. BIBLIOGR. PAMIATKA. Frunze: (Gos. Resp. B-ka Kirgiz. SSR im. N. G. Chernyshevskogo. Russkie Pisateli o Kirgizii, No. 3), 1957, 14 pp. [Russ. text; 47 Russ. titles, pub.: 1925-1930]

MUKAI ELEBAEV, PAMIATKA. Frunze: (Gos. Resp. B-ka Kirgiz. SSR im. N. G. Chernyshevskogo), 1965, 8 pp. [Kirgiz, Russ. text; 37 Kirgiz Russ. titles, pub.: 1931-1960]

Murataliev, M. PRIDATOCHNYE PREDLOZHENIIA VREMENI V KIRGIZSKOM IAZYKE. Frunze: Kirgizuchpedgiz, 1956. [Russ. text; 36 Kirgiz, Russ. titles, pp. 54-56]

Kirgiz: Language, Literature

*N. D. "KIRGIZSKII IAZYK," BOL'SHAIA SOVETSKAIA ENTSIKLOPEDIIA. Vol. 32. Moscow: Gosudarstvennyi Institut "Sovetskaia Entsiklopediia," (Ogiz RSFSR), 1936, 386-387 pp. [Russ. text; Kirgiz, Russ., Europ. titles p. 387]

*"NOVYE KNIGI," IZVESTIIA AKAD. NAUK KIRGIZ. SSR. SERIIA OBSHCHESTV. NAUK. Vol. 6, No. 1. 1964. [Russ. text; 10 Kirgiz, Dungan, Russ. titles, pp. 105-106, pub.: 1960-1962]

OCHERK ISTORII KIRGIZSKOI SOVETSKOI LITERATURY. Frunze, 1960. [Kirgiz text; ca.500 Kirgiz, Russ. titles, per.: Sov., pub.: 1925-1960, pp. 495-510]

*(Okenova, K.) PEREVODY PROIZVEDENII UZBEKSKIKH PISATELEI NA KIRGIZSKII IAZYK. SPISOK LIT. Frunze: "Kyrgyzstan," (Resp. B-ka Kirg. SSR im. Chernyshevskogo), 1969, 12 pp., 1500 copies. [Kirgiz text; 83 Kirgiz (Russ. trans. of titles), pp. 4-12]

OSMONKUL BOLEBALAEV. PAMIATKA. Frunze: (Gos. Resp. B-ka Kirgiz. SSR. im. N. G. Chernyshevskogo), 1963. [Kirgiz, Russ. text; 32 Kirgiz, Russ. titles, pub.: 1940's - 1960's]

PISATELI KIRGIZII--DETIAM. ANNOT. REKOMEND. UKAZATEL' LIT. DLIA UCHASHCHIKHSIA 5-8 KLASSOV. Frunze: "Kyrgyzstan," 1966, 31 pp. [Russ. text; 32 Russ. titles, pub.: 1956-1964]

PISATELI KIRGIZII--DETIAM. (ANNOT. UKAZATEL' LIT. DLIA DETEI MLADSHEGO SHKOL'NOGO VOZRASTA). Frunze, 1963. [Kirgiz text; 26 Kirgiz titles, pub.: 1956-1961]

"PROIZVEDENIIA RUSSKIKH PISATELEI, PEREVEDENNYE NA KIRGIZSKII IAZYK," RUSSKIE PROSTORY. Frunze, 1962. [Kirgiz text; ca.360 Kirgiz titles, pub.: 1934-1961, pp. 484-493]

RAIKAN SHUKYRBEKOV. (1913-1962) PAMIATKA. Frunze: (Gos. Resp. B-ka Kirgiz. SSR im. N. G. Chernyshevskogo), 1963, 9 pp. [Kirgiz, Russ. text; 34 Kirgiz, Russ. titles, pub.: 1950-1962]

*Rakhmatullin, K.; O. Dzhakishev. "KIRGIZSKAIA LITERATURA," BOL'SHAIA SOVETSKAIA ENTSIKLOPEDIIA. Vol. 32. Moscow: Gosudarstvennyi Institut "Sovetskaia Entsiklopediia" (Ogiz RSFSR), pp. 382-384. [Russ. text; Kirgiz, Russ. titles, p. 384]

Kirgiz: Language, Literature

RUSSKIE SOVETSKIE PISATELI O KIRGIZII. Frunze: (Gos. Resp. B-ka Kirgiz. SSR im. N. G. Chernyshevskogo), 1963, 83 pp. [Russ. text; 133 Russ. titles]

Sadabaev, Alymbek. RAZVITIE KUL'TURY RECHI (LEKSICHESKAIA RABOTA). Frunze: "Mektep," 1967, 83 pp., 1500 copies. [Russ. text; Kirgiz titles, pp. 80-83]

*Sadykov, A. TRADITSII I NOVATORSTVO V POEZII ALYKULA OSMONOVA. Frunze: Izd-vo Akad. Nauk Kirgiz. SSR, 1962, 131 pp., 500 copies. [Kirgiz text; ca.100 Kirgiz, Russ. titles, pub.: 1954-1959, pp. 126-129]

*_____. TRADITSII I NOVATORSTVO V POEZII ALYKULA OSMONOVA. Frunze: Kirgiz SSR Ilimder Akademiyasinin Basmasi, 1962, 131 pp., 500 copies. [Kirgiz text; ca.100 Kirgiz, Russ. titles, pp. 126-129]

Sadykova, Sh. comp. ALYKUL OSMONOV. BIBLIOGRAFII--
PROIZVEDENIIA ALYKULA OSMONOVA I LITERATURA O NEM NA KIRGIZSKOM I RUSSKOM IAZYKAKH. Frunze: Izdatel'stvo "Kyrgyzstan," 1967, 48 pp., 2000 copies. [Kirgiz, Russ. text; 407 Kirg., Russ. titles, pub.: 1932-1966

Samaganov, D. PISATELI SOVETSKOGO KIRGIZISTANA. (BIOBIBLIO. SPRAVOCHNIK). Frunze: Kirgizgosizdat, 1962, 500 pp., 4000 copies. [Kirgiz text; titles Sov. per.]

*Samaganov, Dzh. PISATELI SOVETSKOGO KIRGIZSTANA (BIOBIBLIOGR. SPRAVOCHNIK). Frunze: "Kyrgyzstan," 1969, 643 pp., 24,000 copies. [Russ. text; Kirgiz, Russ. titles, per.: XX c]

Sartbaev, K. K. SINTAKSIS SLOZHNOGO PREDLOZHENIIA V KIRGIZSKOM IAZYKE. Frunze, 1957. [Kirgiz text; 200 Kirgiz, Russ. titles, pub.: 1771-1951, pp. 170-175]

Shamshiev, R. comp. VELIKII OKTIABR' I GRAZHDANSKAIA VOINA V KIRGIZSKOI KHUDOZHESTVENNOI LITERATURE. REK. UKAZATEL' (LITERATURY). Frunze: "Kyrgyzstan," (Gos. Resp. B-ka Kirg. SSR im. Chernyshevskogo), 1967, 39 pp., 600 copies. [Kirgiz text; ca.50 Kirgiz titles, pub.: 1950-1965]

*Shamshiev, R. S. KIRGIZSKOE LITERATUROVEDENIE I LITERATURNAIA KRITIKA. BIBLIOGRAFIIA. (1927-1966). Frunze: "Kyrgyzstan," 1967, 202 pp., 2000 copies. [Kirgiz text; 3166 Kirgiz titles, pub.: 1927-1966]

Kirgiz: Language, Literature

Shemshiev, R.; A. A. Timina. comps. MUKAI ELEBAEV.
BIBLIOGRAFICHESKAIA PAMIATKA. [Frunze] (Gos. Resp.
B-ka Kirgiz. SSR im. Chernyshevskogo. Nashi Pisateli)
[1965] 8 pp., 600 copies. [Kirgiz, Russ. text]

_____. TOKTOGUL SATYLGANOV. 1864-1933.
BIBLIOGRAFIIA PROIZVEDENII TOKTOGULA I LIT. O NEM
NA KIRGIZ., RUSS. I NA DRUGIKH IAZ. NARODOV SSSR.
Frunze: "Kyrgyzstan," 1964, 169 pp., 2000 copies.
[Kirgiz text; 1329 Kirgiz, Russ. other titles,
per.: 1864-1933]

*Sheiman. L. A. PUSHKIN I KIRGIZY. Frunze: Kirgiz.
Uchebno-Pedagogich. Izd-vo, 1963. [Russ. text;
ca.100 Kirgiz, Russ. titles, pub.: 1820-1963, pp. 120-
142]

*Shofler, Z. G. comp. IULIUS FUCHIK V KIRGIZII.
REKOMENDATEL'NYI UKAZATEL'. Frunze: (Gosudarstvennaia
Respublikanskaia Biblioteka Kirgizskoi SSR im. N. G.
Chernyshevskogo), 1963, 31 pp., 600 copies. [Russ.
text; 36 Uzbek, Kirgiz, Russ. titles]

[Smolianskii, I. P. comp.] PISATELI KIRGIZII--DETIAM.
(ANNOT. REKOMEND. UKAZATEL' KNIG DLIA UCHASHCHIKHSIA
1-4KH KLASSOV), Frunze: (Resp. Det. B-ka Kirgiz. SSR),
1963, 22 pp. [Russ. text; 22 Russ. titles, pub.:
1957-1962]

Suprun, A. E. RUSSKOE IAZYKOZNANIE V KIRGIZII (1946-1958)
UKAZATEL' LIT. Frunze: (Kirgiz. Gos. Un-t. Fundament.
B-ka), 1960, 37 pp. [Russ. text; 214 Kirgiz, Russ.
titles, pub.: 1946-1958]

*Suvanbekov, Zhursun. MALYE EPOSY V KIRGIZSKOI LITERATURY.
Frunze: Kirgizstan Mamlekettik Basmasi, 1963, 204 pp.,
3000 copies. [Kirgiz text; Kirgiz, Sov. Asian, Russ.
titles, pp. 199-203]

Sydykbekov, T. ed. OCHERK ISTORII KIRGIZSKOI SOVETSKOI
LITERATURY. Frunze: (Akad. Nauk Kirgiz. SSR. In-t
Iazyka i Lit.), 1960. [Kirgiz text; ca.500 Kirgiz,
Russ. titles, Sov. per., pp. 495-510]

_____. ed. OCHERK ISTORII KIRGIZSKOI
SOVETSKOI LITERATURY. Frunze: (Akad. Nauk Kirgiz. SSR.
In-t Iazyka i Lit.), 1961. [Russ. text; ca.210 Russ.
titles, Sov. per., pub.: 1925-1958, pp. 508-519]

Kirgiz: Language, Literature

*Toichinov, I. "KIRGIZSKAIA LITERATURA," LITERATURNAIA ENTSIKLOPEDIIA. Vol. 5. n.p. Izdatel'stvo Kommunisticheskoi Akademii, 1931, 206-212 pp. [Russ. text; Kirgiz, Russ. titles, p. 212]

Toichubekova, Burulkan. NEKOTORYE VOPROSY IMEN DEISTVIIA V KIRGIZSKOM IAZYKE. Frunze: "Mektep," 1968, 120 pp., 2000 copies. [Russ. text; Kirgiz titles, pp. 112-120]

_____. NEKOTORYE VOPROSY IMEN DEISTVIIA V KIRGIZSKOM IAZYKE. Frunze, 1968. [Kirgiz text; ca.180 titles, pp. 112-119]

Toktobaeva, R. comp. KRATKII SPISOK DETSKOI LITERATURY. Frunze, 1958. [Kirgiz text; 70 Kirgiz titles, pub.: 1948-1953]

_____. LITERATURA KIRGIZSTANA. BIOBIBLIOGR. UKAZATEL'. Frunze: (Gos. Resp. B-ka Kirgiz. SSR im. Chernyshevskogo), 1958, 176 pp., 1050 copies. [Kirgiz text; ca.500 Kirgiz titles, pub.: 1938-1957]

_____. comp. NASIRDIN BAITEMIROV. PAMIATKA. Frunze, 1954. [Kirgiz text; 14 Kirgiz titles, pub.: 1939-1953]

[_____.] PROIZVEDENIIA RUSSKIKH PISATELEI NA KIRGIZSKOM IAZYKE. No. 2. Frunze: (Gos. Publ. B-ka im. Chernyshevskogo), 1954, 8 pp., 1000 copies. [Russ. text; 53 Kirgiz titles]

[_____.] TEMIRKUL UMETALIEV. Frunze, 1954. [Kirgiz text; 17 Kirgiz titles, pub.: 1943-1953]

TUGEL'BAI SYDYKBEKOV. BIBLIOGR. PAMIATKA. Frunze: (Gos. Resp. B-ka Kirgiz. SSR im. N. G. Chernyshevskogo), 1962. [Kirgiz, Russ. text; 21 Kirgiz, Russ. titles, pub.: 1947-1961]

*Tulegabylov, Mukambet. TVORCHESKII PUT' KASYMALY BAIALINOVA. Frunze: "Ilim," Baspasi, 1966, 136 pp., 500 copies. [Kirgiz text; 144 Kirgiz, Russ. titles, pp. 130-135]

TVORCHESTVO MOLODYKH POETOV KIRGIZII. Frunze: (Gos. Resp. B-ka Kirgiz. SSR. im. N. G. Chernyshevskogo), 1964. [Russ. text; ca.30 Russ. titles, pub.: 1958-1963, pp. 10-12]

Kirgiz: Language, Literature

VYDAIUSHCHIISIA MASTER KIRGIZSKOI PROZY. MATERIALY PO
PROPAGANDE PROIZVEDENII LAUREATA LENINSKOI PREMII
1963 G. CHINGIZA AITMATOVA. Frunze: (Gos. Resp. B-ka
Kirgiz.SSR im. N. G. Chernyshevskogo. Nauch.-Metod.
Otd.), 1963, 23 pp. [Russ. text; 90 Russ. titles,
pub.: 1954-1962, pp. 14-21]

*Zhumadylov, S. OTRAZHENIE IDEI DRUZHBY NARODOV V
KIRGIZSKOI SOVETSKOI LITERATURE. Frunze: "Ilim,"
1967, 216 pp., 500 copies. [Kirgiz text; Kirgiz,
Russ. titles, pub.: 1945-1963, pp. 209-215]

*Zvoleva, V. P. BIBLIOGRAFIIA KIRGIZII. V 4-KH T.
Vol. 3, No. 6. LITERATURA, ISKUSSTVO. (1946-1955 GG.)
UKAZATEL' LITERATURY. Frunze: (Ministerstvo Kul'tury
Kirgizskoi SSR. Gos. Resp. B-ka Kirg. SSR. im. N. G.
Chernyshevskogo. Otdel Natsional'noi Bibliografii),
1965, 317 pp., 1000 copies. [Russ. text; 2659+ Russ.
titles, pub.: 1946-1955]

_____. VELIKII OKTIABR' I GRAZHDANSKAIA VOINA
V PROIZVEDENIIAKH PISATELEI KIRGIZII (REK. UKAZATEL'
LITERATURY). Frunze: "Kyrgyzstan," 1967, 40 pp.,
600 copies. [Russ. text; ca.50 Russ. titles, per.:
1917-1921, pub.: 1940-1965]

PHILOSOPHY, RELIGION

Amanaliev, B. IZ ISTORII FILOSOFSKOI MYSLI KIRGIZSKOGO
NARODA. Frunze, 1963. [Russ. text; 59 titles,
pp. 73-75]

Amankanov, Kh. NAUKA I RELIGIIA O PRIRODE. Frunze,
1958. [Russ. text; 44 Kirgiz, Russ. titles,
pub.: 1940's - 1950's, pp. 210-211]

_____. NAUKA I RELIGIIA O PRIRODE. Frunze:
Kirgizgosizdat. (Nauch.-Ateistich. B-ka), 1958.
Kirgiz text; 44 titles, Sov. per., pp. 210-211]

Belimova, A. F. KTO TAKIE MENNONITY? Frunze:
"Kyrgyzstan," 1967, 59 pp., 1500 copies. [Russ. text;
17 titles, at end of book]

Kirgiz: Language, Literature

Izmailov, A. E. ATEISTICHESKOE VOSPITANIE V SHKOLE. Frunze, 1957. [Russ. text; 116 Kirgiz, Russ. titles, pp. 61-66]

Shamshiev, R. S. ATEIZM V KIRGIZSKOI KHUDOZHESTVENNOI LITERATURE. (REK. UKAZATEL' LIT.). Frunze: (Gos. Resp. B-ka Kirg. SSR im. Chernyshevskogo), 1967, 23 pp., 600 copies. [Kirgiz text; 61 Kirgiz titles, pub.: 1941-1966]

Ulasovets, G. N. ATEIZM V KIRGIZSKOI KHUDOZHESTVENNOI LITERATURE (REK. UKAZATEL' LIT.). Frunze: "Kyrgyzstan" (Gos. Resp. B-ka Kirg. SSR im. Chernyshevskogo), 1967, 30 pp., 600 copies. [Russ. text; 39 Russ. titles, pub.: 1941-1964]

POLITICAL SCIENCE, LAW

*Abubakirova, Sofiia Shakirovna. BIBLIOGRAFIIA KIRGIZII V CHETYREKH TOMAKH. Vol. 3., No. 1. KOMMUNISTICHESKAIA PARTIIA KIRGIZII. LENINSKII KOMMUNISTICHESKII SOIUZ MOLODEZHI KIRGIZII (1946-1955). Frunze: (Kyrgyz.SSR N. G. Chernyshevskii Atyndagy Mamlekettik Respublikalyk Kitepkanasy), 1966, 411 pp., 800 copies. [Kirgiz text; 4310 Kirgiz titles, per.: 1946-1955]

*Altmyshbaev, A. LENIN I PROPAGANDA MARKSIZMA V KIRGIZII (1905-1923 GG.). Frunze: "Ilim," 1967, 271 pp., 1000 copies. [Russ. text and titles, per.: 1905-1923, pp. 260-269]

Barsukov, N. METODICHESKIE SOVETY K IZUCHENIIU BIOGRAFII V. I. LENINA V NACHAL'NYKH POLITICHESKIKH SHKOLAKH. Frunze: "Kyrgyzstan," 1968, 140 pp., 2000 copies. [Russ. text; Kirgiz titles at end of subject]

*BIBLIOGRAFIIA KIRGIZII. V 4-KH T. Vol. 3, No. 1. S. SH. ABUBAKIROVA. KOM. PARTIIA KIRGIZII. LENINSKII KOM. SOIUZ MOLODEZHI KIRGIZII. (1946-1955). UKAZATEL' LIT. Frunze: (Gos. Resp. B-ka Kirg. SSR im. Chernyshevskogo), 1966, 411 pp., 800 copies. [Kirgiz text; 4310 Kirgiz titles, per.: 1946-1955]

Kirgiz: Political Science, Law

Dzhamgerchinov, B. DOBROVOL'NOE VKHOZHDENIE KIRGIZII V SOSTAV ROSSII. Frunze, 1963. [Russ. text; ca.220 titles, pp. 427-435]

Ilebaev, U. PRAVOVOI REZHIM OROSHAEMYKH ZEMEL' V KIRGIZSKOI SSR V SOVREMENNYI PERIOD. Frunze: "Ilim," 1966, 187 pp., 500 copies. [Russ. text; ca.240 titles, pp. 176-186]

*Kazakbaev, A. KOMPARTIIA KIRGIZII V BOR'BE ZA DAL'NEISHEE RAZVITIE SOTSIALISTICHESKOI KUL'TURY KIRGIZSKOGO NARODA (1956-1961 GG.). Frunze: Kirgizskoe Gosudarstvennoe Izdatel'stvo, 1963, 247 pp., 3000 copies. [Russ. text; ca.190 Russ. titles (incl. archives), per.: 1956-1961, pp. 237-245]

*Kozhonaliev, S. K. SUD I UGOLOVNOE OBYCHNOE PRAVO KIRGIZOV DO OKTIABR'SKOI REVOLIUTSII. Frunze, 1963, 65 pp. [Russ. text; ca.60 Russ., Kirg. titles, pub.: 1870-1960, per.: pre-1917, pp. 62-65]

*Kulishova, L. ZHIZN' I DEIATEL'NOST' M. V. FRUNZE. Frunze: Kirgizuchpedgiz., 1960, 90 pp. [Russ. text; ca.180 Kirgiz, Russ. titles, per.: before and after Rev., pp. 89-91]

*Libova, F.; P. Shats. NATSIONAL'NYI VOPROS I NATSIONAL'NOE STROITEL'STVO (BIBLIOGRAFIA).--REV. I NATS. 1936. No. 7. 1936. [Russ. text; Russ., other titles, Sov. per., pp. 91-97]

*Malabaev, D. M. UKREPLENIE SOVETOV KIRGIZII V PERIOD STOITEL'STVA SOTSIALIZMA (1917-1937). Frunze: "Ilim," 1969, 492 pp., 700 copies. [Russ. text; ca.400 Russ., Eng., Fr., Turk. titles, per.: 1917-1937, pp. 470-488]

*Mirtov, V. V. IDEINOE I ORGANIZATSIONNOE UKREPLENIE OBLASTNOI PARTORGANIZATSII KIRGIZII (1925-1937 GODY). Frunze, 1966. [Russ. text; ca.200 Russ. titles, pub.: 1920-1963, per.: 1925-1937, pp. 267-277]

Morozov, O. D. GOROD FRUNZE--STOLITSA SOVETSKOGO KIRGIZISTANA. KRATKII UKAZATEL' LIT. Frunze, 1956, 19 pp., 1000 copies. [Russ. text; 126 Kirgiz, Russ. titles]

Kirgiz: Political Science, Law

Narynbaev, A. I. XXIII S"EZD KPSS I PREPODAVANIE OBSHCHESTVOVEDENIIA V SREDNEI SHKOLE. Frunze: "Mektep," 1966, 99 pp., 1900 copies. [Russ. text; Kirgiz titles at end of chapters]

Sadykova, Sh. comp. CHELOVEK VSTUPAIUSHCHII V KOMMUNIZM--VOSPITYVAETSIA SEGODNIA (BESEDY O KNIGAKH). Frunze: (Gos. Resp. B-ka Kirgizskoi SSR im. Chernyshevskogo), 1963, 18 pp., 600 copies]

_____. OSNOVOPOLOZHNIKI MARKSIZMA (PROIZVEDENIIA K MARKSA I F. ENGEL'SA I LITERATURA O NIKH) REKOMEND. UKAZATEL' LIT. Frunze, 1966. [Kirgiz text and titles, pub.: 1958-1965]

_____. PRETVORENIE V ZHIZN' LENINSKIKH IDEI. REKOMEND. ANNOT. UKAZATEL'. Frunze, 1965. [Kirgiz text; 128 Kirgiz titles, pub.: 1953-1964]

_____. PROPAGANDA MATERIALOV XIV S"EZDA KP KIRGIZII. SPISOK LITERATURY. Frunze: (M-vo Kul'tury Kirg. SSR), 1966, 10 pp., 300 copies. [Russ. text; Kirgiz titles]

*Sannikov, V.; V. Semenkov. GEROI SOVETSKOGO SOIUZA-- KIRGIZSTANTSY. Frunze: Kirgizskoe Gosudarstvennoe Izdatel'stvo, 1963, 234 pp., 4000 copies. [Russ. text and titles, per.: 1941-1945, pp. 222-231]

Shofler, Z. G. comp. POBEDNAIA POSTUP' PARTII I NARODA. KRATKII REK. SPISOK LIT. K 40-LETIIU OBRAZOVANIIA KIRGIZSKOI SSR I SOZDANIIA KOMMUNISTICHESKOI PARTII KIRGIZII. Frunze: (Gos. Resp. B-ka Kirgizskoi SSR im. Chernyshevskogo), 1965, 9 pp., 700 copies. [Russ. text; 34 titles, Sov. per.]

Toktobaeva, R. I. V. STALIN (KRATKII UKAZATEL' LIT.). Frunze: Gos. Publ. B-ka Kirgiz. SSR im. Chernyshevskogo), 1953, 8 pp., 920 copies. [Kirgiz text; 55 Kirgiz, Russ. titles]

*Turgunbekov, R. RAZVITIE DEMOKRATICHESKIKH FORM DEIATEL'NOSTI VERKHOVNOGO SOVETA KIRGIZSKOI SSR. Frunze: "Ilim," 1966, 118 pp., 500 copies. [Russ. text; 56 Russ. titles, pub.: 1943-1964, pp. 114-117]

* _____. SOZDANIE I RAZVITIE KONSTITUTSII KIRGIZSKOI SSR. Frunze, 1962, 170 pp. [Russ. text; ca.110 Russ. titles, Sov. per., pub.: 1926-1961, pp. 164-169]

Kirgiz: Political Science, Law

Ulasovets, G. N. comp. IZUCHAITE MATERIALY XIV S"EZDA KOMMUNISTICHESKOI PARTII KIRGIZII. SPISOK LITERATURY. Frunze: (M-vo Kul'tury Kirg. SSR), 1966, 11 pp., 600 copies. [Russ. text]

V. I LENIN V VPSPOMINANIIAKH SOVREMENNIKOV. REKOMEND. UKAZATEL' LIT. Frunze, 1963, 16 pp. [Kirgiz text; 51 Kirgiz titles, pub.: 1955-1963]

Zhantuarov, S. B. GRAZHDANSKAIA VOINA V KIRGIZII (1918-1920 GG.). Frunze: Izdat. Akad. Nauk Kirgizskoi SSR, 1963, 240 pp., 500 copies. [Russ. text; ca.240 Russ. titles, per.: 1918-1921, pub.: 1949-1951, pp. 213-225]

SOCIAL ORGANIZATION

Aidaraliev, A. A. BIBLIOGRAFICHESKIE MATERIALY PO ZDRAVOOKHRANENIIU I ISTORII MEDITSINY KIRGIZSKOI SSR. (VTORAIA POLOVINA XIX V.--1959 G.). Frunze: (Resp. Dom San. Prosveshcheniia), 1962. [Russ. text; pub.: 2nd half of 19th c. to 1959]

*Karakeev, K. K. IZ ISTORII KUL'TURNOGO STROITEL'STVA V KIRGIZISTANE. [Frunze] 1968. [Russ. text; ca.110 titles, pp. 171-175]

Shumakova, T. I.; L. I. Mel'nikova. KOMSOMOL'SKIE ORGANIZATSII V SHKOLAKH KIRGIZII. Frunze: "Mektep," 1968, 100 pp., 1300 copies. [Russ. text; titles pp. 99-100]

Tatybekova, Zh. S. RASPKREPOSHCHENIE ZHENSHCHINY-KIRGIZKI VELIKOI OKTIABR'SKOI SOTSIALISTICHESKOI REVOLIUTSIEI. (1917-1936 GG.) Frunze, 1963. [Russ. text; ca.120 titles, per.: 1917-1936, pp. 132-136]

27 TAJIK

GENERAL

*Akhmedova, M.; R. Kukushkina. comps. KNIGA SOVETSKOGO
TADZHIKISTANA. KATALOG (1957-1961 GG.). Dushanbe:
(Gos. Knizhnaia Palata), 1963, 315 pp., 1,500 copies.
[Tajik, Uzbek, Russ. text; 2968 Tajik, Uzbek, Russ.
titles, pub.: 1957-1961]

*_____.; S. Ibrokhimov. ed.
KNIGA SOVETSKOGO TADZHIKISTANA. KATALOG (1962-1966).
Dushanbe: (Gosudarstvennaia Knizhnaia Palata), 1967,
356 pp., 2000 copies. [Tajik, Russ. text; 2847 Tajik,
Uzbek, Russ. titles, pub.: 1962-1966]

Bektimirov, F. comp. BIBLIOGRAFICHESKII SBORNIK
TADZHIKSKOGO GOSUDARSTVENNOGO UNIVERSITETA IM. V. I.
LENINA. (UKAZATEL' PECH. RABOT PROFESSORSKO-
PREPODAVATEL'SKOGO SOSTAVA UN-TA.). Dushanbe:
(Tadzhikskii Gosudarstvennyi Universitet im. V. I.
Lenina), 1960, 184 pp., 1000 copies. [Russ. text;
1820 Tajik, Russ., Europ. titles]

Betger, E. K. "PERECHEN', POMESHCHENNYKH V TURKESTANSKIKH
VEDOMOSTIAKH STATEI I ZAMETOK OTNOSIASHCHIKHSIA DO
OBLASTEI, NYNE VKHODIASHCHIKH V TADZHIKISTAN,"
BIBLIOGRAFIIA TADZHIKISTANA. Tashkent, 1926. [Russ.
text; 389 titles, pub.: 1870-1917, pp. 1-28]

BIBLIOGRAFIIA TADZHIKISTANA. (MATERIALY PO IZUCHENIIU
TADZHIKISTANA). Tashkent, 1926, 69 pp. [Russ. text;
Russ., other titles, per.: 19th - early 20th c.]

Denisova, V. A. comp. BIBLIOGRAFIIA IZDANII TADZH.
BAZY I TADZHIKSKOGO FILIALA AKADEMII NAUK SSSR.
KNIGI I STAT'I. 1933-1951. Stalinabad: (AN Tadzh.SSR.
Tsent. Nauch. B-ka), 1952, 82 pp., 500 copies.
[Russ. text; 805 titles, pub.: 1933-1951]

Tajik: General

*EZHEGODNIK IZDANII AKADEMII NAUK TADZHIKSKOI SSR. 1959 GOD. (ANNOTIROVANNYI UKAZATEL' LITERATURY). Dushanbe: Izdatel'stvo Akademii Nauk Tadzhiksoi SSR, 1961, 101 pp., 500 copies. [Russ. text; 397+ Tajik, Russ. titles, pub.: 1959]

EZHEGODNIK IZDANII AKADEMII NAUK TADZHIKSKOI SSR. 1960 GOD. (SISTEMATICHESKII UKAZATEL' KNIG I STATEI). Dushanbe: Izdatel'stvo Akademii Nauk, 1962, 67 pp., 260 copies. [Russ. text; 452+Tajik, Russ. titles, pub.: 1960]

EZHEGODNIK IZDANII AKADEMII NAUK TADZHIKSKOI SSR. 1961 GOD. (SISTEMATICHESKII UKAZATEL' KNIG I STATEI). Dushanbe: Izdatel'stvo Akademii Nauk, 1963, 120 pp., 300 copies. [Russ. text; 907+ Tajik, Russ. titles, pub.: 1961]

EZHEGODNIK IZDANII AKADEMII NAUK TADZHIKSKOI SSR. 1963 GOD. Dushanbe: Izdatel'stvo AN Tadzhikskoi SSR, 1965, 83 pp., 500 copies. [Russ. text; pub.: 1963]

*EZHEGODNIK IZDANII AKADEMII NAUK TADZHIKSKOI SSR. 1967. (SIST. UKAZATEL' KNIG I STATEI). Duzhanbe: "Donish," 1970, 166 pp., 500 copies. [Russ. text; 985 Tajik, Russ. titles, pub.: 1967]

*EZHEGODNIK IZDANII AKADEMII NAUK TADZHIKSOI SSR. 1968. (SIST. UKAZATEL' KNIG I STATEI). Dushanbe: "Donish," 1970, 151 pp., 500 copies. [Russ. text; 815 Tajik, Russ. titles, pub.: 1970]

Ivanov, P. P. [see also E. K. Betger] "BIBLIOGRAFIIA TADZHIKISTANA. OPYT SISTEMATICHESKOGO UKAZATELIA KNIG, STATEI I ZAMETOK NA RUSSKOM, ZAPADNO-EVROPEISKIKH IAZYKAKH O TADZHIKISTANE," BIBLIOGRAFIIA TADZHIKISTANA. Tashkent, 1926. [Russ. text; 612 Russ., Europ. titles, pub.: 19th c. - 1925, pp. 1-42]

Karpych, V. "K OBRAZOVANIIU SOIUZNOI TADZHIKSKOI SSR (BIBLIOGRAFICHESKII OBZOR)," KNIGA I REVOLIUTSIIA. (Moscow) No. 24. 1929. [Russ. text; pub.: Sov. books up to 1928, titles pp. 18-19]

Tajik: General

KNIZHNAIA LETOPIS'. ORGAN GOS. BIBLIOGRAFII TADZ. SSR. KNIGI NAPECH. V TADZHIKISTANE V 1937-1938 GG. No. 1. Stalinabad: (Knizhnaia Palata Tadzhikskoi SSR), 1939, 39 pp., 1000 copies. [Tajik, Russ. text; ca.560 Tajik, Russ. titles, pub.: 1937-1938]

KNIZHNAIA LETOPIS'. ORGAN GOS. BIBLIOGRAFII TADZH. SSR (ZA 1939). No. 2. Stalinabad: (Knizhnaia Palata Tadzhikskoi SSR), 1940. [Tajik text; titles, pub.: 1939]

KNIZHNAIA LETOPIS'. ORGAN GOS. BIBLIOGRAFII TADZH. SSR. No. 1-2. Stalinabad: (Knizhnaia Palata Tadzhikskoi SSR), 1941. [Tajik text; titles, pub.: 1940-1941]

KNIZHNAIA LETOPIS'. ORGAN GOS. BIBLIOGRAFII TADZH. SSR. 1938-1948 GG. Stalinabad: (Kn. Palata Tadzh. SSR), 1949, 214 pp., 1500 copies. [Tajik text; 2120 Tajik, Russ. titles, pub.: 1938-1948]

KNIZHNAIA LETOPIS' (TADZHIK SSR) ZA 1949 G. ORGAN GOS. BIBLIOGRAFII. Stalinabad: (Knizhnaia Palata Tadzhikskoi SSR), 1949, 48 pp. [Tajik text; 304 Tajik, Uzbek, Russ. titles, pub.: 1949]

KNIZHNO-ZHURNAL'NAIA LETOPIS'. (ZA 1947 G.) Stalinabad: (Knizhnaia Palata Tadzhikskoi SSR), 1948. [Tajik text; titles, pub.: 1947]

*Kurapova, N. I. comp. EZHEGODNIK IZDANII AKADEMII NAUK TADZHIKOI SSR. 1958 G. Stalinabad: (Akad. Nauk Tadzhik. SSR. Tsentr. Nauch. B-Ka), 1959, 48 pp., 500 copies. [Russ text; 348 Tajik, Russ. titles, pub.: 1958]

_____. comp. EZHEGODNIK IZDANII AKADEMII NAUK TADZHIKSKOI SSR. 1962 G. (SISTEMATICHESKII UKAZATEL' KNIG I STATEI). Dushanbe: (AN Tadzhikskoi SSR), 1964, 117 pp., 525 copies. [Russ. text; 681 Tajik, Russ., other titles, pub.: 1962]

_____. comp. EZHEGODNIK IZDANII AKADEMII NAUK TADZHIKSKOI SSR. 1963 G. Dushanbe: (AN Tadzhikskoi SSR...), 1965, 83 pp., 500 copies. [Russ. text; 598 Tajik, Russ. titles, pub.: 1963]

*Leivi, D. S.; N. S. Nazarova. NAUKA V SOVETSKOM TADZHIKISTANE. BIBLIOGRAFICHESKII UKAZATEL' 1951-1960 GG. Dushanbe: (Akademiia Nauk Tadzhikskoi SSR), 1963, 122 pp. [Russ. text; 741+ Tajik, Russ. titles]

Tajik: General

LETOPIS' GAZETNYKH STATEI. ORGAN GOS. BIBLIOGRAFII
TADZH. SSR. (ZA 1939 G.) No. 1-3. Stalinabad:
Gosudarstvennaia Knizhnaia Palata Tadzhikskoi SSR),
1940. [Tajik, Russ. text; titles, pub.: 1939]

LETOPIS' GAZETNYKH STATEI. ORGAN GOS. BIBLIOGRAFII
TADZH. SSR. (ZA 1939 G.) No. 4. Stalinabad:
(Gosudarstvennaia Knizhnaia Palata Tadzhikskoi SSR),
1941. [Tajik, Russ. text; titles, pub.: 4th quarter
1939]

LETOPIS' GAZETNYKH STATEI. ORGAN GOS. BIBLIOGRAFII
TADZH. SSR. (ZA 1940 G.) No. 1-4. Stalinabad:
(Gosudarstvennaia Knizhnaia Palata Tadzhikskoi SSR),
(1941). [Tajik, Russ. text; titles, pub.: 1940]

LETOPIS' GAZETNYKH STATEI. ORGAN. GOS. BIBLIOGRAFII
TADZH. SSR. 3 Nos. (IANV./MART-IIUN'/SENT.)
Stalinabad: (Gosudarstvennaia Knizhnaia Palata
Tadzhikskoi SSR), 1948. [Tajik, Russ. text; titles,
pub.: 1948]

LETOPIS' GAZETNYKH STATEI. ORGAN GOS. BIBLIOGRAFII
TADZH. SSR. 2 Nos. (IANV./MART; APR./IIUN').
Stalinabad: (Gosudarstvennaia Knizhnaia Palata
Tadzhikskoi SSR), 1949. [Tajik, Russ. text; titles,
pub.: 1949]

LETOPIS' GAZETNYKH STATEI. Stalinabad: (Gos. Kn. Palata
Tadzh. SSR) [1949] (quarterly). [Tajik text; No. 2
1066 Tajik, Russ. titles, pub.: 1949]

LETOPIS' PECHATI TADZHIKISTANA. ORGAN GOS. BIBLIOGRAFII
TADZH. SSR. Stalinabad: (Kn. Palata Tadzh. SSR),
1950 (bimonthly), 400 copies. [Tajik text; titles,
pub.: 1950]

LETOPIS' PECHATI TADZHIKISTANA. ORGAN GOS. BIBLIOGRAFII
TADZH. SSR. Stalinabad: (Kn. Palata Tadzh. SSR), 1951
(quarterly), 400 copies. [Tajik text; titles, pub.:
1951]

LETOPIS' PECHATI TADZHIKISTANA. ORGAN GOS. BIBLIOGRAFII
TADZHIK. SSR. Stalinabad: (Kn. Palata Tadzhik. SSR),
1952 (quarterly), 400 copies. [Tajik text; titles,
pub.: 1952]

LETOPIS' PECHATI TADZHIKSKOI SSR. ORGAN GOS. BIBLIOGRAFII
TADZHIK. SSR. Stalinabad: (Knizhnaia Palata Tadzhik.
SSR), 1953 (quarterly), 500 copies. [Tajik, Russ.
text; titles, pub.: 1953]

Tajik: General

LETOPIS' PECHATI TADZHIKSKOI SSR. ORGAN GOS. BIBLIOGRAFII
TADZH. SSR. Stalinabad: (Knizhnaia Palata Tadzhik. SSR),
1954, 500 copies. [Tajik, Russ. text; titles, pub.:
1954]

LETOPIS' PECHATI TADZHIKSKOI SSR. ORGAN GOS. BIBLIOGRAFII
TADZHIK. SSR. Stalinabad: (Knizhnaia Palata Tadzhik.
SSR), 1955, 400 copies. [Tajik, Russ. text; titles,
pub.: 1955]

LETOPIS' PECHATI TADZHIKSKOI SSR. ORGAN GOS. BIBLIOGRAFII
TADZHIK. SSR. Stalinabad: (Knizhnaia Palata Tadzh. SSR),
1956, 400 copies. [Tajik, Russ. text; titles, pub.:
1956]

LETOPIS' PECHATI TADZHIKSKOI SSR. ORGAN GOS. BIBLIOGRAFII
TADZHIK. SSR. Stalinabad: (Knizhnaia Palata Tadzhik.
SSR), [1957] (quarterly). [Tajik, Russ. text; titles,
pub.: 1957]

LETOPIS' PECHATI TADZHIKSKOI SSR. ORGAN. GOS.
BIBLIOGRAFII TADZHIK. SSR. Stalinabad: (Knizhnaia
Palata Tadzhik. SSR) [1958] (quarterly), 350 copies.
[Tajik, Russ. text; titles, pub.: 1958]

LETOPIS' PECHATI TADZHIKSKOI SSR. ORGAN GOS. BIBLIOGRAFII
TADZHIK. SSR), 1959 (quarterly), 300 copies. [Tajik,
Russ. text; titles, pub.: 1959]

LETOPIS' PECHATI TADZHIKSKOI SSR. ORGAN GOS. BIBLIOGRAFII
TADZHIK. SSR. Stalinabad: (Knizhnaia Palata Tadzhik.
SSR) [1960] (quarterly), 300 copies. [Tajik, Russ.
text; titles, pub.: 1960]

LETOPIS' PECHATI TADZHIKSKOI SSR. ORGAN GOS. BIBLIOGRAFII
TADZHIK. SSR. Dushanbe: (Knizhnaia Palata Tadzhik.
SSR), [1961] (quarterly) 300 copies. [Tajik, Russ.
text; titles, pub.: 1961]

LETOPIS' PECHATI TADZHIKSKOI SSR. ORGAN GOS. BIBLIOGRAFII
TADZHIK. SSR. Dushanbe: (Knizhnaia Palata Tadzhik. SSR)
[1962] (quarterly), 400 copies. [Tajik, Russ. text;
titles, pub.: 1962]

LETOPIS' PECHATI TADZHIKSKOI SSR. ORGAN GOS. BIBLIOGRAFII
TADZHIK. SSR. Dushanbe: (Knizhnaia Palata Tadzhik. SSR)
[1963] (quarterly), 420 copies. [Tajik, Russ. text;
titles, pub.: 1963]

Tajik: General

LETOPIS' PECHATI TADZHIKSKOI SSR. Dushanbe: (Knizhnaia Palata), 1964 (quarterly), 400 copies. [Tajik, Russ. text; titles, pub.: 1964]

LETOPIS' PECHATI TADZHIKSKOI SSR. Dushanbe: (Knizhnaia Palata) [1965; quarterly] 420 copies. [Tajik text; titles, pub.: 1965]

*LETOPIS' PECHATI TADZHIKSKOI SSR (1966); No. 1, No. 2, No. 3, No. 4. Dushanbe: (Knizhnaia Palata Tadzh. SSR) [1966] (quarterly), (1) 182 pp. 500 copies; (2) 209 pp., 420 copies; (3) 202 pp., 420 copies; (4) 218 pp., 500 copies. [Tajik, Russ. text; Tajik, Uzbek, Russ. titles, pub.: 1965-1966]

*LETOPIS' PECHATI TADZHIKSKOI SSR (1967); No. 1, No. 2, No. 3, No. 4. Dushanbe: (Knizhnaia Palata Tadzh. SSR), 1967 (quarterly), (1) 195 pp., 500 copies; (2) 206 pp., 500 copies; (3) 184 pp., 500 copies; (4) 205 pp., 500 copies. [Tajik, Russ. text; Tajik, Uzbek, Russ. titles, pub.: 1966-1967]

*LETOPIS' PECHATI TADZHIKSKOI SSR (1968); No. 1, No. 2, No. 3, No. 4. Dushanbe: (Knizhnaia Palata Tadzhikskoi SSR), 1968 (quarterly), (1) 172 pp., 500 copies; (2) 185 pp., 500 copies. [Tajik, Russ. text; Tajik, Uzbek, Russ. titles, pub.: 1967-1968; NNC has No. 1, No. 2.]

LETOPIS' PECHATI TADZHIKSKOI SSR. Dushanbe: (Knizhnaia Palata Tadzh. SSR) [1969] (quarterly), 500 copies. [Tajik, Russ. text; Tajik, Russ. titles, pub.: 1969]

LETOPIS' PECHATI TADZHIKSKOI SSR. Dushanbe: (Knizhnaia Palata Tadzh. SSR) [1970] (quarterly), 500 copies. [Tajik, Russ. text; Tajik, Russ. titles, pub.: 1970]

LETOPIS' ZHURNAL'NYKH STATEI. No. 1. Stalinabad: (Knizhnaia Palata Tadzhikskoi SSR), 1940. [Tajik, Russ. text; titles, pub.: 1940]

Tajik: General

Nabieva, R. IULIIA ARTEM'EVNA SHIBAEVA. (KRATKII OCHERK ZHIZNI ISTORIKA.) Dushanbe: (M-vo Nar. Obrazovaniia Tadzh.SSR.), 1968, 16 pp., 200 copies. [Russ. text; titles pp. 12-16]

*"OBSHCHESTVO DLIA IZUCHENIIA TADZHIKISTANA I IRANSKIKH NARODNOSTEI ZA EGO PREDELAMI," BIULLETEN' SREDNEAZIATSKOGO GOSUDARSTVENNOGO UNIVERSITETA. (Tashkent) No. 14, 1926; No. 17, 1928; No. 18, 1929. [Russ. text; titles (1926) p. 281; (1928) pp. 177-179; (1929) p. 183, pub.: 1925-1928]

Oranskii, I. M. "BIBLIOGRAFIIA TRUDOV A. A. FREIMANA," PROBLEMY VOSTOKOVEDENIIA. No. 4. Moscow, 1959. [Russ. text; 94 Russ., foreign titles, pub.: 1901-1959, pp. 219-222]

PAMIR, TADHIKISTANA, SREDNIAIA AZIIA. OBZOR TRUDOV I MATERIALOV EKSPEDITSII 1932-1935 I 1928-1932 GG. (AN SSR. TADZHIKSKO-PAMIRSKAIA EKSPEDITSIIA. no. 70. BIBLIOGRAFIIA). Moscow-Leningrad, 1936,251 pp. [Russ. text; ca.840 Russ. titles, per.: 1928-1935]

*Romaskevich, A. A.; P. P. Bushev. "SPISOK NAUCHNYKH RABOT V. A. ZHUKOVSKOGO," OCHERKI PO ISTORII RUSSKOGO VOSTOKOVEDENIIA. SBORNIK 5. Moscow: Izdatel'stvo Vostochnoi Literatury, 1960. [Russ. text; titles pub.: 1883-1926, pp. 140-145]

*Sabirova, N. H. Shcherbakova. comp. SARADZHON IUSUPOVA. (1910-1966). (MATERIALY K BIBLIOGR. UCHENYKH TADZHIKISTANA. No. 10). Dushanbe: "Donish," 1967, 35 pp., 720 copies. [Russ. text; titles per.: 1910-1966]

Sharopov, R. OSNOVANYE ETAPY I ZAKONOMERNOSTI RAZVITIIA TADZHIKSKOI LITERATURNOI BIBLIOGRAFII. Dushanbe: "Ifron," 1970, 112 pp., 1000 copies. [Russ. text; ca.120 Tajik, Russ. titles, pub.: 1926-1969, pp. 90-111]

Tajik: General

Shevchenko, Z. M.; D. S. Leivi. BIBLIOGRAFIIA BIBLIOGRAFII TADZHIKISTANA. Dushanbe: (Izdatel'stvo "Donish"), 1966, 167 pp., 770 copies. [Russ. text; 605 Tajik, Uzbek, Russ. titles, pub.: 1920-1964, pp. 7-141]

──────────────.; A. G. Sizhuk. comp. BIBLIOGRAFIIA IZDANII AKADEMII NAUK TADZHIKSKOI SSR. No. 1. "KNIGI I STAT'I. 1951-1954." Stalinabad: (Akad. Nauk Tadzhik. SSR), 1955, 86 pp., 1000 copies. [Russ. text; 591 Tajik, Russ. titles, pub.: 1951-1954]

* ──────────.; M. V. Nikolaeva. KATALOG KANDIDATSKIKH I DOKTORSKIKH DISSERTATSII ZASHCHISHCHENNYKH NA MATERIALAKH TADZHIKSKOI SSR, 1934-1959 GG.; BIBLIOGRAFICHESKII UKAZATEL' LITERATURY. Stalinabad: Izdatel'stvo AN Tadzhikskoi SSR, 1960, 100 pp., 500 copies. [Russ. text; 746 Russ. titles, pub.: 1934-1959]

* ──────────. KATALOG KANDIDATSKIKH I DOKTORSKIKH DISSERTATSII, ZASHCHISHCHENNYKH NA MATERIALAKH TADZHIKSKOI SSR. 1960-1965 GG. (BIBLIOGR. UKAZ. LIT.) Dushanbe: "Donish," 1970, 133 pp., 500 copies. [Russ. text; 655 Russ. titles, pub.: 1960-1965, pp. 4-110]

Sin'kovskaia, A. S. comp. MUKHAMMEDKUL NARZIKULOVICH NARZIKULOV. (AKAD. NAUK TADZH. SSR. MATERIALY K BIBLIOGRAFIIA UCHENYKH TADZH. No. 5). Dushanbe, 1964, 60 pp., 805 copies. [Russ. text]

[Sizhuk, A. G. comp.] EZHEGODNIK IZDANII AKADEMII NAUK TADZHIKSKOI SSR. 1956 G. Stalinabad: (Akad. Nauk Tadzhik. SSR. Tsentr. Nauch.B-ka), 1956, 42 pp., 500 copies. [Russ. text; 328 Tajik, Russ. titles, pub.: 1956]

──────────.; Z. M. Shevchenko. comps. EZHEGODNIK IZDANII ADADEMII NAUK TADZHIKSKOI SSR. 1955 G. Stalinabad: (Akad. Nauk Tadzhik. SSR. Tsentr. Nauch. B-ka), 1956, 62 pp., 450 copies. [Russ. text; 223 Tajik, Russ. titles, pub.: 1955]

* ──────────. EZHEGODNIK IZDANII AKADEMII NAUK TADZHIKSKOI SSR. 1957 G. Stalinabad: (Akad. Nauk Tadzhik. SSR. Tsentr. Nauch. B-ka), 1959, 56 pp., 200 copies. [Russ. text; 413 Tajik, Russ. titles, pub.: 1957]

Tajik: General

Sizhuk, A. G. comp. EZHEGODNIK IZDANII AKADEMII NAUK TADZHIKSKOI SSR. 1964. Dushanbe:"Donish," ;966, 113 pp., 585 copies. [Russ. text; 832 titles]

* _____. comp. EZHEGODNIK IZDANII AKADEMII NAUK TADZHIKSKOI SSR. 1966 G. Dushanbe: "Donish," (AN Tadzh. Tsentr. Nauch. B-ka), 1968, 162 pp., 455 copies. [Russ. text; 858 Tajik, Russ. titles, pub.: 1966]

* _____. comp. EZHEGODNIK IZDANII AKADEMII NAUK TADZHIKSKOI SSR. (SIST. UKAZATEL' KNIG I STATEI) 1965 G. Dushanbe: "Donish" (AN Tadzh. SSR. Tsentr. Nauch. B-ka), 1967, 85 pp., 970 copies. [Russ. text; 632 Tajik, Russ. titles, pub.: 1965]

* _____. EZHEGODNIK IZDANII AKADEMII NAUK TADZHIKSKOI SSR. (SIST. UKAZATEL' KNIG I STATEI) 1970. Dushanbe: "Donish," 1972, 187 pp., 300 copies. [Russ. text; 921 Tajik, Russ. titles, pub.: 1970]

* _____. EZHEGODNIK IZDANII KADEMII NAUK TADZHIKSKOI SSR (SIST. UKAZATEL' KNIG I STATEI) 1969 G. Dushanbe: "Donish," 1971, 176 pp., 300 copies. [Russ. text; 859 Tajik, Russ. titles, pub.: 1971]

SPISOK LITERATURY PO MARKSISTKO-LENINSKOI FILOSOFII DLIA ASPIRANTOV I SOISKATELEI NEFILOSOFSKIKH SPETSIAL'NOSTEI. Dushanbe: "Donish," 1966, 14 pp., 1000 copies. [Russ. text]

*"TADZHIKSKAIA SOVETSKAIA SOTSIALISTICHESKAIA RESPUBLIKA," BOL'SHAIA SOVETSKAIA ENTSIKLOPEDIIA. Moscow: Gosudarstvennoe Nauchnoe Izdatel'stvo "Bol'shaia Sovetskaia Entsiklopediia," Vol. 41. 1956, 2nd ed., 466-499 pp. [Russ. text and titles, pp. 478-479, 493, 496, 497]

*"TADZHIKSKAIA SOVETSKAIA SOTISALISTICHESKAIA RESPUBLIKA," BOL'SHAIA SOVETSKAIA ENTSIKLOPEDIIA. Moscow: Ogiz RSFSR, Gosudarstvennyi Nauchnyi Institut "Sovetskaia Entsiklopediia," Vol. 53. 1946, 1st ed., 412-448 pp. [Russ. text and titles, p. 448]

Tal'man, R. O.; T. I. Poddymnikova; G. Ia. Iakubov; E. N. Iakovleva; M. Akhmedova; K. Dzhamalov. comps. KATALOG KNIG TADZHIKSKOI SSR (1926-1956). Dushanbe: Tadzhikgosizdat, 1960, 294 pp. [Russ. text; 7342 Tajik, Uzbek, Russ. titles, pub.: 1926-1956]

Tajik: General

Tursunova, L. V. comp. SULTAN UMAROVICH UMAROV. (1908-1964). (AN TADZHIKSKOI SSR. TSENTRAL'NAIA NAUCHNAIA BIBLIOTEKA. MATERIALY K BIOBIBLIOGRAFII UCHENYKH TADZHIKISTANA. No. 5). Dushanbe: Izd-vo AN Tadzh.SSR, 1965, 59 pp., 605 copies. [Russ. text; titles, per.: 1908-1964]

ANTHROPOLOGY, ETHNOGRAPHY

*Bisnek, A. G.; N. M. Zel'dovich. "ETNOGRAFIIA NARODOV PAMIRA. SPISOK LITERATURY NA RUSSKOM IAZYKE," SOVETSKAIA ETNOGRAFIIA. SBORNIK 3. 1940, 245 pp. [Russ. text; 262 Russ. titles, pub.: 1835-1937, pp. 219-246]

*Ginzburg, V. V. GORNYE TADZHIKI. MATERIALY PO ANTROPOLOGII TADZHIKOV KARATEGINA I DARVAZA. Moscow-Leningrad: Izdatel'stvo Akademii Nauk SSR, 1937, 475 pp., 1725 copies. [Russ. text; 194 Russ., Europ. titles, pp. 269-275]

Karmysheva, B. Kh. UZBEKI-LOKAITSY IUZHNOGO TADZHIKISTANA. No. 1. "ISTORIKO-ETNOGRAFICHESKII OCHERK ZHIVOTNOVODSTVA V DOREVOLIUTSIONNYI PERIOD. Stalinabad, 1954, 169 pp. [Russ. text; (footnotes) per.: pre-Rev.]

*Kisliakov, N. A. "IZDANIIA SEKTORA ETNOGRAFII INSTITUTA ISTORII, ARKHEOLOGII I ETNOGRAFII AKADEMII NAUK TADZHIKSKOI SSR (1951-1956)," SOVETSKAIA ETNOGRAFIIA. No. 5. 1957. [Russ. text; Russ. survey, pub.: 1951-1956, pp. 190-194]

*Pisarchik, A. K.; B. Kh. Karmysheva. "ETNOGRAFICHESKAIA RABOTA V TADZHIKISTANE V 1952-1953 GG.," SOVETSKAIA ETNOGRAFIIA. No. 3. 1954, 115-119 pp. [Russ. text; 26 titles, pub.: 1951-1953, pp. 118-119]

ARCHITECTURE, ART, MUSIC

Akhrorov, A.; N. A. Belinskaia; V. A. Meshkeris; N. Nurdzhanov; M. P. Stradomskaia; Z. M. Tadzhikova. comp. "SOVETSKAIA LITERATURA PO VOPROSAM ISKUSSTVA TADZHIKISTANA ZA 1958-1960 GG.," ISKUSSTVO TADZH. NARODA. No. 3. Dushanbe, 1965. [Russ. text; 174 titles, pub.: 1958-1960, pp. 326-348]

Belinskaia N. A.; O. L. Dansker; V. A. Meshkeris; N. Nurdzhanov; M. Khorkashev. comps. "SOVETSKAIA LITERATURA PO VOPROSAM ISKUSSTVA TADZHIKISTANA ZA 1956-1957 GG.," TRUDY. (IN-T ISTORII AKAD. NAUK TADZHIK. SSR), Vol. 29, 1960. [Russ. text; 831 titles, pub.: 1956-1957, pp. 317-375]

Buronina, V. L. NARODNAIA ARKHITEKTURA SEVERNOGO TADZHIKISTANA. Moscow, 1959, 99 pp. [Russ. text; 11 Russ. titles, pub: pre-Rev. & Sov.]

Dansker, O. L.; V. A. Meshkeris; N. Kh. Nurdzhanov. "SOVETSKAIA LITERATURA PO VOPROSAM ISKUSSTVA TADZHIKISTANA ZA 1954-1955 GG.," SBORNIK STATEI, POSVIASHCHENNYKH ISKUSSTVU TADZHIKSKOGO NARODA. (AKADEMIIA NAUK TADZHIKSKOI SSR. TRUDY. Vol. 42. INSTITUT ISTORII, ARKHEOLOGII I ETNOGRAFII). Stalinabad, 1956. [Russ. text; 229 Tajik, Uzbek, Russ. titles, pub.: 1954-1955, pp. 245-256]

Norkallaev, I.; R. Nabieva; S. Mushaeva. comps. KALENDAR' ZNAMENATEL'NYKH I PAMIATNYKH DAT TADZHIKSKOI SSR. ...NA 1966 GOD. Dushanbe: "Irfon," 1966, 56 pp., 2000 copies. [Russ. text; titles at end of chapters]

Tal'man, R. O.; Z. A. Chernykh; T. N. Masevich. comps. KALENDAR' ZNAMENATEL'NYKH I PAMIATNYKH DAT TADZHIKSKOI SSR. ... NA 1958 GOD. Dushanbe: "Irfon," 1968, 73 pp., 1000 copies. [Russ. text; titles at end of chapters]

*Veimarn, B. "TADZHIKSKOE ISKUSSTVO," BOL'SHAIA SOVETSKAIA ENTSIKLOPEDIIA. Vol. 53. 1946, 1st ed., 451-455 pp. [Russ. text and titles, p. 455]

ECONOMICS

Amanullaev, F. RAZVITIE SEL'SKOGO KHOZIAISTVA KOLKHOZOV SOVETSKOGO PAMIRA. (AKADEMIIA NAUK TADZHIKSKOI SSR. OTDEL EKONOMIKI. TRUDY. Vol. 6). Stalinabad, 1960. [Russ. text; 40 Russ. titles, pub.: 1894-1958, pp. 83-84]

Bank, V. E. "OPYT BIBLIOGRAFII TADZHIKISTANA," PROBLEMY TADZHIKISTANA (TRUDY I KONFERENTSII PO IZUCHENIIU PROIZVODITEL'NYKH SIL TADZH.SSR. Vol. 2. Leningrad, 1934. [Russ. text]

Dzhamalov, K. OKTIABR'SKAIA REVOLIUTSIIA I RASTSVET SOVETSKOGO TADZHIKISTANA [BIBLIOGRAFIIA] Stalinabad: (Kitobkhonai Davl. Resp. RSS Tojikiston Ba Nomi Firdavst), 1957, 39 pp. [Tajik text; ca.200 Tajik titles, pub.: 1940's - 1950's]

IBADULLA KASIMOVICH NARZIKULOV. Dushanbe: "Donish," 1969, 59 pp., 600 copies. [Russ. text; 121 Tajik, Russ. titles, pub.: 1946-1970]

Iunusov, B. V. EKONOMICHESKIE PROBLEMY ENERGETIKI TADZHIKISTANA. Part 1. Dushanbe: (M-vo Nar. Obrazovaniia Tadzh. SSR), 1967, 115 pp., 500 copies. [Russ. text; 15 titles, p. 115]

Kapustin, P.; A. Khakimov. VNEDRENIE METODOV SETEVOGO PLANIROVANIIA I UPRAVLENIIA V TADZHIKISTANE. Dushanbe: (In-t Nauch.-Tekh. Informatsii i Propagandy pri Gosplane Tadzh.SSR), 1968, 45 pp., 1000 copies. [Russ. text; 11 titles, p. 44]

Khodzhaev, Kh. K. "IZ ISTORII VOSSTANOVLENIIA I RAZVITIIA KHLOPKOVODSTVA V TADZHIKISTANE (1917-1929 GG.)," UCHENYE ZAPISKI. KULIABSKII PED. INSTITUT. No. 1. 1955. [Russ. text; 33 titles, per.: 1919-1929, pp. 49-50]

*Kholdzhuraev, Kh. KOMMUNISTICHESKAIA PARTIIA TADZHIKISTANA V BOR'BE ZA TEKHNICHESKII PROGRESS V PROMYSHLENNOSTI. Duzhanbe: Izdatel'stvo "Irfon," 1967, 363 pp., 1000 copies. [Russ. text; ca.250 Russ. titles, pp. 345-359]

KONFERENTSIIA MOLODYKH UCHENYKH TADZHIKISTANA. TRUDY.
(VOPROSY SEL. KHOZ-VA). Dushanbe: "Irfon," 1966,
355 pp., 1000 copies. [Russ. text; titles at end of
reports]

Masson, M. E. IZ ISTORII GORNOI PROMYSHLENNOSTI
TADZHIKISTANA. BYLAIA RAZRABOTKA POLEZNYKH
ISKOPAEMYKH. (AKADEMIIA NAUK SSSR. TADZHIKSKO-
PAMIRSKAIA EKSPEDITSIIA. 1933. MATERIALY... No. 20),
Leningrad, 1934. [Russ. text; 181 Russ., Europ.
titles, pp. 98-106]

Li, V. G. RAZVITIE EKONOMIKI UKRUPNENNYKH KOLKHOZOV
TADZHIKSKOI SSR (1950-1958 GODY). Stalinabad, 1959.
[Russ. text and titles, pub.: 1950-1958, pp. 254-258]

Narzikulov, I. K.; E. I. Poliarush. "ISTORIIA
FORMIROVANIIA KHOZIAISTVA ZERAVSHANSKOI DOLINY,"
ISTORIIA RAZVITIIA I SOVREM. SOSTOIANIE KHOZIAISTVA
ZERAVSHANSKOI DOLINY. (TRUDY OTD. EKONOMIKI AN
TADZHIK. SSR.) [MATERIALY PO PROIZVODITEL'NYM SILAM
TADZHIKISTANA. No. 1]. Dushanbe: (AN. Tadzhik. SSR),
1961. [Russ. text; 35 Russ. titles, pub.: 1873-1957,
pp. 51-52]

_____. "KRATKIE SVEDENIIA O DOREVOLIUTSIONNOI
KUSTARNOI PROMYSHLENNOSTI TADZHIKISTANA," TRUDY
AKADEMII NAUK TADZHIKSKOI SSR. [Dushanbe] Vol. 81.
1957. [Russ. text; 23 Russ. titles, p. 67]

*_____.; S. N. Riazantsev, ed. TADZHIKSKAIA
SSR. EKONOMIKO-GEOGRAFICHESKAIA KHARAKTERISTIKA.
Moscow: Gosudarstvennoe Izdatel'stvo Geograficheskoi
Literatury. Akad. Nauk Tadzhik. SSR. In-t Geogr.
Akad. Nauk SSSR), 1956, 228 pp., 7000 copies.
[Russ. text; 57 Russ. titles, pp. 225-227]

*NAUCHNYE TRUDY (TADZHIKSKII NAUCHO-ISSLEDOVATEL'SKII
INSTITUT SEL'SKOGO KHOZIAISTVA) Vol. 3 Dushanbe:
Izdatel'stvo "Ifron," 1967, 220 pp., 600 copies
[Russ. text; Russ., Europ. titles at end of articles]

*Rakhimov, A. SOTSIAL'NO-EKONOMICHESKIE PREOBRAZOVANIIA
V TADZHIKSKOI DEREVNE. Dusanbe: (M-vo Nar.
Obrazovaniia Tadzh. SSR. Kuliab. Gos. Ped. In-t im.
A. Rudaki), Izdatel'stvo "Irfon," 1968, 231 pp.,
1000 copies. [Russ. text and titles, pp. 209-229]

Tajik: Economics

*Sevlikiants, G. S. SOTSIALISTICHESKIE AGRARNYE
OTNOSHENIIA I IKH ORGANIZATSIONNYE FORMY. Dushanbe:
"Irfon," 1966, 171 pp., 1000 copies. [Russ. text;
87 Russ. titles, pp. 166-170]

SOVETSKII TADZHIKISTAN. (OCHERKI PO EKONOMICHESKOI
GEOGRAFII). Stalinabad [Dushanbe] (AN SSSR. Tadzh.
Filial), 1950. [Russ. text; 183 Russ. titles, pub.:
19th c - 1950 (strong on 1920's - 1940's), pp. 166-172]

Tal'man, R. O.; L. V. Tursunova. KAIRAK-KUMSKAIA GES
"DRUZHBA NARODOV." UKAZATEL' LITERATURY. Dushanbe:
(Gosudarstvennaia Respublikanskaia Biblioteka
Tadzhikskoi SSR imeni Firdousi. Leninabadskaia
Mezhraionnaia Biblioteka), 1962, 57 pp. [Russ.
text; ca.230 titles, pub.: up to 1961]

Vasil'ev, P. A. K ISTORII ZAROZHDENIIA FABRICHNO-
ZAVODSKOI PROMYSHLENNOSTI V SEVERNOM TADZHIKISTANE.
SOOBSHCH. TADZH. FILIALA AKAD. NAUK SSSR. No. 18,
55 pp. [Russ. text; 15 titles (incl. archives),
pub.: ca.1872-1921]

_____. TADZHIKISTAN. (EKONOM.-GEOGRAFICHESKOE
OPISANIE). Stalinabad, 1947. [Russ. text; 140 Russ.
titles, pub.: up to 1945, pp. 178-185]

*Zhurin, N. I. SEVERNAIA SHAG PO IL'ICHU (KORENNYE
PREOBRAZOVANIIA V EKONOMIKE I KUL'TURE AKTIUB. OBL.
ZA GODY SOVETSKOI VLASTI). Alma Ata: "Kazakhstan,"
1969, 208 pp., 15,600 copies. [Russ. text; 98 Russ.
titles, pp. 200-205, publ.: thru 1967]

EDUCATION

ANNOTIROVANNYI PERECHEN' IZDANII INSTITUTA. Dushanbe:
(Dushanbinskii Gosudarstvennyi Pedagogicheskii
Institut imeni T. G. Shevchenko), 1962, 39 pp.
[Russ. text; pub.: 1940-1961]

*Aripov (Orifi), M. IZ ISTORII PEDAGOGICHESKOI MYSLI
TADZHIKSKOGO NARODA. Part 1. "(IX-XI VV.)" Dushanbe,
1962. [Russ. text; footnotes, per.: 9th c - 11th c.]

Tajik: Education

Babadzhanova, Zh. M. NOSIRDZHON ASADOVICH MASUMI.
BIBLIOGRAFIIA. Dushanbe: "Donish," 1966, 58 pp.,
575 pp. [Russ. text]

Borovskaia E. M. comp. PAVEL NIKOLAEVICH OVCHINNIKOV.
(MATERIALY K BIBLIOGRAFII UCHENYKH TADZHIKISTANA.
No. 3). Dushanbe: Izd-vo Akad. Nauk Tadzhik SSR.
Tsentr. Nauch B-ka Akad. Na-k Tadzhik SSR, 1963, 83 pp.,
600 copies. [Russ. text]

[Bumagina, L. comp.] KATALOG NAUCHNO-METODICHESKOI
LITERATURY I ZHURNAL'NYKH STATEI, IZDANNYKH NAUCHNO-
ISSLEDOVATEL'SKIM INSTITUTOM SHKOL MINISTERSTVA
PROSVESHCHENIIA TADZHIKSKOI SSR. Stalinabad:
(Instituti Tadqiqoti Ilmii Maktabhoi Vazorati
Maorifi RSS Tojikiston),1957, 49 pp., 1000 copies.
[Tajik, Russ. text; Tajik, Russ. titles, pub.:
1945-1957]

Dun, A. Z.; V. I. Solnyshkina. BIBLIOGRAFICHESKII
UKAZATEL' TRUDOV PREPODAVATELEI INSTITUTA. Leninabad:
(M-vo Nar. Obrazovaniia Tadzh. SSR. Leninabadskii
Pedagogicheskii Institut im. S. M. Kirova), 1967,
58 pp., 500 copies. [Russ. text]

Fel'dshtein, D. I. TRUDOVOE VOSPITANIE UCHASHCHIKHSIA
SOVETSKOI SHKOLY. (IST.-PED. OCHERK). Dushanbe,
1968. [Tajik text; ca.440 titles, pp. 200-218]

GOSUDARSTVENNAIA RESPUBLIKANSKAIA BIBLIOTEKA
TADZHIKSKOI SSR IM. FIRDOUSI. PUTEVODITEL'.
Dushanbe: (Gos. Resp. B-ka Tadzhik. SSR. im.
Firdousi.), 1960. [Russ. text; 109 Tajik, Russ.
titles, pp. 47-58]

IUBILEINYI SBORNIK. Leninabad: (Leniiabad Ped. In-t
im. Kirova), 1958. [Tajik, Russ. text; 175 Tajik,
Russ. titles, pp. 129-139]

KAGALOGI ADABIYOTHOI ILMIMETODIE, KI INSTITUTI
TADQIQOTI ILMII MAKTAB HOI VAZORATI MAORIFI RSS
TOJIKISTON DAR SOLHOI 1945-1951 NASHR KARDAAST.
Stalinabad, 1952, 17 pp. [Tajik text; pub.: 1945-1951]

KATALOGII PREDMETII MAQOLAHOI KORKUNI ILMII INSTITUTI
TADQIQOTI ILMII MAKTABHO, KI DAR ZHURNALI "MAKTABI
SOVETI," DAR SOLHOI. 1945-1951 CHOP SHUDAAST.
Stalinabad, 1952, 20 pp. [Tajik text; pub.: 1945-1951]

Tajik: Education

Kononenko, L. A. comp. BADADZHAN NIIAZOVICH
NIIAZMUKHAMEDOV. BIBLIOGRAFIIA. Dushanbe: "Donish,"
1966, 100 pp., 570 copies. [Russ. text]

Leivi, D. S. comp. ABDUL'GANI MUKHAMMEDOVICH MIRZOEV.
(AN TADZHIKSKOI SSR. TSENTR. NAUCH. B-KA. MATERIALY
K BIOBIBLIOGRAFII UCHENYKH TADZHIKISTANA. No. 4),
1965, 87 pp. (incl. essay), 650 copies. [Russ. text;
213 Tajik, Persian, Russ. English titles, pub.:
1933-1964]

Makhmudov, K. comp. KATALOG NAUCHNO-METODICHESKOI
LITERATURY, IZDANNOI NAUCHNO-ISSLEDOVATEL'SKIM
INSTITUTOM SHKOL MINISTERSTVA PROSVESHCHENIIA
TADZHIKSKOI SSR. Stalinabad, 1954, 32 pp., 500
copies. [Tajik, Russ. text]

"MAKTALI SOVETI," ZHURNAL . Stalinabad: Nauch.-
Issled. In-t Shkol M-va Prosveshcheniia Tadzhikskoi
SSR, 1952, 20 pp., 500 copies. [Tajik, Russ. text;
235 Tajik, Russ. titles, pub.: 1945-1951]

Nelipa, A. A. RUSSKII IAZYK V TADZHIKSKOI SHKOLE.
(BIBLIOGR. UKAZ. METOD. LIT.) Leninabad: (Dushanb.
Gos. Ped. In-t im. Shevchenko. Leninab. Gos. Ped.
In-t im. Kirova), 1970, 55 pp., 1000 copies. [Russ.
text; 501 Tajik, Russ. titles, pub.: 1932-1967]

Nosachenko, G. P. comp. "PERECHEN' NAUCHNO-
ISSLEDOVATEL'SKIKH I METODICHESKIKH RABOT
PROFESSORSKO-PREPODAVATEL'SKOGO SOSTAVA I ASPIRANTOV
DUSHANBINSKOGO GOSPEDINSTITUTA IM. T. G. SHEVCHENKO,
OPUBLIKOVANNYKH V 'UCHENNYKH ZAPISKAKH' I VYSHEDSHIKH
OTDELNYMI IZDANIIAMI V PERIOD S 1940 GODA PO 1957
GOD," IUBILEINYI SBORNIK (MAJMURI IDONA).
Dushanbe: (Dushanbinskii Gos. Ped. In-t), 1958.
[Russ. text; 150 titles, pub.: 1940-1957, pp. 135-142]

O POLITEKHNICHESKOM OBUCHENII UCHASHCHIKHSIA
OBSHCHEOBRAZOVATEL'NOI SHKOLY. Stalinabad: Upr.
Shkol M-va Prosveshcheniia Tadzhik SSR, 1953, 7 pp.,
500 copies. [Tajik, Russ. text; 57 titles]

Obidov, I. ISTORIIA RAZVITIIA NARODNOGO OBRAZOVANIIA
V TADZHIKSKOI SSR (1917-1967 GG.) Dushanbe:
"Irfon," 1968, 295 pp., 1000 copies. [Russ. text;
titles, per.: 1917-1967, pp. 287-294]

Tajik: Education

*_____. KRATKII OCHERK ISTORII NARODNOGO
OBRAZOVANIIA V TADZHIKISTANE. Dushanbe: Nashriyoti
"Irfon," 1965, 206 pp., 2000 copies. [Tajik text;
ca.80 Tajik titles, pp. 201-205]

Rakh, G. I.; M. A. Kudaikulov; B. M. Vakhol'skii.
TEKHNICHESKIE SREDSTVA OBUCHENIIA V SHKOLE. Alma Ata,
1969. [Russ. text; 53 titles, 154-156]

*Sharipov, B.; K. Sabirov. STROITEL'STVO KOMMUNIZMA I
RASTSVET TADZHIKSKOI KUL'TURY. Dushanbe: Nashriyoti
"Irfon," 1965, 134 pp., 5000 copies. [Tajik text;
Tajik, Russ. titles, pp. 127-133]

Tanatin, B. Ia. comp. PERECHEN' OPUBLIKOVANNYKH RABOT
PREPODAVATELEI LENINABADSKOGO GOSUDARSTVENNOGO
PEDAGOGICHESKOGO INSTITUTA. MAJMUAI IDONA (IUBILEINYI
SBORNIK). Leninabad: (Instituti Davl. Pedagogii
Leninobod Ba Nomi S. M. Kirov), 1958. [Russ. text;
Tajik, Russ. titles, pub.: 1948-1958, pp. 129-139]

_____. PERECHEN' OPUBLIKOVANNIKH RABOT
PREPODAVATELEI INST. 5 KN. IUBILEINYI SBORNIK.
Leninabad: (Leninabad Ped. Ins-t. im. Kirova), 1958.
[Russ. text; Sov. per., pp. 129-139]

Tursunova, L. V. comp. KONSTANTIN TITOVICH POROSHIN.
Dushanbe: "Donish," 1967, 48 pp., 600 copies. [Russ.
text]

GEOGRAPHY

*Agakhaniants, O. E.; A. S. Sun'kovskaia. BIBLIOGRAFIIA
PAMIRA. UKAZATEL' LITERATURY. 1920-1965 GG. No. 1.
PRIRODA. Dushanbe: Izdatel'stvo "Donish," (AN Tadzh.
SSR. Tsentr. Nauch. B-ka), 1968, 266 pp., 1115
copies. [Russ. text; 1826 Russ. titles, pub.: 1920-
1964]

_____. OSNOVNYE PROBLEMY FIZICHESKOI
GEOGRAFII PAMIRA. Pt. 2. Dushanbe, 1966. [Russ.
text; ca.360 titles, pp. 219-233]

Tajik: Geography

*Azat'ian, A. A. "BIBLIOGRAFIIA TRUDOV A. P. FEDCHENKO I LITERATURA O EGO ZHIZNI I DEIATEL'NOSTI," A. P. FEDCHENKO-GEOGRAF I PUTESHESTVENNIK. Moscow: Gosudarstvennoe Izdatel'stvo Geograficheskoi Literatury, 1956, 127 pp., 10,000 copies. [Russ. text; 48+ Russ., Europ. titles (incl. archives), pub.: 1863-1951, pp. 115-125]

Beletskii, E. A. PIK LENINA. Moscow: Geografgiz, 1958. [Russ. text; 56 titles, pp. 172-174]

BIBLIOGRAFIIA TADZHIKISTANA. Part 1. "GEOGRAFIIA I GIDROLOGIIA" (AN SSSR. TRUDY SOVETA PO IZUCHENIIU PROIZVODITEL'NYKH SIL. SERIIA TADZHIKSKAIA. No. 1.) Leningrad: Izd. Akad. Nauk SSSR i SNK Tadzhikskoi SSR, 1933, 66 pp. [Tajik, Russ. text; 870 Russ. titles, per.: 19th c. - 1931]

Budanov, V. I. "LITERATURY PO GEOLOGII PAMIRA ZA 10 LET (1953 - 1963 GG.)," MATERIALY PO GEOLOGII PAMIRA. No. 2. Dushanbe, n. d. [Russ. text; pub.: 1953-1963]

*Chumichev, D. A. TADZHIKSKAIA SSR. Moscow: Gosudarstvennoe Izdatel'stvo Geograficheskoi Literatury, 1954, 125 pp., 40,000 copies. [Russ. text; Russ. titles, p. 124]

Golovnina, Iu. D. "LITERATURA O PAMIRAKH," NA PAMIRAKH. ZAPISKI RUSSKOI PUTESHESTVENNITSY. Moscow, 1902. [Russ. text; 38 Russ., foreign titles, pp. 242-244]

*Magidovich, I. "GORNO-BADAKHSHANSKAIA AVTONOMNAIA OBLAST'," BOL'SHAIA SOVETSKAIA ENTSIKLOPEDIIA. Vol. 17. Moscow: Aktsionernoe Obshchestvo "Sovetskaia Entsiklopediia," 1930, 1st ed., 731-736 pp. [Russ. text and titles, p. 736]

*Mamadzhanova, M. Iu.; A. N. Promtov; M. R. Rakhimov, et al. TADZHIKISTAN. Moscow: "Mysl'," 1968, 239 pp., 90,000 copies. [Russ. text; 29 Russ. titles, p. 238]

Norkallaev, I. S.; S. Mushaeva. GORODA TADZHIKISTANA. UKAZATEL' LITERATURY. Dushanbe: "Irfon," (Tadzh. Gos. Resp. B-ka im. Firdousi), 1967, 80 pp., 1000 copies. [Tajik text]

Tajik: Geography

*"PAMIR," BOL'SHAIA SOVETSKAIA ENTSIKLOPEDIIA. Vol. 44.
 Moscow: Gosudarstvennyi Institut "Sovetskaia
 Entsiklopediia," (Ogiz RSFSR)- 1939, 30-34 pp.
 [Russ. text and titles p. 34]

*Selivanov, R. I. "KRATKII OBZOR ISSLEDOVANII PO
 VOPROSAM KOMPLEKSNOGO I SPETSIAL'NOGO RAIONIROVANIIA
 TADZHIKISTANA," (TASHKENT) TRUDY TASHKENTSKOGO
 GOSUDARSTVENNOGO UNIVERSITETA IMENI V. I. LENINA.
 NOVAIA SERIIA. No. 186. GEOGRAFICHESKIE NAUKI.
 Book 22. 1961, 176-187 pp. [Russ. text; 25 Russ.
 titles, pub.: 1953 on, pp. 186-187]

*Shchukin, I. S.; M. A. Giliarova. TADZHIKISTAN
 (FIZIKO-GEOGRAFICHESKII OCHERK). No. 23. MATERIALY
 EKSPEDITSII. Leningrad: Izdanie Tadzhiksko-Pamirskoi
 Ekspeditsii, 1936, 399 pp., 1000 copies. [Russ.
 text; 64 + 48 + 95 Russ., Europ. titles, pp. 82-85;
 162-164; 277-281]

HISTORY, ARCHAEOLOGY

Abaeva, T. G. OCHERKI ISTORII BADAKHSHANA. Tashkent,
 1964. [Russ. text; ca.300 Russ. Europ. titles,
 pub.: 18th c. - 1962, pp. 146-162]

ISTORIIA TADZHIKSKOGO NARODA. Vol. 3, Book 1. PEREKHOD
 K SOTSIALIZMU (1917-1937). Moscow: Izdatel'stvo
 "Nauka," 1964, 376 pp., 2500 copies. [Russ. text;
 ca.200 Russ., Taj. titles, per.: 1917-1937, pp. 6-14]

Belenitskaia I. A. "SOVETSKAIA LITERATURA PO
 ARKHEOLOGII TADZHIKISTANA, OPUBLIKOVANNAIA V 1957 G."
 ARKHEOLOGICHESKIE RABOTY V TADZHIKISTANE V 1957 GODU
 No. 5. TRUDY (AKAD. NAUK TADZHIK. SSR), Vol. 103.
 1959. [Russ. text; 117 Tajik, Russ. other titles, pub.:
 1957, pp. 185-191]

Tajik: History, Archaeology

*"BIBLIOGRAFIIA TADZHIKSKOI ARKHEOLOGICHESKOI
 EKSPEDITSII 1946-1952 GG.," MATERIALY I ISSLEDOVANIIA
 PO ARKHEOLOGII SSSR. No. 37. (TRUDY TADZHIKSKOI
 ARKHEOLOGICHESKOI EKSPEDITSII INSTITUTA ISTORII
 MATERIAL'NOI KUL'TURY AN SSSR, INSTITUTA ISTORII,
 ARKHEOLOGII I ETNOGRAFII AN TADZHIKSKOI SSR I
 GOSUDARSTVENNOGO ERMITAZA. Vol. 2. 1948-1950 GG.
 Moscow-Leningrad, 1953, 314 pp. [Russ. text; 94
 Russ. titles, per.: exped. 1946-1952, pp. 312-314]

*"BIBLIOGRAFIIA TADZHIKSKOI ARKHEOLOGICHESKOI
 EKSPEDITSII ZA 1953-1954 GG." MATERIALY I
 ISSLEDOVANIIA PO ARKHEOLOGII SSSR, No. 66. 1958,
 386 pp. [Russ. text; 68 Russ. titles, pp. 386-387,
 per.: exped. 1953-1954]

*Bubnova, M. A.; T. Dzhalilova; A. Isakova."[SOVETSKAIA]
 LITERATURA PO ARKHEOLOGII TADZHIKISTANA,
 OPUBLIKOVANNAIA V SSSR V 1959 G.," ARKHEOLOGICHESKIE
 RABOTY V TADZHIKISTANE. No. 7. (1959 God)
 (Dushanbe), 1961, 184 pp., 500 copies. [Russ. text;
 91 Tajik, Russ. titles, pub.: 1959, pp. 172-183]

 Chernykh, Z. A.; T. N. Masevich; N. N. Kleman, et al.
 comp. KALENDAR' ZNAMENITEL'NYKH I PAMIATNYKH DAT
 TADZHIKSKOI SSR. ...NA 1967 GOD. Dushanbe: "Irfon,"
 1967, 75 pp., 1500 copies. [Russ. text; titles at
 end of chapters]

 Donish, Akhmad. TRAKTAT AKHMADA DONISHA. Dushanbe:
 "Donish," 1967, 142 pp., 3000 copies. [Russ. text;
 titles, pp. 126-141]

 D'iakonov, M. M.; B. A. Litvinskii. "LITERATURA PO
 ARKHEOLOGII TADZHIKISTANA, OPUBLIKOVANNAIA V 1953 G."
 DOKLADY AKADEMII NAUK TADZHIKSKOI SSR. No. 2.
 1954. [Russ. text; 66 Tajik, Russ. titles, pub.: 1953,
 pp. 81-84]

* _____. U ISTOKOV DREVNEI KUL'TURY
 TADZHIKISTANA. Stalinabad: Tadzhikgosizdat, 1956,
 139 pp., 4000 copies. [Russ. text and titles,
 pp. 135-137]

Tajik: History, Archaeology

*Drikker, Kh. N. "RABOTY PO ISTORII TADZHIKISTANA SOVETSKOI EPOKHI (OBZOR)," SOV. VOSTOKOVEDENIE. No. 5. 1958. [Russ. text and titles, Sov. per., pp. 146-153]

Dzhalilov, A. "SOGD NAKANUNE ARABSKOGO NASHESTVIIA I BOR'BA SOGDIITSEV PROTIV ARABSKIKH ZAVOEVATELEI V PERVOI POLOVINE VIII V.," (AKAD. NAUK TADZHIK. SSR. IN-T ISTORII, ARKHEOLOGII I ETNOGRAFII. TRUDY. Vol. 30). Dushanbe, 1961. [Russ. text; ca.100 Russ., Europ. titles, per.: first half of 8th c., pp. 6-27]

*Dzhamalov, K., Z. Radzhabov. PROSVETITEL' AKHMAD DONISH. Dushanbe: Nashriyoti,"Irfon," 1964, 308 pp., 2000 copies. [Tajik text; ca.300 Tajik, Uzbek, Russ., Europ. titles, pub.: 19th c. - 1963, pp. 289-307]

Faktorovich, P. M. VELIKII BUKHARSKII UCHENYI IBN-SINO (AVITSENNA). TRUDY UZBEKSKOGO GOSUDARSTVENNOGO INSTITUTA. NOVAIA SERIIA 30. BIBLIOGRAFIIA. No. 17. Samarkand, 1941. [Russ. text; 68 Russ., Europ. titles, pub.: 1544-1940, pp. 74-76]

Gafurov, B. G. ISTORIIA TADZHIKSKOGO NARODA. Vol. 1. S DREVNIKH VREMEN DO VELIKOI OKTIABR'SKOI SOTS. REVOL. 1917 G. [Moscow] INSTITUT ISTORII AN TADZHIKSKOI SSR, 1952, 2nd ed. [Russ. text; 600 Tajik, Russ. Persian titles, pub.: 1841-1951, pp. 454-495]

* _____.; B. A. Litvinskii, eds. ISTORIIA TADZHIKSKOGO NARODA. Vol. 1. S DREVNEISHIKH VREMEN DO V V. N. E. Moscow: Izdatel'stvo Vostochnoi Literatury, 1963, 596 pp., 2500 copies. [Russ. text; Russ., Persian, Europ. titles, per.: up to 5th c. A. D., pp. 12-33]

* _____. ; A. M. Belenitskii. eds. ISTORIIA TADZHIKSKOGO NARODA. Vol. 2, Book 1. VOZNIKNOVENIE I RAZVITIE FEODAL'NOGO STROIA (VI-XVI VV.). Moscow: Idatel'stvo "Nauka," 1964, 492 pp., 2500 copies. [Russ. text; Russ., Pers., Europ. titles, per.: 6th - 16th cc., pp. 7-35]

Guliamova, E. "SOVETSKAIA LITERATURA PO ARKHEOLOGII TADZHIKISTANA, OPUBLIKOVANNAIA V 1955 G.," ARKHEOLOGICHESKIE RABOTY V TADZHIKISTANE V 1955 G. (AKADEMIIA NAUK TADZHIKSKOI SSR. TRUDY. Vol. 63. INSTITUT ISTORII, ARKHEOLOGII I ETNOGRAFII), Stalinabad, 1956. [Russ. text; 52 titles, pub.: 1955, pp. 122-126]

Tajik: History, Archaeology

*Ibragimov, S. K. et al. MATERIALY PO ISTORII KAZAKHSKIKH
KHANSTV XV-XVIII VEKOV. Alma Ata: "Nauka," 1969,
652 pp., 1750 copies. [Russ. text; ca.360 Uzbek,
Uigur, Kazakh, Tajik, Tatar, English, French,
German, Arabic, Persian titles, per.: XV - XVIII c,
pp. 633-649]

*Irkaev, M. ISTORIIA GRAZHDANSKOI VOINY V TADZHIKISTANE.
Dushanbe: (Tadzhikskii Gosudarstvennyi Universitet
imeni V. I. Lenina), 1963, 760 pp., 1000 copies.
[Russ. text; ca.430 Tajik, Uzbek, Russ., Europ.,
Turkish titles, per.: 1917-1921, pub.: 1922-1962,
pp. 742-758]

* _____.; Iu. Nikolaev; Ia. Sharapov. OCHERK
ISTORII SOVETSKOGO TADZHIKISTANA. (1917-1957 GG.)
Stalinabad: Tadzhikgosizdat, 1957, 502 pp. [Russ.
text; ca.200 Tajik, Russ. titles, per.: 1917-1957,
pp. 487-499]

* _____. OCHERK ISTORII
SOVETSKOGO TADZHIKISTANA. Dushanbe: Tadzhikgosizdat,
1960, 647 pp., 5000 copies. [Tajik text; ca.230
Tajik, Russ. titles, Sov. per., pp. 629-643]

Isakov, A. "SOVETSKAIA LITERATURA PO ARKHEOLOGII
TADZHIKISTANA, OPUBLIKOVANNAIA V 1958 G.," TRUDY
(IN-T ISTORII AKAD. NAUK TADZHIK SSR). Vol. 27.
Dushanbe: (Int. Istorii Akad. Nauk Tadzhik.SSR),
1961. [Russ. text; 110 Tajik, Russ. titles,
pub.: 1958, pp. 173-179]

*Iskandarov, B. I.; A. M. Mukhatarov. eds. ISTORIIA
TADZHIKSKOGO NARODA. Vol. 2, Book 2. POZDNII
FEODALIZM (XVII v.-1917 G.). Moscow: Izdatel'stvo
"Nauka," 1964, 356 pp., 2350 copies. [Russ. text;
Russ., Persian, Europ. titles, per.: 17th c. - 1917,
pp. 6-20]

* _____. VOSTOCHNAIA BUKHARA I PAMIR V PERIOD
PRISOEDINENIIA SREDNEI AZII K ROSSII. n. p.
Tadzhikskoe Gosudarstvennoe Izdatel'stvo, 214 pp.,
3000 copies. [Russ. text; Russ. survey, per.: 19th c.,
pp. 3-5]

* _____. VOSTOCHNAIA BUKHARA I PAMIR VO
VTOROI POLOVINE XIX V. Part 1. (AKADEMIIA NAUK
TADZHIKSKOI SSR. INSTITUT ISTORII IMENI AKHMADA
DONISHA. TRUDY. Vol. 32). Dushanbe, 1962, 356 pp.,
790 copies. [Russ. text; 26 Russ. survey titles,
pub.: 1879-1960, per.: last half 19th c., pp. 7-10]

Tajik : History, Archaeology

*Ismailova, S.; A. E. Pavlova. "SOVETSKAIA LITERATURA
PO ARKHEOLOGII TADZHIKISTANA, OPUBLIKOVANNAIA V
1960 G.," ARKHEOLOGICHESKIE RABOTY V TADZHIKISTANE.
No. 8 (1960 GOD) (Dushanbe) 1962, 161 pp., 500 copies.
[Russ. text; 95 Tajik, Russ. titles, pub.: 1960,
pp. 155-160]

* _____. "[SOVETSKAIA] LITERATURA PO
ARKHEOLOGII TADZHIKISTANA, OPUBLIKOVANNAIA V SSSR V
1961 G.," ARKHEOLOGICHESKIE RABOTY V TADZHIKISTANE.
No. 9 (1961 GOD) (Dushanbe) 1964, 140 pp., 500
copies. [Russ. text; 86 Tajik, Russ. titles,
pub.: 1961, pp. 135-139]

ISTORIIA TADZHIKSKOGO NARODA. Vol. 3. "TADZHIKISTAN
V PERIOD PEREKHODA K SOTSIALIZMU (1917-1937 GG.)"
Moscow-Stalinabad: (Akad. Nauk Tadzhik.SSR. In-t
Istorii, Arkheol. i Etnografii), 1960. [Russ.
text; ca.170 titles, per.: 1917-1937, pp. 276-281]

Iusupov, Sh. OCHERKI ISTORII KULIABSKOGO BEKSTVA V
KONTSE XIX I NACHALE XX VEKA. (TRUDY. INSTITUT
ISTORII IM. DONISHA. Vol. 41). Dushanbe, 1964.
[Russ. text; titles, per.: ca.1900, pp. 5-11]

*Kabo, R. OCHERKI ISTORII I EKONOMIKI TUVY. CHAST'
PERVAIA: DOREVOLIUTSIONNAIA TUVA. (NAUCHNO-ISSLED.
ASSOTS. PO IZUCH. NATSIONAL'NYKH I KOLONIAL'NYKH
PROBLEM. No. 12). Moscow-Leningrad: Gosudarstvennoe
Sotsial'no-Ekonomicheskoe Izdatel'stvo, 1934, 202 pp.
[Russ. text; 185 Russ., Europ. titles, per.: pre-1917,
pp. 196-202]

Kadyrov, A.; Sh. Dzhalilov. MAKSUD RAKHMATULLAEVICH
SHUKUROV. Dushanbe: (Tadzh. Gos. Un-t im. Lenina),
1970, 38 pp., 500 copies. [Russ. text; 149 Tajik,
Uzbek, Russ. titles, pub.: 1949-1970]

*Karimov, T. POBEDA VELIKOI OKTIABR'SKOI
SOTSIALISTICHESKOI REVOLIUTSII I RESHENIE AGRARNOGO
VOPROSA V TADZHIKISTANE. Part 1. Dushanbe: "Irfon,"
1968, 467 pp., 1000 copies. [Russ. text; ca.140
Russ. titles, per.: 1917-1921, pp. 459-466]

*Khaidarov, G. Kh. BOR'BA ZA USTANOVLENIE I UPROCHENIE
SOVETSKOI VLASTI V SEVERNOM TADZHIKISTANE. (1917-1923
GG.), Dushanbe: "Irfon," 1966, 183 pp., 1000 copies.
[Russ. text; 45 Russ. titles, per.: 1917-1923,
pp. 180-182]

Tajik: History, Archaeology

Kholdzhuraev, Kh. DISSERTATSII ISTORIKOV PO MATERIALAM TADZHIKISTANA. Dushanbe: (Tadzh. Gos. Un-t im. Lenina), 1970, 281 pp., 1000 copies. [Russ. text; 142 titles, pub.: 1947-1969]

_____. KAFEDRA ISTORII KPSS K 50-LETIIU SOVETSKOI VLASTI. (SPRAVOCHNI-KATALOG). Dushanbe: (Tadzh. Gos. Un-t im. Lenina), 1967. [Russ. text; ca.660 titles, pp. 46-106]

Kisliakov, N. A. OCHERKI PO ISTORII KARATEGINA. K ISTORII TADZHIKISTANA. Stalinabad: Tadzhikgosizdat, 1954, 2nd ed. (corrected and supplemented). [Russ. text; ca.150 Russ., Europ. titles, pp. 215-222]

*Litvinskii, B. A. ARKHEOLOGICHESKOE IZUCHENIE TADZHIKISTANA SOVETSKOI NAUKOI (KRATKII OCHERK). AN TADZHIKSKOI SSR. INSTITUT ISTORII, ARKHEOLOGII I ETNOGRAFII. TRUDY. Vol. 24. 1954, 83 pp., 700 copies. [Russ. text; Russ. survey titles, p. 56 and scattered]

_____. MATERIAL'NAIA KUL'TURA TADZHIKISTANA. No. 1. Dushanbe: (AN Tadzh.SSR In-t Istorii im. A. Donisha), 1968, 243 pp., 1000 copies. [Russ. text; titles at end of articles]

_____; E. Guliamova. "SOVETSKAIA LITERATURA PO ARKHEOLOGII TADZHIKISTANA, OPUBLIKOVANNAIA V 1954 G.," ARKHEOLOGICHESKIE RABOTY V TADZHIKISTANE V 1954 G. AKADEMIIA NAUK TADZHIKSKOI SSR. TRUDY. Vol. 37. INSTITUT ISTORII, ARKHEOLOGII I ETNOGRAFII. Stalinabad, 1956. [Russ. text; 107 titles, pub.: 1954, pp. 105-110]

Machalisov, O. KRAEVEDCHESKII MATERIAL PO ISTORII TADZHIKISTANA. Part 1. Stalinabad: (Resp. In-t Usovershenstvovaniia Uchitelei), 1957. [Tajik text; 81 Tajik titles, pp. 123-126]
*Madzhlisov, Adil. AGRARNYE OTNOSHENIIA V VOSTOCHNOI BUKHARE V XIX--NACHALE XX VEKA. Dushanbe-Alma Ata: Izdatel'stvo "Irfon," 1967, 331 pp., 1000 copies. [Russ. text; ca.190 Tajik, Uzbek, Russ. titles, per.: 19th - 20th c., pp. 319-329 (incl. archives)]

Marsakova, K. P. ed. OCHERK ISTORII KOLKHOZNOGO STROITEL'STVA V TADZHIKISTANE (1917-1965 GG.) Dushanbe: "Donish," 1968, 434 pp., 4000 copies. [Russ. text; titles, pub.: 1917-1965, pp. 385-431]

Tajik: History, Archaeology

Mukhtarov, A. OCHERK ISTORII URA-TIUBINSKOGO VLADENIIA V XIX V. Dushanbe, 1964. [Russ. text; titles, per.: 19th c., pp. 4-12]

Nabiev, R. DZHURA USMANOVICH USMANOV. (OCHERK O ZHURNALISTE I ISTORIKE). Dushanbe: (M-vo Nar. Obrazovaniia Tadzh.SSR), 1968, 28 pp., 200 copies. [Russ. text; 245 titles, pp. 9-26]

Nevskii, V. A. "VELIKII TADZHIKSKII VRAZH ABU-ALI IBN SINO (AVITSENNA) BIBLIOGRAFIIA," SBORNIK RABOT PO ISTORII MEDITSINY I ORGANIZATSII ZDRAVOOKHRANENIIA V TADZHIKISTANE. TRUDY TADZHIKSKOGO GOS. MED. INSTITUTA IMENI ABU-ALI IBN-SINO. Vol. 28. Stalinabad, 1957. [Russ. text; 203 Sov. Asian, Russ. titles, pp. 61-67]

Norkallaev, I. S.; S. D. Mushaeva. comps. KALENDAR' ZNAMENATEL'NYKH I PAMIATNYKH DAT TADZHIKSKOI SSR. ...NA 1967 G. Dushanbe: "Irfon," 1967, 84 pp., 2000 copies. [Russ. text; titles at end of chapters]

*_____. VLADIMIR IL'ICH LENIN I TADZHIKISTAN. KRATKII REK. UKAZ. LIT. (POSVIASHCHAETSIA 100-LETIIU SO DNIA ROZHDENIIA V. I. LENINA). Dushanbe: (Tadzh. Gos. Resp. B-ka im. Firdousi), 1970, 35 pp., 1000 copies. [Tajik text; ca.340 Tajik titles, pub.: 1953-1970, pp. 7-30]

*OCHERKI ISTORII KOLKHOZNOGO STROITEL'STVA V TADZHIKISTANE (1917-1965 GG.) Dushanbe: "Donish," 1968, 435 pp., 4000 copies. [Russ. text; ca.220 Tajik, Russ. titles, pub.: 1926-1966, per.: 1917-1965, pp. 379-384]

Pavlova, A. E. comp. BIBLIOGRAFIIA KNIG I STATEI PO ARKHEOLOGII, NUMIZMATIKE I ETNOGRAFII IZDANNYKH TADZHIKSKOI BAZOI, TADZHIKSKIM FILIALOM AN SSR I AKADEMIEI NAUK TADZHIKSKOI SSR. (1934-1956 GG.) Stalinabad: (Akad. Nauk Tadzhik.SSR), 1956, 20 pp., 350 copies. [Russ. text; 168 titles, pub.: 1934-1956]

Pripisnov, V. I. PROBLEMY SUB"EKTIVNOGO FAKTORA V ISTORICHESKOM MATERIALIZME. Dushanbe: "Donish," 1966, 136 pp., 1050 copies. [Russ. text; titles pp. 131-135]

Tajik: History, Archaeology

*Radzhabov, S. A.; Iu. A. Nikolaev. eds. ISTORIIA
TADZHIKSKOGO NARODA. Vol. 3, Book 2. PERIOD
SOTSIALIZMA I PEREKHOD K KOMMUNIZMU (1938-1963 GG.)
Moscow: Izdatel'stvo "Nauka," 1965, 283 pp., 2500
copies. [Russ. text; Tajik, Russ. titles, per.:
1938-1963,, pp. 5-8]

*Radzhabov, Z. IZ ISTORII OBSHCHESTVENNO-POLITICHESKOI
MYSLI TADZHIKSKOGO NARODA VO VTOROI POLOVINE XIX I
V NACHALE XX VV. Stalinabad: Tadzhikskoe
Gosudarstvennoe Izdatel'stvo, 1957, 459 pp., 5000
copies. [Russ. text; ca.300 (incl. archives),
per.: 2nd half 19 c. - begin. 20 c., pp. 445-457]

_____. IZ ISTORII OBSHCHESTVENNO-POLITICHESKOI
MYSLI TADZHIKSKOGO NARODA VO VTOROI POLOVINE XIX I
V NACHALE XX V. Stalinabad: Tadzhikgosizdat, 1959.
[Tajik text; ca.300 Tajik, Uzbek, Tatar, Russ.
titles (incl. archives), per.: second half 19th c.-
begin. 20th c., pp. 436-446]

*_____. ed. ISTORIIA TADZHIKSKOI SSR.
Dushanbe: Izdatel'stvo "Irfon," 1965, 451 pp.,
8000 copies. [Russ. text; 58 Tajik, Russ. titles,
per.: up to 1964, pp. 444-447]

_____. RAZVITIE OBSHCHESTVENNOI MYSLI
TADZHIKSKOGO NARODA VO VTOROI POLOVINE XIX V. I V
NACHALE XX V (KRATKII OCHERK). Stalinabad:
Tadzhik. Gos. Int., 1951. [Russ. text; 19 Tajik,
Russ. titles (in footnotes), per.: 19th - 20th cc.,
pp. 4-5]

Ranov, V. ARKHEOLOGI NA "KPYSHE MIRA," Dushanbe, 1967.
[Russ. text; per.: Stone Age, 14 titles]

*Safarova, S.; S. Ibragimov. IZDANIE PROIZVEDENII
VLADIMIRA IL'ICHA LENINA NA TADZHIKSKOM IAZYKE I
LITERATURA O NEM. BIBLIOGR. UKAZ. 1928-1968.
Dushanbe: "Irfon," (Knizhnaia Palata Tadzh.SSR. In-t
Istorii Partii pri Tsk KP Tadzhikistana), 1970,
79 pp., 3000 copies. [Tajik text; 280 Tajik
titles, pp. 16-72]

*Sadykov, M. S. ISTORICHESKII OPYT KPSS PO STROITEL'STVU
SOTSIALIZMA V TADZHIKISTANE. (1917-1959 GG.).
Dushanbe: Izdatel'stvo "Irfon," 1967, 434 pp.,
2000 copies. [Russ. text; 550 Tajik, Russ. titles,
per.: 1917-1959, pp. 407-432]

Tajik: History, Archaeology

Saltovskaia, E. D. "SOVETSKAIA LITERATURA PO ARKHEOLOGII TADZHIKISTANA, OPUBLIKOVANNAIA V 1956 G.," ARKHEOLOGICHESKIE RABOTY V TADZHIKISTANE V 1956 GODU. No. 4. TRUDY (AKAD. NAUK TADZHIK.SSR), Vol. 91. INSTITUT ISTORII, ARKHEOLOGII I ETNOGRAFII. 1959. [Russ. text; 162 titles, pub.: 1956, pp. 181-191]

*Shcherbakova, N. G. comp. ZARIF SHARIPOVICH RADZHABOV. Dushanbe: Izdatel'stvo "Donish," 1966, 60 pp., 1100 copies. [Russ. text; 206+ Tajik, Russ. Europ. titles, pub.: 1932-1966, pp. 16-40]

Semenov, A. A.; V. A. Kozachkovskii. "ISTORICHESKAIA NAUKA V TADZHIKISTANE ZA 25-LET," DOKLADY AN TADZH. SSR. No. 12. Dushanbe, 1954. [Russ. text; 30+ titles, pub.: 1924-1954, pp. 9-14]

Shevchenko, Z. M. comp. BOBODZHAN GAFUROVICH GAFUROV. Dushanbe: "Donish," 93 pp., 700 copies. [Russ. text; 339 + 46 titles, per.: 1935-1968]

*Smirnova-Rakitina, V. AVITSENNA (ABU-ALI IBN-SINO). Moscow: Izdatel'stvo TsK VLKSM "MOLODAIIA GVARDIIA," 1958, 236 pp., 30,000 copies. [Russ. text; 37 Russ. titles, pp. 231-233]

*"SREDNEAZIATSKAYA EKSPEDITSIYA AKADEMII NAUK. PAMIR, TADZHIKISTAN, SREDNIAIA AZIIA," TRUDY I MATERIALY. No. 70. Moscow: Izd-vo AN SSSR, 1936, 250 pp., 1000 copies. [Russ. text; titles, pub.: 1928-1935]

TADZHIKSKII RESP. OB"EDINENNYI MUZEI ISTORIKO-KRAEVEDCHESKII I IZOBRAZITEL'NYKH ISKUSSTV. No. 4. Dushanbe: "Irfon," 1966, 178 pp., 1000 copies. [Russ. text; 19 titles, p. 58]

TADZHIKSKII UNIVERSITET IM. V. I. LENINA. KAFEDRA ISTORII KPSS K 50-LETIIU SOVETSKOI VLASTI. Dushanbe: (M-vo Nar. Obrazovaniia Tadzh.SSR), 1967, 107 pp., 300 copies. [Russ. text]

*[Tal'man, R. O.] GORODA TADZHIKISTANA. UKAZATEL' LITERATURY. Dushanbe: Izdatel'stvo "Irfon," 1967, 88 pp., 1000 copies. [Russ. text and titles, pub.: 1954-1965, titles at end of articles).

UCHENYI PEDAGOG I PROPAGANDIST [MULLO IRKAEVICH IRKAEV. AVT. KH. KHOLDZHYRAEV]. Dushanbe: (Tadzh. Gos. Un-t im. Lenina), 1970, 43 pp., 400 copies. [Russ. text; 202 Tajik, Uzbek, Russ. titles, pub.: 1942-1969]

Tajik: History, Archaeology

Zavadovskii, Iu. N. "MATERIALY DLIA BIBLIOGRAFII
ABU 'ALI IBN SINY. SPISOK SOCH. ABU 'ALI IBN SINY
V RAZLICHNYKH REDAKTSIIAKH EGO BIOGRAFII, SOSTAVLENNOI
ABD AL-UAKHIDOM AL-DZHUZDZHANI." IZVESTIIA OTD.-NIIA
OBSHCHESTV. NAUK. No. 2. n. p., (Akad. Nauk Tadzhik.
SSR), 1958. [169 titles, pp. 91-112]

LANGUAGE, LITERATURE

*A. N. "LAKHUTI, ABDUL KASI," LITERATURNAIA
ENTSIKLOPEDIIA. Vol. 6. Moscow: Gosudarstvennoe
Slovarno-Entsiklopedicheskoe Izdatel'stvo
"Sovetskaia Entsiklopediia," 1932, 124-127 pp.
[Russ. text; Tajik, Russ., Persian titles, p. 127]

*Abdullaev, A. ADIB SABIR TIRMIZI (EPOKHA, ZHIZN' I
TVORCHESTVO). Dushanbe: "Donish," 1969, 199 pp.,
1810 copies. [Tajik text; ca.180 Tajik, Russ.,
Persian, W. Europ. languages, pub.: to 1966, pp.
191-197]

Abramov, P. Ia.; M. Kosimova. MIRZO TURSUN-ZADE--
LAUREAT STALINSKOI PREMII. BIBLIOGRAFICHESKII
UKAZATEL'. Stalinabad: Tadzhikgosizdat (Kom. po
Delam Kul't.-Prosvet. Uchrezhdenii pri Sovete
Ministrov Tadzhik. SSR. Gos. B-ka im. Firdousi).
1953, 64 pp., 2000 copies. [Tajik text; 248 Tajik
titles, pub.: 1932-1952]

*"AINI," LITERATURNAIA ENTSIKLOPEDIIA. Vol. 1. n. p.,
Izdatel'stvo Kommunisticheskoi Akademii, 1929,
59-60 pp. [Russ. text; Tajik, Russ. titles, p. 60]

Aini, Kh. S. BEDIL'; EGO POEMA "IRFON." Stalinabad:
Tadzhikgosizdat, 1956. [Russ. text; 66 Tajik, Uzbek,
Russ., Persian, other titles, pp. 123-126]

_____. BADRIDDIN KHILOLI. Stalinabad: (Akad.
Nauk Tadzhik. SSR. In-t Iazyka i Lit.), 1957.
[Russ. text; 133 Tajik, Sov. Asian, Russ., Europ.
titles, pp. 191-198]

Tajik: Language, Literature

* _____. "BIBLIOGRAFIIA," SMERT' ROSTOVSHCHIKA. Moscow: Sovetskii Pisatel', 1946, 318 pp. [Russ. text; 24 Russ. titles, pub.: 1929-1944, pp. 318-319]

Akhmadova, U. FORMA VSPOMOGATEL'NYKH GLAGOLOV V SOVREMENNOM TADZHIKSKOM IAZYKE. Dushanbe, 1961. [Tajik text; 63 titles, pp. 121-123]

_____. GLAGOL'NYE FORMY S "ISTODAN" V SOVREMENNOM TADZHIKSKOM IAZYKE. Dushanbe, 1961. [Tajik text; 63 Tajik, Russ. titles, pub.: 19th c - 1956, pp. 121-123]

*Amirkulov, S. DZHUNAIDULLO KHOZIK I EGO POEMA "IUSUF I ZULAIKHA." Dushanbe: "Irfon," 1967, 94 pp., 1000 copies. [Tajik text; 94 Tajik, Uzbek, Russ. titles, pub.: 1927-1962, pp. 91-93]

*Amonov, R. TADZHIKSKAIA NARODNAIA LIRIKA. Dushanbe: "Donish," 1968, 412 pp., 2560 copies. [Tajik text; ca.130 Tajik, Russ. titles, pub.: 1936-1964, pp. 407-411]

Azizkulov, Dzh.; Z. Mullodzhanova. BIBLIOGRAFIIA PROIZVEDENII S. AINI I LITERATURY O NEM DO KONTSA 1961 G. Dushanbe: Izd-vo AN Tadzhik.SSR, 1963, 326 pp., 500 copies. [Tajik text; 2623 Tajik, Uzbek, Russ. titles, pub.: to 1961]

*Babadzhanova, Zh. M. comp. NOSIRDZHON ASADOVICH MASUMI. Dushanbe: Izdatel'stvo "Donish," 1966, 57 pp., 575 copies. [Russ. text; Tajik, Russ. titles, pub.: 1934-1966]

Babaev, Iu. MIRZO TURSUN-ZADE. Dushanbe, 1961. [Tajik text; ca.350 Tajik, Sov. Asian, Russ., Europ. titles, pub.: 1932-1961, pp. 290-306]

Bakhriddinova, Kh. comp. "KRATKAIA BIBLIOGRAFIIA TADZHIKSKOI SOVETSKOI LITERATURY," OCHERK ISTORII TADZHIKSKOI SOVETSKOI LITERATURY. Part 1. Stalinabad: (AN Tadzhik.SSR. In-t Iazyka i Lit.), 1955. [Russ. text; ca.700 Tajik, Uzbek, Russ. titles, Sov. per., pp. 275-303]

_____. "KRATKAIA BIBLIOGRAFIIA TADZHIKSKOI SOVETSKOI LITERATURY," OCHERK ISTORII TADZHIKSKOI SOVETSKOI LITERATURY. Part 1. Stalinabad, 1956. [Tajik text; ca.700 Tajik, Uzbek, Russ. titles, Sov. per., pp. 283-311]

Tajik: Language, Literature

Bakoev, M. KHUSRAV DEKHLAVI I EGO POEMA "DUVAL'RONI I KHYZRKHAN." Stalinabad: (Tadzhik. Gos. Un-t im. Lenina. Otd. Vostokovedeniia i Pis'm. Naslediia AN Tadzhik. SSR), 1958. [Tajik text; ca.130 Tajik, Russ., other titles, pp. 127-132]

*[Bektemirova, Z.] PISATELI TADZHIKISTANA O VLADIMIRE IL'ICHE LENINE. UKAZ. LIT. Dushanbe: (Gos. Resp. B-ka im. Firdousi), 1970, 12 pp., 1000 copies. [Russ. text; 100 Russ. titles, pub.: 1957-1969, pp. 4-12]

Berdyeva, T. LEKSIKA I GRAMMATICHESKIE ELEMENTY ARABSKOGO IAZYKA V TADZHIKSKOM. Dushanbe: "Donish," 1968, 27 pp., 500 copies. [Russ. text; titles, per.: 1920s, pp. 23-27]

*Belan, V. G. TADZHIKISTAN V LITERATURE NA INOSTRANNYKH IAZYKAKH. 1961-1965 GG. Dushanbe: (Gos. Resp. B-ka Tadzh. SSR im. Firdousi), 1969, 193 pp., 1000 copies. [Russ. text; 920 various foreign titles, pub.: 1961-1965]

*Bertel's, E. "FIRDOUSI, ABUL-KASIM," LITERATURNAIA ENTSIKLOPEDIIA. Vol. 11. Moscow: Gosudarstvennoe Izdatel'stvo "Khudozhestvennaia Literatura," 1939, 753-757 pp. [Russ. text; Iranian, Russ., Europ. titles, p. 757]

Bertel's, E. E. "PROIZVEDENIIA ABDURRAKHMANA DZHAMI I RABOTY O NEM," IZBR. TRUDY. NAVOI I DZHAMI. Moscow, 1965. [Russ. text; 72 Tajik, other Soviet, Russ., Persian titles, pp. 470-473]

"BIBLIOGRAFICHESKII UKAZATEL' PO TADZHIKSKOI DRAMATURGII PERIODA 1929-1941 GG.--STAT'I I OTDEL'NYE RABOTY PO VOPROSAM TADZHIKSKOI DRAMATURGII I TEATRA," VOPROSY ISTORII TADZHIK. SOVETSKOI DRAMATURGII I TEATRA. No. 1. Stalinabad: (Akad. Nauk Tadzhik. SSR. In-t Iazyka i Lit.), 1957. [Russ. text; 114 Tajik, Russ. titles, pub.: 1929-1941, pp. 273-284]

Boboev, Iu. "BIBLIOGRAFIIA ASARHOI M. TURSUNZODA VA DAR BORAI EJODIYOTI U," MIRZO TURSUNZODA. HAYOT VA EJODIYOTI U. Dushanbe, 1961. [Tajik text; Tajik, Russ. titles, pp. 290-306]

Boldyrev, A. N.; R. Khozhima. "K TYSIACHELETIIU FIRDOUSI," BAROYII ADABIYYOTI SOTSIALISTI. No. 9/10, 1934, 12-20 pp. [Tajik text; titles pp. 18-20]

Tajik : Language, Literature

*Boldyrev, A. N. "NAUCHNOE NASLEDIE EVGENIIA EDUARDOVICHA BERTEL'SA," Bertel's, E. E. IZBRANNYE TRUDY. ISTORIIA PERSIDSKO-TADZHIKSKOI LITERATURY. Vol.1. Moscow: Izdatel'stvo Vostochnoi Literatury, 1960, 556 pp., 2400 copies. [Russ. text; Russ., Europ. survey, pp. 9-15]

*Braginskii, I. S. IZ ISTORII TADZHIKSKOI NARODNOI POEZII. ELEMENTY NARODNO-POETICHESKOGO TVORCHESTVA V PAMIATNIKAKH DREVNEI I SREDNEVEKOVOI PISMENNOSTI. Moscow: (Izdatel'stvo Akademii Nauk SSSR. Institut Vostokovedeniia. Institut Mirovoi Lit. im. Gor'kogo), 1956, 495 pp., 2500 copies. [Russ. text; 940 Tajik, Pers., Russ., Europ. titles, per.: ancient, medieval, up to 18th c., pub.: up to 1956, pp. 423-471]

Braginskii, I. SADRIDDIN AINI. MATERIALY K BIBLIOGRAFII I TVORCHESKOI KHARAKTERISTIKE. Stalinabad, 1948. [Russ. text; 39 Tajik, Uzbek, Russ. titles, pub.: 1926-1948, pp. 118-120]

Braginskii, I. S. "SPISOK OSNOVNYKH (RABOT) PROIZVEDENII S. AINI (NA TADZHIKSKOM IAZYKE). SADRIDDIN AINI. OCHERK ZHIZNI I TVORCHESTVA. TRUDY. Vol. 24. Stalinabad: (Akad. Nauk Tadzhik. SSR. In-t Iazyka i Lit.), 1954. [Russ. text; 283 Tajik titles, per.: 1896-1953, pp. 147-154]

*Chaikin, K. "FIRDOUSI" (FIRDAWSI). BOL'SHAIA SOVETSKAIA ENTSIKLOPEDIIA. Vol. 57. Moscow: Gosudarstvennyi Institut "Sovetskaia Entsiklopediia," (Ogiz RSFSR), 1936, 1st ed., 634-636 pp. [Russ. text; Tajik, Russ., Iranian, Europ. titles, pp. 635-636]

_____. "LITERATURY O FIRDOUSI I IZDANIIA EGO PROIZVEDENII," VOSTOK. SBORNIK VTOROI. Moscow-Leningrad, 1935. [Russ. text; Russ., Europ. titles, pub.: 1892-1934, pp. 465-466]

Cherniavskii, S. D. K ISTORII LENINABADSKOGO TEATRA IM. A. S. PUSHKINA. Dushanbe, 1962. [Russ. text; 67 Tajik, Russ. titles, pub.: 1938-1961, pp. 68-71]

Tajik: Language, Literature

Demidchik, L. N. "STAT'I I OTDEL'NYE RABOTY PO
VOPROSAM TADZHIKSKOI DRAMATURGII I TEATRA," VOPROSY
ISTORII TADZHIKSKOI SOVETSKOI DRAMATURGII I TEATRA.
Stalinabad, 1957. [Russ. text; 70 Tajik, Russ.
titles, pub.: 1929-1954, pp. 281-284]

Dodykhudoev, R. Kh. MATERIALY PO ISTORICHESKOI FONETIKE
SHUGNANSKOGO IAZYKA. Dushanbe, 1962. [Russ. text;
ca.40 survey titles, pp. 1-13]

*Dun, A. Z.; L. A. Remizova. RAKHIM DZHALIL NA STRANITSAKH
LENINABADSKOI PECHATI. BIBLIOGR. UKAZ. Leninabad:
(Leninabad. Mezhraionnaia B-ka im. Asiri. Leninabad:
Gos. Ped. In-t im. Kirova), 1969, 47 pp., 1500 copies.
[Tajik, Russ. text; 333 Tajik, Russ. titles]

Dzhamalov, K. SADRIDDIN AINI. BIBLIOGRAFICHESKII
UKAZATEL'. Stalinabad: (Gos. Resp. B-ka im. Firdousi),
1956, 40 pp., 700 copies. [Tajik text; 247 Tajik
titles]

Dzhuraev, R.; A. Iunusov. DADADZHAN TADZHIEVICH
TADZHIEV. Dushanbe: (Tadzhik. Gos. Un-t im. Lenina),
1965, 27 pp., 500 copies. [Russ. text; 51 titles,
pub.: 1947-1965]

Edel'man, D. I. "K SOVREMENNOMU SOSTOIANIIU IZUCHENIIA
PAMIRSKIKH IAZYKOV," IZVESTIIA AKADEMII NAUK
TADZHIKSKOI SSR. OTDELENIE OBSHCHESTVENNYKH NAUK.
(Dushanbe) No. 1(36). 1964. [Russ. text; ca.70 survey
Russ., Europ. titles, pub.: 19th c.-1963, pp. 70-78]

Esenov, Kh. USLOVNYE I USTUPITEL'NYE PRIDATOCHNYE
PREDLOZHENIIA V SOVREMENNOM KAZAKHSKOM IAZYKE. Alma
Ata, 1969. [Kazakh text; ca.200 titles, pp. 184-192]

*Firdousi. SHAKHNAME. Vol. 1. Moscow: Izdatel'stvo
Akademii Nauk SSSR, 1957, 675 pp., 16,000 copies.
[Russ. text; ca.140 Russ., Europ. titles, pub.: up to
1956, pp. 645-652]

*Freiman, A. "TADZHIKSKII IAZYK," BOL'SHAIA SOVETSKAIA
ENTSIKLOPEDIIA. Vol. 53. 1946, 1st ed., pp. 450-451.
[Russ. text; Russ., German titles, p. 451]

Freitag, K. "BIBLIOGRAFIIA K KHAFEZU," VOSTOK.
SBORNIK VTOROI. Moscow-Leningrad, 1935. [Russ. text;
Europ., Mid. East. titles, pp. 467-469]

Tajik: Language, Literature

*Gaffarov, R. IAZYK I STIL' RAKHIMA DZHALILA. (NA MATERIALE ROMANA "PULAT I GUL'RU"). Dushanbe: "Donish," 1966 (Vyp. Dan. 1967), 225 pp., 1550 copies. [Tajik text; 158 Tajik, Russ. titles, pub.: 1929-1963]

Iunusov, A. AKHMAD DONISH. (UKAZATEL' LITERATURY). Dushanbe: (Gos. Resp. B-ka Tadzhik. SSR im. Firdousi), 1960, 27 pp., 1500 copies. [Tajik, Russ. text; 123 Tajik Russ. titles, pub.: 1871, 1926-1960]

Iusupov, K. S. ULUG-ZODA I EGO AVTOBIOGRAFICHESKAIA POVEST' "UTRO NASHEI ZHIZNI." Dushanbe, 1968. [Tajik text; 208 titles, pp. 110-117]

*Kadyrov, Rashid. DOREVOLIUTSIONNYI OBRIADOVYI FOL'KLOR TADZHIKOV BASSEINA KASHKA-DAR'I. Dushanbe: (Akademiyai Fanhoi RSS Tojikiston. Institut i Ta"rikhi Ba Nomi Ahmadi Donish), 1963, 153 pp., 1600 copies. [Tajik text; 82 Tajik, Uzbek, Russ. titles, pp. 149-152]

*Kolontarov, Ia. I. TADZHIKSKIE POSLOVITSY I POGOVORKI V ANALOGII S RUSSKIMI. Dushanbe: Izdatel'stvo "Irfon," 1965, 535 pp., 9000 copies. [Tajik, Russ. text; 70 Tajik, Russ. titles, pp. 531-534]

*(Kamoliddinov, B.) "UKAZATEL' PROIZVEDENII KHAKIMA KARIMA.--PEREVODY KHUDOZHESTVENNYKH PROIZVEDENII, NAUCHNYKH STATEI I UCHEBNIKOV," KHAKIM KARIM. Dushanbe: "Irfon," 1965, 81 pp. [Tajik text; 131 Tajik, Uzbek, Russ. titles, pub.: 1930-1965, pp. 71-81]

*Karneev, S. B. "PERSIDSKAIA POEZIIA. MATERIALY K BIBLIOGRAFII RUSSKIKH PEREVODOV," BIBLIOGRAFIIA VOSTOKA. No. 10. (Moscow-Leningrad) (1936) 1937, 208 pp. [Russ. text; 111 Russ. titles, pub.: 17th c.- 1934, pp. 101-110]

Khadi-Zade, R. "ISTOCHNIKI K IZUCHENIIU TADZHIKSKOI LITERATURY VTOROI POLOVINY XIX VEKA," (AKAD. NAUK TADZHIK. SSR. IN-T IAZYKA I LIT. TRUDY. Vol. 56). Stalinabad, 1956. [Russ. text; 7 lists, appendix, Tajik, Russ. titles, per.: last half of 19th c., pp. 117-131]

*_____. TADZHIKSKAIA LITERATURA VTOROI POLOVINY XIX VEKA. Part 1. Dushanbe: "Donish," 1968, 295 pp., 1600 copies. [Tajik text; 395 Tajik titles, per.: 1850-1900, pp. 263-273]

Tajik: Language, Literature

*Khaiiam, Omar. TRAKTATY. (PAMIATNIKI LITERATURY NARODOV VOSTOKA. TEKSTY. MALAIA SERIIA, III). Moscow: Izdatel'stvo Vostochnoi Literatury, 1961, 338 + 225 pp., 3200 copies. [Russ. text; ca.125 Russ., Europ. titles, pp. 334-338]

Khamrakulov, Kh. TADZHIKSKIE GOVORY BAISUNSKOGO RAIONA UZBEKSKOI SSR. Dushanbe, 1961. [Tajik text; 88 Tajik, Russ. titles, pp. 269-272]

*Khashimova, Z. "KRATKAIA BIBLIOGRAFIIA TRUDOV O TADZHIKSKOI SOVETSKOI LITERATURE," OCHERK ISTORII TADZHIKSKOI SOVETSKOI LITERATURY. Moscow: Izdatel'stvo Akademii Nauk SSR. (In-t Mirovoi Lit. im. Gor'kogo. In-t Iazyka i Lit. im. Rudaki), 1961, 479 pp., 2200 copies. [Russ. text; ca.280 Tajik, Russ. titles, Sov. per., pp. 466-478]

Khuseinov, Kh. SLOZHNOPODCHINENYE PREDLOZHENIIA S VREMENNYMI PRIDATOCHNYMI V SOVREMENNOM TADZHIKSKOM LITERATURNOM IAZYKE. [Dushanbe] 1960. [Tajik text; 111 Tajik, Russ., Europ. titles, pub.: 19th c.- 1959, pp. 111-117]

Kraulin', Karl. TADZHIKSKAIA LITERATURA. Riga: (Fak. Istorii i Filologii Latv. Gos. Un-ta), 1966, 174 pp., 400 copies. [Russ. text; Latvian titles, pp. 169-172]

*Kulmatov, N. A. ETICHESKIE VZGLIADY SAADI. Dushanbe: (AN Tadzh.SSR. Otd. Filosofii), 1968, 129 pp., 2135 copies. [Russ. text; titles, pp. 117-128]

*Lakhuti, Abdul'kasim. SOBRANIE SOCHINENII V SHESTI TOMAKH. Vol. 6. Dushanbe: Nashriyoti Davlatii Tojikiston, 1963, 335 pp., 3000 copies. [Tajik text; Tajik, Uzbek, Russ., Mid-East titles, pp. 330-331]

Levshina, I. S. TADZHIKSKIE SOVETSKIE PROZAIKI. KRITIKO-BIBLIOGRAFICHESKIE OCHERKI. Stalinabad: Gosudarstvennaia Respublikanskaia Biblioteka Tadzhikskoi SSR imeni Firdousi), 1957, 92 pp. [Tajik text; 4 lists Tajik, Russ. titles, pub.: 1927-1955]

_____. TADZHIKSKIE SOVETSKIE PROZAIKI. KRITIKO-BIBLIOGRAFICHESKIE OCHERKI. Stalinabad: (Gosudarstvennaia Respublikanskaia Biblioteka Tadzhikskoi SSR imeni Firdousi), 1958, 90 pp. [Russ. text; 4 lists Tajik, Russ. titles, pub.: 1927-1955]

Tajik: Language, Literature

*Melekh, N. A. "TADZHIKSKIE GOVORY I IKH RASPROSTRANENIE," VESTNIK LENINGRADSKOGO UNIVERSITETA. No. 14. SERIIA ISTORII, IAZYKA I LITERATURY. No. 3. 1960, pp. 149-151. [Russ. text; 18 Russ. titles, pub.: 1928-1956, pp. 150-151]

Miliband, S. L.; L. B. Tursunova. comp. IOSIF SAMUILOVICH BRAGINSKII. (AKAD. NAUK. TADZH. SSR. TSENTR. NAUCH. B-KA: MATERIALY K BIOBIBLIOGRAFII UCHENYKH TADZH. No. 8). Dushanbe, 1966, 94 pp., 570 copies. [Russ. text; 345 Tajik, Russ., Europ. titles, pub.: 1920-1966]

MIRSAID MIRSHAKAR. UKAZATEL' LITERATURY. Dushanbe: (Gos. Resp. B-ka Tadzhikskoi SSR im. Firdousi. Spravochno-Bibliograficheskii Otdel.), 1961, 67 pp., 2000 copies. [Russ. text; ca.292 Sov. Asian, Russ. titles, pub.: 1934-1960]

Mirzo-Zade, Kh. MATERIALY IZ ISTORII TADZHIKSKOI LITERATURY. Dushanbe, 1962. [Tajik text; 36 titles, pp. 136-137]

Mirzoev, A. BINOI. Stalinabad: (Akad. Nauk. Tadzhik. SSR. In-t Iazyka i Lit.), 1957. [Tajik text; 259 titles, pp. 470-486]

*Mirzoev, A. M. RUDAKI. ZHIZN' I TVORCHESTVO. Moscow: "Nauka," 1968, 318 pp., 8000 copies. [Russ. text; Tajik, Russ., Western titles, pp. 295-302]

*Mirzoev, Abdulghani. ABU ABDULLO RUDAKI. Stalinabad: Nashriyati Davlati Tajikistan. (Akad. Nauk Tadzhik. SSR. Otd. Vostokovedeniia i Lit. Pamiatnikov), 1958, 439 pp., 5000 copies. [Tajik text; ca.150 Tajik, Sov. Asian, Arab, Russ. titles, per.: 19th c., pp. 425-437]

Nabieva, R. comp. MIRSAID MIRSHAKAR. BIBLIOGR. UKAZATEL'. Dushanbe: (Gos. Resp. B-ka im. Firdousi), 1960, 40 pp., 2000 copies. [Tajik text; 348 titles, pub.: 1934-1958]

*Negmat-Zade, T. VOZEKH (TADZH. POET XIX V.) Dushanbe: "Irfon," 1967, 229 pp., 1000 copies. [Tajik text; 162 Tajik, Russ. titles, per.: 19th c., pp. 220-226]

Niiazmukhammedova, B.; M. Ismatullaeva, eds. GRAMMATIKA TADZHIKSKOGO IAZYKA. SINTAKSIS. Dushanbe, 1963. [Tajik text; ca.200 Tajik, Russ. titles, pub.: 19th c.-1962, pp. 171-179]

Tajik : Language, Literature

*Otakhonova, Khursheda. RAKHIM DZHALIL I EGO TVORCHESTVO.
Dushanbe: (Akademiyai Fanhoi RSS Tojikiston. Institut
Zabon Va Adabiyoti Ba Nomi Rudaki), 1962, 159 pp.,
900 copies. [Tajik text; 11 lists Tajik, Russ.
titles, pub.: 1931-1961, pp. 148-157]

*Nurdzhanov, N. TADZHIKSKII TEATR. OCHERK ISTORII.
Moscow: Izdatel'stvo "Iskusstvo," 1968, 262 pp.,
3000 copies. [Russ. text; 59 Tajik, Russ. titles,
pp. 251-253]

*Pakhalina, T. N. PAMIRSKIE IAZYKI. Moscow: "Nauka,"
1969, 163 pp., 1400 copies. [Russ. text; 65 Russ.,
Eng., Ger., Fr. titles, pub.: 1866-1967, pp. 156-160]

*"PAMIRSKIE IAZYKI," BOL'SHAIA SOVETSKAIA ENTSIKLOPEDIIA.
Vol. 44. Moscow: Gosudarstvennyi Institut "Sovetskaia
Entsiklopediia," (Ogiz RSFSR), 1939, 1st ed., 34-36 pp.
[Russ. text; Russ., Iranian, Europ. titles, pp. 35-36]

Petrushkov, V. POETIKA K. M. STANIUKOVICHA-MARINISTA.
(OSOBENNOSTI KHUDOZH. IZOBRAZITEL'NOSTI I STILIA.)
Dushanbe: "Irfon," 1966, 156 pp., 1000 copies.
[Russ. text; titles, pp. 143-155]

*Ponomareva, Z. V.; Z. A. Chernykh. TADZHIKSKAIA
LITERATURA. REKOMENDATEL'NYI UKAZATEL'. Moscow:
Gosudarstvennaia Ordena Lenina Biblioteka SSSR imeni
V. I. Lenina), 1961, 148 pp., 2150 copies. [Russ. text;
14 Tajik, Russ. titles, pub.: pre- and post-1917]

*Pulatova Sh. PIS'MA MIRZO GALIBA NA IAZYKE URDU.
Dushanbe: "Donish," 1966, 138 pp., 1110 copies.
[Tajik text; Tajik, Urdu, Russ., Eng. titles, pp. 125-
127, pub.: 1865-1961]

*Radzhabov, L. Sh. OSNOVNYE PRINTSIPY KHIMICHESKOI
TERMINOLOGII NA TADZHIKSKOM IAZYKE. Dushanbe:
Izdatel'stvo "Donish," 1967, 105 pp., 1000 copies.
[Russ. text; 70 Russ. titles, pp. 102-104]

Radzhabov, M. MIROVOZZRENIE UBAIDA ZOKONI. Stalinabad:
(Akad. Nauk Tadzhik. SSR. Otd. Filosofii), 1958.
[Russ. text; 44 Tajik, Russ., other titles, pp. 111-113]

*Rastogueva, V. S. OCHERKI PO TADZHIKSKOI DIALEKTOLOGII.
No. 1. VARZOBSKII GOVOR TADZHIKSKOGO IAZYKA.
Moscow: Izdatel'stvo Akademii Nauk SSSR, 1952, 206 pp.,
1500 copies. [Russ. text; ca.40 survey Tajik, Russ.
titles, pub.: 1861-1951, pp. 9-19]

Tajik: Language, Literature

*Rastorgueva, V. S. OPYT SRAVNITEL'NOGO IZUCHENIIA TADZHIKSKIKH GOVOROV. Moscow: Izdatel'stvo "Nauka," 1964, 188 pp., 1000 copies. [Russ. text; ca.60 Tajik, Russ. titles, pub.: 1901-1963, pp. 3-10; 183-184]

* _____.; A. A. Kerimova. SISTEMA TADZHIKSKOGO GLAGOLA. Moscow: Izdatel'stvo "Nauka," 1964, 291 pp., 1200 copies. [Russ. text; ca.50 Tajik, Russ. titles, survey, pub.: 1861-1960, pp. 3-6]

*Rustamov, Sh. SLOZHNYE PREDLOZHENIIA S PRIDATOCHNYMI PRICHINAMI V SOVREMENNOM TADZHIKSKOM IAZYKE. Dushanbe: "Donish," 1968, 124 pp., 2000 copies. [Tajik text; 77 Tajik, Russ. titles, pub.: 1847-1966, pp. 111-114]

Semenova, S. F. SADRIDDIN AINI. (1878-1954). KRATKII BIBLIOGRAFICHESKII UKAZATEL'. L'vov: (M-vo Kul'tury USSR. L'vovskaia Gos. Nauch. B-ka), 1968, 11 pp., 500 copies. [Ukrainian text]

Sharofov, R. comp. OBRAZ LENINA V KHUDOZHESTVENNOI LITERATURE. UKAZATEL' LITERATURY. Dushanbe: "Irfon," 1965, 49 pp., 2000 copies. [Tajik text; ca.400 titles]

*Sharofov, Rakhimdzan. comp. TADZHIKSKAIA KHUDOZHESTVENNAIA LITERATURA I KRITIKA. BIBLIOGRAFIIA. Dushanbe: Nashriyati "Irfon," 1967, 160 pp., 2000 copies. [Tajik text; 2113 Tajik titles, pub.: 1955-1960]

Sirus, B. I. RIFMA V TADZHIKSKOI POEZII. TRUDY. IN-T IAZYKA I LITERATURY. Vol. 18. Stalinabad:(AN Tadzhikskoi SSR), 1953. [Russ. text; 50 Tajik, Russ. titles, pp. 83-84]

*Sirus, Bakhram. TRAKTAT OB ARUZE. Dushanbe: Nashriyoti Davlatii Tojikiston, 1963, 287 pp., 2000 copies. [Tajik text; 65 Tajik, Russ., Persian, Europ. titles, pp. 282-284]

*Sokolova, V. S. FONETIKA TADZHIKSKOGO IAZYKA. Moscow-Leningrad: Izdatel'stvo Akademii Nauk SSSR, 1949, 167 pp., 1200 copies. [Russ. text; Russ., Europ. titles, pp. 5-15]

Tabarov, S. PAIRAV SULAIMONI. (OCHERKI HAYOT VA EJODIYOT). Dushanbe, 1962. [Tajik text; 155 Tajik, Russ., Europ. titles, pp. 388-393]

Tajik: Language, Literature

*"TADZHIKSKII IAZYK," BOL'SHAIA SOVETSKAIA ENTSIKLOPEDIIA. Vol. 41, 1956, 2nd ed., 500-501 pp. [Russ. text and titles, p. 501]

*"TADZHIKSKII IAZYK," LITERATURNAIA ENTSIKLOPEDIIA. Vol. 11. Moscow: Gosudarstvennoe Izdatel'stvo "Khudozhestvennaia Literatura," 1939, 1st ed., 173-174 pp. [Russ. text; Tajik, Russ., Europ. titles, p. 174]

Tal'man, R. O.; M. M. Iavich. MIRZO TURSUN-ZADE--LAUREAT STALINSKOI PREMII. BIBLIOGRAFICHESKII UKAZATEL'. Stalinabad: Tadzhikgosizdat, 1953, 68 pp. 3000 copies. [Russ. text; ca.260, 420 Russ. titles, pub.: up to 1953]

_____.; A. Iunusov. RUDAKI. (UKAZATEL' LITERATURY). Dushanbe: (Gos. Resp. B-ka im. Firdousi. Otd. Vostokovedeniia i Pis'm. Naslediia AN Tadzhik. SSR), 1965, 218 pp., 2000 copies. [Tajik text; 1254 Tajik, Sov. Asian, Russ. titles, pub.: up to 1964]

_____. SADRIDDIN AINI. (1878-1954). BIBLIOGRAFICHESKII UKAZATEL'. Stalinabad: (Gosudarstvennaia Respublikanskaia Biblioteka imeni Firdousi. Otdelenie Kraevedeniia), 1956, 49 pp., 2000 copies. [Russ. text; ca.341 Russ. titles, pub.: 1939-1955]

*Tilavov, Bozor. POETIKA TADZHIKSKIKH NARODNYKH POSLOVITS I POGOVOROK. Dushanbe: "Donish," 1967, 123 pp., 2375 copies. [Russ. text; ca.320 Tajik, Russ. Arab, Western titles, pp. 95-107]

"UKAZATEL' LITERATURY PO [TADZHIKSKOI] DIALEKTOLOGII ZA DESIAT' LET. (1959-1969)," VOPR. TADZH. DIALEKTOLOGII. No. 1. 1970. [Tajik text; ca.130 Tajik, Russ. titles, pub.: 1959-1969, pp. 275-289]

"UKAZATEL' PROIZVEDENII RAKHIMA DZHALILA," Otakhonov, Kh. RAKHIM DZHALIL I EGO TVORCHESTVO. Dushanbe, 1962. [Tajik text; 170 titles, pub.: 1931-1961, pp. 148-152]

Usman, T. DVADTSAT' TRI POETESSY. Stalinabad: Tadzhikgosizdat, 1957, [Tajik text; 42 titles, pp. 122-124]

_____. POETESSA MAKHASTI. Dushanbe, 1963. [Tajik text; 46 titles, per.: 12th c., pp. 117-119]

Tajik: Language, Literature

*Veksler, L. F. "ABUL'-KASIM FIRDOUSI (BIBLIOGRAFIIA),"
BIBLIOGRAFIIA VOSTOKA. No. 8/9. Moscow-Leningrad,
(1935) 1936. [Russ. text; 114 Russ. titles, pp. 61-68]

PHILOSOPHY, RELIGION

*Ashurova, G. FILOSOFSKIE VZGLIADY NOSIRI KHISRAVA.
Dushanbe: (Akademiia Nauk Tadzhikskoi SSR. Otdel
Filosofii), 1965, 113 pp., 1200 copies. [Russ.
text; ca.77 Russ. titles, pp. 110-112]

*Boltaev, M. N. VOPROSY GNOSEOLOGII I LOGIKI V
PROIZVEDENIIAKH IBN-SINY I EGO SHKOLY. Dushanbe:
Izdatel'stvo "Irfon," 1965, 600 pp., 1000 copies.
[Russ. text; ca.250 Azeri, Uzbek, Tajik, Persian,Turk.,
Europ., Russ. titles, pp. 589-598]

*Dinorshoev, M. FILOSOFIIA NASIRIDDINA TUSI. Dushanbe:
Izdatel'stvo "Donish," 1968, 157 pp., 1400 copies.
[Russ. text and titles, pp. 153-156]

Molchanova, L. S.; V. D. Kachalo. comp. V
POMOSHCH' NAUCHNO-ATEISTICHESKOI RABOTE MASSOVYKH
BIBLIOTEK. SBORNIK METOD. I BIBLIOGR. MATERIALOV.
Dushanbe, 1961, 93 pp., 2000 copies. [Russ. text;
ca.650 titles, Sov. per.]

*Radzhabov, M. ABDURAKHMAN DZHAMI I TADZHIKSKAIA
FILOSOFIIA XV VEKA. Dushanbe: Izdatel'stvo "Irfon,"
1968, 317 pp., 3000 copies. [Russ. text; ca.230
Cent. Asian, Arab, Russ., Europ. titles, per.: 15th c.,
pp. 303-314]

Tajik

POLITICAL SCIENCE, LAW

Bazarov, A. B.; M. E. Shabinskii. PRAVOVYE OSNOVY
SVOBODY SOVESTI V TADZHIKSKOI SSR. Dushanbe: "Irfon,"
1968, 81 pp., 1000 copies. [Russ. text; titles at
end of book]

Isamutdinova N.; R. Sharopov. K 40-LETIIU [SOROKALETIIU]
LENINSKOGO KOMSOMOLA. [Dushanbe] (Kitobkhonai Davl.
Resp. Ba Nomi Firdavsi), 1958, 115 pp. [Tajik text;
Tajik titles, per.: 1917-1957]

Khamrakulov, R. VOPROSY TEORII I PRAKTIKI KODIFIKATSII
UGOLOVNOGO ZAKONODATEL'STVA SOIUZNOI RESPUBLIKI (PO
MATERIALAM TADZHIKSKOI SSR), 1962. [Russ. text and
titles, pp. 152-159]

*Makashov, A. V. PARTIINAIA ORGANIZATSIIA TADZHIKISTANA
V 1924-1926 GODAKH. BOR'BA PARTIINOI ORGANIZATSII
TADZHIKISTANA ZA LIKVIDATSIIU BASMACHESKOI
KONTRREVOLIUTSII I UKREPLENIE SOVETSKOI VLASTI V
RESPUBLIKE. Dushanbe: Tadzhikgosizdat, 1964, 207 pp.,
2000 copies. [Russ. text; ca.100 Tajik, Russ.
titles, per.: 1924-1926, pp. 202-206]

Mukhamedov, Kh. BOR'BA PARIINOI ORGANIZATSII
TADZHIKISTANA ZA UKREPLENIE KOLKHOZOV (1933-1935 GG.).
Dushanbe, 1963. [Russ. text; ca.150 Tajik, Russ.
titles, per.: 1933-1935, pub.: 1933-1962, pp. 109-118]

Nazarshoev, M. RAZVERNUTOE STROITEL'STVO
KOMMUNISTICHESKOGO OBSHCHESTVA I DAL'NEISHEE SBLIZHENIE
SOTSIALISTICHESKIKH NATSII. Dushanbe, 1962. [Russ.
text; ca.180 titles, pp. 134-143]

Nikolaeva, M. KOMMUNISTICHESKAIA PARTIIA TADZHIKISTANA.
ANNOT. UKAZATEL' LITERATURY. Dushanbe: (Gos. Resp.
B-ka. Tadzhik. SSR im. Firdousi), 1962, 330 pp.,
1500 copies. [Russ. text; [1076] 2067 Russ. titles,
pub.: up to 1961]

Tajik: Political Science, Law

Nikolaeva, M. UCHASTNIKI GRAZHDANSKOI VOINY I BOR'BY ZA LIKVIDATSIIU BASMACHESTVA V TADZHIKISTANE (UKAZATEL' LITERATURY). Stalinabad: (Gosudarstvennaia Respublikanskaia Biblioteka Tadzhikskoi SSR imeni Firdousi), 1957, 32 pp., 2000 copies. [Russ. text; 118 Russ. titles, pub.: from 1930's]

PIONERSKII LAGER'. [SBORNIK] Stalinabad: Tadzhikgosizdat, 1954, 276 pp. [Tajik text; Tajik titles, 4 lists]

Ponomareva, Z.; E. Rudenko. [SOROK] 40 LET LENINSKOMU KOMSOMOLU (1918-1958 GG.) (SBORNIK METODICHESKIKH I BIBLIOGRAFICHESKIKH MATERIALOV). Dushanbe: (Gosudarstvennaia Respublikanskaia Biblioteka imeni Firdousi), 1958, 42 pp. [Russ. text and titles, pub.: mainly 1957-1958, per.: 1918-1958]

_____.; N. Sadullaeva. VELIKAIA OKTIABR'SKAIA SOTSIALISTICHESKAIA REVOLIUTSIIA I RASTSVET SOVETSKOGO TADZHIKISTANA (ANNOTIROVANNYI UKAZATEL' LITERATURY). Stalinabad: (Gosudarstvennaia Respublikanskaia Biblioteka Tadzhikiskoi SSR imeni Firdousi. Otdel Spravochno-Bibliograficheskoi Raboty), 1957, 80 pp. [Russ. text; 220 Russ. titles, per.: 1917-1957, pub.: 1940s-1950s]

Radzhabov, S. TADZHIKSKAIA SSR--SUVERENNOE SOVETSKOE GOSUDARSTVO. Stalinabad: Tadzhikgosizdat, 1957. [Russ. text; ca.175 titles, Sov. per., pp. 340-347]

* _____. TORZHESTVO VSEPOBEZHDAIUSHCHIKH IDEI NAUCHNOGO KOMMUNIZMA. Dushanbe: (O-vo "Znanie" Tadzh. SSR) "Donish," 1968, 81 pp., 3000 copies. [Tajik text; 18 Tajik titles, p. 81]

Serebrennikov, L. F.; Iu. T. Petrishchev. MARKSIZM-LENINIZM O STANOVLENII SOTSIALISTICHESKOGO GOSUDARSTVA. Dushanbe: (O-vo "Znanie" Tadzh. SSR), 1968, 38 pp., 5000 copies. [Russ. text; 52 Tajik titles, pp. 35-37]

SOLI ASHURKHODZHAEVICH RADZHABOV. MATERIALY K BIBLIOGRAFII UCHENYKH TADZHIKISTANA. No. 2. (Tsentr. Nauch. B-ka AN Tadzhik. SSR). Dushanbe, 1962, 88 pp., 500 copies. [Russ. text; 241 Tajik, Uzbek, Russ., Europ. titles, per.: 1932-1962]

Tal'man, R.; N. Razheva; S. Ikramova. KRASNAIA ARMIIA NA STRAZHE SOTSIALISTICHESKOI RODINY. Stalinabad: (Bibliotekai Umumii Davlati), 1941, 22 pp. [Tajik text; Tajik, Russ., titles, per.: WW II]

Tajik

SOCIAL ORGANIZATION

*Kisliakov, N. A. SLEDY PERVOBYTNOGO KOMMUNIZMA U
GORNYKH TADZHIKOV VAKHIO-BOLO. (AN SSSR. TRUDY
INSTITUTA ANTROPOLOGII, ETNOGRAFII I ARKHEOLOGII.
Vol. 10. ETNOGRAFICHESKAIA SERIIA NO. 2).
Moscow-Leningrad: Izdatel'stvo Akademii Nauk SSSR,
1936. [Russ. text; 89 Russ., Europ. titles, per.:
19th - 20th c., pp. 157-159]

*Nevskii, V. A. MEDITSINA V TADZHIKISTANE:
BIBLIOGRAFICHESKII UKAZATEL' LITERATURY PO ISTORII I
SOVREMENNOMU SOSTOIANIIU MEDITSINY I ZDRAVOOKHRANENIIA
V TADZHIKSKOI SSR. Stalinabad: Ministerstvo
Zdravookhraneniia Tadzhikskoi SSR. Nauchnaia
Meditsinskaia Biblioteka, 1959, 381 pp., 1100 copies.
[Russ. text; 4329 Russ., French, Eng. titles,
pp. 7-343]

_____. MEDITSINA V TADZHIKISTANE. DOPOLNENIE I
BIBLIOGR. UKAZATEL'. LITERATURA SO 2-I POLOVINY
1957 G. DO 2-I POLOVINY 1961 G. Dushanbe: Gos.
Nauch. Med. B-ka Tadzh. SSR, 1962, 198 pp. [Russ.
text; titles pub.: 1957-1961]

28 TURKMEN

GENERAL

ADRES-SPRAVOCHNIK PO ZAKASPIISKII OBLASTI NA 1915 G.
Ashkhabad, 1915. [Russ. text; 134 titles, per.: 1915]

Akieva, A. KNIZHNAIA PALATA TURKM. SSR. K 35-LETIIU
SO DNIA ORGANIZATSII. Ashkhabad: (Gos. Knizhnaia
Palata Turkm. SSR), 1961 [Turkmen, Russ. text; 32
titles, per.: 1925-1960, pp. 36-38]

*Akieva, Amangul'. KNIZHNOI PALATE TURKMENSKOI SSR. 40
LET. Ashkhabad: Izdatel'stvo "Turkmenistan," 1966,
31 pp., 500 copies. [Turkmen text; Turkmen, Russ.
titles, per.: 1924-1964, pp. 15-17; 29-31]

"BIBLIOGRAFICHESKII UKAZATEL' STATEI
NAUCHNOISSLEDOVATEL'SKOGO I OPYTNOGO KHARAKTERA,
POMESHCHENNYKH V 'TURKMENSKOI ISKRE'," TURKMENOVEDENIE.
No. 7/9. 1931. [Russ. text; 29 titles, pub.:
Aug. - Oct. 1931, pp. 109-112]

Burov, N. "GOD RABOTY TURKMENSKOI KNIZHNOI PALATY,"
BIBLIOGRAFIIA V SSSR I KNIZHNYE PALATY. SBORNIK.
Khar'kov, 1928. [Turkmen, Russ. text; 69 titles,
pub.: 1926-1927, pp. 173-184]

Dolgova, M. A.; A. Pirliev; K. P. Shelevaia. comps.
PERIODICHESKIE IZDANIIA TURKMENSKOI SSR. 1920-1958.
BIBLIOGR. UKAZATEL'. Ashkhabad: Turkmengosizdat,
1962, 73 pp., 500 copies. [Turkmen, Russ. text;
271 titles, pub.: 1920-1958]

[Iakubson, Ia.] "KNIGA V TURKMENII," TURKMENOVEDENIE.
No. 10/11. 1928. Turkmen, Russ. text; 51 titles,
per.: 1927, pp. 97-98]

KATALOG GAZET I ZHURNALOV TURKMENSKOI SSR....NA 1967
GOD. Ashkhabad: "Soiuzpechat'," 1966, 30 pp.,
10000 copies. [Russ. text; Turkmen, Russ. titles]

KATALOG KNIG, VYPUSHCHENNYKH IZDATEL'STVOM AKADEMII NAUK
TURKMENSKOI SSR... ...V 1949-1953 G.G. ...V (1953-
1956 G. G.). Ashkhabad: Izdatel'stvo Akademii Nauk
Turkmenskoi SSR, 1953, 1956; (1953) 21 pp., (1956)
16 pp., 1000 copies. [Russ. text; pub.: 1949-1956]

Turkmen: General

KNIZHNAIA I ZHURNALNAIA LETOPIS'. No. 3/4, July-Dec., 1941. [Turkmen, Russ. text; titles, pub.: 1940]

KNIZHNAIA LETOPIS'. No. 3/4. Askhabad: (Knizhnaia Palata Turkmenskoi SSR), July-Dec., ca.1939. [Turkmen, Russ. text; titles, pub.: 1939]

KNIZHNAIA LETOPIS'. ORGAN GOS. BIBLIOGRAFII. TURKM. SSR. 1941-1945. Ashkhabad: (Gos. Kn. Palata Turkm. SSR), 1951, 500 copies. [Turkmen text; 561 Turkmen titles, pub.: 1941-1945]

KNIZHNAIA LETOPIS'. 1946-1950. Ashkhabad: (Knizhnaia Palata Turkm. SSR), 1955, 132 pp., 500 copies. [Turkmen, Russ. text; 1013 titles, pub.: 1946-1950]

*Kudelina, V. A.; F. Sh. Abramova, (Comp.); D. Seitniiazov, ed. TURKMENSKAIA SSR--IARKII MAIAK SOTSIALIZMA I KOMMUNIZMA NA VOSTOKE. BIBLIOGRAFICHESKII UKAZATEL' LITERATURY. Ashkhabad: (Turkmenskaia Gosudarstvennaia Respublikanskaia Biblioteka im. Karla Marksa), 1964, 42 pp., 1500 copies. [Russ. text; ca.400 Russ. titles, Sov. per.]

*Kuvadova, M.; V. Panova; A. Pirliev. comp. KNIGA SOVETSKOGO TURKMENISTANA. SVODNAIA BIBLIOGRAFIIA. Book 1, 1920-1960. Ashkhabad: Izdatel'stvo "Turkmenistan," 1965, 707 pp., 1000 copies. [Turkmen text; 7020 Turkmen, Russ. titles, pub.: 1920-1960]

* _____. comp. KNIGA SOVETSKOGO TURKMENISTANA. SVODNAIA BIBLIOGRAFIIA. 1920-1960. Book 2, VSPOMOGATEL'NYE UKAZATELI. Ashkhabad: (Gos. Kom. Soveta Ministrov Turkm. SSR po Pechati. Gos. Knizhnaia Palata Turkm. SSR), 93 pp., 500 copies. [Turkmen, Russ. text and titles, pub.: 1920-1960]

LETOPIS' GAZETNYKH STATEI. (GAZET MAKALALARYNYN LETOPISI]. No. 3/4, Jan.-Dec. 1939. Ashkabad: (Knizhnaia Palata Turkmenskoi SSR), 1941. [Turkmen, Russ. text; titles, pub.: 1939]

LETOPIS' GAZETNYKH STATEI. Nos. 1, 3/4: 1940. Ashkhabad: (Knizhnaia Palata Turkmenskoi SSR), 1941. [Russ. text; titles, pub.: 1940]

LETOPIS' GAZETNYKH STATEI. (GAZET MAKALALARYNYN LETOPISI). 1941. Ashkhabad: 1941. [Turkmen text; titles, pub.: 1941]

Turkmen: General

LETOPIS' PECHATI TURKMENISTANA. TURKMENSKIE KNIGI NA STAROM ALFAVITE POSTUPIVSHIE V KNIZHNUIU PALATU DO 30/XII - 1928 G. Ashkhabad, 1930, 176 pp. [Turkmen text; 313 titles, pub.: 1920-1928]

LETOPIS' PECHATI TURKMENISTANA. No. 2. Ashkhabad: Turkmenistan Metbughat Kitabiyati, 1930, 34 pp., 350 copies. [Russ. text; 207 Russ. titles, pub.: to Dec. 31, 1928]

LETOPIS' PECHATI TURKMENISTANA. No. 3. Ashkhabad: (Gos. Knizhn. Palata Turkmenistana), 1931, 54 pp. [Turkmen text; 224 titles]

LETOPIS' PECHATI TURKMENISTANA. No. 4. Ashkhabad: Turkmenistan Metbughat Kitabiyati, 1932, 36 pp., 200 copies. [Russ. text; 119 Russ. titles, pub.: 1929, 1930]

LETOPIS' PECHATI TURKMENISTANA. No. 5. Ashkhabad: (Gos. Knizhn. Palata Turkmenistana, 1932, 42 pp. [Turkmen text; 174 titles]

LETOPIS' PECHATI TURKMENISTANA. No. 6. Ashkhabad: Turkmenistan Metbughat Kitabijati, 1932, 15 pp., 250 copies. [Russ. text; 45 Russ. titles, pub.: up to Dec. 30, 1931]

LETOPIS' PECHATI. ORGAN GOS. BIBLIOGRAFII TURKM. SSR. [ZA 1938] Ashkhabad: (Knizhnaia Palata Turkmenskoi SSR), 1939 (quarterly). [titles pub.: 1938]

LETOPIS' PECHATI. 1938 G. No. 3/4. Ashkhabad: Turkmengiz, 1939, 20 pp., 200 copies. [Turkmen, Russ. text; ca.100 Turkmen, Russ. titles, pub.: 1938]

LETOPIS' PECHATI TURKMENSKOI SSR. 1941-1945. 1951. [titles pub.: 1941-1945]

LETOPIS' PECHATI TURKMENSKOI SSR, 1946-1950. 1955. [titles, pub.: 1946-1950]

LETOPIS' PECHATI TURKMENSKOI SSR. ORGAN GOS. BIBLIOGRAFII TSSR. No. 1, 2. Ashkhabad: (Gos. Knizhnaia Palata Turkm. SSR), 1952-1953, 500 copies. [Turkmen, Russ. text; titles, pub.: 1951]

LETOPIS' PECHATI TURKMENSKOI SSR. No. 3, 1951 G. Ashkhabad: (Knizhnaia Palata Turkm. SSR), 1954, 500 copies. [Turkmen, Russ. text; titles, pub.: 1951]

Turkmen: General

LETOPIS' PECHATI TURKMENSKOI SSR. ORGAN GOS.
BIBLIOGRAFII TURKM. SSR. 1952. Nos. 1-4. Ashkhabad:
(Knizhnaia Palata Turkm. SSR), 1957, 500 copies.
[Turkmen, Russ. text; titles, pub.: 1952]

LETOPIS' PECHATI TURKMENSKOI SSR. ORGAN GOS.
BIBLIOGRAFII TURKM. SSR. Nos. 1-4, 1953. Ashkhabad:
(Knizhnaia Palata Turkm. SSR), 1954, 500 copies.
[Turkmen, Russ. text; titles, pub.: 1953]

LETOPIS' PECHATI TURKMENSKOI SSR. ORGAN GOS.
BIBLIOGRAFII TURKM. SSR, Nos. 1-2, 1954 G. Ashkhabad:
(Knizh. Palata Turkm. SSR), 1956, 500 copies.
[Turkmen, Russ. text; titles, pub.: 1954]

LETOPIS' PECHATI TURKMENSKOI SSR. ORGAN GOS. BIBLIOGRAFII
Turkm. SSR. 1954, Nos. 3-4. Ashkhabad: (Knizhnaia
Palata Turkm. SSR), 1956, 500 copies. [Turkmen, Russ.
text; titles, pub.: 1954]

LETOPIS' PECHATI TURKMENSKOI SSR. ORGAN GOS. BIBLIOGRAFII
TURKM. SSR, Nos. 1, 2, 3, 4: 1955. Ashkhabad:
(Knizh. Palata Turkm. SSR), 1956 (No. 1 appeared in
1955), 500 copies. [Turkmen, Russ. text; titles,
pub.: 1955]

LETOPIS' PECHATI TURKMENSKOI SSR. ORGAN GOS. BIBLIOGRAFII
TURKM. SSR. 1956. Nos. 1, 2. Ashkhabad: (Knizhnaia
Palata Turkm. SSR), 1956, 500 copies. [Turkmen, Russ.
text; titles, pub.: 1956]

LETOPIS' PECHATI TURKMENSKOI SSR. ORGAN GOS. BIBLIOGRAFII
TURKM. SSR. Nos. 3, 4: 1956; Nos. 1-4: 1957.
Ashkhabad: (Knizhnaia Palata Turkm. SSR), 1958
(monthly), 500 copies. [Turkmen, Russ. text; titles,
pub.: 1956-1957]

LETOPIS' PECHATI TURKMENSKOI SSR. ORGAN GOS. BIBLIOGRAFII
TURKM. SSR. Ashkhabad: (Knizhnaia Palata Turkm. SSR),
1958 (monthly), 700 copies. [Turkmen, Russ. text;
titles, pub.: 1958]

LETOPIS' PECHATI TURKMENSKOI SSR. ORGAN GOS. BIBLIOGRAFII
TURKM. SSR. Ashkhabad: (Knizhnaia Palata Turkm. SSR),
1959 (monthly), 550 copies. [Turkmen, Russ. text;
titles, pub.: 1959]

LETOPIS' PECHATI TURKMENSKOI SSR. ORGAN GOS. BIBLIOGRAFII
TURKM. SSR. Ashkhabad: (Knizhnaia Palata Turkm. SSR),
[1960] (monthly), 550 copies. [Turkmen, Russ. text;
titles, pub.: 1960]

Turkmen: General

LETOPIS' PECHATI TURKMENSKOI SSR. ORGAN GOS. BIBLIOGRAFII
TURKM. SSR. Ashkhabad: (Knizhnaia Palata Turkm. SSR),
[1961] (monthly), 500 copies. [Turkmen, Russ. text;
titles, pub.: 1961]

LETOPIS' PECHATI TURKMENSKOI SSR. ORGAN GOS. BIBLIOGRAFII
TURKM. SSR. Ashkhabad: (Knizhnaia Palata Turkm. SSR),
[1962] (monthly), 500 copies. [Turkmen, Russ. text;
titles, pub.: 1962]

LETOPIS' PECHATI TURKMENSKOI SSR. ORGAN GOS. BIBLIOGRAFII
TURKM. SSR. Ashkhabad: (Knizhnaia Palata Turkm. SSR)
[1963] (monthly), 500 copies. [Turkmen, Russ. text;
titles, pub.: 1963]

LETOPIS' PECHATI TURKMENSKOI SSR. Ashkhabad: Knizhnaia
Palata Turkmenskoi SSR), 1964 (monthly), 500 copies.
[Turkmen, Russ. text; titles, pub.: 1964]

LETOPIS' PECHATI TURKMENSKOI SSR. Ashkhabad: (Knizhnaia
Palata Turkmenskoi SSR), [1965; (monthly)] 500 copies.
[Turkmen, Russ. text; titles, pub.: 1965]

LETOPIS' PECHATI TURKMENSKOI SSR. Ashkhabad: (Gos.
Knizhnaia Palata Turkm. SSR) [1966](monthly), 500
copies. [Turkmen, Russ. text; titles, pub.: 1966]

LETOPIS' PECHATI TURKMENSKOI SSR. Ashkhabad: (Gos.
Knizhnaia Palata Turkm. SSR) [1967] (monthly), 500
copies. [Turkmen, Russ. text; titles, pub.: 1967]

LETOPIS' PECHATI TURKMENSKOI SSR. Ashkhabad: (Gos.
Knizhnaia Palata Turkm. SSR) 1968 (monthly), 500
copies. [Turkmen, Russ. text; titles, pub.: 1968]

LETOPIS' PECHATI TURKMENSKOI SSR. Ashkhabad: (Gos.
Knizhnaia Palata Turkm. SSR) [1970] (monthly), 500
copies. [Turkmen, Russ. text; titles, pub.: 1970]

LETOPIS' ZHURNAL'NYKH STATEI. (ZHURNAL MAKALALARYNYN
LETOPISI). No. 1/2, Jan.-June; No. 3/4, July.-Dec.
Ashkhabad: (Knizhnaia Palata Turkmenskoi SSR), 1939.
[Turkmen, Russ. text; titles, pub.: 1939]

LETOPIS' ZHURNAL'NYKH STATEI. (ZHURNAL MAKALALARYNYN
LETOPISI). No. 1/2, Jan.-June; No. 3/4, July-Dec.
Ashkhabad, 1940. [Turkmen text; titles, pub.: 1940]

LETOPIS' ZHURNAL'NYKH STATEI. (1941-1945). ORGAN GOS.
ANALIT. BIBLIOGRAFII TURKM. SSR.Ashkhabad: (Gos.
Kn. Palata Turkm. SSR), 1951, 68 pp., 600 copies.
[Turkmen text; 1001 Turkmen titles, pub.: 1941-1945]

Turkmen: General

LETOPIS' ZHURNAL'NYKH STATEI. 1946-1947 GG. ORGAN GOS. ANALIT. BIBLIOGRAFII TURKM. SSR. Ashkhabad: (Gos. Kn. Palata Turkm. SSR), 1951, 32 pp., 600 copies. [Turkmen text; titles, pub.: 1946-1947]

*Mikhailov, M. "NATSIONAL'NAIA PECHAT' TURKMENII," REVOLIUTSIIA I NATSIONAL'NOSTI. No. 4(13). 1931. [Russ. text; titles pub.: 1927, pp. 99-105]

Nasyrli, Ia. "NATSPECHAT' V TURKMENISTANE. (KRATKII OCHERK ISTORII PERIODICHESKOI PECHATI), TURKMENOVEDENIE. No. 5. 1929. [Russ. text; 14 titles, pub.: 1918, pp. 15-20]

NOVYE KNIGI, IZDANNYE V TURKMENSKOI SSR. [Ashkhabad]: (Knizhnaia Palata Turkm. SSR), 1963 [monthly], 150 copies. [Turkmen, Russ. text]

*Orakov, E. IZ ISTORII BIBLIOTECHNOGO DELA V TURKMENISTANE (KRATKIE OCHERKI). Ashkhabad: "Turkmenistan," 1966, 148 pp., 1500 copies. [Turkmen text; 210 Turkmen titles, pub.: 1900-1965, pp. 138-144]

*Panova, V.; A. Pirliev. comp. KNIGA SOVETSKOGO TURKMENISTANA. 1961-1965. Ashkhabad: Izdatel'stvo "Turkmenistan," 1969, 238 pp., 1000 copies. [Turkmen, Russ. text; 1848 Turkmen, Russ. titles, pub.: 1961-1965, pp. 7-201]

*Panova, V. P. comp. PERIODICHESKIE IZDANIIA TURKMENSKOI SSR. 1959-1965. BIBLIOGR. UKAZ. Ashkhabad: "Turkmenistan," (Gos. Knizhnaia Palata TSSR), 1970, 82 pp., 1000 copies. [Turkmen, Russ. text; 215 Turkmen, Kazakh, Uzbek, Russ. titles, pub.: 1959-1965, pp. 13-69]

*PECHAT' TURKMENSKOI SSR V 1959 GODU. STATISTICHESKIE MATERIALY. Ashkhabad: Izdanie Knizhnoi Palaty Turkmenskoi SSR, 1962, 75 pp., 500 copies. [Russ. text; 68 + 42 Turkmen, Russ., titles, pub.: 1959, pp. 61-72]

Shelevaia, K. P., et al. comps. LETOPIS' ZHURNAL'NYKH I GAZETNYKH STATEI TURKMENSKOI SSR. 1941-1950. Ashkhabad: (Knizhnaia Palata Turkm. SSR), 1961, 250 pp., 300 copies. [Turkmen, Russ. text and titles, pub.: 1941-1950]

Turkmen: General

"SODERZHANIE ZHURNALA 'TURKMENOVEDENIE' ZA 1927-1928 GG.,"
TURKMENOVEDENIE. Nos. 2, 7/8, 12, 1928. [Russ.
text; 49 titles, (No. 2) pp. 59-62; (No. 7/8) p. 01;
(No. 12) pp. 01-02; 01-04]

*"TURKMENSKAIA SOVETSKAIA SOTSIALISTICHESKAIA
RESPUBLIKA," BOL'SHAIA SOVETSKAIA ENTSIKLOPEDIIA.
Moscow: Gosudarstvennoe Nauchnoe Izdatel'stvo
"Bol'shaia Sovetskaia Entsiklopediia," Vol. 23, 1956,
2nd ed., 444-475 pp. [Russ. text; Turkmen, Russ.
titles, pp. 457-458, 465, 470, 472, 473]

*"TURKMENSKAIA SOVETSKAIA SOTSIALISTICHESKAIA
RESPUBLIKA," BOL'SHAIA SOVETSKAIA ENTSIKLOPEDIIA.
Moscow: Gosudarstvennyi Nauchnyi Institut "Sovetskaia
Entsiklopediia," Vol. 55, 1947 1st ed., 250-308 pp.
[Russ. text and titles, pp. 307-308]

UKAZATEL' RESPUBLIKANSKIKH TEKHNICHESKIKH USLOVII
TURKMENSKOI SSR. Ashkhabad: "Turkmenistan," 1966,
24 pp., 500 copies. [Russ. text]

ANTHROPOLOGY, ETHNOGRAPHY

*Agadzhanov, S. G. "NOVYE MATERIALY O PROISKHOZHDENII
TURKMEN," IZVESTIIA AKAD. NAUK TURKM. SSR (SERIIA
OBSHCHSTV. NAUK). No. 2. 1963, 194 pp. [Russ.
text; 73 Russ., other titles,   per.: Ancient,
pp. 24-26]

Miller, V. F. SISTEMATICHESKOE OPISANIE KOLLEKTSII
DASHKOVSKOGO ETNOGRAFICHESKOGO MUZEIA. No.1; No. 2.
Moscow: (No. 1) 1887; (No. 2) 1889. [Russ. text;
(No. 1) 86 titles, pub.: 1755-1887, (No. 1) pp. 83,
96, 109]

Turkmen: Anthropology, Ethnography

Rosliakov, A. A. K VOPROSU OB ETNOGENEZE TURKMEN. (O VREMENI I USLOVIIAKH OBRAZOVANIIA TURKM. NARODNOSTI). IZVESTIIA TURKM. FILIALA AKAD. NAUK SSSR. No. 5. n. p., (Turkm. Filial Akad. Nauk SSSR), 1950. [Russ. text; 32 titles, pp. 18-19]

*"TURKMENY," BOL'SHAIA SOVETSKAIA ENTSIKLOPEDIIA. Vol. 43. Moscow: Gosudarstvennoe Nauchnoe Izdatel'stvo "Bol'shaia Sovetskaia Entsiklopediia," (OGIZ SSSR), 1956, 2nd ed., pp. 476-478. [Russ. text and titles, p. 478]

ARCHITECTURE, ART, MUSIC

BACHINSKII, I. M. comp. ARKHITEKTURNYE PAMIATNIKI TURKMENII. No. 1. Moscow-Ashkhabad: (Turkmen. Gos. N.-i In-t Istorii, Sektor Istorii Material'noi Kul'tury), 1939. [Russ. text; 59 titles, pub.: 1821-1931, pp. 120-121]

Masson, V. M. KHUMY NISY (O NEKOTORYKH FORMAKH NEPOLIVNOI KERAMIKI). TRUDY IUZHNO-TURKMENISTANSKOI ARKHEOL. KOMPLEKSNOI EKSPEDITSII. Vol. 2. Ashkhabad: (Akad. Nauk Turkm. SSR), 1951 (binding gives 1953). Russ. text; ca.40 titles (in notes), pp. 434-436]

Rempel', L. I. "NOVYE MATERIALY K IZUCHENIIU DREVNEI SKULPTURY IUZHNOI TURKMENII," TRUDY IUZHNO-TURKMENISTANSKOI ARKHEOL. KOMPLEKSNOI EKSPEDITSII. Vol. 2. Ashkhabad: (Akad. Nauk Turkm. SSR) 1951 (cover-1953) 189-191 pp. [Russ. text; ca.50 titles, per.: ancient]

*Repin, I. L. KINEMATOGRAFIIA TURKMENISTANA. BIBLIOGRAFICHESKII UKAZATEL'. 1926-1963. Ashkhabad: (Turkmenskaia Gosudarstvennaia Biblioteka imeni Karla Marksa) 1963, 68 pp., 1500 copies. [Russ. text; 657 Turkmen, Russ. titles, per.: 1926-1963]

Turkmen: Architecture, Art, Music

Saurova, G. SOVREMENNYI TURKMENSKII KOVER I EGO TRADITSII. Ashkhabad: "Ylym," 1968, 164 pp., 1000 copies. [Russ. text; titles pp. 162-163]

Uspenskii, V.; V. Beliaev. "UKAZATEL' LITERATURY (GLAVNEISHIE ISTOCHNIKI)," TURKMENSKAIA MUZIKA. STAT'I I 115 P'ES TURKMENSKOI MUZIKI. Moscow: Narkompros Turkmenskoi SSR, 1928. [Russ. text; 19 titles, pub.: 1867-1927, pp. 364-366]

*V.B.; L. S. "TURKMENSKAIA MUZYKA," BOL'SHAIA SOVETSKAIA ENTSIKLOPEDIIA. Vol. 55. Moscow: Gosudarstvennyi Nauchnyi Institut "Sovetskaia Entsiklopediia," (Ogiz SSSR), 1947, 1st ed., 248-250 pp. [Russ. text; Turkmen, Russ., Europ. titles, p. 250]

*Veimarn, B. "TURKMENSKOE ISKUSSTVO," BOL'SHAIA SOVETSKAIA ENTSIKLOPEDIIA. Vol. 55. Moscow: Gosudarstvannyi Nauchnyi Institut "Sovetskaia Entsiklopediia," (Ogiz SSSR), 1947, 1st ed., 311-314 pp. [Russ. text and titles, pp. 313-314]

ECONOMICS

Agadzhanov, S. G. "K VOPROSU O TORGOVOI I DIPLOMATICHESKOI PRAKTIKE OGUZO-TURKMENSKIKH PLEMEN X-XI VV.," IZVESTIIA AKAD. NAUK TURKM. SSR. No. 3. [Ashkhabad] 1957. [Russ. text; 45 Russ., other titles, per.: 10-11 c., pp. 80-81]

Turkmen: Economics

*Freikin, Z. G. TURKMENSKAIA SSR. EKON.-GEOGR. KHARAKTERISTIKA. Moscow: Geografgiz, 1957, 2nd ed., 450 pp. [Russ. text; ca.150 Turkmen, Russ. titles, Sov. per., pp. 442-449]

*Gosteva, M. N. "INFORMATSIONNYI SPISOK LITERATURY O KARAKUMSKOM KANALE I ZONE EGO VLIANIIA ZA 1955 G.," IZVESTIIA AKAD. NAUK TURKM. SSR. No. 1. Ashkhabad, 1956. [Russ. text; 36 Russ. titles, per.: 1955, pp. 82-84]

*Leizerovich, E. E. EKONOMIKO-GEOGRAFICHESKIE PROBLEMY OSVOENIIA PUSTYN'. Moscow: "Mysl," 1968, 158 pp., 2500 copies. [Russ. text and titles, pub.: 1952-1965, pp. 155-157]

*Manakov, V. S.; A. I. Duplonozhenko; L. V. Gudzhalova. EFFEKTIVNOE ISPOL'ZOVANIE TRUDYVYKH RESURSOV TSSR. Ashkhabad: Izdatel'stvo "Turkmenistan," 1966, 74 pp., 600 copies. [Russ. text and titles, pub.: 1956-1963, pp. 72-73]

Oraev, N. PRIRODNYE USLOVIIA, RESURSY I NASELENIE CHARDZHOUSKOI OBLASTI. CHARDZHOU-Leningrad, 1961. [Russ. text; 212 titles, pp. 51-59, 101-103]

Seidov, A. comp.; D. Seitniiazov, ed. TURKMENSKAIA SSR-- IARKII MAIAK SOTSIALIZMA I KOMMUNIZMA NA VOSTOKE. SPISOK REKOMENDATEL'NOI LITERATURY. Ashkhabad: (Turkmenskaia Gosudarstvennaia Biblioteka im. Karla Marksa), 1964, 52 pp., 2000 copies. [Turkmen text; ca.400 Turkmen titles]

SOVETSKII TURKMENISTAN. Ashkhabad, 1968. [Russ. text; 43 titles, pp. 329-331]

Tashliev, Sh.; S. Kakabaev. eds., E. N. Kuprikova. comp. KOLLEKTIVIZATSIIA SEL'SKOGO STROIA V TURKMENISTANE (1930-1937 GG.) Ashkhabad: "Ylym," 1968, 647 pp., 1700 copies. [Russ. text; titles per.: 1927-1937, 1930-1937, pp. 645-646]

TURKMENSKII S.-KH. INSTITUT IM. M. I. KALININA. TRUDY. Vol. 14. Ashkhabad: "Turkmenistan," 1966, (Vyp. Dan. 1967), 262 pp., 500 copies. [Russ. text; titles at end of articles]

Volkova, A. Ia. POLEZNYE ISKOPAEMYE TURKMENSKOI SSR. NEFT' I GAZY. (1958-1963). Ashkhabad: "Turkmenistan," 1965, 202 pp., 1000 copies. [Russ. text; titles per.: 1958-1963]

Turkmen: Economics

_____. POLEZNYE ISKOPAEMYE TURKMENSKOI SSR. NEFT' I GAZY. MATERIALY DLIA BIBLIOGRAFII. Ashkhabad: (Turkmenskaia Gos. B-ka im. Karla Marksa), 1958, 76 pp., 1000 copies. [Russ. text]

VOPROSY KHIMIZATSII SEL'SKOGO KHOZIAISTVA TURKMENISTANA. Ashkhabad: "Turkmenistan," 1967, 176 pp., 1000 copies. [Russ. text; titles at end of articles]

Zakhidov, T. Z. ed. ZONA TURKMENSKOGO KANALA I RAIONY K NEI PRILEGAIUSHCHIE (UKAZATEL' LIT.) Tashkent: Izd-vo SAGU, 1951, 32 pp., 500 copies. [Uzbek, Russ. text; 417 Uzbek, Russ. titles, pub.: 1950-1951]

Zavarykin, F. I. ZHELEZNODOROZHNIKI ASHKHABADSKOI MAGISTRALI V GODY VELIKOI OTECHESTVENNOI VOINY (1941-1945 GG.) Chardzhou: (Turkmen. Gos. Ped. In-t im. Lenina), 1961. [Russ. text; ca.160 titles, per.: 1941-1945, pp. 165-173]

EDUCATION

Amangel'dyev, S. NEKOTORYE VOPROSY ATEISTICHESKOGO VOSPITANIIA V SHKOLE. Ashkhabad, 1967. [Turkmen text; 79 titles, pp. 165-167]

Annakurdov, M. D. OCHERKI PO ISTORII LIKVIDATSII NEGRAMOTNOSTI V SOVETSKOM TURKMENISTANE. Ashkhabad, 1960. [Turkmen text; 45 Turkmen, Russ. titles, Sov. per., pp. 376-377]

*Azimov, P.; A. A. Kurbanov. TURKMENSKII GOSUDARSTVENNYI UNIVERSITET. Ashkhabad: Turkmenuchpedgiz, 1960, 131 pp., [Russ. text; ca.600 Turkmen, Russ. titles, pub.: 1950-1960, pp. 91-126]

Bogdanov, A. I. METODIKA RUSSKOGO IAZYKA V TURKMENSKOI NACHAL'NOI SHKOLE. Ashkhabad, 1939, 137 pp. [Russ. text; 24 titles, pub.: 1928-1939]

Turkmen: Education

Frolov, I. "TURKMENGOSIZDAT. IZDANIIA 1925-1926 GG.," TURKMENOVEDENIE. No. 1. 1927. [40 titles, pub.: 1925-1926, pp. 42-44]

*Khan'ko, V. F. comp. BIBLIOGRAFIIIA IZDANII NAUCHNO-ISSLEDOVATEL'SKOGO INSTITUTA SHKOL MINISTERSTVA NARODNOGO OBRAZOVANIIA TURKMENSKOI SSR. 1955-1961. Ashkhabad: (Nauchno-Issledovatel'skii Institut Shkol Ministerstva Narodnogo Obrazovaniia TSSR), 1963, 55 pp., 2000 copies. [Turkmen, Russ. text; 222 Turkmen, Russ. titles, pub.: 1955-1961]

Kurbansakhatovaia, M. K. comp. SHADZHA BATYROVYCH BATYROV. (1908-1965). Ashkhabad: "Ylym," 1968, 43 pp., 5000 copies. [Russ. text]

Orakov, E. KPSS O ZNACHENII I ZADACHAKH BIBLIOTEK. Ashkhabad: (M-vo Kul'tury TSSR. Kul't.-Prosvet. Tekhnikum), 1958. [Turkmen text; ca.50 Turkmen, Russ. titles, pp. 38-40, Sov. per.]

Redzhepov, Dzh. PODGOTOVKA K VVEDENIIU VSEOBSHCHEGO OBIAZATEL'NOGO OBUCHENIIA V TURKMENISTANE. Chardzhou: (Turkm. Gos. Ped. Institut im. Lenina), 1960. [Turkmen text; ca.120 Turkmen, Russ. titles, pp. 278-282]

RUSSKII IAZYK V TURKMENSKOI SHKOLE. Ashkhabad, 1966, 238 pp. [Russ. text; titles at end of articles]

Takoeva, T. Ia. CHTENIE I RABOTA NAD LITERATURNO-KHUDOZHESTVENNYM PROIZVEDENIEM NA RUSSKOM IAZYKE V TURKMENSKOI SHKOLE. Ashkhabad: Turkmenuchpedgiz, 1953, 2nd ed. [Russ. text; ca.100 titles, pp. 258-261]

TURKMENISTAN SSR KHALK MAGARYF MINISTRLIGINING MEKDEPLER YLMY-BARLAG INSTITUTYNYNG NESHIRLERINING BIBLIOGRAFIIASY. 1955-1961. Ashkhabad, 1963, 52 pp., 2000 copies. [Turkmen, Russ. text; 254 titles, pub.: 1955-1961]

Volkova, A. Ia. KUL'TURNOE STROITEL'STVO I NARODNOE ZDRAVOOKHRANENIE TURKMENSKOI SSR (1924-1957 G.G.), ANNOT. UKAZATEL' LITERATURY. Ashkhabad: (Turkm. Gos. B-ka im. Karla Marksa), 1957, 43 pp., 1000 copies. [Russ. text; 238 titles, per.: 1924-1957]

GEOGRAPHY

Chariev, G. Ch.　KARA BOGAZ KOL. ISTORIIA ISSLEDOVANIIA I PROM, OSVOENIIA. Ashkhabad: (Turkm. Filial Akad. Nauk SSSR), 1950. [Russ. text; 66 titles, pub.: 1850-1950, pp. 59-62]

*Freikin, Z. G.　TURKMENSKAIA SSR. EKON.-GEOGR. KHARAKTERISTIKA. Moscow: Akad. Nauk SSR. In-t Geografii. Akad. Nauk Turkm. SSR, 1954, 315 pp. [Russ. text; 122 Russ., other titles, pp. 309-314]

*Kitaigorodskii, A.　"KARA-BOGAZ-GOL" (KARA-BOGAZ). BOL'SHAIA SOVETSKAIA ENTSIKLOPEDIIA. Vol. 31. Moscow: Gosudarstvennyi Institut "Sovetskaia Entsiklopediia," (OGIZ RSFSR), 1937, 1st ed. 420-422 pp. [Russ. text and titles, p. 422]

Kniazhetskaia, E. A.　LITERATURA O ZAPADNOM UZBOE. 1714-1950. BIBLIOGR. UKAZATEL'. Ashkhabad: Izdatel'stvo Akademii Nauk Turkmenskoi SSR, 1956, 136 pp., 1000 copies. [Russ. text; 551 Russ., Europ., other titles, pub.: 1714-1950]

Kopekov, Ch. B.　LANDSHAFTY SEVERNOI TURKMENII I IKH KHOZIAISTVENNAIA OTSENKA. Ashkhabad, 1970. [Russ. text; 54 titles, pp. 216-218]

Kunin, V. I. ed.　OCHERKI PRIRODY KARA-KUMOV. Moscow: (AN SSSR in-t Geografii, 1955. [Russ. text; 190 titles, pp. 388-397]

Miagkov, N. Ia.　BIBLIOGRAFICHESKII UKAZATEL' LITERATURY PO KLIMATU TURKMENII. Ashkhabad: (Ashkhabad. Gidrometeorol. Observatoriia), 1957, 106 pp., 500 copies. [Russ. text; 1429 titles, pub.: before 1957]

Muradov, N.　"IZ ISTORII GEOGRAFICHESKOGO ISSLEDOVANIIA ZAPADNOGO KOPET-DAGA (1886-1949 GG.)," UCHEN. ZAP. (TURKM. UN-T). No. 52. SERIIA ESTESTV. NAUK. Ashkhabad: "Ylym," 1968. [Russ. text; 31 titles, per.: 1886-1949, pp. 48-49]

Turkmen: Geography

Obruchev, V. A. PO GORAM I PUSTYNIAM SREDNEI AZII.
Moscow-Leningrad: Izdatel'stvo Akademii Nauk SSSR,
1948, 244 pp., 7000 copies. [Russ. text and titles,
pp. 241-242]

Ovezov, B. KARAKUMSKII KANAL I RAZVITIE EKONOMIKI
TURKMENISTANA. Ashkhabad: "Ylym," 1967, 238 pp.,
5000 copies. [Russ. text; ca.120 titles, pp. 232-237]

Petrov, M. P. "MATERIALY K ISTORII GEOGRAFICHESKOGO
IZUCHENIIA TURKMENISTANA," TRUDY TURKM. GEOGR. O-VA.
No. 1. n. p., (Akad. Nauk Turkm. SSR), 1958.
[Russ. text; 54 titles, pp. 65-67]

Rakhimbekov, R. "IZUCHENNIE PRIRODY TSENTRAL'NYKH
KARAKUMOV UCHENYMI SREDNE-AZIATSKOGO GOSUDARSTVENNOGO
UNIVERSITETA (PO REZUL'TATAM EKSPEDITSII TURKMENKUL'TA
V TSENTRAL'NYE KARAKUMY V 1927 G.)," IZV. UZBEKIST.
GEOGR. O-VA. Vol. 9. 1966. [Russ. text; 36
titles, per.: 1927, pp. 122-123]

Teletov, A. S. "BIBLIOGRAFICHESKII UKAZATEL' PO
POLEZNYM ISKOPAEMYM TURKMENSKOI SSR,"
POLEZNYE ISKOPAEMYE TURKMENSKOI SSR. Ashkhabad,
1928. [Russ. text; 265 titles, pp. 71-82]

*Veisov, K. "FIZIKO-GEOGRAFICHESKII OCHERK TASHAUZSKOGO
OAZISA," UCHEN. ZAPISKI (TURKM. UN-T), No.9,Part I, 1959,
204 pp. [Russ. text; 67 Russ., other titles, pp. 106-109]

*   FIZICHESKAIA GEOGRAFIIA TURKMENSKOI SSR.
Ashkhabad: "Turkmenistan," 1969, 176 pp., 5000
copies. [Turkmen text; 72 Turkmen, Russ. titles,
pub.: 1887-1968, pp. 174-176]

Viazigin, S. A. MATERIALY PO ISTORICHESKOI GEOGRAFII
TURKMENISTANA. SOOBSHCH. 2. IZVESTIIA TURKM.
FILIALA AKAD. NAUK SSSR. No. 1. [Russ. text;
21 titles, pub.: 1877-1940, pp. 20-21]

*Vitver, I. "AKHAL-TEKINSKAIA VOENNAIA EKSPEDITSIIA,"
BOL'SHAIA SOVETSKAIA ENTSIKLOPEDIIA. Vol. 4.
Moscow: Aktsionernoe Obshchestvo "Sovetskaia
Entsiklopediia," 1926, 156-157 pp. [Russ. text;
Russ., Europ. titles, p. 157]

Volkova, A. Ia. POLEZNYE ISKOPAEMYE TURKMENSKOI SSR.
ESTESTV. STROITEL'STV. MATERIALY. BIBLIOGR.
UKAZATEL' LITERATURY. Ashkhabad: (Turkm. Gos. Resp.
B-ka im. Marksa), 1964, 147 pp., 1500 copies.
[Russ. text; 710 titles, pub.: up to 1963]

Turkmen: History, Archaeology

HISTORY, ARCHAEOLOGY

*Agadzhanov, S. G. "IZ ISTORII OGUZO-TURKMENSKIKH PLEMEN RANNEGO SREDNEVEKOV'IA," IZVESTIIA AKAD. NAUK TURKM. SSR. No. 2. Ashkhabad, 1959. [Russ. text; 57 Russ., other titles, pp. 38-39]

* _____. OCHERKI ISTORII OGUZOV I TURKMEN SREDNEI AZII IX-XIII VV. Ashkhabad: "Ylym," 1969, 296 pp., 1500 copies. [Russ. text; 796 Turkmen, Persian, Arabic, Russ., Fr., Ger., Eng. titles, per.: IX-XIII c., pp. 268-291]

Akieva, A. KNIZHNOI PALATE TURKMENSKOI SSR 40 LET. Ashkhabad: "Turkmenistan," 1966, 31 pp., 500 copies. [Russ. text; Turkmen, Russ. titles, pp. 29-31]

*Annanepesov, M. UCHASTIE SOLDATSKIKH MASS V REVOLIUTSII 1905-1907 GODOV V TURKMENISTANE. Ashkhabad: Izdatel'stvo "Turkmenistan," 1966, 172 pp., 1000 copies. [Russ. text; 53 Russ. titles, per.: 1905-1907, pp. 168-171]

*Beliaev, V. I. "ARABSKIE ISTOCHNIKI PO ISTORII TURKMEN I TURKMENII IX-XIII VV.," MATERIALY PO ISTORII TURKMEN I TURKMENII. Vol. 1. VII-XV VV. (TRUDY IN-TA VOSTOKOVEDENIIA, XXIX). (Moscow-Leningrad) 1939. [Russ. text; 126 Arabic, Russ. titles, pub.: 1923-1939, per.: 9 - 13 c., pp. 12-40]

*Durdyev, T. "IZ PREDYSTORII TURKMENSKOI NATSIONAL'NOI INTELLIGENTSII," IZVESTIIA AKADEMII NAUK TURKMENSKOI SSR. SERIIA OBSHCHESTVENNYKH NAUK. No. 2. 1968, 24-32 pp. [Russ. text; 14 Russ. titles, p. 32]

*Bregel', Iu. E. KHOREZMSKIE TURKMENY V XIX VEKE. Moscow: (Akad. Nauk SSR. In-t Narodov Azii), 1961, 441 pp. [Russ. text; ca.220 Russ., other titles, per.: 19th c., pp. 383-395]

Turkmen: History, Archaeology

ENEOLIT IUZHNYKH OBLASTEI SREDNEI AZII. Part I. I. N. Khlopin, "PAMIATNIKI RANNEGO ENEOLITA IUZHN. TURKMENII" (1963). Part II. Y. M. Masson, "PAMIATNIKI RAZVITOGO ENEOLITA IUGO-ZAP. TURKMENII." Moscow-Leningrad, 1962-1963. [Russ. text; (Part I) 94 titles, pp. 27-28; (Part II) 64 titles, p. 29, per.: Aeneolithic Age (Copper Age)]

Ershov, S. A.; G. A. Pogosian. BIBLIOGRAFICHESKII UKAZATEL' LITERATURY PO TURKMENII. No. 1. Ashkhabad: Turkmengiz, 1937. [Turkmen text; 1055 titles, pub.: second half 19th c. - 1930's]

_____. "UKAZATEL" LITERATURY PO ARKHEOLOGICHESKOMU IZUCHENIIU TURKMENII," TURKMENOVEDENIE. No. 1/2. 1931. [Russ. text; 50 titles, pp. 79-80]

Frolov, I.; A. Oblonskii; A. Olevich; A. E. P. "ISTORIKO-KRAEVEDCHESKII MATERIAL O TURKMENII IMEIUSHCHIISIA V GAZETE TURKMENSKAIA ISKRA [I 'TURKMENOVEDENIE']" TURKMENSKAIA ISKRA, No. 1-274 (1927-1929); TURKMENOVEDENIE, No. 1, 1927, pp. 42-44; No. 2/3, 1927, pp. 59-63; No. 4, 1927, pp. 53-57; No. 2, 1928, pp. 55-58; No. 3/4 (7/8) 1928, pp. 69-71; No. 5/6 (9/10), 1928, pp. 95, 101-103; No. 7/8, 1928, pp. 105-110; No. 10/11, 1928, pp. 134-136; No. 12, 1928, pp. 77-79; No. 1, 1929, pp. 145-148; No. 2/3, 1929, pp. 56-57; No. 4, 1929, pp. 36-38; No. 5, 1929, pp. 52-54; No. 6/7, 1929, pp. 57-60; No. 8/9, 1929, pp. 64-67; No. 10/11, 1929, pp. 82-84 (84); No. 12, 1929, pp. 39-40; No. 1, 1930, pp. 39-40; No. 2/3, 1930, pp. 55-57. [Russ. text; titles pub.: 1924-1930]

Iakunicheva, A. S. "BIBLIOGRAFIIA PO ISTORII TURKMENISTANA (1917-1957 GG.)," ISTORIIA TURKMENSKOI SSR. Ashkhabad: (Akad. Nauk Turkm. SSR. In-t Istorii, Arkheologii i Etnografii), 1957. [Russ. text; ca.550 titles, per.: 1917-1957, pp. 684-714]

ISTORIIA RABOCHEGO KLASSA SOVETSKOGO TURKMENISTANA (1917-1965 GG.) Ashkhabad: "Ylym," 1969, 496 pp., 1000 copies. [Russ. text and titles, per.: 1917-1965, a bibl. essay w/footnotes]

Turkmen: History, Archaeology

Khudaiberdiev, Iazkuli. MARKSISTSKO-LENINSKII AVANGARD TURKMENSKOGO NARODA. (OBRAZOVANIE I RAZVITIE KOMMUNIST. PARTII TURKMENISTANA.) Ashkhabad: "Turkmenistan," 1967, 299 pp., 4000 copies. [Russ. text; ca.170 titles, pp. 291-297]

*Kononov, A. N. RODOSLOVNAIA TURKMEN. SOCHINENIE ABU-L-GAZI KHANA KHIVINSKOGO. Moscow-Leningrad: Izdatel'stvo Akademii Nauk SSSR, 1958, 192+ 94 pp. [Russ. text; Chaghatay, Russ., Europ., Turkish titles, pp. 181-190]

Kuprikova, E. N. SOIUZ RUSSKOGO RABOCHEGO KLASSA I TURKMENSKOGO TRUDOVOGO DAIKHANSTVA V PERIOD VELIKOI OKTIABR'SKOI SOTSIALISTICHESKOI REVOLIUTSII I GRAZHDANSKOI VOINY. (1917-1920 GG.) Ashkhabad: (Akad. Nauk Turkmen. SSR. In-t Istorii, Arkheol. i Etnogr.), 1960. [Russ. text; ca.180 titles, per. 1917-1920, pp. 151-160]

Levina, V. A. "ZHILISHCHE ANAU:" POZDNEE GORODISHCHE ANAU," TRUDY IUZHNO-TURKM. ARKHEOL. KOMPLEKSNOI EKSPEDITSII. Vol. 2. Ashkhabad: (Akad. Nauk Turkm. SSR), 1951 [Russ. text; ca.100 titles, pp. 376-378 + 394-395]

"LITERATURA O REVOLIUTSII 1905-1907 GG. V TURKMENISTANE," TRUDY (TURKM. FILIAL IN-TA MARKSIZMA-LENINIZMA PRI TSK KPSS). No. 2. 1956. [Russ. text; 43 titles, per.: 1905-1907, pp. 123-124]

Litvinskii, B. A. "OCHERK O RABOTE ARKHEOLOGICHESKOI GRUPPY V OTRIADA IUTAKE V 1947 G.," TRUDY IUZHNO-TURKM. ARKHEOL. KOMPLEKSNOI EKSPEDITSII. Vol. 2. Ashkhabad: Akad. Nauk Turkm. SSR, 1951. [Russ. text; 130 titles, per.: 1947, pp. 309-314]

Logvinova, T. G.; M. A. Semichaevskii. KHRESTOMATIIA PO ISTORII KPSS. Ashkhabad: "Turkmenistan," 1968, 479 pp., 5000 copies. [Russ. text; Turkmen titles, pp. 437-471]

Masson, M. E. ed. ISTORIIA TURKMENSKOI SSR. Vol. 1. Book 2. S NACHALA XIX VEKA DO VELIKOI OKTIABR'SKOI SOTSIALISTICHESKOI REVOLIUTSII. Ashkhabad: (Akad. Nauk Turkm. SSR. In-t Istorii, Arkheologii i Etnografii), 1957, 487 pp. [Russ. text; ca.1400 USSR lang, Russ., other titles, per.: begin 19 c. - 1917, pp. 403-486]

Turkmen: History, Archaeology

_____. ed. ISTORIIA TURKMENSKOI SSR. Vol. 1, Book 2. "S NACHALA XIX VEKA DO VELIKOI OKTIABR'SKOI SOTS. REVOLIUTSII." Ashkhabad: (Akad. Nauk Turkmen. SSR. In-t Istorii, Arkheol. i Etnografii), 1960. [Turkmen text; ca.1500 Turkmen, Russ., other titles, per.: 18th c. to 1917, pp. 430-500]

_____. ed. "MATERIALY PO ISTORII DREVNEI TEKHNIKI IUZHNOGO TURKMENISTANA," TRUDY IUZHNO-TURKMENISTANSKOI ARKHEOLOGICHESKOI KOMPLEKSNOI EKSPEDITSII. Vol. 8. Ashkhabad: Akad. Nauk Turkm. SSR, 1958, 406 pp. [Russ. text; Russ., other titles]

_____. SREDNEVEKOVYE TORGOVYE PUTI IZ MERVA V KHOREZM I V MAVERANNAKHR. (V PREDELAKH TURKM. SSR.) TRUDY IUZHN.-TURKMENISTANSKOI ARKHEOL. KOMPLEKSNOI EKSPEDITSII. Vol. 13. (Ashkhabad): "Turkmenistan," (1966), 298 pp., 320 copies. [Russ. text; 193 titles, pp. 274-280]

Moshkova, V. G. "OTCHET O RABOTE ETNOGRAFICHESKOI GRUPY V OTRIADA IUTAKE 1947 G. V BAKHARDENSKOM RAIONE TSSR," TRUDY IUZHNO-TURKMENSK. ARKHEOLOGICH. KOMPLEKSNOI EKSPEDITSII. Vol. 2. Ashkhabad: (AN Turkm. SSR), 1951. [Russ. text; ca.60 titles, per.: 1947, pp. 341-343]

Muratgel'dyev, T. VNEKSLASSNAIA RABOTA PO ISTORII. Ashkhabad, 1962. [Turkmen text; 30 titles, pp. 58-59]

*(Ovezov, D. M) AKADEMIK AKADEMII NAUK TURKMENSKOI SSR MIKHAIL EVGEN'EVICH MASSON. Ashkhabad: (AN TSSR. Iuzh.-Turkmenistan. Arkheol. Kompleksnaia Ekspeditsiia), 1970, 59 pp., 500 copies. [Russ. text; 346 Turkmen, Uzbek, Russ., Eng., Ger., Fr., It., Pers., Chin., Esperanto titles, pub.: 1923-1969, pp. 10-12, 27-55,]

Pugachenkova, G. A. "ARKHITEKTURNYE PAMIATNIKI DAKHISTANA, ABIVERDA, SERAKHSA. TRUDY IUZHNO-TURKMENISTANSKOI ARKHEOL. KOMPLEKSNOI EKSPEDITSII. Vol. 2. Ashkhabad: (AN Turkm. SSR), 1951 [cover: 1953] [ca.90 Russ., foreign titles, pp. 250-252]

*Romaskevich, A. A. "PERSIDSKIE ISTOCHNIKI PO ISTORII TURKMEN I TURKMENII X-XV VV. Vol. 1. VII-XV VV. ARABSKIE I PERSIDSKIE ISTOCHNIKI," (TRUDY IN-TA VOSTOKOVEDENIIA, XXIX). Moscow, 1939. [Russ. text; 77 Arabic, Persian, Russ., foreign titles, pub.: 1836-1937, per.: 12-15th cc., pp. 40-60]

Turkmen: History, Archaeology

*Rosliakov, A. A.   KRATKII OCHERK ISTORII TURKMENISTANA
(DO PRISOEDINENIIA K ROSSII). Ashkhabad:
Turkmengosizdat, 1956, 191 pp. [Russ. text; ca.500
Turkmen, Russ. titles (footnotes), pp. 172-192]

_____. REVOLIUTSIONNOE DVIZHENIE I SOTSIAL-
DEMOKRATICHESKIE ORGANIZATSII V TURKMENISTANE V
DOOKTIABR'SKII PERIOD (1900 - MART 1917). Ashkhabad:
(In-t Istorii Partii pri TsK KP Turkmenistana),
1957. [Russ. text; 78 titles, per.: 1900-March 1917,
pp. 261-265]

Sarianidi, V. I.; I. N. Khlopin. "ARKHEOLOGIIA
TURKMENSKOI SSR. (OBZOR STATEI V IZVESTIIAKH AN TSSR
ZA 1951-1959 GG.)" SOVETSKAIA ARKHEOLOGIIA. No. 2.
1962. [Russ. text; titles, pub.: 1951-1959,
pp. 262-267]

_____. PAMIATNIKI POZDNEGO ENOLITA IUGO-
VOSTOCHNOI TURKMENII. Moscow, 1965. [Russ. text;
ca.130 titles, pp. 51-52]

*Seiidov, A.; R. Sh. Bainurov; V. A. Kudelina; et al
comps. VELIKAIA OKTIABR'SKAIA SOTSIALISTICHESKAIA
REVOLIUTSIIA I GRAZHDANSKAIA VOINA V TURKMENISTANE.
BIBLIOGRAFICHESKII UKAZATEL'. Ashkhabad:
"Turkmenistan," 1968, 187 pp., 1500 copies.
[Turkmen, Russ. text; 520 + 779 Turkmen, Russ. titles]

*"SPISOK LITERATURY PO ISTORII ISSLEDOVANIIA TURKMENII,"
TURKMENIIA. (LENINGRAD: AKADEMIIA NAUK KOMISSIIA
EKSPEDITSIONNYKH ISSLEDOVANII). Vol. 1.   1929.
[Russ. text and titles, pp. 120-121]

*Stroeva, L. V. MATERIALY PO ISTORII TURKMEN I TURKMENII.
Vol. 2. XVI-XIX VV. IRANSKIE, BUKHARSKIE I
KHIVINSKIE ISTOCHNIKI. Moscow-Leningrad:
Izdatel'stvo Akademii Nauk SSSR. (In-t Vostokovedeniia
AN SSSR i In-t Istorii pri TsIK Turk. SSR), 1939,
700 pp., 3725 copies. [Russ. text; 151 Chaghatay,
Russ. Europ., Middle East. titles, pub.: 1770-1936;
per.: 16th - 19th c., pp. 687-692]

_____. "(SPISOK LIT-RY, ISPOL'Z. DLIA
PRIMECHARII)" MATERIALY PO ISTORII TURKMEN I TURKMENII
Vol. 1. VII-XV VV. ARAB I PERSID. ISTOCHNIKI.
(TRUDY IN-TA VOSTOKOVEDENIIA XXIX. ISTOCHNIKI PO
ISTORII NARODOV SSSR). (Moscow-Leningrad) 1939.
[Russ. text; 132 Russ., Europ., Eastern titles,
per.: 7th - 15th c., pub.: 1851-1938, pp. 602-605]

Turkmen: History, Archaeology

*Tashliev, Sh., et al. ed.; A. S. Iakunicheva. comp.
OCHERKI ISTORII KOMMUNISTICHESKOI PARTII TURKMENISTANA.
Ashkhabad: Izdatel'stvo "Turkmenistan," 1965, 816 pp.,
5000 copies. [Russ. text; ca.250 Russ. titles,
per.: 1900-1964, pp. 794-810]

TRUDY IUZHNO-TURKMENISTANSKOI ARKHEOL. KOMPLEKSNOI
EKSPEDITSII. Vol. 5. [1948-1952] Ashkhabad:
(Akad. Nauk Turkm. SSR), 1955. [Russ. text; ca.130
Turkmen, Russ. titles, pub.: 1948-1952, pp. 254-259]

Turkmenneshir, A.; A. S. Yakunicheva. comps.
TURKMENISTAN KOMMUNISTIK PARTIYASINING OCHERKLERI.
905 pp. [Turkmen text; titles, pp. 879-897]

*"TURKMENSKAIA SOVETSKAIA SOTSIALISTICHESKAIA RESPUBLIKA,"
BOL'SHAIA SOVETSKAIA ENTSIKLOPEDIIA. Vol. 55.
Moscow: Gosudarstvennyi Nauchnyi Institut "Sovetskaia
Entsiklopediia," (Ogiz SSSR), 1947, 250-308 pp.
[Russ. text; Turkmen, Russ. titles, pp. 307-308]

*Vasianin, N. Ia. "ROL' KOMMUNISTICHESKOI PARTII
TURKMENISTANA V RAZVITII GEOLOGOPOISKOVYKH I
RAZVEDOCHNYKH RABOT V NEFTIANOI PROMYSHLENNOSTI
RESPUBLIKI V 1933-1940 GG.," IZVESTIIA AKADEMIIA
NAUK TURKMENSKOI SSR. SERIIA OBSHCHESTVENNYKH NAUK.
No. 5. 1966, 3-10 pp. [Russ. text; 7 Russ. titles,
per.: 1933-1940, p. 10]

Vinberg, N. A.; Aga Karryev, eds. "OSNOVNAIA LITERATURA
PO ISTORII TURKMENII (VIII-XIX VV.)" OCHERKI IZ
ISTORII TURKM. NARODA I TURKMENISTANA V VIII-XIX VV.
MATERIALY DLIA OBSUZHDENIIA. Ashkhabad: (Akad. Nauk
Turkm. SSR. In-t Istorii, Arkheologii i Etnografii),
1954. [Russ. text; ca.700 Russ., foreign titles,
per.: VIII-XIX c., pp. 368-404]

LANGUAGE, LITERATURE

Abdullaev, O. OBRAZ KOLKHOZNIKA V POSLEVOENNOI TURKMENSKOI SOVETSKOI PROZE. Ashkhabad: (Turkm. Gos. Un-t im. Gor'kogo), 1957. [Turkmen text; ca.75 Turkmen, Russ. titles, per.: post-WW II, pp. 142-145]

Abramova, F. Sh. ATA SALIKH - NARODNYI SHAKHIR TURKMENISTANA. 50 LET SO DNIA ROZHDENIIA. 1908-1958. PAMIATKA CHITATELIU. Ashkhabad: (Turkm. Gos. B-ka im. Karla Marksa), 1958, 19 pp., 2500 copies. [Russ. text; titles, per.: 1908-1958]

──────────────. MAKHTUMKULI (FRAGI). 225 LET SO DNIA ROZHDENIIA VELIKOGO KLASSIKA TURKM. LIT. UKAZATEL' LITERATURY. Ashkhabad: (Turkm. Gos. B-ka im. Karla Marksa), 1959, 27 pp., 1500 copies. [Russ. text; 98 titles, pub.: 1936-1956]

Achilova, G. OPREDELITEL'NYE SLOVOSOCHETANIIA V SOVREMENNOM TURKMENSKOM IAZYKE. Ashkhabad: (Turkm. Filial Akad. Nauk SSSR. In-t Istorii, Iazyka i Lit.), 1951, 1000 copies. [Turkmen text; ca.100 titles, pp. 84-86]

Akhally, S. SLOVAR' MAKHMUDA KASHGARSKOGO I TURKMENSKII IAZYK. Ashkhabad: (Akad. Nauk Turkm. SSR. In-t Iazyka i Lit.) Izdatel'stvo Akademii Nauk Turkmenskoi SSR, 1958, 207 pp., 1000 copies. [Turkmen text; ca.110 Turkmen, Russ., Mid-East titles, pp. 200-205]

*Allakov, Dzh. OBRAZ RABOCHEGO V TURKMENSKIKH ROMANAKH. Ashkhabad: (Ministerstvo Narodnogo Obrazovaniia TSSR. Turkmenskii Gosudarstvennyi Universitet im. A. M. Gor'kogo), 1962, 177 pp., 1000 copies. [Turkmen text; ca.130 Turkmen, Russ. titles, pp. 173-176]

Altaev, S. EVFEMIZMY V TURKMENSKOM IAZYKE. Ashkhabad: (Akad. Nauk Turkm. SSR. In-t Iazyka i Lit.), 1958. [Turkmen text; ca.100 Turkmen, Russ. titles, pp. 87-90]

Turkmen: Language, Literature

*Annaberdiev, S. ZHIZN' I TVORCHESTVO DOSMAMEDA.
Ashkhabad: Turkmenuchpedgiz, 1963, 76 pp., 2000
copies. [Turkmen text; 28 Turkmen, Russ. titles,
p. 75]

*Annanurov, A. VOPROSY SINTAKSISA V PLANE PEREVODA S
RUSSKOGO NA TURKMENSKII IAZYK. Ashkhabad:
(Turkm. Filial IMELS pri TsK KPSS), 1956, 190 pp.
[Russ. text; 157 Turkmen, Russ. titles, pp. 184-189]

Arazkuliev, S. GOVORY TURKMEN TURTKUL'SKOGO RAIONA
KARA-KALPAKSKOI ASSR. Ashkhabad: (Turkmen. Gos.
Ped. Institut im. Gor'kogo), 1961. [Turkmen text;
60 Turkmen, Russ. titles, pp. 265-267]

Ashirov, Z. N. ed. OCHERK PO ISTORII TURKMENSKOI
SOVETSKOI LITERATURY. Part 2. Ashkhabad, 1962.
[Turkmen text; ca.360 titles, Sov. per., pp. 383-394]

Ataeva, Kh. A. RAZVITIE LEKSIKI TURKMENSKOGO IAZYKA ZA
SCHET VNUTRENNIKH RESURSOV. Chardzhou: (Turkmen.
Gos. Ped. In-t im. Lenina), 1961. [Turkmen text;
ca.70 Turkmen, Russ. titles, pp. 123-125]

Azimov, P. TURKMENSKII IAZYK. Ashkhabad:
Turkmenuchpedgiz, 1950. [Turkmen text; ca.200
Turkmen, Russ., foreign titles, pp. 212-222]

*Babaev, Kakadzhan. IDIOMY V TURKMENSKOM IAZYKE.
Ashkhabad: (Turkmenskii Gosudarstvennyi Universitet
imeni A. M. Gorkogo. Kafedra Turkmenskogo Iazyka),
1962, 199 pp., 1000 copies. [Turkmen text; ca.100
Turkmen, Russ. titles, pp. 193-197]

Baskakov, N. A. K ISTORII IZUCHENIIA TURKMENSKOGO
IAZYKA. Ashkhabad: "Turkmenistan," 1965, 35 pp.,
1500 copies. [Russ. text]

_____. Ia. M. Khamzaev, ed. SRAVNITEL'NAIA
GRAMMATIKA RUSSKOGO I TURKMENSKOGO IAZYKOV. Vol. 1.
FONETIKA I MORFOLOGIIA. Ashkhabad, 1964. [Russ.
text; 76 titles, pp. 376-378]

*Batyrov, Sh. B. ed. MAKHTUMKULI. IUBILEINYI SBORNIK
POSVIASHCHENNYI 225-LETIIU SO DNIA ROZHDENIIA
VELIKOGO TURKMENSKOGO POETA. Ashkhabad:
(Institut Lit. im. Makhtumkuli), Izdatel'stvo
Akademii Nauk Turkmenskoi SSR, 1961, 352 pp., 4500
copies. [Turkmen text; titles, per.: 225th
anniversary, pp. 345-346]

Berdyev, D. "KATEGORIIA GLAGOL'NYKH VIDOV V
SOVREMENNOM TURKMENSKOM IAZYKE," TRUDY
CHARDZHOUSKOGO GOS. PED. IN-TA. No. 5, Vyp. 7.
Chardzhou, 1959. [Turkmen text; ca.100 Turkmen,
Russ. titles, per.: contemporary, pp. 141-147]

*Berdyev, R.; S. Kurenov. IZ ISTORII IZUCHENIIA
DIALEKTOV TURKMENSKOGO IAZYKA. IZVESTIIA AKADEMII
NAUK TURKMENSKOI SSR. SERIIA OBSHCHESTVENNYKH
NAUK. No. 6. 1967, 49-56 pp. [Russ. text; 68 Russ.
titles, pub.: 1845-1967, pp. 54-56]

*Berdyev, Redzhep. SLOZHNYE SLOVA V SOVREMENNOM IAZYKE.
Ashkhabad: (Turkmenistan SSR. Ilimlar Akademiyasining
Neshriyati) Izdatel'stvo Akademii Nauk Turkmenskoi
SSR, 1958, 128 pp., 500 copies. [Turkmen text;
Turkmen, Russ. titles, pp. 123-127]

_____. SLOZHNYE SLOVA V SOVREMENNOM TURKMENSKOM
IAZYKE. Ashkhabad: (Akad. Nauk Turkm. SSR. In-t
Iazyka i Lit.), 1958. [Turkmen text; 75 Turkmen,
Russ. titles, pp. 123-126]

Charyiarov, B. KATEGORIIA ZALOGA V SOVREMENNOM
TURKMENSKOM IAZYKE. Ashkhabad: (Akad. Nauk Turkm.
SSR. In-t Iazyka i Lit.), 1957. [Turkmen text;
104 Turkmen, Russ. titles, per.: contemporary,
pp. 162-166]

*D'iachenko, V. P. RUSSKII DRAMATICHESKII TEATR V
TURKESTANSKOM KRAE. Tashkent: Izdatel'stvo "Fan,"
1966, 180 pp., 800 copies. [Russ. text; Russ.
titles, pub.: 1897-1960, pp. 176-180]

Durdyev, T. ROMANY ATA KAUSHUTOVA. Ashkhabad, 1962.
[Turkmen text; ca.110 titles, pp. 224-228]

Gafurova, Kh. NARECHIE V SOVREMENNOM TURKMENSKOM
IAZYKE. Ashkhabad: (Akad. Nauk Turkm. SSR. In-t
Iazykoznaniia), 1959. [Turkmen text; ca.100
Turkmen, Russ. titles, per.: contemporary, pp. 105-108]

Karryev, B. A. "BIBLIOGRAFICHESKII OBZOR RABOT
POSVIASHCHENNYKH MAKHTUM-KULI," IZVESTIIA TURKMEN.
FILIALA AN SSSR. No. 3. 1950, 89-94 pp. [Russ.
text; 33 Turkmen, Russ. titles]

* _____. IZUCHENIE TURKMENSKOI LITERATURY ZA GODY
SOVETSKOI VLASTI. IZVESTIIA AKADEMII NAUK TURKMENSKOI
SSR. SERIIA OBSHCHESTVENNYKH NAUK. No. 5. 1967,
84-90 pp. [Russ. text; 95 Turkmen, Russ. titles,
pp. 88-90]

Turkmen: Language, Literature

*Karryev, Meretkuli. SEIDI (ZHIZN' I TVORCHESTVO). Ashkhabad: Izdatel'stvo Akademii Nauk Turkmenskoi SSR, 1962, 151 pp., 1600 copies. [Turkmen text; ca.120 Turkmen, Russ. titles, pp. 147-150]

Kekilov, A.; R. Redzhepov; K. Dzhumaev. VOZNIKNOVENIE I RAZVITIE KRITICHESKOI MYSLI V TURKMENISTANE. Ashkhabad, 1969. [Turkmen text; ca.160 titles, pp. 147-153]

Kerimi, K. TURKMENSKII TEATR. OCHERK ISTORII. Moscow: Izdatel'stvo "Iskusstvo," 1964, 227 pp., 1400 copies. [Russ. text; 80 Turkmen, Russ. titles, pp. 217-220]

Khodzhakuliev, A. ZHIZN' I TVORCHESTVO KHADZHI ISMAILOVA. Chardzhou: (Turkm. Gos. Ped. In-t im. Lenina), 1960. [Turkmen text; ca.180 Turkmen, Russ. titles, pp. 158-163]

*Khudaikuliev, M. PODRAZHATEL'NYE SLOVA V TURKMENSKOM IAZYKE. Ashkhabad, 1962, 134 pp. [Russ. text; ca.135 Turkmen, other titles, pp. 6-12, 128-133]

Khydyrov, E. OBRAZ SOVETSKOGO VOINA V TURKMENSKOI SOVETSKOI LITERATURE. Chardzhou: (Chardzhouskii Gos. Ped. In-t), 1958. [Turkmen text; 86 Turkmen, Russ. titles, Sov. per., pp. 133-137]

Kulieva, G. NURMURAD SARYKHANOV--NOVELLIST. Ashkhabad: 1967. [Russ. text; 73 Turkmen, Russ., other titles, pp. 99-103]

Kul'-Mukhamedov, Abdul-Khekim. ...MATERIALY PO SREDNEAZIATSKIM LITERATURNYM PAMIATNIKAM. KRATKAIA OPIS' RUKOPISEI PRIOBRETENNYKH AVTOROM LETOM 1928 GODA... Ashkhabad: Turkmenskoe Gosudarstvennoe Izdatel'stvo, 1931, 65 + 1 pp., 2000 copies. [Russ. text; 47 + 67 mss., 2 doc., 1 yar. Turkmen, Russ. titles, p. 66]

Kurbanov, K. TURKMENSKIE NARODNYE ZAGADKI. Chardzhou: (Turkm. Gos. Ped. Institut im. Lenina), 1960. [Turkmen text; ca.120 titles, pp. 276-281]

*Kurbansakhatov, Mukhammed. TVORCHESTVO RAKHMETA SEIDOVA. Ashkhabad: Izdatel'stvo Akademii Nauk TSSR, 1963, 147 pp., 1000 copies. [Turkmen text; 331 Turkmen, Russ. titles, pub.: 1932-1954, pp. 139-146]

Turkmen: Language, Literature

Meredov, A. IZ ISTORII LITERATURY SEL'DZHUKSKOGO PERIODA. Ashkhabad: "Ylym," 1968, 221 pp., 4000 copies. [Russ. text; Turkmen titles, pp. 217-220]

_____. POET-SATIRIK KEMINE. Ashkhabad: (Akad. Nauk Turkm. SSR. In-t Iazyka i Lit.), 1958. [Turkmen text; ca.200 USSR lang., Russ. titles, pp. 261-267]

_____. SHEIDAI. Ashkhabad, 1964. [Turkmen text; ca.170 titles, pp. 338-343]

Muradov, A. K. K ISTORII VZAIMOSVIAZI RUSSKOI I TURKMENSKOI SOVETSKOI LITERATURY. Ashkhabad: (Turkm. Gos. Un-t im. Gor'kogo), 1959. [Turkmen text; ca.120 Turkmen, Russ. titles, pp. 117-122]

Oraztaganov, A. ZHIZN' I TVORCHESTVO BAIRAM-SHAKHIRA. Ashkhabad: Turkmenuchpedgiz, 1961. [Turkmen text; 35 Turkmen, Russ. titles, pp. 82-83]

Penzhiev, M. IMENA CHISLITEL'NYE V SOVREM. TURKMENSKOM IAZYKE. Chardzhou, 1962. [Turkmen text; ca.120 titles, pp. 209-213]

*POETY TURKMENSKOI LITERATURY IX-XVII VV. (SPRAVOCHNIK). Ashkhabad: "Ylym," 1967, 110 pp., 10,000 copies. [Turkmen text; Turkmen, Russ., titles, per.: 9-17th c., pp. 105-106]

*Potseluevskii, A. "TURKMENSKII IAZYK," BOL'SHAIA SOVETSKAIA ENTSIKLOPEDIIA. Vol. 55. Moscow: Gosudarstvennyi Nauchnyi Institut "Sovetskaia Entsiklopediia," (OGIZ SSSR), 1947, 1st ed., pp.310-311. [Russ. text; Turkmen, Russ. titles, p. 311]

Sakali, M. A. "SIUZHETY TURKMENSKIKH SKAZOK," IZV. TURKM. FILIALA AKAD. NAUK SSSR. No. 1. Ashkhabad: (Turkm. Filial Akad. Nauk SSSR), 1946. [Russ. text; 25 Turkmen, Russ. titles, pp. 16-17]

Sakhedov, Kh. ATA SALIKH--NARODNYI SHAKHIR TSSR. BIBLIOGR. UKAZATEL' PROIZVEDENII. Ashkhabad: (Turkm. Gos. B-ka im. Marksa), 1958, 36 pp., 2500 copies. [Turkmen text; ca.274 titles, pub.: 1919-1957]

Seidov, Ashir. ALEKSEI MAKSIMOVICH GOR'KII. (1868-1969). BIBLIOGR. UKAZATEL'. K 100-LETIIU SO DNIA ROZHDENIIA. Ashkhabad: (M-vo Kul'tury Turkm. SSR. Gos. B-ka Turkm. SSR. im. Karla Marksa), 1968, 47 pp., 1000 copies. [Russ. text; Turkmen titles, per.: 1868-1969]

Turkmen: Language, Literature

_____. BIBLIOGRAFICHESKII SPRAVOCHNIK DOREVOLIUTSIONNYKH TURKMENSKIKH POETOV. Ashkhabad: "Turkmenistan," 1965, 150 pp., 1300 copies. [Russ. text; per.: pre-1917]

_____. BIOBIBLIOGRAFICHESKII SPRAVOCHNIK DOREVOLIUTSIONNYKH TURKMENSKIKH POETOV. BIBLIOGRAFIIA NA TURKM. I RUS. IAZ.) Ashkhabad: "Turkmenistan," (Turkm. Resp. B-ka im. Marksa), 1965, 150 pp., 1300 copies. [Turkmen text; ca. 190 Turkmen, Russ. titles, per.: 15th - 19th c.]

Seiidov, A. comp. V. I. LENIN V TURKMENSKOI SOVETSKOI LITERATURE. BIBLIOGRAFICHESKOI UKAZATEL'. Ashkhabad: "Turkmenistan," 1965, 62 pp., 1200 copies. [Turkmen text; ca.900 titles, pub.: 1941-1964]

Seiitniiazov, Dzh. VELIKII TURKMENSKII POET MAKHTUMKULI (FRAGI). K 225 - LETIIU SO DNIA ROZHDENIIA. BIBLIOGR. UKAZATEL'. Ashkhabad: (Turkmen. Gos. B-ka im. Marksa), 1959, 50 pp., 1500 copies. [Turkmen text; ca.332 Turkmen, other titles]

Sevortian, E. V. "SOVREMENNOE SOSTOIANIE I NEKOTORYE VOPROSY ISTORICH. IZUCHENIIA TIURKSKIKH IAZYKOV V SSSR." VOPROSY METODOV IZUCHENIIA ISTORII TIURKSKIKH IAZYKOV. Ashkhabad: (Institut Iazykoznaniia Akad. Nauk SSSR. Institut Iazykoznaniia Turkmen. SSR), 1961. [ca.290 Russ., other titles, pp. 28-41]

*Seyitniyazov, J. AMAN KEKILOV. 50 LET SO DNIA ROZHDENIIA. BIBLIOGR. UKAZATEL'. Ashkhabad: (Turkm. Gos. B-ka im. Marksa) (TSSR Medeniet Ministrligi), 1962, 20 pp., 1000 copies. [Turkmen text; pub.: 1938-1961; 110 Turkmen titles, pp. 9-20]

*Seyitniyazov, J. MAKHTUMKULI. Ashkhabad: K. Marks Adindaki Turkmen Dovlet Kitapkhanasi, 1959, 50 pp., 1500 copies. [Turkmen text; 338 Turkmen, Sov. Asian, Russ. titles, pp. 12-47, per.: 225th anniv.]

Shamuradov, B. ZHIZN' I TVORCHESTVO POETA-DRAMATURGA K. BURNOVA. Ashkhabad: (Institut Lit. im. Makhtumkuli), 1961. [Turkmen text; ca.300 titles, pp. 117-25]

SLAV'SIA, KRAI MOI BARKHATISTYI-KARAKUMSKAIA ZEMLIA! (PAMIATKA DLIA UCHASHCHIKHSIA SRED. I STARSH. SHKOL VOZRASTA). Ashkhabad, 1968. [Russ. text; titles, p. 14]

Turkmen: Language, Literature

Tangrykuliev, Kaium. POSLEVOENNAIA TURKMENSKAIA
SOVETSKAIA DETSKAIA LITERATURA. POET. ZHANR.
(1945-1960). Ashkhabad: "Turkmenistan," 1966, 119 pp.,
2500 copies. [Russ. text; Turkmen titles, per.:
1945-1960, pp. 115-118]

Tarasenko, L. S.; I. A. Meredova; N. Reimov. PISATELI
TURKMENISTANA--DETIAM. ANNOT. UKAZATEL' KNIG DLIA
UCHASHCHIKHSIA. Ashkhabad: Turkmenuchpedgiz, 1959,
57 pp., 3000 copies. [Turkmen, Russ. text; 72
Turkmen, Russ. titles, pub.: 1940-1958]

Ulugberdiev, A. POET--PATRIOT SHALI KEKILOV.
Ashkhabad: (Akad. Nauk Turkmen. SSR. In-t Iazyka i
Lit.), 1957. [Turkmen text; 145 Turkmen, Russ.
titles, pp. 121-126]

*Veselkov, G. OCHERKI TURKMENSKOI LITERATURY.
Ashkhabad: Turkmengiz, 1945, 153 pp., 6000 copies.
[Russ. text and 106 Russ. titles, per.:19th c.-20th c.,
pub.: 1928-1945, pp. 148-151]

VESELKOVA, I. G.: A. Pirliev; V. P. Panova. comps.
PROIZVEDENIIA PISATELEI TURKMENSKOI SSR. 1928-1957.
Ashkhabad: (Knizh. Palata Turkm. SSR), 1958, 72 pp.,
3000 copies. [Turkmen text; ca.500 Turkmen, Russ.,
other titles, pub.: 1928-1957]

*Voronina, N. A.; G. Ch. Gel'dyeva; G. G. Makhova, comp.
BIBLIOGRAFICHESKII UKAZATEL' LITERATURY PO
TURKMENSKOMU IAZYKOZNANIIU (1924-1964 GG.) Ashkhabad:
Izdatel'stvo "Turkmenistan," 1966, 120 pp., 500
copies. [Russ. text; 914 Turkmen, Russ. titles,
pub.: 1924-1964]

PHILOSOPHY & RELIGION

OCHERKI ISTORII FILOSOFSKOI I OBSHCHESTVENNO-POLITICHESKOI
MYSLI V TURKMENISTANE. Ashkhabad, 1970. [Russ. text;
ca.510 titles, pp. 584-604]

Turkmen: Philosophy, Religion

Sosonkin, I. L. IZ ISTORII ESTETICHEWKOI MYSLI V
TURKMENISTANE. (MAKHTUMKULI, KEMINE, MOLLANEPES).
Ashkhabad: Ylym, 1969. [Russ. text; ca.300 titles,
pp. 328-338]

POLITICAL SCIENCE, LAW

Babaev, A.; R. Bazarova; K. Mamieva; M. Charyev.
SOVETSKII TURKMENISTAN. Ashkhabad: "Turkmenistan,"
1968, 333 pp., 5000 copies. [Russ. text; pp. 329-331]

*Batyrova, Sh. B. FORMIROVANIE I RAZVITIIE
SOTSIALISTICHESKIKH NATSII V SSSR. Ashkhabad-Moscow,
1962 (in Russ.); 1961 (in Turkmen), 368 pp. [Turkmen,
Russ. text; ca.200 Russ., other titles, Sov. per.,
pp. 361-368, NNC has 1962]

IZDANIE PROIZVEDENII MARKSA, ENGEL'SA, LENINA, STALINA V
TURKMENSKOI SSR. BIBLIOGRAFICHESKII UKAZATEL'.
1925-1954. Ashkhabad: Gos. Knizhnaia Palata Turkmenskoi
SSR, 1955, 46 pp., 500 copies. [Turkmen text;
Turkmen, Russ. titles, pub.: 1925-1954]

Khudaiberdiev, Ia. OBRAZOVANIE KOMMUNISTICHESKOI
PARTII TURKMENISTANA. Ashkhabad, 1964. [Russ. text;
ca.180 titles, pp. 209-215]

Krevskikh, E. G. KOMMUNISTICHESKAIA PARTIIA TURKMENISTANA
V BOR'BE ZA VYPOLNENIE III PIATILETNEGO PLANA. (1938-
IIUN' 1941 G.) (TRUDY. Vol. 5. IN-T ISTORII PARTII
PRI TSK KP TURKMENISTANA--FILIAL IN-TA MARKSIZMA--
LENINIZMA PRI TSK KPSS. Ashkhabad: (In-t Istorii
Partii pri TsK KPTurkm.), 1960. [Russ.
text; ca.150 titles, per.: 1938-1941, pp. 177-186]

Turkmen: Political Science, Law

Kurbansakhatovoi, M. K. comp. SHADZHA BATYROVICH BATYROV. (1908-1965). VSTUPIT. STAT'IA SH. TASHLIEVA. BIBLIOGRAFIIA SOST. M. K. KURBANSAKHATOVOI. (AN TURKM. SSR. TSENTR. NAUCH. B-KA. MATERIALY K BIOBIBLIOGRAFII UCHENYKH TURKM. SSR. No. 1), 1968, 43 pp., 5000 copies. [Russ. text; 124 titles]

Kuznetsov, Iu. S. KOMMUNISTICHESKAIA PARTIIA (BOL'SHEVIKOV) TURKMENISTANA V 1925-1929 GODAKH. Ashkhabad: (Turkm. Filial In-ta Marksizma-Leninizma pri TsK KPSS), 1960. [Russ. text; ca.220 titles, per.: 1926-1929, pp. 245-256]

*Mel'kumov, V. G. OCHERK ISTORII PARTORGANIZATSII TURKMENSKOI OBLASTI TURKESTANSKOI ASSR. (1920-1924). Ashkhabad: (In-t Istorii Partii pri TsK KP Turkmenistana. Filial In-ta Marksizma-Leninizma pri TsK KPSS),1959, 336 pp. [Russ. text; ca.250 Turk., Russ. titles, per.: 1920-1924, pp. 224-237]

Nepesov, G. POBEDA SOVETSKOGO STROIIA V SEVERNOM TURKMENISTANE. (1917-1936 GG.) Ashkhabad: (Turkm. Filial Akad. Nauk SSSR), 1950. [Russ. text; 295 titles (includes archives), pp. 391-398]

Petrov, A. P. KHRESTOMATIIA PO OSNOVAM POLITICHESKIKH ZNANII. Ashkhabad: "Turkmenistan," 1968, 460 pp., 2500 copies. [Russ. text; Turkmen titles, pp. 446-458]

Redzhenov, A. R. IZ ISTORII SOZDANIIA MARKSISTSKOI LITERATURY NA TURKMENSKOM IAZYKE. Ashkhabad, 1969. [Russ. text; ca.120 titles, pp. 186-192]

*Redzhepov, P. "RABOCHIE KIZYLARVATSKIKH GLAVNYKH ZHELEZNO-DOROZHNYKH MASTERSKIKH V PERIOD PERVOI RUSSKOI REVOLIUTSII 1905 G. [(1906-1907 GG.)]" IZVESTIIA AN TURKM. SSR. (SERIIA OBSHCHESTV. NAUK), Nos. 5-6. 1963. pp. (5) 16-31; (6) 31-38. [Russ. text; 30; 9 Russ. titles, per.: 1905-1907, pp. 31; 38]

Rosliakov, A. A. BOL'SHEVIKI TURKMENISTANA V BOR'BE ZA VLAST' SOVETOV. Vol. 1. "OKTIABR'SKAIA REVOLIUTSIIA I NACHALO BOR'BY ZA UPROCHENIE SOVETSKOI VLASTI. (1917-IIUN' 1918)." Ashkhabad: (Institut Istorii Partii pri TsK KP Turkmenistana), 1961. [Russ. text; per.: 1917-1918, pp. 5-42]

Turkmen: Political Science, Law

———————— "OSNOVNYE CHERTY VOENNOI SISTEMY AZIATSKIKH STEPNIAKOV." IZVESTIIA TURKM. FILIALA AKAD. NAUK SSSR. No. 2. n. p. (Filial Turkm. Akad. Nauk SSSR), 1951. [(Russ.) text; 51 titles, pp. 16-17]

*Shikhmuradov, O. O.; A. A. Rosliakova. eds. OCHERKI ISTORII KOMMUNISTICHESKOI PARTII TURKMENISTANA. Ashkhabad: (Institut Istorii Partii pri TsK KP Tadzhikistana--Filial Marksizma-Leninizma pri TsK KPSS), 1961 685 pp. [Russ. text; ca.250 Turk., Russ. titles, Sov. per., pp. 668-681]

Zyrin, A. A. comp. ZA SOVETSKII TURKMENISTAN. (1917-1920). VOSPOMINANIIA UCHASTNIKOV REVOLIUTSII I GRAZHDANSKOI VOINY. Ashkhabad, 1963. [Russ. text; ca.150 titles, per.: 1917-1920, pp. 417-425]

SOCIAL ORGANIZATION

*Abramova, F. Sh.; V. A. Kudelina. comps. KUL'TURNOE STROITEL'STVO I NARODNOE ZDRAVOOKHRANENIE TURKMENSKOI SSR. BIBLIOGRAFICHESKII UKAZATEL' LITERATURY. No. 2. Ashkhabad: "Turkmenistan," 1965, 60 pp., 1100 copies. [Russ. text; 366 Russ. titles, pub.: 1957-1964]

Annakuliev, K. KOMSOMOL'SKAIA DVUKHLETKA. DVUKHLET. POKHOD KOMSOMOL'TSEV TURKMENISTANA ZA KUL'TURU I SOTS. BYT V KOLKHOZ. SELE. Ashkhabad: "Turkmenistan," 1966, 183 pp., 500 copies. [Russ. text; titles pp. 180-182]

Annamuradov, N.; B. A. Beder. KURORTY TURKMENSKOI SSR. BIBLIOGRAFICHESKII UKAZATEL' (1901-1958 GG.) (RESPUBLIKANSKAIA NAUCH.-MED. BIBLIOTEKA. No. 1). Ashkhabad, 1959, 58 pp., 1000 copies. [Russ. text: titles, per.: 1901-1958]

*Durdyev, T. POD"EM KUL'TURNOGO UROVNIA TURKMENSKOGO DAIKHANSTVA V POSLEVOENNYI PERIOD. (1946-1955 GODY.) Ashkhabad: Izdatel'stvo Akademii Nauk Turkmenskoi SSR, 1962, 175 pp., 400 copies. [Russ. text; ca.150 Turkmen, Russ. titles, per.: 1946-1955, pp. 168-174]

Turkmen: Social Organization

Durdyeva, N. comp. ZHENSHCHINY SOVETSKOGO TURKMENISTANA. BIBLIOGRAFICHESKII UKAZATEL'. Ashkhabad: (Turkmenskaia Gos. B-ka im. Marksa), 1964, 32 pp., 1200 copies. [Turkmen text; ca.340 titles]

Iakubson, Ia. "UKAZATEL' LITERATURY O TURKMENII. (PO MATERIALAM TURKMENSKOI GOSUDARSTVENNOI KNIZHNOI PALATY). TURKMENOVEDENIE. No. 10/11, 12 (1929); No. 1 (1930). 1929-1930. [Russ. text; 271 titles, (1929) pp. 79-81; 37-38; (1930) pp. 37-38]

*Seyidov, Anna comp. PROPAGANDA KNIGI SREDI ZHENSHCHIN (SBORNIK METODIKO-BIBLIOGRAFICHESKIKH MATERIALOV). Ashkhabad: "Turkmenistan Neshriyati," 1965, 56 pp., 1250 copies. [Turkmen text; 6 lists, Turkmen titles]

29 UYGHUR

ANTHROPOLOGY, ETHNOGRAPHY

Oshanin, L. V.; V. Ia. Zezenkova. "K PROBLEME ETNOGENEZA UIGUROV," VOPROSY ETNOGENEZA NARODOV SREDNEI AZII V SVETE DANNYKH ANTROPOLOGII. Tashkent: AN UzSSR, In-t Istorii i Arkheologii, 1953. [Russ. text; 33 Russ., foreign titles, pp. 72-73]

ECONOMICS

*Tikhonov, D. I. KHOZIAISTVO I OBSHCHESTVENNYI STROI UIGURSKOGO GOSUDARSTVA X-XIV VV. Moscow-Leningrad: Izdatel'stvo "Nauka," 1966, 287 pp., 900 copies. [Russ. text; Uyghur, Russ., Europ. titles, per.: 10-14th c., pp. 265-276]

HISTORY, ARCHAEOLOGY

Kabirov, M. N. PERESELENIE ILIISKIKH UIGUR V SEMIRECH'E. Alma Ata: (Sektor Uiguro-Dungan. Kultury pri Prezidiume AN Kaz. SSR), 1951. [Russ. text; 180 Uyghur, Russ. titles, pp. 146-153]

*Tikhonov, D. I. KHOZIAISTVO I OBSHCHESTVENNYI STROI UIGURSKOGO GOSUDARSTVA X-XIV VV. Moscow-Leningrad: "Nauka" (Leningr. Otd-Nie.) 1966, 287 pp., 900 copies. [Russ. text; Russ., Western titles, per.: 10-14th c., pp. 265-276]

Uyghur

LANGUAGE, LITERATURE

Amitin-Shapiro, Z. L. "OB UIGURSKOI BIBLIOGRAFII," BELEK S. E. MALOVU. Frunze, 1946. [Russ. text; titles, pp. 9-14]

*Borovkov, A. "UIGURSKII IAZYK," BOL'SHAIA SOVETSKAIA ENTSIKLOPEDIIA. Vol. 55. Moscow: Gosudarstvennyi Nauchnyi Institut "Sovetskaia Entsiklopediia," (OGIZ SSSR), 1947, pp. 718-720. [Russ. text; Uighur, Russ., Europ. titles, p. 720]

Kaidarov, A. UIGURSKII IAZYK I LITERATURA. ANNOT. BIBLIOGR. UKAZATEL'. Vol. 1. Alma Ata: (AN Kaz. SSR. In-t Iazykoznaniia), 1962, 140 pp., 550 copies. [Russ. text; 824 Uyghur, Turkic, Russ., other titles, per.: pre-Rev., Sov.]

*Khamraev, M. K. OSNOVY TIURKSKOGO STIKHOSLOZHENIIA (NA MATERIALE UIGURSKOI KLASSICHESKOI I SOVREMENNOI POEZII). Alma Ata: Izdatel'stvo Akademii Nauk Khazakhskoi SSR, 1963, 215 pp., 2000 copies. [Russ. text; Uyghur, Kazakh, Kirgiz, Uzbek, Tatar, Russ. titles, pp. 173-176]

*Nasilov, V. M. GRAMMATIKA UIGURSKOGO IAZYKA. Moscow: Izdanie Moskovskogo Instituta Vostokovedeniia, 1940, 152 pp., 750 copies. [Russ. text; Russ., Europ. titles, p. 4]

*Talipov, T. GLASNYE ZVUKI UIGURSKOGO I KAZAKHSKOGO IAZYKOV. Alma Ata: "Nauka," 1968, 108 pp., 1100 copies. [Russ. text; Uyghur, Kazakh, Russ. titles, pp. 101-107]

*Tenishev, E. R.; B. Kh. Todaeva. IAZYK ZHELTYKH UIGUROV. Moscow: Izdatel'stvo "Nauka," 1966, 84 pp., 1700 copies. [Russ. text; Russ., Western titles, pp. 82-83]

*"UIGURSKII IAZYK I LITERATURA," LITERATURNAIA ENTSIKLOPEDIIA. Vol. 11. Moscow: Gosudarstvennoe Izdatel'stvo "Khudozhestvennaia Literatura," 1939, pp. 502-503. [Russ. text; Uigur, Russ., Europ. titles, p. 503]

30 UZBEK

GENERAL

*Ageev, A. I. ed. BIBLIOGRAFIIA IZDANII AKADEMII NAUK
UZBEKSKOI SSR. KNIGI I STAT'I ZA 1958-1960 GG.
Tashkent: Izdatel'stvo Akademii Nauk Uzbekskoi SSR,
1963, 370 pp., 650 copies. [Russ. text; 2960 Uzbek,
Karakalpak, Russ. titles, pub.: 1958-1960]

Avsharov, M P.; M. S. Viridarskii. "BIBLIOGRAFICHESKII
SPISOK RABOT E. K. BETGERA," EVGENII KARLOVICH BETGER
(1887-1956). OCHERK ZHIZNI I DEIATEL'NOSTI.
Tashkent: Gosizdat UzSSR, 1960, 43 pp. [Russ. text;
titles, per.: 1887-1956, pp. 27-43]

*Baibekova, F. I.; R. V. Saidakhmedova. comps.
UZBEKISTAN. 1960. BIBLIOGRAFICHESKII UKAZATEL'
LITERATURY. Tashkent: "Ozbekistan" Nashriyati, 1966,
262 pp., 1500 copies. [Uzbek text; 2091 Uzbek titles,
pub.: 1960, pp. 5-234]

Betger, E. K. UZBEKISTAN NA STRANITSAKH SOVETSKIKH
ZHURNALOV. n. p. 1932. 22 pp. [Russ. text; 81 titles]

BIBLIOGRAFICHESKII UKAZATEL' IZDANII... No. 1. Tashkent:
Uzgiz, n. d., 203 pp., 1620 copies. [Russ. text;
pub.: ca.1935]

BIBLIOGRAFICHESKII UKAZATEL' K VYPUSKAM 1-94 (1939-1959)
TRUDY UZBEKSKOGO GOSUDARSTVENNOGO UNIVERSITETA [IMENI
ALISHERA (NOVAIA SERIIA) NAVOI] 1935-. [Russ. text;
pub.: 1939-1959]

"BIBLIOGRAFIIA," DESIAT' LET. MATERIALY DLIA PROVEDENIIA
V KRASNOARMEISKIKH, RABOCHIKH I DEKHKANSKIKH KLUBAKH.
Tashkent, 1928. [Russ. text; 7 titles, pp. 153-157]

*BIBLIOGRAFIIA IZDANII AKADEMII NAUK UZBEKSKOI SSR. SIST.
UKAZATEL' KNIG I STATEI (1961-1963). Tashkent: "Fan"
(AN UzSSR. Fundam. B-ka), 1967, 543 pp., 650 copies.
[Russ. text; 3979 Uzbek, Karakalpak, Russ. titles,
pub.: 1961-1963]

Uzbek: General

*"BIKHBUDI, MUKHAMMED KHODZHA," LITERATURNAIA ENTSIKLOPEDIIA. Vol. 1. n. p. Izdatel'stvo Kommunisticheskoi Akademii, 1929. [Russ. text; Uzbek, Russ. titles, p. 501]

Dalymov, A.; F. Uzbaibullaev. POLNAIA NAUCHNAIA BIBLIOGRAFIIA. PECHATNAIA PRODUKTSIIA NA UZBEKSKOM IAZYKE (1925-1931). Tashkent: Gosizdat UzSSR, 1934, 252 pp., 2600 copies. [Uzbek text and titles, pub.: 1925-1931]

*Deviatkina, A. V. ed. BIBLIOGRAFIIA IZDANII AKADEMII NAUK UZBEKSKOI SSR. SISTEMATICHESKII UKAZATEL' KNIG I STATEI. (1961-1963 GG.) Tashkent: Izdatel'stvo "Fan" Uzbekskoi SSR, 1967, 543 pp., 650 copies. [Russ. text; 3979+ Karakalpak, Uzbek, Russ. titles, pub.: 1961-1963, pp. 6-495]

GAZETY I ZHURNALY UZBEKSKOI SSR. 1959. Tashkent: Ob"edin. Izd. "Kzyl Uzbekistan," "Pravda Vostoka," i "Uzbekistoni Surkh," 1958, 20 pp. [Uzbek, Russ. text; pub.: 1959]

Izosimova, M. P. comp. BIBLIOGRAFICHESKII SBORNIK NAUCHNYKH TRUDOV SAMARKANDSKOGO GOSUDARSTVENNOGO UNIVERSITETA IMENI ALISHERA NAVOI. Samarkand: (Samarkandskii Gosudarstvennyi Universitet im. Navoi), 1964, 194 pp., 1000 copies. [Russ. text; 578, 1272 Uzbek, Tajik, Russ., foreign titles, pub.: 1959-1963]

_____. BIBLIOGRAFICHESKII UKAZATEL' TRUDOV NAUCHNYKH RABOTNIKOV SAMARKANDSKOGO GOSUDARSTVENNOGO UNIVERSITETA IMENI ALISHERA NAVOI (1964-1966 GG.) Samarkand: (Samark. Gos. Un-t im. Navoi. Fundam. B-ka), 1969, 222 pp., 700 copies. [Russ. text; 1501 Uzbek, Russ., other titles, pub.: 1964-1966]

Kasymova, A. comp. UZBEKISTAN. 1958-1959 GG. BIBLIOGR. UKAZATEL' LIT. Tashkent: Gosizdat UzSSR, 1962, 339 pp., 1000 copies. [Uzbek text; 2744 Uzbek titles, pub.: 1958-1959]

*KATALOG GAZET I ZHURNALOV UZBEKSKOI SSR. ...NA 1967 GOD. Tashkent: (Upr. Rasprostraneniia Pechati "Soiuzpechat'") 1966, 27 pp., 50000 copies. [Russ. text; Uzbek, Russ., titles]

KATALOG IZDANII BYVSHEGO KOMITETA NAUK UZSSR. No. 1. n. p. (Uzbekskii Filial Akademii Nauk SSSR), 1940, 32 pp.

Uzbek: General

KATALOG IZDANII, IMEIUSHCHIKHSIA NA SKLAD IZDATEL'STVA UZBEKISTANSKOGO FILIALA AKADEMII NAUK SSSR. No. 2. n. p. (Uzbekskii Filial Akademii Nauk SSSR), 1940, 4 pp.

KATALOG IZDANII UZBEKISTANSKOGO FILIALA AKADEMII NAUK SSSR. No. 3. n. p. (Uzbekskii Filial Akademii Nauk SSSR), 1940, 32 pp.

KATALOG KNIG I ZHURNALOV AKADEMII NAUK UZBEKISTANA. No. 2. Tashkent: Izdatel'stvo Akademii Nauk Uzbekskoi SSR (Akademiia Nauk UzSSR), 1949, 67 pp., 1000 copies. [Russ. text]

*Keizer, S. I. comp.; M. P. Avsharova, ed. UZBEKISTAN 1956 G. BIBLIOGR. UKAZATEL' LIT. Tashkent: Gosizdat UzSSR, 1960, 279 pp., 2000 copies. [Russ. text; 2082 Russ. titles, pub.: mainly 1956]

"KNIGI K 25-LETIIU UZBEKSKOI SSR," ZVEZDA VOSTOKA. No. 1. 1950. [Russ. text; 80 Uzbek, Russ. titles, pp. 200-203]

KNIZHNAIA LETOPIS' UZBEKISTANSKOI GOS. KNIZHNOI PALATY. Samarkand: (Gos. Knizhnaia Palata UzSSR), No. 1, 1928; Nos. 2-3, 1929; No. 4, 1930, 191 pp. [Uzbek, Russ. text; 737 titles, pub.: 1928]

KNIZHNAIA LETOPIS' UZBEKISTANSKOI GOS. KNIZHNOI PALATY. Nos. 1-4. Samarkand: (Gos. Knizhnaia Palata UzSSR), 1929 (quarterly), 118 pp. [Uzbek, Russ. text; 524 titles, pub.: 1929]

KNIZHNAIA LETOPIS' (KITAB LETOPISI). Nos. 1-4. Tashkent: (Ozbekistan Dawlat Kitab Palatasining Matbuati Kitabiyati), 1935. [Uzbek, Russ. text; titles, pub.: 1930]

KNIZHNAIA LETOPIS' UZBEKISTANSKOI GOS. KNIZHNOI PALATY. Nos. 1-4. Samarkand: Gos. Knizhnaia Palata UzSSR), Nos. 1, 3, 1932; No. 2, 1934, No. 4, 1936, (1-2) 181 pp. [Uzbek, Russ. text; (Nos. 1-2) 842 titles, pub.: 1932]

KNIZHNAIA LETOPIS'. ORGAN GOS. BIBLIOGRAFII UZSSR. Nos. 1-12. Tashkent: Gostekhizdat UzSSR (Gos. Knizhnaia Palata UzSSR), 1939, 300 copies. [Russ. text; titles, pub.: 1938]

KNIZHNAIA LETOPIS'. ORGAN GOS. BIBLIOGRAFII UZSSR. Tashkent: (Gos. Knizhnaia Palata UzSSR) Gostekhizdat UzSSR, Nos. 1-2, 1939; Nos. 3-12, 1940, 300 copies. [Russ. text; (No. 1-2) 88 Uzbek, Russ. titles, pub.: 1939]

Uzbek: General

KNIZHNAIA LETOPIS'. Tashkent: (Gos. Knizhnaia Palata UzSSR), Nos. 1-7, 1940; Nos. 8-12; 1941. [Uzbek, Russ. text; titles, pub.: 1940]

KNIZHNAIA LETOPIS'. Nos. 1-4. Tashkent: Gos. Knizhnaia Palata UzSSR), 1948. [Uzbek, Russ. text; titles, pub.: 1947]

KNIZHNAIA LETOPIS'. Nos. 1-3. Tashkent: (Gos. Knizhnaia Palata UzSSR), No. 1, 1948; Nos. 1-3, 1950. [Uzbek, Russ. text; titles, pub.: 1948]

KNIZHNAIA LETOPIS'. Nos. 1-4. Tashkent: (Gos. Knizhnaia Palata UzSSR), Nos. 1, 3, 4, 1952; No. 2, 1956. [Uzbek, Russ. text; titles, pub.: 1949]

KNIZHNAIA LETOPIS'. ORGAN GOS. BIBLIOGRAFII UZSSR. Nos. 3-4, 1950. Tashkent: (Gos. Knizh. Palata UzSSR), 1955-1956 [quarterly] 500 copies. [Uzbek, Russ. text; titles, pub.: 1950]

KNIZHNAIA LETOPIS'. ORGAN GOS. BIBLIOGRAFII UZSSR. Tashkent: (Gos. Kn. Palata UzSSR), 1952 (quarterly), 500 copies. [Uzbek text; titles, pub.: 1952]

KNIZHNAIA LETOPIS'. ORGAN GOS. BIBLIOGRAFII UZSSR. Tashkent: (Knizhnaia Palata UzSSR), 1953 (quarterly), 500 copies. [Uzbek, Russ. text; titles, pub.: 1953]

KNIZHNAIA LETOPIS'. ORGAN GOS. BIBLIOGRAFII UZSSR. Nos. 1, 2, 3, 4, 1954. Tashkent: (Gos. Knizh. Palata UzSSR), 1955-1956 (quarterly), 500 copies. [Uzbek, Russ. text; titles, pub.: 1954]

KNIZHNAIA LETOPIS'. ORGAN GOS. BIBLIOGRAFII UZSSR. Nos. 1-2, 3-4, 1955. Tashkent: (Gos. Knizh. Palata UzSSR), 1955-1956 (quarterly), 500 copies. [Uzbek, Russ. text; titles, pub.: 1955]

KNIZHNAIA LETOPIS'. ORGAN GOS. BIBLIOGRAFII UZSSR. Tashkent: Gos. Knizh. Palata UzSSR), 1956 (monthly),500 copies. [Uzbek, Russ. text; titles, pub.: 1956]

KNIZHNAIA LETOPIS'. ORGAN GOS. BIBLIOGRAFII UZBEK. SSR. ZA 1957 G. Tashkent: (Knizhnaia Palata UzSSR), 1958-1959 (monthly), 500 copies. [Uzbek, Russ. text; titles, pub.: 1957]

KNIZHNAIA LETOPIS'. ORGAN GOS. BIBLIOGRAFII UZBEK. SSR. ZA 1958 G. Tashkent: (Knizhnaia Palata UzSSR), 1959 (monthly), 500 copies. [Uzbek, Russ. text; titles, pub.: 1958]

Uzbek: General

KNIZHNAIA LETOPIS'. ORGAN GOS. BIBLIOGRAFII UZSSR. ZA 1959 G. Tashkent: (Knizhnaia Palata UzSSR), 1959 (monthly), 500 copies. [Uzbek, Russ. text; titles, pub.: 1959]

KNIZHNAIA LETOPIS'. ORGAN GOS. BIBLIOGRAFII UZSSR. Tashkent: (Gos. Knizhnaia Palata UzSSR), [1960] (monthly), 500 copies. [Uzbek, Russ. text; titles, pub.: 1960]

KNIZHNAIA LETOPIS'. ORGAN GOS. BIBLIOGRAFII UZSSR. Tashkent: (Gos. Knizhnaia Palata UzSSR), [1961] (monthly), 500 copies. [titles, pub.: 1961]

KNIZHNAIA LETOPIS'. ORGAN GOS. BIBLIOGRAFII UZSSR. Tashkent: (Gos. Knizhnaia Palata UzSSR) [1962] (monthly), 500 copies. [Russ. text; titles, pub.: 1962]

KNIZHNAIA LETOPIS'. ORGAN GOS. BIBLIOGRAFII UZSSR. Tashkent: (Gos. Knizhnaia Palata UzSSR), [1963] (monthly), 500 copies. [Uzbek, Russ. text; titles, pub.: 1963]

KNIZHNAIA LETOPIS'. Tashkent: (Gos. Knizhnaia Palata UzSSR), 1964 (monthly), 400 copies. [Uzbek, Russ. text; titles, pub.: 1964]

KNIZHNAIA LETOPIS'. Tashkent: (Gos. Knizhnaia Palata UzSSR) [1965; (monthly)] 400 copies. [Uzbek, Russ. text; titles, pub.: 1965]

KNIZHNAIA LETOPIS'. Tashkent: (Gos. Knizhnaia Palata UzSSR), [1966] (quarterly), 600 copies. [Uzbek, Russ. text and titles, pub.: 1966]

KNIZHNAIA LETOPIS'. Tashkent: (Gos. Knizhnaia Palata UzSSR), [1967] (quarterly), 800 copies. [Uzbek, Russ. text and titles. pub.: 1967]

Kormilitsyn, A. I. comp. ALEKSANDR SERGEEVICH UKLONSKII. Tashkent: "Fan," 1968, 45 pp., 500 copies. [Russ. text]

Kross, Kh. comp. UZBEKSKAIA SSR. SPISOK LIT. Tallin: (Gos. B-ka Est. SSR im. Kreitsval'da), 1968, 12 pp., 1000 copies. [Russ. text; 63 Estonian titles]

*Kudimova, E. P. comp. **UZBEK**ISTAN 1961 GOD. BIBLIOGRAFICHESKII UKAZATEL" LITERATURY. Tashkent: (Gosudarstvennaia Biblioteka UzSSR im. A. Novoi) Izdatel'stvo "Uzbekistan," 1967, 838 pp., 1500 copies. [Russ. text; 5540 Russ. titles, pub.: 1961]

Uzbek: General

[Kul'tiasova, N. M.] UZBEKISTAN. BIBLIOGR. UKAZATEL'
   LIT. 1953-1955 GG. Tashkent: Gosizdat UzSSR, 1958,
   383 pp., 750 copies. [Russ. text; ca.3000 Russ.
   titles, pub.: 1953-1955]

* _____. comp.; S. I. Keizer, ed. UZBEKISTAN.
   1957 G. BIBLIOGRAFICHESKII UKAZATEL' LITERATURY.
   Tashkent: Gosizdat UzSSR, 1961, 467 pp., 2000 copies.
   [Russ. text; 3089 Russ. titles, pub.: 1957]

* _____. comp.; R. A. Reznik, ed. UZBEKISTAN.
   1958 G. BIBLIOGRAFICHESKII UKAZATEL' LITERATURY.
   Tashkent: Gosudarstvennoe Izdatel'stvo Uzbekskoi SSR,
   1962, 607 pp., 2000 copies. [Russ. text; 4330 Russ.
   titles, pub.: 1958]

LETOPIS' PECHATI UZBEKSKOI SSR. Nos. 1-4. Tashkent:
   Gos. Knizhnaia Palata UzSSR, No. 1, 1937; Nos. 2-4,
   1938. [Uzbek, Russ. text; titles, pub.: 1937]

LETOPIS' PECHATI UZBEKSKOI SSR. Tashkent: (Gos.
   Knizhnaia Palata UzSSR) [1968] (quarterly), 1100
   copies. [Uzbek, Russ. text and titles, pub.: 1968
   (starting again 1968)]

LETOPIS' PECHATI UZBEKSKOI SSR. Tashkent: (Gos.
   Knizhnaia Palata UzSSR) [1969] (quarterly), 1100
   copies. [Uzbek, Russ. text and titles, pub.: 1969]

LETOPIS' PECHATI UZBEKSKOI SSR. Tashkent: (Gos.
   Knizhnaia Palata UzSSR) [1970] (quarterly), 1100
   copies. [Uzbek, Russ. text and titles, pub.: 1970]

LETOPIS' ZHURNAL'NYKH STATEI. SBORNIK...ZA 1931-1935 GG.
   Tashkent: (Gos. Knizhnaia Palata UzSSR), 1941.
   [Uzbek, Russ. text; titles for selected articles,
   pub.: 1931-1935]

LETOPIS' ZHURNAL'NYKH STATEI. SBORNIK...ZA 1936-37 GG.
   Tashkent: (Gos. Knizhnaia Palata UzSSR), 1940.
   [Uzbek, Russ. text; titles for selected articles,
   pub.: 1936-1937]

LETOPIS' ZHURNAL'NYKH STATEI. ORGAN GOS. BIBLIOGRAFII
   UZSSR. Nos. 1, 2, IANV.-IIUN' 1938. Tashkent:
   (Gos. Knizhnaia Palata UzSSR) Gostekhizdat UzSSR,
   1939-1940, (No. 1) 29 pp., 300 copies. [Russ. text;
   (No. 1) 216 Russ. titles, pub.: Jan.-June, 1938]

LETOPIS' ZHURNAL'NYKH STATEI. Nos. 1-2. Tashkent:
   Gos. Knizhnaia Palata UzSSR], 1940. [Uzbek, Russ.
   text; titles, pub.: 1939]

Uzbek: General

LETOPIS' ZHURNAL'NYKH STATEI. Nos. 1-4 IANV.-APR.
Tashkent: (Gos. Knizhnaia Palata UzSSR), 1940.
[Uzbek, Russ. text; titles, pub.: 1940]

LETOPIS' ZHURNAL'NYKH STATEI. 1948, No. 1 IANV.-IIUN.
Tashkent: (Gos. Kn. Palata UzSSR), 1951, 500 copics.
[Uzbek text; 330 Uzbek, Russ. titles, pub.: 1948]

LETOPIS' ZHURNAL'NYKH STATEI. ORGAN GOS. BIBLIOGRAFII
UZSSR. Nos. 1, 3, 4. Tashkent: (Gos. Knizhnaia
Palata UzSSR), 1960, 500 copies. [Uzbek, Russ. text;
titles, pub.: 1958]

LETOPIS' ZHURNAL'NYKH STATEI. ORGAN GOS. BIBLIOGRAFII
UZSSR. No. 1. Tashkent: (Gos. Knizhnaia Palata
UzSSR), 1960, 500 copies. [Uzbek, Russ. text; titles,
pub.: 1959]

LETOPIS' ZHURNAL'NYKH STATEI. ORGAN GOS. BIBLIOGRAFII
UzSSR. 1959, Nos. 2-3. Tashkent: (Gos. Knizhnaia
Palata UzSSR), 1961, 500 copies. [Uzbek, Russ. text;
titles, pub.: 1959]

LETOPIS' ZHURNAL'NYKH STATEI. ORGAN GOS. BIBLIOGRAFII
UZSSR. Nos. 1-3 (1960); No. 1 (1961). Tashkent: (Gos.
Knizhnaia Palata Uz.SSR), 1960-1962, 500 copies.
[Uzbek, Russ. text; titles, pub.: 1960-1961]

LETOPIS' ZHURNAL'NYKH STATEI. ORGAN GOS. BIBLIOGRAFII
UZSSR. No. 2, 1961; Nos. 1-8, 1962; Nos. 2-6, 1963.
Tashkent: (Gos. Knizhnaia Palata UzSSR), 1963, 500
copies. [Uzbek, Russ. text; titles, pub.: 1961-1963]

LETOPIS' ZHURNAL'NYKH STATEI. Tashkent: (Gos. Knizhnaia
Palata UzSSR), No. 9, 1962; No. 7/8, 1963, 500 copies.
[Uzbek, Russ. text; titles, pub.: 1962-1963]

LETOPIS' ZHURNAL'NYKH STATEI. Nos. 10, 11, 1962;
Nos. 1-5, 1964. Tashkent: (Gos. Knizhnaia Palata
UzSSR), 1965, 400 copies. [Uzbek, Russ. text; titles,
pub.: 1962-1964]

LETOPIS' ZHURNAL'NYKH STATEI. Tashkent: (Gos. Knizhnaia
Palata UzSSR), 1964-1965 (quarterly), 400 copies.
[Uzbek, Russ. text; titles, pub.: 1964-1965]

LETOPIS' ZHURNAL'NYKH STATEI. Tashkent: (Gos. Knizhnaia
Palata UzSSR), [1966] (monthly), 400 copies. [Uzbek,
Russ. text; titles, pub.: 1966]

LETOPIS' ZHURNAL'NYKH STATEI. Tashkent: (Gos. Knizhnaia
Palata UzSSR), [1967] (monthly), 400 copies. [Uzbek,
Russ. text; titles, pub.: 1967]

Uzbek: General

* _____. "BIBLIOGRAFICHESKII UKAZATEL'
LITERATURY PO ARKHEOLOGII, ISTORII, ETNOGRAFII,
FILOSOFII I PRAVU UZBEKISTANA, VYSHEDSHEI V SVET V
1962 GODU," OBSHCHESTVENNYE NAUKI V UZBEKISTANE.
No. 12. 1963. [Russ. text; 590, 170 Uzbek, Russ.
titles, pub.: 1962, 1959-1961, pp. 23-59]

* _____. "BIBLIOGRAFICHESKII UKAZATEL'
LITERATURY PO ARKHEOLOGII, ISTORII, ETNOGRAFII,
FILOSOFII I PRAVU UZBEKISTANA, VYSHEDSHEI V SVET V
1963 GODU," OBSHCHESTVENNYE NAUKI V UZBEKISTANE.
No. 12. 1964. [Russ. text; ca.630; 20 Uzbek, Russ.
titles, pub.: 1955-1963, pp. 34-62]

* _____. "BIBLIOGRAFICHESKII UKAZATEL'
LITERATURY PO ARKHEOLOGII, ISTORII, ETNOGRAFII,
FILOSOFII I PRAVU UZBEKISTANA, VYSHEDSHEI V SVET V
1964 GODU," OBSHCHESTVENNYE NAUKI V UZBEKISTANE.
No. 12. 1965. [Russ. text; ca.700 Uzbek, Russ.
titles, pub.: 1964, pp. 31-57]

* _____. "BIBLIOGRAFICHESKII UKAZATEL'
LITERATURY PO ARKHEOLOGII, ISTORII, ETNOGRAFII,
FILOSOFII I PRAVU UZBEKISTANA, VYSHEDSHEI V SVET V
1965 GODU," [CONTINUED IN No. 1 (1967)],
OBSHCHESTVENNYE NAUKI V UZBEKISTANE. No. 12. 1966.
[Russ. text; Uzbek, Russ. titles, pub.: 1965, pp. 44-55]

* _____. "BIBLIOGRAFICHESKII UKAZATEL'
LITERATURY PO ARKHEOLOGII, ISTORII, ETNOGRAFII,
FILOSOFII I PRAVU UZBEKISTANA, VYSHEDSHEI V SVET V
1965 GODU (OKONCHANIE. NACHALO SM. V No. 12 ZA
1966 G.)," OBSHCHESTVENNYE NAUKI V UZBEKISTANE. No. 1.
1967, 71 pp., 1420 copies. [Russ. text; Uzbek, Russ.
titles, pub.: 1964-1965, pp. 43-67]

_____. "BIBLIOGRAFICHESKII UKAZATEL'
LITERATURY PO ARKHEOLOGII, ISTORII, ETNOGRAFII,
FILOSOFII I PRAVU UZBEKISTANA, VYSHEDSHEI V SVET V
1966 GODU. [NACHALO]," OBSHCHESTVENNYE NAUKI V
UZBEKISTANE. No. 12. 1967. [Russ. text; titles
pp. 21-32]

* _____. "BIBLIOGRAFICHESKII UKAZATEL'
LITERATURY PO ARKHEOLOGII, ISTORII, ETNOGRAFII,
FILOSOFII, I PRAVU UZBEKISTANA, VYSHEDSHEI V SVET V
1967 GODU," OBSHCHESTV. NAUKI V UZBEKISTANE. No. 12,
1968; No. 1, 1969, (No. 12) pp. 38-46, 1320 copies.
(No. 1) 31-53 pp., 1522 copies. [Russ. text; ca.660
Uzbek, Russ. titles, pub.: 1967]

Uzbek: General

*Lunin, B. V. "BIBLIOGRAFICHESKII UKAZATEL' LITERATURY PO ARKHEOLOGII, ISTORII, ETNOGRAFII, FILOSOFII I PRAVU UZBEKISTANA, VYSHEDSHEI V SVET V 1955 G." IZVESTIIA AN UZSSR (SER. OBSHCHESTV. NAUK). No. 3. 1957. [Russ. text and titles, pub.: 1955, pp. 65-71]

* _____. "BIBLIOGRAFICHESKII UKAZATEL' LITERATURY PO ARKHEOLOGII, ISTORII, ETNOGRAFII, FILOSOFII I PRAVU UZBEKISTANA, VYSHEDSHEI V SVET V 1958 G." IZVESTIIA AKAD. NAUK UZSSR. SERIIA OBSHCHESTV. NAUK. No. 6. 1959. [Russ. text; ca.515 Uzbek, Russ. titles, pub.: 1955-1958, pp. 44-73]

* _____. "BIBLIOGRAFICHESKII UKAZATEL' LITERATURY PO ARKHEOLOGII, ISTORII, ETNOGRAFII, FILOSOFII I PRAVU UZBEKISTANA, VYSHEDSHEI V SVET V 1956[-1957 GG.]," IZVESTIIA AKAD. NAUK UZSSR. SERIIA OBSHCHESTV. NAUK. No. 4 (1957); No. 4 (1958). [Russ. text; ca.850 Uzbek, Russ. titles, pub.: 1956[-1957], (1957, No. 4) pp. 81-91; (1958, No. 4) pp. 57-79]

* _____. "BIBLIOGRAFICHESKII UKAZATEL' LITERATURY PO ARKHEOLOGII, ISTORII, ETNOGRAFII, FILOSOFII I PRAVU UZBEKISTANA, VYSHEDSHEI V SVET V 1959 G.," IZVESTIIA AKAD. NAUK UZSSR. SER. OBSHCHESTV. NAUK. No. 5. 1960. [Russ. text; ca.500 titles, pub.: 1959, pp. 55-76]

* _____. "BIBLIOGRAFICHESKII UKAZATEL' LITERATURY PO ARKHEOLOGII, ISTORII, ETNOGRAFII, FILOSOFII I PRAVU UZBEKISTANA, VYSHEDSHEI V SVET V 1960 G.," OBSHCHESTV. NAUKI V UZBEKISTANE. No. 6. 1961. [Russ. text; ca.740 titles, pub.: 1960 (also 1956-1959), pp. 32-61]

* _____. "BIBLIOGRAFICHESKII UKAZATEL' LITERATURY PO ARKHEOLOGII, ISTORII, ETNOGRAFII, FILOSOFII I PRAVU UZBEKISTANA, VYSHEDSHEI V SVET V 1961 GODU," OBSHCHESTV. NAUKI V UZBEKISTANE. No. 12. 1962. [Russ. text; 700 Uzbek, Russ. titles, pub.: 1956-1958, 1961, pp. 42-69]

Uzbek: General

*   . BIBLIOGRAFICHESKII UKAZATEL'
 LITERATURY PO ARKHEOLOGII, ISTORII, ETNOGRAFII,
 FILOSOFII I PRAVU UZBEKISTANA, VYSHEDSHEI V SVET V
 1968 GODU. OBSHCHESTV. NAUKI V UZBEKISTANE. No. 1.
 Tashkent: "Fan," 1970, 46-75 pp., 1571 copies.
 [Russ. text; ca.600 Uzbek, Russ. titles, pub.: 1968,
 pp. 46-75]

*   . "BIBLIOGRAFICHESKII UKAZATEL'
 LITERATURY PO ISTORII SAMARKANDA. LIT. PO ISTORII
 SAMARKANDA S DREVNEISHIKH VREMEN DO VELIKOI
 OKTIABR'SKOI SOTS. REVOLIUTSII," ISTORIIA SAMARKANDA.
 Vol. 1. Tashkent: "Fan," 1969, 484 pp., 10000
 copies. [Russ. text; ca.900 Russ. titles, pub.:
 1843-1969, per.: Ancient - 1917, pp. 409-458]

*   . "BIBLIOGRAFICHESKII UKAZATEL'
 LITERATURY PO ISTORII SOVETSKOGO SAMARKANDA,"
 ISTORIIA SAMARKANDA. Vol. 2. Tashkent: "Fan,"
 1970, 496 pp., 10000 copies. [Russ. text; ca.140
 Russ. titles, pub.: 1922-1967, pp. 467-474]

Magnus, O. "BIBLIOGRAFICHESKII UKAZATEL' LITERATURY PO
 ARKHEOLOGII, VYSHEDSHEI V SSSR ZA 1918-1928 GG.,"
 IZVESTIIA GOS. AKADEMII ISTORII MATERIAL'NOI
 KUL'TURY. Vol. 8, No. 4-7. Leningrad, 1931, 116 pp.
 [Russ. text; ca.50 titles]

*Malysheva, N. Ia. comp. UZBEKISTAN V KHUDOZHESTVENNOI
 LITERATURE. (ANNOTIROVANNYI UKAZATEL' LITERATURY).
 Tashkent: (Gosudarstvennaia Biblioteka UzSSR, im.
 A. Navoi. Otdel Natsional'noi Bibliografii. K 50-
 Letiiu Velikogo Oktiabria), 1967, 104 pp., 400
 copies. [Russ. text; 195 Russ. titles, pp. 4-79]

Morozov, I. S. SPISOK NAUCHNYKH RABOT I PUBLIKATSII
 ZASLUZHENNOGO DEIATELIA NAUKI UZBEKSKOI SSR, DOKTORA
 ISKUSSTVOVEDENIIA, PROFESSORA L. I. REMPELIA. K 60-
 LETIIU SO DNIA ROZHDENIIA I K 40-LETIIU NAUCH.-ISSLED.
 DEIATEL'NOSTI. BIBLIOGR. UKAZATEL'. Tashkent:
 In-t Iskusstvovedeniia im. Khamzy Khakim-Zade
 Niiazi....), 1968, 13 pp., 150 copies. [Russ. text]

N. P. "UKAZATEL' STATEI, POMESHCHENNYKH V BIULLETENIAKH
 TsSU TURKRESPUBLIKI ZA 1921-1924 GG.," BIULLETEN'
 TSENTRAL'NOGO STATISTICHESKOGO UPRAVLENIIA UZBEKISTANA.
 No. 1. Tashkent, 1925. [Russ. text; 169 titles, pub.:
 1921-1924, pp. 53-56]

Uzbek: General

*Nasirova, M. Ia.; F. I. Baibekova. comps.; F. I.
Baibekova ed. UZBEKISTAN - 1961. BIBLIOGRAFICHESKII
UKAZATEL' LITERATURY. Tashkent: Ozbekistan SSR.
Davlat Nashriyati, 1967, 287 pp., 1500 copies.
[Uzbek text; 2216 Uzbek titles, pub.: 1961]

NAUCHNAIA ORGANIZATSIIA TRUDA. REK. UKAZATEL'
LITERATURY. Tashkent: (Resp. Nauch.-Tekhn. B-ka
UzSSR), 1968, 15 pp., 1500 copies. [Russ. text]

Nevzorova, M. P.; E. M. Subbotina. LITERATURA O
SOVETSKIKH SOTSIALISTICHESKIKH RESPUBLIKAKH. No. 4.
UZBEKISTAN. TADZHIKISTAN. Moscow: (Narkompros
RSFSR. Nauchno-Issledovatel'skii Institut
Bibliotekovedeniia i Rekomendatel'noi Bibl.), 1936,
32 pp., 6000 copies. [Russ. text]

NOVAIA LITERATURA OB UZBEKISTANE. I. POLUGODIE 1962 G.
Tashkent: (Gos. Biblioteka UzSSR im. Navoi. Fundam.
B-ka AN UzSSR), 1962, 217 pp., 130 copies. [Russ.
text; 1696 titles, pub.: 1962]

Pankov, A. V. "EVGENII KARLOVICH BETGER (BIBLIOGRAFIIA
1887-1956. NEKROLOG)," IZVESTIIA AKADEMII NAUK UZSSR.
No. 9. 1956. [Russ. text; pp. 91-93]

*Rasulova, H. comp. OZBEKISTAN BADIIY ADABIYATDA
(ADABIYATLARNING ANNOTATSIYALI KORSATKCHI). Tashkent:
(Alisher Nawaiy Namli OzSSR Dawlat Kutubkhanasi.
Milliy Bibliografiya Bolimi Ulugh Oktyabrning 50
Yilligiga), 1967, 106 pp., 400 copies. [Uzbek text;
213 Uzbek titles, pp. 4-81]

Said, Ziya. OZBEK WAQTLI MATBU'ATI TA'RIKHIGA
MATIRIYALLAR. 1870-1927. Samarkand-Tashkent:
Ozbekistan Dawlat Nashriyati, 1927. [Uzbek text;
pub.: 1870-1927]

Salikova, A. P. comp. TRUDY UZBEKSKOGO GOSUDARSTVENNOGO
UNIVERSITETA IM. A. NAVOI. BIBLIOGR. UKAZATEL'
K VYPUSKAM 1-94 (1935-1959 GG.) Samarkand: Izd-vo
Uzbek. Un-ta, 1960, 91 pp., 300 copies. [Russ. text;
674 titles, pub.: 1935-1959]

*Shnaiderman, F. A.; V. G. Bek-Nazarova. comps.
BIBLIOGRAFIIA IZDANII AKADEMII NAUK UZBEKSKOI SSR.
SIST. UKAZATEL' KNIG I STATEI. (1943-1952).
Tashkent: Izdatel'stvo Akademii Nauk Uzbekskoi SSR,
1956, 257 pp., 650 copies. [Russ. text; 2847 Uzbek,
Russ. titles, pub.: 1943-1952]

Uzbek: General

* _____. BIBLIOGRAFIIA IZDANII AKADEMII NAUK UZBEKSKOI SSR. SISTEMATICHESKII UKAZATEL' KNIG I STATEI (1953-1957). Tashkent: Izdatel'stvo Akademii Nauk Uzbekskoi SSR. (AN UzSSR. Fundamental'naia Biblioteka), 1959, 331 pp., 850 copies. [Russ. text; 3318 Uzbek, Russ. titles, pub.: 1953-1957]

SPISOK NAUCHNYKH PUBLIKATSII BORISA VLADIMIROVICHA LUNINA K 60-LETIIU SO DNIA ROZHDENIIA. Tashkent: (AN UzSSR. In-t Istorii i Arkheologii), 1967, 32 pp., 290 copies. [Russ. text]

Tarnovskii, G. V. "PERECHEN' STATEI POMESHCHENNYKH V GAZETE OKRAINA ". Nos.: 3, 5, 8, 12. Samarkand, 1891. [Russ. text; 439 titles, pub.: 1890-1891]

TRUDY ASPIRANTOV TASHGU. No. 325. Tashkent: Tashkenskii Universitet im. V. I. Lenina, 1968, 196 pp., 500 copies. [Russ. text and titles, bibliography at end of articles]

TRUDY ASPIRANTOV TASHGU. NAUCHNYE TRUDY. No. 338. Tashkent: Tashkentskii Universitet im. V. I. Lenina, 1968, 142 pp., 500 copies. [Russ. text; titles at end of articles]

*UKAZATEL' DOKTORSKIKH I KANDIDATSKIKH DISSERTATSII, ZASHCHISHCHENNYKH V UZBEKISTANE V 1936-1951 GG. OBSHCHESTVENNYE NAUKI, ESTESTVENNYE NAUKI. MATEMATIKA. Tashkent: Izdatel'stvo Sredneaziatskogo Gosudarstvennogo Universiteta, 1954, 174 pp., 500 copies. [Russ. text; 595, 234 Uzbek, Russ. titles (incl. hum. & soc. sci.), pub.: 1936-1951, pp. 7-69 (hum. & soc. sci.); pp. 7-165]

"UKAZATEL' SOOBSHCHENII, OPUBLIKOVANNYKH V 'DOKLADAKH AKADEMII NAUK UZSSR' V 1961 G.," DOKLADY AN UZSSR. No. 12. 1961. [Russ. text; titles, pub.: 1961, pp. 62-69]

*"UZBEKSKAIA SOVETSKAIA SOTSIALISTICHESKAIA RESPUBLIKA," BOL'SHAIA SOVETSKAIA ENTSIKLOPEDIIA. Vol. 55. Moscow: Gosudarstvennyi Nauchnyi Institut "Sovetskaia Entsiklopediia" (Ogiz SSSR), 1947, 1st ed., 620-693 pp. [Russ. text; Uzbek, Russ. titles, pp. 692-693]

Uzbek: General

"UZBEKSKAIA SOVETSKAIA SOTSIALISTICHESKAIA RESPUBLIKA,"
BOL'SHAIA SOVETSKAIA ENTSIKLOPEDIIA. Vol. 44.
Moscow: Gosudarstvennoe Nauchnoe Izdatel'stvo
"Bol'shaia Sovetskaia Entsiklopediia," 1956, 2nd ed.,
6-42 pp. [Russ. text; titles pp. 19, 29, 39, 40]

*Zezenkova, Liudmila Iakovlevna; Evgeniia Grigor'evna
Belen'kaia, comps.; Stanislava Ivanovna Keizer, ed.
UZBEKISTAN. 1960 G. BIBLIOGRAFICHESKII UKAZATEL'
LITERATURY. Tashkent: Gosizdat UzSSR, 1962, 735 pp.,
1000 copies. [Russ. text; 4844 Russ. titles, pub.:
1960]

ANTHROPOLOGY, ETHNOGRAPHY

*Borozna, N. "ETNOGRAFICHESKOE IZUCHENIE UZBEKOV
DASHTIKIPCHAKSKOGO PROISKHOZHDENIIA," SOVETSKAIA
ETNOGRAFIIA. No. 3. 1964, 210 pp. [Russ. text;
Russ., foreign titles, pp. 147-153]

Gazi-Iunucov. "OPIS' MATERIALOV PO ETNOGRAFII UZBEKOV,
SOBRANNYKH V SAMARKANDSKOI OBLASTI I
UEZDAKH TASHKENSKOI I GOLODKOSTENSKOI SYR-DAR'II
OBL.," NAUKA I PROSV. No. 2. Tashkent, 1922.
[Russ. text; titles pp. 47-50]

Pisarchik, A. K. "MIKHAIL STEPANOVICH ANDREEV (1873-
1948)," TRUDY AKAD. NAUK TADZHIKSKOI SSR. Vol. 120.
1960, 3-29 pp. [Russ. text; titles pp. 20-23; 23-29
(archives), per.: 1873-1948]

*Shaniiazov, K. UZBEK-KARLUKI (ISTORIKO-ETNOGRAFICHESKII
OCHERK). Tashkent: Izdatel'stvo "Nauka," Uzbekskoi
SSR, 1964, 195 pp., 800 copies. [Russ. text; Russ.,
Europ. titles, pp. 184-194]

Uzbek

ARCHITECTURE, ART, MUSIC

Akhmedov, Akbar. ORATORSKOE ISKUSSTVO. Tashkent: "Uzbekistan," 1967, 56 pp., 10,000 copies. [Russ. text; Uzbek titles, pp. 54-55]

Alimbaeva, K.; M. Akhmedov. NARODNYE MUZYKANTY UZBEKISTANA. [Tashkent] (In-t Iskusstvoznaniia Akad. Nauk UzSSR) [1959]. [Russ. text; 17 titles, pub.: 1924-1957, pp. 126-127]

Asinovskaia A.; I. Akbarov. KOMPOZITORY SOVETSKOGO UZBEKISTANA. Tashkent: (Soiuz Sovetskikh Kompozitorov Uzbekistana), 1959. [Russ. text; titles Sov. per., pp. 127-150]

Biriukov, V. S. POSOBIE PO KURSOVOMU PROEKTIROVANIIU OBSHCHESTVENNYKH ZDANII KURSA. Tashkent: (Trest "Uzorgtekhstroi"), 1967, 62, 73 pp., 1000 copies. [Russ. text; 20 titles at end of book]

*Dolinskaia, V. G. PLAKAT UZBEKISTANA. Tashkent: Izdatel'stvo "Fan," 1968, 118 pp., 1000 copies. [Russ. text; 41 Russ. titles, pub.: 1919-1968, pp. 116-118]

*_____. PLAKAT UZBEKISTANA. Tashkent: "Fan," 1968, 211 pp., 1000 copies. [Russ. text; 41 Uzbek, Russ. titles, publ: 1919-1968, pp. 116-118]

*Grazhdankina, N. S.; M. K. Rakhimov; I. E. Pletnev. ARKHITEKTURNAIA KERAMIKA UZBEKISTANA. Tashkent: Izdatel'stvo "Fan," 1968, 156 pp., 800 copies. [Russ. text; 53 Russ. titles, pp. 153-155]

*Keizer, S. I. comp. [see also Eshonkhuzhaeva, S.] GORODA UZBEKISTANA (UKAZATEL' LITERATURY). Tashkent: Gosudarstvennoe Izdatel'stvo Uzbekskoi SSR, 1964, 96 pp., 1000 copies. [Russ. text; Russ., other titles]

Uzbek: Architecture, Art, Music

Klimkina, R. D.; V. R. Kosenko. RAIONNAIA PLANIROVKA, ZEMLEUSTROISTVO, PLANIROVKA I ARKHITEKTURA NASELENNYKH MEST UZBEKISTANA. BIBLIOGR. UKAZATEL'. Tashkent: (Tashk. In-t Inzhenerov Irrigatsii i Mekhanizatsii Sel. Khoz-va. (Fundam. B-ka) Uzgiprozem. Sredneaz. NII Ekonomiki Sel. Khoz-va. K 100-Letiu so Dnia Rozhdeniia V. I. Lenina), 1969, 303 pp., 705 copies. [Russ. text; ca.2500 Russ., other titles, pub.: 1917-early 1968]

Korsakova, A. UZBEKSKII OPERNYI TEATR. OCHERK ISTORII. Tashkent, 1961. [Russ. text; 46 titles pp. 485-487]

*Masson, M. E. "MATERIALY PO BIBLIOGRAFII MAVZOLEIA ISHRATKHANA," MAVZOLEI ISHRATKHANA. Tashkent: Goslitizdat UzSSR, 1958. [Russ. text; 33 Russ., foreign titles, pp. 149-152]

*_____. "SAMARKANDSKII REGISTAN," TRUDY SREDNEAZ. GOS. UN-TA. NOVAIA SERIIA. No. 11. (GUMANITARNYE NAUKI), Book. 3. 1950. [ca.30 Russ. titles (in notes), pp. 87-90]

MATERIALY I ISSLEDOVANIIA PO ISTORII I RESTAVRATSII ARKHITEKTURNYKH PAMIATNIKOV UZBEKISTANA. No. 1. Tashkent: Izd. Khudozh. Lit., 1967, 160 pp., 1000 copies. [Russ. text; 18 titles at end of articles]

*Meshkeris, V. A. TERRAKOTY SAMARKANDSKOGO MUZEIA. KATALOG. Leningrad, 1962, 106 pp. [Russ. text; 53 Russ., other titles, pp. 6-8, 9-14]

NARODNOE DEKORATIVNOE ISKUSSTVO SOVETSKOGO UZBEKISTANA. TEKSTIL'. Tashkent: (Akad. Nauk Uzbek. SSR. In-t Istorii i Arkheologii...), 1954. [Russ. text; 33 titles, Sov. per., pp. 191-192]

*Pekker, Ia. V. "SPISOK SOCHINENII V. A. USPENSKOGO," V. A. USPENSKII. MUZ.-ETNOGR. I KOMPOZITORSKAIA DEIATEL'NOST' V UZBEKISTANE I TURKMENII. Moscow: Muzgiz, 1953, 154 pp. [Russ. text; 25 Russ. titles, pp. 150-152]

*Pugachenkova, G. A. SAMARKANDSKAIA KERAMIKA XV VEKA. TRUDY SREDNEAZ. GOS. UN-TA. NOVAIA SERIIA. No. 11. GUMANITARNYE NAUKI. Book 3. 1950. [Russ. text; ca.40 Uzb., Russ. titles, per.: 15th c., pp. 118-120]

Uzbek: Architecture, Art, Music

*Rakhimov, M. K. KHUDOZHESTVENNAIA KERAMIKA UZBEKISTANA. Tashkent: (In-t Iskusstvovedeniia im. Khamzy), 1961, 243 pp. [Russ. text; 60 Russ., other titles, pp. 6-11; 241-243]

*Ratiia, Sh. E. MECHET' BIBI-KHANYM V SAMARKANDE. Moscow: Gos. Izd. Arkhitektury i Gradostroitel'stva, 1950, 106 pp. [Russ. text; 78 Uzbek, Russ. titles pp. 105-106]

Rempel', L. I. ed. REZ'BA I ROSPIS' PO GANCHY I DEREVU. Tashkent, 1962. [Russ. text; 56 titles pp. 129-131]

Tatur, P. K. "PLANIROVKA I ZASTROIKA OBSHCHESTVENNYKH TSENTROV SEL'SKOKHOZIAISTVENNYKH NASELENNYKH PUNKTOV V OROSHAEMYKH RAIONAKH UZBEKISTANA," TRUDY. TIIIMSKH. No. 3. 1956. [Russ. text; 33 titles, pp. 140-141]

_____. PLANIROVKA KOLKHOZNYKH POSELKOV V OROSHAEMYKH RAIONAKH UZBEKISTANA. Tashkent: (Tashk. In-t Inzhenerov Irrigatsii i Mekhanizatsii Sel'skogo Khoziaistva) [1949]. [Russ. text; ca.120 titles, pub.: 1914-1947, pp. 176-178]

Umarov, A. PORTRETNAIA ZHIVOPIS' UZBEKISTANA. Tashkent: "Fan," 1968, 133 pp., 1000 copies. [Russ. text; titles pp. 126-129]

*"UZBEKSKOE ISKUSSTVO," BOL'SHAIA SOVETSKAIA ENTSIKLOPEDIIA. Vol. 55. Moscow: Gosudarstvennyi Nauchnyi Institut "Sovetskaia Entsiklopediia," (Ogiz SSSR), 1947, 1st ed., 698-702 pp. [Russ. text and titles, p. 702]

*Veimarn, B. V. ARKHITEKTURNO-DEKORATIVNOE ISKUSSTVO UZBEKISTANA. Moscow, 1948, 107 pp., 4000 copies. [Russ. text; 14 Russ. titles, pub. 1883-1947, p. 105]

Veimarn, B. V.; N. B. Cherkasova. ISKUSSTVO SOVETSKOGO UZBEKISTANA. OCHERKI. Moscow: (Akad. Khudozhestv. SSSR. Nauch.-Issled. In-t Teorii i Istorii Izobrazit. Iskusstv), 1960. [Russ. text; ca.130 titles, Sov. per., pp. 111-115]

Veksler, S. M. OCHERK ISTORII UZBEKSKOI MUZYKAL'NOI KUL'TURY (DO VELIKOI OKTIABR'SKOI SOTS. REVOLIUTSII). Tashkent, 1965. [Russ. text; ca.150 titles, per.: pre-1917, pp. 236-241]

Uzbek: Architecture, Art, Music

Voitsekhovskaia, E. A. comp. KALENDAR' ZNAMENATEL'NYKH I PAMIATNYKH DAT UZBEKSKOI SSR. 1966 G. Tashkent: "Uzbekistan," 1966, 79 pp., 7000 copies. [Russ. text; titles at end of articles, per.: 1966]

_____.; M. Ia. Iarovinskaia. comps. KALENDAR' ZNAMENATEL'NYKH I PAMIATNYKH DAT UZBEKSKOI SSR. ...NA 1966 GOD. Tashkent: "Uzbekistan," 1966, 79 pp., 7000 copies. [Russ. text; titles at end of chapters]

*Voronina, V. L. NARODNYE TRADITSII ARKHITEKTURY UZBEKISTANA. Moscow: Gos. Izd., Arkhitektury i Gradostroitel'stva, 1951, 166 pp. [Russ. text; 36 Uzbek, Russ., other titles, pp. 162-163]

Zakhidov, P. "OSNOVNAIA LITERATURA PO VOPROSAM NARODNOI ARKHITEKTURY SREDNEI AZII XIX-NACHALA XX V.," SAMARKANDSKAIA SHKOLA ZODCHIKH. XIX-NACHALO XX V. Tashkent, 1965. [Russ. text; 83 titles, per.: 19th - 20th cc., pp. 171-174]

*Zotov, A. N. TASHKENT V SHESTOI PIATILETKE (PROSHLOE, NASTOIASHCHEE I BUDUSHCHEE GORODA). Tashkent: Gosudarstvennoe Izdatel'stvo Uzbekskoi SSR, 1958, 96 pp., 5000 copies. [Russ. text; 21 Russ. titles, pp. 94-95]

ECONOMICS

Abduganiev, A. A.; U. N. Mirzakhodzhaev; V. A. Osminin. OBSHCHESTVENNYI PRODUKT I NATSIONAL'NYI DOKHOD UZBEKSKOI SSR. Tashkent: (Akad. Nauk UzSSR. In-t Ekonomiki), 1960. [Russ. text; 56 titles, Sov. per., pp. 178-180]

Abdullaev, Sh. IZ ISTORII BOR'BY ZA LIKVIDATSIIU FAKTICHESKOGO NERAVENSTVA NARODOV UZBEKISTANA. Tashkent: Gosizdat UzSSR, 1959. [Uzbek text; ca.175 Uzbek, Russ. titles (incl. archives), Sov. per., pp. 271-279]

Uzbek: Economics

Abdurazakov, V.; F. Abdullaev. MATEMATICHESKIE METODY V PLANIROVANII I PROEKTIROVANII KHLOPKOVODCHESKIKH SVOISTV UZBEKSKOI SSR. Tashkent: "Fan," 1967, 94 pp., 650 copies. [Russ. text 47 titles, pp. 90-92]

Abdushukurov, T., M. Zaidov. NEKOTORYE PROBLEMY POVYSHENIIA PROIZVODITEL'NOSTI TRUDA V PROMYSHLENNOSTI UZBEKISTANA. Tashkent, 1970. [Russ. text; ca.270 titles, pp. 372-386]

*Aiupov, M. T. NEKOTORYE VOPROSY ISTORII PROFSOIUZNOGO DVIZHENIIA V UZBEKISTANE. Tashkent: "Uzbekistan," 1969, 270 pp., 3000 copies. [Russ. text; ca.210 Russ. titles, per.: 1941-1965, pub.: 1927-1967, pp. 259-268]

Akhmedov, S. I. KOMMUNISTICHESKAIA PARTIIA UZBEKISTANA V BOR'BE ZA DAL'NEISHEE RAZVITIE KHLOPKOVODSTVA V GODY CHETVERTOI PIATILETKI (1946-1950). Tashkent: (Akad. Nauk UzSSR), 1959. [Russ. text; 32 titles, (including archives), per.: 1946-1950, pp. 123-125]

*Akhun, M. I.; K. A. Petrov. comps. MATERIALY PO ISTORII NARODOV SSSR. No. 3. MATERIALY PO ISTORII UZBEKSKOI, TADZHIKSKOI I TURKMENSKOI SSR. Part 1. Leningrad: Izdatel'stvo Akademii Nauk SSSR, 1932, 504 pp., 1500 copies. [Russ. text; 232 Russ. titles, per.: 16th - 17th c.c., pp. 492-504]

Akramov, Z. M. NAMANGANSKAIA OBLAST'. EKON.-GEOGR. OCHERK. Tashkent, 1955. [Russ. text; 114 titles, pp. 170-174]

Allamuradov, D. DEIATEL'NOST' SOVETOV UZBEKISTANA PO VOSSTANOVLENIIU NARODNOGO KHOZIAISTVA RESPUBLIKI (1921-1924 GG.) Tashkent, 1965. [Russ. text; ca.130 titles (incl. archives), per.: 1921-1924, pp. 152-157]

Aminov, A. M. EKONOMICHESKOE RAZVITIE SREDNEI AZII (SO VTOROI POLOVINY XIX STOLETIIA DO PERVOI MIROVOI VOINY). Tashkent: Gosizdat UzSSR, 1959. [Russ. text; ca.340 titles (incl. archives), per.: 2nd half 19th c. - W. W. I., pp. 5-20, 282-296]

Aminova, R. Kh. AGRARNAIA POLITIKA SOVETSKOI VLASTI V UZBEKISTANE (1917-1920 GG.) Tashkent, 1963. [Russ. text; ca.220 titles, per.: 1917-1920, pp. 27-53, 332-343]

Uzbek: Economics

*Batrakov, V. S. OSOBENNOSTI RAZVITIIA SEL'SKOGO KHOZIAISTVA BUKHARSKOGO KHANSTVA S POLOVINY XVIII DO 70-KH GG. XIX VEKA. NAUCHN. TRUDY TASHK. UN-TA. No. 193, 1962. Tashkent: (Tashkent Un-t), 1962, 221 pp. [Russ. text; ca.50 titles, per.: 18th - 19th c., pp. 183-184]

BIBLIOGRAFICHESKII UKAZATEL' NAUCHNYKH RABOT, OPUBLIKOVANNYKH V TRUDAKH. Tashkent:(Tashkentskii Institut Inzhenerov Irrigatsii i Mekhanizatsii Sel'skogo Khoziaistva) (MSKH SSSR), 1967, 48 pp., 330 copies. [Russ. text; 345 titles, pub.: 1955 - May 1967]

*Chikaev, Kh. F. "K ISTORII BOR'BY ZA RAZRESHENIE AGRARNOGO VOPROSA I ZEMEL'NYKH OTNOSHENII V UZBEKISTANE (1917-1921)," TRUDY UZBEK. UN-TA. No. 51. 1952, 218 pp. [Russ. text; ca.70 Russ., other titles, per.: 1917-1921, pp. 82-84]

Davydov, A. M. AGRARNYE PREOBRAZOVANIIA I FORMIROVANIE SOTSIALISTICHESKOGO ZEMLEPOL'ZOVANIIA V UZBEKSKOI SSR. Tashkent, 1965. [Russ. text; ca.190 titles, pp. 264-270]

Dosumov, R. Ia. PROBLEMY ORGANIZATSII I PLANIROVANIIA RITMICHNOSTI PROIZVODSTVA NA PROMYSHLENNYKH PREDPRIIATIIAKH. Tashkent: "Fan," 1968, 136 pp., 650 copies. [Russ. text; titles pp. 134-135]

Dvorkina, E. A. "IZ ISTORII BOR'BY NARODNYKH MASS ZA VYPOLNENIE TRET'EI PIATILETKI UZBEKSKOI SSR," TRUDY SREDNE-AZIAT. UN-TA. No. 75. (EKON. NAUKI), Book 1. 1955. [Russ. text; 67 titles, Sov. per., 3rd 5-year plan, pp. 91-92]

*Dzhamalov, O. B. ed. ISORIIA NARODNOGO KHOZIAISTVA UZBEKISTANA. Vol. 1. OT OKTIABR'SKOI REVOLIUTSII DO VELIKOI OTCHESTVENNOI VOINY. Tashkent, 1962, 385 pp. [Russ. text; ca.250 Uzbek, Russ. titles, per.: 1917-1941, pp. 375-385]

_____. SOTSIAL'NO EKONOMICHESKIE PREDPOSYLKI SPLOSHNOI KOLLEKTIVIZATSII SEL'SKOGO KHOZIAISTVA V UZBEKISTANE. Tashkent: Gosizdat UzSSR, 1950. [Russ. text; ca.85 titles (incl. archives), pp. 120-123]

*EKONOMICHESKOE RAIONIROVANIE UZBEKISTANA. Tashkent: Izdatel'stvo "Fan" Uzbekskoi SSR, 1966, 246 pp., 1000 copies. [Russ. text; 58 Russ. titles, pp. 243-245]

Uzbek: Economics

Frolov, S. I.; Iu. I. Krivonogov. "UKAZATEL' LITERATURY I MATERIALOV," UZBEKISTAN. Moscow-Samarkand, 1930. [Russ. text; 64 titles, pp. 273-278]

* _____. UZBEKISTAN. POSOBIE PO IZUCHENIIU EKONOMIKI KRAIA. Moscow: Uzgosizdat, 1930, 276 pp. [Russ. text and titles, pp. 273-275]

Gel'berg, B. T.; G. D. Pekelis. REMONT PROMYSHLENNOGO OBORUDOVANIIA. Tashkent: "Uchitel'," 1966, 420 pp., 3000 copies. [Russ. text; Uzbek titles, p. 414]

*Iakovkin, I. I. "OPYT BIBLIOGRAFICHESKOGO UCHETA RUKOPISNYKH I VEDOMSTVENNYKH MATERIALOV PO SODERZHANIIU SVOEMU OTNOSIASHCHIKHSIA K UZBEKSKOI SSR," MATERIALY 1-I KONFERENTSII PO IZUCHENIIU PROIZVEDITEL'NYKH SIL UZBEKSKOI SSR. No. 2. 1932. [Russ. text; titles pp. 46-48]

*Iarovinskaia, M. Ia. "V POMOSHCH' IZUCHAIUSHCHIM ISTORIIU NARODNOGO KHOZIAISTVA UZBEKISTANA. (OBZOR BIBLIOGR. UKAZATELEI)," OBSHCHESTVENNYE NAUKI V UZBEKISTANE. No. 2. 1968. [Russ. text; 4 Russ. titles, p. 78]

Iusupov, K. RAZVITIE SEL'SKOKHOZIAISTVENNOGO PROIZVODSTVA UZBEKISTANA V PERIOD PEREKHODA OT FEODALIZMA K SOTSIALIZMU. Tashkent, 1965. [Russ. text; ca.200 titles (incl. archives), pp. 122-130]

K [DVADTSAT] 25-LETNEMU IUBILEIU UZBEKSKOI SSR. SPISOK LITERATURY. Tashkent: (Uzb. Gos. Publ. B-ka im. Navoi), 1949, 14 pp., 500 copies. [Uzbek text; 68 Uzbek titles, per. 1925-1950]

Kaiumov, F. EFFEKTIVNOST' KAPITAL'NYKH VLOZHENII V OSVOENIE ZEMEL'. Tashkent: "Fan," 1968, 103 pp., 650 copies. [Russ. text; 41 titles, pp. 101-102]

KASHKA-DAR'INSKAIA OBLAST'. Vol. 2: "EKON.-GEOGR. KHARAKTERISTIKA," (SREDNEAZIAT. GOS. UN-T IM. LENINA. TRUDY. [NOVAIA SERIIA]. No. 156. [GEOGR. NAUKI]. Book 15.) Tashkent, 1959. [Russ. text; 65 titles, pp. 241-243]

Khodzhaev, S. RAZVITIE TRANSPORTA V UZBEKISTANE. Tashkent: Gosizdat UzSSR, 1957. [Russ. text; 30 titles, pp. 109-110]

Uzbek: Economics

Lapkin, K. I. RAZMESHCHENIE I SPETSIALIZATSIIA
SEL'SKOKHOZIAISTVENNOGO PROIZVODSTVA PO ZONAM I
RAIONAM UZBEKSKOI SSR. Tashkent, 1966. [Russ. text;
ca.260 titles, pp. 375-387]

MATERIALY PO PROIZVODITEL'NYM SILAM UZBEKISTANA. No. 16.
GOLODNAIA STEP'. OPYT PROEKTIROVANIIA, STROITEL'STVA
I KHOZ. OSVOENIIA TSELINNYKH ZEMEL'. Tashkent,
1964. [Russ. text; titles scattered at end of
chapters]

Muminov, N. M. BOR'BA SOVETOV ZA INDUSTRIALIZATSIIU
UZBEKISTANA. (1928-1932 GG.) Tashkent: Gosizdat
UzSSR, 1959. [Uzbek text; 52 titles, per.: 1928-1932,
pp. 108-110]

Mukminova, R. G. K ISTORII AGRARNYKH OTNOSHENII V
UZBEKISTANE XVI V. PO MATERIALAM "VLAKF-NAME".
Tashkent: "Nauka," 1966, 354 pp., 1000 copies.
[Russ. text; titles, pp. 331-337]

Nasyrova, M. REKOMENDATEL'NYI SPISOK LITERATURY K
30-LETIIU UZBEKSKOI SSR. Tashkent: Gosizdat UzSSR,
1954, 44 pp., 1000 copies. [Uzbek text; 145 titles,
Sov. per.]

NAUCHNAIA KONFERENTSIIA PO SEL'SKOMU KHOZIAISTVU, 3-IA
MATERIALY. Tashkent: "Fan," 1968, 219 pp., 700
copies. [Russ. text; titles at end of reports]

Nurullaev, A. FORMIROVANIE KADROV RABOCHIKH
SOTSIALISTICHESKOGO SEL'SKOGO KHOZIAISTVA UZBEKISTANA.
Tashkent, 1965. [Russ. text; ca.130 titles (incl.
archives), pp. 108-114]

*Pavlov, E. A.; N. N. Trotskii. UZBEKISTAN. SPRAVOCHNIK.
Tashkent: Gosudarstvennoe Izdatel'stvo Uzbekskoi SSR,
1959, 279 pp., 20,000 copies. [Russ. text and titles]

PROBLEMY ISPOL'ZOVANIIA ZEMEL'NO-VODNYKH RESURSOV
UZBEKSKOI SSR. Tashkent, 1969. [Russ. text; titles
at end of articles]

Proshliakov, V. P. MEZHKHOZIAISTVENNOE ZEMLEUSTROISTVO
V USLOVIIAKH OROSHAEMOGO ZEMLEDELIIA. Tashkent:
"Ukituvchi," 1967, 156 pp., 5500 copies. [Russ. text;
Uzbek titles, pp. 154-155]

"REKOMENDUEMAIA LITERATURA (K 40-LETIIU OBRAZOVANIIA
UZSSR I KOMPARTII UZBEKISTANA)," KOMMUNIST UZBEKISTANA.
No. 9. 1964. [Russ. text; 48 titles, per.: 1925-1964,
pp. 73-74]

Uzbek: Economics

*Saidov, Kh. BOR'BA ZA OSUSHCHESTVLENIE LENINSKIKH IDEI V RAZVITII SOVETSKOGO KHLOPKOVODSTVA. Tashkent:"Fan," 1966, 115 pp., 650 copies. [Russ. text; 250+ Russ. titles, pp. 102-114]

_____ LICHNOE MATERIAL'NOE STIMULIROVANIE TRUDA V KOLKHOZAKH. Tashkent, "Fan," 1968, 127 pp., 1000 copies. [Russ. text; titles at end of book]

Shappo, A. F. ZEMLEUSTROISTVO OVTSEVODCHESKIKH SOVKHOZOV UZBEKSKOI SSR. Tashkent, 1968, 142 pp., 1000 copies. [Russ. text; 25 titles at end of book]

*Smirnov, N. V. GORODA FERGANSKOI DOLINY. (EKON-GEOGR. OCHERK) (SREDNE-AZIAT. GOS. UN-T IM. LENINA. TRUDY. NOVAIA SERIIA. No. 95. GEOG. NAUKI. Book 9.) Tashkent, 1957. [Russ. text; 62 Uzbek, Russ. titles, Sov. per., pp. 149-151]

SURKHAN-SHIRABADSKAIA DOLINA. (EKON.-GEOGR. KHARAKTERISTIKA). (NAUCHNYE TRUDY. TASHKENTSKII GOSUDARSTVENNYI UNIVERSITET IM. LENINA I PROEKTNYI INSTITUT "UZGIPROZEM," No. 217), 1964. [Russ. text; 55 titles, pp. 245-247]

Talipov, M. OSUSHCHESTVLENIE LENINSKIKH IDEI ELEKTRIFIKATSII V UZBEKISTANE. Tashkent, 1970. [Russ. text; ca.150 titles, pp. 169-176]

TASHKENTSKII S.-KH. INSTITUT. TRUDY. No. 20. Tashkent: "Fan," 1968, 299 pp., 1000 copies. [Russ. text; titles at end of articles]

Tatarnikova, M. M.; N. K. Eremiants. VILT KHLOPCHATNIKA I BOR'BA S NIM. UKAZATEL' OSNOVNOI LITERATURY, IZD. V SSSR. 1930-1966. Tashkent: (M-vo Sel. Khoz-va UzSSR), 1967, 148 pp., 1000 copies. [Russ. text; titles per.: 1930-1966]

Tatur, P. K. "OSNOVNYE VOPROSY RAIONNOI PLANIROVKI, ORGANIZATSII TERRITORII I RAZMESHCHENIIA NASELENNYKH PUNKTOV V GOLODNOI STEPI UZBEKSKOI SSR. TRUDY TASHKENSTSKOGO INSTITUTA INZHENEROV IRRIGATSII I MEKHANIZATSII SELSKOGO KHOZIAISTVA. No. 5. 1957. [Russ. text; 49 titles, pp. 260-261]

UZBEKISTAN. EKON.-GEOGR. KHARAKTERISTIKA. Tashkent: (AN UzSSR. In-t Ekonomiki), 1950. [Russ. text; 189 titles, pp. 294-300]

Uzbek: Economics

Valiev, A. Kh. SOTRUDNICHESTVO RABOCHIKH I KREST'IAN V UZBEKISTANE 1951-1965 GG. Tashkent, 1969. [Russ. text; ca.190 titles, per.: 1951-1965, pp. 11-20; 215-223]

*Ubaiduliaeva, R. A. ZHENSKII TRUD V SEL'SKOM KHOZIAISTVE UZBEKISTANA. Tashkent: "Fan," 1969, 123 pp., 650 copies. [Russ. text; ca.130 Russ. titles, pub.: 1886-1967, pp. 116-121]

VOPROSY ZEMLEUSTROISTVA, RAIONNOI PLANIROVKI, PLANIROVKI NASELENNYKH MEST I GEODEZII. TRUDY TIIMSKH. No. 27. Tashkent: "Fan," 1966, 149 pp., 650 copies. [Russ. text; titles at end of articles]

Zakirov, Sh. N. VOPROSY RAZVITIIA I RAZMESHCHENIIA PROMYSHLENNOSTI UZBEKISTANA. Tashkent, 1965. [Russ. text; 108 titles, pp. 137-142]

Ziiadullaev, S. K. PROMYSHLENNOST' UZBEKISTANA I OSNOVNYE EKONOMICHESKIE PROBLEMY EE RAZVITIIA. Tashkent: "Fan," 1967, 331 pp., 2000 copies. [Russ. text; ca.330 titles, pp. 318-330]

Uzbek

EDUCATION

*Kocharov, V. T. IZ ISTORII ORGANIZATSII I RAZVITIIA NARODNOGO OBRAZOVANIIA V DOREVOLIUTSIONNOM UZBEKISTANE (1865-1917 GG.) Tashkent: Izdatel'stvo "Fan," 1966, 124 pp., 650 copies. [Russ. text and ca.130 titles, per.: 1865-1917, pp. 119-124]

Ageev, A.; F. Baibekova, comps. REKOMENDATEL'NYI KATALOG SEL'SKOI I KOLKHOZNOI BIBLIOTEKI. Tashkent: Gosizdat UzSSR, 1955, 335 pp., 5000 copies. [Uzbek text]

ALFAVITNO-PREDMETNYI UKAZATEL' PECHATNYKH MATERIALOV NA RUSSKOM IAZYKE PO NARODNOMU OBRAZOVANIIU NA TERRITORII UZBEKISTANA ZA 1917-1931 GG. 1932/1933. [Russ. text and titles, pub.: 1917-1931]

Arkhangel'skii, Nik. UCHEBNAIA LITERATURA NA UZBEKSKOM IAZYKE," NAUKA I PROSVESHCHENIE. No. 2. 1922 (Oct.-Dec.) [Uzbek text; 61 Uzbek titles, per.: 1907-1922, pp. 34-41]

Bilialov, G. M. IZ ISTORII KUL'TURY I PROSVESHCHENIIA V KHOREZMSKOI NARODNOI SOVETSKOI RESPUBLIKE. (1920-1924 GG.) Tashkent: "Fan," 1966, 126 pp., 2000 copies. [Russ. text; ca.250 titles, per.: 1920-1924, pp. 115-125]

Dumenko, M. F. ed. VOPROSY VOSPITANIIA I OBRAZOVANIIA. (SBORNIK STATEI. NAUCH. TRUDY. No. 324.) Tashkent: Tashk. Gos. Un-t im. V. I. Lenina, 1968, 134 pp., 500 copies. [Russ. text and titles at end of articles]

Faktorovich, Ia. "Turkgosizdat," NAUKA I PROSVESHCHENIE. No. 2. [Tashkent] 1922 (Oct.-Dec.) [Russ. text; 38 titles, p. 163]

Gel'mont, A. M.; D. I. Paltorak. TELEVIDENIE V SHKOL'NOM OBRAZOVANII. Tashkent, 1967. [Uzbek text; 38 titles pp. 150-151]

Uzbek: Education

Kary-Niiazov, T. N. IZBRANNYE TRUDY V 8-MI T. Vol. 5. OCHERKI ISTORII KUL'TURY I NAUKI SOVETSKOGO UZBEKISTANA. 1917-1953. Tashkent: "Fan," 1967, 558 pp., 3000 copies. [Russ. text; titles, per.: 1917-1953, pp. 554-556]

*_____. OCHERKI ISTORII KUL'TURY SOVETSKOGO UZBEKISTANA. Moscow: (Akad. Nauk SSSR. Akad. Nauk Uzbek. SSR), 1955, 560 pp. [Russ. text; 62 Uzbek, Russ. titles, Sov. per., pp. 556-558]

_____. OCHERKI ISTORII KUL'TURY SOVETSKOGO UZBEKISTANA. Tashkent: (Akad. Nauk SSSR. Akad. Nauk Uzbek. SSR. Dekada Uzbek. Iskusstva i Lit. Moskva 1956), 1956. [Uzbek text; 42 Uzbek, Russ. text; Sov. per., pp. 511-512]

Khairullaev, M. M.; R. I. Khamidov. comps. IBRAGIM MUMINOVICH MUMINOV. Tashkent: "Fan," 1968, 52 pp., 1000 copies. [Russ. text]

Khushbekov, A. IZ ISTORII KUL'TURNOGO STROITEL'STVA V UZBEKISTANE V GODY PERVOI PIATILETKI. Samarkand: (Sredneaziat. Gos. Un-t im. Lenina), 1959. [Russ. text; 65 titles, per.: 1928-1931, pp., 86-91]

*[Kormilitsyn, A. I.; D. F. Zhelezniakov; S. Kh. Khalbaev] MATERIALY K ISTORII TASHKENTSKOGO GOSUDARSTVENNOGO UNIVERSITETA IM. LENINA. ANNOT. BIBLIOGR. UKAZ. (1920-1966). NAUCH. TURDY TASHK. GOS. UN-TA IM. LENINA. No. 385. MATERIALY K BIBLIOGR. No. 15. Tashkent, 1970, 271 pp., 500 copies. [Russ. text; 1542 Tajik, Uzbek, Russ. titles, per.: 1920-1966, pp. 20-261]

Ledenev, V. G. LITERATURNO-TVORCHESKIE SOCHINENIIA NA RUSSKOM IAZYKE V STARSHIKH KLASSAKH UZBEKSKOI SHKOLY. Tashkent, 1967. [Russ. text; 57 titles, pp. 63-65]

"MATERIAL, POMESHCHENNYI V ZH. 'SOTSIALISTICHESKAIA NAUKA I ZHIZN'' ZA 1939 G." SOTSIALISTIK FANWA TURMUSH. No. 12. 1939. [Uzbek text; 132 Uzbek titles, pub.: 1939, pp. 31-32]

Mirochnik, V. Sh.; S. P. Vinogradenko. V POMOSHCH' UCHITELIU RUSSKOGO IAZYKA V UZBEKSKOI SHKOLE. No. 1. Tashkent: Uchpedgiz UzSSR, 1954. [Russ. text; 131 Uzbek, Russ., other titles, pp. 48-55]

Uzbek: Education

NARODNOE PROSVESHCHENIE UZBEKISTANA. BIBLIOGRAFICHESKII
UKAZATEL' SOSTAVLENNYI BRIGADOI SOTRUDNIKOV GOS.
PUBLICHNOI BIBLIOTEKI UZBEKISTANA. Part 1-2. n. p.,
n. d., (1) 143 pp.; (2) 389 pp. [Russ. text; (1)
2290 titles, (2) 3922 titles, pub.: before and after
1917]

"PROIZVODSTVENNYI PLAN UZBEKSKOGO NAUCHNO-
ISSLEDOVATEL'SKOGO INSTITUTA KUL'TURNOGO STROITEL'STVA
NA 1933 G.," SBORNIK NAUCHNYKH TRUDOV. Vol. 1, No. 2.
Tashkent: Narkompros UzSSR. Uzbekskii Nauchno-
Issledovatel'skii Institut Kul'turnogo Stroitel'stva,
1934. [Russ. text; 47 titles, pp. 89-91]

*Pulatov, Kh. KUL'TURNO-VOSPITATEL'NAIA DEIATEL'NOST'
SOVETSKOGO GOSUDARSTVA V UZBEKISTANE (PERIOD BOR'BY
ZA POSTROENIE FUNDAMENTA SOTSIALIZMA). Tashkent:
Gosudarstvennoe Izdatel'stvo Uzbekskoi SSR, 1959,
142 pp., 3000 copies. [Russ. text; Uzbek, Russ.
titles, per.: 1917-1932, pp. 137-141]

Saidakhmedova, R. V. comp. VOSPITYVAEM CHELOVEKA
KOMMUNISTICHESKOGO OBSHCHESTVA. ANNOT. REK. SPISOK
LIT. Tashkent: Gosizdat UzSSR, 1963, 39 pp., 2000
copies. [Uzbek text; ca.170 titles]

Salikova, A. P. comp. KRATKII BIBLIOGRAFICHESKII
UKAZATEL'. K 40-LETIIU. Samarkand: (Samarkandskii
Universitet im. Alishera Navoi...Fundamental'naia
Biblioteka), 1968, 29 pp., 500 copies. [Russ. text]

_____. SAMARKANDSKII GOSUDARSTVENNYI
UNIVERSITET IMENI ALISHERA NAVOI. KRATKII BIBLIOGR.
UKAZATEL'. K 40-LETIIU [UN-TA]. Samarkand:
(Samarkandskii Gos. Un-t im. Navoi. Fundam. B-ka), 1968,
29 pp., 500 copies. [Russ. text; 243 Uzbek, Tajik,
Russ. titles]

Shukur, Sagdulla. PAMIATKA CHITATELIU 3-4 KLASSOV.
Fergana: (Gos. Resp. Det. B-ka UzSSR), 1968, 22 pp.,
5000 copies. [Russ. text; Uzbek, Russ. titles]

"SODERZHANIE NOMEROV ZHURNALA ZA 1939 G." BOL'SHEVISTIK
MATBUAT. No. 12. 1939. [Uzbek text; 34 titles,
pub.: 1939, p. 47]

VOPROSY ISTORII FIZICHESKOI KUL'TURY SPORTA V
UZBEKISTANE. Tashkent: (Trudy In-ta [Uzb. Gos. In-t
Fiz. Kul'tury] No. 4), 1968, 268 pp. [Russ. text;
titles at end of articles]

GEOGRAPHY

GEOGRAFICHESKOE OBSHCHESTVO SSSR. IZVESTIIA UZBEKISTANSKOGO GEOGRAFICHESKOGO OBSHCHESTVA. Vol. 11. Tashkent: "Fan," 1968, 143 pp., 1000 copies. [Russ. text; titles at end of articles]

GEOGRAFICHESKOE OBSHCHESTVO SSSR. UZBEKISTANSKII FILIAL. IZVESTIIA UZBEKISTANSKOGO GEOGRAFICHESKOGO OBSHCHESTVA. Vol. 9. Tashkent: "Fan," 1966, 134 pp., 650 copies. [Russ. text; titles at end of articles]

Ianitskii, N. "CHIRCHIKSKII ELEKTROKHIMICHESKII KOMBINAT," BOL'SHAIA SOVETSKAIA ENTSIKLOPEDIIA. Vol. 61. Moscow: Gosudarstvennoe Slovarno-Entsiklopedicheskoe Izdatel'stvo "Sovetskaia Entsiklopediia," (Ogiz RSFSR), 1934, 616-617 pp. [Russ. text and titles, p. 617]

*Kes', A. S. RUSLO UZBOI I EGO GENEZIS. TRUDY IN-TA GEOGRAFII AKAD. NAUK SSSR. No. 30. Moscow-Leningrad, 1939, 220 pp. [Russ. text; 133 Uzbek, Russ. titles, pub.: 1822-1935, pp. 114-118]

*"KHOREZM," BOL'SHAIA SOVETSKAIA ENTSIKLOPEDIIA. Vol. 60. Moscow: Gosudarstvennoe Slovarno-Entsiklopedicheskoe Izdatel'stvo "Sovetskaia Entsiklopediia," (Ogiz RSFSR), 1934, 95 pp. [Russ. text and titles, pp. 95-96]

*Korzhenevskii, N. L. ed. UZBEKSKAIA SSR. Moscow: Gosizdat Geograficheskoi Literatury. (Sredneaziat. Un-t im. Lenina), 1956, 471 pp., 6000 copies. [Russ. text; ca.120 Russ. titles, Sov. per., pp. 464-469]

LANDSHAFTY UZBEKISTANA. No. 1. Tashkent, 1966, 136 pp. [Russ. text; titles at end of articles]

Malysheva, N. Ia. comp. PO RODNYM PROSTORAM UZBEKISTANA (ANNOTIROVANNYI REKOMENDATEL'NYI SPISOK LITERATURY). Tashkent: (Gosudarstvennaia Biblioteka UzSSR imeni Alishera Navoi. Otdel Natsional'noi Bibliografii...), 1966, 29 pp., 300 copies. [Russ. text; ca.170 titles]

Uzbek: Geography

MATERIALY PO FIZICHESKOI GEOGRAFII UZBEKISTANA.
Tashkent, 1966, 134 pp. [Russ. text; titles at end of articles]

PRIRODNYE USLOVIIA I RESURSY IUGO-ZAPADNOGO UZBEKISTANA.
Tashkent, 1965, 403 pp. [Russ. text; titles at end of articles]

*[Shul'ts, V. L. ed.] KASHKA-DAR'INSKAIA OBLAST'.
Vol. 1. "PRIRODA." SREDNEAZIAT. GOS. UN-T IM.
LENINA. TRUDY. [NOVAIA SERIIA] No. 155, [GEOGR. NAUKI] 2, Book 14. Tashkent, 1959, 278 pp. [Rus. text; 76 Russ; other titles, pp. 277-279]

VOPROSY EKONOMICHESKOI GEOGRAFII UZBEKISTANA. NAUCH.
ZAPISKI. No. 34. Tashkent: "Fan," 1968, 152 pp., 2000 copies. [Russ. text; titles at end of articles]

VOPROSY FIZICHESKOI I EKONOMICHESKOI GEOGRAFII
UZBEKISTANA. NAUCH. TRUDY. No. 310. Tashkent: (Tashk. Gos. Un-t im. V. I. Lenina), 1967, 176 pp., 500 copies. [Russ. text; titles at end of articles]

HISTORY, ARCHEOLOGY

Abduraimov, M. A. OCHERKI AGRARNYKH OTNOSHENII V BUKHARSKOM KHANSTVE V XVI-PERVOI POLOVINE XIX VEKA.
Vol. 1. Tashkent: Izdatel'stvo "Fan," Uzbekskoi SSR, 1966, 370 pp., 650 copies. [Russ. text; ca.680 Uzbek, Tajik, Russ., Persian, Turkish, Europ. titles, per.: XVI - 1st half XIX c., pp. 321-349]

* ——————————. OCHERKI AGRARNYKH OTNOSHENII V BUKHARSKOM KHANSTVE V XVI-PERVOI POLOVINE XIX VEKA.
Vol. 2. Tashkent: Izdatel'stvo "Fan," Uzbekskoi SSR, 1970, 286 pp., 650 copies. [Russ. text; Tajik, Russ., Persian, Arabic titles, per.: 16th - 19th cc., pp. 271-272]

Uzbek: History, Archaeology

*[Ageev, A. I.; R. Guliamova; E. I. Duborvina] LENIN V PECHATI UZBEKISTANA. BIBLIOGRAFIIA. 1954-1968. Tashkent: "Fan," 1969, 151 pp., 1200 copies. [Uzbek, Russ. text; 869 Uzbek, Russ. titles, pub.: 1954-1968, p. 151]

Ageeva, E. I. "K ISTORII IZUCHENIIA ARKHEOLOGICHESKIKH PAMIATNIKOV SREDNEGO TECHENIIA SYRDAR'I I KARATAU," IZVESTIIA AKAD. NAUK KAZSSR. No. 67. SERIIA ARKHEOLOGICHESKAIA. No. 2. 1949. [Russ. text; 151 titles, pp. 138-142]

*Akbarov, A. I. ROL' GAZETY "PRAVDA" V POBEDE SOTSIALISTICHESKOI REVOLIUTSII V TURKESTANE. Tashkent: "Uzbekistan,' 1968, 304 pp., 3000 copies. [Russ. text; titles pp. 297-303]

*Akhmedov, Boris Akhmedovich. GOSUDARSTVO KOCHEVYKH UZBEKOV. Moscow: Izdatel'stvo "Nauka," 1965, 195 pp., 1650 copies. [Russ. text; ca.270 titles, pp. 6, 165-176]

Akramov, A.; M. Saliamova. NOVYE KNIGI PO ISTORII KOMPARTII UZBEKISTANA. (OBZOR). UCHEN. ZAPISKI (TASHK. PED. IN-T). Vol. 40, No. 4. 1963. [Russ. text; titles pp. 145-151]

Alekseenkov, P. KOKANDSKAIA AVTONOMIIA. Tashkent: Uzgiz, 1931, 72 pp. [Russ. text; titles per.: 1917-1918, p. 71]

*Aminova, R. Kh. AGRARNYE PREOBRAZOVANIIA V UZBEKISTANE NAKANUNE SPLOSHNOI KOLLEKTIVIZATSII (1925-1929 GG.) Tashkent: "Fan," 1969, 472 pp., 650 copies. [Russ. text; ca.220 Russ. titles, pub.: 1925-1967, pp. 458-468]

* _____. AGRARNYE PREOBRAZOVANIIA V UZBEKISTANE V GODY PEREKHODA SOVETSKOGO GOSUDARSTVA K NEPU. Tashkent: Izdatel'stvo "Nauka," Uzbekskoi SSR. Institut Istorii i Arkheologii, 1965, 347 pp., 1000 copies. [Russ. text; 318 Russ. titles, incl. archives, per.: 1920's, pp. 8-35, 331-346]

* _____.; A. F. Iatsyshina. ISTORIIA RABOCHEGO KLASSA UZBEKISTANA. Vol. 3. Tashkent: Izdatel'stvo "Fan" Uzbekskoi SSR, 1966, 238 pp., 1000 copies. [Russ. text; Uzbek, Russ. titles, pp. 234-237]

Uzbek: History, Archaeology

_____. ISTORIIA RABOCHEGO KLASSA UZBEKISTANA. Vol. 3. (1956-1965). 1966. [Russ. text; 85 titles, per.: 1956-1965, pp. 18-22; 234-237]

*Aminova, R. Kh. ed. ISTORIIA UZBEKSKOI SSR. Vol. 1. S DREVNEISHIKH VREMEN DO SEREDINY XIX VEKA. Tashkent: Izdatel'stvo "Fan," 1967, 770 pp., 5000 copies. [Russ. text; Uzbek, Russ. titles, pp. 710-730]

* _____. ed. ISTORIIA UZBEKSKOI SSR. Vol. 2. OT PRISOEDINENIIA UZBEKSKIKH KHANSTV K ROSSII DO VELIKOI OKTIABR'SKOI SOTSIALISTICHESKOI REVOLIUTSII. Tashkent: Izdatel'stvo "Fan," 1968, 662 pp., 5000 copies. [Russ. text; Uzbek, Russ. titles, pp. 597-615]

* _____. ed. ISTORIIA UZBEKSKOI SSR. Vol. 3. POBEDA VELIKOI OKTIABR'SKOI SOTSIALISTICHESKOI REVOLIUTSII I POSTROENIE SOTSIALIZMA V UZBEKISTANE (1917-1937). Tashkent: Izdatel'stvo "Fan," 1967, 707 pp., 5000 copies. [Russ. text; Uzbek, Russ. titles, per.: 1917-1937, pp. 669-684]

* _____. et al. eds. ISTORIIA UZBEKSKOI SSR. Vol. 4. PERIOD ZAVERSHENIIA STROITEL'STVA SOTSIALIZMA I PEREKHOD K KOMMUNIZMU. (1938-1965 GG.). Tashkent: Izdatel'stvo "Fan," 1968, 583 pp., 5000 copies. [Russ. text; Uzbek, Russ. titles, per.: 1938-1965, pp. 553-561]

ARKHEOLOGIIA SREDNEI AZII. TRUDY TASHK. GOS. UN-TA V. I. LENINA. 7 (...No. 295). Tashkent: "Fan," 1966, 128 pp., 500 copies. [Russ. text; titles at end of articles]

*Avsharova, M. P.; A. I. Alashnikova; S. I. Keizer. ISTORIIA UZBEKISTANA. UKAZATEL' SOVETSKOI LITERATURY. 1917-1952 GG. Part 1.--S DREVNEISHIKH VREMEN DO VELIKOI OKTIABR'SKOI SOTSIALISTICHESKOI REVOLIUTSII. Tashkent: Izdatel'stvo "Uzbekistan," (Gos. B-Ka UzSSR im. Navoi K 50-Letliu Velikogo Oktiabra) 1968, 167 pp., 2000 copies. [Russ. text; 1194 titles, per.: 1917-1952]

Uzbek: History, Archaeology

Azadaev, F. OCHERKI IZ ISTORII TASHKENTA. (SOTS.-EKON. I POLIT. ISTORIIA GORODA VO VTOROI POLOVINE XIX V.) Tashkent: (Akademiia Nauk Uzbekskoi SSR. Institut Istorii i Arkheologii.), 1960. [Uzbek text; 115 Uzbek, Russ. titles, per.: second half of 19th c., pp. 5-10, 261-266]

* _____. TASHKENT VO VTOROI POLOVINE XIX VEKA. Tashkent: (Akad. Nauk UzSSR, In-t Istorii i Arkheologii), 1959, 223 pp. [Russ. text; ca.125 Russ., other titles, per.: second half of 19th c., pp. 5-10, 236-241]

*"BABUR, ZEKHIR-ED-DIN MUKHAMMED," BOL'SHAIA SOVETSKAIA ENTSIKLOPEDIIA. Vol. 4. Moscow: Aktsionernoe Obshchestvo "Sovetskaia Entsiklopediia," 1926, 276 pp. [Russ. text; Russ., Europ. titles, p. 276]

Baisheva, M. M.; M. A. Dzhalalova; A. Kh. Nigmanova; L. P. Derkach; A. T. Aiupov. comps. VLADIMIR IL'ICH LENIN. BIBLIOGR. UKAZ. (1918-1968 GG.) Tashkent: (Gos. Knizhnaia Palata UzSSR), 1970, 196 pp., 3000 copies. [Uzbek, Russ. text; 1209 Uzbek, Russ., other Sov. titles, pub.: 1918-1968]

*Bek-Nazarova, V. I. comp. ISTORIIA UZBEKISTANA. BIBLIOGRAFICHESKII UKAZATEL' KNIG I STATEI V IZDANIIAKH KOMITETA NAUK PRI SOVETE NARODNYKH KOMISSAROV UZ SSR UZBEKISTANSKOGO FILIALA AKADEMII NAUK SSSR I AKADEMII NAUK UZ SSR (1933-1957 GG.) Tashkent: Izdatel'stvo Akademii Nauk Uzbekskoi SSR, 1960, 119 pp., 1000 copies. [Russ. text; 1122+ Uzbek, Russ. titles, pub.: 1933-1957]

Bernshtam, A. N. "PREDVARITEL'NYE ZAMETKI I PUBLIKATSII OB EKSPEDITSIIAKH 1944-1948 GG.," DREVNIAIA FERGANA. Tashkent: (Akad. Nauk UzSSR. In-t Istorii i Arkheologii), 1951. [Russ. text; 40 titles, Ancient per., pp. 44-45]

_____. "OSNOVNYE PECHATNYE RABOTY M. E. VORONTSA," SOV. ETNOGRAFIIA. No. 3. 1956. [Russ. text; 20 Russ. titles, pub.: 1917-1954, pp. 153-154]

*Chebotareva, V. G. TASHKENT V PROSHLOM I NASTOIASHCHEM. Tashkent: (Tashk. Gor. Organizatsiia O-va "Znanie,") 1968, 42 pp., 2000 copies. [Russ. text; 10 Russ. titles, pub.: 1957-1966, p. 42]

Uzbek: History, Archaeology

*Denike, B. "BUKHARA STARAIA," BOL'SHAIA SOVETSKAIA
 ENTSIKLOPEDIIA. Vol. 8. Moscow: Aktsionernoe
 Obshchestvo "Sovetskaia Entsiklopediia," 1927, 267-
 269 pp. [Russ. text; Uzbek, Russ. titles p. 269]

DOKUMENTY ARKHIVA KHIVINSKIKH KHANOV PO ISTORII I
 ETNOGRAFII KARAKALPAKOV. Moscow: "Nauka," 1967,
 539 pp., 1600 copies. [Russ. text; titles
 pp. 331-333]

Eraliev, E. K VOPROSU ISTORIOGRAFII DRUZHBY NARODOV
 UZBEKISTANA I KIRGIZII. SBORNIK RABOT ASPIRANTOV
 (KIRG. UN-T). No. 3. 1967. [Russ. text; titles
 pp. 18-24]

Fazylkhodzhaev, K. ODNA RODINA, ODNA SUD'BA.
 Tashkent: "Uzbekistan," 1968, 318 pp., 3000 copies.
 [Russ. text; titles pp. 301-316]

Gentshke, L. V. ed. OCHERKI ISTORII PROFSOIUZOV
 UZBEKISTANA. NAUCH. TRUDY. no. 328. Tashkent:
 (Tashk. Gos. Un-t im. V. I. Lenina), 1967, 429 pp.,
 1000 copies. [Russ. text; titles at end of articles]

Godkina, S. A. comp. UZBEKISTAN V GODY VELIKOI
 OTECHESTVENNOI VOINY. (1941-1945). Tashkent: "Fan,"
 1966, 207 pp., 1000 copies. [Russ. text; ca.330
 titles, per.: 1941-1945, pp. 7-11, 193-206]

*Gremiatskii, M. A. ed. TESHIK-TASH. PALEOLITICHESKII
 CHELOVEK. Moscow: Izdatel'stvo Moskovskogo
 Gosudarstvennogo Universiteta, 1949, 183 pp., 2000
 copies. [Russ. text; scattered lists, Russ., Europ.
 titles, per.: Ancient, pp. 84-85, 99, 108, 182]

*Guliamov, Ia. G. ISTORIIA OROSHENIIA KHOREZMA S
 DREVNEISHIKH VREMEN DO NASHIKH DNEI. Tashkent:
 (Akad. Nauk Uzbek. SSR. In-t Istorii i Arkheologii),
 1957, 313 pp. [Russ. text; ca.480 Russ., other
 titles, per.: antiquity to present, pp. 299-315]

* _____. ISTORIIA OROSHENIIA KHOREZMA S
 DREVNEISHIKH VREMEN DO NASHIKH DNEI. Tashkent:
 (Akad. Nauk UzSSR. In-t Istorii i Arkheologii),
 1959. [Russ. text; ca.480 Uzbek, Russ., foreign
 titles, per.: Antiquity to Present, pp. 310-323]

Uzbek: History, Archaeology

Guliamov, Ia. G.; U. Islamov; A. Askarov.
PERVOBYTNAIA KUL'TURA I VOZNIKNOVENIE OROSHAEMOGO
ZEMLEDELIIA V NIZOV'IAKH ZARAFSHANA. Tashkent: "Fan,"
1966, 267 pp., 650 copies. [Russ. text; ca.290
titles, pp. 257-265]

*I. Kh. "KHIVA," BOL'SHAIA SOVETSKAIA ENTSIKLOPEDIIA.
Vol. 59. Moscow: Gosudarstvennyi Institut "Sovetskaia
Entsiklopediia," (Ogiz RSFSR), 1935, 528-535 pp.
[Russ. text and titles, p. 535]

Iakubov, B. IZ ISTORII PARTIINOI ORGANIZATSII FERGANY.
Tashkent, 1967. [Russ. text; 49 titles, pp. 220-222]

*Iarovinskaia, M. Ia. "V POMOSHCH' IZUCHAIUSHCHIM
ISTORIIU UZBEKISTANA," OBSHCHESTV. NAUKI V
UZBEKISTANE. No. 6. n. p. "Fan," 1969, 1623 copies.
[Russ. text; 11 Uzbek, Russ. titles, pub.: 1926-1963,
pp. 57-58]

Iakubovskii, A. Iu. SAMARKAND PRI TIMURE I TIMURIDAKH.
Leningrad: (Gosudarstvennyi Ermitazh, Muzei Istorii
Kul'tury i Iskusstva), 1933, 67 pp., 3000 copies.
[Russ. text and titles, per.: 14th - 16th cc., pub.:
1881-1928, pp. 65-66]

*ISTORIIA GRAZHDANSKOI VOINY V UZBEKISTANE. Vol. 1.
Tashkent: Izdatel'stvo "Nauka" Uzbekskoi SSR, 1964,
438 pp., 1200 copies. [Russ. text and titles, pp. 6-19]

ISTORIIA RABOCHEGO KLASSA UZBEKISTANA. Vol. 1. Tashkent,
1964. [Russ. text; ca.320 titles, pp. 10-19, 324-337]

*ISTORIIA UZBEKISTANA. UKAZ. SOVETSKOI LIT. 1917-1966 GG.
Part 2. VELIKAIA OKTIABR'SKAIA SOTS. REVOLIUTSIIA V
UZBEKISTANE. UZBEKISTAN V PERIOD GRAZHD. VOINY I
INOSTR. VOEN. INTERVENTSII. Tashkent: "Uzbekistan,"
1969, 344 pp., 2000 copies. [Russ. text; 2382 Russ.
titles, per.: 1917 - early 1920's, pub.: 1917-1966,
pp. 7-313]

*ISTORIIA UZBEKSKOI SSR. Vol. 1, Book 2. Tashkent:
(Akad. Nauk Uzbekskoi SSR. Inst. Istorii i Arkheologii),
1956, 2nd ed., 494 pp. [Russ. text; ca.1000 Uzbek,
Russ., other titles, per.: mid.-18th c. to 1917,
pp. 464-495]

Uzbek: History, Archaeology

*ISTORIIA UZBEKSKOI SSR. Vol. 2. Tashkent: Ozbekistan
SSR Fanlar Akademiyasi Nashriyati, 1958, 681 pp.,
10,000 copies. [Uzbek text; ca.750 Uzbek, Russ.
titles, per.: 1917-1957, pp. 657-680]

*Iuldashev, M. Iu. K ISTORII KREST'IAN KHIVY XIX VEKA.
Tashkent: Izdatel'stvo "Fan," Uzbekskoi SSR, 1966,
136 pp., 1000 copies. [Russ. text; 44+ Uzbek, Russ.
titles, incl. archives, per.: 19th c., pp. 133-135]

IZ ISTORII PARTIINOGO STROITEL'STVA V UZBEKISTANE. (NAUCH.
TRUDY. No. 312). Tashkent: (Tashk. Gos. Un-t im. V. I.
Lenina), 1967, 118 pp., 500 copies. [Russ. text;
titles at end of articles]

Kalymbetov, Zh. KOMMUNISTICHESKAIA PARTIIA UZBEKISTANA
V BOR'BE ZA RAZVITIE PROMYSHLENNOSTI I TRANSPORTA V
GODY VELIKOI OTCHESTVENNOI VOINY. Tashkent: "Fan,"
1966, 174 pp., 500 copies. [Russ. text; titles pp. 163-
173]

*Kel'diev, T. Kh. RAZGROM KONTRREVOLIUTSII V FERGANSKOI I
SAMARKANDSKOI OBLASTIAKH TURKESTANSKOI ASSR (1918-1923
GG.) Tashkent: Gosizdat UzSSR, 1959, 148 pp. [Russ.
text; ca.140 titles, incl. archives, per.: 1918-1923,
pp. 142-149]

*Khafiz, Tanysh Bukhari. ABDULLANAME. SHARAFNAME SHAKHI.
(IST. ISTOCHNIK PO ISTORII NARODOV SRED. AZII XVI V.)
Vol. 1. Tashkent: "Fan," 1966, 399 pp., 3000 copies.
[Russ. text; Uzbek titles, pp. 387-393]

*Khairullaev, M. M. MIROVOZZRENIE FARABI I EGO ZNACHENIE
V ISTORII FILOSOFII. Tashkent: Izdatel'stvo "Fan,"
Uzbekskoi SSR, 1967, 355 pp., 2000 copies. [Russ.
text; Uzbek, Kazakh, Tajik, Russ., Europ., Turk.,
Arabic, Persian titles, pp. 340-353]

Korovnikova, N. I. NACHALO RABOCHEGO DVIZHENIIA I
RASPROSTRANENIE MARKSIZMA-LENINIZMA V ROSSII. (1883-
1894 GG.) Tashkent: Ob"edin. Izd. TsK KP Uzbekistana,
1966, 83 pp., 30,000 copies. [Russ. text; Uzbek
titles, per.: 1883-1894, pp. 55, 62]

Kunakova, L. Z. ZEMEL'NO-VODNAIA REFORMA V UZBEKISTANE
(1925-1929 GG.) Frunze: "Mektep," 1967, 300 pp.,
1000 copies. [Russ. text; titles per.: 1925-1929,
pp. 8-21]

Uzbek: History, Archaeology

Kvasnitskii, D. P.; A. V. Shenrok. "NAUCHNAIA I NAUCHNO-POPULIARNAIA KNIGA UZBEKISTANA," SOTSIALISTICHESKAIA NAUKA I TEKHNIKA. (SOTSIALISTIK ILM VA TEKHNIKA) No. 8. n. p. (Uzb. Gos. Knizhnaia Palata), 1934. [Russ. text; 137 titles, pp. 85-95]

[Lunin, B. V.] SPISOK NAUCHNYKH PUBLIKATSII AKADEMIKA AN UZSSR IA. G. GULIAMOVA (K 60-LETIIU SO DNIA ROZHDENIIA). Tashkent: (AN UzSSR. In-t Istorii i Arkheologii), 1968, 16 pp., 500 copies. [Russ. text; 86 titles pub.: 1931-1968]

*_____. "SPISOK NAUCHNYKH RABOT DOKTORA ISTORICHESKIKH NAUK, ARKHEOLOGA VASILIIA AFANAS'EVICHA SHISHKINA (S 1925 PO 1964 G.)," ISTORIIA MATERIAL'NOI KUL'TURY UZBEKISTANA. No. 6. 1965. [Russ. text; 79 titles, pub.: 1925-1964, pp. 12-16]

*_____. "SPISOK PECHATNYKH RABOT PROF. L. V. OSHANINA (1922-1960)," ISTORIIA MATERIAL'NOI KUL'TURY UZBEKISTANA. No. 2. Tashkent: Izd-vo Akad. Nauk Uzbek. SSR, 1961, 5-17 pp., 1000 copies. [Russ. text; 32 Russ. titles, pub.: 1922-1960, pp. 13-17]

*_____. "SPISOK PECHATNYKH RABOT VSEVOLODA DANILOVICHA ZHUKOVA (1934-1961 GG.)," ISTORIIA MATERIAL'NOI KUL'TURY UZBEKISTANA. No. 4. Tashkent: Izdatel'stvo Akademii Nauk Uzbekskoi SSR, 1963, 159 pp., 1000 copies. [Russ. text; Uzbek, Russ. titles, pub.: 1934-1961, pp. 156-157]

*Masson, M. E. AKHANGERAN. ARKHEOL. TOPOGR. OCHERK. Tashkent: (AN UzSSR. In-t Istorii i Arkheologii), 1953, 143 pp. [Russ. text; ca.150 Uzbek, Russ., other titles, per.: 5th c. - 1939, pp. 139-144]

_____. ; G. A. Pugachenkova. "SHAKHRISIABZ PRI TIMURE I ULUGBEKE," TRUDY SREDNEAZIAT. UN-TA. No. 49 (GUMANITARNYE NAUKI] Book 6, 1953, 143 pp. [Russ. text; ca.150 Uzbek, Russ; other titles, per.: 5th c. -1939, pp. 139-144]

*Masson, V. M. "GORUDISHCHE KHANABAD [TASHKENT. OBLAST']." SBORNIK STUDENCH. RABOT SREDNEAZ. GOS. UN-TA. No. 3, 1951. [Russ. text; 44 titles (in notes), pp. 86-87]

Uzbek: History, Archaeology

Mirza 'Abdal'azim Sami. TA'RIKH-I SALATIN-I MANGITIIA. (ISTORIIA MANGYTSKIKH GOSUDAREI). Moscow, 1962. [Russ., Persian text; ca.160 titles, pp. 171-178]

Mukhamedov, Kh. IZ ISTORII DREVNIKH OBORONITEL'NYKH STEN UZBEKISTANA. (S III V. DO NASHEI ERY DO X V. NASHEI ERY). Tashkent: Izd-vo AN UzSSR, 1961. [Uzbek text; 52 Uzbek, Russ. titles, per.: 3rd c. B. C. - 10th c. A. D., pp. 99-101]

*Mukminova, R. G. K ISTORII AGRARNYKH OTNOSHENII V UZBEKISTANE XVI V. PO MATERIALAM "VAKF-NAME." Tashkent: Izdatel'stvo "Nauka" Uzbekskoi SSR, 1966, 354 pp., 1000 copies. [Russ. text; Uzbek, Tajik, Chaghatay, Russ., Mideast, Europ. titles, per.: 16th c., pp. 331-337]

Munirov, K. ISTORICHESKIE TRUDY MUNISA, AGAKHI I BAIANI. Tashkent: (In-t Vostokovedeniia im. Abu Reikhan Biruni), 1960. [Uzbek text; ca.320 Uzbek, Russ., other titles, per.: pre-Sov., pp. 156-170]

Nasyrkhodzhaev, S. INTELLIGENTSIIA UZBEKISTANA V PERIOD KOMMUNISTICHESKOGO STROITEL'STVA. Tashkent, 1968. [Uzbek text; ca.170 titles, pp. 264-270]

Nasyrova, M.; O. Kasimova; M. Olimkhuzhaeva. comps. UZBEKISTAN. BIBLIOGR. UKAZATEL' LIT. 1957. Tashkent: Gosizdat UzSSR, 1961, 191 pp., 1000 copies. [Uzbek text; 1526 Uzbek titles, pub.: 1957]

Nepomnin, V. Ia. OCHERKI ISTORII SOTSIALISTICHESKOGO STROITEL'STVA V UZBEKISTANE (1917-1937 GG.) Tashkent: (Akad. Nauk Uzbek. SSR. In-t Istorii i Arkheologii), 1957. [Russ. text; ca.150 titles, per.: 1917-1937, pp. 211-218]

Obel'chenko, O. V. KURGANNYE POGREBENIIA PERVYKH VEKOV N. E. I KENOTAFY KUIU-MAZARSKOGO MOGIL'NIKA V BUKHARSKOI OBLASTI. TRUDY SREDNEAZIAT. UN-TA. No. 111. (IST. NAUKI), Book 25. 1957. [Russ. text; titles per.: 1st cc. A. D., pp. 130-132]

OCHERKI ISTORII UZBEKSKOI SOVETSKOI LITERATURY. I. Tashkent: Inst. Iazyka i Lit. im. Pushkina), 1961. [Uzbek text; ca.750 Uzbek, Russ., other titles, per.: Sov., pp. 387-410]

Uzbek: History, Archaeology

"PERECHEN' TRUDOV IULDASHA AKHUNBABAEVA--TRUDY O IULDASHE AKHUNBABAEVE," VALIEV V. IULDASH AKHUNBABAEV. EGO ROL' V SOTS. PREOBRAZOVANIIAKH V UZBEKISTANE. Tashkent, 1968, 188-189 pp. [Russ. text; 19 titles, pub.: 1926-1967, pp. 188-189]

PODGOTOVKA I PROVEDENIE VELIKOI OKTIABR'SKOI SOTSIALISTICHESKOI REVOLIUTSII. KRATKII REK. SPISOK LIT. DLIA RAION. I SEL. BIBLIOTEK. Tashkent: (Tashk. Obl. B-ka), 1957, 15 pp., 500 copies. [Uzbek text; 66 titles, per.: 1st quarter 20th c.]

Rabich, R. comp. ISTORIIA RABOCHEGO KLASSA UZBEKISTANA. Vol. 2. [1941-1955 GG.] Tashkent: Izdatel'stvo "Nauka" Uzbekskoi SSR, 1965, 379 pp., 1500 copies. [Russ. text; ca.200 Russ. titles, per.: 1941-1955, pp. 370-378]

Radzhabova, M. D. "K VOPROSU O RAZRABOTKE ISTORII UZBEKISTANA V SOVETSKOI ISTORICHESKOI NAUKE V 30-E GODY," NAUCHN. RABOTY I SOOBSHCH. Book 6. 1963. [Russ. text; titles, per.: 1930s, pp. 269-281]

Rashidov, G. ISTORIIA SOTSIALISTICHESKOGO TASHKENTA. Vol. 1. Tashkent, 1965. [Russ. text; ca.310 titles (incl. archives), pp. 18-38, 452-467]

Razzakov, A. BOR'BA TRUDIASHCHIKHSIA UZBEKISTANA ZA DOSTIZHENIE KHLOPKOVOI NEZAVISIMOSTI SSSR. Tashkent, 1968. [Russ. text; ca.220 titles, pp. 261-269]

*"REKOMENDATEL'NYI SPISOK LITERATURY DLIA VYSTAVKI. ISTORIIA FERGANY....NARODNOE KHOZIAISTVO FERGANY," TRUD KAZHDOGO--NA BLAGO VSEKH. (IZ OPYTA RABOTY BIBLIOTEK UZBEKISTANA). SBORNIK 2. Tashkent: Izdatel'stvo "Uzbekistan," 1966, 54 pp., 1500 copies. [Russ. text and titles, pp. 39-40]

Romodin, V. A. NEKOTORYE ISTOCHNIKI PO ISTORII FERGANY I KOKANDSKOGO KHANSTVA (16-GO - 19 GO VV.) V RUKOPISNYKH SOBRANIIAKH LENINGRADA. Moscow: Izd. Vost. Lit., 1960, 20 pp., 350 copies. [English text; titles, per.: 16th - 19th cc.]

Rustamov, M. UZBEKSKAIA KNIGA. Tashkent: "Uzbekistan," 1968, 160 pp., 5000 copies. [Russ. text; 26 Uzbek titles, pp. 159-160]

Uzbek: History, Archaeology

Semenov, A. A. "UKAZATEL' PERSIDSKOI LITERATURY PO ISTORII UZBEKOV V SREDNEI AZII," TRUDY BIBLIOGRAFICHESKOI KOMISSII BYVSH. PRI SNK TURKRESPUBLIK. Tashkent, 1926, 31 pp. [Russ. text; 125 titles, per.: from 15th c. - 1918]

*Shamagdiev, Sh. A. OCHERKI ISTORII GRAZHDANSKOI VOINY V FERGANSKOI DOLINE. Tashkent: (Akademiia Nauk Uzbekskoi SSR. Institut Istorii i Arkheologii), 1961, 386 pp. [Russ. text; ca.500 Uzbek, Russ. titles, per.: 1918-1922, pp. 365-387]

[Shamardiev, Sh. A. ed.] MATERIALY K ISTORII SOVETSKOGO UZBEKISTANA. Tashkent: (Akad. Nauk UzSSR. In-t Istorii i Arkheologii), 1957, 298 pp. [Russ. text; titles, Sov. per.]

Sultanov, M. Z. UZBEKISTAN V DNI OTECHESTVENNOI VOINY. BIBLIOGRAFICHESKII UKAZATEL'. Tashkent: GPB UzSSR, n. d. [Russ. text; titles, per.: 1941-1945]

Svidina, E. D. comp. UZBEKISTAN. BIBLIOGR. UKAZATEL' LIT. 1959 G. Tashkent: Gosizdat UzSSR, 1961, 624 pp., 2000 copies. [Russ. text; 4304 Russ. titles, pub.: 1959]

TASHKENT V PROSHLOM I NASTOIASHCHEM. BIBLIOGRAFICHESKII UKAZATEL'. Tashkent: Gosizdat UzSSR, 1964, 60 pp. [Russ. text]

*Terenozhkin, A. LITERATURA PO ARKHEOLOGII V UZBEKISTANE. VESTNIK DREVNEI ISTORII. No. 1 (6). 1939. [Russ. text; 32 Russ., other titles, pub.: 1930-1938, pp. 186-191]

*Tolstov, S. P. ed. ISTORIIA UZBEKSKOI SSR. Vol. 1. Book 1. Tashkent: Izdatel'stvo Akademii Nauk Uzbekskoi SSR (AN UzSSR In-t Istorii i Arkheologii), 1955. [Russ. text; ca.1200 Uzbek, Russ., Mid-East., Europ. titles, per.: up to middle of 18th c., pp. 504-542]

*Trever, K. V.; A. Iu. Iakubovskii; M. E. Voronets. eds. ISTORIIA NARODOV UZBEKISTANA. Vol. 1. S DREVNEISHIKH VREMEN DO NACHALA XVI V. Tashkent: AN UzSSR. In-t Istorii i Arkheologii, 1950. [Russ. text; ca.670 Russ., other titles, per.: up to 16th c., pp. 449-472]

*"UZBEKI," BOL'SHAIA SOVETSKAIA ENTSIKLOPEDIIA. Vol. 55. Moscow: Gosudarstvennyi Nauchnyi Institut "Sovetskaia Entsiklopediia" (Ogiz SSSR), 1947, 1st ed., 607-609 pp. [Russ. text and titles, p. 609]

Uzbek: History, Archaeology

Vakhabov, M. TASHKENT V PERIOD TREKH REVOLIUTSII.
Tashkent: Gosizdat UzSSR, 1957. [ca.250
Uzbek, Russ. titles, per.: 1905-1917, pp. 269-282]

Zadneprovskii, Iu. A. DREVNEZEMLEDEL'CHESKAIA
KUL'TURA FERGANY. MATERIALY I ISSLEDOVANIIA PO
ARKHEOLOGII SSSR. No. 118. Moscow-Leningrad: (AN
SSSR), 1962, 235-248 pp. [Russ. text; ca.550 Russ.,
Europ. titles, per.: Ancient, pub.: 1851-1962]

*Zevelev, A. I. IZ ISTORII GRAZHDANSKOI VOINY V
UZBEKISTANE. Tashkent: Gosizdat UzSSR, 1959, 606 pp.
[Russ. text; Uzbek, Russ. titles, per.: 1918-1921,
pp. 16-49]

*Zhitov, K. E.; M. Iu. Iuldashev; V. V. Ershov; V. Ia.
Nepomnina; Kh. T. Tursunov, eds. ISTORIIA
UZBEKSKOI SSR. Vol. 2. Tashkent: Izdatel'stvo
Akademii Nauk Uzbekskoi SSR, 1957, 654 pp., 10,000
copies. [Russ. text; Uzbek, Russ. titles, per.: 1917-
1957, pp. 628-651]

_____. POBEDA VELIKOI OKTIABR'SKOI
SOTSIALISTICHESKOI REVOLIUTSII V UZBEKISTANE.
Tashkent: (Akad. Nauk Uzbek. SSR. In-t Istorii i
Arkheologii), 1957. [Russ. text; ca.120 Uzbek, Russ.
titles per.: 1917-, pp. 225-230]

Zhuramardyeb, A. ZEMEL'NO-VODNYE OTNOSHENIIA FERGANY
XVI-XIX VV. Tashkent, 1965. [Uzbek text; ca.130
titles, per.: XVI-XIX c., pp. 176-181]

*Ziiaev, Khamid. SREDNIAIA AZIIA I POVOLZH'E (VTORAIA
POLOVINA XVI-XIX VV.) Tashkent: Ozbekistan SSR "Fan,"
Nashriyati, 1965, 237 pp., 650 copies. [Uzbek text;
Uzbek, Russ. titles, incl. archives, per.: 16th - 19th
c., pp. 226-236]

Uzbek

LANGUAGE, LITERATURE

*Abdullaev, F. A. FONETIKA KHOREZMSKIKH GORODOV. OPYT MONOGRAFICHESKOGO OPISANIIA OGUZSKOGO I KIPCHAKSKOGO NARECHII UZBEKSKOGO IAZYKA. Tashkent: Izdatel'stvo "Fan," Uzbekskoi SSR, 1967, 246 pp., 1500 copies. [Russ. text; Russ., Sov., Western titles, pp. 229-244]

Abdurakhmanov, G. SINTAKSIS SLOZHNOGO PREDLOZHENIIA. Tashkent, 1964. [Uzbek text; ca.150 titles, pp. 159-164]

Abdurakhmanov, N. PARNYE SLOVA V UZBEKSKOM IAZYKE. Samarkand, 1969. [Uzbek text; ca.110 titles, pp. 83-87]

*Abrarov, A. "YAZUWCHI SHARAF RASHIDOVNING OZBEK TILIDA BASILGAN ASARLARINING QISQA BIBLIOGRAFIYASI," PISATEL' I SOVREMENNOST'. Tashkent: Izdatel'stvo "Nauka," UzSSR, 1964, 175 pp., 2000 copies. [Uzbek text and titles, pp. 171-174]

*Abrazhev, A. I.; P. A. Danilov; R. I. Bigaev. OCHERKI PO SOPOSTAVITEL'NOI GRAMMATIKE RUSSKOGO I UZBEKSKOGO IAZYKOV. Tashkent: (Akademiia Nauk UzSSR. Institut Iazyka i Literatury im. A. S. Pushkina), 1960, 189 pp., 3000 copies. [Russ. text; 65 Uzbek, Russ. titles, pp. 184-186]

Alimdzhanova, Khul'kar. STRUNY MYSLI. (K 60-LETIIU SO DNIA ROZHDENIIA IZVESTNOGO UZB. POETA M. SHEIKHZADE). Tashkent: Ob"edin. Izd. TsK KP Uzbekistana, 1968, 37 pp., 21,090 copies. [Russ. text; Uzbek titles, p. 37]

"ALISHER NAVOI," KHRESTOMATIIA PO LITERATURY NARODOV SSSR. Moscow, 1959. [Russ. text; titles, pp. 929-931]

"ALISHER NAVOI (BIBLIOGRAFIIA)," KLASSIKI KHUDOZHESTVENNOI LITERATURY NARODOV SSSR. Moscow, 1965. [Russ. text; titles pp. 45-50]

Uzbek: Language, Literature

ALISHER NAVOI. 1441-1501 (525 LET SO DNIA ROZHDENIIA). PAMIATKA CHITATELIU. Samarkand: (Samark. Obl. Upr. Kul'tury. Samark. Obl. Biblioteka im. A. S. Pushkina), 1966, 4 pp. [Russ. text; titles per.: 1441-1501]

Askarova, M. A. FORMY PODCHINENIIA I TIPY PRIDATOCHNYKH PREDLOZHENII V SOVREMENNOM UZBEKSKOM IAZYKE. Tashkent: "Fan," 1966, 345 pp., 1000 copies. [Uzbek text; 172 Uzbek titles, pp. 337-343]

*Avsharova, M. P.; E. D. Svidina. UZBEKSKAIA LITERATURA. REKOMENDATEL'NYI UKAZATEL'. Moscow: (Gosudarstvennaia Ordena Lenina Biblioteka SSSR imeni V. I. Lenina), 1959, 133 pp., 3000 copies. [Russ. text and titles]

Baibekova, F. I. CHTO CHITAT' DETIAM. (BIBLIOGR. UKAZATEL'). Tashkent: (Uzbek. Gos. Publ. B-ka im. Navoi), 1957, 72 pp., 5000 copies. [Uzbek text; ca.270 titles, pub.: 1945-1956]

*_____.; R. V. Saidahmedova. comps. V. I. LENIN V UZBEKSKOI LITERATURE. BIBLIOGRAFICHESKII UKAZATEL'. Tashkent: Goslitizdat UzSSR. Oz SSR Dawlat Badiiy Adabiyat Nashriyati, 1962, 42 pp., 1500 copies. [Uzbek text; 570 titles]

*_____.; M. Sultanova; M. Nasyrova; M. Alimkhozhaeva. UZBEKSKAIA LITERATURA. BIBLIOGRAFIIA. 1940-1958 G. Tashkent: Goslitizdat UzSSR, 1963, 1079 pp., 1000 copies. [Uzbek text; 14,000 Uzbek titles, pub.: 1940-1958]

Baltabaeva, Kh. OSLOZHNENNOE PROSTOE PREDLOZHENIE V UZBEKSKOM IAZYKE (SINTAKSIS). Tashkent, 1969. [Uzbek text; ca.230 titles, pp. 164-172]

*"BATU, MAKHMUD KHADIEV," LITERATURNAIA ENTSIKLOPEDIIA. Vol. 1. n. p. Izdatel'stvo Kommunisticheskoi Akademii, 1929. [Russ. text; Uzbek titles, p. 368]

BIBLIOGRAFICHESKII UKAZATEL'. UZBEKSKOE ISKUSSTVO (TEATR, MUZYKA, KINO NA STRANITSAKH PECHATI). Tashkent: GPB Uz UzSSR, 1936.

"BIBLIOGRAFIIA LITERATURY OB 'ALPAMYSHE'," Mirzaev, T. UZB. VARIANTY DASTANA "ALPAMYSH." Tashkent, 1968. [Uzbek text; ca.190 Uzbek. Russ. titles, pub.: 1890-1967, pp. 151-160]

Uzbek: Language, Literature

*Borovkov, A. "UZBEKSKII IAZYK," BOL'SHAIA SOVETSKAIA
ENTSIKLOPEDIIA. Vol. 55. Moscow: Gosudarstvennyi
Nauchnyi Institut "Sovetskaia Entsiklopediia," (Ogiz
SSSR), 1947, pp. 696-698. [Russ. text; Uzbek, Russ.
Europ. titles, p. 698]

DRUZHBA NARODOV - DRUZHBA LITERATUR. (OCHERKI IZ ISTORII
UZBEK. LIT. SVIAZIEI). (NAUCH. TRUDY. TASHK. GOS.
UN-T IM. LENINA. No. 258. FILOL. NAUKI. Book 30).
Tashkent, 1964, 231 pp. [Uzbek, Russ. text; scattered
titles]

Dzhumaniiazov, R. KRATKII BIBLIOGRAFICHESKII UKAZATEL'
LITERATURY PO IAZYKOZNANIIU. Tashkent: Izd-vo Akad.
Nauk UzSSR, 1956, 144 pp., 2000 copies. [Russ. text;
ca.2000 Russ., other titles, pub.: 1950-1952]

Ernazarov, T. RASTSVET NARODNOI PECHATI V UZBEKISTANE.
Tashkent: "Uzbekistan," 1968, 184 pp., 5000 copies.
[Russ. text]

Fazylov, E. ISTORICHESKAIA MORFOLOGIIA UZBEKSKOGO IAZYKA.
Tashkent, 1965. [Russ. text; ca.180 titles, pp. 162-
169]

*_____. STAROUZBEKSKII IAZYK. Vol. 1.
KHOREZMIISKIE PAMIATNIKI XIV VEKA. Tashkent:
Izdatel'stvo "Fan," 1966, 650 pp., 1200 copies.
[Russ. text; Uzbek, Russ., Europ. titles, per.: XIV c.,
pp. 8-12]

Guliamov, A. G.; M. A. Askarova. SOVREMENNYI UZBEKSKII
IAZYK. SINTAKSIS. Tashkent, 1961. [Uzbek text;
60 titles, per.: contemporary, pp. 275-277]

*Guliamov, Aiub; Mazluma Askarova. SOVREMENNYI UZBEKSKII
LITERATURNYI IAZYK. SINTAKSIS. Tashkent: Izdatel'stvo
"Uchitel'," 1965, 2nd ed., 315 pp., 12,500 copies.
[Uzbek text; 66 Uzbek, Russ. titles, pp. 311-313]

Guliamova, Ia. G. GRAMMATIKA TASHKENTSKOGO GOVORA. Ch. 1.
Tashkent, 1968. [Russ. text; ca.100 titles, pp. 158-161]

Ibragimova, R. A. LITERATURA ZARUBEZHNYKH STRAN NA
UZBEKSKOM IAZYKE (1961-1965). BIBLIOGR. UKAZ. Tashkent:
(AN UzSSR. Fundam. B-ka. Filial No. 3.), 1969, 70 pp.
[Uzbek text; 526 Uzbek titles, pub.: 1961-1965]

*_____. LITERATURNAIA ZHIZN'. 1967. (UKAZ.
MATERIALOV PO UZB. LIT.) (AN UZSSR. FUNDAM. B-KA.
FILIAL No. 3). Tashkent, 1970, 84 pp. [Uzbek text; 759
Uzbek, Russ. titles, pub.: 1967]

Uzbek: Language, Literature

Kabilov, N. POET-PATRIOT (LIT.-KRITICH. OCHERK O SULTANE DZHURE). Tashkent, 1961. [Uzbek text; 19 titles, pp. 68-69]

*Kadyrov, Mukhsin. ALISHER NAVOI I ISKUSSTVO. Tashkent: Ob"edin. Izd. TsK KP Uzbekistana, 1968, 40 pp., 21,080 copies. [Uzbek text; 38 Uzbek titles, sources: pp. 39-40]

Kaiumov, L. "PROIZVEDENIIA ZUL'FII.--LITERATURA O TVORCHESTVE ZUL'FII," POETESSA ZUL'FIIA. Tashkent, 1965. [Uzbek text; 44 Uzbek, Russ. titles, pp. 111-113]

*Kadyrova, Makhbuba. NADYRA. ZHIZH' I TVORCHESTVO. Tashkent: Ozbekistan SSR "Fan," Nashriyati, 1965, 101 pp., 1000 copies. [Uzbek text; 49 Uzbek, Tajik titles, incl. archives, MSS, per.: 19th c., pp. 99-100]

_____. NADIRA. OCHERK ZHIZNI I TVORCHESTVA. Tashkent, 1967. [Russ. text; 53 titles, pp. 185-186]

Karimov, G. K.; Sh. Rakhmattulaev. eds. NEKOTORYE VOPROSY UZBEKSKOI FILOLOGII. Tashkent: "Fan," 1968, 170 pp., 500 copies. [Russ. text; Uzbek titles at end of articles]

Kasymkhodzhaeva, A. MORFOLOGICHESKAIA STRUKTURA SLOVA. Tashkent, 1963. [Uzbek text; 127 tiles, pp. 126-130]

Kasymov, A. KHAMZA KHAKIMZADE NIIAZI [1889-1929]. BIOBLIOGR. I METODICHESKIE MATERIALY V POMOSHCH' BIBLIOTEKARIU. Tashkent: Goslitizdat UzSSR, 1960, 63 pp., 3000 copies. [Uzbek, Russ. text; titles per.: 1889-1929]

*Khadzhiev, Azim. SLOZHNYE, PARNYE SLOVA I SLOVA-POVTORY V UZBEKSKOM IAZYKE. Tashkent: Izdatel'stvo Akademii Nauk UzSSR, 1963, 145 pp., 1000 copies. [Uzbek text; Uzbek, Kazakh, Russ. titles, pp. 143-144]

*Khanazarov, K.Kh. SBLIZHENIE NATSII I NATSIONAL'NYE IAZYKI V SSSR. Tashkent: Izdatel'stvo Akademii Nauk Uzbekskoi SSR, 1963, 244 pp., 3000 copies. [Russ. text; Russ. titles (incl. archives), pp. 233-241]

_____. STROITEL'STVO KOMMUNIZMA I NATSIONAL'NYE IAZYKI. Tashkent, 1965. [Uzbek text; ca.320 titles (incl. archives), pp. 392-408]

Uzbek: Language, Literature

*Khasanova, Kh. TALANTLIVAIA PISATEL'NITSA (SAIDA ZUNNUNOVA). Tashkent: Ob"edin. Izd. TsK KP Uzbekistana,1968, 32 pp., 20,510 copies. [Russ. text; 13 Uzbek titles, pub.: 1948-1967, p. 31]

KHUDOZHESTVENNAIA LITERATURA OB OKTIABR'SKOI REVOLIUTSII V UZBEKISTANE. BESEDA O KNIGAKH. Tashkent: (Gos. Publ. B-ka k 40-Letiiu Velik. Oktiabr. Sots. Rev.), 1957, 14 pp., 1500 copies. [Uzbek text; titles, per.: 1917]

Khusainova, Z. UZBEKSKIE ZAGADKI. Tashkent: "Fan," 1966, 114 pp., 6000 copies. [Uzbek text; 35 Uzbek titles, pp. 110-111]

*Koklianova, A. A. KATEGORIIA VREMENI V SOVREMENNOM UZBEKSKOM IAZYKE. Moscow, 1963, 122 pp. [Russ. text; ca.130 Uzbek, Russ. titles, pp. 119-123]

*Kononov, A. N. GRAMMATIKA SOVREMENNOGO UZBEKSKOGO LITERATURNOGO IAZYKA. Moscow-Leningrad: Izdatel'stvo Akademii Nauk SSSR, 1960, 446 pp., 3500 copies. [Russ. text; titles, per.: contemporary, pp. 60-62, 69-70, 72-73, 85-86, 88-90, 103-104, 139-141, 144, 165, 171-172, 186, 197-198, 200, 236-237, 258-259, 271, 295, 327, 337, 340, 344, 348, 358, 360, 386-387, 391, 397, 406, 446, 423-424]

*Kor-Ogly, Kh. G. UZBEKSKAIA LITERATURA. Moscow: Izdatel'stvo "Vysshaia Shkola," 1968, 292 pp., 5000 copies. [Russ. text; 101 Russ. titles, pub.: 1934-1965, pp. 289-291]

Korshunova, A. V. KHUDOZHESTVENNAIA LITERATURA OB OKTIABR'SKOI REVOLIUTSII V UZBEKISTANE. Tashkent: (Gos. Publ. B-ka UzSSR. im. Navoi), 1957, 19 pp., 1500 copies. [Russ. text; titles, Sov. per.]

Kungurov, R. IZOBRAZITEL'NYE SLOVA V SOVREMENNOM UZBEKSKOM IAZYKE. Tashkent: "Fan," 1967, 155 pp., 1500 copies. [Russ. text; ca.150 Uzbek titles, pp. 149-154]

Kunina, A.; Z. Shalashova. "ALISHER NAVOI (BIBLIOGRAFIIA)," KLASSIKI LITERATURY NARODOV SSSR. Moscow, 1961. [Russ. text; titles, p. 35]

*L'vov, N. "UZBEKSKII TEATR," BOL'SHAIA SOVETSKAIA ENTSIKLOPEDIIA. Vol. 55. Moscow: Gosudarstvennyi Nauchnyi Institut "Sovetskaia Entsiklopediia," (Ogiz SSSR), 1947, 1st ed., 693-696 pp. [Russ. text and titles, p. 696]

Uzbek: Language, Literature

Madaliev, B. SLOZHNYE SLOVA V SOVREMENNOM UZBEKSKOM IAZYKE. Tashkent: "Fan," 1966, 182 pp., 650 copies. [Uzbek text; ca.150 Uzbek titles, pp. 176-181]

*Madzhidii, Rakhmat. LIRIKA AGAKHI. Tashkent: Izdatel'stvo Akademii Nauk UzSSR, 1963, 138 pp., 1500 copies. [Uzbek text; Uzbek, Russ. titles (incl. MSS), pp. 135-138]

Makhmudov, A. SLOVESNOE UDARENIE V UZBEKSKOM IAZYKE. Tashkent: (Akad. Nauk UzSSR. In-t Iazyka i Lit. im. Pushkina), 1960. [Uzbek text; ca.150 titles, pp. 65-70]

_____. GLASNYE UZBEKSKOGO IAZYKA. Tashkent: "Fan," 1968, 60 pp., 500 copies. [Russ. text; 108 titles, pp. 55-59]

Mallaev, N. GENIAL'NYI POET I MYSLITEL'. (K 525-LETIIU SO DNIA ROZHDENIIA ALISHERA NAVOI). Tashkent: "Fan," 1968, 53 pp., 10,000 copies. [Russ. text; 83 Uzbek titles, pp. 47-52]

*Mallaev, Natan Muradovich. ISTORIIA UZBEKSKOI LITERATURY. Part 1. (XVII ASRGACHA). Tashkent: Izdatel'stvo "Uchitel'," 1965, 2nd ed., 746 pp., 20,000 copies. [Uzbek text; ca.180 Uzbek, Russ. titles, per.: up to 17th c., pp. 739-745]

*Malyshev, N. Ia. UZBEKISTAN V KHUDOZHESTVENNOI LITERATURE. ANNOTIROVANNYI UKAZATEL' LITERATURY. Tashkent: Gosudarstvennaia Biblioteka UzSSR, im. A. Navoi, 1967, 102 pp. [Russ. text; 194 Sov. Lang. titles]

Mirzaev, N. M. BUKHARSKAIA GRUPPA GOVOROV UZBEKSKOGO IAZYKA. Tashkent, 1969. [Uzbek text; ca.130 titles, pp. 149-153]

Mirzaev, T. "BIBLIOGRAFIIA TRUDOV KH. T. ZARIFOVA," UZBEKSKOE NARODNOE TVORCHESTVO. Tashkent, 1967. [Uzbek text; 103 titles, pub.: 1927-1965, pp. 17-22]

*Mirzaeva, N.; Z. Polvanova. ALISHER NAVOI. BIOBIBLIOGRAFIIA (1917-1966). K 525-LETIIU SO DNIA ROZHDENIIA. Tashkent: Izd. Khudozhestvennoi Literatury, 1968, 67 pp., 3000 copies. [Uzbek text; 650 Sov., Russ. titles, pub.: 1917-1966]

Uzbek: Language, Literature

*Narzullaeva, Saida. ALISHER NAVOI. (IZ TVORCHESKOI BIOGRAFII). Tashkent: Izdatel'stvo "Fan," 1966, 155 pp., 500 copies. [Uzbek text; 115 Uzbek, Russ. titles, pub.: 1928-1963, pp. 151-154]

NEKOTORYE VOPROSY FILOLOGII I METODIKA PREPODAVANIIA INOSTRANNYKH IAZYKOV. Tashkent: "Fan," 1966, 160 pp., 1500 copies. [Russ. text; titles, at end of articles]

*Niiazov, Kh. N. "SPISOK POETICHESKIKH PROIZVEDENII S. AINI," PUT' SADRIDDINA AINI--POETA. Moscow: Izdatel'stvo "Nauka," 1965, 143 pp., 2200 copies. [Russ. text; 211 Tajik, Uzbek, Russ. titles, pp. 133-142]

Nizamiddinova, S. CHISLITEL'NYE V SOVREMENNOM UZBEKSKOM IAZYKE. Tashkent, 1963. [Uzbek text; ca.120 titles, pp. 92-95]

"NOVYE KNIGI O NIZAMI I NAVOI," PRAVDA VOSTOKA. Oct. 7, 1940; Jan. 2, 1941. KOMSOMOLETS UZBEKISTANA. Feb. 3, 1941. LIT. AZERBAIDZHAN. No. 2, 1941. [Russ. text]

O PROVEDENII NEDELI DET. KNIGI. Tashkent: (M-vo Prosveshcheniia Uzbek. SSR. Upr.Shkol. Nauch.-Issled. In-t Ped. Nauk), 1957. [Uzbek text; ca.650 titles, pp. 19-52]

Pinkhasov, Ia. D. LEKSIKA SOVREMENNOGO UZBEKSKOGO IAZYKA. Tashkent: (Resp. Nauch.-Metod. Kabinet po Zaoch. Obucheniiu), 1960. [Uzbek. text; 50 Uzbek, Russ. titles, pp. 77-79]

PROIZVEDENIIA KLASSIKOV RUSSKOI LITERATURY V PEREVODAKH NA UZBEKSKII IAZYK. Tashkent: (Uzb. Gos. Publ. B-ka im. Navoi), 1951, 32 pp., 1000 copies. [Uzbek text; 119 Uzbek titles]

Rakhimov, N. IZ ISTORII UZBEKSKOI SOVETSKOI SATIRY (1917-1959). Tashkent, 1962. [Uzbek text; 67 titles, per.: 1917-1959, pp. 164-166]

Rakhmanov, M. ISTORIIA UZBEKSKOGO TEATRA. (TVORCHESKII PUT' UZB. TEATR. ISKUSSTVA S XVIII PO XX V.) Tashkent: "Fan," 1968, 430 pp. [Russ. text; 395 Uzbek titles, per.: 18th - 20th cc., pp. 417-428]

Uzbek: Language, Literature

Rakhmatullaev, Sh. NEKOTORYE VOPROSY UZBEKSKOI
FRAZEOLOGII. Tashkent: "Fan," 1966, 262 pp., 650
copies. [Russ. text; Uzbek titles, pp. 258-260]

*Rasulii, M. PROIZVEDENIIA V. MAIAKOVSKOGO NA
UZBEKSKOM IAZYKE. Tashkent: Ozbekistan SSR Fanlar
Akademiyasi Nashriyati, 1961, 209 pp., 1000 copies.
[Uzbek text; Uzbek, Tajik, Russ. titles, pp. 200-208]

*[Rasulova, Kh. comp.] UZBEKISTAN V KHUDOZHESTVENNOI
LITERATURE. (ANNOT. UKAZATEL' LIT.) Tashkent: (Gos.
B-ka UzSSR im. Navoi k 50-Letiiu Velikogo Oktiabria),
1967, 106 pp., 400 copies. [Uzbek text; 213 titles]

Razzakov, Kh. SATIRA I IUMOR V UZBEKSKOM USTNOM
NARODNOM TVORCHESTVE. Tashkent, 1965. [Uzbek text;
57 titles, pp. 142-143]

*Sabirov, Tursun. ed. OCHERKI ISTORII KINODRAMATURGII
UZBEKISTANA. Tashkent: Izdatel'stvo Akademii Nauk
UzSSR, 1963, 296 pp., 1000 copies. [Uzbek text and
titles, pp. 274-295]

*_____. TVORCHESKII PUT' KAMIL'A IASHENA.
(SBORNIK STATEI). Tashkent: Izdatel'stvo Akademii
Nauk Uzbekskoi SSR, 1963, 173 pp., 1000 copies.
[Uzbek text; Uzbek, Russ. titles, pp. 164-172]

Safaev, A. S. ISSLEDOVANIIA PO SINTAKSISU UZBEKSKOGO
IAZYKA. Tashkent: "Fan," 1968, 161 pp., 2500 copies.
[Russ. text; 86 titles, pp. 158-160]

Said-Nasyrova, Z. N.; T. V. Derkunskaia. RUSSKO-
UZBEKSKII KRATKII TOLKOVII SLOVAR' PO KHIMII.
Tashkent: Uchpedgiz, 1954. [Uzbek, Russ. text; 64
Russ. titles, pp. 645-647]

Saifullaev, A. R. OBRASHCHENIE V SOVREMENNOM
UZBEKSKOM LITERATURNOM IAZYKE. Tashkent, 1968. [Uzbek
text; 76 titles, pp. 72-74]

Seiidov, A. LITERATURA I ISSKUSSTVO SOVETSKOGO
UZBEKISTANA. (BIBLIOGR. UKAZATEL').
Ashkhabad: (Turkm. Resp. Gos. B-ka im. Marksa k Dekade
Uzb. Lit. i Iskusstva v Turkmenii), 1967, 35 pp.,
200 copies. [Turkmen text; ca.460 titles]

Uzbek: Language, Literature

Seiidov, Ashir. comp. UZBEKSKAIA LITERATURA OT NAVOI...
(BIBLIOGRAFICHESKII UKAZATEL'). Ashkhabad: (M-vo
Kul'tury TSSR. Turkmenskaia Respublikanskaia
Gosudarstvennaia Biblioteka im. Karla Marksa. K
Dekade Uzbekskoi Literatury i Iskusstva v Turkmenii),
1967, 35 pp., 200 copies. [Turkmen text]

Semenov, A. A. MATERIALY K BIBLIOGRAFICHESKOMU UKAZATELIU
PECHATNYKH PROIZVEDENII ALISHERA NAVOI I LITERATURY O
NEM. (TRUDY SREDNEAZIAT. GOS. UN-TA. SERIIA 2.
ORIENTALIIA. No. 5. IZ RABOT FUND. B-KA SAGU. No. 2).
Tashkent, 1940, 38 pp. [Russ. text]

_____. OPISANIE RUKOPISEI PROIZVEDENII NAVOI,
KHRANIASHCHIKHSIA V GOSUDARSTVENNOI PUBLICHNOI
BIBLIOTEKE UZSSR. Tashkent: Gosizdat UzSSR
(Iubileinyi Komitet Navoi. Gos. Publichnaia
Biblioteka UzSSR), 1940, 45 pp. [Russ. text]

Shaabdurakhmanov, Sh. UZBEKSKII LITERATURNYI IAZYK I
UZBEKSKIE NARODNYE GOVORY. OPORNYE GOR. GOVORY I
VOPROSY IKH VZAIMOSVIAZI V SOVREM. UZBEK. LIT. IAZYKE.
Tashkent, 1962. [Uzbek text; ca.150 titles, pp. 365-370]

[Shakirov, U.] IZZAT ATAKHANOVICH SULTANOV. Tashkent:
"Fan," 1970, 44 pp., 300 copies. [Russ. text; 322
Uzbek, Russ., other Sov. titles, pub.: 1930-1970]

Sharafutdinov, A. ALISHER NAVOI. EGO EPOKHA, ZHIZN'
TVORCHESTVO I SMERT'. Tashkent, 1939, 70 pp.
Uzbek text; 14 titles, pub.: 1856-1939]

Sharipov, D. IZ ISTORII PEREVODA V UZBEKISTANE.
DOREVOLIUTSIONNYI PERIOD. Tashkent, 1965. [Uzbek
text; ca.300 titles, per.: pre-Rev., pp. 465-478]

*Sharipov, Dzhumaniiaz Sharipovich. NEKOTORYE PROBLEMY
POETICHESKOGO PEREVODA S RUSSKOGO NA UZBEKSKII IAZYK.
Tashkent: Izd-vo Akad. Nauk UzSSR, 1958, 144 pp.
[Russ. text; ca.100 Uzbek, Russ. titles, pub.: Sov.
per., pp. 139-144]

* _____. NEKOTORYE PROBLEMY POETICHESKOGO
PEREVODA S RUSSKOGO NA UZBEKSKII IAZYK. Tashkent:
Izdatel'stvo Akademii Nauk Uzbekskoi SSR, 1959, 153 pp.,
2000 copies. [Uzbek text; ca.100 Uzbek, Russ. titles,
pp. 146-152]

Uzbek: Language, Literature

SHUKUR SARDULLA. PAMIATKA CHITATELIU 3-4 KLASSOV.
Fergana: (Gos. Resp. Det. B-ka UzSSR. Fergan. Obl.
Det. B-ka. K 50-Letiiu Oktiabr'skoi Revoliutsii),
1968, 22 pp., 5000 copies. [Uzbek, Russ. text]

*Shukurov, Sh. ISTORIIA RAZVITIIA GLAGOL'NYKH FORM
UZBEKSKOGO IAZYKA. (NASTOIASHCHEE I BUDUSHCHEE
VREMENA). Tashkent: Izdatel'stvo "Fan," Uzbekskoi SSR,
1966, 138 pp., 1000 copies. [Russ. text; ca.180
Uzbek, Russ., West. titles, pp. 129-137]

*[SVIDINA, E. D. COMP.] ISTORIIA UZBEKSKOI SOVETSKOI
LITERATURY. Moscow: Izdatel'stvo "Nauka," 1967, 794 pp.,
4100 copies. [Russ. text; ca.300 Sov., Russ., West.
titles, pp. 781-792]

*Svidina, Evgeniia Dmitrievna. comp. ALISHER NAVOI.
BIOBIBLIOGRAFIIA (1917-1966 GG.) Tashkent:
Izdatel'stvo Khudozhestvennoi Literatury imeni
Gafura Guliama, 1968, 107 pp., 3000 copies. [Russ.
text; Russ., other Sov.people, foreign titles,
pub.: 1917-1966]

*Tajiyeva, Lala. "A"QAHHAR FEL'ETONLARINING GHAYAVIY VA
BADIIY KHUSUSIYATLARI," V. I. LENIN NAMIDAGI ORTA
ASIYA DAVLAT UNIVERSITETINING ILMIY ASARLARI. OZBEK
ADABIYATI. n. s. CXVIII, FILOLOGIYA FANLARI: 15 Kitab.
(Tashkent) 1957, 117-141 pp., 500 copies. [Uzbek
text; 76 Uzbek, Russ. titles, pp. 139-141]

"TSENNYI UKAZATEL' PROIZVEDENII NAVOI (SOSTAVLENNYI
FUNDAMENTAL'NOI BIBLIOTEKOI SAGU)," PRAVDA VOSTOKA.
May 11, 1939. [Russ. text]

Turdyev, Sh.; B. Karyev. BIBLIOGRAFIIA PO UZBEKSKOMU
LITERATUROVEDENIIU I KRITIKE. (1918-1941).
Tashkent: "Fan," 1967, 179 pp., 650 copies. [Uzbek
text; 2535 titles]

Umarbekova, Z. KHAMID ALIMDZHAN. (BIBLIOGRAFICHESKII
UKAZATEL'.) Tashkent: Izd-vo Akad. Nauk UzSSR, 1960,
27 pp., 1000 copies. [Uzbek text; ca.380 Uzbek, Russ.
titles, pub.: 1926-1958]

Usmanov, S. NEKOTORYE VOPROSY UZBEKSKOI TERMINOLOGII.
Tashkent: "Ukituvchi," 1968, 32 pp., 5000 copies.
[Russ. text; Uzbek titles, p. 32]

Uzbek: Language, Literature

UZBEKSKAIA LITERATURA. (TASHK. GOS. UN-T IM. LENINA. NAUCH. TRUDY. [NOVAIA SERIIA]. No. 162. [FILOL. NAUKI] Book 20). Tashkent, 1960, 219 pp. [Uzbek text; ca.130 Uzbek, Russ., other titles, pp. 208-220]

UZBEKSKOE ISKUSSTVO (TEATR, MUZYKA, KINO NA STRANITSAKH PECHATI). BIBLIOGRAFICHESKII UKAZATEL'. Tashkent: GPB UzSSR, 1936. [Uzbek text]

Vladimirova, N. NEKOTORYE VOPROSY KHUDOZHESTVENNOGO PEREVODA S RUSSKOGO NA UZBEKSKII IAZYK. Tashkent: (In-t Iazyka i Lit. im. Pushkina), 1957. [Russ. text; ca.130 Uzbek, Russ. titles, pp. 121-125]

VOPROSY FRAZEOLOGII I GRAMMATICHESKOGO STROIA IAZYKA. Tashkent: "Fan," 1967, 171 pp., 1000 copies. [Russ. text; titles, pp. 114, 121]

Zarikov, M. MAKSUD SHEIKHZADE. OCHERKI ZHIZNI I TVORCHESTVA. Tashkent, 1969. [Uzbek text; 126 titles, pub.: 1932-1967, pp. 185-189]

PHILOSOPHY, RELIGION

Ageev, A.; F. Baibekova. V POMOSHCH' NAUCHNO-ATEISTICHESKOI PROPAGANDE. REK. UKAZATEL'. Tashkent: (Tashk. Obl. B-ka), 1956, 38 pp., 500 copies [Uzbek text; ca.170 titles]

Akhmedov, A. "O NEKOTORYKH RABOTAKH PO ISTORII FILOSOFII, OPUBLIKOVANNYKH V SOVETSKOM UZBEKISTANE V 20-KH GODAKH. [OBZOR]."OBSHCHESTV. NAUKI V UZBEKISTANE. No. 10. Tashkent, 1962. [Russ. text; titles, pub.: 1920s, pp. 59-62]

*Ismailov, B. IAZYK I POZNANIE MIRA. Tashkent: "Fan," 1969, 148 pp., 2000 copies. [Russ. text; ca.160 Russ. titles, pub.: 1888-1968, pp. 138-145]

Karimov, R. K.; A. K. Valiev. MARKSISTSKII ATEIZM--VYSSHAIA FORMA ATEIZMA. Samarkand, 1962. [Uzbek text; 45 titles, pp. 46-47]

Uzbek: Philosophy, Religion

[Khairullaev, M. M.; R. I. Khamidov. comps.] IBRAGIM
MUMINOVICH MUMINOV. Tashkent: "Fan," (AN UzSSR. Fundam.
B-ka. Deiateli Nauki i Kul'tury UzSSR), 1968, 52 pp.,
1000 copies. [Russ. text; 198 Uzbek, Russ. titles,
pub.: 1939-1968]

Mirzaev, S. PROIZVEDENIIA IBN-SINY V INSTITUTE
VOSTOKOVEDENIIA. BIBLIOGRAFIIA. Tashkent: Akad.
Nauk Uzbek. SSR. In-t Vostokovedeniia, 1955, 72 pp.,
2000 copies. [Uzbek text; ca.350 Tajik, Chaghatay,
Arabic, other titles, per.: Middle Ages]

VOPROSY PSIKHOLOGII I LOGIKI (NAUCH. TRUDY. No. 327.)
Tashkent: (Tashk. Gos. Un-t im. V. I. Lenina), 1968,
160 pp., 500 copies. [Russ. text; titles at end of
articles]

POLITICAL SCIENCE, LAW

Abdullaev, G. Kh.; B. K. Akhunov. NEKOTORYE
TEORETICHESKIE VOPROSY STROITEL'STVA KOMMUNIZMA.
Tashkent: "Fan," 1967, 177 pp., 3000 copies.
[Russ. text; Uzbek titles, at end of chapters]

*Abdushukurov, R. Kh. OKTIABR'SKAIA REVOLIUTSIIA.
RASTSVET UZBEKSKOI SOTSIALISTICHESKOI NATSII I
SBLIZHENIE EE S NATSIAMI SSSR. Tashkent: Gosizdat
UzSSR, 1962, 727 pp., 10,000 copies. [Russ. text and
titles, Sov. per., pp. 709-725]

[Ageev, A. I.] KLASSIKI MARKSIZMA-LENINIZMA I
LITERATURA O NIKH. Tashkent: (Resp. Bibliotech.
Kollektor Uzglavknigotorga. Gos. Publ. B-ka UzSSR im.
Navoi), 1953, 36 pp., 3000 copies. [Uzbek text; 119
Uzbek titles]

_____. KLASSIKI MARKSIZMA-LENINIZMA V
PEREVODAKH NA UZBEKSKII IAZYK, 1925-1940 GG. Tashkent:
Gosudarstvennaia Publichnaia Biblioteka UzSSR, 1941.
[Russ. text]

Uzbek: Political Science, Law

Agaronian, A. S. MIROVOZRENIE V SISTEME OBSHCHESTVENNOGO SOZNANIIA I PUTI FORMIROVANIIA NAUCHNOGO MIROVOZZRENIIA TRUDIASHCHIKHSIA UZBEKISTANA. Tashkent: "Fan," 1968, 156 pp., 1000 copies. [Russ. text; titles, pp. 147-156]

Agzamkhodzhaev, A.; Sh. Urazaev. RAZVITIE KONSTITUTSII UZBEKSKOI SSR. Tashkent: Gosizdat UzSSR, 1957. [Russ. text; ca.120 titles, Sov. per., pp. 169-174]

Allamuradov, D. SOVETY V BOR'BE ZA POBEDU SOTSIALIZMA V UZBEKISTANE. (1924-1937 GG.) Tashkent, 1970. [Russ. text; ca.120 titles, per.: 1924-1937, pp. 268-274]

*Azimov, O. MESTNYE SOVETY DEPUTATOV TRUDIASHCHIKHSIA. (PO MATERIALAM SAMARKANDSKOI OBL.) Tashkent: "Fan," 1969, 168 pp., 7000 copies. [Uzbek text; ca.130 Uzbek, Russ. titles, pub.: 1920-1968, pp. 163-167]

*Baibekova, F. I. comp. BIBLIOGRAFICHESKII UKAZATEL' PROIZVEDENII MARKSA-ENGEL'SA-LENINA, PEREVEDENNYKH NA UZBEKSKII IAZYK (1950-1963). Tashkent: Gosizdat UzSSR. Ozbekistan SSR Dawlat Nashriyati, 1964, 24 pp., 2000 copies. [Uzbek text; 104 Uzbek titles, pub.: 1950-1963]

Benediktova, N. N. "UZBEKISTAN V DNI OTECHESTVENNOI VOINY," BIBLIOGRAFICHESKII UKAZATEL'. Tashkent: GPB UzSSR im. Navoi, 1945. [Russ. text; titles, per.: 1941-1945]

Dzhalilov, I. VOZNIKNOVENIE I RAZVITIE SOVETSKOGO ZEMEL'NOGO PRAVA V UZBEKISTANE. Tashkent, 1970. [Russ. text; ca.480 titles, pp. 254-271]

Fuzulkhodzhaev, K. ODNA RODINA, ODNA SUD'BA. (K ISTORII DRUZHBY UZB. NARODA S BRATSKIMI NARODAMI SSSR). Tashkent, 1968. [Russ. text; ca.370 titles, pp. 301-316]

Garritskii, A. A. "KRATKII BIBLIOGRAFICHESKII UKAZATEL' PO BASMACHESTVU V VOSTOCHNOI BUKHARE," BIBLIOGRAFIIA VOSTOKA. No. 7. Leningrad: Izd-vo AN SSSR, 1935. [Russ. text; ca.200 titles]

*Glass, Iu. "IZDANIE PROIZVEDENII IL'ICHA V TURKESTANE," NARODNOE KHOZIAISTVO SREDNEI AZII. No. 4. 1964, 210 pp. [Russ. text; Russ., other titles, pub.: 20th c., pp. 16-17]

Uzbek: Political Science, Law

Inoiatov, Kh. Sh. ed. KHRONIKA SOBYTII VELIKOI OKTIABR'SKOI SOTSIALISTICHESKOI REVOLIUTSII V UZBEKISTANE. FEBR.-NOIABR' 1917 G. Tashkent, 1962. [Russ. text; ca.130 titles, per.: Feb.-Oct. 1917, pp. 278-285]

*Ishanov, A. I. SOZDANIE BUKHARSKOI NARODNOI RESPUBLIKI. (1920-1924 GG.) Tashkent: (Akad. Nauk Uzbek. SSR. In-t Istorii i Arkheologii), 1955, 178 pp. [Russ. text; 44 Uzbek, Russ. titles, per.: 1920-1924, pp. 178-179]

Iuldashev, M. Iu. ZEMLEVLADENIE I GOSUDARSTVENNOE USTROISTVO, O FEODAL'NOI KHIVY. Tashkent: Gosizdat UzSSR, 1959. [Uzbek text; ca.400 Uzbek, Russ. titles, Pre-Sov. per., pp. 337-362]

IZ DEIATEL'NOSTI KOMMUNISTICHESKOI PARTII UZBEKISTANA V PERIOD STROITEL'STVA KOMMUNIZMA. TASH. GOS. UN-T IM. V. I. LENINA. NAUCH. TRUDY. No. 294. Tashkent: "Fan," 1967, 104 pp., 500 copies. [Russ. text; titles at end of articles]

*Khakimov, M. Kh. RAZVITIE NATSIONAL'NOI SOVETSKOI GOSUDARSTVENNOSTI V UZBEKISTANE V PERIOD PEREKHODA K SOTSIALIZMU. OSNOVNYE PROBLEMY. Tashkent: Izdatel'stvo "Nauka," Uzbekskoi SSR, 1965, 504 pp., 1500 copies. [Russ. text; ca.520 Russ., Europ. titles (incl. archives), pp. 7-22, 477-502]

*Kharin, V. P. "OKTIABR'SKAIA SOTSIALISTICHESKAIA REVOLIUTSIIA V UZBEKISTANE," TRUDY SREDNEAZIAT. UN-TA. No. 101. (INST. NAUKI). Book 19. 1957. [Russ. text; ca.75 Uzbek, Russ. titles, Sov. per., pp. 59-62]

Khasanov, K. TSK VKP(B) V BOR'BE ZA POSTROENIE SOTSIALIZMA V SREDNEI AZII (1924-1937 GG.) Tashkent: "Fan," 1968, 219 pp., 1000 copies. [Russ. text; titles per.: 1924-1937, pp. 201-217]

*KRITIKA SOVREMENNOI BURZHUAZNOI POLITICHESKOI EKONOMII I REVIZIONIZMA. Tashkent: (Otd. Propagandy i Agitatsii TsK Kompartii Uzbekistana), 1958, 95 pp. [Uzbek text; 92 Russ., Europ. titles, contemporary per., pp. 11-15]

METODIKA PARTIINOI PROPAGANDY. Tashkent: "Uzbekistan," 1966, 210 pp. 10,000 copies.

Uzbek: Political Science, Law

*METODIKA PARTIINOI PROPAGANDY. Tashkent: "Uzbekistan,"
 1966, 204 pp., 10,000 copies. [Russ. text; titles,
 pp. 200-203]

*Mukhammedberdyev, K. KOMMUNISTICHESKAIA PARTIIA V BOR'BE
 ZA POBEDU NARODNOI SOVETSKOI REVOLIUTSII V KHOREZME.
 Ashkhabad: Turkmenskoe Gosudarstvennoe Izdatel'stvo
 (In-t Istorii Partii pri TsK KP Turkmenst.--Filial
 In-ta Marks-Len.), 1959, 278 pp. [Russ. text; ca.300
 Turkmen, Russ. titles, per.: early 1920's, pp. 260-277]

Musaev, M. D. BOR'BA PARTORGANIZATSII FERGANSKOI
 OBLASTI ZA VOSSTANOVLENIE I POD"EM SEL'SKOGO
 KHOZIAISTVA V GODY CHETVERTOI PIATILETKI (1946-1950 GG.)
 Farghana, 1962. [Russ. text; ca.60 titles, per.:
 1946-1950, pp. 123-126]

Nepesov, G. IZ ISTORII KHOREZMSKOI REVOLIUTSII. 1920--
 1924 GG. Tashkent, 1962. [Russ. text; ca.290 titles,
 per.: 1920-1924, pp. 344-356]

*Nishanov, R. INTERNATSIONALIZM--ZNAMIA NASHIKH POBED.
 (IZ OPYTA DEIATEL'NOSTI PART. ORGANIZATSII
 UZBEKISTANA PO INTERN. VOSPITANIIU TRUDIASHCHIKHSIA).
 Tashkent: "Uzbekistan," 1970, 320 pp., 15,000 copies.
 [Russ. text; ca.240 Russ. titles, per.: Sov., pub:
 1915-1969, pp. 310-318]

O PROIZVEDENII K. MARKSA I F. ENGEL'SA. Tashkent: (Gos.
 Publ. B-ka UzSSR im. Navoi) [1952] 15 pp., 500 copies.
 [Uzbek, Russ. text; 64 titles]

O RABOTAKH V. I. LENINA "SHAG VPERED DVA SHAGA NAZAD;"
 I. V. STALINA "KLASS PROLETARIEV I PARTIIA
 PROLETARIEV." Tashkent: (Gos. Publ. B-ka UzSSR im.
 Navoi), 1952, 14 pp. [Uzbek, Russ. text; 33 titles]

"PERECHEN' TRUDOV IULDASHA AKHUNBABAEVA--TRUDY O
 IULDASHE AKHUNBABAEVE," Valiev, V. NARODNYI AKSAKAL.
 Tashkent, 1962. [Russ. text; 18 titles, pub.: 1926-
 1942, pp. 102-103]

PRAVOVEDENIE. NAUCH. TRUDY. No. 313. Tashkent: (Tashk.
 Gos. Un-t im. V. I. Lenina), 1968, 243 pp., 500 copies.
 [Russ. text; titles at end of articles]

PRIMERNYE SPISKI LITERATURY REKOMENDUEMOI SAMOSTOIATEL'NO
 IZUCHAIUSHCHIM MARKSISTKO-LENINSKUIU TEORIIU.
 Tashkent, [1949]. [Uzbek, Russ. text; 24 Uzbek, Russ.
 titles]

Uzbek: Political Science, Law

RABOTA V. I. LENINA "CHTO DELAT'?" Tashkent: Uzb. Gos. Publ. B-ka im. Navoi, 1952, 10 pp., 300 copies. [Uzbek, Russ. text; 29 Uzbek, Russ. titles]

RABOTA V. I. LENINA "DVE TAKTIKI SOTSIAL-DEMOKRATII V DEMOKRATICHESKOI REVOLIUTSII." Tashkent: Kom. po Delam Kult-Prosvet. Uchrezhdenii pri Sovete Ministrov UzSSR, 1952, 14 pp., 300 copies. [Uzbek, Russ. text; 37 Uzbek, Russ. titles]

RABOTA V. I. STALINA "OB OSNOVAKH LENINIZMA." Tashkent: Gos. Publ. B-ka UzSSR im. Navoi, 1952, 16 pp., 300 copies. [Uzbek, Russ. text; 44 Uzbek, Russ. titles]

Rasulev, A. Kh. SOZDANIE I RAZVITIE SOVETSKOGO SUDA V UZBEKISTANE. Tashkent: Gosizdat UzSSR, 1957. [Russ. text; 184 titles, Sov. per., pp. 184-187]

Tursunov, Kh. T. OBRAZOVANIE UZBEKSKOI SOVETSKOI SOTSIALISTICHESKOI RESPUBLIKI. Tashkent: (Akad. Nauk Uzbek. SSR. In-t Istorii i Arkheologii), 1957. [Russ. text; ca.150 Uzbek, Russ. titles, pp. 235-242]

——————————. OBRAZOVANIE UZBEKSKOI SOVETSKOI SOTSIALISTICHESKOI RESPUBLIKI. Tashkent: Izdatel'stvo Akademii Nauk Uzbekskoi SSR, 1958, 249 pp., 3000 copies. [Uzbek text; Uzbek, Russ. titles, pp. 241-248]

Tutundzhan, T. A. 50 LET VOSSTANIIA TURKESTANSKIKH SAPEROV. Tashkent, 1962. [Russ. text; ca.130 titles, per.: 1912, pp. 83-90]

*Umurzakova, O. P. "OBZOR LITERATURY PO VOPROSU O FORMIROVANII UZBEKSKOI BURZHUAZNOI NATSII," IZVESTIIA AN UZSSR. SERIIA OBSHCHESTVENNYKH NAUK. No. 3. 1960. [Russ. text and titles, pp. 53-55]

*Valiev, A. K. SOVETSKAIA NATSIONAL'NAIA INTELLIGENTSIIA I EE SOTSIAL'NAIA ROL'. Tashkent: "Fan," 1969, 227 pp., 1000 copies. [Russ. text; ca.330 Russ., Eng. titles, pub.: 1919-1969, pp. 216-226]

Valiev, V. NARODNYI AKSAKAL. Tashkent: Gosudarstvennoe Izdatel'stvo Uzbekskoi SSR, 1962, 103 pp., 5000 copies. [Russ. text; 18 Russ. titles, pp. 102-103]

Uzbek

SOCIAL ORGANIZATION

Avsharova, M. P. comp. UZBEKSKAIA ZHENSHCHINA V PROSHLOM I NASTOIASHCHEM. Tashkent: Gosizdat UzSSR, 1958, 176 pp., 1500 copies. [Russ. text; ca.1000 titles, pub.: 1919-1956]

[Kasimova, O] CHTO CHITAT' O ZHENSHCHINE UZBEKISTANA. Tashkent: Gosizdat UzSSR, 1957, 37 pp., 5000 copies. [Uzbek text; ca.200 titles, per.: pre-Rev., post-Rev.]

*Nepomnin V. Ia. ISTORICHESKII OPYT STROITEL'STVA SOTSIALIZMA V UZBEKISTANE (1917-1937). Tashkent: Gosudarstvennoe Izdatel'stvo Uzbekskoi SSR, 1960, 382 pp., 5000 copies. [Russ. text and titles, per.: 1917-1937, pp. 367-380]

Strelkova, M. S. O RUKOVODIASHCHEI ROLI KOMMUNISTICHESKOI PARTII SOVETSKOGO SOIUZA V ORGANIZATSII SOVETSKOGO ZDRAVO-OKHRANENIIA NA PRIMERE UZBEKISTANA. (1917-1928). (TRUDY SAMARK. MED. IN-TA IM. PAVLOVA. Vol. 18. No. 1.) Samarkand, 1960. [Russ. text; 156 titles, per.: 1917-1928, pp. 109-120]

PART V

SIBERIA & MONGOLIA

31 ALTAY

GENERAL

*"ALTAI," SIBIRSKAIA SOVETSKAIA ENTSIKLOPEDIIA. Vol. 1.
Novosibirsk: Sibirskoe Kraevoe Izdatel'stvo, 1929,
62-83 pp. [Russ. text and titles, pp. 82-83]

"ALTAI. MATERIALY DLIA BIBLIOGRAFIIA ALTAIA 1891-1893,"
ALTAISKII SBORNIK. Vol. 1. (Tomsk) 1894. [Russ.
text; titles, pub.: 1891-1893, pp. 9-48]

*Iukhen, P. M. "ALTAISKII OKRUG," SIBIRSKAIA SOVETSKAIA
ENTSIKLOPEDIIA. Vol. 1. Novosibirsk: Sibirskoe
Kraevoe Izdatel'stvo, 1929, 85-87 pp. [Russ. text
and titles, p. 87]

Kon, F. Ia. "IZDANIIA MINUSINSKAGO MUZEAIA,"
MINUSINSKII MUZEI. Kazan, 1902. [Russ. text]

"MATERIALY DLIA BIBLIOGRAFII ALTAIA (1891-1893),"
ALTAISKII SBORNI. Vol. 1. 1894. [Russ. text;
106 titles, pp. 7-48]

Rybachenko, V. I.; E. R. Smirnova; I. Ia. Sterlin. comp.
ALTAISKII KRAI. BIBLIOGRAFICHESKII UKAZATEL'.
Barnaul: Altaiskoe Knizhnoe Izdatel'stvo, 1957, 127 pp.,
2000 copies. [Russ. text; ca.450 titles, pub.: after
1945, mainly 1953-1956]

Shishkin, B. K. "LITERATURA OB URIANKHAISKOI ZEMLE I
SOPREDEL'NYKH SAIANAKH," OCHERKI URIANKHAISKAGO KRAIA.
(IZVIESTIIA TOMSKAGO UNIVERSITETA. Book 60). Tomsk,
1914. [Russ. text; 140 titles]

[Vokhrysheva, M. G.; E. G. Glaz; L. V. Dobrokhotova;
R. M. Zhil'tsova; L. S. Pankratova; V. M. Posashkova.
comps.] LITERATURA OB ALTAISKOM KRAE. BIBLIOGR.
UKAZATEL'. Barnaul: Alt. Kn. Izd., 1968, 220 pp.,
5000 copies. [Russ. text; 1235 titles, pub.: 1917-
1965]

*Zalesskii, P. "BARNAUL'SKII OKRUG," SIBIRSKAIA
SOVETSKAIA ENTSIKLOPEDIIA. Vol. 1. Novosibirsk:
Sibirskoe Kraevoe Izdatel'stvo, 1929, 245-253 pp.
[Russ. text and titles, pp. 252-253]

Altay

ANTHROPOLOGY, ETHNOGRAPHY

*A. Sh. "ALTAITSY," SIBIRSKAIA SOVETSKAIA ENTSIKLOPEDIIA. Vol. 1. Novosibirsk: Sibirskoe Kraevoe Izdatel'stvo, 1929. [Russ. text and titles, p. 89]

*Ivanovskii, Al. "ALTAISKII MISSIONER, PROTOIEREI V. I. VERBITSKII (NEKROLOG)," ETNOGRAFICHESKOE OBOZRIENIE. No. 1. 1891, 176-179 pp. [Russ. text; 28 Russ. titles, pp. 178-179]

*Tokarev, Sergei A. DOKAPITALISTICHESKIE PEREZHITKI V OIROTII. Leningrad: Sotsial'no-Ekonomicheskoe Izdatel'stvo, Leningradskoe Otdelenie, 1936, 155 pp., 1250 copies. [Russ. text and titles, pp. 147-151]

ARCHITECTURE, ART, MUSIC

Shul'gin, B. O MUZYKAL'NOI KUL'TURE ALTAITSEV. (Barnaul): Gorno-Altaisk, (Alt. Kn. Izd.), 1968, 88 pp., 500 copies. [Russ. text; 28 titles, p. 87]

ECONOMICS

AGRONOMIIA I EKONOMIKA. TRUDY ALT. S.-KH IN-TA. No. 8. Barnaul: Alt. Kn. Izd., 1966, 263 pp., 1000 copies. [Russ. text; titles at end of articles]

*"ALTAI," BOL'SHAIA SOVETSKAIA ENTSIKLOPEDIIA. Vol. 2. 1950, 2nd ed., 136-141 pp. [Russ. text and titles, pp. 139, 141]

*[ALTAISKII S.-KH INSTITUT.] SBORNIK NAUCHNO-ISSLEDOVATEL'SKIKH RABOT ASPIRANTOV. No. 1. MATERIALY KONFERENTSII MOLODYKH UCHENYKH. Barnaul: Altaiskoe Knizhnoe Izdatel'stvo, 1966, 91 pp., 500 copies. [Russ. text and titles at end of articles]

ALTAISKII S.-KH. INSTITUT. SBORNIK NAUCHNO-ISSLEDOVATEL'SKIKH RABOT ASPIRANTOV I MOLODYKH UCHENYKH. No. 2. MATERIALY KONFERENTSII. Barnaul: Alt. Kn. Izd., 1966, 144 pp., 500 copies. [Russ. text; titles at end of articles]

ALTAISKII S.-KH. INSTITUT. SBORNIK NAUCHNO-ISSLEDOVATEL'SKIKH RABOT ASPIRANTOV I MOLODYKH UCHENYKH. No. 6. Barnaul: (Alt. Kraev. Pravl. NTO Sel. Khoz-va), 1968, 141 pp., 500 copies. [Russ. text; titles at end of articles]

Kukis, S. I. ed. AGRONOMIIA I EKONOMIA. TRUDY ALT. S.-KH. IN-TA. No. 14. Barnaul: (M-vo Sel. Knoz-va SSSR), 1968, 328 pp., 500 copies. [Russ. text; titles at end of articles]

*Lizinaia, A. I.; T. M. Makeev. eds. RAZVITIE EKONOMIKI I KUL'TURY ALTAISKOGO KRAIA ZA 40 LET. SOVETSKOI VLASTI. Barnaul: Alt. Kn. Izd., 1957, 231 pp., 15,000 copies. [Russ. text; ca.60 Russ. titles, Sov. per., pp. 228-230]

Makeev, T. M. MIROVAIA SOTSIALISTICHESKAIA SISTEMA KHOZIAISTVA. (Barnaul) (Dom Polit. Prosveshcheniia Alt. Kraikoma KPSS), 1968, 36 pp., 1500 copies. [Russ. text; 13 titles, pp. 3-4]

Altay: Economics

*Obruchev, V.; A. Iarkho. "ALTAI," BOL'SHAIA SOVETSKAIA
ENTSIKLOPEDIIA. Vol. 2. 1926, 1st ed., 265-274 pp.
[Russ. text; Russ., Europ. titles, p. 274]

*_____.; A. Sakharov; M. Uroev. "OIROTSKAIA
AVTONOMNAIA OBLAST'," BOL'SHAIA SOVETSKAIA
ENTSIKLOPEDIIA. Vol. 42. 1939, 1st ed., 787-798 pp.
[Russ. text; titles, pp. 794, 797]

*Tokarev, S. A. DOKAPITALISTICHESKIE PEREZHITKI V
OIRATII. Leningrad: Sotsial'no-Ekonomicheskoe
Izdatel'stvo, 1936, 155 pp. [Russ. text and titles,
per.: 1932, pp. 147-151]

EDUCATION

KRAEVEDCHESKAIA RABOTA V SEL'SKIKH KUL'TURNO-
PROSVETITEL'NYKH UCHREZHDENIIAKH. Barnaul:
Altkraiizdat, 1952, 28 pp. [5 lists]

VOPROSY RAZVITIIA SEL'SKOGO KHOZIAISTVA GORNOGO ALTAIA.
Novosibirsk: "Nauka," 1968, 358 pp., 1000 copies.
[Russ. text; titles at end of articles]

GEOGRAPHY

Gebler, I. V. SOVETSKII GORNYI ALTAI. Tomsk:
(Tomskii Politekhn. In-t im. Kirova), 1956. [Russ.
text; 48 titles, pp. 75-76]

*GEOGRAFICHESKOE OBSHCHESTVO SSSR. ALTAISKII OTDEL.
IZVESTIIA... No. 7. Barnaul: Alt. Kn. Izd., 1966,
124 pp., 500 copies. [Russ. text; titles at end of
articles]

Altay: Geography

Iavorskii, V. I.; P. I. Butov. "SPISOK NOVEISHEI
LITERATURY PO KUZNETSKOMU BASSEINU," KUZNETSKII
KAMENNOUGUL'NYI BASSEIN. (TRUDY GEOLOGICHESKOGO
KOMITETA. No. 177). Leningrad, 1927. [Russ. text;
titles, pub.: since 1901]

Kambalov, N. PO INTERESNYM MESTAM ALTAISKOGO KRAIA.
Barnaul: Alt. Kn. Izd., 1956. [Russ. text; 55 titles,
pp. 130-132]

Pilipenko, P. P. "LITERATURA PO MINERALOGII, GEOLOGII
I GEOGRAFII ZAPADNAGO ALTAIA," MINERALOGIIA
ZAPADNAGO ALTAIA, (IZVIESTIIA TOMSKAGO UNIVERSITETA,
Book 62.) Tomsk, 1915. [Russ. text; 313 + 71 titles]

Pitter, T. M. "BIBLIOGRAFIIA IZDANII ALTAISKOGO OTDELA
GEOGRAFICHESKOGO OBSHCHESTVA SOIUZA SSR," IZV. ALT.
OTD. GEOGR. O-VA SSSR. No. 10. 1969. [Russ. text;
25 titles, pp. 115-126]

Rozen, M. F. OCHERKI I BIBLIOGRAFIIA ISSLEDOVANII
PRIRODY ALTAIA. (IZV. ALT. GEOGR. O-VA SSSR. No. 12.)
[Barnaul] Alt. Kn. Izd-vo, 1970. [Russ. text; titles
pub.: 1667-, p. 255]

Shafranovskii, K. I.; V. A. Feider; T. G. Maziukevich;
E. P. Faidel'; L. M. Garkavi; E. I. Gol'tsman; V. P.
Alekseeva. comps. "MATERIALY DLIA BIBLIOGRAFII
ALTAISKO-IRTYSHSKOGO RAIONA. SISTEMATICHESKII
UKAZATEL' LITERATURY. SOSTAVLENNYI BIBLIOTEKOI
AKADEMII NAUK SSSR," BOL'SHOI ALTAI. SBORNIK
MATERIALOV PO PROBLEME KOMPLEKSKOGO IZUCHENIIA I
OSVOENIIA PRIRODNYKH RESURSOV ALTAISKO-IRTYSHSKOGO
RAIONA. TRUDY KAZAKHSTANSKOI BAZY AN SSSR. Vol. 3.
No. 6. (Moscow-Leningrad) 1936. [Russ. text; 3221
Russ. titles, pub.: up to 1934, pp. 261-576]

"UKAZATEL' LITERATURY PO GEOLOGII I GEOGRAFII
ALTAISKAGO OKRUGA," TRUDY GEOLOGICHESKOI CHASTI
KABINETA E. I. V. Vol. 1. No. 1; Vol. 3. Part 1.
1895. [Russ. text; 410 Russ., Europ. titles
(1) pp. 15-104; (3) pp. 122-131]

Altay

HISTORY, ARCHAEOLOGY

Borodkin, P. A. S. I GULIAEV. Barnaul: Alt. Kn. Izd., 1960. [Russ. text; 39 titles, pub.: 1839-1884, pp. 108-109]

Demidov, V. A. PEREKHOD ALTAITSEV NA OSEDLOST'. Barnaul: Alt. Kn. Izd., 1968, 103 pp. [Russ. text; titles, pp. 97-102]

Filov, V. PUGACHEVTSY NA ALTAE. Barnaul: Alt. Kn. Izd., 1955. [Russ. text; ca.130 titles, per.: 18th c., pp. 214-227]

*Gavrilova, A. A. MOGIL'NIK KUDYRGE. KAK ISTOCHNIK PO ISTORII ALTAISKIKH PLEMEN. Leningrad: Izdatel'stvo "Nauka," 1965, 143 pp., 1200 copies. [Russ. text; ca.175 Russ., Europ. titles, pub.: 1825-1962, pp. 107-110]

*Iarkho, A. "ALTAI-ALTAISKAIA GUBERNIIA," BOL'SHAIA SOVETSKAIA ENTSIKLOPEDIIA. Vol. 2. Moscow: Aktsionernoe Obshchestvo "Sovetskaia Entsiklopediia," 1926, 265-274 pp. [Russ. text; Altai, Russ., Europ. titles, p. 274]

Potapov, P. P. ed. DOKLADY SOVETSKOI DELEGATSII NA XXIII MEZHDUNARODNOM KONGRESSE VOSTOKOVEDOV. SEKTSIIA ISSLEDOVANII PO ALTAISTIKE. OSNOVNYE PROBLEMY IZUCHENIIA NARODOV ALTAIA V SOVETSKOI IST. NAUKE. n. p. Akad. Nauk SSSR, 1954. [Russ., English text; 42 titles, pp. 29-31]

Potapov, L. P. "IZUCHENIE ALTAITSEV RUSSKIMI UCHENYMI V DOREVOLIUTSIONNYI PERIOD. [OBZOR]" UCHEN. ZAPISKI GORNO-ALT. NAUCH.-ISSLED. IN-TA ISTORII, IAZYKA I LIT. No. 2. 1958. [Russ. text; titles, per.: pre-1917, pp. 3-23]

*Rudenko, S. I. ISKUSSTVO SKIFOV ALTAIA. Moscow: Izdatel'stvo Gosudarstvennogo Muzeia Izobrazitel'nykh Iskusstv imeni A. S. Pushkina, 1949, 91 pp., 5000 copies. [Russ. text; 27 Russ., Eng. titles, p. 90]

Altay: History, Archaeology

* _____. KUL'TURA NASELENIIA GORNOGO ALTAIA V SKIFSKOE VREMIA. Moscow-Leningrad: (Akad. Nauk SSSR. In-t Isorii Material'noi Kul'tury) Izdatel'stvo Akademii Nauk SSSR, 1953, 401 pp., 3000 copies. [Russ. text; 92 Russ., foreign titles, per.: ancient, pp. 377-380]

*Umanskii, A. PAMIATNIKI KUL'TURY ALTAIA. Barnaul: Altaiskoe Knizhnoe Izdatel'stvo, 1959, 252 pp., 3000 copies. [Russ. text; ca.100 titles (incl. archives), pp. 248-252]

LANGUAGE, LITERATURE

Baskakov, N. A. "K ISTORII IZUCHENIIA ALTAISKOGO IAZYKA. [OBZOR]," UCHEN. ZAPISKI GORNO-ALT. NAUCH.-ISSLED. IN-TA ISTORII, IAZYKA I LIT. No. 2. 1958. [Russ. text; titles, pp. 24-38]

* _____.: T. M. Toshchakova. OIROTSKO-RUSSKII SLOVAR'. Moscow: Gos. Izd. Inostr. i Nats. Slovarii, 1947, 312 pp. [Oirat, Russ. text; 27 titles, pp. 7-8]

*Dmitriev, N. "ALTAISKIE IAZYKI," BOL'SHAIA SOVETSKAI ENTSIKLOPEDIIA. Vol. 2. Moscow: Aktsionernoe Obshchestvo "Sovetskaia Entsiklopediia," 1926, 1st ed., 275-276 pp. [Russ. text; Altai, Russ., Europ. titles, p. 276]

*Katanov, N. Th. OPYT IZSLIEDOVANIIA URIANKHAISKAGO IAZYKA S UKAZANIEM GLEVNIESHIKH RODSTVENNYKH OTNOSHENII EGO K DRUGIM IAZYKAM TIURKSKAGO KORNIA. Kazan: Tipo-Litografiia Imperatorskago Kazanskago Universiteta, 1903, 487 pp. [Russ. text; 84 Russ., Europ. titles, pub.: 1768-1902, pp. 317-472]

*N. B. "OIROTSKII IAZYK," BOL'SHAIA SOVETSKAIA ENTSIKLOPEDIIA. Vol. 42. Moscow: Gosudarstvennyi Institut "Sovetskaia Entsiklopediia," (Ogiz RSFSR), 1939, 2nd ed., 798-799 pp. [Russ. text; Altai, Oirot, Russ., Europ. titles, p. 799]

Altay: Language, Literature

*Ramstedt, G. J. VVEDENIE V ALTAISKOE IAZYKOZNANIE. Moscow: Izd-vo Inostrannoi Literatury, 1957, 254 pp. [Russ. text; titles, pp. 5-11]

Surazakov, S. PAVEL VASIL'EVICH KUCHIIAK. Gorno-Altaisk: Kn. Izd., 1957. [Altay text; 32 Altay, Russ. titles, pub.: 1932-1955, pp. 58-59]

Vokhrusheva, M. G.; L. S. Pankratova. comps. PISATELI ALTAIA. BIOBIBLIOGRAFICHESKII SPRAVOCHNIK. Barnaul: Altaiskoe Knizhnoe Izdatel'stvo, 1967, 151 pp., 8000 copies. [Russ. text]

32 BURIAT

GENERAL

AKADEMIIA NAUK SSSR. BURIATSKII FILIAL KNIGI
BURIATSKOGO FILIALA SIBIRSKOGO OTDELENIIA AN SSSR.
1967 GOD. Ulan-Ude, 1967, 51 pp., 5000 copies.
[Russ. text]

*Azheeva, R. B.; M. M. Spektor; E. M. Zharkova.
LITERATURA O BURIATSKOI ASSR. REK. UKAZATEL. Ulan-
Ude: Buriat. Kn. Izd., 1968, 227 pp., 1500 copies.
[Russ. text; 1262 Buriat, Russ. titles, pub.: 1958-
1967]

*_____.; O. D. Tarmakhanova; M. M. Spektor;
V. M. Chemeris. comps. 300 LET G. ULAN-UDE. (KRATKII
REK. UKAZATEL' LIT.) Ulan-Ude: (M-vo Kul'tury Buriat.
Assr) (Resp. B-ka im. Gor'kogo BuraSSR), 1966, 28 pp.,
500 copies. [Russ. text; ca.290 titles]

"BIBLIOGRAFICHESKII UKAZATEL' NA STAT'I, POMESHCHENNYE V
ZHURNALE 'ZHIZN' BURIATII' ZA 1928 GOD," ZHIZN'
BURIATII. No. 10/12. 1928. [Russ. text; 78 titles,
pub.: 1928, pp. 223-225]

"BIBLIOGRAFICHESKII UKAZATEL' STATEI ZHURNALA 'ZHIZN'
BURIATII' ZA 1924-1927 GG." ZHIZN' BURIATII. No. 11/12.
1927. [Russ. text; 356 titles, pub.: 1924-1927,
pp. 115-126]

"BIBLIOGRAFIIA BURIAT," BURIATOVEDCHESKII SBORNIK. No. 2.
Irkutsk, 1926. [Russ. text]

BURIAT-MONGOL'SKAIA ASSR. (BIBLIÓGRAFICHESKII
UKAZATEL'.) Ulan-Ude: (Respublikanskaia Biblioteka
Buriat-Mongol'skoi ASSR), 1957, 97 pp. [Russ. text;
ca.1300 titles, pub.: ca. 1950-1957]

*BURIATSKII PEDAGOGICHESKII INSTITUT IM. DORZHI BANZAROVA.
UCHENYE ZAPISKI. No. 28. Ulan-Ude: Buriatskoe
Knizhnoe Izdatel'stvo, 1967 (Vyp. DAN 1968), 310 pp.,
1000 copies. [Russ. text and titles at end of
articles]

Buriat : General

Dorzhinov, S. "BIBLIOGRAFIIA MESTNOI PECHATI BURIAT-MONGOL'SKOI ASSR (1938)," ZAPISKI BURIAT MONGOL'SKOGO NAUCHNO-ISSLEDOVATEL'SKOGO INSTITUTA IAZYKA, LITERATURY I ISTORII. No. 1. 1939. [Russ. text; 101 Buriat, Russ. titles, pp. 135-150]

* _____. "PECHATNYE RABOTY BURIATSKOGO KOMPLEKSNOGO NAUCHNO-ISSLEDOVATEL'SKOGO INSTITUTA SIBIRSKOGO OTDELENIIA AKADEMII NAUK SSSR," KRATKIE SOOBSHCHENIIA BURIATSKOGO KOMPLEKSNOGO NAUCHNO-ISSLEDOVATEL'SKOGO INSTITUTA. No. 1. (Ulan Ude), 1959, 172 pp., 1000 copies. [Russ. text; 24+ Buriat, Russ. titles, pub.: 1957-1959, pp. 155-162]

Florensov, A. NOVYE RABOTY O BURIATII I MONGOLII. (BIBLIOGRAFICHESKIE ZAMETKI). KHOZIAISTVO MONGOLII. No. 3. May-June 1926. [titles, pp. 196-199]

Kazarinov, P. K. "O BIBLIOGRAFII BURIAT-MONGOLOV I IKH KRAIA," BURIATOVEDCHESKII SBORNIK. No. 1. (Irkutsk), 1926, 3-23 pp. [Russ. text; Russ. survey, pub.: up to 1925, pp. 5-16]

_____. O BIBLIOGRAFII BURIAT-MONGOLOV I IKH KRAIA. Irkutsk, 1926. [Russ. text]

LETOPIS' PECHATI BURIATSKOI ASSR. Ulan Ude: Buriatskoe Knizhnoe Izdatel'stvo, 1926, 52 pp., 1000 copies. [Buriat, Russ. text and titles, pub.: 1958-1959]

LETOPIS' PECHATI BURIATSKOI ASSR. LITERATURA O BURIATSKOI ASSR. Ulan Ude: Buriatskoe Knizhnoe Izdanie, 1962 (annual), 175 pp., 500 copies. [Buriat, Russ. text and titles, pub.: 1960]

LETOPIS' PECHATI BURIATSKOI ASSR. Ulan Ude: Buriat. Kn. Izd., 1966, 226 pp., 800 copies. [Russ. text; titles, pub.: 1961]

LETOPIS' PECHATI BURIATSKOI ASSR. Ulan Ude: (Resp. B-ka im. Gor'kogo), 1968, 280 pp. [Russ. text; titles, pub.: 1962]

LETOPIS' PECHATI BURIATSKOI ASSR. Ulan Ude: (Resp. B-ka im. Gor'kogo), 1968, 239 pp. [Russ. text; titles, pub.: 1963]

LETOPIS' PECHATI BURIATSKOI ASSR. Ulan Ude: (Resp. B ka im. Gor'kogo), 1970, 274 pp. [Russ. text; titles, pub.: 1964]

Buriat: General

LETOPIS' PECHATI BURIATSKOI ASSR. Ulan Ude: (Resp. B-ka im. Gor'kogo), 1970, 352 pp. [Russ. text; titles, pub.: 1965]

LETOPIS' PECHATI BURIATSKOI ASSR. Ulan Ude: (Resp. B-ka im. Gor'kogo), 1966-1967 (quarterly), 800 copies. [Russ. text; titles, pub.: 1966]

Mangutov, N. R. "BIBLIOGRAFIIA LITERATURY, IZDANNOI V BURIAT-MONGOL'SKOI ASSR V 1949 I 1950 GG.," ZAPISKI BURIAT-MONGOL'SKOGO NAUCHNO-ISSLEDOVATEL'SKOGO INSTITUTA KUL'TURY. No. 16. 1952. [Russ. text; 122 Buriat, Russ. titles, pub.: 1949-1950, pp. 100-127]

Matrosova, N. A. "BIBLIOGRAFIIA LITERATURY, IZDANNOI V BURIAT-MONGOL'SKOI ASSR V 1948 GODU," ZAPISKI BURIAT MONGOL'SKOGO NAUCHNO-ISSLEDOVATEL'NOGO INSTITUTA KUL'TURY. No. 10. (Ulan-Ude), 1950. [Russ. text; 146 titles, pub.: 1948, pp. 157-178]

Matveev, N. CHTO CHITAT' O DAL'NEM VOSTOKE. Vladivostok, 1925. [Russ. text]

NOVYE KNIGI BURIATSKOGO KOMPLEKSNOGO NAUCHNO-ISSLEDOVATEL'SKOGO INSTITUTA. Ulan Ude: (Akademiia Nauk SSSR. Sibirskoe Otdelenie), 1960, 15 pp. [Russ. text; 29 titles, pub.: 1958-1960]

"PERIODICHESKAIA PECHAT' NA DAL'NEM VOSTOKE V PERIOD REVOLIUTSII 1917-1918 G. G.," IZVESTIIA . PRIMORSKOE GUBERNSKOE ARKHIVNOE BIURO. Vol. 1, No. 3. 1923. [Russ. text]

*Pomus, M.; B. Klobukov. "BURIAT-MONGOL'SKAIA AVTONOMNAIA SOVETSKAIA SOTSIALISTICHESKAIA RESPUBLIKA," SIBIRSKAIA SOVETSKAIA ENTSIKLOPEDIIA. Vol. 1. Novosibirsk: Sibirskoe Kraevoe Izdatel'stvo, 1929, 405-419 pp. [Russ. text and titles, p. 419]

Shirabon, Sh. "BURIATSKAIA LITERATURA," SIBIRSKAIA SOVETSKAIA ENTSIKLOPEDIIA. Vol. 3. Novosibirsk: Sibirskoe Kraevoe Izdatel'stvo, 1931, 221-226 pp. [Russ. text and titles, p. 226]

*Shperk, F. "BURIATY," ENTSIKLOPEDICHESKII SLOVAR'. Vol. 5. St. Petersburg: Izdateli: F. A. Brokgauz; I. A. Efron, 1891, 59-64 pp. [Russ. text; Russ., Europ. titles, pub.: 1751-1891, p. 64]

Buriat: General

*Smolin, G. Ia.; K. I. Shafranovskii. eds. UKAZATEL'
BIBLIOGRAFII PO MONGOLOVEDENIIU NA RUSSKOM IAZYKE,
1824-1960. Leningrad: (Akademiia Nauk SSSR.
Biblioteka Akademii Nauk), 1962, 89 pp., 650 copies.
[Russ. text; 201 Russ. titles, pp. 23-73]

ANTHROPOLOGY, ETHNOGRAPHY

Bliumenfel'd, O. ETNOGRAFICHESKIE EKSPEDITSII I
POEZDKI, ORGANIZOVANNYE VOSTOCHNO-SIBIRSKIM OTDELOM
RUSSKOGO GEOGRAFICHESKOGO OBSHCHESTVA. UKAZATEL'
LITERATURY. 1851-1926. IZVESTIIA VOSTOCHNO-
SIBIRSKOGO OTDELA RUSSKOGO GEOGRAFICHESKOGO
OBSHCHESTVA. Vol. 50. 1926. [Russ. text; 90 Russ.
titles, per.: 1851-1926, pp. 38-41]

*BURIATOVEDCHESKII SBORNIK. Irkutsk, 1929 - III/IV; 1930-
V. [Russ. text; Russ., Europ. titles, pp. 100-101,
86-88]

Daurskii, V. "LITERATURA O TIBETSKOI I NARODNOI
MEDITSINE BURIAT-MONGOLOV, MONGOLOV, TIBETSEV,"
SOVREMENNAIA MONGOLIIA. No. 3 (22). 1937, 92-106 pp.
[Russ. text; 132 titles, pp. 99-106]

Kazantsev, A. I. "MATERIALY K IZUCHENIIU BURIATSKIKH
CHEREPOV," BURIATOVEDCHESKII SBORNIK. No. 3/4.
(Irkutsk) 1927, 90-100 pp. [Russ. text; 16 Russ.,
Europ. titles, pp. 99-100]

Khoroshikh, P. P. "LITERATURA O NARODNOI I TIBETSKOI
MEDITSINE BURIAT-MONGOLOV. (NA RUSSKOM IAZYKE),"
BURIATOVEDCHESKII SBORNIK. No. 1. (Irkutsk), 1926.
[Russ. text; 59 Russ. titles, pp. 42-45]

Petrova-Smagina, V. O. "ETNOGRAFIIA V TRUDAKH
VOSTOCHNO-SIBIRSKOGO OTDELA RUSSKOGO GEOGRAFICHESKOGO
OBSHCHESTVA. BIBLIOGRAFICHESKII UKAZATEL'. 1851-1926,"
SIBIRSKAIA ZHIVAIA STARINA. No. 2 (VI). 1926.
[Russ. text; ca.400 Russ. titles, pub.: 1851-1926,
pp. 63-84]

Buriat : Anthropology, Ethnography

*Rumiantsev, G. N. PROISKHOZHDENIE KHORINSKIKH BURIAT. Ulan Ude: Buriatskoe Knizhnoe Izdatel'stvo, 1962, 267 pp., 1000 copies. [Russ. text; survey + ca.380 Buriat, Mongol, Russ., Europ. titles (incl. archives), pp. 5-63, 64-82, 248-264]

*Tugutov, I. E. MATERIAL'NAIA KUL'TURA BURIAT. ETNOGRAFICHESKOE ISSLEDOVANIE. Ulan Ude: (Akademiia Nauk SSSR. Sibirskoe Otdelenie. Buriatskii Kompleksnyi Nauchno-Issledovatel'skii Institut), 1958, 215 pp., 800 copies. [Russ. text; titles (incl. archives), pp. 201-214]

Vinogradov, G. ETNOGRAFICHESKIE IZUCHENIIA VOSTOCHNO-SIBIRSKOGO OTDELA RUSSKOGO GEOGRAFICHESKOGO OBSHCHESTVA. 1851-1926. KRATKII OBZOR. IZVESTIIA VOSTOCHNO-SIBIRSKOGO OTDELA RUSSKOGO GEOGRAFICHESKOGO OBSHCHESTVA. Vol. 50. 1926. [Russ. text; titles, pp. 3-37]

ARCHITECTURE, ART, MUSIC

Khoroshikh, P. P. "LITERATURA O MUZYKE, TEATRE, PESNIIAKH I NARODNYKH RAZVLECHENIIAKH BURIAT-MONGOLOV (NA RUSSKOM IAZYKE)," BURIATOVEDCHESKII SBORNIK. No. 1. (Irkutsk), 1926. [Russ. text; 91 Russ. titles, pp. 65-68]

_____. "ZADACHI IZUCHENIIA IZOBRAZITEL'NOGO ISKUSSTVA BURIAT," ZHIZN' BURIATII. No. 6. 1925, 83-89 pp. [Russ. text; ca.20 titles]

Kunitsyna, I.; O. Kunitsyn. MUZYKA SOVETSKOI BURIATII. Ulan Ude: Buriat. Kn. Izd., 1968, 112 pp., 3000 copies. [Russ. text; titles p. 111]

Murueva, V. P.; S. G. Ulakhanov. comps. V POMOSHCH' AGITBRIGADAM. REPERTUARNO-METOD. SBORNIK. Ulan Ude: Buriat. Kn. Izd., 1967, 35 pp., 500 copies. [Russ. text; 87 titles, pp. 11-15]

Buriat: Architecture, Art, Music

Tarmakhanova, O. D. comp. KALENDAR' ZNAMENATEL'NYKH
I PAMIATNYKH DAT...PO BURIATII. ...NA 1966 GOD.
Ulan Ude: Buriat. Kn. Izd., 1966, 72 pp., 750 copies.
[Russ. text; titles at end of chapters]

ECONOMICS

Aiushiev, A. D.; V. N. Petrov. VNUTRIPROIZVODSTVENNYE
REZERVY I METODY IKH VYIAVLENIIA. Ulan Ude: Buriat.
Kn. Izd., 1968, 71 pp., 2000 copies. [Russ. text
and titles, at end of articles]

*Buiantuev, B. R.; G. Sh. Radnaev. SOVETSKAIA BURIAT-
MONGOLIIA (EKONOMIKO-GEOGRAFICHESKII OBZOR). Ulan
Ude: Buriat-Mongol'skoe Knizhnoe Izdatel'stvo, 1957,
352 pp., 3000 copies. [Russ. text; ca.100 Russ.
titles, pp. 347-351]

*Deriugina, V. N. PROIZVODSTVENNYE TIPY KOLKHOZOV I
SOVKHOZOV BURIATSKOI ASSR. Ulan Ude: Buriat. Kn.
Izd., 1968, 123 pp., 1000 copies. [Russ. text;
titles, pp. 121-122]

Ivanov, B. I. ISPOL'ZOVANIE OSNOVNYKH PROIZVODSTVENNYKH
FONDOV V KOLKHOZAKH I SOVKHOZAKH BURIATII. Ulan Ude:
Buriat. Kn. Izd., 1966, 110 pp., 1000 copies.
[Russ. text; titles pp. 108-109]

Khomkholov, B. Kh. SOVETSKAIA BURIAT-MONGOLIIA V
EDINOI SEM'E NARODOV SSSR. Ulan Ude: Buriat-
Mongol'skoe Knizhnoe Izdatel'stvo, 1958. [Russ. text;
127 titles, pp. 391-398]

*Koz'min, N. "BURIATO-MONGOL'SKAIA AVTONOMNAIA
SOVETSKAIA SOTSIALISTICHESKAIA RESPUBLIKA," BOL'SHAIA
SOVETSKAIA ENTSIKLOPEDIIA. Vol. 8. Moscow:
Aktsionernoe Obshchestvo "Sovetskaia Entsiklopediia,"
1927, 221-233 pp. [Russ. text; Buriat, Russ. titles,
p. 233]

Buriat: Economics

*Mangutov, N. R. AGRARNYE PREOBRAZOVANIIA V SOVETSKOI
BURIATII. (1917-1933 GG.) Ulan Ude: (Akademiia Nauk
SSSR. Sibirskoe Otdelenie. Buriatskii Kompleksnyi
Nauchno-Issledovatel'skii Institut), 1960, 215 pp.,
1000 copies. [Russ. text; ca.100 Russ. titles,
per.: 1917-1933, pp. 209-214]

*Rumiantsev, N. N. OPISANIE ARKHIVA U. TS. ONGODOVA.
(IZ SOBRANIIA RUKOPISNOGO OTDELA BURIATSKOGO
KOMPLEKSNOGO INSTITUTA). Ulan Ude:(Akademiia Nauk
SSSR. Sibirskoe Otdelenie. Buriatskii Kompleksnyi
Nauchno-Issledovatel'skii Institut), 1959, 78 pp.
[Russ. text; 302 titles (incl. archives)]

*Tugutov, I. E. MATERIAL'NAIA KUL'TURA BURIAT.
ETNOGRAFICHESKOE ISSLEDOVANIE. Ulan Ude: (Akademiia
Nauk SSSR. Sibirskoe Otdelenie. Buriatskii
Kompleksnyi Nauchno-Issledovatel'skii Institut),
1958, 215 pp., 800 copies. [Russ. text; ca.320
Russ. titles (incl. archives), pp. 201-214]

*Zdobnov, N. V. comp. BIBLIOGRAFIIA BURIAT-MONGOLII ZA
1890-1936. BIBLIOGRAPHY OF BURIAT-MONGOLIA 1890-1936.
Vol. 1. ESTESTVOZNANIE; [Vol. 2. GUMANITARNAIA LIT.
not published] Vol. 3. SEL'SKOE, LESNOE, PUSHNO-
ZVEREVOE I RYBNOE KHOZIAISTVO; Vol. 4.
ZDRAVOOKHRANENIE. Moscow-Leningrad: Izdatel'stvo
Akademii Nauk SSSR, (Vol. 1) 1939; (Vol. 4) 1940,
220 pp., 2000 copies; (Vol. 3) 1946, 534 pp., 2000
copies. [Russ. text; (Vol. 3) 2527 Russ. titles;
(Vol. 4) 977 Russ. titles, pub.: 1890-1936]

Zubatova, L. E. comp. BIBLIOGRAFIIA IRKUTSKOI OBLASTI.
TRUDY NAUCHNOI BIBLIOTEKI IRKUTSKOGO GOSUDARSTVENNOGO
INSTITUTA IMENI A. A. ZHDANOVA. No. 13. FIZICHESKAIA
GEOGRAFIIA. n. p. 1957, 173 pp. [Russ. text;
2358 Russ., other titles, pub.: 18th c.-1950]

EDUCATION

*Andreev, V. I. ISTORIIA BURIATSKOI SHKOLY (1804-1926 GG.)
Ulan Ude: Buriatskoe Knizhnoe Izdatel'stvo, 1964,
567 pp., 1500 copies. [Russ. text; ca.580 Buriat,
Russ. titles (incl. archives), per.: 1804-1962,
pp. 543-567]

Buriat: Education

Badmatsyrenov, S. S. OKTIABR' I VSEOBUCH V BURIATII. Ulan Ude, 1968. [Russ. text; ca.190 titles, pp. 234-241]

Nikorov, A. V. OBUCHENIE RUSSKOI ORFOGRAFII V V-VIII KLASSAKH BURIATSKOI SHKOLY. Ulan Ude, 1964. [Russ. text; ca.110 titles, pp. 177-182]

Sandanov, B. FIZICHESKAIA KUL'TURA I SPORT V BURIATII. Ulan Ude, 1968. [Russ. text; 68 titles, pp. 160-162]

Semichov, B. V. "BIBLIOGRAFICHESKII UKAZATEL' IZDANII BURIAT-MONGOL'SKOGO NAUCHNO-ISSLEDOVATEL'SKOGO INSTITUTA KUL'TURY ZA 35 LET," K 35 LETIIU INSTITUTA KUL'TURY. SBORNIK STATEI. Ulan Ude: (Buriat-Mongol'skii Nauchno-Issledovatel'skii Institut Kul'tury), 1958. [Russ. text; 302 Buriat, Russ. titles, pp. 257-305]

Tsydypov, Ts. PREPODAVANIE FONETIKI I MORFOLOGII. POSOBIE DLIA UCHITELEI V-VI KLASSOV. Ulan Ude: (Ministerstvo Prosveshcheniia Buriatskoi ASSR), 1961. [Buriat text; ca.50 Buriat, Russ. titles, pp. 92-94]

GEOGRAPHY

*Bashkuev, B. V.; R. F. Tugutov. PO BURIATII. TURISTSKIE MARSHRUTY. Ulan Ude: Buriatskoe Knizhnoe Izdatel'stvo, 1961, 89 pp., 2000 copies. [Russ. text and titles, p. 88]

*Buiantuev, B. R. BARGUZINSKAIA DOLINA. OBZOR PRIRODY, KHOZIAISTVA I PERSPEKTIV RAZVITIIA RAIONA. Ulan Ude: (Buriatskii Filial Geograficheskogo Obshchestva SSSR) Buriatskoe Knizhnoe Izdatel'stvo, 1959, 60 pp., 2000 copies. [Russ. text; 50 Russ. titles, pp. 57-59]

Buriat: Geography

*Murzaev, E. M. GEOGRAFICHESKIE ISSLEDOVANIIA MONGOL'SKOI NARODNOI RESPUBLIKI. Moscow-Leningrad: (Akademiia Nauk SSSR. Institut Geografii i Mongol'skoi Komissii. Seriia, Itogi i Problemy Sovremennoi Nauki) Izdatel'stvo Akademii Nauk SSSR, 1948, 210 pp., 3000 copies. [Russ. text; ca.380 Russ., Europ. titles, pub.: 1706-1948, pp. 185-203]

TIPY MESTNOSTI I PRIRODNOE RAIONIROVANIE BURIATSKOI ASSR. Moscow: (Akademiia Nauk SSSR. Institut Geografii), 1959. [Russ. text; ca.120 titles, pp. 212-216]

HISTORY, ARCHAEOLOGY

Banzarov, D. "SPISOK SOCHINENII BANZAROVA--BIBLIOGRAFIIA LITERATURY O D. BANZAROVE," SOBRANIE SOCHINENIIA. Moscow: (Akademiia Nauk SSSR. Institut Vostokovedeniia. Buriat-Mongol'skii Nauchno-Issledovatel'skii Institut Kul'tury), 1955. [Russ. text; 200 Russ. titles, pub.: 1846-1852; 1836-1953, pp. 352-372]

Batotsyrenov, V. B. SOVETSKAIA ISTORIOGRAFIIA OKTIABR'SKOI REVOLIUTSII I GRAZHDANSKOI VOINY V BURIATII. (1917-1965 GG.) Ulan Ude: Buriat. Kn. Izd-vo, 1967, 71 pp., 1000 copies. [titles, pub.: 1917-1965]

"BIBLIOGRAFIIA PECHATNYKH RABOT ISTORIKA F. A. KUDRIAVTSEVA," ZAPISKI BURIAT-MONGOL'SKOGO GOSUDARSTVENNOGO NAUCHNO-ISSLEDOVATEL'NOGO INSTITUTA IAZYKA, LITERATURY I ISTORII. No. 3/4. 1941. [Russ. text; titles, pub.: 1924-1940, pp. 283-301]

*Chernoiarova, A. A. MUISKAIA DOLINA. (PRIRODA, LIUDI, KHOZ-VO) Ulan Ude: Buriat. Kn. Izd., 1966, 100 pp., 1000 copies. [Russ. text and titles, pub.: 1875-1964, pp. 96-100]

Buriat: History, Archaeology

*Dikov, N. N. BRONZOVYI VEK ZABAIKAL'IA. Ulan Ude:
(Akademiia Nauk SSSR. Sibirskoe Otdelenie.
Buriatskii Kompleksnyi Nauchno-Issledovatel'skii
Institut), 1958. 105+ pp., 500 copies. [Russ. text;
239 Russ., Europ. titles, (incl. 9 mss), per.: Ancient,
pp. 73-81]

Egunov, N. P. PERVAIA RUSSKAIA REVOLIUTSIIA I VTOROI
ETAP NATSIONAL'NOGO DVIZHENIIA V BURIATII. Ulan
Ude: 1970. [Russ. text; ca.300 titles, pp. 188-198]

[Girchenko, V. P.; A. N. Turunov. comps.]
BIBLIOGRAFIIA BURIATII. ZA 1890-1931 GG. No. 5.
ISTORIIA DOREV. BURIATII, OKTIABR'SKOI REVOLIUTSII I
OBRAZOVANIE BM ASSR. Ulan Ude: Buriat Kn. Izd-vo, 1970,
167 pp.[Russ. text; ca.1050 titles, per.: 1890-1931]

Girchenko, V. P. "BIBLIOGRAFIIA PO ISTORII I EKONOMIKE
BRIBAIKAL'IA," PRIBAIKAL'E. KRATKII ISTORICHESKII
OCHERK. Verkhneudinsk, 1922. [Russ. text; ca.150
titles, pp. 25-26]

_____. "IZDANIIA I STAT'I PO ISTORII
REVOLIUTSIONNOGO DVIZHENIIA V PRIBAIKAL'E," ZHIZN'
BURIATII. No. 2/3. 1924. [Russ. text; 16 titles,
pub.: 1917-1923, pp. 101-103]

*ISTORIIA BURIATSKOI ASSR. Vol. 2. Ulan Ude:
Buriatskoe Knizhnoe Izdatel'stvo, 1959,
643 pp., 5000 copies. [Russ. text; Buriat, Russ.
titles, pp. 617-629]

Iumozhapov, A. B. "DOPOLNENIIA (PO 1965 G.) K
'BIBLIOGRAFIIA LITERATURY O BURIATSKOM UCHENOM DORZHI
BANZAROVE' O. G. TROITSKAIA," TRUDY VOST.-SIB.
IN-TA KUL'TURY. No. 6. 1970. [Russ. text; 22
titles, pub.: 1965, pp. 183-185]

Khaptaev, P. T. BURIATIIA V GODY GRAZHDANSKOI VOINY.
Ulan Ude: Buriat. Kn. Izd., 1967, 264 pp., 2000
copies. [Russ. text; titles, pp. 241-251]

* _____. ed. ISTORIIA BURIATSKOI ASSR. 2 Vols.
Ulan Ude: Buriatskoe Knizhnoe Izdatel'stvo.
(Akademiia Nauk SSSR. Sibirskoe Otdelenie.
Buriatskii Kompleksnyi Nauchno-Issledovatel'skii
Institut), 1959, 643 pp., 5000 copies. [Russ. text,
ca. 400 Russ. titles, per.: up to 1955; pub.: 1774-
1958, pp. 617-629 (for Vols. 1 & 2.)]

Buriat: History, Archaeology

*Khaptaev, P. T. ed. ISTORIIA BURIATSKOI ASSR. V DVUKH TOMAKH. Vol. 2. Ulan Ude: Buriatskoe Knizhnoe Izdatel'stvo, 1959, 643 pp., 5000 copies. [Russ. text and titles, per.: 1917-1955, pp. 617-629]

Khoroshikh, P. "UKAZATEL' ISTORIKO-ETNOGRAFICHESKOI LITERATURY O BURIATSKOI NARODNOSTI," SIBIRSKAIA ZHIVAIA STARINA. ETNOGRAFICHESKII SBORNIK. No. 1. (Irkutsk), 1923, (separately) 28 pp. [Russ. text; 432 Russ. titles, pub.: 1774-1923, pp. 154-178]

Kim, N. V. OCHERKI ISTORII ULAN-UDE. (XVII--NACHALO XX VV.) Ulan Ude: Buriat. Kn. Izd., 1966, 115 pp., 1000 copies. [Russ. text; 110 titles, pp. 110-114]

*Kiuner, N. "BURIATY," BOL'SHAIA SOVETSKAIA ENTSIKLOPEDIIA. Vol. 8. Moscow: Aktsionernoe Obshchestvo "Sovetskaia Entsiklopediia," 1927, 237-241 pp. [Russ. text; Buriat, Russ. titles, p. 241]

*Kolodina, I. A.; S. B. Tsibikzhapova. comps. UKAZATEL' IZDANII BURIATSKOGO KOMPLEKSNOGO NAUCHNO-ISSLEDOVATEL'SKOGO INSTITUTA SO AN SSSR. (1959-1962 GG.) Ulan Ude: Akademiia Nauk SSSR. Sibirskoe Otdelenie. (Buriatskii Kompleksnyi Nauchno-Issledovatel'skii Institut), 1964, 96 pp., 1000 copies. [Russ. text; 74 Buriat, Russ. titles, pub.: 1959-1962, pp. 5-68]

Koz'min, N. N. comp. "BIBLIOGRAFICHESKII UKAZATEL' LITERATURY I ISTOCHNIKOV PO ISTORII BURIATSKOGO NARODA." Bogdanov, M. N. OCHERKI ISTORII BURIAT-MONGOL'SKOGO NARODA. Verkhneudinsk, 1926. [Russ. text; ca.250 titles, pp. 184-191]

*Kudriavtsev, F. A.; G. A. Vendrikh. IRKUTSK. OCHERKI PO ISTORII GORODA. n. p. Irkutskoe Knizhnoe Izdatel'stvo, 1958, 515 pp., 10,000 copies. [Russ. text; 538+ Russ., Europ. titles, pp. 488-512]

*Manzhigeev, I. M. IANGUTSKII BURIATSKII ROD. (OPYT ISTORIKO-ETNOGRAFICHESKOGO ISSLEDOVANIIA). Ulan Ude: (Akademiia Nauk SSSR. Sibirskoe Otdelenie. Buriatskii Kompleksnyi Nauchno-Issledovatel'skii Institut). Buriatskoe Knizhnoe Izdatel'stvo, 1960, 232 pp., 1000 copies. [Russ. text; ca.115 Buriat, Russ. titles, (incl. archives), pp. 227-231]

Buriat: History, Archaeology

MATERIALY PO ISTORII I FILOLOGII TSENTRAL'NOI AZII.
TRUDY BURIAT. IN-TA OBSHCHESTV. NAUK. No. 3.
SERIIA VOSTOKOVEDENIIA. Ulan Ude: Buriat. Kn. Izd.,
1968, 202 pp., 1000 copies. [Russ. text; titles
at end of articles]

Matveev, Z. "BIBLIOGRAFIIA PO ISTORII REVOLIUTSII I
INTERVENTSII NA RUSSKOM DAL'NEM VOSTOKE," DAL'ISPART.
No. 2. Vladivostok, 1924. [Russ. text]

*Matveev, Z. N. ISTORIIA DAL'NEVOSTOCHNOGO KRAIA.
Vladivostok: Izdanie Vladivostokskogo Otdela
Gosudarstvennogo Russkogo Geograficheskogo
Obschestva. (Zapiski Vladivostokskogo Otdela
Gosudarstvennogo Russkogo Geograficheskogo
Obshchestva), 1929, 341-377 pp., 250 copies. [Russ.
text and titles, p. 377]

*Okladnikov, A. P. ed. ISTORIIA BURIAT-MONGOL'SKOI
ASSR. Vol. 1. Ulan Ude: Buriat-Mongol'skoe
Gosudarstvennoe Izdatel'stvo, 1951, 574 pp., 5000
copies. [Russ. text; Russ. survey, per.: up to 1917,
pp. 9-23]

"PERECHEN' STATEI I SOOBSHCHENII, POMESHCHENNYKH V
ZHURNALE 'KUL'TURA BURIATII' ZA 1932 G.," KUL'TURA
BURIATII. No. 4. 1932. [Russ. text and 51 Russ.
titles, pp. 37-39]

"POSOBIE I ISTOCHNIKI DLIA IZUCHENIIA ISTORII BURIAT.
(SPISOK SOSTAVLEN PO MATERIALAM M. N. BOGDANOVA I
N. N. KOZ'MINA)," VESTNIK AZII. No. 48, Vyp. 1.
(Harbin), 1922. [Russ. text; 132 titles, pp. 169-173]

*Pozdnieev, A. MONGOLIIA I MONGOLY. REZUL'TATY POIEZDKI
V MONGOLIIU, ISPOLNENNOI V 1892-1893 GG.... Vol. 1.
DNEVNIK I MARSHRUT 1892 GODA. St. Petersburg:
Izdanie Imperatorskago Russkago Geograficheskago
Obshchestva, 1896, 696 pp. [Russ. text; 68 Russ.
titles, pp. XIII-XV]

*Rumiantsev, G. N. PROISKHOZHDENIE KHORINSKIKH BURIAT.
Ulan Ude: Buriatskoe Knizhnoe Izdatel'stvo, 1962,
267 pp., 1000 copies. [Russ. text; Buriat, Russ.,
Europ., Mongol titles (incl. archives), pp. 5-63,
64-82, 245-264]

Buriat: History, Archaeology

Shofman, A. S.   KAZANSKII PERIOD ZHIZNI I
DEIATEL'NOSTI DORZHI BANZAROVA.   Ulan Ude: (Buriat-
Mongol'skii Nauchno-Issledovatel'skii Institut
Kul'tury), 1956.   [Russ. text; 73 titles, pp. 161-163]

*Shperk, F. "BURIATY," ENTSIKLOPEDICHESKII SLOVAR'.
Vol. 5. St. Petersburg: F. A. Brokgauz, I. A. Efron,
1891, 59-64 pp. [Russ. text; Russ., Europ. titles,
p. 64]

*Sydenov, K. comp. "BIBLIOGRAFIIA RABOT IAPONSKIKH
UCHENYKH PO MONGOLOVEDENIIU," MATERIALY PO ISTORII
I FILOLOGII TSENTRAL'NOI AZII. (TRUDY BURIATSKOGO
KOMPLEKSNOGO NAUCHNO-ISSLEDOVATEL'SKOGO INSTITUTA:
No. 8; SERIIA VOSTOKOVEDENIIA.)   (Ulan Ude) 1962.
[Russ. text; Japanese, Europ. titles, pp. 199-200]

Troitskaia, O. G. "BIBLIOGRAFIIA LITERATURY O
BURIATSKOM UCHENOM DORSHI BANZAROVE," TRUDY VOST.-
SIB. IN-TA KUL'TURY. No. 6. 1970. [Russ. text;
98 titles, pub.: 1955-1964, pp. 172-182]

Turunov, A. PROSHLOE BURIAT-MONGOL'SKOI NARODNOSTI.
Irkutsk, 1922. [Russ. text; ca.30 titles, (prilozhenie)
pp. 43-48]

Zolotoev, A. K. "SOVETSKII VOSTOKOVED G. N. RUMIANTSEV,"
K [TRIDTSAT PIAT'] 35-LETIIU INSTITUTA KUL'TURY.
Ulan Ude: (Buriat-Mongol'skii Nauchno-Issledovatel'skii
Institut Kul'tury), 1958. [Russ. text; 41 titles,
pub.: 1937-1957, pp. 253-255]

LANGUAGE, LITERATURE

*Buraev, I. D.   ZVUKOVOI SOSTAV BURIATSKOGO IAZYKA.
Ulan Ude: (Akademiia Nauk SSSR. Sibirskoe
Otdelenie. Buriatskii Kompleksnyi Nauchno-
Issledovatel'skii Institut), 1959, 195 pp., 500
copies. [Russ. text; 110 Russ., Europ. titles,
pp. 191-194]

Buriat: Language, Literature

Dondukov, U.-Zh. Sh. AFFIKSAL'NOE SLOVOOBRAZOVANIE CHASTEI RECHI V BURIATSKOM IAZYKE. Ulan Ude, 1964. [Russ. text; 108 titles, pp. 239-244]

*Dugar-Nimaev, Ts.-A. ZHAMSO TUMUNOV, KRITIKO-BIOGRAFICHESKII OCHERK. Ulan Ude: (Akademiia Nauk SSSR. Sibirskoe Otdelenie. Buriatskii Kompleksnyi Nauchno-Issledovatel'skii Institut), 1960, 156 pp., 1000 copies. [Russ. text; 172 Buriat, Russ., Europ. titles, pub.: 1939-1959, pp. 147-155]

*Dugarov, N. B. comp. BIBLIOGRAFIIA LITERATURY PO BURIATSKOMU IAZYKOZNANIIU. Ulan Ude: (Akademiia Nauk SSSR. Sibirskoe Otdelenie. Buriatskii Kompleksnyi Nauchno-Issledovatel'skii Institut), 1964, 165 pp., 1000 copies. [Russ. text; 877 Buriat, Russ. titles, pp. 5-136]

_____. "SPISOK OPUBLIKOVANNYKH RABOT A. D. ABASHEEVA," K IZUCHENIIU BURIAT. IAZ. (TRUDY BURIAT. IN-TA OBSHCHESTV. NAUK. No. 6.) Ulan Ude, 1969. [Russ. text; 30 titles, pub.: 1927-1969, pp. 152-153]

*Eliasov, L. E.; V. A. Abramov; A. A. Belousov; Ts.-A. Dugar-Nimaev; G. O. Tudenov. eds. OCHERK ISTORII BURIATSKOI SOVETSKOI LITERATURY. Ulan Ude: Buriatskoe Knizhnoe Izdatel'stvo, 1959, 275 pp., 2000 copies. [Russ. text; 146 Buriat, Russ. titles, per.: Sov. up to 1955, pp. 265-273]

Evgrafova, R. comp. DANRI, DANILOVICH KHITUKHIN. K 50-LETIIU SO DNIA ROZHDENIIA. Ulan Ude: (M-vo Kul'tury Buriat. ASSR), 1966, 16 pp., 1500 copies. [Russ. text; titles pp. 14-16]

Iarnevskii, I. Z. USTNYI RASSKAZ KAK ZHANR FOLK'LORA. Ulan Ude, 1969. [Russ. text; 260 titles, pp. 222-230]

*Kim, I. BURIATSKAIA SOVETSKAIA POEZIIA DVADTSATYKH GODOV. Ulan Ude: Buriat. Kn. Izd., 1968, 252 pp., 1000 copies. [Russ. text; 124 Buriat, Russ. titles, pp. 248-252]

[Madasoi, I. N. comp.] ISTORIIA BURIATSKOI SOVETSKOI LITERATURY. Ulan Ude, 1967. [Russ. text; ca.470 titles, pp. 459-473]

Buriat: Language, Literature

*"POPPE, NIKOLAI NIKOLAEVICH," BOL'SHAIA SOVETSKAIA ENTSIKLOPEDIIA. Vol. 46. Moscow: Gosudarstvennyi Institut "Sovetskaia Entsiklopediia," (Ogiz RSFSR), 1940, 1st ed. [Russ. text; Buriat, Mongol, Russ., titles, p. 425]

*Poppe, N. "BURIATSKAIA LITERATURA," LITERATURNAIA ENTSIKLOPEDIIA. Vol. 1. n. p ., Izdatel'stvo Kommunisticheskoi Akademii, 1929, 624-626 pp. [Russ. text; Buriat, Russ. titles, p. 626]

* _____. "BURIATSKII IAZYK," LITERATURNAIA ENTSIKLOPEDIIA. Vol. 1. n. p. Izdatel'stvo Kommunisticheskoi Akademii, 1929, 626-628 pp. [Russ. text; Russ., Europ. titles, p. 628]

* _____. "BURIATSKII IAZYK I LITERATURA," BOL'SHAIA SOVETSKAIA ENTSIKLOPEDIIA. Vol. 8. Moscow: Aktsionernoe Obshchestvo "Sovetskaia Entsiklopediia," 1927, 234-237 pp. [Russ. text; Buriat, Russ., Europ. titles, pp. 236-237]

*Rudnev, A. D. KHORI-BURIATSKII GOVOR. (OPYT IZSLIEDOVANIIA, TEKSTY, PEREVOD I PRIMIECHANIIA.) No. 3. PEREVOD I PRIMIECHANIIA. St. Petersburg: Tipografiia V. Th. Kirshbauma, 1913-1914, 137 pp. [Russ. text; 62 Russ., Europ. titles, pp. 0126-0133]

Shagdarov, L. D. "RAZRABOTKA VOPROSOV FONETIKI, DIALEKTOLOGII, LEKSIKI, I ORFOGRAFII BURIATSKOGO IAZYKA ZA SOVETSKII PERIOD," K IZUCHENIIU BURIAT. IAZ. (TRUDY BURIAT. IN-TA OBSHCHESTV. NAUK. No. 6.) Ulan Ude, 1969. [Russ. text; 62 titles, per.: Sov., pp. 17-18, 27-28]

Shagdarov, L. Sh. IZOBRAZITEL'NYE SLOVA V SOVREMENNOM BURIATSKOM IAZYKE. Ulan Ude: Buriatskoe Knizhnoe Izdatel'stvo, 1962, 149 pp. [Russ. text; 47 titles, pp. 146-148]

*Sharakshinova, N. O. BURIATSKII FOL'KLOR. n. p. Irkutskoe Knizhnoe Izdatel'stvo, 1959, 227 pp., 3000 copies. [Russ. text; Buriat, Russ., German titles, pp. 221-226]

_____. KHOTSA NAMSARAEV. Ulan Ude: Buriat-Mongol'skoe Knizhnoe Izdatel'stvo, 1958. [Russ. text; 68 Buriat, Russ. titles, pp. 155-157]

Buriat: Language, Literature

Sherkhunaev, R. A. "PROIZVEDENIIA P. P. PETROVA-- LITERATURA O ZHIZNI I DEIATEL'NOSTI," SKAZITEL' PEOKHON PETROV. Irkutsk, 1969. [Russ. text; 46 Buriat, Russ. titles, pub.: 1938-1967, pp. 88-92]

_____.; B. M. Shkol'nik. "BURIAT-MONGOL'SKII NARODNYI SKAZITEL' I POET A. A. TOROEV. BIBLIOGRAFIIA," ZAPISKI BURIAT-MONGOL'SKOGO NAUCHNO-ISSLEDOVATEL'SKOGO INSTITUTA KUL'TURY. Vol. 18. 1954. [Russ. text; 183 Buriat, Russ. titles, pp. 117-127]

Shkol'nik, B. M. APOLLON ANDREEVICH TOROEV. BURIAT- MONGOL'SKII NARODNYI SKAZITEL'-POET. PAMIATKA CHITATELIU. Irkutsk: Knizhnoe Izdatel'stvo, 1954, 16 pp., 1000 copies. [Russ. text; 26 Buriat, Russ. titles]

Sorokovikov-Magai, E. I. SKAZKI I PREDANIIA MAGAIA. Ulan Ude: Buriat. Kn. Izd., 1968, 371 pp., 1500 copies. [Russ. text; titles pp. 368-370]

Tarmakhanova, O. D. BURIATSKOMU TEATRU DRAMY 30 LET. BIBLIOGRAFICHESKII UKAZATEL'. Ulan Ude: (Respublikanskaia Biblioteka imeni Gor'kogo), 1962, 23 pp., 500 copies. [Russ. text; 61 Buriat, Russ., titles]

* _____.; L. V. Makhneeva; D. S. Zharkov; N. S. Kartashov; I. V. Shubina; Iu. A. Kharaev. PISATELI SOVETSKOI BURIATII. BIO-BIBLIOGRAFICHESKII SPRAVOCHNIK. Ulan Ude: Buriatskoe Knizhnoe Izdatel'stvo, 1959, 186 pp., 3000 copies. [Russ. text; 58 lists; + 100 Buriat, Russ. titles]

*Tudenov, G. O.; B. V. Semichov. "BIBLIOGRAFIIA OSNOVNYKH IZDANII BURIATSKOI SOVETSKOI LITERATURY NA BURIATSKOM I RUSSKOM IAZYKAKH (VKLIUCHITEL'NO PO 1955 G.)," OCHERK ISTORII BURIATSKOI SOVETSKOI LITERATURY. Ulan Ude: (Buriatskoe Knizhnoe Izdatel'stvo. Buriatskii Kompleksnyi Nauchno-Issledovatel'skii Institut), 1959, 275 pp., 2000 copies. [Russ. text; 146 Buriat, Russ. titles, pub.: up to 1955, pp. 265-275]

Buriat: Language, Literature

*Ulanov, A. I. ed. ISTORIIA BURIATSKOI SOVETSKOI
LITERATURY. Ulan-Ude: Buriatskoe Knizhnoe
Izdatel'stvo, 1967, 474 pp., 1200 copies. [Russ.
text and titles, per.: 1920-1965, pp. 459-473]

*Voskoboinikov, M. G. FOL'KLOR EVENKOV BURIATII.
Ulan Ude: Buriatskoe Knizhnoe Izdatel'stvo, 1958,
187 pp., 1500 copies. [Russ. text; 36 Evenkii,
Russ. titles, pp. 184-185]

*Zhamtsaranov, Tsyben. "MATERIALY K IZUCHENIIU USTNOI
LITERATURY MONGOL'SKIKH PLEMEN. (OBRAZTSY NARODNOI
LITERATURY BURIAT-EKHRID I BULDTHAD," ZAPISKI
VOSTOCHNAGO OTDIELENIIA RUSSKAGO ARKHEOLOGICHESKAGO
OBSHCHESTVA. Vol. 17, No. 4 ZA 1906. 1907,
0109-0128 pp. [Russ. text; 21 Russ., Europ. titles,
pp. 0127-0128]

PHILOSOPHY, RELIGION

*Khadalov, P. I.; L. Zh. Iampilov; B. D. Dandaron.
OPISANIE SOCHINENII GUNCHEN=CHZHAM'IAN-SHADPA-DORCHZHE.
1649-1723. Ulan Ude: (AN SSSR. Sibirskoe Otdelenie,
Buriatskii Kompleksnyi Nauchno-Issledovatel'skii
Institut), 1962, 126 pp., 500 copies. [Russ. text;
143 Tibetan, Sanskrit MSS., per.: 1649-1723]

POLITICAL SCIENCE, LAW

ALFAVITNYI UKAZATEL' K IZVIESTIIAM IRKUTSKOI
GORODSKOI DUMY ZA TREKHLIETIE IKH SUSHCHESTVOVANIIA,
S 1886 PO 1888 GG. VKLIUCHITEL'NO. Irkutsk, 1889.
[Russ. text and titles, pub.: 1886-1888]

Buriat: Political Science, Law

ALFAVITNYI UKAZATEL' K IZVIESTIIAM IRKUTSKOI GORODSKOI DUMY ZA TREKHLIETIE IKH SUSHCHESTVOVANIIA, ZA 1903 I 1904 GG. Irkutsk, 1907. [Russ. text and titles, pub.: 1903-1904]

ALFAVITNYI UKAZATEL' K PROTOKOLAM IRKUTSKOI GORODSKOI DUMY 1879-1885 GG. Vol. 1. Irkutsk, 1908, 352 pp. [Russ. text; titles pub.: 1879-1885]

Badmatsyrenov, S. S. OKTIABR' I VSEOBUCH V BURIATII. Ulan Ude: Buriat. Kn. Izd., 1968, 242 pp., 800 copies. [Russ. text; titles pp. 234-241]

*Bartanova, A. A. OBRAZOVANIE BURIATSKOI AVTONOMNOI SOVETSKOI SOTSIALISTICHESKOI RESPUBLIKI. Ulan Ude: Buriatskoe Knizhnoe Izdatel'stvo, 1964, 133 pp., 1500 copies. [Russ. text and titles, (incl. archives), per.: late 19th c. - 1963, pp. 128-132]

*Egunov, N. P. KOLONIAL'NAIA POLITIKA TSARIZMA I PERVYI ETAP NATSIONAL'NOGO DVIZHENIIA V BURIATII V EPOKHU IMPERIALIZMA. Ulan Ude: Buriatskoe Knizhnoe Izdatel'stvo, 1963, 316 pp., 1500 copies. [Russ. text and titles (incl. archives), per.: 19th & 20th cc., pp. 304-316]

Khaptaev, P. T. OKTIABR'SKAIA SOTSIALISTICHESKAIA REVOLIUTSIIA I GRAZHDANSKAIA VOINA V BURIATII. Part 1/2. Ulan Ude, 1964. [Russ. text; ca.280 titles, pp. 320-329]

Khoroshikh, P. P. "LITERATURA O REVOLIUTSIONNOM I OBSHCHESTVENNOM DVIZHENII V BURIATII," BURIATOVEDCHESKII SBORNIK. No. 2. (Irkutsk), 1926, (separately) 13 pp. [Russ. text; 222 Russ. titles, pp. 14-24]

*Ochirov, Ts. O. PARTIINAIA ORGANIZATSIIA BURIATII V BOR'BE ZA NOVYI POD"EM KUL'TURY (1956-1960 GG.) Ulan Ude: Buriatskoe Knizhnoe Izdatel'stvo, 1960, 244 pp., 1500 copies. [Russ. text; Russ., Europ. titles, per.: 1956-1960, pp. 236-243]

OTVAZHNYE SYNY I DOCHERI BURIATII--GEROI VELIKOI OTECHESTVENNOI VOINY 1941-1945 GG. (REKOMENDATEL'NYI UKAZATEL' DLIA UCHASHCHIKHSIA 7-8 KL.) Ulan Ude: (Ministerstvo Kul'tury Buriatskoi ASSR. Detskaia Respublikanskaia Biblioteka), 1966, 16 pp., 1500 copies. [Russ. text]

Buriat: Political Science, Law

Sikorskii. "OKTIABR'SKAIA REVOLIUTSIIA I GRAZHDANSKAIA
VOINA V BURIATII (OPYT BIBLIOGRAFII)," KUL'TURA
BURIATII. No. 1. 1932. [Russ. text; 73 titles,
pp. 52-58]

Tarmakhanova, O. D.; Iu. A. Kharaev. comps.
NERUSHIMAIA DRUZHBA RUSSKOGO I BURIATSKOGO NARODOV.
REKOMENDATEL'NYI UKAZATEL' LITERATURY. Ulan Ude:
(Respublikanskaia Biblioteka Buriatskoi ASSR imeni M.
Gor'kogo), 1958, 26 pp., 1000 copies. [Russ. text;
41 Buriat, Russ. titles]

*Troitskaia, O. G.; A. K. Potapova. comps. "BOR'BA ZA
SOVETSKUIU VLAST' V IRKUTSKOI GUBERNII. (1918-1920 GG.)
MATERIALY K BIBLIOGRAFII," BOR'BA ZA VLAST' SOVETOV V
IRKUTSKOI GUBERNII (1918-1920 GG.) (PARTIZANSKOE
DVIZHENIE V PRIANGAR'E). SBORNIK DOKUMENTOV. n. p.
Irkutskoe Knizhnoe Izdatel'stvo, 1959, 276 pp.,
3000 copies. [Russ. text; 205 Russ. titles, per.:
1918-1920, pp. 256-263]

33 DOLGAN

GENERAL

*"DOLGANY," BOL'SHAIA SOVETSKAIA ENTSIKLOPEDIIA.
Vol. 15.   n.p.   Gosudarstvennoe Nauchnoe
Izdatel'stvo "Bol'shaia Sovetskaia Entsiklopediia,"
1952, 2nd ed., 12 pp. [Russ. text and titles, p. 12]

*Levin, M. G.; L. P. Potapov. "DOLGANY," NARODY SIBIRI.
Moscow-Leningrad: Izdatel'stvo Akademii Nauk SSSR,
1956, 746, 1010 pp., 5000 copies. [Russ. text and
titles, p. 1010]

34 KHAKASS

GENERAL

Averikhin, V. comp. "KNIZHNYI ZNAK," VYSTAVKA PUTEVODITEL' PO VYSTAVKE. ABAKAN. 1967. Kyzyl: Tuvknigoizdat, 1967, 78 pp., 1000 copies. [Russ. text; titles, per.: 1967]

*Ivanov, S. N. NIKOLAI FEDOROVICH KATANOV. (1862-1922). OCHERK ZHIZNI I DEIATEL'NOSTI. Moscow-Leningrad: Izdatel'stvo Akademii Nauk SSSR. (Akademiia Nauk SSSR. Khakasskii Nauchno-Issledovatel'skii Institut Iazyka, Literatury i Istorii), 1962, 107 pp., 2500 copies. [Russ. text; 192 + 25 Russ., Europ. titles, pub.: 1885-1921, pp. 94-106]

*"KHAKASSKAIA AVTONOMNAIA OBLAST'," BOL'SHAIA SOVETSKAIA ENTSIKLOPEDIIA. Moscow: Gosudarstvennyi Institut "Sovetskaia Entsiklopediia," (Ogiz RSFSR). Vol. 59. 1935, 1st ed., 389-396 pp. [Russ. text and titles, p. 396]

SPISOK KNIG, IZDANNYKH KHAKASSKIM KNIZHNYM IZDATEL'STVOM V 1961 GODU. Abakan, 1962, 9 pp., 500 copies. [Russ. text; titles pub.: 1961]

*Tokarev, S. "KHAKASSKAIA AVTONOMNAIA OBLAST'," BOL'SHAIA SOVETSKAIA ENTSIKLOPEDIIA. Vol. 59. Moscow: Gosudarstvennyi Institut "Sovetskaia Entsiklopediia" (Ogiz RSFSR), 1935, 1st ed., 389-396 pp. [Russ. text and titles, p. 396]

*_____. "KHAKASY," BOL'SHAIA SOVETSKAIA ENTSIKLOPEDIIA. Vol. 59. Moscow: Gosudarstvennyi Institut "Sovetskaia Entsiklopediia," (Ogiz RSFSR), 1935, 1st ed., p. 397 [Russ. text; Russ. titles, p. 397]

*VOPROSY SOTSIAL'NO-EKONOMICHSKOGO RAZVITIIA KHAKASII. (ISTORIIA, EKONOMIKA, KUL'TURA, NAUKA.) Abakan: Krasnoiar. Kn. Izd., Khakas. Otd-nie, 1968, 180 pp., 2000 copies. [Russ. text; 176 Russ. titles, pp. 170-179]

Khakass

ECONOMICS

Kolobkov, M. N.; N. N. Protopopov. KHAKASSKAIA
AVTONOMNAIA OBLAST'. Novosibirsk, 1949, 142 pp.
[Russ. text; 266 pp.]

*_____. "SOVETSKAIA KHAKASIIA," IZVESTIIA
VSESOIUZ. GEOGR. O-VA. Vol. 83, No. 1. (Moscow-
Leningrad), 1951, 54-65 pp. [Russ. text; 45 Russ.
titles, pp. 64-65]

Nikol'skaia, L. A. KHAKASIIA. EKON.-GEOGR. OCHERK.
Abakan: Khakknigizdat, 1960. [Russ. text; 79 titles,
pp. 163-167]

_____. KHAKASIIA. EKON-GEOGR. OCHERK.
Krasnoiarsk, 1968. [Russ. text; ca.280 titles,
pp. 230-242]

HISTORY, ARCHAEOLOGY

Kiuner, N. V. "KITAISKIE ISTORIKI-LETOPISTSY O
KHAKASAKH. (BIBLIOGR. OBZOR)," ZAPISKI (KHAKAS.
NAUCH.-ISSLED. IN-T IAZYKA, LITERATURY I ISTORII),
No. 3. 1954. [Russ. text; Chinese, Russ., other
titles, pp. 110-159]

*Levasheva, V. P. IZ DALEKOGO PROSHLOGO IUZHNOI CHASTI
KRASNOIARSKOGO KRAIA. n. p. Krasnoiarskoe Kraevoe
Gosudarstvennoe Izdatel'stvo, 1939, 68 pp., 4000
copies. [Russ. text; 11 Russ., Europ. titles, per.:
ancient, p. 68]

Khakass: History, Archaeology

"SPISOK NAUCHNYKH TRUDOV K. G. CHAPTYKOVA," UCHEN.
ZAPISKI (KHAKAS. NII IAZYKA, LITERATURY I ISTORII.
No. 10. 1964. [Russ. text; 12 titles, pub. 1955-
1963, pp. 162-163]

Ulturgashev, S. P. "OPYT PERIODIZATSII ISTORIOGRAFII
KHAKASII," UCHEN. ZAP. KHAKAS. NII IAZ., LIT. I
ISTORII. No. 13. 1969. [Russ. text; 281 titles,
pp. 118-137]

LANGUAGE, LITERATURE

"BIBLIOGRAFIIA PROIZVEDENII KHAKASSKIKH PISATELEI
(1927-1964)," LIT-KHUDOZH. AL'MANAKH. No. 12. 1966.
[Khakass text; 91 Khakass titles, pub.: 1927-1964,
per.: 1927-1964, pp. 120-122]

Bushueva, E. I.; M. B. Volostnova. SLOVAR'
GEOGRAFICHESKIKH TERMINOV I DRUGIKH SLOV,
VSTRECHAIUSHCHIKHSIA V TOPONOMII KHAKASSKOI
AVTONOMNOI OBLASTI. Moscow: (Glav. Upr. Geodezii i
Kartografii pri Sovete Ministrov SSSR), 1968, 79 pp.,
500 copies. [Russ. text; 44 titles, pp. 74-46]

Donidze, G. I. BEZLICHNYE PREDLOZHENIIA V KHAKASSKOM
IAZYKE. Abakan: (Khakass Nauch.-Issled. In-t Iazyka,
Lit. i Istorii), 1957. [Russ. text; 32 titles,
pp. 90-91]

_____. "IZDANIIA KHAKASSKOGO NAUCHNO-
ISSLEDOVATEL'SKOGO INSTITUTA IAZYKA, LITERATURY I
ISTORII (1947-1956 GG.) (BIBLIOGR. SPRAVKA),"
ZAPISKI (KHAKAS. NAUCH-ISSLED. IN-T. IAZYKA,
LITERATURY I ISTORII. No. 5. 1957. [30 Khakass,
Russ. titles, pub.: 1947-1956, pp. 186-190]

*N. D. "KHAKASSKII IAZYK," BOL'SHAIA SOVETSKAIA
ENTSIKLOPEDIIA. Vol. 59. Moscow: Gosudarstvennyi
Institut "Sovetskaia Entsiklopediia" (Ogiz RSFSR),
1935, 1st ed., 396 pp. [Russ. text; Khakass, Russ.,
Europ. titles, p. 396]

Khakass: Language, Literature

Tanzybaeva, N. A. comp. NASHEMU TEATRU 30 LET.
(UKAZATEL' LIT.) Abakan: (Khakas. Obl. B-ka), 1961,
19 pp., 200 copies. [Russ. text; ca.150 titles, per.:
1930-1960]

Tenishev, E. R. "TRUDY FAZYLA GARIFOVICHA ISKHAKOVA,"
UCHENYE ZAPISKI KHAKAS. N.I.I. IAZYKA LIT. I ISTORII.
No. 9. 1963. [Russ. text; 35 titles, pub.: 1934-
1961, pp. 124-126]

Troiakov, P. A. comp. LITERATURA SOVETSKAIA KHAKASII.
Abakan, 1962. [Russ. text; 177 Khakass, Russ.
titles, Sov. per., pp. 145-151]

VOPROSY KHAKAS. IAZYKA I LIT. Abakan: (Khakas. Nauch.-
Issled. In-t Iazyka, Lit. i Istorii), 1955.
[Khakass, Russ. text; 47 titles, pub.: 1926-1954,
pp. 10-12]

35 MONGOLIA

GENERAL

*Baldaev, R. L.; N. N. Vasil'ev. comps. BIBLIOGRAFIIA MONGOL'SKOI NARODNOI RESPUBLIKI. KNIGI I STAT'I NA RUSSKOM IAZYKE (1951-1961.) Moscow: Izdatel'stvo Vostochnoi Literatury, 1963, 119 pp., 1350 copies. [Russ. text; 1798 Russ. titles, pub.: 1951-1961, pp. 9-96]

*"BIBLIOGRAFIIA," SOVETSKOE VOSTOKOVEDENIE. No. 5. 1955. [Russ. text; 123 titles, pub.: 1938-1953, pp. 185-190]

BIBLIOGRAFIIA O MONGOLII. OTCHET O RABOTAKH MONGOL'SK. EKSPED. MOLODYKH. Irkutsk, 1919. [Russ. text]

*Cheboksarova, N. N. et al., ed. NARODY VOSTOCHNOI AZII. Moscow-Leningrad: Izdatel'stvo "Nauka," 1965, 1024 pp., 2700 copies. [Russ. text and titles, pp. 974-976]

"CHTO CHITAT' O MONGOL'SKOI NARODNOI RESPUBLIKE," PROPAGANDIST. No. 11. (Moscow), 1936. [Russ. text; 36 titles, pub.: 1936, pp. 62-63]

*Iakovleva, Ekaterina Nilovna. BIBLIOGRAFIIA MONGOL'SKOI NARODNOI RESPUBLIKI. (SISTEMATICHESKII UKAZATEL' KNIG I ZHURNAL'NYKH STATEI NA RUSSKOM IAZYKE.) IZDANIE NAUCHNO-ISSLEDOVATEL'SKOI ASSOTSIATSII PO IZUCHENIIU NA NATSIONAL'NYKH I KOLONIAL'NYKH PROBLEM. (TRUDY...No. 18.) Moscow, 1935, 230 pp., 1500 copies. [Russ. text; 2422 Russ. titles, pub.: 18th c. -1934]

Il'in, K. "KRATKAIA SPRAVKA O PERIODICHESKOI PECHATI MONGOLII," SOVREMENNAIA MONGOLIIA. No. 3. 1933. [Russ. text; Mongol titles, pub.: ca.1933, pp. 76-78]

KATALOG KNIGAM I RUKOPISIAM NA KITAISKOM, MAN'CHZHURSKOM, MONGOL'SKOM, TIBETSKOM I SANSKRITSKOM IAZYKAKH NAKHODIASHCHIMSIA V BIBLIOTEKIE AZIATSKAGO DEPARTAMENTA. St. Petersburg, 1844, 69 + 13 pp. [Russ. text; 590 Mongol, Tibetan, Chinese, Manchu, Sanskrit titles (incl. mss.)]

Mongolia: General

KATALOG KNIGAM, RUKOPISIAM I KARTAM NA KITAISKOM, MANCHZHURSKOM, MONGOL'SKOM, TIBETSKOM I SANSKRITSKOM IAZYKAKH, NAKHODIASHCHIMSIA V BIBLIOTEKE AZIATSKAGO DEPARTAMENTA. St. Petersburg, 1843, 102 pp. [Russ. text; 609 (43 in Mongol) Mongol, other titles]

Khokhriakova-Simonova, L. Kh. BIBLIOGRAFIIA RABOT I STATEI PO ZABAIKAL'IU I MONGOLII V IZDANIIAKH VOSTOCHNO-SIBIRSKAGO OTDIELA RUSSKAGO GEOGRAFICHESKAGO OBSHCHESTVA. (1851-1901) TRUDY TROITSKO-SAVSKO-KIAKHTINSKAGO OTDIELENIIA PRIAMURSKAGO OTDIELA RUSSKAGO GEOGRAFICHESKAGO OBSHCHESTVA. Vol. 4. No. 2. 1901 [Russ. text; 180 Russ. titles, pub.: 1851-1901, pp. 127-137]

*Kazakevich, V. A. "BIBLIOGRAFIIA TRUDOV P. K. KOZLOVA," BIBLIOGRAFIIA VOSTOKA. No. 8/9. (Moscow-Leningrad) (1935) 1936. [Russ. text; 69 Russ., Europ. titles, pp. 41-47]

*Kotovich, Vl. IAPONSKIE IZDANIIA NA MONGOL'SKOM IAZYKE. ZAPISKI VOSTOCHNAGO OTDIELENIIA IMPERATORSKAGO RUSSKAGO ARKHEOLOGICHESKAGO OBSHCHESTVA. Vol. 18 [za] 1907-1908. (St. Petersburg), 1908. [Russ. text; Mongol survey, pp. 0195-0200]

Krylov, V. N. KNIGI I BROSHIURY O KITAE, MAN'CHZHURII, VNUTRENNEI MONGOLII. BIBLIOGRAFICHESKII BIULLETIN. Vol. 3, No. 2. 1930. [Russ. text; titles pp. 24-29]

──────────. KNIGI I BROSHIURY O KITAE, MONGOLII I VNUTRENNOI MONGOLII. VESTNIK MAN'CHZHURII. No. 6. 1930. [Russ. text; titles pp. 111-116]

──────────. "LITERATURA NA IAPONSKIM IAZYKE O MONGOLII I SOPREDEL'NYKH STRANAKH," VESTNIK MAN'CHZHURII. No. 6, No. 11/12. 1928. [Russ. text; Japanese titles, (6) pp. 1-16; (11/12) pp. 4-10]

*"MONGOL'SKAIA NARODNAIA RESPUBLIKA," (MNR), BOL'SHAIA SOVETSKAIA ENTSIKLOPEDIIA. Vol. 40. Moscow: Gosudarstvennyi Institut "Sovetskaia Entsiklopediia," (Ogiz RSFSR), 1938, 68-74 pp. [Russ. text; Russ., Europ. titles, p. 74]

Mongolia: General

MONGOL'SKAIA NARODNAIA RESPUBLIKA. BIBLIOGRAFICHESKAIA SPRAVKA. Rostov N/D: (Rostovskaia Gosudarstvennaia Nauchnaia Biblioteka imeni Karla Marksa), 1950, 8 pp. [Russ. text]

*MONGOL'SKAIA NARODNAIA RESPUBLIKA. BIBLIOGRAFIIA KNIZHNOI I ZHURNAL'NOI LITERATURY NA RUSSKOM IAZYKE. 1935-1950 GG. (TRUDY MONGOL'SKOI KOMISSII. No. 42.) Moscow: Izdatel'stvo Akademii Nauk SSSR, 1953, 87 pp., 3000 copies. [Russ. text and titles, pub.: 1934-1950]

OSNOVNYE RABOTY PO MONGOLII, OPUBLIKOVANNYE V 1945-1961 GG. KRATKIE SOOBSHCHENIIA INSTITUTA NARODOV AZII. No. 54. 1962. [Russ. text; titles, pub.: 1945-1961]

"PERECHEN' STATEI PO KITAIU, MAN'CHZHURII I MONGOLII, POMESHCHENNYKH V 1925 G. V RAZLICHNYKH IAPONSKIKH PERIODICHESKIKH ORGANAKH PECHATI," VESTNIK MAN'CHZHURII. No. 1/2. 1926. [Russ. text; Japanese titles, pub.: 1925, pp. 106-110]

Sh[astina], N. [P.] "KNIZHNYE I ZHURNAL'NYE NOVOSTI O MONGOL'SKOI NARODNOI RESPUBLIKE. (MATERIALY PO BIBLIOGRAFII)," SOVREMENNAIA MONGOLIIA. No. 3(6). 1934. [Russ. text; 69 titles, pub.: 1932-1933, pp. 106-114]

_____. "MATERIALY PO BIBLIOGRAFII MONGOLII: (PO MATERIALAM BIBLIOTEKI NAUCHNO-ISSLEDOVATEL'SKOGO KOMITETA MNR)," SOVREMENNAIA MONGOLIIA. No. 4(11). 1935. [Russ. text; 61 titles, pub.: 1934, pp. 84-92]

_____. "OSNOVNAIA LITERATURA O MONGOLII," SOVREMENNAIA MONGOLIIA. No. 1, 2. 1933. [Russ. text; 119 titles, (1) pp. 82-94; (2) pp. 92-105]

_____. "OSNOVNAIA LITERATURA O MONGOLII," SOVREMENNAIA MONGOLIIA. No. 4, 1935; No. 6, 1936. [Russ. text; titles, (4) pub.: 1935, pp. 84-90; (6) pp. 98-113]

*Skachkov, P. E. BIBLIOGRAFIIA KITAIA. SISTEMATICHESKII UKAZATEL' KNIG I ZHURNAL'NYKH STATEI O KITAE NA RUSSKOM IAZYKE. 1730-1930. Moscow-Leningrad: (Kommunisticheskaia Akademiia. Nauchno-Issledovatel'skii Institut po Kitaiu) Gosudarstvennoe Sotsial'no-Ekonomicheskoe Izdatel'stvo, 1932 (1948 2nd ed. in U.S.A.), 842 pp., 2175 copies. [Russ. text; 350 (re. Mong.) Russ. titles, esp. pp. 368-373]

Mongolia: General

*"SODERZHANIE ZHURNALA 'KHOZIAISTVO MONGOLII',"
BIBLIOGRAFIIA VOSTOKA. No. 1. (Leningrad), 1932.
[Russ. text; 229 Russ. titles, pp. 119-131]

"SPISOK MATERIALAM ZHAMTSARANOVA I B. BARADIINA,"
IZVIESTIIA AKADEMII NAUK. 1903-1904. [Russ. text;
titles, pp. 049-084]

*Tiuliaeva, V. P. MONGOL'SKAIA NARODNAIA RESPUBLIKA:
BIBLIOGRAFIIA KNIZHNOI I ZHURNAL'NOI LITERATURY NA
RUSSKOM IAZYKE, 1935-1950 GG. (TRUDY MONGOL'SKOI
KOMISSII. No. 42.) Moscow: Izdatel'stvo Akademii
Nauk SSSR, 1953, 87 pp., 3000 copies. [Russ. text;
ca.860 Russ. titles, pub.: 1934-1950, pp. 7-78]

"V. A. OBRUCHEV. (KRATKAIA BIOGRAFIIA SO SPISKOM
NAUCHNYKH TRUDOV)," SEVERNAIA AZIIA, No. 2. 1927.
Russ. text; titles, pp. 14-22]

Vdovenko, G. D. comp. LITERATURA O MONGOL'SKOI
NARODNOI RESPUBLIKE (V POMOSHCH' AGITATORU). Tomsk:
Tomskoe Izdatel'stvo "Krasnoe Znamia," 1939, 6 pp.
[Russ. text; 37 titles]

*Vladimirtsov, B. Ia. "PREDISLOVIE," Laufer, B.
OCHERK MONGOL'SKOI LITERATURY. Leningrad: Izdanie
Leningradskogo Vostochnogo Instituta imeni A. S.
Enukidze, 1927, 95 pp., 1000 copies. [Russ. text; Russ.,
Europ, titles, pp. IV-XXI]

Zaderman, L. I. MONGOL'SKAIA NARODNAIA RESPUBLIKA.
REKOMENDATEL'NYI SPISOK LITERATURY K LEKTSII.
Moscow: Izdatel'stvo TsPB, 1951, 5 pp. [Russ. text]

ANTHROPOLOGY, ETHNOGRAPHY

*Cheboksarova, N. N.; S. I. Bruka; R. F. Itsa; G. G.
Stratanovicha. eds. "MONGOL'SKIE NARODY [KITAIA]....
MONGOLY I DRUGIE NARODY MNR," NARODY VOSTOCHNOI AZII.
Moscow-Leningrad: Izdatel'stvo "Nauka," 1965, 1027 pp.,
2700 copies. [Russ. text; Russ., Europ. titles,
pp. 974-976]

Mongolia: Anthropology, Ethnography

*D. A. "MONGOLY," ENTSIKLOPEDICHESKII SLOVAR'.
Vol. 19 A. St. Petersburg: F. A. Brokgauz, I. A.
Efron, 1896, 751-752 pp. [Russ. text; Russ., Europ.
titles, p. 752]

ARCHITECTURE, ART, MUSIC

*Rudnev, A. D. "MELODII MONGOL'SKIKH PLEMEN," SBORNIK V
CHEST' SEMIDESIATILIETIIA GRIGORIIA NIKOLAEVICHA
POTANINA. ZAPISKI IMPERATORSKAGO RUSSKAGO
GEOGRAFICHESKAGO OBSHCHESTVA. OTD. ETNOGRAFII.
Vol. 34. St. Petersburg, 1909, 395-430 pp. [Russ.
text; Russ., Europ. titles, pp. 396-399]

ECONOMICS

Derevianko, P. A. SEL'SKOKHOZIAISTVENNOE
VODOSNABZHENIE MONGOL'SKOI NARODNOI RESPUBLIKI.
Moscow: Izdatel'stvo Akademii Nauk SSSR, 1959, 132 pp.
[Russ. text; 76 titles, end of book]

Kormazov, V. A. BARGA. EKONOMICHESKII OCHERK.
Kharbin: (Ekonomicheskoe Biuro KVZHD), 1928. [Russ.
text; 45 titles, pp. V-VII]

*Shubin, V. F. ZEMLEDELIE MONGOL'SKOI NARODNOI
RESPUBLIKI. BUGD NAIRAMDAKH MONGOL ARD ULSYN
TARIALANG. (TRUDY MONGOL'SKOI KOMISSII. No. 52).
Moscow: Izdatel'stvo Akademii Nauk SSSR, 1953,
346 pp., 1500 copies. [Russ. text; ca.150 Mongol,
Russ. titles, (incl. archives), pp. 342-346]

Mongolia: Economics

*Skachkov, P. E. VNUTRENNAIA MONGOLIIA. (EKONOMIKO-GEOGRAFICHESKII OCHERK). Moscow: Izdanie Nauchno-Issledovatel'skoi Assotsiatsii po Izucheniiu Natsional'nykh i Kolonial'nykh Problem, 1933, 151 pp., 2500 copies. [Russ. text; Russ., Europ. titles, pp. 139-149]

_____. VNUTRENNAIA MONGOLIIA. (EKONOMIKO-GEOGRAFICHESKII OCHERK). Moscow-Leningrad, 1937, 261 pp. [Russ. text; 216 Russ., Chinese, Europ. titles, pp. 243-255]

Ulymzhiev, D-ts. B. SOTSIALISTICHESKOE PEREUSTROISTVO SEL'SKOGO KHOZIAISTVA V MNR. Ulan Ude: Buriat. Kn. Izd., 1968, 268 pp., 1000 copies. [Russ. text; titles, pp. 4-21]

EDUCATION

Baldaev, R. L. "NARODNOE OBRAZOVANIE V MONGOL'SKOI NARODNOI RESPUBLIKE," SOVETSKAIA PEDAGOGIKA. No. 11. 1958. [Russ. text; 33 Mongol, Russ. titles, p. 128]

Ishidordzhi, "UCHEBNAIA LITERATURA MNR," SOVREMENNAIA MONGOLIIA. No. 3(6). 1934. [Russ. text; titles pub.: 1921-1934, pp. 86-95]

GEOGRAPHY

Borzov, A. A.; F. Aristov. "BIBLIOGRAFIIA P. K. KOZLOVA," ZEMLEVEDENIE: GEOGRAFICHESKII ZHURNAL. Vol. 32. 1930. [Russ. text]

Mongolia: Geography

*Kazakevich, V. A. "NOVYE MATERIALY PO KARTOGRAFII MONGOLII," BIBLIOGRAFIIA VOSTOKA. No. 8/9. 1935. [Russ. text; Mongol, Russ. survey, pp. 131-138]

*Kozlov, P. K. MONGOLIIA I KAM TREKHLETNEE PUTESHESTVIE PO MONGOLII I TIBETU (1899-1901 GG.) Moscow: Ogiz. Gosudarstvennoe Izdatel'stvo Geograficheskoi Literatury, 1947 (2nd ed.; 1st ed. 1905), 437 pp., 15,000 copies. [Russ. text and titles, pub.: 1895-1941, pp. 427-430, 431-433]

_____. RUSSKII PUTESHESTVENNIK V TSENTRAL'NOI AZII. IZBRANNYE TRUDY. K STOLETIIU SO DNIA ROZHDENIIA (1863-1963). Moscow: Izdatel'stvo Akademii Nauk SSSR, 1963, 523 pp., 3000 copies. [Russ. text; 81+35+53 Russ., Europ. titles, per.: 1863-1963, pp. 510-518]

_____. "SPISOK PECHATNYKH RABOT, IAVIVSHIKHSIA REZUL'TATOM IZUCHENIIA MATERIALOV, PRIVEZENNYKH EKSPEDITSIEI," PUTESHESTVIE V MONGOLIIU. 1923-1926. DNEVNIKI. ZAPISKI VSESOIUZNOGO GEOGRAFICHESKOGO OBSHCHESTVA. NOVAIA SERIIA. Vol. 7. Moscow, [ca.1950] [Russ. text; 39 Russ., Europ. titles, pub.: 1924-1947, per.: 1923-1926, pp. 231-232]

*"MONGOLIIA," VOENNAIA ENTSIKLOPEDIIA. Vol. 16. Petersburg: T-vo I. D. Sytina, 1914, 387-391 pp. [Russ. text and titles, p. 391]

*"MONGOL'SKOE NASHESTVIE," VOENNAIA ENTSIKLOPEDIIA. Vol. 16. Petersburg: T-vo I. D. Sytina, 1914, 391-396 pp. [Russ. text and titles, p. 396]

*Murzaev, E. M. MONGOL'SKAIA NARODNAIA RESPUBLIKA. FIZIKO-GEOGRAFICHESKOE OPISANIE. Moscow: Ogiz. Gosudarstvennoe Izdatel'stvo Geograficheskoi Literatury, 1948, 314 pp., 10000 copies. [Russ. text; Russ., Europ. titles, pp. 293-302]

_____. "OSNOVNYE PROBLEMY FIZIKO-GEOGRAFICHESKOGO IZUCHENIIA MONGOL'SKOI NARODNOI RESPUBLIKI," PROBLEMY FIZICHESKOI GEOGRAFII. No. 12. 1946. [Russ. text; 18 titles (incl. MSS), pp. 79-80]

_____. SPISOK PECHATNYKH RABOT. 1930-1960. Moscow: (Akademiia Nauk SSSR. Institut Geografii), 1961, 77 pp. [Russ. text]

Mongolia: Geography

*Obruchev, V. "MONGOLIIA VNUTRENNAIA," BOL'SHAIA SOVETSKAIA ENTSIKLOPEDIIA. Vol. 40. Moscow: Gosudarstvennyi Institut "Sovetskaia Entsiklopediia," (Ogiz RSFSR), 1938, 34-35 pp. [Russ. text; Russ., Europ. titles, p. 35]

*_____. ISKOPAEMYE BOGATSTVA POGRANICHNOI DZHUNGARII. Moscow: Gosudarstvennoe Nauchno-Tekhnicheskoe Izdatel'stvo Tsvetnoi i Zoloto-Platinovoi Promyshlennosti, 1932, 68 pp., 2200 copies. [Russ. text; 46 Russ. titles, pp. 67-68]

_____. IZBRANNYE TRUDY. Vol. 1. Moscow: Izdatel'stvo Akademii Nauk SSSR, 1958. [Russ. text; 95 Russ., Europ. titles, pp. 29-47]

*_____. POGRANICHNAIA DZHUNGARIIA. Vol. 3-- GEOGRAFICHESKOE I GEOLOGICHESKOE OPISANIE. No. 1-- OBZOR LITERATURY OROGRAFIIA, GIDROGRAFIIA. Leningrad: Izdatel'stvo Akademii Nauk SSSR, 1932, 311 pp. [Russ. text; 173 Russ., Europ. titles, pp. 4-86]

*_____. VOSTOCHNAIA MONGOLIIA. GEOGRAFICHESKOE I GEOLOGICHESKOE OPISANIE. CHASTI 1/2--OBZOR LITERATURY. OROGRAFICHESKII I GIDROGRAFICHESKII OCHERKI. Moscow-Leningrad: Izdatel'stvo Akademii Nauk SSSR, 1947, 351 pp. [Russ. text; 574 Russ., Europ. titles, pp. 10-138]

_____. VOSTOCHNAIA MONGOLIIA. CHAST' 3-- GEOLOGICHESKOE OPISANIE. TRUDY MONGOL'SKOI KOMISSII AKADEMII NAUK SSSR. No. 6. 1954. [Russ. text; titles, pp. 5-23]

*Pevtsov, M. V. "TRUDY M. V. PEVTSOVA," PUTESHESTVIIA PO KITAIU I MONGOLII. Moscow: Gosudarstvennoe Izdatel'stvo Geograficheskoi Literatury, 1951, 283 pp., 1500 copies. [Russ. text; 27 Russ. titles, pub.: 1879-1905, pp. 275-276]

*Przheval'skii, N. M. MONGOLIA I STRANA TANGUTOV. TREKHLETNEE PUTESHESTVIE V VOSTOCHNOI NAGORNOI AZII. Moscow: Ogiz. Gosudarstvennoe Izdatel'stvo Geograficheskoi Literatury, 1946, 333 pp., 15,000 copies. [Russ. text; 110 + 12 Russ., Europ. titles, (incl. maps), pp. 325-330]

Mongolia: Geography

Tkachenko, M. I. comp. "MATERIALY PO BIBLIOGRAFII I
KARTOGRAFII VNUTRENNEI I VNESHNEI MONGOLII,
URIANKHAISKOGO KRAIA I OTCHASTI POGRANICHNOI S NIMI
POLOSY," Molody, I. F., SELENGA V PREDELAKH
MONGOLII. KRATKII OTCHET O RABOTAKH MONGOL'SKOI
EKSPEDITSII 1919 GODA POD NACH. I. F. MOLODYKH.
Irkutsk, 1920. [Russ. text; 608 + 63 titles,
pp. 131-176]

Zaderman, L. I. ISSLEDOVANIE TSENTRAL'NOI AZII RUSSKIMI
PUTESHESTVENNIKAMI. REKOMENDATEL'NYI SPISOK
LITERATURY. Moscow: Izdatel'stvo TsPB, 1953, 12 pp.
[Russ. text]

HISTORY, ARCHAEOLOGY

*A. P. "KALMYKI," ENTSIKLOPEDICHESKII SLOVAR'. Vol. 14.
St. Petersburg: F. A. Brokgauz, I. A. Efron, 1895,
57-64 pp. [Russ. text; Russ., Europ. titles, p. 64]

*ARMIANSKIE ISTOCHNIKI O MONGOLAKH. IZVLECHENIIA IZ
RUKOPISEI XIII - XIV VV. Moscow: Izdatel'stvo
Vostochnoi Literatury, 1962, 155 pp., 3200 copies.
[Russ. text; Armen., Russ. titles (incl. archives)
per.: 13th - 14th cc., pp. 135-140]

*Bartol'd, V. "CHINGIZ-KHAN," ENTSIKLOPEDICHESKII
SLOVAR'. Vol. 38 A. St. Petersburg: F. A.
Brokgauz, I. A. Efron, 1903, 841-843 pp. [Russ.
text; Russ., Europ. titles, p. 843]

*BIBLIOGRAFIIA. "VOSTOCHNAIA EVROPA. SREDNIAIA AZIIA I
ZAKAVKAZ'E POD VLAST'IU MONGOLO-TATARSKIKH
ZAVOEVATELEI," BOL'SHAIA SOVETSKAIA ENTSIKLOPEDIIA.
TOM   SOIUZ SOVETSKIKH SOTSIALISTICHESKIKH RESPUBLIK.
Moscow: Gosudarstvennyi Nauchnyi Institut "Sovetskaia
Entsiklopediia," (Ogiz SSSR), 1947, p. 52.
[Russ. text and titles, p. 52]

"BURIATO-MONGOL'SKAIA ASSR," SOVETSKAIA VOENNAIA
ENTSIKLOPEDIIA. Vol. 2. Moscow: Gosudarstvennoe
Slovarno-Entsiklopediia   Izdatel'stvo "Sovetskaia
Entsiklope-iia," Ogiz RSFSR, 1933, p. 858. [Russ.
text and titles, p. 858]

Mongolia: History, Archaeology

*[Dorzh, D.; Ts. Khandsuren. comps.] ISTORIIA MONGOL'SKOI NARODNOI RESPUBLIKI. Moscow: Izdatel'stvo "Nauka," 1967, 537 pp., 5500 copies. [Russ. text; ca.550 Mongol, Russ., West. titles, pp. 515-532]

Gol'man, M. I. KRATKIE SOOBSHCHENIIA INSTITUTA NARODOV AZII. No. 85. 1964. [Russ. text]

"KNIGI I STAT'I O MONGOL'SKOI NARODNOI RESPUBLIKE," SOVREMENNAIA MONGOLIIA. No. 1. 1941. [Russ. text; 31 Russ. titles, pp. 75-79]

*Munkuev, N. Ts. KITAISKII ISTOCHNIK O PERVYKH MONGOL'SKIKH KHANAKH. NADGROBNAIA NADPIS' NA MOGILE ELIUI CHU-TSAIA. PEREVOD I ISSLEDOVANIE. Moscow: Izdatel'stvo "Nauka." Glavnaia Redaktsiia Vostochnoi Literatury, 1965, 224 pp., 1400 copies. [Russ. text; Mongol, Russ., Europ., Chinese, Japan. titles, pp. 202-211]

*"OSNOVNAIA LITERATURA PO ISTORII MNR," ISTORIIA MONGOL'SKOI NARODNOI RESPUBLIKI. Moscow: (Akad. Nauk SSSR. Kom. Nauk MNR) Izdatel'stvo Akademii Nauk SSSR, 1954, 422 pp., 10,000 copies. [Russ. text; 326 Mongol, Russ., Chinese, Europ. titles, pp. 395-408]

*Pozdneev, A. "MONGOLIIA," ENTSIKLOPEDICHESKII SLOVAR'. Vol. 19A. St. Petersburg: F. A. Brokgauz, I. A. Efron, 734-751 pp. [Russ. text; Russ., Europ. titles, p. 751]

"SAD AD-DAULA," EVREISKAIA ENTSIKLOPEDIIA. Vol. 13. St. Petersbug: Izdanie Obshchestva Dlia Nauchnykh Evreiskikh Izdanii i Izdatel'stva Brokgauz-Efron, n. d., 820-821 pp. [Russ. text; Europ. titles, p. 821]

*Simkhovich, M. "MONGOLO-TATARSKOE NASHESTVIE," BOL'SHAIA SOVETSKAIA ENTSIKLOPEDIIA. Vol. 40. Moscow: Gosudarstvennyi Institut "Sovetskaia Entsiklopediia," (Ogiz RSFSR), 1938, 48-58 pp. [Russ. text and titles, p. 58]

*Tokarev, S. "MONGOLY," BOL'SHAIA SOVETSKAIA ENTSIKLOPEDIIA. Vol. 40. Moscow: Gosudarstvennyi Institut "Sovetskaia Entsiklopediia," (Ogiz RSFSR), 1938, 58-59 pp. [Russ. text; Russ., Europ., Chinese titles, p. 59]

Mongolia: History, Archaeology

*Zhukov, E. M. et al. ed. ISTORIIA MONGOL'SKOI
NARODNOI RESPUBLIKI. Moscow: "Nauka," 1967, 537 pp.,
5500 copies. [Russ. text; titles, pp. 515-532]

LANGUAGE, LITERATURE

*Badmaev, A. V. "SPISOK OPUBLIKOVANNYKH NAUCHNYKH
TRUDOV G. I. MIKHAILOVA," UCHEN. ZAP. KALM. NII IAZ.,
LIT. I ISTORII. No. 9. Elista, 1970, 352-362 pp.,
500 copies. [Russ. text; 85 Buriat, Mongol, Russ.,
Chinese titles, pub.: 1932-1968, pp. 359-362]

*Cheremisov, K. M.; G. N. Rumiantsev. MONGOL'SKO-RUSSKII
SLOVAR'. (PO SOVREMENNOI PRESSE) S PREDISLOVIEM N. N.
POPPE.) (TSIK SSSR. LENINGRADSKII VOSTOCHNYI
INSTITUT. 62.) Leningrad: Izdanie Leningradskogo
Vostochnogo Instituta, 1937, 562 pp., 1000 copies.
[Russ. text; 28 Mongol, Russ. titles, pub.: 1927-
1935, pp. XI-XIV]

*Gerasimovich, L. K. LITERATURA MONGOL'SKOI NARODNOI
RESPUBLIKI. 1921-1964 GODOV. n. p. Izdatel'stvo
Leningradskogo Instituta, 1965, 311 pp., 1800 copies.
[Russ. text; Mongol, Russ. titles, per.: 1921-1964,
pp. 288-310]

*_____. LITERATURA MONGOL'SKOI NARODNOI
RESPUBLIKI 1921-1926 GODOV. n. p. Izdatel'stvo
Leningradskogo Universiteta, 1965, 311 pp., 1800
copies. [Russ. text; Mongol, Russ. titles,
pp. 288-310]

*Laufer, B. [SEE ALSO "PREDISLOVIE"] OCHERK MONGOL'SKOI
LITERATURY. (PEREVOD V. A. KAZAKEVICHA. POD RED.
I S PREDISLOVIEM B. IA. VLADIMIRTSOVA). Leningrad:
(TsIK SSSR. Leningradskii Vostochnyi Institut
imeni A. S. Enukidze), 1927, 95 pp. [Russ. text;
Mongol, Russ., Europ. survey]

*Mikhailov, G. I. OCHERK ISTORII SOVREMENNOI
MONGOL'SKOI LITERATURY. Moscow: Izdatel'stvo
Akademii Nauk SSSR, 1955, 216 pp., 5000 copies.
[Russ. text; Mongol, Russ. titles, pp. 198-206]

Mongolia: Language, Literature

*Mikhailov, G. I. OCHERK ISTORII SOVREMENNOI
MONGOL'SKOI LITERATURY. Moscow: Izdatel'stvo
Akademii Nauk SSSR, 1955, 216 pp., 5000 copies.
[Russ. text; Mongol, Russ. titles, pp. 198-206]

*N. P. "MONGOL'SKIE IAZYKI," BOL'SHAIA SOVETSKAIA
ENTSIKLOPEDIIA. Vol. 40. Moscow: Gosudarstvennyi
Institut "Sovetskaia Entsiklopediia," (Ogiz RSFSR),
1938, 90-93 pp. [Russ. text; Mongol, Kalmuk, Russ.
Europ. titles, pp. 92-93]

*Poppe, N. "MONGOL'SKAIA LITERATURA," LITERATURNAIA
ENTSIKLOPEDIIA. Vol. 7. Moscow: Gosudarstvennoe
Slovarno-Entsiklopedicheskoe Izdatel'stvo
"Sovetskaia Entsiklopediia," 1934, 446-451 pp.
[Russ. text and titles, p. 451]

*_____. "MONGOL'SKII IAZYK," LITERATURNAIA
ENTSIKLOPEDIIA. Vol. 7. Moscow: Gosudarstvennoe
Slovarno-Entsiklopedicheskoe Izdatel'stvo
"Sovetskaia Entsiklopediia," 1934, 451-453 pp.
[Russ. text; Russ., Europ. titles, p. 453]

*Pozdneev, A. "KALMYTSKIE IAZYKI I LITERATURA,"
ENTSIKLOPEDICHESKII SLOVAR'. Vol. 14. St. Petersburg:
F. A. Brokgauz, I. A. Efron, 1895, 71-72 pp.
[Russ. text; Russ., Europ. titles, p. 72]

*_____. "MONGOL'SKIE IAZYKI I LITERATURA,"
ENTSIKLOPEDICHESKII SLOVAR'. Vol. 19A. St.
Petersburg: F. A. Brokgauz, I. A. Efron, 1896,
752-755 pp. [Russ. text; Russ., Europ. titles,
pp. 752-755]

Rudnev, A. D. LEKTSII PO GRAMMATIKE MONGOL'SKAGO
PIS'MENNAGO IAZYKA, CHITANNYE V 1903-1904
AKADEMICHESKOM GODU. No. 1. St. Petersburg, 1905,
95 pp. [Russ. text; 46 titles, pp. IV-VI]

_____. MATERIALY PO GOVORAM VOSTOCHNOI MONGOLII.
St. Petersburg, 1911. [Russ. text; 62 titles]

*Sanzheev, G. "MONGOL'SKAIA LITERATURA," BOL'SHAIA
SOVETSKAIA ENTSIKLOPEIIA. Vol. 40. Moscow:
Gosudarstvennyi Institut "Sovetskaia Entsiklopediia"
(Ogiz RSFSR), 1938, 66-67 pp. [Russ. text; Mongol,
Russ. titles, p. 67]

*Sanzheev, G. D. SOVREMENNYI MONGOL'SKII IAZYK.
Moscow: Izdatel'stvo Vostochnoi Literatury, 1960
(2nd ed., revised), 104 pp., 1000 copies. [Russ.
text; Mongol, Russ., Europ. titles, pp. 102-103]

Mongolia: Language, Literature

*"SPISOK NAUCHNYKH TRUDOV AKADEMIKA B. IA.
VLADIMIRTSOVA," Mikhailov, G. I; N. P. Shastina. eds.
FILOLOGIIA I ISTORIIA MONGOL'SKIKH NARODOV. PAMIATI
AKADEMIKA BORISA IAKOVLEVICHA VLADIMIRTSOVA.
Moscow: (Akademiia Nauk SSSR. Institut
Vostokovedeniia) Izdatel'stvo Vostochnoi Literatury,
1958, 348 pp., 1100 copies. [Russ. text; 69 + 25
Mongol, Russ., Europ. titles, pp. 8-11]

*Todaeva, B. Kh. MONGOL'SKIE IAZYKI I DIALEKTY KITAIA.
Moscow: Izdatel'stvo Vostochnoi Literatury, 1960,
137 pp., 1600 copies. [Russ. text; Russ., Western
titles, pp. 135-136]

*Vinogradov, V. V. IAZYKI NARODOV SSSR. Vol. 5.
MONGOL'SKIE, TUNGUSO-MAN'CHZHURSKIE I PALEOAZIATSKIE
IAZYKI. Leningrad: "Nauka," 1968, 524 pp., 6200
copies. [Russ. text; titles at end of chapters]

*Vladimirtsov, B. [Ia.] "BIBLIOGRAFIIA MONGOL'SKOI
SKAZKI," ZHIVAIA STARINA. No. 2/4. Vol. 21, 1912.
1914. [Russ. text; 81 Russ., Europ. titles,
pp. 521-528]

* _____. MONGOL'SKII SBORNIK RASSKAZOV IZ
"PANCATANTRA," SBORNIK MUZEIA ANTROPOLOGII I
ETNOGRAFII...PRI AKADEMII NAUK SSSR. Vol. 5.
Petrograd, 1921, 162 pp. [Russ. text; 247 titles,
pp. 156-162]

PHILOSOPHY, RELIGION

Gerasimova, K. M. LAMAIZM I NATSIONAL'NO-KOLONIAL'NAIA
POLITIKA TSARIZMA V ZABAIKAL'E V XIX I NACHALE XX
VEKOV. Ulan Ude: Buriat-Mongol'skii Nauchno-
Issledovatel'skii Institut Kul'tury), 1957. [Russ.
text; ca.130 Mongol, Russ. titles, per.: 19th c. -
1917, pp. 143-159]

*Pozdneev, A. "KALMYTSKOE VIEROUCHENIE,"
ENTSIKLOPEDICHESKII SLOVAR'. Vol. 14. St. Petersburg:
F. A. Brokgauz, I. A. Efron, 1895, 72-74 pp. [Russ.
text; Russ., Europ. titles, p. 74]

Mongolia

POLITICAL SCIENCE, LAW

*Berzhanskii, M. "SUKHE-BATOR," BOL'SHAIA SOVETSKAIA ENTSIKLOPEDIIA. Vol. 53. Moscow: Gosudarstvennyi Nauchnyi Institut "Sovetskaia Entsiklopediia," (Ogiz RSFSR), 1946, 251-252 pp. [Russ. text; Mongol, Russ. titles, p. 252]

Khoroshikh, P. P. "LITERATURA O REVOLIUTSIONNOI MONGOLII," ZHIZN' BURIATII. No. 9/12. 1925. [Russ. text; 20 titles, pub.: 1922-1925, pp. 173-174]

Kondrat'eva, M. I. "MATERIALY DLIA BIBLIOGRAFII MONGOLII (IZ RABOT BIBLIOTEKI UCHENOGO KOMITETA MNR)," KHOZIAISTVO MONGOLII. No. 5(18), 1929; No. 3(21), 1930. [Russ. text; 332; 164 titles, per.: hist. up to 1930, (1929) pp. 75-96; (1930) pp. 88-89]

*Krol, M. "ULUS," ENTSIKLOPEDICHESKII SLOVAR'. Vol. 34A. St. Petersburg: F. A. Brokgauz, I. A. Efron, 1902, 698-700 copies. [Russ. text; Russ., Europ. titles, p. 700]

MONGOL'SKAIA NARODNAIA RESPUBLIKA. SPRAVKA. Rostov Na Donu: (Rostovskaia Gosudarstvennaia Nauchnaia Biblioteka imeni Karla Marksa), 1950, 8 pp., 1500 copies. [Russ. text; 15 titles, pub.: 1945-1950]

*Zhamtsarano, Ts.; A. Turunov. "OBOZRENIE PAMIATNIKOV PISANOGO PRAVA MONGOL'SKIKH PLEMEN," SBORNIK TRUDOV PROFESSOROV I PREPODAVATELEI GOSUDARSTVENNOGO IRKUTSKOGO UNIVERSITETA. OTDEL I--NAUKI GUMANITARNYE. No. 1. (Irkutsk) 1921, 1-13 pp. [Russ. text; Mongol, Russ., Europ. titles, p. 11]

Mongolia

SOCIAL ORGANIZATION

Borodkin, P. A. et al. comps. BOR'BA TRUDIASHCHIKHSIA
ZA USTANOVLENIE SOVETSKOI VLASTI NA ALTAE (1917-1920
GG.) Barnaul: (Part. Arkhiv Alt. Kraikoma KPSS.
Gos. Arkhiv Alt. Kraia), 1957. [Russ. text; 133
titles, per.: 1917-1920, pp. 495-503]

Lantsov, V. I. OT SOTSIALIZMA K KOMMUNIZMU. (METOD.
POSOBIE PO POLIT. EKONOMII DLIA SHKOL OSNOV
MARKSIZMA-LENINIZMA.) Barnaul: (Dom Polit.
Prosveshcheniia Alt. Kraikoma KPSS), 1968, 26 pp.,
1500 copies. [Russ. text; titles at end of book]

*Vladimirtsov, B. Ia. OBSHCHESTVENNYI STROI MONGOLOV.
MONGOL'SKII KOCHEVOI FEODALIZM. Leningrad:
Izdatel'stvo Akademii Nauk SSSR, 1934, 223 pp.,
3175 copies. [Russ. text; 302 Mongol, Russ., Europ.
titles, pub.: 1909-1931, pp. 197-207, IX-XI]

36 SIBERIA

GENERAL

Adgokov, A. N. SOVETSKAIA PRESSA V SIBIRI V
1917-1818 G. G. (MATERIALY K BIBLIOGRAFICHESKOMU
OBZORU). Irkutsk: Gosudarstvennoe Izdatel'stvo,
Irkutskoe Otdelenie, 1922, 24 + 3 pp., 1000 copies.
[Russ. text; 14 + survey titles, pp. 1917-1918]

Adrianov, A. V. GOROD TOMSK V PROSHLOM I NASTOIASHCHEM.
Tomsk, 1890. [Russ. text; titles, pp. I-XII, 1-433]

_____. PERIODICHESKAIA PECHAT' V SIBIRI. S
UKAZATELEM IZDANII V 1918 GODU. Tomsk, 1919, 31 pp.
[Russ. text; survey + list, pub.: 1918]

Avdeev, I. A. DRUZHBA I BRATSTVO NARODOV SSSR--VELIKOE
ZAVOEVANIE OKTIABRIA. Omsk: (Omskii Obkom KPSS. Otd.
Propagandy i Agitatsii), 1967, 19 pp., 1200 copies.
[Russ. text; titles at end of book]

*Azadovskii, Mark K. "BIBLIOGRAFIIA SIBIRSKOGO
FOL'KLORA, 1917-1926," SLAVIA. Vol. 7, No. 1.
Prague, 1928. [Russ. text; 198 Russ. titles,
pub.: 1917-1926, pp. 201-213]

*_____. OBZOR BIBLIOGRAFII SIBIRI. (TRUDY
OBSHCHESTVA ETNOGRAFII, ISTORII I ARKHEOLOGII PRI
TOMSKOM UNIVERSITETE. No. 1.) TOMSK: Tipolit.
Tomskoi Zheleznoi Dorogi, 1920, IV + 46 pp. [Russ.
text; 133 Russ. titles]

*B. A. "PERESELENIE ILI KOLONIZATSIIA. (NOVEISHAIA
LITERATURA VOPROSA O KOLONIZATSII SIBIRI)," RUSSKAIA
MYSL'. Book 8. 1913. [Russ. text; Russ., Europ.
titles, per.: 1913, pp. 3-9]

*Batorov, V. V. "SPISOK KNIG, NAPECHATANNYKH V TOMSKOI
GUBERNSKOI TIPOGRAFII," IZ ISTORII KNIGI, BIBLIOTECH.
DELA I BIBLIOGRAFII V SIBIRI. Novosibirsk: "Nauka,"
1969, 284 pp., 900 copies. [Russ. text; 38 Russ.
titles, pub.: 1861-1876, pp. 32-35]

Siberia: General

Belov, Aleksei M. MATERIALY K UKAZATELIU LITERATURY O
SIBIRI NA EVROPEISKIKH IAZYKAKH S 1917 G. PO 1930 G.
Leningrad: Izdatel'stvo Akademii Nauk SSSR, 1931,
35 pp., 1000 copies. [Russ. text; 494 European titles,
pub.: 1917-1930]

"BIBLIOGRAFICHESKII OTDEL' TEKUSHCHEI LITERATURY O
IAKUTSKOI OBLASTI," LENSKIIA VOLNY. No. 1.- 1915.
[Russ. text; titles at end of every issue]

*"BIBLIOGRAFICHESKII SPISOK KNIG I BROSHIUR O SIBIRI ZA
1884-1887 G.," SIBIRSKII SBORNIK. Book 1, 2, 4.
1886. [Russ. text; ca.50 titles, pub.: 1884-1887,
(I) pp. 214-216; (2) 182-184 pp., (4) 160-168 pp.]

"BIBLIOGRAFICHESKII UKAZATEL' DLIA NACHINAIUSHCHIKH
KRAEVEDOV PO IZUCHENIIU ZAPADNOI SIBIRI I OMSKOGO
OKRUGA," MATERIALY OMSKOGO OBSHCHESTVA
KRAEVEDENIIA. No. 1. 1926. [Russ. text]

"BIBLIOGRAFICHESKII UKAZATEL' SIBIRSKIKH OGNEI ZA 1931 G.,"
SIBIRSKIE OGNI. No. 11/12, 1931, 107-108 pp.;
No. 11/12, 1932, 113-114 pp. [Russ. text and titles]

"BIBLIOGRAFICHESKII UKAZATEL' STATEI, POMESHCHENNYKH V
ZHURNALE 'SIBIRSKIE VOPROSY'," SIBIRSKIE VOPROSY. (A)
ZA 1905-1908 GG.; (B) ZA 1909 G.; (C) ZA 1910-1911 GG.;
(D) ZA 1912 G. 1908 (1909-1913, annually). [Russ.
text; titles, pub.: 1905-1908, 1909-1913, (A) 1908
49-52; I-XX pp.; (B) 1910 No. 3, pp. 52-58; (C) 1912
No. 9, 10, pp. 1-12; (D) 1913 No. 1, pp. 71-76]

"BIBLIOGRAFIIA," SIBIRSKAIA GAZETA. 1885, No. 33, 39,
47, 49; 1886, No. 6, 9, 13, 17, 18, 25, 28, 29, 30,
35, 41, 42, 44, 48; 1887, No. 3, 4, 6, 13; 1888 No. 7,
20, 23, 36, 45, 47. [Russ. text]

*BIBLIOGRAFIIA IZDANII ZAPADNO-SIBIRSKOGO FILIALA AKADEMII
NAUK SSR 1944-1956 GG. Novosobirsk: Izdatel'stvo
Zapadno-Sibirskogo Filiala AN SSSR, 1957, 90 pp.
[Russ. text; 568 titles, pub.: 1944-1956 GG.]

"BIBLIOGRAFIIA KNIG I STATEI, KASAIUSHCHIKHSIA SIBIRI,"
IZVIESTIIA SIBIRSKAGO OTDIELA IMPERATORSKAGO RUSSKAGO
GEOGRAFICHESKAGO OBSHCHESTVA. Vol. 1. 1870. [Russ.
text; titles pp. 31-43]

Busse, F. F. UKAZATEL' LITERATURY OB AMURKSOM KRAIE.
St. Petersburg: Tipografiia Imperatorskago Russkago
Geograficheskogo Obshchestva, 1874, No. 1, 42 pp.;
1882, No. 2, I-IV, 1-80 pp. [Russ. text; (No. 1) 522
Russ., foreign titles; (No. 2) 1416 Russ., foreign
titles, pub.: 1881 and before]

Siberia: General

Cherdantsev, A. UKAZATEL' K TOMAM I-XXX 'ZAPISOK URAL'SKAGO OBSHCHESTVA LIUBITELEI ESTESTVOZNANIIA' EKATERINBURGIE S 1871 PO 1910. Ekaterinburg: (Otd. Prilozhenie K Tom XXX 'Zapiski Ural'skago Obshchestva Liubitelei Estestvoznaniia'), 1911, 58 pp. [Russ. text; titles pub.: 1871-1910]

Ch[eremnykh], G. IZDANIIA VOSTOCHNO-SIBIRSKOGO OTDELA RUSSKOGO GEOGRAFICHESKOGO OBSHCHESTVA. SIBIRSKIE OGNI. No. 2. 1925. [Russ. text; survey, pub.: 1924-1925, pp. 264-265]

Cherepanova, M. "LITERATURA, VYPUSHCHENNAIA TIUMENSKIM KNIZHNIM IZDATEL'STVOM V 1951-1960 GG.," EZHEGODNIK TIUMEN. OBL. KRAEVED. MUZEIA. No. 2. Tiumen', [Russ. text; titles, pub.: 1951-1960, pp. 135-149]

Dmitriev - Mamonov, A. I. NACHALO PECHATI V SIBIRI. PECHAT' V TOBOL'SKOM NAMIESTNICHESTVIE V KONTSIE XVIII STOLIETIIA. ISTORIKO-BIBLIOGRAFICHESKIIA IZSLIEDOVANIIA. n. p., Izd. Akmol. Obl. Stat. K. O., 1891. [Russ. text; titles pub.: 1891 and before, p. 82]

_____. "PECHAT' V TOBOL'SKOM NAMIESTNICHESTVIE V KONTSIE XVIII STOLIETIIA. ISTORICHESKAIIA I BIBLIOGRAFICHESKIIA ROZYSKANIIA," PAMIATNAIA KNIZHKA TOBOL'SKOI GUBERNII NA 1884 G. Tobol'sk, 1884. [Russ. text; titles pub.: 18th c., pp. 258-358]

DOPOLNITEL'NYI SPISOK' KNIG', KART' I BROSHIUR' O SIBIRI I SOPREDIEL'NYKH FI STRANAKH, IZDANNYKH V 1884 G. SIBIRSKII SBORNIK. Book 1. 1886. [Russ. text; titles pub.: 1884, pp. 182-184]

*Filimonov, M. R.; D. P. Maslov. comps. TRUDY UCHENYKH V IZDANIIAKH TOMSKOGO UNIVERSITETA ZA 70 LET (1889-1958). SISTEMATICHESKII UKAZATEL' K PERIODICHESKIM IZDANIIAM I SBORNIKAM TGU. Tomsk: Izdatel'stvo Tomskogo Universiteta, 1962, 292 pp., 750 copies. [Russ. text; 4255 + 22 Russ. titles, pub.: 1889-1958, pp. 15-268]

Gedroits, K. I. SISTEMATICHESKII UKAZATEL' VSIEKH IZDANII [VOST.-SIB.] OTDIELA POMIESHCHENNYKH V NIKH STATEI, ZAMIETOK I MELKIKH IZVESTII I SOOBSHCHENII SDIELANNYKH V OBSHCHIKH SOBRANIIAKH I ZASIEDANIIAKH RASPORIADITEL'NAGO KOMITETA ZA DESIATILIETIE (1901-1911). Irkutsk: Vost.-Sibir. Otdiel Imperatorskago Russkago Geograficheskogo Obshchestva, 1912, 15 pp. [Russ. text; titles, pub.: 1901-1911]

Siberia : General

Girchenko, V. P.; K. M. Vil'min; A. P. Bazhin. comps.
UKAZATEL' LITERATURY PO PRIBAIKAL'IU. Verkhneudinsk,
1923, 38 pp. [Russ. text; 604 titles]

Golodnikov, K. UKAZATEL' STATEI, POMIESHCHENNYKH V
TOBOL'SKIKH GUBERNSKIKH VIEDOMOSTIAKH ZA 1889 G.
n.p.; n.d. [Russ. text; titles pub.: 1889]

Guliaeva, M. G., et al. comps. LITERATURA O ZAPADNOI
SIBIRI. Novosibirsk: (Novosibirsk. Obl. B-ka. Otd.
Zonal'noi Kraeved. Bibliografii), 1962, 364 pp.,
1000 copies. [Russ. text; 3648 titles]

Iakovleva, K. A. VSEVOLOD IVANOVICH VAGIN.
BIBLIOGRAFIIA. Vol. 19, No. 5. Vost.-Sib. Otdiel
Imperatorskago Russkago Geograficheskogo Obshchestva.
[Russ. text; titles pp. 83-96]

Iakubovich, S. P. BIBLIOGRAFIIA
SIBIRI, MONGOLII, MAN'CHZHURII I KOREI ZA [1897, 1898].
IZVIESTIIA VOSTOCHNO-SIBIRSKAGO OTDIELA
IMPERATORSKAGO RUSSKAGO GEOGRAFICHESKAGO OBSHCHESTVA.
Vol. 29-30, No. 2; 1-2/3. 1898-1899. [Russ. text;
711 Russ. titles, pub.: 1897-1898, Vol. 29: (1898) (2)
1-17 pp.; Vol. 30: (1899) (1) 19-33 pp., (2/3) 1-18 pp.]

Ishevskaia, V.; V. Nikolaeva comps. PEREKHOD NA
NOVUIU SISTEMU PLANIROVANIIA I EKONOMICHESKOGO
STIMULIROVANIIA PROIZVODSTVA ZA 1966-1967 GG.
Khabarovsk: (Khabar. TSBTI), 1967, 27 pp., 4000 copies.
[Russ. text; titles per.: 1966-1967]

Ivanovskii, A. A. "K BIBLIOGRAFII SIBIRI,"
BIBLIOGRAFICHESKIE ZAPISKI. No. 2. 1892. [Russ.
text; 171 titles, pp. 117-183]

_____. PAMIATNAIA KNIZHKA IRKUTSKOI GUBERNII
NA 1891 G. ETNOGRAFICHESKOE OBZORENIE. No. 1. 1892.
[Russ. text; 30+ titles, pub.: 1891, pp. 26-28]

IZDANIIA VOSTOCHNO-SIBIRKOGO OTDELA GOSUDARSTVENNOGO
RUSSKOGO GEOGRAFICHESKOGO OBSHCHESTVA ZA PIAT' LET.
1921-1926. Irkutsk: Izd. Tipografiia Izdatel'stva
"Vlast' Truda," 1926, 40 pp. [Russ. text]

Katanov, N. F. SVIEDIENIIA O TIURKAKH ENISEISKOI
GUBERNII. BIBLIOGRAFIIA. SIBIRSKII SBORNIK. 1887.
[Russ. text; Russ., foreign titles, p. 278]

Siberia: General

Kazarinov, P. K. "SIBIRSKOE KRAEVEDENIE. KRATKII BIBLIOGRAFICHESKII OBZOR POSLEDNIKH LET. 1920-1923," SIBIRSKAIA ZHIVAIA STARINA. No. 2. (Irkutsk: Izd. Vost.-Sib. Otd. Russ. Geogr. Obshch.), 1924, 34 pp. [Russ. text; titles, pub.: 1920-1923, pp. 159-190]

KHRONOLOGICHESKII UKAZATEL' K "IZVIESTIIAM IRKUTSKOI GORODSKOI DUMY" ZA 10 LIET. 1886-1895. Irkutsk, 1896. [Russ. text; pub.: 1886-1895]

Kirsanova, M. I. SOSTOIANIE I PROBLEMATIKA BIBLIOGRAFII NARODNOGO KHOZIAISTVA SIBIRI I DAL'NEGO VOSTOKA. (OBZOR BIBLIOGR. 1917-1968 GG.) Novosibirsk: (GPNTB Sib. Otd.-niia AN SSSR), 1969, 143 pp., 800 copies. [Russ. text; 289 titles, pub.: 1917-1968]

"KNIGI TSENTRAL'NYKH IZDATEL'STV O SIBIRI I DAL'NEM VOSTOKE," SIBIRSKIE OGNI. No. 9, 1963; No. 11, 1963; No. 8, 1964. [Russ. text; titles (No. 9) pp. 188-192; (No. 11) pp. 188-192; (No. 8) pp. 184-190]

KNIZHNAIA LETOPIS' DAL'NEVOSTOCHNOI KNIZHNOI PALATY PRI GOSUDARSTVENNOI PUBLICHNOI BIBLIOTEKE. Books 1-3 VESTNIK PROSVESHCHENIIA (ZHURN.) (CHITA), 1922. [Russ. text; titles pub.: 1922]

KNIZHNAIA LETOPIS' IRKUTSKA ZA GODY REVOLIUTSII (1917-1919). Irkutsk: Tip. Gubernskaia, 1920, 76 pp. [Russ. text; titles pub.: 1917-1919]

KNIZHNAIA LETOPIS' IRKUTSKA ZA GODY REVOLIUTSII (1920). Irkutsk: Tip. Gubernskaia. [Russ. text; titles pub.: 1920]

Kosovanov, V. P. BIBLIOGRAFIIA PRIENISEISKOGO KRAIA. SISTEMATICHESKII UKAZATEL' KNIG I STATEI NA RUSSKOM I INOSTRANNYKH IAZYKAKH, OPUBLIKOVANNYKH S 1612 PO 1923 G. VKLIUCHITEL'NO. [Vol. 1 not listed in sources] Vol. 2, FILOLOGIIA, CHISTYE NAUKI I PRIKLADNYE ZNANIIA. 1923. Vol. 3, ISKUSSTVA, LITERATURA, ISTORIIA, OPISATEL'NAIA GEOGRAFIIA, KARTOGRAFIIA I BIOGRAFIIA. 1930. Krasnoiarsk: Izdanie Eniseiskogo Gub. Ekon. Sov. Sibirskogo Kraev. Izdatel'stva, 1923-1930, (1923) 296+27 pp; (1930) 348+30 pp. [Russ. text; (Vol. 2) 6088 Russ., Europ. titles; (Vol. 3) 6317 Russ., Europ. titles, pub.: 1912-1923]

Siberia: General

Kozhevnikov, P. I. "UKAZATEL' STATEI 'RUDOKOPA',"
TRUDY PERMSKOI UCHENOI ARKHIVNOI KOMISSII. No. 7.
1904. [Russ. text; titles, pub.: 1898-1899, pp. 96-99]

KRASNOIARSKAIA KRAEV. MEZHVUZOVSKAIA STUDENCHESKAIA
KONFERENTSIIA 1966. MATERIALY MEZHVUZOVSKOI
STUDENCHESKOI KONFERENTSII 1966 GODA. Krasnoiarsk:
(Krasnoiar. Kraev. Sovet. Nauch.-Tekhn. O-v), 1967,
139 pp., 500 copies. [Russ. text; titles at end of
reports]

[Kudinova, N. I. comp.] BIBLIOGRAFICHESKII UKAZATEL'
TRUDOV PREPODAVATELEI DVGU (1956-1966 GG.) No. 2.
Vladivostok: (Dal'nevost. Gos. Un-t B-ka), 1967,
128 pp., 300 copies. [Russ. text; 71 titles,
pub.: 1956-1966]

Kuznetsov, E. NOVYIA IZDANIIA, KASAIUSHCHIIACIA SIBIRI.
1893, Nos. 1-3, 10, 13, 24, 27, 29-30, 35-36, 38, 40,
43, 45, 48, 50; 1894, Nos. 1, 5-11, 13, 16-17, 20,
24-25, 27, 31, 33, 36, 39, 42, 46, 50; 1895, Nos. 3,
7, 18, 21, 24, 37, 43. TOBOL'SKIIA GUBERNSKIIA
VIEDOMOSTI. 1893, 1894, 1855. [Russ. text; pub.:
1892-1895]

K[uznetsov], E. V. "UKAZATEL' STATEI, POMIESHCHENNYKH
V NEOFITSIAL'NOI CHASTI 'TOBOL'SKIKH GUBERNSKIKH
VIEDOMOSTEI' S NACHALA IKH IZDANIIA (27 APRELIA
1857 G.)," TOBOL'SKIIA GUBERNSKIIA VIEDOMOSTI.
Nos. 5-11, 15-17, 19. 1871. [Russ. text; pub.:
1857-1859, etc.]

_____.; UKAZATEL' STATEI POMESHCHENNYKH V
TOBOL'SKIKH GAZETAKH ZA 1891-1892 G. KATALOG TOB.
GUB. n. d. [Russ. text; titles pub.: 1891-1892]

Lavrov, V. M. ed. SIBIR' V 1923-1924 GODU.
Novonikolaevsk, 1925, 266 pp. [Russ. text and titles,
per.: 1923-1924]

Lezhin, P. D. "KRATKII UKAZATEL' LITERATURY O SIBIRI I
DAL'NEM VOSTOKE," DAL'NII VOSTOK. Chita, 1922.
[Russ. text; titles (appendix)]

"LITERATURA O SIBIRI I RUSSKOM DAL'NEM VOSTOKE,"
BIBLIOGR. VIESTN. T-VA 'V. A. BEREZOVSKII,' No. 246.
1918. [Russ. text; titles pp. 49-50]

Siberia: General

LITERATURA OB OMSKOI OBLASTI. PO POLUGODIIAM. 1964 G.
Omsk: (Omskaia Obl. Biblioteka im. Pushkina), 1964,
1000 copies. [Russ. text; titles pub.: 1964]

Mameev, S. N. "PERIODICHESKAIA PECHAT' SIBIRI,"
SIBIRSKII LISTOK. No. 39, 1891; No. 63, 1893.
[Russ. text; titles pub.: 1891-1893]

_____. "PERIODICHESKAIA PECHAT' SIBIRI,"
TOBOL'SKIE GUBERNSKIE VIEDOMOSTI. No. 18, 1892;
No. 72, 1896. [Russ. text; titles, pub.: 1892, 1896]

_____. MATERIALY DLIA BIBLIOGRAFII SIBIRI.
UKAZATEL' IZDANII, VYSHEDSHIKH V 1892 G. GOD PERVYI,
1892 G.--Nos. 1-15. Tobol'sk: Izd. A. A.
Syromiatnikova, 1892, 22 pp. (also as separate Nos.
3 pp. each). [Russ. text; titles pub.: 1892]

_____. UKAZATEL' KNIG O SIBIRI, VYSHEDSHIKH V
1892 G. Nos. 1-6. Tobol'sk: (Izdanie Vtoroe
Ispravlennoe), 1893, 12 pp. [Russ. text; pub.: 1892]

*Manasein, V. S. SIBIR' V KAZANSKOI PERIODICHESKOI
PECHATI PERVOI POLOVINY XIX-GO STOLETIIA
(BIBLIOGRAFICHESKII UKAZATEL'). (PRILOZHENIE K T.
XIII "SBORNIK TRUDOV IRKUTSK. GOSUD. UN-TA,"
FAKUL'TET PRAVA I MESTNOGO KHOZIAISTVA), Irkutsk: Izd.
Irkutsk. Un-t., 1927. 1-37 pp., 250 copies. [Russ.text;
151 Russ. titles, per.: 19th c.. pub.: 1811-1860]

Maslov, D. P.; M. R. Filimonov. comps. "BIBLIOGRAFIIA
NAUCHNYKH RABOT, OPUBLIKOVANNYKH V IZDANIIAKH
TOMSKOGO GOSUDARSTVENNOGO UNIVERSITETA IMENI V. V.
KUIBYSHEVA ZA 1889-1950 GG. SISTEMATICHESKII UKAZATEL',"
No. 1 [GEOGRAPHY], VOPROSY GEOGRAFII SIBIRI.
SBORNIK 3. 1953. [Russ. text; titles, pub.: 1889-
1950, pp. 305-318]

"MATERIALY DLIA BIBLIOGRAFICHESKAGO UKAZATELIA STATEI
I SOCHINENII, ZAKLIUCHAIUSHCHIKH V SEBIE SVIEDIENIIA
O PERMSKOI GUBERNII," PERMSKIE GUBERNSKIE VIEDOMOSTI.
No. 51. 1866. [Russ. text; 31 titles]

MATERIALY DLIA BIBLIOGRAFII SIBIR. UKAZATEL' IZDANII,
VYSHEDSHIKH S 1892 G. Tobol'sk: A. A. Syromiatnikov,
1892. [Russ. text; titles pub.: 1892]

Matveev, Z. N. CHTO CHITAT' O DAL'NE-VOSTOCHNOI
OBLASTI. OPYT SISTEMATICHESKOGO UKAZATELIA
LITERATURY (KLASSIFITSIROVAN PO MEZHDUNARODNOI
DESIATICHNOI SISTEME). Vladivostok, 1925, 248 pp.
[Russ. text; 3973 Russ. titles]

Siberia: General

_____. SOSTOIANIE BIBLIOGRAFICHESKOI LITERATURY DAL'NEVOSTOCHNOGO KRAIA. Vladivostok, 1926. [Russ. text]

*"MESTNAIA PECHAT' SIBIRSKOGO KRAIA V 1927 G. BIBLIOGRAFICHESKIE MATERIALY," SIBIRSKIE OGNI. (Novosibirsk) No. 5, 1927; Spisok 2, No. 3, 1928; Spisok 3, No. 6, 1928. [Russ. text; 749 Russ. titles, (No. 5) p. 37; (No. 3) pp. 37-68; (No. 6) pp. 70-103]

Migirenko, G. S. OKTIABR'. NAUKA. SIBIR. Novosibirsk: Zap.-Sib. Kn. Izd., 1967, 52 pp., 2000 copies. [Russ. text; titles, p. 52]

Mikhlina, I. I. "CHTO CHITAT' OB ORENBURGSKOI OBLASTI." ORDENONOSNOE ORENBURGZH'E. Cheliabinsk, 1968. [Russ. text; 216 titles, pp. 378-392]

Miliutin, A. N. "UKAZATEL' K SIBIRSKIM IZDANIIAM V RABOTE N. M. LISOVSKOGO 'RUSSKAIA PERIODICHESKAIA PECHAT' 1703-1900 GG.,'" TRUDY TOMSKOGO KRAEVOGO MUZEIA. Vol. 1. 1927. [Russ. text; Russ. titles pub.: up to 1900]

*NOVOSIBIRSKII PEDAGOGICHESKII INSTITUT. NAUCHNAIA SESSIIA POSVIASHCHENNAIA 50-LETIIU VELIKOI OKTIABR'SKOI SOTSIALISTICHESKOI REVOLIUTSII. No. 4. RUSSKII IAZYK. Novosibirk: (M-vo Prosveshcheniia RSFSR), 1967, 111 pp., 500 copies. [Russ. text; titles at end of reports]

Obruchev, V. A., ed. SISTEMATICHESKII UKAZATEL' VSEKH IZDANII OTDIELA, POMIESHCHENNYKH V NIKH STATEI, ZAMIETOK I MELKIKH IZVESTII I SOOBSHCHENII SDELANNYKH V OBSHCHIKH SOBRANIIAKH ZASEDANIIAKH RASPORIADITEL'NAGO KOMITETA I OTDELENII ZA SOROKALETIE 1851-1891. Irkutsk: Vost.-Sibir. Otdiel Imeratorskago Russkago Geograficheskogo Obshchestva, 1891. [Russ. text; titles pub.: 1851-1891, pp. 11 + 76 + VI + III]

OGLAVLENIE GAZETY "SIBIR'" 1875-1885. Supplement to "Sibir." 1886. [Russ. text; titles pub.: 1875-1885, p. 90]

Siberia: General

"PECHATNYE TRUDY OTDIELA," IUBILEINYI SBORNIK
ZAPADNO-SIBIRSKAGO OTDIELA IMPERATORSKAGO RUSSKAGO
GEOGRAFICHESKAGO OBSHCHESTVA. Omsk, 1902. [Russ.
text; titles pp. 147-172]

Pechenkina, V. A. comp. SVODNYI KATALOG INOSTRANNOI
PERIODICHESKOI LITERATURY, VYPISANNOI DLIA GPNTB I
BIBLIOTEK NAUCHNYKH UCHREZHDENII SIBIRSKOGO
OTDELENIIA AKADEMII NAUK SSSR NA 1968 G. Part 1.
Novosibirsk: (Gos. Publ. Nauch.-Tekhn B-ka Sib.
Otd.-niia ANSSSR), 1968, 62 pp., 430 copies. [Russ.
text]

Penkina, Z. M. ZAKASPIISKII KRAI. 1865-1885 G.
SISTEMATICHESKII SBORNIK KNIG I STATEI O
ZAKASPIISKOM KRAE I SOPREDEL'NYKH STRANAKH.
St. Petersburg: Tip. S. Mullera i I. Bogel'mana, 123 pp.
[Russ. text]

"PERIODICHESKAIA PECHAT' V SIBIRI," DAL'NII VOSTOK.
No. 79. 1893. [Russ. text]

Petriaev, E. D. ISSLEDOVATELI I LITERATORY STAROGO
ZABAIKAL'IA. OCHERKI IZ ISTORII KUL'TURY KRAIA.
Chita: Chitinskoe Knizhnoe Izdatel'stvo, 1954, 260 pp.
10,000 copies. [Russ. text; 124 Russ. titles, per.:
17th-19th cc., pp. 254-259+]

Petukhov, F. [Sulotskii, A. I] N. A. ABRAMOV (S
PERECHNEM EGO PROIZVEDENII). n. p., 1870, 12 pp.

Porshnev, G. I. KNIZHNAIA LETOPIS' [G.] IRKUTSKA ZA
GODY REVOLIUTSII. (1917-1919 GG.) Irkutsk, 1920,
75 pp. [Russ. text; 913 titles pub.: 1917-1919]

Potapova, N. K. et al. CHTO CHITAT' OB IRKUTSKOI
OBLASTI. UKAZATEL' LITERATURY. Irkutsk: Knizhnoe
Izdatel'stvo, 1958, 52 pp. [Russ. text]

Romanov, N. "PERIODICHESKAIA PECHAT' G. IRKUTSKA.
SPISOK IZDANII PERIODICHESKOI PECHATI G. IRKUTSKA S
1857 G.," SIBIRSKAIA LETOPIS'. (SIBIRKII ARKHIV).
(Irkutsk) No. 9/10. 1916. [Russ. text; 146 titles,
pub.: 1857-1916, pp. 389-448]

Rubtsova, M. D. ENISEISK. REK. UKAZATEL' (LITERATURY).
GORODA NASHEGO KRAIA. No. 5. Krasroiarsk: (Krasnoiar.
Kraev. Nauch. B-ka im. V. I. Lenina), 1967, 46 pp.,
300 copies. [Russ. text; ca.240 titles]

Siberia: General

Semenov, V. F. "OCHERK PIATIDESIATILETNEI
DIEIATEL'NOSTI ZAPADNO-SIBIRSKAGO OTDIELA
[GOSUDARSTVENNAGO] IMPERATORSKAGO RUSSKAGO
GEOGRAFICHESKAGO OBSHCHESTVA. 1877-1927," ZAPISKI
ZAPADNO-SIBIRSKAGO OTDIELA IMPERATORSKAGO RUSSKAGO
GEOGRAFICHESKAGO OBSHCHESTVA. Vol. 39. (Omsk), 1927.
[Russ. text; titles, pub.: 1877-1927]

*Semenov-Tian-Shanskii, V. P. ed. ROSSIIA. POLNOE
GEOGRAFICHESKOE OPISANIE NASHEGO OTECHESTVA. Vol. 16.
ZAPADNAIA SIBIR'. St. Petersburg: Izdanie A. F.
Devriena, 1907, 591 pp. [Russ. text and titles,
pp. 542-551]

Shcheglov, I. V. "BIBLIOGRAFICHESKII UKAZATEL' KNIG I
ZHURNAL'NYKH STATEI, KASAIUSHCHIKHSIA SIBIRI, ZA
1880 G.," SIBIR', Nos. 2,3,5,6,8,14. 1881 [Russ.
text; titles pub.: 1880]

Shchukin, N. "MATERIALY DLIA SIBIRSKOI BIBLIOGRAFII.
(ISTORIIA, GEOGRAFIIA, ETNOGRAFIIA, PUTESHESTVIIA,
STATISTIKA, TEKHNOLOGIIA I GEOGRAFICHESKIE KARTY),"
PMIATNAIA KNIGA IRKUTSKOI GUBERNII NA 1865 GOD.
Irkutsk: Izdanie Irkutskago Statisticheskago
Komiteta. [ca.1865] [Russ. text; 250 titles, pub.:
1750-1864, pp. 29-62]

*"SIBIRSKIE OGNI," ZHURN. UKAZATEL' SODERZHANIIA.
(1922-1964 GG.) Novosibirsk: Zap.-Sib. Kn. Izd.,
1967, 431 pp., 3000 copies. [Russ. text; per.:
1922-1964]

Simonov, E. OPYT BIBLIOGRAFII "OBSHCHESTVA IZUCHENIIA
KRAIA" PRI MUZEE TOBOL'SKOGO SEVERA ZA 1921 G.
Tobol'sk, 1922. [Russ. text]

Slobodskii, M. A. BIBLIOGRAFICHESKII OCHERK NARYMSKOGO
KRAIA. MATERIALY PO IZUCHENIIU SIBIRI. Vol. 4.
1933. [Russ. text; titles pp. 107-130]

Slovtsov, Iv. MATERIALY DLIA BIBLIOGRAFII TOBOL'SKOI
GUBERNII. 1800-1889. Vol. 1. PUTESHESTVIIA I
NAUCHNYE TRUDY. KALENDAR' TOBOL'SKOI GUBERNII NA
1890 GOD. Tobol'sk: Izd. Tobol'skoi Gubernskoi
Tipografii, ca.1889. [Russ. text; Russ., Europ.
titles, per.: 1800-1889, pp. 269-292]

Siberia: General

_____. STEPAN IVANOVICH GULIAEV.
BIBLIOGRAFICHESKII OCHERK. Omsk, 1891. [Russ. text;
titles pp. 67-69]

Smirnov, V. A. VVEDENIE V IZUCHENIE PRIENISEISKOGO
KRAIA. Krasnoiarsk: Biuro Kraevedeniia pri
Krasnoiarsk. Otdele Russ. Geogr. O-va, 1926, 19 pp.
[Russ. text; 111 titles]

Smyshliaev, D. D. ISTOCHNIKI I POSOBIIA DLIA
IZUCHENIIA PERMSKAGO KRAIA [SUPPL. IN: SBORNIK
PERMSKAGO ZEMSTVA No. 5/6 1882 (IV OTDIEL), 124
TITLES] (PRILOZHENIE K SBORNIKU PERMSKAGO ZEMSTVA).
Perm', 1876, 278+4 pp. [Russ. text; 1386 titles]

_____. "ISTOCHNIKI I POSOBIIA DLIA
IZUCHENIIA PERMSKAGO KRAIA," PERMSKIE GUBERNSKIE
VIEDOMOSTI. 1870--Nos. 47-59, 61-63; 1871--Nos. 8, 9,
11-17; 1873--Nos. 67, 68, 71, 72, 75-78, 81-83, 85,
90, 91; 1874--Nos. 14-18, 21, 22, 24, 29, 31, 32;
1875--Nos. 57-59. 1870-1875. [Russ. text; 1405
titles, pub.: up to 1866]

Sokolova, V. P. KEMEROVSKAIA OBLAST'. ANNOTIROVANNYI
UKAZATEL' LITERATURY. Kemerovo: Knizhnoe Izdatel'stvo
(Kemerovska Oblastnaia Biblioteka), 1955, 73 pp.
[Russ. text]

Spektor, I. V. comp. PUBLICHNAIA NAUCHNO-TEKHNICHESKAIA
BIBLIOTEKA. SVODNYI KATALOG INOSTRANNOI PERIODICHESKOI
LITERATURY, VYPISANNOI DLIA GPNTB I BIBLIOTEK
NAUCHNYKH UCHRAZHDENII SIBIRSKOGO OTDELENIIA AKADEMII
NAUK SSSR NA 1966 G. Part 2. SISTEMATICHESKII
UKAZATEL'. Novosibirsk: Gos. Publ. Nauch-Tekhn.
B-ka Sib. Otd.-niia AN SSSR), 1966, 192 pp., 400
copies. [Russ. text]

SPISOK IZDANII TROITSKOSAVSKO-KIAKHTINSKAGO OTDIELENIA
PRIAMURSKAGO OTDIELA IMPERATORSKAGO RUSSKAGO
GEOGRAFICHESKAGO OBSHCHESTVA. 1894-1904. TRUDY
TROITSKOSAVSKO-KIAKHTINSKAGO OTDIELENIIA PRIAMURSKAGO
OTDIELA IRGO. Vol. 7, No. 2. 1904. [Russ. text;
Russ. titles pub.: 1894-1904, pp. 60-64]

Siberia: General

"SPISOK IZDANII VOSTOCHNAGO INSTITUTA," SPRAVOCHNAIA KNIZHKA PO VOSTOCHNOMU INSTITUTU NA 1909 GOD. Vladivostok, 1909. [Russ. text]

"SPISOK STATEI, POMIESHCHENNYKH V KALENDARIAKH NA 1888 I 1889 G.," KALENDAR' TOBOL'SKOI GUBERNII NA 1890 GOD. Tobol'sk: Izd. Tobol'skoi G. Tipografii (B. G. P.) [ca.1889]. [Russ. text; titles pub.: 1888-1889]

SPISOK STATEI, POMIESHCHENNYKH V 'SIBIRSKOM LISTKIE' ZA VREMIA S 1-GO IIULIA 1896 PO 1-E IIULIA 1897 G. SIBIRSKII LISTOK (PRILOZHENIE). No. 51. 1897, 16 pp. [Russ. text; titles pub.: 1896-1897]

STAT'I, POMIESHCHENNYIA V 'SIBIRSKOM LISTKIE' ZA 1891-1893 G. SIBIRSKII LISTOK. (PRILOZHENIE). n. p. [ca.1893] 17 pp. [Russ. text]

Ternovskii, A. A. K BIBLIOGRAFII SIBIRI. UKAZATEL' STATEI I GLAVNIEISHIKH ZAMIETOK, KASAIUSHCHIKHSIA SIBIRI I POMIESHCHENNYKH V SIBIRSKIKH PERIODICHESKIKH IZDANIIAKH 1893 G. EZHEGODNIK TOBOL'SKAGO GUBERNSKAGO MUZEIA. Vol. 3. 1895. [Russ. text; 1559 titles, pub.: 1893, pp. 1-110]

_____. "MATERIALY DLIA BIBLIOGRAFII SIBIR. UKAZATEL' STATEI I GLAVNIEISHIKH ZAMIETOK, KASAIUSHCHIKHSIA SIBIRI I POMIESHCHENNYKH V SIBIRSKIKH PERIODICHESKIKH IZDANIIAKH 1892 G.," EZHEGODNIK TOBOL'SKAGO GUBERNSKAGO MUZEIA. No. 1. (Tobol'sk) 1893. [Russ. text; 818 Russ. titles, pub.: 1892, pp. 1-52]

UKAZATEL' LITERATURY, IZDANNOI NA IAZYKAKH NARODOV SEVERA V 1931-1933 GG., 1934; 1931-1934 GG., 1935. Leningrad, 1934-1935. [Russ. text; titles local langs.]

"UKAZATEL' STATEI GAZETY 'SIBIR'' ZA 10 LIET EE SUSHCHESTVOVANIIA," SIBIR' (GAZETA) (PRILOZHENIE K No. 27+) 1885-1886. [Russ. text; titles pub.: 1875-1885, pp. 1-85]

"UKAZATEL' STATEI, NAPECHATANNYKH V ZHURNALE ZHIZN' SIBIRI ZA 1930 G.," ZHIZN' SIBIRI. No. 5/6. 1931, 146-148 pp. [Russ. text and titles pub.: 1930]

Siberia: General

"UKAZATEL' STATEI POMIESHCHENNYKH V ZHURNALE 'ZHIZN' SIBIRI' V 1924 G." "V 1925, 1926 G.," ZHIZN' SIBIRI. No. 5-6. Novosibirsk, 1926. [Russ. text; titles pub.: 1924-1926, pp. 156-159, 159-163]

UKAZATEL' STATEI VOSTOCHNOGO OBOZRIENIIA ZA 1887 G. VOSTOCHNOE OBOZRIENIIE. No. 51-52. 1887. [Russ. text; titles pub.: 1887]

"UKAZATEL' STATEI, ZAMIETOK, RASSKAZOV, OCHERKOV, STIKHOTVORENII, VIDOV, PORTRETOV I PR. POMESHCHENNYKH V 'SIBIRSKOM NABLIUDATELE' (VYKHODIVSHEM S IANVARIA 1899 DO MAIA 1901 POD NAZVANIEM 'DOROZHNIK PO SIBIRI I AZIATSKIM VLADENIIAM ROSSII'), ZA PERVYE CHETYRE GODA EGO SUSHCHESTVOVANIIA," SIBIRSKII NABLIUDATEL'. (PRILOZHENIE). 1903. [Russ. text; titles pub.: 1899-1901, pp. I-XIV]

Vasilev, V. DORDZHI BANZAROV (S BIBLIOGRAFICHESKIM UKAZATELEM RABOT). St. Petersburg, 1890. [Russ. text; titles pp. 85-90]

Vegman, V. "PARTIINO-SOVETSKAIA PRESSA V SIBIRI," TRI GODA BOR'BY ZA DIKTATURU PROLETARIATA. Omsk, 1920. [Russ. text; titles pub.: 1919-1920]

Vorob'eva, T. A. SOSTOIANIE I PROBLEMATIKA BIBLIOGRAFII RASTITEL'NOSTI SIBIRI I DAL'NEGO VOSTOKA. (ANALIT. OBZOR). Novosibirsk: (GPNTB Sib. Otd.-niia AN SSSR), 1970, 66 pp., 600 copies. [Russ. text; 70 titles]

Zakharova, H. CHTO CHITAT' O KAMCHATKE. REK. UKAZ. LIT. Petropavlovsk-Kamchatskii: (Dal'nevost. Kn. Izd-vo), 1970, 124 pp., 1000 copies. [Russ. text; 1200 titles]

*Zdobnov, N. "BIBLIOGRAFIIA," SIBIRSKAIA SOVETSKAIA ENTSIKLOPEDIIA. Vol. 1. Novosibirsk: Sibirskoe Kraevoe Izdatel'stvo, 1929, 292-307 pp. [Russ. text; 213 Russ. titles, pp. 294-307]

*_____. "BIBLIOGRAFIIA I BIBLIOTEKOVEDENIE...," PECHAT' I REVOLIUTSIIA. Book 3. Apr.-May 1923, 227-230 pp. [Russ. text; 24 Russ. titles, pp. 228-230]

_____. SISTEMATICHESKII UKAZATEL' STATEI I ZAMETOK, POMESHCHENNYKH V ZHURNALE, SEVERNAIA AZIIA V 1925 I 1926 GG. SEVERNAIA AZIIA. Book 5/6. (Moscow) 1926, 203-214 pp. [Russ. text; 176 Russ. titles, pub.: 1925-1926]

Siberia: General

Zvenigorodskaia, E. Ia. comp. OMSK. KRATKII REK. SPISOK LITERATURY V SVIAZI S 250-LETIEM GORODA. (1716-1966). Omsk: (Omskaia Obl. Nauch. B-ka im. A. S. Pushkina), 1967, 59 pp., 2000 copies. [Russ. text; titles per.: 1716-1966]

Zvierinskii, V. "BIBLIOGRAFICHESKII UKAZATEL' SOCHINENII I STATEI O TOBOL'SKOI GUBERNII," SPISOK NASELENNYKH MIEST. Vol. 60--TOBOL'SKAIA GUBERNIIA. St. Petersburg: Izd. Tsentral'nago Statisticheskago Komiteta, 1871. [Russ. text; titles pp. CCLXVII-CCLXXII]

_____. BIBLIOGRAFICHESKII UKAZATEL' SOCHINENII I STATEI O TOMSKOI GUB. SPISKI NASELENNYKH MIEST PO SVEDYENIIAM 1859 G. Vol. 60--TOMSKAIA GUB. St. Petersburg: Izd. Tsentral'nago Statisticheskago Komiteta, 1868. [Russ. text; titles pub.: 1858-1867, pp. CXIX-CXXII]

ANTHROPOLOGY, ETHNOGRAPHY

Anuchin, D. N. MATERIALY DLIA ANTROPOLOGII VOSTOCHNOI AZII. PLEMIA AINOV. (supplement to 1st part) ISTOCHNIKI DLIA IZUCHENIIA PLEMENI AINOV. Vol. 20. IZVESTIIA OB-VA LIUBITELEI ESTESTVOZNANIIA, ANTROPOLOGII I ETNOGRAFII. 1876. [Russ. text; 141 titles, pp. 117-123]

Azadovskii, M. K. "ETNOGRAFIIA V KRAEVYKH BIBLIOGRAFICHESKIKH UKAZATELIAKH. 1918-1925 G. G." ETNOGRAFIIA. No. 1-2. Moscow-Leningrad, 1926. Russ. text; titles,pub.: 1918-1926, pp. 247-257]

_____. "ETNOGRAFIIA V SIBIRI. OBZOR ETNOGRAFICHESKIKH IZUCHENII V SIBIRI ZA 1918-1925," SEVERNAIA AZIIA. Nos. 5-6. 1926. [Russ. text; titles,pub.: 1918-1925, pp. 111-132]

Siberia: Anthropology, Ethnography

Azadovskii, Mark. "LITERATURA PO ETNOGRAFII SIBIRI ZA POSLEDNEE DESIATILETIE XIX VEKA. (PERECHEN' STATEI V PERIODICHESKIKH IZDANIIAKH 1891-1900," SIBIRSKAIA ZHIVAIA STARINA. No. 2. (Irkutsk): Izd. Vostochno-Sibirskogo Otdela Russkogo Geograficheskogo Obshchestva, 1924, (separately) 34 pp. [Russ. text; 740 Russ. titles, pub.: 1891-1900, pp. 191-222]

Bliumenfel'd, O. M. "ETNOGRAFICHESKIE EKSPEDITSII I POEZDKI, ORGANIZOVANNYE VOSTOCHNO-SIBIRSKIM OTDELOM RUSSKOGO GEOGRAFICHESKOGO OBSHCHESTVA. 1851-1926 GG.," IZVESTIIA VOSTOCHNO-SIBIRSKOGO OTD. RUSSKOGO GEOGRAFICHESKOGO OBSHCHESTVA. Vol. 50. (Irkutsk), 1926. [Russ. text; 90 titles, pub.: 1851-1926, pp. 38-41]

Bogdanov, V. V. "PECHATNYE TRUDY D. N. ANUCHINA," SBORNIK V CHEST 70-I LETIIA PROF. D. N. ANUCHINA. Moscow, 1913. [Russ. text; titles,pp. XX-XI]

*Eliasov, L. E. RUSSKII FOL'KLOR VOSTOCHNOI SIBIRI. 2 pts. CHAST' 1--SOBIRATELI I ISSLEDOVATELI RUSSKOI NARODNOI POEZII VOSTOCHNOI SIBIRI. CHAST' 2--NARODNYE PREDANIIA. Ulan Ude: (Akademiia Nauk SSSR. Sibirskoe Otdelenie. Buriatskii Kompleksnyi Nauchno-Issledovatel'skii Institut), 1958-1960, (I) 183 pp., 1000 copies; (II) 480 pp., 1000 copies. [Russ. text; ca.210 Russ. titles,(I) pp. 166-173; (II) pp. 453-459]

*Golovachev, P. SIBIR'. PRIRODA. LIUDI. ZHIZN'. Moscow: Tipografiia T-va I. D. Sytina, 1905, 2nd ed., 401 pp. [Russ. text and titles,pp. 399-400]

Iakovlev, E. K. "ETNOGRAFICHESKII OBZOR INORODCHESKOGO NASELENIIA DOLINY IUZHNOGO ENISEIA I OB'IASNITEL'NYI KATALOG ETNOGRAFICHESKOGO MUZEIA," OPISANIE MINUSINSKOGO MUZEIA. No. 4. Minusinsk, 1900. [Russ. text; Russ., foreign titles, pp. 197-212]

_____. "PERECHEN' KNIG, ZHURNALOV I GAZETNYKH STATEI O KACHINTSAKH, SAGAITSAKH, BEL'TIRAKH, KOIBALAKH I SOIOTAKH," (ETNOGRAFICHESKII OBZOR INORODCHESKAGO NASELENIIA IUZHNAGO ENISEIA). OPISANIE MINUSINSKAGO MUZEIA. No. 4. Minusinsk, 1900. [Russ. text; ca.210 titles]

Iokhel'son--Brodskaia, D. L. "K ANTROPOLOGII ZHENSHCHIN PLEMEN KRAINIAGO SIEVERA SIBIR," RUSSKII ANTROPOLOGICHESKII ZHURNAL. No. 1/2. (St. Petersburg) n. d., 1-87 pp. [Russ. text; 33 Russ., Europ. titles, pp. 86-87]

Siberia: Anthropology, Ethnography

_____. "K ANTROPOLOGII ZHENSCHIN PLEMEN KRAINEGO SEVERO-VOSTOKA SIBIR," RUSSKII ANTROPOLOGICHESKII ZHURNAL. No. 1/2. 1907. [Russ. text; 33 titles]

Ivanovskii, A. A. "NASELENIE ZEMNOGO SHARA OPYT ANTROPOLOGICHESKOI KLASSIFIKATSII," IZVESTIIA OB-VA LIUBITELEI ESTESTVOZNANIIA, ANTROPOLOGII, I ETNOGRAFII. Vol. 121. 1911. [Russ. text]

_____. OB ANTROPOLOGICHESKOM SOSTAVIE NASELENIIA ROSSII. Vol. 105. IZVESTIIA OB-VA LIUBITELEI ESTESTVOZNANIIA, ANTROPOLOGII I ETNOGRAFII. 1904. [Russ. text; Russ., foreign titles, pp. 211-287]

_____. "PERIODICHESKIE IZDANIIA SIBIRI I SREDNEI AZII (1789-1891). UKAZATEL' STATEI PO ETNOGRAFII," BIBLIOGRAFICHESKIE ZAPISKI. No. 7. Moscow, 1892. [Russ. text; 480 titles, pub.: 1789-1891, (supplement) pp. 1-14]

*_____. "UKAZATEL' ETNOGRAFICHESKIKH STATEI I ZAMIETOK SODERZHASHCHIKHSIA V SIBIRSKIKH IZDANIIAKH OT NACHALA IKH SUSHCHESTVOVANIIA," ETNOGRAFICHESKOE OBOZRENIE. 1890, Nos. 2, 3, 4; 1891, Nos. 1, 2, 3, 4; 1892, No. 1. [Russ. text; titles pub.: up to 1888, (1890 No. 2, pp.237-248; No. 3, pp. 220-230; No. 4, pp. 244-261; (1891) No. 1, pp. 246-249; No. 2, pp. 198-200; No. 3, pp. 219-226; No. 4, pp. 269-279; No. 1, pp. 39-56]

*Kamenetskaia, R. V. comp. "NOVAIA LITERATURA PO NARODAM SIBIRI I SEVERA. SOVETSKAIA ETNOGRAFIIA. No. 4. 1967, pp. 180-186. [Russ. text and titles, pub.: 1966]

*_____. "NOVAIA LITERATURA PO NARODAM SIBIRI I SEVERA," SOVETSKAIA ETNOGRAFIIA. No. 5. Moscow: "Nauka," 1968, 176-189 pp., 1990 copies. [Russ. text; ca.290 Tuvan, Buriat, Iakut, Russ. titles, pub.: 1965-1968, pp. 176-189]

Keppen, F. P. "UCHENYE TRUDY P. S. PALLASA," ZHURNAL MINISTERSTVA NARODNOGO PROSVESHCHENIIA. No. 4. 1895. [Russ. text; titles pp. 400-437]

Khoroshikh, P. P. "LITERATURA O ZNAKAKH SOBSTVENNOSTI, TAVRAKH, TAMGAKH," SIBIRSKAIA ZHIVAIA STARINA. No. 8-9. 1929. [Russ. text; 141 titles, pp. 213-218]

Siberia: Anthropology, Ethnography

Krushanov, A. I.; Iu. A. Sem; E. V. Shavkunov.
"NAUCHNYE RABOTY A. P. OKLADNIKOVA PO ISTORII DAL'NEGO
VOSTOKA, OPUBLIKOVANNYE ZA PERIOD S 1957 PO 1967 GOD,"
NARODY SOVETSKOGO DAL'NEGO VOSTOKA V DOOKTIABR'SKII
PERIOD ISTORII SSSR. [TRUDY (DAL'NEVOST. FILIAL
IM. KOMAROVA SO AN SSSR) SERIIA IST. Vol. 6]
Vladivostok, 1968, 6-7 pp. [Russ. text; 30 titles
pub.: 1957-1967]

Kuznetsova, A. A.; P. E. Kulakov. MINUSINSKIE I
ACHINSKIE INORODTSY. Krasnoiarsk: Izd. Enis. Gub.
Stat. Kom. Krasn., 1898. [Russ. text; 110 titles,
pp. 295-298]

*Levin, M. G.; L. P. Potapova. eds. NARODY SIBIRI.
Moscow-Leningrad: Izdatel'stvo Akademii Nauk SSSR
(Institut Etnografii im. Miklukho-Maklaia), 1956,
1083 pp., 5000 copies. [Russ. text; 840 Russ.,
Europ. titles, pp. 993-1016]

MATERIALY DLIA BIBLIOGR. SLOVARIA VOSTOCHNO-SIBIRSKIKH
ETNOGRAFOV. Irkutsk: Izd. "Vlast Truda," 1926,
150 copies. [Russ. text; titles pp. 194-210]

*MATERIALY DLIA BIO-BIBLIOGRAFICHESKOGO SLOVARIA
VOSTOCHNO-SIBIRSKIKH ETNOGRAFOV. PREDVARITEL'NYI
SPISOK. (VOSTOCHNO-SIBIRSKII OTDETL GOSUDARSTVENNOGO
RUSSKOGO GEOGRAFICHESKOGO OBSHCHESTVA. SEKTSIIA
ETNOGRAFII) (IZVESTIIA. Vol. 51, pp. 193-210).
Irkutsk, 1926, 20 pp., 150 copies. [Russ. text and
titles, pp. 5-20]

Mezhov, V. I. LITERATURA PO RUSSKOI GEOGRAFII,
ETNOGRAFII I STATISTIKE (ZA 1859-1880 G.) Vol. 1-9.
St. Petersburg, 1864-1884. [Russ. text; titles
pub.: 1859-1880]

*Mirotvortsev, K. "LITERATURA O KARAGASAKH," SBORNIK
TRUDOV PROFESSOROV I PREPODAVATELEI GOSUDARSTVENNOGO
IRKUTSKOGO UNIVERSITETA. No. 2. Irkutsk, 1921,
66 90 pp. [Russ. text; 32 Russ., Europ. titles,
pp. 66-90]

Petri, B. E. "BIBLIOGRAFIIA ZA 1911 GOD PO ETNOGRAFII,
RELIGII, IAZYKOZNANIIU I FOL'KLORU," ZHIVISHAIA
STARINA. Vol. 3-4. 1913. [Russ. text; 485 titles
pub.: 1911, pp. 44-468]

_____. "BIBLIOGRAFIIA ZA 1911 G., PO ETNOGRAFII,
RELIGII, IAZYKOZNANIIU I FOL'KLORU," ZHIZN' SIBIRI.
No. 3-4. 1913. [Russ. text; titles,pub.: 1911,
pp. 440-468]

Siberia: Anthropology, Ethnography

Petrova-Smagina, V. L. "ETNOGRAFIIA V TRUDAKH VOSTOCHNO-
SIBIRSKOGO OTDELA RUSSKOGO GEOGRAFICHESKOGO
OBSHCHESTVA. BIBLIOGRAFICHESKII UKAZATEL' 1851-1926 GG.,"
SIBIRSKAIA ZHIVAIA STARINA. (SBORNIK). No. 2(6)
Irkutsk, 1926. [Russ. text; 367 Russ. titles, pub.:
1851-1920, pp. 63-847]

Samoilovich, E. Ia. "BIBLIOGRAFICHESKIE MATERIALY
DLIA IZUCHENIIA RUSSKIKH SVADEBNYKH OBRIADOV V SIBIRI,"
SIBIRSKAIA ZHIVAIA STARINA. Nos. 3-4. Irkutsk: Izd.
Vostochno-Sibirskogo Otdela Russkogo Geograficheskogo
Obshchestva, 1925, (separately) 14 pp. [Russ. text;
72 titles, pp. 205-216]

Slobodskii, M. A. "LITERATURA PO ETNOGRAFII SIBIRI
ETNOLOGO-GEOGRAFICHESKIKH POVREMENNYKH IZDANIIAKH
1901-1917 GG.," CHAST' I. PERIODICHESKIE IZDANIIA
EVROPEISKOI ROSSII. SIB. ZHIVAIA STARINA. Nos. 3-4
(also separately) (Irkutsk) 1924-1925, (separately)
24 pp. [Russ. text; 342 Russ. titles, pub.: 1901-
1917, pp. 217-240]

_____. "LITERATURA PO ETNOGRAFII SIBIRI V
ISTORICHESKIKH ZHURNALAKH 1901-1917 G.," SIBIRSKAIA
ZHIVAIA STARINA. No. 7. [Separate Offprint, Irkutsk,
1928] 1928, 12 pp. [Russ. text; 145 Russ. titles,
pub.: 1901-1917, pp. 145-155]

*"SPISOK NAUCHNYKH TRUDOV L. P. POTAPOVA," IZVESTIIA
SIBIRSKOGO OTDELENIIA AKADEMII NAUK SSSR. No. 9.
SERIIA OBSHCHESTVENNYKH NAUK. No. 3. 1966, 149-154 pp.
[Russ. text; 150 Russ., Europ. titles, pub.: 1928-1965]

Vinogradov, Georgii Semenovich. KRATKII OBZOR
ETNOGRAFICHESKIKH IZUCHENII VOSTOCHNO-SIBIRSKAGO
OTDELA GOS. RUSSKOGO GEOGRAFICHESKOGO OB-VA.
Irkutsk, 1926, 41 pp. [Russ. text]

Siberia

ARCHITECTURE, ART, MUSIC

Azadovskii, Mark. comp. NARODNOE ISKUSSTVO V IZDANIIAKH VOSTOCHNO-SIBIRSKOGO OTDELA GOSUDARSTVENNOGO RUSSKOGO GEOGRAFICHESKOGO OBSHCHESTVA. 1922-1927. Irkutsk: Izdanie Vostochno-Sibir. Otdela Gos. Rus. Geografich. O-va, 1927, 31 pp., 400 copies. [Russ. text; 29 titles, pub.: 1922-1927]

Blagodatov, G. I. "MUZYKAL'NYE INSTRUMENTY NARODOV SIBIRI," SBORNIK MUZEIA ANTROPOLOGII I ETNOGRAFII. (IN-T ETNOGRAFII IM. MIKLUKHO-MAKLAIA) Vol. 18. 1958. [Russ. text; 18 titles, pp. 187-188]

*Eval'd, Z.; V. Kosovanov; S. Abaiantsev. "MUZYKA I MUZYKAL'NYE INSTRUMENTY," SIBIRSKAIA SOVETSKAIA ENTSIKLOPEDIIA. Vol. 3. Novosibirsk: Sibirskoe Kraevoe Izdatel'stvo, 1932, 577-596 pp. [Russ. text and titles, p. 596]

ISKUSSTVO ZABAIKAL'IA (BIBLIOGR. UKAZATEL'). Chita: (Chit. Obl. B-ka im. A. S. Pushkina), 1967, 19 pp., 1000 copies. [Russ. text]

Marshalkova, M. I.; V. I. Kurtseva; E. M. Gontarovskii. comps. KALENDAR' ZNAMENATEL'NYKH I PAMIATNYKH DAT PO KRASNOIARSKOMU KRAIU. ...NA 1966 GOD. Krasnoiarsk: (Krasnoiar. Kraev. B-ka), 1966, 46 pp., 1000 copies. [Russ. text; titles at end of chapters, per.: 1966]

Pivkin, V. M. ORIENTATSIIA ZHIL'KH ZDANII V USLOVIIAKH SREDNEI POLOSY SIBIRI. Moscow: (Tsentr. Nauch.-Tekh. Informatsii po Grazhd. Stroitel'stvu i Arkhitekture), 1968, 76 pp., 2000 copies. [Russ. text; 70 titles, pp. 73-75]

Sapozhnikova, K. L.; L. K. Pak. comp. KALENDAR ZNAMENATEL'NYKH I PAMIATNYKH DAT PO CHITINSKOI OBLASTI... ...NA 1966 GOD. Chita: (Chit. Obl. B-ka im. A. S. Pushkina), 1966, 67 pp., 1000 copies. [Russ. text; titles at end of articles]

Siberia: Architecture, Art, Music

"SPISOK NAUCHNYKH RABOT I. V. AREMBOVSKOGO," BIULLETEN' KOMISSII PO IZUCHENIIU CHETVERTICHNOGO PERIODA. No. 21. 1957. [Russ. text; 19 titles, pub.: 1937-1954, pp. 142-143]

ECONOMICS

ALTAISKII S-KH. INSTITUT. SBORNIK NAUCHNO-ISSLEDOVATEL'SKIKH RABOT ASPIRANTOV I MOLODYKH UCHENYKH. No. 3. Barnaul: Alt. Kn. Izd., 1967, 215 pp., 500 copies. [Russ. text; titles at end of articles]

Andronova, L. T. et al. comps. SIBIRSKAIA SEL'SKOKHOZIAISTVENNAIA NAUKA ZA 50 LET. "SPISOK NAUCH. RABOT IZD. SIB. NII SEL. KHOZ-VA ZA 1917-1967 GG." Omsk: (M-vo Sel. Khoz-va RSFSR), 1968, 274 pp., 1200 copies. [Russ. text; titles at end of articles, per.: 1917-1967]

Aniskov, V. T. KOLKHOZNOE KREST'IANSTVO SIBIRI I DAL'NOGO VOSTOKA-FRONTA 1941-1945 GG. Barnaul: Alt. Kn. Izd., 1966, 371 pp., 1000 copies. [Russ. text; ca.130 titles, per.: 1941-1945, pp. 363-369]

Azadovskii, Mark. "MATERIALY DLIA BIBLIOGRAFII SIBIRI. BIBLIOGRAFICHESKII PERECHEN' STATEI PO VOPROSAM NARODNOGO KHOZIAISTVA SIBIRI V PERIODICHESKIKH IZDANIIAKH 1891-1900 G.," OCHERKI PO ZEMLEVEDENIIU I EKONOMIKE VOSTOCHNOI SIBIRI. No. 2. (Irkutsk) (Izd. Vost.-Sib. Otd. Russ. Geogr. O-va), 1926, 15; 153-167 pp. [Russ. text; titles, pub.: 1891-1900]

Bagashev, I. MINERAL'NYE ISTOCHNIKI ZABAIKAL'IA. Moscow, 1905, 159 pp. [Russ. text; 227 Russ., Europ. titles]

Balyko, N. N.; E. N. Morachevskaia. comps. BIBLIOGRAFIIA KRASNOIARSKOGO KRAIA. (1924-1960 GG.) V 2-KH T. T. I. PRIRODNO-EKONOMICHESKIE USLOVIIA I RAZVITIE NARODNOGO KHOZIAISTVA. Krasnoiarsk: Kn. Izd., 1963, 569 pp., 500 copies. [Russ. text; titles per.: 1924-1960]

Siberia: Economics

Belous, N. Kh. VAZHNEISHIE MINERAL'NO-SYR'EVYE BAZY
SIBIRI I PUTI IKH EFFEKTIVNOGO ISPOL'ZOVANIIA.
Novosibirsk: "Nauka," 1967, 330 pp., 600 copies.
[Russ. text; 55 titles, pp. 322-327]

BLAGOVESHCHENSKII S.-KH. INSTITUT. TRUDY.... Vol. 4.
No. 2. (AGRONOMICHESKII FAKUL'TET). Khabarovsk:
Khabarovsk. Kn. Izd., 1967, 95 pp., 1000 copies.
[Russ. text; titles at end of articles]

*Bogatova, G. P. OSVOIM PRIRODNYE BOGATSTVA SIBIRI I
DAL'NEGO VOSTOKA. BESEDA O KNIGAKH. Moscow:
(Ministerstvo Kul'tury RSFSR. Gosudarstvennaia
Ordena Lenina Biblioteka SSSR imeni V. I. Lenina),
1956, 30 pp., 30,000 copies. [Russ. text and
titles, pp. 6-26]

*Bogorad, D. R. VOPROSY SPETSIALIZATSII I KOMPLEKSNOGO
RAZVITIIA NARODNOGO KHOZIAISTVA SIBIRI. Moscow:
Izdatel'stvo "Nauka," 1966, 195 pp., 2000 copies.
[Russ. text and titles, pp. 191-194]

Brok, A. A. OSNOVY TEKHNIKI BEZOPASNOSTI I
PROTIVOPOZHARNOI TEKHNIKI (OKHRANA TRUDA.) Tomsk:
Izd. Tomskogo Un-ta, 1967, 178 pp., 178 copies.
[Russ. text; 22 titles, p. 177]

CHELIABINSKAIA OBL. KONFERENTSIIA UCHENYKH. DOKLADY NA
KONFERENTSII UCHENYKH OBLASTI, POSVIASHCHENNOI 50-LETIIU
SOVETSKOI VLASTI. Cheliabinsk: "Znanie," 1968, 503 pp.
[Russ. text; titles at end of reports]

CHITINSKAIA OBL. S.-KH OPYTNAIA STANTSIIA. TRUDY.
Vol. 1. Chita: (M-vo Sel. Khoz-va RSFSR), 1967,
168 pp., 1500 copies. [Russ. text; titles at end of
articles]

Davidenkova, V. S. EKONOMICHESKAIA GEOGRAFIIA SSSR PO
RAIONAM. SIBIR'. Moscow-Leningrad: Gosudarstvennoe
Izdatel'stvo, ca.1927/1928, 112 pp. [Russ. text]

Dolzhnykh, V. N. INDUSTRIIA PRIBAIKAL'IA I EFFEKTIVNOST'
EE RAZVITIIA. (Irkutsk): Vost.-Sib. Kn. Izd., 1967,
184 pp., 2000 copies. [Russ. text; titles, pp. 181-182]

EKONOMIKA, RAZMESHCHENIE I ORGANIZATSIIA PROMYSHLENNOGO
PROIZVODSTVA SIBIRI I DAL'NEGO VOSTOKA. BIBLIOGR.
(1917-1965 GG.) Ch. 2. 1946-1965 GG. Novosibirsk:
(GPNTB Sib. Otd-niia AN SSSR), 1969, 387 pp., 700
copies. [Russ. text; 2267 titles, pub.: 1946-1965]

Siberia: Economics

Golovachev, D. BIBLIOGRAFICHESKII UKAZATEL' STATEI, KORRESPONDENTSII I ZAMIETOK V SIBIRSKOI PERIODICHESKOI PECHATI PO VOPROSU O ZOLOTOPROMYSHLENNOSTI SIBIRI. St. Petersburg: Tip. N. I. Skorokhodova, 1890, 60 pp. [Russ. text; 759 Russ. titles, pub.: 1856-1889]

Golovin, M. M. "SPISOK LITERATURY PO VOPROSU O KEDROVOM PROMYSLE I O LESOVODSTENNYKH SVOISTVAKH SIBIRSKOGO KEDRA," MATERIALY DLIA IZUCHENIIA EST.-PROIZV. SIL LES. No. 43. Petrograd, 1922. [Russ. text]

Golubnichii, V. F. POLNEE ISPOL'ZOVAT' EKONOMICHESKIE STIMULY V RAZVITII SEL'SKOGO KHOZIAISTVA. Orenburg: (Orenb. Obl. Organizatsii O-va "Znanie"), 1966, 37 pp., 1000 copies. [Russ. text; 12 titles, p. 36]

Gul'chenko, A. EKONOMICHESKAIA REFORMA I PARTIINOE RUKOVODSTVO PROMYSHLENNOST'IU I STROITEL'STVOM (V PRIMORSKOM KRAE). Vladivostok: Dal'nevost. Kn. Izd., 1968, 48 pp., 3000 copies. [Russ. text; titles pp. 47-48]

Iankevich, P. F. SOTSIAL'NYE IZMENENIIA V KREST'IANSTVE ZAPADNOI SIBIRI V PROTSESSE KOMMUNISTICHESKOGO STROITEL'STVA. Moscow, 1970. [Russ. text; ca.530 titles, pp. 275-294]

Ivanov, B. V. EDINAIA TRANSPORTNAIA SET' I VZAIMODEISTVIE RAZLICHNYKH VIDOV TRANSPORTA SSSR. Novosibirsk, 1968, 45 pp., 500 copies. [Russ. text; 12 titles at end of book]

Kalmyk, V. A.; Z. V. Kupriianova. SOTSIAL'NO-EKONOMICHESKIE PROBLEMY TRUDOVYKH RESURSOV. No. 7. Novosibirsk: (AN SSSR. Sib. Otd-nie.In-t. Ekonomiki...) 1968, 220 pp., 600 copies. [Russ. text; titles at end of articles]

Kirsanova, M. I.; G. P. Latushkina; N. N. Rechkina; N. P. Galitskaia. comps. EKONOMIKA, RAZMESHCHENIE I ORGANIZATSIIA PROMYSHLENNOGO PROIZVODSTVA SIBIRI I DAL'NEGO VOSTOKA.BIBLIOGRAFIIA 1917-1965. Ch. 1. LITERATURA, IZDANNAIA V 1917-1945 GG. Novosibirsk: (Gos. Nauch.-Tekhn. Biblioteka Sib. Otdeleniia AN SSSR. Otd. Nauchn. Bibliogr.), 1968, 452 pp., 650 copies. [Russ. text; titles,per.: 1917-1945]

Kolobkov, M. N. KEMEROVSKAIA OBLAST'. (PRIRODNYE I EKONOMICHESKIE RESURSY I PERSPEKTIVY RAZVITIIA KHOZIAISTVA). Novosibirsk, 1950, 204 pp. [Russ. text; 205 titles]

Siberia: Economics

Konoplev, I. I. PROMYSHLENNOST' AMURSKOI OBLASTI V RAZVITII. Khabarovsk: Kn. Izd., 1966, 143 pp., 10,000 copies. [Russ. text; titles, pp. 141-142]

Kosovanov, V. P. "SPISOK VAZHNEISHEI EKONOMICHESKOI LITERATURY, KASAIUSHCHEISIA PRIENISEISKOGO KRAIA ZA PIATILETIE 1917-1921 GG.," VESTNIK ENISEISKOGO EKONOMICHESKOGO SOVESHCHANIIA. Krasnoiarsk, 1921. [Russ. text; titles, per.: 1917-1921]

Kozicheva, N. A.; S. M. Meiler; N. A. Shokina: A. M. Shtutina. comp. CHTO CHITAT' O SIBIRI I DAL'NEM VOSTOKE. UKAZATEL' LITERATURY. Moscow: Gosudarstvennoe Izdatel'stvo Kul'tprosveticheskoi Literatury, 1956, 34 pp. [Russ. text; 227 titles]

*Krotov, V. A. "EKONOMIKO-GEOGRAFICHESKIE PROBLEMY VOSTOCHNOI SIBIRI," SIBIRSKII GEOGRAFICHESKII SBORNIK. No. 4. 1965, 6-41 pp. [Russ. text; 51 Russ. titles, pp. 40-41]

* _____.; M. I. Pomus; G. D. Rikhter; V. B. Sochava. ed. VOSTOCHNAIA SIBIR'. EKONOMIKO-GEOGRAFICHESKAIA KHARAKTERISTIKA. Moscow: Gosudarstvennoe Izdatel'stvo Geograficheskoi Literatury, 1963, 888 pp., 4000 copies. [Russ. text and titles, pp. 866-886]

*Khakhlov, V. A. ed. PRIRODA I EKONOMIKA PRIVASIUGANIIA. Tomsk: Izd. Tomskogo Un-ta, 1966, 347 pp., 1000 copies. [Russ. text; ca.320 Russ. titles, pp. 333-345]

Mamieev, S. N. BIBLIOGRAFIIA ZHELIEZNO-DOROZHNAGO VOPROSA V SIBIRI. UKAZATEL' STATEI, KORRESPONDENTSII I ZAMIETOK, POMESHCHENNYKH V SIBIRSKIKH PERIODICHESKIKH IZDANIIAKH I SBORNIKAKH ZA 1857-1894 GG. Tobol'sk, 1895, IV+56 pp. [Russ. text; 969 titles, pub.: 1857-1894]

MATERIALY BURIATSKOGO REGIONAL'NOGO SOVESHCHANIIA KONFERENTSII PO RAZVITIIU PROIZVODITEL'NYKH SIL VOSTOCHNOI SIBIRI. Ulan Ude: (Akademiia Nauk SSSR. Sibirskoe Otdelenie.Buriatskii Kompleksnyi Nauchno-Issledovatel'skii Institut), 1959, 658 pp. [Russ. text and titles, at end of reports]

METODICHESKIE POLOZHENIIA PO OPTIMAL'NOMU OTRASLEVOMU PLANIROVANIIU V PROMYSHLENNOSTI. Novosibirsk: "Nauka" Sib. Otd-nie, 1967, 174 pp., 5900 copies. [Russ. text; 104 titles, pp. 167-173]

Siberia: Economics

Nedeshev, A. A.; I. M. Osokin; V. V. Vorob'ev.
VOSTOCHNOE ZABAIKAL'E. Irkutsk-Chita: Vost.-Sib.
Kn. Izd., 1968, 188 pp., 1500 copies. [Russ. text;
titles pp. 182-187]

OCHERK NASELENIIA I KHOZIAISTVA ZAPADNOI SIBIRI.
Novosibirsk, 1965, 95 pp. [Russ. text; titles at end
of articles]

OMSKII S.-KH. INSTITUT IM. S. M. KIROVA. TRUDY. Vol. 69.
No. 2. SBORNIK ASPIRANTSKIKH RABOT ZEMLEUSTROITEL'NOGO
FAKUL'TETA. Omsk: (M-vo Sel. Khoz-va SSSR....),
1967, 38 pp., 500 copies. [Russ. text; titles at end
of articles]

OMSKII S.-KH INSTITUT IM. S. M. KIROVA. TRUDY. Vol. 69.
No. 5. Omsk:(M-vo Sel. Khoz-va SSSR...), 1967,
103 pp., 500 copies. [Russ. text; titles at end of
articles]

Patrushev, V. D. METODIKA IZUCHENIIA BIUDZHETOV VREMENI
TRUDIASHCHIKHSIA. SBORNIK MATERIALOV. Novosibirsk:
(AN SSSR. Sib. Otd-nie. In-t Ekonomiki i Organizatsii
Prom. Proizvodstva), 1966, 299 pp., 510 copies.
[Russ. text; titles at end of works]

*Pomus, M. I. ZAPADNAIA SIBIR' (EKONOMIKO-GEOGRAFICHESKAIA
KHARAKTERISTIKA). Moscow: Gosizdat Geograficheskoi
Literatury, 1956, 643 pp., 5000 copies. [Russ. text
and titles, pp. 624-641]

[Potapova, N. K.] RAZVITIE PROIZVODITEL'NYKH SIL
VOSTOCHNOI SIBIRI. (MATERIALY K BIBLIOGR.) Irkutsk:
(Vost.-Sib. Sovet Koordinatsii i Planirovaniia Nauch.-
Issled. Rabot po Gumanitarnym Naukam. Irkut. Gos.
Un-t im. Zhdanova. Vost.-Sib. Otd-nie Geogr. O-va SSSR),
1970, 101 pp., 1000 copies. [Russ. text; 1200 titles,
pub.: after 1917]

PRIMORSKAIA KRAEV. NAUCHNO-TEKHNICHESKAIA KONFERENTSIIA
PO NAUCHNOI ORGANIZATSII TRUDA, 2-IA. MATERIALY....
Vladivostok: (Dal'nevost. TSBTI DV Filial NII Truda),
1968, 116 pp., 3000 copies. [Russ. text; 40 titles,
pp. 113-115]

*SEL'SKO-KHOZIAISTVENNAIA LITERATURA ZAPSIBKRAIA ZA 1 POL.
1932 G. ALFAVITNYI UKAZATEL'. SOTSIALISTICHESKOE
ZEMLEDELIA. No. 8/9. 1932. 120 pp. [Russ. text;
116 Russ. titles, pub.: 1932, pp. 3-4, 93-96]

Siberia: Economics

SEL'SKOE KHOZIAISTVO ZABAIKAL'IA. (BIBLIOGR. UKAZATEL').
Chita: (Chit. Obl. B-ka im. A. S. Pushkina), 1967,
11 pp., 1000 copies. [Russ. text]

SHAGI ZABAIKAL'SKOI INDUSTRII. (BIBLIOGR. UKAZATEL').
Chita: (Chit. Obl. B-ka im. A. S. Pushkina), 1967,
8 pp., 1000 copies. [Russ. text]

Shinderman, B. M. ANALIZ RENTABEL'NOSTI PROMYSHLENNOGO
PREDPRIIATIIA. Sverdlovsk: (MV i SSO RSFSR.
Ural'skii Gos. Un-t im. A. M. Gor'kogo), 1966, 40 pp.,
500 copies. [Russ. text; 13 titles, p. 31]

Shotskii, V. P. PRIRODNYE USLOVIIA
SEL'SKOKHOZIAISTVENNOGO PROIZVODSTVA I
ESTESTVENNOISTORICHESKIE RAIONY IRKUTSKOI OBLASTI.
(AKAD. NAUK. SSSR. VOST-SIB. FILIAL. MATERIALY PO
S.-KH. RAIONIROVANIIU IRKUT. OB. No. 1). Irkutsk:
1956. [Russ. text; 179 titles, pp. 119-127]

SIBIRSKII NAUCHNO-ISSLEDOVATEL'SKII INSTITUT SEL'SKOGO
KHOZIAISTVA SBORNIK NAUCHNYKH RABOT. No. 14. Omsk:
(M-vo Sel. Khoz-va RSFSR), 1968, 222 pp., 1000
copies. [Russ. text; titles at end of articles]

SISTEMA VEDENIIA SEL'SKOGO KHOZIAISTVA DAL'NEGO VOSTOKA.
Khabarovsk, 1968. [Russ. text; 66 titles, pp. 522-524]

Smirnov, V. D.; A. A. Grishin. OPTIMAL'NOE PLANIROVANIE
SEL'SKOKHOZIAISTVENNOGO PROIZVODSTVA V SOVKHOZAKH.
Novosibirsk: "Nauka," 1968, 142 pp., 600 copies.
[Russ. text; 32 titles, pp. 137-140]

*Stepichev, I. S. POBEDA LENINSKOGO KOOPERATIVNOGO
PLANA V VOSTOCHNO-SIBIRSKOI DEREVNE. Irkutsk: Vost.-Sib.
Kn. Izd., 1966, 742 pp., 2000 copies. [Russ. text and
titles, pp. 735-741]

Tarasov, G. L. VOSTOCHNAIA SIBIR'. Moscow, 1964.
[Russ. text; 47 titles, pp. 228-229]

Ugarov, A. N. VOPROSY EKONOMIKI I ORGANIZATSII
SEL'SKOKHOZIAISTVENNOGO PROIZVODSTVA. Irkutsk: Vost.-Sib.
Kn. Izd., 1967, 246 pp., 500 copies. [Russ. text;
titles, pp. 180-181]

Vereshchagin, G. Iu. "OPYT SVODA LITERATURY PO BAIKALU
I EGO POBEREZH'IU," TRUDY KOMISSII PO IZUCHENIIU
OZERA BAIKALA. Vol. 2. Leningrad, 1929. [Russ.
text; 884 titles, pub.: up to 1926, pp. 187-222]

Siberia: Economics

VOPROSY EKONOMIKI I ORGANIZATSII SOTSIALISTICHESKOGO
PROIZVODSTVA. No. 2. Tomsk: Izd. Tomskogo Un-ta,
1967, 197 pp., 700 copies. [Russ. text; titles at
end of articles]

ZAPADNO-SIBIRSKII EKONOMICHESKII RAION. Moscow: "Nauka,"
1967, 251 pp., 2500 copies. [Russ. text; titles,
pp. 245-246]

*Zaslavskaia, T. I. ed. SOTSIAL'NYE PROBLEMY TRUDOVYKH
RESURSOV SELA. (NA MATERIALAKH ZAPADNOI SIBIRI).
Novosibirsk: Izdatel'stvo "Nauka," Sibirskoe
Otdelenie, 1968, 348 pp., 500 copies. [Russ. text;
Russ. titles at end of articles]

*Zhilinskii, A. A. ROSSIIA NA SIEVERIE (K OPISANIIU
ZHIZNI I DIEIATEL'NOSTI M. K. SIDOROVA). Arkhangel'stk:
Izdanie Komiteta po Uviekoviecheniiu Pamiati M. K.
Sidorova, 1918, 155 pp. [Russ. text and titles,
pp. 147-150]

EDUCATION

Lushnikov, M. "UKAZATEL' STATEI PO VOPROSAM KUL'TURNO-
PROSVETITEL'NOI DEIATEL'NOSTI, POMESHCHENNYKH V
ZHURNALAKH I GAZETAKH, IZDANNYKH SIBIRSKOI
POTREBITEL'SKOI KOOPERATSIEI V 1917-18 GG. I V
IANVARE-APRELE 1919 G.," SIBIRSKAIA KOOPERATSIIA.
No. 4/6. 1919. [Russ. text; titles pp. 156-182]

NOVOSIBIRSKII PEDAGOGICHESKII INSTITUT. XI NAUCHNAIA
SESSIIA... POSVIASHCHENNAIA VELIKOI OKTIABR'SKOI
SOTSIALISTICHESKOI REVOLIUTSII. No. 8. FILOSOFIIA.
Novosibirsk: (M-vo Prosveshcheniia RSFSR), 1967,
42 pp., 500 copies. [Russ. text; titles at end of
reports]

NOVOSIBIRSKII PEDAGOGICHESKII INSTITUT. XI NAUCHNAIA
SESSIIA. No. 10. PEDAGOGIKA. Novosibirsk: (M-vo
Prosveshcheniia RSFSR), 1968, 158 pp., 500 copies.
[Russ. text; titles at end of reports]

Siberia: Education

Shamakhov, F. F. NARODNOE OBRAZOVANIE V ZAPADNOI SIBIRI V KONTSE XIX--PERVYE GODY XX VV. (S 90-KH GODOV DO PERVOI RUSSKOI REVOLIUTSII. 1905-1907 GG.) UCHEN. ZAPISKI. Vol. 15. (TOMSKII PED. IN-T). 1956. [Russ. text; 300 titles, per.: 1890-1907, pp. 92-103]

*_____. SHKOLA ZAPADNOI SIBIRI MEZHDU DVUMIA BURZHUAZNO-DEMOKRATICHESKIMI REVOLIUTSIIAMI. (1907-1917 GG.) Tomsk: Izdatel'stvo Tomskogo Universiteta, 1966, 192 pp., 500 copies. [Russ. text; 157 Russ. titles, per.: 1907-1917, pp. 186-191]

_____. SHKOLA ZAPADNOI SIBIRI V KONTSE XIX-NACHALE XX VEKOV. Tomsk: (Tomskii Gos. Ped. In-t), 1957, 268 pp. [Russ. text and titles, per.: end XIX c.-begin. XX c., scattered]

Ternovskii, A. A. BIBLIOGRAFIIA I IKONOGRAFIIA TOBOL'SKAGO GUVERNSKAGO MUZEIA. EZHEGODNIK TOBOL'SKAGO GUBERNSKAGO MUZEIA. Vol. 2. 1894. [Russ. text; titles, pp. 1-33]

*"UKAZATEL' STATEI, POMESHCHENNYKH V ZHURNALE PROSVESHCHENIE SIBIRI ZA 1931 GOD," PROSVESHCHENIE SIBIRI. No. 12, 1931, I-VIII pp.; No. 8, 1933, 66-67 pp.; No. 16/18, 1933, 105-112 pp. [Russ. text and titles, pub.: 1931-1933]

Usova, A. V. ORGANIZATSIIA SAMOSTOIATEL'NOI RABOTY PO KURSU FIZIKI V VOS'MILETNEI SHKOLE. Cheliabinsk, 1968. [Russ. text; 85 titles, pp. 232-235]

Vasil'eva, N. A. comp. CHELIABINSKII POLITEKHNICHESKII INSTITUT. PECHATNYE RABOTY PROFESSORSKO-PREPODAVATEL'SKOGO SOSTAVA....ZA 1966 GOD. Cheliabinsk, 1967, 64 pp., 150 copies. [Russ. text]

Vradii, V. P. "GLAVNEISHAIA LITERATURA O SIBIRSKIKH MUZEIAKH," ORUZHEINYI SBORNIK. (St. Petersburg), No. 4. 1908. [Russ. text; 107 titles]

Siberia:

GEOGRAPHY

*Agafonov, Nikolai Timofeevich. OSNOVNYE PROBLEMY
FORMIROVANIIA PROMYSHLENNYKH KOMPLEKSOV V VOSTOCHNYKH
RAIONAKH SSSR. Part 1. OSOBENNOSTI RAZVITIIA I
RAZMESHCHENIIA PROMYSHLENNOSTI. Leningrad:
Izdatel'stvo Leningradskogo Universiteta, 1970, 168 pp.,
1280 copies. [Russ. text; ca.260 Russ. titles, per.:
1920s-1960s, pp. 159-167]

Alekseev, Mikhail P. SIBIR' V IZVESTIIAKH ZAPADNO-
EVROPEISKIKH PUTESHESTVENNIKOV I PISATELEI XIII-XVII V.
Irkutsk: Oblastnoe Izdatel'stvo, 1941, 2nd ed.,
612 pp. [Russ. text]

*Andreev, A. I; A. I. Baklanova. "TRUDY G. F. MILLERA O
SIBIRI," Miller, G. F. ISTORIIA SIBIRI. V TREKH
TOMAKH. Vol. 1. Moscow-Leningrad: Izdatel'stvo
Akademii Nauk SSSR, 1937, 5000 copies. [Russ. text;
Russ., Europ. titles, survey, inc. mss., pp. 57-144;
543-569]

Arkhipov, A. I. [et al.] ZAPADNO-SIBIRSKAIA RAVNINA.
Moscow, 1970. [Russ. text; ca.600 titles, pp. 259-278]

*"BAIKAL," ENTSIKLOPEDICHESKII SLOVAR', Vol. 2A.
St. Petersburg: F. A. Brokgauz, I. A. Efron, 1891,
715-717 pp. [Russ. text; Russ., Europ. titles, p. 717]

*"BAIKAL'SKIIA GORY," ENTSIKLOPEDICHESKII SLOVAR'.
Vol. 2A. St. Petersburg: F. A. Brokgauz, I. A. Efron,
1891, 717-718 pp. [Russ. text; Russ., Europ. titles,
p. 718]

*"BAIKAL'SKOE OZERO," VOENNAIA ENTSIKLOPEDIIA. Vol. 4.
St. Petersburg: T-vo I. D. Sytina, 1931, 344-345 pp.
[Russ. text and titles, p. 345]

*Beliavskii, P. E. "IRTYSH," ENTSIKLOPEDICHESKII SLOVAR',
Vol. 13. St. Petersburg: F. A. Brokgauz, I. A. Efron,
1894, 347-355 pp. [Russ. text and titles, p. 355]

Siberia: Geography

Bielkin, D. Z.; A. V. Trirogov. VOSTOCHNO-SIBIRSKII
OTDIEL IMPERATORSKAGO RUSSKAGO GEOGRAFICHESKAGO
OBSHCHESTVA. 1891-1901. SISTEMATICHESKII UKAZATEL'
VSIEKH IZDANII OTDIELA... Irkutsk: Parovaia
Tipo-Litografiia P. I. Makushina, 1901, 22 pp. [Russ.
text; 240 titles, pub.: 1891-1901]

*BIBLIOGRAFIIA DAL'NEVOSTOCHNOGO KRAIA. Vol. 1.
FIZICHESKAIA GEOGRAFIIA. Moscow: Izdatel'stvo
Vsesoiuznaia Assotsiatsiia S.-kh. Bibliografii, 1935,
377 pp., 2000 copies. [Russ. text; 2106 Russ.
titles, per.: 1890-1931, pp. 1-284]

*Boiarshinova, Z. Ia. NASELENIE ZAPADNOI SIBIRI DO
NACHALA RUSSKOI KOLONIZATSII (VIDY KHOZIAISTVENNOI
DEIATEL'NOSTI I OBSHCHESTVENNYI STROI MESTNOGO
NASELENIIA). n.p., Izdatel'stvo Tomskogo Universiteta,
1960, 151 pp., 1000 copies. [Russ. text and titles,
pp. 149-150]

*Borzova, A. A. "SIBIR' (GEOGRAFICHESKII OBZOR),"
KRITICHESKOE OBOZRENIE. No. 7. 1908, 5 pp. [Russ.
text; 5 Russ. titles, pub.: 1892-1908]

Chekanovskii, A. L. SBORNIK NEOPUBLIKOVANNYKH MATERIALOV
A. L. CHEKANOVSKOGO: STAT'I O EGO NAUCHNOI RABOTE.
Irkutsk: Irkutskoe Knizhnoe Izdatel'stvo, 1962,
364 pp., 2000 copies. [Russ. text; Russ., Polish,
Europ. titles (incl. archives), pp. 321-351]

Gedroits, K. I. comp. VOSTOCHNO-SIBIRSKII OTDIEL
IMPERATORSKAGO RUSSKAGO GEOGRAFICHESKAGO OBSHCHESTVA.
1901-1911. SISTEMATICHESKII UKAZATEL' VSIEKH IZDANII
OTDIELA... Irkutsk: I. P. Kazantsev, 1912, 15 pp.
[Russ. text]

GEOGRAFICHESKOE OBSHCHESTVO SSSR. CHELIABINSKII OTDEL.
DOKLADY NAUCHNO-KRAEVEDCHESKOI KONFERENTSII. No. 2.
Cheliabinsk: Geograficheskoe Obshchestvo SSSR, 1966,
133 pp., 800 copies. [Russ. text; titles at end of
reports]

GEOGRAFICHESKOE OBSHCHESTVO SSSR. PRIMORSKII FILIAL.
Zapiski. No. 25. Vladivostok: Dal'nevost. Kn. Izd.,
1966, 175 pp., 1000 copies. [Russ. text; titles at
end of articles]

*GEOGRAFICHESKOE OBSHCHESTVO SSSR. ZABAIKAL'SKII FILIAL.
Vol. 2. No. 1. Chita: Vost.-Sib. Kn. Izd. Chit.
Otd-nie, 1966, 112 pp., 600 copies. [Russ. text;
titles at end of articles]

Siberia: Geography

*GEOGRAFICHESKOE OBSHCHESTVO SSSR. ZABAIKAL'SKII FILIAL. IZVESTIIA... Vol. 2. No. 2. Chita: (AN SSSR), 1966, 103 pp., 600 copies. [Russ. text; titles at end of articles]

*GEOGRAFICHESKOE OBSHCHESTVO SSSR. ZABAIKAL'SKII FILIAL. IZVESTIIA. Vol. 2. No. 3. Chita: (AN SSSR. Geogr. O-vo SSSR), 1966, 140 pp., 600 copies. [Russ. text; titles at end of articles]

*GEOGRAFICHESKOE OBSHCHESTVO SSSR. ZABAIKAL'SKII FILIAL. IZVESTIIA. Vol. 2. No. 4. Chita: Izd. Zabaikal. Filiala Geogr. O-va SSSR, 1966, 112 pp., 600 copies. [Russ. text; titles at end of articles]

*GEOGRAFICHESKOE OBSHCHESTVO SSSR. ZABAIKAL'SKII FILIAL. IZVESTIIA. Vol. 4. No. 2. Chita: Izd. Zabaikal. Filiala Geog. O-va SSSR, 1968, 115 pp., 800 copies. [Russ. text; titles at end of articles]

*GEOGRAFICHESKOE OBSHCHESTVO SSSR. ZABAIKAL'SKII FILIAL. IZVESTIIA. Vol. 4. No. 3. Chita: Izd. Zabaikal. Filiala Geogr. O-va SSSR, 1968, 117 pp., 700 copies. [Russ. text; titles at end of articles]

*GEOGRAFICHESKOE OBSHCHESTVO SSSR. ZABAIKAL'SKII FILIAL. IZVESTIIA. Vol. 4. No. 4. Chita: Izd. Zabaikal. Filiala Geogr. O-va SSSR, 1968, 99 pp., 700 copies. [Russ. text; titles at end of articles]

*GEOGRAFICHESKOE OBSHCHESTVO SSSR. ZABAIKAL'SKII FILIAL. IZVESTIIA. Vol. 4. No. 5. Chita: Izd. Zabaikal. Filiala Geogr. O-va SSSR, 1968 (Vyp. Dan 1969), 95 pp., 700 copies. [Russ. text; titles at end of articles]

GEOGRAFICHESKIE OSOBENNOSTI OSVOENIIA TAEZHNYKH RAIONOV ZAPADNO-SIBIRSKOI NIZMENNOSTI. (MATERIALY OB'-IRTYSH. EKSPEDITSII IN-TA GEOGRAFII SIBIRI I DAL'NEGO VOSTOKA. No. 1.) 1969. [Russ. text; ca.140 titles, pp. 263-269]

*GEOGRAFIIA NASELENIIA VOSTOCHNOI SIBIRI. Moscow: Izdatel'stvo Akademii Nauk SSSR, 1962, 164 pp., 2000 copies. [Russ. text and titles, scattered]

*GEOGRAFIIA ZAPADNOI SIBIRI. NOVOSIBIRSKII GOSUDARSTVENNYI PEDAGOGICHESKII INSTITUT. UCHENYE ZAPISKI. No. 21. Novosibirsk: Zapadno-Sibirskoe Knizhnoe Izdatel'stvo, 1965, 204 pp., 1000 copies. [Russ. text and titles, at end of articles]

Siberia: Geography

Gerasimov, A. S. "UKAZATEL' MATERIALOV PO KARTOGRAFII VOSTOCHNOI SIBIRI I SMEZHNYKH S NEIU TERRITORII." REZUL'TATY DEIATEL'NOSTI VOSTOCHNO-SIBIRSKOGO OTDELA RUSSKOGO GEOGRAFICHESKOGO OBSHCHESTVA V OBLASTI KARTOGRAFII ZA 75 LET. 1851-1926 GG. IZVESTIIA VOSTOCHNO-SIBIRSKOGO OTDELA RUSSKOGO GEOGRAFICHESKOGO OBSHCHESTVA. Vol. 50. No. 2. (Irkutsk) 1928. [Russ. text; 130 + 173 titles, pub.: 1851-1926]

*Granina, A. N. "BIBLIOGRAFICHESKIE RABOTY V VOSTOCHNO-SIBIRSKOM OTDELE GEOGRAFICHESKOGO OBSHCHESTVA SSSR. (VSORGO). (OBZOR)," IZ ISTORII KNIGI, BIBLIOTECH. DELA I BIBLIOGRAFII V SIBIRI. Novosibirsk, 1969. [Russ. text]

Gusev, O. K.; S. K. Ustinov. PO SEVERNOMU BAIKALU I PRIBAIKAL'IU. (PUTEVODITEL' I MARSHRUTY). Moscow: "Fizkul'tura i Sport," 1966, 103 pp., 17000 copies. [Russ. text; titles at end of book]

[Iakhnenko, V. I. comp.] FIZICHESKAIA GEOGRAFIIA IRKUTSKOI OBLASTI. (BIBLIOGRAFIIA). No. 2. (1951-1962). Irkutsk: Vost. Sib. Kn. Izd. (In-t Geografii Sibiri i Dal'nego Vostoka), 1965, 140 pp., 1100 copies. [Russ. text; 1139 titles]

INSTITUT GEOGRAFII SIBIRI I DAL'NEGO VOSTOKA. DOKLADY. No. 11. Irkutsk: (Akademiia Nauk SSSR. Sibirskoe Otdelenie), 1966, 83 pp., 1100 copies. [Russ. text; 103+ scattered Russ., French titles, at end of articles, pp. 74-81]

INSTITUT GEOGRAFII SIBIRI I DAL'NOGO VOSTOKA. No. 14. Irkutsk: (AN SSSR. Sib. Otd-nie), 1967, 92 pp., 1200 copies. [Russ. text; titles at end of articles]

INSTITUT GEOGRAFII SIBIRI I DAL'NEGO VOSTOKA. DOKLADY. No. 18. Irkutsk: (AN SSSR. Sib. Otd.-nie), 1968, 84 pp., 1200 copies. [Russ. text; titles at end of articles]

INSTITUT GEOGRAFII SIBIRI I DAL'NOGO VOSTOKA. DOKLADY. No. 19. Irkutsk: (AN SSSR. Sib. Otd-nie), 1968, 83 pp., 1200 copies. [Russ. text; titles at end of articles]

INSTITUT GEOGRAFII SIBIRI I DAL'NOGO VOSTOKA. DOKLADY. No. 20. Irkutsk: (AN SSSR. Sib. Otd.-nie), 1968, 80 pp., 1200 copies. [Russ. text; titles at end of articles]

Siberia: Geography

IRKUTSKII PEDAGOGICHESKII INSTITUT. UCHENYE ZAPISKI.
No. 24. Ch. 2. SERIIA GEOGRAFICHESKAIA. (Irkutsk)
Vost.-Sib. Kn. Izd., 1967, 118 pp., 700 copies.
[Russ. text; titles at end of articles]

*Kaufman, A. "AMURSKAIA OBLAST'," ENTSIKLOPEDICHESKII
SLOVAR'. DOPOLNITEL'NYI TOM I. St. Petersburg: F. A.
Brokgauz, I. A. Efron, 1905, 102-104 pp. [Russ. text
and titles, p. 104]

Khomentovskii, A. S. ed. VOPROSY GEOGRAFII DAL'NEGO
VOSTOKA. SB. 8. Khabarovsk: Khabarovsk. Kn. Izd.,
1967, 302 pp., 1000 copies. [Russ. text; titles at
end of articles]

Khoroshikh, P. P. LITERATURA K TURISTSKIM EKSKURSIIAM
PO PRIBAIKAL'IU. Irkutsk: Izdatel'stvo Vostochno-
Sibirskogo Otdela Russkogo Geograficheskogo Obshchestva,
1929, 16 pp. [Russ. text and titles]

Kirillov, M. V. "KRATKAIA KHARAKTERISTIKA ISTORII
FORMIROVANIIA SOVREMENNYKH FIZIKO-GEOGRAFICHESKIKH
USLOVII V RAIONE G. KRASNOIARSKA," UCHENYE ZAPISKI.
Vol. 8. (Krasniarsk: Ped. In-t), 1957. [Russ. text;
36 titles, pp. 56-57]

Kirillova, G. K.; Iu. A. Shcherbekov. "VLIIANIE
EKSPOZITSII NA PRIRODNYE USLOVIIA SKLONOV V GORAKH
IUZHNOI SIBIRI," UCHEN. ZAP. (PERM. UN-T). No. 196.
1968. [Russ. text; 45 titles, pp. 42-44]

*Kunitsyn, L. F. "OSVOENIE ZAPADNOI SIBIRI I PROBLEMY
VZAIMODEISTVIIA PRIRODNYKH KOMPLEKSOV I TEKHNICHESKIKH
SISTEM," IZV. AN SSSR. SERIIA GEOGR. No. 1. n. p.
"Nauka," 1960, 37-48 pp., 1610 copies. [Russ. text;
30 Russ. titles, pub.: 1946-1969, p. 48]

[Kurbatova, V. S. comp.] KATALOG IZDANII INSTITUTA
GEOGRAFII SIBIRI I DAL'NEGO VOSTOKA. (1959-1968 GG.)
Irkutsk: (In-t Geografii Sibiri i Dal'nego Vostok),
1968, 20 pp., 400 copies. [Russ. text; 60 titles]

Ladnov, I. K. OPISANIE KARTOGRAFICHESKAGO MATERIALA,
NAKHODIASHCHEGO V KAZENNYKH UCHREZHDENNIIAKH
ZABAIKAL'SKOI, AMURSKOI I PRIMORSKOI OBLASTI I U
UCHASTNYKH LITS. (PRILOZHENIE 3 K VYP. 1, TRUDY
AMURSKOI EKSPEDITSII). St. Petersburg, 1911. [Russ.
text]

Siberia: Geography

*Luchinskii, G. "SIBIR'," ENTSIKLOPEDICHESKII SLOVAR'.
Vol. 29 A. St. Petersburg: F. A. Brokgauz, I. A.
Efron, 1900, 748-814 pp. [Russ. text and titles,
pp. 813-814]

*Lutskii, S. L. GEOGRAFICHESKIE OCHERKI RUSSKOI TAIGI.
Moscow: Ogiz, Gosudarstvennoe Izdatel'stvo
Geograficheskoi Literatury, 1947, 183 pp., 10,000
copies. [Russ. text; 77 Russ. titles, pp. 180-182]

*Mikhailov, N. I. SIBIR'. FIZIKO-GEOGRAFICHESKII
OCHERK. Moscow: Gosudarstvennoe Izdatel'stvo
Geograficheskoi Literatury, 1956, 382 pp., 15,000
copies. [Russ. text and titles, pp. 370-372]

*Murzaev, E. M.; V. V. Obruchev; G. E. Riabukhin.
VLADIMIR AFANAS'EVICH OBRUCHEV. ZHIZN' I DEIATEL'NOST'.
Moscow: Izdatel'stvo Akademii Nauk SSSR, 1959, 302 pp.,
15000 copies. [Russ. text and titles, pp. 295-301]

NAUCHNOE SOVESHCHANIE GEOGRAFOV SIBIRI I DAL'NEGO
VOSTOKA 3-E OMSK 1966 MATERIALY. No. 1. Omsk: Zap.-
Sib. Kn. Izd., 1966, 118 pp., 500 copies. [Russ. text;
titles at end of reports]

Obruchev, V. A. "OBZOR GEOLOGICHESKOI I GEOGRAFICHESKOI
LITERATURY PO IUGO-ZAP. ZABAIKAL'IU (SELENGINSKOI
DAURII)," OROGRAFICHESKII I GEOLOGICHESKII OCHERK
IUGO-ZAPADNAGO ZABAIKAL'IA. Part 1. (GEOLOGICH.
ISSLED. I RAZVED. RABOTY PO LINII SIBIRSKOI ZHELEZNOI
DOROGI. No. 22, Part 1). St. Petersburg, 1914.
[Russ. text; 176 titles, pub.: up to 1909, pp. 1-55]

*_____. "OBZOR LITERATURY O POGRANICHNOI
DZHUNGARII I SOSEDNIKH CHASTIAKH SEMIPALATINSKOI
OBLASTI I SEMIRECH'IA," POGRANICHNAIA DZHUNGARIIA.
Vol. 3. GEOGRAFICHESKOE I GEOLOGICHESKOE OPISANIE.
No. 1. OBZOR LITERATURY, OROGRAFIIA, GIDROGRAFIIA.
Leningrad: Izdatel'stvo Akademii Nauk SSSR, 1932,
311 pp., 1000 copies. [Russ. text; 173 Russ., Europ.
titles, pp. 3-86]

_____. "OBZOR GEOLOGICHESKOI I GEOGRAFICHESKOI
LITERATURY IUGO-ZAPADNAGO ZABAIKAL'IA (SELENGINSKOI
DAURII)," GEOLOGICHESKIE IZSLIEDOVANIIA I
RAZVIEDOCHNYE RABOTY PO LINII SIBIRSKOI ZHELEZNOI
DOROGI. No. 22, Part 1. St. Petersburg, 1914.
[Russ. text; 176 titles, pub.: 1675-1909, pp. 1-55]

Siberia: Geography

_____. VOSTOCHNO-SIBIRSKII OTDEL IMPERATORSKAGO RUSSKAGO GEOGRAFICHESKAGO OBSHCHESTVA. 1851-1891. SISTEMATICHESKII UKAZATEL' VSIEKH IZDANII OTDIELA, POMESHCHENNYKH V NIKH STATEI, ZAMIETOK I MELKIKH IZVIESTII I SOOBSHCHENII. Irkutsk: Tipografiia K. I. Vitkovskii, 1891, 76 pp. [Russ. text; 969+ titles]

Obruchev, V. V.;:N. M. Asafova. comp. VLADIMIR AFANAS'EVICH OBRUCHEV. Moscow-Leningrad: Izdatel'stvo Akademii Nauk SSSR, 1946, 88 pp., 2500 copies. [Russ. text]

Ogurtsov, S. A. "M. B. PEVTSOV I EGO DEIATEL'NOST' V ZAPADNO-SIBIRSKOM OTDELE RUSSKOGO GEOGRAFICHESKOGO OBSHCHESTVA," IZVESTIIA OMSKOGO OTDELA GEOGR. O-VA SSSR. No. 1. 1956, 14 pp. [Russ. text; 14 titles]

*Orlova, V. ZAPADNAIA SIBIR'. KLIMAT SSSR. No. 4. Leningrad: Gidrometeorologicheskoe Izdatel'stvo, 1962, 360 pp., 1500 copies. [Russ. text and titles, pp. 311-316]

Petriaev, E. D. KRAEVEDY I LITERATORY ZABAIKAL'IA. MATERIALY DLIA BIOBIBLIOGRAFICHESKOGO SLOVARIA. Part 1. DOREVOLIUTSIONNYI PERIOD. (ZAPISKI ZABAIKAL'SKOGO OTDELENIIA GEOGR. O-VA SSSR. No. 25.) Irkutsk-Chita: Vost.-Sib. Kn. Izd. (Chit. Obl. B-ka im. Pushkina), 1965, 87 pp., 600 copies. [Russ. text; titles, per.: pre-1917]

*Postupal'skaia, M.; S. Ardashnikova. OBRUCHEV. (ZHIZN' ZAMECHATEL'NYKH LIUDEI. SERIIA BIOGRAFII. No. 13 [369].) Moscow: Izdatel'stvo TsK VLKSM "Molodaia Gvardiia," 1963, 431 pp., 65,000 copies. [Russ. text and titles (incl. archives),pp. 428-430]

PREDBAIKAL'E I ZABAIKAL'E. Moscow, 1965. [Russ. text; ca.660 titles, pp. 457-478]

PRIRODA I KHOZIAISTVO SIBIRI. VOPROSY PREPODAVANIIA GEOGRAFII. UCHEN. ZAPISKI. No. 31. SERIIA GEOGR. Irkutsk: (Gos. Ped. In-t.), 1968, 241 pp., 1500 copies. [Russ. text; titles at end of articles]

Semenov, V. F. "SPISOK STATEI, DOKLADOV, SOOBSHCHENII, REFERATOV, LEKTSII I DRUGOGO KRAEVEDNOGO MATERIALA, OPUBLIKOVANNYKH V IZDANIIAKH ZAPADNO-SIBIRSKOGO OTDELA RUSSKOGO GEOGRAFICHESKOGO OBSHCHESTVA V G. OMSKE," ZAPISKI ZAPADNO-SIBIRSKOGO OTDELA RUSSKOGO GEOGRAFICHESKOGO OBSHCHESTVA. Vol. 39. 1927. [Russ. text; 606 titles, pp. 93-131]

Siberia: Geography

Sizikov, A. I. "SODERZHANIE ZAPISOK ZABAIKAL'SKOGO OTDELA GEOGRAFICHESKOGO OBSHCHESTVA. No. 1-17 (1894-1930 GG.)," ZAPISKI ZABAIKAL'SKOGO OTDELA GEOGRAFICHESKOGO OBSHCHESTVA SSSR. No. 24. 1964. [Russ. text and titles, pub.: 1894-1930, pp. 143-146]

TELETSKOE OZERO. (OPISANIE I MARSHRUTY). Barnaul: Alt. Kn. Izd., 1966, 112 pp., 20,000 copies. [Russ. text; titles, pp. 107-111]

"UKAZATEL' SOCHINENII I STATEI, NAPECHATANNYKH SIBIRSKIM OTDELENIEM ROSSIISKAGO GEOGRAFICHESKAGO OBSHCHESTVA OSOBO I POMESHCHENNYKH V EGO IZDANIIAKH," OCHERK [DVADTSAT PIAT] 25-LETNEI DEIATEL'NOSTI SIBIRSKAGO OTDIELA R. G. OBSHCHESTVA. Omsk, 1876. [Russ. text; 239 titles, pub.: ca.1850-1875, (appendix) pp. 1-10]

*VODNYE RESURSY I VODNOE KHOZIAISTVO SIBIRI. Novosibirsk: "Nauka," 1968, 115 pp., 1200 copies. [Russ. text and titles, at end of articles]

*VOPROSY GEOGRAFII SIBIRI SBORNIK SHESTOI. Tomsk: Izdatel'stvo Tomskogo Universiteta, 1966, 182 pp., 700 copies. [Russ. text and titles, at end of articles]

*VOPROSY GEOGRAFII VERKHNEGO PRIAMUR'IA. (SBORNIK STATEI.) BLAGOVESHCH. GOS. PED. IN-T IM. M. I. KALININA. UCHEN. ZAPISKI. Vol. 12). Blagoveshchensk: (Blagoveshch. Gos. Ped. In-t.), 1968, 111 pp., 600 copies. [Russ. text; titles at end of articles]

*Vorob'ev, V. V.; L. P. Litvintseva. GEOGRAFIIA NASELENIIA SIBIRI I DAL'NEGO VOSTOKA. Irkutsk: (AN SSSR. Sib. Otd.-nie), 1968, 223 pp., 700 copies. [Russ. text; 2212 Russ. titles, pub.: 1917-1965, Bibliogr. Ukazatel']

Vorobev, Vladimir Vasilevich. GORODA IUZHNOI CHASTI VOSTOCHNOI SIBIRI: ISTORIKO-GEOGRAFICHESKIE OCHERKI. Irkutsk: Irkutskoe Knizhnoe Izdatel'stvo, 1959, 147 pp. [Russ. text; 394 titles, pp. 136-146]

*Vrangel', F. P. PUTESHESTVIE PO SEVERNYM BEREGAM SIBIRI I PO LEDOVITOMU MORIU SOVERSHENNOE V 1820, 1821, 1822, 1823 I 1824 GG. Moscow: Izdatel'stvo Glavsevmorputi, 1948, 455 pp., 15,000 copies. [Russ. text; 103 Russ., Europ. titles, per.: 1820-1824, pp. 687-692]

Siberia

HISTORY, ARCHAEOLOGY

Akulov, M. R. PROMYSHLENNOE RAZVITIE SIBIRI V GODY
VELIKOI OTECHESTVENNOI VOINY (1941-1945 GG.)
Stavropol', 1967. [Russ. text; 112 titles, per.:
1941-1945, pp. 6-16, 313-318]

Aleksandrov, Al. K BIBLIOGRAFII PO ISTORII SIBIRI.
KNIGOVEDENIE. No. 2. 1894. [Russ. text; 22 titles,
pp. 13-16]

"BAIKAL," SOVETSKAIA VOENNAIA ENTSIKLOPEDIIA. Vol. 2.
Moscow: Gosudarstvennoe Slovarno-Entsiklopedicheskoe
Izdatel'stvo "Sovetskaia Entsiklopediia," Ogiz RSFSR,
1933, 96-97 pp. [Russ. text and titles, p. 97]

*Bakhrushin, S. V. NAUCHNYE TRUDY. Vol. 1. Moscow:
Izdatel'stvo Akademii Nauk SSSR, 1952, 264 pp.,
5000 copies. [Russ. text and titles, pub.: 1909-1952,
per.: 16th - 17th cc., pp. 9-20]

* _____. NAUCHNYE TRUDY. Vol. 3. IZBRANNYE
RABOTY PO ISTORII SIBIRI XVI-XVII VV. CH. 2. ISTORIIA
NARODOV SIBIRI V XVI-XVII VV. Moscow: Izdatel'stvo
Akademii Nauk SSSR, 1955, 299 pp., 2500 copies.
[Russ. text and titles,   pub.: 1916-1955, per.:
16th - 17th c., pp. 273-276]

Belikova, L. I. KOMMUNISTY PRIMOR'IA V BOR'BE ZA
VLAST' SOVETOV NA DAL'NEM VOSTOKE. (PRIMOR.
ORGANIZATSIIA RKP(B) V 1917-1922 GG.) Khabarovsk:
(Kn. Izd.), 1968, 287 pp., 1500 copies. [Russ. text;
titles, pub.: 1917-1922, pp. 256-279]

*Belitser, V. "SIBIRSKIE TATARY," BOL'SHAIA SOVETSKAIA
ENTSIKLOPEDIIA. Vol. 53. Moscow: Gosudarstvennyi
Nauchnyi Institut "Sovetskaia Entsiklopediia,"
(Ogiz RSFSR), 1946, 666 pp. [Russ. text; Tatar, Russ.,
titles, p. 666]

Ber, Nadezhda S. "SIBIRSKAIA ZHIVAIA STARINA   ZA PIAT'
LET, 1923-1928. BIBLIOGRAFICHESKII UKAZATEL',"
SIBIRSKAIA ZHIVAIA STARINA. No. 8/9. 1929.
[Russ. text; 201 Russ. titles, pub.: 1923-1928,
pp. 267-283]

Siberia: History, Archaeology

Bezgin, I. G. SIBIRSKAIA ZHELEZNAIA DOROGA.
BIBLIOGRAFICHESKAIIA IZYSKANIIA O PROEKTAKH ZHELEZNOI
DOROGI I K GOR. SIMBIRSKU. (MATERIALY DLIA
BIBLIOGRAFICHESKOGO SLOVARIA, No. 2.) St. Petersburg:
Tip. Iu. Erlikha, 26 pp. [Russ. text]

BOR'BA KOMMUNISTICHESKOI PARTII ZA OSUSHCHESTVLENIE
DEKRETA O ZEMLE. Omsk: (Otd. Propagandy i Agitatsii
Obkoma KPSS), 1967, 30 pp. [Russ. text; titles,
pp. 29-30]

DAL'NEVOSTOCHNAIA MEZHVUZOVSKAIA NAUCHNAIA
KONFERENTSIIA PO ISTORII SOVETSKOGO DAL'NEGO VOSTOKA.
MATERIALY... Khabarovsk: (M-vo Prosveshcheniia
RSFSR. Khabar. Gos. Ped. In-t), 1967, 294 pp., 1000
copies. [Russ. text; titles at end of reports]

Dresvianskii, F. D. IZMENENIIA V GEOGRAFII SEL'SKOGO
KHOZIAISTVA PREDBAIKAL'IS V DOREVOLIUTSIONNYI PERIOD.
UCHENYE ZAPISKI (IRKUT. PED. IN-T) No. 24. Ch. 2.
1967. [Russ. text; 30 titles, pp. 116-117]

Dulov, V. I. KREST'IANSTVO VOSTOCHNOI SIBIRI V GODY
PERVOI RUSSKOI REVOLIUTSII. Irkutsk: Kn. Izd., 1956.
[Russ. text; ca.150 titles, per.: 1905-1907, pp. 263-269]

*Evseev, E. N.; M. A. Pletneva; O. K. Sosnenko. comps.
IZ ISTORII OMSKA. (1716-1917 GG.) OCHERKI, DOKUMENTY,
MATERIALY. Omsk: Zap.-Sib. Kn. Izd., 1967, 223 pp.,
5000 copies. [Russ. text; titles, per.: 1716-1917,
pp. 214-218]

*Fetisov, A. P. OKHOTSKAIA PRELIUDIIA. RASSKAZ ISTORIKA
O PODVIGE KOMMUNAROV SEVERNOGO POBEREZH'IA. Khabarovsk:
Khabarovskoe Knizhnoe Izdatel'stvo, 1967, 96 pp.,
3000 copies. [Russ. text and titles, pub.: 1957-1967,
p. 91]

*GEROICHESKIE GODY BOR'BY I POBED. DAL'NII VOSTOK V OGNE
GRAZHDANSKOI VOINY. Moscow: Izdatel'stvo "Nauka,"
1968, 390 pp., 7000 copies. [Russ. text; ca.260 Russ.
titles, per.: 1917-1921, pp. 382-388]

Girchenko, V. P.; K. I. Vel'min; A. P. Bazhin. comps.
KRATKII UKAZATEL' LITERATURY PO PRIBAIKAL'IU.
Verkhneudinsk: Izd. Pribaikal'skogo Narodnogo
Universiteta. (Pribaikal'skii Narodnyi Institut i
Pribaikal'skoe Gubernoe Vystavochnoe Biuro), 1923,
38+1 pp., 500 copies. [Russ. text; 604 titles]

Siberia: History, Archaeology

Glushchenko, N. A. BOL'SHEVITSKAIA PECHAT' DAL'NEGO
VOSTOKA V GODY PERVOI RUSSKOI REVOLIUTSII (1905-1907 GG.)
Vladivostok, 1970. [Russ. text; ca.320 titles,
per.: 1905-1907, pp. 205-230]

Golosov, V. TRUD I CHELOVEK. OCHERKI PO ISTORII
VOZNIKNOVENIIA I RAZVITIIA GUMANISTICH. IDEOLOGII
TRUDIASHCHIKHSIA MASS. Krasnoiarsk: Kn. Izd., 1966,
510 pp., 4500 copies. [Russ. text; 294 titles,
pp. 498-507]

Golubev, I. K. "SIBIRSKAIA PERIODICHESKAIA PECHAT'.
SPISOK IZDANII, VYKHODIASHCHIKH V 1895 G.," KNIGOVEDENIE.
No. 4/5. 1895. [Russ. text; 40 titles, pp. 54-59]

Gurvich, I. S. ETNICHESKAIA ISTORIIA SEVERO-VOSTOKA
SIBIRI. (TRUDY IN-TA ETNOGRAFII IM. N. N. MIKLUKHO-
MAKLAIA. NOVAIA SERIIA. Vol. 89.) Moscow: "Nauka,"
1966, 269 pp., 1700 copies. [Russ. text; titles
pp. 3-8]

*Gudoshnikov, M. A. OCHERKI PO ISTORII GRAZHDANSKOI
VOINY V SIBIRI. Irkutsk: Irkutskoe Knizhnoe
Izdatel'stvo, 1950, 206 pp., 5000 copies. [Russ.
text and titles, pub.: 1924-1956, pp. 202-205]

Iak. Andr. "SIBIRSKAIA BIBLIOGRAFIIA," TOMSKIE
GUBERNSKIE VIEDOMOSTI. Nos. 26-45. 1860. [Russ.
text]

IRKUTSKII OBL. KRAEVEDCHESKII MUZEI. OTCHETY
ARKHEOLOGICHESKIKH EKSPEDITSII ZA 1963-1965 GODY.
Irkutsk: In-t Arkheologii AN SSSR, 1966, 71 pp.,
1000 copies. [Russ. text; titles, per.: 1963-1965,
at end of reports]

*"ISTOCHNIKI DLIA IZUCHENIIA ISTORII SIBIRI," SIBIRSKAIA
SOVETSKAIA ENTSIKLOPEDIIA. Vol. 2. Novosibirsk:
Sibirskoe Kraevoe Izdatel'stvo, 1932, 399-402 pp.
[Russ. text; Russ., Europ. titles, pp. 400-402]

ISTORIIA KRASNOIARSKOGO KRAIA. Krasnoiarsk: (Kn. Izd.),
1967, 312 pp., 15,000 copies. [Russ. text; titles
at end of chapters]

*"ISTORIIA SIBIRI," SIBIRSKAIA SOVETSKAIA ENTSIKLOPEDIIA.
Vol. 2. Novosibirsk: Sibirskoe Kraevoe Izdatel'stvo.
1932, 380-399 pp. [Russ. text and titles, p. 399]

*ISTORIOGRAFIIA SOVETSKOI SIBIRI. (1917-1945 GG.)
Novosibirsk: "Nauka," (AN SSSR. Sib. Otd-nie. In-t
Istorii, Filologii i Filosofii), 1968, 3200 copies.
[Russ. text; titles per.: 1917-1945]

Siberia: History, Archaeology

IZ ISTORII DREVNEGO MIRA I SREDNIKH VEKOV. Krasnoiarsk:
(M-vo Prosveshcheniia RSFSR), 1967, 72 pp., 500
copies. [Russ. text; titles at end of articles]

IZ ISTORII SEL'SKOGO KHOZIAISTVA SOVETSKOI SIBIRI.
UCHEN. ZAPISKI. No. 30. SERIIA IST. Irkutsk:
(M-vo Prosveshcheniia RSFSR. Irkut. Gos. Ped. In-t),
1967, 117 pp., 700 copies. [Russ. text; titles at
end of articles]

Karpenko, Z. G. RABOCHIE I KREST'IANE KUZBASSA
NAKANUNE I V GODY PERVOI RUSSKOI REVOLIUTSII 1905-
1907 GG. Kemerovo: Kn. Izd., 1956. [Russ. text;
ca.100 titles, pp. 88-93]

*Kashlakova, O. M. comp. OPYT EKONOMIKO-
SOTSIOLOGICHESKIKH ISSLEDOVANII V SIBIRI.
Novosibirsk: "Nauka," Sib. Otd-nie., 1966, 152 pp.,
1600 copies. [Russ. text; ca.130 Russ. titles,
pp. 145-151]

*Khaninson, Ia. G. comp. "SIBIR' V GODY VELIKOI
OKTIABR'SKOI SOTSIALISTICHESKOI REVOLIUTSII I
GRAZHDANSKOI VOINY," SIBIRKIE OGNI. No. 2. 1958.
[Russ. text and titles, pp. 189-190]

Khaslavskii, L. A. comp. KRASNYI OSTROV. VOSPOMINANIIA,
OCHERKI, DOKUMENTY O BOR'BE ZA VLAST' SOVETOV NA
AMURE. 1918-1922. Khabarovsk: Kn. Izd., 1967,
358 pp., 15,000 copies. [Russ. text; titles, per.:
1918-1922, pp. 355-356]

*Khaziakhmetov, E. BOL'SHEVIKI V NARYMSKOI SSYLKE.
Novosibirsk: Zap.-Sib. Kn. Izd., 1967, 187 pp., 8000
copies. [Russ. text; 12 Russ. titles, pub.: 1954-1963,
p. 186]

KOMMUNISTICHESKAIA PARTIIA V BOR'BE ZA SOZDANIE
SOVETSKOGO APPARATA I VOVLECHENIE MASS V UPRAVLENIE
GOSUDARSTVOM. Omsk: (Otd. Propagandy i Agitatsii
Omskogo Obkoma KPSS. V Pomoshch' Lektoru), 1966,
27 pp., 1200 copies. [Russ. text; titles, pp. 26-27]

Khoroshikh, P. P. "UKAZATEL' LITERATURY PO ARKHEOLOGII
IRKUTSKOGO KRAIA," IZVESTIIA BIOLOGO-GEOGRAFICHESKOGO
NAUCHNO-ISSLEDOVATEL'SKOGO INSTITUTA PRI GOSUDARSTVENNOM
IRKUTSKOM UNIVERSITETE. Vol. 1, No. 1. (Irkutsk),
1924, (separately) 8 pp. [Russ. text; 104 Russ.
titles, pub.: to 1923]

Siberia: History, Archaeology

*KOMMUNISTY ZAPADNOI SIBIRI. (1917-1967). Tiumen: (Otdely Shkol, Propagandy i Agitatsii Tiumenskogo Obkoma KPSS), 1967, 245 pp., 1500 copies. [Russ. text; 60 Russ. titles, per.: 1917-1967, pp. 239-243]

Kosovanov, V. P. "UKAZATEL' VAZHNEISHEI LITERATURY PO ISTORII GORODA KRASNOIARSKA," SPRAVOCHNIK PO GORODU KRASNOIARSKU NA 1923 G. Krasnoiarsk, 1923. [Russ. text; 73 titles]

Kutsyi, G. BOR'BA RABOCHEGO KLASSA DAL'NEGO VOSTOKA PROTIV INTERVENTOV I VNUTRENNEI KONTRREVOLIUTSII. 1918-1920 GG. Vladivostok: Dal'nevost. Kn. Izd., 1967, 302 pp., 1000 copies. [Russ. text; titles, per.: 1917-1920, pp. 297-300]

Krushanov, A. N. OKTIABR' NA DAL'NEM VOSTOKE. CH. 1. PUS. DAL'NII VOSTOK V PERIOD IMPERIALIZMA (1908-MART 1917 GG.) Vladivostok, 1968. [Russ. text; ca.450 titles, per.: 1908-1917, pp. 117-133]

Krushanov, A. I. OKTIABR' NA DAL'NEM VOSTOKE. Ch. 2. POBEDA VELIKOI OKTIABR'SKOI REVOLIUTSII. Vladivostok, 1969. [Russ. text; ca.550 titles, per.: 1917-1918, pp. 158-175]

*Kulikova, L. K.; A. N. Maslova. DAL'NII VOSTOK V PERIOD VELIKOI OKTIABR'SKOI SOTSIALISTICHESKOI REVOLIUTSII I GRAZHDANSKOI VOINY. (1917-1922 GG.) UKAZATEL' LIT. Khabarovsk: (Khabarovskaia Kraevaia Nauchnaia Biblioteka.Zonal'noe Ob"edinenie Bibliotek Dal'nego Vostoka), 1968, 287 pp., 2500 copies. [Russ. text; 2737 Russ. titles, per.: 1917-1922, pub.: 1917-1966]

Kuznetsov, E. "UKAZATEL' SIBIRSKIM LIETOPISIAM," TOBOL'SKAIIA GUBERNSKIIA VIEDOMOSTI. Nos. 1-2, 5-6, 9-10, 20-21, 26. 1894. [Russ. text]

Kuznetsov, E. V. UKAZATEL' SOCHINENII ISTORIKA SIBIRI P. A. SLOVTSOVA. TOBOL'SKIIA GUBERNSKIIA VIEDOMOSTI. No. 12. 1893. [Russ. text]

K. [Kuznetsov, E. V.] "UKAZATEL' STATEI PO ARKHEOLOGII, ISTORII I ETNOGRAFII SIBIRI, POMIESHCHENNYKH V TOBOL'SKIKH GAZETAKH 1891-1892 G.," KALENDAR' TOBOL'SKOI GUBERNII NA 1893 G. Tobol'sk. [ca.1892] [Russ. text; ca.150 titles, pub.: 1891-1892, pp. 126-133]

Siberia : History, Archaeology

*Kuznetsov, I. I. ZASHCHISHCHAIA OTECHESTVO. Irkutsk:
Vosto.-Sib. Kn. Izd., 1968, 272 pp., 15,000 copies.
[Russ. text; 28 Russ. titles, per.: 1941-1945, p. 270]

Larichev, V. SOROK LET SREDI SIBIRSKIKH DREVNOSTEI.
MATERIALY K BIOGR. AKAD. A. P. OKLADNIKOVA.
Novosibirsk: Zap.-Sib. Kn. Izd-vo, 1970, 239 pp.,
1000 copies. [Russ. text; ca.600 titles]

*Lichkov, L. "IAKUTY," ENTSIKLOPEDICHESKII SLOVAR'.
Vol. 41A. St. Petersburg: F. A. Brokgauz, I. A.
Efron, 1904, 631-634 pp. [Russ. text; Russ., Europ.
titles, p. 634]

* _____. "TUNGUZY," ENTSIKLOPEDICHESKII SLOVAR.
Vol. 34. St. Petersburg: F. A. Brokgauz, I. A. Efron,
1902, 65-68 pp. [Russ. text; Russ., Europ. titles,
p. 68]

*Maksakov, V.; A. Turunov. KHRONIKA GRAZHDANSKOI VOINY V
SIBIRI. (1917-1918). Moscow-Leningrad:
Gosudarstvennoe Izdatel'stvo, 1926, 301 pp., 3000
copies. [Russ. text; Russ., Europ. titles, per.:
1917-1918, pp. 280-288]

*Maslov, D. P.; I. A. Sychev; V. S. Flerov; A. T. Koniaev;
M. S. Kuznetsov. comps. LENIN I SIBIR'. BIBLIOGR.
UKAZ. (2nd ed.) Novosibirsk: Zap.-Sib. Kn.
Izd.-vo, 1970, 304 pp., 3000 copies. [Russ. text;
1966 Russ. titles, pp. 11-262]

MATERIALY DLIA BIBLIOGRAFICHESKAGO UKAZATELIA
SOCHINENII I ZHURNAL'NYKH STATEI O SIBIRI I
SOPREDIEL'NYKH EI STRAN. SBORNIK ISTORIKO-
STATISTICHESKIKH SVIEDIENII O SIBIRI I
SOPREDIEL'NYKH EI STRAN. Vol. 1. 1875. [Russ. text;
titles, pp. 1-32]

MATERIALY DLIA BIBLIOGRAFII SIBIRI. UKAZATEL'
LITERATURNYKH TRUDOV E. V. KUZNETSOVA. TOBOL'SKIIA
GUBERNSKIIA VIEDOMOSTI. No. 24-26. 1896. [Russ. text]

*Merkur'ev, S. A.; A. Ia. Shapranova. comps. OCHERKI
PO ISTORII IRKUTSKOI ORGANIZATSII KPSS. Ch. 1.
(1901-1920.) Irkutsk: Vost.-Sib. Kn. Izd., 1966,
382 pp., 5000 copies. [Russ. text and titles,
per.: 1901-1920, pp. 366-381]

Siberia: History, Archaeology

Mezhov, V. I. SIBIRSKAIA BIBLIOGRAFIIA. UKAZATEL'
KNIG I STATEI O SIBIRI NA RUSSKOM IAZYKIE I ODNIEKH
TOL'KO KNIG NA INOSTRANNYKH IAZYKAKH ZA VES' PERIOD
KNIGOPECHATANIIA. Vol. 1.:ISTOCHNIKI I MATERIALY
DLIA ISTORII SIBIRI: BIBLIOGRAFICHESKIE UKAZATELI,
ISTORICHESKIE I ISTORIKO-IURIDICHESKIE AKTY I
DOKUMENTY, PIS'MA I MEMUARY: Vol. 2.: ISTORIIA.
BIOGRAFIIA. GEOGRAFIIA. PUTESHESTVIIA. STATISTIKA.
ETNOGRAFIIA. KARTOGRAFIIA: Vol. 3.: PEDAGOGIKA.
PRAVOVIEDIENIE I GOSUDARSTVENNYIA NAUKI.
POLITICHESKIIA I SOTSIAL'NYIA NAUKI. SEL'SKOE
KHOZIAISTVO I ZEMLEDIELIE. TEKHNOLOGIIA. ASTRONOMIIA.
GEODEZIIA I MEKHANIKA. ESTESTVENNYIA NAUKI. MEDITSINA.
IAZYKOZNANIE. SLOVESNOST'. ISKUSSTVO. Suppl.:
AZBUCHNYE UKAZATELI IMEN, AVTOROV I PREDMETOV....
St. Petersburg: I. M. Sibiriakov, 1891-1892 (Vols. 1,
2, 1891; Vol. 3, suppl. 1892),(Vol. 1) XII+485 pp.;
(Vol. 2) X+470 pp; (Vol. 3) X+303 pp.; (suppl.) 188 pp.
[Russ. text; 25,250 Russ., Foreign lang. titles]

*_____. SIBIRSKAIA BIBLIOGRAFIIA. UKAZATEL'
KNIG I STATEI O SIBIRII NA RUSSKOM IAZYKIE I
ODNIEKH TOL'KO KNIG NA INOSTRANNYKH IAZYKAKH ZA VES'
PERIOD KNIGOPECHATANIIA. St. Petersburg: Sklad
Izdaniia v Knizhnom Magazinie Th. A. Semenova.
Vols. 1-3. 1903 [Re-issue of 1891-1892 ed.],
485 pp.; 470 pp.; 303 pp. [Russ. text; Russ., Europ.
titles]

*Miller, G. F. ISTORIIA SIBIRI. Vol. 1. Moscow-
Leningrad: Izdatel'stvo Akademii Nauk SSSR, 1937,
607 pp., 5000 copies. [Russ. text; 30 European
titles, per.: up to 18th c., pp. 327-328]

[Miliutin, B.] "MATERIALY DLIA BIBLIOGRAFII SIBIRI,
SREDNEAZIATSKIKH VLADENII ROSSII I SOPREDEL'NYKH EI
STRAN," SBORNIK IST. STAT. SVEDENII O SIBIRI. Vol. 1.
(St. Petersburg) 1875-1876, 135 pp. [Russ. text;
2108 titles]

Mukhin, A. A. "K ISTORII IZUCHENIIA PROLETERIATA
SIBIRI EPOKHI KAPITALIZMA. ISTORIOGR. OBZOR," VOPROSY
ISTORII SIBIRI. Irkutsk, 1967. [Russ. text; 150
titles, per.: pre-1917, pp. 105-127]

Naiakshin, K. Ia. comp. BOR'BA ZA SOVETSKUIU VLAST'
V SAMARSKOI GUBERNII. Kuibyshev. Kn. Izd., 1957.
[Russ. text; ca.100 titles, Sov. per., pp. 286-289]

Siberia: History, Archaeology

Nikolaev, P. F. SOVETSKAIA MILITSIIA SIBIRI. (1917-1922). Omsk, 1967. [Russ. text; 94 titles, pp. 14-27, 277-282]

Obruchev, V. A. ISTORIIA GEOLOGICHESKOGO ISSLEDOVANIIA SIBIRI. PERIOD PIATYI (1918-1940). No. 9.: OBZOR LITERATURY, SODERZHASHCHEI OPISANIE VSEI SIBIRI ILI KRUPNYKH EE CHASTEI, A TAKZHE SVODKI PO MESTOROZHDENIIAM POLEZNYKH ISKOPAEMYKH, FLORE I FAUNE, GEOGRAFII, GEOMORFOLOGII, GEODEZII I DRUGIM SOPRIKASAIUSHCHIMSIA NAUKAM. Moscow: Izdatel'stvo Akademii Nauk SSSR, 1959, 199 pp. [Russ. text; 1300 titles, per.: 1918-1940]

_____. ISTORIIA GEOLOGICHESKOGO ISSLEDOVANIIA SIBIRI. PERIOD PIATYI (1918-1940). No. 1. VVEDENIE. OBSHCHII OBZOR ISSLEDOVANII SIBIRI S 1918 PO 1940 G. I IKH REZUL'TATOV.KRATKIE BIOGRAFII GLAVNYKH ISSLEDOVATELEI SIBIRI. UKAZATELI K VYPUSKAM 2-8. Moscow-Leningrad: Izdatel'stvo Akademii Nauk SSSR, 1949, 59 pp. [Russ. text]

_____. ISTORIIA GEOLOGICHESKOGO ISSLEDOVANIIA SIBIRI. PERIOD CHETVERYI (1889-1917). (SISTEMATICHESKIKH GOSUDARSTVENNYKH ISSLEDOVANII). Moscow-Leningrad: Izdatel'stvo Akademii Nauk SSSR, 1937, 573 pp. [Russ. text; 2567 titles, pub.: 1889-1917, pp. 87-213]

_____. ISTORIIA GEOLOGICHESKOGO ISSLEDOVANIIA SIBIRI. PERIOD PIATYI (1918-1940). No. 4.: ALTAISKO-SAIANSKAIA GORNAIA STRANA. Moscow-Leningrad: Izdatel'stvo Akademii Nauk SSSR, 1944, 239 pp. [Russ. text; 1919 titles, pp. 178-239]

_____. ISTORIIA GEOLOGICHESKOGO ISSLEDOVANIIA SIBIRI. PERIOD PIATYI (1918-1940). No. 6.: PRIBAIKAL'E, BAIKAL'SKOE NAGOR'E, ZABAIKAL'E I ALDANSKAIA PLITA. Moscow-Leningrad: Izdatel'stvo Akademii Nauk SSSR, 1945. [Russ. text; 844 titles, per.: 1918-1940, pp. 89-118]

"'OBZOR STATEI I ZAMIETOK' SIBIRSKAGO I AZIATSKAGO VIESTNIKOV. 1818-1822 GG." VOSTOCHNOE OBOZRENIE. Nos. 27, 29. 1885. [Russ. text; Russ. survey, pub.: 1818-1822]

OCHERK EKONOMICHESKOGO RAZVITIIA SIBIRI. (2-IA POLOVINA XIX V.) Irkutsk: (M-vo Vyssh. i Sred. Spets. Obrazovaniia RSFSR), 1967, 148 pp., 700 copies. [Russ. text; titles, pp. 143-145]

Siberia: History, Archaeology

*Ogorodnikov, Vl. I. OCHERK ISTORII SIBIRI DO NACHALA
XIX STOL. Part 1. VVEDENIE. ISTORIIA DO-RUSSKIKH
SIBIRI. Irkutsk: Tipografiia Shtaba Voennogo
Okruga, 1920, 289 pp. [Russ. text and titles, per.:
pre-19th c., scattered]

*_____. OCHERK ISTORII SIBIRI DO NACHALA
XIX STOL. Part 2. No. 1. Vladivostok:
Tipografiia Gosudarstvennogo Dal'nevostochnogo
Universiteta, 1924, 108 pp. [Russ. text and
titles, scattered]

*Oksenov, A. "SVIEDIENIIA O NEIZDANNYKH SIBIRSKIKH
LIETOPISIAKH. (S BIBLIOGRAFICHESKIM UKAZATELEM
NAPECHATANNYKH SIBIRSKIKH LIETOPISEI I NIEKOTORYKH
INYKH ISTOCHNIKOV," LITERATURNYI SBORNIK.
St. Petersburg: Izdanie Redaktsii "Vostochnago
Obozreniia," 1885, 446-455 pp. [Russ. text; 18
Russ. titles, pp. 451-455]

*Pabetskaia, Z. I. "PROBLEMY SEL'SKOGO KHOZIAISTVA V
TRUDAKH ISTORIKOV VOSTOCHNOI SIBIRI (1956-1965 GG.),"
IZ ISTORII SEL'SKOGO KHOZIIAISTVA SOVETSKOI SIBIRI.
(UCHENYE ZAPISKI. IRKUTSKII PEDAGOGICHESKII
INSTITUT. No. 30.) Irkutsk: (Ministerstvo
Prosveshcheniia RSFSR), 1967, 117 pp., 700 copies.
[Russ. text; 50 Russ. titles, pub.: 1956-1965,
pp. 114-116]

Palenko, I. A. AMURSKAIA OBLAST'. KRATKII OCHERK
ISTORII, GEOGRAFII, EKONOMIKI. Khabarovsk: Kn. Izd.,
1966, 94 pp., 15,000 copies. [Russ. text; titles,
pp. 90-93]

"PECHATNYE RABOTY DOKTORA ISTORICHESKIKH NAUK S. A.
TOKAREVA, KASAIUSHCHIESIA ISTORII I ETNOGRAFII
NARODOV SIBIRI," UCHENYE ZAPISKI. No. 4. (INSTITUT
IAZYKA, LIT. I ISTORII IAKUT. FILIALA AKAD. NAUK
SSSR), 1956. [Russ. text; 38 titles, pub.: 1930-
1955, pp. 142-144]

*Petrova, T. N. DEIATEL'NOSTI PARTIINYKH ORGANIZATSII
ZAPADNOI SIBIRI PO USILENIIU TVORCHESKOGO
SODRUZHESTVA NAUKI S PROIZVODSTVOM V GODY VELIKOI
OTECHESTVENNOI VOINY (1941-1945 GG.) Tomsk:
"Izdatel'stvo Tomskogo U-ta," 1968, 390 pp., 600
copies. [Russ. text; ca.300 Russ. titles, per.:
1941-1945, publ.: 1939-1967, pp. 368-380]

Siberia: History, Archaeology

PO STRANITSAM ISTORII ZABAIKAL'IA. (BIBLIOGR. UKAZATEL'.)
Chita: (Chit. Obl. B-ka im. A. S. Pushkina), 1967,
25 pp., 1000 copies. [Russ. text; titles]

[Rudykh, Z. S.; P. I. Shvarts. comps.] IZ ISTORII
IRKUTSKOI OBLASTNOI PARTIINOI ORGANIZATSII. UKAZATEL'
LIT. Part 2. (1921-1966 GG.) (IRKUT. GOS. UN-T
IM. ZHDANOVA. NAUCH. B-KA. TRUDY. No. 19), 1967,
62 pp., 300 copies. [Russ. text; ca.720 titles]

*Samoilov, V. A. SEMEN DEZHNEV I EGO VREMIA. Moscow:
Izdatel'stvo Glavsevmorputi, 1945, 151 pp., 15,000
copies. [Russ. text; 41+ Russ. titles, per.: 17th c.,
pp. 116-120]

Semenov-Tiashanskii, V. P. ed. ROSSIIA. POLNOE
GEOGRAFICHESKOE OPISANIE NASHEGO OTECHESTVA. Vol. 16.
ZAPADNAIA SIBIR'. St. Petersburg, 1907. [Russ. text;
300 titles, Russ. (273), foreign (27)]

*Serebrennikov, I. I. SIBIREVIEDIENIE. Kharbin, 1920,
213 pp. [Russ. text; 17 Russ. titles, pp. 211-212]

*Shchapov, A. P. SOBRANIE SOCHINENII. DOPOLNITEL'NYI
TOM K IZDANIIU 1905-1908 GG. Irkutsk:
Vostochnosibirskoe Oblastnoe Izdatel'stvo, 1937,
380 pp., 3000 copies. [Russ. text; 122 Russ. titles,
pub.: 1861-1937, pp. 363-379]

SIBIREVEDENIE. KATALOG KNIG, KNIZHNYKH MAGAZINOV
SIBKRAIIZDATA. Novosibirk, 1929, 68 pp. [Russ.
text]

"SIBIRSKIE OGNI." 1922-1947. BIBLIOGRAFICHESKII
UKAZATEL'. Novosibirsk, 1947, 48 pp., 250 copies.
[Russ. text and titles, pub.: 1922-1947]

*Simchenko, Iu. B. TAMGI NARODOV SIBIRI XVII VEKA.
Moscow: Izdatel'stvo "Nauka," 1965, 226 pp., 1200
copies. [Russ. text and titles, per.: Ancient,
pp. 222-226]

Skalon, V. N. RUSSKIE ZEMLEPROKHODTSY--ISSLEDOVATELI
SIBIRI S XVII V. Moscow, 1951, 198 pp. [Russ. text;
280 titles, per.: 17th c., pp. 190-198]

Siberia: History, Archaeology

*Soustina, A. F.; A. V. Suvorova. comps. SIBIRSKIE OGNI. LITERATURNO-KHUDOZHESTVENNYI I OBSHCHESTVENNO-POLITICHESKII ZHURNAL. UKAZATEL' SODERZHANIIA. 1922-1964 GG. Novosibirsk: Zapadno-Sibirskoe Knizhnoe Izdatel'stvo, 1967, 431 pp., 3000 copies. [Russ. text; 8538 Russ. titles, pub.: 1922-1964, pp. 19-350]

*Stepanov, N. P. A. SLOVTSOV (U ISTOKOV SIBIRSKOGO OBLASTNICHESTVA.) Leningrad: Izdatel'stvo Instituta Narodov Severa TsIK SSSR, 1935, 44 pp., 1500 copies. [Russ. text; 52 Russ. titles, pp. 41-43]

*Studentsova, S. V.; A. P. Slivina; I. A. Priadko. comps. SOLDATY VELIKOI BOR'BY. Krasnoiarsk: Krasnoiarsk. Kn. Izd., 1968, 167 pp., 2000 copies. [Russ. text and titles, pub.: 1934-1964, pp. 163-165]

[Sycheva, L.] BOR'BA ZA USTANOVLENIE SOVETSKOI VLASTI V SAMARSKOI GUBERNII. KRATKII REK. UKAZATEL' LIT. Kuibyshev: (Kuibyshevskaia Obl. B-ka), 1957, 12 pp., 1200 copies. [Russ. text; 31 titles, Sov. per.]

Tiukavkin, V. G. "SPISOK NAUCHNYKH TRUDOV V. I. DULOVA," VOPROSY ISTORII I METODIKI PREPODAVANIIA ISTORII V SHKOLE. Irkutsk, 1966. [Russ. text; 62 titles, pub.: 1940-1964, pp. 10-13]

_____. OKTIABR' I VOSTOCHNAIA SIBIR'. Irkutsk: (M-vo Prosveshcheniia RSFSR. Irkut. Gos. Ped. In-t), 1968, 162 pp., 700 copies. [Russ. text; titles at end of articles]

_____. "V. I. LENIN O PERESELENII KREST'IAN V SIBIR'," OCHERKI ISTORII SIBIRI. Vol. 1. (UCHEN. ZAP. IRKUTS. PED. IN-TA. No. 39), (Irkutsk), 1970, 114-126 pp., 1000 copies. [Russ. text; 33 Russ. titles, pub.: 1905-1968, pp. 125-126]

Tomashevskii, V. V. MATERIALY K BIBLIOGRAFII SIBIRI I DAL'NEGO VOSTOKA. (XV--PERVAIA POLOVINA XIX VEKA.) Vladivostok: (Akademiia Nauk SSSR. Dal'nevostochnyi Filial im. V. L. Komarova), 1957, 213 pp. [Russ. text; ca. 4000 copies; per.: 15th - 19th cc.]

Turunov, A. N.; T. N. Popova. 1905 GOD V SIBIRI. MATERIALY K BIBLIOGRAFICHESKOMU OBZORU KNIG I ZHURNAL'NYKH STATEI. Moscow: Izdatel'stvo "Sovetskaia Aziia," 1930, 24 pp., 1000 copies. [Russ. text; 214 Russ. titles, per.: 1905]

Siberia: History, Archaeology

Vasil'ev, Iu. A. "KOMMUNISTY SIBIRI V PERIOD VELIKOI OTECHESTVENNOI VOINY," IZ ISTORII PART. ORGANIZATSII ZAP. SIBIRI (1917-1967) (UCHEN. ZAP. TIUMEN. PED. IN-TA. SB. 87). Sverdlovsk, 1969. [Russ. text; titles, per.: WW II, pp. 5-24]

Vasilevskii, V. I.; G. V. Grunin; V. G. Izgachev. et al. BOR'BA ZA VLAST' SOVETOV V VOSTOCHNOM ZABAIKAL'E. (Irkutsk): Vost.-Sib. Kn. Izd., 1967, 365 pp., 3000 copies. [Russ. text; 140 titles, pp. 356-363]

*[Vinogradova A.; I. Iakhnina; N. Balyko] NASH KRAI. REK. UKAZATEL' LIT. Krasnoiarsk: (Kraev. B-ka), 1957, 59 pp., 1500 copies. [Russ. text; 278 titles]

*Vnotchenko, L. N. POBEDA NA DAL'NEM VOSTOKE. VOEN.-IST. OCHERK O BOEVYKH DEISTVIIAKH SOVETSKIKH VOISK V AVG.-SENT. 1945 G. Moscow: Voenizdat, 1966, 328 pp., 19,000 copies. [Russ. text and titles, per.: Aug.-Sep. 1945, pp. 323-324]

VOPROSY ISTORII SIBIRI. UCHEN. ZAPISKI. No. 28. SERIIA IST. Irkutsk: (M-vo Prosveshcheniia RSFSR. Irkut. Gos. Ped. In-t.), 1967, 217 pp., 700 copies. [Russ. text; titles at end of articles]

*Vorob'ev, V. V.; G. V. Sdasiuk. IRKUTSK. (EKONOMIKO-GEOGRAFICHESKAIA KHARAKTERISTIKA.) (Irkutsk) Vostochno-Sibirskoe Knizhnoe Izdatel'stvo, 1966, 77 pp., 2000 copies. [Russ. text; 17 Russ. titles, pp. 75-76]

LANGUAGE, LITERATURE

*Avrorin, V. A. et al. ISSLEDOVANIIA PO IAZYKU I FOL'KLORU. No.1. Novosibirsk: "Nauka," 1966, 267 pp., 510 copies. [Russ. text and titles at end of articles]

Siberia: Language, Literature

Azadovskii, M. SIBIR' V KHUDOZHESTVENNOI LITERATURE. OPYT BIBLIOGRAFICHESKOGO UKAZATELIA. No. 1.: PERIODICHESKAIA LITERATURA EVROPEISKOI ROSSII ZA 1890-1917 GG. Irkutsk: Izd. Vostochnogo Sibirskogo Otdela Russkogo Geograficheskogo Obshchestva, 1927 (Also: IZVESTIIA VOSTOCHNO-SIBIRSKOGO OTDELA VGO, 1926, Vol. 51.), 49 pp., 550 copies. [Russ. text; 447 Russ. titles, pub.: 1890-1917]

*_____. "SIBIRSKIE TEMY V IZUCHENII RUSSKOGO USTNOGO TVORCHESTVA," SBORNIK TRUDOV GOSUDARSTVENNOGO IRKUTSKOGO UNIVERSITETA (PEDAGOGICHESKII FAKUL'TET). No. 9. VOPROSY NOVOI SHKOLY. (Irkutsk) 1925, 181 pp. [Russ. text; 61 Russ. lists, pp. 143-163]

Bondarko, L. V.; N. G. Zagoruiko; V. A. Kozhevnikov. et al. MODEL' VOSPRIIATIIA RECHI CHELOVEKOM. Novosibirsk: "Nauka," 1968, 59 pp., 600 copies. [Russ. text; 97 titles, pp. 51-58]

*Eliasov, L. E. NARODNAIA REVOLIUTSIONNAIA POEZIIA VOSTOCHNOI SIBIRI EPOKHI GRAZHDANSKOI VOINY. Ulan-Ude: Buriat-Mongol'skoe Knizhnoe Izdatel'stvo, 1957, 278 pp., 2000 copies. [Russ. text; 1072 Russ. titles, pp. 270-276]

*Fateeva, T. I. comp.; N. S. Ber, ed. ISAAK GRIGOR'EVICH GOL'BERG. K 30-LETIIU LITERATURNOI DEIATEL'NOSTI 1903-1933. (BIBLIOGRAFICHESKII UKAZATEL'.) TRUDY NAUCHNOI BIBLIOTEKI VOSTOCHNOSIBIRSKOGO KRAIA. No. 4.) Irkutsk, 1934, 11 pp., 250 copies. [Russ. text and titles, pub.: 1903-1933]

Gladkii, A. V. LEKTSII PO MATEMATICHESKOI LINGVISTIKE. DLIA STUDENTOV NGU. Novosibirsk: (Novosib. Gos. Un-t), 1966, 189 pp., 350 copies. [Russ. text; 24 titles, pp. 184-187]

*Gurevich, Aleksandr. comp. VOSTOCHNAIA SIBIR' V RANNEI KHUDOZHESTVENNOI PROZE. Irkutsk: Irkutskoe Oblastnoe Izdatel'stvo, 1938, 135 pp., 8000 copies. [Russ. text; 6 Russ. lists, pp. 131-134]

*Ivanovskii, N. N. ed. PISATELI SIBIRI. (KRATKII BIBLIOGRAFICHESKII UKAZATEL'). Novosibirsk: Novosibirskoe Knizhnoe Izdatel'stvo, 1956, 76 pp., 3000 copies. [Russ. text and titles]

Siberia: Language, Literature

*[Ianovskii, N. N. comp.] PISATELI-SIBIRIAKI.
LITERATURNO-KRITICHESKIE OCHERKI. No. 1. Novosibirsk:
Novosibirskoe Knizhnoe Izdatel'stvo, 1956, 344 pp.,
5000 copies. [Russ. text; titles, pp. 322-343]

IAZYK KHUDOZHESTVENNYKH PROIZVEDENII. SBORNIK STATEI.
Omsk: Zap.-Sib. Kn. Izd. Omskoe Otd-nie, 1966,
184 pp., 1000 copies. [Russ. text; titles, p. 122]

*Ivanov, S. N. NIKOLAI FEDOROVICH KATANOV (1862-1962).
OCHERK ZHIZNI I DEIATEL'NOSTI. Moscow-Leningrad:
Izdatel'stvo Akademii Nauk SSSR, 1962, 107 pp., 2500
copies. [Russ. text; 117 Russ., Europ. titles,
pub.: 1885-1952, pp. 95-106]

*Khovratovich, B. M. comp. POLE LIUBIT TRUD. RUS.
RUSSKIE NARODNYE POSLOVITSY I POGOVORKI O SEL'SKOM
KHOZIAISTVE. Krasnoiarsk: Krasnoiarskoe Knizhnoe
Izdatel'stvo, 1966, 143 pp., 30,000 copies. [Russ.
text and titles, pub.: 1869-1965, pp. 140-142]

KHUDOZHESTVENNAIA LITERATURA V SIBIRI. Novosibirsk,
1927. [Russ. text; 5 Russ. lists, pub.: 1922-1927 and
before]

Korshunova, L. A. SIBIR' V KHUDOZHESTVENNOI LITERATURE.
(BIBLIOGRAFICHESKII UKAZATEL'.) Novosibirsk:
(Novosibirskaia Oblastnaia Biblioteka), 1953, 80 pp.
[Russ. text]

LITERATURNAIA CHITA. (BIBLIOGR. SPISKI.) Chita:
(Chit. Obl. B-ka im. A. S. Pushkina), 1968, 39 pp.,
3000 copies. [Russ. text]

[Maklakova, I. V. comp.] SIBIRSKIE PISATELI--DETIAM.
PAMIATKA DLIA UCHASHCHIKHSIA 3-4-KH KLASSOV.
Novosibirsk: Zap.-Sib. Kn. Izd. (Novosib. Obl. Det.
B-ka im. Gor'kogo), 1968, 40 pp., 1000 copies.
[Russ. text]

*MATERIALY TRET'EI DAL'NEVOSTOCHNOI ZONAL'NOI NAUCHNOI
KONFERENTSII, POSVIASHCHENNOI 50-LETIIU SOVETSKOI
VLASTI....SERIIA FILOLOGII. Vladivostok: (M-vo
Vyssh. i Sred. Spets. Obrazovaniia RSFSR), 1968, 196 pp.,
1000 copies. [Russ. text; titles at end of reports]

Siberia: Language, Literature

Mezherova, L.; A. Nagibina. "LITERATURNYI OTDEL GAZETY
   VOSTOCHNOE OBOZRENIE (1882-1906). BIBLIOGRAFICHESKIE
   MATERIALY," SIBIRSKII LITERATURNO-KRAEVEDCHESKII
   SBORNIK. Irkutsk: Vostochno-Sibirskii Otd. Gosud.
   Russk. Geografich. O-va, 1928, (separate) 32 pp.
   [Russ. text; 717 Russ. titles, pub.: 1882-1906,
   pp. 93-122]

Mikhaleva, S. P. IRKUTSKIE POETY. (Irkutsk): Vost.-Sib.
   Kn. Izd., 1966, 27 pp., 2000 copies. [Russ. text]

Moskovskii, A. P. O PRIRODE KOMICHESKOGO. (Irkutsk):
   Vost.-Sib. Kn. Izd., 1968, 96 pp., 1000 copies.
   [Russ. text; 84 titles, pp. 94-96]

Palagina, V. V. "IZUCHENIE RUSSKIKH NARODNYKH GOVOROV
   TERRITORII TOMSKOI OBLASTI (KRATKII OBZOR I
   BIBLIOGRAFIIA)," VOPROSY RUS. IAZYKA I EGO GOVOROV.
   (TRUDY TOMSKOGO UN-TA IM. KUIBYSHEVA. Vol. 197.)
   Tomsk, 1968, 93-99 pp. [Russ. text; 70 titles]

*PISATELI O SEBE. (SBORNIK STATEI.) Novosibirsk: Zap.-Sib.
   Kn. Izd., 1966, 215 pp., 7000 copies. [Russ. text;
   titles, pp. 171-214]

PISATELI ZABAIKAL'IA. (BIBLIOGR. UKAZATEL'.) Chita:
   (Chit. Obl. B-ka im. A. S. Pushkina), 1967, 16 pp.,
   1000 copies. [Russ. text]

*Sergeev, M. "LITERATURA NARODOV SIBIRI. (MATERIALY K
   BIBLIOGRAFII)," LITERATURA NARODOV SIBIRI. SBORNIK
   STATEI. n. p. Novosibirskoe Knizhnoe Izdatel'stvo,
   1956, 184 pp., 3000 copies. [Russ. text and titles,
   pp. 169-178]

SIBIRSKIE PISATELI ZA 30 LET. (BIBLIOGRAFICHESKII
   UKAZATEL'.) Irkutsk, 1947. [Russ. text]

*Sidel'nikov, V. BYLINY SIBIRI. Tomsk: Izdatel'stvo
   Tomskogo Universiteta, 1968, 420 pp., 2000 copies.
   [Russ. text; 71 Russ. titles, pp. 414-417]

[Sycheva, L.] PROIZVEDENIIA KUIBYSHEVSKIKH PISATELEI.
   BIBLIOGR. UKAZATEL'. No. 2. 1952-1956. Kuibyshev:
   (Kuibyshevskaia Obl. B-ka. Kuibyshevskoe Ob. Otd-nie
   Soiuza Sovetskikh Pisatelei), 1957, 21 pp., 1000
   copies. [Russ. text; 29 titles, pub.: 1952-1956]

Siberia: Language, Literature

TRUDY KAFEDR RUSSKOGO IAZYKA VUZOV VOSTOCHNOI SIBIRI I DAL'NEGO VOSTOKA. No. 4. Ulan-Ude: Buriat. Kn. Izd., 1966, 226 pp., 500 copies. [Russ. text; titles, pp. 90-91]

*Tsomakion, N. A. TURUKHANSKIE GOVORY V IKH ISTORII I SOVREMENNOM SOSTOIANII. Krasnoiarsk: Krasnoiarskoe Knizhnoe Izdatel'stvo, 1966, 494 pp., 500 copies. [Russ. text and titles, at end of chapters]

Veisberg, G. P.; G. M. Pushkarev. SIBIR' V KHUDOZHESTVENNOI LITERATURE. Moscow-Leningrad, 1927. [Russ. text; titles scattered]

[Vorob'eva, T. A. et al. comp.] PISATELI SIBIRI. (KRATKII BIBLIOGR. UKAZATEL'). Novosibirsk: Kn. Izd. (Novosib. Obl. B-ka. K Soveshchaniiu Sib. Pisatelei), 1956, 76 pp., 3000 copies. [Russ. text]

*Zaitseva, S. PISATELI MALYKH NARODOV DAL'NEGO VOSTOKA. BIOBIBLIOGR. SPRAVOCHNIK. Khabarovsk: Kn. Izd., 1966, 120 pp., 2000 copies. [Russ. text; titles, pub.: 1936-1965]

Zdobnov, N. V. "MATERIALY DLIA SIBIRSKOGO SLOVARIA PISATELEI. (PREDVARITEL'NYI SPISOK POETOV, BELLETRISTOV, DRAMATURGOV, KRITIKOV)," SEVERNAIA AZIIA. (PRILOZHENIE). Book 1, 2. 4-6. Moscow: (Izdatel'stvo "Severnaia Aziia"), 1927, (Separately) 61 pp., 300 copies. [Russ. text; ca.6000 Russ. titles]

Zelenkina, O. "N. A. KOSTROV," ETNO. BIULLETEN'. No. 4. (Irkutsk), 1923, 1-7 pp. [Russ. text]

PHILOSOPHY, RELIGION

Gagarin, Dm. UKAZATEL' K IRKUTSKIM EPARKHIAL'NYM VIEDOMOSTIAM ZA DVADTSAT' PIAT' LIET (1863 PO 1888). Irkutsk, 1889, 264 pp. [Russ. text; titles, pub.: 1863-1888]

Siberia: Philosophy, Religion

Gagarin, Dm. UKAZATEL' K IRKUTSKIM EPARKHIAL'NYM
VIEDOMOSTIAM ZA SHESTNADTSAT' LIET (1888-1904).
Irkutsk,1905, 135 pp. [Russ. text; titles, pub.:
1888-1904]

Ivashevskii, L. I. comp. METODICHESKOE POSOBIE PO
FILOSOFII. Irkutsk: (Vost.-Sib. Filial SO AN SSSR.
Kafedra Filosofii), 1968, 48 pp., 1000 copies. [Russ.
text; 150 titles, pp. 33-48]

Kuliev, N. ANTINAUCHNAIA SUSHCHNOST' ISLAMA I ZADACHI
ATEISTICHESKOGO VOSPITANIIA TRUDIASHCHIKHSIA V
USLOVIIAKH SOVETSKOGO TURKMENISTANA. Ashkhabad:
(Akad. Nauk Turkm. SSR. Otd. Filosofii i Prava),
1960. [Russ. text; ca.130 titles, pp. 161-165]

Kuznetsov, E. V. UKAZATEL' 'TOBOL'SKIKH EPARKHIAL'NYKH
VIEDOMOSTEI' 1882-1896 G. G. TOBOL'SKIE EPARKHIAL'NYE
VIEDOMOSTI. (PRILOZHENIE). (Tobol'sk), 1898, 66 pp.
[Russ. text; titles, pub.: 1882-1896]

Lazarev, D. N. OGLAVLENIE STATEI, POMESHCHENNYKH V
'ENISEISKIKH EPARKHIAL'NYKH VIEDOMOSTIIAKH' ZA 1884-
1895 GG. Krasnoiarsk, 1896. [Russ. text; titles
pub.: 1884-1895]

POLITICAL SCIENCE, LAW

Ageev, A. I. BIBLIOGRAFICHESKII UKAZATEL'. KLASSIKI
MARKSIZMA-LENINIZMA V PEREVODAKH NA UZBEKSKII IAZYK.
(1925-1940). Tashkent: Gos. Publichnaia Biblioteka
Uzbekskoi SSR, 1941. [Titles pub.: 1925-1940]

*Astrakhantseva, I. F.; A. A. Dudoladov; M. I. Timoshenko.
comps. ADMINISTRATIVNO-TERRITORIAL'NOE DELENIE SIBIRI.
(AVGUST 1920 G.-IIUL' 1930 G.) ZAPADNOI SIBIRI
(IIUL' 1930 G.-SENTIABR' 1937 G.) Novosibirsk:
Zapadno-Sibirskoe Knizhnoe Izdatel'stvo, 1966, 220 pp.,
2000 copies. [Russ. text and titles, per.: 1920-1937,
p. 190]

Siberia: Political Science, Law

Azadovskii, M.; M. Slobodskii. "DEKABRISTY V SIBIRI. BIBLIOGRAFICHESKIE MATERIALY," SIBIR' I DEKABRISTY. STAT'I, MATERIALY, NEIZDANNYE PIS'MA, BIBLIOGRAFIIA. Irkutsk: Izdanie Irkutskogo Gubernskogo Ispolnitel'nogo Komiteta, 1925, 208 pp., 1500 copies. [Russ. text; 384 Russ. titles, pp. 166-182]

Bessel', L. "BIBLIOGRAFIIA SSYLKI," SIBIRSKAIA SSYLKA. Moscow, 1927. [Russ. text]

*Bondarev, A. VALENTIN IAKOVLEV. (1892-1918). Krasnoiarsk: Krasnoiarskoe Kn. Izd., 1966, 39 pp., 10,000 copies. [Russ. text and titles, pub.: 1911-1963, pp. 37-38]

Budarin, Mikhail. BYLI O SIBIRSKIKH CHEKISTAKH. (Omsk) Zap.-Sib. Kn. Izd. Omskoe Otd-nie, 1968, 270 pp., 30,000 copies. [Russ. text; 36 titles, pp. 264-266]

*Flerov, V. S. ed. TOMSKAIA GORODSKAIA PARTIINAIA ORGANIZATSIIA V GODY VELIKOI OTECHESTVENNOI VOINY. 1941-1945. SBORNIK DOKUMENTOV. n. p. Tomskoe Knizhnoe Izdatel'stvo, 1962, 487 pp., 3000 copies. [Russ. text and titles, per.: 1941-1945, pp. 467-470]

Ianchenko, N. N. ISSLEDOVANIE PROTSESSA PERERABOTKI GRUZOV NA VOENNYKH SKLADAKH. Novosibirsk: Novosib. In-t Inzhenerov Zh-d. Transporta), 1967, 73 pp., 500 copies. [Russ. text; 35 titles, pp. 72-73]

*Kadeikin, V. A. RABOCHIE SIBIRI V BOR'BE ZA VLAST' SOVETOV I OSUSHCHESTVLENIE PERVYKH SOTSIALISTICHESKIKH PREOBRAZOVANII (NOIABR' 1917-AVGUST 1918 GG.) Kemerov: Kemerovskoe Knizhnoe Izdatel'stvo, 1966, 370 pp., 3000 copies. [Russ. text; 2063 Russ. titles (incl. archives), per.: 1917-1918, pp. 360-369]

KHABAROVSKII POLITEKHNICHESKII INSTITUT. MATERIALY VI NAUCHNO-TEKHNICHESKOI KONFERENTSII (KAFEDRY OBSHCHESTV. NAUK). Khabarovsk: (M-vo Vyssh. i Sred. Spets. Obrazovaniia RSFSR), 1968, 158 pp., 600 copies. [Russ. text and titles, at end of reports]

*Kolosov, E. E. SIBIR' PRI KOLCHAKE. VOSPOMINANIIA, MATERIALY, DOKUMENTY. Petrograd: Izdatel'stvo "Byloe," 1923, 190 pp., 4000 copies. [Russ. text; Russ. survey, per.: 1918-1920, pp. 34-36]

Siberia: Political Science, Law

Lazo, O. SERGEI LAZO. Krasnoiarsk: Kn. Izd., 1966, 20 pp., 10,000 copies. [Russ. text; titles at end of book]

NASHI ZEMLIAKI-GEROI SOVETSKOGO SOIUZA. Irkutsk: (Irkutsk. Obl. Organizatsiia O-va "Znanie" v Pomoshch' Lektoru), 1967, 38 pp., 600 copies. [Russ. text; 34 titles, pp. 36-37]

Nikitin, E. "BIBLIOGRAFICHESKII SPRAVOCHNIK PO ISTORII NERCHINSKOI KATORGI," KARA I DRUGIE TIUR'MY NERCHINSKOI KATORGI. Moscow, 1927. [Russ. text]

*Popov, I. I. SAMOUPRAVLENIE I ZEMSKAIA UCHREZHDENIIA (PO POVODU VVEDENIIA ZEMSTVA V SIBIRI). Moscow: Izdanie S. Dorovatovskago i Charushnikova, 1906, 55 pp. [Russ. text and titles, pp. 53-54]

Potapova, A. V.; N. N. Balyko; E. N. Mel'nikova; O. D. Tarmakhanova; R. I. Tsuprik; A. N. Alekseev. comps. BOR'BA ZA VLAST' SOVETOV V VOSTOCHNOI SIBIRI (1917-1922). BIBLIOGRAFICHESKII UKAZATEL'. Irkutsk: Knizhnoe Izdatel'stvo, 1962, 202 pp., 1000 copies. [Russ. text; ca.2800 titles, pub.: ca.1917-1960]

REVOLIUTSIONNOE DVIZHENIE V SIBIRI V PERIOD PERVOI RUSSKOI REVOLIUTSII (1905-1907 GG.). REKOMENDATEL'NYI UKAZATEL' LITERATURY. Novosibirsk: (Novosibirskaia Oblastnaia Biblioteka), 1957, 73 pp. [Russ. text; titles, per.: 1905-1907]

*REVOLIUTSIONNOE DVIZHENIE V ZABAIKAL'E, 1905-1907 GG. SBORNIK DOKUMENTOV I MATERIALOV K PIATIDESIATILETIIU PERVOI RUSSKOI REVOLIUTSII. Chita: Chitinskoe Knizhnoe Izdatel'stvo, 1955, 447 pp., 5000 copies. [Russ. text; 60 Russ. titles, per.: 1905-1907, pp. 434-437]

Rudykh, Z. S.; P. I. Shchvarts. comps. IZ ISTORII IRKUTSKOI OBLASTNOI PARTIINOI ORGANIZATSII. (UKAZATEL' LITERATURY). NAUCH. B-KA. TRUDY. Part 2. 1921-1966 G. No. 19. Irkutsk: (Irkut. Gos. Un-t im. A. A. Zhdanova), 1967, 62 pp., 300 copies. [Russ. text; titles, per.: 1921-1966]

Shakhmatov, V. P. SDELKI, SOVERSHENNYE S TSEL'IU, PROTIVNOI INTERESAM GOSUDARSTVA I OBSHCHESTVA. Tomsk: Izd. Tomskogo Un-ta, 1966, 140 pp., 1000 copies. [Russ. text; titles at end of chapters]

Siberia: Political Science, Law

[Shatunova, A.] DEKABRISTY V SIBIRI. KRATKII REK. SPISOK LIT. Novosibirsk: (Novosibirskaia Obl. Det. B-ka im. Gor'kogo), 1957, 11 pp., 1000 copies. [Russ. text; 25 titles]

Timofeeva, A. V. VOPROS O VOINE I MIRE--OSNOVNOI VOPROS SOVREMENNOSTI. Omsk: (Otd. Propagandy i Agitatsii Omskogo Obkoma KPSS), 1967, 24 pp., 1200 copies. [Russ. text; titles at end of book]

Turunov, A. N.; V. D. Vegman. REVOLIUTSIIA I GRAZHDANSKAIA VOINA V SIBIRI. UKAZATEL' KNIG I ZHURNAL'NYKH STATEI. Novosibirsk: Sibkraiizdat, 1928, 136 pp. [Russ. text; 870 Russ., Czech., Europ. titles]

*Vedernikov, N. T. IZUCHENIE LICHNOSTI PRESTUPNIKA V PROTSESSE RASSLEDOVANIIA. Tomsk: Izd. Tomskogo Un-ta, 1968, 84 pp., 1200 copies. [Russ. text; ca.120 Russ. titles, pub.: 1924-1966, pp. 79-83]

SOCIAL ORGANIZATION

Bondarovskaia, S. B. 25 SLAVNYKH LET. (IZ ISTORII NORIL. KOMSOMOL'SKOI ORGANIZATSII.) MONOGRAFIIA. Krasnoiarsk: (Kn. Izd.) 1966, 55 pp., 2000 copies. [Russ. text; 122 titles, per.: 25 years, pp. 53-55]

"CHTO CHITAT' O KUIBYSHEVSKOM KOMSOMOLE," LET LEGENDARNYKH PEREKLUCHKOV. Kuibyshev, 1968. [Russ. text; 42 titles, pp. 422-426]

DOROGOI BOR'BY I POBED. (AMURSKII OBKOM VLKSM. OCHERKI PO ISTORII AMURSKOI KOMSOMOL'SKOI ORGANIZATSII. 1918-1964.) Khabarovsk: Kn. Izd., 1966, 173 pp., 3000 copies. [Russ. text; 129 titles, per.: 1918-1964, pp. 169-172]

*Futorianskii, L. I. DELA VECHNO ZHIVYE. KOMSOMOL I MOLODEZH'. ORENBURZH'IA V GODY GRAZHD. VOINY. (Cheliabinsk): Iuzhn.-Ural. Kn. Izd., 1968, 103 pp., 8000 copies. [Russ. text; 17 Russ. titles, pub.: 1957-1960, p. 102]

Siberia: Social Organization

[Lebedeva, E. comp.] DOROGOI OTTSOV IUNOST' IDET. (KRATKII REK. SPISOK LIT. O SLAVNYKH DELAKH I TRADITSIIAKH KOMSOMOL'TSEV I MOLODEZHI KUIBYSHEVSKOI OBL.) Kuibyshev: (Kuibyshevskaia Obl. B-ka. K 50-Letiiu VLKSM), 1968, 1000 copies. [Russ. text; 21 titles]

Prikhod'ko, P. T. OKHRANA ZDOROV'IA, TRUD I BYT TRUDIASHCHIKHSIA SIBIRI. SISTEMATICHESKII UKAZATEL' LITERATURY ZA 1776-1929 GG. (PRILOZHENIE K TRUDAM TOMSKOGO GOSUDARSTVENNOGO MEDITSINSKOGO INSTITUTA. Vol. 2.) Tomsk, 1930, 106 pp. [Russ. text; 2016 titles, pub.: 1776-1929]

Shpisman, I. I.; D. D. Iablokov. BIBLIOGRAFICHESKII UKAZATEL' PO KURORTAM SIBIRI I SMEZHNYKH OBLASTEI. Tomsk: (Tomskoi Oblastnoi Nauchno-Issledovatel'skii Institut Fizicheskikh Metodov Lecheniia i Kurortologii), 1951, 183 pp. [Russ. text; ca.2000 titles, pub.: mainly 1929-1949]

37 TUVAN

GENERAL

*Andreev, A. I. OCHERKI PO ISTOCHNIKOVEDENIIU SIBIRI.
XVII VEK. Vol. 1-2. Leningrad: Glavsevmopput',
1960-65. [Russ. text; titles, per.: 17th c.]

*Dulov, V. I.; E. N. Morachevskaia; Kh. M. Seifulin;
P. A. Shakhunova. comps. BIBLIOGRAFIIA TUVINSKOI
AVTONOMNOI OBLASTI (1774-1958 GG.) Moscow:
Izdatel'stvo Akademii Nauk SSSR. (Akad. Nauk SSSR.
Sovet po Izucheniiu Proizvodit. Nauch.-Issled. In-t
Iazyka, Lit. i Istorii), 1959, 167 pp., 1500 copies.
[Russ. text; ca.1200 Russ. titles, pub.: 1774-1958]

LITERATURA O TUVE, ULUG-KHEM. No. 3. 1956, 197 pp.
[Russ. text; 21 Tuvan, Russ. titles]

*"OBSHCHAIA BIBLIOGRAFIIA...MONGOL'SKAIA NARODNAIA
RESPUBLIKA...TUVINSKAIA RESPUBLIKA...,"
BIBLIOGRAFIIA VOSTOKA. No. 1. 1932. [Russ. text
and titles, pp. 137-139]

Ondur, D. D.; L. M. Soboleva. comps. CHTO CHITAT' O
TUVE. REKOMENDATEL'NYE SPISKI LITERATURY. Kyzyl:
[Tuvknigoizdat] (Tuvinskaia Respublikanskaia
Biblioteka imeni A. S. Pushkina), 1966, 36 pp.,
1000 copies. [Russ. text]

*"TUVINSKAIA AVTONOMNAIA OBLAST'," BOL'SHAIA SOVETSKAIA
ENTSIKLOPEDIIA. Vol. 55. Moscow: Gosudarstvennyi
Nauchnyi Institut "Sovetskaia Entsiklopediia,"
(Ogiz SSSR), 1947, 110-116 pp. [Russ. text; Tuvan,
Russ., Europ. titles, pp. 115-116]

*"TUVINSKAIA AVTONOMNAIA OBLAST'," BOL'SHAIA SOVETSKAIA
ENTSIKLOPEDIIA. Vol. 43. Moscow: Gosudarstvennoe
Nauchnoe Izdatel'stvo "Bol'shaia Sovetskaia
Entsiklopediia," 1956, 2nd ed., 352-358 pp. [Russ.
text; titles pp. 356, 358]

"UKAZATEL' NAUCHNYKH TRUDOV, IZDANNYKH TNIIIALI (1946-
1964 GG.); UKAZATEL' STATEI OPUBLIKOVANNYKH V
UCHENYKH ZAPISKAKH TNIIIALI (1953-1963 GG.)"
20 LET SOVETSKOI TUVY. (UCHEN. ZAPISKI TUVIN. NII
IAZYKA, LITERATURY I ISTORII. No. 11). Kyzyl,
1964. [Russ. text; 70+ Tuvan, Russ. titles, pub.:
1945-1964, pp. 391-394, 382-390]

ANTHROPOLOGY, ETHNOGRAPHY

Katanov, Nikolai F. "BIBLIOGRAFICHESKII UKAZATEL' LITERATURY OB URIANKHAITSAKH I IKH ZEMLE," OPYT ISSLEDOVANIIA URIANKHAITSKAGO IAZYKA. Part 4. Kazan: (Uchenye Zapiski Kazanskago Universiteta za 1902), 1903. [Russ. text; 84 Russ., Europ. titles, pub.: 1768-1902, pp. 317-472; 1369-1524]

*Vainshtein, S. I. TUVINTSY-TODZHINTSY. ISTORIKO-ETNOGRAFICHESKIE OCHERKI. Moscow: Izdatel'stvo Vostochnoi Literatury, 1961, 218 pp., 1000 copies. [Russ. text; Russ., Europ. titles, pp. 205-209]

* _____. TUVINTSY-TODZHINTSY. IST.-ETNOGR. OCHERKI. Moscow: (Akad. Nauk SSSR. Institut Narodov Azii. Tuvin. Nauch.-Issled. Institut Iazyka, Literatury i Istorii), 1961, 216 pp. [Russ. text; ca.200 Russ., other titles, pp. 205-209]

ECONOMICS

*Obruchev, V. A. "ESTESTVENNYE BOGATSTVA TANNU-TUVINSKOI RESPUBLIKI I STEPEN' IZUCHENNOSTI POSLEDNEI," NOVYI VOSTOK. Book 13/14, 1926. 1926, 426 pp. [Russ. text; 45 Russ. titles, pub.: Sov. per., pp. 425-427]

Shakhunova, P. A.; B. N. Likhanov. SOVETSKAIA TUVA (PRIRODA, NASELENIE, KHOZIAISTVO). Kyzyl: (Tuvin. Nauch.-Issled. In-t Iazyka, Lit. i Istorii), 1955, [Russ. text; 98 titles, Sov. per., pp. 150-156]

Tuvan

GEOGRAPHY

*Grumm-Grzhimailo, G. E. OPISANIE PUTESHESTVIIA V
 ZAPADNYI KITAI. Moscow: Geografgiz, 1948, 2nd
 abridged ed., 685 pp. [Russ. text; Russ., other
 titles, pub.: 1920, pp. 667-674]

Obruchev, S. V. V SERDTSE AZII. Moscow, 1965. [Russ.
 text; 41 titles, pp. 125-127]

Obruchev, V. A. ed. GEOGRAFICHESKOE OBSHCHESTVO,
 VOSTOCHNO-SIBIRSKII OTDIEL. SISTEMATICHESKII
 UKAZATEL' VSIEKH IZDANII OTDIELA...ZA SOROKA-LIETIE
 1851-1891 [1891-1901 GG.; 1901-1911] Irkutsk,
 1891, 1901, 1912, (1891) p. 89; (1901) p. 24;
 (1912) p. 15. [Russ. text; titles, pub.: 1851-1911]

Shakhunova, P. A. comp. "PRIRODNYE USLOVIIA
 TUVINSKOI AVTONOMNOI OBLASTI," TRUDY TUVIN.
 KOMPLEKSNOI EKSPEDITSII. No. 3. Moscow, 1957.
 [Russ. text; ca.340 titles, pp. 265-276]

URIANKHAISKII KRAI. SVIEDENIIA O GOSUDARSTVAKH
 DAL'NEGO VOSTOKA. (OBZOR PERIODICHESKOI PECHATI)
 ZA FEVRAL' MESIATS 1912 G. Irkutsk, 1912. [Russ.
 text; titles pp. 13-16]

HISTORY, ARCHAEOLOGY

*Dulov, V. I. SOTSIAL'NO-EKONOMICHESKAIA ISTORIIA
 TUVY. XIX--NACHALO XX V. Moscow: (Akad. Nauk SSSR.
 In-t Istorii. Tuvin. Nauch.-Issled. In-t Iazyka,
 Lit. i Istorii), 1956, 608 pp. [Russ. text; ca.470
 Russ., other titles, per.: 19th - beginning of 20th c.,
 pp. 564-585]

Tuvan: History, Archaeology

*Potapov, L. P. ed. ISTORIIA TUVY. Vol. 1, 2.
Moscow: Izdatel'stvo Nauka. Vol. 1, 1964, 410 pp.;
Vol. 2, 1964, 455 pp., 8000 copies. [Russ. text;
Tuvan, Russ., Europ., Turkish titles (incl. archives),
per.: (1) up to 1917; (2) 1917-1961, (1) pp. 11-16;
(2) pp. 448-452]

*Stepanova, A. V. "LITERATURA O V. I. LENINE NA
TUVINSKOM IAZYKE," UCHEN. ZAP. TUVIN. NII IAZ.,
LIT., I ISTORII. No. 14. Kyzyl, 1970, 264-265 pp.,
1500 copies. [Russ. text; 22 Tuvan titles, pub.:
1931-1969, pp. 264-265]

*"TUVINSKAIA AVTONOMNAIA OBLAST'," BOL'SHAIA SOVETSKAIA
ENTSIKLOPEDIIA. Vol. 55. 1947, 1st ed., 110-116 pp.
[Russ. text; Russ., Europ. titles, pp. 115-116]

LANGUAGE, LITERATURE

Izyneeva, M. A. "BIBLIOGRAFICHESKII UKAZATEL'
KHUDOZHESTVENNO-KRITICHESKOI LITERATURY O TUVE.
(NA RUS. IAZ.)," UCHEN. ZAPISKI (TUVIN. NAUCH.-
ISSLED. IN-T IAZYKA, LIT. I ISTORII). No. 4. 1956.
[Russ. text; 130 Russ. titles, pub.: 1944-1956,
pp. 188-192]

*Iskhakov, F. G.; A. A. Pal'mbakh. GRAMMATIKA TUVINSKOGO
IAZYKA. Moscow: Akad. Nauk SSSR, 1961, 471 pp.
[Russ. text; ca.190 Russ., other titles, pp. 464-470]

Mongush, D. A. FORMY PROSHEDSHEGO VREMENI
IZ"IAVITEL'NOGO NAKLONENIIA V TUVINSKOM IAZYKE.
Kyzyl, 1963. [Russ. text; ca.150 titles, pp. 158-164]

*Pal'mbakh, A. "TUVINSKII IAZYK," BOL'SHAIA SOVETSKAIA
ENTSIKLOPEDIIA. Vol. 55. Moscow: Gosudarstvennyi
Nauchnyi Institut "Sovetskaia Entsiklopediia,"
(Ogiz SSSR), 1947, 116-117 pp. [Russ. text; Tuvan,
Russ. titles, p. 117]

*_____.: Iu. L. Akanchyn; A. K. Kalzang. eds.
OCHERKI TUVINSKOI LITERATURY. Kyzyl: Tivaning Nom
Undurer Cheri, 1964, 239 pp., 1000 copies. [Tuvan
text; Tuvan, Russ. titles, pp. 231-239]

Tuvan: Language, Literature

*Sat, Shuluu Chyrgal-Oolovich. OCHERK ISTORII IZUCHENIIA TUVINSKOGO IAZYKA. Kyzyl: Tuvinskoe Knizhnoe Izdatel'stvo, 1964, 114 pp., 1000 copies. [Tuvan text; Tuvan, Russ., Europ. titles, pp. 103-113]

*_____. SOVREMENNYI TUVINSKII LITERATURNYI IAZYK. Kyzyl: Tyvanyng Nom Undurer Cheri, 1966, 144 pp., 2000 copies. [Tuvan text; Tuvan, Russ. titles, pp. 141-142]

*_____. SOVREMENNYI TUVINSKII LITERATURNYI IAZYK. SINTAKSIS. Kyzyl: Tuvknigoizdat, 1966, 144 pp., 2000 copies. [Tuvin text; Tuvin, Russ. titles, pub.: 1945-1966, pp. 141-142]

*Soboleva, L. M. "BIBLIOGRAFICHESKII UKAZATEL' KHUDOZHESTVENNO-KRITICHESKOI LITERATURY O TUVE. (1960-1967 GG.) KHUDOZH. PROZA. PUTEVYE ZAMETKI. PUBLITSISTIKA. STIKHI. FOL'KLOR," UCHEN. ZAP. TUVIN. NII IAZ., LIT. I ISTORII. No. 13. Kyzyl, 1968, 344-353 pp., 1000 copies. [Russ. text; ca.150 Russ. titles, pub.: 1960-1967, pp. 344-353]

_____.: A. A. Stepanova. comps. PISATELI TUVY. Kyzyl: Tuvknigoizdat, 1970, 115 pp., 1500 copies. [Russ. text]

"SPISOK LITERATURY, IZDANNOI TUVINSKIM NAUCHNO-ISSLEDOVATEL'SKIM INSTITUTOM IAZYKA, LITERATURY I ISTORII ZA 10 LET--1946-1956 GG. (BEZ UCHEBNIKOV)," UCHEN. ZAPISKI (TUVIN. NAUCH.-ISSLED. IN-T IAZYKA, LIT. I ISTORII), No. 5. 1957. [Russ. text; 32 Tuvan, Russ. titles, pub.: 1946-1956, pp. 249-250]

Stepanova, A. V. "PROIZVEDENIIA KHUDOZHESTVENNOI LITERATURY V PEREVODAKH NA TUVINSKII IAZYK. (1938-1960 GG.)," UCHEN. ZAPISKI (TUVIN. NAUCH.-ISSLED. IN-T IAZYKA, LIT. I ISTORII), No. 9. 1961. [Russ. text; ca.180 titles, pub.: 1938-1960, pp. 275-281]

_____. "TUVA V KHUDOZHESTVENNOI LITERATURE," UCHEN. ZAPISKI. (TUVIN. NAUCH.-ISSLED. IN.-T IAZYKA, LIT., I ISTORII), No. 8. 1960. [Russ. text; 83 Russ. titles, pub.: 1943-1959, pp. 254-259]

*Tolgar-Ool, O. A. comp. RUSSKO-TUVINSKII SLOVAR'. OBSHCHESTVENNO-POLITICHESKIKH TERMINOV. Kyzyl: Tuvknigoizdat, 1966, 364 pp., 1000 copies. [Tuvin, Russ. text; 16 Tuvin, Russ. titles, pub.: 1953-1964, pp. 9-10]

Tuvan: Language, Literature

TUVINSKAIA LITERATURA. KRATKAIA ISTORIIA. Kyzyl,
  1964. [Tuvan text; ca.170 titles, pp. 231-239]

*"UKAZATEL' NAUCHNYKH TRUDOV, IZDANNYKH TNIIIALI
  (1964-1969 GG.)," UCHEN. ZAP. TUVIN. NII IAZ.,
  LIT. I ISTORII. No. 14. Kyzyl, 1970, 274-275 pp.,
  1500 copies. [Russ. text; 16 Tuvan, Russ. titles,
  pub.: 1964-1969, pp. 274-275]

PHILOSOPHY, RELIGION

Sermavkin, T. V. comp. PRAVDA O TSERKOVNIKAKH I
  SEKTANTAKH TUVY. Kyzyl, (Otd. Propagandy i Agitatsii
  Tuvin. Obkoma KPSS), 1961. [Russ. text; ca.70
  titles, pp. 174-182]

POLITICAL SCIENCE, LAW

*"BIBLIOGRAFIIA PO TANNU-TUVINSKOI RESPUBLIKE," NOVYI
  VOSTOK. No. 13/14. 1926, 426 pp. [Russ. text and
  titles, pub.: Sov. per., pp. 425-427]

Sat, Sh. Ch.; A. V. Stepanova. "PROIZVEDENIIA V. I.
  LENINA NA TUVINSKOM IAZYKE," UCHEN. ZAPISKI (TUVIN.
  NAUCH-ISSLED. IN-T IAZYKA, LIT. I ISTORII). No. 8.
  1960. [Russ. text; 22 titles, pub.: 1951-1959]

_____. "SPISOK PROIZVEDENII V. I. LENINA I I. V.
  STALINA, IZDANNYKH NA TUVINSKOM IAZYKE ZA PERIOD S
  1931 G. DO IIULIA 1953 GODA," UCHENYE ZAPISKI
  TUVIN. NAUCH.-ISSLED IN-T IAZYKA, LIT. I ISTORII.
  No. 1. 1953. [Russ. text; 55 Tuvan titles, pub.:
  1931-1953, pp. 111-116]

38 YAKUT

GENERAL

*Azadovskii, M. "NEKROLOG. E. K. PEKARSKII 1858-1934,"
SOVETSKAIA ETNOGRAFIIA. No. 5. 1934, 105-108.
[Russ. text and titles, pp. 107-108]

Ber, N. S. IZDANIIA IRKUTSKOGO GOSUDARSTVENNOGO
UNIVERSITETA ZA DESIAT' LET EGO SUSHCHESTVOVANIIA.
1918-1928. BIBLIOGRAFICHESKII UKAZATEL'. Irkutsk:
Izdatel'stvo Irkutskskogo Universiteta. (Trudy
Biblioteki Irkutsk. Gos. Un-ta. No. 2), 1930, 49 pp.
[Russ. text; 293 Russ. titles, pub.: 1918-1928]

Bialetskii, K. A.; S. S. Krivtsov. et al. IAKUTIIA.
Moscow-Leningrad, Moskovskii Rabochii, 1929, 117 pp.
[Russ. text]

Buchenkov, A. N. "IAKUTSKII KRAI V RUSSKOI LITERATURE
(BIBLIOGRAFIIA)," SOTSIALISTICHESKAIA IAKUTIIA.
Sept. 25, 1945. [Russ. text and titles]

Esipov, V. "IZDANIIA AKADEMII NAUK SSSR PO
ISSLEDOVANIIU IAKUTSKOI ASSR. (VTOROI
BIBLIOGRAFICHESKII OBZOR)," SOVETSKII SEVER. No. 1.
1934. [Russ. text; titles pp. 158-160]

_____. "IZDANIIA KOMISSII PO IZUCHENIIU IAKUTSKOI
ASSR PRI AKADEMII NAUK SSSR ZA 1925-1930 GG.
(KRATKII BIBLIOGRAFICHESKII OBZOR)," SOVETSKII SEVER.
No. 6. 1931. [Russ. text; titles, pp. 117-125]

Gribanovskii, N. N. "MATERIALY DLIA BIBLIOGRAFII
IAKUTSKOI OBLASTI ZA 1914-1915 GG.," IZVESTIIA
IAKUTSKAGO OTDIELENIIA RUSSKAGO GEOGRAFICHESKAGO
OBSHCHESTVA. Vol. 1. 1915. [Russ. text; titles
pub.: 1914-1915, pp. 119-127]

*Grigor'ev, A. "IAKUTSKAIA AVTONOMNAIA SOVETSKAIA
SOTSIALISTICHESKAIA RESPUBLIKA," (IAASSR).
BOL'SHAIA SOVETSKAIA ENTSIKLOPEDIIA. Vol. 65.
Moscow: Gosudarstvennoe Slovarno-Entsiklopedicheskoe
Izdatel'stvo "Sovetskaia Entsiklopediia," (Ogiz
RSFSR), 1931, 473-479 pp. [Russ. text and titles,
p. 479]

Yakut: General

*"IAKUTY," BOL'SHAIA SOVETSKAIA ENTSIKLOPEDIIA. Vol. 65.
Moscow: Gosudarstvennoe Slovarno-Entsiklopedicheskoe
Izdatel'stvo "Sovetskaia Entsiklopediia," (Ogiz
RSFSR), 1931, 507-509 pp. [Russ. text; Iakut, Russ.,
Europ. titles, p. 509]

Iavlovskii, Prokopii. SISTEMATICHESKII UKAZATEL'
STATEI POMIESHCHENNYKH V NEOFFITSIAL'NOI CHASTI
IAKUTSKIKH EPARKHIAL'NYKH VIEDOMOSTEI ZA PERVOE
DESIATILIETIE IZDANIIA (1887-1897). n. p. 1898.
[Russ. text]

*Karamyshev, E. "UKAZATEL' KNIZHNOI LITERATURY PO
IAKUTII S 1926 G.," SOVETSKOE KRAEVEDENIE. No. 8.
1935, 82-83 pp. [Russ. text; 66 titles]

Kosven, M. IAKUTSKAIA RESPUBLIKA. Moscow-Leningrad:
Izd. "Zemlia i Fabrika," 1925, 155 pp. [Russ. text]

LETOPIS' PECHATI IAKUTSKOI ASSR. ORGAN GOS.
BIBLIOGRAFII IAKUT. ASSR. ZA 1958-1959 GODY.
Yakutsk: Kn. Izd., 1960, 600 copies. [Yakut, Russ.
text; titles, pub.: 1958-1959]

LETOPIS PECHATI IAKUTSKOI ASSR. ZA 1960 G. Yakutsk:
Kn. Izd., 1961, 52 pp., 500 copies. [Yakut, Russ.
text; pub.: 1960]

LETOPIS' PECHATI IAKUTSKOI ASSR. ORGAN GOS.
BIBLIOGRAFII IAKUT. ASSR. Yakutsk: (Iakut. Resp.
B-ka im Pushkina), 1962, 53 pp., 600 copies. [Yakut,
Russ. text; titles, pub.: 1961]

LETOPIS' PECHATI IAKUTSKOI ASSR. ORGAN GOS.
BIBLIOGRAFII IAKUT. ASSR ZA 1962 G. Yakutsk: Kn. Izd.,
1963, 47 pp., 600 copies. [Yakut, Russ. text;
titles, pub.: 1962]

LETOPIS' PECHATI IAKUTSKOI ASSR. ZA 1963 G. Yakutsk:
Knizhnoe Izdatel'stvo, 1964, 50 pp., 600 copies.
[Yakut, Russ. text; titles, pub.: 1963]

LETOPIS' PECHATI IAKUTSKOI ASSR. ZA 1964 G. Iakutsk:
Kn. Izd., 1965, 40 pp., 600 copies. [Yakut, Russ.
text; titles, pub.: 1964]

LETOPIS' PECHATI IAKUTSKOI ASSR. Yakutsk: Kn. Izd.,
1966, 49 pp., 600 copies. [Yakut, Russ. text and
titles, pub.: 1965]

Yakut: General

LETOPIS' PECHATI IAKUTSKOI ASSR. YAKUTSK: Kn. Izd., 1968, 44 pp., 600 copies. [Yakut, Russ. text; Yakut, Russ. titles, pub.: 1967]

LETOPIS' PECHATI IAKUTSKOI ASSR. Yakutsk: Iakutknigoizdat, 1969, 30 pp., 600 copies. [Yakut, Russ. text and titles, pub.: 1968]

LETOPIS' PECHATI IAKUTSKOI ASSR. Yakutsk: Iakutknigoizdat, 1970, 30 pp., 1000 copies. [Yakut, Russ. text and titles, pub.: 1969]

Matveev, Z. N. BIBLIOGRAFIIA DAL'NEVOSTOCHNOGO KRAIA. UKAZATEL' LITERATURY O DVK, VYSHEDSHEI V 1931 G. V PREDELAKH DVK I VNE EGO. VESTNIK DAL'NEVOSTOCHNOGO FILIALA AKADEMII NAUK SSSR. No. 3/4. 1932, 87-93 pp. [Russ. text; titles, pub.: 1931]

[Oleinikov, N. E.] "BIBLIOGRAFICHESKII UKAZATEL' LITERATURY OB IAKUTSKOI OBLASTI [ZA 1913-1916 GG.]," LENSKIE VOLNY, 1914-1916. [Russ. text]

_____. BIBLIOGRAFICHESKII UKAZATEL' STATEI NAPECHATANYKH V IAKUTSKIKH EPARKHIAL'NYKH VIEDOMOSTIAKH ZA 2-E DESIATILIETIE IKH IZDANIIA (1897-1907). n. p. Izdanie 1-e Iakutskikh Eparkhial'nykh Viedomostiei. 1915, 40 pp. [Russ. text; titles, pub.: 1897-1907]

_____. "BIBLIOGRAFICHESKII UKAZATEL' TEKUSHCHEI LITERATURY OB IAKUTSKOI OBLASTI," LENSKIE VOLNY. (1915) Nos. 13-25, etc. (1916). 1914-1916. [Russ. text; ca.500 titles, end of each no.]

_____. [PERECHNI TEKUSHCHEI LITERATURY OB IAKUT. OBL.] LENSKIE VOLNY (ZHURN.) 1914-1916. [Russ. text; ca.500 titles, pub.: contemporary]

Petrova, G. I. comp. "BOL'SHEVIKI-LENINTSY V IAKUTSKOI SSYLKE. Iakutsk: (Iakutknigoizdat), 1968, 22 pp., 600 copies. [Russ. text]

Priklonskii, V. L. MATERIALY DLIA BIBLIOGRAFII IAKUTSKOI OBLASTI. PRILOZHENIE K GAZ. "VOSTOCHNOE OBOZRENIE," Tipografiia K. I. Vitkovskoi, 1893, 83 + I-VI. [Russ. text; 1688 Russ. titles]

Yakut: General

Romanov, N. S. "K ISTORII PERIODICHESKOI PECHATI V G. IAKUTSKE," IZVESTIIA VOSTOCHNO-SIBIRSKOGO OTDELA RUSSKOGO GEOGRAFICHESKOGO OBSHCHESTVA. Vol. 48, No. 1. (Irkutsk) 1924. [Russ. text]

*"SHALAUROV, NIKITA," BOL'SHAIA SOVETSKAIA ENTSIKLOPEDIIA. Vol. 61. Moscow: Gosudarstvennoe Slovarno-Entsiklopedicheskoe Izdatel'stvo "Sovetskaia Entsiklopediia," (Ogiz RSFSR), 1934, 796 pp. [Russ. text and titles, p. 796]

"SPISOK OSNOVNYKH STATEI, KORRESPONDENTSII, OCHERKOV A. A. SEMENOVA, OPUBLIKOVANNYKH V PERIODICHESKOI PECHATI S 1911 PO 1931 GOD," IAKUT. DRUZ'IA A. M. GOR'KOGO. Iakutsk, 1970. [Russ. text; 129 titles, pub.: 1911-1931, pp. 302-307]

Tarskii, G. "NOVYE BIBLIOGRAFICHESKIE RABOTY O IAKUTII," SOTSIALISTICHESKAIA IAKUTIIA. No. 75. April 1, 1940. [Russ. text]

*Tokarev, S. "NOVAIA NAUCHNAIA LITERATURA O IAKUTII," PROPAGANDIST. No. 13. 1945, 182 pp. [Russ. text and titles, Sov. per., pp. 57-62]

TRUDY I MATERIALY. Leningrad: Akademiia Nauk. Iakutskaia Komissiia. [Yakut text]

ANTHROPOLOGY, ETHNOGRAPHY

Ergis, G. U. "SPISOK RABOT A. A. POPOVA.--OB A. A. POPOVE," SBORNIK STATEI I MATERIALOV PO ETNOGRAFII NARODOV IAKUTII. No. 2. 1961. [Russ. text; 46 titles, pub.: 1928-1959, pp. 104-106]

Yakut: Anthropology, Ethnography

*"IAKUTY," BOL'SHAIA SOVETSKAIA ENTSIKLOPEDIIA.
Vol. 49. 1957, 549-551 pp. [Russ. text and titles,
p. 551]

*Khoroshikh, P. P.; E. K. Pekarskii. eds. IAKUTY. OPYT
UKAZATELIA ISTORIKO-ETNOGRAFICHESKOI LITERATURY O
IAKUTSKOI NARODNOSTI. IZVESTIIA VOSTOCHNO-SIBIRSKOGO
OTDELA RUSSKOGO GEOGRAFICHESKOGO OBSHCHESTVA. Vol. 48,
No. 1. [also separately] Irkutsk, 1924, (separately)
48 pp. [Russ. text; 829 Russ. titles, pub.: 19th - 20th
cc., pp. 1-48]

*Okladnikov, A. P. "IZ OBLASTI DREVNEI KULTURY IAKUTOV,"
SOV. ETNOGRAFIIA, 1946. No. 3. n. p., 1946,
113-122 pp. [Russ. text; ca. 40 titles (footnotes),
pub.: 1851-1943, per.: ancient]

P[ekarskii], E. IAKUTSKIIA GAZETY ZA 1907-1909 G. n. p.
1909. [Russ. text; 9 Russ., 15 Iakut titles, pub.:
1907-1909, pp. 108-110]

Popov, G. A. IAKUTSKII KRAI. Nos. 1, 2. Yakutsk, 1926.
[Russ. text; (1) 147 titles, (2) 477 titles]

ARCHAEOLOGY, ARCHITECTURE, ART

*Gribanovskii, N. N. "SVEDENIIA O PISANITSAKH
[NASKAL'NYKH RISUNKAKH] IAKUTII," SOV. ARKHEOLOGIIA.
Vol. 8. 1946, pp. 281-284]

KALENDAR' ZNAMENATEL'NYKH I PAMIATNYKH DAT IAKUTSKOI ASSR.
...NA 1966 GOD. Iakutsk: Iakutknigoizdat, 1966,
121 pp., 2000 copies. [Russ. text; titles at end of
articles]

[Potapov, I. A.] AFANASII MUKHALOV. BIO-BIBLIOGR.
UKAZ. Yakutsk: Iakutknigoizdat, 1969. [Russ. text;
66 Yakut, Russ. titles, 600 copies]

Yakut

ECONOMICS

Arzhakov, S. T. DVIZHENIE, USTREMLENNOE V BUDUSHCHEE.
Iakutsk, 1969. [Russ. text; 88 titles, pp. 108-111]

*Basharin, G. P. ISTORIIA AGRARNYKH OTNOSHENII V
IAKUTII (60-E GODY XVIII - SEREDINA XIX V.) Moscow:
(AN SSSR. Inst. Istorii), 1956, 427 pp. [Russ.
text; ca.160 Russ., other titles, per.: 1760's -
middle of 19th c., pp. 405-409]

*"EKONOMICHESKII OCHERK," BOL'SHAIA SOVETSKAIA
ENTSIKLOPEDIIA. Vol. 65. Moscow: Gosudarstvennoe
Slovarno-Entsiklopedicheskoe Izdatel'stvo "Sovetskaia
Entsiklopediia," (Ogiz RSFSR), 1931, 1st ed., 481-490 pp.
[Russ. text; Yakut, Russ. titles, p. 490]

Kurbatov, Kh. ISTORIIA ALFAVITA I ORFOGRAFII TATARSKOGO
IAZYKA. Kazan: (AN SSSR. Kazan. Filial. In-t Iazyka,
Lit. i Istorii), 1960. [Tatar text; ca.130 Tatar,
Russ. titles, pp. 127-130]

Gribanovskii, N. N. BIBLIOGRAFIIA IAKUTII. Part 2,
No. 2. EKONOMIKA: PROMYSHLENNOST'...Moscow-Leningrad,
1935, 220 pp. [Russ. text; Russ., Europ. titles]

*Guchek, T. S., et al. comps. BIBLIOGRAFIIA IAKUTSKOI
ASSR. (1931-1959). Vol. 2. "PRIRODNYE USLOVIIA,
RESURSY I NAR. KHOZIAISTVO," Moscow: (AN SSSR.
Sektor Seti Spets Bibliotek. Gosekonomsovet SSSR...),
1962, 225 pp., 1100 copies. [Russ. text; ca.4000
titles, pub.: 1931-1959]

IAKUTSKII NAUCHNO-ISSLEDOVATEL'SKII INSTITUT SEL'SKOGO
KHOZIAISTVA. TRUDY. No. 8. Yakutsk: Iakutknigoizdat,
1966, 219 pp., 1000 copies. [Russ. text; titles
at end of articles]

Yakut: Economics

IAKUTSKII NAUCHNO-ISSLEDOVATEL'SKII INSTITUT
SEL'SKOGO KHOZIAISTVA. TRUDY. No. 9. Yakutsk:
Iakutknigoizdat, 1968, 215 pp., 1000 copies. [Russ.
text; titles at end of articles]

IAKUTSKII UNIVERSITET. UCHENYE ZAPISKI. No. 17.
SERIIA SEL'SKOKHOZIAISTVENNYKH NAUK. Yakutsk:
Iakutknigoizdat,1967, 128 pp., 600 copies. [Russ.
text; titles at end of articles]

Maksimova, E. G.; S. E. Mostakhov. comps. SEVERO-
VOSTOCHNYI EKONOMICHESKII RAION RSFSR (PRIRODA I
KHOZIAISTVO). REKOMENDATEL'NYI UKAZATEL'. Yakutsk:
Iakutknigoizdat, 1964, 20 pp., 1000 copies. [Russ.
text; 113 titles]

Mirotvortsev, K. N. BIBLIOGRAFICHESKIE ZAMETKI O
ZHURNALE KHOZIAISTVO IAKUTII. Irkutsk: Ocherki po
Izucheniiu Iakutskogo Kraia. No. 2. 1928. [Russ.
text; titles,pp. 155-163 (11 pp. sep.)]

*Mitiushkin, V. V. SOTSIALISTICHESKAIA IAKUTIIA.
Yakutsk: Iakutskoe Knizhnoe Izdatel'stvo, 1960,
359 pp., 5000 copies. [Russ. text; ca.90 Russ.
titles, incl. archives, Sov. per., pp. 354-357]

Mostakhov, S. E.; L. T. Ivanova, comps. IAKUTIIA--
KRAI NESMETNYKH BOGATSTV. (V POMOSHCH'
IZUCHAIUSHCHIM SVOIU RESPUBLIKU). REK. UKAZATEL'.
Yakutsk: (Iakut. Resp. B-ka im. Pushkina), 1962, 30 pp.,
600 copies. [Russ. text; 70 titles]

*Naumov, G. V. ZAPADNAIA IAKUTIIA (EKON.-GEOGR.
KHARAKTER.) Moscow: 1962, 140 pp. [Russ. text;
61 Russ. titles, pp. 139-141]

Petrov, V. T. GEROI SOTSIALISTICHESKOGO TRUDA
IAKUTSKOI ASSR. (BIOBIBLIOGRAFICHESKII SPRAVOCHNIK).
Yakutsk: Iakutknigoizdat, 1968, 139 pp., 2000
copies. [Russ. text]

Sidorov, P. K. VOPROSY KAPITAL'NYKH VLOZHENII V
SEL'SKOE KHOZIAISTVO IAKUTII. Yakutsk:Iakutknigoizdat,
1963, 64 pp., 3000 copies. [Russ. text; 37 titles,
pp. 62-63]

Yakut : Economics

Vasil'eva, L. F. PUSHNOI PROMYSEL I ZVEROVODSTVO IAKUTSKOI ASSR. UKAZATEL' LIT. Yakutsk: (Iakut. Resp. B-ka im. Pushkina), 1957, 22 pp. [Russ. text; ca.280 Yakut, Russ. titles, pub.: mainly after 1950]

EDUCATION

Afanas'ev, V. F. SHKOLA I RAZVITIE PEDAGOGICHESKOI MYSLI V IAKUTII. Yakutsk: Iakutknigoizdat, 1966, 344 pp., 5000 copies. [Russ. text; 232 titles, pub.: 1946-1966, pp. 330-342]

_____. VETERANY PEDAGOGICHESKOGO TRUDA. Yakutsk, 1965, 56 pp. [Russ. text; titles, per.: pre- & post 1917]

*Gribanovskii, N. N. BIBLIOGRAFIIA IAKUTII. Part 3. NARODNOE PROSVESHCHENIE. Yakutsk: Iakutskoe Knizhnoe Izdatel'stvo, 1965, 198 pp., 1000 copies. [Russ. text; 3532 Russ., Europ. titles, pub.: 1791-1931]

_____. "MATERIALY DLIA BIBLIOGRAFII IAKUTSKOGO MUZEIA," SAKHA-KESKILE [ZHURNAL] No. 3. Yakutsk, 1926. [Russ. text]

GEOGRAPHY

Gakkel', Ia. Ia.; E. S. Korotkevich. eds. SEVERNAIA IAKUTIIA. (FIZ.-GEOGR. KHARAKTERISTIKA). (TRUDY ARKT. I ANTARKT. NAUCH.-ISSLED. IN-TA. Vol. 236). Leningrad, 1960. [Russ. text; 224 titles, pp. 274-280]

Yakut : Geography

Gerasimov, A. S. OPISANIE KARTY 1924 G. IAKUTSKOI ASSR. Leningrad: Izd. Partii po Issledovaniiu Rek Lensko-Baikal'skogo Basseinov Upravleniia Vodnymi Putiami Sibiri, 1924, 46 + 2 pp. [Russ. text]

Gribanovskii, N. N. BIBLIOGRAFIIA IAKUTII. Part 1. PRIRODNYE RESURSY I NASELENIE IAKUTSKOGO KRAIA. 1932. Part 2. EKONOMIKA. No. 1: EKONOMICHESKOE POLOZHENIE, EKONOMICHESKAIA POLITIKA, SEL'SKOE KHOZIAISTVO IAKUTII. 1933. TRUDY SOVETA PO IZUCHENIIU PROIZVODITEL'NYKH SIL: SERIIA IAKUTSKAIA. No. 9, 15. Leningrad, 1932-1933. (1) 127 pp. (2) 232 pp. [Russ. text; Russ., Europ. titles]

IAKUTSKII RESP. KRAEVEDCHESKII MUZEI IM. EMEL'IANA IAROSLAVSKOGO. SBORNIK NAUCHNYKH STATEI. No. 4. Yakutsk: Iakutknigoizdat, 1966, 231 pp., 3000 copies. [Russ. text; 24 titles, pp. 168-169]

*Korzhuev, S. S. et al. IAKUTIIA. PRIRODNYE USLOVIIA I ESTESTVENNYE RESURSY SSSR. Moscow: Izdatel'stvo "Nauka," 1965, 467 pp., 2100 copies. [Russ. text; ca.420 titles, pp. 441-455]

Molodoi, I. F. BIBLIOGRAFICHESKII UKAZATEL' PO KOLYMSKOMU KRAIU IAKUTSKOI ASSR. Irkutsk: (Nar. Kom. Vod. Transporta...), 1931, 104 pp. [Russ. text]

SEM'DESIAT PIAT' LET VOSTOCHNO-SIBIRSKOGO OTDELA GOSUDARSTVENNOGO RUSSKOGO GEOGRAFICHESKOGO OBSHCHESTVA. 1851-1926. IZVESTIIA VOST.-SIB. OTD. GOSUD. RUSSK. GEOGR. O-VA. Vol. 50. Irkutsk, 1926, 3-142; 143 pp. [Russ. text; 116 titles, per.: 1851-1926]

SYROVATSKII, A. D. IAKUTSK-STOLITSA ALMAZNOGO KRAIA. PUTEVODITEL'. Yakutsk: Iakutknigoizdat, 1968, 52 pp., 15,000 copies. [Russ. text; titles, pp. 50-51]

*Vittenburg, P. V. ed. IAKUTIIA. SBORNIK STATEI. Leningrad: Izdatel'stvo Akademii Nauk SSSR, 1927, 752 pp., 1500 copies. [Russ. text; ca.600 scattered Russ., Europ. titles]

HISTORY, ARCHAEOLOGY

Afanas'ev, V. F. ZASLUZHENNYI DEIATEL' NAUKI
IAKUTSKOI ASSR PROFESSOR G. P. BASHARIN.
(BIBLIOGRAFICHESKII UKAZATEL'.) Yakutsk:
Iakutknigoizdat (Iakut. Resp. B-ka im. A. S.
Pushkina), 1967, 28 pp., 1000 copies. [Russ. text;
186 Iakut, Russ. titles]

Antipin, V. N. et al. eds. ISTORIIA IAKUTSKOI ASSR.
Vol. 3. "SOVETSKAIA IAKUTIIA." Moscow, 1963.
[Russ. text; ca.340 titles, Sov. per., pp. 353-362]

*Bakhrushin, S. V. ISTORICHESKIE SUD'BY IAKUTII.
Leningrad: Izdatel'stvo Akademii Nauk, 1927, 48 pp.
[Russ. text and titles, Sov. per., pp. 47-48]

*Basharin, G. P. OBOZRENIE ISTORIOGRAFII
DOREVOLIUTSIONNOI IAKUTII. Yakutsk: Iakutskoe
Knizhnoe Izdatel'stvo, 1965, 70 pp., 300 copies.
[Russ. text; Russ., Europ. essay & notes, per.: pre-
1917, pp. 5-36]

*Braginskii, M.; G. Lur'e. "IAKUTSKAIA SSYLKA,"
BOL'SHAIA SOVETSKAIA ENTSIKLOPEDIIA. Vol. 65.
Moscow: Gosudarstvennoe Slovarno-Entsiklopedicheskoe
Izdatel'stvo "Sovetskaia Entsiklopediia," (Ogiz
RSFSR), 1931, 1st ed., 503-506 pp. [Russ. text and
titles, p. 506]

*Chemezov, V. N. IZ ISTORII IAKUTSKOI ORGANIZATSII RKP(B)
(8 FEVRALIA 1919 - 6 IIUNIIA 1920 GG.) Yakutsk:
Iakutskoe Knizhnoe Izdatel'stvo, 1967, 215 pp.,
4000 copies. [Russ. text and titles, per.: 1919-1920,
pp. 205-209]

_____.; L. T. Ivanova; P. V. Gogolev. comps.
KUL'TURNAIA REVOLIUTSIIA V IAKUTII (1917-1937 GG.)
SBORNIK DOKUMENTOV I MATERIALOV. Yakutsk:
Iakutknigoizdat, 1968, 610 pp., 1000 copies. [Russ.
text; 54 titles, per.: 1917-1937, pp. 607-609]

Yakut : History, Archaeology

Chemezov, V. N. PLAMENNYI BOL'SHEVIK (O ZHIZNI I
DEIATEL'NOSTI S. IU. SHIROKIKH-POLIANSKOGO). Yakutsk,
1969. [Russ. text; 40 titles, pp. 77-79]

Dmitrieva, L. V. RUKOPISNYE MATERIALY N. A.
VITASHEVSKOGO. KRATKIE SOOBSHCH. IN-TA VOSTOKOVEDENIIA.
No. 16. n. p. AN SSSR, 1955. [Russ. text; 85
titles, pub.: 1885-1929, pp. 72-79]

Ivanova, A. A. IAKUTSKAIA PARTIINAIA ORGANIZATSIIA V
PERIOD VOSTANOVLENIIA NARODNOGO KHOZIAISTVA (1923-1925).
Yakutsk: Iakutknigoizdat, 1968, 126 pp., 3000 copies.
[Russ. text; titles per.: 1923-1925, pp. 118-125]

*Ivanov, V. N. SOTSIAL'NO-EKONOMICHESKIE OTNOSHENIIA U
IAKUTOV XVII V. Yakutsk: Iakutskoe Knizhnoe
Izdatel'stvo, 1966, 423 pp., 2000 copies. [Russ.
text; ca.160 Russ. titles, per.: 17th c., pp. 401-406]

Korzhikhina, T. P. et al. comps. DOKUMENTY O
REVOLIUTSIONNYKH SOBYTIIAKH 1905-1907 GG. V IAKUTII.
Yakutsk: (Akad. Nauk SSSR. Iakut. Filial. In-t
Iazyka, Lit. i Istorii. Tsentr. Gos. Arkhiv IaASSR),
1957. [Russ. text; 85 titles, per.: 1905-1907,
pp. 189-192]

Makarov, G. G. OBRAZOVANIE IAKUTSKOI AVTONOMNOI
SOVETSKOI SOTSIALISTICHESKOI RESPUBLIKI. Yakutsk:
Iakutknigoizdat, 1957. [Russ. text; ca.100 titles,
Sov. per., pp. 202-206]

*Makarov, I. G. VLADIMIR IL'ICH LENIN I IAKUTIIA.
BIBLIOGR. UKAZ. Yakutsk: Iakutknigoizdat, 1970,
349 pp., 2000 copies. [Russ. text; 2061 Yakut,
Russ. titles, pub.: 1917-1969, pp. 17-265]

*Mamet, L. "ISTORICHESKII OCHERK IAASSR," BOL'SHAIA
SOVETSKAIA ENTSIKLOPEDIIA. Vol. 65. Moscow:
Gosudarstvennoe Slovarno-Entsiklopedicheskoe
Izdatel'stvo "Sovetskaia Entsiklopediia," (Ogiz RSFSR),
1931, 1st ed., 492-502 pp. [Russ. text; Yakut,
Russ. titles, pp. 501-502]

Nevskii, V. I. ed. LENSKII RASSTREL. BIBLIOGRAFIIA.
Moscow-Leningrad: Gosudarstvennoe Ekonomicheskoe
Izdatel'stvo, 1932, 70 pp. [Russ. text]

Yakut: History, Archaeology

*Novgorodov, A. I. OKTIABR'SKAIA SOTSIALISTICHESKAIA
REVOLIUTSIIA I GRAZHDANSKAIA VOINA V IAKUTII.
Novosibirsk: "Nauka" (Sibir. Otd.), 1969, 400 pp.,
2000 copies. [Russ. text; 142 Yakut, Russ. titles,
per.: 1917-1920, pp. 386-390]

Okladnikov, A. P. ISTORIIA IAKUTSKOI ASSR. Vol. 1.
"IAKUTIIA DO PRISOEDINENIIA K RUSSKOMU GOSUDARSTVU."
Moscow-Leningrad: (Akad. Nauk SSSR. In-t Iazyka,
Literatury i Istorii Iakut. Filiala AN SSSR), 1955,
2nd ed., 432 pp. [Russ. text; (footnotes) per.:
before Russ. annexation]

Petrov, P. "CHTO CHITAT' O REVOLIUTSIONNYKH SOBYTIIAKH
1905-1907 GG. V IAKUTII," PO LENINSKOMU PUTI. No. 11.
1955. [Russ. text; ca.30 titles, per.: 1905-1907,
pp. 46-52]

Petrov, P. U. RAZGROM PEPELIAEVSKOI AVANTIURY.
Yakutsk: Kn. Izd., 1955. [Russ. text; ca.100
titles, pp. 108-113]

_____. USTANOVLENIE SOVETSKOI VLASTI V IAKUTII.
Yakutsk: Iakutknigoizdat, 1957. [Russ. text; ca.150
titles, Sov. per., pp. 256-264]

_____. ed. ZA VLAST' SOVETOV V IAKUTII. BIOGR.
SBORNIK O BORTSAKH, POGIBSHIKH V 1918-1925 GG.
Yakutsk: (Part. Arkhiv Iakut. Obkoma KPSS), 1958,
2nd ed. [Russ. text; ca.250 titles, per.: 1918-1925,
pp. 250-258]

[Petrova, G. I. comp.] BOL'SHEVIKI-LENINTSY V
IAKUTSKOI SSYLKE. (BESEDA O KNIGAKH). Yakutsk:
(Iakut. Resp.B-ka im. Pushkina), 1968, 600 pp.
[Russ. text; 21 titles]

Safronov, F. G. DEKABRISTY V IAKUTSKOI SSYLKE.
Yakutsk: Kn. Izd., 1955. [Russ. text; 31 titles,
pp. 79-81]

* _____. RUSSKIE KREST'IANE V IAKUTII. (XVII-
NACHALO XX VV.) Yakutsk: Iakutknigoizdat, 1961,
494 pp. [Russ. text; ca.250 Yakut., Russ. titles,
per.: 17th - beginning of 20th c., pp. 3-8, 486-491]

*Syrovatskii, A. "KNIGI PO ISTORII IAKUTII," SIBIRSKIE
OGNI. No. 8. 1958. [Russ. text; Russ. survey,
pp. 184-185]

Yakut

LANGUAGE , LITERATURE

*Afanas'ev, Petr Savich. GOVOR VERKHOIANSKIKH IAKUTOV.
Yakutsk: Iakutskoe Knizhnoe Izdatel'stvo, 1965,
174 pp., 1000 copies. [Russ. text; Russ., Europ.
titles, pp. 3-6]

Argunov, F. S. "PROIZVEDENIIA UKRAINSKIKH PISATELEI NA
IAKUTSKOM IAZYKE," K 300-LETIIU VOSSOEDINENIIA
UKRAINY S ROSSIEI. Yakutsk: (Akad. Nauk SSSR.
Iakut. Filial. In-t Iazyka, Lit., i Istorii), 1954.
[Yakut text; 163 Yakut titles, pp. 77-94]

Alekseev, N. M. CHTO CHITAT' IZ PROIZVEDENII
IAKUTSKIKH PISATELEI NA RUSSKOM IAZYKE. Yakutsk:
Kn. Izd., 1954, 11 pp., 500 copies. [Russ. text;
ca.110 titles, pub.: 1951-1954]

[_____.] D. K. SIVTSEV (SUORUN OMOLLOON)
UKAZATEL' LIT. Yakutsk: Iakutgiz, 1949, 9 pp.,
1500 copies. [Russ. text; 31 titles, pub.: 1936-1949]

[_____.] N. E. MORDINOV (AMMA ACHCHYGYIA).
UKAZATEL' LIT. Yakutsk: Iakutgiz, 1949, 12 pp.,
1500 copies. [Russ. text; 44 titles, pub.: 1927-1948]

_____.; V. A. Protod'iakonov. N. E. MORDINOV
(AMMA- ACHCHYGYIA). UKAZATEL' LIT. Yakutsk: (Iakut.
Resp. B-ka im. Pushkina), 1956, 27 pp., 600 copies.
[Russ. text; 53 Yakut, Russ. titles, pub.: 1927-1955]

[_____.] N. G. ZOLOTAREV (NIKOLAI IAKUTSKII).
UKAZATEL' LIT. Yakutsk: Iakutgiz, 1949, 8 pp.,
1500 copies. Russ. text; 30 titles, pub.: 1939-1948]

[_____.] NOVIKOV. (KIUNNIUK URASTYROV).
Yakutsk: Iakutgiz, 1949, 8 pp., 1500 copies. [Russ.
text; 27 Yakut, Russ. titles, pub.: 1932-1949]

[._____.] S. R. KULACHIKOV (ELLIAI).
UKAZATEL' LIT. Yakutsk: Iakutgiz, 1949, 9 pp.,
1500 copies. [Russ. text; 34 Yakut, Russ. titles,
pub.: 1929-1949]

Yakut: Language, Literature

[Alekseev, N. M.] S. S. IAKOVLEV. (ERILIK ERISTIN).
Yakutsk: Gosizdat Iakutskoi ASSR, 1952, 11 pp.,
500 copies. [Russ. text; 35 Yakut, Russ. titles,
pub.: 1924-1951]

[_____.] S. S. VASIL'EV (BOROGONSKII).
UKAZATEL' LIT. Yakutsk: Iakutgiz, 1949, 8 pp.,
1500 copies. [Russ. text; 20 Yakut, Russ. titles,
pub.: 1935-1949]

Antonov, N. K. LEKSIKA SOVREMENNOGO IAKUTSKOGO IAZYKA.
Yakutsk: Iakutknigoizdat, 1967, 102 pp., 3000 copies.
[Russ. text; 24 Yakut titles, pp. 100-101]

[Barashkov, I. I.] A. G. KUDRIN-ABAGINSKII. UKAZATEL'
LIT. Yakutsk: (Iakut. Gos. Nauch. B-ka im. Pushkina),
1949, 18 pp., 1500 copies. [Russ. text; 101 Yakut,
Russ. titles, pub.: 1927-1946]

[_____.] I. D. VINOKUROV-CHAGYLGAN.
UKAZATEL' LIT. Yakutsk: Gosizdat IaASSR, 1952,
15 pp., 500 copies. [Russ. text; 127 Yakut, Russ.
titles, pub.: 1931-1950]

[_____.] IAKUTSKAIA KHUDOZHESTVENNAIA
LITERATURA V BOR'BE ZA MIR. 1950-1951. Yakutsk:
Iakutgosizdat, 1952, 20 pp., 500 copies. [Russ.
text; 140 Yakut titles, per.: 1950-1951]

[_____.] V. A. PROTOD'IAKONOV, (V. KULANTAI).
UKAZATEL' LIT. Yakutsk: Iakutgiz, 1949, 8 pp.,
1500 copies. [Russ. text; 39 Yakut, Russ. titles,
pub.: 1929-1949]

Basharin, G. P. "SOCHINENIIA A. E. KULAKOVSKOGO.
(BIBLIOGRAFIIA)," KULAKOVSKII. Yakutsk:
Iakutknigoizdat, 1964. [Russ. text; 41 Yakut, Russ.
titles, per.: 1908-1947, pp. 85-87]

Boeskorov, G. K. RAZVITIE ZHANROV PROZY V IAKUTSKOI
SOVETSKOI LITERATURE. Yakutsk: (Akad. Nauk SSSR.
Sib. Otd-nie. Iakut. Filial In-t Iazyka, Lit. i
Istorii), 1961. [Russ. text; 130 Yakut, Russ.
titles, Sov. per., pp. 302-308]

Chernykh, P. IZBRANNOE [STIKHI]. Yakutsk: Nauch.-
Issled. In-t Iazyka, Lit-ry i Istorii Ia. S.S.R,
1945. [Russ. text; 19 titles, per.: 1913-1944,
pp. 134-135]

Yakut: Language, Literature

Emel'ianov, N. V. IAKUTSKIE POSLOVITSY I POGOVORKI.
Yakutsk, 1962. [Russ. text; 39 titles, pp. 93-94]

_____. comp. SBORNIK IAKUTSKIKH POSLOVITS
I POGOVOROK. Yakutsk: Iakutskoe Knizhnoe
Izdatel'stvo, 1965, 246 pp., 5000 copies. [Yakut,
Russ. text; 41 Yakut, Russ. titles (incl. archives),
pp. 228-232]

*Ergis-Germogenov, G. "OIUNSKII, PLATON ALEKSEEVICH,"
LITERATURNAIA ENTSIKLOPEDIIA. Vol. 8. Moscow:
Gosudarstvennoe Slovarno-Entsiklopedicheskoe
Izdatel'stvo "Sovetskaia Entsiklopediia," (Ogiz
RSFSR), 1934, 1st ed., 266-268 pp. [Russ. text; Yakut,
Russ. titles, p. 268]

*Ergis, G. U. SPUTNIK IAKUTSKOGO FOL'KLORISTA.
Yakutsk: Gosizdat IaASSR, 1945, 97 pp., 2000 copies.
[Russ. text; Yakut, Russ. titles, pp. 78-94]

*"IAKUTSKII IAZYK," BOL'SHAIA SOVETSKAIA ENTSIKLOPEDIIA.
Vol. 65. Moscow: Gosudarstvennoe Slovarno-
Entsiklopedicheskoe Izdatel'stvo "Sovetskaia
Entsiklopediia," (Ogiz RSFSR), 1931, 1st ed.
506-507 pp. [Russ. text; Yakut, Russ., Europ.
titles, p. 507]

"IZDANIIA INSTITUTA IAZYKA, LITERATURY I ISTORII
IAKUTSKOGO FILIALA AKADEMII NAUK SSSR," UCHEN.
ZAPISKI (IN-T IAZYKA, LITERATURY I ISTORII IAKUT.
FILIALA AKAD. NAUK SSSR), No. 4. n. p., 1956.
[Russ. text; 138 Yakut, Russ. titles, pub.: 1937-1956,
pp. 123-130]

*Kanaev, N. P. TVORCHESTVO V. M. NOVIKOVA-KIUNNIUK
URASTYROVA. Yakutsk: Iakutknigoizdat, 1968, 160 pp.,
3000 copies. [Yakut text; 29 Yakut, Russ. titles,
pub.: 1932-1961, pp. 158-159]

Kopyrin, N. Z. POEZIIA ELLIAIA. Yakutsk, 1964.
[Russ. text; 70 Yakut, Russ. titles, pp. 170-174]

Maksimov, D. K. "KUZNETS KIUKIUR" I "SAISARY" (DRAMY
D. K. SIVTSEVA). Yakutsk: Iakutknigoizdat, 1967,
79 pp., 3000 copies. [Russ. text; 31 titles,
pp. 77-78]

*Morozova, L. M.; V. F. Afanas'ev; G. S. Tarskii. comps.
GOR'KII I IAKUTIIA. Yakutsk: Iakutknigoizdat, 1968,
184 pp., 5000 copies. [Russ. text; titles pp. 154-184]

Yakut: Language, Literature

Ors, Z. N. "O RABOTE KRUZHKA DETSKOI T EATRAL'NOI SAMODEIATELNOSTI," V POMOSHCH' UCHITELIU. SBORNIK METOD. STATEI. Yakutsk: (Int. Usovershenstvovaniia Uchitelei pri Narkomprosv. Ia. A.SSR), 1946. [Russ. text; 51 titles, pub.: 1941-1945, pp. 112-113]

Pavlov, N. "BIBLIOGRAFIIA." E. ERISTIN. IZBRANNYE PROIZVEDENIIA. Yakutsk, 1948. Yakut text; 23 Yakut, Russ. titles, pub.: 1928-1948, pp. 349-350]

*Pekarskii, Ed. "BIBLIOGRAFIIA IAKUTSKOI SKAZKI," ZHIVAIA STARINA. Vol. 21. 1912. 1914. [Russ. text; 17 Yakut, Russ. titles, pp. 529-532]

_____. PERECHEN' ISTOCHNIKOV SLOVARIA IAKUTSKOGO IAZYKA, S DOPOLNENIEM K. ZALEMANA. IZVIESTIIA AKADEMII NAUK. No. 2. 1905. [Russ. text]

* _____. SLOVAR' IAKUTSKOGO IAZYKA. 3 Vols. St. Petersburg-Leningrad: Akademiia Nauk SSSR, 1907-1930 [reprint 1958-1959] (Vol. 1) 1280 pp.; (Vol. 3) 3858 pp., 750 copies. [Russ. text and titles, pub.: 1851-1930, (Vol. 1) pp. X-XVIII; the end, (Vol. 3) pp. I-VIII]

Petrov, N. E. IAKUTSKII IAZYK. (UKAZATEL' LIT.) Yakutsk: (Iakut. Filial Akad. Nauk SSSR. In-t Iazyka, Lit. i Istorii. Iakut. Resp. B-ka im. Pushkina), 1958, 96 pp., 1250 copies. [Russ. text; 891 Yakut, Russ., other titles]

"PLATON ALEKSEEVICH OIUNSKII (1893-1939). UKAZATEL' LIT.," PLATON ALEKSEEVICH OIUNSKII. Yakutsk: (Akad. Nauk SSSR. Sib. Otd-nie. Iakut. Filial In-t Iazyka, Lit. i Istorii), 1959. [Russ. text; 213 Yakut, Russ. titles, pp. 78-87]

"PROIZVEDENIIA A. I. SOFRONOVA I LITERATURA O NEM," Basharin,G. P., A. I. Safronov. Yakutsk, 1969. [Russ. text; 176 Yakut, Russ. titles, pp. 56-63]

*Protod'iakonov, V.; N. Alekseev. PISATELI IAKUTII. (KRATKII BIO-BIBLIOGR. SPRAVOCHNIK). Yakutsk: Iakutknigoizdat, 1963, 168 pp., 3000 copies. [Russ. text; 84, 57 Russ. titles, per.: pre-1917]

Sivtsev, D. K. comp. IAKUTSKII FOL'KLOR. SBORNIK. Yakutsk, 1970. [Yakut text; 90 titles, pub.: 1890-1967, pp. 328-333]

Yakut: Language, Literature

*Sleptsov, P. A. RUSSKIE LEKSICHESKIE ZAIMSTVOVANIIA V IAKUTSKOM IAZYKE. (DOREVOLIUTSIONNYI PERIOD). Yakutsk: Iakutskoe Knizhnoe Izdatel'stvo, 1964, 196 pp., 2000 copies. [Russ. text; 71 Russ., Europ. titles, pp. 4-7, 192-194]

SOFRON DANILOV. BIOBIBLIOGR. UKAZATEL'. Yakutsk: Iakutknigoizdat, 1969, 43 pp., 1000 copies. [Russ. text; 369 Yakut, Russ. titles]

[Tarskii, G. S.; G. P. Tikhonov] P. N. CHERNYKH-IAKUTSKII. UKAZATEL' LIT. Yakutsk: Iakutgosizdat, 1953, 27 pp., 500 copies. [Russ. text; 115 Yakut, Russ. titles]

Tarskii, G. "PROIZVEDENIIA P. CHERNYKH-IAKUTSKOGO. (BIBLIOGRAFICHESKII UKAZATEL') - LITERATURA O P. CHERNYKH-IAKUTSKOM," P. CHERNYKH-IAKUTSKII. Yakutsk, 1964. [Russ. text; 196 Yakut, Russ. titles, per.: 1907-1962, pp. 47-64]

Ubriatova, E. I. OCHERK ISTORII IZUCHENIIA IAKUTSKOGO IAZYKA. Yakutsk, 1945.

Vasil'ev, G. M.; G. U. Ergis; N. P. Kanaev. OCHERK ISTORII IAKUTSKOI SOVETSKOI LIT. Moscow: (In-t Mirovoi Lit. im. Gor'kogo. Filial AN SSSR. In-t Istorii, Iazyka i Lit.), 1955. [Russ. text; 70 titles, pub.: 1940-1955, pp. 193-195]

PHILOSOPHY, RELIGION

Iavlovskii, P. SISTEMATICHESKII UKAZATEL' STATEI, POMESHCHENNYKH V NEOFITSIAL'NOI CHASTI 'IAKUTSKIKH EPARKHIAL'NYKH VIEDOMOSTIAKH' ZA PERVOE DESIATILETIE IZDANIIA (1887-1897). Sergiev-Posad, 1898. [Russ. text; titles pub.: 1887-1897]

Yakut: Philosophy, Religion

Oleinikov, N. E. [BIBLIOGRAFICHESKII] SISTEMATICHESKII UKAZATEL' STATEI [NAPECHATANNYKH] POMESHCHESNNYKH V NEOFITSIAL'NOI CHASTI "IAKUTSKIKH EPARKHIAL'NYKH VIEDOMOSTIAKH" ZA 2-E DESIATILIETIE IKH IZDANIIA (1897-1907 GG.) Yakutsk, 1915. [Russ. text; titles pub.: 1897-1907]

*Tokarev, S. A. SHAMANSTVO U IAKUTOV XVII V. SOV. ETNOGRAFIIA. Vol. 2. 1939. [Russ. text; 37 (notes) per.: 1730, 1878-1931, pp. 88-103]

POLITICAL SCIENCE, LAW

*Alekseev, E. E. ROL' V. I. LENINA V USTANOVLENII I UKREPLENII SOVETSKOI VLASTI V IAKUTII. Yakutsk: Iakutskoe Knizhnoe Izdatel'stvo, 1962, 159 pp., 1500 copies. [Russ. text; ca.115 Russ. titles, per.: late 19th - 20th c., pp. 147-151]

V. N. Chemezov. et al. comps. "BOR'BA ZA USTANOVLENIE I UPROCHENIE SOVETSKOI VLASTI V IAKUTII." Part 2. Book 2. "RAZGROM PEPELIAEVSKOI AVANTIURY." Yakutsk, 1962. [Russ. text; 645 titles, Sov. per., pp. 365-392]

Fedorov, M. RAZVITIE SOVETSKOI GOSUDARSTVENNOSTI V IAKUTII (1918-1937). Yakutsk: Iakutknigoizdat, 1968, 339 pp., 3000 copies. [Russ. text; titles, per.: 1918-1937, pp. 318-337]

IAKUTIIA OT S'EZDA K S'EZDU. 1959-1961 GG. REK. SPISOK LIT. Yakutsk: (Iakut. Resp. B-ka im. Pushkina), 1962, 21 pp., 600 copies. [Russ. text; ca.100 Yakut, Russ. titles, per.: 1959-1961]

Ivanova, A. A. IAKUTSKAIA PARTIINAIA ORGANIZATSIIA V PERIOD VOSSTANOVLENIIA NARODNOGO KHOZIAISTVA. (1923-1925). Yakutsk, 1968. [210 titles, per.: 1923-1925, pp. 118-125]

Yakut: Political Science, Law

Matveev, Z. N. MATERIALY K BIBLIOGRAFICHESKOMU
OPISANIIU LITERATURY O 1905 G. NA DAL'NEM VOSTOKE.
REVOLIUTSIONNOE DVIZHENIE 1905 G. NA DAL'NEM
VOSTOKE (SBORNIK). Vladivostok, 1925. [Russ.
text]

[Mestnikova, Z. R. comp.] SLAVNYI PUT'. (BESEDA O K
KNIGAKH). Yakutsk: (Iakut. Resp. B-ka im. Pushkina),
1969, 8 pp., 600 copies. [Russ. text]

*NEKOTORYE VOPROSY METODIKI SAMOSTOIATEL'NOI RABOTY NAD
POLITICHESKOI LITERATUROI. Yakutsk: Iakutknigoizdat,
1967, 48 pp., 3000 copies. [Russ. text and titles,
pub.: 1952-1965, pp. 41-46]

Nikolaev, V. "MATERIALY DLIA BIBLIOGRAFII IAKUTSKOI
POLITICHESKOI SSYLKI " V IAKUTSKOI NEVOLE. Moscow,
1927. [Russ. text; 109 titles]

Petrov, P. U. O REVOLIUTSIONNYKH SOBITIIAKH 1905-
1907 GG. V IAKUTII. Yakutsk: (Vsesoiuz. O-vo po
Rasprostraneniiu Polit. i Nauch. Znanii. Iakut.
Otd-nie), 1955. [Russ. text; 44 titles, per.: 1905-
1907, pp. 59-62]

_____. STEPAN ARZHAKOV. [IAKUT. REVOLIUTSIONER]
Yakutsk. 1962. [Russ. text: 33 titles, pp. 56-59]

Petrov, V. S. SLAVNYI PUT' BOL'SHEVIKA. (O ZHIZNI I
DEIATEL'NOSTI I. N. BARAKHOVA). Yakutsk:
Iakutknigoizdat, 1961. [Russ. text; 39 titles,
pub.: 1920-1927, pp. 74-75]

Syrovatskii, A. D. O REVOLIUTSIONNOI RABOTE SSYL'NYKH
BOL'SHEVIKOV SREDI MOLODEZHI IAKUTII. Yakutsk:
(Vsesoiuz. O-vo. po Rasprostraneniiu Polit. i
Nauch. Znanii. Iakut. Otd-nie), 1956. [Yakut text;
50 titles, per.: pre-Sov., pp. 51-54]

_____. STRANITSY KOMSOMOL'SKOI SLAVY (IZ
ISTORII IAKUT. ORGANIZATSII VLKSM ZA 1920-1945 GG.)
Yakutsk, 1961. [Russ. text; 36 titles, per.:
1920-1945, pp. 98-99]

*Tarasov, I. A. KPSS-ORGANIZATOR SOTSIALISTICHESKOGO
PREOBRAZOVANIIA KHOZIAISTVA MALIKH NARODNOSTEI
SEVERA. (NA MATERIALAKH IAKUT ASSR 1930-1940 GG.)
Yakutsk: Iakutknigoizdat, 1967, 175 pp., 3000
copies. [Russ. text; titles, per.: 1930-1940,
pp. 171-174]

Yakut: Political Science, Law

VOPROSY MATODIKI PROPAGANDISTSKOI RABOTY. Yakutsk:
(Otdel. Propagandy i Agitatsii Iakut. Obkoma KPSS),
1962. [Russ. text; 36 titles, pp. 83-84]

SOCIAL ORGANIZATION

*Basharin, G. P. "O PATRIARKHAL'NO-FEODAL'NYKH
OTNOSHENIIAKH V IAKUTII KONTSA XVIII--PERVOI POLOVINY
XIX VEKA," VOPROSY ISTORII. No. 3. 1955. [Russ.
text; footnotes, per.: 18-19th cc., pp. 80-89]

SOVIET ASIA

Beliaev, E. "BIBLIOGRAFIIA PO ISLAMU NA NEMETSKOM, ANGLIISKOM, FRANTSUZSKOM I ITAL'IANSKOM IAZYKAKH," ISLAM. Moscow, 1931. [Sov. Asia religion, Russ. text; 197 Europ. titles, pub.: mid-19th c. - end of 1920s, pp. 168-173]

_____.; A. M. Arsharuni. "BIBLIOGRAFIIA PO ISLAMU NA RUSSKOM IAZYKE. DOREVOLIUTSIONNYE IZDANIIA," ISLAM. Moscow, 1931. [Sov. Asia religion; Russ. text; 159 + 87 Russ. titles, pub.: up to 1930, pp. 131-155; 156-167]

* _____. "ISLAM," BOL'SHAIA SOVETSKAIA ENTSIKLOPEDIIA. Vol. 29. Moscow: Gosudarstvennyi Institut "Sovetskaia Entsiklopediia," (OGIZ RSFSR), 1935, 1st ed., pp. 371-406. [Sov. Asia religion, history, literature; Russ. text; Russ., Europ. titles, pp. 405-406]

*"BUDDIZM," ENTSIKLOPEDICHESKII SLOVAR'. Vol. 4A. St. Petersburg: F. A. Brokgauz, I. A. Efron, 1891, pp. 839-848. [Sov. Asia religion; Russ. text; Russ., Europ. titles, pp. 847-848]

*"GEOGRAFICHESKAIA LITERATURA ROSSII EVROPEISKOI I AZIATSKOI I PRILEZHASHCHIKH STRAN, PO DANNYM BIBLIOTEKI IMPERATORSKAGO GEOGR. O-VA," IZVESTIIA IMP. RUSSK. GEOGR. O-VA. Vol. 27, 1891; Vol. 28, 1892, Vol. 29, 1893. [Sov. Asia geography; Russ. text; titles (Vol. 27, 1891) pp. 94-96, 164-167, 245-248, 352-355, 456-459, 632-636; (Vol. 28, 1892) pp. 142-147, 251-252, 345-346, 428-432, 523-527, 659-660; (Vol. 29, 1893) pp. 48-51, 107-108, 212-216, 343-346, 489-494, 682-689]

*"ISLAM," ENTSIKLOPEDICHESKII SLOVAR. Vol. 13. St. Petersburg: F. A. Brokgauz, I. A. Efron, 1894, pp. 384-387. [Sov. Asia religion; Russ. text; Russ., Europ. titles, p. 387]

*"ISLAMA ISKUSSTVO," BOL'SHAIA SOVETSKAIA ENTSIKLOPEDIIA. Vol. 29. Moscow: Gosudarstvennyi Institut "Sovetskaia Entsiklopediia" (OGIZ RSFSR), 1935, p. 406. [Sov. Asia art history; Russ. text; Russ., Europ. titles, pp. 406-407]

Supplement: SOVIET ASIA

Kagarov, Evg. "OBZOR NOVEISHEI INOSTRANNOI LITERATURY PO VOPROSAM EKONOMIKI I ETNOGRAFII SEVERA. NO. 4," SOVETSKII SEVER. No. 10/11, 1931, pp. 147-152. [Sov. Asia general; Russ. text; 48 Europ. titles, pub.: ca.1930]

*Keppen, Petr. comp. KHRONOLOGICHESKII UKAZATEL' MATERIALOV DLIA ISTORII INORODTSEV EVROPEISKOI ROSSII. St. Petersburg: Tipografiia Imperatorskoi Akademii Nauk, 1861, 510 pp. [Sov. Asia history; Russ. text and titles,(Tatar) pp. 429-477; (Chuvash) pp. 502-507; (Kazakh) pp. 312-344; (Bashkir) pp. 28-59]

*Krymskii, A. "MOKHAMMED," ENTSIKLOPEDICHESKII SLOVAR'. Vol. 20. St. Petersburg: F. A. Brokgauz, I. A. Efron, 1897, pp. 47-55. [Sov. Asia religion; Russ. text; Russ., Europ. titles, pp. 54-55]

*Latyshev, V. V. comp. "SPISOK TRUDOV N. I. VESELOVSKOGO," ZAPISKI VOSTOCHNOGO OTDIELENIIA IMPERATORSKOGO RUSSKOGO ARKHEOLOGICHESKOGO OBSHCHESTVA. Vol. 25, No. 1/4, 1921. [Sov. Asia history, geography, anthropology; Russ. text; 177 + 125 Russ. titles, pp. 387-398]

*Reisner, M. "BUDDIZM," BOL'SHAIA SOVETSKAIA ENTSIKLOPEDIIA. Vol. 7. Moscow: Aktsionernoe Obshchestvo" Sovetskaia Entsiklopediia," 1927, 1st ed., pp. 777-792. [Sov. Asia religion, Russ. text; Asian, Russ., Europ. titles, p. 792]

*Skladanek, B. "ANANIASH ZAIONCHKOVSKII (K SHESTIDESIATILETIIU SO DNIA ROZHDENIIA)". NARODY AZII I AFRIKI, No. 6, 1963, pp. 272-274. [Sov. Asia language; Russ. text; Russ. Polish titles, pp. 273-274]

Vishnevskii, B. N. "[NOVAIA] LITERATURA PO KRAEVEDENIIU [ZA POSLEDNIE GODY]" KRAEVEDENIE. No. 1, 1923, pp. 70-82; No. 2, 1923, pp. 193-198; No. 3, 1924, pp. 326-338. [Sov. Asia geography, economics, anthropology; Russ. text]

*Voznesenskii, S. V. MATERIALY DLIA BIBLIOGRAFII PO ISTORII NARODOV SSSR XVI-XVII VV. AN SSSR. TRUDY ISTORIKO-ARKHEOGRAFICHESKOGO INSTITUTA. Vol. 7. No. 4. Leningrad: Izdatel'stvo Akademii Nauk, 1933, 353 pp., 3000 copies. [Sov. Asia history; Russ. text and titles, per.: 16th-17th cc., pp. 74-101, 266-307]

Supplement: BLACK SEA & WEST CASPIAN LITTORAL

BLACK SEA & WEST CASPIAN LITTORAL
Azerbaijan

Abdullaev, B. A. UKAZATEL' KHUDOZHESTVENNOI
[AZERBAIDZHANSKOI] LITERATURY (ZA 1951 G.) Baku:
(M-vo Kul'tury Azer. SSR), 1955, 24 pp., 1000 copies.
[Azerb. literature; Azerb text; 393 titles, pub.: 1951]

Arsharuni, A. "AZERBAIDZHANSKAIA KHUDOZH. LIT-RA I
FOL'KLOR."--CHTO CHITAT', No. 10/11, 1939. [Azerb.
literature; Russ. text; 10 titles, pub.: 1935-1939,
pp. 49-51]

*Danilov, D. Kh. FIKRET AMIROV. Moscow: "Sov. Kompozitor,"
1959, 68 pp., 1210 titles. [Azerb. music, compositions;
Russ. text; 50 Azerb., Russ. titles, Sov. per.,
pp. 65-68]

*Gadzhieva, N. Z. SINTAKSIS SLOZHNOPODCHINENNOGO
PREDLOZHENIIA V AZERBAIDZHANSKOM IAZYKE (V ISTORICHESKOM
OSVESHCHENII). Moscow: Izdatel'stvo Akademii Nauk
SSSR, 1963, 220 pp., 1000 copies. [Azerb. language;
Russ. text; 60 Azerb., Russ., Turkish, Europ. titles,
pp. 213-219]

Gavrilova, S. A. "GRUZINSKAIA SSR, AZERBAIDZHANSKAIA
SSR, ARMIANSKAIA SSR," EKONOMICHESKIE ADMINISTRATIVNYE
RAIONY SSSR: UKAZATEL' NOVOI LITERATURY PO PRIRODE,
RESURSAM I KHOZIAISTVU. No. 13. Moscow:
Izdatel'stvo Akademii Nauk SSSR, 1957, 122 pp.
[Azerb. Economics; Russ. text]

Ibragimov, D. PUTESHESTVIE AFANASIIA NIKITINA V
AZERBAIDZHAN. Baku: (O-vo po Rasprostraneniiu Polit.
i Nauch. Znanii Azerbaidzh. SSR), 1956. [Azerb.
history; Azerb. text; 43 Azerb., Russ. titles, per.:
Middle Ages, pp. 36-37]

Iuzbashev, Ramzi Mavsun Ogly. "DOSTIZHENIIA TOPONOMIKI
V AZERBAIDZHANE ZA 50 LET. REZIUME," AKADEMIIA NAUK
AZERBAIDZHANSKOI SSR. INSTITUT GEOGRAFII. TRUDY.
Vol. 18. 1971, pp. 302-306. [Azerb. geography; Russ.
text; titles, Sov. per., pp. 303-306]

Kagramanov, A. G. AZERBAIDZHANSKAIA LITERATURA V DNI
VELIKOI OTECHESTVENNOI VOINY. (1941-1948 GG.)
BIBLIOGR. UKAZATEL'. Baku: (Azerb. Gos. Knizh. Palata),
1946, 161 pp., 1000 copies. [Azerb. literature; titles,
pub.: during W. W. II]

Supplement: BLACK SEA & WEST CASPIAN LITTORAL

*Kashkai, M. A.; P. M. Alampiev. eds. AZERBAIDZHANSKAIA
SSR: EKONOMIKO-GEOGRAFICHESKAIA KHARAKTERISTIKA.
Moscow: Geografgiz, 1957, 445 pp., 5000 copies.
[Azerb. economics; Russ. text; ca.200 Russ. titles,
per.: 20th c., pp. 434-443]

KATALOG OBSHCHESTVA OBSLEDOVANIIA I IZUCHENIIA
AZERBAIDZHANA NA TIURKSKOM I RUSSKOM IAZYKAKH.
1925-1929 GG. Baku: Izd. Obshchestva Obsledovaniia i
Izucheniia Azerbaidzhana, 1930, 16 pp. [Azerb. general;
Russ. text; 38 Azerb., Russ. titles, pub.: 1925-1929]

*"UKAZATEL' STATEI, POMESHCHENNYKH V PERIODICHESKIKH
IZDANIIAKH ASSR, VYKHODIVSHCHIKH V NEOPREDELENNYE
SROKI, KOTORYE OPISANY V NASTOIASHCHEM (NO. 9/10)
NOMERE 'LETOPISI'," LETOPIS' PECHATI AZERBAIDZHANA.
No. 9/10, 1929. [Azerb. general; Azerb., Russ. text;
Russ. titles, serial contents, pub.: Sept.-Oct. 1929,
pp. 161-164]

Caucasus

"AZOVSKOE MORE," SOVETSKAIA VOENNAIA ENTSIKLOPEDIIA.
Vol. 1. Moscow: Gosudarstvennoe Slovarno-
Entsiklopedicheskoe Izdatel'stvo "Sovetskaia
Entsiklopediia," OGIZ RSFSR, 1932, pp. 351-357.
[Caucasus geography, history; Russ. text and titles,
p. 357]

"D'IACHKOV-TARASOV, A. S. A. N. (K TRIDTSATILETIIU EGO
NAUCHNOI DEIATEL'NOSTI)." BIULLETEN' SEVERO-KAVKAZSKOGO
KRAEVOGO GORSKO-NAUCHNO-ISSLEDOVATEL'SKOGO INSTITUTA
KRAEVEDENIIA. Nos. 2/4. 1927. [Caucasus general;
Russ. text; 27 titles, p. 78]

Eritsov, A. D. "UKAZATEL' SOCHINENII, IMEIUSHCHIKH
OTNOSHENIE K IZUCHENIIU EKONOMICHESKOGO BYTA
GOSUDARSTVENNYKH KREST'IAN ZAKAVKAZSKOGO KRAIA,"
MATERIALY PO IZUCHENIIU EKONOMICHESKAGO BYTA
GOSUDARSTVENNYKH KREST'IAN ZAKAVKAZSKAGO KRAIA. Vol. 1,
No. 2. Tiflis, 1885. [Caucasus economics, social
organization; Russ. text; 150 Russ. titles, pp. XII-XXV]

Supplement: BLACK SEA & WEST CASPIAN LITTORAL

Melikset-Bekov, L. "MATERIALY DLIA BIBLIOGRAFICHESKAGO
UKAZATELIA BELLETRISTICHESKIKH PROIZVEDENII RUSSKIKH
PISATELEI, POSVIASHCHENNYKH KAVKAZU I EGO
OBITATELIAM," IZVESTIIA ODESSKAGO BIBLIOGRAFICHESKAGO
OBSHCHESTVA, Vol. 3, No. 3, 1914. [Caucasus general;
literature; Russ. text; 13 Russ. lists, pp. 161-163]

"NOVOE OBOZRENIE" ZA 20 LET (1884-1903), KRATKII
ISTORICHESKII OCHERK. PERECHEN' STATEI,
PECHATAVSHIKHSIA V "NOVOM OBOZRENII" V 1884-1903 GG.
Tiflis, 1904. [Caucasus general; Russ. text and
titles, pub.: 1884-1903]

"SPISOK GLAVNEISHIKH STATEI I ZAMIETOK, POMESHCHENNYKH V
'KAVKAZSKOM KALENDARE' ZA 67 LET EGO IZDANIIA (S
1846 PO 1913 G.)," KAVKAZSKII KALENDAR' NA 1913 G.
[Caucasus general; Russ. text and titles, pub.: 1846-
1913, pp. 165-]

Dagestan

*"DAGESTANSKAIA AVTONOMNAIA SOVETSKAIA SOTSIALISTICHESKAIA
RESPUBLIKA," BOL'SHAIA SOVETSKAIA ENTSIKLOPEDIIA.
Vol. 13. Moscow: Gosudarstvennoe Nauchnoe
Izdatel'stvo "Bol'shaia Sovetskaia Entsiklopediia,"
1952, 2nd ed., pp. 272-294. [Dagestan general; Russ.
text and titles, pp. 277, 283, 285, 289-290, 292, 293]

"SPISOK IZDANII DAGNARKOMZEMA," PLANOVOE KHOZIAISTVO
DAGESTANA. No. 7/8. 1928. [Dagestan economics;
Russ. text; 32 Azerb., Kumyk, Sov. Asian, Russ.
titles, pub.: 1924-1928, pp. 101-104]

Karachay-Balkar

*Akbaev, Shakman Khuseinovich. FONETIKA DIALEKTOV
KARACHAEVO-BALKARSKOGO IAZYKA. Cherkessk: Karachaevo-
Cherkesskoe Knizhnoe Izdatel'stvo, 1963, 165 pp.,
1000 copies. [Karachay-Balkar language; Russ. text;
titles, pp. 159-164]

Supplement: BLACK SEA & WEST CASPIAN LITTORAL
N. Caucasus

*Maslov, E. P.; A. I. Gozulov; S. N. Riazantsev, eds.
SEVERNYI KAVKAZ. Moscow: Geografgiz, 1957, 507 pp.,
5000 copies. [North Caucasus geography, economics;
Russ. text; ca.140 Russ. titles, pub.: mainly 1950s,
pp. 500-505]

Ozerova, G. A. SEVERNYI KAVKAZ. BIBLIOGRAFIIA
KRAEVEDCHESKOI BIBLIOGRAFII RSFSR: ANNOTIROVANNYI
UKAZATEL'. No. 6. Leningrad: (Gosudarstvennaia
Publichnaia Biblioteka Imeni M. E. Saltykova-Shchedrina),
1963, 445 pp. [North Caucasus general, Russ. text;
1259 titles]

Parkhomenko, I. I. RAIONY NIZHNEGO DONA I SEVERNOGO
KAVKAZA. EKONOMICHESKIE ADMINISTRATIVNYE RAIONY
SSSR: UKAZATEL' NOVOI LITERATURY PO PRIRODE, RESURSAM
I KHOZIAISTVU. Vol. 4. Moscow: Izdatel'stvo
Akademii Nauk SSSR, 1958, 100 pp. [North Caucasus
geography; Russ. titles]

VOLGA BASIN

Pokshishevskii, V. V. RAIONY POVOLZH'IA. EKONOMICHSKIE
ADMINISTRATIVNYE RAIONY SSSR: UKAZATEL' NOVOI
LITERATURY PO PRIRODE, RESURSAM I KHOZIAISTVU.
Vol. 3. Moscow: Izdatel'stvo Akademii Nauk SSSR,
1958, 84 pp. [Volga basin economics; Russ. text]

Bashkir

Khismatov, Mukhamed'ian Fazyl'ianovich. OCHERKI PO
GEOGRAFII BASHKIRII. Ufa: (Bashkirskii Gosudarstvennyi
Universitet. Bashkirskii Institut Usovershenstvovaniia
Uchitelei), 1963, 104 pp. [Bashkir geography; Russ.
text; ca.140 titles, pp. 98-104]

KNIZHNAIA LETOPIS'. Ufa: Bashknigoizdat, 1967, 107 pp.,
1000 copies. [Bashkir general; Bashkir, Russ. text and
titles, pub.: 1966]

Supplement: VOLGA BASIN

Chuvash

*"ISAEV, DMITRII EFREMOVICH," BOL'SHAIA SOVETSKAIA ENTSIKLOPEDIIA. Vol. 29. Moscow: Gosudarstvennyi Institut "Sovetskaia Entsiklopediia" (OGIZ RSFSR), 1935, p. 282. [Chuvash literature; Russ. text; Chuvash, Russ. titles, p. 282]

Kalmyk

Dzhimbin, S. M. KALMYTSKAIA ASSR. EKONOMIKO-GEOGRAFICHESKII OCHERK. Elista: Kalmizdat, 1960. [Kalmyk economics, geography; Russ. text; 55 titles, pp. 143-145]

Urals

*Buchinskaia, K.; B. Smirnova, ed. STALINSKII URAL; ANNOTIROVANNYI UKAZATEL' LITERATURY. Moscow: (Gosudarstvennaia Biblioteka SSSR im. V. I. Lenina), 1943, 47 pp., 2000 copies. [Urals general; Russ. text and titles, pub.: 1904-1943]

I. O. "K IZUCHENIIU PERMSKOI GUBERNII. UKAZATEL' KNIG I STATEI, KASAIUSHCHIKHSIA PERMSKOI GUBERNII," PERMSKIE GUBERNSKIE VIEDOMOSTI. Nos. 29, 30, 1892. [Urals general; Russ. text]

Iofa, Leonid E. GORODA URALA. Part 1. FEODAL'NYI PERIOD. Moscow: Geografgiz, 1951, 422 pp. [Urals Geography; Russ. text; ca.700 titles, pub.: up to 1861, pp. 385-421]

*Komar, Igor Valerianovich. URAL: EKONOMIKO-GEOGRAFICHESKAIA KHARAKTERISTIKA. Moscow: Izdatel'stvo Akademii Nauk SSSR, 1959, 367 pp., 2500 copies. [Urals economics; Russ. text; ca.575 Russ., Europ. titles, per.: 17th - 20th c.; mainly 1950s, pp. 352-366]

Parkhomenko, I. I. RAIONY URALA. EKONOMICHESKIE ADMINISTRATIVNYE RAIONY SSSR: UKAZATEL' NOVOI LITERATURY PO PRIRODE, RESURSAM I KHOZIAISTVU. Vol. 5. Moscow: Izdatel'stvo Akademii Nauk SSSR, 1957, 48 pp. [Urals economics; Russ. text]

Supplement: VOLGA BASIN

Volga Tatar

Izbekov, I. N. VYBOROCHNYI PRINTSIP POSTROENIIA OTVETA PRI PROGRAMMIROVANNOM KONTROLE USVOENIIA. Kazan: Tatknigoizdat, 1968, 36 pp., 2000 copies. [Volga Tatar education; Russ. text; 15 titles, pp. 34-35]

Khabibullina, Z. Sh. KHUDOZHESTVENNAIA LITERATURA K 30 LETIIU TATARSKOI ASSR. (REK. SPISOK LIT.) Kazan: (Resp. B-ka TatASSR im. Lenina), 1950, 7 pp. [Volga Tatar Literature; Tatar text; 36 Tatar titles, per.: 1920-1950]

Nadzhmi, K. SVETLAIA TROPA. Kazan: Tatgosizdat, 1951. [Volga Tatar literature; Tatar text; 113 Tatar, Russ. titles, per.: 1924-1951, pp. 539-344]

CENTRAL ASIA

Azatian, Armen; Zoia Dontsova; Vera Fedchina. "ISTORIIA ISSLEDOVANIIA SREDNEI AZII," RUSSKIE GEOGRAFICHESKIE ISSLEDOVANIIA KAVKAZA I SREDNEI AZII V XIX--NACHALE XX V. Moscow: Izdatel'stvo "Nauka," 1964, pp. 61-157. [Central Asia history; Russ. text; 133 titles, per.: 19th - early 20th cc.]

[Dmitrovskii, N. V.] "BIBLIOGRAFICHESKII UKAZATEL' KNIG I STATEI O SREDNEI AZII ZA 1871 G.," TURKESTANSKIE VIEDOMOSTI. 1871, Nos. 33, 36, 39, 43, 44; 1872, Nos. 7, 16. [Central Asia general; Russ. text; 123 titles, pub.: 1871]

Gavrilova, S. A.; I. I. Parkhomenko. UZBEKSKAIA SSR, KIRGIZSKAIA SSR, TADZHIKSKAIA SSR, TURKMENSKAIA SSR. EKONOMICHESKIE ADMINISTRATIVNYE RAIONY SSSR: UKAZATEL' NOVOI LITERATURY PO PRIRODE, RESURSAM I KHOZIAISTVU. Vol. 11. Moscow: Izdatel'stvo Akademii Nauk SSSR, 1958, 161 pp. [Central Asia economics; Russ. text]

Kunavina, G. S. FORMIROVANIE ZHELEZNODOROZHNOGO PROLETARIATA V TURKESTANE. (1881-1914 GG.) Tashkent, 1967. [Central Asia history; Russ. text; ca.220 titles, per.: 1881-1914, pp. 181-190]

*"KUROPATKIN, ALEKSIEI NIKOLAEVICH," VOENNAIA ENTSIKLOPEDIIA. Vol. 14. St. Petersburg: T-vo I. D. Sytina, 1914, 410-416 pp. [Russ. text and titles, p. 416]

Supplement: CENTRAL ASIA

Maslova, O. V. "OBZOR RUSSKIKH PUTESHESTVII I
EKSPEDITSII V SREDNIUIU AZIIU. MATERIALY K ISTORII
IZUCHENIIA SREDNEI AZII. CHAST' 1-3," MATERIALY K
BIBLIOGRAFII. Nos. 5, 7, 9. Tashkent:
(Sredneaziatskii Gosudarstvennyi Universitet), 1955,
1956, 1962, pp. 83, 102, 181. [Central Asia history;
Russ. text; titles, per.: 1715-1880]

*Mints, A. A. ed. SREDNIAIA AZIIA: EKONOMIKO-
GEOGRAFICHESKAIA KHARAKTERISTIKA I PROBLEMY
RAZVITIIA KHOZIAISTVA. Moscow: Izdatel'stvo "Mysl',"
Geografiz, 1969, 504 pp., 4000 copies. [Central
Asia, economics; Russ. text; ca.175 Russ. titles,
per.: 20th c. (ca.1905 on), pp. 493-502]

*Tolstov, S. P. ed. TRUDY KHOREZMSKOI ARKHEOLOGO-
ETNOGRAFICHESKOI EKSPEDITSII. Vol. 1.
ARKHEOLOGICHESKIE RABOTY KHOREZMSKOI EKSPEDITSII.
1945-1948. Moscow: (In-t Etnografii im. Miklukho-
Maklaia), 1952. [Central Asia history, archaeology;
Russ. text; 98 titles, pub.: 1945-1948, pp. 648-651]

Kazakh

*Baishev, S. B. ed. RAZVITIE I RAZMESHCHENIE
PROIZVODITEL'NYKH SIL KAZAKHSKOI SSR. Moscow:
Izdatel'stvo "Nauka," 1967, 259 pp., 2600 copies.
[Kazakh geography, economics; Russ. text; 72 Russ.
titles, per.: 1950s-1960s, pp. 251-253]

*Baranskii, N. N.; O. R. Nazarevskii, eds. KAZAKHSKAIA
SSR: EKONOMIKO-GEOGRAFICHESKAIA KHARAKTERISTIKA.
Moscow: Geografgiz, 1957, 734 pp., 10000 copies.
[Kazakh economics; Russ. text; ca.600 Russ. titles,
per.: 20th c., pp. 701-732]

*Cherepanov, M. B. OTRAZHENIE PRINTSIPOV KAZAKHSKOI
LINGVISTICHESKOI SHKOLY V ISSLEDOVANIIAKH N. B.
KRUSHENSKOGO. Saratov: (Ministerstvo Prosveshcheniia
RSFSR), 1969, 52 pp., 2000 copies. [Kazakh language;
Russ. text; 52+ Russ., Polish, German titles, pp. 50-52]

Chernavskii, N. M. "ORENBURGSKIE EPARKHIAL'NYE
VIEDOMOSTI," TRUDY ORENBURGSKOI UCHENOI ARKHIVNOI
KOMISSII. No. 12. 1903. [Central Asia religion;
Russ. text; titles, pp. 175-188]

Supplement: CENTRAL ASIA, Kazakh

Pal'gov, N. N. ed. TSELINNYI KRAI. KRATKIE OCHERKI O PRIRODE, NASELENII I KHOZIAISTVE. Alma Ata, 1962. [Kazakh economics, geography; Russ. text; 45 titles, pp. 188-189]

Parkhomenko, I. I. KAZAKHSKAIA SSR. EKONOMICHESKIE ADMINISTRATIVNYE RAIONY SSSR: UKAZATEL' NOVOI LITERATURY PO PRIRODE, RESURSAM I KHOZIAISTVU. Vol. 12. Moscow: Izdatel'stvo Akademii Nauk SSSR, 1958, 143 pp. [Kazakh economics; Russ. text]

Pokrovskii, S. N. POBEDA SOVETSKOI VLASTI V SEMIRECH'E. Alma Ata: (Akad. Nauk Kaz. SSR. Institut Istorii, Arkheologii i Etnografii), 1961. [Kazakh pol. sci.; Russ. text; ca.250 titles, per.: Civil War, pp. 3-15, 350-357]

*Sabitov, N. "BIBLIOGRAFICHESKII UKAZATEL' MATERIALOV O ZHIZNI I DEIATEL'NOSTI KAZAKHSKOGO UCHENOGO CHOKANA CHINGIZOVICHA VALIKHANOVA," VESTNIK AN KAZ. SSR. No. 2. 1950. [Kazakh history; Russ. text; ca.100 Kazakh, Russ., German titles, pp. 118-121]

Sarybaev, Sh. "BIBLIOGRAFIIA PO ISTORII I DIALEKTOLOGII KAZAKHSKOGO IAZYKA," KAZAKHSKAYA DIALEKTOLOGIIA. No. 1. Alma Ata, 1965. [Kazakh language, history; Kazakh, Russ. text; 97 Kazakh, Russ. titles, pp. 287-292]

SOVET KHALQINING ULI OTAN SOGHISI (QAZAQ SSR KITAP PALATASI). Vol. 1. Alma Ata: Qazmembirikken Baspasi, 1948, 99 pp. [Kazakh general; Kazakh text; titles, per.: W.W. I]

SOVET KHALQINING ULI OTAN SOGHISI (QAZAQ SSR KITAP PALATASI). Vol. 2. Alma Ata: Qazmembirikken Baspasi, 1943, 164 pp. [Kazakh general; Kazakh text; titles, per.: W.W. II]

*Trunova, E. E.; U. Kudekova; N. P. Nesterov. comp. BIBLIOGRAFICHESKII UKAZATEL' TRUDOV SOTRUDNIKOV KAZAKHSKOGO GOSUDARSTVENNOGO UNIVERSITETA IM. S. M. KIROVA. Alma Ata: (Kazakhskii Gosudarstvennyi Universitet im. S. M. Kirova. Fundamental'naia Biblioteka), 1961 2nd ed., revised, 373 pp., 1000 copies. [Kazakh general; Russ. text; 378 Kazakh, Russ. titles, per.: 1934-1960, pp. 5-356]

Supplement: CENTRAL ASIA

Kirgiz

*Riazantsev, Sergei Nikolaevich; Viktor Fedorovich
 Pavlenko. KIRGIZSKAIA SSR: EKONOMIKO-GEOGRAFICHESKAIA
 KHARAKTERISTIKA. Moscow: Geografgiz, Ak. N. SSSR. Ins.
 Geo., 1960, 485 pp., 6000 copies. [Kirgiz economics;
 Russ. text; ca.150 Russ. titles, per.: 1913-1958,
 pp. 479-484]

Tajik

*Narzikulov, I. K.; S. N. Riazantsev, eds. TADZHIKSKAIA
 SSR: EKONOMIKO-GEOGRAFICHESKAIA KHARAKTERISTIKA.
 Moscow: Geografgiz, 1956, 228 pp., 7000 copies.
 [Tajik economics; Russ. text; 57 Russ. titles, per.:
 mainly 1920s-1950s, pp. 225-227]

*Rakhimov, M. R. "ZEMLEDELIE TADZHIKOV BASSEINA R.
 KHINGOU V DOREVOLIUTSIONNYI PERIOD. (IST.-ETNOGR.
 OCHERK)," TRUDY. AKAD. NAUK TADZHIK. SSR. IN-T
 ISTORII, ARKHEOLOGII I ETNOGRAFII. Vol. 43. 1957,
 221 pp. [Tajik history; Russ. text; Tajik; Russ.
 titles, per.: pre-1917, pp. 5-12]

[Semenova, S. F.] SADRIDDIN AINI. (1878-1954). KRATKII
 BIBLIOGR. UKAZATEL' LIT. Lvov:(Lvovskaia Gos. Nauch.
 B-ka), 1968, 11 pp. [Tajik literature; Ukrainian,
 text; 35 Ukrainian, Russ. titles, pub.: 1931-1965]

Turkmen

Azymov, M. "SOVREMENNYI TURKMENSKII IAZYK," Kh. Bailiev,
 KRATKII KURS GRAMMATIKI SOVREMENNOGO TURKMENSKOGO
 IAZYKA. Part 1. MORFOLOGIIA. Ashkhabad: (Zaoch.
 Ot. Ashkhab. Gos. In-ta im. Gor-kogo), 1948,
 pp. 138-141. [Turkmen language; Turkmen text; 40
 Turkmen, Russ. titles, pub.: 1936-1947]

*Freikin, Zakhar G.; V. N. Kunin, ed. TURKMENSKAIA SSR:
 EKONOMIKO-GEOGRAFICHESKAIA KHARAKTERISTIKA. Moscow:
 Geografgiz, 1957, 2nd ed., 451 pp., 8000 copies.
 [Turkmen economics; Russ. text; ca.150 Russ. titles,
 per.: 19th-20th c., pp. 442-449]

Meredov, A. IZ ISTORII LITERATURY SEL'DZHUKSKOGO
 PERIODA. Ashkhabad: "Ylym," 1969. [Turkmen
 literature; Turkmen text; 80 titles, per.: Seldzhuk,
 pp. 217-220]

Supplement: CENTRAL ASIA, Turkmen

TURKMENISTAN SSR-NING TARIKHI. Vol. 2. APREL' 1917-
1957-NZHI YILLAR. Ashkhabad: TSSR Ia Neshiryati,
1959, 808 pp. [Turkmen history; Turkmen text;
titles, per.: Rev. & Civil War, pp. 171-803]

Uzbek

*Bek-Nazarova, V. G. comp. BIBLIOGRAFIIA IZDANII
AKADEMII NAUK UZBEKSKOI SSR. KNIGI I STAT'I V
IZDANIIAKH KOMITETA NAUK PRI SNK UZSSR I
UZBEKISTANSKOGO FILIALA AKADEMII NAUK SSSR. 1933-
1942 GG. Tashkent: Izdatel'stvo "Nauka," Uzbekskoi
SSR, 1965, 243 pp., 650 copies. [Uzbek general;
1737 Uzbek, Russ. titles, pub.: 1933-1942]

GEOGRAFICHESKOE OBSHCHESTVO SSSR. UZBEKISTANSKII
FIFLIAL. IZVESTIIA UZBEKISTANSKOGO GEOGRAFICHESKOGO
OBSHCHESTVA. Vol. 10. Tashkent: "Fan," 1967, 132 pp.,
650 copies. [Uzbek geography; Russ. text; titles at
end of articles]

KATALOG VOENNOI LITERATURY. (K OBSLUZHIVANIIU LAGERNYKH
SBOROV). Tashkent: Gosizdat Uzbekskoi SSR, 1933,
19 pp., 500 copies. [Uzbek pol. sci.; Uzbek, Russ.
text]

Kvasnitskii, D. "UZBEKSKAIA KNIZHNAIA PALATA,"
BIBLIOGRAFIIA SSSR I KNIZHNYE PALATY. SBORNIK.
Kharkov, 1928. [Uzbek general; Russ. text; 35
titles, pub.: Apr. 1925-Sept. 1927, pp. 165-171]

Nasyrkhodzhaev, S. Kh. INTELLIGENTSIIA UZBEKISTANA V
PERIOD KOMMUNISTICHESKOGO STROITEL'STVA. Tashkent:
"Uzbekistan," 1968, 271 pp., 4000 copies. [Uzbek
history; Russ. text; Uzbek titles, pp. 264-270]

Pankov, A. V. SISTEMATICHESKII UKAZATEL' K IZDANIIAM
UZBEKISTANSKOGO GEOGRAFICHESKOGO OBSHCHESTVA I EGO
PREDSHESTVENNIKOV, SOSTAVLENNYI K 50-LETIIU OBSHCHESTVA.
(1897-1947 GG.) Vol. 2(22). Tashkent: SAGU. Trudy
Uzbekistanskogo Geograficheskogo Obshchestva, 1948.
[Uzbek geography, anthropology, economics; Russ. text;
323 mainly Russ. titles, per.: 1897-1947, pp. 171-201]

Supplement: SIBERIA & MONGOLIA

SIBERIA & MONGOLIA

Altay

*"ALTAISKII KRAI," BOL'SHAIA SOVETSKAIA ENTSIKLOPEDIIA.
Vol. 2. Moscow: Gosudarstvennyi Institut
"Sovetskaia Entsiklopediia"(OGIZ RSFSR), 1950, 2nd ed.,
pp. 142-151. [Altay economics, geography; Russ. text
and titles, p. 151]

Mongolia

*Obruchev, Vladimir A. VOSTOCHNAIA MONGOLIIA:
GEOGRAFICHESKOE I GEOLOGICHESKOE OPISANIE. Part 1 &
2. OBZOR LITERATURY. OROGRAFICHESKII I
GIDROGRAFICHESKII OCHERK. Moscow-Leningrad:
Izdatel'stvo Akademii Nauk SSSR, 1947, 351 pp., 2500
copies. [Mongol geography; Russ. text; 574 Russ.
titles, pp. 10-138]

Shastina, N. P. "OBZOR LITERATURY O MONGOLII ZA 1935 GOD.
(PO MATERIALAM BIBLIOTEKI UCHENOGO KOMITETA MNR),"
SOVREMENNAIA MONGOLIIA. No. 6(19), 1936. [Mongol
general; Russ. text; 142 Russ., Europ. titles, pub.:
1935, pp. 94-113]

Siberia

Bandman, M. K. ed. PROBLEMY RAZMESHCHENIIA I
FORMIROVANIIA TERRITORIAL'NO-PROIZVODSTVENNYKH
KOMPLEKSOV SIBIRI. Novosibirsk: (AN SSSR. Sib.
Otd-nie), 1968, 68 pp., 600 copies. [Siberia economics;
Russ. text and titles at end of reports]

Dmitriev-Mamonov, A. I. NACHALO PECHATI V SIBIRI.
St. Petersburg: Tovarishchestvo "Khudozhestvennoi
Pechati," 1900, 72 + 3 pp. [Siberia general; Russ.
text; titles, pub.: 1900 & before, appendix]

Gavrilova, S. A. RAIONY DAL'NEGO VOSTOKA. EKONOMICHSKIE
ADMINISTRATIVNYE RAIONY SSSR: UKAZATEL' NOVOI
LITERATURY PO PRIRODE, RESURSAM I KHOZIAISTVU. Vol. 8.
Moscow: Izdatel'stvo Akademii Nauk SSSR, 1958, 43 pp.
[Siberia economics; Russ. text]

_____. RAIONY ZAPADNOI SIBIRI. EKONOMICHESKIE
ADMINISTRATIVNYE RAIONY SSSR: UKAZATEL' NOVOI
LITERATURY PO PRIRODE, RESURSAM I KHOZIAISTVU. Vol. 6.
Moscow: Izdatel'stvo Akademii Nauk SSSR, 1958, 62 pp.
[Siberia economics; Russ. text]

Supplement: SIBERIA & MONGOLIA

Glazyrina, N. G. comp. PUBLICHNAIA NAUCHNO-
TEKHNICHESKAIA BIBLIOTEKA. KATALOG BIBLIOGRAFICHESKIKH
UKAZATELEI I SPRAVOK....VYPOLNENNYKH V 1967 G.
Novosibirsk: (Gos. Publ. Nauch-Tekhn. B-ka Sib.
Otd-nie AN SSSR), 1968, 21 pp., 700 copies. [Siberia
general; Russ. text; titles, pub.: 1967]

Kirillov, Mikhail Vasilevich; Iurii Adrianovich
Shcherbakov. KRASNOIARSKII KRAI: PRIRODNOE I
EKONOMIKO-GEOGRAFICHESKOE RAIONIROVANIE. Krasnoiarsk:
Knizhnoe Izdatel'stvo, 1962, 404 pp. [Siberia
economics; Russ. text; ca.400 titles, pp. 384-402]

*Krotov, V. A.; M. I. Pomus; G. D. Rikhter; V. B. Sochava,
eds. VOSTOCHNAIA SIBIR': EKONOMIKO-GEOGRAFICHESKAIA
KHARAKTERISTIKA. Moscow: (Gosudarstvennoe Izdatel'stvo
Geograficheskoi Literatury, 1963, 888 pp., 4000
copies. [Siberia economics; Russ. text; ca.500 Russ.
titles, historical review: 17th - 19th c.; main book:
since the revolution, pp. 866-886]

*Margolin, A. B. ed. ZAPADNO-SIBIRSKII EKONOMICHESKII
RAION. Moscow: Izdatel'stvo "Nauka," 1967, 521 pp.,
2500 copies. [Siberia economics; Russ. text; 32 Russ.
titles, per.: 1930s-1960s but mainly 1950s-1960s, pp.
245-246]

Mel'kheev, Matvei Nikolaevich. GEOGRAFICHESKIE NAZVANIIA
VOSTOCHNOI SIBIRI. Irkutsk: Vostochno-Sibirskoe
Knizhnoe Izdatel'stvo, 1969, 121 pp. [Siberia
geography; Russ. text; titles, pp. 118-120]

*Moshinskaia, V. I. ARKHEOLOGICHESKIE PAMIATNIKI SEVERO-
ZAPADNOI SIBIRI. Moscow: Izdatel'stvo "Nauka,"
1965, 88 pp., 900 copies. [Siberia history,
archaeology; Russ. text; Russ., Europ. titles, pub.:
1833-1961, pp. 45-46]

ODINATSATAIA NAUCHNAIA SESSIIA...POSVISHCHENNAIA 50-
LETIIU VELIKOI OKTIABR'SKOI SOTSIALISTICHESKOI
REVOLIUTSII. No. 1. ISTORICHESKIE NAUKI.
Novosibirsk: Novosibirskii Pedagogicheskii Institut,
1967, 200 pp., 500 copies. [Siberia history; Russ.
text; titles at end of reports]

Pokshishevskii, V. V. RAIONY VOSTOCHNOI SIBIRI.
EKONOMICHESKIE ADMINISTRATIVNYE RAIONY SSSR:
UKAZATEL' NOVOI LITERATURY PO PRIRODE, RESURSAM I
KHOZIAISTVU. Vol. 7. Moscow: Izdatel'stvo Akademii
Nauk SSSR, 1958, 75 pp. [Siberia economics; Russ.
text]

Supplement: SIBERIA & MONGOLIA

*Pomus, Moisei Isaakovich. ZAPADNAIA SIBIR': EKONOMIKO-
GEOGRAFICHESKAIA KHARAKTERISTIKA. Moscow: Geografgiz.
Akademiia Nauk SSSR. Institut Geografii, 1956,
643 pp., 5000 copies. [Siberia economics; ca.425
Russ. titles, mainly 1950s, pp. 624-641]

Sergeev, Mikhail. NARODNOE KHOZIAISTVO KAMCHATSKOGO
KRAIA. Leningrad: Izdatel'stvo Akademii Nauk SSSR,
1936, 815 pp. [Siberia economics; Russ. text; 399
titles, pp. 799-809]

Skalon, Vasilii. RUSSKIE ZEMLEPROKHODTSY--ISSLEDOVATELI
SIBIRI XVII VEKA. (MOSKOVSKOE OBSHCHESTVO
ISPYTATELEI PRIRODY. ISTORICHESKAIA SERIIA. NO. 44).
Moscow, 1952, 198 pp. [Siberia history; Russ. text;
280 titles, per.: 17th c., pp. 190-198]

Spidchenko, Konstantin Ivanovich. GORODA KUZBASSA:
EKONOMIKO-GEOGRAFICHESKII OCHERK. Moscow: Geografiz,
1947, 147 pp. [Siberia economics; Russ. text; 217
titles, pp. 138-145]

Stepanov, A. A. comp. KHABAROVSKII KRAI, DAL'NII
VOSTOK. UKAZATEL' TRUDOV PRIAMURSKOGO (KHABAROVSKOGO)
FILIALA GEOGRAFICHESKOGO OBSHCHESTVA SSSR. 1962-
1967 GG. Khabarovsk: (Priamurskii [Khabarovskii]
Filial Geograficheskogo Obshchestva SSSR), 1968, 54 pp.
[Siberia geography; Russ. text; 540 titles, pub.:
1962-1967]

Tomashevskii, V. V. MATERIALY K BIBLIOGRAFII SIBIRI I
DAL'NEGO VOSTOKA: XV-PERVAIA POLOVINA XIX V.
Vladivostok: Izdatel'stvo Akademii Nauk SSSR, 1957,
213 pp. [Siberia, geography, history; Russ. text;
ca.3500 titles, per.: 1400-1850]

Vakhlamov, B. A. REZERVY I EKONOMIKA. IZ OPYTA RABOTY
PREDPRIATII ZAP. SIBIRI. Novosibirsk: Zap.-Sib. Kn.
Izd., 1966, 83 pp., 2000 copies. [Siberia economics;
Russ. text; titles, pp. 80-82]

Vorobev, Vladimir V.; N. I. Vershinskaia. PUBLIKATSII
SIBIRSKIKH I DAL'NEVOSTOCHENYKH ORGANIZATSII
GEOGRAFICHESKOGO OBSHCHESTVA SSSR. 1945-1963 GG.
Irkutsk: (Akademiia Nauk SSSR. Sibirskoe Otdelenie.
Institut Geografii Sibiri i Dal'nego Vostoka,
Geograficheskoe Obshchestvo SSSR, Biuro Sibirskikh i
Dal'nevostochnykh Organizatsii), 1966, 167 pp.
[Siberia geography; Russ. text; 1495 titles, pub.:
1945-1963]

Supplement: SIBERIA & MONGOLIA

VOSTOCHNOE ZABAIKAL'E. (PERSPEKTIVY RAZVITIIA
PROIZVODIT. SIL CHIT. OBL.) Irkutsk-Chita, 1968.
[Siberia economics; ca.180 titles, pp. 182-187]

Zakharova, H. CHTO CHITAT' O KAMCHATKE. REK. UKAZ.
LIT. Petropavslovk-Kamchatskii: Dal'nevost. Kn.
Izd-vo, 1970, 124 pp., 1000 copies. [Siberia general;
Russ. text; 1200 titles]

Tuva

*Nordega, Igor Glebovich. "ISTORIIA GEOGRAFICHESKOGO
IZUCHENIIA TUVY VO VTOROI POLOVINE XIX I PERVOI
POLOVINE XX V.," AKADEMIIA NAUK SSSR. INSTITUT
ISTORII ESTESTVOZNANIIA I TEKHNIKI. TRUDY. Vol. 27,
1959, pp. 67-111. [Tuva geography, history; Russ.
text; 192 Russ., French, English, German titles,
pub.: 1850-1950, pp. 103-111]

ABOUT THE AUTHOR

EDWARD ALLWORTH, Ph.D. in Slavic and Central Asian literature, Columbia University, is Professor of Turco-Soviet Studies in the Department of Middle East Languages and Cultures, and Director of the Program on Soviet Nationality Problems, Columbia University. Dr. Allworth has travelled and conducted research throughout the Soviet Union, Turkey, and Europe. Among his numerous publications is "The 'Nationality' Idea in Czarist Central Asia," in Erich Goldhaben (ed.), ETHNIC MINORITIES IN THE SOVIET UNION (Praeger, 1968).

In addition to the present volume, the Program on Soviet Nationality Problems has copublished with Praeger Special Studies the following works: Edward Allworth (ed.), THE NATIONALITY QUESTION IN SOVIET CENTRAL ASIA (1973); Ralph S. Clem (ed.), THE SOVIET WEST (1975); and Robert A. Lewis, Richard H. Rowland, and Ralph S. Clem, POPULATION, NATIONALITY, AND MODERNIZATION IN RUSSIA AND THE USSR (forthcoming, 1976).

RELATED TITLES
Published by
Praeger Special Studies

THE SOVIET WEST: INTERPLAY BETWEEN NATIONALITY
AND SOCIAL ORGANIZATION
      edited by Ralph S. Clem

THE NATIONALITY QUESTION IN SOVIET CENTRAL
ASIA
      edited by Edward Allworth

DEVELOPMENT REGIONS IN THE SOVIET UNION AND
EASTERN EUROPE
      edited by Andrew F. Burghardt

THE SOVIET ECONOMY IN REGIONAL PERSPECTIVE
      edited by V. N. Bandera
      and Z. L. Melnyk

THE INFLUENCE OF EAST EUROPE AND THE SOVIET WEST ON
THE USSR
      edited by Roman Szporluk

Z
3414
M54
A44